Genealogies of
BARBADOS FAMILIES

From Caribbeana *and* The Journal of the
Barbados Museum and Historical Society

Genealogies of
BARBADOS FAMILIES

From Caribbeana *and* The Journal of the
Barbados Museum and Historical Society

Compiled by
JAMES C. BRANDOW

With an Index by Robert & Catherine Barnes

Baltimore
GENEALOGICAL PUBLISHING CO., INC.
1983

Preface

FAMILY HISTORY is a compulsive interest to many of us; we want to trace our origins and learn about our ancestors. It is astonishing how often the trail leads to Barbados. Fortunately, Barbados has good records from as far back as 1640, or even earlier, and most of these are well preserved and easily accessible to researchers. Within the last few years a lot of the information from these records has been published in summarized form. But, of course, official records give only part of the story; they have to be supplemented by information from other sources.

The Journal of the Barbados Museum and Historical Society has been published continuously since 1933 and in its early years devoted much space to the history of Barbados families. The issues containing most of these articles have long been out of print and the decision to republish the articles, together with articles from *Caribbeana,* is most welcome. James Brandow, in the course of his extensive research into the Carrington family, has become familiar with most of those whose story is told in these pages and he must be warmly congratulated on taking the initiative in bringing all this material together in a single volume.

Family connections between Barbados and North America are of very long standing. A son of John Winthrop, Governor of Massachusetts, was among those who arrived from England to settle Barbados, then uninhabited, in 1627, and close ties between the two countries have existed ever since. In the seventeenth and eighteenth centuries Barbados had connections with almost every point of the Atlantic seaboard from the Piscataqua River in the north to Charleston in the south. We know of persons from the Piscataqua who immigrated to Barbados in the 1640s, and in the 1670s a Barbadian was Governor of South Carolina. Americans went to Barbados to trade, and population pressures at home (for Barbados has an area of only 166 square miles) led hundreds of Barbadians to seek their fortunes in America. Many of these persons and their descendants achieved distinction in their new home. Two of the signatories of the American Declaration of Independence, for example, Lewis Morris and Arthur Middleton, were descended from men who had arrived from Barbados a century earlier.

I hope this book will provide answers to those wanting information about the origins of their families. I hope also that it will make them wish to learn more about an island with a long and most interesting history.

P. F. CAMPBELL, Editor
*Journal of the Barbados
Museum and Historical Society*

Foreword

INTEREST in Barbados family history has always been keen because of the unique role Barbados played in the settlement of America. For 350 years the flow of emigrants from that island to these shores has been continuous. Many Americans engaged in genealogy have discovered distant cousins in Barbados or traced an ancestor back to Great Britain by way of "Little England." In general, though, researchers have been frustrated in their efforts to obtain information on Barbados families because of the inaccessibility of published materials. What has been published is either out of print or found only in a handful of specialized libraries.

In 1909 Vere Langford Oliver, an English genealogist, commenced the publication of *Caribbeana,* a quarterly journal concerned solely with West Indian genealogy. Many articles on Barbados families were printed in this magazine, but after six volumes and three supplements it ceased publication in 1919. A second periodical, *The Journal of the Barbados Museum and Historical Society,* under the scholarly influence of Eustace Maxwell Shilstone, began printing records and articles on Barbados families in 1933, and for five decades it has made a significant contribution, though it has not had a wide circulation in the United States. With this present publication, however, genealogists will have access to both these periodicals, for this compilation contains every article dealing with Barbados family history ever published in these journals. The combined articles include genealogies, pedigrees, will abstracts, extracts from parish registers, Bible records, genealogical notes and even queries. An appendix is also included: four lists of Quakers who lived in Barbados from 1677 to 1761. Many of these dissenters migrated to Philadelphia and to other Quaker centers in America.

Principal Contributors

VERE LANGFORD OLIVER (1861-1942) of Weymouth, Dorsetshire, devoted his entire life to the research and writing of West Indian genealogy. During an early visit to Antigua he abandoned thoughts of a medical career and set out to record the history of that island and its most important families. Today, his three-volume *History of the Island of Antigua* (London, 1894-99) is recognized as a standard work. He launched *Caribbeana* in 1909 but the World War increased publication costs and the lack of subscribers finally brought about its demise in 1919. He also edited *The Monumental Inscriptions in the Churches and Churchyards of the Island of Barbados, British West Indies* (London, 1915).

EUSTACE MAXWELL SHILSTONE (1889-1969), one of the founders and later President of the Barbados Museum and Historical Society, was a prolific and frequently anonymous contributor to the *Journal*. He was privately educated, became a successful solicitor, and for a time served as Clerk of the House of Assembly. A diligent researcher known for his accuracy, Mr. Shilstone's knowledge of local history and island families was said to be "second to none." In 1924 he edited Richard Hall's *A General Account of the First Settlement . . . of Barbados* (Bridgetown) and in 1933 published *Notes on Controverted Elections* (Bridgetown). His *Monumental Inscriptions in the Burial Ground of the Jewish Synagogue at Bridgetown, Barbados* (London and New York, 1956) includes an interesting history of Jews in Barbados.

Contents

———————————————— ❦ ————————————————

Genealogies of
BARBADOS FAMILIES

From Caribbeana and The Journal of the
Barbados Museum and Historical Society

Adams, Maxwell and Walker of Barbados.[*]

In looking over an old Law Book, entitled "Cases with opinions of eminent Counsel in matters of Law Equity and Conveyancing," I came across the following two items:—

Vol. I., p. 358. Elizabeth Maxwell, widow, late of the Island of Barbadoes, deceased, by her will disposed of the residue of her Estate, which she left to her "grand nephew Thomas Maxwell Adams, an infant son of my nephew Thomas Adams, Esq.," in tail general, whom failing to "Frances Adams, sister to the said T. M. Adams," whom failing to my brother in law George Graeme and his heirs and assigns for ever." The said T. M. Adams was living in 1768, and had issue a son and a dau., infants of tender years. The said Frances Maxwell was also living but sans issue.

Vol. I., p. 314. Alexander Walker, Esq., being then (*i.e.*, 19 May 1742) in Barbadoes, made his will whereby he bequeathed to his dau. and only child Newton Walker all his estate in the Island and elsewhere in the world, to be delivered to his said dau. on attaining 21 years of age or on marriage, whichever should first happen, but should she die s.p. then to his brother William Walker, but should William Walker die s.p. living at his death then to his brother in law Captain Thomas Walker, but should he also die s.p. surviving, then to his cousin George Walker. Alexander Walker died in 1759, and soon after his death Newton Walker married John Walter, Esq., and died in 1772 without ever having had issue. [This corrects the pedigree *ante*, p. 186.] William Walker predeceased his brother Alex. Walker. Thomas Walker was apparently living at the date of Newton's death in 1772.

Notes by the Editor.

"*Maxwells*" is a well-known plantation in the parish of Christ Church, close to the high road running from Hastings to Oistins.

In 1680 Tho. Maxwell owned 24 acres, 2 white servants and 30 negroes.

In 1715 the Hon. Lt.-Gen. Tho. Maxwell, Eliz. his lady, one son and five daughters were entered in the census.

Thomas son of Tho. Maxwell of Christ Church, Barbadoes, Esq., matriculated from Christ Church, Oxford, 23 Aug. 1717, aged 14. "*Graemes*" was an adjoining estate.

The family of Adams was also an old one in the parish.

Williams Adams, who had recently purchased a very considerable estate, was in 1701 recommended for the Council. He is stated to have married Frances, only child and heir of Col. Tho. Walrond by Frances his wife daughter of Sir Jonathan Atkins, Knt. (Burke's "L.G.")

The Hon. Tho. Adams of *Adams Castle* was buried at St. Michael's, 4 Sept. 1764. Margaret his wife died 30 June 1743 (?), aged 38, and was also buried there with several of her children, in the McNemara vault.

Their son, Tho. Maxwell Adams, entered Eton School 24 Jan. 1760; was admitted a student of Lincoln's Inn 21 Jan. 1762, and matriculated from Merton Coll., Oxford, 13 Aug. 1764, aged 19. This would give his birth about 1745, two years after his mother's death, so the year 1743 on her tombstone must be wrong. He married in 1770 Anne Foublanque, and she died his widow at Brompton, 27 March 1812. See his book-plate No. 160. Mr. Austen-Leigh in his MS. list of Etonians has a note of an earlier Adams, who entered Eton in Jan. 1753; perhaps William, elder brother of Tho. Maxwell Adams.

* Contributed by Mr. Erskine E. West of Dublin.

A will of Eliz. Maxwell, probably the one in question, was recorded in 1750.

Alex. Walker was son of Alex. W. of St. Peter's, a Judge, and grandson of the Rev. Wm. W., the Bishop of London's Commissary in this Island. He and his brother Wm. matriculated at Oxford on 17 Dec. 1715, aged respectively 18 and 17, but he did not graduate. He died 23 May, and was buried in Westminster Abbey 2 June 1757, aged 60, the date of 1759 in the legal case being therefore incorrect. His will was proved 21 Feb. 1758 by his daughter, then wife of John Walter, Esq. (59, Hutton.)

ALLEYNE OF BARBADOS.

CONTRIBUTED BY LOUISE R. ALLEN.

ARMS. Per chevron Gules and Ermine, in chief, two lions heads erased Or.

CREST. Out of a ducal coronet Or a horse's head Argent.

MOTTO. Non tua ta moveat sed publica vota.

REYNOLD ALLEYNE, the progenitor of the Barbados family, a youthful emigrant who arrived within three years of the first settlement of the island, was the son of Rev. Richard Alleyne, D.D., Rector of Stowting in the county of Kent.

A Pedigree of the family of ALLEN of Lincolnshire appeared in Vol. 50 of the Harleian Society's publication *Lincolnshire Pedigrees* (vide p. 8 et seq) which gives Richard Alleyn, D.D., rector of Stowting, Kent, as the son of Richard Allen of Skillington Lincs, by his wife Margaret, daughter of John Wisdome of London. This statement has been questioned by the writer of an article on the subject in *Miscellanea Genealogica et Heraldica** who has submitted that Richard of Stowting was the son of Richard Allen of Hundleby, Lincs, at one time vicar of Skillington, and that it was this Richard of Hundleby who married Margaret Wisdome. It is suggested that the error which also occurs in Burke's *Baronetage* etc. in the ancestry of Sir John Meynell Alleyne, Bart., was due to the curious coincidence that both Richard of Skillington and Richard of Hundleby died in 1616 leaving an eldest son, Richard, by a wife Margaret.

The present writer has made extensive searches amongst the English records referred to in the above-mentioned article, and has come to the conclusion that the facts sought to be proved have not been established, and having discovered other records which point to a different conclusion, the quest for a final solution of the problem has not yet been abandoned.

A seal with the above described arms and crest and the words *Johanis Allyn Armi Sigillum* within a circle was entered with the pedigree of the branch of the Alleyn family of Richard Alleyn, D.D., rector of Stowting. The same seal is also found on Deeds and notes of Henricus Allen, Staffordshire, 47 Edward III (1375); Thomasia Alleyn of Garingshale meo filio Robto Alleyn of Broomshill, 5 Edw II (1312); and Thome Alleyne of Garingshalle, 16 Henry 6 (1445). The Alleyne family probably originated in Staffordshire, but as yet no definite proof of connection between the family of that county and the Barbados branch has been found. It has been established beyond all doubt that Rev. Richard Alleyn, D.D., of Stowting, Kent,

*Fifth Series Vol VIII Part VII, page 211 et seq contributed by C. A. Higgins Esqre.

3

was the father of Reynold Alleyne, the emigrant, which for the purposes of this pedigree is as far as we need go.

1. RICHARD ALLEYNE[1] D.D., of Stowting, Kent, England. Born 1572. Possibly 9 Nov. 1572, at Skillington, Linc. Died 25 Oct. 1651 at Stowting, Kent. Married Christian dau of . . . ? She was living 1650.

Alumni Oxonienses—George Foster, gives ALLEN, RICHARD (ALLYN) of co. Lincoln, cler. fil. Corpus Christi Coll., Matric. 23 Feb., 1587—8, aged 15; B.A. 5 Feb., 1590—1, M.A. 12 Dec., 1594, B.D. 7 July, 1603, D.D. 30 June 1608. See Foster's *Index Ecclesiasticus*.

Mr. H. Oswell, rector of St. Mildred's, Canterbury, 14 Oct. 1930, kindly copied these records. Richard Alleyn D.D. of Stowting, Kent 1634. Rector of St. Mildred's, Canterbury, 1601—1637; also rector of Stowting. Richard Alleyn, his son, rector of St. Mildred's, Canterbury, 1637—1654.

Richard Alleyn was instituted to the Rectory of Stowting 6 May 1605. He possessed lands in the Manor of East Greenwich which belonged to his great-grandfather, as well as other property, as shown by the following deeds:

In the Close Rolls of 2 Charles I (1627) (Part 24) is a deed of bargain and sale of lands in Hundlebie, Lincolnshire, held in fee simple by Richard Alleyn of Stowting, Doctor of Divinity, and sold by him to Timothy Allen the elder, merchant of Dublin, Ireland, and Timothy Allen the younger, his son and heir. The two Timothys are sometimes called Allen, sometimes Alleyn. There is a full description of the property, and the purchase price was £800.

Indenture made the 20 June 1643 between Abell Aleyn, Citizen and Haberdasher of London, of the one part, and Richard Alleyn, Doctor of Divinity and Rector of the Parish Church of Stowting, Kent, and Abell Alleyne his sonne, of the other part, Witnesseth that in consideration of £250 Sterling and for divers other good causes him thereunto specially moving, Abell Alleyn grants and conveys and sells to Richard Alleyn and Abell his sonne, all the freehold messuage with the appurtenances in the Parish of St. Martin in Stamford Baron, Northants, now in the tenure or occupation of Lady Frances Wingfield or her assignes, together with the Dovecott, barnes, stables, etc., and all those 7 acres of arable land in the fields of Stamford Baron, and all that close of pastures are in the occupation of William Crane, or his assignes, and all hedgerows, Woods, Trees, etc., and all other lands and premises of Abell Alleyn lately purchased to him and his heires, of William Alleyn, late of Stamford, in the countie of Lincolne, Gentleman, and all reversions and remainders, and all deeds and evidences, to have and to hold to Richard Alleyn and Abell his sonne and to their heires and assignes forever, to the only use and behoofe of Richard Alleyn and Abell Alleyn.

(Close Roll. 19. C.1.. Part 8. No. 3. Alleyn & Alleyn, Northants.)

4

The will of Richard Alleyn. clerk, Dr. in Divinity and Rector of the parish of Stowting. is dated 21 April 1650. To be buried in the chancel next my children lying there. Poor 40s. To Christian, my wife. a bed and one-third linen. Ann. my daughter. wife of George Lawe £10. Reynold, my son, whom God hath blessed with abundance of temporal goods far beyond my abilitie to apportion £50 in plate. £100 to Margt. my daughter, wife of Wm. Culpepper, to be paid to Sir Cheyney C. (Culpepper) and Dr. Steed £200, I have secured by lands to them. My son Abell £10. To Allyn Culpepper. son of my dau. Margt. £10. 4 servants 10s each. All residue to Richard Alleyn, my son and sole Executor. 50s to the poor of the parish of St. Mildred's and St. Margt. Castle in Canterbury. Christian. daughter of my son Abell, a calf.

Codicil 22 May 1650. Proved 16 March 1651 by Richard Allen (52 Bowyer.)

George Lawe married Anne daughter of Richard Allen D.D. and great-grand-daughter of John Allen, 26 Dec. 1628.

The following entries were copied from the Register of Stowting. Kent. and testified by the Rev. William Warren, Minister, Sept. 1771.

John Allien, son of Richard Allien, Bapt 23 Mar. 1607.

Benjamin Allyen son of Master Doctor Allyen, Bapt 2 June 1612.

Benjamin Allyen, son of Mr. Doctor Allyen, buried 1 June 1611.

Children of Richard Alleyn[1] of Stowting, and Christian his wife.

i. JOHN [2], bapt 23 March 1607 at Stowting Kent, and buried there 3 May 1639.
There seems to have been a son before John according to the following record.
ALLEYNE. JOHN 2nd son of Richard of Stowting, Kent. S.T.D. Oriel Coll. Matriculated 17 Jan. 1622—3. aged 16 ; B.A. 7 July 1625. M.A. 15 May 1628. One of these names Vicar of Marston, Oxon. 1627. (Alumni Oxonienses.)

ii. ANNE, Married 26 Dec. 1628 George Lawe, Citizen & Mercer of London. She was living 1650.

2. iii. REYNOLD, bapt Aug. 1609 at Stowting Kent, died 17 Dec. 1651 in Barbados B.W.I. Married Mary Skeet.

iv. RICHARD, born—1610 at Stowting, Kent, Eng., Married Elizabeth dau of Mrs. Bennet Hales.
Richard Alleyne M.A. Rector of St. Mildred's, Canterbury. Marriage license 10 April 1640 to marry Elizabeth Hales, daughter of Mrs. Bennet Hales. He a bachelor aged 30. She aged 18, at Stowting Kent. Married 13 April 1640. He was rector of St. Mildred's, Canterbury, Kent, 1637 to 1654.

v. BENJAMIN, buried 1 June 1611 at Stowting, Kent.

vi. BENJAMIN, bapt. 2 June, 1611 at Stowting, Kent.

vii. MARGARET, b. 29 June 1613 at Stowting. Kent. Married 30 April 1633 at Stowting. Kent. Rev. Wm. Culpepper, of Wichling, Co. Kent. Cousin of Sir Thomas Culpepper of Hollingborne. She was

5

living in 1650, and had issue :—

(1) *Abel*   *Culpepper*

(2) *Alleyne*   ,,   *Mentioned in grfather's will*

(3) *John Alleyne* ,,

(4) *Francis*   ,,

(5) *Margaret*   ,,   *Married 10 Nov. 1667 Reynold Skeet of Barbados.*

viii. ABEL, bapt 1 Dec. 1616 at Stowting, Kent, Married 29 Sept. 1646 Frances Berks

ix. THOMAS, b. 26 Sept. 1620 at Stowting, Kent, buried there 12 Oct. 1637.

2. REYNOLD ALLEYNE.[2] (*Richard.*[1])   Born Aug. 1609 at Stowting, Kent, England, Died 17 Dec. 1651 at Barbados, B.W.I. Married Mary daughter of . . . . . Skeet of Three Houses, St. Philip, Barbados, and Sister of Capt. Francis Skeet.

Reynold Alleyne is first mentioned in the records of Barbados as one of the Councillors in the government under Captain Henry Hawley who went to Barbados as Governor June 1630 and held the first session on the 5th of July (1630): Reynold Alleyne was then not quite 21 years old. His name appears in a list of owners of more than ten acres of land in Barbados in 1638, as Reynold Allen. Other persons of the same surname included in the list are William Allen, John Allen and Richard Allen.

He returned to England, and left again for Barbados in 1639. In Hotten's *"Original List of Emigrants"* are these records: "Portus Southton, 28 June 1639. Regnald Allen of Kent of 30 yeares gent, Gerrard Haughton of 30 yeares com. Oxon. gen, David Bixe of 35 years com Kanc. gen. free planters of Barbathoes," with five persons named as servants to the planters abovenamed, "they passe in the Boldadventure of Hampton for the Isle of Guarnzey from thence they take shipping for the Barbathoes, who have taken the Oaths." His associations with David Bixe continued over the space of many years.

Between 1641 and 1648 several deeds are recorded from which it appears that Capt. Alleyne traded in cotton and tobacco, and acted as agent for Constant Silvester, a London merchant. He also bought and sold land in St. Philip and Christ Church parishes in the neighborhood of *Staple Grove* plantation, which is mentioned in one of the deeds.

On the 14 July 1643 Reynold Alleyne sold 20 acres of land in Christ Church, Barbados, for 2600 pounds of cotton and tobacco.

On 3 Jan 1642 3 Captain Reynold Allen sold 50 acres in Christ Church to Captain Hilliard for 10,000 pounds of cotton.

In the struggle between the Royalists and Roundheads for supremacy, Reynold Alleyne was an adherent to the Commonwealth. Oldmixon in his *'History of the British West Indies'* says: "The system of arbitrary rule which, under King Charles I (crowned 2 Feb. 1626, decapitated 30 Jan 1648/9) and the system of open opposition to it in arms, which had been carried to such excess in

6

England, did not fail to raise among the colonists similar animosi-
ties; but the success of the republicans in Europe gave such advantage to that party in the Barbadoes as occasioned an unqualified
opposition to Lord Willoughby, the governor, against whom a depu-
tation of principal inhabitants, requesting assistance, was sent to
England in 1650. Among these was Colonel Reynold Allen. Their
expectation was fully answered; for by a commission from Oliver
Cromwell, a considerable military, as well as naval force was sent
to them under the command of Sir George Ascough." They reached
Barbados on 15 Oct. 1651.

For weeks the fleet beat up and down the coast, and it was not
until Dec. 7th that, early in the morning, under cover of darkness,
a force of between 400 and 500 men, of whom about 130 were Scots
taken out of the Virginia Fleet, was landed under the command of
Col. Alleyne, who having, as Oldmixon says: "a considerable interest in the island, was supposed to be the fittest man to lead the
soldiers to gain it."

They were met by 1200 foot and troop of horse under Col.
Gibbes which had been assembled to oppose them. The Commonwealth men made good their footing; the fort was taken and afterwards razed to the ground; four houses burned and four great guns
thrown into the sea. Of the landing party, six or eight were killed
and thirty wounded, among the latter was Col. Alleyne, who received a musket shot when landing. Mrs. Alleyne was granted a pass to
go on board the *Rainbow* to visit her husband who succumbed to his
wound, being lamented as "a man of worth and honour."

Reynold Alleyne's estate was sequestrated with that of others
of the same party by Act of Legislature dated 12 Sept. 1651, towards defraying the cost of the defences by the Royalists, one-fifth
only being reserved for the relations of those dispossessed.

He made his will on 16 June 1650, being then a resident of
Barbados, but "by Divine Providence appointed to depart this
Island." Mentions: Deare wife Mary Allen one-third part of all
moveable estate, and one-third part of all lands and profits of same
during her natural life, after debts are paid. To sonne Abell, one-
third part of all lands and goods when he is 21 years of age. To
sonnes Reynold and Dix and "ye child my wife now goeth with"
one-third part of whole estate. To daughter Mary, out of profits of
his estate during his son's minority and over and above their "bringing up" £500 Sterling on her marriage or at her age of 18 years.
"and the like proportion to ye child my wife now goeth with if a
daughter." Wife, Mary Alleyne sole executrix. "I earnestly in-
treate Collo. Henry Hawley and Major Valentine Hawley, Lt.
Thomas Lukumb and Mr. Thomas Sayer to be assistant unto my
said wife and to be guardians of my children in their minority."
Witnesses : Bartine Clarke, aged about 40 years. Will Howe, aged
about 30 years. Proved: 14 June 1652.

Children of Reynold[2] and Mary (Skeet) Alleyne, born in Barbados :—

3. i. ABEL 3,

ii. REYNOLD, of St. Philip, Barbados. Will dated 25 Oct 1675 proved 1688 at Barbados. Abstract; Eliza and Edward Skeat, children of Col. Fdward Skeat. My sister Mrs. Mary Rous. My sister Elizabeth Alleyne. Brother Abel Alleyne Mrs. Mary Skeat. Mr. Alleyne. Culpepper and Francis Culpepper. Nephew Reynold Alleyne.

iii. DIX. The name Dix appears in the copied record of his father's will but in the entry of his marriage to Priscilla Benson he is named Lt. Bix Allen. He was probably named after his fathers' friend David Bixe*

iv. MARY, Married Major Thomas Rouse of the *Cliff*, St, John, Barbados. Living in 1662.

v. ELIZABETH, born soon after 16 June 1650 and referred to in father's will, then unborn.

Mary (Skeet) Alleyne, widow of Reynold Alleyne,[2] married secondly John Turner of St. Philip, Barbados, and predeceased him, leaving issue named in her husband's Will dated 26 Nov. 1673 Pr. 14th June 1675.

Children of Mary (Skeet) Alleyne and John Turner:

(1) ANNE TURNER, Md. Tobias Frere, their son John Frere, Lieut General and President of the Council of Barbados, Married Elizabeth his cousin.

(2) MARY TURNER Md. 1st. Col. Thomas Farmer, Md. 2nd. Col. Thomas Spiar whose will dated 28 Nov. 1682 mentions Abel Alleyne brother-in-law. Mary Spiar daughter, and to her heirs the plantation etc., called Mount standfast, Barbados. Thomas and Mary Spiar had issue :—

(i) *Mary Spiar*, married Robert Stewart, whose child, Mary Stewart, married Sir Mark Pleydell Bart.

(ii) *Elizabeth Spiar* Md. John Frere aforesaid son of Tobias Frere & Anne Turner his cousin.

(iii) *Rebecca Spiar* Md. William Terrill of Cabbage Tree Hall, St. Lucy Barbados and had issue a Daughter. Mary Terrill, Md. John Alleyne her cousin. Their son Sir John Gay Alleyne.

(3) ABIGAIL or ELEANORA TURNER Md—Lighthouse of Bridgetown, Barbados.

3. ABEL ALLEYNE[3] (*Reynold[2] Richard.[1]*) Married 12 Jan. 1665/6 Elizabeth Denzy, daughter of Thomas Denzy, at St. John, Barbados.

Elizabeth Denzy, Bapt 27 July 1652, daughter of Thomas Denzy, whose will is dated 1674, Barbados. She died 25 Sept 1705 at St. James, Barbados.

Children :

4. i. THOMAS 4, bapt. April 1668 at St. Philip, Barbados. Died 10 Feb. 1717 at Barbados, Married Judith Thornhill.

5. ii. REYNOLD Born 1672 at Barbados. Died 2 Oct. 1722 at St. James , Barbados Married Elizabeth Isabella Gay.

6. iii. BENJAMIN Buried 22 April 1721 at St. James, Barbados. Married (1) Arabella Pilgrim, (2) Anne Kirton.

*Priscilla Benson was the only daughter of Robert Benson of St. John, Gent and Katharine his wife.

iv. ELIZABETH Married 13 June 1697, Richard Parsons of *Mount Misery*,
   St. Thomas, Barbados, and had issue : —
   (1) *Elizabeth Parsons,*
   (2) *Lucy Parsons*
v. LUCY. Married 22 April 1697, at St. James Barbados, John Walter
   Esq. of Bushbridge, Surrey, England, who died 12 May 1736.
vi. MARY. Married 15 Jan 1703/4 William Dottin of Grenade Hall
   St. Peter, Barbados. William Dottin of Yeamans Plantation, St.
   Andrew, Barbados. Born 1684 Matric. at Christ church, Oxford
   1701 aged 17. Buried 22 Dec. 1737.
vii. ARABELLA Born 1694 Married 26 Feb 1707 at St. James,
   Barbados, Hon. Timothy Salter, of *Salters*, St. George, Bar-
   bados. He was born 1684.
   Abstract of will of Timothy Salter of Barbados. Proved 15 Dec.
   1730. I do hereby nominate and appoint my cousins Reynold
   Alleyne, the son of Brigadier Thomas Alleyne, and my cousin
   Reynold Alleyne, the son of Honourable Reynold Alleyne, Esq.
   deceased, to be executors etc. (Barbados Records Vol. 34. pp 553.)
viii. CATHERINE Buried 14 Nov. 1695 at St. James Barbados.
   Immediately following this entry of burial in the Register of St.
   James is the following record : —
   Christian, daughter of Col. Abel Alleyne and Elizabeth, who had
   been buried many years in the church (S. James) was taken up
   and buried in the vault.

3.   ABEL ALLEYNE owned considerable property in Barbados.
In 1666 he purchased from his step-father, John Turner of St.
Philip, for £5,728 sterling one-half share of a plantation in the
parish of St. Andrew of 421 acres (? Turner's Hall) with the following boundaries:—Bounded on the east by lands of Thomas Lake
and a river called the Sea River, on the south by lands of Thomas
Johnson and the lands of one Woodward then in possession of Mr.
Ralph Fretwell, on lands of Col. Lewis Morris, on lands of Capt.
William Porter, on the West on lands of the said Col. Morris and a
river which is the bounds of part of the lands of Mr. John Bawden
and Mr. John Sparkes, on the north on lands of the said John Bawden and John Sparkes unto the corner of the aforesaid Thomas
Lake; together with a moiety of all houses, buildings, mill, mill
works, coppers, stills, sugar works, woods, timber trees, and of all
negroes, horses, cattle, and assenegoes. This plantation is said to be
the family estate known as Mount Alleyne in the XVII and XVIII
centuries.
   He was one of the Assistant Judges of the Court of Common
Pleas for the precinct of St. Andrew and St. Joseph 1683, Major of
Militia, afterwards Colonel 1689, and later Lieut. General in the
Island. Member of Assembly for St. Andrew in 1684—5, Member
for St. James 1686—1701. Speaker 1690 and other occasions, and
Old Planter and Member of Council 1701.
   10 June 1692 Governor Kendall recommended for the Council,
Abel Alleyne, Colonel of a regiment of foot—"A sober, discreet
gentleman of great estate." (Col. Cal. pp 649).
   30 Jan. 1700. List of Gentlemen recommended for Councillors
by the Governor of Barbados, Col. Abel Alleyne, Commander of

9

Leeward Regiment of Foot. An old Planter who by his own industry, has acquired a very considerable estate. (Ibid pp 44).

Abel Alleyne left a will which is not recorded. He died on 12 June 1706 and was buried the same day at St. James. Barbados.

4. THOMAS ALLEYNE[4](*eldest son of Abel,*[3]*Reynold,*[2]*Richard,*[1]) Bapt. April 1668 at St. Philip. Barbados. Died 10 Feb. 1717 aged 52 years at Barbados. Married 5 July 1688 Judith Thornhill daughter of Colonel Timothy Thornhill and sister of Sir Timothy Thornhill Bart., of Barbados and Kent, England.

Colonel Timothy Thornhill died in Barbados on 1 August 168! leaving £1,000 to his youngest daughter Judith "at 18, which will be the 29th of March 1685."

The Settlement on the marriage of Thos. Alleyne with Judith Thornhill is dated 30 June 1688, and made between Sir Timothy Thornhill, Bart, of the first part, Col. Abel Alleyne of the second part, and Rev. Zachariah Legard as trustee (the Rector of the parish and a kinsman of Sir Timothy's wife) of the third part, whereby Sir Timothy settled a plantation in St. Peter of 164 acres with its windmill and sugar works on Thomas Alleyne to be held in trust for him until he came of age, and securing a jointure to Judith in case she survived her husband. The consideration to be paid or secured by Abel Alleyne on the settlement was £3,280. Of this sum Sir Timothy was to receive £780 by instalments out of the proceeds of the plantation, £1,500 was to remain in Col. Alleyne's hands for Thomas as Judith's marriage portion, and in full of all legacies and interest given her by the will of her late father which was due by Sir Timothy, and £1,000 was secured to Sir T. by the bond of Col. Alleyne to be paid on 1 July 1689, at which date he agreed to surrender the plantation, having by then manufactured the crop of sugar, molasses and rum. Col. Alleyne agreed to settle £1,500 on each child of the marriage as it came of age, but not more than £4,000 if the number exceed two. Sir Timothy agreed to build a mansion house on the plantation for Thomas and Judith of the same dimensions as the free school near Speights Bay, only "the cellars and conveniences" which were under the free school to be adjoining the new house. Col. Alleyne agreed to furnish bullet tree beams 24 feet in length for the house and sufficient timber for making the doors and windows. The old Great House on the plantation was to be pulled down and the materials used again. The boundaries of the plantation were as follows:—East on a broad path leading from other lands of Sir Timothy to Mr. William Walker's plantation, north on lands of the said Walker, and on lands of Mr. Johnson to the bottom of the gulley, west on Robert Maxwell, Thomas Plunkett George Gray and John Haywood, south to the bottom of the great gulley, on lands of Henry Clinckett and on other lands of Sir Timothy, which was formerly of Cap. James Clinckett, then in possession of Sir Timothy. This plantation was afterwards known as *Four Hills* and took its name from its situation.

Thomas Alleyne succeeded his father at Mount Alleyne, St.

James, Barbados. He was Member of the General Assembly for St. James 1704—1706.

In the Barbados census Oct. and Nov. 1715 St. James: The Honourable Thomas Alleyne Esq., 8 men. 6 women, 2 boys, 1 girl. From an old book at Tissington Hall Co. Derby, the following is taken: Thomas Alleyne, aged 20 years and 3 mo. and Judith Thornhill aged 21 and 4 mos. were joined together in the holy state of matrimony at St. Peters, Barbados, by the Rev. Zachary Legrand, (Legard) minister of the parish of St. Peter's, Barbados, on the 5th of July 1688. They had 9 children. the youngest born 30 Jan 1704, married Littleton Poyntz Meynell, of Bradley Co. Derby. Her daughter Mary, married William Fitz-Herbert. great-grandfather of the wife of Sir John Gay Newton Alleyne.

Record taken from a stone in the middle isle of St. Dunstan's in the East, London.

Here lies the body of Mr. Denzie Alleyne, son of the Honble Brigadr Thomas Alleyne Esq. Of the Island of Barbados in America, who departed this life The 3rd day of March 1712/13 In the 16th year of his age. Here lies the body of Mr. Thomas Alleyne another Son of the said Honourable Brigadier Thomas Alleyne Who departed this life the 20 Of December 1715 aged 20 years. Also the body of Mr. Robert Johnstoun Esq. of the Island of Barbados, who departed this Life the 3rd of March 1720 aetatis suæ. 19.

Denzie Alleyne, son of Thos Alleyne of the island of Barbados, Esq., apprenticed to Richard Filden, Citizen and embroiderer of London, 3 Dec. 1712. Consideration £200.

Children of Thomas Alleyne [4] and Judith Thornhill.

7.   i.   ABEL [5], born 1689 in Barbados. Died 1727 Married Elizabeth Booth dau of Sir William Booth of Barbados.

8.   ii.   TIMOTHY. born 1691 at Barbados. Buried 3 March 1722. Married 12 Feb. 1713 Elizabeth (Buttals) Holder.

     iii.   THOMAS born 27 Oct. 1695. Died 20 Dec. 1715 aged 20 yrs. Buried in St. Dunstan's in the East, London.

     iv.   DENZIE born 1696/7 Died 5 March 1712/13 aged 15 yrs. Buried in St. Dunstan's in the East, London.

9.   v.   REYNOLD. born 23 Jan. 1699 Died 17 June 1749, Married Elizabeth Price 12 Nov. 1721.

10.   vi.   JOHN. born 1 Jan. 1702, Died Oct. 1737 in London, Married 1st Mary Peers, Married 2nd Mary Alleyne 15 Jan. 1736/7.

     vii.   JUDITH. born 30 Jan. 1703, Married Littleton Poyntz Meynell of Bradley, Co. Derby, England.

     viii.   LUCY. died 8 Aug. 1703 at St. James Barbados.

Will of Thomas Alleyne [4] of the parish of St. James, Barbados, dated 1 June 1713. To be decently interred by my father's, without any needless ceremony or extraordinary expense. It is my will and charge that whatsoever of my father's will (father's will not in the records in Barbados) shall be remaining unperformed at the time of my death, be duly observed and punctually complyed with as it becomes due.

Dear and loving wife Judith Alleyne, all her jewels, one-half of all my plate (except my Monteth, that I give particularly to my son Abel) Household stuff, the new charriott and furniture, with four of the best horses which usually draw it. The use of my dwelling-house, house negroes etc. of *Mount Alleyne* Plantation, at the plantation charge. £200 current money p. ann. this being only a legacy I leave her in remembrance of me over and above her joynter settled by a certain deed in lieu and full recompense of dower upon our intermarriage, bearing date the thirty day of June 1688.

To son Timothy Alleyne and daughter (Judith) £50 each.

To son Thomas Alleyne, my Four Hills Plantation Etc. when he shall attain the full age of 21 years, which is on the 27 day of Oct. 1716. Also £80 p. ann. during his minority and one of the negroe boys, etc.

To son Reynold Alleyne when he attain the age of 21 years which will be the 23rd day of January 1720. My Mount Alleyne Plantation, etc. Also £60 p. ann. for his education and maintenance until he attains the age of 18 years and then £80 untill the age of 21 years. "Tis my will and meaning that after my said son Reynold shall be possesst of my said Mount Alleyne Plantation, that he shall have nothing to do with the dwelling-house farther than by his mother's permission, during her continuing a widow. I having before given her the use of it."

To son John when he attain the age of 21 years which will be on ye 1st day of January 1722, £3,000. Also £50 current money of England p. ann. for his education and maintenance in England till he goes to the University of Oxford or Cambridge (he did not go to either) and then the sum of £80 like money p. ann. during his minority.

To daughter Judith Alleyne when she shall attain the age of 18 years, which will be on the 30th Jan. 1721, £2,520. Also £100 paid her mother for her maintenance and education p. ann. Also her nurse Philips with all her increase which she now hath or shall have. Mulatto Billy, Young Jean (Ubballi's child) and Indian Gabriel.

I give and bequeath to all mine and my wife's brothers and sisters, each of them a ring of 25s price.

To my cousin Edward Skeete £50 when he attains the age of 21 years.

To niece Ann Strode £10 to buy her a suit of mourning.

To son Abel Alleyne all the rest and residue of estate real and personal and mixed not already bequeathed.

Wife Judith Alleyne and son Abel Alleyne guardians of my children during their minority.

Son Abel Alleyne sole executor with this charge, that he be particularly tender and careful of his mother, and always see that her annuity be punctually complyed with and paid during her widow-hood. Signed Thomas Alleyne.

Witnesses: Charles Staughan. Tho: Ward, Samuel Treasurer. Proved 21 May 1717. (Barbados Records Vol. 4. pp 132.)

The Honourable Brigadier Thomas Alleyne died 10 Feby. 1717 aged 52 and was buried in the family vault at St. James Church, Barbados. His widow, Judith Alleyne, did not long survive him, and was buried in the same vault on 30 April 1717.

5. REYNOLD ALLEYNE[4] (*second son of Abel[3], Reynold[2], Richard[1],*) Born 1672. Buried 2 Oct. 1722, Honourable Reinold Alleyne Esq. buried at St. James, Barbados. Married Elizabeth Isabella daughter and co-heiress of John Gay of Dymocks, Barbados. Reynold Alleyne was seated at Four Hills, Barbados. Member of the Assembly for St. Andrew and Chief Justice of the Bridge Court of Barbados. His younger brother, Benjamin Alleyne, left him by Will his plantation Mount Standfast, St. James.

Barbados census taken Oct. and Nov. 1715. Reynold Alleyne aged 43, John Alleyne aged 20, Reynold Alleyne aged 9, Able Alleyne aged 18, Thomas Alleyne aged 7, Iszabella aged 14, Christian Alleyne aged 12.

Children :

11. i. JOHN ALLEYNE, Born 23 Dec. 1695. Buried at Bath Abbey 20 April 1730. Married Mary Terrill, 24 Nov. 1718.

ii. ELIZABETH ALLEYNE, Born 18 April, 1697. Married George Forster of Forster Hall Barbados. Eliz ye daughter of Capt. Reynold and Isabella Alleyne, christened 18 April 1697 at St. James Barbados.

12. iii. ABEL ALLEYNE, Bapt. 16 Feb. 1698/9 at St. James, Barbados, Died 1747. Married 16 July 1719 Mary Woodbridge.

iv. ISABELLA ALLEYNE, Born 1701. Married Joseph Gibbes of Plum Tree, Barbados.

v. CHRISTIAN ALLEYNE, Born 1703 Died 22 Feb. 1780 aged 77 years in Barbados Married John Gibbes of the Castle, Barbados. In St George's Church Barbados, is a fine marble oval surmounted by an urn wreathed and with a shield of arms in the centre. Arms : Argent, three battle axes sable. (Gibbes) : impaling : Per Chevron Gules and Ermine in chief two lions heads erased Or. (Alleyne) Sacred to the memory of Christian Gibbes Consort of John Gibbes Daughter of the Honourable Reynold Alleyne (34 lines) The Baronetcy of Gibbes of Barbados was created in the person of Philip Gibbes 30 May 1774, great-grandson of Philip Gibbes who who settled in Barbados In 1635. (Monumental Inscriptions of B. W. I. Archer p 373)

13. vi. REYNOLD ALLEYNE Born 1706. Died 17 Aug. 1735 at St. James, Barbados. Married 30 Oct 1729 Elizabeth Ward.

14. vii. THOMAS ,, Born 1707. Buried 9 Nov. 1753 Married 1st. Lucy Dottin " 2nd Susanna Gibbes

viii RUTH ,, Bapt 20 Aug. 1708 at St. James, Barbados. Married John Holder of Joes River, Barbados
(1) *John Alleyne Holder.*
(2) *Henry Evans Holder,* Married Abel Dudley 6th dau of Abel Alleyne of Mount Standfast, Barbados.
(3) *Isabella Christian Holder.*
(4) *Anna Maria Holder.*

13

Will of 5. Reynold Alleyne [4] dated 18 March 1720.
Reynold Alleyne of the Parish of St. Andrew, Barbados. To
daughter Elizabeth Forster wife of George Forster Esq. negro woman
Frances. To daughter Isabella Gibbes wife of Joseph Gibbes 2
negro girls. To dau Christian Gibbes wife of John Gibbes, negro
woman. To dau Ruth Alleyne when 21 years old or at marriage
£2,000 and £50 more to buy her a horse and saddle. Also a negro
woman. To son Reynold Alleyne at age 21 years £4,000 and negro
woman and her children. To son Thomas Alleyne at age of 21
years £4,000 and negro woman and her children.

Son Reynold Alleyne to be paid £40 every three months for
his maintenance and accommodation in dwelling house. Also accommodation for his horse and negros. "My own horse and best
saddle to be delivered to him immediately after my decease." Son
Thomas Alleyne to be educated in England until he attain the age
of 21 yrs. "I leave it to the discretion of his guardians to have him
bound to a merchant, attorney-at-law or bred at the university" to
be paid for by the estate.

"I will and appoint that my daughter Ruth Alleyne be rendered the care and discretion of my Mother Elizabeth Gay and do appoint that she be allowed out of my whole estate £175 p. annum
current money of this Island to be paid Quarterly into the hands of
my said Mother, which is for the maintenance and accommodation of
her negroes which is to continue untill her legacy aforesaid becomes
due, not doubting but if that is more than will bring her up handsomely, My Mother will preserve it to be an addition to her fortune. If my said Mother should dye before she attain the age of
21 years or day of marriage, then I desire my Daughter Alleyne
(my son John's wife) to take the trouble of bringing up my said
Daughter Ruth and I charge my son John Alleyne that he supply
my place to her." To each grandchild £50. To brother Samuel
Osborne gold headed cane. Mother Elizabeth Alleyne £50. All
sons and sons-in-law, daughters and daughters-in-law £25 for mourning. The same to brothers and sisters and nephew Timothy Alleyne
and his wife. Guardians of the children: Brothers Benjamin and
Samuel Osborne. Sons John and Abel Alleyne. All residue of
estate to son John Alleyne. Son John Alleyne sole executor and
charge him to be particularly careful of his brothers and sisters and
to be a father to them all as well as a brother. Signed Reynold
Alleyne.

Witnesses: John Wilde. Thomas Scott. John Harrison.
Proved 16 Nov. 1722. (Barbados Records Vol. 6 p 486.)

Letter from the Hon. Reynold Alleyne Esq. refusing post of
Chief Judge of Precinct of Saint Michael, Barbados.
To the Honourable the President,
Sir,
I need not take any pains to convince Your Honour how great
a misfortune it is to live in a constant ill state of health. The in-
conveniency is so great even in my private affairs, that I find myself

14

under a necessity of banishing all thoughts of acting in any publick Post whatever; I am very well assur'd I should never be able to discharge my Duty to my Country with the least Pleasure or satisfaction to my self, since I can have no hopes of exerting my self with that Vigour and application, which is so indispensably neces-sary to every man, who values his own Reputation, or has the interest of his Countrey at heart.

I think my selfe under a great many obligations for the Honour designed me, and tho' with the greatest reluctancy, yet I must beg leave to be excused from obeying Your Commands, and am Your Honour's

Most obedient Humble servant,

REYNOLD ALLEYNE.

Four Hills,
December ye 12th, 1721.

6. BENJAMIN ALLEYNE [4] (*3rd son of Abel* [3] *Reynold* [2] *Richard.* [1]) Married 1st Arabella Pilgrim of St. George, Bdos. Married 2nd Anne Kirton 17 Nov. 1710 at Christ Church, Bdos. He was of Mount Standfast, St. James, Bdos. Hon. Benjamin Alleyne Esq. Buried April 1721 in vault at St. James, Barbados.

Barbados Census Oct. and Nov. 1715 :—

Benjamin Alleyne Esq. St. James. 14 men. 5 Women. 4 boys.
Child of the second marriage :—

    i. BENJAMIN ALLEYNE, born 2 July 1713 Bapt. 3 July St. James, Barbados, Died 3 Aug 1713 Buried 4 Aug 1713 in Vault St James.

Will of Benjamin Alleyne dated 1 June 1715. Pr. 18 July 1721.

Benjamin Alleyne of the parish of Saint James, and Island of Barbados. Debts and funerall expenses be first paid. Wife two best beds and furniture for two chambers. All plate, jewells charriot and four such horses as she shall chuse. Her accommodation at Mount Standfast Plantation, the keeping of her foure horses with sufficient green meat and corne, with the use of all my dwelling house, household stuff and negroes. To kinsman Edward Skeete the eldest, £150 English money and £10 Barbados money for mourning. To nieces Elizabeth and Lucy Parsons at age of 18 years £500. To kinsman Timothy Alleyne, son of my brother Thomas Alleyne, £500 money of England. The rest and residue of my Estate both reall and personall, to my brother Reynold Alleyne and his heirs, and doe appoint him my sole executor.
Dated 1 June 1715. Signed Benjamin Alleyne.
Witnesses : Jno. Glasgow. John Reese. Thos. Salmon. (Barbados Records Vol. 6. p 252.)

Benjamin Alleyne was buried at St. James, Barbados, on 22 April 1721.

7. ABEL ALLEYNE [5] (*Eldest son of Thomas* [4] *Abel* [3] *Reynold* [2] *Richard* [1].) Born 1689 at Barbados. Died 1727.

Married Elizabeth, only daughter and sole heiress of Sir William Booth of Black Jacks, Barbados. No issue. Madame Elizabeth Alleyne aged 49 died of a jaundice. Buried 6 Nov. 1746 at St. James, Barbados.

Allen or Alleyne (aged 16) at Trinity Coll. Cambridge. 5 July 1705. Son of Thomas, of Barbados. M.I. School, Blackheath, Kent. Matri. 1705; B.A. 1708—9.

Abel Alleyne owned Turners Hall, Barbados and Squerries Court, Co. Kent. England. He was Colonel of the Hole Town regiment, and Member of the Assembly for St. Andrews, Barbados. Barbados Census Oct. and Nov. 1715. Col. Abel Alleyne Esq. St. James. 14 men. 2 boys. 8 girls.

On his marriage in 1713 to Elizabeth Booth, Abel Alleyne purchased from Dame Rosamond Booth, widow of Sir William Booth and Mother of Elizabeth, three plantations in St. James, St. Peter, and St. Andrew, containing together four hundred and ninety five acres of land with two dwellinghouses, two stone windmills, two boilinghouses, and a large number of slaves, cattle. and sheep for £11,000 currency. He settled these plantations on his wife to secure to her a jointure of £400 per annum if he predeceased her.

The plantation in St. James was described in the deeds as bounding on lands of John Scott, John Harrison, Arthur Slingsby, Henry Taitt, Thomas Fullerton (then in possession of Samual Osborne), Francis Gamball. and Samuel Richards. The plantation in St. Peter was said to be bounding on lands of Hon. Reynold Alleyne, Thomas Rollston, John Gibbons, Jacob Scott, Henry Baker, Melisha Holder, William Davis, and John Scott; and the plantation in St. Andrew was adjoining lands of Richard Edwards, Senior, of George Walker, William Benjamin, and Thomas Merrick, deceased. Reference to Mayo's Map of Barbados (1717—1721) shows that the plantations in St. James and St. Peter were situated about where Sion Hill and Black Bess plantations are to be found on modern maps, and are almost certainly identical with those estates.

In the will of Dame Rosamond Booth is mentioned Hon. Abel Alleyne, son-in-law, wife Elizabeth Booth. Debts to be paid, one of £4,000 to son Alleyne and his wife, by her (Booth) bond. Died 1756. (Dame Rosamond Booth was daughter of Littleton Meynell, of Bradley, Co. Derby, Eng.)

Will of 7. Abel Alleyne[5] . Dated April 6, 1726.

I Abel Alleyne of the Parish of St. George, Hanover Sq. London, England. All debts paid and all real estate in England sold. Wife Elizabeth £200 a year. Directions for disposal of the estate if his wife has a child, if no child, then real estate in Barbados and use of personal estate to nephew Thomas Alleyne son of late brother Timothy Alleyne and his heirs. If he should die then to brother Reynold Alleyne (Abel's brother). If he should die then to his (Abel's) brother John. If he should die to nephew Thomas and his heirs. Poor of parish of St. Andrew Barbados £20 a year. Nephew

16

Thomas Alleyne to pay each of his two uncles Reynold and John Alleyne £2,000 a piece when he shall arrive at age of 21, and to his Aunt Judith Meynell £1,000.

When said Nephew Thomas Alleyne comes of age he to release all right to lands which his uncles Reynold and John Alleyne are in possession and occupation of. namely estates called Mount Alleyne and the Four Hills, and "in case he shall think fit to disturb them he shall be obliged to pay his uncle Reynold £500 and his uncle John £1,000 above their respective legacys." Very minute instructions as to what shall be done with the estate in case of the death of his nephew Thomas Alleyne. Executors.—John Walter, Littleton Meynell. Brothers Reynold and John Alleyne. To have £50 apiece for their trouble. Signed Abel Alleyne.

Witnesses. Samuel Forster. Thomas Oliver. Henry Stocker. Codicil 6 July 1726. Wife £2.000 English money. Had given brothers Reynold and John Alleyne £2,000 apiece. Left them £1,500 additional. Estate in Surrey to be sold. Brother Meynell, my uncle Walters and George Jeffreys Esq. to sell estate. Codicil sealed and published 7 July 1727 in presence of Francis Hall. William Wood. John Murry.
To friend Mrs. Margaret Mathews 100 gs. Coachman Ned and my man Will 5 gs. to man Frank all clothes, linnen, Wiggs. To Susan Smith 5 gs. All servants 40s each. To poor of Albury 5 gs. Signed 8 July 1727. Abel Alleyne. Proved 20 March 1727. (P.C.C. Farrant 1727, 8). Also proved at Barbados. (Barbados Records Vol. 2 p 469).

Will of Elizabeth Alleyne wife of 7 Abel Alleyne [5] Dated 15 Oct 1746. Elizabeth Alleyne of the Parish of St. Andrews, Barbados. Widow of the late Coll. Abel Alleyne. Executors to sell house in Brook St. St. James's Westminster, London, and to sell all pictures except family pictures. To nephew Thomas Alleyne, his own and his sister's pictures in one frame. Also silver Montiff that was my grandfather Alleyne's. To friend Samuel Forster of Gt Britain Esq. £500. To friend and good servant, Susannah Smith £100. All Real, personal and mixed estate to trustees and executors to dispose of as she directs. Sugar Plantation to nephew Thomas Alleyne. If nephew Thomas Alleyne dies, estate to go to niece Mary Fitz Herbert of kingdom of Gt. Britain. Executors: Rowland Blackman, Robert Warren, George Walker, and John Gay Alleyne Esq. Signed Elizabeth Alleyne.
Witnesses: James Bruce, Joseph Gamble, Reynold Skeete, Richard Richards, William Duke.
Proved 12 Nov. 1746. (Barbados Records. (Vol. 26. p. 28.)

(To be Continued.)

ALLEYNE OF BARBADOS

(SECOND INSTALMENT).

CONTRIBUTED BY LOUISE R. ALLEN.

8. TIMOTHY ALLEYNE.⁵ (*second son of Thomas,*¹ *Abel,*³ *Reynold,*² *Richard*¹) of Black Jack's, Barbados, was born in 1691. He matriculated at Queen's College, Oxford, on 27 March 1708 at the age of seventeen, and was admitted a student of the Middle Temple. On 12 February 1713-4 he married at St. James, Barbados, Elizabeth Buttals (born 1675) daughter of Charles and Mary Buttals. Mary Buttals (born 1652) had married first . . . . . Holder, and secondly Charles Buttals. Their second daughter Jane Buttals who was 37 in 1715 married Henry Peers, her junior by six years. The Will of Mary Buttals of Morgan's, St. George, dated 21 May 1718, was proved in 1720. In it she mentions her grandson, Thomas Alleyne, to whom she left one-half of Morgan's plantation, and also her daughter, Elizabeth, wife of Timothy Alleyne.

In a Census taken in Barbados in the months of October and November 1715, are mentioned Timothy Alleyne Esq. aged 24, his wife Elizabeth aged 40, and their son Thomas, then one year old.

Children of Timothy Alleyne and Elizabeth, his wife :—

15.   i. THOMAS ALLEYNE,⁶ born 25th, baptised 27th April 1714 at St. James, Barbados. Married Jane Rolleston and died at Barbados in 1752.

     ii. MARY ALLEYNE, born 6th April 1719, and baptised at St. James, Barbados, on the following day, being "sick of fits." She married first Joseph Ball on 3 June 1735, secondly Robert Hooper on 7 January 1745, and thirdly Jonas Maynard of Passage, Barbados, who was Member of Assembly for St. Michael. Jonas Maynard died 3rd August 1781 aged 86, and Mary Maynard predeceased him dying sometime before the year 1777.

Timothy Alleyne was buried at St. James, Barbados, on 3rd March, 1722, having died the previous day "of a surfeit" at the age of thirty years. By his Will dated 27 February 1721, Timothy Alleyne gave his wife, Elizabeth his coach and six horses, her riding horse, plate, jewels, etc., besides her accommodation in his dwelling-house and £100 per annum. To his daughter Mary at age of 18, £2,500. To his son Thomas Alleyne all his real estate etc. Executors : Wife Elizabeth Alleyne, and Brothers Abell, Reynold, and John Alleyne, who were also to be guardians of his infant children. Signed Timothy Alleyne.

Witnesses : John Alleyne, Richard Towne. William Paterson. Proved at Pilgrim 16 Nov. 1722. (Barbados Records Vol. 6. p. 489.)

Will dated 10 June 1728 of Elizabeth Alleyne of the Parish of

---

In the first instalment of this compilation a mistake occurs at page 106. The text reads as follows :—
"This plantation is said to be the family estate known as Mount Alleyne in the XVII and XVIII centuries." For "Mount Alleyne" please read : "Turner Hall."

18

St. James, Barbados, widow of Timothy Alleyne. [5] In case my son, Thomas Alleyne, refuses to confirm gift of negro slaves by my husband Timothy Alleyne to our daughter Mary. she is to have £150 out of the estate for each negro Thomas refuses to give her. To daughter Mary at age of 16 or marriage £1.500. also an Indian Cabinet and dressing-box. calico worked counter-pin, half of my jewels, plate etc. Appoint friend Mrs. Ann Richards and niece Mary Alleyne to divide the same. To my brother Henry Peers Esq. £25. To Mrs. Ann Richards the wife of Samuel Richards £50 to buy a piece of plate. To Henry Risbon £50 for care of my son. To brother John Alleyne two silver cups with handles marked E.B., and £10. To my brother Reynold Alleyne £10. I give my negro women Bess and Katie their freedom and £5. To ten poor housekeepers 40s. To son Thomas Alleyne all my real estate. If both children, Thomas and Mary die, their estates to be equally divided between my nephews Peers and Thomas Alleyne. sons of brother John Alleyne. Executors. Brothers Coll. Henry Peers, Reynold Alleyne, and John Alleyne Esqs., Kinsmen Mr. John and Abel Alleyne Esq. Signed E. Alleyne. Witnesses—Francis Skeete, Henry Rishton, Wm. Woollvin.

Proved at Pilgrim 18 July 1730. (Barbados Records Vol. 34. p. 496.)

9. REYNOLD ALLEYNE,[5] (*fifth son of Thomas*,[4] *Abel*,[3] *Reynold*,[2] *Richard*[1]), born 23 Jan. 1699. was educated at Westminster School. The school records show : Alleyne, Reynold. fifth son of Thomas Alleyne of the parish of St. James in the island of Barbados; B. Adm. (aged 15) Sept. 1715: in under school list 1716; inherited the plantation of Mount Alleyne in Barbados. Mar. a daughter of Lawrence Price; d. in Barbados June 30, 1749. (The Records of the Old Westminsters, Vol. I. pp. 14. G. F. R. Barker & Alan H. Stenning.)

He was married 12 Nov. 1721 at S. Michael's Parish Church to Elizabeth Price, daughter of Lawrence Price.

The marriage certificate reads : Reynold Alleyne Esq. of St. James Parish and Miss Elizabeth Price of Christ Church parish married 12 Nov. 1721 by Mr. Gordon.

Reynold Alleyne was Member of the Assembly for St. James 1723—1725, 1734—1744.

Children of Reynold and Elizabeth Alleyne :—

i. ELIZABETH ALLEYNE, Born 6 Feb. 1724 at Christ Church, Barbados. Married 2 Oct. 1740 at Christ Church, Barbados, John Newton of Newton's, Barbados, and Spittsbury Co. Dorset, Eng. and Abbots Bromley, Co., Staff. Eng.
John Newton, dying without issue, left Mount Alleyne and other property in Barbados, acquired by his marriage to Elizabeth Alleyne, to Sir John Gay Alleyne, Bart.

ii. JUDITH ALLEYNE Born 1727. She died unmarried 11 July 1763 aged 36, and was buried in Bristol Cathedral, Eng , where in the wall of the North Cloister is a marble memorial with the following inscription :—Sacred to the Memory of/Judith Alleyne/Daughter of Reynold Alleyne/of Mount Alleyne/in the Island of Barbados Esqr./who departed this life, July 11 1763/Aged 36 years.

1763 July 14. Judith Alleyne was buried and Funeral Sermon preached by the Precentor. (Bristol Cathedral Burial Register.)
Reynold Alleyne died in Barbados, 30 June 1749.

In Christ Church, Barbados, is a blue marble tablet with this inscription. Crest : Out of a ducal coronet a horse's head over a wreath and helmet. Arms : Per chevron gules and ermine two lions heads erased Or. Here lies interred the body of Reynold Alleyne of Mount Alleyne in the Parish of St. James Esq. who departed this Life the thirtieth Day of June Anno Domini 1749 aetatis 49.

The will dated 29 June 1749 of Reynold Alleyne[5] of the Parish of St. James. Barbados. To my daughter Judith Alleyne £2,000 to make her equall with my daughter Elizabeth Newton, wife of John Newton Esq.. to whom I gave the like sum upon her marriage with the said John Newton. My daughters Elizabeth Newton and Judith Alleyne to share equally in my real estate etc.

Executors—John Newton, son-in-law, Daughters Elizabeth Newton and Judith Alleyne. Signed Reynold Alleyne.

Witnesses. John Mower, Faithful Adams, Anthony Lynch.

Codicil. To wife Elizabeth Alleyne chariot and chariot horses, her living at Mount Alleyne, and one-third part of all money. Dated 29 June 1749. Signed Reynold Alleyne.

Witnesses. John Mower, Faithful Adams, Anthony Lynch.

Proved at Pilgrim Barbados, 11 July 1749, before H. Grenville.

Will of Elizabeth Hannay of Christ Church, Barbados, Widow. Dated 12 Nov. 1755. Entered 27 Nov. 1755. Proved 28 Sept. 1756 by John Newton Esq. Power reserved to the others.

£100 to Poor of Parish of Christ Church. Grand-daughter Judith Alleyne £100 a year and £12,000, plate, furniture, chariot and four horses. Mrs. Prudence Hart widow £6 a year. All residue to my grand-daughter Elizabeth wife of John Newton Esq. The latter and Judith Alleyne, Executors. Witnesses :—John Philips, Henry Durant. John Ramsey. (247 Glazier. Somerset House. London Eng.)

10. JOHN ALLEYNE[5] (*sixth son of Thomas,[4] Reynold,[3] Abel,[2] Richard[1]*) of Rock Hall, Barbados, was born 1 Jan. 1701/2. He married first Mary daughter and co-heiress of General Henry Peers, of Martin Castle. Barbados. She "died of a fever," and was buried 27 Oct. 1735 at St. James, Barbados, aged 29 years.

John Alleyne married secondly Mary, eldest daughter of his first cousin Abel Alleyne 15 Jan. 1737 at St. James, Barbados. She was 17 and he was 35 years old. His eldest son was almost her age.

Children of John Alleyne and Mary Peers, his wife :—

i. JUDITH ALLEYNE Married.........Fercharson of Sandy Lane.

ii. PEERS ALLEYNE, born 1724, Died Unmarried 1747 at Calebs, Barbados. He matriculated at Queen's College, Oxford, 12 March 1742/3 aged 18
Will of Peers Alleyne dated 24 July 1747. To sister Judith Alleyne £1000 at age of 20 years. To relation Thomas Alleyne of St. James, £2300. To friend John Eyre of Wynchester, Eng. Clerk, £300. To Friend and relation John Lyte Esq. £100. To six friends to be appointed and approved by executors £20 apiece for mourning

20

Servant Thomas Osborne £50 All real estate to brother Thomas Alleyne at 21. Executors: John Lyte. relation Thomas Alleyne. Uncle Reynold Alleyne, until brother Thomas is 21 years, then he to be sole executor. To executors and friends John Gay Alleyne and Dr. Reynold Alleyne £20 apiece to buy mourning. Signed Peers Alleyne. Witnesses: Reynold Alleyne, Joseph Blackman, Thomas Cantwell Walter Bennet. Proved at the Mount Plantation 29 Aug. 1747.
(Barbados Records Vol. 26 pp 160).

16 iii. THOMAS ALLEYNE Born 1728. Married 1st Hannah Downe-, married 2nd Margaret, widow of Lieut Alexander Mc Carthy.

In 1775 John Alleyne went to England and died soon after arriving in London. A notice of his death appeared in the Gentlemen's Magazine. "Col. John Alleyne of Bockhall (Rock Hall) Barbados, died in Gracechurch Street. Lately arrived. 29 Nov. 1737.

Will of John Alleyne dated 22 Aug. 1737.

John Alleyne of the Parish of St. Peter's, Barbados. To be "buried in a prudent frugal manner." Gives his wife Mary Alleyne her riding horse and saddle, gold watch and chain, diamond rings. locket and jewels etc. besides slaves; and her accommodation in his mansion house. Gives executors power to buy and sell sugar, slaves, etc. To son Thomas Alleyne at 21 years £1,800, also negroes. To daughter Judith Alleyne at 18 years £1,200, also negroes. His children to be maintained and educated. Residue of estate to son Peers Alleyne. Executors and guardians of minor children, Honourable Henry Peers, Abel Alleyne Esq. my father-in-law. Reynold Alleyne Esq., my brother, until son Peers Alleyne is of age. Signed John Alleyne.

Proved 14 Jan. 1737 (Barbados Records Vol. 27. p. 371).

11. JOHN ALLEYNE[5] (eldest son of Reynold,[1] Abel,[3] Reynold[2] Richard[1]). Born 23 Dec. 1695. Married 24 Nov. 1718 in Bedford St., Covent Garden, London, Mary, daughter of William Terrill of Cabbage Tree Hall. sole heiress of her mother. Rebecca, daughter and co-heiress of Colonel Thomas Spiar of Mount Standfast, by Mary, daughter and co-heiress of John Turner, of the Three Houses in the Thickets, by his wife Mary, daughter of   Skeet. and relict of Colonel Reynold Allen. Mary Alleyne died in 1742 and was buried at St. Nicholas Church, Guilford, Surrey, England.

Cabbage Tree Hall was so named because it had a double row of "cabbage trees" (royal palms) at the sides of the drive. which were destroyed in the hurricane of 1780. and later it was called Alleynedale Hall. It was supposed to be haunted, because Mr. William Terrill committed suicide by cutting his throat in one of the servant's rooms. He walked up the stairs and opened doors.

John Alleyne inherited from his father the seat at Four Hills, Barbados. He received his education at Magdalen College, Oxford. Matric. 14 Jan. 1711—12 aged 15 and received honorary degree of M.A. Admitted to Middle Temple 29 April 17 ?

On his return to Barbados, although frequently pressed to take part in public affairs he declined to do so. He died at Bath, and was buried at Bath Abbey on 20 April 1730.

21

Children of John and Mary Alleyne :—

i. REYNOLD ALLEYNE Died aged 5 years in Barbados.

ii. MARY ALLEYNE Born 6 Nov. 1721. Died 16 March 1742. Married
Capt. Charles Knowles 23 Dec 1740.
Capt. Charles Knowles of Lovell Hill, Wingfield, Berkshire. Capt.
of the "Litchfield" belonging to Sir Chaloner Ogle's Squadron.
M. P. for Galton, Surrey, 1749—52. Later Rear Admiral of Great
Britain. Created baronet 31 Oct. 1765. He died 1777.
Their child EDWARD KNOWLES Born 1742 Died Jan 1762. Lost at
sea while in command of H. M Ship Peregrine in a storm off Belle
Isle.
At St. Nicholas Church, Guildford, Surrey, on a marble tablet
against a pier in the nave: To the Memory of Mrs. Mary Knowles,
daughter of John and Mary Alleyne, of Barbados, and wife of
Capt. Charles Knowles, who departed this life March the 16th
1741/2 in the 22nd year of her age. Prov. 31 verse 26. "When
she opened her mouth it was with wisdom and in her tongue
was the law of kindness." Below in relief is a small figure recum-
bent, a child in her lap, and below "jurando consumior."
Admiral Sir Charles Knowles married Maria Magdalena Theresa
Bouquet, a lady of an old Lorraine family, as his second wife ; their
son was Sir Charles Henry Knowles second Bart. born 24 Aug. 1754
in Jamaica, when Sir Charles was Governor. Sir Charles Henry
Knowles died 28 Nov. 1831 aged 77 years. Buried at St. Nicholas
Church, Guilford, Surrey, Eng.

17. iii. SIR JOHN GAY ALLEYNE6 Born 28th April 1724. Buried 7 Dec.
1801 at St. James, Barbados. Married first Christian Dottin
Married secondly Jane Abel Alleyne.

iv. REBECCA ALLEYNE Born 11 Oct. 1725 St. James. Barbados,
Died 4 May 1764 Married William. Viscount Folkstone 5 Sept 1751.
Hon. William Bouverie, second Lord Folkstone was born 26 Feb.
1725. Created, 31 Oct 1765, Baron Pleydell Bouverie of Coleshill,
Berkshire, and Earl of Radnor. He died 28 June 1776,
Lord Folkstone married first 14 Jan. 1747/8 Harriet only daughter
of Sir Mark Stuart Pleydell, Bart. of Coleshill Berks. Had only
son Jacob 2nd Earl. Rebecca Alleyne was his second wife.
He married thirdly 22nd July 1765 Anne, Dowager Lady Fever-
sham, daughter of Sir Thomas Hales, Bart. They had two sons.
both of whom died in infancy.
Rebecca Alleyne and Lord Folkstone had several childen.

v. REYNOLDIA ALLEYNE, Died aged 6 yrs. Buried at Hambledon,
Surrey, Eng.

Will of *John Alleyne*5 dated 8 May, proved 15 Dec. 1730.

John Alleyne in the Parish of St. James in the Island of Barbados. To wife Mary Alleyne besides her jointure all plate, household goods, jewels, her living and accommodation in dwellinghouse
at Four Hills, chariot, chaise, coach horses, her riding-horse, furniture, also her mourning. Negro man Harry.
To three daughters Mary, Rebecca. Renoldia at their ages of
21 or mariage £1,500, also one negro woman cach. Their education
and maintenance out of the whole estate. Gives executors authority
to sell plantation called *Christopher Jackson's* to pay debts. Owned
plantations called *Bawdens, Four Hills* and *Skeets*. Order "debt
due to me from my brother Abel Alleyne to be at 8% interest untill
tis paid." Son John Gay Alleyne all rest and residue of estate.
Wife Mary Alleyne executrix. Executors in trust until son John Gay
Alleyne is of age : Father, Honourable William Terrill, my uncle

Samuel Osbourne, Brothers Abel, Reynold, and Thomas Alleyne, my kinsmen Reynold and John Alleyne. Signed, John Alleyne. Witnesses : Hen. Peers, Thomas Lake, H. Gibbes. Proved at Pilgrim 15 Dec. 1730 by Doctor Higinbotham Gibbes. Signed. Hen. Worsley. (Barbados Records Vol. 34 p. 555.)

Will of Mary Alleyne wife of *John Alleyne*,[5] dated March 1741, proved 19 Dec. 1745.

Mary Alleyne in the Parish of St. James, Barbados.

"All debts and funeral expenses be paid by selling my plate which I purchased from my dear Mr. Alleyne's creditors." To son John Gay Alleyne, to son-in-law Charles Knowles Esq. and to daughter Mary Knowles his wife, and daughter Rebecca Alleyne, mourning. To daughter Mary Knowles diamond earings. To daughter Rebecca, negro wench Peggy, also all my finger rings and half my wearing apparel. The other half with £5 to faithful servant Sarah Dix. Money now at interest in the hands of friend and relation Tobias Frere Esq. be kept in his hands until son John Gay Alleyne attains his age of 21 years. Bequeath one quarter part thereof to son-in-law Charles Knowles and my daughter Mary his wife and their heirs. Another one quarter part to daughter Rebecca. The remaining one half part to son John Gay Alleyne and his heirs. To son John Gay Alleyne the place in Gloucestershire called *Langley* and all rest and residue of estate. Recommends son John Gay Alleyne to care of worthy friend and relation Sir Mark Pleydel. Daughter Rebecca Alleyne recommended to care of her brother-in-law and sister (Capt. Charles Knowles and Mary Alleyne Knowles) Negro man Harry and old negro woman named Pothena not to be sold but to be cared for by children.

Executors : Friend and relation Sir Mark Pleydel, son-in-law Charles Knowles Esq., my brother Joseph Terrill Esq., friend and relation Tobias Frere Esq. Signed Mary Alleyne. Witnesses : Elizabeth Alleyne, Eliza Barwick. (Barbados Records Vol. 36 p. 44).

12. ABEL ALLEYNE[5] (*second son of Reynold*,[4] *Abel*,[3] *Reynold*,[2] *Richard*,[1]) born and bapt. 16 Feb. 1699 at St. James, Barbados. Married 16 July 1719 at St. Philip, Barbados, Mary daughter of Honourable Dudley Woodbridge, of *Kensington* and *Mount Standfast*, Barbados, and Jane Willey, relict of Edward Willey.

Dudley Woodbridge was Jane Willey's fourth husband.

Children of Abel and Mary Alleyne :—

    i.   MARY ALLEYNE Bapt. 4 June 1720 at St. Michael, Barbados. Died in Boston, Mass., and is supposed to be buried under King's Chapel, though there is no record of her either under the Chapel or in the graveyard adjoining.
Married first 15 Jan. 1737 at St. James, Barbados, John Alleyne[5] of Rock Hall, Barbados, fourth son of Thomas Alleyne[4] her cousin as his second wife. She was 17 and he was 35 years old. His oldest child was almost her age. No issue. He died in London 29 Nov. 1737. She married secondly Sept. 2 1750 Peter Chardon of Boston Mass. No issue. Her portrait was in possession of Mr. Clarke Gamble of Toronto, Canada.

23

In a number of the '*Massachusetts Gazette*' for Jan. 1767, may be found the following obituary notice from '*The Gazette*' of Dominica, W.I. Charlottetown, Oct 1766. "Last night about 11 o'clock died here, Peter Chardon, Esq., barrister-at law. It is hard to say whether a thorough knowledge of his profession or the unblemished integrity and nonour with which he acted was the greatest. In him were joined the finished scholar and the complete gentleman, and he is not only universally lamented as such, but as a real loss to the colony." (Ms. of Mr. W. G. Brooks, New England Historical & Genealogical Register, Vol. 8, p. 258.)

Peter Chardon was the son of an eminent Boston merchant, belonging to one of the French protestant families which had taken refuge in America after the revocation of the Edict of Nantes. The family residence was on Bowdoin Sq., on the spot where the Baptist Church now stands at the corner of Chardon St.

Peter Chardon and Sarah Colman married 6 Dec 1733 by Rev. Benj. Colman D. D. (Boston marriage record 1733-34).

Peter Chardon and Mary Alleyne married 2 Sept. 1750 at King's Chapel, Boston, Mass. (Boston Marriages 1700-51).

ii   REYNOLD ALLEYNE born 15 June 1721 and bapt. on the following day at St. Michael, Barbados. Buried 17 Jan. 1758 at St. James, Barbados. Married 16 July 1744 Christian Mercy Forster. No issue. She married secondly 6 Aug 1761 Jonas Maynard at Cnrist Church, Barbados.

Will of Reynold Alleyne dated 7 Sept. 1756. Of the Parish of St. James and Island of Barbados. To be buried in the family vault at St. James Church All my father's debts and all my own debts be paid out of Mount Standfast estate. To my dearly beloved and most affectionate wife, Christian Mercy Allyeue, all negro slaves, all plate, jewels, household goods, property, money etc. Be queath slaves Pretty Boy and Jenny to eldest son of friend John Denny Esq. and Eliza Denny wife. Wife £2,000. To much respected and esteemed Mother Mary Alleyne of New England £100 for mourning. To sister Jane Isabella Winston (Winslow) £400. To sister Benjamina Woodbridge Alleyne £400 To brother Thomas Alleyne £400. To brother Timothy Henry Peers Alleyne £500 and a negro man of £40 value to be bought out of the yard. To sister Abel Dudley Alleyne £500 and 2 negro girls of £25 value to be bought out of the yard. To sister Isabella Elizabeth Alleyne £400. To good friend Robert White £50 for mourning. To good friend Richard Denny £50 for mourning. To brother John Alleyne Esq. all the rest and residue of estate real and personal. I advise and direct him as a friend and tender brother that as soon as some difficulties may arise in the performance of this my will and testament and intention that on the decease of my respected Mother he sell the estate for its full value and make himself and his friends herein mentioned easy and satisfied that he may live with a calm breast and with a quiet mind. Executors and Executrix : Brother John Alleyne, friend John Collins Esq Wife Christian Mercy Alleyne.

Signed Reynold Alleyne.
Witnesses : Robert Ferchardson, John Waite.
Proved at Pilgrim 6 April 1758. (Barbados Records Vol. 3. p. 341).

iii. ABEL ALLEYNE, born 20 Sept. 1722, bapt. 22 Sept. 1722 at St. James, Barbados. Died of a malignant fever aged 16. Buried 2 Dec 1738 at St. James, Barbados.
Alleyne, Abel. 2nd son of Abel Alleyne of *Mount Standfast* Plantation, Barbados, and Boston, New England by Mary Woodbridge of Kensington, Barbados. B—Adm. (aged 8) Oct. 1730 : Left 1732. Died young. (Records of the Old Westminsters. Vol. I. 14).

iv.   DUDLEY ALLEYNE, born 2 Sept. 1724 in Barbados. The tradition in the family is that Dudley and Abel were lost at sea on their way

24

to school in England. I have not been able to get any further record of Dudley but evidently Abel was not lost at sea as the above record shows he was buried in Barbados.

v. JANE ISABELLA ALLEYNE, born 22 Oct. 1726, bapt. 23 Oct. 1726 at St. James, Barbados. Died in North or South Carolina, U.S A. Married 16 July 1745 Rev. Edward Winslow, at St. Philip, Barbados. Issue :—

    (i)   Jane Isabella Winslow, bapt. Nov. 1756.
    (ii)   Elizabeth   ,,   ,,   Sept. 1758.
    (iii)   Anne   ,,   ,,   Aug. 1760.
    (iv) { Catharine Isabella ,,   ,,   Feb. 1763. } Twins.
           { Isabella Catherine ,,   ,,   ,,   ,,

Rev. Edward Winslow, grandson of Col. Edward Winslow of Boston, Mass., born 8 Nov. 1722 in Boston Mass. Graduate of Cambridge University, England, 1741. Went to Barbados in 1754 then back to England 1754. Ordained Deacon and Priest 1754 by Bishop of London. While there appointed missionary to Stratford. Conn. Later went to Braintree, Mass. and officiated at Christ Church, then to New York City. In 1774 Chaplain of H.M.S. *Mercury* in Boston Bay. On 31 Oct. 1780 on returning from a funeral he expired on the steps of his house at the corner of Pearl and Cherry Sts. in New York City. His remains are entombed under the altar of St. George's Church, New York City. (Winslow Family. Holton Vol. I p. 61).

vi. BENJAMINA WOODBRIDGE ALLEYNE, born 20th and bapt. 21st Novem, ber 1728 at St. James, Barbado-. Died suddenly at Quincy-Mass., U.S.A. 19 Feb. 1782. Single. Called "Aunt Benjy."

vii. JOHN ALLEYNE, born 22 Jan. 1730 in Barbados. Married Elizabeth Fercharson daughter of Bowden Fercharson of St. James, Barbados. Alleyne, John brother of Abel (Q. V.) B. Adm. aged 16 ? (19) July 1749. In school List 1752. Married Elizabeth Ferguson. (Fercharson) The records of the Old Westminsters Vol. 1 p. 14) John Alleyne lived and died in Barbados. He was Captain of the Sea Service 1771.
Children of John and Elizabeth Alleyne :—

(1) ABEL ALLEYNE, Bapt 12 April 1752 at St. James. Buried 2 May 1752 at St James

(2) ELIZABETH YEAMANS ALLEYNE, Bapt 16 Sept. 1753 at St. James Bdos. Married first 2 April 1778 at St. Michael, Bdos., John Lespenosse Governor of Demerara. Married secondly ....Buxton.
Jan L'Espinasse was appointed Directeur-General of the Colony of Essequebo-Demerara (then the property, under charter, of the Dutch West India Company) in September 1784. He took up his appointment in February 1785. In his time, Stabroek (now Georgetown) at the mouth of the Demerara river was finally settled upon as the seat of government, and was much enlarged. He resigned about May, 1789. (*ex rel. J.* Graham Cruickshank).

(3) MARY WOODBRIDGE ALLEYNE, Bapt. 7 Sept. 1755 at St. James, Bdos. Died 31 Oct. 1756.

(4) JOHN ALLEYNE bapt. 7 Oct. 1757 at St. James, Bdos.

(5) ANNA MARIA ALLEYNE, born 14 June 1761 Bapt. 30 June 1761 Married first James Marshail, secondly McGrath.

(6) REBECCA ALLEYNE Married Graw ?

(7) JANE KNOWLES ALLEYNE, Married at Demerara

18. viii. THOMAS ALLEYNE, 6 born 28 bapt. 29 Aug. 1733 at St. James Barbados. Died 9 Aug. 1787 at sea or North or South Carolina, U. S. A. Married Dorothy Harbin Forster.
Thomas Alleyne of Braintree. Co. Suffolk, Mass., and Dorothy Harbin Alleyne his wife so'd for £1,600 to Thomas Fayerweather of Cambridge, Co. Middlesex, Mass., farm and tract of land in

25

Braintree containing 400 acres more or less with mansion house and three other houses and two barns and outbuildings. 18 April 1786. Signed Thomas Alleyne, Dorothy Harbin Alleyne his wife, Entered 28 Nov. 1786.

ix. TIMOTHY HENRY PEERS ALLAYNE, born 28 Jan. 1735, bapt. 8 Feb. 1735 at St. James, Bdos. Died 10 July 1808 aged 73 yrs. Married 26 Sept. 1757 at St. James, Barbados, Thomasine, daughter of John Waite of Barbados.
13 July 1808. Died on Saturday last, Timothy Henry Peers Alleyne Esq. Collector of H M. Customs at the Port of Hole Town and Captain Gunner of St. James Fort. This gentleman, of a branch of one of the most ancient families in this Island, uniformly studied to preserve and support the dignity of his respectable descent, retired in the 74th year of his age. (Signed "Amicus." in Barbados Chronicle.)
Children of Timothy Henry Peers Alleyne and Thomasine, his wife :—
(i) Mary Honor Alleyne bapt. 27 April 1758 at St. James, Bdos. Married 2 July 1780 Samuel Battaley at St. James, Bdos.
(ii) Susanna Alleyne bapt. 6 March, 1761 at St. James, Bdos.

x LUCRETIA ALLEYE, born 4, bapt. 5 April 1738 at St. James, Barbados. Married John Waite and had issue one daughter, Rebecca Alleyne Waite

xi. ABEL DUDLEY ALLEYNE, born 14 April 1740, Barbados. Married first 3 March 1756 Brig. Gen. Henry Evans Holder a Judge of Joes River, Bdos., her first cousin. He died 1771.
Children of Henry Evans Holder and Abel Dudley, his wife :—
(i) Henry Holder
(ii) John Holder
(iii) William Holder
She married secondly ....Fitchett.
Mrs. Abel Dudley Holder of Barbados, now resident of Braintree (Mass) baptised Sunday evening Nov. 7 1778 at residence of Madam Alleyne, Braintree.

xii. ISABELLA ELIZABETH ALLEYNE, born 4 Nov. 1743 at Milton, Mass., U.S.A. Died 8 Dec. 1813 at Maugersville, New Brunswick, Canada. Married 27 Oct. 1760 Joseph Clarke, M D. of Stratford, Connecticut, U.S.A.

Abel Alleyne5 = Mary Woodbridge

Isabella Elizabeth Alleyne = Joseph Clarke, M.D.

Isabella Elizabeth Clarke = John Gamble, Surgeon

Sarah Hannah Boies Gamble = James Geddes   Leah Tyrer Gamble = Wm. Allan

John Gamble Geddes = Susan Stewart   George Wm, Allan = Adelaide Schreiber

Susan Stewart Geddes = Charles Phipps Maude Allan — Allan Casse's

Daughter   3 sons

Mrs. Phipps was living in Victoria B.C. April 1930 aged 85 yrs.
This pedigree was made by Mrs. Allan Cassels 6 May 1930.
John Gamble had 12 children, James Geddes had 12 children and
Allan Geddes, one of his sons had 12 childen.

On the failure of his health, Abel Alleyne was advised to try
the cooler climate of New England, so he went to Boston, Mass. with
his family in 1739. afterwards removing to Braintree, later called
Quincy, Mass. ("Antiently known by the name of Mount Wollaston.")

He built a large house on Milton Hill. Milton, Mass. which was
afterwards demolished.

His widow, Mary Alleyne, bought an estate in Braintree from
James Bradford 2 Jan. 1770 for £2.800 sterling, the fine mansion
house of which was originally built by William Coddington in 1636
and was remodelled by Judge Edmund Quincy in 1706. It had 400
acres of land surrounding it. The timbers of which the house was
built were cut from trees that grew in State Street, Boston, and were
rafted across the bay to Quincy. There is a hidden room lighted
from the upper panes of the windows of the kitchen below, and
shafts with ropes for drawing up provisions from the cellar.

Just behind the house is a rising ground commanding a view
of the ocean. This has been laid out in building lots and named
Alleyne Terrace. Imbedded over the door in the rear of the house
is a cannon ball.

The house was sold several times and finally bought by the
Metropolitan Park Commission in 1906. The Massachusetts Society
of Colonial Dames leased it for an indefinite period, using it as
a museum and calling it "The Dorothy Q. House," because it had
belonged to the Quincy family at one time.

Pasted on the back of a picture of the "Dorothy Q. House" in
the possession of Miss Edith Doane Beck, 40 Hawthorne Road,
Brookline, Mass. in 1930 was the following from a Braintree Newspaper of Dec. 8, 1787 :

The Mansion House and Out-Houses together with as much
land adjoining the same as will bring the sum of £1,614. 0. 0. it
having been the property of Mrs. Mary Alleyne, late of Braintree,
widow, deceased, at her death and lying in the North of Parish of
Braintree adjoining to the estate formerly belonging to Mr. Burland.
The fertility of the soil, its contiguousness to the salt water, together
with its beautiful situation for a gentleman's Country Seat, it is presumed will be sufficient inducement for many purchasers to attend
the sale which will be at the Dwelling House on the premises.

Administrators with the will annexed. Signed : Abel Alleyne,
Jeremiah S. Boies. By order of the Supreme Judicial Court.

Mary Alleyne, Widow, will dated 3 June 1775, pr. 16 Oct. 1781.

I Mary Alleyne late of Barbados but now residing in Braintree,
County of Suffolk, Province of Massachusetts. Debts and funeral
expenses to be paid. To be buried in plain and frugal manner. To
son John Alleyne £20. Son Timothy Henry Peers Alleyne £20. To
daughter Jane Isabella Winston (Winslow) pair of silver candle-

27

sticks and snuffers. To daughters Benjamina Woodbridge Alleyne all wearing apparell, etc. Half of furniture and chinaware and Negro girl Patience, and right to live in house while she is unmarried, and suit of mourning. To daughter Abel Dudley Holder wrought silver cup and cover. To daughter Isabella Elizabeth Clarke my wrought silver coffee pot and wrought silver sugar chest. To grandson Abel Alleyne the son of my son Thomas Alleyne £150 at age of 21 years. All gilt plate consisting of large cup and cover, one large salver, two smaller salvers and two canns, also negro boy Hannibal. Suit of mourning. To grand-daughter Sarah Hannah Clarke, the daughter of Isabella Elizabeth Clarke £150 at age of 18 years. Also gold watch and diamond ring that has her Grandfather's hair set under it and her mother's picture. Suite of mourning. To son Thomas Alleyne all that farm which I purchased of James Brandford (Bradford) Esq. which lays in Braintree with all the stock of every kind and sort on it with all utensils etc. and all estate and interest both real and personal in New England or Barbados or any part of the world. Son Thomas Alleyne sole executor. 3 June 1775. Signed Mary Alleyne.

Witnesses : Ebenezer Miller, Elyat Underwood, Seth Copeland. Proved at Boston 16 Oct. 1781 O Wendell. Jud : Probate. Att. Wm. Cooper, Regt.

Given at Pilgrim this 27 day of Nov. 1783. D. Parry.

Abel Alleyne of Braintree, Co. Suffolk, Mass; Gentleman, and Jeremiah Smith Boies of Milton, Co. Suffolk, Mass., Gent., Administrators of estate of Mrs. Mary Alleyne late of Braintree, Widow. Sold by order of the Supreme Judicial Court dated 1 Wed. Dec. 1787, authorising them to sell as much of said Mary's estate as will amount to £1,614 for purpose of paying her lebts. Sold Jan. 29, 1788 at public Auction at Mansion House for sum of £981. 1s. 6d. to Benjamin Beale of Dorchester, highest bidder, 258 acres, 2 Quarters and 15 rods, together with dwelling houses, barns, outhouses. 29 Jan. 1788.

Entered 12 Feb. 1788.

This is the "Dorothy Q. House" in Quincy, Mass.

Boston record of deed to land at Braintree, Mass., bought by Mary Alleyne, widow of Abel Alleyne 2 Jan. 1770. (Vol. 116. p. 56.)

James Bradford of Braintree, Co. Suffolk, Province of Mass. Bay. in New England, Esq. sells for £2,800 paid by Mary Alleyne of Braintree, 400 acres with mansion house and three other houses, two barns bounded by . . . . James Bradford swears he is the true owner of the land through inheritance. Sarah wife of James Bradford. 24 Nov. 1769.

Witnesses : Ebenezer Miller, Edward Winslow.

Acknowledged before Ebenezer Miller, Justice of Peace. Jan. 2, 1770. Ezekl Goldthwait, Registrar.

At a special meeting of the Congregation of Whitsunday, after divine service in the afternoon May 30, 1773. Voted "That ground sufficient for building a tomb under the south side of the new part of the church be appropriated and assigned together with said tomb to Mrs. Mary Alleyne her heirs and assigns forever." (Episcopal Church, Braintree, Mass.)

Anna Wentworth, daughter of George Henry Apthorp, aged 10 buried in the Tomb belonging to the Alleyne family. Oct. 12, 1817.

Elizabeth W. wife of Dr. William Lee Leskins or Perkins, formerly of Hampton Court, England, buried in the same tomb 1802.

Bristol, a negro child of Philip, servant to Mrs. Mary Alleyne was baptised privately July 2nd, 1765.

Phebe, a negro child of Philip servant to Mrs. Mary Alleyne and Tipp his wife servant to Mr. Ephraim Thayer was baptised at church on Sunday, June 1st, 1766.

Patience a negro infant daughter of June servant to Miss Benjamina Woodbridge Alleyne of Braintree, was baptised privately at the house of Madam Alleyne Sunday evening Nov. 7, 1773.

Mrs. Abel Dudley Holder of Barbados now resident in Braintree, baptised at the same time and place.
(Episcopal Church Records, Braintree, Mass.)

Will dated 10 Oct. 1744 of Abel Alleyne of the Parish of St. John, Barbados. To be buried in the vault in St. James Church as near my father as possible. I give to the best of women and most affectionate wife and tenderest parent Mary Alleyne all my plate, jewels, etc., whatever money I have by me at my death or what is owing me then. Profits on my estate called *Mount Standfast* to be divided among children after paying wife's marriage settlement of £400 per annum. Wife and children to have accommodation in dwelling house at *Mount Standfast*. I would be understood in regard to my children living on my Estate or in my dwelling-house, that my meaning is not that if they should marry that they then should live there and no longer than they are single, excepting my son Reynold who shall not be master of my house, but my best of Wives, Mistress. But no other child shall have the liberty of bringing his wife or her husband there to live. N.B. I do not mean that whether it be agreeable to my dear wife or not that my son Reynold and his wife shall live on my Estate or in my dwelling-house with her, but it shall be at her election whether she will consent to or admit of it.

Executrix and Executor, Wife and son Reynold Alleyne ; in case of both their deaths, then sons John Alleyne, Thomas Alleyne, and Timothy Henry Peers Alleyne. Signed Abel Alleyne.

Witnesses : William Gall Jr., Christopher Estwick Gall.

Proved at Pilgrim 18 Sept. 1747. Henry Grenville. (Barbados Records. Vol. 26. p. 190.)

13. REYNOLD ALLEYNE,[5] (*third son of Reynold,*[4] *Abel,*[3] *Reynold,*[2] *Richard*[1]), was born in 1706. Married 30 Oct. 1729 Elizabeth, daughter of Thomas Ward Esq. of *Glen Hall,* Barbados, at St. Michael, Barbados, by Mr. Hotchkis.

He was seated at *Jacksons*, St. James. Barbados, and "died of a fever" and was buried on 17 August. 1736. at St. James, Barbados. Children of Reynold Alleyne [5] and Elizabeth, his wife :—

   i. ELIZABETH REYNOLDIA ALLEYNE, born 1730, died 7 Aug. 1808. Married 30 May 1749 Rev. John Carter, Rector of St. George, Barbados, at St. Michael, Barbados. He died 21 Oct. 1796 aged 90 years. No issue.

19. ii REYNOLD ALLEYNE,[6] born 1732 died 2 April 1765 Married 7 July 1750 Lucy daughter of Thomas Alleyne his uncle.

Will of Elizabeth Alleyne (wife of Reynold Alleyne[5]) dated 19 April 1750.

Parish of St. Michael, Barbados. Elizabeth Alleyne, widow, relict of Reynold Alleyne and dau. of Thomas Ward Esq. To be buried with father and mother in parish of St. Michael. Sister Sarah Nicholls £5 to buy her a ring. Cousin William Duke £5. Son Reynold Alleyne who is to marry niece Lucy Alleyne daughter of brother-in-law Thomas Alleyne. Daughter Elizabeth Reynoldia Carter wife of Rev. Mr. John Carter. Signed Elizabeth Alleyne. Witnesses : Christian Gibbes, Thomas Mapp, William Duke. Proved at Pilgrim 14 Oct. 1751. (Barbados Records. Vol. 21. p. 549.)

14. THOMAS ALLEYNE[5] (*fourth son of Reynold,[4] Abel,[3] Reynold,[2]Richard.[1]*), born 1707. buried 9 Nov. 1753 at St. James. Barbados, aged 46 years. Married first Lucy, daughter of William Dottin and his wife Mary Alleyne Dottin of Granade Hall, Barbados, buried 14 March, 1835. She was daughter of Abel Alleyne.[3]

Mrs. Lucy Alleyne wife of Thomas Alleyne buried 14 March 1735 at St. James, Barbados, aged about 18 years. Died of a fever. (B'dos. Records.)

Children of Thomas and Lucy Alleyne :—

20. i. ABEL ALLEYNE [6] Married Jane Skeet.

   ii. LUCY ALLEYNE, bapt 22 Aug. 1734 at Thomas, Barbados. Died 5 Dec. 1795. Married her cousin Reynold Alleyne son of Reynold Alleyne of *Jacksons*, Barbados.

Thomas Alleyne married, secondly, Susanna, daughter and heiress of William Gibbes of *Black Rock*, Barbados, and Relict of—Walker, at St. Thomas, Bdos.

Thomas Alleyne and Susannah Walker, widow, married at St. Thomas, Barbados 9 Sept. 1736. (Barbados Record.)

Children of Thomas and Susannah Alleyne :—

   i SUSANNA ALLEYNE bapt. 15 July 1737 St. Thomas Bdos.

21 ii. WILLIAM GIBBES ALLEYNE[6] bapt. 18 June 1738 St. Thomas, Bdos. Bur. 19 Sept. 1783 St. Thomas, Bdos, aged 45 yr. Married first Mercy Dottin. and secondly Elizabeth Lane.

22 iii. THOMAS ALLEYNE, bapt. 9 March 1739 St. Thomas, Bdos. Married Mary Gibbes

23 iv. JOHN HOLDER ALLEYNE buried 16 June 1794. Married Marian Alleyne Skeet.

   v. REYNOLD ALLEYNE bapt. 8 July 1744 St. Thomas, Bdos. buried 25 July 1773 St. James, Bdos. Aged 29 years, single

   vi. THOMASIN ISABELLA ALLEYNE, bapt. 23 Nov. 1746 St. Thomas, Bdos. Married Thomas Carmichael.

Children of Thomas and Thomasin Isabella Carmichael :—

    (i)   Francis Carmichael
    (ii) Susannah Carmichael
    (iii) Christian Carmichael
    (iv) Lucy Carmichael

vii. TIMOTHY ALLEYNE, bapt. 17 Dec. 1749 St. Thomas, Barbados, Buried 16 July 1751 St. James, Barbados, aged "near 2 years."

Will of Thomas Alleyne[5] dated 4 Feb. 1753. Parish of St. Thomas, Barbados. To be buried in vault in St. James Church in a plain cedar coffin without any funeral pomp and to be carried there by my nephews. Wife Susanna estate called *Dymocks*. Plate, jewels, household furniture etc. As my eldest son Abel Alleyne is now in England for his education tis my desire he may be allowed his necessary maintenance and that my wife shall also look upon him as her eldest son.

Executrix wife Susanna Alleyne. Signed Thomas Alleyne. Witnesses : Reynold Alleyne, Thomas Alleyne. Proved at Pilgrim 5 Jan. 1754. Ralph Weeks.

Codicil. Son Abel Alleyne £100 at age of 21 yrs, and two riding horses to be delivered to him on his arrival on this island for his own use and benefit.

Dated 6 Nov. 1753 the mark of Thomas X Alleyne. Witness : Littler Roe. Proved at Pilgrim 5 Jan. 1754. (Barbados Records. Vol. 22. 335.)

Alleyne, Thomas son of Reynold Alleyne of Barbados. B; Adm. (aged 13) July 1723; Queens Coll. Oxon. Matric. Nov. 2, 1725; Adm. to the Middle Temple April 6, 1726. (Record of the Old Westminsters. Vol. I.)

Alleyne, Thomas S. Reynold of the Isle of Barbados. Arm. Queen's Coll. matric. 2 Nov. 1725 aged 18 years, admitted to the Middle Temple 6 April, 1726. (Alumni Oxonienses, 1715—1886.)

Seated at *Dymocks*, Barbados.

W. Dotin, the chief-gunner of James Fort, near Holetown, having been accused of embezzling gunpowder from the public stores, Colonel T. Alleyne applied to Mr. J. Dotin, the chairman of commissioners of fortifications and a brother of the accused, to convene a board for the purpose of investigating the charges; but this application was not attended to. Colonel Alleyne therefore suspended the chief gunner until he had cleared himself of the charges brought against him, and desired that the keys of the fort should be delivered up to a person whom he appointed. The chief gunner, accompanied by his brother, hastened to the Governor, and succeeded in influencing him to write a letter to Colonel Alleyne, in which his Excellency denied that Colonel Alleyne possessed any authority to suspend the chief gunner, and forbidding the Colonel to interfere with the gunners and matrosses of his division, further than to inform him of any misconduct.

On the receipt of this letter, Colonel Alleyne hastened to the Governor's residence for the purpose of entering into some explanation, when the irritable temper of the Governor rendered matters much worse by his adding insult, which induced Colonel Alleyne to tear his cockade from his hat and indignantly surrendering his commission, he observed that he disdained to hold it under such terms. Mr. Alleyne laid his complaints before the Assembly, who resolved on an address to the Governor praying that his Excellency would order the chairman to the commissioners of fortifications for St. James to convene a Board for investigation of the charges brought against the chief-gunner. This produced the necessary investigation and Captain Dotin was fully convicted and dismissed from the service. (History of Barbados by Sir R. H. Shomburgk, p. 334.)

Will dated 1 Decr. 1753 of William Gibbes (Not Alleyne) of St. Michael, Barbados, leaves everything to wife Alice Christian Alleyne (during her widowhood) including the *Spring, Black Rocks,* and *Small Hopes* Plantations. If grandson William Gibbes Alleyne shall attain the age of 23 during wife's widowhood she shall deliver to him either the *Spring* Plantation or the *Black Rock* Plantation which she shall think fit. If grandson Thomas Alleyne shall attain the age of 23 years during wife's widowhood she shall deliver to him *Small Hopes* Plantation. Bequeaths money due from son-in-law Thomas Alleyne to wife Alice Christian Alleyne during widowhood, ceasing to be widow, unto daughter Susanna Alleyne, widow, if she marries, to her children. My several grandchildren Vizt. Susanna Alleyne, Reynold Alleyne.

To grand-daughter Alice Christian Walker, £2,000. Grand-daughter Susanna Alleyne £2,000. John Holder Alleyne grandson £2,000. Reynold Alleyne, grandson, £2,000. Thomazin Isabella Alleyne, grand-daughter, £2,000. Grand-daughter-in-law Lucy Alleyne wife of Mr. Reynold Alleyne £100. Store at Reids Bay belonging to Plantation *Small Hopes* be always kept in repair. William Gibbes nephew £10 per annum. Gives wife authority to sell any of the old or bad slaves.

Executor : William Gibbes Alleyne, Grandson. Signed William Gibbes.

Proved 22 Aug. 1754. (Barbados Records, Vol. 22. pp. 464.)

15. THOMAS ALLEYNE[6] (*only son of Timothy,[5] Thomas,[4] Abel,[3] Reynold,[2] Richard[1]*) was born 25th and bapt. 27th April 1714 at St. James, Barbados. Died 1752 St. James Barbados. Married Jane daughter of Rolleston. She married secondly 21 April 1752 at St. James, Barbados, Robert Fercharson of Sandy Lane Barbados.

Thomas Alleyne Matric. Queens College, Oxford, 24 Aug. 1731 aged 17, and was of *Black Jacks,* Barbados, and Member of the Assembly for St. Andrew 1742—44. No issue.

Thomas Alleyne was nephew and heir of his uncle Abel Alleyne and heir of his Aunt Elizabeth, wife of Abel Alleyne in 1746. He also inherited one half of *Morgan's,* Barbados, from his grandmother, Mary Buttals. The other half went to Henry Peers.

Will dated 7 Jan. 1745, of Thomas Alleyne of the Parish of St. James, Barbados. To wife Jeane Alleyne my moiety of a house in Swan St., Bridgetown, tenanted by Jacob Valverde. Household furniture, plate, jewels, chaise, chaise horses, her riding horse and saddle and 8 house negroes. To poor of Parish of St. James £10. To wife Jane £2.000 per annum. If there are no children. If there were children, other arrangements were made.

Executors : Wife, Jane Alleyne, Honourable Thomas Applewhaite; John Frere Esq. Signed, Thomas Alleyne.

Witnesses : John Odwin, Senior, Edward Gill Jr., Joseph Marshall.

Proved at Pilgrim 28 April 1752. (Barbados Records Vol. 25. pp. 81.)

16. THOMAS ALLEYNE [6](second son of John,[5] Thomas[4] Abel,[3] Reynold,[2] Richard [1]), born 1728. Married first Hannah, daughter of John Downes of The Spring, St. Thomas, Barbados, 10 Dec. 1747. She died 10 Feb. and was buried 13 Feb. 1762 in the Cathedral Church, Bath, England.

On the south wall of the south aisle opposite the 5th bay in Bath Abbey is a shield with the Alleyne arms impalling : *Three wavy lines paly* only visible, the paint having worn off. Beneath :—

Here lies/the body of Mrs. Hannah Alleyne/Wife of Thomas Alleyne Esqr./of the Island of Barbadoes./nine lines/February the 10th 1762 aged 35 years.

Children of Thomas and Hannah Alleyne :—

24. i. JOHN ALLEYNE,[7] born 25 Sept. 1748, bapt. 9 Oct., 1748 at St. Peter, Barbados. Died 11 July 1777 at home in Hackney, England. Married Anne Roswell.

ii. ELIZABETH ALLEYNE, born 22 Nov. 1749, bapt. 30 Dec. 1749 St. Peter, Barbados. Died 28 Jan. 1752 and buried St. James, Barbados

Thomas Alleyne married secondly Margaret widow of Lieut. Alexander McCarty. No issue.

Will dated 25 Feb. 1775 of Thomas Alleyne [6] Esq. of the Inner Temple. Son John Alleyne all estate whatsoever and to be sole executor.

Witnesses : John Hogarth, Moses B chen.

Proved 25 May 1775 by John Alleyne, son. (Alexander 168. Somerset House.)

(*To be Continued.*)

SIR REYNOLD ABEL ALLEYNE
2nd Baronet

SIR JOHN GAY ALLEYNE
1st Baronet

ALLEYNE OF BARBADOS.

(THIRD INSTALMENT).

CONTRIBUTED BY LOUISE R. ALLEN.

17. SIR JOHN GAY ALLEYNE, BART[6] *(second son of John[5], Reynold[4], Abel[3]. Reynold[2], Richard[1])*, born April 28th, 1724, at St. James, Barbados. Buried December 7, 1801 at St. James, Barbados.

Married first, Oct. 19. 1746, at St. James Church, Barbados, Christian Dottin, fourth daughter of Joseph Dottin of *Black Rock* and *St. Nicholas* Plantations, Barbados, (by Anne, sole daughter and heiress of Major Edward Jordan of *Black Rock*) by whom he had one son :—

 i. GAY ALLEYNE, bapt. 20 April, 1747, at St. Philip, Barbados. No record of his death.

Married, secondly, 29 June 1786 (he was 62 years old) at St. James, Barbados, by license, Jane Abel his cousin, daughter of Abel Alleyne M.D. of *Mount Standfast*. (Her mother was Jane daughter of Francis Skeet of *Mangrove*, Barbados.) Jane Abel was 21 years old. She was buried 29 Aug. 1800 at St. James, Barbados.

Children of Sir John Gay Alleyne and Jane Abel his wife :—

 i. JOHN GAY NEWTON ALLEYNE, born 18 Feb. 1787, bapt. 10 June 1787 at St. Peter, Barbados. Died 1800 at Eton College, England, aged 13 from illness brought on by over bathing.

 ii. MARY SPIRKS (SPIAR) ALLEYNE, born 21 May 1788, bapt. 13 July 1788 at St. James, Barbados. Died 10 June 1862.

25. iii. SIR REYNOLD ABEL ALLEYNE, born 10 June 1789, bapt. 16 July 1789 at St. James, Barbados. Died 14 Feb. 1870. Married 20 Sept. 1810 Rebecca Olton.

 iv. JANE GAY ALLEYNE, born 11 Nov. 1790, bapt. 9 Jan. 1791 at St. Peter, Barbados. Died 23 Nov. 1836 at Clevedon, Co. Somerset, Eng.
 On Wednesday last at Clevedon, near Bristol, Jane Gay Alleyne, second daughter of the late Hon. Sir John Gay Alleyne, Bart. of the island of Barbados. (Death notice in "The Times," London, Eng. Died 23 Nov. 1836.)

 v. REBECCA BRAITHWAITE ALLEYNE, born 18 Nov 1792, bapt. 5 Jan. 1793 at St. Peter, Barbados, Died 13 March 1846. Married 20 Nov. 1810 as his second wife, Dr. John William Bovell at St. James Church, Barbados.
 At St. James Church on the 17 inst. John W. Bovell Esq. M.C.P. Major Commandant of the St. Peter's Battalion of Militia, to Rebecca Brathwaite, third daughter of the late Sir John Gay Alleyne Bart and sister of the present Sir Reynold Alleyne, Bart. who lately married Rebecca, (now Lady Alleyne) third daughter of the late John Allen Olton Esq. Deceased. (Barbados Mercury 20 Nov. 1810)
 At the northeast portion of the church-yard, Clifton, England : Died March 13th 1846/Rebecca Braithwaite Bovell/aged 51 years/ Daughter of/sir John Gay Alleyne Bart./of the Island of Barbados and Relict of/John William Bovell Esqr. M.D./of Demerara.

35

(Barbados Mercury and Bridgetown Gazette 1847)
Lately deceased at Gloucester aged 36 J. W. Bovell Esq. only child
of Rebecca Braithwaite Bovell of Bath
(Gentlemen's Magazine. 667).
Issue :—
JOHN WILLIAM BOVELL Died 1847.

vi.   CHRISTIAN DOTTIN ALLEYNE, born 12 Jan. 1795. Died 11 Feb·
1873. Married Rev. Henry Withy of Trinity Church, Huddersfield
26 March 1829.
At Cheltenham on the 26th inst. by the Rev. J. D. Ostrehan A.B.
the Rev. Henry Withy A. M. to Christian Dottin, fourth daughter
of the late Hon. Sir John Gay Alleyne Bart of Barbados.
('The Times' London 27 March 1829)
vii.   ABEL ALLEYNE, born 18 March 1796, bapt 9 June 1796 at St. Peter
Barbados. Buried 6 Jan 1812 at St George, Barbados.
Miss Abel Alleyne buried 6 Jan. 1812 at St. George, sister to Sir
Reynold A. Alleyne, Baronet, and niece to Richard Cobham of this
parish.

Sir John Gay Alleyne (1724—1801), perhaps the most illus-
trious member of the Alleyne family, was created a Baronet of
Great Britain by His Majesty King George III on April 8, 1769 (at
the age of 45).   The son of John Alleyne (1695—1730 : See 11 of
the 2nd Instalment of the Alleyne pedigree—May 1936 Journal)
he succeeded to his father's estates at the age of 6.

He was first elected to the General Assembly in 1757, at the
age of 33, as one of the two members for the Parish of St. Andrew,
in which he owned two sugar plantations Bawdens and the River;
and he was re-elected annually—with only a single break of one
annual session (1771—72)—until he resigned his seat in 1797, at
the age of 73.   After only 10 years service, the House of Assembly
unanimously elected him its Speaker on June 3, 1767 (at the age
of 43), and he was regularly re-elected (except during his absence
of one session) to the Speaker's chair until his resignation from the
Assembly thirty years later.

In 1759, two years after his election to the General Assembly,
Mr. J. G. Alleyne attracted public attention by his defence of the
conduct of Barbados in connection with naval operations against
Martinico (Martinique) and Guadeloupe. John Poyer in his "History of Barbados (London, 1808)" pages 319—320, states :—

"The British armament left Carlisle Bay on the thirteenth day of January,
and entered the harbour of Fort Royal, at Martinico two days afterwards,
when the troops were disembarked at Point des Negroes. But in consequence of some difference in opinion between general Hopson and Commodore Moore, they were re embarked within twenty-four hours after their
landing, at the very moment when the principal inhabitants were employed
in arranging a plan for the surrender of the island. The British fleet then
proceeded to Bassetere at Guadeloupe, where, though they experienced a
vigorous resistance, they were ultimately successful.

"During the progress of the siege, the commodore, having received intelligence of the arrival of M. de Bompart, with nine sail of the line at Martinico, left the troops to protect themselves, and retired to Dominica with his
squadron, consisting of ten line of battle ships. With this superior force
Moore ingloriously lay at anchor in Prince Rupert's Bay, above eleven weeks
in which time upwards of ninety sail of English merchantmen were captured and carried into Martinico. The inactivity of the commodore excited
considerable murmurings in Barbados, where he was burnt in effigy; his

36

person treated with indignity, and his name held in absolute detestation. This occasioned some ill-blood between the inhabitants and the officers of the navy ; and the character of the country was afterwards grossly calumniated, in a pamphlet, published by Captain Gardner ;* which produced a spirited reply from the classical pen of Sir John Gay Alleyne,* who, for his judicious defence, was honoured with the public thanks to the general assembly."

Mr. Alleyne was the first Speaker of the Barbados House of Assembly to claim for its members parliamentary privileges.

"The commencement of Mr. Rous's administration was marked by the assembly's first claim to parliamentary privileges. Mr. John Gay Alleyne, having been called to the speaker's chair, [*June 3. 1767] on the death of Mr. Lyte, determined to remedy the omission of which his predecessors had been guilty. Mr. Alleyne possessed great talents and extensive erudition. He was thoroughly acquainted with the principles of the English constitution, and with the forms and practice of the house of commons. With an incorruptible integrity, he had understanding to discover, and spirit to assert, the rights of the people. His chief fault. if it be one, was that of a great mind, an insatiable thirst of praise; and though he pursued the phantom popularity, with unceasing ardour, he assiduously strove to attain it by the noblest means, the welfare of his country. His appointment having been confirmed by the president, the speaker, in an appropriate speech, demanded of his honour the privileges to which the assembly were entitled. First, security to their persons and servants from all arrests and other disturbances, that may obstruct their regular attendance on the house : secondly freedom of speech in their proceedings ; and lastly, free access at all times, to the commander in chief. The president was a little startled at the novelty of the demand, and excused himself from giving an immediate answer. The house sat again the next day, when, receiving no answer to the speaker's demand, they resolved to enter on no business till they had obtained satisfaction on this important point. On the next meeting of council, the president commanded the attendance of the assembly, in the council chamber ; and, after an apology for the delay, 'granted them, as far as was consistent with the royal prerogative, and the laws and constitution of the island, every privilege and liberty which had been enjoyed by any former assembly.'" (Poyer's History of Barbados, pages 338-339).

The Speaker's action invoked the disapprobation of the Author of "A Short History of Barbados, from its first discovery and settlement, to the end of the year 1767." [London : Printed for J. Dodsley, in Pall Mall, 1768.] which although published anonymously was known to be the work of Mr. George Frere of Barbados. A scathing criticism of the book followed from the pen of Sir John Alleyne in a pamphlet entitled :—"Remarks upon a Book entitled, A Short History of Barbados : in which the Partial and unfair Representations of the Author upon the Subjects of his History in general, and upon that of the demand of Privileges in particular, are detected and exposed. Barbados : Printed by Esmand, and Walker. 1768." in which Mr. Frere's unjust assertions were refuted. A duel between the two gentlemen followed, and, (as Poyer observes) though it ended without bloodshed, the dispute laid the

---

*He wrote and published a pamphlet in 88 pages entitled A DEFENCE of the Conduct of BARBADOS during the late Expedition to Martinique and Guadeloupe in a letter to the Right Hon. Gen Barrington By a Native. Resident in the Island. London Printed for R. and J Dodsley, in Pall mall, MDCCLX (1760).

*Poyer erroneously ascribes the occurrence of these events to the year 1766.

37

foundation of an enmity which had a visible influence on the politics of the literary antagonists during their lives.

Undoubtedly the most conspicuous and distinguished figure in the public life of Barbados during the Eighteenth Century, John Gay Alleyne enjoyed the entire confidence of the general public and his constituents and of his fellow members of the Assembly.

The following incidents narrated by Poyer (pp. 348/9) illustrate this :

"The following year (1770) was productive of an extraordinary dispute between the house of assembly, and the free holders of Saint Andrew's parish. By a law of the island, the assembly were restricted from allowing more than two of their members to be absent from the country at the same time. The speaker, however finding his health impaired, was desirous of trying the effect of a voyage to Europe ; but as two members were already absent, he was precluded from obtaining the same indulgence, by the ordinary means. To remove this obstacle, a bill was introduced by the attorney-general, Henry Beckles, to empower Sir John Alleyne to leave the island, without vacating his seat, and to extend the permission to four members at a time. The bill was passed unanimously, by both houses ; but it appeared to be a measure of so unusual a nature, that the governor suspended his assent until the King's pleasure could be known.

' Sir John Alleyne, nevertheless, left the island and the assembly, at their next meeting, addressed the governor to issue a writ for the election of a member in his room. On the day appointed, the freeholders of Saint Andrew's appeared at the poll, refused to make choice of another representative : and presented an address to Mr. Maycock, the sitting member, explaining the reason of their refusal. They could not be persuaded that Sir John Alleyne had vacated his seat, by his absence ; and could not, therefore, with propriety proceed to another election. It would, in the first place, they said, imply a forgetfulness of his former services. and a willingness to deprive him of the benefit intended him, by two branches of the legislature. Secondly, they affected an apprehension of violating a plain law, since, by electing a new member, they would, in the event of the old one's return, be represented by a greater number than they were legally entitled to. From these considerations, they determined to imitate the governor's example and await the result of the reference to the crown.*"

In 1772 "a law was enacted to empower the general assembly to permit any of their members, not exceeding four at a time, to be absent from the island. The propriety of such an indulgence is at best highly questionable. Many members of the house of commons, it is true, are frequently employed on foreign service, without producing any national inconvenience by their absence ; but in a colony whose representative body consists only of twenty two members, the absence of nearly one-fourth of the number may justly be apprehended to impede the progress of public business, and to facilitate the sinister views of a venal faction. The law, as we have already seen, originated in the partial design of granting a particular indulgence to Sir John G. Alleyne ; but, from the failure of that attempt, and the baronet's jealousy of Mr. Spry, the proposal was not revived until after his excellency's death. Nor was this the only innovation introduced for the personal gratification of Sir John Alleyne. It had ever been a standing rule of the assembly, that the speaker, like the speaker of the house of commons, should vote only in case of an equal division of the house. Such a rule did not suit Sir John

---

" *The act was rejected by the King on the recommendation of the lords of trade who reported to His Majesty that as Sir John Alleyne had already come to England, and vacated his seat, they conceived that the confirmation of the act would involve the legislature in difficulties, in case of the election of another member, without benefiting the person in whose favour it had been proposed ; to whose merits Mr. Spry had borne such ample testimony, as to occas on a wish that the indulgence could have been granted consistently with the constitution of the country " *Poyer's History of Barbados, pages 348/9.*

Alleyne's ardent, active mind. Anxious to distiuguish himself upon every question in which the interest of his country was involved, he could not bear to be fettered by a rule which confined the exercise of his intellectual powers, and obstructed the r.pid flow of patriotic eloquence which he poss-essed. The restraiut was, therefore, removed, and he was permitted to speak or vote, upon all occasions, as any other member might do." (*Poyer's History of Barbados, pp. 358—359*).

At present, there are certain restrictions on the activities of the Speaker, who does not take any part in debate and who has only a casting vote in divisions taken in the House.

After the hurricane of 1780, a bill was introduced by Judge Gittens which suspended, for a limited number of years, legal pro-ceedings for debt against landowners.

"The second reading of the bill was ably opposed by Sir John Gay Alleyne. He commenced an eloquent, argumentative speech, with observing, that the feelings of compassion, like all other affections of the human soul, ought to be regulated by the principles of natuial justice ; and that even the love of his country, however ardent, must yield to those superior obligations. He could not consent to countenance a measure which tended to establish an unworthy and unwarrantable distinction between the landholder and the other classes of society, who were all entitled to the equal protection of wise and equitable laws. No partial regard to the embarrassments of men of landed property should ever influence the deliberations of that house ; there were others who ought to be considered with an equal degree of ten derness. The man who had no other property than money ient out at inter-est, and who, by the late dreadful visitation from heaven, was probably deprived of a place of rest and shelter, ought not to be excluded from the benefit which the law had given him of procuring a habitation, or food for his family. In this class there were many young ladies whose whole fortune consisted in debts and legacies, and who perhaps, had been left by the storm, with no other cloaths than those on their backs. Shall the condition of these helpless females, he asked, be rendered more destitute by a law, that would deprive them of the means of procuring the decent habiliments of their sex ? Neither could the merchants and tradesmen of the several towns, sharers in the common calamity, be debarred, without justice, from recovering what was due to them, for their immediato subsistence, or the support of that credit on which their mercantile existence depended. Still less should those, who, in their several departments and professions, earn their livelihood by their manual labour, their learning, or their mental ingenuity, be denied the legal right of enforcing their just demands to enable them to rebuild their houses, and to furnish themselves with food and raiment.

"Nor did Sir John Alleyne think the bill calculated for the real and per-manent advantage of those whom it favoured most, unless it were those whose debts exceeded the value of their property. None others could benefit by a suspensicn of justice. But to pass an act which should afford debtors, of this description, an opportunity of enjoying their plantation a few years longer, to the prejudice of their creditors, would be to establish iniquity by law. To debtors of every other class, the honourable baronet contended, the bill would eventually prove injurious as it must effectually destroy all confidence in those whose unfortunate circumstances more par-ticularly required credit to enable them to repair their works, and restore their plantations to a proper state of cultivation. Sir John Alleyne offered a variety of arguments to prove, that the operation of the bill would not only be prejudicial to those for whose benefit it was intended, but that it would be inconsistent with the honour of that house, and injurious to the character of the country." .... " The venerable speaker of the assembly again exerted his patriotic eloquence in supporting the claim s of justice ; and, rather than suffer any imputation on his gocd faith, moved an additional clause, excluding himself, by name, from any benefit to be derived from

39

the operation of the law.........But finding the powerful opposition which he had to encounter, Mr. Gittens withdrew the bill without putting it to the vote." *(Pages 463—465, Poyer's History of Barbados).*

Sir Charles Pitcher Clarke, Kt., K.C., late Attorney-General of Barbados, in his pamphlet "The Tercentenary of the First Settlement of Barbados, February 1927" states of Sir John Alleyne :

"His imagination was clouded by an idea of the poverty of the country, which led him to draw gloomy pictures of distress, a state of mind perhaps warranted by the very hard times due to drought and cane disease in the seventies of the 18th century. He did not hesitate to declare in the House of Assembly his disapproval of the system of slavery, which he described as a lawful and necessary yet unhappy sight which leaves an immense debt upon us to clear the obligation of human nature. At the time (1774) the abolition of slavery was quite beyond the scope of the imagination of any ordinary slave owner. John Gay Alleyne was a very great man."

Sir R. H. Schomburgh in his History records two further examples of Sir John Gay Alleyne's independence of character and judgment :

"Numerous American privateers infested the seas materially injuring the trade and capturing boats. Sir John Alleyne, the Speaker of the House, disregarding the usual custom of applying through the Governor, addressed himself directly to Admiral Young, the naval commander on the station, soliciting protection, who promised to station a frigate to cruise round the Island."

* * * * *

"Sir Ralph Abercrombie had received His Majesty's commands to raise five regiments of black troops in the West Indies. The frightful mortality amongst the white soldiers induced the British ministers to adopt the plan of recruiting the army with men better able to stand the influence of the climate. The West India governors were instructed to bring this project before their respective legislatures. This plan was strenuously opposed by the respective legislatures, who with the example of San Domingo before their eyes, saw nothing but ruin and death in a proposal for putting arms into the hands of slaves. When Governor Rickets communicated the proposition in a message to the House on January 17, 1797, the Speaker, Sir John Gay Alleyne, opposed the measure, and a number of resolutions condemning it were unanimously adopted, and a copy of them sent to the Governor in reply to his message."

Of Sir John Gay Alleyne's retirement from the House of Assembly and the Speaker's Chair on June 6, 1797, Poyer the historian writes (pages 647—648) :—

"The house was now doomed to sustain the privation of those talents by which it had long been illumined, and of that wisdom which had often guided its deliberations. Worne down by the heavy hand of time and the increase of infirmities, Sir John Gay Alleyne was now compelled to quit the service of his country, whose rights he had vindicated with equal spirit and ability, and whose prosperity he had promoted for nearly forty years with the most

40

disinterested zeal and integrity. Led by that hope which never forsakes us till we die, Sir John Alleyne vainly sought in an European climate, a renovation of that health and vigour which age alone had exhausted. Sir John Alleyne was not permitted to carry into retirement with him any testimonies of public favour or gratitude. Even the poor unsubstantial tribute of a vote of thanks was withholden from the venerable patriot, whose life had been spent in a series of meritorious exertions for the benefit of the happy spot which gave him birth. In other men various passions alternately rule the soul and direct their actions ; but one uniform principle governed the whole of Sir John Alleyne's political conduct. The welfare of his country was the primary wish of his heart ; and, however mistaken he might sometimes have been as to the means of attaining his object, he ever steadily kept the end in view. The sun, which decorated the horizon, was no sooner withdrawn, than the light and warmth which it afforded were forgotten. No other notice was taken of the Speaker's letter of resignation than to appoint a successor."

Mr. Poyer's strictures regarding the lack of courtesy shewn to Sir John Alleyne by his fellow-members of the General Assembly are not borne out by the records of the House. When Sir John was re-elected Speaker on October 25, 1796, he made an eloquent speech of thanks in which he refers to a recent "bitter calamity" which had befallen him; and in presenting himself as Speaker to the Governor he spoke of "the disadvantages I lie under from a late Calamity that nearly cost me my life and which has left me still in a disabled state." He actually presided for the last time as Speaker of the House of Assembly on January 17, 1797. At the meeting held on February 11, the Clerk read a letter from him excusing his non-attendance owing to indisposition. Lt. Col. Mayers was about to move that the House should adjourn to another day, when a message arrived from the Governor concerning some pressing business, and in the circumstances Judge Gittens was forthwith elected Speaker pro tem. Sir John Alleyne continued to be absent from the meetings of the House until June 6, 1797 when his letter of resignation of the Speaker's chair was laid by the Clerk before the Assembly. This letter, which is recorded in full in the Minutes, contains the following reference to his ill-health : " . . . but such has become the miserable decrepitude of my limbs, aggravated by incessant pain day and night; so that I am driven as a refuge from these miseries to resolve upon a voyage to England for the benefit of the Bath waters." And his letter makes no mention of resigning from the House but on the contrary requests "a leave of absence from the House for the remainder of their term, that I might prosecute my voyage without a forfeiture of my legal seat in it." Judge Gittens was then chosen Speaker pro tem and immediately addressed the House : "This House, I am convinced, considers itself somewhat obliged to the late Speaker for his long and faithful services in the public duties of his country, that they must receive with the sincerest regret his official notification to retire from them, and be ready to anticipate me in every compliment they can pay him by expressing this wish that he may be continued to hold his seat as Speaker during his residence. I therefore move that Sir John Gay Alleyne be continued Speaker of this House during his residence in this Island." Colonel Beckles seconded the motion which was unanimously agreed to, leave being granted until the end of the Session.

Sir John in a letter of acknowledgment which was read at the next meeting of the House (July 11) states that he was embarking for England on July 23, and suggests that at their next meeting the members "proceed to the appointment of an established Speaker." This letter was written from *Nicholas*, on June 19, 1797, and addressed to Samuel Moore Esquire, Clerk of the Assembly. Nicholas Plantation belonged to Sir John's first wife, Christian Dottin, who had inherited the estate from her father, Joseph Dottin. In 1782, Lady Alleyne, being in poor health and wishing to dispose of the plantation, settled it upon her nephews and nieces (subject to Sir John's life interest therein) children of her three sisters, Mrs. Blenman, Mrs. Husbands, and Mrs. Beckles.

The plantation Great House—now called St. Nicholas Abbey— is an ancient stone mansion resembling an English manor house of the 17th century. Although nothing is known of its history or date of erection it is believed that the mansion was built by Sir John Gay Alleyne. The only example of its style of architecture in the Island, it is also unique in that it contains chimneys and flues for fireplaces, two of the bedrooms having been provided with these furnishings though wholly unnecessary in a tropical climate.

* * * * *

In the records of the Society for the Propagation of the Gospel is a letter from John Gay Alleyne dated April 23, 1774. The seal affixed is spade-shaped, suspended by a ribbon. Arms : Quarterly 1 & 4 Per chevron gules and ermine in chiel two lions heads erased Or. (Alleyne). 2 & 3 Two Chevronels between three trefoils (Terrill).

Between 1770 and 1783, Sir John Gay Alleyne founded a school in St. Andrew's Parish which was originally called 'The Seminary', later the name was changed to 'Alleyne School.' Motto : *aliis non sibi* (For others, not for self). The Deed of Settlement for this school was written 30 Dec. 1783 and was still at the school in March 1928. A bond of £750 was given 7 July 1770 which was part of the salary Sir John had received during his tenure of Churchwardenship of the Parish, to be applied for the maintenance, support and education of poor boys of the parish of St. Andrew. The bond secured an annuity or yearly rent charge of £60 from his plantation called '*Bawdens*' in St. Andrew, containing 350 acres. This is perpetual and stands as a debt against the plantation whenever it is sold. The school was intended for white boys but, there being very few, permission was obtained to allow colored boys to enter, and in March 1928 the school was being very efficiently conducted by the headmaster, Mr. J. I. C. Howard, with about sixteen boys. On a white

marble tablet at one side of the schoolroom is the following inscription :

Barbados.   Parish of St. Andrews.

To lead to useful knowledge,
To sow the early seeds of Virtue
In the minds of Youth,
To improve the present and
To benefit future Generations,
The Honourable Sir John Gay Alleyne,
                    Baronet,
Speaker of the House of Assembly,
            In this Island,
Influenced by that benevolent and patriotic Spirit
Which has ever marked with distinguished lustre,
His disinterested and beneficent Actions
            in public life,
And those amiable Virtues which adorn
            His private Character,
Founded, erected and endowed this school,
With permanent Salary to the Master
            of Sixty pounds per Annum,
In the Year of our Redemption,
            1785.
The Reverend Mr. Joseph Hebson,
Being Rector of the said Parish.

Will of Sir John Gay Alleyne dated 13 Oct. 1798. Proved 25
May 1802.
Sir John Gay Alleyne of the Island of Barbados at present residing in Albermarle St., St. James, Westminster, London, now about
to return to Barbados.
Wife Jane Abel Alleyne £500 and all jewels, rings, watches
and trinkets, usually worn by her, and my post chaise and any two
carriage horses and a saddle horse. Use of all plate, making an inventory thereof for the trustees. After her death all plate to eldest
son John Gay Newton Alleyne. Mourning rings value 10 gs to each
executor. Son Reynold Abel Alleyne £4000 at 21 yrs. Daughters
Mary Spire Alleyne, Jane Gay Alleyne, Rebecca Braithwaite Alleyne, Christian Dottin Alleyne, and Abel Alleyne, £3000 apiece at
21 years or day of marriage provided they marry wtih consent of
their mother, or if she is dead, with consent of their guardians. If
they marry without consent then payment of money to be postponed
until they are 21 yrs.
Plantation called 'Bawdens' in Parish of St. Andrews, Barbados charged with payment of all debts, funeral expenses and legacies. Wife Jane Abel to have annuity of £600 without deductions
of any taxes.
Emancipate my old and faithful slave Henry Buckingham and
give him annuity of £16.
Estate called Bawdens with all buildings etc. charged with an-

nuity to my wife and the said legacies to the Right Honourable Alleyne Lord St. Helens, The Honourable William Henry Bouverie of Dover St. Piccadilly, Co. Middlesex. The Honourable Bouverie of Edward St. Co Middlesex, Henry Cally of Great Russell St. Bloomsbury Co. Middlesex and Honourable John Forster Alleyne of Island of Barbados Esq. as trustees . . . . to pay out of profits of the estate for maintenance support and education of daughters and younger sons during their minorities not to exceed £300 apiece for sons and £200 apiece for daughters, and subject thereto to the use of my said son John Gay Newton Alleyne at 21, any sum of money not exceeding one third portion intended for son Reynold Abel Alleyne or any son I may hereafter have to be advanced for purchasing or procuring him or them any civil or military employment or promotion or placing him or them in any profession or business or otherwise for his or their advancement in the world.

And whereas my estate and plantation called Mount Alleyne situate in the Parish of St. James in the island of Barbados, is in settlement and I have purchased sundry slaves for the use of the said last mentioned plantation all to belong to the same person or persons and in the same order and course of succession as such last mentioned estate and plantation shall by virtue of the limitation in the said settlement go and belong to or as near and similar thereto as circumstances will permit and the law allow.

Residue to son John Gay Newton Alleyne at 21 years if he should die to son Reynold Abel Alleyne at age 21 years.

Trustees directed to mortgage Bawdens to pay legacies instead of selling securities if they think it wise.

In one skin of parchment I set my hand and seal this 13th day of Oct. 1798. Signed— John Gay Alleyne.
Witnesses : Gilbert Jones, Salisbury Sq. Fleet St. London. William Green, Salisbury Sq. William Yeo, clerk to Mr. Jones. Entered 27 Feb. 1802. Given at Pilgrim, Barbados 25 May 1802.

Codicil 9 May, 1801. Whereas it has pleased God to take from me my dearest son John Gay Newton so that his younger brother Reynold Abel will of course succeed to the possession of my estate in the room of his eldest brother.... the trust created for purpose of raising £4000 as his fortune shall cease as he receives the estate. To sister *(sister-in-law)* Judith Alleyne spinster, £50 per annum for life or so long as my debts remain unpaid but from that happy period I give her £50 more per annum £100 in all as some recompense for her parental attention to my younger children since the death of their poor mother as well as for her kind regard to myself since that fatal loss and wound felt to all my future happiness in life. (His second wife Jane Abel was buried 29 Aug. 1800.)

To faithful female servant Marianne Burton £25 annually. Apprehensive of the absence of my friend John Foster Alleyne from the island .... I hereby nominate my two relations Richard Cobham Esq. and Joseph Terrill Esq. to be additional executors. Sister Judith to be guardian and to superintend the education of my

44

daughters jointly with other nominated friends on both sides of the ocean. 9 May 1801 and the 76th year of my age.

(Signed) J. G. Alleyne.

Codicil 22 May 1801. Probate granted at Pilgrim Barbados 31 Dec. 1801. Whereas the Legislature of this Island have increased by act the fine upon freeing slaves to such an amount as may make it inconvenient for my estate to afford, incumbered with debts perhaps as well as legacies, for purchasing the freedom of my man slave Harry Buckingham, I therefore hereby revoke that part of my will in ordering him to be freed, yet as a reward for his fidelity I give him the same sum Yearly for his better support which is specified in the will of £16 for and during his natural life and in order to exempt him from the hand and direction of the executors and trustees named in my will for the use of my estate in general I do hereby instead thereof give and bequeath my said slave Harry Buckingham to my son Reynold and to his heirs forever.

There are two cases of extraordinary fine Noyau in the garret that which is marked of different sorts. I beg may be presented John Forster Alleyne Esq. for Mrs. Alleyne. The other case divided between Mr. Cobham and Mr. Terrill; and all the Malmsey wine particularly reserved for my children as also all the Madeira and Port wine that may not be required for my funeral. No furniture to be sold but bed in hall chamber and easy chair. I give Harry the laced and embroidered cloths in the trunk upstairs and the trunk also, and all my loose clothes about my chamber the rest of my clothes I desire may be preserved.

I give Richard Wood, Thomas Mahon, and Thomas Challenor £50 each six months after my death in token of my regard for them. 28 May 1801. (Seal) Witness : Judith Alleyne.

Codicil 26 November 1801. I give to my daughter Mary Spire £500 stlg. in addition to £3000 already given her by my Will. To my worthy friend Arthur Piggott Esqre of Powis Place, London, £100 stlg. in grateful remembrance of both his and Mrs. Piggott's parental care of my two dear boys when I was absent from them.

* * * * *

On a tablet east of the north door of St. James Church, Hole Town, Barbados. Sacred to the Memory of/Dames/Christian and Jane Abel/successively the consorts/of Sir John Gay Alleyne Baronet;/Women in whose praise Encomium has to borrow no false colouring/from Flattery; and of whom no language/describes the loss./With the former he lived six and thirty years/of unspeakable Felicity/and but little more than fourteen/with the latter./In that short period/She bless'd him with the Birth/of seven lovely infants;/the eldest of which/John Gay Newton Alleyne/a Boy of Hopes commensurate/to the fondest wishes of a Father/in thirteen summers was too ripe for immortality/for longer Continuance upon Earth./The afflicting intelligence of his death/at Eton School/arrived but one Day late enough/to spare his expiring Mother,/such

Pangs as she was incapable of feeling/for her own Dissolution/but such, as the mournful Erecter of/this three fold Monument/of the Instability of all human/Enjoyments,/for the Sake of his surviving children/and in silent Resignation/to the Wisdom that ordains it; must labour to/endure./

(The above Monumental Inscription is said to have been written by the Rector of St. James, Rev. Francis Fitchatt, a copy of the inscription was contributed to the West Indian Committee Circular (Vol. 27 pp 233) by the late Mr. Forster M. Alleyne.)

In the south porch of St. James Church, Hole Town, Barbados, is a white marble ledger with a long inscription of 42 lines. (Worn in places.) To the Memory/of Dame Christian Alleyne/the beloved Wife of Sir John Gay Alleyne, Bart./who (6 lines) died on the 2nd day of . . . of our Lord 1782. (Married life—36 years.)

(To be Continued).

———————

ALLEYNE OF BARBADOS.

(Fourth Instalment).

Contributed by Louise R. Allen.

18. Thomas Alleyne[6] (*fourth son of Abel*[5] *, Reynold*[4], *Abel*[3] *, Reynold*[2] *, Richard*[1]), born 28th, baptised 29th Aug. 1733 at St. James, Barbados. Died 9th Aug. 1787 at sea or in South or North Carolina, U.S.A.

Married Dorothy Harbin, daughter of John Forster of Forster Hall, St. Joseph, Barbados, and Harbin, his wife who was the daughter of Isaac Thorpe of St. Philip, and grand-daughter of Joseph Harbin of St. Michael, Merchant. The marriage ceremony was performed by the Rev. Haynes Gibbes at the home of Mrs. Sarah Osborne, Barbados on Thursday, 2 Jan. 1754. Dorothy Harbin Forster was born 1735.

Dorothy Harbin (Forster) Alleyne is said to have been a very beautiful woman. She died at Dedham, Mass., 14 Nov. 1814, and was buried in the family vault in the Quincy Church, Mass. She is the lady who said she never indulged her children, but let little Thomas bring the chickens into the parlour to play with.

The picture of the "Barbados Beauties" belonged to Dorothy Harbin (Forster) Alleyne who gave it to her grand-daughter, Sarah Hannah Boies Alleyne (Beck) and it is to go to her children. This picture was owned by Edith Doane Beck daughter of Frederick Beck, and grand-daughter of Sarah Hannah Boies Alleyne Beck who lived in Boston in 1931. It was painted by "Harris 1716." The tradition in the family is that the girls were Mary and Rebecca Alleyne, daughters of John Alleyne, and sisters of Sir John Gay Alleyne, but they could not be because Mary Alleyne, the elder, was not born until 1721. They may have been Forster children as they do not correspond with the ages of any Alleyne children.

Children of Thomas and Dorothy Harbin Alleyne:—

26. i.   Abel Alleyne Born 19 May 1757 at Salem, Mass. Died 7 Dec. 1807 at Dedham, Mass. Married Anna Chase.

     ii. Thomas Alleyne Born 9 July 1758 being Sunday. Bapt. by the Rev. Dr. Miller in Braintree, Mass. (Bible Record.) Bapt. Thomas ye son of Thomas Alleyne by Dorothy Harbin, his wife. Born 9 July & Bapt. 22 July 1758. Died 30 Sept. 1765 aged 7 yrs. at Braintree, Mass. Buried in the church in Braintree 2 Oct 1765.

27. iii. John Forster Alleyne Born 22 April 1762 at Braintree, Mass. Died 29 Sept. 1823 at Porter's, St. James, Barbados. Married Elizabeth Gibbes Willing.

James Brackett of Braintree, Co. Suffolk, Mass., Innholder, and Mary his wife, administrators of the estate of Capt. Richard Brackett deceased, sold to Thomas Alleyne of Braintree, Gent, for £253. 6s. 8d. by Order of the Superior Court of Judicature at Boston 3 Tuesday of Feb. 1762 a messuage and tenement being part of estate of Capt. Richard Brackett lying in Braintree containing 6 acres with house and shop and two barns etc., 7 June 1762. Braintree Road to the landing. (*Boston Records Vol. 98. p. 96.*)

Thomas Alleyne of Braintree, Gent, and Dorothy Harbin Alleyne, his wife, sold for £306 13s. 4d. to William Vesey and Oliver Gay, Wardens of the Episcopal Church of Braintree, for the residence of the minister of said church, 6 acres, house, shop and one barn. 'Northly part of road leading from the landing Place. Signed at Braintree 2 April, 1765. Entered 23 May, 1765. (*Suffolk Deeds Vol. 104. p. 138.*)

Thomas Alleyne and Mary Alleyne £5 each toward Hous glebe. 1764-1765. Voted that the ground in the gallery be disposed of for the building of four pews of 6 feet square, to be assigned as follows: One for the minister, the second for Mr. Thomas Alleyne Esq., the third to Mr. Peter Etler (Episcopal Church, Braintree, Mass.)

1767. Mr. Alleyne and others resigned their pews in the gallery.

Voted that a small pew built at the expense of Major Miller, Thomas Alleyne Esq. Mr. William Vesey Jr. being at the end of the gallery at the north side of the church, be assigned, appropriated to the service of those gentlemen for their servants. (*Episcopal Church Records, Braintree, Mass.*)

Among the names of families belonging to the church in Braintree and Milton, Mass., 1764 and after were Thomas Alleyne, Mary Alleyne, Dorothy Harbin Alleyne and Benjamina Woodbridge Alleyne.

DEBORAH FORSTER: *Will* dated 1 Dec. 1790. Pr. 5 April, 1794. (Sister of Dorothy Harbin (Forster) Alleyne, wife of Thomas Alleyne.) Deborah Forster of Bristol, Eng., Spinster. To James Houlder of Ashpart, Co. Hants., Eng. £400. Bank annuities to pay the interest to my sister Dorothy Harbin Alleyne of Braintree, near Boston, in America, widow, for life and at her death for Deborah Forster Alleyne of Braintree, Spr., grand-daughter of the said Dorothy Forster Alleyne and great niece to me, at 18. All residue of my bank annuities to my nephew, John Forster Alleyne of the Island of Barbados Esq., in trust for his daughter Sarah Gibbes Alleyne. My silver spoons marked D.T. to Deborah Thorpe, Island of Barbados now of Taunton, Co. Somerset, Spr. All residue to my great niece Deborah Forster Alleyne, her father's and mother's receipt to be sufficient. T. to be Executor. Codicil. £200 in the hands of Messrs. Horway Mason & Co. to my niece Deborah Forster Alleyne, daughter of Abel Alleyne in America. Jan. 10, 1793. Sworn 3 Dec. 1793. Proved 5 April 1794 by James Houlder Esq. (*196 Holman, Somerset House.*)

DEBORAH FORSTER was born 4 Dec. 1728 bapt. 5 Dec. 1728 in Barbados, daughter of John and Harbin Forster. Mr. Isaac Thorpe, John Ashley Esq., Godfathers, Mrs. Deborah Thorpe and Mrs. Mercy Clarke, Godmothers.

19. REYNOLD ALLEYNE[6] (*only son of Reynold* [5], *Reynold* [4], *Abel* [3], *Reynold* [2], *Richard* [1].) Born 1732. Died 2 April, 1765.

48

Buried 4 April, 1765 at St. James, Barbados. Married 7 July, 1750 at St. Thomas, Barbados, Lucy, daughter of his uncle Thomas Alleyne by his first wife Lucy Dottin. She died 5 Dec. 1795. Married by Rev. Mr. John Carter, Reynold Alleyne's brother-in-law.

Children of Reynold and Lucy Alleyne:—

i. LUCY DOTTIN ALLEYNE, born 10 March 1757, bapt. 11 March 1757 at St. Michael, Bdos., buried 22 Feb. 1764 at St. James, Bdos. aged 7 years.

ii. ELIZABETH REYNOLDIA ALLEYNE, born 5 Nov. 1758, Married 23 Feby. 1775. Dr. Grant Elcock. (b. 1744) son of Grant Elcock (1690—1744) of S. John, Barbados, and his wife Ann Sieuzac, who was a daur. of John and Ann (Morris) Sieuzac. Their daughter—Lucy Reynold Elcock, Married first, Dr. George Wilson 1 Sep. 1796, and secondly, 12 Sep. 1807 Rev. Mark Nicholson M.A. (b. 1770 at Barton, Westmorland) Principal of Codrington College, Barbados, (1797—1821). by whom she had issue.

iii. REYNOLD THOMAS ALLEYNE, bapt. 29 Aug. 1762 at St. Michael, Bdos. Buried 9 Feb. 1764 at St. Michael, Bdos. aged 15 Months.

iv. CHRISTIAN ANN ALLEYNE. The Family Bible which belonged to Eliz Reynoldia (Alleyne) Ellcock records the name of this child as Susanna Christian Alleyne and the dates of her birth & death as 12 Feby 1765, & 12 Sep. 1818 respectively. The entry in the Baptismal Register of St. James, Barbados, is as follows:— "1765 Feby 15, Christian Ann daughter of Reynold & Lucy Alleyne, born about two weeks before." She died on 12 Sep. & was buried the following day at S. James, Barb. "19 Feby 1818. Died on Saturday last. Miss Susanna C Alleyne, Aunt of R. A. Ellcock Esq."—*Extract from Newspaper.*

Will of Susanna Christian Alleyne (dated 5 Sept. 1810. Proved 9 Nov. 1818) of the Parish of St. Michael, Barbados.

Sum of £1,100 due from my brother, Doctor Grant Ellcock as my moiety of £2,200 due my mother against the Sugar Work Plantation called *Jacksons* which I give to my niece Christian Gibbes Ellcock. Also set of dressing plate. Niece Elizabeth Ward Ellcock £100. Niece Anne Pilgrim £200. Niece Lucy Reynold Nicholson, slaves. Great Nephew John Grant Wilson. Niece Elizabeth Alleyne Pilgrim Sister Elizabeth Reynoldia Ellcock. Nephew Reynold Alleyne Ellcock. Friend Miss Judith Alleyne. Sole Executor, nephew Reynold Alleyne Ellcock. Signed—Susanna Christian Alleyne.

Codicil. Niece Christian Gibbes Maynard, Great niece Elizabeth Alleyne Pilgrim, daughter of Rev. John F. Pilgrim. £25 to Doctor Parris Greaves. 10 gas. to Dr. Philip Caddell. Proved 9 Nov. 1818. (*Barbados Records Vol. 61. pp. 251-2*).

Will dated 31 March 1765. Pr. 20 June 1765 of Reynold Alleyne[6] of the Parish of St. Michael, Barbados. It is my direction that my body be deposited in the plainest manner in St. James Vault wherein my children now lie and that my coffin does not exceed the sum of £6. No rings or scarves on any account to be given at my funeral. Wife Lucy Alleyne £100 per annum. £50 per annum to be paid wife at death of my mother, Elizabeth Alleyne, Wife all real and personal estates.

Executrix. Wife Lucy Alleyne. Executors. Brother (in-law)
Rev. Mr. Carter. Uncle Samson Wood. Brother Thomas Alleyne.
Signed Reynold Alleyne. Witnesses: Thomasin Isabella Alleyne.
Thomas Alleyne: *(Barbados Records. Copied Vol. 17. p. 247).*

20. ABEL ALLEYNE [6] *(eldest son of Thomas [5], Reynold [4],
Abel [3], Reynold [2], Richard [1],)* Married Jane (Born 1667) daughter
of Francis Skeete of *Mangrove Plantation,* Barbados.
Abel Alleyne was an M.D. of Mount Standfast, St. James,
Barbados.

Children of Dr. Abel Alleyne and Jane (Skeete) Alleyne, his
wife:—

i. CHRISTIAN ALLEYNE, born 14 May 1757, bapt 21 May 1757 at St.
Michael, Barbados. Married William White 19 May 1785 at St.
James, Barbados. Issue:—
  (1) Jane Skeete White
  (2) Wilhelmina White
  (3) Abel Alleyne White

ii. LUCY ALLEYNE, bapt 31 July 1758 at St James, Bdos. Married
James Hendy 31 May 1776 at St James, Barbados. Issue:—
  (i) James Alleyne Hendy.

iii. JUDITH SUSAN ALLEYNE, Bapt 25 January 1760 at St. James, Bdos.

iv. THOMAS ALLEYNE bapt. 30 Sept. 1761 at St. James, Barbados.
Died 1 Oct. 1761.

v. SUSAN ALLEYNE, bapt. 27 Feb. 1763 at St. James, Bdos. Married
25 Jan. 1787 Richard Cobham at St. James, Bdos, by whom she had
Issue:--
  (i) Mary Jane Cobham
Susanna Cobham of Barbados died 1806. (1 & 4 Cobham. 2 & 3
Dottin. Impaling Jordan.) *(*Monumental inscription in Bristol
Cathedral, England.)

vi. JANE ABEL ALLEYNE, bapt. 2 Oct. 1765 at St. James, Barbados.
Buried 29 Aug. 1800 at St. James, Barbados. Married 29 June 1786
at St. James, Bdos. Sir John Gay Alleyne, her cousin.

vii. ABEL ALLEYNE, born 2 July 1768, bapt. 16 Sept. 1769 at St. James,
Barbados. Married Jane Rolleston Alleyne, his cousin, daughter
of John Holder Alleyne 6.
Issued :—
  (1) Marian Skeete Alleyne.

Will of Jane Alleyne, widow of Abel Alleyne [6] of the Parish
of St. Thomas, Barbados. I give to my son Abel Alleyne a mulatto
boy slave named Tom. To my Grand-daughter Mary Jane Cobham,
a slave girl named Betty Jane. All real estate to be sold by executors and debts paid. Daughter Judith Alleyne £15 for mourning.
All the rest and residue and remainder of my estate I give, devise
and bequeath to my said son Abel Alleyne, to my son-in-law Richard
Cobham, to my son-in-law Sir John Gay Alleyne, to my said daughter Judith Alleyne, to my grandson James Alleyne Hendy, and to my
grand-daughter Jane Skeete White to be equally divided among
them share and share alike. Grand-daughter Wilhemina White,
Grandson Abel Alleyne White. Executors. Son Abel Alleyne, son-
in-laws Richard Cobham and Sir John Gay Alleyne. Dated 27 Sept.
1897. Signed.—Jane Alleyne. Witnesses:—John Cobham, Thomas

50

Burnett. Proved at Pilgrim 31 October 1797. *(Barbados Records. Vol. 38. p. 447.)*

21. WILLIAM GIBBES ALLEYNE[6] (*second son of Thomas[5], Reynold [4], Abel[3], Reynold [2], Richard [1]*), bapt. 18 June, 1738 at St. Thomas, Barbados, buried 19 Sept. 1783 at St. James, Barbados aged 45 years. Married first, 4 June 1761, at St. Thomas, Barbados, Mercy daughter of General John Dottin of Mt. Edge Plantation, Barbados. Mercy Alleyne died 25 August 1774 aged 30 years and was buried at St. James, Barbados.

Married secondly, Elizabeth, daughter of John Lane 14 Nov., 1776 at St. Thomas, Barbados.

Elizabeth Lane had Black Rock Plantation from her uncle, William Maynard after his wife's death.

Died on the 12th inst. (May 1828) at Upton Gray, Hants, in the 85th year of her age, Elizabeth Alleyne widow of the late William Gibbes Alleyne Esq. of the island of Barbados. (G. M. Magazine.)

William Gibbes Alleyne was seated at Black Rock Plantation and he served as Member of the Assembly for St. Thomas, Barbados, from 1762 until his death. There was no issue of either marriage.

Tablet on the north wall of the nave of St. James Church at Hole Town, Barbados with arms and inscription: *Gules, per chevron Ermine and Gules two lions' heads erased.* On an inescutcheon: *Gules, two lions passant.* (Dottin). Motto: Aptissima Quaeque. Crest of Alleyne.

To record the Virtues and perpetuate the Memory /of*Mercy*, his dear beloved Consort/*William Gibbes Alleyne Esqr.* as a testimony of/ Sincere Affection has erected this/Monument. /After thirteen years of constant uninterrupted/Bliss with a Partner, who by every Endearment/sweetened the Joys, alleviated the Cares and/ heightened the Pleasures of the nuptial State; to/his inexpressible Sorrow and Concern She was/separated from him on Thursday/ Aug. 25th 1774 aged thirty years. /Her descent from a Race of worthy Ancestry/deriving her Lineage from the Honourable/*James Dottin* who was President of the Island/three different times and being the daughter of the/Honourable *John Dottin,* a gentleman who for a/series of years filled the most distinguished civil and/ military Stations in our Community/Gave her that Consequence among us, which is due/to Birth and Rank. (8 lines).

(Monumental Inscriptions of the British West Indies. By Vere Langford Oliver, M.R.C.S.)

Will of William Gibbes Alleyne, of the Parish of St. Thomas, Island of Barbados. My funeral expenses to be fully paid and satisfied, and it is my will and desire that my funeral be plain and decent without pomp or show and that the price of my coffin be £10 and that the same be made by Francis Williams and that there be no funeral sermon preached for me. I confirm to wife Elizabeth, my Spring plantation which I settled on her on our marriage and I also give her my Black Rock Plantation with all slaves etc. for her life and at her death to be disposed of by her to such of my family as she think fit. At death of wife bequeath unto each of brother Thomas Alleyne's sons, to wit:—Thomas and William Gibbes Alleyne £200. To each of the other children of said brother Thomas Alleyne, to wit—John Collyns, Benjamin Bostock Marshall and Isabella Susannah and Mary, the sum of £100. Upon death of said wife, bequeath unto each of my brother John Holder Alleyne's sons, to wit—Thomas and William, £200. To daughter of said brother John Holder Alleyne, Jane Alleyne £100. To each of sister Carmichael's children to wit—Francis, Christian, Susannah and Lucy the like sum—£100. Authorize executrix to sell 10 acres in Dymocks Plantation, formerly Susannah Alleyne's, 8 acres situated in Irishtown now in the tenure of Thomas Redman and 43 acres near Chalky Mount. Money to be applied to debts. To wife Elizabeth Alleyne all plate, furniture, horses and all personal and real estate. Executrix—Wife Elizabeth Alleyne. Dated 25 August 1783. Signed William Gibbes Alleyne. Witnesses: Jane Hendy, William Thomas, Philip Seymore.

Codicil. To sister Tomasin Isabell Carmichael an annuity of £20. To Damaris Carter annuity of £20 for life. All legacies to children to be paid at their ages of 21 years. Dated 25 Aug. 1783. Signed William Gibbes Alleyne. Proved at Pilgrim, Barbados 27 Sept. 1783. (*Barbados Records. Vol. 28. p. 145.*)

Will of Elizabeth Alleyne (widow of William Gibbes Alleyne[6]) formerly of the Island of Barbados but now residing in the Parish of Odiham, Co. Southampton, England.

Nephew Rev. William Maynard Payne, Rector of Parish of St. Andrew, Barbados, son of late Brother-in-law and sister John and Martha Payne. 30 acres of land part of the Black Rock Estate, St. Michael, Barbados, which belonged to my late husband which was by me purchased after his death, together with 6 slaves. Niece Rebecca Payne, spinster. Good friends Rev. Thomas Salmon of Odiham, Clerk, and Thomas James, and James Winter.

Great nieces Agnes Payne daughter of late nephew Capt. John Payne, brother of Rebecca Payne. Great nephew John Payne brother of Rebecca Payne, nephew Charles Payne brother of Rebecca Payne. Late husband William Gibbes Alleyne Esq. My estate called *Clermont* in Barbados charged with £3,000 given to friend John Hanbury Beaufoy, of Upton Gray, Co. Southampton, England. George Gibbes the younger of City of Bristol, merchant and Thomas Salmon. My niece Agnes Beaufoy, wife of said John Hanbury Beaufoy. Great nephew William Maynard Payne the younger and Elizabeth Alleyne Payne son and daughter of nephew William Maynard Payne.

Capt. John Payne, brother, Rev. William Maynard Payne, Rebecca Payne, their sister. John and Agnes Payne £1,000 each. Nephew Charles Payne £500. Mrs. Ismena Payne widow of Capt. John Payne £100.

Executors. John Hanbury Beaufoy, George Gibbes the younger,

Thomas Salmon. Signed Elizabeth Alleyne. Dated 12 January, 1819.

Witnesses: Richard Raggett, John Cole, Solrs, Odiham, Elizabeth Rogers, servant to Mrs. Alleyne.

Codicil. 14 Feb. 1820. Agent Messrs. Gibbs Sons and Bright, Bristol, England. Revokes bequest to Charles Payne and gives it to John Hanbury Beaufoy.

Codicil. 7 Nov. 1820. Changing bequests. Revokes gift to nephew Rev. William Maynard Payne of 30 acres of land late part of Black Rock Esatte who was then dead. Another codicil 9 Oct. 1827.

Will and Codicils Proved 2 June, 1828 in Prerog. C.C. (*Barbados Records. Vol. 66. p. 7.*)

Will of John Lane, brother of Elizabeth (Lane) Alleyne wife of William Gibbes Alleyne[6], dated 3 Oct. 1801, proved 30 Aug. 1802.

John Lane of the Island of Barbados now of Clifton, England, Esq. To wife Mary, Black Rock Plantation. Daughter Elizabeth Lane. Daughter Agnes Lane. Son John Branford Lane.

Codicil 9 Oct. 1801. For many years I have rented the Spring Plantation from my sister Elizabeth Alleyne.

Proved 30 Aug. 1802. (*632 Kenyon*) Somerset House, London.

22. THOMAS ALLEYNE[6] (*third son of Thomas*[5], *Reynold*[4], *Abel*[3], *Reynold*[2], *Richard*[1]) baptised 9 March 1739 at St. Thomas, Barbados.

Married 21 April 1763 Mary Gibbes, daughter of Reynold Gibbes of Plumtree, Barbados, at St. James.

Children of Thomas[6] and Mary Alleyne:—

i. ANN ISABELLA ALLEYNE,[7] born 21 Jan 1764, bapt 28 Jan. 1764 at St. James, Bdos. Married, 21 Jan. 1784, John Glasow Lewis at St. James, Barbados.

ii. SUSANNA GIBBES ALLEYNE, bapt. 7 Oct. 1765 at St. James, Barbados. Married George Maynard at St. James, Bdos. 20 March 1786. After her death he married her sister Mary, widow of William W. Williams.

iii. THOMAS ALLEYNE, born 19 Nov. 1767, bapt. 22 Nov. 1767 at St. James, Bdos.

iv. REYNOLD GIBBES ALLEYNE, born 17 April 1769, bapt. 27 April 1769 at St James, Bdos.

v. WILLIAM GIBBES ALLEYNE, born 25 Oct. 1770, bapt 4 Nov. 1770 at St. James, Bdos. Married. 28 July 1796, Isabella Piercy Selman at St. Thomas, Bdos. Resided in Demerara, British Guiana.

vi. MARY GIBBES ALLEYNE, bapt. 12 Oct. 1772 at St. James, Bdos. Married first, 5 June 1791, William Wiltshire Williams at St James, Bdos. Married secondly George Maynard her brother in-law.

vii. JOHN COLLINS ALLEYNE, born 1 Aug. 1776, bapt. 11 Aug. 1776 at St. James, Bdos. Married 30 July 1803 Sarah Christian Rolestone of Airy Hall, St. Thomas, Bdos.

Will, dated 14 March 1812, pr. 28 June, 1819 of John Collins Alleyne. Wife Sarah Christian Alleyne, formerly Sarah Christian Rollstone. *Airy Hall*, St. Thomas, Barbados, to be sold and money to brother William Gibbes Alleyne resident of Demerara, British Guiana.

Executrix and executor Wife and friend Dr. Samuel Forte. Signed
John Collins Alleyne. Witness: James Thurbarne Jones, Samuel
Fercharson. *(Barbados Records. Vol. 62. p. 30).*

viii. LUCY CHRISTIAN ALLEYNE, born 19 April 1779, bapt. 2 May 1779
at St. James, Barbados. Buried 8 Sept. 1794 aged 14 years at St.
James, Barbados.

ix BENJAMIN ROSTOCK MARSHALL ALLEYNE, bapt. 26 May 1782 at St.
James, Bdos.

x. ELIZABETH CARTER ALLEYNE, born 25 Aug. 1784 at St. James, Bdos.
Buried 25 May 1808 at St. James, Bdos.

Jonas Maynard =	Christian Mercy dau of.... Clarke & widow
married 6 Aug. 1761 as	of Reynold Alleyne 6, son of Abel Alleyne 5,
his fourth wife. Died 3	who was buried 17 Jan. 1758. She died 23 March
August 1781 aged 86	1777 aged 52 years.
years.	

George Maynard = 1st Susanna	Capt. Forster Maynard	Elizabeth Christian
Born 1765 Gibbes Alleyne	Born 1768. Married	Maynard. Born 1769
dau. of Thomas	Newland Mary Raines	Married Francis
Alleyne 6.		Ford Pinder of
= 2nd Mary Gibbes		Hothersal Estate,
Alleyne dau. of		Barbados.
Thomas Alleyne 6		
sister of Susanna & widow		
of William Wiltshire		
Williams.		

23. JOHN HOLDER ALLEYNE[6] , *(fourth son of Thomas[5] Rey-
nold[4] , Abel[3] , Reynold[2] , Richard[1] ,)*Buried 16 June 1794 at
St. James, Barbados. Married 16 May 1765, at St. James, Barbados.
Marian Alleyne daughter of Francis Skeete, of Mangrove Planta-
tion, Barbados. She was buried 6 Sept. 1809 at St. Thomas,
Barbados.

Children of John Holder Alleyne and Marian Alleyne, his
wife:—

i. JANE ROLLESTONE ALLEYNE, born 31 Dec 1767, bapt. 10 March 1768
at St. James, Barbados. Died 18 March 1838. Married her cousin
Abel Alleyne 7 son of Abel Alleyne 6 by whom she had a daughter
Marian Skeete Alleyne On Sunday the 18 inst. (March 1838) in
Aldersgate St. in the 70th year of her age, Jane, relict of the late
Abel Alleyne Esq. of Demerara. *(The Times,* London, 19 March
1838.)

ii. THOMAS ALLEYNE, bapt. 10 Aug. 1769 at St James, Barbados.
Married Elizabeth Lynch

iii. WILLIAM GIBBES ALLEYNE,

Will of John Holder Alleyne[6] of the Parish of St. George, Barbados. To be buried at the nearest Church for the ease and con-
venience of my dear family, in a plain coffin not to exceed in price
£10. All debts paid so that no one may suffer one farthing by my
death. Wife Marian Alleyne Alleyne household furniture. Grand-
daughter Marian Skeete Alleyne daughter of my daughter Jane
Rolleston Alleyne £200 at age of 14 years, interest amounting thereon to be paid to her mother Jane Rolleston Alleyne for her maintenance and education. To friend Miss Sarah Nowell £100. To three
children, Jane Rolleston, Thomas Alleyne and William Gibbes

Alleyne all I die possessed of or by virtue of my marriage articles in equal shares. I also give and bequeath unto my sons Thomas and William Gibbes Alleyne a bed, bolster and two pillows each. Executrix. Wife Marian A. Alleyne. Executors sons Thomas Alleyne and William Gibbes Alleyne. Dated 18 July 1793. Signed John Holder Alleyne. Witnesses: John Isaac Redman, Nathaniel Nowell. Proved at Pilgrim, Barbados, 28 Aug. 1794. *(Barbados Records. Vol. 29. p. 371.)*

24. JOHN ALLEYNE[7] , *(only son of Thomas[6] , John[5] , Thomas[4] , Abel[3] , Reynold[2] , Richard[1] .)* born 25 Sept. 1748, bapt. 2 Oct. 1748 at St. Peter, Barbados. Married 29 May 1768 Anne daughter of Benjamin Roswell of Hackney. He was of Lincoln's Inn, barrister-at-law, and Boswell Court, London. Children:

   i. HANNAH ALLEYNE, born 8 April 1769, bapt. 8 May 1769 at Hackney, England.

   ii. ANNE ALLEYNE, born 11 May 1770, at Boswell Court, bapt. 9 Dec. 1770 at St. Clement's Danes,

John Alleyne was educated at Eton 1761-3. He was entered on 16 Jany. 1761 as John Allen son and heir of Thomas Allen of Queen's Street, Westminister. (Fee paid £220. Eton Records-Harding.) Was at one time clerk in the office of Benjamin Roswell, attorney in Angel Court, Throgmorton Street, whose daughter he married. He was admitted student of the Middle Temple 27 April 1767, Barrister 8 May 1772..

In 1774 he published, "Legal Degrees of Matrimony stated and considered in series of letters to a Friend etc." He died at his home in Hackney 11 July 1777.

25. SIR REYNOLD ABEL ALLEYNE[7] , second Bart. *(second son of Sir John Gay[6] , John[5] , Reynold[4] , Abel[3] ,Reynold[2] ,Richard[1].)* born 10 June 1789, bapt. 16 July 1789 at St. Peter, Barbados. Died 14 Feb. 1870. Buried at Barton-under-Needwood, England. Married Rebecca Olton of Barbados, at St. Philip Church, Barbados, by license 20 Sept. 1810. Rebecca Olton (born 23 Aug. 1794, died 5 June 1860) third daughter (youngest) of John Allen Olton (by Anne daughter of Alexander Kirton, widow of Henry Peter Simmons of Barbados) of *Harrow* Barbados.

Children of Sir Reynold Abel Alleyne and Rebecca his wife:—

   i. JOHN GAY ALLEYNE, bapt. 29 July 1811 at St. James, Barbados, and died 31 July 1811.

   ii. PHILIPPA COBHAM ALLEYNE, born 17 Feb. 1813 Died 5 Jan. 1889 Married 6 July 1831 at St. Peters, Bdos. Hampden Clement Esq of 20 Wilton Crescent, S. W. London who died 4 Feb. 1880.

   Issue:—

   (i) *Reynold Alleyne Clement* Born 3 March 1834. Mar. 20 July 1867 Louisa Cecilia dau. of Sir Henry Martin Blackwood, Bart. Major late 68th Regt. New Zealand 1864—6. One of H. M. Gentlemen-at-Arms 1876 Served with 13th Hussars. She died 2 Oct. 1905 Leaving issue.

   (ii) *Rosalie Philippa Hampden Clement*

   (iii) *Helena Rebecca Clement*

   (iv.) *Son.*

iii. ANN ALLEYNE, born 9 Nov 1814. Died 14 Dec. 1864. Married 20 Feb. 1836 at St. Lucy, Barbados. William Fitz Herbert, eldest son of Sir Henry Fitz Herbert, who afterwards succeeded his father in the Baronetcy. He died 12 Oct. 1896.

Marriage record – William Fitz Herbert of St. Lucy and Anne Alleyne of St. Lucy. License. 20 Feb. 1836. Witnesses : R. A. Alleyne, Hampden Clement.

Issue : —

(i) *William Cromwell Fitz Herbert*, born 30 Jan. 1842. Died 24 Jan. 1874. Unmarried.

(ii) *Beresford Fitz Herbert*. Born 11 Sept. 1844. Died 25 May 1873 s p.

(iii.) *Rev. Sir Richard Fitz Herbert*, Born 12 April 1846. Md. 10 Oct. 1871 Mary Anne Arkwright, youngest dau. Edw. Arkwright of Fatten, Derby.

(iv) *Hugo Meynell Fitz Herbert*, Born 24 Dec. 1847 Died 6 Aug. 1864.

(v.) *Agnes Rebekah Fitz Herbert*, Died 4 Jan. 1921 Md. 16 Oct. 1867 Maj Gen. Wm. Reid Martin, Bengal Lancers.

(vi.) *Ida Fitz Herbert*. Died 25 Nov. 1890 s.p. Md. 30 Jan 1890 Edward Fletcher.

(vii.) *Frances Theresa Fitz Herbert*, Md. 22 Aug. 1883 Charles Edward Evelyn Harcourt – Vernon.

(viii) *Mina Fitz Herbert*, Died Unmarried.

iv. REBECCA ALLEYNE, born 25 Sept. 1816, bapt. 30 Oct. 1816 at St. Peter Barbados. Died 25 April 1894. Married 20 June 1837 Lieut. Col. Robert Fanshawe Martin 3rd son of Admiral Sir Byam Martin. No children.

Robert Fanshawe Martin, Lieut. Col. and Deputy Adjutant Quartermaster General at Bombay. Of Oriel Coll. Oxon. Matric. 18 Feb. 1823 age 17. Died 13 July 1836 at Poonah. s.p.

v. CAROLINE ALLEYNE, born 1st Oct. 1818, bapt. 18 Jan. 1819 at St. Peter Bdos. Died 27 July 1820

28. vi. SIR JOHN GAY NEWTON ALLEYNE, 8 born 8 Sept. 1820 at Alleynedale Hall, Barbados Died 20 Feb. 1912 at Falmouth, England. Married Augusta Isabella FitzHerbert.

vii. CAROLINE RYCROFT ALLEYNE, born 11 Dec. 1822. Privately bapt. 22 Dec. 1822 at 51 Upperton Gardens, Eastbourne, England. Publicly bapt. 10 Feb. 1823 at St. Peter, Barbados. She was Living 1870.

29 viii. REYNOLD FITZHERBERT BERESFORD ALLEYNE, born 7 Aug. 1825 at Alleyncdale Hall, Barbados. Died 24 Sept. 1889 at Barbados. Married Anna Maria Best Clarke.

30. ix. BOUVERIE ALLEYNE, Born 19 July 1828 at Alleynedale Hall, Barbados. Died 25 Oct. 1861 at St. Vincent, B. W. I. Married Charlotte Agnes Emma Colebrooke.

Sir Reynold Abel Alleyne succeeded to the Baronetcy at the age of twelve and was educated at Eton. He was Member of the Council of Barbados for 30 years and Colonel of Militia there.

As the only surviving son and heir-at-law of his father, he became entitled to *Bawdens* and *The River* plantations, the slaves, and all of his father's estate, charged with the payment of sums of £3,000 to each of his five sisters. During his minority the estates were held in trust, while he and his sisters derived income for their support out of the profits of the plantations. The family estate *Mount Alleyne* had descended through Thomas[4] Alleyne, and his son Reynold[5] and eventually passed to Elizabeth and Judith Alleyne, daughters of Reynold [5]. Judith Alleyne died unmarried, and Elizabeth her sister married John Newton and had no issue. John Newton by will dated August 8, 1782, created an entail of the plantation in settling it on Sir John Gay Alleyne and his heirs male; thus, it passed with all the working slaves with which Sir John had stocked it to Sir Reynold, who on attaining his majority executed a deed dated February 7, 1811, barring the entail and thenceforth holding the estate in fee simple. At that time the plantation was described as containing 357 acres of land, bounding on Lancaster plantation (then the property of Hon. John Alleyne Beckles) on Porter's and Mount Standfast plantations (belonging to Hon. John Forster Alleyne) on Westmorland plantation (then owned by Mr. William Prescod) on Apes Hill plantation, and on a place called Cabbage Tree belonging to George James Esq. The mansion house in which Reynold[5] Alleyne and his wife Elizabeth (Price) had resided was apparently then standing, and the plantation had a windmill and sugar works and was stocked with 102 slaves. The dwelling house was probably destroyed in the hurricane of 1831, and perhaps the windmill as well. The site of the windmill and sugar works and the mansion house is marked by the remains of the stone foundations but the lands of the plantation were very many years ago divided up and sold to the owners of adjoining estates, a large area being added to Lancaster plantation.

He bought Cabbage Tree Hall in the Parish of St. Peter, Barbados in 1810 and changed the name to *Alleynedale Hall.* Cabbage Tree Hall belonged to William Terrill whose daughter Mary married John Alleyne[5] grandfather of Sir Reynold Abel Alleyne. He also owned Barton Hall, Staffordshire, England.

On Jan. 6, 1826 the St. Peter and St. Lucy Battalion of Militia met at Cabbage Tree Hall plantation (the residence of Sir Reynold Abel Alleyne, Bart). *Barbadian Newspaper 1826.*

May 23 1826. Sir Reynold Abel Alleyne, Bart. presided as Chief Justice of the Grand Sessions. (*Ibid.*)

The following extracts from an "Account of the Fatal Hurricane by which Barbados suffered in August 1831" published in Bridgetown by Samuel Hyde in 1831, have reference to Sir Reynold A. Alleyne:—

"Six Men's Estate, the property of Lieutenant General Sir F. T. G. Maclean, Bart. was completely ravaged; not a building escaped total ruin. The mansion, built in the ancient style, and one of the most spacious in the colony, was the residence of the gallant General's daughter Mrs. John Alleyne" (wife of John Gay Alleyne, the son of John Forster Alleyne) "and family..... The highly respectable lady mentioned, her two sons and four daughters were there during that awful night exposed to the greatest misery that human nature could sustain; as the water poured from the heavens it

57

accumulated in the pit until it was up to the waists of the sufferers. In this dreadful situation, with almost all their clothes beaten off and without refreshment, they were compelled to remain until the forenoon of the 11th, when having collected some pieces of negro clothing that were strewed about, they proceeded in an almost exhausted state through mud and water to the seat of Sir R. A. Alleyne, Bart., about a mile distant, where 'they arrived at 2 p.m. in a most dreadful plight."

"In the second despatch of His Excellency Sir James Lyon to Lord Viscount Goderich the Secretary of State for the Colonies, dated Aug. 30, 1831 the disobedient and even rebellious conduct of the slaves was referred to........ Induced by evil disposed persons of whom members are not wanting in any community, these misguided people thought to take advantage of the universal devastation and commenced a course of plunder..... The particulars of this misconduct have not generally transpired, and it is less publicly known to whom the colonists are indebted for the suppression of the rebellious spirit which was manifested in no small degree on several estates in the leeward part of the Island. To the patriotism and decisive conduct of the Honourable Sir Reynold A. Alleyne, it was owing that the sparks of insurrection were promptly extinguished, otherwise the flame would soon have been kindled, and would have spread with rapidity into every part of the Island."

Here are other incidents in Sir Reynold A. Alleyne's life. He fought a duel with Mr. Downes and shot him through the lungs from which he died, Sir Reynold Abel being wounded in the leg. He ordered a gold tea service from England; the ship that brought it was wrecked and a case of teaspoons was washed ashore. Sir Reynold once rode a horse up the stairway of St. Nicholas Abbey, St. Peter, Barbados. It was his custom to send 16 horses for the Governor, Lord Combermere, whenever the latter visited him at his home Alleynedale Hall.

In 1823 Sir Reynold Abel Alleyne writes to Mr. Francis that: "Mr. Simmons is embarrased and under all circumstances a tardy Paymaster." John Simmons was youngest son of Henry Peter Simmons and Anne Kirton. Rebecca Olton, wife of Sir Reynold Abel Alleyne, was John Simmons' half sister, youngest daughter of Anne Kirton (Simmons) and John Allen Olton. John Simmons bought Harrow Plantation, Barbados from Mr. John Olton in 1811.

In St. Lucy's Church, Barbados, on the east wall of the nave, north side, is a Gothic brass in colours on black marble:—Crest of Alleyne. Arms of Alleyne. Quartering: *Argent, two chevronels between three trefoils azure* (Terrill). Impaling, *Gules, a lion rampant Or* (Olton). Motto—Non tua sed publica vota. Badge of Ulster.

Sacred to the loved/memory of Sir Reynold/Abel Alleyne, Bart./Born June 10th 1789/Died Feb. 14th 1870/and Rebecca, his wife/Born Aug. 23rd 1794/Died June 5th 1860/ (2 Lines).

Oliver's M.I. op. cit.

Will of SIR REYNOLD ABEL ALLEYNE[7] .

Sir Reynold Abel Alleyne, Bart. late of Nuttal House, Barton-under-Needwood, Co. Stafford, Eng. Died at Nuttall House 14 Feb. 1870. Will proved by his son Sir John Gay Newton Alleyne and Thomas Hill, 21 March 1870. Executors John Gay Newton Alleyne, Thomas Daniel Hill, Henry Bridges.

Whereas I have already made provision for several of my children. House and lands, Nuttal, to daughter Caroline Rycroft Alleyne. Also £3,000 to her. Son John Gay Newton Alleyne £3,000 before estates in Barbados are sold, they to be offered for sale to son Reynold Beresford FitzHerbert Alleyne at a fair valuation. Had already given son furniture, effects etc. which he shall keep. Dated 10 May, 1867. Signed Reynold Abel Alleyne. Witnesses: John Richardson, William Small.

Codicil. All ready money to daughter. All silver plate to son John Gay Newton Alleyne. Signed Reynold Abel Alleyne. Recorded in Barbados 29 April, 1870. (*Barbados Records Vol. 80 p. 146.*)

Will of John Allen Olton dated 9 Nov. 1809. Proved 1811.

John Allen Olton of Marylebone London, Eng. Taking a voyage to Barbados. My daughter Margaret Ann Olton £10,000. My dau. Mary Dunkin wife of Thomas Dunkin Lieut. of the 4th Dragoons £250 a year. My dau. Rebecca Olton £10,000 at 21 yrs. To son John Allen Olton plantation called *Allens* in parish of St. Philip of 380 acres. To brother Henry Olton all lands and slaves in Surinam, in trust to sell. Mother Mary Olton £500.

Signed John Allen Olton.

P.C.C. 246 Crockett.

Tablet in St. James' Piccadilly, London to Ann Olton wife of John Allen Olton of Barbados. Died 22 June 1804 aged 20 years.

ALLEYNE OF BARBADOS.

(FIFTH INSTALMENT.)

CONTRIBUTED BY LOUISE R. ALLEN.

26. ABEL ALLEYNE[7] (*eldest son of Thomas*[6], *Abel*[5], *Reynold*[4], *Abel*[3], *Reynold*[2], *Richard*[1]), born 19 May, 1757 at Salem, Mass., being Thursday; bapt. 27 May, 1757 at St. Peter Episcopal Church, Salem, Mass., U.S.A. by the Rev. Mr. Gilchrist. His godfathers were his father's brothers Reynold and John Alleyne, the Rev. Edward Winslow and his father standing proxy for them. Mrs. Mary Alleyne was his godmother. Died 7 Dec., 1807 of apoplexy. Buried at the Episcopal Church, Dedham, Mass.

He was married at Bolton, Mass., to Anna Chase, daughter of Thomas Chase of Bolton, Mass., by the Rev. Phineas Wright at Mrs. Elizabeth Chase's on Thursday evening 22 Nov., 1787.

Anne, widow of Abel Alleyne, born 10 Aug., 1765, died 6 Nov., 1812, aged 47 years, at Milton, Mass. Buried 9 Nov. at the Episcopal Church Quincy, Mass.

Abel Alleyne owned a paper mill on the Neponset River, in Mattapan, Mass.

Abel Alleyne and George Clarke both of Milton, Mass., were chosen wardens of St. Paul's Church, Dedham, Mass., 6 April, 1801. Later it was decided wardens must live in Dedham. Abel Alleyne moved to Dedham and died there.

Children of Abel and Anna Alleyne:—

i. DOROTHY DEBORAH FORSTER ALLEYNE, born 24 Sept. 1788, at Braintree, Mass. Died 30 July 1843, at Roxbury, Mass. Married Jabez Chickering, Jr.

ii. MARY BENJAMINA WOODBRIDGE ALLEYNE, born 29 May, 1791. Died at Quincy, Mass. Married first, 30 Nov. 1806, John Jacob Gourgas. Married second, 16 Nov. 1823, John Avery Coffin Esq.

31. iii. THOMAS HARBIN ALLEYNE, born 14 Nov. 1792, at Milton, Mass., Died 25 June 1839, at St. James, Barbados. Married Elizabeth Frere Williams.

iv. SARAH HANNAH BOIES ALLEYNE, born 24 Aug. 1794, at Milton, Mass., Died 13 Jan. 1864. Married Frederick Beck.

32. v. JAMES HOLDER ALLEYNE, born 30 May 1798, at Milton, Mass. Died 1876—7 in London, England. Married Caroline Robertson.

vi. ABEL DUDLEY ALLEYNE, born 9 July 1796, at Milton, Mass. Died 11 Sept. 1828 at Woodstock, Vermont, aged 31 yrs. Born at Milton, Mass on Saturday, 9 July 1796, at 4 o'clock A. M. Bapt. by Rev. Mr. Montague and named for his father and Aunt Clarke, a daughter of Dr. Joseph Clarke of St. John's River, (Maugersville) New Brunswick, Canada. (Bible Record.)

33. vii. JEREMIAH SMITH BOIES ALLEYNE, born 5 Dec. 1800, at Milton, Mass. Bapt 22 Dec. 1801, at Episcopal Church, Dedham, Mass. Married Lydia Stedman 11 Dec. 1825, in Boston, Mass. born in Milton (Mass.) on Friday Dec. 5, 1800, at half past 1 o'clock A. M. Bapt. by Rev. Wm. Montague and named for his Uncle Boies. (Bible Record.)

viii. GEORGE JOHN FORSTER ALLEYNE, born 23 Jan. 1803, at Dorchester, Mass. Bapt. 7 Feb. 1803, at Episcopal Church, Dedham, Mass.

Died   1848 in New Orleans, U.S.A. George John Forster
Alleyne aged 12 years, left Boston 29 Oct. 1815 for Barbados.
John George born in Dorchester, (Mass,) on Sunday. Jan. 23 1803
at half past 9 o'clock A. M. Bapt. by Rev. Mr. Montague and
named for his Uncle Alleyne of Barbados, and a son of his that
died in Bristol, England. Died New Orleans (U S. A.) 1848.
(Old Alleyne Bible.)

27. JOHN FORSTER ALLEYNE[λ] (*second son of Thomas* [6] *
Abel* [5], *Reynold* [4], *Abel* [3], *Reynold* [2], *Richard* [1]), born 22 April
1762 at Braintree, Mass., U.S.A., died 29 Sept., 1823 at Porters,
Barbados. Married 10 June, 1782 Elizabeth Gibbes Willing, daughter of Charles Willing of Philadelphia, Penn., U.S.A.

John Forster Alleyne, born at Braintree, Mass., 22 April, 1762
being Thursday. Bapt. by Rev. Mr. Miller an hour after his birth
being very ill. (Alleyne Bible Record.)

John Forster Alleyne was adopted by his aunt, Mrs. Sarah
Forster Osborne, (his mother's sister) in Barbados, who left him
her property. She was "Aunt Osbourne." Her sister, Deborah
Forster, never married, and by her will left Mrs. Sarah Forster
Osborne the income from her property; the principal went to her
great niece, who was born while Deborah Forster was on a visit to
England. She said she would leave the money to her if they named
her Deborah; the child's first name, Dorothy, was added by her
father, Abel Alleyne, for his mother, Dorothy Harbin Forster
Alleyne. This Dorothy Deborah Forster Alleyne married Jabez
Chickering and was called "Aunt Chickering."

John Forster Alleyne was appointed Chief Judge of the Court
of Common Pleas for the precinct of St. James on 31 July, 1798
by Governor Ricketts, in which office he served for many years. He
was also a member of His Majesty's Council for Barbados during
a long period, eventually attaining the high office of President of
the Council. During his Presidency he twice acted as Governor
of Barbados in 1817, in the absence of Lord Combermere.

Elizabeth Gibbes Willing daughter of Charles Willing of
Bridgetown, Barbados, and Hannah Carrington of Carrington's
Estate, Barbados, was born in Philadelphia, Penna., U.S.A., 1 Oct.,
1764. She died 12 Feb., 1820 at 28 York Crescent, Clifton, Bristol,
England, aged 56 years. Her remains were transported to Barbados
and interred in the family cemetery in St. James Church-yard.
Her mother Elizabeth Hannah Willing, died 12 Oct., 1795 at St.
James, Barbados, and was buried in St. James Church-yard where
a stone with the following inscription marks her place of burial
in the Gibbes family enclosure.

UNDERNEATH THIS STONE ARE DEPOSITED/THE REMAINS/OF/MRS.
ELIZ. HANNAH WILLING/RELICT OF CHARLES WILLING ESQR./LATE OF
THE CITY OF PHILADELPHIA/IN THE STATE OF PENNSYLVANIA/IN NORTH
AMERICA/SHE WAS BORN THE 12TH OF MARCH 1739/AND/DIED THE
12TH OF OCTOBER 1795.

Two other vaults in the same enclosure in the churchyard are
marked with the following inscriptions:—

61

HERE LIE THE REMAINS OF/THE HON'BLE JOHN. FORSTER
ALLEYNE/WHO DIED ON THE 29TH SEPT. 1823/AGED 63 YEARS/AND
OF HIS BELOVED WIFE/ELIZ. GIBBES ALLEYNE/WHO DIED ON THE 12TH
FEB. 1820/AGED 55 YEARS/ALSO THOSE OF/MANY OF THEIR CHILDREN
/WHO WERE PREVIOUSLY INTERRED/IN THE SAME GRAVE.

SACRED/TO THE MEMORY OF MARY/FOURTH DAUGHTER OF/THE
HON'BLE JOHN FORSTER ALLEY,NE/AND ELIZABETH GIBBES ALLEYNE/
OF PORTERS, IN THIS PARISH/WHO DEPARTED THIS LIFE/THE 6TH
NOVEMBER 1835/AGED 40 YEARS. (2 LINES.)

(Monumental Inscriptions of Barbados by V. L. Oliver.)

Hon. John Forster Alleyne bore the arms of his family quartered with the Willing (? Lowle) arms—Sable, a dexter cubit arm
couped, the hand grasping three arrows, one pale, two saltire. Per
chevron gules and ermine in chief two lions' heads erased Or.
(Alleyne). Motto—Je crains Dieu et n'ai point d'autre crainte.

Children of John Forster Alleyne and Elizabeth Gibbes
Alleyne, his wife:—

34. i. HAYNES GIBBES ALLEYNE, born 14 May 1783, Barbados, bapt. 5
June 1783, St Michael, Bdos. Died at sea 23 July 1813 Married
Georgiana Yea 21 May 1804.

35. ii. JOHN GAY ALLEYNE, born 21 July 1785, bapt. 13 Sept. 1785, St.
James, Bdos. Died 10 March 1821, Married 1 July 1807, Johanna
Bishop.

36. iii. SARAH GIBBES ALLEYNE, born 11 Sept. 1787, bapt 15 Oct. 1787,
St. James, Bdos. Died   Sept 1876. Married 19 May 1808, Capt
Alex. McGeachy.

37. iv. JAMES HOLDER ALLEYNE, born 13 March 1790. Died 2 July, 1842.
Married   1815, Elizabeth Mary Lowe James.

      v. ELIZABETH ALLEYNE, born 4 April 1792, bapt. 30 May 1792, at
St. James, Bdos. Died 13 Nov. 1806 at Porters, Barbados. aged
14 years 7 mo.

      vi. MARGARET SALTER ALLEYNE, born 16 Jan. 1794, bapt. 21 April
1794, at St. James, Bdos Died 7th May 1823 in London, England.
Married 25 May 1811, David Hall Esq. of *Locust Hall*, Barbados,
at St. James, Church, by Rev. Mr. Pilgrim.

      vii. MARY ALLEYNE, born 25 Sept. 1795. bapt. 26 Dec. 1795, at St.
James, Bdos. Died at Porters 6 Nov. 1835 of heart disease. Buried
at St. James, Bdos. Single.

Will of Mary Alleyne dated 16 May, 1833. Proved 30 Jan.,
1836. Residing in village of Clifton, Co., Gloucester, Eng.

In consequence of the altered state of affairs in the West Indies,
I am led to apprehend that many of my nearest relatives may be
reduced to much pecuniary distress and I therefore feel myself
called upon to make a different disposal of my fortune to that
which I made some years ago etc. Regrets omitting the names of
others to whom in a former will she had bequeathed legacies, but
they have other resources, and these need it more. Dear sister
Charlotte Emily Alleyne, use of interest on £1,200, late a debt owing
me from my brother Charles Thomas Alleyne but recently paid me.
At her death to be divided between my brothers Rev. John Forster
Alleyne and Henry Alleyne. Of the mortgage given by my brother
Hon. John Forster Alleyne on his estate of *Coxes* in Barbados for

something above the sum of £5,200. I give my brother Rev. John Forster Alleyne £1,500. Youngest brother Henry Alleyne £1,500. The daughters of my late brother John Gay Alleyne £1,500 equally. Nephew Alexander McGeachy Alleyne, son of Brother James Holder Alleyne £500. And also the remainder of sum due to me on the mortgage of his father Hon. James Holder Alleyne.

Give brother Henry Alleyne right and title to sum of money which I became entitled to by the will of the late Paul Bedford and now owing me from the estate of my Father. Also six silver table and six teaspoons with my crest and initials engraved on them. God-daughter Joana Bishop Alleyne gold watch.

Sister Charlotte Emily right and property in any slaves in Barbados also any money, jewels, plate, or property not otherwise disposed of.

Executors:—Brothers James Holder Alleyne, Charles Thomas Alleyne, Henry Alleyne. Signed Mary Alleyne.

Codicil dated 8 February, 1834:—About to embark on voyage to Barbados in Ship *Steadfast*. Instructions for manumission of child of servant Carlyon Wilson who accompanied her on the voyage. Adds brother Rev. John Forster Alleyne as executor.

Sum of money bequeathed to sister C. E. Alleyne at her death to go to my brothers John Forster Alleyne and Henry Alleyne or survivor is £1,346. 14s. 4d. in 3% reduced stock and was purchased for me by Robert Bright Esq.

The will first proved in England 22 January, 1836 on the testimony of David Hall of Chertsey, Surrey and Charles Thomas Alleyne of Barbados.

viii. CHARLOTTE WILLING ALLEYNE, born 18 March 1797, bapt. 20 Mar. 1797. Buried 8 Oct. 1797 at St. James, Barbados.

38. ix. CHARLES THOMAS ALLEYNE, born 1 May 1798. bapt. 9 July 1798 at St. James, Bdos. Died 15 April 1872, Married Margaret Frances Bruce Pryce

x. THOMAS ALLEYNE, born 13 July 1799. bapt. 30 Sept. 1799 at Clifton Eng. Died 14 Feb. 1807, at Porters, Bdos, aged 7 yrs. 7 mo.

xi. GEORGE FORSTER ALLEYNE, born 20 Oct. 1801 at Westbury College, Eng., bapt. Nov. following. Died 29 Sept. 1802.

39. xii. JOHN FORSTER ALLEYNE, born 3 Feb. 1804, at Westbury College, Eng. bapt 30 March 1805, Died 16 Dec. 1884, Married Helen Maria Gore.

xiii. CHARLOTTE EMILY ALLEYNE, born 28 June 1805 at Berkeley Square, Bristol, Eng., bapt. 25 May 1808 at St. James, Bdos. Died 1884. 25 May 1808. Received into the church (St. James, .Bdos.; Charlotte Emily daughter of John Forster & Elizabeth Gibbes Alleyne. Born 28 June 1805 & privately baptized at St. Augustine Chapel in the Bristol, Eng. by name of Charlotte alone. (Record St. James Church, Bdos.)

xiv. DOUGLAS ALLEYNE, born 2 Jan. 1807, at Porters. Bdos. bapt. 25 May 1808. Died 1820 at Clifton, Bristol, Eng. 25 May 1808. Received into the church (St. James, Bdos.) Douglas son of John Forster & Elizabeth Gibbes Alleyne Born Jan. 2 1807 & privately baptized by me on the 15th (Jan.) Signed J. Pilgrim,

40. xv. HENRY ALLEYNE, born 2 Jan. 1808, bapt. 25 May 1808, at St. James,

Bdos. Died 3—4 Jan. 1852. Drowned when the "Amazon" burned in the Bay of Biscay. Married Mary Reeve.

xvi. Sophia Alleyne, bapt. March 1810, St. James, Bdos. Buried 22 March 1810 at St. James, Bdos.

Will (dated 9 June, 1823. Proved 13 Oct., 1823) of John Forster Alleyne [7] of the Parish of St. James, B'dos. Grandsons Forster Alleyne McGeachy, son of daughter Sarah Gibbes McGeachy, widow, and John Forster Alleyne, son of late son John Gay Alleyne £500 each. Son Charles Thomas Alleyne watch made by Roskell, chain and seals. Son John Forster Alleyne watch made by Ellicott. Nephews Abel Dudley Alleyne, Jeremian Smith Boies Alleyne. Nieces Deborah Forster Chickering, Mary Woodbridge Gourgas and Sarah Hannah Beck sons and daughters of my late brother Abel Alleyne, resident in the United States of America, 30 gs. each. Executors empowered to sell two Sugar Work Plantations known as *Porters* and *Mount Standfast* etc., also all plate, silver, jewels, pictures, horses and all other property etc. in this island, or United States or England for the most money that can be obtained. After all debts and legacies are paid I then give my two daughters Sarah Gibbes McGeachy, widow, and Margaret Salter Hall, wife of David Hall, Esq. £1,000 each. Daughter Mary Alleyne, Spinster, £7,000. Youngest daughter Charlotte Emily, spinster, £6,000. Residue equally divided between four sons, James Holder Alleyne, Charles Thomas Alleyne, John Forster Alleyne, and Henry Alleyne. Taking out the sum of £5,000 from share of James Holder Alleyne which was given him at his marriage to Elizabeth Mary James, relict of George James Esq. Three youngest children John Forster Alleyne, Henry Alleyne, Charlotte Emily Alleyne.

Executors:—Sons James Holder Alleyne, Charles Thomas Alleyne, son-in-law David Hall, daughter Sarah Gibbs McGeachy, Mary Alleyne, guardians of the three youngest children.

Signed Jno. F. Alleyne.

Sister-in-law Mrs. Ann Morris, widow, of the City of Philadelphia in U.S.A. £100.

Witnesses:—Moses Ward, Alexander Trotter, Edward Coleton. Probate granted at Government House 13 Oct., 1823.

(*Barbados Records Vol. 63, p. 14*).

The following records have been taken from a Bible presented to Elizabeth Gibbes Alleyne by her Uncle Rev. Francis Fitchatt, 23 Oct., 1793.

John Forster Alleyne married Elizabeth Gibbes, daughter of Charles Willing of Philadelphia, Penn., U.S.A., 10 June, 1782.

Mary born 25 Sept. 1795, being Friday, at half after six in the evening.

Charlotte Willing born 18 March being Saturday 1797 at 8 o'clock in the morning. Died 8 Oct., 1797.

Charles Thomas Born 1 May, 1798 at 11 o'clock at night. Bapt. 9 July.

Thomas born in the village of Clifton, near Bristol at 6 o'clock in the morning 13 July, 1799. Bapt. 30 Sept. at the parish church of Clifton. Died a quarter before three Thursday afternoon 14 Feb., 1807 aged 7 years 7 mo.

George Forster born in the Parish of Westbury-upon-Trym at the College House, in Co. Gloucester, at three quarters after six in the evening on Tuesday, 20 Oct., 1801. Bapt. 29 Nov. following. Died at a quarter before 1 Wednesday morning 29 Sept., 1802.

John Forster born Parish of Westbury etc. at 7 o'clock in the evening 3 Feb., 1804. Bapt. in Westbury Church 30 March, 1805.

Charlotte Emily born in Parish of St. Augustine, in City of Bristol, at Friday noon, one o'clock June 28, 1804. Bapt. at St. James in the Island of Barbados, 25 May 1808 by Rev. J. F. Pilgrim.

Douglas, born at Porters, St. James, Barbados, Friday morning at 7 o'clock 2 Jan., 1807. Bapt at St. James, 25 May, 1808.

Henry born Saturday afternoon at 2 o'clock 2 Jan., 1808. Bapt. at St. James 25 May 1808.

Alexander McGeachy married Sarah Gibbes Alleyne. Married by Rev. Mr. Pilgrim at Porters 19 May, 1808.

John Forster son of Thomas Alleyne and Dorothy his wife born in the village of Braintree, Mass., North America on the 22 day of April, 1762,

Elizabeth Gibbes daughter of Charles Willing and Elizabeth Hannah his wife born in the City of Philadelphia in the State of Pennsylvania in North America on the 1 Day of October, 1764.

John Forster Alleyne and the above Elizabeth Gibbes Willing were married in the Parish Church of St. Michael in the Island of Barbados by the Rev. Doctor Thomas Wharton on the 10th day of June, 1782.

Haynes Gibbes son of John Forster Alleyne and Elizabeth Gibbes, born 14 May, 1783 being Wednesday at three quarters before 10 o'clock in the morning and Baptized the 5 June by Rev. Dr. Thomas Wharton. Sponsors, Sir John Gay Alleyne, William Thorpe Holder Esq. Mrs. Sarah Gibbes, Miss Abigall Willing, Mrs. Francis Straker.

John Gay born July 28, 1785 at six o'clock in the morning. Bapt. in Sept. by Rev. Fras. Fitchatt. Sponsors His Excellency Gov. Parry, Sir John Gay Alleyne, Mrs. J. C. Parry, Mrs. Abel (?Alleyne). [The Church record states that he was born on July 21.]

Dudley Fitchatt married Johanna Bishop 1 July, 1807 by Rev. Mr. Caddell at Reid's Bay House, St. James, Barbados. (This is evidently an error. It was John Gay Alleyne, second son of Hon. John Forster Alleyne, who on that date married Johanna Bishop.)

Sarah Gibbes born Tuesday 11 Sept., 1787 at six o'clock in the evening. Baptized 15 Oct.

James Holder born 13 March, 1790 at half past two in the morning.

Elizabeth born 4 April, 1792 being Thursday at 11 o'clock at night. Died 13 Nov., 1806 Thursday afternoon at a quarter before 3. Aged 14 years 7 mo.

Margaret Salter born 16 Jan. being Thursday 1794 at a quarter after two in the morning. Baptized 21 April.

James Holder married Elizabeth Mary Lowe of Gregg Farm, Barbados.

Joseph Lowe Married Julia daughter of J. A. Holder of Lemon Arbor, Barbados.

Alexander McGeachy married Henrietta daughter of Rev. R. Wood of Husbands, Bosworth, Leicestershire.

Arthur married Rosalie daughter of Admiral White.

Haynes Gibbes (Alleyne) born 14 May, 1783, died 1813, married Georgiana Yea daughter of Wm. Yea of Purland, Co. Somerset. Were married Monday morning 25 May 1804 by Rev. George Trevyllian in the parish church of Bishop Hull in above mentioned Co.

Charles Thomas married Margaret daughter of John Bruce Pryce, Duffryn, Co. Glamorgan, Wales.

John Forster married Helen daughter of Gen. Arthur Gore, (She was born 5th Feb., 1814. Died Dec., 1894) at Church, Cookham, Hants.

Margaret Salter (born 16 Jan. 1794) married David Hall Esq. Died 1823 leaving a son A. Hall Esq., who married Caroline Hanky, leaving 4 sons and 4 daughters.

Douglas, his wife ran away with another man who blew his brains out on the steps of a club.

Henry Nelson died about 1820 married Constance Knyvett daughter of Sir . . . . Knyvett.

John Forster 2nd son of Thomas, born at Braintree near Boston in North America, 22 April 1762 married 10 June 1782. Died at Barbados 29 Sept. 1823. Married Elizabeth Willing of Philadelphia who was born 1 Oct. 1764. Died 12 Feb. 1820.

Thomas married Mary daughter of Reynold Gibbes Esq. of Plumtree, Barbados.

John Holder married Mary Anne daughter of Francis Skeet of Mangrove, Barbados.

Joseph Lowe born Nov. 1820 married Julia daughter of J. A. Holder, of Lemon Arbor, Barbados.

Caroline married J. D. Maycock, son of James D. Son Frederick and daughter Eleanor.

Forster McGeachy married Elsinora Alma.

Herbert Percy, married Amy daughter of R. Bright.

Arthur Gore, son of John Forster, Born 14 Dec. 1841 died 26 Jan. 1861 at Montevideo. Midshipman H.M.S. Curacoa.

Charles Stuart Forster son of John Forster, born 17 March 1844, died 15 Nov. 1863. Ensign 92nd Gordon Highlanders.

Alice Maria daughter of John Forster born 19 Oct. 1845, married 12 April 1866 to G. W. Marker, who died 12 Oct. 1904.

John married Mary daughter of Wm. Terrill sole heir of her mother, Rebecca, co-heir of Col. Thomas Spire, married 24 Nov. 1718 in Bedford Street, Covent Garden. Buried at Guilford, Co. Surrey.

Elizabeth daughter of Reynold of Mt. Alleyne, son of Thomas, son of Abel, married John Newton of Newtons, and Mt. Alleyne and Spitsbury Co. Dorset. Living 1771.

The following information concerning the Willing family has been extracted from papers and records in the possession of the descendants of Charles Willing, the father of Mrs. John Forster Alleyne.

Charles Willing was the second son of Charles Willing and Anne his wife, formerly Anne Shippen. He was born in Philadelphia on May 30, 1738, and became a prominent merchant in that city, but he also carried on business in Barbados where he resided for many years. He married at Barbados May 24, 1760, Elizabeth Hannah Carrington, (born at Barbados March 12, 1739) daughter of Paul and Elizabeth Carrington, and later returned to Philadelphia, where his daughters, Elizabeth Gibbes Willing, and Anne Willing were born. He continued to reside there until his death in 1788 in his fiftieth year. An excellent portrait of him by Benjamin West is in the possession of Charles Willing Littel of Baltimore. His widow, returned to Barbados after his death and died there in 1795. Their daughter Anne Willing (born 1767, died January 11, 1853) married March 9, 1786, Luke Morris, son of Anthony and Elizabeth (Hudson) Morris. Her only son, Thomas Willing Morris of Waterloo Farm, Baltimore, was at one time Lafayette's A.D.C.

Charles Willing the elder, father of the abovenamed Charles Willing, was born in Bristol, England, on May 18, 1710, but he settled in Philadelphia in 1728 when he was only eighteen years of age. His parents were Thomas Willing, a merchant of Bristol, and Anne his wife, formerly Anne Harrison, who was a granddaughter of two regicides, Major General Thomas Harrison, and Simon Mayne, both members of the court who had condemned Charles I. Thomas Willing was the child of Joseph Willing of Gloucester, and his second wife, Ava Lowle.

28. SIR JOHN GAY NEWTON ALLEYNE [8] *eldest surviving son of Reynold Abel* [7] *, John Gay* [6] *, John* [5] *, Reynold* [4] *, Abel* [3] *. Reynold* [2] *, Richard* [1] *)*, born 8 Sept. 1820 in Barbados, died 20 Feb. 1912 at Cambridge Place, Falmouth, Eng. Aged 92 yrs. Married 11 March 1851 Augusta Isabella 6th daughter of Sir Henry Fitz Herbert 3rd Bart. of Tissington Hall, Derbyshire. She died at Falmouth 9 Sept. 1910.

Children of Sir John Gay Newton Alleyne and Augusta Isabella his wife.

41.   i.   REYNOLD HENRY NEWTON ALLEYNE, born 16 May 1852 at Barbados, died 6 April 1908 at Falmouth, England. Married 4 January 1879 Susanna Meynell, daughter of John Meynell of Meynell Lang'ey, Derbyshire.

      ii.   AGNES REBECCA AUGUSTA ALLEYNE, born 8 June 1855. Married 7 Sept. 1880 Frederick Channer Corfield, J. P , of Ormonde Fields, Derby, and Chatwell Hall, Leebotwood, Salop. Eldest son of Rev. Frederick Corfield, Vicar of Shirley Co. Derby.

SIR JOHN MEYNELL ALLEYNE
4th Baronet

SIR JOHN GAY NEWTON ALLEYNE
3rd Baronet

Issue :

(1) *Frederick Alleyne Corfield,* born 1884 Married Mary Graham, daughter of T. Bowater Vernon, 1907.

(2) *Richard Fitzherbert Corfield,* born 1892. Married Beth daughter of J. W, Rynam-Smith.

(3) *John Wilmot Corfield,* born 1893. Married 1919 Jean daughter of J. J. Beringer.

(4) *Ralph Tregoning Channer Corfield,* born 1895.

(5) *Agnes Sarah Augusta Corfield,* Married 1906 Ivan Fitz Herbert Wright.

(6) *Lucy Mary Corfield,* Married 1905 Kenneth Hepburn Wright.

(7) *Margaret Emily Corfields,* Married 1917, Edward Wheatly Kilby.

(8) *Kitty Conyngham Corfield,* Married 1911 Rev. Arthur Clement Buss.

iii. JUDITH ALLEYNE, born 27 Dec. 1856. Married 7 Sept. 1880 William de Burgh Jessop, J. P. He died 10 April 1894.

Issue :

(1) *John De Burgh Jessop,* D. S. O. Lieut. Commander Royal Navy Died a few years after the Great War.

(2) *Mabel Alleyne Jessop,* born 6 March 1883. Married Commander Henry Albert Le Fowne Hurt, C. M. G., R. N. 1906.

(3) *Dorothy Babington Jessop.* Married 1910 Maj. James Gerald Thewlis Johnson D. S. O.

(4) *Eva FitzHerbert Jessop.* Married Com. Phillip Acheson Warre O. B. E., R. N. 1921.

iv. ANTHONY FITZ HERBERT ALLEYNE, born 25 Oct. 1858. Died 30 Dec. 1859. Buried at Barton-Under-Needwood, Staff.

v. REBECCA OLTON ALLEYNE, born 20 June 1860. Married 7 Nov. 1883, Frederick Charles Arkwright J. P., D. L. He died 18 July 1923.

Issue :—

(1) *Richard Alleyne Arkwright,* born 1 Sept. 1884. Married 1912, Marjorie daughter of Captain Frank Hardcastle, Coldstream Guards.

(2) *Frederick George Alleyne Arkwright,* born 23 Oct. 1885. In the World War 1914—1918. Lieut. 11th Hussars 1905 and R. F. Corps. Killed in flying accident in the Great War.

(3) *Katharine Rebecca Arkwright,* born 16 July 1890 Married Capt. Guy Bonham-Carter. 19th Hussars, Killed in Action 1915.

vi. MAUD ALLEYNE, born 30 Aug. 1862. Died 1863.

vii. MARY ALLEYNE, born 24 Nov. 1863.

viii. GRACE ALLEYNE, born 30 May 1866

ix. AUGUSTA ALLEYNE, born 17 Dec. 1867.

x. KATHARINE OCTAVIA ALLEYNE born 28 April 1870. Residence 3 Cambridge Place, Falmouth, England.

John Gay Newton Alleyne was educated at Harrow and Bonn University. He was entered at Harrow as Alleyne, John Gay Newton, son of Sir Reynold A. Alleyne, 2nd Bart. Alleyne Dale Hall, Barbados. Entrance Easter. Midsummer 1837. (The Grove.)

Left Mids. 1840. (Mr. Street) (Harrow School Registers). He was Warden of Dulwich College 1843-51. He drove a tandem, and shot woodcock over what is now the most crowded part of Dulwich. Manager of Sugar Works Plantation in Barbados 1851-2. Engineer and Manager of the Butterley Iron Works 1852-80. Vice-President of the Iron and Steel Institute, M.I.C.I., M.I.M.E. (He refused the Presidency of the Institute.) County Alderman and J.P. Derby. Succeeded as third Baronet 14 Feb. 1870. He possessed mechanical genius in a high degree and his engineering was entirely self-taught while he was Warden of Dulwich College. It was while he was manager of the Butterley Company in 1868 that he engineered the construction and erection of St. Pancras Station at that time the greatest span in the world.

On the occasion of the golden wedding of Sir John and Lady Alleyne in 1901 there were assembled children, grandchildren, sons-in-law and daughters-in-law to the number of 35.

For many years Sir John lived at Chevin House, about a mile from the village of Hazelwood in Derbyshire, and took an active part and interest in county affairs. He established an observatory at Chevin, with the then second largest telescope in the world. He learned to bicycle after he had passed his eightieth year and he owned and sailed his yacht the 'Wave Queen.' In 1875 he was appointed a county magistrate and he regularly attended the Court of Quarter Sessions and the Belper Police Court, where his wide experience and business ability made his advice and opinion very acceptable to his colleagues. When County Councils were established Sir John was honoured by being appointed one of the first Aldermen and retained that post until his death.

ALLEYNE OF BARBADOS.

(Sixth Instalment.)

Contributed by Louise R. Allen.

---

29. **Reynold Fitzherbert Beresford Alleyne**[8] *(third son of Sir Reynold Abel , Sir John Gay*[6]*, John*[5]*, Reynold*[4]*, Abel*[3]*, Reynold , Richard*[1]*)*, born 7 Aug., 1825, at Alleyne-dale Hall, Barbados, died 24 Sept., 1889 in Barbados. Married 23 March, 1854, at St. John, Barbados, Anna Maria Best Clarke, second daughter of Sir Robert Bowcher Clarke, K.C.B., Chief Justice of Barbados. She died 3 June, 1913.

Children of R. F. B. Alleyne and his wife Anna M. B. Alleyne:—

   i. **Emily Rebecca Alleyne**, born 25 Jany. 1855, Married 5 July 1876 Henry Alleyne Pile cf Warleigh, Barbados, son of Hon. Nathaniel Jones Pile, M. L. C. He died 5 March 1923 and was buried in the family vault under the chancel of the Parish Church of St. Peter. Issue :—

      (1) Anna Rachael Pile, born 28 June 1877. Married 1890 Godfrey White FitzHerbert, and has issue four daughters and one Son.

      (2) Agnes Elise Pile, born 6 Augt. 1878. Married 25 June 1912 Anthony Fenwick of Kogeria Kyambu, Nairobi, Kenya Colony, South Africa. No Issue.

      (3) Rosalie Augusta Pile. born (1885 ?). Died 1907. Married Colonel Arthur Spooner. Issue, one daughter.

   ii. **Agnes Martin Alleyne**, born 17 April 1856, bapt. 22 May 1856 at St. Lucy, Barbados. Married 20 Dec. 1882 James Francis Browne of Merton Lodge, Barbados. She later lived in London. Issue :—

      (1) Francis Reynold Browne, born 13 Sept. 1883. Lieut. 6th Bat. Worcester Regt. Sub-inspector of Constabulary, Trinidad. Served in South Africa 1901. Medal with 2 clasps. On tea plantation in Ceylon, India.

      (2, Eleanor Anna Alleyne Browne, born 27 July 1885. Married 17 April 1913, Herbert Athelston Hughes who died 12 Oct. 1919. Their children :—

         (1) Anthony Francis Alleyne Hughes, born 27 Nov. 1917.

         (2) Cecily Mary Agnes Hughes. born 1 March 1914.

   iii. **Reynold Beresford Senhouse Alleyne**, born 1 March 1858, bapt. 4 April 1858 at Alleynedale. St. Lucy, Barbados. Died a Bachelor 6 July 1898 at Sedge Pond Plantation, St. Peter.

   iv **William Newton Alleyne**, born 25 Dec. 1860 at Alleynedale. St. Lucy. Barbados. Died 6 Sept. 1910 in Barbados. Married 18 March 1903 Florence Ethel Mason, daughter of John Mason Esq. of Bulkeley plantation, Barbados. They had Issue a Son :—

      (1) William Norman Alleyne, born 8 Oct. 1903, bapt. 4 Nov. 1903 at St. Peter, Barbados. Married 6 Oct. 1936 Dorothy Muriel Armstrong eldest daughter of Rev. Arthur Evelyn Armstrong M. A. by his first marriage.

Alleyne, William Newton, in care of Sir R. B Clarke, Ecc'eston
Sq. S.W. London, Class Lower IIIrd Lower IV. Left Mids. 1877.
Plantation in Barbados. Belcher (Entries May 1876 of Malvern
School, England).
William Newton Alleyne buried 6 Sept., 1910. Interred in the
vault under the chancel of St Peter. Proprietor. Abode Sedge
Pond, St. Andrew. Born Alleynedale. (Barbados Records).
William Newton Alleyne was a planter and Parochial Treasurer
for St. Andrew. He was an enthusiastic cricketer and on many
occasions represented the island in tournaments.

Will of Reynold FitzHerbert Beresford Alleyne. Proved
4 October 1889. To wife Anna Maria Best Alleyne all
linen, china, etc. except silver plate and plated articles. Also
horses etc. £300. Silver plate and plated articles to sons-in-law
Henry Alleyne Pile and James Francis Browne in trust, after wife's
death, to be divided equally between my sons Reynold Beresford
Senhouse Alleyne and William Newton Alleyne. Real and personal
estate to trustees, H. A. Pile and J. F. Browne in trust for widow
for life, after her death or marriage, capital and annual income to
be divided equally between my children, Emily Rebecca Pile, wife
of Henry Alleyne Pile, Agnes Martin Browne, wife of James Francis
Browne, Reynold Beresford Senhouse Alleyne and William Newton
Alleyne.

No sale of my Sugar Works Plantation called *Kensington* shall
be made in the life of my wife, where she may live. Trustees to
manage it. Any money in Colonial Bank to be retained by trustees
not exceeding £500 as a fund to assist trustees in managing Plantations. Money to be repaid out of profits of Plantations and to
go back to estate. These provisions for wife in satisfaction of dower.
Signed Reynold FitzHerbert Beresford Alleyne.
Witnesses: J. W. C. Catford, W. H. Seale.

30. BOUVERIE ALLEYNE[6], *(fourth son of Sir Reynold Abel[7],
Sir John Gay[6], John[5], Reynold[4], Abel[3], Reynold[2], Richard[1],
Born 19 July, 1828 at Alleynedale Hall, Barbados, Died 25 Oct.,
1861 at St. Vincent, B.W.I. Married Charlotte Agnes Emma Cole-
broke, youngest daughter of Lieut. Genl. Sir William Colebrooke, .
C.B., K.H., Governor of Barbados. She died 24 April, 1895.

Bouverie Alleyne was Colonial Secretary of Grenada and afterwards of St. Vincent, B.W.I.
Children of Bouverie and Charlotte A. E. Alleyne:—
    i. CHARLOTTE ALLEYNE, Died young.
    ii. GERTRUDE ALLEYNE,
    iii. BOUVERIE COLEBROOKE ALLEYNE, born 14 Jan. 1861, died 19 Feb.
    1901. Married 17 Aug. 1892 Frances Ada Clement, dau. of Henry
    Lincoln Clement of Yarmouth, England.

Bouverie Colebrooke Alleyne was in the Merchant Service.
Lieut. Royal Reserve. He joined an expedition to Benin in 1897,
when the King, Overanie, was captured. This town was found to
be an absolute shambles, reeking with the victims of Juju butchery.
He and all who took part in the expedition were awarded medals.
    Issue:—

(1) *Mabel Charlotte Alleyne*, born 31st March 1896 at Southampton, England. Her pictures have been exhibited in the Academy, London.

Frances Ada Clement Alleyne, widow of Bouverie Colebrooke Alleyne died 7 December, 1935 at 33 Park Road, Forest Hill, S.E., London.

31. THOMAS HARBIN ALLEYNE [8], *(eldest son of Abel* [7], *Thomas* [6], *Abel* [5], *Reynold* [4], *Abel* [3], *Reynold* [2], *Richard* [1]), born in Milton, Mass., on Wednesday 14 Nov., 1792 at 12 o'clock at night. Bapt. by Rev. Mr. Montague and named for his Grandfather and Grandmother. Died 25 June, 1839 at Alleyne Cottage, St. James, Barbados. Married 19th Sept., 1816 at St. James Church, Barbados, Elizabeth Frere Williams, daughter of Robert Williams of Bristol, England.

Thomas Harbin Alleyne left Dorchester, Mass., 23 Nov., 1802 (he was 10 years old) for New London, Conn., and sailed from there Dec. 19, 1802, arriving at Barbados Jan. 3rd, 1803 after a passage of 18 days.

He was a planter and later Officer of Customs in Barbados. For many years he resided at Alleyne Cottage, Holetown, which has since been demolished although it withstood the hurricane of 1831, the Chaise-house alone being destroyed and Mr. Alleyne's gig blown into a gulley three or four hundred yards away. The house stood near to St. James Church, where there are several *Alleyne* tablets and a private burying ground of the Alleyne's in one corner of the cemetery, surrounded by cement walls, with an iron gate which is kept locked. Sir John Gay Alleyne and several others of the family are buried there.

Will of Thomas Harbin Alleyne dated 20 Feb, 1839, proved 14 Aug., 1839. Barbados, Parish of St. James. Wife Elizabeth Frere Alleyne household furniture, plate etc., and horse and gig. I am indebted to my son, Thomas Abel Forster Alleyne £200 with interest from 1 Oct., 1818, being legacy bequeathed to him by his aunt Sarah Williams. My wife; my brother James Holder Alleyne Esq., Doctor of Medicine of the colony of Demerara, and relation Henry Alleyne Esq., of Barbados to be Executors. Sons Thomas Abel Forster Alleyne, Robert Harbin Alleyne, Frederick William Alleyne, and Alexander Hall Alleyne; daughters mentioned but not named. Dated 20 Feb., 1829. Signed Thos. H. Alleyne. Witnesses. James H. Alleyne, Richard W. Layne. (Barbados Records Vol. 69 p. 57).

Children of Thomas Harbin and Elizabeth Frere Alleyne:—

i. THOMAS ABEL FORSTER ALLEYNE, born 24 Aug. 1817, bapt. 25 Oct. 1817, Buried 18 Sept. 1839 at St. James, Barbados, aged 22 yrs.

ii. SARAH MARSHALL ALLEYNE, born 3 Sept. 1819. bapt. 24 Sept. 1819 at St James, Barbados Died 19 May 1890. Single.

iii. CHARLES ALLEYNE, born 13 July 1821. bapt. 22 Sept. 1821 at St. James, Barbados. Buried 16 Nov. 1821 at St. James, Barbados.

42. iv. ROBERT HARBIN ALLEYNE, and

v. DAMARIS ELIZABETH ALLEYNE, twin children, born 27 Aug. 1823 at Porters, St. James, Barbados, bapt. 12 Sept. 1823.
Damaris Elizabeth Alleyne, married first, 15 July 1843, Capt. Henry DeCourcy Carleton, son of Admiral Carleton at St. James. Bdos. Witnesses: Robert H. Alleyne, Frederick W. Alleyne. She married secondly, 17 Dec. 1859 Timothy Barnes Mahon, Bachelor, Planter, at St. Michael. Barbados Chapel of St. Stephen. Residence Welches. Witnesses: Frederick William Alleyne, John G. Alleyne,

43. vi. FREDERICK WILLIAM ALLEYNE, bapt. 25 Sept. 1825 at St. James. Barbados. Died 25 June 1910, at St. Michael. Married Mary Sophia Earle

vii. ANNA CHASE ALLEYNE, bapt. 10 July 1828 at Porter's, St. James, Barbados, died 14 Feb. 1910, at St. Michael.

viii. ALEXANDER HALL ALLEYNE, bapt. 19 Aug. 1829 at Porter's St James, Barbados, died 1840.

ix. CHARLOTTE EMILY ALLEYNE, bapt. 27 May 1831 at Alleyne Cottage, St. James, Barbados, died unmarried 6 May 1896. Will proved 19 June 1896.
Will of Charlotte Emily, daughter of Tnomas Harbin Alleyne (dated 6 Nov. 1889. Proved 19 June, 1896) of the Parish of St. Michael, Barbados.
Plate, household belongings and furniture to sister Anna Chase Alleyne. Rents, interest and profits from estate to sister Anna Chase Alleyne. After her death following legacies. To sister Elizabeth Hall Roach $50. To niece Inez McGeachy Louise Roach $75, Niece Elizabeth Frere Roach $75. Niece Alice Amelia Thomas $30. Niece Kate Williams Alleyne $30. Niece Mary Parry Alleyne $30. Nephew Forster McGeachy Alleyne $30. Grand niece Elsinora Alma Jemmott $30. Niece Eliza Dallas Alleyne. Nephew Rev. Innes Milton Alleyne.
Executors. Brother-in-law Joseph Williams Roach. Friend Charles Newton Callender Roach. Signed Charlotte Emily Alleyne. Proved 19 June, 1896 (Barbados Records Vol. 99, p 282.

x. ELIZABETH HALL ALLEYNE, bapt 6 April at Alleyne Cottage, St. James, Barbados, died 2 Oct. 1920. Married, 10 Nov. 1864, Joseph William Roach, son of Isaac Newton Roach of Barbados. Issue:—

(1) Inez McGeachy Louise Roach, born 30 March 1867. Married 19 Jan. 1892 James Pearce Austin son of James Dear Austin of Barbados.
(2) Rosa Mary Roach.
(3) Edith Frere Roach.
(4) Ethel Frost Roach.

xi. CHARLES ALLEYNE, and
xii. WILLIAM ALLEYNE, twin children, William Alleyne died in infancy.

32. JAMES HOLDER ALLEYNE S (*second son of Abel[7]*, *Thomas [6]*, *Abel[5]*, *Reynold[4]*, *Abel[3]*, *Reynold[2]*, *Richard[1]*,) born 30 May, 1798 at Milton, Mass., died 1876–7 in London, England. Married 9 Feb. 1829 Caroline Robertson at Demerara, British Guiana.

James Holder, born at Milton, (Mass.) Wednesday 30 May, 1798 at half past 11 o'clock p.m. (Being General Election of Massachusetts) Bapt. at Quincy on Sunday June 3rd 1798 by the Rt. Rev. Bishop Edward Bass of Newburyport, and named for his Cousin James Holder Esq. (He died 1818 without issue) of Ash Park, Hants, England. His sponsors were his father, Major Eben

Miller, his grandmother and his aunt Boies. He was married to Caroline Robertson at Demerara 9 Feb., 1829. He afterwards removed to England. (Old Alleyne Bible).

James Holder Alleyne, aged 13 years left Dedham, (Mass.) 21st May, 1811 for Hartford, (Conn.) sailed from Middletown (Conn.) 30 May, 1811; arrived in Barbados July 10, 1811, after a passage of 6 weeks. Heard from him 29 Aug., 1811. (Old Alleyne Bible.)

James Holder Alleyne, who was a medical practitioner, lived at 27 Gloucester Place, Hyde Park Gardens, England in 1856, and must not be confused with James Holder Alleyne third son of John Forster Alleyne, who was born 13 March, 1790 and died 2 July, 1842 at Cheltenham, England.

Children of James Holder Alleyne and Caroline, his wife:—

i. ANNA MARIA ALLEYNE, born 23 June 1830 at Demerara, British Guiana.

ii. OSMOND ALLEYNE, born 20 Oct. 1832 at Demerara. Died 1853 in London aged 20 yrs.

iii. CAROLINE HENRIETTA ALLEYNE, born 31 Oct. 1834 in Demerara.

iv JAMES ROBERTSON ALLEYNE, born 4 Aug. 1837 in Demerara.

v. FRANCIS GEORGE ALLEYNE, born 9 July 1840 at Gloucester Place, Hyde Park Gardens, London, Eng.

33. JEREMIAH SMITH BOIES ALLEYNE[8] (*third son of Abel*[7],) *Thomas* [6] , *Abel*[5] , *Reynold*[4] , *Abel*[3] , *Reynold*[2] , *Richard*[1], born 5 Dec., 1800 at Milton, Mass. Bapt. 22 Dec., 1801 at Episcopal Church, Dedham, Mass. Died at St. Louis, Mo., U.S.A. Married 11 Dec., 1825 Lydia Stedman.

Jeremiah Smith Boies (Alleyne) born in Milton on Friday Dec. 5, 1800 at half past 10 o'clock a.m. Bapt. by Rev. Wm. Montague and named for his Uncle Boies. (Old Alleyne Bible.)

He went to St. Louis Mo., U.S.A. with his family in 1850.

Children of Jeremiah Smith Boies Alleyne and Lydia his wife:—

i. JEREMIAH SMITH BOIES ALLEYNE, born 11 Dec. 1826. He was an M. D. in St. Louis, Mo. 1851—1895.

ii. EMILY ANNA CLARKE ALLEYNE, born 10 Jan. 1831 in Boston, Mass., died 26 April 1837 in Boston, aged 5 yrs. Buried at Mount Auburn

iii. ARABELLA DUDLEY ALLEYNE, born 10 April 1835 in Boston, Mass., died 15 April 1850 at St. Louis, Missouri, aged 15 years.

34. HAYNES GIBBES ALLEYNE[8] (*eldest son of John Forster* [7] *Thomas* [6] , *Abel*[5] , *Reynold*[4] , *Abel* [3] , *Reynold* , *Richard*[1]), born 14 May, 1783 at Porter's, Barbados, bapt. 5 June, 1783 at St. Michael, Barbados, died 23 July, 1813 at sea. Married 21 May, 1804 Georgiana Yea daughter of William Walter Yea, son of Sir William Yea, of Pyrland, Co. Somerset, England.

Alleyne, Haynes Gibbes s. John of Barbados, West Indies, Arm., Christ Church. Matric 22 Oct., 1801 aged 18. Died 23 July, 1813. (Alumni Oxonienses.)

Children of Haynes Gibbes Alleyne[8] and Georgiana, his wife:—

i. GEORGIANA ALLEYNE, born 12 May 1805, died, 26 July 1867, aged 62 years. Married, 7 June 1825, George 2nd son of George Sydenham Fursdon Esq. Fursdon, Cadbury, Devon. as his first wife. Issue :—

    (1) *Margaret Grace Fursdon*, born 17 Nov. 1826, died 14 Feb. 1901.

    (2) *Ellen Fursdon*, born 11 March 1828, died 9 March 1880 Md. 17 Nov. 1868 Rev. James Senior, of Compton Pauncefoot, Somerset.

    (3) *Charles Fursdon*, born 31 July 1829, died 7 April 1912. Md. 2 Dec. 1858 Eliza dau. Henry Willis.

    (4) *Lucy Fursdon*, born 19 Feb. 1831, Died 29 Oct. 1838.

    (5) *Alice Fursdon*, born 4 June 1832, died 18 Jan, 1913. Md. 15 Oct. 1872 Philip Haughton James of Jamaica, B.W.I.

    (6) *Walter Fursdon*, born 27 Dec. 1833, died 2 Mar. 1876. Md 5 Sept. 1863 Sarah Anna dau. of Rev. G. Hole.

    (7) *George Edward Fursdon*, born 21 Mar 1840, died 18 June 1892 Md. April 1868 Elizabeth dau of George Grant.

ii. HAYNES WALTER FORSTER ALLEYNE, born 21 July 1806, bapt. 2 Sept. 1806, Buried 10 Sept. 1806 at St. James, Barbados.

iii. ELIZABETH JANE ALLEYNE, born 21 July 1807, bapt. 23 May 1808 at St. James, Barbados. Died.

iv. AUGUSTA LOUISA ALLEYNE, bapt 31 May 1810 at St. James Barbados. Died.

v. MARIA LOUSIA ALLEYNE, born 18 June 1812, bapt. 9 Aug. 1812 at St. James, Barbados. Died in India. Married 16 March 1842 Capt. John Fordyce.

On the 16th inst. (16 March 1842) at the British Embassy, Parris, by the Rev. Dr. Halfhead, Capt. John Fordyce of the Bengal Artillery and Maria Louisa, youngest daughter of the late Haynes Gibbes Alleyne, Esq of the Island of Barbados. (London Times, Monday 21 March 1842.)

Will of Haynes Gibbes Alleyne dated 20 June, 1813.

If I die in England I wish to be buried as near as may be to the spot where my respected and highly valued Friend and Father-in-law, Walter Yea, Esq., lies interred. I give to my dear father, the Honourable John Forster Alleyne, for whom I feel the warmest filial affection and deepest sense of gratitude and whose happiness and comfort, if it should please God to spare my life, it will be my earnest study to promote by every means in my power my library elbow chair and round mahogany table. My cattle on *Sandy Lane* Plantation also 10 acres of land etc. Expresses great affection for mother and leaves her edition of Plutarch's Lives and £10 to buy a piece of Plate. Brothers, John Gay Alleyne, James Holder Alleyne, Henry Alleyne, £10 each to buy plate as a remembrance. Brother Charles Thomas Alleyne to have English Horse, Eclipse. Sisters, Mary Alleyne, Charlotte Emily Alleyne, £10 each for plate. Sister Sarah Gibbes McGeachy, widow. Margaret Salter Hall, wife of David Hall £5 each. Relation Thomas Harbin Alleyne £5. Daughter Georgiana Alleyne gold watch. Youngest daughter Maria Louisa

Alleyne, gold watch worth 20 gs. to be bought for her. I arrived at age 21 on 14 May, 1804 and had legacy of £6,000 bequeathed by Rev. Haynes Gibbes, "Charged on his plantation called Porters in the parish of St. James, which my father did on my marriage the same year, with Miss Georgiana Yea, 2nd daughter of Walter Yea, of Taunton, Co. Somerset, Esq. agree to make and did actually make £5,000. £4,000 of which said money was by deed of settlement secured at marriage on wife. The other £1,000 father gave me his sealed note on interest at 5% which note I still hold, so I am fully paid and satisfied etc."

Executrix and executors: Father Hon. John Forster Alleyne, Wife, Georgiana. Dated 20 June, 1813.

'Signed Haynes Gibbes Alleyne.

Witnesses: Mathew Chapman, Robert B. Garrett.

Entered 28 May, 1814, Barbados.

(Barbados Records, Vol. 60 p. 44.).

(To be continued).

ALLEYNE OF BARBADOS.

(SEVENTH INSTALMENT).

CONTRIBUTED BY THE LATE LOUISE R. ALLEN.

The Compiler evidently intended the following sketch pedigrees of Anna Chase who married Abel Alleyne [7] to be printed immediately after the records of the children of their marriage, which appeared in the Fifth Instalment on page 85 of the Journal for February, 1937, Volume IV, part 2. Being inadvertently omitted, this seems to be a convenient place to insert it, before the Alleyne Pedigree is continued. *

Pedigree of ANNA CHASE who married ABEL ALLEYNE.

THOMAS CHASE = ELIZABETH PHILBRICK dau of Thomas Philbrick and Died before 5 Octr. 1652. Of Hampton, New Hampshire, U.S.A. | Elizabeth his wife, who settled in Watertown, Mass, 1636. She married, secondly, 26 Ocr. 1654, John Garland. Thirdly, 19 Feb. 1674 Henry Roby. She died 11 Feb. 1677.

1. MARY PERKINS dau Isaac Perkins, of Hampton, N. H. Born 23 July 1658, died 1674, Md. 20 Feb. 1673. = LIEUT ISAAC CHASE Born 1 April 1650 died 19 May 1727. Will pr. 7 July 1727. Of Hampton, N. H. then of Edgartown, Martha's Vineyard. Owned most of Vineyard Haven Village. Quaker and blacksmith. = 2. MARY TILTON, dau. of Wm. and Susanna Tilton of Lynn, Mass. She died 14 June 1746. Md. 5 Dec. 1675 in Tisbury, Mass.

JOSEPH CHASE = LYDIA COFFIN dau of Nathaniel Born 26 Feb. 1689 in Tisbury, Mass. Died 1 May 1749 in Edgartown, Martha's Vineyard. Md. 16 Sept. 1714 in Nantucket. Moved to Nantucket before 1729. Edgartown 1737. He was a hatter, and lived in 'Homes Hole'. | Coffin and Damaris (Gayer) his wife. Born 16 May, 1697 in Nantucket. Died 17 July, 1749 in Edgartown.

1. ANNA FIELD Born 1738 Died 21 Oct. 1769 aged 31. = THOMAS CHASE Bapt. 24 June 1739 in Edgartown. Died 17 May 1787 in Boston, Distiller Dep. Quarter Master of Troops, 1779. = 2. ELIZABETH BAGNALL Md. 10 Oct 1771. Secondly Wm. Greenleaf in Bolton Mass.

ANNA CHASE = ABEL ALLEYNE, son of Thomas Alleyne Born 10 August 1765. Died 6 Novr. 1812 Buried at Quincy, Md. 22 Novr. 1787 at Bolton, Mass. | and Dorothy Harbin (Forster) Alleyne of Braintree, Mass. Md. 22 Novr. 1787 at Bolton, Mass.

* Page 60, this volume.

COFFIN pedigree of ANNA CHASE who married ABEL ALLEYNE.

NICHOLAS COFFIN = JOAN
Of Braxton, Co. Devon,
Born c. 1550. Will proved
3 Novr. 1613.

PETER COFFIN = JOAN THEMBER
Will proved 13 March 1628, of Braxton | Born 1584. Died 1661 in Nantucket,
Co. Devon. | aged 77.

TRISTRAM COFFIN = DIONIS STEVENS
Born 1605 at Braxton, co Devon. Died 3 Octr. | dau. of W. Stevens, ship's car-
1681 at Nantucket, Mass He came to America | penter of Braxton, Co. Devon.
1642 with his wife and 5 children, his mother
aged 58 yrs. and two unmarried sisters. Went
to Salisbury, Mass., where he had an Inn and
ferry across Merrimac river. Went to Nantucket 1659 Owned one fourth of Nantucket

JUDGE JAMES COFFIN = MARY SEVERANCE
Born in England, probably in Braxton, Devon. | dau. of John S. of Salisbury,
Judge of the Common Pleas and Probate Court. | Mass.

NATHANIEL COFFIN =DAMARIS GAYER, dau. of Wm. Gayer and Dorcas
Born 166-, died 1721. | Starbuck, his wife. She lived to be 90.

LYDIA COFFIN = JOSEPH CHASE, son of Lieut
Born 16 May, 1696 in Nantucket. Died 17 July, | Isaac Chase of Hampton, N. H.
1749 at Edgartown, Mass. Married 16 Sept. 1714
at Nantucket.

THOMAS CHASE = ANNA FIELDS
Bapt. 24 June, 1739 at Edgartown. Died 17 | Born 1738 Died 21 Octr. 1769
May, 1787 in Boston. Distiller, Dep. Quarter- | aged 31 years.
Master General of Mass. Troops 1779.

ANNA CHASE = ABEL ALLEYNE son of Thomas
Born 10 Aug. 1765 in Boston. Died 6 Nov. 1812 | Alleyne of Braintree, Mass.
Buried at Quincy, Mass. Married 22 Nov. 1787,
at Bolton, Mass.

35.   JOHN GAY ALLEYNE[8] *(second son of John Forster[7] , Thomas[6] ,
Abel[5] , Reynold[4] , Abel[3] , Reynold[2] , Richard[1]);* born 21 July, 1785,
bapt. 13 Sept., 1785 at St. James, Barbados, died 10 March, 1821 at Sandy
Lane, Barbados, aged 37 years. Buried 11 March, 1821 at St. James, Barbados.
Married 1 July, 1807 Joanna, daughter of John Bishop, at St. James, Barbados.
On the first instant at Reid's Bay Plantation John Gay Alleyne, Esq., son
of the Hon. John Forster Alleyne to Miss Johanna Bishop, daughter-in-law
(step-daughter) of Brig. Gen. Maclean on the staff of H.M. Army in this island.
(Barbados Mercury, 7 July, 1807).
Children of John Gay Alleyne and Joanna his wife:—
   i   ELIZABETH ALLEYNE, born 3 July 1808, bapt. 7 Aug. 1808 St James.
   ii. JOHN GAY ALLEYNE, born 1 May 1810 Bapt. 1 May 1810 Died a bachelor. 4 July
        1885 aged 76 yrs. He was an Ensign in the 35th Regt. of Foot, stationed at
        Barbados in 1827.

79

iii. JOANNA BISHOP ALLEYNE, born & bapt. 27 Oct. 1810 St. James, Barbados. Died 7 July 1868. Married 10 Aug. 1836 Lieut. Philip Chetwode, R. N. Bart. who died 1844.
John Gay son, & Joanna Bishop dau. of John Gay Alleyne & Joanna Bishop his wife, were baptized in St. Peters Parish & registered here (St. James) at the request of their parent. John Gay was born & bapt. 1 May 1810 Joanna Bishop was born & Bapt. 27 Oct. 1810.

iv. SARAH McGEACHY ALLEYNE, born 4 Jan 1812 bapt. 9 Aug. 1812 St. James.

v. HAYNES GIBBES ALLEYNE, born 14 Oct 1813, bapt 20 Sept. 1814 St. James. Died a bachelor 9 Sept. 1882 at Sydney, Australia.
Haynes Gibbes Alleyne studied Medicine at Edinburgh University, having obtained a scholarship for 4 years at £100 a year.
The following details of his career have been taken from an article entitled *An Early Australian Quarantine Officer*. By F. McCallum, M.B., D.P.H., D.T.M. & H., Quarantine Officer, Commonwealth Department of Health, published in the journal *"Health,"* dealing with developments in the field of Public Health in Australia. Issued by the Commonwealth Department of Heath. Vol. IV. No. I. Jan. 1926.
Haynes Gibbes Alleyne, M.D., L.R.C.S. (Edin.) arrived in Australia in 1851 from New Zealand, where he had served in the first Maori War. He was appointed Health Officer of Port Jackson, and later became Chief Medical Officer to the Government in succession to Dr. Arthur Savage, R.N., the first Health Officer of New South Wales (1839—1852). He was an honorary physician to the Sydney Hospital from 1855 to 1873, and honorary consulting physician from 1875 to 1882. He was for many years president of the Medical Board and one of the medical examiners of the University of Sydney. Dr. Watson in his *History of The Sydney Hospital, 1811—1911*, has recorded that : " In the year 1852 the first administration of chloroform was made by Dr. H. G. Alleyne. Although not a member of the staff in this year, he successfully administered it to a girl during an operation for amputation of the left leg for strumous disease." Dr. Alleyne possessed a general knowledge of natural history, especially Ichthyology ; possibly he founded the piscatorial tradition that has persisted amongst Australian health officers to this day. However, he compiled an excellent monograph of the fishes of Port Jackson, which was published by the Linnaean Society. Dr. Alleyne retired in July 1882 after 30 years devoted to the public service, during which his only leave of absence was a period of two days in July 1881 when he was "Out of Health." He died suddenly following an apoplectic fit on 9th Sept., 1882. In an obituary notice in the Melbourne *Argus* it is recorded that "Apart from his official position, Dr. Alleyne was in many ways intimately connected with the welfare of Sydney, having taken an active part in promoting the philanthropic, scientific, and social institutions of the city."
The records of Dr. Alleyne's service as port health officer are contained in his annual reports and in the Minutes of Evidence of the Select Committee which inquired into the Quarantine Laws in 1853 and of the Royal Commission of 1881 which inquired into the management of the Quarantine Station. These papers are all contained in the Parliamentary Votes and Proceedings of the Colony at that time. The earlier period of his service as port health officer is an exceptionally interesting record of the time.

vi. MARY CARTHCART ALLEYNE, born 14 Dec. 1814, bapt. 31 March 1815 St. James. Buried 1st Sept 1836 at St. James, Bdos

vii. CHARLES KYD ALLEYNE, born 25 March 1817, bapt 23 April 1817 St. James.

viii. JOHN FORSTER ALLEYNE,

80

Will of John Gay Alleyne[8] , dated at Barbados 2nd Aug., 1819, pr. 10 April, 1821. Living on my estate called *Sandy Lane* and about to make a voyage to England. To my wife, Joanna, £3500, in addition to the like sum of £3500 already settled on her in this estate; all furniture, chaise and chaise horses and any other horse she may choose; and all silver and plated articles during her life. I give my Breakfast Service consisting of a silver coffee pot, teapot, sugar basin, milk pot, and one dozen teaspoons, to my daughter Elizabeth, in case of her death to my eldest daughter living. Remainder of silver and plate articles to son John or to the eldest of living sons.

Estate *Sandy Lane* to be kept together until it shall have paid off balance due from it on Mr. James Holder Alleyne's execution and funded a sufficient sum annually to meet Mrs. Haynes Alleyne's execution, and then to be sold, but to advantage. Money to be divided among my children. Executors: Wife, Joanna, and Father, Hon. John Forster Alleyne. Signed: John Gay Alleyne. Witnesses: I. Pairman, William Blanchett.

Codicil: I give to my son John my gold watch, chain and seals, and gold ring containing his mother's hair. Daughter Elizabeth gold brooch containing hair of my esteemed friend and relation Mary S. Alleyne. To Thomas H. Alleyne my Gun and Pistols. Signed: John Alleyne.

36. SARAH GIBBES ALLEYNE [8] *(eldest daughter of John Forster* [7] *Thomas* [6] *, Abel* [5] *, Reynold* [4] *, Abel* [3] *, Reynold* [2] *Richard* [1]*)*, Born 11 Sept., 1787 at Porters, Barbados. Bapt. 15 Oct , 1787 at St. James, Barbados. Died Sept., 1876 at Clifton, Bristol, England aged 89 years. Married 19 May, 1808 Captain later Major, Alexander McGeachy at Porters, St. James, Barbados, by Rev. Mr. Pilgrim.

Issue :—

(1) *Forster Alleyne McGeachy*, of Chenley Hill, Hertfordshire, M. P. for Honiton, 1841—7. Married first Anna Maria Letitia Adderley, sister of Sir Charles Adderley, first Lord Norton. She died s. p. 30 Jan 1841. Married secondly 1848, Clara, daughter of Rev. Thomas Newcome. Rector of Shenley and widow of Rev W. R. Hall.

Mrs. Leonora Blanche (Alleyne) Lang daughter of Charles Thomas Alleyne, widow of Andrew Lang, the author, was kind enough to write the following statement for me (Louise R. Allen) when I was in London in 1928.

Statement made to me, Leonora Blanche Alleyne (Mrs. Andrew Lang) by my Aunt, Sarah McGeachy, née Alleyne, as to the circumstances of her marriage with Alexander McGeachy.

It was about the year 1866 or 7 that I was talking to my aunt, then aged 79, about her girlhood in Barbados. She told me many little things of interest, soon we came to her marriage. As she always referred to her husband as "Major" McGeachy, I cannot be sure whether at the time it took place he really was "Major" or merely Captain, but this is immaterial to the story.

The officers of the British Regiment then stationed at Barbados were welcomed at all of the principal houses, amongst others, *Porter's*, one of the estates belonging to the Alleynes, a household

81

including many young people, with Sarah as the eldest and prettiest daughter. The attraction between her and young McGeachy, aged, I think about 28, was mutual, but in proposing for her hand in marriage, he had little to offer, and was promptly rejected. The blow was severe, but, fortunately for him, orders came for the regiment to embark at once for Madeira, in case it might be necessary for it to proceed later to Portugal.

The ship put out to sea immediately, but in a few hours a violent storm arose and the vessel was so badly knocked about that she had to put back for repairs. The Major went ashore and up to the nearest planter's house to ask for hospitality, quite ignorant of the fact that Mrs. Alleyne had taken Sarah to this very place in order to cheer up her spirits, which were woefully distressed.

Well, the coincidence was too much even for the stern parents; the mother, I gathered, being the more severe of the two. Consent was given, the marriage was hurried on, and when the ship again set sail it had Sarah for a passenger.

The McGeachys remained in Madeira for about 18 months, then orders came for the regiment to proceed to Portugal to join Wellington's army in fighting the French.

Sarah was ill in bed when her husband came to say goodbye. His farewell could only be brief, and after he had gone, she saw he had left his sword belt behind him. A gleam of gladness shot through her.

"He cant do without it," she said to herself. "If I leave it he will have to come back and fetch it, and I shall see him again." And then another thought came to her. No, they shall not say he is a coward and afraid to leave his wife." And she sent it after him.

As soon as possible she came home to England, where a few months later her son was born. Their son lived to be an old man but never saw his father who was killed at the siege of Badajoz in 1811.

Mrs. Sarah McGeachy received a pension of £300 a year from the Portuguese Government till her death at Clifton in Sept. 1876 at the age of 89. Though 60 years have passed since she told me that story, it is as fresh in my mind as though I had heard it yesterday. I still retain the vivid impression I received at the moment that she was telling, not her own tragedy, but the love tale of someone hardly known to her, but with whom she had no personal concern. And indeed, it must have seemed so to her, for what connection could she have felt between the placid old lady who for 50 years had lived with her sister above the banks of the Avon, and the tragic girl widow of 23? L. B. Lang. June 12, 1928. London, England.

37. JAMES HOLDER ALLEYNE [8] *(3rd son of John Forster[7], Thomas[6], Abel[5], Reynold[4], Abel[3], Reynold[2], Richard[1].)* born 13 March, 1790, died 2 July, 1842 suddenly of apoplexy at Cheltenham, England, aged 52 yrs. Married 1815 Elizabeth Mary, daughter of Joseph Lowe M.D. and widow of George James. She died 25 February, 1877.

Issue :—

i. MARGARET HALL ALLEYNE, born   July 1816, bapt. 4 April 1817.
at St. James Barbados. Died 10 June 1870.
Will dated 12 Aug. 1863. (Pr. 3 March, 1871) of Margaret Hall
Alleyne of 9 Upper Brunswick Place, Hove, Sussex, England,
Spinster.
£2,500 part of £5,000 Bank annuities bequeathed to me by my
father to Sister Caroline Maycock, free from all the debts, control
and engagements of any husband. The other £2,500 to half-sister,
Elizabeth Georgiana, wife of William Clarke, M.D. £500 to William
Clarke. Lieut. in H M 73 Regt eldest son of Elizabeth Georgiana
Clarke. £1,300 Bank Annuities to Brother Arthur Osbourne Gibbes
Alleyne. Brother Alexander McGeachy Alleyne £300. If he is
bankrupt or has assigned to creditors, it to be left to Arthur
Osbourne Gibbes Alleyne. Half sister Mary Reeve Alleyne, widow
£500. After her death to Douglas Alleyne Lieut. 37 Regt. eldest
son of Mary Reeve Alleyne. All my shares in Coxe's and Spa
estates, Barbados, to be sold and paid to Mother Elizabeth Mary
Alleyne.
Executors: Mother, Elizabeth Mary Alleyne, widow, sister Caroline
Maycock, widow, brother Rev. Arthur Osborne Gibbes Alleyne,
uncle Rev. John Forster Alleyne. Signed Margaret Hall Alleyne.
Witness I. W. Howlett, Solicitor, Brighton, England. E. H.
Stacey, his clerk.
Codicil. Margaret Hall Alleyne, now living at 32 East Southernhay,
Exeter. 9 July, 1868   Brother Alexander McGeachy Alleyne since
died. His share to brother Arthur Osborne Gibbes Alleyne.
(Signed) Margaret Hall Alleyne.
Sworn under £8,000 (Barbados Record, Vol. 80, p. 343)

ii. CAROLINE ALLEYNE, born 27 Dec. 1817, bapt. 24 Jan. 1819 St.
James, Barbados. Married James Dottin Maycock who died 1877.
Issue :—
  (1) James Dottin Maycock
  (2) Frederick Maycock
  (3) Eleanor Maycock

45. iii. JAMES HOLDER ALLEYNE, born 27 May 1819, bapt. 23 Sept 1819
St. James, Barbados. Died 28 Jan. 1862 Married first Louisa
Fisher, Secondly Ellen Sarah Crutchley.

46. iv. JOSEPH LOWE ALLEYNE, born 8 Nov. 1820, died 3 July 1858
Married Julia Holder.

47. v. ALEXANDER McGEACHY ALLEYNE, bapt. 24 July 1825 St James,
Barbados, died 5 Jan. 1867. Married Henrietta Maria Wood. She
married Secondly Col. Frederick Bassett Wingfield.

48. vi. ARTHUR OSBORNE GIBBES ALLEYNE, born 22 March 1833, died
11 Feb. 1905 Married 13 Sept. 1870 Rosalie Sophia White.

Elizabeth Mary, daughter of Joseph Lowe M.D. of Gregg Farm
Estate, Barbados, widow of George James, Esq., who married James
Holder Alleyne, had two daughters by her first husband: Georgiana
Mary James, who married William Clarke, M.D., and Mary Reeve
James, (born 18 May, 1811) who married Henry Alleyne. Mary
Reeve Alleyne died 9 December, 1896. See M.I. in Clifton Church,
Bristol.

James Holder Alleyne [3] was a Member of the Council of Barbados. He later lived in Clifton, near Bristol, England. A monument to his memory in the north transept of Bath Abbey bears the
following inscription:—

Sacred to the memory/of James Holder Alleyne Esq./of the
Island of Barbados/for many years member/of her Majesty's Coun-

83

cil in that Island/who died at Cheltenham/on the 2nd of July 1842 aged 51. (4 lines. Erected by his widow and children.) Will dated 4 March, 1842. (Proved 5 January, 1844) of James Holder Alleyne [8] of Barbados and Cheltenham, Co. Gloucester, England.

Wife, Elizabeth Mary, money credited for *Greggs* Plantation with Messrs George Gibbs & Robert Bright, Merchants, Bristol, England. Plantations called *Spa* and *Cox's* in Barbados with all sugar, stock, funds and personal estate of every sort to brother, Thomas Alleyne, of Clifton, Co. Gloucester, England.

Daughter, Margaret Hall Alleyne, son Joseph Alleyne £5,000, $3\frac{1}{2}\%$ consols. Daughter, Caroline Alleyne, son Arthur Osborne Gibbs Alleyne. £5,000. Son James Holder Alleyne £6,000. Lieut. 52 Regt. Can advance money to pay for his Captaincy or Majority in Army. Son Joseph, until he complete his education at Cambridge, £250 per annum, when at death of his mother he becomes entitled to sum of £200 per annum. To purchase ensign's commission for son Alexander McGeachy also a Lieutenancy, Captaincy, and Majority not more than £5,000. Wife use of plate and plated goods bearing my crest, to go to eldest son on her death; if he die, to second son. Step-daughter Georgiana Mary Clarke, wife of William Clarke, Esq. M.D., of Barbados, and Mary Reeve Alleyne wife of Henry Alleyne of Barbados, Esq. £500 each. John Alleyne Holder Esq. and Jane Hagget Holder his wife. guardians of estate of Julia Holder, John Alleyne Holder, and Henry Holder, their children. Executors: Charles Thomas Alleyne, Robert Bright, Margaret Hall Alleyne, Joseph Alleyne. (Signed) James Holder Alleyne.

Witnesses: John Bubb, Robert Sole Lingwood, Solicitors, Cheltenham. (Barbados Records Vol. 71 p. 55).

38. CHARLES THOMAS ALLEYNE [8] *(fourth son of John Forster* [7] *, Thomas* [6] *, Abel* [5] *, Reynold* [4] *, Abel* [3] *, Reynold* [2] *, Richard* [1]) born May 1, 1798, bapt. July 9, 1798 at St. James, Barbados. Died April, 15, 1872 at Clifton in Bristol. Married October 22, 1835, Margaret Frances, eldest daughter of John Knight Bruce of Aberdare (who afterwards assumed the additional surname of Pryce) and sister of Lord Aberdare. The ceremony was performed at the parish church of Aberdare, Glamorgan, Wales.

Charles Thomas Alleyne was the owner of several large sugarworks plantations in Barbados, of which may be mentioned Porter's, Mount Standfast, Carmichael's, Hannays, Dunscombe and Lewis. He resided at Porter's for many years, afterwards settling in England, where he purchased 2, Litfield Place, Clifton, Bristol, which was his home until the time of his death. In Clifton Church, Bristol, there is a mural tablet recording the dates of his birth and death, as well as those of his wife Margaret Frances (b. May 24, 1811, d. July 18, 1862) and his son Henry Wyndham Alleyne.

(To be continued.)

ALLEYNE OF BARBADOS.

(Eighth Instalment).

Contributed by the late Louise R. Allen.

Continuing the record of 38, Charles Thomas Alleyne [8] (fourth son of John Forster Alleyne [7]), born May 1, 1798.

Mr. C. T. Alleyne was elected a member for the parish of Saint Joseph in the Barbados House of Assembly in the year 1834, but he withdrew from that constituency in 1837, and was returned to the Assembly in the same year for his native parish of Saint James. During his long years of residence in Barbados he identified himself with the affairs of the colony and was a well-known public figure.

An inscription on a brass plate in the floor of St. James's parish church, Barbados, records the fact that the chancel was enlarged and beautified in the year 1874 as a tribute to his memory.

Children of Charles Thomas Alleyne and Margaret Frances, his wife:—

i. Sarah Frances Alleyne, born 15th Oct. 1836, bapt. 18th Oct 1836 at St. James's. Will of Sarah Frances Alleyne of 2 Litfield Place, Clifton, Bristol, England. Brothers, Forster McGeachy A. and Herbert Percy A.; sisters, Elizabeth Willing A, Annabella A, Leonora Blanche Alleyne Lang, and Elizabeth Willing Grieve; cousins Mary Alleyne A., Elizabeth A., Sarah A.; niece Alma Margaret A.; sister-in-law Elsinora Alma A.; sister-in-law Amy Constance A. Brothers-in-law Charles J. Grieve and Andrew Lang. Nieces, Frieda A and Evelyn Grieve. God-daughters, Katherine Symonds, Margaret Frances Daleyns and Beatrice Marshall, Cousin Helen Margaret A. Aunt Helen and Aunt Emily. Kate Grieve, Margaret Grieve, Henrietta Marshall, Emma Marshall, Janet Catherine Symonds, Margaret Symonds, John Addington Symonds.

"The antique ruby ring (oval shape with *Peace* holding an olive branch for the signet) to be buried with me on the third finger of my left hand." My three aunts, Mary, Elinor, and Gertrude Bruce.

Will dated 11th July, 1884. Proved in England.

The signet ring was given her by a great friend and was not a family ring, although the crest which it bore was used by an Irish branch of the Alleyne family.

Sarah Frances Alleyne wrote several books of poems and was a great classical scholar. She was one of the pioneers of advanced education for women, and was a very cultured woman.

ii. Charles Bruce Knight Alleyne, born 12th Aug., 1839, died 7th April, 1861, unmarried. "Alleyne, Charles Bruce Knight, son of C. T. Alleyne Esq., Litfield Place, Clifton, (Mrs. Drury's). Entered Jan. 1852, left Dec. 1853. Died 1861." (*Harrow School Entries.*)

iii. ELIZABETH WILLING ALLEYNE, born 3rd Jan., 1841, married 26th April, 1870, Charles John Grieve of Branxholn Park, Roxburgh, Scotland, by whom she had thirteen children.

iv. HENRY WYNDHAM ALLEYNE, born 29th Nov., 1843, died 24th Sep. 1863. Single. Matric. Exeter Col., Oxford, 29th Jan., 1862, aged 18. A tablet on the north side of Clifton Church, Bristol, records the dates of his birth and death.

49. v. FORSTER McGEACHY ALLEYNE, born 1st July, 1845, died 22nd Nov., 1913. Married 16th May, 1872 Elsinora Alma Taylor.

vi. ANNABELLA ALLEYNE, born 3rd Oct., 1847. Died single.

vii. LEONORA BLANCHE ALLEYNE, born 18th March, 1851 at Clifton, died 10th July, 1933 in London. Funeral services at St. James's, Piccadilly. Buried in the Cathedral Precincts, St. Andrews, Fife. Long obituary notice in *The Times*, 12th July, 1933. She married Andrew, son of John Lang of Selkirk, N.B., (1844-1912) who wrote many delightful books.

viii. HERBERT PERCY ALLEYNE, born 5th March, 1855, died 25th Nov., 1884 at Derby Hall, Matlock Bridge, Derby. Married 14th April, 1880, Amy Constance Bright, eldest daughter of George Bright, Esq. "Alleyne, Percy Herbert, 1871, son of C. T. Alleyne of Clifton, 1869-1873. Eton XI., 1873. Merton Coll., Oxford, B.A. 4th Class Lit. Hum. 1877. Called to the Bar of Inner Temple 1878. Died 25th Nov., 1884. (*Eton School Register*). Issue:

(1) *Stella Margaret Alleyne*, born 19th March, 1883. Educated at Clifton Hall High School and Lady Margaret Hall, Oxon. During World War she worked in the Admiralty and Ministry of Munitions. Afterwards had a permanent post in the Ministry of Agriculture and Fisheries. Controller of Women's staff. Died single.

Will of Herbert Percy Alleyne. Dated 14th April, 1880. Proved 8th Sep., 1905. To wife, Amy Constance A., household effects etc. All plate to trustees upon trust to permit wife to have use thereof during widowhood, and then for eldest son at 21, and failing a son upon trust for his brother Forster Mc Geachy A. Wife an immediate legacy of £200, and annuity of £300 during widowhood. To god-son and nephew James Wyndham Grieve and nieces Alma Margaret A., and Thyra Blanche A., £500 each. To sister Sarah Frances A., £500. To Elizabeth Burnham, old and valued servant £500. To Preston Bruce Austin, of St. Philip, Barbados, £200. Residue to the use of my brother Forster McGeachy A., of Inner Temple, London, Barrister-at-law, The Hon. Henry A. Adderly of Filloughley Hall, Coventry, Warwick, and Rev. John H. J. Ellison of Haseley Rectory, Fetworth, Oxon, upon trust to pay income to wife during widowhood, and at her death to divide capital among my children, whom failing, to Forster Mc Geachy A. Sgd. Herbert Percy Alleyne, between one and 2 o'clock of afternoon of Wednesday 14th Aprl, 1880 after solemnizaton that day of marriage between the said Herbert Percy A. and Amy Constance A. previously A. C. Bright. Witnesses James B. Cook, Solicitor, Bristol, Charles J. Grieve, Branxholn Park, Hawick, N.B. Codicil, 15 Augt., 1880, giving £200 to each executor. Will and Codicil proved 3 June, 1905. Barbados Records Vol. 95. 319.

39. JOHN FORSTER ALLEYNE 8 (*fifth son of John Forster* 7, *Thomas* 6, *Abel* 5, *Reynold* 4, *Abel* 3, *Reynold* 2, *Richard* 1), born 3rd Feb. 1804 at Westbury College, bapt. 30th March, 1805. Died 16th Dec. 1884. Married 31st March 1835 Helen Maria, daughter of Brig. Gen. Arthur Gore. She was born 5th Feb. 1814. Died in Dec. 1894. Brig. Gen. Arthur Gore was killed at the battle of Bergen.

Children of John Forster Alleyne and Helen Maria, his wife:—

   i. ARTHUR GORE ALLEYNE, born 14 Dec., 1841. Died 26 Jan., 1861 at Montevideo, Argentine. Midshipman H.M.S. *Curacoa*. Single.

   ii. CHARLES STUART FORSTER ALLEYNE, born 17 March, 1844. Died 15 Nov., 1863 of a low fever aged 19. Ensign 92nd Gordon Highlanders. Single.

   iii. ALICE MARIA ALLEYNE, born 19th Oct., 1845. Married 12th April, 1866 George W. Marker of Grantlands, Devon, J.P., Lieut. North Devon Hussars. He died 12th Oct., 1904. She was living in London in 1934. No issue.

   iv. GEORGIANA MARY ALLEYNE, died 7th March, 1871. Single.

   v. HELEN JANE MARGARET ALLEYNE.

40. HENRY ALLEYNE 8 (*sixth son John Forster* 7, *Thomas* 6, *Abel* 5, *Reynold* 4, *Abel* 3, *Reynold* 2, *Richard* 1), born 2nd Jan. 1808. Died 3rd Jan. 1852 at sea, in the Bay of Biscay. Married 25th Feb. 1836 Mary Reeve born 18th May 1811, died 9th Dec., 1896, younger daughter of George James, Esq., at St. James, Barbados.

Her marriage was the occasion of a double wedding, her sister, Georgiana James, being married to Dr. Clarke at the same ceremony.

Children of Henry and Mary Reeve Alleyne:—

   i. DOUGLAS ALLEYNE, born 17th Dec., 1836, at Porters, Barbados. Died 2nd March, 1908 at Clifton, Bristol, England. Married 12th Jan., 1865, Ada daughter of Charles Twisleton Graves, Esq.

Children of Douglas and Ada Graves:

     (1) *Evelyn Helen Maude Alleyne*, born 1865. Drowned, aged 18 in 1883 at Westward Ho.

     (2) *Mildred Eliza Florence Alleyne*, md. Bernard Londsdale.

     (3) *Ethel Lisley Alleyne*, died aged 6 years.

Alleyne, Douglas, son of H. Alleyne, Esq., Barbados. Born 17th Dec., 1836. Entered Feb. 1849. Left Midsummer 1853. C.E. (*Marlborough College Register*).

Lieut. Col. Douglas Alleyne, formerly of the 79th Highlanders and 37th Regt. died at Clifton, Bristol, Eng. on the 2nd inst., aged 71. (*The Times* London, 2nd March, 1908).

Col. Alleyne entered the 79th Queens Own Cameron Highlanders as ensign, Feb. 23rd, 1855 and became Lieut. Nov. 2nd, 1855. Exchanging to the 37th Regt. 1860. He became Captain Jan. 24th, 1865. Major Sept. 9th., 1871. Lieut. Col. Oct. 1st, 1879, and retired, receiving the value of his commission Nov. 30th., 1879.

He served with the 79th Highlanders in the Crimea from 16th Aug. to Dec. 1855, including the siege and fall of Sebastopol and assault on Redan Sept. 8th. (Medal with clasp and Turkish medal). Also during the Indian Mutiny Campaign 1858-59, including the affair of Secundra near Allahabad; the siege and capture of Lucknow, the attack on the Fort of Rooyah, the action of Allygunge, Barielly and Shahjehanpore, the capture of Forts Bunnai and Mahomdee, and the passage of the Gogra at Fyzabad. He acted as Adjutant at the capture of Rampore Kussiah and during the subsequent operations in Oude across the Gogra and Raptee Rivers. (Medal with clasp.) *(Army and Navy Gazette, 14th March, 1908).*

Douglas. His wife ran away with another man who blew his brains out on the steps of a club. (From old Alleyne bible.) Col. Lawrence was the other man.

ii. MARY ALLEYNE, born 21st Jan., 1839, bapt. 27th March, 1839 at St. James, Barbados. Died 25th Nov., 1928. Single. Buried in Clifton Parish Churchyard.

iii. HENRY ALLEYNE, born 14th Oct., 1840, bapt. 31st May, 1841 at St. James, Barbados.

iv. JAMES ALLEYNE, born 13th Jan., 1842 at Porters, Barbados, bapt. 21st Sept., 1842, at St. James, Barbados. Died 23rd April, 1899 at Clifton, Bristol, Eng aged 57 years. Single. Entered Cheltenham College, Aug. 1854. Left June 1858.

James Alleyne passed for Royal Military College, Sandhurst, 1859, did not proceed there, but attended Royal Military Academy, Woolwich 1860. Lieut. Royal Artillery 1862. Captain 1875. Adjutant 1877-79. Brevet-Major 1879. Major 1882. Brevet Lieut. Col. 1882. Colonel 1885. Major General 1895. Brigade Major, Royal Artillery, Aldershot 1882. Deputy Assistant Adjutant and Quartermaster General, Egypt Aug. to Oct. 1884-1885. Assistant Adjutant General Woolwich District, 1886-91. Assistant Adjutant General Aldershot District 1893-95. Major General on Staff, commanding Royal Artillery Aldershot 1895-97. Served in command of the Detachment of Royal Artillery and 7 pounder mountain guns, which accompanied the Red River Expedition from Canada in 1870. Served in the Zulu War of 1879 and was present at the battle of Ulundi (mentioned in despatches, Brevet Major, Medal with clasp.) Subsequently was a commissioner for the sub-division of Zululand, and in the following year, 1880, was commssioner to delineate the Transvaal, Swaziland Boundary. Served in the Egyptian War of 1832 as Deputy Assistant Adjutant and Quartermaster General on the Lines of Communication and Base, and was present in the engagement at Tel-el-Mahuta, and at the battle of Tel-el-Kebir. (Mentioned in despatches, Brevet of Lieut. Col, Medal with clasp, 4th Class. Osmanieh and Kedive's Star.) Served with the Nile Expedition in 1884-85 as Director of River Transport and Assistant Adjutant and Quartermaster General at Headquarters, and was

present at the action of Kirbekan, in command of a detached force.
(Twice mentioned in despatches, Brevet Col. two clasps.)
C.B. 1891. K.C.B. 1897. Also received Queen's Jubilee Medal in
1897. General Sir James Alleyne died at Clifton, Bristol, England
on the 23rd April, 1899.

v. HENRY NELSON ALLEYNE, born 17th May, 1844, bapt. 17th May, 1844
at St. James, Barbados. Died 17th Jan. 1917 at Clifton, Bristol, Eng.
aged 72 years. Married 18th July, 1893 Constance Noel Weddubun,
daughter of Sir Carey John Knyvett, K.C.B., and Lady Knyvett,
nee Weddubun.

He was educated in the British Navy, becoming a cadet 1858.
Sub. Lieut. 1865. Lieut. 1867. Commander 1881. Retired Capt.
1893. Appointed Sec. to R.N. Fund 1893.

Children of Captain Henry Nelson Alleyne and Constance Noel,
his wife:—

(1) *Winifred Mary Constance Alleyne,* born 16th Nov., 1900 at
London.

(2) *Henry Guy Knyvett Alleyne,* born 23rd April, 1905 in
London. Died single 17th Aug. 1935. Farming in South
Africa.

ALLEYNE. On Aug. 17th, 1935 at Edenbridge Hospital,
HENRY GUY KNYVETT (Bonzo) aged 30. Only son of the
late Captain H. N. Alleyne R.N., and the late Mrs.
Alleyne. Cremation Golders Green 12.30 to-morrow (Tues-
day, Aug. 20). No mourning. Flowers at Crematorium.
South and East African papers please copy.
(*The Times.* London Aug., 19th 1935).

vi. ALICE ALLEYNE, bapt. 21st Jan., 1847 at St. James, Barbados. Died
20th April, 1853 at Tunbridge aged 6 years.

On a long slate ledger over a vault enclosed by an iron railing
at Clifton Church, Bristol, Eng. is the following:

IN MEMORY OF/ALICE/YOUNGEST DAUGHTER OF THE LATE
HENRY ALLEYNE, ESQ'RE/OF THE ISLAND OF BARBADOS/OBIIT 20TH
APRIL 1853/AGED 6 YEARS/ALSO OF/MARY REEVE, WIFE OF THE ABOVE
HENRY ALLEYNE, BORN 18 MAY, 1811/DIED 9TH DEC. 1896. ALSO OF/
JAMES ALLEYNE/DIED APRIL 23RD 1899/AGED 56 YEARS/SON OF
HENRY ALLEYNE AND MARY REEVE ALLEYNE.

On the south wall of the nave of St. James's Church,
Barbados:—

CREST: *A horse's head out of a ducal coronet.*

ARMS: *Quarterly, 1 & 4, Per chevron gules and ermine, two lions'
head erased Or* (ALLEYNE): *2 & 3, Sable, a hand issuing from
sinister side couped, grasping three arrows, one in pale and two
saltire (Willing), all Or: impaling quarterly of 4: 1. Argent, two
bars doubly embattled Gules.* (JAMES *of Ightham, Kent*); *2. Argent,
a chevron Sable between three millrinds transverse (James);
3, Barrywavy of six Argent and Azure, on a chief or three swallows
volant; 4. Ermine, on a bend engrailed Azure three cinquefoils Or:*

MOTTO: *Je crains Dieu et n'ai point d' autre crainte.*

SACRED/TO THE MEMORY OF/THE HONOURABLE HENRY ALLEYNE
/MEMBER OF HIS MAJESTY'S COUNCIL/IN THIS ISLAND/YOUNGEST SON

OF/THE HONOURABLE JOHN FORSTER ALLEYNE/OF PORTERS, IN THIS
PARISH/WHO WAS BORN ON THE 2ND JANUARY 1808/AND PERISHED
AT SEA/BY THE BURNING OF/THE ROYAL MAIL STEAMER AMAZON/OFF
USHANT IN THE BAY OF BISCAY, DURING THE NIGHT OF THE 3RD AND
4TH JANUARY, 1852.

TO THE INEXPRESSIBLE GRIEF AND SORROW OF THIS ENTIRE
COMMUNITY, AS WELL AS OF HIS OWN IMMEDIATE FAMILY AND
FRIENDS. TO PERPETUATE THE REMEMBRANCE OF SUCH HIGH IN-
TEGRITY, WORTH AND EXCELLENCE AS ARE RARELY EXEMPLIFIED IN
EITHER PUBLIC OR PRIVATE LIFE, THIS MONUMENT IS ERECTED BY HIS
BEREAVED AND DEEPLY AFFLICTED WIDOW.

Henry Alleyne was a planter and lived at Porters, Barbados.
Will of Henry Alleyne dated 17th June, 1847. Pr. 21 Jan., 1852.

Brother Charles Thomas Alleyne all Hole Town property
which he purchased from him years ago, consisting of stores, timber
yard and other premises. Wife Mary Reeve Alleyne plate linen
furniture, carriages, horses, etc. Also during life interest on £3,400.

Estate called Lancaster in parish of St. James containing 480
acres, to be sold and money invested for wife.

If no children then after death of wife all property for sister
Charlotte Emily Alleyne. After her death to brother John Foster
Alleyne. Executrix: Wife Mary Reeve Alleyne. Signed Henry
Alleyne.

Witnesses: Jno. Pitcher Jr. Jno. W. Gill. (Barbados Record.
Vol. 74 p. 261).

'The Times' London 7th January, 1852.

Destruction of the Steamship *Amazon* by fire at the entrance to the Bay
of Biscay, 2—3 Jan., 1852. Narrative by Vincent, Midshipman on the
Amazon, who was saved.

"We left Southampton with the West Indian and Mexican mails on board
on Friday the 2nd inst. On the 3rd at noon, we were in latitude 49.12 north,
longitude 4.57 west. At 9.30 p.m. we stopped with hot bearings. At 11.2)
we proceeded, wind still increasing. About 20 minutes to one Sunday
morning fire was observed bursting through the hatchway forward of the fore-
funnel. Every possible exertion was made to put out the fire, but all was ineffectual. The mail boat was lowered with 20 or 25 persons in it, but was
immediately swamped and went astern, the people clinging to one another.
They were all lost. The pinnace was next lowered, but she hung by the fore
tackle, and being swamped, the people were all washed out of her. In
lowering the second cutter the sea raised her and unhooked the fore tackle,
so that she fell down perpendicularly and all but two of the persons in her
were washed out.

"Capt. Symons was all this time using his utmost exertions to save his
passengers and crew. 16 men, including 2 passengers, succeeded in lowering
the life boat, and about the same time, I (Mr. Vincent) with 2 men, the
steward and a passenger, got into and lowered the dingy. In about half an
hour the life boat took the dingy's people into her, but the sea increasing,
and being nearly swamped, they were obliged to cast the dingy off and bring
the boat head to the sea. The masts went, first the foremast and then
the mizenmast.

"About this time a barque past astern of the life boat, we hailed her with united 21 voices and thought she answered us, but she wore and stood under the stern of the burning vessel and immediately hauled her wind and stood away again.

"The gig with 5 hands was at this time some little way from us, but the sea was running so high we could not render her any assistance and shortly afterwards lost sight of her.

"About 4 a.m. (Sunday) it was raining heavily and the wind shifted to the northward; sea confused, but decreasing; put the boat before the sea. At 5 o'clock the ship's magazine exploded and about half an hour afterwards the funnels went over the sides and she sunk.

"At noon we were picked up by the "Marsden" of London, Capt. Evans, by whom we were treated in the kindest manner possible. Put in at Plymouth 10.50 Jan. 5th and were most hospitably and kindly received by the landlord of the Globe Hotel, Mr. Radmore."

Out of the 156 people on board only 21 were saved. Mr. Henry Alleyne was one of the passengers lost.

There is a tradition in Barbados that the night the 'Amazon' was blown up on her maiden trip to the West Indies, and Mr. Henry Alleyne lost his life, his wife, who was living at Porters, was sitting at a table playing a game of cards with Mr. Charles Alleyne, her brother-in-law, when they heard a terrible explosion. Everyone jumped up and searched the whole place, even the cellar, but there was nothing to be seen.

He had sent his wife a packing case, not to be opened until he arrived, as he had the key. After his death, when his wife opened the case the first thing she saw was the song, 'What are the Wild Waves Saying.' It was a popular song which had just come out and he had bought it for her.

Another tradition is that whenever a member of the family was going to die, a white bird would perch on one of the family portraits, of which there were several.

Porters is a charming old house which has been added to several times and the floors are on different levels and the ceiling low. There is a long winding drive to the house through a grove of mahogany trees which are inhabited by lots of monkeys who used to look in at the windows. Some of them were still there in 1930.

At the back of the house there is a lovely garden marked off with olive hedges, and beyond a large paddock. At the side of the garden is the swimming bath which looks like a small chapel covered with vines. Dudley Woodbridge was drowned in it at the age of 17 years, and there is an inscription in latin on the wall, which, freely translated, is:

'Against the will of Dudley Woodbridge Esquire,
notwithstanding that he was a lover of cleanliness,
this chamber was transformed into a bath by an
inundation 24 March, 1735.'

ALLEYNE OF BARBADOS.

(Ninth Instalment).

41. Reynold Henry Newton Alleyne 9 (*eldest son of Sir John Gay Newton* 8, *Sir Reynold Abel* 7, *Sir John Gay* 6, *John* 5, *Reynold* 4, *Abel* 3, *Reynold* 2, *Richard* 1), born 16 May 1852, bapt. 1 July 1852 at Turner's Hall, Barbados. Died 6 April 1908 at Falmouth, England. Married 4 January 1879, Susanna, third daughter of John Meynell, eldest son of Godfrey Meynell, of Meynell Langley Park, Co. Derby. She was born 13 May 1849 at Tapton Grove, near Chesterfield, Derby. Residences Cheven House, Belper, Derbyshire, 27, Drayton Court, South Kensington, S.W. 10 London, England.

Children of Reynold Henry Newton Alleyne and Susanna, his wife:—

i. Augusta Alleyne, born 21 Nov., 1881 at Codnor Park, Derbyshire, Single.

ii. Eleanor Alleyne, born 13 May, 1883 at Coxbench Hall, Derbyshire.

iii. Alice Alleyne, born 22 Dec., 1884 at Thorner, near Leeds, Yorkshire. Married 10 June 1911 Charles Tertius Maclean Plowright, M.B., B.C., Capt. R.A.M.C. during European War. King Street, King's Lynn, Norfolk.

> (1) *Mary Alice Alleyne Plowright*, born 16 Jan., 1913; married Jack Storey.

> (2) *Susie Vere Alleyne Plowright*, born 11 Oct., 1919.

iv. Ida Alleyne, born 26 May, 1886 at Thorner, Leeds, Yorks.

v. Sir John Meynell Alleyne, of whom later.

vii. Reynold Meynell Alleyne, born 6 March, 1892 at Thorner, near Leeds, Yorks. Lieut. R.N. 1914. Lieut. Com. 1923. European War 1914-1918.

During the World War 1914--18 Lieut. Reynold Meynell Alleyne served (from 4 Aug., 1914 to Oct., 1915) in H.M.S. *Seagull*, a mine sweeper sweeping in the North Sea and English Channel and was present at the first bombardment of Ostend in which his brother, Sir John Meynell Alleyne also took part in H.M.S. *Lord Clive*. The *Seagull* was damaged by a mine in 1915 and towards the end of the war was sunk in collision, after Reynold Alleyne had left her. From Nov., 1915 to Oct., 1917 he was in H.M.S. *Britannia*, Battleship, engaged in escorting Australians and New Zealand troops from Cape of Good Hope to Sierra Leone, and later was working in conjunction with the Italian Fleet in the Mediterranean. H.M.S. *Britannia* was torpedoed and sunk a few weeks after Reynold M. Alleyne left her. He served in H.M.S. *New Zealand*, Battleship, for the remainder of the war in the North Sea, and was present at the surrender of the German Fleet on 21 Nov., 1918.

Reynold Henry Newton Alleyne was born at Turner's Hall, Barbados, on 16th May 1852. He was educated at Winchester College from 1866 to 1870 and then was apprenticed to Messrs. Napier and Son, ship builders and engineers of Glasgow. The last year of his apprenticeship (1873) was served in the works of the Butterley Co., at Codnor Park, where he had charge of the first open hearth regenerative Siemens still furnace, and subsequently he became manager of the works. In 1883 he went to Leeds to take the management of a machine tool business purchased by a relative, but owing to a serious illness he was compelled to relinquish it in 1892. In 1896, having somewhat regained his health, he was elected a Director of the Norfolk Estuary Co., which had been incorporated many years before for reclaiming and embanking from the sea two large tracts of lands situated in the great estuary of the Wash between the counties of Norfolk and Lincoln. In 1898 he became Managing Director of the Works. He was actively engaged in this connection up to his death. Among other works designed by him was a large sluice intended to be constructed in one of the sea banks which would provide for the drainage out-fall of the Company's embanked lands. In 1905 he introduced a system of bank protection known as the Villa Mantle, which consisted of a special kind of covering extensively used in Holland. In Feb. 1908 he was called before the Royal Commission on Coast Erosion and gave evidence as to the nature of the Company's operations. He was a partner in Messrs. Scriven & Co., Engineers and Machine Tool Makers, Leeds, from 1883. His death took place at Falmouth on 6th April 1908 in his fifty-sixth year.

42. SIR JOHN MEYNELL ALLEYNE 10 (*eldest son of Reynold Henry Newton* 9, *Sir John Gay Newton* 8, *Sir Reynold Abel* 7, *Sir John Gay* 6, *John* 5, *Reynold* 4, *Abel* 3, *Reynold* 2, *Richard* 1), born 11 Aug. 1889 at Thorner near Leeds, Yorks. Married 20 Dec. 1920, Alice Violet, daughter of James Campbell of Cornwall Gardens, S.W. 7. London, and Mary daughter of Gen. Sir William Olpherts, V.C., K.C.B. She was born Jan. 1895 at Sheen, Surrey, England.

"The marriage took place yesterday (20 Dec. 1920) at St. Saviour's, Walton Street, of Lieutenant-Commander Sir John Alleyne, Bt., D.S.O., D.S.C. of H.M.S. *Dunedin*, eldest son of the late Mr. Reynold Henry Newton Alleyne and of Mrs. Alleyne of Langley, Derbyshire, and Alice Violet daughter of the late Mr. James Campbell and Mrs. James Campbell, of 12 Cornwall Gardens, S.W. The bride was given away by her brother Captain James Campbell. Her three bridesmaids, Miss Kathleen and Ida Alleyne, sisters of the bridegroom and Miss Campbell, (her sister). Master Christopher Olpherts was page. The Rev. F. W. Meynell, Vicar of Stapenhill, officiated and Maj. Meynell was best man."

('*The Times*' London Dec. 21, 1920).

Seat Chevin House, Belper, Derby. Town residence 27 Drayton Court, South Kensington, S.W. 10, London.

Children of Sir John Alleyne and Alice Violet, his wife:—

i. EILEEN VIOLET ALLEYNE, born 11 May 1923 at 12 Cornwall Gardens, London.

ii. ROSEMARY ALLEYNE, born 26 April, 1925 at 12 Cornwall Gardens, London.

iii. JOHN OLPHERTS CAMPBELL ALLEYNE, born 18 Jan., 1928 at 12 Cornwall Gardens, London. He received the names of Campbell after his mother's family, and of Olpherts after his maternal grandfather, Gen. Sir William Olpherts, who received the Victoria Cross in the Indian Mutiny.

Sir John Meynell Alleyne succeeded his grandfather, Sir John Gay Newton Alleyne as fourth Baronet on 20 Feb. 1912.

Sir John Alleyne went to sea from the *Britannia* in September 1905, joining H.M.S. *Hindustan*, Captain A. G. Tate, in the Channel Fleet. When the War began he was navigator of the *Hebe*, submarine parent ship. Later he joined the monitor, *Lord Clive* and served in action off the Belgian coast, for which he was awarded the D.S.C. in May 1917. Joining the *Vindictive* for the Ostend raid, he was severely wounded there during the abandonment of the ship. He was badly hit before he could be got over the side, fell into the water, and was rescued by a motor-launch. The D.S.O. was awarded him, and in the official dispatch Sir Roger Keyes stated that Lieutenant Alleyne had been most useful in fitting up the navigational instruments destroyed in the previous raid on April 23, and had asked to be allowed to navigate the *Vindictive* in the the second operation. Sir Roger Keyes approved of this, "feeling that this officer's experience and intimate knowledge of the shoals and currents on the Belgian coast would be of great value to the Commander of the *Vindictive*."

He showed great coolness under a very heavy fire, and most skillfully navigated the *Vindictive* to the entrance to Ostend harbour. He was severely wounded and rendered unconscious when his Captain was killed. He was with *Vindictive's* commander on the upper steering position when the attack on Ostend was opened.

Sir John Alleyne was promoted as Commander in December 1924, and later graduated at the Staff College and served in the Operations and Plans Divisions. He commanded H.M.S. *Lupin* in the Persian Gulf in 1928-30.

Sir John Alleyne was King's Harbour Master at Singapore, but retired at his own request after 32 year's service in the Navy.

Copy of a letter written by Lieut. Sir John Meynell Alleyne to his brother Lieut. Reynold Alleyne from No. 30 General Hospital A. E. F. France. May 23, 1918.

My dear White:

I was so awfully pleased to get your letter this afternoon, thank you very much for it; but I am seriously afraid that I have not done anything brilliant or even clever. I think that as it has all come out in the papers, I may as well spin the whole yarn now, such as it is, as the official account was not quite right as far as I was concerned, as of course, I did not have any say in the report, being in hospital in Dunkerque.

As I expect you know, in the first show, the *Vindictive* and blockships were all manned by people from the Grand Fleet, or somewhere, and we were not given a chance to volunteer, which "Seeing as how" it was on our preserves, I thought a bit rough.

However, after we heard that the *Vindictive* was going to try again, manned by the people from the *Brilliant* and *Serious*, I found quite by accident, that they had no Lieutenant (N), so after talking a lot of hot air about that, of course, being the reason they missed the entrance (of course it really had nothing to do with it) I got taken on for the job.

It was an almost perfect evening for the show when we started. When we began to get close to Ostend all the shore batteries opened fire, but I don't think they could see us as they seemed to be putting up a barrage, as the stuff was no thicker around us than anywhere else, and the smoke screen seemed very good; but when, by dead reckoning, we ought to have arrived at the pier heads, to our horror and dismay, we could not see a blessed thing except shell and fog.

We turned parallel to the coast and steamed up and down about a mile or so either way three or four times, until suddenly we sighted the pier heads close to S.W. and I think they must have seen us about the same time, as the fire began to concentrate on us then, and we started getting hit. We made for the entrance and just as we were coming up to the piers, they opened a pretty hot fire on us with machine guns. Crutchley was in the conning tower then, and the Captain and I were on the bridge, so as we came up to the piers, the Captain said we would go down to the conning tower; so we started down, but I got hit by a machine gun bullet just as I got down the first ladder. It hardly hurt at all, but made me feel horribly sick and shaky at the knees almost at once.

I managed to get on into the conning tower, but am a bit hazy as to exactly what happened after that, except that I kept nearly going off and trying not to, and I remember the P.O. saying it was time to abandon ship and carrying me aft to where two M.L's were along side.

As there were only ropes ends etc. to get down with, wounded had to be thrown overboard and picked up, so I was chucked into the ditch, which revived me considerably. I got hold of the life line of one of the M.L's. but could not climb up the side and she shoved off before I could get anyone to haul me on board.

As she went astern, she scraped up against the other boat so I had to let go to save myself being jammed, and the other boat went off before I could get hold of her, so I swam back to the ship. I found the whaler hanging by the after falls with her bows in the water, so I managing to climb into her, intending to wait till the Huns came off in the morning. However, I found an A.B. in the boat who was not wounded, so I told him to try to climb up and cut the after fall, hoping we might lie in the bottom of the boat and let her drift out of the harbour on the ebb tide.

Just as he was climbing up, another M.L. suddenly appeared, heroically dashing in through the machine gun fire, and as you can imagine we were pretty pleased to see her. They pulled us on board and got out again all right though they had an officer and several men killed.

They could not put me below as they had their acid tank shot through and the cabin was full of fumes; at least they did put me below for a bit, but I had to be hauled out again half suffocated.
cabin was full of fumes; at least they did put me below for a bit, but I had to be hauled out again half soffocated.

We eventually fell in with one of the monitors, by which time I was pretty frozen, but they could not give me anything to drink till they were certain what the damage was, but they warmed me with hot water bottles and things.

I was landed at Dunkerque and sent to the Queen Alexandra Hospital, where they X-rayed me right away and found the bullet had gone through and out the other side and just missed everything that mattered. (A button deflected the bullet). I had a small operation of some sort as the top of my hip bone is chipped.

I was awfully well done there, though of course, one gets sick of lying in bed.

I came on here Tuesday afternoon, which is the first stage toward crossing to England and I am hoping to go across to-morrow. I do not know where I shall go when I get across, but I expect Chatham. I hope they will let me go home in ten days or so, as soon as I can get on my feet a bit. I hope I shall be at home during your leave anyhow. The doctor says I shant be fit for duty for about six weeks yet, so I am pretty sure to see you, aren't I? I am still getting on very well and dont feel at all ill, thank you very much.

Hoping to see you soon,

Your affectionate brother,

JACK.

43. ROBERT HARBIN ALLEYNE 9, (*third son of Thomas Harbin* 8, *Abel* 7, *Thomas* 6, *Abel* 5, *Reynold* 4, *Abel* 2, *Richard* 1,) born August 27, 1823, baptized at *Porter's*, Barbados. Married January 14, 1845 at St. Michael, Barbados, Mary daughter of .... Woodley Esq., who was of Irish descent. Died July 14, 1890.

Robert Harbin Alleyne was Agricultural Attorney of *Porter's* and other plantations owned by Charles Thomas Alleyne, and resided at *Porter's*, St. James. He held the rank of Captain in the Barbados Yeomanry Cavalry. He was returned to the House of Assembly at a by-election in the parish of St. James in February 1866 and served until the end of the Session when he retired.

Children of Robert Harbin Alleyne and Mary his wife:—

    i. ROBERT HARBIN ALLEYNE, born at Hothersal, St. John, Barbados, baptized July 31, 1847, died July 25, 1886 in Wesley, Kossuth Co. Iowa, U.S.A. Unmarried.

96

Dr. Robert Harbin Alleyne was educated at the Lodge School, Barbados, and studied medicine at the University of Edinburgh, taking his degree on August 1, 1871. He returned to Barbados and practised his profession there for some years. but left for United States about 1880, owing to a love affair, it was said. He settled in the little Town of Wesley, and continued to practise medicine, living at a hotel, and not communicating with his relatives in Barbados. The records of the State Dept. of Health, Des Moines, Iowa, show that in 1886 he had been practising in Iowa five and one-half years. He was very popular in Wesley, and regarded as a very clever physician.

An inscription on the stone over his grave in Wesley shows that he was a member of the Masonic Fraternity, and it reads as follows:—

"IN MEMORY OF DR. H. ALLEYNE, DIED JULY 25, 1886, AGED 40 YEARS. ERECTED BY FRIENDS. BY STRANGERS HONOURED AND BY STRANGERS MOURNED."

ii. ELIZA DALLAS ALLEYNE, bapt. 26 Sept., 1848 at St. John Barbados. Died 7 July, 1890. Single.

iii. HENRY ALLEYNE, bapt. 2 Sept., 1849, St. John, Barbados. Married Mrs. Jane Harriet Laurie King Watson.

iv. JAMES HOLDER ALLEYNE, bapt. 19 July, 1851, St. John, Barbados, died 22 Dec., 1876.

v. MARY WOODLEY ALLEYNE, born 31 May, 1855, bapt. 1 Sept., 1855, died 11 April, 1926, single.

vi. ALICE MATILDA ALLEYNE, born 25 Aug., 1856, bapt. 22 Sept., 1856, died 30 Nov., 1925, single.

vii. FRANCES BRUCE ALLEYNE, born 19 Dec., 1859 at Porter's, Barbados, bapt. 20 Dec., 1858, St. James, Barbados, died 25 Feb., 1914, single.

viii. CHARLES KNIGHT BRUCE ALLEYNE, bapt. 23 Jan., 1862 at St. James, Barbados, died 2 Nov., 1891, in Trinidad, B.W.I.

Will of Robert Harbin Alleyne, dated 31 Aug., 1876. Proved 21 Nov., 1890. Barbados, Parish of St. James.

Plantations called *Buckden, Saltram* and the *Union* and my place called *Binfield*, also place called *Alleynedale*, all situate in this island. All personal estate to use of sons Robert Harbin Alleyne, Henry Alleyne, and James Holder Alleyne, daughter Elizabeth Dallas Alleyne. Friends Edward Braithwaite Skeete, John Henry Thomas, both of St. Philip. Shares of any married daughter or grand-daughter to be her sole and separate use free from marital control.

Notwithstanding the trust aforesaid, if my son Charles Knight Bruce, shall survive me and be under 25 years at my decease, he shall be entitled to same provisions for maintenance as the daughters.

Signed Robert Harbin Alleyne.

Witnesses: Chas. T. Cottle. J. W. C. Catford.

44. FREDERICK WILLIAM ALLEYNE 9, (second son of Thomas Harbin 8, Abel 7, Thomas 6, Abel 5, Reynold 4, Abel 3, Reynold 2, Richard 1), born at Porter's, Barbados, bapt. 25 Sept., 1825, St. James, Barbados. Married 9 April, 1845 Mary Sophia Earle. He was a planter and lived at Carmichael's, St. George, Barbados.

Children of Frederick William Alleyne and Mary Sophia, his wife:—

    i. JULIA DECOURCEY ALLEYNE, born 18 Sept., 1845, married 22 Feb., 1866, George James Jemmott. (Julia DeCourcey Alleyne aged 20, spinster. Married 22 Feb., 1886 at St. George, Barbados, to George James Jemmott, aged 30 bachelor, planter. Residence Parks, Carmichael's. Her father Frederick W. Alleyne, Planter. His father, Conrade Jemmott, Planter.) There were 10 children of the marriage.

    ii. JOSEPH CARLETON ALLEYNE, born 5 April, 1847, at Hole Town, Barbados, single.

    iii. MARGARET ELIZABETH ALLEYNE, born 1 June, 1849 at Hole Town, Barbados, Married William Thomas.

50. iv. INNES MILTON ALLEYNE, born 26 Nov. 1851 at Hole Town, Barbados, died 17 May, 1930, married 14 June, 1877, Laura, daughter of John Berryman.

    v. ALICE AMELIA ALLEYNE, married Urban Thomas.

    vi. KATE ALLEYNE, single.

    vii. GEORGE ALLEYNE, Married, first issue:
        (1) Lizzetta Alleyne.
        (2) Dora Alleyne.
        (3) Emily Alleyne.
    Married secondly, Mrs. Buchanan, widow. Lived at Stockton, New Jersey, U.S.A.

    viii. WILLIAM ALLEYNE, Single.

    ix. MARY PARRY ALLEYNE, born 12 May, 1870, died 26 Jan., 1929, in Barbados, Married 1895, Ernest Jones.

    x. FORSTER MCGEACHY ALLEYNE, Single.

    xi. MARY BRUCE ALLEYNE, born 6 May, 1863, bapt. 26 July, 1863 at St. James, Barbados.

45. JAMES HOLDER ALLEYNE JR 9, (eldest son of James Holder 8, John Forster 7, Thomas 6, Abel 5, Reynold 4, Abel 3, Reynold 2, Richard 1), born 27 May, 1819, bapt. 23 Sept. 1819 at St. James, Barbados. Died 28th Jan. 1862. Married first, 21 Sept. 1850, Louisa Fisher. Died 11 April, 1852.

21 Sept. 1850 at St. George, Hanover Square, London, Eng. James Holder Alleyne Esq., late Capt. 52 Light Infantry, to Louisa

daughter of William Fisher Esq. of Walsworth Hall Gloucester, and of Kings Clere, Hants, and Ebury St. London, S.W.

James Holder Alleyne, M.D., was Capt. 52 Light Infantry and went through the Peninsular War. He also was Colonial Surgeon of British Guiana and later lived at 27 Gloucester Place, Hyde Park W. London, Eng.

Child of James Holder Alleyne Jr., and Louisa, his wife:—

51.   i. EDWARD WENTWORTH FISHER HOLDER ALLEYNE, born 30 March, 1852, Died Dec., 1897. Married Emily Alicia Katherine Addison.

James Holder Alleyne Jr. married, secondly, 2 Feb., 1853, Ellen Sarah, daughter of Colonel Robert Crutchley, of Princes Terrace, Marylebone, London.

Child of James Holder Alleyne Jr. and Ellen Sarah, his wife:—

   i. WALTER PERCY ALLEYNE, born 17 Dec., 1858 at Florence, Italy. Married 2 October, 1884, Marian Georgiana Haig, second daughter of John Haig of Bray Court, Maidenhead. He was educated at Winchester College.
       Issue:—

   i. *Lilith Alleyne*, born 20 April, 1885. Living in Victoria, B.C. in 1929; in London, 1933.

   ii. *Victor Percy Alleyne*, born 21 April, 1887. Married June 19, 1929 at Victoria, B.C., Elizabeth, second daughter of Dr. Cyril Wace of Victoria, B.C. Commander R.N. (Retired 1927). Living in Victoria, B.C.

   iii. *Nellie Alleyne*, born 1 Aug., 1889. Married 3 Dec., 1915, William Sprague Swinscow. Lived at Torquay, Devon, Eng.
        Issue:—

        (1) Thomas Douglas Victor Swinscow, born 10 July, 1917.

        (2) Alleyne Godfrey Swinscow, born 29 March, 1919.

ALLEYNE OF BARBADOS.
(Tenth Instalment.)

46. Joseph Lowe Alleyne 9 *(second son of James Holder 8, John Forster 7, Thomas 6, Abel 5, Reynold 4, Abel 3, Reynold 2, Richard 1)*, born 8 Nov. 1820, died 3 July, 1858. Married Julia, daughter of John Holder Esq. of Lemon Arbor, Barbados. She died in 1858.

Joseph Lowe Alleyne, matric. at St. John's Coll., Cambridge, 1840. L.L.B. Magdalene, Cambridge 1851.

He was of Buttals Plantation, Barbados, and 4, Oxford Square, Hyde Park, London, England.

Children of Joseph Lowe Alleyne and Julia, his wife:—
  i. James Alexander McGeachy Alleyne, born 12 April 1850.
  ii. Joseph Lowe Alleyne, born 1852.
  iii. Mary Elizabeth Josephine Alleyne, born Dec. 1856. Married Bruno Digby Beste.

Will of Rev. Joseph Lowe Alleyne dated 1st July, 1858. Late of Buttals, Barbados, now of 4, Oxford Square, Hyde Park, Co. Middlesex, London, England. Household effects except plate to wife. Plate to son Alexander Alleyne, if he dies, then to son Joseph Lowe Alleyne, if he dies then to daughter Mary Elizabeth Josephine Alleyne. ¼ part of estate of Buttals, in Barbados, to wife and £2,000. Other ¾ divided between children. Estate called Greggs (which was bequeathed to me by my maternal grandfather) one moiety to Alexander Alleyne, one moiety to son Joseph Alleyne. To daughter Mary Elizabeth Josephine £1,000. Wife to receive two-thirds and profits of estates called Burrels and Greggs or two-thirds if sold.

Children must be instructed and educated in conformity with the Creed, Doctrine and Faith of the established Church of England and in no other faith or religion whatsoever.

Executors: Wife, Julia, and brother Alexander McGeachy Alleyne of 4 Oxford Square, Gent., and Brother Arthur Osborne Gibbes Alleyne of Brighton, Co. Sussex, Eng. Clerk. Signed Joseph Lowe Alleyne.

Witnesses: William Dickens, the Cambridge Street chemist. Thomas Philips, Butler, 4 Oxford Square.

Codicil 2 July, 1858. Insurance and plate to son. Also add Robert Alleyne of Porters, Barbados, Planter to Executors.

Signed Joseph Lowe Alleyne.

Witnesses: Elizabeth Mary Alleyne. Will Maxwell, Clerk to C. Lewis, 1 Albany Court Yard, Piccadilly. Proved 3 Aug. 1858. Entered 25 March 1859. (Barbados Records. Vol. 77. pp. 34).

In the High Court of Justice, Chancery Division, Mr. Justice Chitty. (1882 A. No. 39) Fos. 55. Filed 28 March 1882. Estate of Joseph Lowe Alleyne. Between Julia Alleyne, widow, Plaintiff and Robert Alleyne, James Alexander Alleyne, Joseph Lowe Alleyne and the Rev. Kenelm Digby Beste. Defendants.

Joseph Lowe Alleyne, formerly of Buttals, Barbados, late of Oxford Square, Hyde Park, Co. Middlesex. Will dated 1 July,

1958. Brothers, Alexander McGeachy Alleyne, Arthur Osborne Gibbes Alleyne, Executors and trustees. Greggs' Estate bequeathed to him by his maternal grandfather. Son Alexander Alleyne. Son Joseph Lowe Alleyne. Daughter Mary Elizabeth Josephine Alleyne. Robert Alleyne "relative."

Alexander McGeachy Alleyne died 5 Jan. 1867. Joseph Lowe Alleyne's surviving children, James Alexander Alleyne, born 1850. Joseph Lowe Alleyne of Greggs Estate born 1852. Josephine Mary Elizabeth Alleyne Beste, wife of Bruno Digby Beste, born 1856. 21 in Dec. 1877.

Buttals and Greggs plantations 442 acres in St. George and St. Andrews, Barbados. Mrs. Elizabeth Alleyne, mother of testator who died 25 Feb. 1877. Special Case under order 34. G. T. Woodrooffe, 1 New Square, Lincoln's Inn. Plaintiff's solicitor.

G. T. Woodrooffe, 1 New Square, Lincoln's Inn. Plaintiff's solicitor.

47. ALEXANDER McGEACHY ALLEYNE 9 *(third son of James Holder* 8, *John Forster* 7, *Thomas* 6, *Abel* 5, *Reynold* 4, *Abel* 3, *Reynold* 2, *Richard* 1)*, bapt. 24 July, 1825 at St. James, Barbados, died 5 Jan. 1867. Married Henrietta Maria daughter of Rev. R. Kendall Wood of Husbands Bosworth, Leicestershire. A famous beauty. She later married Col. Frederick Bassett Wingfield, Colonel of the 7th Dragoon Guards.

Children of Alexander McGeachy Alleyne and Henrietta Maria, his wife: i. CECIL HOWARD ALLEYNE.

ii. FRANCES MARY ELIZABETH ALLEYNE, married Oct. 1878 Col. Fleming George Gill at St. George's, Hanover Square, London.

Frances Mary Elizabeth Alleyne, eldest daughter of Capt. A. McGeachy Alleyne late 7th Dragoon Guards, married Maj. Fleming George Gill, R.A. of Remembrance House, Wraysbury, and Yeovency Hall, Middlesex, at St. George's Chapel, Hanover Square, London. Amongst the guests were Col. and Mrs. D. Alleyne, Capt. J. Alleyne, R.A., Mr. and Mrs. E. Alleyne, Mr. Cecil Alleyne, Mrs. Henry Alleyne, Mr. Herbert Percy Alleyne. *(Morning Post,* Oct. 1878).

iii. NINA ALLEYNE, married Reginald Russell.

(1) Muriel Russell.

iv. FRANCIS EDMUND ALLEYNE, born 18 March, 1864, died 12 Jan., 1924. Married Rebekah Ellett, daughter of Francis Marion Ellett, of Baltimore, Maryland, U.S.A. No issue.

Educated at St. Paul's, Stoney Strafford, England, Eton College, and finally at University of London, where he received the degree of B.D.

Was in the siege of Alexandria in 1880 in H.M.S. *Condor.* Retired voluntarily, with rank of Captain.

He went to America about 1883 and received holy orders in 1892 from Bishop Tuttle of Missouri. In charge of a boy's school at Portland. Missouri, near St. Louis, Mo., 1891—1899. Afterwards Rector of All Hallows Church. Davidsonville, Maryland, U.S.A.

48. ARTHUR OSBORNE GIBBES ALLEYNE 9 *(fourth son of*

James Holder[8], *John Forster* [7], *Thomas* [6], *Abel* [5], *Reynold* [4], *Abel* [3], *Reynold* [2], *Richard* [3]), born 22 March 1932, died 11 Feb. 1905. Married 13 Sept. 1870, Rosalie Sophia, daughter of Rear Admiral Richard Dunning White, R.N.

Arthur Osborne Gibbes Alleyne was educated at Marlborough College, 1845—1849, and matriculated at Oriel College, Oxford, 13 March, 1851 aged 18. B.A. 1855. M.A. 1857. Rector of St. Edmund's Exeter, Co. Devon, 1863. British Chaplain in Florence, Italy.

Children of A. O. G. Alleyne and Rosalie Sophia, his wife:—

i. MARGARET TERESA ROSALIE MARY ALLEYNE, married 10 Aug. 1907, Arthur Grey, Barrister-at-law.

ii. AGNES ELIZABETH MARY ALLEYNE, marrièd 25 April, 1906 Richard H. Kirkwood, of Devon Regiment.
   Issue:—
   (1) Osborne Kirkwood. (2) Hugh Kirkwood. (3) Tristram Kirkwood.

iii. BEATRICE GABRIELLE MARIE ALLEYNE, married 26 July, 1906 Charles Goring, D.L., J.P., of Wiston Park, Sussex.

49. FORSTER MCGEACHY ALLEYNE [9] (*third son of Charles Thomas* [8], *John Forster* [7], *Thomas* [6], *Abel* [5], *Reynold* [4], *Abel* [3], *Reynold* [2], *Richard* [1]), born 1 July 1845, died 22 Nov. 1913, aged 68 in London, England. Married 16 May 1872 Elsinora Alma, fifth daughter of Bridges Taylor, Esq., H.B.M. Consul at Elsinore, Denmark, and 41 Cadogan Place, London.

Children of Foster McGeachy Alleyne and Elsinora Alma his wife:—

i. ALMA MARGARET ALLEYNE, born 25 April, 1873. Married 28 Dec. 1911 Athelston Simey M.D., son of Ralph Simey, Deputy Lieut. of Durham County, at Durham Cathedral, by her uncle George Kitchin, Dean of Durham.

ii. THURA BLANCHE ALLEYNE, born 9 April 1875. Single. Warden of College Hall, University of London, England. M.Litt. of Durham University.

iii. ELSINORA ALLEYNE, born April 1876 at 41 Cadogan Place, London. Died July 1876.

iv. FRIEDA MARION ALLEYNE, born 18 Feb. 1879 at 41 Cadogan Place, London. Single. After her father's death she was Home Teacher to the blind for Oxfordshire, and lived with her mother in Oxford.

v. ELSIE ALLEYNE, born 8 Aug. 1880 at 41 Cadogan Place, London. Married Oct. 1911 Reginal Weeks, son of Rev. Weeks at Nairobi Cathedral, East Africa.
   Issue:—
   (1) Reginal Alleyne Weeks, born 11 Oct. 1912 at Horley, Africa.
   (2) Vivien Mary Weeks, born 8 July, 1915 at Port Hall, Kenya, Africa.
   (3) Forster Brian Weeks, born 16 Oct., 1919 at Mombasa, Kenya, Africa.

vi. CHARLES FORSTER ALLEYNE, born 8 Oct., 1882 at 41 Cadogan Place, London. Educated at Eton College, April 1896. Lieut. 5th Bn. Middlesex Regt. Militia Houndslow, 1898.

Married, first, Nov. 1906 Dorothy, daughter of Samuel Herbert Cox, at St. Barnabas, Addison Road, London, Eng.

Married, secondly, Marjorie, sister of his first wife, and widow of Cecil Morris of Albion, Berbice, Demerara, British Guiana. She had two children, Joan Audrey Morris and Geoffrey Morris. He was A.D.C. to Sir Frederic Hodgson, Governor of British Guiana.

vii. DORA FRANCES ALLEYNE, born 17 July, 1888 at 2 Litfield Place, Clifton, Bristol, England. Died 7 Nov. 1919 at 21 Overstrand Mansions, Battersea Park, London, Eng.

Mr. Forster McGeachy Alleyne was educated at Day's House at Eton, and at Merton College, Oxford, where he graduated with honours, taking his M.A. in due course. He was called to the Bar by the Inner Temple and practised in England for ten years; during which period he was greatly responsible for the inception of the National Bounty Movement aimed against the foreign sugar bounty system, which was ruining the sugar industries of the West Indies. Towards this movement, which paved the way for the suppression of bounties and cartels by international agreement in 1902, he devoted large sums of money. In 1886 he proceeded to Barbados, and thence forward he lived at Porters, where he endeavoured to retrieve the family fortunes, but the abolition of bounties came too late. In Barbados his ability was soon recognized and his assistance was always the first to be sought in any political movement. For many years he filled the position of Honorary Correspondent to the West India Committee. Mr. Alleyne was Commissioner for Barbados at the Colonial and Indian Exhibition of 1886 and again in 1905, and he represented the island at various inter-colonial conferences. In 1902 he was appointed a member of the Legislative Council, a position which he filled with much ability.

He was a stanch churchman and while living at Clifton was a church warden under Dean Randall and Canon Bromly of All Saints, whose history he wrote, and he was appointed by Bishop Bree, Chancellor of the diocese of Barbados.

Mr. Alleyne was also a gifted amateur actor and a founder of a company well known in the eighties as the "Shooting Stars" which benefitted charities by many hundreds of pounds.

Mr. Forster Alleyne lived at Porter's Estate, Barbados from 1897 to 1908. By the will of his father, Charles Thomas Alleyne, one-half of the estates, Porter's, Mount Standfast, Hannays, Dunscombe Lewis, Carmichael's, and The Ridge in Barbados, and 2, Litfield Place, Clifton, Bristol, was left to him, and the other half to his brother, Herbert Percy Alleyne, whose interest passed, on his decease to his daughter, Stella Margaret Alleyne.

Owing to the decline in sugar prices, the estates became heavily involved, and Mr. Forster Alleyne, retired from the management of the sugar plantations and returned to England, where he resided until his death on November, 22, 1913. He died at his residence, Challenor Street, West Kensington, London at the age of 68, and was buried at Brompton Cemetery.

(To be continued).

103

ALLEYNE OF BARBADOS.

(FINAL INSTALMENT)

Contributed by the late LOUISE R. ALLEN.

50. HENRY ALLEYNE [10] (*second son of Robert Harbin,* [9] *Thomas Harbin* [8], *Abel* [7], *Thomas* [6], *Abel* [5], *Reynold* [4], *Abel* [3]. *Reynold* [2], *Richard* [1]), born 2 Sept., 1849, and baptised same day. Married, 9 Feb., 1875, Jane Harriet Laurie Watson, daughter of James W. King, and widow of John Henry Watson. She died 10 March, 1909 of yellow fever at St. Ann's Garrison, Barbados. aged 59 years. Mr. Henry Alleyne is a retired sugar planter and resides with his eldest son at Friendly Hall, St. Lucy, Barbados.

Children of Henry Alleyne and Jane Harriet Laurie Alleyne, his wife:—

i. HENRY ALLEYNE, born 22 March 1876 at Saltram, St. Joseph, Barbados, bapt. 8 April, 1876 at St. Michael, Barbados. Married 13 April, 1904 at St. Lucy, Barbados, Rosalie Estelle Ann, daughter of Thomas Edward Norton Deane and Mary Adelaide (Yearwood) Deane, his wife.

Children of Henry Alleyne and Rosalie Estelle Ann, his wife:—

(1) Theodore Woodley Alleyne, born 14 Dec., 1908 at Hannays, St. Lucy, Barbados. Educated at the Lodge School, St. John, Barbados. His first position was in Barclays Bank (D. C. & O.), Bridgetown, afterwards removed to Grenada branch of the Bank.

(2) John Reynold Alleyne, born 17 Feb., 1920 at Bromefield, St. Lucy, Barbados.

(3) Marian Elsie Alleyne, born 19 Dec., 1921 at Bromefield, St. Lucy, Barbados.

Henry Alleyne, jnr., was educated at The Lodge School and Harrison College, Barbados. He is a sugar-planter and owner of Bromefield, Hannays, and Friendly Hall plantations in St. Lucy, Barbados. Mr. Alleyne represented the parish of St. Lucy in the House of Assembly from 1929-1937 and served as Chairman of Committees of the House from 1934-1937. Mr. Alleyne is a Justice of the Peace, and resides at Friendly Hall.

ii. JAMES DOUGLAS ALLEYNE, born 7 Oct., 1877 at Lemon Arbor, St. John, Barbados, bapt. 25 Nov., 1877 at St. John, Barbados. Married 15 June, 1904 Mary Agnes, daughter of William Fitzgerald of Peabody, Mass., U.S.A.

Children of James Douglas Alleyne, and Mary Agnes his wife:—

(1) Mary Fitzgerald Alleyne, born 22 March, 1905 at Boston, U.S.A.

(2) Julia Marian Alleyne, born 15 April, 1907 at Salem, Mass., U.S.A.

(3) Agnes Paula Alleyne, born 15 Jan., 1910 at Bridgetown, Barbados.

(4) Hannah Frances Alleyne, born 2 Sep., 1912 at Bridgetown, Barbados.

(5) Elizabeth Jane Alleyne, born 5 May, 1914 at Bridgetown, Barbados.

Dr. James Douglas Alleyne studied at Harrison College, Barbados. In 1893 at the age of sixteen he sailed in a Schooner. to the United States and travelled, working his way, for three years. He joined the gold rush to the Klondike in Alaska in 1896 where he remained five months. Later he went to Boston and studied as a nurse for two years at the Boston City Hospital. Then he took the medical course of four years at Tufts College, Boston, Mass. He was resident at the Boston City Hospital for one year and practised in Boston two years, returned to Barbados in 1909 where he had a private practice for twelve years. He was Visiting Physician to the Leper Asylum in 1917. In 1919 he was appointed Assistant Health Officer; and on 11th April, 1921, Port Health Officer, a position which he continues to fill with conspicuous success, combining with it the office of Acting Chief Medical Officer of the Island. In January 1935 he received the Honour from His Majesty the King of the membership of the Most Excellent Order of the British Empire in recognition of his public services. He was Transport Doctor for the troops from Trinidad and Barbados in 1916 in the World War and went to England where he stayed for three months.

When Dr. Alleyne arrived in Barbados in 1909 he was met with the sad news that his brother, Dr. Charles Beresford Alleyne had died of yellow fever on 4th February, 1909. On March 10, 1909 his mother died of the same disease, and on 17th April, 1909 his sister, Helen Marian Levitt, was also a victim of the same disease.

iii. CHARLES BERESFORD ALLEYNE, born 28 Aug., 1879, bapt. 16 Oct., 1879, at St. John, Barbados. Died 4 Feb., 1909 aged 29 years. Married Dorothy Doherty of Baltimore, Md., U.S.A., who died of yellow fever in 1908.

Charles Beresford Alleyne went to America and studied nursing at the Boston City Hospital for two years, then he enlisted in a New York Regiment for the Spanish-American War and went to camp in Virginia, but was invalided to a camp in New Mexico. Later he went to Baltimore Medical School and graduated as a surgeon. Afterwards he established a private practice in Barbados. At the time of his death he was resident surgeon of Barbados General Hospital, where he died.

iv. HELEN MARIAN ALLEYNE, born 2 Jan., 1883, bapt. 24 Feb., 1883 at St. John, Barbados. Died 27 April, 1909 of yellow fever in Barbados. Married 12 Nov., 1903, Albert Francis Levitt.

Issue:—

(1) Daphney Alleyne Levitt, born 3 Nov., 1904, bapt. 22 Dec., 1904. After her mother died her father married a second time, and she went to live with her Aunt, Mrs. Maurice Burt Carroll, (Florence Bouverie Alleyne) in New Jersey, U.S.A.

v. FLORENCE BOUVERIE ALLEYNE, born 16 Jan., 1884, bapt. 2 Sep., 1884 at St. James, Barbados. Married Maurice Burt Carroll,

Engineer, Harvard University, son of Rev. Vernon Burton Carroll and Cordelia Burt. They live at Tenafly, New Jersey, U.S.A.—

Issue:—

(1) Maurice Burt Carroll, (2) Roger Alleyne Carroll.

51. INNES MILTON ALLEYNE [10], *(second son of Frederick William* [9], *Thomas Harbin* [8], *Abel* [7], *Thomas* [6], *Abel* [5], *Reynold* [4], *Abel* [3], *Reynold* [2], *Richard* [1])*, born 26 Nov., 1851 at Holetown, Barbados. Died 17 May, 1930 at Christ Church, Barbados. Married 14 June 1877 Laura, daughter of John Perryman. She died 13 October, 1933 in Barbados aged 79 years.

Innes Milton Alleyne was educated at the Lodge School and Codrington College, Barbados, Ordained Deacon in 1875 and Priest 1877. Vicar of St. Saviour in Barbados 1880, and of All Saints in 1881 where he served 17 years. In 1898 he was appointed Rector of St. Andrew where he served 27 years, until his retirement.

Children of Rev. Innes Milton Alleyne and Laura his wife:—

i. JOHN MILTON CARLISLE ALLEYNE, Married first Daisy Deane, daughter of Thaddeus Deane of Barbados. Married secondly, Annie Alleyne, daughter of Charles Alleyne of Philadelphia, Penn., and his wife Janet Ellis, daughter of James Ellis of Prince Edward Island. These Alleynes are no relation to the Alleynes of this genealogy.

Issue of the first marriage:—

(1) Dorothy Carlisle Alleyne, (2) Harold Carlisle Alleyne, (3) Marguerite Carlisle Alleyne, (4) Maurice Carlisle Alleyne.

No issue of the second marriage.

ii. HERBERT MILTON DECOURCEY ALLEYNE, married Edith, daughter of Conrad Jemmott. He studied at Codrington College, Barbados. Ordained at St. Michael's Cathedral, Bridgetown. Rector of St. Lucy, Barbados, 1929.

Issue:—

(1) Theodore Alleyne. *(2) Murray Alleyne,* *(3) Douglas Alleyne, (4) Jean Alleyne.*

iii. ANNIE MAUD ALLEYNE, married Nathan Archibald Seale, and had issue three sons and five daughters.

iv. FRANCIS MILTON OSBORNE ALLEYNE, born 7 Nov., 1884. Married 27 April, 1907 at the Church of the Redeemer, New York City, Mabel Louise Greaves Mahon, daughter of Augustus Mahon.

Dr. Alleyne studied dentistry at the Brooklyn School of Dental Surgery, New York, and practises dentistry at Bridgetown, Barbados. There is issue of the marriage four daughters and three sons.

v. IDA MILLICENT ALLEYNE.

vi. LAURA EULALIE ALLEYNE. Married Henry St. John Greaves Mahon, son of Augustus Mahon, and has issue four sons and one daughter.

vii. FREDERICK MILTON STANLEY ALLEYNE, born in 1893. Died 19 April, 1931 in Barbados. Married Alice Gore of Antigua, B.W.I. He became an American Citizen and fought in the

World War, and was gassed in the last battle. Buried at Westbury Cemetery, Barbados.

Issue:—

(1) Lawrence Stanley Gore Alleyne.

52. EDWARD WENTWORTH FISHER HOLDER ALLEYNE [10] *(eldest son of James Holder [9], James Holder [8], John Forster [7], Thomas [6], Abel [5], Reynold [4], Abel [3], Reynold [2], Richard [1]),* born 30 March, 1852. Died in Decr. 1897 of pneumonia after a journey to the Klondike. Married Emily Alicia Katherine, youngest daughter of Rev. John Dupré Addison, Vicar of Weymouth.

Edward W. F. H. Alleyne was at Eton in 1868, and afterwards held a commission in 12th Regt. Royal Lancers. He lived at Taunton, Somerset, and had an income of £1,700 a year and a stable of seventeen horses.

Children of Edward W. F. H. Alleyne and his wife:—

i. AUDLEY HELEN CAROLINE WENTWORTH ALLEYNE, born 24 Octr., 1876.

ii. WENTWORTH HOLDER ALLEYNE, born 21 July, 1878, twin brother of Evelyn Addison Wentworth Alleyne. Married Hazel Forrest Fleming, widow of Major Fleming.

Major Alleyne was a member of the force which covered the evacuation of Antwerp. He was an "Old Contemptible", being a member of the famous 7th Division, and owing to the terrible casualties amongst the officers of his regiment, was in actual command of it for two days previous to being wounded and then taken prisoner. Before his capture he was twice mentioned in despatches. There is an account in Sir Arthur Conan Doyle's "The Seventh Division" of his stand together with Lieut. Valentine on the Menin Road, but in it he was erroneously reported killed.

iii. EVELYN ADDISON WENTWORTH ALLEYNE, born 21 July, 1878, twin brother of Wentworth Holder Alleyne.

Dr. Evelyn Addison Wentworth Alleyne, M.R.C.S., L.R.C.P., had two very severe illnesses shortly after qualifying in medicine, which precluded him from practising. In 1928 he went to the Island of St. Lucia, B.W.I., in search of health.

THE END.

APPLEWHAITE OF BARBADOS.

WILL of THOMAS APPLEWHAITE of Barbados, dated December 10, 1674. To my wife Mary the best bed and furniture and plate in my dwellinghouse, two men and two women negroes, and the gelding with the furniture she is accustomed to ride, and the choice of one-third of my real and personal estate or £100 per annum and £500 within one year after my debt due to John Miller of London is paid. Also the living in a chamber in my mansion house during her widowhood.

To my daughter Margarett £1,000 to be paid as follows: £300 at her age of 19, £300 at 20, and £400 at 21, and £30 per annum until she is 19, for her maintenance.

To my grandson Philip Kirton £50 at 21. To my friend Thomas Cole £10 for his care and pains for me.

To my son Henry all my estate, and if he shall die without issue to my daughter Margarett and failing her to my daughter Mary Kirton during her life, and then to my loving cousin Henry Applewhaite now resident in Virginia. My son Henry to be sole executor and my friends William Sharpe and John Morgan, Esq. to be supervisors and £10 each.

God hath furnished me with an estate far beyond my desert, I require my executor within two years of my decease to take what care he possibly can to see that the poor of the parish wherein I was born (being a country village in the county of Suffolk in England called Stoke Ash) to receive £20 out of my estate to be equally divided between them. (Sd.) Tho. Applewhaite. Wits: John Benham, Tho. Coulton, Jno. Gibson, Richard Nokes, Tho. Cole.

Memo. That I Thomas Applewhaite do give my daughter Margarett £200 more to be paid out of my estate within 5 years. Proved March 19, 1678 before J. Atkins.

Will of HENRY APPLEWHAITE of St. Thomas, Barbados, Esquire. Dated November 16, 1703. To my wife Hester an annuity or jointure which I settled on her before marriage, and the use of my mansion and furniture therein during her widowhood. My wife to have the care of my five children, Thomas, Hester, Margarett, Elizabeth, and Frances, and to have their maintenance out of my plantation in St. Thomas and St. George's parishes. To my wife the choice of my best horse and furniture, and the use of my coach and horses when she pleases to ride out, and two negro women and any boys she may select to wait upon her.

One-half of all such silver and gold plate as I die possessed of to be by her disposed of except what money is reserved for my daughter Hester's portion.

To my dau. Hester £1,000 (£500 at 18 and £500 at 21). To my daughter Margarett £1,000 at 21. To my daughter Elizabeth £1,000 at 18, and my daughter Frances £1,000 at 18 and a negro to wait upon each of them and a good horse of £20 and £6 for furniture. To my said daughters the other half of my plate share and share alike.

To my nephew Philip Kirton £100. To my son Thomas all my plantation, negroes, and the residue of my personal estate, and I appoint him sole executor at 17 years, in the meantime my wife executrix during her widowhood, and Philip Kirton, Thomas Maxwell, and Coll. Richard Downes Esq., executors in trust, and to be guardians of my children until they attain 18 years. Rings of £5 to each executor-in-trust.

Sd. Hen: Applewhaite. Wits: Wm. Henry, Thomas Barnard, Philip Lewis Proved 1705 (no date) Recorded July 6, 1705.

Will of HESTER APPLEWHAITE of St. George, dated July 26, 1727.

To my daughter Hester Pare £100, to my dau. Margarett A., one negro wench named Sofiah and her children. To my daughter Frances A. two negroes named Sambo and Nanny and £500 on her marriage. To my grandson Edward Pare one negro boy named Peter. To my granddaughter, Hester Pare, one negro wench named Molly. To my niece Mary Lot £30. My loving son Thomas A. to be executor. Sd. H. Applewhaite. Wits: Richard Stanton, Jona. Francklin. Proved December 10, 1728.

Will of THOMAS APPLEWHAITE of St. George, Barbados, Esq., dated June 12, 1749. My debts to be paid out of the profits of my plantation.

To my wife Elizabeth all my plate (except my gold watch and silver monteith) together with my chariot, chaise, and household stuff and certain named slaves. I give my wife my whole Spring plantation as well as the part I bought of Mrs. Elizabeth Nanfanas as the part I had before, with negroes and stock for her life in lieu of dower.

I give the said plantation and premises to my grandson Henry Frere and also my land at New Barbados in the Jerseys. To my daughter Susannah Frere after my debts and legacies are paid all my windward plantation called Kingslands, with all the negroes, stock etc for her life and then to my grandson Tobias Frere and his heirs, and I give him my land in Bridgetown over against the land of Mr. John Shurland decd.

109

To my son-in-law Hon. John Frere my gold watch and silver monteith. To my sister Margaret Doldarne £100. To my sister Frances Carmichael £100. To my niece Hester Pare £300. To my nephew Thomas Carmichael £200. To my nephew Archibald Carmichael £200. To my nephew Edward Pare, son of my nephew Edward Pare £50. To my cousin Mary Parsons £50. To my brother Archibald Carmichael £25 for mourning. To my nephew Edward Pare £25 for mourning. To my granddaughter Elizabeth Frere £100 at 16, charged upon my Spring plantation. To my granddaughter Hester Susannah Frere at 16 £1,000 charged upon my windward plantation. To my granddaughter not yet bap--tised, daughter of my daughter Susanah Frere £1,000 at 16, charged upon my Windward and Spring plantations. To my relations and friends—my brother and sister Gibbes, by nephew Holder, and Mr. James Carter and Mr. Samuel Husbands a handsome mourning ring each, Residue of my estate to my wife absolutely and I appoint her executrix. Sd. Thom. Applewhaite. Wits: Gedney Clarke, Richard Stanton, Sam. Husbands. Proved September 26, 1749.

Will of EDWARD APPLEWHAITE of Christ Church, Barbados, gent. Dated February 6, 1803. To my father Thomas A. and to my mother Mary A. £50 each. To my mother-in-law, Mercy Lytcott. £25. To my bros. Thomas and Samuel A. £50 each. To my Aunt Frances Archer £25 for mourning. To Mr. Gilbert Ripnol £50 To my friend James Crichlow Trotman £10 to buy a ring. To my godson, the second son of Peter Depuis Abbott, Esq., of Powis Place, London, £25. All my right in the Library Society of Barbados to my son Thomas. My law books and half my stock of madeira wine to be sold for payment of my funeral expenses and legacies. To my wife, Mary, all my plate etc., and the other half of my stock of madeira, my post chaise and two-wheel chaise, the horse at present used as a chaise horse and another a match for him.

The slaves on my plantation called Bentleys. I give my wife a rent charge of £220 per annum in addition to her jointure of £180 per annum and the use of my place at the Castle during her widowhood and then to my son Thomas, and a proportion of sugar and rum etc., from Bentleys while it remains unsold. My plantation Bentleys to be sold at the discretion of my executors and proceeds invested.

To my sons, Thomas, Philip and Edward, £5,000 each at 21, and to my daughters, Mary Ellen, Sarah, Frances, Louisa, and Ann £3,000 each at 18.

My good father has by Will made provision for my children, but any child of which my wife may be now enciente, I give any such child £6.000 if a boy, £3,000 if a girl.

Residue of my estate, half to my son Thomas, one-fourth to son Philip, and one-fourth to son Edward.

My wife during widowhood, my father Thomas A., and my bro. Thomas A. and each of my sons at 21 to be executors, and my wife, father, and brother guardians. sd. Edward Applewhaite, Wits. : Henry T. Crane, Philip Lytcott. Proved September 10, 1804.

Will of THOMAS APPLEWHAITE of St. George, Barbados, Esq. Dated September 26, 1815. To be buried in family vault in the parish of St. George with my beloved wife and that my body be put in a lead coffin. £18 per annum to the Boy's Charity School of the parish of St. George charged upon my plantation called Walkers and slaves and stock thereon.

To each of my executors £50. To my son Samuel A. £1,000 to be paid out to him out of any monies in my house at the time of my decease.

To my daughters-in-law Sarah Ward Applewhaite widow of my son Thomas A. and to Mary Applewhaite, widow of my son Edward A. £100.

To Frances Archer, sister of my deceased wife and of Edward Archer late of Virginia, U.S.A., decd. £25 per annum for life. To Richard Archer and Samuel B. Archer sons of the said Edward Archer, decd. £50.

To my grandsons in law James Bovell and John Chase Eversley all monies and securities on account of the partnership in which I have been a partner with them.

My little slave Frances to be manumitted within six years, and an annuity of £6 to her charged on Walkers. I request my granddaughters Mary Elizabeth Bovell, Eleanor Eversley, Sarah Applewhaite, Frances Applewhaite, Ann Applewhaite and Louisa Applewhaite to take care of the said Frances.

All my plantations in the co. of Isle of Wight in Virginia (Mr. Lawrence tenant) to my relations Thomas Applewhaite and Henry Applewhaite to them equally who were sons of Josiah Applewhaite, and which said Henry A. was sometime past released by me from prison in Liverpool. My executors in U.S.A. to sell my real estate there and apply proceeds as follows : To my relation Henry Wells Applewhaite, a son of Captain John Applewhaite £300 currency of Virginia; to my relation George Applewhaite son of Captain Arthur Applewhaite and his two sisters, Nancy A. and Ridley A. £300 like money, each; to my relation William Orr of Worsington. North Carolina, the son of my relation Polly Applewhaite £300. To . . . Orr, sister of the said William Orr to Polly A. and Judith A. daughters of the said Captain John Applewhaite £300. To the said Thomas Applewhaite and his sister Peggy A. £ 300. To the said Henry Applewhaite £300 and as a mark of my respect to Mr. John Barber of Smithfield, Virginia,

£50. To my goddaughter, Sarah Thomas, daughter of Rev. Anthony Keighley Thomas £50; to my goddaughter Elizabeth Oxley, daughter of William Oxley, Esq., £50; to my godson, Robert Gill, son of William Gill, Esq. £50. My madeira and other wines at Walkers to my son Samuel A.

To my daughter-in-law, Mary A. and my grandsons-in-law James Bovell and John Chase Eversley all my madeira and other wines and liquors in my house and stores in Bridgetown. To my grandchildren, sons and daughters of my son Edward A. £10,000. To my granddaughter, Eleanor Eversley, wife of the said John Chase Eversley, £150 only, because I gave her on her marriage the money I intended to leave her. To my granddaughter Sarah A. £7,000, granddaughter Frances A £7,000, granddaughter Ann A. £7,000, granddaughter Louisa A. £7,000 each at 21. To my granddaughter Mary Elizabeth Bovell, wife of James Bovell, £1,000, and to each of her first four children £1,000 at 18. I gave Mary Elizabeth Bovell on her marriage, £3,000. I give £5,000 to the first five children of my granddaughter, Mary Mercy Ellcock equally, and if more than five, £1,000 to each additional child.

To my granddaughter Sarah A. my four-wheel carriage and pair of grey horses. To my friend Claborne Blagrove Lamprey £100 when he shall have brought up the books of Walkers and Bentleys plantations to date of my death and £25 per annum instead of the present salary for posting the books.

To my son Samuel all my plate and furniture etc., in Walkers (save my old silver grace cup and two new porter cups given me by my friend George Blackman, Esq., to my grandsons in law James Bovell and John Chase Eversley to be divided as they like.

To my friends Hon. Samuel Hinds and William Eversley, Esq., and my grandson Edward A. all that my plantation called Walkers and Braces or Workmans added to Walkers in St. George with mills, buildings and slaves upon trust for my son Samuel Applewhaite for life and then to the use of the first and every other son of the said S.A. in tail male, to the use of my grandson Edward A. for ever, charged with £3,000 to each of the daughters of my sd. son Samuel A. at 18 or marriage and if only one daughter then £5,000. If no sons, then my son Samuel may appoint £10,000 and charge it on Walkers. If my grandson Edward A. shall die, my exors. to sell the plantation and divide the proceeds (less the charges thereon) to my granddaughters Mary Elizabeth Bovell, Eleanor Eversley, Sarah Applewhaite, Frances Applewhaite, Ann Applewhaite and Louisa Applewhaite equally.

My executors to sell my dwellinghouse in Broad Street and the purchase money to form part of my residuary estate. If my grandson Edward A. shall desire to carry on the mercantile business then I recommend him to purchase at fair appraisement.

My decd. son Edward A. by his Will gave his wife Mary a dwellinghouse adjoining St. Ann's Castle which I had given him by deed of gift; and his son Thomas was to have the house at Mary's death. Thomas has since died under 21, and his brother

112

Philip is entitled. I have conveyed the said house to King George III for £4,125 and placed out the money with David and George Hall on judgment.

To my grandson in law John Chase Eversley £1,000 out of moneys due me from my deceased son Edward, and the remainder to my grandson Edward A. and if he shall die, to Eleanor, Sarah, Frances, Ann and Louisa A. equally.

The residue of my estate to my grandson Edward A. at 21.

Appoint Samuel Hinds, Wm. Eversley, and grandson Edward A. exors., in Great Britain and West Indies, and George Newton of Norfolk. Virginia. Samuel B. Archer, and grandson Edward A. exors., in U.S.A.

Sd. Thos. Applewhaite. Wits. : Gabriel Jemmett, F. A. Walrond. Wm. Crane. Proved August 5, 1816.

Holograph Will of SARAH WARD APPLEWHAITE of St. Michael, widow, dated June 6, 1816. To my daughter Mary Elizabeth Bovell all my estate, and in case of her death, to my niece Keturah Shepherd Davidson, wife of Alexander Grey Davidson of Brompton near London, one half of my estate, the remaining half to be divided between Henry Barker, son of Mary Ann Umphrey of St. George, and my six relations, Elizabeth Martha Carter, wife of Timothy Cheesman Carter of St. Michael, Sarah and Elizabeth Carter, daughters of the said E.M.C., William Wells Worrell, Eliza Julia Ward Worrell and Eliza Jane Shepherd. I appoint William Murrey and John Bovell of St. Michael, executors.

Sd Sarah Ward Applewhaite. Testator's signature proved by Philip Lytcott Applewhaite 10 Nov. 1817.

Will of MARY APPLEWHAITE of St. Michael, widow of Edward A. late of this island, Barrister-at-law, dated March 17, 1821.

To son-in-law John Bovell two slaves. To daughter Frances A. table linen etc. and to all my daus. living at my death my silver etc.

Sets free from slavery a negro called Dennis and the sum to be paid out of her estate. All other slaves and residue of estate to John Chase Eversley, son-in-law, and appoints him sole executor.

Sd Mary Applewhaite. Wits: Wm. Walrond jnr. Conrade A. Howell, jr Proved March 18, 1822.

Will of PHILIP LYTCOTT APPLEWHAITE of St. Michael, about to go to England, dated Novr. 10, 1835.

My estate to be kept together and after the death of my wife to be divided equally between my children except Kirton plantation in St. Philip which belongs to my sons James Nathaniel Crichlow A. and William Bovell A. equally. My children Edward

113

A., John A., Mary A., Eleanor A., Judith A., James Nathaniel Crichlow A. and William Bovell A.

To my wife Ann A. all household furniture, plate etc. for her life and then for my children equally. Wife Ann and brother-in-law John Bovell executors. Sd. P. L. Applewhaite. Wits: John Crichlow. Proved Novr. 24, 1841.

Will of EDWARD ARCHER APPLEWHAITE late of South Pickenham Hall, Norfolk, who died 8 Novr. 1889. Will dated Feby. 14, 1889, proved at Norwich February 17, 1890 by Charles Mundy A. son of decd., and Henry Blake executors.

Appoints Son Charles Mundy A. and Henry Blake exors.

Recites marriage settlement April 19, 1820 between himself of first part, Judith Frewin Wood, an infant, spr. 2nd pt., Cumberbatch Sober 3rd pt., Samson Senhouse Esq. Rev. Samson Wood Sober and Francis Onslow Trent 4th pt. declaring trust of £10,000. There are 3 children of the marriage between his late wife and himself, namely, C.M.A., Henry Hanson A. Sarah Hartopp wife of Edward Samuel Evans Hartopp all of full age. Appoints £4,000 part of trust funds to sd. C.M.A. and residue to H.H.A.

Mansion called Pickenham Hall to be in trust to pay an annuity of £60 to H.H.A. and £200 to S.H. and to the use of C.M.A. in fee simple.

Plantation Walkers in Barbados and interest in Mount Gay plantation to which he is entitled under deed of arrangement dated Decr. 30, 1854, between his late wife of 1st pt., Thomas Thornhill 2nd pt., Harry Spencer Waddington 3rd pt., and Windham Berkeley Portman 4th pt., to his trustees upon trust for sale and to fall into residue. Legacies of £2,000 to grandson Edward A. eldest son of late son Edward Thornhill A. £1,000 to each of other children of sd. son, namely Harry, Frederick, Mabel, Cora A., £1,000 to grandson Cecil Hay, son of late dau. Julia Hay, £1,000 to grandson Churchill A. only son of late Ernest Bassett Gaskin A. (sd.) E. A. Applewhaite. Wits: Robert Buchanan Marriott, Surgeon, John Raymer.

Will of CHARLES MUNDY APPLEWHAITE of Pickenham Hall, Norfolk. dated Febry. 14, 1890.

Appoint my wife Mary Florence A. Hanson Henry A., and Henry Blake exors. Devise Pickenham Hall and estate subject to annuities to wife for life and then to children equally. If no children, then to be held in trust for Hanson Henry A. My plantation in Barbados Mount Gay or share therein to my bro. H.H.A.

Sd. Chas. M. Applewhaite. Proved 13 June, 1898.

(To be continued.)

114

APPLEWHAITE OF BARBADOS.

Parish.	Date of Marriage.	Names.
St. John	16 April 1668	Mary Applewhaite to Capt. Philip Kirton.
Ch. Christ	27 Nov. 1684	Henry Applewhaite to Hester Kingsland.
St. Michael	4 October 1787	Thomas Applewhaite jnr. to Sarah Ward Devonish.
"	4 August 1791	Edward Archer Applewhaite to Mary Lycott.
"	1 July, 1811	Mary Elizabeth Applewhaite to James Bovell.
Ch. Church	15 October 1811	Mary Mercy Applewhaite to Reynold Alleyne Elcock.
St. George	1 July 1811	Mary Elizabeth Applewhaite to James Bovell, Barrister-at-Law, (dau. of Thomas A.)
Ch. Church	8 July 1814	Eleanor Applewhaite to John Chase Eversley of St. Michael.
St. Michael	13 March 1817	Philip Lycott Applewhaite to Susannah Todd.
Ch. Church	20 Jan. 1817	Sarah Applewhaite to John Bovell.
St. Thomas	13 March 1817	Philip Lycott Applewhaite to Susannah Todd.
St. George	7 Sept. 1820	Ann Applewhaite to William Maynard Pinder.
"	2 Nov. 1820	Louisa Applewhaite to Edmund John Eversley.
St. Michael	24 July 1827	Philip L. Applewhaite to Ann Crichlow, Spinster, married in Church.
"	18 Dec. 1834	Mary Frances Applewhaite to Samuel Thomas Morris.
"	21 May 1836	Mary Applewhaite to John Reynold Campbell (the contracting parties could not write).
St. Joseph	27 Aug. 1836	William Applewhaite of St. Michael to Mercy Dinah Mellowes.
St. George	2 April 1836	Denis Francis Applewhaite to Mary Susan Rupell (married in Church).
"	19 Nov. 1836	James Henry Applewhaite to Margaret Ann Bourne.
St. Michael	13 Sept. 1837	William Applewhaite, apprenticed labourer of the Kew estate, to Amelia King.

Parish.	Date of Baptism.	Date of Birth.	Names.
St. Michael	3 June 1772	5 June 1772	William Applewhaite, son of Thomas & Mary.
„	23 Feb. 1775		Samuel Applewhaite, son of Thomas & Mary.
Ch. Church	27 Nov. 1788		Jane Abigail Applewhaite, d. of Edward Archer & Mary A.
St. Michael	21 March 1789	9 Feb. 1789	Mary Elizabeth Applewhaite, d. of Thomas jnr. & Sarah Wood, wife.
„	30 June 1790	3 May 1790	Thomas Applewhaite, son of Thos. & Sarah Wood, his wife.
„	25 June 1792	23 May 1792	Mary Elizabeth Applewhaite, d. of Thomas & Sarah Wood, wife.
Ch. Church	19 Sept. 1795	30 Aug. 1794	Eleanor Applewhaite, d. of Edward Archer & Mary A.
„	16 Aug. 1795	19 Sept. 1795	Eleanor, daughter of Edward Archer Applewhaite and Mary.
„	16 Aug. 1795	16 Aug. 1795	Mary Mercy, d. of Edward Archer and Mary Applewhaite.
„	27 Nov. 1795	27 Nov. 1795	Thomas, son of Edward & Mary Applewhaite.
„	28 Dec. 1796	6 Dec. 1796	Philip Lytcott, s. of Edward Archer & Mary Applewhaite.
„	28 Feb. 1798	19 Jan. 1798	Sarah, d. of Edward & Mary Applewhaite.
„	11 May 1799	18 April, 1799	Edward Archer, s. of Edward Archer & Mary Applewhaite.
„	24 Aug. 1800	17 July, 1800	Frances, d. of Edward & Mary Applewhaite.
„	14 Nov. 1801	10 Oct. 1801	Ann, d. of Edward & Mary Applewhaite.
„	26 Dec. 1802	26 Nov. 1802	Louisa, d. of Edward & Mary Applewhaite.

Parish and Date	Name and Place
St. M. 9 June 1672	Mr. John Applewhaite, church.
„ 16 Octr. 1677	Mr. Thomas Applewhaite, in the church.
„ 30 July 1684	Mrs. Mary Applewhaite, in ye church.
St. T. 15 June 1749	The Hon'ble Genl. Thos. Applewhaite buried at St. George, parishioner of St. Thomas.
St. M. 30 Novr. 1775	William the son of Thomas Applewhaite.
„ 5 Dec. 1775	John, son of Thomas Applewhaite.
„ 27 Sep. 1789	Mary, daughter of Thomas Applewhaite junr.
St. G. 29 May 1808	This day was duly buried by me, Thomas Applewhaite, oldest son of Edward Applewhaite decd., and grandson of Thomas Applewhaite Esq., Walkers estate. Anthony Keighley Thomas, A. B. Rector.
„ 12 March 1809	Elizabeth Devonish, widow of Mr. T. Applewhaite, St. George's parish.
„ 14 Aug. 1809	Thomas Applewhaite, son of Thomas and Sarah Applewhaite, Green's estate.
„ 14 Oct. 1809	the wife of Thomas Applewhaite Esq. of Walkers estate.
„ 28 Nov. 1810	Mary the wife of Samuel Applewhaite Esq. from Bridgetown.
„ 12 Jan. 1814	This day was duly buried by me in the family vault, Thomas Applewhaite Esq., aged 50 years, owner of Green's estate, husband of Mrs. Sarah W. Applewhaite.
„ 8 July 1816	Thomas Applewhaite Esq. of this parish.
„ 13 Nov. 1819	Samuel Applewhaite, a vestryman, 44 years old.
St. M. 28 July 1821	Mary Applewhaite.
„ 20 Apl. 1826	Thomas Applewhaite.
„ 28 Apl. 1826	Susan Applewhaite, aged 28.

ST. GEORGE'S CHURCH, BARBADOS.

In the nave, south wall, is a large marble tablet with the following inscription:—

SACRED to the Memory / of the Hon'ble THOMAS APPLE-WHAITE ESQR / one of the Hon'ble MEMBERS of his Majesties / Council, in this Island, Lieut. GENERAL, of the / Forces here. President of the Councils of War / Master GENERAL, of the Ordnance. and / Colonel, of the Windward / Regiment of Foot / He Died the 14 day of Iune / 1749 / Aged 59 Years / Also Mrs. ELIZABETH APPLEWHAITE Wife / of the above-mentioned THOS. APPLEWHAITE / Esqr. She Died the 11 April 1750 / Aged 59 Years.

In the churchyard a grave to the south of the Chancel enclosed by railing, with a white marble slab:—

Here Lieth Interred the Body of / The Honourable THOMAS APPLEWHAITE ESQ / obiit Iune 14th 1749 / Ætatis 59. / Also MRS. ELIZABETH APPLEWHAITE Wife of / the above mentioned THOMAS APPLEWHAITE / ESQ. obiit the 11th of April 1750 / Ætatis 59 Years.

Barbados Census, 1679.

Parish of St. George, Mrs. Applewhaite widdoe, owned 169 acres.
„ ., St. Thomas, Lt. Henry Applewhaite, owned 272 acres,
9 bought servants, 4 hired servants, 216
negroes.
Colonel Thornhill's Regiment. A list of officers and soldiers belonging to Capt. George Lillington: Lt.
Applewhaite 5 men. Col. Carter's troop —
Lt. Henry Applewhaite, 2 horse.
List of Persons who left Barbados in 1679. May 6. Burne, Denis,
a servant belonging to Mr. Henry Apple-
whaite, in Ketch *Prosperous* (David Fogg,
Commander,) for Virginia.
May 6. Rainey, Luke, a servant belonging
to Mr. Henry Applewhaite, in Ketch *Prosperous* (David Fogg, Commander) for Virginia.
Barbados Census 1715. St. George. Hester Applewhaite, aged
49, Thomas Applewhaite Esq., 25, Eliza.
Applewhaite, 24, Margaret Applewhaite, 20,
Eliza. Applewhaite, 16, Frances Applewhaite, 14, Susanna Applewhaite, 1½.

APPLEWHAITE DEEDS RECORDED IN BARBADOS.

25 July 1 Ano. R.R.S Caroli. Lieut. Coll. Tho. Ellice of Barbados, for 35 lbs merchantable tobacco in role, 140 lbs. indigo,
& 4000 lbs. of sugar to me by Thomas Applewhaite of Barbados
gent. secured to be paid, sell my plantation 127 ac. of land in
the p. of St. James, adjoining the plantation whereon Ensign
Edward Crofte lately lived. sd. Tho. Ellice. Wits: John Read,
Wm. Read, Rich. Bishop. Recorded 12 die 9 bris 1644.

1 March 1643, 19th yr. of Charles. Capt. James Holdipp of
Barbados Esq. sells to Thomas Applewhaite, citizen and cloth-
worker of London, All those plantations with houses etc. 200
acres at least, situate in Barbados Island, three score acres
whereof by estimation being heretofore the plantation of Ensign
Edward Crofte, adjoining on one side by plantation called Locust
Hall and on the other side the plantation now or late of Capt.
Thomas Ellis, and the other 140 acres adjoining the 60 acres
aforesaid. Also pasturage for 20 cattle on other ground of
Holdipp, Applewhaite providing two servants to look after them.
Holdipp covenants to deliver to T.A. so many good sugar canes
to plant upon the premises sold ·as shall be needful. The consideration for this lease being that T.A. will send 25 men servant
immediately after arrival there of good ship *Victory of London*,
350 tons, John Ruband, Master, to go with the ship to the island,
to be chosen by lot, and of the company of men servants which
the said T.A. shall transport thither, and to pay the passage of
4 maid servants for the said Holdipp. T.A. to transport 40 men
servants at least for the service of the island. The sale to be
void if the said ship shall not arrive there. sd. James Holdipp.

118

Wits: Thomas Peade, John Warson, William Brewer, Richard Ellice, Michael Goodall. Recorded 15 Decr. 1644.

14 April 1645. Rice Evans of Barbados, gent. to Thomas Applewhaite merchant, my plantation 50 acres lying between the plantation whereon Tho. Evans is now resident, William Trottles ground, and Capt. Matthew Wood his 100 acres. sd. Rice Evans. Wits: William Chibnall, Richard Jones.

28 Sep. 1648. Thomas Applewhaite of London, merchant, to John Bentham of Barbados, appointing him an additional attorney with Edward Herbert and Richard Ellis of Barbados, merchants. sd. Thomas Applewhaite. Wits: Roger Kemp, James Bartlett.

22 Aug. 1649. Notarial Act. Thomas Applewhaite and Thomas Pead of London. merchants, appointing John Bentham and Roger Heymish, merchants in Barbados, attorneys of Endeavour plantation, then in the possession of Richard Ellis and Edward Herbert, and revoking their attorneyship. Recorded 2 Mar. 1649.

7 Decr. 1659. Thomas Pead and Thomas Applewhaite of Barbados. Agreement that all the estate in Barbados belonging to them in partnership shall be deemed to be held in tenancy in common, with a declaration against right of survivorship. Sd. Thomas Peade. Wits: John Benham, Rich Glascock scr. Recorded 2 March 1659/60.

14 March 1667/8. John Bentham and Elizabeth Bentham, sister of the said J. B. release Henry Applewhaite of Barbados, gent., of their interest in the plantation called Endeavour, parish of St. Thomas, lately in the tenure and occupation of Thomas Applewhaite & Thomas Pead decd., holden betwixt them in joint common tenancy, together with the plantation called Apter's Farme lying in the parish of St. Joseph, bounding on the plantation of Thomas Wardall Esq., John Worsham, and Jacob Lucye. sd. John Benham, Elizabeth Benham. Wits: William Kirton, Philip Kirton. Recorded 14 July 1668.

16 March 1667/8. John Benham of St. Thomas, Barbados, gent, and Elizabeth Benham of Christ Church, Spinster, the son and daur. of John and Elizabeth B. lately of London, merchant taylor, which said E. B. was heretofore called E. Pead, late sister to Wm. Pead late of St. Thomas, merchant, decd. The parties release Thomas Applewhaite from all claims to the plantation in St. Thomas and St. George, 540 acres, of land called Endeavour plantation. Butting on lands of Humphry Hooke Esq. .. .. .. Richardson, John Silkham. John Jennings, Thomas Hayes, William Musgrove, John Bread, planters, Edward Thompson, Thomas Wardall Esq., Edward Thornborough Esq., Thomas Holdipp gent, John Bonner, James Butler, John Barnes, John de la hugh, George Sanders, and Richard Hawkins Esq. and is the land and plantation which the said Thomas Applewhaite

and our late decd. uncle Thomas Pead lately held together. sd. John Benham, Elizabeth Benham. Wits: William Kirton, Philip Kirton, Richard Seawell.

1 May 1683. Henry Applewhaite Esq. to Charles Lewis, farrier, lease of plantation of 17 acres, Bounding on John Battin, Thomas Lewis, Elizabeth Gittens; for rent £28 per an. sd. Henry Applewhaite. Wits: John Bentham, John Hyland. Recorded 12 July 1686.

Endorsed. Assignment of the lease from Charles Lewis to Nathaniel Maverick.

13 March 1687. Henry Applewhaite Esq. to Hon. Col. John Hallett. Assignment of two sums of £2,000 each held against Mary Kingsland, widow and exx. of Will of Nathaniel Kingsland decd. sd. Henry Applewhaite, John Hallett. Mary Kingsland. Wits: Joseph Alford, Abra: Bueno Demsey, Nicholas Sayers.

26 Sep. 1691. John Hyland of St. Michael to Henry Applewhaite, sale of a parcel of land in St. Michael and 9 slaves. sd. John Hyland. Wits: Jon. Ridgeway. Recorded 8 Oct. 1691.

Major 15 Oct. 1722. Thomas West of St. Michael, gent, Esther his wife, to Thomas Applewhaite. for £115 paid, sell T. A. 5 negro slaves. sd. Thomas West, Esther West. Wits: Edward Pare. Recorded 5 Dec. 1722.

24 March 1723-4. Nathaniel Kingsland of St. Margaret Westmister gent to Thomas Applewhaite of Barbados Esq. Whereas T. A. and Edward Pare of Barbados, gent, and George Lascelles of London, merchant, on behalf of and as surety for T. A. by bond dated 16 Sep. 1719 became bound to Nathaniel Kingsland £700 to secure an annual sum of £100 for his life. And whereas in consideration of such bond N. K. on 15 Sep. 1719 conveyed Kingsland plantation and all his estate in Barbados to T. A. And Whereas E. P. and G. L. both reside in Barbados and N. K. requires security given him in London. George Newport of London, mercht., for account of sd. T. A. hath agreed to give security £1,500 to secure the annuity, and T. A. now requires further assurance of the said plantation and premises from N. K. In consideration of the new bond N. K. conveys unto T. A. Kingsland pltn. 160 acres by estimation, in Christ Church, butting on William Carter Esq., Thomas Maxwell Esq., Conrade Adams Esq., Richard Callender and other land of T. A. formerly part of Kingsland, together with mills, and buildings and all other plantations in Barbados, white servants, negroes, cattle, horses, sheep, pigs, and utensils and implements. Sd. by Robert Warren, attorney of N. K. Wits: Humphrey Cockeram, R. Morris. *Endorsed.* Letter of Attorney to Robert Warren and Henry Lascelles of Barbados Esqs. to execute the deed. sd. 11 Jan. 1723 Nathl. Kingsland. Wits: Thomas Hawys, Simon Clarke, Tho. Newson, Tho. Tryon, John Page. Proved in Barbados by Thomas Newson. Recorded 31 Mar. 1724.

24 March 1730. Sir Jermyn Davers of Rushbrook co. Suffolk, Bart. eldest surviving son and heir of Robert Davers, late of same place, Bart. and of Dame Mary Davers, his late wife both decd. and also brother and h at 1 of Sir Robert Davers late of same place Bart. who whilst living was eldest son and h at 1 of said Sir R. D. the father, and of the said Dame Mary. of the 1 part, The Hon. Thomas Davers late of Rushbrook aforesaid but since of Barbados youngest brother of said Sir J. D. 2nd part, The Honble John Frere of Barbados Esq. 3rd part and The Honble Thomas Applewhaite of Barbados Esq. and Robert Warren of same Island 4th part. Reciting deed 30 June 1727 whereby J. D. sold pltn. called St. Paul pltn., 479 acres 3rds partly in St. Michael and a strip in St. George for £8,000 to Thomas Davers. The purchase money still remains unpaid, and convey same to use of T. A. and R. W. to the use of J. D. for 1,000 years and then for John Frere.

13 July 1745. Bill of Lading. The Honble Thomas Applewhaite Esq. & Archibald Carmichael Esq. on *Charming Sally*, John Davidson, Master, now at anchor in Carlisle Bay, sailing for London, 3 hhds. of coarse clayed sugar on account of Richard Worsam Esq., freight 7/6 per 100. Recorded 18 August 1746.

27 July 1747. Deed executed by Honble Thomas Applewhaite Esq. and Samuel Husbands executors of the Will of Hon. James Dottin late of Barbados decd. (not of interest.)

25 Aug. 1747. Edward Pare of St. George Esq. and Lucretia his wife, 1. The Hon. Thomas Applewhaite of St. Thomas, The Honble John Frere of St. George, and Thomas Finlay of St. M. Esq. 2. and Thomas Tunckes of St. M. Esq. 3. Reciting deed 16 Jan. 1739 between Edward Pare, Eliza Shawe of St. M., widow, Samuel Salmon of St. M. Esq. and the said T. A., J. F. and T. F., whereby in consideration of the marriage then to be solemnized between E. P. and Lucretia Salmon, one of the daurs of the said S. S. and Sarah, his wife, a pltn. in St. George 220 ac., butting on George Walker decd. and the Glebe land of St. George, Major Neale, Richard Worsam, Sir Willoughby Chamberlaine decd. Edwin Carter decd., together with windmill, slaves, cattle, etc. was conveyed upon trust for E. P. and L. P. Since then Shawe and S. Salmon both decd. Edward Thomas Pare issue of the marriage and heir at law. L. P. now confirms the settlement and releases part of her jointure. Recorded 2 Sep. 1747.

The following Applewhaite records have been kindly furnished by Mrs. Amabel St. Hill who has made extensive searches in the records of this family.

JOHN APPLEWHAITE of Stoke Ash, the elder, yeoman, Will dated 1632. Proved P.C.C. 1634/5. My freehold and coppiholde lands lying in Stoake Ashe, Wetheringsett and Thorndon which were devised to me by the last Will and Testament of William

Applewhaite to my eldest son John and his heirs. Land in the Manor of Brockford. My sons Henry, Thomas, and Edmond, each £400. My coz. Robt. Sheppe of Wichfield, 40/-. My wife Lydia. THOMAS APPLEWHAITE of Limehouse, Stepney, alias Steboniheath, Middlx, mariner. My son Thomas A. £250 to be paid into the hands of my friends Mr. Barnaby Dunch of London, merchant, and James Conaway of Redcliff, mariner, for the use of my son Thomas during his minority. My dau. Elizabeth A. £200 when 21. My brother William Applewhaite £5. Residue to my wife Elizabeth. Written on five sheets of paper by my owne hand.

HENRY APPLEWHAITE of Isle of Wight Co. Virginia, Will dated 26 August 1703, proved 8 May 1704. Son Henry executor. Sons Thomas, William, and John. Daughter Ann Applewhaite. Grandson Henry Applewhaite. Wife mentioned but not named.

Alumni Cantab:—JOHN APPLEWHAITE, Adm. pens. Caius aet. 17, son of John A. of Stoke Ash, Suffolk, gent., matriculated 1626. Scholar 1627/8. Grays Inn 1633. Died circa 1679. JOHN APPLEWHAITE, mat. 1654, adm. pens. Corpus Cristi, perhaps son and heir of John of Stoke Ash. Adm. Lincolns Inn 1661. JOHN APPLEWHAITE, adm. pens, St. Catherine 1680, of Suffolk.

Thomas Applewhaite of Le Charles Barbados died unmd. and admin. granted to his sister Elizabeth, wife of Thomas Evans. P.C.C. 1693.

John Applewhaite of Stoke Ash £10 Suffolk Subsidy Roll anno 1612.

Thomas Applewhaite of I of Wight, Virginia, Will made Octr. 1770 proved Jan. 1771. My sons Henry, Josiah, my daurs. Sally, Mary Robertson, and my son Thomas Applewhaite living in Barbados.

Other Wills proved in I of Wight, Virginia—Thomas A. 1732, John A. 1736, Martha A. 1739, Henry A. 1741, Ann A. 1747, John A. 1759, Arthur A. 1766, Henry A. 1770.

Mrs. Lovett Frescoln, of Pennsylvania, U.S.A., a professional genealogist and an authority on the *Applewhite* family, has kindly sent us the following records:—

Register of St. Dionis Backchurch, London.

MARRIAGES.

1639, Feb. 26—Thomas Applewhaite and Mary Pead.

CHRISTENINGS.

1617, Oct. 14—Elizabeth Pead, daughter of Thomas Pead, Apothecary.

1619, Nov. 7—Mary, dau. of Thomas Peede.

1622/23, March 23—Anne Peade, dau. of Thomas Pead.

BURIALS.

1638, April 3—Thomas Pead.

1646, April 9—Elizabeth, dau. of Thomas Applewhaite.

1650, Feb. 18—Widow Pead.

"St. Dionis Backchurch, dedicated to Dionysius the Areopagite, who was one of St. Paul's first converts at Athens, and who, under the name of St. Denis, became the patron saint of France. This church was situated at the south west corner of Lime Street, and was called "Backchurch" from its position behind "Fenchurch", which, standing in the middle of the street, was sometimes designated "Forechurch".

St. Dionis was pulled down in 1878 and its parish united with that of All Hallows, Lombard St."

London City Churches—Daniell.

The above Thomas Applewhaite died in Barbados before March 19, 1677, on which date his will was proved. His widow Mary survived.

"Registers of Bramfield"   Suffolk, England.

Arthur Applewhaite—(He was married at Thorington, Dec. 31, 1728, to Bridgett Nelson of Bramfield.)   Buried Sept. 12, 1733.

The following inscription to his memory is on a large flat stone in the chancel floor of Bramfield Church.

Here lies the body of Arthur Applewhaite Second Son of Henry Applewhaite of Huntingfield in this County, Gent. (who was Favorite and Bayliff to Henry Heveningham, Henry Heron, and John Bence. Deceased, and remains so to Alexander Bence and George Dashwood, all Esquires, and successively owners of the Heveningham Hall Estate) who died on the ninth day of September A.D. 1733. And in the 39th year of his age. He married Bridgett the Eldest Daughter And at length, Sole Heiress of Lambert Nelson, late of this Parish Gent. By whom he had no Issue and to whom (Having, by his Father's Instigation made no will) He left no Legacy but a Chancery Suit with his Eldest Brother for her own Paternal Estates in this Town and Blyford

Burials: Sep. 15, 1737. Mrs. Bridget Applewaithe.

The following inscription to her memory is inscribed on a large flat stone on the floor of the chancel of Bram. Ch.

M.S.

Between the Remains of her Brother Edward & Husband Arthur
Here lies the Body of Bridgett Applewhaite
once Bridgett Nelson
After the Fatigues of a Married Life
Borne by her with Incredible Patience
for Four Years and Three Quarters, bating three weeks,
and After the Enjoinment of the Glorious Freedom
of an easy and Unblemisht widowhood
For four years and upwards
She resolved to run the Risk of a second Marriage Bed
But Death forbad the Banns
and having with an Apoplectick Dart
(The same Instrument with which he had
Formerly
Dispatcht her Mother)
Toucht the most vital part of her Brain:
She must have fallen Directly to the Ground
(as one Thunderstrook)
If she had not been catcht and Supported
by her Intended Husband
of which Invisible Bruise
After a struggle for above sixty Hours
With that grand enemy to Life.

(But the certain and Merciful Friend to Helpless Old Age) In Terrible Convulsions Plaintive Groans or Stupefying sleep. Without Recovery of her Speech or Senses She dyed on the 12th day Sep'r. in ye year of our Lord 1737 of her own age 44.

123

ARNOLD, ARNOLL

WILLS RECORDED IN BARBADOS

11 Feb. 1688. REBECKAH ARNOLL. My father William A. My three sisters, Ann, Susanna, & Katherine. My brother, William. Susannah, Rebecca and Elizabeth, daughters of my brother, Robert. To my brother Samuel's daughter, Rebecca, a Jacobus piece of gold; and to his sons William and Matthew. My three sisters-in-law, Elizabeth, wife of Robert; Anne, wife of Samuel; Rebecca wife of Jacob. To Mr. William Walker, Minister, a piece of gold, and he to preach my funeral sermon. My brothers, Robert, Samuel, and Jacob to be executors. sd. Rebekah Arnoll. Witnesses: Edmund Gaskin, Henry Carmill (?). Recorded 23 June 1690.

2 Oct. 1679. Will of THOMAS ARNOLD, mariner. Gives all to his shipmates. Recorded 5 Oct. 1697.

24 July 1690. WILLIAM ARNOLL of St. Peter's All Saints, gent. My father. William A. My three sisters Ann, Susannah, and Katherine. My cousin, Susanna, daughter of my brother Robert. Cousin, Rebeckah, daughter of my brother Samuel. Cousins William, son of my brother, Robert, and William, son of my brother Samuel. My brothers Robert & Samuel as executors. sd William Arnoll, Witnesses: Edmund Gaskin, Richard Farjeon. Recorded 17 Feb. 1690/1.

13 August 1690. Will of WILLIAM ARNOLL, gent. My grandchildren, Rebecca, Susanna, Elizabeth and William, children of my son Robert and Elizabeth his wife. Grandchild, Rebecca, daughter of my son Jacob. Son Robert as executor. sd. William Arnoll. Witnesses: Caesar Marlton. Peter Dakers. Recorded 6 Aug. 1691.

8 Sep. 1690. JACOB ARNOLL of St. Andrew Overhills, gent. My daughter, Rebekah, at 21 or marriage. My two cousins, William Arnoll, son of my brother Robert and Matthew Arnoll, son of my brother Samuel. Brothers Robert & Samuel as executors. sd. Jacob Arnoll. Witnesses: Thomas Reason, Robert Gore. Recorded 16 Dec. 1690.

6 May 1704. Will of EDWARD ARNELL of St. Michael, gent. My brother, William Arnell, hatmaker, of city of London. My sister, Margaret wife of William Luntly, shipwright, now of city of Dublin. Brother-in-law, John Wadsworth: sister-in-law, Elizabeth Wadsworth. Daughter-in-law, Barbary Grace, spinster. My late wife, Ann, the late wife of Benj. Grace, sr., decd. My son John Arnell. Benjamin Grace. George Hogshard, Col. Tobias Frere, Capt. Robert Arnell. my namesake, Thos. Fry, Master of my Brig., Charles Thomas, Edward Chilton, James Cowse, John Walter Lawer, John Le Gay, William Chearnley, John Goby, Joane Shiller, Francis, Mead, Francis Man, Mary Devereux, John Dymes, Abfiah Gibbs, ye wife of Henry Gibbs. Executors—Samuel Dursaw, Robert Cotlett, John Wadsworth, Geo. Hogshard, Mrs. Eliza Wadsworth. sd. Edward Arnell. Witnesses: William King, Thomas Cooper, Will: Walker.

Codicil. 20 May 1704. Charles Thomas to be executor. sd. Edward Arnell. Witnesses: James Cowse, Wm. Roberts, Thos. Cooper. Recorded 22 May 1704.

8 Dec. 1713. Will of JOHN ARNELL of St. Michael. To kinsman Benjamin Grace, son of Benjamin. James Matthews, John Anderson and John Smith, gift of mourning rings. Residue to John Wadsworth and my Aunt Eliza Bullock and to be executors. sd. John Arnell. Witnesses: John Jennings, Gidn. De Verde John House, John Smith. Recorded 16 June 1714.

26 Nov. 1710. Will of ELIZA ARNOLL of St. Peter, widow. Daughters, Eliza Gibbs, Susanna, Anne and Katherine Arnoll. Granddaughters, Rebecca and Mary Ball. Residue to son, William Arnoll and he to be executor. sd. Eliza Arnoll by her mark. Witnesses : Phill. Collyns, Thos. Merrick. Recorded 9 Aug. 1714.

8 June 1725. Will of MATTHEW ARNOLL, of St. Peter—All Saints. To poor of St. Peter's parish £5. To All Saints Chapel £25 towards buying a pulpit. Rings to brothers, William and Robert Arnoll and sister Rebecca Hawkesworth. Daughter, Ann Arnoll, £400. To son, John Arnoll, residue at 21, and to be apprenticed at 15. Failing his children surviving, then his estate between children of brothers, William and Robert, and sisters Rebecca Hawkesworth and Ann Hawkesworth decd. Executors—Philip Jackman, Philip Thomas and Robert Arnoll. sd. Matthew Arnoll. Witnesses: Benjamin Lopez, Andrew Trent jr., Henry Hough. Recorded 4 Jan. 1725/6.

28 Feb. 1724. Will of WILLIAM ARNOLL of St. Peter, esq. Wife (not named) annuity of £100 charged on estate in satisfaction of dower and jointure under marriage settlement with her and Sarah Daniel, widow. Son, William, £500 at 21. Daughter, Alice £500 at 20. Eldest son Robert at 21. Sister, Elizabeth Gibbs, £12. Residue to son, Robert, at 21. Appoints brothers, John Gibbs, Mr. Timothy Thornhill, and John Forster executors and guardians. Friends, Samuel Osborne and Matthew Grey esqs., to aid executors. sd. Wm. Arnoll. Witnesses : Simon Scantlebury, John Husbands, Giles Scantlebury. Recorded 18 Dec. 1725.

11 June 1733. Will of ROBERT ARNOLL of St. Peter, Esq. Wife, Elizabeth, £30 Kinswoman, Ann, daughter of my brother, William. Estate to son, Samuel at 21; failing him, to son, William, and failing him, equally between daughters, Rebecca and Jean. Wife, Elizabeth, brother, William, friend, John Battaley, and brother-in-law, William Bovell, executors. sd. Robert Arnoll. Witnesses: Samuel Mayhew, George King. Recorded 20 Febry. 1733.

3 June 1741. Will of WILLIAM ARNOLL of St. Peter. To Mrs. Rebecca Rumball, 4 acres and a house where my mother lives, to her and her children Robert Arnoll and Rebecca Arnoll. Residue to Ann Wells and Susanna Mayhew. Sons-in-law, Nicholas Wells and Samuel Mayhew, executors, and Rebecca Rumball, exx. sd. Will: Arnoll. Witnesses: Jos. Waterman, James Clarke, Saml. Arnoll sr. Recorded 14 July 1741.

27 June 1772. Will of SAMUEL ARNOLL of St. Peter, esq. To Thomas Sober Holloway and Elizabeth Burchall, dau. of Humphrey Burchall decd. £50 each. My 3 daughters, Sarah, Elizabeth, and Mary. Executors—John Wickam sr., Jos. Leacock, and daus. Sarah & Elizabeth. sd. Samuel Arnoll. Witnesses : Wm. Sandiford, James Hendy, and Jonas Yearwood. Recorded 27 Sep. 1774.

1 Aug. 1776. Will of ROBERT ARNOLL of St. Peter. My son, William and my daus. Sarah & Rebecca. My sister, Rebecca Arnoll £25. To my wife, Mary and my 4 children residue of my estate. Executors—Benony Waterman, William Arnoll Wells, and my son William, at 21. mark of X Robt. Arnoll. Witnesses : Joseph Hutchins, Henry Barnwell, Thomas Whitney. Recorded 9 Aug. 1776.

15 Nov. 1783. Will of WILLIAM ARNOLL of Town of Speights, St. Peter. It is my desire that my body be interred at some hour of the night when it may be reasonably supposed the old women of both sexes are happily snoring in their beds in as private a manner and with as little expense as possible in the grave on the south side of the church porch with the bodies of my father and sister, and that no person be requested to attend my funeral (besides the necessary ones) but my most particular friends and connections.

To my dear sister, Rebecca, at 21 or marriage my stonewall messuage in the Town of Speights, bounding on lands of William Prescod, of James Hinkson, on Vinegar Alleyne. My mother and Aunt Rebecca, to have their living in the house as in my lifetime. To my brother, Robert, £40. To my friend Mr. William Bycraft my Rolts Dictionary of Trade & Commerce and the works of Dr. Jonathan Swift in 13 vols. Residue to my sister, Rebecca. John Brathwaite Skeete, Wm. Bycraft, and Aunt Rebecca Arnoll, exors. sd Wm. Arnoll. Witns : Henry Bishop Wells, John Jackman, Recorded 20 Oct. 1784.

2) July 1791. Will of SARAH ARNOLL of St. Peter, spinster. My mansion house in Speightstown. My sister, Mary Cozier; my bro-in-law, Edward Cozier; my niece. Mary Sober Cozier. James O'Neal, cordwainer, £20. My relation, Sarah Maycock, £20. To my friend Elizabeth Burchall, spinster, £10. Exors :—Edward Cozier, John Peter. sd. Sarah Arnoll. Witns : Edward Licorish, Benj. Leacock. Recorded 16 Aug. 1791.

27 Nov. 1789. Will of MARY ARNOLD of Town of Speights, St. Peter, widow. Aged & infirm. To my son-in-law, Thomas Thoney, 5 slaves, and all my estate and he to be exor. sd by her mark. Witns : Richd. John Farre, Benj. Beard jr., Edward Licorish. Recorded 20 Aug. 1792.

DEEDS RECORDED IN BARBADOS

24 March 1644. William Arnold of Barbados, planter, sells Elice Price 4 acres in St. Lucy, bounding on lands of John Walker, Thomas Fletcher, the said Price and John Branton.

18 July 1662. Robert Downeman, sen., and Priscilla, his wife, in consideration of their natural love and affection for their dau., Judith, wife of Samuel Arnoll grant one-third part of that plantation we now live on in St. Lucy containing 100 acres of land, bounding south on Capt. Thos. Maycock, north of Matthew Hardacre, and west on the sea; together with one-third part of 7 head of cattle, 2 horses, 5 negroes, and 2 mulattoes, 4 coppers, one still and worm one mill with gudgeons and braces, 15 swine, with the houses etc.

8 April 1669. Richard Arnold of Barbados to Teague O'Morrean; one acre in St. Peter, bounding on lands of James Simson, John Maynard, Steven Stevens.

10 April 1685. William Arnoll, junior, of St. Peter All Saints, gent. sells to Robert Arnoll of same parish, gent. for £228 stlg. 10 acres and 6 chains situate in said parish, bounding west on Thomas Jones decd. and James Bullen, south on lands of the said Robert Arnoll, north on lands of Matthew Gray & Thomas Harris, and east on land of Morgan Lewis.

7 June 1680. James Bullen of Barbados, planter, sells William Arnoll, jun. planter, three acres of land in St. Peter All Saints adjoining lands of said William Arnoll east; upon lands of Thomas Jones west; upon lands of Matthew Gray and Jonathan Cloys north; and on James Bullen south.

1 May 1684. Thomas Norvell of St. Peter, gent, and Elizabeth, his wife, sell Robert Arnoll of same parish, merchant, for £1,350 stlg. sixty acres commonly called Easons & Tysons estate in St. Peter All Saints, bounding on Edward Hughes, Jacob Scantlebury, Christian Horwood, Wm. Arnoll, Lt. Thos. Jones, Wm. Arnoll jnr. & . . . Lewis; together with houses etc.

3 April 1685. Edward Hughes and William Hughes of St. Peter All Saints, sell Robert Arnoll of same parish, merchant, 6 acres in St. Peter, bounding on lands of Jacob Scantlebury, Morgan Lewis, and the said Arnoll.

20 Oct 1687. William Arnold of St. Peter All Saints gives son Robert Arnold 7 acres of land in St. Peter, bounding west on lands of the said William Arnold, east and north on lands of the said Robert Arnold, south on Francis Cussock and Charles Herline. And also 4 slaves.

26 Oct. 1687. William Arnold of St. Peter, gent, gives son, Jacob, 7 acres of land in St. Peter, bounding west on lands of said William Arnold, east on Samuel Arnold and Robert Arnold, south on Nicholas Hutchinson, with 4 slaves.

3 Novr. 1687. William Arnold of St. Peter, gives daughter Rebecca 7 acres of land in St. Peter, bounding west on Richard Farr, east Jacob Arnold, north on Catherine Arnold, south on Ann Arnold, with 4 slaves.

3 Nov. 1687. William Arnold of St. Peter, gives dau. Ann, 7 ac. of land in St. Peter, bounding west on lands of Rich. Farr, & Josiah Gosling, gent., east on Jacob Arnold, north on Rebecca Arnold; south on Nicholas Hutchins, and Joseph Gosling and also 4 slaves.

5 Nov 1687. William Arnold of St. Peter gives daughter, Susannah Arnold 7 ac of land in St. Peter, bounding west on lands of Michael Tyrill, east on Jacob Arnold, north on Thos. Jones, south on Catherine Arnold, and also 4 slaves.

4 Novr. 1687. William Arnold of St. Peter gives Catherine Arnold 7 ac of land in St. Peter, bounding west on lands of Richd. Farr and Michael Tyril, east on Jacob Arnold, north on Susanna Arnold and south on Rebecca Arnold, and also 4 slaves.

14 April 1685. Robert Arnoll sells Lewis Perrin of St. Peter for £30 one acre in St. Peter, bounding, south-east on the broad path, south-west on lands of the said Perrin, north-west on lands of Jacob Scantlebury, north-east on Francis Shorey.

3 Dec. 1687. Jacob Arnold to Samuel Arnold of St. Peter, sale of 7 ac of land given him by his father William Arnold.

5 Dec 1687. Samuel Arnold of St. Peter to Robert Arnold of the same, sale of 3½ ac of land in St. Peter, bounding east on lands of William Arnold, west on Susannah and Catherine Arnold, south on lands of the said Samuel Arnold, north on lands of the said Robert Arnold.

30 Jan. 1686. John Berringer to Robert Arnold, sale of 5 slaves.

5 June 1688. John Dickenson of St. Peter, gent, to Robert Arnold of St. Peter All Saints, Lease of a house in Speights Bay alias Little Bristol, bounding on a road leading to the Church and Churchyard, and on lands of Captain John Dickenson, Captn. Thomas Merrick, on the broad road leading from the Bay to the Great Fort called the Orange Fort, for 31 years.

5 June 1688. The same to the same, Release of the above described freehold property.

31 March 1688. John Dickenson to son-in-law Robert Arnold, sale of six slaves.

16 Nov 1695. Thomas Merrick to Captain Samuel Arnold of St. Peter, sale of 10 ac. of land in St. Andrew, bounding on lands of Thos. Beresford, Walter Scott, the said Merrick, and the sea.

25 Oct. 1695. Benjamin Hall of St. Michael to Edward Arnold sale of land in Palmetto Street, Bridgetown, bounding on lands of Hugh Hall and Hon Francis Bond.

Austin, Austyn, Astin, or Oistin of Barbados.*

WILLS.

1671-2, Jan. 11. Edmund, of St Michael's, Merchant. Brother Joseph of London, Woollen Draper.

1672, March 23. Thomas, of St Philip, Gent. To be buried in St Philip's Churchyard. Daughter Jane Coffin, wife of Wm Coffin. Cousin Ann Borden; "Old Mrs Bowden." Brother-in-law Samuel Williams, Thomas Forcherson. Son Edward. A witness, Edward Mayo.

1680-1, Feb. 21. Nicholas Austyn. Wife Susannah. Daughter Gollinery. Bro.-in-law Edward Baxter. "All my children."

1694-5, March 5. James Oistin, of Christ Church, Gent. Wife Angelletta. Son James. Daughters, Elizabeth, Angelletta.

1709, Aug. 23. Edward. Sons, John, Edward, William. Brother Thomas.

1714, Feb. 15. John, of Christ Church, Planter. Wife Susan. Sons, Thomas, Philip. Daughter Elinor Ford. Grandchildren, not named. A witness, John Wilshire.

1714, Feb. 16. John, of Christ Church, Planter. Wife Susan. Sons, Thomas, Philip. Daughter Elinor Ford. Grandchildren, unnamed. Witnesses, Thomas Lewis, Wm Addison.

1714-15, July 13. Philip Astin, of St George's. Brothers, John, Joseph, Jonathan, William. Sisters, Martha (wife of William Roberts), Mary (wife of John Linton), Elizabeth Astin. Nephews, Robert and William Linton. Niece Sarah Roberts. Cousins, Sarah, Frances, and Henrietta Ridgway, widow. A witness, John Wilshire.

1716, Aug. 20. Philip, of St Thomas. Wife Mary. Sons, William, John, Francis, James, Thomas, Philip. Daughter Mary.

1719, July 8. Thomas, Millwright. Daughter Susanna, wife of John Belcher (dau. Elizabeth). Brothers, Edward (children, William, Elizabeth), William (daus. Sarah, Elizabeth), Philip (children—? John). Nephew Edward, son of Edward.

1719, July 25. Elizabeth, of St John's, Spinster. Sister Anne Austin, now living in London.

1734, Dec. 14. Mary, of St Philip, Widow. Grandchildren, Ralph, Nathaniel, and Edward Weekes, Jane, Mary, Susanna Dempster (children of John and Mary Dempster), Enoch Forte, Jane Forte, Samuel Gretton, Elizabeth Gretton.

1736, June 30. James, of St James. Jonathan Tremaine, residuary legatee.

1737, May 10. Sarah Astin, Widow. Sister Elizabeth Maverick, widow. Cousins, Ellinor Curtis, Sarah Butler, Samuel Belgrave, Mary Maverick, widow, Robert Belgrave, J^r, Maverick Belgrave, Sarah Belgrave, and Robert Belgrave, Senr.

1737, Oct. 7. Abraham, of St James, Labourer. Heir, William Horne.

* Communicated by Mr. N. Darnell Davis.

1740, May. Joseph Astin, of St Peter. Sons, Joseph, Edward, Jonas. Wife Elizabeth.

1741. Feb. Richard, of St Peter's. Sons, William, Thomas.

1748, April 28. Francis, of St Thomas. Brothers, John, James, Philip. Sister Mary, wife of Benjamin Niblett (son Samuel).

1753, March 24. John, of Christ Church. Wife Ann. Daughter Elizabeth. Sons, Edward, Samuel, Josias, John, Abraham.

1758, Oct. Joseph, of St Peter. Wife Elizabeth. Sons, Joseph, Edward, John.

1767, June 29. Sarah Astin (widow of John of Christ Church). Sons, Benjamin, John. Daughter Mary, wife of John Ramsay.

1769, April. Edward, of St Peter's. Brother Jonas Maynard Austin. Cousin Thomas Lang.

1779, May. George, of St Peter, Cordwainer. Son George Hutchins Austin. Grandchildren, George Hutchins, Henry, and Elizabeth Ann.

1788, July 22. Elizabeth, of St Peter. Sons, John, Thomas, George. Daughter Katherine Lewis.

1789, Oct. Abraham, Practitioner in Physic and Surgery. Wife Elizabeth. Brother John. Daughters, Elizabeth Ann, Lucy.

1791, March 10. Benjamin, of Christ Church. Son Benjamin. Others, William Earle, J^r, son of W^m and Eliz. Earle.

1794, July 6. Thomas, J^r, of St Michael, Practitioner of Physick. Wife Charlotte. Son William. Brothers, Hugh Williams, William. A witness, John Austin.

1795. John, of Christ Church. Wife Sarah. Son Edward Samuel. Daughter Ann. Executor, Dr. John Austin.

1797, Oct. 6. John, of St Thomas. Brother William. Brother-in-law Wm Moore. Nieces, Jane Byshley, Mary Riley.

1797, Aug. 31. William Wentworth, of St Michael's and Surinam. Wife Jane. Daughter Joanna, wife of Rev. Richard Austin. Catherine Sims Wentworth, Paul Wentworth. A witness, John Austin.

MARRIAGES—AUSTIN.

Year and Day.		Christian Names.	To whom Married.
1659	Feb. 27	Elizabeth	Henry Stokes.
1660	Nov. 27	Dorothy	Edward Nevill.
1674	Sept. 3	Thomas	Margaret Gay.
1674	Aug. 16	Elizabeth	Robert Harrison.
1678	Jan. 6	Jane	Samuel Ketro.
1686	Sept. 3	Susanna	Owen Davis.
1687	Oct. 6	Francis	Margaret Davis.
1690	July 24	Eleanor	Thomas Field.
1691	July 16	Nicholas	Alice Loflin
1692	Dec. 29	Margaret	Charles Prigg.
1693	Sept. 5	Elizabeth	Edward Arther.
1693	Mar. 18	Samuel	Frances Borradell.
1693	July 25	Jane	William Greenidge.

130

Year and Day.	Christian Names.	To whom Married.
1694 Jan. 24	Thomas	Sarah Copp.
1694 —	Jane	Enoch Gretton.
1695 June 13	Thomas	Ann Corkman.
1696 Dec. 17	Susanna	Henry Clarke.
1696 Oct. 10	Ann	John Rose.
1696 July 5	Owen	Ann Nicholas.
1698 Mar. 14	Edward	Elizabeth Ockman.
1702 July 9	Elizabeth	John Outram.
1703 Sept. 30	Edward	Mary Drayton.
1703 Aug. 9	Thomas	Mary Lanier.
1704 April 20	Cornelius Astin	Elizabeth Thomas.
1706 Aug. 25	Edward	Sarah Edwards.
1709 Sept. 8	Elizabeth	Frederick Bixe.
1713 Aug. 26	Sarah	Maurice Evans.
1713 Aug. 22	Susanna	John Batcher.
1755 June 27	Thomas	Mary Williams.
1756 Nov. 4	Gabriel	Edward Butler.
1757 May 26	Elizabeth	John Ward.
1759 April 12	John	Ann Robinson.
1760 June 17	John	Sarah Ruck.
1761 June 26	Sarah	Morgan Dowling.
1762 July 5	Ann	Richard Merifield.
1763 Dec. 8	Mary Astin	James Robertson.
1763 —	George Hutchins	Sarah Keene.

MARRIAGES—OISTINE.

Year and Day.	Christian Names.	To whom Married.
1655 Mar. 27	Joana	John Blagrove.
1659 Mar. 1	Edward	Sarah Emperor.
1664 Feb. 4	Elizabeth	Daniel Gilbert.
1664 —	Huncks	Joan Russell.
1670 Aug. 30	Sarah	William Leigh.
1674 Mar. 24	Susannah	Henry Holmes.
1679 Sept. 25	Sarah	Francis Emperor.
1681 April 7	Joanna	Henry Rennter.
1681 May 19	Gollifrey	Dennis Halsy.
1681 June 2	Sarah	James Marshart.
1681 Nov. 10	Jane	Roger Talbot.
1684 Oct. 18	Maria	Samuel Ward.
1695 July 17	Elizabeth	Edward Stevens.
1697 —	James	Mary Thomson.
1699 Sept. 29	James	Mary Callander.
1703 Mar. 24	Nicholas	Martha Miles.
1711 July 24	Angeletta	John Tappin.
1716 May 20	Mary	John Bullias.
1723 Aug. 11	Sarah	Richard Ince.
1724 Mar. 13	Jonathan	Margarit Higgins.
1724 Oct. —	Elizabeth	John Carr.
1725 Jan. 24	Edward	Elizabeth Oistine.
1725 Jan. 24	Elizabeth	Edward Austin.
1728 Nov. 9	Rebecca	Jules Dewee.
1730 Nov. 10	James	Sarah Linton.
1743 Nov. 19	Sarah	Francis Draycott.
1750 Aug. 23	Mary	John Olton.
1756 Feb. 28	Sarah	Richard Catlewell.
1761 Sept. 6	Henrietta	John Brand.

Date of Baptism.		Christian Names.	Parents.
1646	April 5	Mary	Henry and Joan.
1653	Nov. 17	Margaret	Thomas.
1656	July 25	John	John & Susan.
1657	April 17	Rebecca	Thomas & Elizabeth.
1658	Aug. 3	d. of Nicholas	Mother Susanna.
1659	May 26	Susan	John & Susan.
1660	Sept. 30	Elizabeth	William.
1660	Oct. 25	Susan,	Nicholas & Susanna.
1661	May 26	Thomas	John & Susan.
1662	April 18	Jane (Astin)	John Astin
1662	Dec. 4	Mary	Nicholas & Susan.
1662	Nov. 13	Eleanor	John & Susan.
1663	—	d. of Wᵐ Astin.	
1665	May 18	Francis	John & Susan.
1665	May 16	Nicholas	Nicholas & Susan.
1666	Feb. 17	Nicholas.	
1666	—	Charles	John & Susan.
1667	Nov. 6	Mary (Austen).	
1668	May 13	Owen	Nicholas & Susan.
1669	—	Son of John.	
1670	April 9	John Austen.	
1670	June 13	Sarah	Nicholas & Susanna.
1672	July 12	Thomas Assten.	
1672	Mar. 28	Eliz. Austine	John & Susan.
1672	Mar. 28	Ann Austine.	
1674	July 12,	William Austen.	
1674	Mar. 30	Mary	John & Susanna.
1675	April 8	Elizabeth	Nicholas & Susanna.
1685	Feb. 25	Jane	Elias & Mary.
1687	July 3	George	George & Alice.
1691	May 26	Susanna	Thomas & Ann.
1694	Nov. 14	Samuel	Samuel & Frances.
1696	May 8	Ann	A woman of Sᵗ Philip's.
1699	April —	John	Edward & Elizabeth.
1700	Oct. 13	Thomas	George & Mary.
1702	Nov. 14	Ann	Samuel & Frances.
1702	Sept. 26	William	Edward & Elizabeth.
1703	Mar. 17	Susan	Thomas & Mary.
1705	May 13	Samuel	Thomas & Mary.
1706	July 13 born 16 April	}Child of	Thomas & Mary.
1708	—	William	Samuel & Frances.
1708	—	William	Edward & Sarah.
1709	—	Elizabeth.	
1716	Nov. 27	William	John & Judith.
1717	Nov. 7	Richard.	
1720	Feb. 22	Thomas.	
1721	Dec. 15	Thomas.	
1722	—	Astin, William.	
1725	—	„ Joseph	Mʳ Joseph & Mʳˢ Frances.
1726	—	„ Thomas.	
1726	Sept. 8	„ Sarah	Mʳ Joseph & Mʳˢ Frances.
1726	—	Mary Austin	Edward & Elizabeth.
1726	—	Joan.	

Date of Baptism.		Christian Names.	Parents.
1729	—	Astin, Frances.	
1730	—	„ Martha.	
1730	—	Austine.	
1732	—	Astin, Mary.	
1733	—	„ David ⎫	Mulattoes belonging to Phœbe
	—	„ Robert ⎬	Haynes, widow.
	—	„ Margareta ⎭	
	—	Austin, Mary.	
1734	—	Astin, Timothy	A. Mulatto.
1737	—	„ Elizabeth.	
1737	Oct. 29	Austin, Sarah	William.
1743	—	Astin, Elizabeth	A free Negro.
1744	Oct. 22	Mary	John & Sarah.
1747	Feb. 13	Astin, Elizabeth	William & Elizabeth.
1748	June 9	Son of John	John & Ann.
1749	June 20	Philip	Philip & Mary.
1749	June 5	„	„ „
1753	Sept. 9	Mary	„ „
1753	Nov. 4	Astin, Samuel	William & Elizabeth.
1786	—	Mary Ann Williams	Thomas & Mary.
1757	Oct. 12	Hugh William	„ „

BIRTHS—OISTINE.

Date of Baptism.		Christian Names.	Parents.
1645	Dec. 16	Elizabeth	Edward & Jane.
1645	Feb. 8	Thomas	„ „
1660	May 29	Edward	Edward & Sarah.
1663	April 13	Edward	„ „
1663	April 13	Sarah	„ „
1665	Jan. 16	Elizabeth	„ „
1671	Oct. 15	Edward	James & Angeletta.
1674	Feb. —	Elizabeth	„ „
1679	July 4	James	„ „
1682	Nov. 28	Sarah	„ „
1687	Sept. 17	Angeletta	„ „
1694	—	James.	
1701	Sept. —	William	James & Mary.
1706	Dec. 24	James	„ „
1711	Nov. 17 ⎱ 1708* ⎰	Elizabeth	„ „
1713	Mar. 21	Angeletta	„ „
1737	July 13 ⎱ 1735* ⎰	James	James & Sarah.
1737	Oct. 28	Henry	„ „
1741	Nov. 15	John	John & Ann.
1742	Feb. 25	Samuel	„ „

DEATHS—AUSTINS.

1657	May 8	John.	1670	Feb. 2	Samuel.
1661	Nov. 18	Henry.	1671	Jan. 6	Edmund.
1666	Sept. 1	Elizabeth.	1673	Mar. 31	Elizabeth.
1668	Mar. 12	Mary.	1673	April 23	Thomas.
1670	Jan. 29	William.	1674	April 1	Mary, d. of John A.

* These years refer to the date of birth.

1677	Sept. 27	John, a cooper.	1703	Dec. 11	Ann, an infant.
1678	June 28		1704	May 14	John, mariner.
1680	Mar. 9	Wife of John Austin.	1704	June 1	Elizabeth.
1681	June 16		1705	Nov. 7	Child of Thomas
1682	Oct. 2	Jone.			Austin.
1687	Nov. 8	George, son of George.	1705	—	
1689	—	George & Alice.	1706	Aug. 16	William.
1689	Aug. 30	From Howell & Guys.	1708	Jan. 3	Mary, widow.
1691	Aug. 3		1708	Feb. 13	William, child.
1691	Aug. 24	Richard.	1709	Aug. 8	Edward.
1691	June 14	John.	1711	July 26	Child of Edward.
1691	Dec. 3	Francis.	1711	July 19	Mary, wife of Edward.
1692	Dec. 16	Mary, a child.	1713	Oct. 23	John.
1693	Dec. 16	Joan, a child.	1714	July 31	Edward, cooper.
1693	May 16	Ann.	1714	July 30	Philip.
1694	Mar. 13	Thomas.	1714	July 8	Sarah.
1696	May 16	Ann.	1718	? —	Richard, J. & Judith.
1698	Dec. 27	Alice, wife of Nicholas.	1719	Sept. 3	Marke.
1698	July 16	Samuel.	1722	Nov. 19	William, from ye Pine
1699	Nov. 16	Susan.			Pln.
1700	Aug. 29	Owen.	1725	Feb. 26	Martha.
1701	July 29	Thomas, a child.	1726	Mar. 17	About 40 years.
1703	April 13	Samuel, a child.			

DEATHS—ASTIN.

1673	Dec. 5	Joane.	1713	Jan. 18	Thomas, merchant.
1678	July 28	William.	1729	Jan. 6	Thomas, a child.

BALL OF BARBADOS.

Extracts From Wills in the Record Office.

RICHARD BALL. (Portions only of) Will dated 9th, Septr. 1647, in which he mentions his mate Roger Burnett, and Avis Doronton.

JOHN BALL of St. Peter, B'dos. Will dated 12th Octr 1657. My brother William B. of Ross in Hereford, Esq., 500 lbs in sugar. My sister Joane Fade of Kensington 500 lbs in sugar. My brother George B. his freedom after my decease. My wife, Frances B, all ye estate I had with her. My friends Richard Backford and John Swinstead to be Overseers. My two children John and James B. (Sgd.) John Ball (his mark). Witnesses, John Wilkins and John Murphie (mark), John Roope. Recorded 3 Feb. 1657.

JOHN BOLLS of Town of St. Michaels. Will dated 21st May, 1683. My four children, son Robert (if he claims in person within 3 years after my decease), daughter Agnes Jackson, daughter Mary at sixteen or marriage, son Charles, a minor. Friends Captain John Stewart and Mr. James Taggart executors, to whom 40/- each for mourning rings. (Sgd.) John X Bolls. Witnesses, William Read, James Viccars, John Cocke. 4th June 1683, Memo : bequeathing whole estate to sons Robert and Charles. Ellinor Mackey, mother of Charles, to have management of his half till he comes of age. (Sgd) John X Bolls. Witnesses, John X Robinson, John Bailey, Lachlan Bayne. Recorded 17th April, 1684.

EDWARD BALL of the parish of Saint Michael, Carpenter. Will dated 10th July 1695. To wife, Prudence Ball, my whole estate, and she executrix. Friends Adams Barrs and Thomas Husse executors in trust. (Sgd.) Edward Ball. Witnesses Thomas Burrow and John Griffith. Recorded 17th Novr. 1696.

MARGARET BALL of St. Peter All Saints. Will dated 12th Novr., 1695. My son, Capt. Charles Sandiford, the plantation where I now live. My dau. Dorothy Ball, for the use of Anne Sandyford, a minor, dau. of William Sandiford decd. Annuity due to me from my son Charles Sandiford and my dau-in-law Frances Sandiford, executrix to her late husband Edmund Sandiford. I have £100 sealed up in a bag in the house ; it is my wish that £10 thereof be laid out in a piece of plate for the service of the Church of this parish, leaving £90 to be laid out in my funeral expenses and, if any residue, to poor of the parish. My son Capt. Charles Sandiford and son-in-law Benjamin Ball, executors. Witnesses, John Ifill, Philip Jones, Peter Deane, Peter Barker. Recorded 21st Septr., 1700.

JOSEPH BALL. Will dated 15th Sept, 1703. My master, Lt. Col. William Allemby, executor, and all my estate to him. (Sgd.) Joseph X Ball. Witness, John Mackeny. Recorded 8th Feb., 1704.

HON. GUY BALL of Christ Church, Esqre. Will dated 20th Novr 1719. To my wife household goods, furniture and plate, chariot and six coach-horses. To son Joseph at 21, £2000 Cy. To son Benjamin at 21, £2000 Cy. To dau. Catherine at 21 or marriage £2000 Cy. To dau Mary at 21 or marriage £2000 Cy. Wife, and father-in-law, Jos Hole, and friends Major Genl. Maxwell and Ralph Weeks executors, and £50 each. Residue to son Richard, a minor. I direct that my sons be bred in England. Witnesses Faithful Adams, A. Reid. Robert Warren. Recorded 30th April 1722.

HONOR BALL of St Michael. Widow. Will dated 18th Dec. 1727. My grandson, Humphrey Ball, 5 acres in St Michael. Son Humphrey B., grand-daus, Dicksfield Ball, Honor Mayer, Elizabeth Lewis, Mary Lewis, Ann Kelly, Honor Kelly. Four grandsons, Benjamin Lewis, John Lewis, William Lewis and Nathanial Lewis, and David Lewis. (sgd) Witnesses Jos. Whit, John Arnot. John Flowerdewe. Recorded 10 Sep., 1728

WALTER BALL of St. Peter, Planter. Will dated 6 Nov. 1733. Wife Ann one-third of my estate for life. Three daus. Ann, Charity, and Dorothy, £30 each at 21. Son Benjamin residue at 21. Brothers, John and Charles, Brothers-in-law Simeon Edwards and Thomas Agard executors. (sgd). Walter Ball. Witnesses, William Burnett, William Waterman, John Piercy, James Clarke. Recorded 14th Octr. 1734.

JOSEPH BALL late of Christ Church, Barbados, but now of Billiter square, London. Exemp. from P.C. of Canterbury of Will dated 24th March 1742. My wife Mary, annuity £400 Cy, payable out of estate in Barbados. Dau. Elizabeth Ball £4000 Cy at 18. My late sister Mary Rawlins decd. Friends John Lyte, Edmund Jenkins and Edward Lascelles Esq. all of Barbados guardians of my dau. My wife Mary, my brother George of Barbados, John Lyte, Edmund Jenkins, and William Whittaker of London, Mercht. and Henry Whittaker of Tewksbury, Gloucester Co., Gent, to be executors, and I give them £50 each. My bros. Benjamin and Chapman £500 each. To my bro. George, all my estates and plantations in Barbados and Gr. Britain. (sgd). Joseph Ball. Proved by George Ball, executor, in England, 19 April 1743.

HUMPHRY BALL of St. Michael, Mason. Will dated 11th July, 1745. My wife Jane Ball my plantation in St. Michael with dwellinghouse where I now reside, and my slaves. My son, Humphrey, and daus. Dixwell and Jane. To Humphry 5 acres in S. Michael which were my Mother's, Mrs. Honor Ball decd. House in High St. to two daus. Wife Jane, Friend,

136

William Simms, and daus. Jane and Dixwell Ball, executors. Wits. Jos. Taylor, Thomas Waterman, Peter Barker. Recorded 24 August, 1745.

GEORGE BALL of St. Michael. Will dated 22 August 1746. My wife Margaret Ball my whole estate in this Island and Gt. Britain, and to be executrix. (sgd). George Ball. Wits. William Maynard and Thomas Finlay. Recorded 27 June, 1747.

JANE BALL of St. Michael, Widow. Will dated 8 Augt. 1748. To son Humphry a coat, wig, and some shirts that were his Father's, with £5 Cy. in full of all claims against my estate. To dau. Dixwell Ball £10 Cy. These amounts due from James Grasett. Residue to dau. Jane B. and to be executrix. (Sgd). Jean Ball. Wits. Elizabeth Jones, Thomas Waterman, Thomas Sol (?). Recorded 21 Dec., 1750.

ELIZABETH BALL. Will dated 1 Aug. 1753. To nephew Robert Babb (son of Robert Babb). (sgd). Eliza X Ball. Wits. H. Sacheverell Smith, James Kelly. Recorded 20 March 1754.

BENJAMIN BALL of St. Peter. Will dated 3 Dec. 1764. My wife Elizabeth, my whole estate and to be executrix. (sgd) Benja. Ball. Wits. Jno. Smith, Jur. James Bullen and John X Bullion. Recorded 27 June, 1766.

ANN BALL of St. Peter. Will dated 6 June 1760. To my Grand dau. Martha King, dau. of William and Ann King. Grandchildren Samuel Bowen, son of Sam Bowing and Dorothy, and the said Martha King. To Elizabeth Balls 20/-. Executors—William Pearen and grdson, Samuel Bowen. (sgd). Ann X Ball. Wits. Philip Pearen, Joseph Salmon, Thomas Denner. Recorded11 Jany., 1770.

JAMES BALL of St. Peter. Will dated 13 Octr. 1770. To my dau. Mary B., £20 Cy @ £5 per an. To said dau. and son Benjamin my household furniture after death of wife. Wife to have life interest in whole est. in lieu of dower. House and land over gully adjoining estate of Benony Waterman to be kept rented for maintenance of children. Dau. Mary to have advantage during her single life of the said house etc. for support of herself and two brothers Jamey and John. Desire that my sister Mary B be buried out of my estate. My estate, after death of Wife, to go in tail to children Benjamin, James, John and Mary. My wife and Capt. Saml. Hinds exors. (sgd). James Ball. Wits. William Kenn, Samuel Arnoll, Benjamin Jones. Proved 29 Dec. 1770.

DIXWELL BALL of St. Thomas. Will dated 22 Decr. 1773. Estate to Thomas and James Partridge, sons of Thomas P. and Christian his wife. Executors—John Grasett and Christian Partridge. (sgd). Dixwell Ball. Wits. Thos. West and Samuel Johnson. Recorded 21 July 1774.

The following extracts have been taken from the Volume of Census Papers deposited in the Registration Office, Barbados, copied from the returns made by the Governor to the Council of Trade and Plantations in the years 1679 and 1715, and now preserved in the Public Record Office, London.

Census of 1679.

Burials. St. Michael.	1678 June 19, Thomas Bal.
	1679 Augt. 26, John Bal.
Baptism, do.	1678 Augt. 1, Mary ye da. of Humphrey and Elizabeth Ball.
Parish of St. James.	John Ball decd., his widow is pore. 3 acres, 1 negro.
St Peter.	Capt. James Ball, 2 servts., 80 negroes, 211 acres.
	Benjamin Ball, 3 servts., 20 negroes, 80 acres.
Baptism, St. Peter.	James Ball, (in a list of baptisms between 25 March 1678 and 29 Sept. 1679).
1679 Apl. 19.	Ticket granted to James Ball in the ship *Pelican* for London, John Cocke, Commander.
Apl. 22.	The ship *Hope* for London, Joseph Ball, Commander.
Oct. 11.	William Ball, Roger Ball, and John Ball, soldiers in Lt. Col. Baylie's Regt.
	Francis Ball, soldier in Col. Thornhill's Regt.
	In Col. Standfast's Regt. Capt. James Ball, 117 acres, 2 tenants, 2 freemen, 1 servant.

Census of 1715.

Parish of Ch. Church	The Honble. Guy Ball Esq. aged 41 yrs.
	Katherine Ball his Lady ,, 27
	Richard Ball his son „ 7
	Katherine Ball his da. ,, 6
	Joseph Ball his son ,, 4
	Mary Ball his da. ,, 9 mths.
Par. of St. Peter.	John Ball aged 22 years.
„ „ „	Mrs. Elizabeth Ball 38 ,,
	her son 12 ,,
Par. of St. Mich.	Humphrey Ball aged 26¼ .,
	his wife 27
	son 15
	daughter 3
	Prudence Ball aged 101 years.

In a list of persons of 1638 who owned more than 10 acres :—
Ambrose Ball, Thomas Ball.

MARRIAGES *entered in Parish Registers to 1800.*

1644 Sept. 5 ....Ball and Peter Jones
1671 Oct. 15 Edward Ball and Prudence Waters
1673 Jany. 15 John Ball and Lidia Osburne
1677 May 2 Humphrey Ball and Elizabeth Haddock
1682 Decr. 28 Jane Ball and William Powell both of St. Thomas Parish.
1683 Decr. 27 Susanna or Elizabeth Ball to Robert Turner
1685 Apl. 27 Eleanor Boll and Mr Ham Noy
1689 Augt. 8 Humphrey Ball and Honnor Leddra
1692 Mar. 20 John Ball and Ann Meade
1694 Augt. 5 Hannah Ball and Edward Rouse
1711 July 22 Ann Ball and Anthony Steptoe
1712 April 6 Humphrey Ball and Mrs. Jane Bromfield
1715 Augt. 27 Elizabeth Ball and Edward Fitz-Gerald
1717 Feb. 16 Richard Ball and Mary Browne, Spinster
1719 Feb. 22 Mirtilla Ball and John Harbinson
1724 Augt. 9 Catherine Ball and Edward Chambers
1725 June 20 Catherine Ball and Samuel Maynard
1733 Jany. 1 Frances Ball and Edward Lascelles
1733 Jany. 7 Mrs. Mary Ball, Spinster, and William Rollin
1735 June 3 Joseph Ball and Mary Allen
1741 June 1 Sarah Ball and Rev. Mr. John Huxley. Rector of St. Michael
1745 Augt. 24 Capt George Ball and Mrs. Margret Young
1745 Jan. 7 Mary Ball and Robert Hooper
1745 Dec. 24 George Ball and Mary Young, Spinster
1750 Feby. 10 Mary Ball and .... Johnstone Esqre.
1750 Ann Ball and.........
1753 Jany. 25 Sarah Ball and Samuel Smith
1756......... Charity Ball and Hugh Edwards
1756......... Dorothy Ball and Thomas.........
1756......... Benjamin Ball and Elizabeth Dowrich
1768 May 7 Jane Ball, Spinster, and James Crichlow Grasett

BURIALS *entered in the Parish registers to 1800.*

1648 Novr. 26 Daughter of William Ball
1649 Jany. 15 Servant of Frances Ball
1662 Novr. 17 Carolina da. of William Ball, buried at St. Michael's Church.
1674 Dec. 16 Sarah Ball
1676 Apl. 4 Alice Boll wife of Henry Boll
1676 May 30 Mrs. Eliza Boll
1678 June 19 Thomas Ball
1679 Augt. 26 John Ball
1680 Augt 23 William, son of John Ball
1683 May 26 Mary, da. of John Boll
1683 June 5 John Bolls Senior, being the last of the family
1685 Sept. 27 Mary Ball
1685 Jany 25 Philip Ball, the blind man
1685 Sept. 27 William Ball

```
1689 July  10   Elizabeth Ball
1690 Dec.  27   Robert Ball, a child
1690 May   21   Henry Ball, cooper of the Bristol Frigate
1691 July  18   Richard Ball, from Capt. Bowdidge
1691 Oct.  16   James Ball, a sailor
1693 May   31   James Ball, a cooper
1695 Sept. 12   Sergeant Edward Ball
1698 Jany.  7   Zabulon Ball, mariner
1699 Octr. 23   Capt. Edmund Ball
1701 Octr.  3   Ann Ball of old age
1702 Jany. 14   John Ball, planter
1710  „    „    James Ball
1713 Augt. 16   Thomas Ball, a child
1714 May   10   Richard Ball
1715 Aug.  20   Honnor Ball, a child
1718 June   2   Joseph Ball, mariner
1718 Dec.  12   Prudence Ball, widow
1722 Apl.  21   Guy Ball
1724 May   18   Mary, wife of Richard Ball
1724 Dec.  21   Richard Ball, tailor, drowned
1725 Feb.  10   Pickford, s. of Humphrey Ball
1725 Feb.  26   John, s. of Humphrey Ball
1727 Jany.13    Mrs. Honor Ball.
1728 Aug. 22    Richard, s. of Richard Ball
1728 July 18    Henry s. of Richard Ball
1730 June 26    Jonathan Ball, pauper
1735 Oct.  10   Ann, wife of Christ. Ball
1737 Feb.  12   Jeremiah, s. of Jeremiah Ball
1738 July  28   John Ball, a tailor
1741 Feb,  13   Margaret Ball, widow
1743 Aug.  19   Benjamin Ball, in the church
1745 July  20   Humphrey Ball, a mason
1748 Oct.   4   Ann Ball
1750 Nov   17   Jane Ball, widow
1755 June  22   Elizabeth Ball
1757 Oct.  15   James Ball, a tailor
1759 Jan.  17   Joseph Ball
1770 Sept.  4   Hester Ball
1780 Apl.  10   John Ball, a soldier in the 89th Regt.
1782 Apl.  30   Elizabeth Ball
1782 Dec.   8   Christian, da. of James and Ann Ball, born
                2 Decr. 1780, bapt. 8 June 1782.
1786 Feb.   8   William Ball
1787 Nov.   2   John Ball
1788 May   10   Thomas Ball
1789 Mar.  21   Elizabeth Ball
1794 Nov.  30   Sarah Ball
1796 Jan.  14   John Ball
1799 June  27   Ann Ball
1799 Oct.  13   James Ball, alias Meares.
```

Ball Deeds, Recorded in Registration Office.

20 Sept. 1641. Capt, Christopher Codrington of Barbados Esq. sells to Thos. Ball and Robert Rabie of Barbados Planters, 50 ac., part of 820 ac, in St. John formerly in possesion of Capt. William Hawley.

22 Oct. 1640. Certificate by Thomas Horne. Surveyor, of having laid off for purchaser, Thomas Ball, 31 poles of land adjoining the Indian River. Also 15 ft. in length 66 ft. in breadth next adjoining to Capt. James Drax's Storehouse at the Bridge, and to Mr. Thomas .. Storehouse.

7 March 1642. Thomas Ball of Barbados planter sells to Thomas Bishop, planter. 20 acres part of 820 acres in St. John formerly belonging to Capt. William Hawley.

11 Sept. 1643. Richard Hyler to William Ball, Assigns a Bill of Sale.

(No date) Certificate by John Hapcott, Surveyor, of having laid off 50 sq. ft of land near to Indian Bridge lately in possession of Thomas Ball.

25 July 1653 John Walker and Bridget his wife sell to John Ball, planter, 5 acres of land in St. Thomas.

9 April 1654. Nicholas Dupless, alias Plusey, and John Corbett and Damaris his wife of St. Lucy sell to Thomas Ball, Merchant, plantation of 20 acres bounding on lands of Jos. Pickering.

31 Jany. 1679/80. Thomas Collins St Peter, planter, sells to John Ball one acre of land in St. Peter.

10 April 1675. Edward Jacob of St. Peter sells to James Ball of same parish 38½ acres in St. Peter.

10 April 1675 Giles Keyse of Bristol Mercht. atty. of James Richard of Carlyon, co. Monmouth, yeoman, and Winifred, his wife, sister and heir of Philip Green, late of St. Peter's, All Saints, Barbados, gent. decd sells, to James Ball of same parish 50 acres in St. Peter.

16 April 1686. James Ball of St. Peter, Barbados gent, sells to Charles Sandyford of St. Andrew gent 50 acres land in St. Peter

10 Oct. 1682. Richard Heard and Alice his wife of St. Thomas, Barbados sell to John Ball of St. Micheal a small dwellinghouse in town of St. Michael.

10 Nov. 1678. Richard Farr of St. Peter sells to Benjamin Ball of same parish 5 acres, of land there.

4 July 1685. Humphrey Ball of Barbados, Cirurgeon, and Elizabeth his wife sell to Tobias Frere, 20 ac. in Ch. Ch.

27 May 1659 Thomas Ball sells to Richard Feifeild a piece of land, (particulars destroyed).

21 Mar 1677. George Huit, St Peter, gent to James Ball, Settlement of 30 ac. in trust for Ann, wife of George Huit the Younger and daughter-in-law (?step daughter) of the said James Ball.

John Nelson, St. Michael, Mason, sells to Edward Ball, Carpenter, and Prudence his wife a parcel of land in Reed St. in town of St. Michael.

28 Dec. 1688. Richard Walters, Mercht. atty. of John Godfrey, Son of the prov. of Caroline. sells to 'Benjamin Ball of St. Peter a plantn there of 50 acres which was formerly let to farm by sd Godfrey, to Capt James Ball father of sd Benjamin

14 July 1694 William Whitehall of St. Michael distiller and Jeane his wife to Edward Ball St Michael carpenter and Prudence his wife a piece of land in Read's Street.

7 July 1714 Alex Cunningham, Chief Marshal of Court of Com. Pleas for precinct of St. Michael, to Guy Ball Esq of 17 acres 3 roods 36 p and 18 acres 3 roods 10 p in St. John.

20 July 1714. Guy Ball Esq. of Christ Church sells to James Drinkwater of St John 2½ acres in St. John.

12 Sep. 1720. Hon. Edmund Sutton of St. Michael to Hon. Guy Ball of Christ Church, planter sells 105 acres of land in St. Thomas for £2,100.

13 Sep. 1720. Hon. Guy Ball of Christ Church to William Warrener of Christ Church planter sells one acre of land in Christ Church for £25.

7 Sep., 1720. Hon. Guy Ball of Christ Church sells to John Mills of St. Andrew, 10 acres in St. Joseph.

7 Sept., 1720. Hon. Guy Ball of Christ Christ to Richard Alder of St. Joseph sells 10 acres in St. Joseph.

8 Sep., 1720. Hon. Guy Ball of Christ Church to Henry Hawl 3 acres of land in St. Joseph.

7 Sep., 1720. Hon. Guy Ball of Christ Church sells John Lewis 10 acres in St. Joseph.

7 Sep., 1720. Hon. Guy Ball of Christ Church sells Capt. John Swan 10 acres in St. Joseph

7 Sept. 1920. Hon. Guy Ball of Christ Church to John Cobham sells 10 ac. in St. Joseph.

20 Dec., 1718. Hon. Guy Ball of Christ Church sells a piece of land (no description) to Edward Lovell of St. James.

1 Sep., 1722. Bridget Walrond of St. John, spinster, to Catherine Pall of Christ Church, widow and exx. of Will of Hon. Guy Ball, decd., lease for 4 years of land in St. John.

4 Sep., 1730. John Hamilton of St. Michael, gent, sells Humphry Ball of St. Michael, merchant, 23 acres in St. Michael with dwelling house.

20 Novr., 1666. James Ball of Barbados, gent, and Margaret, his wife, to John Swinstead, Snr. of Barbados, merchant, of a plantation of 42 acres in St. Peter for £160 stlg. and 70,000 lbs. of muscovado sugar.

20 March 1666. Thomas Ball of St. Lucy, Mercht, to Capt. Thomas Dowden of a plantation of 20 ac, in St. Lucy whereon the sd Thomas B was living.

25 June 1671. James Ball of St. Peter, gent, sells to

Margaret Sandyford of same parish, widow, 13 acres of land in St. Peters for 22,000 lbs muscovado sugar.

12 January 1684. Philip Ball of town of St. Michael exor of Will of Thos Ball decd sells to John Manning of St. Michael a house and land in Palmetto St. for the life of sd Philp Ball in consideration of sd John M. furnishing him with sufficient meat, drink, lodging and decent clothing etc suitable to his condition, and providing someone to lead him about his occasions, he being afflicted for want of sight.   (Philip Ball died 25th Jany 1685.)

8 June 1704.   Guy Ball of St. Michael and Catherine his wife to Benjamin Matson, Settlement of the Guinea plantation St. John 317 acres, bounding on lands of Gen. Codrington, together with Mill etc and slaves in consideration of marriage already solemnized between sd Guy and Catherine, formerly C. Duboys, spinster, daughter of Thomas Duboys decd. and of £3000 Currency received with her : Upon Trust for the said Guy for life, then for Catherine for life. then to the first and other sons in tail.

1 June 1708.   Guy Ball of London, Merchant, to Edward Lascelles of London, Mercht, sale of plantation called the Netherlands in St. Philip Barbados, 250 acr and a plantation called the Guinea, St. John. Barbados subject to jointure of £400 in favour of Catherine, wife of sd Guy Ball.

29 April 1712.   Guy Ball Christ Church to John Spooner of St. Michael, gent. sale of 10 acr in Christ Church a portion of the estate of the sd Guy Ball for £450 Currency.

21 August 1746.   George Ball of St Michael. gent, and Margaret, his wife, formerly M. Young spinster, only daughter of Joseph Young.   Mortgages to Edward Lascelles Esq, Canewood plantation in St. Michael and St. Thomas which Margaret had inherited from her father, and also several small properties in the Town of St. Michael.

143

BALL OF BARBADOS. **

Extracts from Barbados Records continued from Vol. II. No. 1 p. 22.

BAPTISMS entered in Parish Registers to 1750.

1661	April 8	Penelope dau, of James & Bridgett Ball.
1664	(July 3?)	John Ball.
1666	Sep. 27	Ruth Ball.
1667	Decr. 5	John son of John Ball.
1671	Oct. 24	Mary Balle.
1678	Apr. 15	Maria dau of Humphrey and Elizabeth Ball.
1679	Dec. 27	Charles son of John & Elinor Balls.
1691	Mar. 30	Alice dau of James & Hannah Ball born 26th.
1711	Dec. 19	Joseph son of Guy and Catherine Ball.
1712	Feb. 24	Dickfield dau of Humphrey & Jane Ball, born 18th.
1713	Aug. 3	Thomas son of Guy and Catherine Ball.
1715	Jan. 12	Honnor dau of Humphrey & Jane Ball, born 11th.
1715	Feb. 14	Mary dau of Guy and Catherine Ball.
1716	Sep. 9	Humphrey son of Humphrey and Jane Ball, born 8th.
1716	Apr. 7	George son of Guy and Catherine Ball.
1718	Nov. 4.	Ann dau of Humphrey and Jane Ball.
1718	Mch. 2	Frances* dau of Guy and Catherine Ball.
1719	Apl. 24	Mary Ball a poor child, at church.
1719	May	Benjamin son of Guy and Catherine Ball.
1722	Nov 11	John son of Humphrey and Jane Ball born 8th.
1724	Mar. 7	Pickford son of Humphrey and Jane Ball, born 4th August.
1728	Oct. 6	Elizabeth dau of Henry and Elizabeth Ball, born 21st August.
1731	July 12	Margaret dau of Richard and Elizabeth Ball born 10 June.
1736	Oct. 15	Elizabeth dau of Joseph & Mary Ball.
1740	Jan. 27	Esther Ball a child 8 mos. old.
1746	Aug. 22	Christian Ball dau of James Grassett and Dickfield Ball.
1750	Sep. 1	Mary dau of Humphrey Ball.

*She was the mother of the first Earl of Harewood.
**Page 143, this volume.

Bayley, or Bailey, of Barbados.‡

WILLS.

1682, July 19. Richard, Colonel, St Peter's. Sons, Richard, John, William, Edward Simon. Daughters, Abigail, Anne. Sisters, Jane Hobson, Anna Bayley. Kinsm . Nathaniel Snow. Granddaughters, Elizabeth Hayman, Ann Morgan. Son-in-law Richard Morgan, Esquire.

1682, Dec. 19. Richard, Gent., St Peter's. Sisters, Jane Morgan, Elizabeth Birchall. Nieces, Elizabeth Hayman, Ann Morgan. Nephews, Richard Hayman,

‡ Communicated by Mr. N. Darnell Davis.

James Hayman, Richard Morgan, Laurence Price. Brother-in-law Richard Morgan.

1686, Feb. 7. Ann, Widow, St Michael's   Heir, John Freeman, son of Henry Freeman of St Michael's Town, Cooper.

1688, March 12. John, Captain. Sons, John, Thomas. Margaret, daughter of Richard Morris.

1696, May 8. John, Esquire. Brothers, William (wife Anne), Edward (wife . . . .), Simon. Sisters, Abigail, Anne. Brother-in-law Colonel John Farmer. Cousins, Thomas Forghardson (wife Joyce), Philip Philips (wife . . . .), John Farmer, J^r. Friend, Capt. Christopher Portman. Executors, Col^l John Eggerton, Capt. Tho. Myers, Esquires. Witnesses, Colonel John Frere, Mathew Kenn, Thomas Reeve, Thomas Foulerton.

1702, August. William, St Thomas, Mason. Wife Mary. Sons, William, John. Daughters, Margaret, Jane.

1706, Dec. 11. Joseph, Senior, Planter, St Philip's. Son Joseph, J^r; his children, John and Alice. Wife Elizabeth. Daughter-in-law Elizabeth.

1706, Dec. 11. Joseph, Senior, St Michael, Planter. Wife Elizabeth. Son Joseph (children, John, Alice).

1715, Jan. 21. Margaret, Widow. Son Abraham, now resident in Bermuda. Daughter Rachel Adams. Grandchildren, Adams, Robert John, Margaret, Mary, Sarah, Rebecca, Richard.

1715, June 1. Abigail, Spinster, St James, "being suddenly bound off this Island." Nieces, Mrs Elizabeth Baylie, Damaris Baylie, Anne Hayman daughter of Capt. James Hayman. Cousins, John Gibbes son of Willoughby Gibbes, Philip Gibbes and Yeamans Gibbes sons of Willoughby Gibbes. John Baylie.

1717, Sept. 27. Mary. Son John. Daughters, Margaret Hafferman, Jane Snow.

1726, May. Oliver, Town of St Michael's. Daughters, Elizabeth Rybery, Hannah Butler, Ann.

1726, Dec. 15. Frances, Widow, St. Thomas. Daughter Ann Niccolls.

1751, March 12. Thomas, St Michael. Son Davis. Wife Christian. Daughters, Ann, Elizabeth, Jane.

1757,* April 7. Love, St Michael's. Son James Jacson. Daughter, wife of Captain Thomas Carew. Executors, Hon. Henry Pears and James Bunce. Witnesses, Wm Sidney and Leon L. Boyd.

1766, June 27. Jean, St James. Daughter, wife of William Wiltshire. Son John Bayley (his children not named). Relatives and Friends, Rev. Hayman Gibbes, Thomas Gibbes, and William Cox, Esquires.

1767, March 27. John. Wife Elizabeth. Nephew Thomas Harding.

1772, Dec. 10. Joseph Bayley, St Philip. Son John. Daughters, Mary (wife of Thomas Franklyn), Elizabeth (wife of Enoch Forte). Grandson Joseph Bayley Franklyn. Granddaughters, Mary (wife of Thomas Wiltshire), Elizabeth (wife of James Griffiths), Rebecca and Jane Forte, Eliza Forte, Mary Austin Forte. Great-granddaughters, Rebecca Wiltshire, Margaret Wiltshire, Maria Wiltshire, Mary Griffiths. Great-grandson John Bayley Wiltshire.

1778, April 29. Thomas, St John. Sons, William, John. Daughters, Katherine, Elizabeth.

1779, April 9. Christian, Widow, St Michael. Daughters, Elizabeth Baylie, spinster; Jane Gibson, widow. Witnesses, Richard Butcher, Hugh Jackman.

1779, Sept. 8. Rebecca Bayley, Widow, St George. Sisters, Elizabeth Edwards, Margaret Jones. Nephews, Samuel Edwards, James Garner. Niece Elizabeth Rebecca Garner.

* The year may be 1737. The writing is difficult to read.

BECKLES OF BARBADOS.

1. RICHARD[1] BECKLES of Crosgate near the City of Durham, England, dyer, in 1670 was in Barbados on a visit to his son, ROBERT[2] then residing there.   Information concerning both father and son is gathered from Oliver's *Caribbeana*, Volume V, page 298, quoting from original documents recorded in Durham Chancery Proceedings (References 7/51, 2/68, 119 and 281) in which Robert[2] was complainant and Timothy Wittingham Esq., of Holmside, county Durham, was defendant.   The suit was brought to recover £62, expenses incurred at defendant's request in redeeming and transporting defendant's son, William Whittingham, from slavery in Barbados.   William had been bound by indenture as servant apprentice to Thomas Berisford of Barbados for three years, but having committed some misdemeanour and being imprisoned was then sold for £18 by his master as a slave to go to Jamaica. ROBERT[2] paid £20 for William's release and incurred other expenses in paying his passage to England and fitting him out for the voyage. RICHARD[1] BECKLES was about to take ship for England and undertook to see William safely landed there.   They embarked on the ship *William and James,* but during the voyage the vessel sprang a leak and was broken in pieces by the violence of the weather.   The two travellers escaped with their lives and landed at Fayal, where they spent a month until they obtained passage for England by a Dutch vessel. The voyage was again disastrous, and RICHARD[1] BECKLES was obliged to engage another vessel named the *Fortune of Dover,* William Hare, Master, by which he and his young companion were safely landed at Dover in the month of December, 1670.

2. ROBERT[2] BECKLES (*Richard[1]*) was probably born in England and about the year 1650. He must have settled in Barbados at an early age as he was only twenty years old when his father came to visit him in Barbados in 1670.   He married at St. Michael's Parish Church, Barbados, 8 November 1671, Susannah Stokes, daughter of John Stokes and Ann, his wife.[1] Ann Stokes became a widow, and married secondly

---

1. The marriage record reads as follows—8 November 1671, Robert Beckles & Mrs. Susanna Stoake. ''Stoake'' is a variation of the name Stokes. Susannah Stokes was then a spinster: the title ''Mrs.'' was usually given to a single woman of rank as a mark of distinction.

Her father, John Stokes died on 22 January 1671 and was buried at St. Michael's parish. His burial is recorded in the parish register as ''Mr. John Strakes'', an error for ''Stokes'. He is named John Stokes in his Will dated 17 January 1671 and is described as a vintner. His wife, Ann, and his daughter Susan (?Susannah) are named as beneficiaries of his whole estate.

146

Captain William Povey, Provost Marshal of Barbados 1655-60.[2]

The name ROBERT BECKLES appears in the Census of Barbados taken in the year 1679. He and his wife and three children are recorded as residents in the town of St. Michael. By the same Census records it appears that he was then a Lieutenant serving in Colonel Bates's Regiment of Militia, and later he became a Captain in the same regiment.

ROBERT[2] was a merchant in Barbados, and certainly a man of substance. He died in 1682 at the early age of 32 years and was buried in the Churchyard of St. Michael (now the Cathedral). His tomb is in the southside of the churchyard and bears the following inscription:

Here lyeth Interred the Body of CAPTN ROBERT BECKLES Merchant: who departed this life the 19th day of July 1682 Aged 32 yeares. As also SUSANNAH the wife of the Abovesaid ROBERT BECKLES Who departed this life the 8th day of September, 1683 Aged 27 yeares (sic) As also two of their children. Here also Lyeth Inter'd the Body of Madame ANN POVEY wife of WILLIAM POVEY Esq. and Mother to ye Abovesaid SUSANNAH BECKLES who Dyed the 22th (sic) day of February 1700 Aged ....7 years.

The burials of ROBERT[2] and Susannah Beckles are recorded in the Parish Register of St. Michael under the respective dates given in the Monumental inscription copied above.

ROBERT[2] BECKLES was not the only member of the Beckles family residing in Barbados in the XVII century· There is a Will on record dated 31 December, 1667, of Thomas Beckles of Barbados, merchant, in which the testator mentions "my kinsman Robert Beckles" to whom he left a legacy of £600. The exact relationship between Thomas and ROBERT[2] has not been determined—they were probably cousins. Thomas Beckles died on 10 January 1668 (burial register) and was buried in the parish Church of St. Michael, in accordance with instructions to his executors.

Children of Robert[2] and Susannah Beckles, born in Barbados and the record of their baptisms at St. Michael in the following order—

      i. ANNE, born 31 January, 1673, baptised 9 February 1673. Married .... Haggarty. She died 7 February 1747 aged 76 years.

3. ii. THOMAS[3], born and baptised 11 January 1675.,

2. The Poveys were much interested in the Plantations. William Povey's grandfather, Justinian, was a Commissioner in the Caribbees in 1637 for the Earl of Carlisle. William's brother, Thomas Povey, was clerk to the Council for Plantations (see D.N.B.). Another brother, Major Richard Povey, was Secretary of Jamaica 1661—74, and a nephew, William Blaythwayt, M.P. was a commissioner for the Plantations and clerk to the Privy Council.

iii. SUSANNA, baptised 8 February 1677. Married 14 April 1700. ALEXIS LESBRIS.
Children born in Barbados:
(1) *Anne Lesbris*, b. 29 August 1701, bap. 31 August 1701.
(2) *Thomas Lesbris*, b. 24 October 1703, bap. 7 December, 1703.
(3) *Eleanor Lesbris*, b· June 1705, bap. 6 January, 1706.

iv. ELIZABETH, born 24 August and baptised 28 August 1679. She died, and was buried at St. Michael 10 June 1680.

v. ELIZABETH, born 14 August and baptised 28 August 1681. She died, and was buried at St. Michael 13 September, 1682. These two children, both named Elizabeth, are those referred to in the monumental inscription

It will be seen from the above records that on the death of the Widow, Susannah Beckles, in 1683 her three surviving children were left, as orphans, about 11, 9 and 7 years of age respectively, evidently in the care of their grandmother, Madam Povey.

3. THOMAS³ BECKLES (*Robert²*, *Richard¹*,), born in Barbados and baptised there 11 January 1675. He was at various times residing in the parishes of St. Michael and Christ Church, and described in the records first as a Captain and later as a Major in the Militia and lastly as the honourable Thomas Beckles. He was one of the members for the parish of St. Michael in the House of Assembly from 1708 to 1710, and for some years held the important position of Chief Judge of the Common Pleas for St. Michael.

Hon: Thomas³ Beckles was thrice married. His first wife was Mary, daughter of John Forde and Mary his wife. Mary Beckles died 3 May 1700 without issue and Major Thomas³ Beckles married secondly, MAUD COX, born in Barbados 15 December 1688, daughter of Samuel and Elizabeth Cox. The marriage took place at St. Michael on 3 January 1706 and the entry reads—"Major Thomas Beckles and Mrs. Maud Cox." Maud Beckles died on 23 December, 1725 and was buried at Christ Church, Barbados. She made a Will dated 20 December 1725 with the consent of her husband, giving the reversion in several slaves (which she owned before her marriage) subject to her husband's life interest therein, to her daughters, Mary, Sarah, Susanna, and Anne. The Will was not proved until 13 May 1734, after the death of her husband Thomas³.

Hon. Thomas³ Beckles married thirdly, MARGARET INCE, at Christ Church on 17 August 1727. She was born in January 1696 the daughter of John and Rachael Adams and had married

148

first, 13 May 1713, John Ince of Christ Church, Barbados, who was then a widower with one child, Ann. John and Margaret Ince had five children, all named in the Will dated 29 October 1724 of their father.

Children of Hon: Thomas[3] Beckles by his second wife, Maud:—

    i. ELIZABETH, baptised at St. Michael, 17 October, 1706. Buried at St. Michael's Church on 7 August, 1710.

    ii. THOMAS[4], born 30 December, 1708, baptised at St. Michael, 9 January, 1709. His portrait was paint-ed in London by Achmann in 1725. He was called to the bar by one of the Inns of Court, and died and was buried in the Temple, London, in 1732.

    iii. MARY, born 3 April, 1710, baptised 8 April, 1710 buried at St. Michael 11 March, 1758. Her Will dated 13 February 1758 was recorded on 30 March, 1758. In it are named her brothers Robert, Richard and Henry, her sisters Rachael Beckles and Sarah Harris, wife of James Harris, her nephew John Gill and nieces Sarah Gill and Sarah West Gill (children of Sarah's first marriage) and William Fortescue Harris and Mary Beckles Harris, children of the second marriage·

    iv. SAMUEL, baptised at Christ Church on 13 March, 1715, died 17 August, 1716 and buried at St Michael.

    v. SARAH, born 29 August, 1716, baptised at Christ Church 3 September, 1716. Married 25 December, 1732 Edward Gill, by whom she had issue—
        (1) *John Gill*, (2) *Sarah Gill*, and (3) *Sarah West Gill*. Sarah Gill married secondly James Harris, by whom she had issue —
        (4) *William Fortescue Harris*, (5) *Mary Beckles Harris*, and
        (6) *Susannah Harris*.

    vi. SUSANNA, baptised June 1718 at Christ Church. Died 23 December, 1725 and buried at Christ Church. This was also the date of her mother's death and burial.

4. vii. ROBERT, born 8 June, 1720, Married 17 April, 1743, Elizabeth, daughter of John and Margaret Ince.

    viii. RICHARD, born 31 July, 1722, baptised the day following in St. Michael. His sponsors were Dr. Patrick Horne, Mr. Isaac Crumpt and Madam Elizabeth Grayham. Married first Sarah Rycroft at Christ Church on 21 February 1754. She died 11 March 1755 and Richard Beckles married secondly Sarah Sisnett, 1 May, 1761, who died 5 January, 1779. Richard Beckles died in 1791 aged 70 and was buried at St. Philip.

Child of the second marriage—

(1) *Thomas Graeme Beckles,* born 11 July 1763, died 7 November 1763 and buried at St. Philip.

ix. CHARLES, born 6 January, 1724 and baptised 23 February, 1724 at St. Michael. His sponsors were William Haggardy, Mr. James Hassell, and Madam Elizabeth Cox. Died 4 November, 1751.

x. ANN, born 7 November, 1725.

Children of the second marriage between Thomas² Beckles and Margaret Ince—

xi. JOHN, baptised at Christ Church 28 September, 1729 and died and was buried in that parish 8 May, 1736.

xii. RACHAEL, born about 1730, whose baptism is not recorded. Named in contemporary family Wills. Died unmarried 26 August 1796. By her Will dated 19 August, 1796 she gave her property to her niece Mary Ann Beckles, and failing her to her nephew John Beckles.

xiii. HENRY, born 3 April, 1732, concerning whom there is also no baptismal record. He matriculated at Queen's College, Oxford, 1751, aged 19 and was called to the bar in England. Elected as a member of the House of Assembly for Christ Church parish and took his seat on 6 November 1765 and was annually returned to the house until his death 18 January 1772. He was Attorney General of Barbados from 1770 to 1772. Married Elizabeth Maxwell at Christ Church 30 December, 1762, and her dowry was said to have been £30,000, a considerable fortune in those days.

xiv. THOMAS, born 1733, lived for 9 days.

Hon. Thomas³ Beckles died in 1734 and was buried at the parish church of Christ Church. By his Will dated 29 January, 1734 he bequeathed his household goods and his chariot and four horses to his wife, Margaret, with the use of his dwellinghouse during her widowhood. He left legacies of £500 each to his daughters, Mary Beckles and Sarah Gill; £300 to each of his sons, Richard, Charles, John and Henry on their attaining their majority, and £300 to each of his daughters Ann and Rachael at 18. He bequeathed the residue of his estate to his son and heir Robert, failing him, to his (testator's) son John. He appointed his brothers in law Hon. Henry Peers and George Graeme and his wife Margaret guardians of his children³. The Will was proved 23 May, 1734.

Margaret Beckles, widow of Hon. Thomas[3] Beckles, survived her husband by thirty-eight years. She died at the age of 77 and was buried at the parish church of Christ Church 21 November 1772. By her Will dated 7 August 1772 she gave a legacy to her grandson John Ince, son of her late son Thomas Ince, a child of her first marriage. She left her slaves to her grandson Fortescue Beckles, son of her step-son Robert Beckles, her daughter Rachael, her grand-daughters Mary Ann Beckles, Sarah Beckles and Elizabeth Christian Beckles, children of her step-son Robert Beckles and Elizabeth his wife, and her daughter Mary Perry.

4. ROBERT[4] BECKLES (Thomas[3], Robert[2], Richard[1]) son and heir of Hon. Thomas Beckles and Maud (Cox) his wife Married ELIZABETH INCE on 17 April, 1743 daughter of John and Margaret Ince. He died in October, 1791 at St. Michael, Barbados, and was buried in the Churchyard of the parish Church of St. Michael as appears by the entry in the parish register. By his Will dated 12 May, 1790 he directed his body to be interred in the grave with his grandfather, Robert[2] Beckles in St. Michael's churchyard under the tombstone, and he desired his name and age to be engraved on the said stone. The tombstone is still in place (see the inscription above recorded) but without the desired addition. He insisted that there should not be a sermon preached nor wine of any sort served at his funeral nor scarves furnished but only gloves supplied to the bearers; his coffin not to exceed £10 in cost and to be carried by the black coats immediately to the grave who were to be paid double wages for their trouble as the distance between his place of residence and the churchyard was very great. Hearses were not yet in use in Barbados. To his wife, Elizabeth, he bequeathed the use of his jewels and household effects for her life and then to his unmarried daughters, if any, otherwise to his son John £1,200 for his wife's use in lieu of dower. His slaves amongst his daughters, Elizabeth Christian Potts, Mary Ann Beckles, and Sarah Beckles, and £1,000 to be invested and the interest paid to his wife for life and at her death £500 to be paid to his son Charles, failing him, £200 to Susannah Croft Beckles, Charles's daughter and £300 to such of his daughters as might then be living and £500 to his three daughters named. His brother Richard to enjoy a sum then invested for his life and the residue of his estate to his son John. He appointed his wife Elizabeth, son John and son-in-law William Potts as executors. The Will was proved in Barbados on 13 October, 1791.

Children of Robert[4] and Elizabeth Beckles; all born in Barbados.

---

3. Hon. Henry Peers and George Graeme both married daughters of Samuel Cox, sisters of Thomas[3] Beckles's second wife.

I THOMAS, born 25 February 1744, baptised at Christ Church 25 March 1744. Died in 1745.

II FORTESCUE, born 14 May 1746, baptised there 25 May 1746. Died unmarried in 1791 and buried at St. Philip. Will dated in 1783 was proved 9 August 1791.

III MARGARET, born 18 December 1748.

5. iv. JOHN[5], born 29 April 1751, baptised at Christ Church in May 1752, of whom later.

V CHARLES, born 10 December 1752. Married Sarah Welch and had issue one daughter —
   (1) *Susan Croft Beckles*, born 25th December 1778, married Daniel Parsons 13 Septr. 1803.

VI ELIZABETH CHRISTIAN, baptised at St. Philip 24 August 1759. Married William Potts 5 September 1784 at the parish church of St. Michael. William Potts was a merchant of Baltimore, Maryland, and he took his wife to America and their children were born there. Mrs. Potts's sister, Sarah, seems to have made her home with them in Baltimore and she mentions the names of her nieces and nephews in her will.
   Children of William and Elizabeth Christian—
   (1) *Dr. William Potts*, (2) *Sarah Lee Potts*, (3) *Elizabeth Christian Potts*.

VII MARY ANN, named in her parent's Wills, born 2 April 1757.

VIII SARAH, named in the aforesaid Wills, born 16 July, 1759. She was residing in Frederick County, Maryland, when she made her Will on 22 May, 1812. She gave legacies to her nephew John Alleyne Beckles, her niece Elizabeh Christian Beckles, niece Susannah Croft Beckles daughter of her brother Charles, her cousins Mary Beckles and Susanna Maud Cox. She directed £100 to be invested and the income paid to her negro servant Moll for her life and at her death the sum to be divided between her brother John, sister Elizabeth Christian Potts and sister Mary Ann Beckles, to whom also she gave her Barbados estate. Her shares in the Bank of Maryland and other property in that State to Sarah Lee and Elizabeth Christian, daughters of William Potts, and her nephew Dr. William Potts. The Will was recorded in Barbados on 19 June 1813.

5. JOHN[5] BECKLES (*Robert[4], Thomas[3], Robert[2], Richard[1]*) born 29 April 1751, married before 1778 ELIZABETH HUSBANDS, daughter of Samuel and Susannah Husbands at St. Marylebone Church, London. John[5] Beckles was called to the bar in England, and after the birth of his first child he returned to Barbados to practise his profession.

John[5] Beckles was elected as a member of the House of Assembly of Barbados for the parish of St. Michael on 6 August 1872, being then 31 years of age. His ability was soon recognised, as the records of the House will prove. Poyer, the Historian of Barbados, refers to his powers of eloquence in relating the debates of the House in the year 1784 on certain resolutions put forward in connection with the conduct of Mr. Estwick the Agent of Barbados in London. Poyer says—"The debate was rendered more remarkable by the distinguished part taken by Mr. John Beckles, a young member, who, in support of the motion, gave an early specimen of those commanding powers of eloquence which have since secured him a deserved pre-eminence in the senate and at the bar." Again in the year 1788, Poyer, in referring to the laws generally respecting larceny and the receiving of stolen goods which had proved insufficient to prevent the infamous practice of the community in purchasing cotton and other stolen crops, to the manifest injury of the planters, and the ineffectual efforts of the legislature to remedy those evils, records the part which Beckles took in framing the new laws. Poyer says— "It was reserved for the comprehensive genius and intellectual acumen of Mr. Beckles to devise an effectual remedy for an evil which menaced the industrious planter with ruin; and, if he had given no other proofs of his talents for legislation, his bill to encourage the planting of cotton is sufficient to establish his fame on the firmest basis." The statute in question provided for the appointment of cotton inspectors to guard against fraud by ascertaining the property, growth and produce of the crop, and to issue certificates which would entitle the owner to dispose of the produce. It is interesting to note that this salutary law is still effective, and is the basis on which cotton is still grown and marketed in Barbados.

An interesting sidelight on the character and disposition of John Beckles may be gathered from Poyer's account of his conduct in the House on a particular occasion, when, although he was Solicitor General of the Island he vigorously opposed a measure brought forward by the Government of the time. It seems that a squadron of warships under the command of Sir John Jervis had arrived early in the year 1794 along with a considerable body of troops under the orders of Sir Charles Grey designed to make war upon the French in the West Indies. Mr. Bishop, the President of the Council who was then administering the government had led these veteran commanders to expect considerable reinforcements of men for the navy and the army pressed into service from the local inhabitants. Legislation was passed compelling the owners of slaves to furnish a contingent drawn mainly from slave labour for which they would be compensated, but the suggestion that an Act should be passed to strengthen the hands of the civil power by enabling the magistrates to apprehend seamen of all descriptions met with the blunt refusal of the House. Admiral Jervis's disappointment found expression in a letter to the President, a copy of which accompanied the latter's message to the House. According to Poyer, the letter treated the President and the whole legislature with "equal indelicacy and disrespect", and showed in the strongest terms a degree of impatience for the powerful aid which Sir Charles Grey and he had been taught to expect. The message having been read, Mr. Solicitor General Beckles after some just and spirited remarks on the offensive insinuations thrown out by the admiral, expressed his doubts concerning the propriety of the President's proposals. Willing at all times to afford every necessary aid to His Majesty's forces, the House should take care Mr. Beckles said, not to lose sight of constitutional rights of the subject. Although the impressment of seamen had been sanctioned by custom he was not aware of any act of parliament by which it was expressly authorised. To take up all seamen indiscriminately and send them on board His Majesty's ships would be a most glaring infringement on the liberty of the subject.

Appointed Solicitor General in 1807 and later in the same year Attorney General, Mr. Beckles had a most successful career, continuing in the office until the time of his death on 4 December 1823 in his 73rd year. He had represented the parish of St. Michael in the Assembly from 1782 to 1819, a period of 37 years, and was Speaker of the House fourteen years.

Hon. John Beckles was the owner of the plantations Baxters in St. Andrew and the Bay Estate in St. Michael. The Bay Estate was then a large sugar plantation with its lands stretching from the high ridge on which is the Garrison Savannah down to the sea as far as Charles Fort, and thence in the direction of the town past the Bay Mansion and back to Culloden Farm. About 1789 the War Department acquired about 20 acres of this land in the Garrison District divided off and sold to them by Mr. Beckles. Other portions of the Estate in and around Upper Bay Street were sold off for building purposes, and eventually the area of the plantation under cultivation became considerably reduced. On the death of John[5] Beckles, his son John Alleyne[6] became possessed of the property, and again on the latter's death in 1840 it passed to his children, subject to charges which their grandfather, John[5] Beckles had made upon it for legacies under his Will. In 1842 the property consisted of 107 acres, and through the fall in the price of sugar the plantation was placed in Chancery and was appraised to £16,425.

The Estate was purchased out of Chancery by Robert Hunte, (son-in-law of John Alleyne[6] Beckles) and John S. Sainsbury, and afterwards Robert Hunte became the sole owner by purchase of his co-owners share. Robert Hunte died in 1864 and left the plantation to his only child Robert Beckles Hunte, whose descendants are still the owners of the Estate.

There is an ancient and imposing mansion fronting on Bay Street which was occupied by Hon. John[5] Beckles and his family and afterwards by his son John Alleyne[6] Beckles as his principal place of residence. It was one of the very few houses in that part of St. Michael which withstood the hurricane of 1831, only the roof sustaining damage.

To the south of the mansion was the well-known Beckles Spring, a major source of supply of water to the inhabitants of the town before the water mains were laid from country reservoirs. It was also the source of the supply of water to ships in the bay, which were brought to anchor as near to the shore as possible and the water was raised by windmills and delivered to the vessels.

The Bay Estate sugar works stood on high ground at the top of Beckles Road near the present Wanderer's Cricket Fields. Sugar cultivation and manufacture were abandoned some years ago, and the lands of the Estate are now let in allotments to tenants.

Children of John[5] and Elizabeth Beckles:

6 I JOHN ALLEYNE[6], born 10 June 1778 in Saville Row, St. James's, London.

II SUSANNA MARY DEHANY, born 3 January 1780, baptised 19 January. Married WILLIAM HENERY 6 March 1800 at St. Michael, Barbados.
Children named in Will of Grandfather, John Beckles —

(1) *Susannah Beckles Henery*, married her cousin Samuel Husbands Beckles, son of John Alleyne[6] Beckles.

(2) *Mary Elizabeth Graeme Henery*, died single 3 October 1851.

(3) *William*, died in Barbados November 1817 of yellow fever.

III ELIZABETH CHRISTIAN, born 21 February 1781, baptised 26 March at St. Peter's parish, Barbados. Married 22 January 1807 Robert Augustus Hyndman, then a member of the Council of the Island of Dominica, B.W.I. The Hyndmans came from Nevis and Antigua. Hon. Robert A. Hyndman died 24 July 1814 at his plantation Rome in the colony of Demerara. His widow, Elizabeth Christian, died in London on 9 September 1834. See the Gentleman's Magazine for that year.

155

Hon. John Alleyne Beckles

She was living at Gloucester Lodge, Old Brapton, near London, on 6 October 1828 when her Aunt, Miss Mary Ann Beckles (her father's sister) died there.
Children of Robert A. and Elizabeth Christian Hyndman —

(1) *John Beckles Hyndman* of Botley's Park, Surrey, England. Married 1 January 1839 at Cheltenham, England, Caroline, Seyliard, second daughter of the late Henry Adams Mayers of Redland, near Bristol, formerly of Barbados.

(2) *Elizabeth,* probably born in Demerara. Died in 1835 at Torquay, Devon, England, of a decline. She is said to have left by Will a trust fund of £80,000 for building Churches in England.

IV MARGARET ANN, born 7 September 1782, baptised at St. Michael 2 October. Died 2 September 1785 and buried at St. Michael.

V SARAH ANN, born 22 September 1785, baptised at St. Michael 3 October and buried there 6 October 1785.

VI MARY ANN, born 29 December 1789, baptised 21 January 1790 at St. Michael. She was always called Margaret Ann, although baptized Mary Ann. Died 1 May 1868.

6. JOHN ALLEYNE[6] BECKLES, (*John[5]*, *Robert[4]*, *Thomas[3]*, *Robert[2]*, *Richard[1]*) born 10 June 1778 at Saville Row, London. Married 8 February 1800 ELIZABETH SPOONER, youngest daughter of Hon. John Spooner, President of H.M. Council of Barbados. Died 14 July 1840. His widow, Elizabeth Beckles, died 25 August 1868 at Durham Villa, Adelaide Road, (?London).

Nothing is recorded of his early life except that he is said to have received his education in England and became a student at one of the Inns of Court, but he left England to return to Barbados without having been called to the bar. In 1800 soon after he attained his majority, he received a license from the Governor of Barbados admitting him to practise as a barrister in the Courts of the Island. Later in the year 1807 he was appointed as Assistant Registrar of the Courts, that is, as deputy to the holder of the patent office who resided in England. In 1804 he secured the important office of Secretary of the Island and Remembrancer. In those days the Island Courts of Common Pleas were divided into five precincts each presided over by a Chief Judge (not necessarily a legally trained man) and a number of assistants, the office of Chief Judge being regarded as a high place of honour as well as profit. Relinquishing his post as Deputy Secretary he was presented with the office of Chief Judge of the St. Andrew precinct in 1807, but was transferred later in the same year to the Court of St. Peter, afterwards being appointed to Christ Church (1822) and lastly to the highest office in the precincts, namely, St. Michael, which he received in July 1829. In 1807 he had also been granted the important and lucrative position of Chief Judge of the Court of Vice Admiralty of Barbados. He was called to a seat in H.M. Council of Barbados in about the year 1830 and the Presidency of the Council falling vacant in 1833 he was appointed to that office as the crowning feature of his distinguished career. In 1836, having resigned the lucrative position of Chief Judge of the Court of Common Pleas for St. Michael, he was voted an annuity of £500 per annum as President of the Council, which he was to receive whether he was administering the Government of the Island in the absence of the Governor or not. He retained his Presidency and his Judgeship of the Court of Vice Admiralty until his death.

President Beckles administered the Government of Barbados as acting Governor on three occasions during the absence abroad of the Governor.

Hon. John Alleyne[6] Beckles was initiated into the order of Freemasonry by the Albion Lodge No. 333 of Barbados, and such was his interest and proficiency in the craft that not many years after, he was appointed Right Worshipful Provincial Grand-Master of Freemasons on the English Registry in Barbados. His installation as Provincial Grand-Master took place at the Temple in Bridgetown on Saint John the Evangelist's Day, 27 December, 1817. He continued to hold that high office until his death, having filled it with the greatest dignity and wisdom and contributing largely to the flourishing condition of the craft in Barbados during the period of his leadership.

On 14 July, 1840, at the age of sixty-two, he closed a career noted for its brilliance and devotion to public duty. It seems that on the previous morning, as he sat to breakfast, apparently in perfect health, he was seized with a fit of apoplexy, and became totally paralysed, being unable to speak again, and he died on the following morning about nine o'clock. In recording his death, the editor of a local newspaper stated that he would long be remembered for his truly charitable and benevolent heart, his great urbanity of manners, amiable temper and great humility. The newspaper was printed within heavy black borders and gave an account of the funeral which took place at the Cathedral and Parish Church of St. Michael. The cortege took its way from the Bay Mansion to the Church, forming a long procession comprising the Members of the Council, most of the public officers, heads of military and naval departments, and the entire Masonic Body, arriving at the church at 1.30 p.m. The service was performed by the Ven.

Archdeacon, the Rector of St. Michael, and Rev. Cummins. Masonic Services then concluded the ceremonies.

The actual place of interment in the graveyard is not marked, but there is an imposing monument to the memory of the deceased on the wall of the Cathedral Church east of the north door:—

ARMS.—On a shield, the Arms of the United Grand Lodge of England.

Below the tablet is—

CREST.—A dexter arm in armour, in the hand a cross pattée fitchée.

ARMS.—Argent, a chevron between three like crosses, all Gules; impaling: Azure, in bend a boar's head couped guttee de sang.

MOTTO.—QUOD POTES ID TENTES.

SACRED TO THE MEMORY OF
THE HONOURABLE JOHN ALLEYNE BECKLES
FOR MANY YEARS PRESIDENT OF THIS ISLAND;
JUDGE OF THE COURT OF VICE ADMIRALTY,
AND PROVINCIAL GRAND-MASTER
OF THE FREE AND ACCEPTED MASONS OF BARBADOS
HE DEPARTED THIS LIFE ON THE FOURTEENTH DAY OF JULY
ONE THOUSAND EIGHT HUNDRED AND FORTY
AGED SIXTY TWO YEARS.

Anxious on all occasions to promote
the general welfare of the craft
ever foremost to stretch forth
the hand of fellowship
and minister to the wants of a distressed brother
His easiness of access and urbanity of manners
won for him the affections of the whole masonic body
by whom this marble is erected
as a sincere but trifling token
of their deep regret for the loss
and great esteem and regard for the character
of their departed grand master.
"Let us hold Fast the profession of our faith".

Children of John Alleyne[6] and Elizabeth Beckles :
  i. SARAH ELIZABETH SPOONER[7], born 12 December, 1800, baptised at St. Michael, 12 February, 1801. Married 2 December, 1830 at St. Michael to Rev. Thomas Rochford Redwar, Master of the Boys' Central School and Curate of St. Matthew's Chapel. They went to reside in England where he died 1 January, 1866 and she died 23 December, 1866.

ii. SUSANNA MARY, born 10 March, 1802, baptised at St. Michael, 7 April, 1802. Died a spinster in England, 5 August, 1866.

iii. CHRISTIAN MARGARET MAXWELL, born...................... baptised 16 January, 1806, at St. James's parish, Barbados. Died unmarried at St. Michael, 11 October, 1821.

iv. HANNAH MARIA HUSBANDS, born........................, baptised 24 October, 1807. Married 20 July, 1826 at St. Michael to Robert Hunte of St. Philip, Barbados. Robert Hunte died at Ryde, Isle of Wight, on 28 August, 1864. Mrs. Hunte was living at South Norwood, Surrey, in 1869. Their only child was *Robert Beckles Hunte*, born at St. Michael, 20 April, 1831.

v. JOHN ALLEYNE, born 22 June, 1810, baptised 15 August, 1810 at St. James's parish, Barbados. Married Mary Lee Hill, second daughter of the late William Hill of H.M. Customs in Trinidad and formerly of Barbados, at St. Pancras Church, London, on 16 May, 1836. John Alleyne Beckles, the younger was called to the bar in England, and succeeded his father in 1840 as Judge of the Court of Vice Admiralty in Barbados. In the following year he went to England, and on 2 September, 1841, six days after his arrival there, he died at Preston.

Children of the marriage :

(1) *John Alleyne[8] Beckles,* born at the Bay Estate, 13 April, 1837, baptised at St. Michael, 17 May, 1837. Married Ellen Gall. Died in England on 27 June, 1867. Ellen Beckles was living in Islington, Middlesex, England, in 1869.

(2) *William Augustus Beckles,* baptised at St. Michael, 2 January, 1839.

(3) *Henry Cromartie,* born August, 1840, baptised 6 September, 1840. Died 11 September, 1840. having lived only 24 days.

vi. WILLIAM AUGUSTUS, born 12 August, 1812, baptised at St. James's Church, 6 September, 1812. Married 12 January, 1836, Mary Anne Smith King, who predeceased him. He was educated at Codrington College, Barbados, and ordained a Priest of the Church of England at the Cathedral on 7 January 1837. He was presented to a benefice in the colony of Berbice, where he died on 23 October 1840 after three days illness of fever. He had married secondly Sarah Saunders, who bore him two girl children. These facts appear in the documents of title of the Bay Estate. In one

160

of these documents made in 1842 one of the parties *Sarah Catherine Beckles* is named as the widow and relict of Rev. Wm. Augustus Beckles late of the Colony of British Guiana, and it is recited that he had died leaving two infant children named Sarah Elizabeth Bruce Beckles and Augusta Ann Beckles, who were then entitled to his share in the Bay Estate under his father's Will, subject to the dower of their mother, Sarah Christian therein. Mrs. Sarah Christian Beckles afterwards married ———— McNaughton and resided at St. Anne's, near Montreal, Canada. Her daughter Augusta Ann Beckles was living at Bout de Lisle, Montreal, in 1869.

   vii. SAMUEL HUSBANDS, born 12 April 1814, baptised 16 May at St. Michael. He was called to the bar by the Middle Temple, London, and was F.R.S., F.R.G.S., etc. Married on 17 July 1838 at Christ Church, Mary-le-bone, London, to his cousin, Susannah Beckles Henery, daughter of William Henery, then deceased. They were living at No. 9, Grand Parade, St. Leonard's on Sea, Sussex, in 1869.

7. viii. EDWARD HYNDMAN, born 14 February 1816, baptised at St. James, Barbados, 10 March 1816.

   ix. CAROLINE FRANCES ANN, born 29 May 1818. Was a spinster living with her sister Julia Amelia at South Norwood, Surrey, in 1860. Died in 1884.

   x. JULIA AMELIA WORRELL, born 30 December 1820, baptised at St. Michael, 17 March 1821. Living at South Norwood, Surrey in 1869. Died in 1888.

  7. EDWARD HYNDMAN BECKLES[7], (*John Alleyne*[6], *John*[5], *Robert*[4], *Thomas*[3], *Robert*[2], *Richard*[1]), born 14 February 1816, baptised at St. James, Barbados, 10 March 1816. Married first 29 August 1837, at St. Michael's Cathedral, Margaret Simpson Walcott, youngest daughter of Edward Brace Walcott, then deceased. Served in Her Majesty's Customs in Barbados from the year 1836 until 1841. Ordained Deacon in 1843 by the Bishop of Barbados, who presented him with a curacy at the Church of the Holy Trinity in Trinidad. Ordained Priest 4 May 1844, and appointed incumbent of St. Michael's parish, Trinidad, at the special request of Sir Henry McLeod, the governor; was also Chaplain to the troops stationed in that island; laboured for some time in the diocese of London, returned to the West Indies and served as Rector of a Church in St. Christopher, returned to England in 1858 and officiated for a short time in the diocese of Winchester, where his unceasing and indefatigable labours brought him under the special notice of the Archbishop of Canterbury. On 17 November 1859 he was nominated by the Archbishop as

RT. REV. EDWARD HYNDMAN BECKLES

bishop of Sierra Leone and consecrated on 2 February 1860 at Lambeth. He resigned that see in 1869 and in the same year he was appointed Minister of Berkeley Chapel, Mayfair, then in 1870 rector of Wooten, Dover, and in 1873 rector of St. Peter's Bethnal Green, London. In February 1877 he was appointed Superintendent Bishop of the English Episcopalian Congregation in Scotland[4].

Bishop Beckles's first wife died in England in 1900, and he married, secondly, in 1901, Selina Mary, eldest daughter of Peter Blake, then deceased. He died at the age of eighty-six in England on 5 December 1902.

Children of the first marriage:—

8. i. EDWARD HYNDMAN[8], born at the Bay Estate, baptised at St. Michael, 29 August 1838.

ii. JOHN ALLEYNE, born 28 February 1840 at the Bay Estate, baptised 22 April 1840 at St. Michael. Died 26 August 1840 aged six months.

9.iii. JOHN ALLEYNE, no record of birth or baptism. Married Harriett Harrison and had issue.

iv. MARGARET SIMPSON, born in Trinidad 5 July 1844.

v. HENRY MC LEOD, born 28 May 1846. Married Charlotte Victoria Dodson and had issue.

vi. WILLIAM AUGUSTUS, born 7 November 1849, married Helen Maud Sainsbury.

vii. SAMUEL HUSBANDS, died within twelve hours of birth.

viii. SAMUEL HUSBANDS, born 27 May 1852, married Caroline Jane Terry and had issue.

ix. ROBERT BRACE FISK, born 2 October 1854, married Mrs, —— Rogers.

x. MARY ELIZABETH, born 10 January 1857.

8. EDWARD HYNDMAN[8] BECKLES (*Edward Hyndman[7], John Alleyne[6], John[5], Robert[4], Thomas[3], Robert[2], Richard[1].*) born at the Bay Estate, Barbados, 23 July, 1838, baptised at St. Michael, 29 August, 1838. Educated at London House, London, and also at Morden Hall, Surrey; Served in the Commissariat and H.M. Civil Service, Control Staff in Sierra Leone. Married on 14 July, 1862, in England Elizabeth Reece Haynes, youngest daughter of Henry Husbands Haynes of The Bath plantation, Barbados. He died at Sierra Leone, 23 July, 1872. Mrs. Edward Hyndman Beckles died in Barbados.

---

4. Authorities: Crockford; Men of the Time, 1887. Who Was Who, 1897—1916. The statement in these publications that Bishop Beckles was educated at Codrington College, Barbados, appears to be incorrect. His name is not on the College Rolls, although we find that of his brother, William Hyndman Beckles. He received the Lambeth Degree of D.D. on his consecration.

Children of the marriage:—

i. EDWARD HYNDMAN[9], born 22 May, 1863, died 11 August, 1863.

ii. EDWARD HYNDMAN HAYNES HUNTE, born 12 August, 1867. Married 6 April, 1903, Frances Wilhelmina Woodfall. They had issue one son who died in infancy. He died in Australia, about 1928.

iii. ELIZABETH REECE, born 13 July, 1864. Married 10 October, 1894 at St. Paul's, Grove Park, Chiswick, by Rt. Rev. Bishop Beckles, her grandfather, Earwaker Carrington Haynes, second son of John Torrance and Catherine Garrett Haynes of Bush Hall, Barbados. Elizabeth Reece Haynes died in Barbados on 26 July, 1930. Earwaker Carrington Haynes married secondly Gertrude Jones, daughter of Hon. Thomas Jones and Annie Blades his wife. He died in Barbados on 12 September, 1933.

Only child of the first marriage:—

(1) *Edward John Earwaker Haynes,* born 3 December, 1903. Married 14 June, 1930, Marie Thelma Archer, daughter of Tom Archer.

9. JOHN ALLEYNE BECKLES[8], (*Edward Hyndman[7], John Alleyne[6], John[5], Robert[4], Thomas[3], Robert[2], Richard[1]*), born at the Bay Estate, Barbados. Married Harriett Harrison, daughter of Sir John Harrison. Educated at Christ's Hospital and King's College, London. Appointed to a clerkship in ordnance survey department, Southampton, 1859; private secretary to the Governor of Gambia, 1860; gazetted as lieutenant in the Gambia Militia Artillery, and served in the expedition against the robber king of Baddiboo, was present at the taking of Kinto, Cunda, and Sabba, 1861; Lieut. of the Sierra Leone Militia, served under Colonel Hill against the King of the Quiah country, acting as quarter-master and adjutant; 1862 appointed private secretary to the Governor of Lagos. Ordained deacon July 1864; priest January 1866; appointed curate of St. Ambrose, Barbados, August 1864; transferred to curacy in St. George same year, and thence to the curacy of St. Paul, Grenada, in February 1867; appointed rector of the united parishes of St. John, St. Mary and St. Paul in Island of Tobago in August, 1867. Afterwards Canon of Singapore.

Died (date unknown) and left issue surviving him.

BECKLES:

AN INTERESTING ACQUISITION

Whilst on a visit to London last year, Mr. J. E. Warmington, a member of the Society, discovered an 18th, century mourning ring with the name of a member of the Beckles family of Barbados, which he purchased on behalf of the Museum Collections Fund for 15 guineas.   The ring is 22 carat gold and is set with a square-cut crystal between two smaller diamonds. The design of the surrounding ring is a series of 8 scrolls enamelled in white and inscribed:

CHA: | BECKLES | OB: 24 | NOV: 1751 | : AE 27

According to the parish register of St. Philip's Church, Charles Beckles was buried there on 25th, November 1751.   He was unmarried and left no will. He was the 9th Child of Hon. Thomas Beckles by his second wife Maud, daughter of Samuel and Elizabeth Cox.   Hon. Thomas Beckles represented St. Michael in the House of Assembly from 1708 to 1710 and until his death in 1734 was Chief judge of the Common Pleas of St. Michael.

*See "Beckles of Barbados", *B M.. & H. S. Journal*, Vol. XII, pp. 3—19.   At page 7. there is an omission of a figure in the date of the death of Charles Beckles which is given as 4 November 1751, instead of 24 November 1751. **

** Page 150, this volume.

Beddall, or Biddle, of Barbados.[†]

DEATHS.

1665	Jan. 6	Mary.	1704	July 1	James, a child.
1670	July 15	John, a child.	1706	April 25	Jeri.
1674	Oct. 11	John.	1715	Oct. 23	Jacob, child.
1677	Dec. 17	Robert Bidwell, a seaman.	1716	July 3	Thomas.
			1717	July 13	James, a child.
1680	Mar. 23	William Biddale.	1719	Dec. 29	John Beedle.
1690	Jan. 13	William Biddale.	1724	Feb. 27	Sarah Biddle (Mrs., widow).
1697	Oct. 19	Mrs. Biddle.			
1700	Nov. 5	Mary Ann, child.	1726/7	Feb. 25	Anne, wife of Capt. Jacob Boddle, in their garden.
1702	Nov. 17	Jeremiah, child.			
1703	May 12	Joseph, child.			
—	May 25	Solomon (Mrs.).	1726*	—	Benjamin.

BIRTHS.

1662	Mar. 30	William son of William.
1663	Dec. 29	Mary dr of William.
1665	June 11	William.
1668	April 5	John.
1670	May 10	Jeremiah.
1673	June 29	John.
1700	Oct. 13	Mary Ann dr of Jeremiah and Sarah.
1702	Sept. 27	Jeremiah s. of Jeremiah and Sarah.
1703	April 23	Joseph Mr Solomon and Mrs Elizabeth.
1703	Aug. 25	James s. of Jeremiah and Sarah.
1704	June 12	Benjamin s. of Captain Jacob and Mrs Ann.
1706	June 4	Sarah dr of Jeremiah and Sara.
1706	—	Henry s. of Captain Jacob and Mrs Ann.
1708	May 29	Joseph s. of Captain Jacob and Mrs Ann.
1726	—	Mahittabell ⎫
	—	Esther ⎪ Children of Captain Jacob and Mrs Ann.
	—	Eliza ⎬ Mrs Mary Boddle one of the godmothers.
	—	Ann ⎭

* Or 1716.   † Communicated by Mr. N. Darnell Davis.

BENSON RECORDS

The name BENSON often occurs in the records of the XVII century in Barbados.

In a list of the inhabitants who owned more than ten acres of land in the year 1638 given in *Memoirs of the First Settlement of the Island of Barbados* is the name Robert Benson. It is uncertain whether this Robert Benson is identical with (1) Robert Benson of St. Peter who made his will in 1673 and died later in the same year, (2) Ensign [1] Robert Benson, senior, whose name figures in several title deeds of land and whose will, dated 2 October, 1667, was proved and recorded in the year 1674, or with (3) Robert Benson, who was buried in St. John on 15 December 1667.

Robert Benson of St. Peter left two sons, Thomas and Benjamin and a daughter, Mary. Ensign Robert Benson and Katherine, his wife, had issue four sons and one daughter, namely, (Captain) Robert, William, Miles, Francis and Priscilla. Captain Robert Benson married Mary Cheeswright, a widow with two children, and had issue an only child, Mary, who married Captain Thomas Downes. William Benson married Elizabeth Eastmond and had issue a son James and a daughter, Elizabeth. His widow Elizabeth married James Kincaed, 23 August, 1683. He died on 21 April, 1686 and she died on 19 Dec. following. Her will is indexed under the letter B. as she is therein referred to as Elizabeth Kinked alias Benson. Priscilla Benson married, first, Lieut. Bix Alleyne, son of Reynold and Mary (Skeet) Alleyne, [2] and secondly, Jeffrey Battaley of St. Peter, 3 January, 1678. Battaley died in 1695. [3]

Francis Benson appears in the Census Records of the year 1679 as living in the Parish of St. John and owning 6 negroes and 15 acres of land. The only other Benson named in the Census Records is Mary, then living in St. Peter, with 2 Christian servants, 22 negroes and 40 acres of land. She was almost certainly the daughter of Robert Benson of St. Peter who succeeded to his plantation and other property.

BENSON WILLS

Will of ROBERT BENSON of St. Peter, Barbados.

To wife, Mary, all my estate for her life provided she does not marry; otherwise to my daughter, Mary Benson, to be immediately divided on my said wife's marriage, i.e. 50 acres of land, together with all my houses etc. situate in the parish of St. Peter, bounding on lands of William Davis, of John Maniford, of John Tothill. west upon the sea, together with 36 negroes, cattle and utensils upon my said plantation, to her and her heirs for ever. To my son Thomas Benson, 10,000 lbs. [4] to be paid one year after my decease and likewise 10,000 lbs to my son Benjamin. Daughter, Mary, to be sole executrix immediately after her mar-

---

1. Title of rank denoting the lowest commissioned officer of foot.
2. See *Alleyne Pedigree, B.M. & H.S. Journal,* Vol. 3, P. 105.*
3. The name Battaley survived as that of a plantation of 64 acres in St. Peter.
   Extracts from Will of Jeffrey Battaley — The last July 1694 I. Jeffreys Battalley of St. John. To wife Priscilla all my estate during widowhood she maintaining and educating my two youngest children, John and Katherine and if she remarry to have only one-third for her life in lieu of dower. After wife's death estate to be divided amongst my four children, Samuel, Edward, John and Katherine at 21. Appoint my trusty friends Mr. Henry Combes and Mr. Thomas Fox executors; each to have a gold ring of 20/- (sd) Jeffereys Battalley. Witnesses: mark of Thomas Wickham, mark of Mary Connell, Francis Mellichame. Proved by Oath of both witnesses 18 July 1695 and recorded same day.
4. Evidently lbs. of muscovado sugar.

*Page 8, this volume.

riage or when she becomes 16 years, and in the meantime Colonel Richard Bayne to be executor and guardian of Mary during her minority.

Dated 12 June 1673. (sd.) Robert Benson. Witnesses: Wm. Baylie, Richard Baylie. Proved by Oath of William Baylie, 30 Sep. 1673. Recorded 15 Novr., 1673.

Will of GRACE BENSON of St. Michael, Barbados.

To son-in-law, John Frederick, 500 lbs. sugar. To Judith, daughter of Henry Hunt; to Elizabeth Goddin and Henry Hunt jr. and his brother, Richard Hunt, and to Roger Rumbolt, various articles.

Appoints Henry Hunt sole exor.

Dated 4 Feb. 1672. (sd.) Grace Benson by her mark.

Witnesses: Bryan Roach, Wm. Goddin, and Mary Wakefield.

Proved 4 August, 1674, by Bryan Roach and Mary Wakefield.

Will of ROBERT BENSON, senior, of St. John, Barbados.

To my eldest son, Robert Benson, the plantation whereon I now live and all my estate both real and personal both here and in England, except what I hereby dispose of, to him and the heirs of his body and in default of issue then to my son, William Benson and his heirs and in default of issue to my son Miles Benson, and then to my son Francis Benson and his heirs and in default of heirs to my daughter Priscilla and her heirs.

Appoint son, Robert, sole executor. To wife, Katherine, if it should please God to restore her to her understanding, one-third of the plantation whereon I now live for her life, but if she does not so recover to be decently kept and maintained at the discretion of my executor.

To son, William £440. To son, Miles, £600 to be paid when he comes out of his apprenticeship. To daughter, Priscilla, all her mother's clothes, jewels, and 50,000 lbs of muscovado sugar at the age of 21 or six months after marriage.

To friends, Lieut. William Consett, Mrs. Elizabeth Consett, Mrs. Sweete, Christopher Codrington Esq., Gaustine Codrington, Thomas Hothersall and his wife, a mourning ring of 10/- each. To Mrs. Deborah Walrond a ring of 10/- price. To Henry Sweete one beaver hat and a ring worth 10/- To William Lesley[5] 1,000 lbs of muscovado sugar. To the poor of St. John's [parish] 2,000 lbs. of like sugar to be paid one year after my decease to the Churchwarden of the said parish for the use of the poor.

If my estate should descend to my younger children before they attain 21 years or marry, then I appoint Henry Sweete Esq., and Henry Walrond, jr. gent, to manage same in the meantime.

Dated 2 October, 1667. (sd) by the mark of Robert Benson.[6] Witnesses: Henry Walrond jr. John Pearnoll, Leonard Duffield. Proved 25 April, 1674; recorded 29 October, 1674.

Codicil to will of ROBERT BENSON, senior. 50,000 lbs of sugar given to my daughter, Priscilla, is now in possession of Henry Sweete, and to remain in his and Henry Walrond jr., hands to get interest for the benefit of my daughter.

Dated 2 October, 1667. (sd.) by mark of Robert Benson. Witnesses: as in the will. Proved and recorded, as in the will.

Will of Captain ROBERT BENSON of St. John, Barbados, Gent. To daughter-in-law,[7] Elizabeth Cheeswright, 30,000 lbs of muscovado sugar, 10,000 to be

---

5. Rector of the parish of St. John, died December 1674.
6. It is remarkable that the testator, being a man of property with prominent connections could not sign his Will and many executed deeds on record otherwise than by his mark.
7. i.e. step-daughter.

168

paid her at age 15, 10,000 at 16, and 10,000 lbs at 17. Likewise two negro women. To son-in-law,[8] John Cheeswright, 20,000 lbs of sugar and six negroes at the age of 21. To daughter, Mary Benson, my plantation of 100 acres of land, together with houses crops, utensils &c., at 21 or marriage, except that one-third is for wife, Mary, during her natural life. Appoint wife sole executrix.

To friends, Henry Sweet and Henry Walrond jr. the best beaver hat each that can be procured. To poor of St. John's parish 1000 lbs. of muscovado sugar to be paid within two years after my decease. To my servant Ann Pouncer 500 lbs. of sugar to be paid her six months after she is free having lawfully served out her time.

Dated 27 November, 1675. (sd.) Robert Benson.
Witnesses: Christopher Codrington, Emanuel Wolfe, Ja. Kyth, Wm. Haynes. Proved by Oath of Henry Walrond Jr. and William Haynes 7 Feb., 1675/6, Recorded 8 Feb., 1675/6.

Will of ALEXANDER BENSON of St. George, Barbados.

To wife, Mary Benson, my plantation in Carolina so long as she is my widow, also the net proceeds of my negroes here in Barbados, but if she shall marry again then to have one-third part of such produce. Should she relinquish her one-third part aforesaid then I give her my plantation in Carolina aforesaid together with the stock thereon for her natural life. None of my negroes to be sold or sent out of the island, but they may be hired out. Negro woman, Jane, to have her freedom with one year after my decease. To friend, Henry Evans, son of Henry Evans, one negro girl. Gives other two thirds of plantation in Carolina to John Best, Susan Perrin (wife of John Perrin) Joseph Best, Alexander Perrin and their heirs to be equally divided between them. One-third of the plantation to wife if she will not take the whole plantation in lieu of the produce of negroes aforesaid. If my wife marries, then I give my sisters, Jane Hodgerson (Hodkinson) and Ellen Ford living in Ireland two-thirds of produce of negroes aforesaid; but if wife takes the plantation in Carolina, then produce of all negroes to be equally divided between aforesaid sisters.

To friend, Peter Evans, 1000 lbs of sugar and appoint him sole executor.
Dated 6 July, 1681. (sd.) Alexand. Benson. Witnesses: John Ellis, James Fenty, Thomas Gibbes. Proved by Oath of Fenty 10 Sep., 1681.

Will of ELIZABETH KINKED alias BENSON, widow.

To son, James Benson, two negroes at 18 years. To daughter, Elizabeth, three negroes and money due me from the estate of my deceased brother, James Eastmond, at 18 years or marriage. Appoint friend and brother-in-law Alexander Parris executor in trust for my children.

Dated 1 Dec., 1686. (sd.) Elizabeth Kinked alias Benson her mark. Witnesses: Alexander Kidney, Christian Holmes, Sa. Williams Proved by Kidney and Williams 30 March 1687. Recorded 29 April, 1687.

BENSON DEEDS

10 March 1640/41. I, Ensign ROBERT BENSON of Barbados, bind myself to pay to Adam Thompson of Barbados, gent, 3600 lbs. of good merchantable cotton woolle cleared from the seeds and other filth or 10,000 lb. of good merchantable tobacco well made up in role at or before 1 June 1642 at some convenient storehouse at ye Indian Bridgetown, for the performance whereof I bind myself

8. i.e. step-son.
9. Otherwise Kincaed.

and my plantation of 50 acres or thereabouts whereon I now live adjoined to the land of Mr. Thomas Hothersall and to the land of Clement Roberts, together with three servants for the full times they have to serve, by name under John Coalte, Xtopher Priskett, with three assinegoes which are now in my possession, by way of mortgage and in default of the premises it shall be lawful for the said Adam Thompson to enter into the premises aforesaid and to enjoy forever without suit of law. (sd). Robert Benson. Witnesses: Xtopher Thompson, John Spence. Recorded 27 August, 1641.

13 January 1643/4. This bill bindeth us, ROBERT BENSON and JOHN CHEESWRIGHT of Barbados, in the sum of 24,000 lbs. of good dye [10] and well cleared cotton wool together with one indigo workhouse and three assinegoes lately purchased with all ye whole estate of either plantation or servants or cattle if we have or enjoy in the said island of Barbados to be paid unto ROBERT HAYNES and FRANCIS DICKENSON the full and just sum of 12,000 lbs. of ye like cotton wool or ye quantity of so much indigo as it will yield in cotton from man to man at ve sea side due to be paid at or before ye last day of June 1645 at some convenient storehouse at ye Indian Bridge. (s) the mark of Robert Benson, John Cheswright. Witnesses: Thomas Kitchin, William Haynes.

9 October 1647. I, Ensign ROBERT BENSON of Barbados, Gent. sell to Capt. CHRISTOPHER CODRINGTON of ye same Island esq., all my right and interest in ye half part of my plantation containing 110 acres lying in ye parish of St. John, together with certain negroes, Christian servants, assinegoes and other cattle as per Schedule, and ye half-part of all profits &c. thereunto belonging. (sd) X of Robert Benson. Witnesses: Miles X Middleton, Edmund Fayrehurst.

Schedule — 6 negroes and one child, 2 Christian servants, 5 assinegoes and one foal, one cow, one heifer, one bull calf, (6 brand hoes, (4) narrow hoes, 2 axes, one hatchet, 4 bills, 2 potts, 3 breeding sows, one boar, one great barrow, 2 sow shoats 3 barrow shoats) (sd) Robert Benson.   All the tools, potts and hogs (within brackets) are agreed to go in partnership between Captain Codrington and Ensigne Benson before ye sealing hereof.

3 September 1656. JOHN RUSSELL of Barbados, sells to Ensigne ROBERT BENSON of Barbados gent. "All that my plantation whereon I now live," 24 acres, bounding east on land of Susan Steede, widow, north on lands of Lt. Col. Wm. Consett, south on land of George Haggice, west on lands of John Padden, with buildings, horses, indigo and timber. Witnesses: Robert Sparrow, Robert Benson, Robert Bond. Recorded 31 October 1656.

6 July. 1657. Ensigne ROBERT BENSON of Barbados, sells THOMAS DUNN of Barbados, planter, All that his plantation lately purchased from John Russell, 24 acres, bounding on lands of Susanna Steed, widow, Lt. Col. Wm. Consett, George Haggies, John Paddine, with houses, woods &c. (sd) X of Robert Benson. Witnesses: Thomas Tuffe, Thomas Cooke, Acknowledged by Robert Benson, 12 May 1658, before Henry Sweete.

11 May, 1659. THOMAS COOPER of Barbados, attorney to Henry Reeves and William Reeves, administrators of ALEXANDER PYOTT and HENRY PYOTT of the One Part and ROBERT BENSON and CHRISTOPHER CODRINGTON, Gent, of the Other Part. Lease of a plantation of 39½ acres, late the plantation of the said Alexander Pyott decd. and late ' in the possession of Captain Thomas Hart, with houses, woods, servants, negroes, hoggs, household stuff, tools &c. as per schedule, for seven years beginning 16 July next ensuing for £40 current money of England to be paid before 15 May in Fenchurch Street,

10. Indigo.

London, at the house of Thomas Cooper. (Here follow terms for maintaining number of slaves, stock &c. otherwise 1000 lbs of muscovado sugar for every negro and 200 lbs. for every hog so wanting) (sd) by Robert Benson and acknowledged by him and Christopher Codrington 11 May 1659 before Henry Sweete. Witnesses: Edward Hussey, Tho. Cooke. Schedule — 39 acres of land, one old dwellinghouse, one table form, one old cook room, one old tobacco house, one small house, one small house for servants to lie in, 3 negro women (named) one negro child, 5 sows, one boar, one copper weighing 70 lb one cross-cut saw, one iron crow, one iron pott, one English servant by name John Bowman to serve, the Said Christopher Codrington paying his wages.

15 February 1660. CHRISTOPHER CODRINGTON of Barbados, Esq. sells ROBERT BENSON of Barbados All that his plantation called Old Guyes plantation, 140 acres in the Parish of St. John, bounding on lands of Henry Sweete Esq. James Goldingham, Lt. Col. Wm. Consett and Henry Coulson. (sd) Christopher Codrington, Witnesses: Fer. Gorges, Phill. Lancaster, Theo Cooke, Recorded 17 July 1661.

1 May, 1670. ROBERT BOWMAN of Barbados, planter, sells to Capt. ROBERT BENSON of Barbados, 2 negro women, by name Maria and Rose, one negro boy named Jack and one negro child named Diana, one milch cow, two breeding sows, one boar, one small goat, three pigs; the said R. Bowman paying to the said R. Benson the yearly rent of 2500 lbs of muscovado sugar according to the time and place mentioned in an indenture of lease made by the said R. Benson bearing even date with these presents, being for ten acres of land for seven years. (sd) Robert Bowman his mark, Witnesses: William Harris, Willian Haynes, Francis Benson. 7 May 1670 acknowledged by Robert Bowman before E. Sweete Recorded 18 May, 1670.

2 October, 1672. Indenture between Captain ROBERT BENSON of St. John, Barbados, of the one part and MARY PYOTT of Tring in the county of Harford, spinster, the only daughter and sole heiress of Major Alexander Pyott late of the said parish of St. John deceased, of the other part. WHEREAS the said Mary Pyott by indenture of lease of even date has let to the said Captain ROBERT BENSON All that plantation in St. John's 39½ acres, which was late the plantation of the said Major Alexander Pyott deceased and late in the tenure of Captain Thomas Harte, and all houses &c. for the term of nine years commencing 6 May last for rent of £30 stlg. payable 16 May every year in the insurance office of the Royal Exchange in London; it was witnessed that the said Robert Benson granted unto the said Mary Pyott and her heirs 6 negroes (named) as security for his due performance of the terms of the said lease. (sd) Robert Benson. Witnesses: William Haynes, Henry Gorges, James Elliott, F. Foster. Recorded 2 June 1683.

Memorandum. Whereas Mary Pyott hath at my request made a lease to Robert Benson of a plantation in Barbados as per an indenture in my hand and I do promise to obtain a mortgage from Captain Robert Benson and to deliver same to her, and I will not deliver the lease until I have procured and delivered the mortgage to Mary Pyott. (sd) Fer Georges.

10 July 1686. GEORGE HANNAY, Marshall of H.M. Court of Common Pleas. in consideration of judgment recovered by Francis Benson, Jeffrey Battalia[11] and Priscilla his wife against Captain Thomas Downes and Mary his wife, executrix of Robert Benson jr. deceased eldest son and sole executor of Robert Benson, his father, deceased, as they the said Francis and Priscilla are the only

11. The correct name was Battaley.

surviving children of the said Robert Benson, senior, deceased, have sold to the said Francis Benson, Jeffrey Battalia and Priscilla his wife eleven acres of land, butting on the north and east on lands of Esther Foster, south on the said Downes and west on Hon. John Hothersall Esq., the said Captain Thomas Downes and the said Hester Forster; being appraised at the rate of £18 stlg. per acre, equal to £198 stlg, as per plot of same hereto annexed by John Combles, Sworn Surveyor, and attached for satisfaction of £198 stlg. (s) George Hannay, Sgt. at Arms. Witnesses: Thomas Walker, Thomas Poore. Memorandum 12 July 1686, quiet and peaceable possession of eleven acres of land within mentioned by tuft and twigge was then given to the said Francis Benson, Jeffrey Battalia and Priscilla his wife. (sd.) George Hannay, Sgt. at Arms. Witnesses: Thomas Miller, Richard Downes. Plan appended.

BENSON BAPTISMS to 1700 — none on record.

BENSON MARRIAGES 1643—1700

Parish	Date	Names of Parties
St. John	3 Feb. 1667	Captain Robert Benson and Mary Cheeswright.
„	3 Sep. 1668	William Benson and Elizabeth Eastmond.
„	6 Jul. 1669	Priscilla Benson and Lt. Bix Allen.
„	23 Aug. 1683	Elizabeth Benson and James Kincaed.
St. M.	19 May 1690	Elizabeth Benson and Richard Painter.

BENSON BURIALS 1643—1700

St. M.	2 Apl. 1651	Ann Benson
„	12 Dec. 1654	Susanna wife of Henry Benson
St. John	30 Dec. 1669	Katherine daughter of William Benson.
„	25 Aug. 1659	Sarah daughter of Robert Benson.
„	15 Dec. 1667	Robert Benson
St. M.	12 Oct. 1672	Henry Benson
„	4 May 1673	Grace Benson
St. Phil.	12 Jul. 1681	Alexander Benson
St. John	28 Aug. 1685	John Benson
„	22 Sep. 1686	William son of Francis Benson
„	19 Dec. 1686	Elizabeth Benson alias Elizabeth Kincaed.
„	7 Oct. 1691	Major Francis Benson
St. M.	24 Dec. 1692	Peter Benson
St. John	28 Apl. 1692	Francis Benson
St. M.	24 Jan. 1696/7	George Benson.

Blackman of Antigua and Barbados.

The following list is written on a double sheet of folio paper, bearing " G.R." on the water-mark. It is unfortunately not signed nor dated, but it was probably drawn up by Rowland Blackman in or soon after 1726, when settling his late father's affairs.

The deeds relate to the Blackmans' plantations in Antigua and Barbados, both called " *Mount Lucie*," which had descended to them by marriage from the family of Messrs. Lucie, who were wealthy Anglo-Dutch merchants, with extensive dealings in the West Indies during the seventeenth century.

Endorsed " a List of papers left in Bdoes."

Counterpart of y[e] Demise from M[r] Prissick to Madam Weyman, 1716.

Lease for a year for One Moiety of a plantation in North Sound Division and of One Other Moyety of a plantation in new Division both in the Isl[d] of Antigua 1724.

Assignment of Arrears of Rent and Other personal Estate of M[r] Christopher Prissick* in Antigua.   M[rs] Prissick to Coll Frye.†

and Indenture of Covenant for Sale of y[e] plantation and real Est[e] of y[e] s[d] M[r] Prissick in Antigua, 1719.   the s[d] M[rs] Prissick to Coll Frye.

Demise from M[r] Prissick to Madam Weyman, 1716.

Assignm[ts] of Arrears of Rent of plantations in Antigua, 1722.

M[rs] Prissick to M[r] Cotton and Frye.

---

* He had married Sarah, dau. of Col. John Codrington of Barbados, & in his will dated in 1717 & p. in 1720 (162, Shaller) describes all his lands in Yorkshire, & states that his wife was entitled to one-third of the Island of Barbuda. He was evidently a retired planter.

† Col. John Frye, d. 1747-8, æ. 78.

Lease for a year of a moyety of two plantations in Antigua, 1722.
Mrs Prissick to Mr Cotton and Mr Frye.
Release of a moyety of two plantations in Antigua, 1722.
Mrs Prissick to Mr Cotton and Mr Frye.
Assignm^t of 1000 years of Mr Prissick's plantation in Antigua, 1722.
Mrs Weyman and al.
to Mr Burgoyne and al. in trust for Mr Cotton and Mr Frye.
Release* of One Moyety of a plantation in North Sound Division and of One
Other Moyety of a plantation in new Division both in ye Island of Antigua, 1724.
Assignm^{ts} of moyetys of plantations in Antigua, 1725.
Mr Duke to Mr Burgoyne and al.
and Copys of ye general Release and acco^t of ye deposition of Mr Jonathan
Ayleworth affixt.
A Writ of Partition of ye plantation in Antigua.
Giles Watkins's acco^t in 1699.
Plantation acco^{ts} of Mrs Mary Gilmore* in 1699 to 1702.
Bills of lading for Sug^{rs} shipt in Antigua.
Edwd Byam and al. Attorneys to Mrs Gilmore and Mrs Weyman their power
to John L. Blackman to repair ye buildings, etc.
Mr Bowyers bill of Sale to Jacob Lucie and Harris of his third part of all y^e
lands in Antigua.
Lucie Blackman's Will.†
Willoughby Byam and Edwd Byam's bill of sale to Jacob Lucie and Rob.
Gilmore of 30 acres of land.
Jacob Lucie & Co's patent.‡
Mr Prissick's Letters and answers to them.
Letters to Capt: Duer.§
Letters from Coll. Frye.
An Acco^t of payments made by Mr Cotton received from Coll. Frye.
Inventory of ye Estate in 1726.
Sundry lists of Negroes and Cattle on ye plantation in Antigua.
The Case of Division of ye Est^e in Antigua stated, and Mr Attorney Genl
Carter's Opinion on ye Queries.
The Petition of Coll. Frye in behalf of John Lucie Blackman against y^e
20 p̄ Cent. being laid on ye non-Residents, granted.
John L. Blackman's Patent.‖
Several Letters to John L. Blackman in Antigua.
Petition to his Excellency Walter Hamilton‖ to confirm ye patent for y^e
Island, granted.
power of Attorney from Rowl^d Blackman to John Frye.
Sundry Acco^{ts} in 2 bundles from Merc^{ts} and tradesmen in Antigua.
Miles Toppin's Acco^t.
Plantation Acco^{ts} in Antigua.
a parcel of loose papers.
the plot of ye plantation in Antigua.
Rowl^d Blackman to John Blackman lease for a year.
Rowl^d Blackman to D^o Mortgage of lands in Antigua for £2000 and
John Lucie Blackman to Rowl^d Blackman Lease for a year.

* See "Antigua," i., 47, for Close Roll indentures of 1703 & 1724, describing the transactions
relating to the plantation of 600 acres in North Sound Division, which Lucie, Harris, & Bowyer
purchased.
† Dated 15 May & p. 27 Aug. 1696 (155, Bond). Estates in Barbados, Antigua, & Jamaica,
Essex, Yorkshire, Lincolnshire, & London, to his eldest son John.
‡ In 1682 Gov. Sir Wm. Stapleton granted a patent to them for 529 acres in Antigua.
"Blackmans," formerly known as "Mount Lucye," is in St. George's parish, reduced in 1852 to
230 acres.   § Major John Duer d. in L. 6 Sept. 1716.
‖ For 6 acres of flashes in Antigua, by Gov. Johnson in 1705; confirmed, together with a
small island, by Gov. Hamilton in 1715-16.

John Lucie Blackman to D° Reconveyance.
Rowl° Blackman's marriage articles.*
Rowl° Blackman to Robᵗ Warren lease for a year.
Rowl° Blackman to D° Release.
Record from Giles Watkins of yᵉ afore sᵈ Lease and Release.
Agreemᵗ between Catherine Weyman and Christopher Prissick.
A List of Mount Lucie Plantation Stock in 1671.
Jacob Lucie's Will in 1686.†
Representation of yᵉ Council to his Exceᵗy. Henry Worsley and Presidᵗ Cox.
the Merchants petition concerning Trade.
Daniel Mackaskill's papers.
a Bill for securing yᵉ Estᵉ and Effects of debtors for yᵉ use of their Creditors.
a bundle with Securitys and bills of Sale.
sundry bundles of Accoᵗˢ and Receipts.
a bundle with sundry accoᵗˢ of my Sisters from Jacob and Sam.
a small bundle of accoᵗˢ of mony pᵈ and disbursed for my Sisters, etc.
3 Lettʳˢ from Lascelles and Maxwell relating to assignmᵗˢ of Alleyne's.
Judgmᵗˢ by Wᵐ Moore as a Collateral Security.
Lettʳˢ from Patrick Grant of Antigua.
Lettʳˢ from Coᵗ. King.
Lettʳˢ from and to Mʳ Reid in a small bundle.
2 bundles of papers relating to Gould, Sᵇ John and al.
a Copy of my Father's Will,‡ and inventory of yᵉ Estᵉ at his death.
Wᵐ Weaver's power of Attorney and papers.
Lease for 3 years Abigˡ Henriques to Rowlᵈ Blackman.
Thruston Blackman's recᵗ for his Father's Legacy of £1000.
Rowlᵈ Blackman and Ux. their Lease and Release to Robᵗ Warren.
two bundles of Mʳˢ Courtney's Accᵗˢ.
Sundry plots of Land.
an Execution agᵗ my Father to Roberts and Withers wᵗʰ satisfaction on it.
Dʳ Lenahan's Accoᵗ and Receipt thereon.
a bundle wᵗʰ sundry bonds paid off.
Geo: Hannay§ to Rowlᵈ Blackman Lease and Release.
Rowlᵈ Blackman to Fr: Blackman Lease and Release of 100 Acres of land.
John Lucie Blackman to Rowlᵈ Blackman Release.
Release of sevˡ Legacys devised by yᵉ Will of Mʳ J. L. Blackman to Mary Blackman and al.
Geo: Hannay and al. Release to Rowlᵈ Blackman.
Thruston Blackman to Rowlᵈ Blackman and al. Release.
Thruston Blackman's Release of a legacy of £1000 to Benjⁿ A. Hole.
Articles of Agreemᵗ between Rowlᵈ Blackman, Benjⁿ A. Hole and J. Barbarie.
Articles of Agreemᵗ between Robᵗ Warren and al. and Jos. Hole's Accoᵗ in a bundle.
Bills of Sale from sundry persons to my Father for Land and Negˢ.
Decree Sᵇ John p̄ Attorney agᵗ Blackman.

---

* Married Priscilla, dau. & h. of Rob. Warren, M.D., of Barbados, & thus acquired "*Blackrock*" or "*Warrens*," which they sold about 1762-3, to Tho. Breuster for £13,700.

† Will dated 21 Sep. 1686, and p. 12 Dec. 1688 (44, Exton). He bequeathed to his dau. Eliz. his plantation in Barbados, called "*The 700 acres*" alias "*Apter's Hill*" alias "*Mount Lucie*," ½ of another in Antigua, & ¼ of another in Jamaica. She m. Gerard Napier, Esq., & d. s.p. before 1688, when all the estates passed by the entail to testator's nephew Lucie Blackman.

‡ John Lucie Blackman. Will dated 5 June 1724, and p. 14 Nov. 1726 (218, Plymouth). He left besides 5 daus., 7 sons: 1. Rowland, b. 1705; 2. John Lucie, b. 1707; 3. Tho., b. 1708; 4. Sam., b. 1709; 5. Thurston, b. 1715; 6. Jacob Lucie, b. 1716; 7. Joseph, b. 1719.

§ Will dated 13 June 1767, & p. 7 Dec. 1776 (495, Bellas). His brother-in-law Rowland Blackman was his h. & residuary legatee. Mrs. Anna Maria Hannay, sister of the latter & relict of testator, d. in Conduit Str. Will p. 1790 (381, Bishop).

plat of Land laid off for Sr Wm Courtnay.

the Ord^r of ye Vestry of St Joseph's* for a pew in ye Church ratified and confirm'd by his Excell^y Robt Lowther Esqre.

An Acco^t of ye Repairs of Pe ... iar's.†

Deed of Exchange of land between Rowl^d Blackman and Edwd Butcher.

Haynes Gibbes's Lease for 3 years.

Indenture to lead to ye use of ye fine of lands in Barbados.

An Acco^t of monys p^d and disbursed by you on acc^t of ye plantation.

a little book with instructions from my father to my Mother.

Counterp^t of Jos. Blackman's indenture of apprenticesp.

a small book wth Town Agent's Acco^{ts}.

two parchment books wth law Acco^{ts}.

Doctor Warren's and Gedney Clarke's Acco^{ts}.

Blenman of Barbados.

1654, Jan. Elianor Blinman. On the 27th adm'on to Roger B. son of E. B. late of Stokewisey, co. Som. fo. 2.

Geo. Blynman l. of the citty of Bristoll linendraper but now resident within the I. of Barbadoes. Will dated 29 Nov. 1702, 1 Q. Anne. To my brothers John B. and Fra. B. my messuage called Buckmans in the town of Watchett, p. of S[t] Decumans, co. Som., given by my l. dec[d] father during my term. My sister Jane Steward wife of Tho. S. of S[t] Malla in France £100. Accounts depending between me and Mary Jones of this I., wid., f. Mary Didras, and bet. me and M[r] Sampson Wood of s[d] I., gent. I desire my friends Joseph Mole of Bridge Town M[t] and Tho. Denny of s[d] p. M[t] and M[r] Adam Shand of s[d] p. to receive all sums due and make them overseers. All residue to my said brothers whom I nominate Ex'ors. Wit. by Edw. Austen, Adam Shand, M: M[c] Kaskell. On 3 Feb. 1706/7 appeared Fra. B. of Williton in the p. of S[t] Decumans, co. Som., Esq., one of the brothers and Ex'ors of test. l. of B'oes, bach., dec[d], and this deponent having been abroad at the siege of Barcelona and in Spain and Portugal came to the city of Exon in Nov. last where lived M[rs] Phillips Salter wife of M[r] Tho. S., goldsmith, sister of dec[d], who gave him the copy of will delivered her by M[r] Hole M[t] of s[d] city, who received it from Joseph Hole of Bridgetown in s[d] I. M[t] his brother and was sworn. Proved 3 Feb. 1706 by F. B., J. B. the other Ex'or renouncing. (26, Poley.)
Will also recorded in B'os.

Edward Warner of Antigua, esq. Will dated 1732. Jonathan Blenman of Barbados, esq., a guardian.

Harry Slingsby of Barbados, esq. Will dated 1746. Hon. Jonathan Blenmau of Barbados, an Ex'or.

Edward Blenman of Tempell in the city of Bristol. Will dated the 4th day of the 7th month 1752. To my dau. Rachel Willett 2 of my shares in the Brass Works. My grands. Jacob Post, gunner, 1 share. My grands. Edw. Post 1 share. My dau. Lidde Holwell 2 shares for her and her husband's life. My tenement in Debtford to my 2 grandsons Jacob Ager and Edw[d] Ager. My kinswomen Eliz. Godwin, Love Peters, Sarah Peters. W[m] Tilly. My dau. Drew, dec[d], without a will. Joseph Loscombe, Rob. Payn, W[m] Tilly and Rob. Peters, all merchants of Bl., to be Ex'ors. On 3 Jan. 1753 ad' to Rachell Willett, widow, the Ex'ors having renounced. (1, Searle.)

Margaret Bevilia Blenman l. of the I. of B'oes, now at Welbeck Str., S[t] Marylebone, spinster, sick. Will dated 29 May 1772. My debts and legacies to be paid by my brother W[m] B., Esq. To my Mother Mary B. the annual interest of what shall be due from my said brother, and after her death I give to my brother Wm., my brother Timothy and sister Caroline £500 each. My nephew Jonathan B. books, nephew W. B. my m. ring for my father, nephew Jos. B. a ring, nephew Timothy B. a ring. My 2 neices Eliz. and Ann B. wearing apparel. Friend Miss Mary Gibbes a ring. My friend the Hon. R[d] Salter, Esq., and Margaret his wife rings. Friend Geo. James of B'es, Esq., my negro woman. Friend W[m] Forbes. Remainder of money to Hon. R[d] Salter and his wife for a charitable purpose, and to be T. for this fund. My Mother and brother W[m] Ex'ors. Proved 23 Sept. 1774 by W. B. the brother p. r. to Mary B. the Mother. (330, Bargrave.)

177

ARMS.—*Per chevron engrailed Azure and Argent two lozenges in chief, a bee in base.*
CREST.—*A dexter arm holding a scroll.*

Thomas Blenman of Croscombe, co. Som.⊤

Jonathan Blenman of Barbados, Attorney-Gen. 1727;=Mary, ..., living 1774. Judge of the Admiralty 1734; Grant of arms 1739; | Arms : *Argent, three* M. of C. 1746. W.I. Bookplate No. 168. | *daggers.*

| William Blenman of Bath. Will dated 13 May 1794; proved 13 Aug. 1800 (576, Adderley). | =Eliz., dau. of Joseph Dotin; born 1728; mar. 1748; died 10 Aug. 1763. M.I. at Clifton (*ante*, II., 371). Had four sons and two daus. | Timothy Blenman, born 1725; of Christ Church, Oxford, matric. 17 Dec. 1741, aged 16; of Gray's Inn 22 Jan. 1741-2; living 1744. ? Will recorded in 1799. | Margaret Bevilia Blenman of Welbeck Street. Will dated 29 May 1772; proved 23 Sept. 1774 (330, Bargrave). | Caroline Blenman of Welbeck Street. Will dated 23 Feb. and proved 23 Sept. 1774 (330, Bargrave). |

| Jonathan Blenman, born 1753; of Christ Coll., Camb., 18 Oct. 1769, aged 16; of Lincoln's Inn 24 Aug.1771; Solicitor-Gen. and Judge of Vice-Admiralty, Barbados; bur. at St. George 14 Feb.1807. Will (363, Ely). | =Anna Maria, born 1759; ? dau. of . . . . Cobham ; died 16 Aug. 1817, aged 58. M.I. in crypt of St. Paul's Cathedral (*ante*, IV., 232). | Joseph Blenman, d.v.p. 1794—8. — Ann Blenman, mar. Tho., son of Alex. Graeme of Barbados ; living 1804. | Rev. Timothy Blenman, ? 5th son, went to Barbados 1783. W.I. Bookplate No. 169, quartering arms of Dotin. | =. . . ., died at Clifton 27 Nov. 1820. ⋏ | Wm. Blenman. Eliz. Blenman. |

| Jonathan Blenman, born 1785; of Christ Church, Oxford, matric. 21 Feb. 1802, aged 17; B.A. 1806; Lincoln's Inn 1803; died at Penzance 22 July 1843, aged 58. | =Sarah Isabella . . . ., died at Tonbridge Wells 4 Sept. 1850. | Timothy Blenman, born 1795; died 28 Dec. 1829, aged 34. M.I. at St. Paul's Cathedral. | John Cobham Blenman, born 1798; died 12 April 1828, aged 30. M.I. in St. Paul's Cathedral. | Anna Maria Blenman, born 4 Feb. 1794; died 26 Aug. 1837. M.I. in St. Paul's Cathedral. |
⋏

Caroline B. of Welbeck Str. Will dated 23 Feb. 1774. To my Mother £500 and all my slaves in the I. of B'oes. Cubbah to be free after her death. Romeo to be free immediately. Friend Mary Gibbes jewels, £300. Mr Farquhar 5 gns. My 2 neices Eliz. and Ann B., Mr Sam. Gibbes a ring. All res. to my bro. Wm B. My friend Mr Geo. James 10 gns. My Mother and Bro. Ex'ors in the p. of Philip Gibbes, jr, Sam. Osborne Gibbes. Proved 23 Sept. 1774 by W. B. Esq., p. r. to Mary B. (330, Bargrave.)

Wm. Dottin Battyn l. of B'os now of Bristol. Will dated 23 Oct. 1798. My relation Jonathan Blenman, Esq., £1000. (14, Howe.)

Ann Battyn l. of B'os now of Bristol, widow. Will dated 3 March 1799. My cousin Jonathan Blenman, Esq., £1000. (246, Howe.)

The will of Timothy B was recorded in 1799 in B'os.

Wm Blenman of Walcot Terr., Bath, Esq. Will dated 13 May 1794. My age. To my friend Mrs Fra. Jones, whose true name is Fyscot, who has lived in my house for 13 years, all my furniture, she paying my debts and funeral. Books on music to my s. Joseph, the rest of my books to my 1st s. Jonathan. Cod. To Mrs F. J. arrears of H.M. bounty and the salary of a little employment I hold in St Jas. Palace. Having agreed for the sale of a farm in N. Wootton in this Co. for £1000, and the books bequeathed to my s. Joseph lately decd to my 1st s. Jonathan. 17 Jan. 1798. Sworn 14 July 1800. On 13 Aug. 1800 ad. of all the est. of testr, widr, decd, gr. to Tho. Greene, Esq., atty of Jon. B., Esq., Fra. Fyscot als. Jones, spr., renouncing. (576, Adderley.)

Jonathan B. of St Mich., B'os, barrister. Will dated 9 June 1804. Wife Anna Maria my Duke's farm. All res. to her and my chn. My sister Ann Graeme. My brothers John and Rd Cobham and Tho. Graeme. Sworn 27 Feb. 1807. Proved 1808. (363, Ely.)

Susanna Christian Cobham late of B'os now of Bristol, widow. Will dated 3 Dec. 1801. My godson Jonathan Blenman £1500 c. My godson John Cobham Blenman £1000 c. (194, Pitt.)

1676, Apr. 3. Francis Blynman of Abbotsleigh and Penelope Payton of ditto. (Bristol Mar. Bonds and Alleg. Glouc. N. and Q., x., 84.)

Deed between Hugh Fortescue of Filleigh, in the co. of Devon, Esq., and Richard Blonman, of the co. of Somerset, clothier, relates to a fulling mill and the land belonging, in the co. of Somerset, with fine signature and seal of Hugh Fortiscue, dated 1700. (Dealer's Catalogue.)

1726-7, Mar. 5. Jonathan Planman (sic), Esq., appointed his Majesty's Attorney-General in the I. of B. (Hist. Reg., 13.)

1728, Mar. 19. Mr. Bloman (sic), Attorney-at-Law, appointed Attorney-General in the I. of B. (Ibid., 18.)

1734, July. Jonathan Blenman, Esq., Attorney-General of B., made sole Judge of the Admiralty there. (Ibid., 19, and "G.M.," 391.)

1741-2, Jan. 22. Timothy Blenman, 2nd s. of Jonathan B., Attorney-General of B'os. (Gray's Inn Admissions.)

Rev. T. Blenman went out to Barbados 27 June 1783. (Fothergill's "Emigrant Ministers.") He was licensed to St George's parish on the 24th inst.

Jonathan B. s. of Wm., arm., b. in B. School, Kensington, under Mr. Lally. Adm. fell. commoner under Dr Shipherd, 18 Oct. 1769. Age 16. Resided till Midsr 1773. Gave two large silver candlesticks as his plate. Adm. at Linc. Inn, 24 Aug. 1771, as s. of W. B. of Welbeck Str. (Christ's Coll., Camb., Regr. II., p. 289.)

1796. William Blenman. (Eton School List, p. 26.)

BOSTOCK OF BARBADOS.

The Barbados family of BOSTOCK are thought to have been descended from the family of that name who were settled in various parts of the county of Chester and bore *Arms*: Sa. a fesse humettée ar., *Crest*: On the stump of a tree eradicated ar. a bear's head erased sa. muzzled or. Similar crest and arms are incised in the marble slab on the tomb of Benjamin Bostock (1716-1785) in the Churchyard of St James's parish church, Barbados, which is still standing although in need of repair.

The first Bostock mentioned in the Barbados records is Edward, most probably the English immigrant.

1. EDWARD BOSTOCK[1], of Holetown, Barbados, gunsmith, in the year 1713, and possibly earlier. In the 1715 census he is recorded as being 51 years of age, his wife 23, and one child, one year.

Married first, Elizabeth (surname unknown) who died in 1729, aged 40 years, and was buried in the north-eastern area of St. James's churchyard according to the entry in the Church Register.

Children of the first marriage: all baptised at St. James's.—

   i. Mary, baptised 19 Jan. 1713; died 11 Sep. 1715.
   ii. Elizabeth, born 26 July 1714, died 30 April 1721 of small-pox.
   iii. Mary, born—died 23 April 1721 of small-pox.
2. iv. BENJAMIN,[2] born 2 Nov, 1716, of whom later.
   v. Edward, born—married Rebecca (surname unknown) and had issue—

     (1) *Elizabeth*, born 8 May 1745.
     (2) *Benjamin*, died 17 Oct. 1752 aged two years and nine months.

Edward Bostock[1] married secondly, 9 Jan. 1730, at St. James's Barbados. Margaret Barnet or Barnett. She was born 14 Jan. 1710/11, child of Thomas Barnett and Ruth (Burrowes) his wife.

Children of the second marriage: all baptised at St. James.—

   vi. Thomas, born 23 April 1731, married 9 Nov. 1752, Anne Hearne Milward, and had issue—

     (1) *Elizabeth*, born 13 Oct. 1754; married 27 May 1773, John Wrong.
     (2) *Benjamin*, born 17 Jan. 1758, died 10 April 1758.
     (3) *Thomas*, bap. 30 March 1760. died 19 Oct. 1787 aged 27 years.
       Thomas Bostock, the father left a will dated 4 May 1769 and made on his deathbed. His wife, Anne Hearne predeceased him, 28 Aug. 1768, aged 36 years.
   vii. John, born 15 Aug. 1732, married 21 Dec. 1754, Elizabeth Goddard, and had issue a son, *Edward* born 6 Dec. 1755.
   viii. Dr. William, born 2 March 1734/5, married 13 March 1756, Mary Freke, and they had issue—

     (1) *Thomas Campbell John*, born 26 Jan. 1757.
     (2) *William*, bap. 7 March 1761, about 8 months old.
     (3) *Mary*, bap. 19 July 1763, married John Poyer, the Barbados historian, 23 July 1780.

Edward[1] Bostock died 27 Aug. 1737 about 75 years of age and was buried in St. James. His widow, Margaret (Barnet) married secondly, 10 Sep. 1743, Richard Edwards of St. James, planter, (d. 1760). She survived him.

Will of Edward[1] Bostock of St. James, Barbados, dated 21 Oct. 1736. To wife, Margaret, £150, furniture, linen china etc. To Bowden Fercharson my best horse. Son, Benjamin, £800 at 21; also tools etc. belonging to the smith's trade, all my smith's negroes; and to pay my son, Edward, one-half the value of the negroes. To three sons, Thomas, John and William, £350 each at 21. If wife marries they must be put in care of their grandmother, Ruth Barnett. To wife's sister, Elizabeth Barnett, £15 to buy a negro. Residue to my five sons. Should they all die, my estate for my friends, Arthur Upton of St. Michael, and William Bryant of St. Andrew, equally; and they to be executors and guardians. sd. Edward Bostock. Witnesses: John Sulevan, James Cocker, Abraham Pile.

2 BENJAMIN[2] BOSTOCK (*Edward[1]*) b. 2 Nov. 1716, married Alice (surname unknown). He owned valuable sugar-work plantations in widely separated districts of Barbados—Yorkshire plantation in the parish of Christ Church, Carlton and Plum Tree (Plumb Tree) in St. James. In 1752 he was coroner of the parish of St. James; collector of customs at Holetown, 1775; member of the House of Assembly for St. James 1779/80 to 1785.

Of his marriage there was one child—

3 EDWARD[3], born 22 Sep. 1737, married Judith Collier, 15 Aug. 1762, and died 17 March 1776, but of whom later.

Benjamin[2] Bostock died on 28 June 1785 leaving his estates to his grandson, Benjamin. His will dated 13 Sep. 1781 describes him as a merchant, of the parish of St. James, and directed his funeral expenses not to exceed £50. Bequest to his wife, Alice, of £2,000 cy. also the house he lived in, furniture, plate, nine negroes (named) £50 to purchase a horse and chaise; and 12 pots of clayed and muscovado sugar, one hhd. of spirit, and ground provisions as in his lifetime, for her absolute use annually, for her life.

"If my grandson, Benjamin Bostock, shall not think it proper to carry on the cooperage in Holetown, then my stores, buildings, cooper negroes, and boat negroes, to be sold and the sum paid to my creditors. If he should carry on the cooperage, then I give him the stores, negroes etc.

Grandsons and granddaughters £100 each at 21, and interest at 4% to be paid to their mother, Judith Bostock, formerly Collier, for their maintenance and education. To the said Judith £25 to purchase mourning. He gave his mulatto slave, Nanny, her freedom, and £50 to be paid to the churchwarden for her manumission. Nanny to have an allowance of 12 pints of corn and 2 lbs. of flesh per week for her life. To grandson, Benjamin Bostock, a mulatto slave named Ned, and the estates, "one called Upper Grays now goes by the name of Yorkshire in Christ Church," and the other Carlton in St. James, together with the windmill, negroes, lands, live and dead stock, at the age of 21; in case of his prior death to go to his (testator's) grandson, Thomas Bostock, allowing his brother, William, £120 per an. for life over and above the legacy of £100 to be paid to him at 21 and interest at 4%; and failing him, the estate to go to grandson, Samuel Bostock, and failing him to two grand-daughters, Jane and Alice Bostock, equally.

"To James Cummins who served his time with me, £20. I appoint my friends, Thomas Daniel Esq., merchant in Bristol, Stephen Morgan, Robert Ewing, and Philip Lytcott, executors, together with my wife, Alice, as executrix, and guardians of the bodies of my grandchildren," sd. B. Bostock. Wits: Phillip Burrowes, Thomas Bostock. Proved 4 July 1785.

Benjamin[2] Bostock is buried in a raised tomb at the north-eastern corner of the churchyard of St. James, enclosed by railings, and with a marble slab with Crest and Arms as noted above and an inscription—

SACRED TO THE MEMORY OF/BENJAMIN BOSTOCK ESQR.,/Member of the Assembly/who Departed this Life the 28th of/June 1785 Aged 69 Years. He died regarded by all as a valuable member of Society/having at all times conducted himself through every/Station of life with the strictest Rectitude of manner/and might with the greatest Propriety have been styled/the noblest Work of GOD an Honest man. / He has left his Relations and Friends to sincerely / Lament the Vicissitudes of human Nature in the / great loss they have sustained/ This tomb was erected as a mark of Esteem and Veneration for his character by his grandson / BENJAMIN BOSTOCK ESQR.

3 EDWARD[3] BOSTOCK (*Benjamin,[2] Edward[1]*) born 22 Sep. 1737; married Judith Collier, 15 August 1762. Children of the marriage—

4   (i)   BENJAMIN[4], born 17 Nov. 1763.
    (ii)   Jane Collier, bap. 18 Dec. 1766, married Samuel Richards, 14 Dec. 1786. They had issue—surname Richards, (1) *Samuel Munckley,* born 1 Mar. 1792, (2) *Mary Judith,* born 2 Jan. 1795, (3) *William Edward,* born 20 May 1797. (4) *Thomas,* born 17 Apl. 1799/
  (iii)   William, born 7 Jan. 1768.
  (iv)   Edward, born 2 Jan. 1769, died 23 Feb. 1769.
  (v)   Thomas, born 18 Feb. 1770.
  (vi)   Samuel, born 19 August 1771, married 24 Jan. 1792, Katherine Ifill, and had issue (1) *Mary Jane,* borne 2 Feb. 1794, (2) *Edward,* born 28 Oct. 1795.
  (vii)   Alice, born 19 Jan. 1776, married 19 Dec. 1793, William Clinckett, (son of William and Eleanor Clinkett) of Speightstown, Barbados.

Edward[3] Bostock being ill, made his last will on 12 March 1776. He left his gold watch and two seals to his son, Benjamin the younger. To his wife, Judith, his dwellinghouse, furniture, and six negroes. To his daughters, Jane Collier and Alice, he gave slave women and their children. The residue of his estate to be divided between his three sons William, Samuel, and Thomas, equally. He left his father, Benjamin[2] Bostock, and his wife, Judith, guardians of his children and to be executor and executrix of his will. He was unable to sign the will and made his mark. He died on 16 March 1776, and the will was proved on 2 May following.

Edward[3] Bostock was buried in St James's churchyard; his burial is recorded under date 17 March 1776, and his age is entered as 40 years. There is no memorial to him.

4 BENJAMIN[4] BOSTOCK, (*Edward[3], Benjamin[2], Edward[1]*), born 17 November 1763, married, 23 February 1789, at Christ Church Philadelphia, U.S.A., Harriett Straker Budden, daughter of Captain James Budden of Philadelphia, and Frances, his wife. Benjamin was living in London in 1785, and was on a visit to Barbados in 1788. On 13 August 1790 he settled Plum Tree plantation of 156 acres with a number of slaves thereon, by conveying the same to his mother-in-law, Frances Budden, widow, in trust for himself the said

Benjamin, for his life, and after his decease, for the use of his wife, Harriett, in lieu of dower.

There were two children of the marriage —

5 (i) BENJAMIN[5] JAMES BOSTOCK, born—   , married Louisa Light-bourne, of Bermuda. Of him later.

(ii) Frances Mary, born—   , living in Philadelphia in November 1817, when she was about to marry William Halstead jr. of New Jersey. The marriage was solemnized by Rev. David Moore on 5 Nov. 1817, and a notice of the event appeared in the New Jersey News for Nov. 11.

On 10 July 1793 Benjamin[4] Bostock, then of Philadelphia made his will. He bequeathed to his two children, Benjamin James and Frances, son and daughter of Harriett Straker Bostock, his carriage and pair of horses and all his household furniture, jewels, plate and linen, and two (named) slaves. He confirmed the gift made to his wife of his sugar-work plantation (in his will called Plumb Tree), in the parishes of St Thomas and St James, with all the slaves, cattle, and stock thereon, in bar of dower.

To his son, Benjamin James[5], his sugar-work plantation called Grays or Yorkshire in Christ Church (Barbados) with the slaves, cattle, stock etc. thereon and also the moneys then due to him from William Prescod [for the unpaid purchase money of Carlton plantation which he had sold him.] To his daughter, Frances, £4000 cy. to be paid at her day of marriage or 21. If the gifts to the children should fail, then he gave his property to his brothers, Thomas and Samuel, and his two sisters, Jane Richards and Alice Bostock and £100 to Richard Bland Esq. of Great Britain, and to each of his children, Kitty, John, and Peter Bland, £100. To his friend Richard Morgan £50. To his executors, £50. To his good friends, Malbro and John Frazier, merchants of Philadelphia, £50 each. and to Elijah Brown, merchant, of the same place, £50. His friends James Went King and John Randall Phillips (both of Barbados) executors. He signed the will in the presence of Thomas Wright and Elijah Brown. Benjamin[4] Bostock died in Philadelphia on 7 Aug. 1793, was buried in Christ Church, Philadelphia, and his will was proved there 23 Decr. following before Isaac Wampole, Deputy Registrar, administration being granted to Malbro Frazier, administrator with the will annexed, 8 Jan. 1794.

His widow, Harriett Straker Bostock, married at Christ Church, Phil., on 3 Apl. 1794, Dr. Plunkett Fleeson Glentworth of Philadelphia, who had attended her husband, Benjamin, in his last illness. Dr. and Mrs. Glentworth sold the Barbados plantation, Plum Tree, to Timothy Thornhill in 1797 but apparently they had some difficulty in recovering the purchase money or some of it, despite a visit made by Dr. Glentworth to Barbados in 1799, and the appointment by him of attorneys to collect the debt.

5 BENJAMIN JAMES[5] Bostock married Louisa Lightbourn, daughter of William Lightbourn of Bermuda. Benjamin James[5] is said to have been admitted to one of the Inns of Court in London, but researches have failed to prove the assertion a fact, although it is certain that he was admitted to practise as a barrister-at-law in the Courts of Barbados in 1817, as the records show. In 1811 he came to Barbados to wind up the estates of his father and great-grandfather. He sold Yorkshire plantation to William Drayton for £22,000. His father had already sold Carlton estate to William Prescod.

Benjamin James[5] Bostock and Louisa (Lightbourn) his wife had issue —

6. (i) WILLIAM LIGHTBOURN[6].

(ii) JAMES.

He died in the United States a few years after his marriage, leaving his widow and the two young sons. She returned with them to Bermuda where they spent their childhood, and then settled in the United States. They went into partnership in the shipping business, but eventually they parted over money differences.

6 WILLIAM LIGHTBOURN[6] BOSTOCK married Roxana Osborn of Nova Scotia, then a widow. She survived her husband, William Lightbourn Bostock, and died in Brooklyn, N.Y.
Their children —
  (i) Alice, married Rev. Edward Love, and had issue —
    (1) *Alfred Love*, (2) *Roxana Bostock Love*, (3) *Oswald Love.*
  (ii) Ida,
  (iii) Louisa
  (iv) Sarah Chipman
  (v) Benjamin, who died in infancy.
William Lightbourn[6] Bostock died at Elizabeth, New Jersey, in 1896.

E. M. S.

Bovell of Barbados.†

WILLS.

1736. July 28. William, S[t] Lucy's, Chirurgeon. Father Finch Bovell. Mother Elizabeth. Sons, John, William, James. Sisters, Esther, Sarah. Brother-in-law John Best. Father-in-law John Jacobs. Will taken down by John Best, brother-in-law.

1771, April 4. John, S[t] Peter's. Wife Elizabeth. Brother Thomas Sober Holloway. Brother-in-law James. Eldest son to come of age at 28 years.

1773. April 30. William, S[t] Lucy. Sons, John, William, James. Brother John (wife Ann). Daughter Elizabeth.

† Communicated by Mr. N. Darnell Davis.

1773, May 17. Elizabeth, Widow, St Michael's. Nephews, John and Samuel Branch (minors). Nieces, Elizabeth Branch the elder, Olive Branch (her grandfather John Branch), Hopey Barkclay (formerly Branch, now wife of Alexander Barkclay), Mary and Elizabeth Branch the younger (their father John Branch). Elizabeth Pott, Spinster, Elizabeth Williams (formerly Goddard, now wife of Samuel Goddard), and Jane Goddard the younger. Daughter-in-law Mary Harris, Widow.

1774, Oct. 25. John, Speight's Town, Practitioner of Physick, &c. Wife Ann. Sons, John, William, James. Daughter Elizabeth. Brother (dead) William.

1790, Jan. 25. Jacobs, Christian, Spinster, St Peter's. Niece Elizabeth Bovell. Nephews, Dr John Bovell (son John William), William Bovell (children Elizabeth, Ann), James (son James).

BIRTHS.

1643 April — Elizabeth child of John and Ann.
1667 May 10 Warren child of Roger and Hannah.
1675 May — Elizabeth child of Richard and Elizabeth.

MARRIAGES.

Year and Day.		Christian Names.	To whom Married
1661	Aug. 3	Elizabeth	Wm Connell.
1752	Mar. 25	Heather	Samuel Perry.
1781	May 10	William	Mary Gaskin.
1782	Feb. 1	James	Elizabeth Griffith.
1795	April 30	Elizabeth	Robert Bowcher Clarke.
1800	Mar. 6	Johnston	Margaret N. Nichell.

BOWEN OF BARBADOS.

Contributed by W. L. McKinstry, Barrister-at-Law.

THIS FAMILY has been settled in Barbados for more than
300 years. There is some evidence to show that it came from
Bristol and probably, originally, from the county of Glamorgan
in Wales, which is near Bristol. There are four Bowen families
referred to in Burke's Landed Gentry one of which settled in
Glamorgan many centuries ago and was thought to be descended
from the Ab Owains who were independent princes in Wales in
the tenth, eleventh, and twelfth centuries. The Barbados branch
is possibly descended from this family.

The first Bowen mentioned in Barbados Records is
ANTHONY BOWEN. His name occurs in "Memoirs of the First
Settlement of the Island of Barbados to the year 1742" as "one
of the inhabitants in the year 1638 who then possessed more
than 10 acres of land". Those were pre-Cromwellian days. Queen
Elizabeth had only been dead 35 years and Shakespeare 22 !

It is interesting to quote from these Memoirs to show the
manner in which the early settlers got possession of land and
the conditions under which they lived and worked.

"In December 1629 Sir William Tufton, Bart. arrived in the
Island as Governor for the Earl of Carlisle and, on the 21st day
of the same month, held a Sessions or Court and this year gave
140 grants to several persons for 15,870 acres of land. By 1633
the Inhabitants had greatly increased and amounted to 766
Possessors of more than 10 acres of land."

We may thus presume that Anthony Bowen came to the
Island sometime between its Settlement in 1627 and 1638.

Whether he came alone or with others of his family is not
known, but as domestic events, such as Baptisms, Burials and
Marriages are chronicled as occurring within twenty years of
the Settlement, it would seem probable that other Bowens came
with him or soon after.

In the "Memoirs" it is stated that the first settlers produced
"Cotton and tobacco by the manual labour of a few white settlers" and the island was described as "one of the riches Spotes
of ground in the wordell and fully inhabited". Another writer,
quoted in this Journal for August 1938 Vol. 5 No. 4 stated, however, that by 1654 it—Barbados—had become the "Dunghill
whereone England doth cast forth its rubidg".

In 1638 there were only a few hundred slaves, but by 1651
they numbered more than 20,000. The reason for this great
increase was due to the introduction of the sugar cane plant
from Brazil, in about 1640, and the great competition between
the British and Portuguese traders for the trade in slaves. So
great had this competition become that in 1651 the iniquitous

Navigation Act was passed permitting West Indian trade to be carried on only in British ships.

It was not until after the battles of Preston, Drogheda, Naseby and Worcester were fought, between the years 1648 and 1658, that white prisoners of war were sold to the Planters in the West Indies as Redemptioners. Previous to this, however, many Englishmen had, voluntarily, bound themselves to serve in the Plantations as Christian servants for terms of years in the hope of becoming landowners on the expiry of their terms of service.

Although there is a family tradition, that the first BOWEN landed from a Pirate Ship near Maycocks Bay in St. Lucy with a bag of doubloons and bought land in that part of the Island. and, although it is true that the Bowen name has always been fairly common in that parish, it seems more likely that they settled in Christ Church at first, as early records of baptisms, marriages and burials occurred mainly in that Parish.

BAPTISMS IN THE 17TH CENTURY. [1]

1645, Jan. 23rd.	Christ Church.	Anthony Bowen, son of Thomas Bowen and Mary his wife who were married in 1644. This Anthony may have been grandson or nephew of the Anthony mentioned in the "Memoirs".
1648, Sept. 9th.	St. Philip.	C of William Bowen.
1654, May 5th.	Christ Church.	Joan daughter of John Powell and his wife Mary Bowen who were married in 1653.
1675, Oct. 8th.	St. Michael.	James ye son of Mr. William Bowen.
1683, Dec. 3rd.	St. Michael.	William the son of Benjamin BOOWEN.

MARRIAGES IN THE 17TH CENTURY. [2]

1644, August 15th.	Thomas Bowen of Christ Church to Mary Brookes.
1649, April 29th.	Eleanor Bowen of Christ Church to Thos. Flambridge.
1653, April 27th.	Mary Bowen of Christ Church to John Powell.
1684, May 22nd.	Ruth Bowen of St. Michael to Samuel Earle.

1. After the year 1683 there are no records of baptisms of Bowens until 1735 although there are records of BOWNS, BORNES, BOWHANES, BOURNS and BORNS— a break of 52 years.

2. Here too there is a break in the marriages of Bowens recorded, of 20 years, 1684 to 1704. As in the previous note there are variations in the spelling of the name in the intervening years.

BURIALS IN THE 17TH CENTURY

1646, Feb. 8th.	Christ Church.	Jane da of Thomas Bowen.
1647, Oct. 21st.	,, ,,	John Bowen.
1679, May 30th.	St. Michael.	James son of Mr. William and Ruth Bowen. This child only lived four years.
1682, Jan. 23rd.	,, ,,	William Bowen.
1682,	St. Philip.	James Bowen.
1695, Jan. 16th.	St. Michael.	Mrs. Ruth Bowen.
1695, Mar. 16th.		Mr. Edward Bowen, Merchant. (See extract from his will).
1696, July 10th.		John Bowen, Mariner.

In the "Census of the Population in 1679", it is stated that John BOWING of St. Lucy owned six acres of land and five negroes. In the same Census it is also stated that in the List of "Souldiers" in Colonel Thornhills Regiment of Guards for H.E. Sir Jonathan Atkins, Captain General and Governor of this Island and the Caribee Islands, at present under the command of Colonel William Bates occur the names of

Richard Bowen under command of Major Tho. Holmes.

Jno. Bowen under command of Captain Jno. Sampson.

William Bowen a clerk in Col. Bates Regiment.

There is no record of the baptism of any of these Bowen "Souldiers" who must have been born in the 1650's and were probably grandsons of the first Anthony.

It was Colonel Sir Timothy Thornhill who, with his Barbadian Volunteers, in 1689, went to the Leeward Islands, "where they signalized themselves at the taking of St. Christopher and in several other enterprizes." (See the Memoirs of the First Settlement quoted above.) No list of the names of these Volunteers appears to be in existence.

BAPTISMS IN THE 18TH CENTURY.

1735, May 27th.	St. Joseph.	Frances Bowen, Mary Ann Bowen. Twin daughters of Richard and Frances Bowen. (See marriages in 1732.)
1737, Sept. 9th.	St. Thomas.	Jane, da of John and Alice Bowen.
1750, Oct. 18th.	St. Lucy.	Samuel [1], son of Samuel Bowen.
1752, July 5th.	St. Lucy.	JOHN, son of John and Mary Bowen.
1754, Oct. 5th.	,, ,,	Samuel, son of John and Mary Bowen.

1. This Samuel is referred to in Ann Balls' Will as her grandson and as son of Samuel Bowing and Dorothy his wife and is appointed one of her executors. See this Journal at Vol. II. No. 1. November 1934. *

*Pages 135-143, this volume.

1755, Aug. 18th.	St. Lucy.	William, son of William and Alice Bowen.
1758, Jan. 10th.	,, ,,	Susanna, da of William and Alice Bowen.
1760, Dec. 25th	,, ,,	Israel, son of John and Mary Bowen.
1761, Aug. 13th.	,, ,,	Alice, da of William and Alice Bowen.
1763, April 10th.	,, ,,	Benjamin, son of John and Mary Bowen.
1764, Oct. 21st.	,, ,,	Elizabeth, da of William and Alice Bowen.
1766, Aug. 19th.	,, ,,	Mary Ann, da of Israel and Ann Bowen.
1768, Oct. 10th.	,, ,,	Thomas Gibbs, son of Israel and Ann Bowen.
1769, Nov. 7th.	St. Michael.	John, son of Benjamin and Alice Bowen.
1769, Nov. 9th.	St. Lucy.	Hy Sacheverell Smith son of John and Mary Bowen.
1772, March 8th.	,, ,,	George Gibson, son of Israel and Ann Bowen.
1773, May 20th.	,, ,,	Elizabeth Ann, da of Jacob and Elizabeth Bowen.
1774, Sept. 13th.	St. Michael.	Benjamin, son of Elizabeth Bowen.
1775, Oct. 11th.	St. Lucy.	Sarah Boyce, da of John and Susanna Bowen.
1776, June 22nd.	Christ Church.	Elizabeth Sasanna, da of Israel and Ann Bowen.
1777, Nov. 4th.	St. Lucy.	JOHN, son of John and Susanna Bowen.
1778, Dec. 11th.	,, ,,	Ann, da of William and Rebecca Bowen.
1779, Aug. 4th.	,, ,,	Mary, da of Joseph and Mary Bowen.
1779, Dec. 15th.	,, ,,	Johnston Wm. son of John and Susanna Bowen.
1783, Feb. 22nd.	,, ,,	Samuel, son of John and Susanna Bowen.
1783, July 4th.	St. Peter.	Jacob, son of Jacob and Elizabeth Bowen.
1784, Feb. 1st.	Christ Church.	William, son of Jacob and Elizabeth Bowen.
1784, Feb. 7th.	St. Lucy.	William, son of Jacob and Elizabeth Bowen.
1784, Oct. 17th.	,, ,,	Elizabeth Seale, da of William and Rebecca Bowen.

1785, May 10th.	St. Lucy.	Hy Sach[1], son of John and Susanna Bowen.
1785, June 3rd.	„ „	Joseph, son of Joseph and Mary Bowen.
1786, Dec. 29th.	„ „	William Carrington, son of Israel and Frances Bowen.
1787, Nov. 9th.	„ „	Mary, da of John and Susanna Bowen.
1788, Jan. 9th.	„ „	Mary Ann, da of Benjamin and Mary Ann Bowen.
1788, Nov. 3rd.	„ „	John Yard, son of Israel and Frances Bowen.
1788, Jan. 14th	„ „	Israel, son of John and Susanna Bowen.
1788, Feb. 10th.	„ „	Rebecca, da of Joseph and Mary Bowen.
1789, Dec. 24th.	„ „	Frances Carrington, da of Israel and Frances Bowen.
1790, May 22nd.	„ „	John, son of Benjamin and Mary Ann Bowen.
1790, April 7th.	„ „	Catherine, da of William and Rebecca Bowen.
1791, Jan. 5th.	St. Michael.	John Marshalls, son of Benjamin and Barbara Bowen.
1791, June 5th.	St. Lucy.	Thos. Bagally, son of John and Susanna Bowen.
1791, March 21st.	„ „	Joseph Farrell, son of William Farrell and Rebecca Bowen.
1792, Sept. 7th.	„ „	Elizabeth Williams, da of Israel and Frances Bowen.
1793, Sept. 6th.	„ „	Samuel, son of Benjamin and Mary Bowen.
1794, May 4th.	St. Michael.	Mary, da of ANTHONY and Winifred Bowen of the 43rd Regiment † (now the Oxfordshire and Buckinghamshire Light Infantry).
1794, May 19th.	St. Lucy.	Mary Greaves, da of Israel and Frances Bowen.
1795, May 1st.	„ „	Benjamin John, son of John and Susanna Bowen.
1795, May 4th.	„ „	Joseph, son of Samuel and Elizabeth Bowen.
1796, May 29th.	„ „	George Gibson ⎫ twin sons of Jacob and Elizabeth
1796, „ „	„ „	Jacob ⎭ Bowen.

† This Regiment has ''Martinique 1794'' subscribed to its titles in the Army list—an Honour awarded in commemoration of its services against that Island. It is known that recruits from this island joined the Expedition.

BAPTISMS IN THE 18TH CENTURY.—*Contd.*

1798, Dec. 18th.	St. Lucy.	John, son of John and Mary Campbell Bowen.
1798, Dec. 8th.	St. Michael.	Harriet Chase, da of Joseph and Rebecca Farrell Bowen.

The following information is taken from "A CENSUS of the Island of Barbados West Indies with the names and ages of all the white Inhabitants of the Island arranged under the several Parishes. A.D. 1715".

CHRIST CHURCH.

Sarah Bowen	1	month.
Henry Bowen	28	years.
Elizabeth his daughter	5	months.
Mary Bowen	3	months.
Nicholas Bowen	36	years.
Ann his wife	34	years.
Margaret his daughter	13	years.
John his son	10	years.
Nicholas his son	5	years.
Sarah his daughter	2	years.
Susannah Bowen	32	years.
Joshna her son	13	years.
Banbridge her son	11	years.
Henry her son	4½	years.
Ruth her daughter	1½	years.

ST. MICHAEL.

Samuel Bowen	35	years.
Mary his wife	30	years.
Thomas his son	9	years.
Elizabeth his daughter	7	years.
Ann his daughter	2	years.

This must have been a very incomplete Census.

MARRIAGES IN THE 18TH CENTURY.

1704, May 6th.	Jane Bowen of St. Michael to Timothy Dunnovan.
1712, July 5th.	Patience Bowen, spinster, of St. Michael to Mr. James Huie.
1732, April 23rd.	Richard Bowen of St. Joseph to Frances Crane. (See Baptisms for 1735 for two of their children.)
1751, April 26th.	JOHN BOWEN of St. Lucy to Mary Farley.
1763, Jan. 22nd.	Samuel Bowen of St. James to Ann Southwood. (pr license.)
1767, Dec. 5th.	Ann Bowen of St. Lucy to John Hayes. (Married by Thos. Harris.)

MARRIAGES IN THE 18TH CENTURY.—*Contd.*

1769, April 11th.	Ann Bowen (widow) of St. Michael to Benjamin Bowen.
1774, Feb. 12th.	Sarah Bowen of St. Lucy to Saml. Williams.
1774, Jan. 30th.	JOHN BOWEN of St. Lucy to Susannah Boyce.
1779, March 16th.	Joseph Bowen of St. Lucy to Mary Ward.
1782, Oct. 17th.	Mary Bowen of St. Michael to James Redman.
1784, Dec. 23rd.	Sarah Bowen of St. Michael to John Wm. Sobers.
1784, Dec. 9th.	Israel Bowen of St. Thomas to Frances Carrington.
1785, June 28th.	Benjamin Bowen of St. Joseph to Mary Ann Gilkes. (Son of John and Mary Bowen born in 1763.)
1789, July 14th.	Benjamin Bowen of St. Michael to Barbara Knight.
1794, Dec. 28th.	Rebecca Bowen (widow) of St. Michael to John Jameson.
1798, May 3rd.	Joseph Bowen of St. Michael to Rebecca Farrell Fletcher.
1798, Sept. 21st.	JOHN BOWEN to Mary Campbell Archer.

BURIALS IN THE 18TH CENTURY.

1712, July 30th.	St. Michael.	Susannah Bowen (Spinster).
1721, March 10th.	St. James.	Evan Bowing.
1748, Feb. 8th.	St. Lucy.	Mary Bowen.
1749, Jan. 3rd.	" "	John Bowen.
1750, July 26th.	" "	Samuel Bowen.
1757, April 11th.	St. John.	Thomasin Bowen. (Wife of Richard Bowen of St. George).
1769, April 24th.	St. Lucy.	John Bowen.
1775, Oct. 31st.	" "	Sarah Boyce Bowen.
1779, Dec. 31st.	St. Michael.	Ann Bowen.
1779, Sept. 15th.	St. Lucy.	Benjamin Bowen.
1779, Oct. 5th.	" "	Dorothy Bowen.
1779, Feb. 13th.	St. Michael.	Benjamin Bowen (an American prisoner).
1782, April 16th.	St. Lucy.	Mary Bowen.
1782, July 12th.	" "	Farnum Richard Bowen.
1783, Sept. 20th.	" "	Jacob Bowen.
1783, Sept. 23rd.	" "	Joseph Bowen (an infant).
1787, July 24th.	" "	Jacob Bowen.
1787, Sept. 23rd.	" "	William Bowen, son of Jacob.
1787, Dec. 12th.	" "	Mary Bowen.
1787, July 14th.	" "	Elizabeth Bowen.
1787, Aug. 21st.	" "	Samuel Bowen.

BURIALS IN THE 18TH CENTURY.—*Contd.*

1788,	St. Peter.	Christian Ann Bowen.
1790, June 4th.	St. Michael.	Thomas Bowen.
1790, August 8th.	St. Lucy.	Sarah Eliza Bowen.
1791, May 4th.	St. Michael.	Barbara Bowen (wife of Benjamin Bowen).
1792, July 4th.	„ „	William Bowen (husband of Rebecca Bowen).
1793, Dec. 10th.	„ „	Mary Bowen (wife of Joseph Bowen).
1794, Jan. 10th.	„ „	William Bowen.
1795, June 6th.	„ „	Sarah Greaves Bowen.
1796, May 2nd.	St. Lucy.	Susannah Bowen[1] (wife of John Bowen).
1797, Jan. 30th.	St. Michael.	Elizabeth Bowen (b. 1764).
1797, Nov. 7th.	St. Lucy.	Alice Bowen.
1798, July 26th.	St. Michael.	Ann Bowen.
1799 March 5th.	„ „	John Bowen.

EXTRACTS FROM BAPTISMS IN THE 19TH CENTURY TO 1840.

(NOTE. In the 19th Century only extracts from the Records are given.)

1801, July 26th.	St. Lucy.	Susannah Greenidge Bowen, daughter of William John and Sarah Thomas Bowen.
1801, Sept. 11th.	„ „	Susannah Boyce Bowen, daughter of John and Mary Campbell Bowen.
1801, July 21st.	„ „	Mary Bowen, daughter of William and Mary Bowen.
1802 May 9th.	„ „	C. of John Bowen, (There is evidence that this refers to ISRAEL BOWEN, founder of the firm of Bowen & Sons.)
1802, March 8th.	St. Michael.	Jane Bowen, daughter of Joseph and Rebecca Farrell Bowen.
1802. Oct. 16th.	St. Lucy.	Susannah Bowen, daughter of Wm. Johnson and Sarah Thos. Bowen.
1803, May 31st.	„ „	Eliza Bowen, daughter of Wm. and Sarah Bowen.

---

1. In "Oliver's Monumental Inscriptions" in Barbados there is mention of her burial in St. Lucy's Churchyard:—No. 1194 white marble.

"This marble is erected to perpetuate the memory of Susannah Bowen wife of John Bowen and Benjamin John Bowen son of the said John and Susannah the former of whom departed this life in giving birth to the latter May 1st, 1796. Aged 41 years."

Date	Church	Name
1804, Jan. 4th.	St Lucy.	Springer Bowen, son of John Bowen Jr. and Mary Campbell Bowen.
1805, July 1st.	„ „	Sarah Frances Bowen.
1813, July 25th.	St. Michael.	Thomas Bowen, son of Israel Bowen.
1814, July 1st.	„ „	William Bowen.
1814, Nov. 14th.	St. Lucy.	Mary Louisa Bowen.
1814, Nov. 14th.	„ „	Alexander Butcher Bowen.
1813, Sept. 20th.	St. Peter.	Senhouse Bowen.
1814, Dec. 1st.	„ „	Frances Carrington Bowen.
1816, May 18th.	„ „	John Walton Bowen.

Children of William Bowen.

Children of Wm. Carrington Bowen and Anna his wife.

1819, March 2nd.	St. Michael.	William Clarke Bowen, son of Jacob and Anna Bowen.
1820, April 12th.	St. Lucy.	Thomas Griffith Bowen b. 1808.
1820, June 15th.	„ „	Mary Eliza Bowen b. 1810.
1820, June 1st.	„ „	Robert James Bowen b. 1812.
1820, Aug. 24th.	„ „	Caroline Johnson Bowen b. 1815.
1820, June 10th.	„ „	Benjamin Alfred Bowen, son of Israel Bowen and Lucretia Jane his wife.
1820, Dec. 27th.	„ „	Charles Thomas Bowen, son of Wm. Johnson Bowen and Sarah his wife.
1813, Dec. 8th.	„ „	John Thomas Bowen, son of Wm. Johnson Bowen and Sarah his wife.
1827, Feb. 14th.	„ „	Mary Bowen, daughter of Wm. Johnson Bowen and Sarah his wife.
1828, March 30th.	St. Michael.	LEWIS NURSE BOWEN, son of Israel and Sarah Frances Bowen.
1830, April 25th.	St. Lucy.	John Richard Bowen, son of Israel and Lucretia Jane Bowen.
1833, April 28th.	„ „	Mary Elizabeth Bowen, daughter of John and Elizabeth Ann Bowen.
1834, Jan. 30th.	„ „	John Bowen, son of Jacob Johnson and Sarah Bowen.
1834, July 19th.	St. Michael.	John Bowen, son of Jacob and Sarah Frances Bowen.

EXTRACTS FROM BAPTISMS IN THE 19TH CENTURY
TO 1840.—*Contd.*

1835, March 3rd.	St. Lucy.	John Bowen, son of John and Elizabeth Ann Bowen.
1837, Feb. 26th.	St. Michael.	GRANT THOMAS BOWEN, son of Israel and Sarah Frances Bowen.
1837, April 11th.	St. Lucy.	Thomas Bowen, son of John and Elizabeth Ann Bowen (John Bowen was a schoolmaster).
1838, Sept. 30th.	St. Michael.	Thomas William Bowen.
1838, Nov. 24th.	St. Lucy.	Mary Elizabeth Bowen, daughter of Richard and Anna Bowen.
1839, June 10th.	St. Michael.	ISRAEL SINDERBY BOWEN, son of Israel Bowen of Trafalgar Street, Bookseller.

EXTRACTS FROM MARRIAGES IN THE 19TH CENTURY

1800, May 24th.	Jacob Bowen of St. Lucy to Sarah Jordan.
1801, July 23rd.	William Johnson Bowen of St. Lucy to Sarah Thomas Archer.
1807, April 7th.	Israel Bowen of St. Peter to Mary Taylor.
1808, Nov. 26th.	Mary Bowen of St. Michael to Wm. Rowe Wildes.
1809, Dec. 23rd.	Katherine Bowen of St. Peter to Lawrance Grogan Skinner.
1810, May 12th.	Mary Bowen of St. Peter to John James Hollingsworth.
1810, Nov. 5th.	Wm. Carrington Bowen of St. Peter to Anna Rowe.
1811, March 5th.	William Bowen of St. Lucy to Elizabeth Butcher.
1816, Sept. 14th.	Sarah Bowen of St. Michael to Andrew Smith.
1818, Jan. 3rd.	Rebecca Bowen of St. Michael to Thomas Hollingsworth.
1818, Jan. 29th.	Jacob Bowen of St. Michael to Anna Benskin.
1818, Dec. 18th.	Joseph Farrell Bowen of St. Michael to Sarah Frances Young.
1820, Feb. 4th.	Israel Bowen of St. Michael to Lucretia Jane Austin.
1825, June 21st.	Keren Bowen of St. Lucy to Thomas Johnson Edwards.
1826, Aug. 19th.	ISRAEL BOWEN of St. Lucy to Sarah Frances Worme at St. Joseph. (This Israel was the founder of the firm of Bowen & Sons.)

EXTRACTS FROM MARRIAGES IN THE 19TH
CENTURY—*Contd.*

1827, Nov. 15th.	Sarah Frances Bowen of St. Lucy to William Benjamin Worme.
1827, May 3rd.	Joan Reynold Bowen of St. Lucy to John Clarke.
1832, May 30th.	John Bowen of St. Lucy to Elizabeth Ann Gilkes.
1833, July 2nd.	Sarah Neville Bowen of St. Lucy to Samuel Bradshaw.
1834, March 5th.	Richard Bowen of St. Lucy to Ann Lawrance.
1835, Feb. 18th.	Jane Ann Bowen of St. Lucy to Benjamin Harris.
1835, July 18th.	William Marshall Bowen of St. Lucy to Mary Elizabeth Wilde.
1839, Nov. 13th.	Mary Rose Bowen of St. Lucy to Samuel Coard.

EXTRACTS FROM BURIALS IN THE 19TH CENTURY TO 1840.

1800, Dec. 5th.	St. Lucy.	Jacob Bowen.
1802, May 9th.	St. Michael.	James Bowen.
1802, Aug. 6th.	St. Lucy.	Susanna Greenidge Bowen.
1802, Dec. 18th.	,, ,,	Mary Bowen.
1803, Dec. 21st.	St. Michael.	Ann Bowen.
1803, June 1st.	,, ,,	Thomas Bowen (mariner).
1803, Aug. 10th.	,, ,,	Jane Bowen.
1804, Aug. 6th.	St. Lucy.	John Bowen (infant).
1804, Nov. 11th.	,, ,,	Frances Bowen.
1806, Dec. 29th.	,, ,,	Jacob Bowen.
1807, Sept. 2nd.	St. Michael.	Ann Bowen.
1809, Feb. 25th.	St. Lucy.	Mary Bowen.
1813, Sept. 15th.	,, ,,	William Bowen.
1814, Dec. 13th.	St. Michael.	Harriett Chase Bowen. (Died at 11 years of age.)
1815, April 2nd.	Christ Church.	Mary Ann Bowen.
1815, Aug. 30th.	St. Lucy.	A. Butcher Bowen.
1816, April 6th.	St. Michael.	John Bowen.
1816, Sept. 13th.	St. Lucy.	William Bowen.
1817, Sept. 1st.	,, ,,	Alexander B. Bowen (infant).
1817, April 9th.	St. Peter.	John Bowen.
1821, Sept. 19th.	St. Michael.	Edward L. Bowen.
1821, Nov. 12th.	,, ,,	Christain Bowen.
1821, Oct. 14th.	St. Lucy.	Elizabeth B. Bowen.
1821, Feb. 23rd.	,, ,,	Samuel Bowen.
1821, April 6th.	,, ,,	Susannah Bowen.
1822, Dec. 4th.	St. Michael.	Thomas Bowen.
1822, Oct. 31st.	St. Lucy.	John Bowen.
1824, Sept. 18th.	,, ,,	Samuel Bowen.

1826, April 9th.	Christ Church.	George Gibson Bowen.
1827, Feb. 27th.	St. Lucy.	John Bowen.
1830, Dec. 4th.	„ „	Rebecca Bowen.
1831, Oct. 13th.	„ „	Susannah Bowen.
1831, June 2nd.	„ „	Henry Sacheverell Bowen.
1831, Feb. 6th.	„ „	John Bowen.
1834, Oct. 13th.	„ „	William Bowen.
1835, Sept 7th.	„ „	Samuel Bowen.
1835, Feb. 5th.	„ „	Benjamin Bowen.
1835, Sept. 8th.	„ „	William Bowen.
1837, Jan. 18th.	„ „	George Walker Bowen.
1838, Dec. 20th.	„ „	Elizabeth Bowen.
1840, Feb. 27th.	„ „	John E. Bowen.
1840, Sept. 30th.	„ „	Anthony Bowen.

EXTRACTS FROM WILLS IN THE REGISTRY.

1. JOHN BOWEN of the Parish of St. Lucies, Planter. His Will is dated 29th March 1656/7. After bequeathing his "Soule unto God who made itt" he gave to his loving wife Ann one halfe or moyety of his whole estate including lambs servants and household stuffe excepting one brass "prott" which he gave to his daughter Katherine and, on his wife's decease, all his estate "to be divided equally between all his children and if any die before they come to receive his or her porcions then his or her share to be equally divided between the rest even to the longest liver." He left to his sister Margery Bowen 1000 lbs. of muscovado sugar and to his friend   one hundred pounds of sugar for his "funerall sermond". He made his wife sole executrix and appointed John Harris and' William Fosnes guardians and tutors of his children.

Witnesses: John Harris, Thomas (signum) Withsmith, and William Jone.

Will proved 10th March 1658 before Daniel Searle [Governor].

(There is no record of his marriage to Ann or of his Burial or of the Baptism of any of his children.)

2. JOHN BOWEN of Christ Church, Planter. Will dated 22nd April 1682. Proved 14th August 1682. To his wife Elizabeth a Plantation of 14 acres until his nephew John reaches the age of 21. Then he is to have 7 acres the remainder divided between the children of his brother William by his first wife. To his deare beloved wife Elizabeth seaven of the said 14 acres which was devised to him by his brother Richard with houses and buildings thereon for life then to go to his nephew John. To wife one negro girl by name Sue—all the rest of his negroes and estate real and personal to his wife for life and on her death to his nephew John. In default of issue to him to his nephew William.

197

To Honble. Richard Howell and Colonel Richard Guy each a ring of 25/- value to be overseers of his will. Other legacies of rings to his friends William Bowen, Thomas Warner, Conrad Adams and Chris Cole appointed his wife executrix.

Witnesses: Ri Cartright, William Wheeler.

John Bowen his X mark.

(There is no record of his baptism, marriage or burial in the Registry.)

3. JOHN BOURN Planter of Christ Church. Will dated 4th July 1684. (In the Index of Wills his name is spelt BOWEN —In an old map of the Island the names BOURN and BOWNE occur as names of Plantations in Christ Church.) Testator left to his beloved wife (unnamed) all his lands and houses for her life and one negro woman named Rose. To his son Samuel 5 acres of land and dwelling house (land carefully defined by Will) on wife's decease to his daughter Joanna Ince in default of issue of his son. To his granddaughter Lucy Addison £5 sterling on reaching the age of 18. To Philip Cammwell and Joseph Carmichael to pay the like to his daughter Deborah Fefeld. The remainder to his son John for life then to go to his son Nicholas. He appointed his wife sole executrix. Witnesses:—John Ruck, Edward Alsop and Robert Aylam.

4. EDWARD BOWEN merchant of St. Michael. Will dated 16th March 1695. Proved 21st July 1696. To his beloved sister Ann Bowen spinster of the city of BRISTOLL all his estate real and personal. Failing which to his loving brother Thomas Bowen mariner his heirs and assigns. He nominated Captain Peter Michell to be executor.

Witnesses:—John Haggard, Edward Dyer and Nicho. Sayers.

5. ANN BOWEN relict and widow of John Bowen deceased. Will dated 16th July 1702—proved 3rd Jan. 1703 before Basell Granville. To her son Jacob 2 acres of land purchased of Abel Poyer and on his death to his sons Samuel and Israel equally and their heirs. Bequests of slaves to sons Samuel, John, Israel and Jacob. She left her cows to her daughter Ann. Executors to be her brother Samuel Armstrong and Thomas Agard.

Witnesses:—Samuel Armstrong, Joseph Almond.

6. ISRAEL BOWIN Planter of St. Lucy. Will dated 1732 "As touching the small estate which the Lord in his mercy hath bestowed upon me" he gave to his Cousin Jacob Bowen son of Jacob Bowen 2 negroes "Little Sarah" a woman and "Cogo" a boy. All the residue of his estate real and personal to the said Jacob. His father Jacob Bowen to be sole executor.

Proved 11th December 1732 before Samuel Barwicke.

7. JACOB BOWEN Planter of St. Lucy. Will dated October 1758. The Petition to Governor Spry of Mary Edwards, his widow, to allow a paper document which was not executed to be his last will is set out. Petition stated that instructions to make

the Will had been given to George Agard and that he had drawn it but that the deceased had died suddenly before signing it.

The draft will was allowed at Pilgrim by Governor Spry on the 7th December 1770. He gave his house called "Goughs" to his wife during widowhood and then to his child Jacob Gibson Bowen. The Will leaves to his brother Israel one negro boy named "Matt". To his mother his cows and, at her death, to his sisters Mary Morrison and Ann Bowen. The residue of his estate to his brother Israel and his heirs.

Executors Henry Sacheverell Smith and John Bowen. Proctor Ed. Harrison who was to present the Petition to the Governor had been taken ill and died without doing so.

8. MARY BOWEN of St. Lucy Parish. Will dated 28th July 1759. Bequeathed all wearing apparell household goods and furniture to daughters Mary Morrison and Ann Bowen equally. Executors to sell 4½ acres of butting and bounding on lands of Jacob Bowen Barrell, Murphy Stephen Agard and Jane Gibson. Proceeds to be divided between all her children viz. William and Benjamin Bowen, Mary Morrison, Ann Bowen, Samuel, John, and Israel Bowen. The x mark of Mary Bowen made in presence of John Seale, Joseph Butcher and Roach Westwood. Proved by Joseph Butcher and given at Pilgrim 27th Nov. 1764. Charles Pinfold.

9. SAMUEL BOWEN of St. Peter. Will dated 17th June 1773. To cousins John Samuel and Sarah Bowen children of John Bowen and to Thomas Babb £2. 10. each to buy mourning rings. To Catherine Barrow one negro man slave named Billey. Said slave to be made free on her death and that £50 currency to be paid for the freedom and manumission of Billey to the Churchwarden of St. Peter. Residue of property for Catherine Barrow and her heirs forever, appointed her executrix of Will.

Witnesses :—Ben Babb, Percival Goulding Archer and Anthony Archer.

Will proved by Anthony Archer.

Given at Pilgrim 20th August 1773.

10. WILLIAM BOWEN of St. Lucy. Will dated 21st May 1786. "Being very aged but in good health" he gave his grandson William Farnell Bowen £50 — all other his real and personal estate to dear son Jacob and his heirs forever. Jacob appointed executor.

Witnesses :—William Frizzle, Thomas Gibbes Farnum and John Mc Geary.

Proved by John Mc Geary, Given at Pilgrim 24th January 1795. G. P. Ricketts.

11. ELIZABETH BOWEN of St. Michael. Will dated 28th Jan. 1797. To daughter Sarah Sober wife of Dr. John Wilson Sober my negro woman slave Grace with her 3 children with their future issue and increase—also a negro man named Ned—other bequests of slaves to grand-daughter and son Benjamin Bowen. To niece Betsy Bowen £40.

Dr. Sobers and Samuel Moore appointed executors.

Witnesses :—Richard Hall, Edmund Eversley.

Given at Pilgrim 8th February 1797. G. P. Ricketts.

12. JACOB BOWEN of St. Lucy Parish. Will dated 3rd October 1799. To my dear wife Sarah Bowen the living in my place and to be supported in an ample manner as in my life and £18 p.a. while my widow, also £300 currency in lieu and bar of dower. To sons Jacob and George Gibson Bowen £1,000 each on attaining 21 years of age. Said sons to be supported educated and maintained at his place out of estate until 21. Various slaves to be given to them. Residue of real and personal property to son William when he is 21. Wife and friends Benjamin Babb and Edward Licorish to be executors.

Witnesses:—John Odwin, Thomas Hollingsworth Jordan.

Will proved by John Odwin at Pilgrim 29th December 1800 before William Bishop.

13. ANN BOWEN (widow of Israel Bowen of St. Michael). Will dated 4th August 1807. To daughter Mary Ann Roach, wife of Robert Roach and to granddaughter Mary Roach, to daughters Elizabeth Rebekah Susannah O'Donald (widow of Jameson O'Donald) certain slaves. Residue of estate to Mary Ann Roach who with John Bowen a relation were appointed executors.

Witnesses:—Joseph Cox and Anthony Wilson.

Proved at Pilgrim before John Spooner 17th Sept. 1807.

14. BENJAMIN BOWEN of St. Michael, mariner. Will dated 10th April 1809. To housekeeper Henrietta Moore, £150 with apparel and household furniture. To son John N. Bowen 10/- excluding him from having anything to do with his estate of whatever kind. Certain slaves to be manumitted, others devised to friends. Residue to nephews Samuel N. Sober and John W. Sober and niece Mary Elizabeth Sober equally.

Executors appointed Thomas Herbert, Irenaeus Mascoll.

Witnesses:—Benjamin Bynoe and Joseph Gibson.

Given at Pilgrim 1st April 1813. George Beckwith.

15. ANN BOWEN of St. Peter. Will dated 9th Sept. 1818. Slaves bequeathed to son in law Mathew Farnum McCoy, to daughter Ann Greaves (wife of Joseph Greaves), to daughter Elizabeth Mahon (wife of Richard Odwin Mahon), to daughter Susannah Chandler (wife of George Chandler), McCoy executor.

Witnesses:—Timothy Mahon, James Whitehead.

Given at Government House 7th February 1820 before LORD COMBERMERE.

PEDIGREE OF ISRAEL BOWEN AND HIS DESCENDANTS.

Owing to the incompleteness of the records for the years from 1683 to 1735 it is difficult to trace descent from the first Anthony Bowen.

As has been stated ANTHONY owned at least 10 acres of land in 1638. This land was probably in Christ Church Parish as old maps show such place names as Bown, Bowne, Borne in that Parish.

It seems likely that he brought 3 sons, John, William and Thomas and a daughter Mary with him to Barbados. Mary was married to John Powell on April 27th 1653 and their child Joan was baptised at Christ Church on May 5th 1654. John died in 1647 and all we know of William is that a son of his was baptised in St. Philip on September 9th 1648 and that he himself was buried in St. Michael in 1682. Thomas married Mary Brookes in Christ Church on August 15th 1644 and their son Anthony was born on January 23rd, 1645. There is no further record of him, or of the name Anthony until we come to 1794 when a child of an Anthony Bowen, named Mary, was baptized in St. Michael. At the time this Anthony was in the 43rd Regiment, and England was at war with France. (See footnote page 51.)

The following line of descent is believed to be correct :—

1. Issue of ANTHONY BOWEN
    i John died 1647.
    ii William died 1682.
  2. iii Thomas married Mary Brookes 1644.
    iv Mary married John Powell 1653.

2. THOMAS BOWEN (Anthony[1]) married Mary Brookes.
    i Anthony born 23rd, January 1645.
  3. ii Benjamin born 1648 (circa).
    iii William born 1650 (circa) died 1682.

3. BENJAMIN BOWEN (Thomas[2] Anthony[1])
  4. i Nicholas born 1679 (See Census 1715).
    ii William born December 3rd. 1683.

4. NICHOLAS BOWEN (Benjamin[3] Thomas[2] Anthony[1]) married Ann (Surname not known) about 1700.
    i Margaret born 1702.
  5. ii John born 1705 died 1769.
    iii Nicholas born 1710.
    iv Sarah born 1713.

5. JOHN BOWEN (Nicholas[4] Benjamin[3] Thomas[2] Anthony[1]) married Mary Farley in 1751 and had issue :
  6. i John born 1752 died 1804.
    ii Samuel born 1754 died 1821.
    iii Israel born 1760 died 1847. He married Frances Carrington in 1784.
    iv Benjamin born 1763.
    v Henry Sacheverell born 1769 died 1831.

6. JOHN BOWEN (John[5] Nicholas[4] Benjamin[3] Thomas[2] Anthony[1]) married Susannah Boyce 1774 and had issue :—

7. i John born 1777 died 1832.
ii William born 1779 died 1789.
iii Henry Sacheverell born 1785.
iv Sarah Boyce born 1786 married Andrew Smith 1816.
v Israel born 1788 died 1820.
7. JOHN BOWEN (John^6 John^5 Nicholas^4 Benjamin^3 Thomas^2 Anthony^1) married Mary Campbell Archer 1798 and had issue:—
i John born 1799. M Elizabeth Ann Gilkes died 1840.
ii Susannah Boyce born 1801.
8. iii Israel born 1802 died 1880.
8. ISRAEL BOWEN (John^7 John^6 John^5 Nicholas^4 Benjamin^3 Thomas^2 Anthony^1) married three times :—
(A) Sarah Frances Worme in 1826 and had issue by her :—
9. i Lewis Nurse born 1828 married Margaret Brathwaite Hunte in 1854. He died in England in 1884.
ii John Packer born 1830 died 1853 while a student at Codrington College.
iii William Turpin born 1834. After being a missionary in British Guiana he went to the U.S.A.
10. iv Grant Thomas born 1837 married Elizabeth Southwell (widow) née Fitzgerald. Vicar of St. Ambrose and St. Cyprian Churches. Died 1918.
(B) Elizabeth Sinderby in 1838 in England and had issue by her :—
11. i Israel Sinderby born 1839 married Margaret Anne Goodridge Simpson 1860. Died 1915.
(C) Annie Howard in 1870 in England. On her husband's death in England in 1880 she went to Vancouver and died there about 1925. Issue by her one daughter who only lived a fortnight.
9. LEWIS NURSE BOWEN (Israel^8 John^7 John^6 John^5 Nicholas^4 Benjamin^3 Thomas^2 Anthony^1) and his wife Margaret Brathwaite Bowen had issue :—
i Louis Nurse born 1855 married Emma Trotman 1912 died 1930. They had issue one son and one daughter.
ii Charles Packer born 1857 married Mary Leila Boxill 1883 died 1921. They had issue two sons and one daughter.
iii Minnie Goding born 1865 married Walter Leonard McKinstry 1892. They had issue one daughter and two sons.
Lewis Nurse Bowen succeeded his father in the Firm in partnership with his half-brother Sinderby Bowen who later retired. On the death of Lewis Nurse Bowen his son Louis Nurse Bowen became head of the firm with his brother and sister as partners.

Charles Packer Bowen practised as a Solicitor in Barbados and was clerk of the House of Assembly. He was also organist of the Cathedral for many years.

10. GRANT THOMAS BOWEN (Israel[8] John[7] John[6] Nicholas[4] Benjamin[3] Thomas[2] Anthony[1]) and his wife Elizabeth Bowen had issue:—

  i Cuthberth Fitzgerald M.D. born 1864 married 1895 Agnes Elizabeth Bonyun (widow) died 1899. At one time he was Senior Resident Medical Officer at the General Hospital.

  ii Arthur Fitzgerald born 1868 died unmarried 1921. Barrister-at-law, Middle Temple, and an accomplished musician. He was a Judge of the Assistant Court of Appeal of Barbados.

  iii Elizabeth Fitzgerald born 1871 married Lisle Evan Boxill 1892 and had issue two sons and three daughters. Died in England 1939.

The Revd. Grant Thomas Bowen married as his second wife Elizabeth Barker Grant, (widow) 1907. There was no issue of this marriage.

11. ISRAEL SINDERRY BOWEN (Israel[8] John[7] John[6] John[5] Nicholas[4] Benjamin[3] Thomas[2] Anthony[1]) and his wife Margaret Anne Goodridge Bowen had issue :—

  i Ernest Francis Sinderby born 1861 died in the U.S.A., where he had gone (after retiring from the Colonial Civil Service) to pursue his love of painting. There are many paintings of his both in water colours and in oils in this island. Married Maud Hodgkinson in England and they had issue.

  ii Eustace Gordon born 1865 married Agnes Lisle Webb 1904. He was a master at the Combermere School and a good classical scholar and had won an Island Scholarship to Codrington College 1883. There was no issue of this marriage.

  iii Florence Glanville born 1866 married Samuel St. Hill. There was no issue of this marriage. Died in U.S.A.

  iv Goodridge Sinderby born in 1868 married in England to Annette Sterner and had issue. Under the name of Julian Pascal he became a famous professional pianist and composer both in London and New York.

  v Charles Inniss born 1869. Went to U.S.A. to study Art.

  vi Henry Farre born 1872. Was employed under the Admiralty at Chatham, England.

  vii Frederick Augustus born 1874. Went to U.S.A.

  viii Kathleen Goding born 1885. Went to the U.S.A. with her sister Florence on the death of the latter's husband.

Israel Sinderby Bowen had great musical talent and played both the organ and piano with exceptional ability.

Israel Bowen died in England on the 18th December 1880 and was buried at Highgate Cemetery where his son Lewis Nurse Bowen was also buried. The latter died in England on the 31st of May 1884.

Israel's first wife Sarah Frances was buried in St. Paul's Churchyard, Barbados, and there is a marble head stone enclosed by an iron railing commemorating her death on the 27th May 1837 aged 33 years.

He first started his bookshop in Church Street in 1834 and the Editor of the "Barbadian" newspaper published the following on February 6th 1835 "Editor notices that the Booksellers shop commenced last year by Mr. Israel Bowen is increasing in extent and respectability. List of books on sale". In the same paper for November 11th 1837 is an advertisement as follows:— "Mr. Israel Bowen opens a bookshop filling a long felt want here". There is also a notice in the same paper of the death on May 27th 1837 "after a severe illness of Mrs. Bowen wife of Mr. Israel Bowen, Bookseller, Church Street". In August 1838 it was also announced in the "Barbadian" that he had married Miss Sinderby in England.

In 1839 Israel Bowen was Secretary of the Barbados Temperance Society which had been in existence for some years. In that year the name was changed to the Barbados Society for the suppression of Drunkenness and Intemperance.

In 1841 Israel Bowen was carrying on his bookshop at 13 Trafalgar Street where he also had a circulating Library.

In 1863 the Barbados Almanac and Diary was published by I. Bowen, Bookseller and Stationer at No. 20 Broad Street, Bridgetown, Barbados. Judging from the preface this was the first issue of the Almanac. In 1866 it was published by I. Bowen and Sons the new title of the Firm. In later years, probably after the death of Israel Bowen the Founder, the Almanac was issued annually by the Firm of Bowen and Sons, its present name, up to at least 1887.

There is a good portrait of Israel Bowen in oils painted by his grandson Ernest Francis Sinderby Bowen late Director of Public Works in Barbados, who was the architect of the Carnegie Public Library and a painter of ability who had exhibited at the Royal Academy in London.

Others of Israel Bowen's descendants have distinguished themselves in the Arts and Music. He himself played the violin and was very musical as his only surviving grandchild in Barbados well remembers. Amusing stories are told of this kindly, interesting and remarkable man—not the least being the consternation of his family at the news of his third marriage in England when he was 68 to a lady of 17. When he brought her back to Barbados she was received by the family with open arms. Their baby girl only lived a fortnight. They retired to England where he died at the age of 78.

ADDENDUM.

DR. THOMAS BOWEN b. April 11th, 1837, was one of the leading physicians of the Island from 1870 to 1920 and was a son of John and Elizabeth Ann Bowen of St. Lucy who were married on May 30th, 1832. John was the eldest brother of Israel, founder of the Firm. Dr. Bowen died 27th Feby., 1926. There is a brass tablet to his memory in St. Leonard's Church. There is also one to his son Francis Goding Bowen, B.A., M.B., B.C., Cantab, M.R.C.S., L.R.C.P., London, who died at Fort Jameson, North Eastern Rhodesia on 17th Feby., 1905.

Dr. Bowen married Mary Challenor in 1868 and had by her 3 sons and one daughter. On her death he married, as his second wife, in 1878, Annie Newbold O'Neal and had 2 daughters by her.

It may be noted that there have been few more popular doctors in the Island than Dr. Thomas Bowen and, after him, his son Dr. Colin Bowen who both had large practices in Barbados.

Carrington of Barbados.*

Nathaniel C. of St. Thomas' Parish. Will proved 30 November 1693. Son William. Brother Paul.

Paul C. (Doctor) of St. Philip's. Will proved 16 December 1724. By common fame testator perished at sea eight years before 17 November 1724. Daus.: Sarah, Elizabeth, Ann, Mary, Hannah. Sons: Nathaniel, Paul, Codrington, Robert and John (twins), George, Joseph, Edward. Wife Hemingham.

Thomazin C. alias Waterland, widow, of St. Philip's. Will proved 14 July 1727. John Perryman alias Carrington alias Waterland of St. Philip's, Francis Perryman alias Carrington alias Waterland, planter. Dau. Sarah Bedford.

John C. of St. Philip's Parish, gentleman. Will proved 15 March 1733. Brothers: Robert, Paul, Codrington, Nathaniel, wife Mary (their children, Elizabeth, Judith, Paul, and John). Brother-in-law John Hearne, wife Hannah (their children, Ann and Ruth Hearne). Sister-in-law Rebeccah Gittens.

Robert C., merchant, at present residing in Antigua. Will proved at Antigua 30 October 1734. Mother Hemingham Carrington of St. Philip's. Brothers: Codrington, St. Michael's; Nathaniel, St. Philip's, planter. Hemingham Hearne, daughter of John Hearne, practitioner in physic and chirurgery.

Hemingham C. of St. Philip's Parish, widow. Will proved 12 February 1744-45. Sons: Nathaniel, eldest (his children, Elizabeth, Judith, Paul, John, Robert, Codrington), Codrington, Paul (his daughter, Eliza Hannah). Dau. Hannah, wife of John Hearne (their children, Ruth, Elizabeth, Codrington, Walter, John, and Nathaniel Hearne). Daus.-in-law (step-daughters?): Elizabeth, spinster, Ann Mayo, Mary Milward.

Edward C., intending a voyage to Virginia. Entered 17 December 1745. Mother Hannah Carrington. Father Paul, deceased. Brothers: Codrington, Paul, Nathaniel. Nephew Paul. Nieces: Elizabeth and Judith Carrington, Ann and Ruth Hearne, Ann Milward. Brother-in-law John Hearne.

Paul C. of St. Michael's Parish. Will proved 5 July 1750. Wife Mary. Brother Codrington. Brother-in-law Benjamin Mellowes ("my children," not named). Dau. Elizabeth Hannah.

* Communicated by Mr. N. Darnell Davis.

205

Thomas C. of St. Peter's Parish. Will entered 30 October 1758. Wife Elizabeth (" all my children," not named).

Elizabeth C., spinster, of St. Philip's. Will dated 8 April 1766. Sister Mary Milward, widow. Nieces: Ann Hearne Bostock, Elizabeth Bostock. Sister Elizabeth Adams (her children, Elizabeth, Lydia, Millicent).

Charles C. of St. Thomas' Parish. Will proved 19 April 1783. Wife Christian, and children (not named).

William C. of St. Thomas', gentleman. Will proved 26 November 1787. Sons: William, Nathaniel, Thomas, Richard Williams, Paul. Daus.: Elizabeth, and Frances, wife of Israel Bowen.

Christian C. of St. Thomas' Parish. Will proved 15 December 1788. Sons: William and Charles Carrington, James and Thomas, Thomas Partridge.

Abel Williams C. of St. Andrew's Parish. Will proved 5 November 1798. Wife Elizabeth. Son Abel. Daus.: Elizabeth, Harriet, Frances. Brother Richard Williams Carrington. Relation Thomas Williams.

John C. of St. John's. Will proved 12 October 1805. Wife Ann Anderson (" children," not named). Christopher E. Gall, a witness.

Elizabeth C. of St. Thomas'. Will proved 3 August 1807. Dau. Francis Elizabeth Carrington *alias* Christie.

William C. of Christ Church. Will proved 9 November 1807. Brother Charles. Sister Christian Carrington. Brother-in-law James Partridge (his children, Thomas, Mercy Evans, Sarah Roswell; Thomas was in the colony of Berbice). Nephew Samuel Thomas Partridge.

Elizabeth C. of St. Thomas', widow. Will proved 8 March 1814. Son Abel. Daus.: Elizabeth, Harriet Frances. Brother-in-law Richard Williams Carrington.

Richard Williams C. of St. Thomas', planter. Will proved 15 September 1817. Sons: John William Worrell Carrington, Nathaniel Thomas Worrell Carrington. Nieces (daughters of sister Elizabeth Matthews) Frances, Elizabeth. Executor, his friend Dr. Thomas Williams.

Charles C. of St. Michael's Parish. Will proved 19 January 1818. Wife Elizabeth. Son James Henry. Daus.: Mary Christian, Elizabeth Alice, Sarah Ann. Brother William, deceased.

Joshua C. of St. Michael. Will proved 21 June 1843. Sister Margaret Ann.

Margaret Ann C. of St. Michael, spinster. Will proved 28 January 1846. Niece Caroline, wife of Henry Affleck Sisnett.

MARRIAGES.

Date.			To whom married.
1661	Feb. 24	Ann	John Thatcher.
1671	Aug. 28	Ann	Nicholas Newton.
1687	May 10	Paul	Thomazine Waterland.
1714	Feb. 27	Sarah	Robert Bedford.

Date.			To whom married.
1716	Sep. 24	Ann	Joseph Mayo.
1725	May 19	Nathaniel	Mary Howell.
1730	July 25	Codrington	Elizabeth Bissell, widow.
1730	Sept. 12	William	Ann Watkins.
1734	Jan. 12	Edward	Jane Gibbes.
1746	Oct. 25	William	Elizabeth Williams.
1756	Dec. 23	Judith	Jonathan Brooke.
1758	Jan. 24	Paul	Mary Ann Howton.
1760	May 24	Eliza Hannah	Charles Willing of.Philadelphia.
1765	April 13	Mary	Cornelius Donovan.
1770	July 12	Judith	Foster Carter Cattlewell.
1775	May 11	Charles	Christian Partridge.
1778	Aug. 1	Elizabeth	David Parris.
1780	Feb. 8	Thomas	Sarah Smith Benjamin.
1782	Dec. 14	William	Martha King.
1784	Dec. 9	Frances	Israel Bowen.
1787	—	Richard Williams	Jane Worrell.
1798	Feb. 16	Sarah Ann	Thomas Alder.
1799	April 6	Paul	Mary Seale Chandler.
1801	Aug. 20	Mary	William Leslie.
1802	Nov. 11	Charles	Elizabeth King.
1806	—	Mary Seale	Benjamin Stroud.
1806	—	Frances Elizabeth	John Matthews.
1809	—	Christian Ann	George Upton Law.
1810	Jan. 6	Charles	Elizabeth Hite.
1815	Aug. 31	Sarah B:	John Worrell Williams.

BAPTISMS.

Year.		Child's Name.	Parents.
1689	Feb. 10	Thomas	Thomas and Mary.
1696	Mar. 14	John William	} Sons of Paul and Thoma.
1702	Oct. 31	Nathaniel	Dr. Paul.
1704	Feb. 22	Hannah	
1706	June 23	Paul	} Dr. Paul and Mrs. Hemingham.
1707	Nov. 21	Codrington	
1710	April 23	William	Paul.
1711	July 8	George	Paul.
1713	July 26	Joseph	Paul.
1714	Feb. 7	Edward	Paul.
1730	Sept. 6	Judith	Nathaniel and Mary.
1731	Jan. 9	Paul	Nathaniel and Mary.
1737	June 2	Christian	William and Anne.
1739	May 6	Charles	William and Anne.
1741	May —	Ann	William and Anne.
1743	—	John	William and Anne (St Thomas). Born 27 June.
1745	Nov. 30	Judith	William and Anne
1746	Oct. 26	Ann	Paul and Mary. Born 20 Oct.
1746	Mar. 8	Antipas	William and Ann.

Year.			Child's Name.	Parents.
1747	Nov.	12	Nathaniel	William and Elizabeth.
1748	Aug.	18	William	William and Elizabeth.
1749	Oct.	3	Thomas	William and Elizabeth
1750	Jan.	4	Codrington	Paul and Mary. Born 5 Oct. 1749.

DEATHS.*

1693	July	20	Thomas, a child.
1698	Jany.	26	Mary, a child.
1700	July	16	Parsis.
1723	July	23	a son.
1729	Aug.	25	Nathaniel son of Nathaniel.

				Reference to Register.	Parish.
1733	Jan.	13	Dr John	25, 42	St Philip.
1738	May	11	Christen, a child	49, 108	St Thos.
1738	May	13	Rebecca, a child	49, 108	St Thos.
1740	Sep.	16	Jane wife of Paul, Esq.	25, 49	St Philip.
1744	Jan.	29	Heningham	25, 52	St Philip.
1745	March	9	Paul, an infant	49, 116	St Thos.
1754	Feb.	17	Miss Ann, a child 7 years old	49, 128	St Thos.
1762	July	21	Mary, from St Michael	25, 67	St Philip.
1764	Sep.	25	Mary, a child	4, 258	St Mich^l.
1764	June	—	Codrington, St Michael	25, 69	St Philip.
1765	May	26	M^{rs}	49, 155	St Thos.
1767	Sep.	11	Frances	4, 363	St Mich^l.
1768	June	25	Robt Codrington	4, 399	St Mich^l.
1769	Feb.	25	Paul	4, 434	St Mich^l.
1769	Feb.	1	Nathl Codrington son of Paul, infant	4, 430	St Mich^l.
1770	Jan.	29	William, from S. Thomas' Parish, aged 89 years	4, 482	St Mich^l.
1772	Jan.	6	Ann	49, 178	St Thos.
1779	May	16	John Natural son of Mary	5, 202	St Mich^l.
1780	Oct.	15	Eliz.	5, 256	St Mich^l.
1780	Jan.	1	Robt son of Rev. Codrington	25, 84	St Philip.
1783	March	31	Charles, Husband of Christian	5, 340	St Mich^l.
1786	March	13	Richd Dowell	5, 409	St Mich^l.
1787	Sep.	6	Edward Codrington	5, 445	St Mich^l.
1788	Oct.	17	Christian, M^{rs}	49, 243	St Thomas.
1789	Jan.	17	Edward Codrington son of William	5, 478	St Mich^l.
1790	Oct.	26	Nathl	49, 250	St Thomas.
1791	Sep.	10	Mary Ann	5, 541	St Mich^l.
1792	June	27	Thos.	46, 620	St James.

---

* Checked and corrected by Mr. E. G. Sinckler.

ALL SAINTS, SOUTHAMPTON.*

South aisle, east wall (vestry) :—

SACRED TO THE BELOVED MEMORY OF THE MOST EXCELLENT PAULINA,
WIFE OF SIR CODRINGTON EDMUND CARRINGTON KN^{HT}.
THE FIRST CHIEF JUSTICE OF CEYLON, APPOINTED IN 1801,
AND DAUGHTER OF JOHN BELLI, ESQ^{RE} OF A NOBLE ITALIAN FAMILY,
AND OF ELIZABETH STUART COCKERELL, HIS WIFE,
SHE WAS MARRIED IN THIS CHURCH, AUGUST 1801,
AND DIED AT NEW HOUSE, CHALFONT ST. GILES, BUCKS,
AUGUST 9TH 1823, AGED 38.
ERECTED BY MARIANNE AND JANE CARRINGTON
TWO OF HER SURVIVING CHILDREN 1872.

Above are ARMS.—*Sable, on a bend Or three lozenges* [CARRINGTON], *impaling :
Or, on a chevron Azure between in base a rose, and in chief three heads (? men's
heads), a mullet between two roses.*
MOTTO above.—SPERO .... Below : SURG ....
The brass shield is very dirty and the paint worn off.

Sir Codrington Edmund Carrington, the son of Codrington Carrington of the
Blackmoor estate in Barbados, by the eldest dau. of the Rev. Edmund Morris,
Rector of Nutshalling, was born at Longwood in Hampshire 22 Oct. 1769. _ He
was educated at Winchester, and called to the Bar at the Middle Temple 10 Feb.
1792, went to India the same year, returned in 1799, codified the laws of Ceylon,
and was knighted and appointed Chief Justice of that Island in 1800. In 1806
he retired and purchased an estate in Bucks, was J.P., D.L., and Chairman of
Quarter Sessions, D.C.L., F.R.S., and F.S.A., and M.P. for St Mawes 1826—1831.
During his last years he resided at St. Helier's, Jersey, and died at Exmouth
28 Nov. 1849, aged 80, leaving two sons, Edmund F. J. Carrington of Park Hill,
Paignton, Devonshire, and the Very Rev. H. Carrington, Dean and Rector of
Bocking, Essex. (See full account in " D.N.B.")
See *ante*, I., 374, for the M.I. to his second wife in Lansdown Cemetery, Bath.
In St. Philip's, Barbados, is a M.I. to Henningham Carrington, widow of
Paul Carrington .... ob. Jan. 28, 1741, æt. 69 (Archer, 386). 1741 is an error
for 1744 [ED.].
1768, Nov. 25. Codrington Carrington, Esq ; of Barbadoes, to Miss Morris
of Havant, Hants. (" G.M.," 590.)
1823, Aug. 9. At New-house-place, Chalfont St. Giles, Bucks, the lady of
Sir Corington (*sic*) Edmund Carrington. (*Ibid.*, 188.)
1834, Ap. 26. The lady of Sir Codrington Edmund C. of Chalfont St. Giles,
Bucks, a dau. (*Ibid.*, 649.)
1834, June 25. At Leamington, aged 15, Amelia, dau. of Sir C. E. Carrington,
of Chalfont St. Giles. (*Ibid.*, 221.)
1840, Ap. 13. At Mount Pleasant, Jersey, the lady of Sir C. E. C., a son.
(*Ibid.*, 535.)
1849, Nov. 28. At Exmouth, a. 80, Sir Codrington Edmund Carrington,
Knt. a Bencher of the Middle Temple, D.C.L., F.R.S., F.S.A., etc. (*Ibid.*, 1850,
92.)
1854, May 24. At Bath, the Rev. Tho. Mordaunt Rosenhagen Barnard, B.A.
of Exeter Coll. Ox. to Charlotte, dau. of the l. Sir Codrington Edmund Carrington, Chief Justice of Ceylon. (*Ibid.*, 189.)
1815, Sep. 2. On Thursday morning in St. Michael's Church, Mr. John W.
Williams to Miss Sarah B. Carrington. (" Barbados Mercury," *ante*, II., 216.)

* Notes added by the Editor.

John Belli of Southampton, Esq. Will dated 24 May 1802. My brothers-in-law Sam. Pepys Cockerell and Chas. Cockerell, Esq^res. My late father-in-law Sam. Blount. My wife and children. Proved 1805 (251, Nelson).

Major Chas. Fred. Napier, R.A., mar. 1804 Cath., dau. of Codrington Carrington of The Chapel and Carrington B., and died March 1812, having had a son afterwards Lord Napier of Magdala.

Sir John Worrell Carrington, Knt., was born 1847 in Barbados, fourth son of Nath. T. W. C. of Industry plantation, St. Joseph's Parish, planter, by Christian Wharton his wife, dau. of Dr. R. Reed of St. Philip's Parish. He matriculated from Lincoln Coll., Oxford, 22 Oct. 1868, aged 21, B.A. 1872, Barrister-at-law, Lincoln's Inn, 1872, Solicitor-General of Barbados 1878, Chief Justice of St. Lucia and Tobago 1882—89, Attorney-General of British Guiana 1889—96, Chief Justice of Hongkong 1826—1902, when he retired. He was knighted in 1897. Married in 1872 Susan Cath., dau. of Wm. Walsh of Norham, Oxford, and resides at Reading. (" Knightage," and Foster's " Alumni Oxonienses.")

A MATRIMONIAL CONUNDRUM

P. F. CAMPBELL

An article by Norma Forde entitled 'The Evolution of Marriage Law in Barbados' appeared in the Journal in 1975 (xxxv.33-46), and at page 42 it was stated (referring to Barbados) that 'there was no legal divorce before 1935 even by Act of Parliament'. This contains a printer's error: 'even' should read 'except'. The error came to light in connection with an investigation into the circumstances surrounding the passing in Barbados on 13 August 1706 of 'An Act to make null and void the marriage of Paul Carrington, Chirurgeon, and Thomazin his wife'. The title is given in Hall's *Laws*, but the text of the Act is not known.

The Act of 1706 appears to be the only one that has ever been passed in Barbados declaring a marriage to be null and void, and it would be of great interest to know the background to the Act and the grounds on which the marriage was nullified. The only small bit of information we have is that in 1701 a petition of Dr. Paul Carrington (who will be referred to here as Dr. Paul) was submitted to the Barbados House of Assembly, but was held over for consideration until the next session.

There is, of course, a distinction between a divorce and a declaration that a marriage is null and void. In Barbados, as stated by Miss Forde in the passage from her article quoted above, there was no divorce in Barbados until 1935 except by Act of Parliament, and after 1773 the Governor was forbidden by his Instructions to assent to any such Act without the permission of the Crown. There is no record of a private Divorce Act in Barbados. In England it was not until 1858 that divorce could be granted by the courts. Before that date the procedure for obtaining a divorce by Act of Parliament was lengthy and expensive; indeed, there were only five such Acts before the reign of George I.

The title of the Barbados Act of 1706 makes it clear that it was not a Divorce Act but an Act to declare the marriage of Dr. Paul and Thomazin null and void; in other words, declaring that there was never a legal marriage. This is doubly perplexing. The first reason is that it is far from clear on what grounds the marriage could have been declared null and void. The grounds recognized

211

at the time were want of proper age (which was then twelve years), consanguinity, absence of consent and the physical incapacity of either spouse. None of these grounds appear to have been applicable in this case. Thomazin was baptized on 3 May 1673 and was at least fourteen years of age at the time of her marriage; it is reasonably certain that there was no relationship between her and Dr. Paul; and the fact that she had borne a child or children to Dr. Paul would have ruled out any plea of absence of consent or physical incapacity.

The other matter that is perplexing is why the nullification of the marriage required an Act of Parliament. An Act would have been necessary to nullify the marriage if the parties had been within the prohibited degrees of consanguinity, but all the evidence is against this. Otherwise nullification was not a matter requiring legislation, as the following extract from the minutes of the Council of 18 May 1670 makes clear:

Upon petition of Mary Ditty alleging, that before she was ten years of age, she was ruled by those her duty taught her to obey, and was married to one Thomas Higham; and that coming to mature years, she found she could not affect the same Thomas Higham, as being a match disproportionate for her: and it appearing to this Board, that as soon as she had power of dissenting, which was presently after she was twelve years of age, she petitioned to the Justices of Quarter Sessions (where she lived), for a separation: and she observing, that the said Higham had never carnally known her, as a wife, and they both appearing this day before this Board; and the said Mary Ditty still averring the same; this Board have ordered, and do order, that the said marriage being under years be and is declared to be a nullity; and the said parties to be separated as if not married; and that the said Higham leave her free; and claim no more the said Ditty as his wife.

Dr. Paul was the second son of a Paul Carrington who died in Barbados in 1666. Dr. Paul himself was born in Barbados about 1665 and was the founder of the St. Philip branch of the family, purchasing the estate now known as Carrington not later than 1707. He married Thomazin Waterland of St. Philip in May 1687.

The matrimonial affairs of Dr. Paul and Thomazin were complex in the extreme; we know of nineteen children of whom one or the other was the parent, and we know that Richard Perryman was the father of some and that Hemingham (or Heningham) Codrington was the mother of others. We also know that Richard Perryman married Ann Haynes in 1678 and had at least two children by her. It is assumed that it was this Ann Perryman who died in 1712.

To assist the reader, a list is now given of the twenty-one known children of whom Dr. Paul, Thomazin, Hemingham or Richard Perryman was one of the parents. The date of birth or baptism is given when this is known; in other cases the date of birth is calculated from the child's age stated in the 1715 census; and this date is printed in italics. Unfortunately, the census age of a person can differ from the baptismal age by a year, depending on the date of the person's birthday, and in some cases the census age is two years less than the baptismal age. The married names (first marriage only) of children are given in brackets.

		Father	*Mother*
1679	Ann Perryman (Beauchamp)	Richard	Ann
	Sarah Carrington (Bedford)	Paul	Thomazin
1695	Elizabeth Carrington	Paul	
1696	Edmund Perryman	Richard	Ann
1697	John Perryman	Richard	Thomazin
1697	William Perryman	Richard	Thomazin
1699	Ann Carrington (Mayo)	Paul	
1699	Mary Perryman (Garey)	Richard	Thomazin
1699	Rachel Perryman	Richard	Thomazin
1701	Mary Carrington (Milward)	Paul	
1702	Nathaniel Carrington	Paul	Hemingham
1705	Francis Perryman	Richard	Thomazin
1705	Hannah Carrington (Hearne)	Paul	Hemingham
1706	Paul Carrington	Paul	Hemingham
1707	Codrington Carrington	Paul	Hemingham
1709	John Carrington	Paul	Hemingham
1709	Robert Carrington	Paul	Hemingham
1710	William Carrington	Paul	Hemingham
1711	George Carrington	Paul	Hemingham
1713	Joseph Carrington	Paul	Hemingham
1715	Edward Carrington	Paul	Hemingham

NOTES

1. It is clear that Edmund was not brought up by his father, Richard Perryman, who made no reference to him in his will. The daughter Ann (baptized 1679) was married in 1693.
2. Sarah was the eldest known child of Dr. Paul and Thomazin. She was married in February 1714/15.

3. John and William Perryman, twins, are entered in the baptismal register as sons of Dr. Paul and Thomazin, but they were certainly the sons of Richard Perryman. They are referred to in Thomazin's will as 'Perryman alias Carrington alias Waterland'.

We are fortunate that most of the persons concerned made wills and mentioned the children by name, and also stated their relationship to the testator. Of the fourteen children in the above list who have Dr. Paul shown as the father, thirteen are mentioned in his will of 1715; the only one omitted is William, who had already died. Similarly, in her will made in 1745, Hemingham names as children all the survivors of the nine boys and a girl whom she bore to Dr. Paul between 1702 and 1715. Richard Perryman, in his will of 1712, refers to 'my much esteemed friend' Mrs. Thomazin Waterland alias Carrington and to her five children John, William, Francis, Mary and Rachel; and Thomazin, in her will made in 1726, describes Sarah as her daughter.

This accounts for everybody in the list except Elizabeth, Ann (Mayo) and Mary (Milward). Who was their mother? The obvious candidates are Thomazin and Hemingham. The evidence will now be examined.

Assuming that Ann was born in 1698 instead of 1699, it would have been physically possible for Thomazin to have been the mother. If that were so, the births between 1695 and 1701 would have been as follows:

		Father	Mother
1695	Elizabeth Carrington	Paul	Thomazin
1696	Edmund Perryman	Richard	Ann
1697	John and William Perryman	Richard	Thomazin
1698	Ann Carrington	Paul	Thomazin
1699	Mary and Rachel Perryman	Richard	Thomazin
1701	Mary Carrington	Paul	Thomazin

There was much promiscuity in Barbados in the seventeenth century, but it would be difficult to find in any civilized society a pattern such as that shown in this list, with Thomazin bearing children in alternate years to Dr. Paul and Richard. However, there are other reasons for thinking that Thomazin was not the mother of the three girls. It will be noted that after Sarah, and with the unimportant exception of the twins John and Robert, all the children known to have been borne to Dr. Paul by either Thomazin

214

or Hemingham were baptized; even the twins John and William, borne by Thomazin to Richard, were baptized as the children of Dr. Paul and Thomazin, indicating that at that date, and after the birth of Elizabeth, Dr. Paul and Thomazin were trying to save their marriage. If the three girls were in fact the daughters of Thomazin, it has to be explained why she never recognized them as such, bearing in mind that she recognized Sarah as her daughter. It is also unusual, to say the least, that Thomazin should have agreed to Mary as the name of her daughter by Dr. Paul in 1701 when she had borne a child of the same name to Richard two years previously. For all these reasons it is unlikely that Thomazin was the mother of Elizabeth, Ann and Mary.

We know from the 1715 census that at that date the three girls were being brought up in the household of Dr. Paul and Hemingham. But in her will made in 1745 Hemingham refers to them as daughters-in-law, which at the time often meant stepdaughters. If she had meant that they were born out of wedlock, she would have had to apply the same description to Nathaniel, Hannah and Paul, all of whom were born before the passing of the Act of 1706.

The conclusion reached is that Elizabeth, Ann and Mary were probably borne to Dr. Paul neither by Thomazin, nor by Hemingham, but by some other woman. The only clue we have to her identity is contained in the will made in 1766 by Elizabeth, who had never married. In the will she left her 'cousin Elizabeth Adams, spinster' £100, and she left smaller amounts to two other Adams cousins. Mrs. Elizabeth Adams, widow, who seems to have been their stepmother is, described as a friend. The term 'cousin' was used in those days to denote any sort of relationship, and since in this will cousins are in any case contrasted with friends one assumes that some relationship did exist. Yet there is no mention of an Adams in any other Carrington will, and it is reasonably certain that there was no relationship between the two families.

The fathering of illegitimate children was common in all ranks of society and did not necessarily result in the breakdown of a marriage. Dr. Paul, for example, condoned the adultery of Thomazin with Richard Perryman when he registered as his own the twins she had borne to Richard. Perhaps she already knew of his own adultery with the mother of Elizabeth. Nevertheless it does seem that Thomazin must have left Dr. Paul for Richard Perryman about 1696-7, and presumably all her children except Sarah were brought up in the Perryman household.

This raises the question of when Dr. Paul started an association with Hemingham, and in what household Elizabeth, Ann and Mary lived. It is unlikely that Dr. Paul's adultery with Hemingham started earlier than 1701; her subsequent record of childbearing supports this view, as also does the fact that 1701 was the year in which Dr. Paul petitioned for the annulment of his marriage to Thomazin. It is possible that Elizabeth, Ann and Mary were taken into the household of Dr. Paul and Hemingham on the death of their mother — or perhaps on her marriage.

How did Dr. Paul manage to get an Act passed to annul his marriage to Thomazin? Everything points to this being a case of the rules being bent to accommodate a person of influence. Dr. Paul was hardly such a person. We know that he was a successful merchant, trading with North America and England, to both of which countries he seems to have paid several visits. He is described as a doctor not long after his marriage, but we do not know where or when he acquired medical qualifications, and there is no record of his ever having practised. Though he was obviously well off, he was never a member of the Council or House of Assembly. It is probably fair to describe him as a respected member of the community, but not as a person of influence.

One would expect to find the influence being exerted by the Codrington family. Until recently none of the theories put forward about Hemingham's ancestory have been at all convincing. J.C. Brandow, who has done a great deal of research into the Carringtons, has now suggested that she may have been descended from Robert Codrington of Didmarton, who married Herningham (perhaps Hemingham) Drewrey of Norfolk, and whose son Robert was baptized in London in 1635. This son may have been the Robert Codrington who was living in Barbados with his wife Elizabeth in 1665. If Hemingham, who was born in 1676, was their daughter — they had another daughter in 1678 — she was a distant relative of Christopher Codrington, and he may have been the person who used his influence.

Richard Perryman and his lawful wife Ann both died in 1712, she predeceasing him by a few months, and Richard therefore never married Thomazin. No record has been traced of the marriage of Dr. Paul and Hemingham. The marriage registers for this period for some parishes (St. Joseph, St. Thomas, St. Lucy, St. Peter, St. George and St. Andrew) are no longer available, and it is possible, but unlikely, that a marriage took place in one of those parishes. Marriages often took place in private houses, but even then the law required them to be registered. When Hannah and Paul, both of whom were born before the 1706 Act, were baptized in 1707 they were described as the children of Dr. Paul and Hemingham Carrington. Thereafter she is always referred to as his wife, and on her tombstone in St. Philip's churchyard she is described as his widow.

In countries whose system of law was based on Roman law it was possible for illegitimate children to be legitimized by the subsequent marriage of their parents. This was not so in England, nor in Barbados, and there was no way in which Hemingham's children born before 1706 could have been legitimized, unless one accepts the possibility that the Act did so retrospectively. Nevertheless, it seems that for all practical purposes the children borne by Hemingham to Dr. Paul before their marriage (if there was a marriage) were regarded as legitimate, and Nathaniel, the eldest of these, succeeded to the Carrington estate on Dr. Paul's death.

ACKNOWLEDGEMENTS

J. C. Brandow continues to be indefatigable in his search for information about the history of the Carrington family, and I am deeply grateful to him for making available to me the results of his research. I am grateful also to Norma Forde for the interest she has taken in this subject, and for her advice.

REV. WILLIAM CHADERTON.

A correspondent has sent us a clipping from the **Montreal Gazette** of an article entitled "ALL OUR YESTERDAYS" By Edgar Andrew Collard which is of distinct Barbadian interest. It is one of a series by the same author on the old burial ground about St. Matthew's Anglican Church in John Street, Quebec City, and the memorials to be there seen. Among the monuments to clergymen of note in Quebec's early days is one bearing the following inscription—

SACRED
TO THE MEMORY
OF
THE REVD. WILLIAM CHADERTON
AN EXEMPLARY PASTOR
AND A DEVOTED SERVANT OF
CHRIST
WHO DIED
OF TYPHUS FEVER
CONTRACTED
IN THE ZEALOUS DISCHARGE
OF HIS SACRED CALLING
ON THE 15TH JULY 1847
AGED 59 YEARS.

Mr. Collard gives an account of the deceased's West Indian origin and his life and ministry, culminating in his falling a victim to the prevailing fever in the course of ministering to the sick in the Marine Hospital.

Research in the Barbados Records has provided additional information regarding birth, parentage and early ministry, and the compass of the original notes on the subject of the memoir has been enlarged for publication in the Journal.[1]

William Chaderton was born in Barbados in the year 1788, the son of John Chaderton, a sugar planter, and manager of Drax Hall plantation in the parish of St. George, Barbados. His mother was Antoinette Lynch,[2] daughter of Dominick and Elizabeth Lynch and a relation of Patrick Joseph Dottin Lynch, one time Prothonotary and Chief Clerk of the Barbados Law Courts. William Chaderton was the eldest of six children of the marriage: one daughter and five sons. There is no record of John Chaderton's origin who seems to have been the progenitor of the Barbados family.

William was sent to Scotland for his education, studying under Rev. James Walker, later Bishop of Edinburgh. He was ordained Deacon by the Bishop of London in 1813, and Priest by the Bishop of Ely in 1814. William's father, John Chaderton died in 1809 leaving by his will a sum of Three

---

1. Rev. Canon A. R. Kelly, Archivist, of Montreal, has kindly furnished the present writer with additional information besides that acknowledged by Mr. Collard and in writing the original article.
2. Barbados Records. Marriage. Parish of St. George, 1785 (date blank) John Chaderton to Antoinette Lynch.

hundred pounds for the completion of his son's education. William return-ed to Barbados in 1814 and soon left for the island of Antigua to assume the Rectory of St. Mary's parish there, to which he had been appointed. He was soon transferred to St. Paul's parish, his patent from Governor Sir James Leith being dated 10 December 1815

In the meantime he had married (wife's name not known) and had two daughters born in Antigua in 1817 and 1818 respectively. In 1822 he and his family left Antigua for the Rectory of St. George in the Island of Tortola to which he had been appointed. His wife died there, and he and his infant children went to live with relations in the United States of America some time after 1824.

On 25 August 1827 he was residing in the borough of Bristol, co of Bucks., State of Penn., and for some years he was assistant to Bishop White in one or more churches in Philadelphia. In 1835 he was in charge of Christ Church, St. Louis, Missouri, and in the following year of St. John's, Northampton, Mass. He was offered greater preferment in the American Church but he refused on account of his desire to return to British Dominions. He applied to Rt. Rev. George Jehoshophat Mountain, Bishop of Quebec, and was appointed curate-in-charge of St. Peter's Chapel in which parish was the Marine Hospital, now the Hospice of St. Charles. There the sick emigrants were taken from the ships and Mr. Chaderton would minister to them. The great crisis of his life came in the summer of 1847 when the Marine Hospital was overflowing with the fever-stricken emigrants who had fled from the typhus in Ireland only to be overtaken by it on the Atlantic, and who arrived desperately ill in a strange country. "It is impossible to conceive anything more disgraceful", wrote Bishop Mountain, "than the manner the poor wretched emigrants have been packed off, and the condition and management of most of the emigrant vessels." Rev. Chaderton was one of the few who went forward to meet this "floodtide of human misery". In the end, after working twelve hours without a rest the fever claimed him. The next day was Sunday July 4. He appeared in St. Peter's Chapel and took the morning service, with the fever already upon him. Eleven days later William Chaderton was dead. It was a new sorrow in a clouded summer. In mourning for his loss the Cathedral was hung in black for three days, and Bishop Mountain wrote: "We have lost in this parish one of the best clergymen and one of the most consistent Churchmen that ever lived".

Rev. Chaderton was twice married. The name of his second wife has not been preserved. The monument to his memory in the Quebec Ceme-tery was erected by her. A younger daughter, Phoebe, bequeathed a sum to the church adjoining the cemetery for the upkeep of her father's grave.

There is a tablet to the memory of the deceased in St. Peter's Church, Quebec.

REV. WILLIAM CHADERTON

In continuation of the notes on this eminent clergyman which appeared in Vol. XVII of the Journal, p. 185, the following particulars are of interest—

Chaderton is mentioned in *BARBADOS and OTHER POEMS* by the Barbadian poet M. J. Chapman, publ. London; James Fraser, Regent Street, 1833. p. 63.

> "But one is absent, whom his country mourns;
> Nor yet her own, her favourite son returns.
> O'er his young lips the bees enchanted hung,
> And, as the Muses spake, the poet sung;
> But soon he brake his all-unwilling lyre.
> Warm from the altar, rapt with holier fire;
> And now with higher inspiration fraught,
> As though the prophet's mantle he had caught,
> He peals the music of his tuneful voice
> Bids the bad tremble and the good rejoice.
> But ah! forgetful of his native dells,
> The holy man in some far country dwells;
> And still the bearded isle regrets her son,
> And calls in vain on absent Chaderton."

In the Author's Notes to his poem, he says—p. 103—"Mr. Chaderton is somewhere in North America. He is one of the most distinguished men the island has produced. With the finest imagination and acutest sensibilities, he has devoted himself with a martyr-like spirit, to his holy calling".

The Barbadian Newspaper for 1833 August 17, commences Extracts from Chapman's poems. He is referred to as Dr. Chapman jr., a native of this island some years resident in Demerara. Then in the issue of August 21, where the portion about Chaderton is reproduced, the Editor notes Chaderton "as the elegant Chaderton who preached in the Cathedral in 1814.[4] He is now somewhere in North America".

---

3. The Barbados Rector also died (England) in 1728, but his Will was proved in London on 18 April 1728, i.e. about six weeks before the death of the Rector of Dyce.

4. The year he returned from England after his ordination and that in which he later departed for Antigua.

Codrington of Barbados.

So much confusion having arisen about this family, owing to the same Christian name having been used in three generations, the Editor attempts to set down what facts are known of them. In 1910 appeared the "Annals of Codrington College," by T. Herbert Bindley, D.D., and the "Memoir of the family of Codrington," by R. H. Codrington, D.D., both interesting works.

CHRISTOPHER CODRINGTON I.

The first settler's name does not appear in the List of Landholders of 1638 ("Memoirs of the First Settlement," p. 73), but he must have landed in or about 1640, the date of his son's birth. His wife's name is not known, but there is good reason to believe that she was a sister of William Drax and Sir James Drax, both wealthy and prominent planters of old standing, as in the next generation the Draxes and Codringtons were cousins.

In 1641, when his land transactions are first recorded, he is styled "Capt. Christopher Codrington, Esq.," and this implies that he was a gentleman of good estate on arrival.

The last reference I noticed to him was in 1653. His will cannot be found. There was an administration in the P.C.C. on 15 June 1656 of the estate of Christopher Codrington of Bath, deceased, to Mary his widow, but there is no proof of identity. He apparently had three if not four sons, viz.:—

1. Christopher II., his successor.
2. John, died 1685, ancestor of the Baronets.
3. Coppleston, manager of John's estates.
4. ? Robert, married and living 1678 in St. Michael's.

CHRISTOPHER CODRINGTON II.

Probably eldest son of the preceding. In 1663 he was one of the Barbadians who purchased St. Lucia from the native chiefs. His name frequently occurs in the State Papers. In lists of the Council of 1666 he is described as: "A young Man borne in the place" (*Ante*, III., 308). This would have been in 1640, as in his deposition on 30 June 1688 he gave his age as 48 ("Memorials of St. Lucia," p. 481).

1671, June 7. Sir Tho. Lynch wrote: "Col. Christopher Codrington, my Lord's deputy, being of a debonaire liberal humour, a native and a planter, they have been kind to, giving him in the two and a half years he has commanded 300 or 400,000 lbs. of sugar."

1672, Nov. 14. Wm. Lord Willoughby writes of the Assembly: "My late Deputy Coll: Codrington hath harrassed them to death wth heedless improssitions." (Egerton MS. 2395, Brit. Museum.)

1673, May 28. Sir Peter Colleton, Dep.-Gov., wrote: "His Excellency when he lay sick put Col. Codrington out of the Council and put his own son in his place. Col. C. and his Lordship had large accounts, which Sir Peter had adjusted, bringing one to give and the other to take £5000 to be paid in time, but his Lordship, finding that C. to avoid being forced to pay his creditors had made over all his estate, grew very jealous, which, and being no freeholder, was, Sir Peter thinks, the cause he was put out."

Having been deprived of his seat in the Council, C. seems to have been annually elected to the Assembly for St. John's Parish 1674—82 and was chosen Speaker by ballot in 1674, 1675, and 1678.

1677, May. Sir Peter Colleton sends an "Account of Judge Sharpe's fraudulent proceedings in reference to a deed he was employed to draw by Conset withdrawing the trust of his estate, one of the best in the island, from one Turner, and to place it in Christopher Codrington then Dep.-Govr. Conset's wife dying left her estate to Lt-Genl Henry Willoughby, who arriving at Barbadoes was invited to supper by Codrington, who had taken possession of the estate, and went from Codrington's house well at night, but after he got to his lodging fell into a violent burning of the stomach and died the next mornin;." *

1677, Nov. 1. Petition of Dame Joan Hall "that she had been in possession of a plantation in Antigua called Bettyes Hope above 14 years when the French in 1667 invaded it. She retired to Nevis, then returned in 1668 when Wm. Lord Willoughby soon after assigned it to Col. C., who has ever since detained the same, but it is now offered for sale."

In a deed of 1684 C. leased his two plantations called "Didmarton" and "Consett" in Barbados, the former being the name of the manor in Gloucestershire owned by the Codringtons.

1686, Feb. 27. The King to Sir Wm. Stapleton directing that Chr. C. shall be sworn of the Council of the Leeward Islands. On July 6 he also took his seat again at the Council of Barbados.

1687, March 17. "Chr. C. left the island last Decr. No knowledge when he may return."

In 1689 Gov. Sir Nath. Johnson quitted the Leeward Islands, deputing Lieut.-Gen. Chr. C. to carry on the government until the King's pleasure might be known. · C. was subsequently appointed by His Majesty Gov.-in-Chief, and continued as such until his death at Antigua on 20 July 1698. Some 25 years ago I copied the entry of his burial from the parish register of St. Philip, where it is very briefly recorded : "1698, July 21. Chris. Codrington in Garden." The "Garden" was a plantation near "Bettys Hope," both of which are still owned by the family.

His wife Gertrude is stated to have been living in 1659, but nothing more is known of her. The Governor's will was made 15 July 1698 and proved 12 Oct. following (P.C.C., 211, Lort), and after providing for natural children and slaves, giving small sums to friends, settling £200 a year on his younger son John, an imbecile, he bequeathed everything to his son Christopher. John died in 1702 a lunatic and intestate. In Dec. 1700 the Assembly voted £500 for a monument to their late Governor in England.

In trying to arrive at an estimate of Codrington's character, compare the fulsome panegyrics of Edwards and Poyer, with the summing up of the Hon. J. W. Fortescue, in his editorial preface to the Colonial Calendar of State Papers for 1697-8, p. xxx.

"It is melancholy that the career of such a man should have had so mean and sordid an end. Codrington had done very good service to the State . . . He was able to exert almost despotic power, and from using it wholly for the public service, soon began to abuse it for his own profit."

Codrington certainly lent large sums out of his private purse for the public service, providing pay and powder for the troops, when none was forthcoming from the home government. He was a strong military governor, one of that band of men of the stamp of Warner, Willoughby, and Stapleton—the builders of Empire. His great policy was to drive the French out of the adjacent islands ; and it was he who recommended that the West Indian Colonies should be annexed to the Crown and be directly represented in Parliament ; an Imperial idea, now over 200 years old, which is still agitating men's minds, and which this present war may bring to fruition.

CHRISTOPHER CODRINGTON III.

Elder son of the preceding, born at Barbados about 1668, matriculated from Christ Church, Oxford, 4 July 1685, aged 17, entered the Middle Temple 1687, Fellow of All Souls 1690, B.A. 1691, M.A. 1694, Capt. of 1st Foot Guards. He succeeded his father in 1698 as Governor of the Leeward Islands.

* 1669 Dec. 1 Lieut. Genl Hen. Willoughby, in the Church. (Burial Register of St. Michael's.)

In 1701 Pere Labat when in St. Kitts was invited with his friend Capt. Lambert to dine at the house of an English officer named Bouriau, where they met Gov. Codrington, his chaplain and Major-Gen. Hamilton. " Le General Codrington me fit cent questions sur mon voiage . . . mais il étoit si vif, qu'il avoit toûjours trois ou quatre questions d'avance, avant que j'eusse eu le tems de repondre à la premiere. Il etoit bien plus sobre que ne le sont d'ordinaire ceux de sa nation." (II., 298.)

In Oct 1703 the Council reported that his request to return to England by reason of ill-health should be granted, but another Governor appointed. Various complaints were also made against him, but they were mostly of a frivolous nature. On 3 Dec. 1703 the Queen had appointed Col. Wm. Mathew *vice* Codrington dismissed.

On 14 Feb. 1703-4 the late Governor wrote attributing the loss of his government to mistakes he acknowledged that he had made.

On 20 July 1704 he complained that he had lost his eyesight and the use of his limbs. On 4 Dec. Gov. Sir Wm. Mathew died and Codrington on 6 Dec. wrote and begged to be re-appointed, but the Queen ignored his petition and nominated Col. Daniel Parke in March 1704-5.

In a letter of 12 Nov. 1706 the writer said that General Codrington and Gov. Parke have already had disagreements and are frequently at variance.

George French gives the following contemporary account of the ex-Governor : " Colonel Christopher Codrington (whether enraged with Envy, at Colonel Parke's being preferr'd before him to that Government he once had the Command of, or whether excited by the wild Starts of a crazy Brain, that much about that Time began to affect him) was the first who infused Fears and Jealousies into the Minds of the People, and stirr'd them up to Division ; which no Person could manage more artfully, as he was superior in Parts as well as Fortune to most, if not all others in America, which begets Respect every where, but a Veneration in those Parts, where his Sentiments met with a general blind Acquiescence from the Multitude.

In the midst of the Distractions he occasion'd, he played the Hypocrite so nicely, that to outward Appearance none carry'd more smoothly, and with a fairer Face, to the General, than Mr. Codrington ; but a requisite Mixture of the Serpent with the Dove meeting in Colonel Parke, he saw into the Proceedings, and made an early Discovery of the vile Practices : And foreseeing the Danger, he concluded to strike at the Root of the Evil, and prevent its Growth : Calling the said Codrington to Account, he warmly reprimanded him for the ill Treatment, telling him how much more consistent it was with his Character, as a Gentleman, and the Generosity of Spirit always suppos'd to accompany a liberal Education, to appear a publick Patriot, than a base Incendiary : Yet as this Reproof begat a present Submission, it occasion'd a Discontent, which 'twas impossible wholly to smother in such a Breast as Mr. Codrington's, but broke out in a violent Relapse, that raged with more Fury : And to shun a just Resentment, he retired to Barbadoes, from whence, by an uninterrupted Correspondence, he continu'd to refresh the Dissensions he had sown, and keep up the Ferment he occasion'd to his Dying Day." G. French's " Answer to a Scurrilous Libel," etc., 1719, p. 24.

He was last present at the Council on 14 July 1706, and after November his name disappears from the Minute Book. It is probable that Christopher had retired to Barbados, where he died 7 April 1710 at the age of 42. He made his will at Antigua on 22 Feb. 1702-03, proved 8 Feb. 1710-11. (P.C.C., 23, Young.) £10,000 was left to All Souls, Oxford, of which £6000 was for a building and £4000 for books. Testator also bequeathed to the college his own library of books then housed at Oxford. The estate at Dodington in Gloucestershire purchased of Sam. Codrington, Esq., Betty's Hope plantation in Antigua, a plantation in St. Christopher, and one moiety of the lease of Barbuda were devised to his 1st cousin Lt.-Col. Wm. C. Two plantations and 300 slaves in Barbados were given to the S.P.G. on trust for the foundation of a college. £500 to a cozen Mrs.

Rachel Courthope. The body of testator's father was to be carried to England and buried in Westminster Abbey. Besides £750 granted by St. Chr. and A. he added £500 for a monument to him. His own body he wished interred in All Souls Chapel, to be covered by a plain black marble of £20 value. For some reason the body of Chr. C. II. was never removed to the Abbey, nor was a monument erected. In 1716 the remains of Chr. III. were interred in All Souls Chapel.

CODRINGTON OF GLOUCESTERSHIRE.

Robert Codrington, gent., 1st son of Simon C. of Wapley, co. Glouc., died v.p. at his residence in the precinct of St. Geo. Cathedral, Bristol, 14 Feb. 1618, aged 46. A large monument to him stands in the cathedral. He made his will 11 Feb. 1618, and after providing portions for his seven daughters of £200 apiece bequeathed to his six younger sons (not named) £10 a year apiece for maintenance and £20 apiece, gave a lease to his eldest son John and all residue to his wife Anne, who proved the will. Anne, after eight and a half years of widowhood, married Ralph Marsh, and against them her children John C., Esq., Nich. C., Christopher C. and others brought an action in the Court of Chancery in 1628, by which it appears that testator was seized of divers lands of the yearly value of £300 and his personal estate amounted to £2272. Testator married about 1594 the above Anne, dau. of Wm. Stubbes, Esq. Robert their 2nd son was born about 1602. In the parish register of St. Augustine's, Bristol, adjoining the cathedral, I found the following entry : "1612 The xvij day of October was baptized Christopher Cotherington the sonne of Mr Robert Cotherington, gent. And Mrs Annes his wyffe." He is supposed to have gone out to Barbados, but no evidence is forthcoming as to his doings between 1628 and 1641. None of the numerous wills of the Codringtons of Gloucestershire makes any allusion to the W.I. Chr. C. the 3rd of Barbados sealed his letters with the arms of C. of Sodbury, differenced by the fesse being Sa, fretty Or. He was evidently unable to prove his descent beyond his grandfather, and his pedigree in the College of Arms bears this out.

The clues in Barbados are equally indefinite. By a deed it appears that one of the plantations in St. John's parish belonging to Chr. C. II. was known in 1684 as "Didmarton." The late Mr. N. D. Davis told me that he recollected seeing in a Calendar a letter from the Countess of Worcester to a statesman applying for the Government of Barbados for Codrington (Chr. C. II.) at the request of his "cozen Codrington of Bristol." Chr. C. III. in his will gave 100 gas. to Mr. Sam. C., from whom he purchased the estate at Dodington, and £500 to his "cozen" Mrs. Rachel Courthope. The term "cousin" is too vague. She was dau. of John, eldest son and heir of Rob. of Bristol, and testator is supposed to have been great-grandson of Robert.

John Drax of the parish of St. Michael, Barbadoes, gent. Will dated 25 July 1671. To my honoured cosen Coll: Christopher Codrington, Dep.-Gov. of this Island, and to his Lady £20 apiece. My cosen John Codrington, Esq., £20 and my silver cimeter. (3, Eure.)

Henry Drax of the parish of St. Giles in the ffeilds, co. Middx., Esq. Will dated 30 June 1682. Plantations in Barbadoes. To my godchildren Christopher Codrington, Eliz. C. and Dorothy C., each £20 for the purchase of a piece of plate. My friends Chr. C. and John C., Ex'ors in B'oes. (107, Cottle.)

224

Dorothy Drax of St. Giles in the Feilds, co. Middx., widow of Henry Drax, Esq., lately deceased. Will dated 26 Oct. 1683. To my goddau. Dorothy Coddrington £10. To my cozen Gartrude Coddrington a clock. (88, Hare.)

Sir James Drax of Hackney, kt. Will dated 22 Feb. 1663. To Chr. Coddrington of the I. of B'oes, Esq., his wife and children £10 apiece. (40, Hyde.)

Wm. Frankland of B'oes. Will dated 10 Oct. 1684. To my honoured kinsman and friend Lt-Col. John Codrington £50 and Ex'or. My couzin Dorothy Codrington, dau. of my couzin Lt-Col. John C., £500. (163, Lloyd.)

Sam. Newton of B'oes, Esq. Will dated 12 Feb. 1683. My goddau. Dorothy Codrington, dau. of Lt-Col. John C., £20 for a piece of plate. (5, Lloyd.)

" Entred the 20th day of Aprill, 1686."
Collonell John Codrington of the parish of St Michaell's in the I. of B'os. Will dated 20 Dec. 1685. To be bur. as my wife shall thinke fitt. To my s. John C. all my est. r. and p. in the I. of Antegua and one moiety of my est. in the I. of Barbuda, but if captured by the enemy he shall have from my est. in B'os £200 st. pr. ann. To my dau. Sarah C. £1500 st. from my est. in B'os at 18 or M^{ge}. To my dau. Dorothy C. £1500 st. from my est. in A. and B'a at 18 or M., if taken by enemy then out of est. in B'os. My brother Coppleston C.* £50 st. pr. ann. out of my est. in B'a, and if he prove serviceable to my wife and ch^n in the managem^t of their est. he shall receive £50 st. pr. ann. more. All res. to my s. Wm. C. My wife to have the G. of my ch^n and managem^t of my est. during their minority. If she marry then to receive £400 st. pr. ann. My loving brothers† and good friends Coll^o Chr. Cod., Coll^o John Hallett, John Hothersall, Esq., John Gibbs, Esq., R^d Bate, gt., Cornwall Summers, Esq., and John Sutton, gt., Ex'ors, and £20 st. ea. In the presence of Mary Davies, Marg^t Morris, John Hillier +. Sworn 9 Jany 1685. Edwyn Stede, Lt-Gov. The will of his widow Sarah was p. in Barbados in 1725, but I have not seen it. (Barbados Record Office.)

See Hawtayne deed reciting deed of sale of 20 March 1641 by which he purchased of Capt. C. C. 100 a. and 8 negroes.
1641, March 26. Proclamation by the Genl Assembly. Signed by Govr Henry Huncks and 30 others of the Council and freeholders, including " Christopher Codrington." (Vol. I., p. 60.)
1641, Sept. 20. He sells 50 a., part of 820 a. in St John's, formerly in the possession of Capt Wm. Hawley. (Ibid., p. 931.)
1641, Nov. 16. Capt Chr. C., Esq., his bond of 4400 lbs. of cotton. (Ibid., p. 894.)
1641, Dec. 11. He sells 20 a. in St George. (Ibid., p. 910.)
1641. Capt. Jas. Drax of B., Esq., sells 225 a. in St John's. Wit. by Chr. C. Recorded 7 Feb. 1641. (Ibid., p. 915.)

* Sir James Drax in his will of 1663 names his uncle Coppleston Horton of co. Som., Esq.
† The plural of this word is doubtful. Chr. was the only brother so far as I know among the executors, and Richard Bate was his wife's brother.

1642, March 3. Capt Chr. Codrington, gent., in consideration of the use of 6 men-servants having 4 years yet to run, delivered by the Right Worshipfull Capt Philip Bell, Govr, and of 20,000 lbs. of cotton and of a mare, sell to P. B. 50 acres which I bought of Mr James Knott. Signed " Christo × Codrington." (*Ibid.*, p. 200.)

1643, April 17. The plantation in St Andrew's late in the possession of Capt Coddrington. (*Ibid.*, p. 178.)

1643, Feb. Capt Xpher Codrington of B., Esq., sale of 30 acres in St John's signed : " Christ^o : Codrington." (*Ibid.*, p. 648.)

1645, May 20. Capt Chr. C., Esq., sells 40 a. in St John's. (*Ibid.*, p. 658.)

1646, Nov. 7. Capt C. C., Esq., sells 40 a. in St Andrew over Hills. (Vol. II., p. 198.)

1647, April 4. Capt C. C., Esq., sells 20 a. in St Andrew. (*Ibid.*, p. 62.)

1647, July 18. I, Capt. Chr. Coderington, Esq., am indebted to Ensign Edward Fairhurst the sum of 1203 pounds of Indicoe or 30,075 pounds of Tobaccoe, payable May next, and bind myself in 2000 pounds of Indicoe, signed " Christo Coderington." (Vol. 2 of Deeds.)

1653, April 30. Tho. Kendall of L., merch^t. Deed witnessed by Chr. Cotrington. (Vol. II., p. 808.)

ST. MICHAEL'S, BARBADOS.

BURIALS.

1667	June 15	Mrs Mary the wife of Mr Robert Codrington.
1670	July 30	Mary the D^a of Coll^o Xtop^r Codrington in Ch.
1678	July 16	Alice C. ye d. of Mr Robert C.
1678	Sept. 8	Frances ye d. of Robert & Elisabeth C.*
1685	Aug. 22	Christopher the s. of John C., Esq., in the Church.
1685	Dec. 26	The Honble John C., Esqr, in the Church.
1694-5	Feb. 25	Mrs Elizab : C.
1710	April 8	Coll^o Christop^r C., Esqr, late Genl of ye Leward Islands, in Church.
1725	Nov. 7	Mad^m Sarah C., wid^o, in the Church.

BAPTISMS.

1678	Sept. 7	Frances ye daughter of Mr Robert Codrington & Elisabeth h. w.*
1680	May 2	William the s. of Lt Coll : Jno C. & Sarah h. w.
1685	Aug. 13	Christopher the s. of Jno Codrington, Esqr.
1681	Sept. 18	John the s. of Lt-Coll : John C. & Sarah his wife.

---

* These two entries from Hotten ; the others I extracted from the books in the Record Office in Bridgetown, but made no complete search.

Estwick of Barbados.

Christopher Estwicke of St John's Parish, Barbadoes. Will dated 17 Jan. 1660-1. My wife Anne Eastwicke. My children, 3 visible, Ellinor, Mary, and Christopher, and a 4th not yet born. My brother Francis. To my uncle Richard E. my gold ring, formerly my father's, with our coat of arms upon it. Proved 28 Jan. 1660-61. Entered 16 April 1662. (N. Darnell Davis.)

———

Chr. Estwick of Stoake in the co. of the citie of Coventry, gent., 20 Maie 1656. To be bur. in the p'sh ch. of S. Wife Elliner use of household stuff and plate. 1st son Chr. ye row of houses in Overstoke and land in Lower S. I had of my F. Walden and £10 a year; dau. Ellenor Grosvenor £5; her husband a gold ring of 20s.; son Adrian £4 a year; son Fra. £200 at 21; dau. Marie E. £250 at 25; son R^d £200 at 23; son Brooke E. £100 at 2. Bro. Fra. E. dwelling at Feversham in Kent 40s. House and land at S. to wife for life then to son Izaack. Lov. Bro. Mr Rob. Phippes a ring of gold of 20s. Uncle Mr Silvester Brooke gloves. Wife E. and son Izaack Ex'ors. My uncle Mr S. Brook and my son Leicester Grosvenor overseers. Wit. by Tho. Wagstaffe, Anne W., Ab. English, Anne Hooke, John Abbott. Proved 12 June 1657 by I. Estwick; power reserved to E. Estwick. (212, Ruthen.)

———

Isaac Estwick of Hackney, Mercht., 29 April 1689. The ch^n of my eldest bro. Chr. E., dec^d, 10^l ea. My bro. Adrian E. 5^s. My bro. Richd E. if living 10^l. My sisters Eleanor Grosvenor and Mary Shuttleworth 10^l ea. My bros. Peter Causton and Daniel Causton and sister Mary Causton 10^l ea. Stoke near Coventry 10^l. All res. to my wife Esther and Ex'trix. Proved 24 Feb. 1689. (21, Dyke.)

———

Esther Estwick of Hackney. Nephew Causton. Proved 1726. (96, Plymouth.)

———

1759. Thomasin Forte of St. George, widow. Dau. Ann Estwick.

———

Tobias Frere, Jun., of Burlington Gardens, co. Middlesex, Esq., 24 March 1763. My sister Eliz. Estwicke, wife of Sam. E., Esq., £300 c. a year for her life, and to him my chariot and 3 horses. Proved 6 April 1763. (177, Cæsar.)

Barbados. Eliz. Estwick, wife of Sam. E. of St. Michael's Parish, Esq.,
8 May 1766. Whereas John Frere, my F., by his will of 3 Jan. 1766 bequeathed
to Eliz. Sus^n and Charlotte, my two ch^n, a bond from Henry Frere, my bro., of
£3869, also another due from the est. of Tobias Frere, my bro., dec^d, of £1366,
I desire that the £5236 be divided betw. my s^d 2 daus. at 21. My dear bro.
Tobias F. by his will, dat. 24 Mch. 1763, left my ch^n £5000 to be divided eq.
My husb^d Sam. E. to be T. and sole Ex'or. Wit.: John Rous Estwick, Wm.
Arewell, Ben. Webster. Sam. Estwick confirmed the will. Proved 9 Dec. 1766
by S. Estwick, the husband. (449, Tyndall.)

Sam. Estwick of Lower Berkeley Street, St. Marylebone, 23 July 1793. My
dau. Eliz. Sus^h Jones £1200 st. and a debt of £1084 due to me from the est. of
Tobias Frere, Senr, Esq., dec^d, part of her Mother's fortune. My dau. Grace
£1200 st. at 21. My dau. Charlotte £1200 st. at 21. To my sons Henry,
Willoughby Bertie, Rich^d £1200 st. ap. My 1st wife's jewels already given to
my dau. Jones. Of my 2^d wife's jewels the diamond sprig to my dau. Charlotte,
the diamond ring given me by Mr Trent to my son Sam., and the rest to my dau.
Grace.
By a deed of sett., dated 13 July 1793, of my plant. in Barb. on the mar. of
my son Sam. with the Hon. Miss Hawke, dau. of the R^t Hon. Lord H., power
was given me to charge it with £7000 st., apart from 2 annuities of £800 st. to
the s^d Sam. E., Junr., and Cassandra Julia Hawke, his wife. To my son Sam. my
s^d est. in B. already settled on him and all res. He and John Trent, Esq., of
Geo. Str., St Marylebone, and Miss Mary Langford of Lower Seymour Str., do.,
Spr., Ex'ors, T., and G.
Wit.: Jos. Lynn, G. Pengant, N. Piesse.
Codicil.—8 April 1795. The £1200 has been already p^d to my dau. Grace on
her mar. with Mr Simpson. Legacies of £60 ea. beq. to my ch^n by their late aunt
Mrs. Langford. My serv^t Nich. Piesse £25. The furn. and effects at my
apartments in Chelsea Hospital have been disposed of by gift. Robt Burnett
Jones of Manch^r Str. to be also an Ex'or.
Proved 3 Dec. 1795 by Sam. E., the son; power reserved to John Trent and
Mary Langford and Robt. Burnett Jones. (682, Newcastle.)

Sam. Estwick, Jun., of Devonshire Str., Portland Pl., St Maryleborne.
6 Dec. 1796. To my wife the Hon. Cassandra Juliana E. all securities, furn.,
jewels, plate, horses, and carriages apart from her joynture of £800 a year. My
plant. c^d Co . . . . Hill in the parish of Christ Church, Barb., of 224 a. ch. with
the s^d joynture and with legacies of £1200 ea. to my 3 younger bros. Henry,
Willoughby Bertie, and Rich^d. I give to my bro. Henry ch. with £200 a year
for my sister Charlotte E., and £800 ap. to my 2 youngest bros., Willoughby
Bertie and Rich^d at 21. My Father-in-law Lord Hawke and my brother-in-law
the Hon. John Simpson and my wife Exors. Wit.: S. Birt, John Birch, Dean
Str., Soho, N. Piesse, Duke Str., Manch. Sq.
Mem. dated at Madeira 11 Feb. 1797. Lord Hawke's house in Portland Pl.
Marquis de Cely occupying my late Father's house in Berkeley Str. My Father's
seals and swords to my bro. Henry. My dear bro. Willoughby, should it please
God to restore him to his friends, his Father's watch. My bro. Rich^d my own
watch. My Spanish gun to my bro. Mr. M. Hawke. £50 to Mrs. Lane and her
passage to England. Thank Miss Gibbs. " Finding very sensibly my health
grow worse and worse and my strength gradually decrease."
Proved 30 April 1798 by the wife, and on 5 Jan. 1799 by the others. (253,
Walpole.)

Richard Estwick of St. George's Parish, Barbados, 1679,=Joan, relict of then owner of 40 acres and 20 negroes. See p. 65. | .... Clerk.

Richard Estwick.	Chr. Estwick=Frances, of Barbados, dau. of Esq. Recom- .... mended for Bond. the Council 30 Jan. 1700. Died 1705.	Eliz. Estwick, mar. Sam. Forte, Sen., who settled at Barbados in 1680, s.p. His 1st wife Ursula died 1700.	Anne Estwick, 2nd dau., mar. Sam. Forte, Jun., son of Sam. Forte, Sen., by his 1st wife. He was born 1685; she died 1720. (Burke's "Colon. Gentry," 437.)

Richard Estwick=Eliz., 1st dau. of Hon. John Rous of Barbados, by Margaret, dau. of Tho. Max-died 1753. well; mar. 1722; living 1736.	Frances Estwick, mar. 1722 Sam. Maynard.	Eliz. Estwick.

Richard Rouse Estwick, living 1750. — Chr. Estwick, 2nd son.	Eliz., 1st dau. of Hon. John Frere, President of Barbados, by Susanna Applewhaite; born 1738; died 1766, aged 28. Will dated 8 May and proved 9 Dec. 1766 (449, Tyndall).	=Samuel Estwick, Esq., born 1736: of Queen's Coll., Oxford, matric. 10 Oct. 1753, aged 17; created M.A. 4 Nov. 1763, D.C.L. 8 July 1773; M.P. Westbury Mch. 1779. In 1783 Registrar of Chelsea Hospital and Searcher of Customs at Antigua; Agent for Barbados; died Nov. 1796. (682, Newcastle.)	=Grace Langford, 6th dau. and co-heiress of Jonas Langford of Antigua and Theobalds, co. Herts; born 23 Nov. 1743; mar. 11 May 1769 at St. Marylebone; died 23 April 1784.

A

Charlotte Estwick, died young. — Eliz. Susannah Estwick, mar. Rob. Burnett Jones of Ades, co. Sussex, Attorney-Gen. of Barbados. He died 5 Aug. 1817. (See Burke's "Landed Gentry.")	1. Samuel Estwick, Jun., born=Cassandra Julia, 22 Jan. 1770; of Queen's Coll., Oxford, matric. 31 Aug. 1787, aged 17; created M.A. 10 March 1791, D.C.L. 5 July 1793; M.P. Westbury Jan. 1795 to May 1796; died 23 Feb. 1797 at Madeira, aged 27. M.I. in Old St. Marylebone Church.	1st dau. of 2nd Lord Hawke; mar. 1st 15 July 1793; 2ndly, Sep. 1800, Rev. Steph. Sloane; 3rdly, Thomas Green. s.p.	2. Henry Estwick, Lieut. 64th Foot; died 18 Aug. 1797.

Rob[t] Denison of Leeds, Esq., £1000 for a mon[t] to be erected near the grave of my late bro. at Ossington, co. Notts. Proved 1785. (183 Ducarel.)

1638. Francis Estwick, owner of more than 10 acres. ("Memoirs of the First Settlement of Barbados," p. 75.)

1641-2, March 11. Capt. Fra. Skeete sold to Rich[d] Estwicke 50 a., being part of that land I had formerly sold to M[r] Tho. Verney, which I took again from him by consent. Deeds, vol. i., fo. 423. See as to Tho. Verney in Barbados in vol. of "Verney Papers," Camden Soc. Pub. (N. Darnell Davis.)

1698, Jan. 25. Minutes of the Council. Major Estwick appointed Assistant at Bridge Court. (W.I. Cal., p. 95.)

1699, Nov. 29. Chr. Estwicke, security for Lt-Col. Richd Downes, the Treasurer. (*Ibid.*, p. 559.)

1700, Jan. 30. Chr. Estwick recommended for the Council. (*Ibid.*, p. 44.)

1704. C. Estwick, then a M. of Assembly for St John's. (Poyer, 178.)

1705. Act N° 526, "for the better enabling the Executors of Christopher Estwicke, Esquire, deceased, to pay the debts of the said Christopher Estwicke, Esq." Repealed Sept. 1712. (Barbados Acts.)

1715. Company under Capt. Jas. Binney: Mr Richard Eastick 1 man; Henry Eastick 3 men.

St. John's parish: Chr. Estwicke 26, Susan E. 20, Frances E. 3, Eliz. E. 1.

1750. Richard Estwick and Richd Rouse Estwick were subscribers to Hughes' "History of Barbadoes."

Estwick, Samuel, s. Richard, of Isle of B., gent.; Queen's Coll., matric. 10 Oct. 1753, aged 17; created M.A. 4 Nov. 1763, and also D.C.L. 8 July 1773, M.P. Westbury in 4 Parliaments March 1779, until his death Nov. 1795. (Foster.)

Estwick, Samuel, s. Samuel, of Marylebone, Middlesex; arm. Queen's Coll., matric. 31 Aug. 1787, aged 17; created M.A. 10 March 1791, and also D.C.L. 5 July 1793, then of Chelsea, Middlesex; M.P. Westbury, Jan. 1795 to May 1796. (*Ibid.*)

In 1780 Govr Cunninghame arbitrarily rejected the Bill of both Houses, re-appointing Mr Estwick to the Agency.

On 26 Nov. 1783 the bill for his re-election was rejected by the Assembly. (Poyer, 436, 541.)

S. Estwick was author of the 4 following tracts, viz. :—

(1.) A Vindication of the Ministry's Acceptance of the Administration, etc. 1765. (2.) Considerations on the Negro Cause. 2^d ed. 1773. (3.) Letter to the Rev. J. Tucker, Dean of Gloucester, etc., with a Postscript, in which the

A

3. Willough-by Estwick, died in the Army 9 Oct. 1799.	4. Richard Estwick, youngest son, of Dublin and Cowes; born 1784; died 1857, aged 73.	Frances, dau. of Major-General Fyers, R.E.; mar. 1817; died 1883.	Grace Estwick, mar. 1793 (as 2nd wife) Hon. John B. Simpson, 3rd son of 1st Earl of Bradford. He was born 13 May 1763 and died 5 June 1850. She died 1839.	Charlotte Estwick, mar. (as 2nd wife) at Babworth, co. Notts, Dec. 1796, John Wilkinson, later Denison, of Ossington Hall, Merchant, of London, and M.P. He died 6 May 1820. Their 1st son John was created Viscount Ossington.

1. Richard Estwick, died 1885.	2. Gustavus Edward Estwick, Capt. 2nd Batt. Connaught Rangers and 3rd Batt. R. Warwickshire, died 6 March 1888, aged 67, at Home Park House, Hampton; bur. 9 March at Hampton Wick.	Sarah Eliz. Nunn, 2nd dau. of Wm. A. D. Nunn; mar. at Whippingham, I. of Wight, 17 Oct. 1848; died Dec. 1887.

Fred. Estwick, 1st son, came home from Canada in 1888 to be mar. in April, and returning there.	Richard Evelyn Estwick, living 1888 on the family plantation of "Charnocks;" died at Little Welches, Barbados, 9 June 1912.	Frances Estwick, joined her bro. Richard at Barbados in May 1889.

A pedigree of Estwick of Old Hays was entered in the Visitation at Market-Bosworth 13 Sept. 1682 by Adrian Estwick, and this is given in Nichol's "Leicestershire," iv., 888, and now printed in italic. The arms recorded were: Quarterly: 1 *and* 4, *Checky Ermine and Gules;* 2 *and* 3, *Per pale Argent and Sable.* CREST.—*A stork close, proper.* The arms used by the later Estwicks were: *Ermine, a fess Gules.* Additions to the pedigree have been made from deeds in Howard's "Misc. Gen. et Her.," i , 195, from wills and family papers.

Christopher Estwick of Milton⚭*Anne Brooke of Great Oakley, co. North-Bryan, co. Bedford, died 1600.* | *ampton,* sister of Mr. Silvester Brooke.

A

Christopher Estwick of Stoke in Coventry,⚭*Eleanor, dau. of* *Francis Estwick* of *co. Warwick, died 1656, aged 56.* Will | *Isaac Walden of* Feversham,co. Kent, dated 20 May 1656; proved 12 June | *Coventry,* alder- 1656; *died s.p.1666,* 1657 (212, Ruthen). | man. *aged about 54.*

B

Christopher Estwick,⚭Anne.	Frances	*Isaac Estwick*⚭*Hester*	Eleanor
mar. in Barbados;	Estwick,	*of Hackney, co.* (? Causton),	Estwick,
died about 1666, and	born 1	*Midd.,* draper, sole Ex'trix	born
left issue. Purchased	Aug.	*living 1682,* 1689. Will	1625.
50 acres in Barbados	1622;	*aged about 45;* proved 1726	—
in 1641-2. In deed	died 11	aged 21 on 13 (96, Ply-	Anne
of 20 Oct. 1648 des-	July	Jan. 1645; mouth).	Estwick,
cribed as late of Lon-	1634.	signed deed of	born 8
don,gent. Will dated		20 Oct. 1648.	Jan.
at St. John's, Bar-		Will dated 29	1629;
bados, 17 Jan.,proved		April 1689;	died 21
28 Jan. 1660-1.		proved 24 Feb.	July
		1689-90 (21,	1637.
		Dyke).	

Christopher⚭	Ellinor	Mary	(?) a 4th	*Elizabeth Estwick,*	Mary
Estwick.	Estwick.	Estwick.	child.	*aged about 10.*	Estwick.

Christopher Estwick of St. John's,⚭Susan, aged 20 Barbados, aged 26 in 1715. | in 1715.

Susan Estwick.	Frances Estwick.	Eliz. Estwick.

Present War against America is shewn to be the effect not of the causes assigned by him and others, but of a fixed plan of administration, founded in system : The Landed opposed to the Commercial Interest of the State. J. Almon, 1776. (4.) The Present Crisis of the Colonies considered, with some Observations on the Necessity of properly connecting their Commercial Interest with Great Britain and America, with a Letter to Lord Penrhyn relative to the distinction between the English and Irish Flag. 2ᵈ ed. 1786. 8vo.

1769, May 11. Sam. Estwick, esq., Cavendish Square—to Miss Grace Langford.

1782, Aug. 22. Samuel Estwick, esq., Member for Westbury, is appointed by the Right Hon. Isaac Barré to the office of Deputy-Receiver and Paymaster General of his Majesty's guards, garrisons, and land forces. ("Bath Chronicle.")

1783, Mch. 14.   Sam. Estwicke, esq; to be secretary and register to the royal
hospital at Chelsea.   (" G.M.," 275, and " B.C.," March 20.)
1783, Mch. 14.   S. Estwick, esq. M.P. to be searcher of the customs of
Antigua.
1784, Ap. 23.   In childbed the lady of Sam. Estwick, esq ; M.P. for Westbury.
(" G.M.," 318, and " T. and C. Mag.," 280.)
1793, July 15.   Sam¹ Estwick, esq. (son of Sam. E. esq. secretary and register
of Chelsea-hospital) to the Hon. Miss Hawke, dau. of Ld. H.   (" G.M.," 670.)
1793, July 5.   Oxford.   Honorary D.C.L. conferred on Samuel Estwick, esq.
(*Ibid.*, 665.)

A
_____

Richard Estwick, named 1660-1	*Henry Estwick of* St. George's⳨	*Anne, wife*
in the will of his nephew Christo-	Parish, Barbados, 1679, then	*of . . . .*
pher ; *a merchant in Barbadoes;*	owner of 50 acres and 37 slaves;	*Woolfe of*
living 1682, aged 70; mar. . . . . .,	*of Barbados 1682, aged 62 ; s.p.*	*Barbados.*
widow of . . . . Clerk.		

B
_____

Adrian⳨*Mary, dau.*	Francis Estwick,	*Richard Est-*	*Eleanor, wife of Leices-*
Estwick	*of Henry*	born 24 April	*wick, a Tur-*	*ter Grosvenor of Bridge-*
of Old	*Whit-*	1637 ; named	*key merchant*	*north* in 1656. She was
Hays,	*church of*	1660 in will of	*1682, aged*	21 on 23 Feb. 1646;
aged 50,	*Somerset-*	his bro. Christo-	*about 40 ;*	signed deed of 1 May
1682 ;	*shire.*	pher of Barbados.	under 23 in	1647 ; living 1689.
born 16			1656.	
April		*Thomas Estwick*	—	*Mary, wife of Cha. Fittle-*
1632;		*of London, drug-*	Brooke Est-	*worth* (? Shuttleworth)
living		*gist, died 1682,*	wick, under	*of Fillingley, co. War-*
1689.		*aged about 45.*	23 in 1656.	*wick.* She was under
				25 in 1656 and alive 1689.

_____

Adrian Estwick, aged 18,	*Henry Estwick,*	*Mary Estwick, aged 16.*	*Susan*
1682.	*aged 4.*		*Estwick,*
		Elizabeth Estwick, aged	*aged 7.*
	—	*13.*	
Christopher Estwick, aged	*Another son,*		—
14.	*born 1682, not*	—	*Lydia*
	christened.	*Eleanor Estwick, aged*	*Estwick,*
—		*9.*	*aged 5.*
Francis Estwick, aged 10.			

1795, Dec. Lately. Samuel Estwick, esq. M.P. for the borough of Westbury,
register of Chelsea hospital, and agent for the island of Barbadoes, in the West
Indies. (" G.M.," 1057.)
1796, Dec. Lately. At Babworth, co. Nottingham, John Denison, esq. of
Osington, to Miss Estwick, daughter of the late Samuel E., esq. (*Ibid.*,
1797, p. 79.)
1797, Feb. 23. At Madeira, whither he went for the recovery of his health,
Samuel Estwick, esq. member in the last parliament for Westbury, Wilts.
(*Ibid.*, 435.)
1797, Aug. 18. At Chelsea, of a decline, Henry Estwick, esq ; lieutenant in
64th reg. of foot. (*Ibid.*, 717.)
1815, Oct. 3. Last week in the parish of St. Thomas, Thomas F. Estwick,
Esq., to Miss Ann Selman. (" Barbados Mercury.")
1816, Aug. 10. Yesterday died T. F. Estwick, Esq. (*Ibid.*)

1817, Jan. Lately. Richard Eastwick, esq. to Frances, youngest dau. of Maj-gen. Fyers. (" G.M.," 82.)

1818, Jan. 3. Died. Richard James Estwick, Esq., many years ag one of His Majesty's Council of this Island. (" Barbados Mercury.")

1839, Feb. Lately. At Bilton-Hall, Grace, wife of the Hon. John Bridgeman-Simpson. She was the dau. of Samuel Estwicke, esq., became the second wife of Mr. Bridgeman Simpson in 1793, and has left a numerous family. (" G.M.," 221.)

1841, Sep. 28. At Cannanore, Fred. Manners Estwick, Ensign in H.M. 94th reg. of Foot, to Miss Johanna Eliz. Thompson, only dau. of Wm. T., M.D., Surgeon of the same Corps. (Ibid., 1842, 321.)

1848, Oct. 17. At Whippingham, I. of W., Gustavus Edw. E. yst s. of Rich. E. of Kingston, Surrey, to Sarah-Eliz. 2d dau. of Wm. A. D. Nunn. (Ibid., 1849, 79.)

1854, March 6. Long obit. of Edwd Denison, Bishop of Salisbury, 2^d son of John D. by his 2^d wife Charlotte Estwick. See " Notes and Queries," 10th S., ix., 428, for inquiry about Charlotte Estwick.

1866, Aug. 8. At Bilton Hall, Rugby, aged 69, Charlotte Bridgman-Simpson. She was the second dau. of the late Hon. John Bridgeman-Simpson by his second wife, Grace, dau. of Samuel Estwicke, esq., and granddau. of Henry, 1st Lord Bradford. She was born April 8, 1797. (Ibid., 422.)

1888, March 6. At Home Park House, Hampton Wick, Captain Gustavus Edward Estwick, late 2nd Battalion Connaught Rangers and 3rd Battalion Royal Warwickshire, younger son of the late Richard Estwick of Dublin, and Cowes, I. of W., aged 67, having survived his wife three months.

1912. On the 9th June, at Little Welches, Barbados, W.I., Richard Evelyn, youngest son of the late Gustavus E. Estwick of Home Park House, Hampton Wick.

MARYLEBONE OLD CHURCH.

On the N. wall, above the gallery :—

Sacred to the Memory of SAMUEL ESTWICK *ESQ^R:*
whofe Remains are depofited in his Family Vault
in the Ground belonging to this Church.
He was Born the 22^d of January 1770, Married the 15th of July 1793,
The Hon. Caffandra Julia Hawke Eldeft Daughter of
The Right Honble Lord Hawke and Died the 23rd of February 1797.
after a Lingering and Painful Illnefs, which he bore with the utmoft
Chriftian Fortitude, and Pious Refignation.
In Memory of his many Virtues and as the laft mournful Tribute
to a Dearly Beloved Husband, his Widow has caused this
Monument to be erected.

Below, painted on a shield, are his arms: *Ermine, a fess Gules* [ESTWICK]; impaling, *Argent, a chevron Erminois between 3 pilgrims' staves Purple* [HAWKE].

Samuel Estwick, Esqr, of this Parish, Widower, and Grace Langford of the same Parish, Spinster, were married in this Church by Licence this Eleventh Day of May in the Year One Thousand Seven Hundred and Sixty-Nine, by me Sambrook Russell, Curate.

This Marriage was solem- { Samuel Estwick.
nized between us { Grace Langford.

In the presence of { Thomas Oliver.
{ Dorothy Frere.

FROM OLIVER PAPERS.

Mr. Estwick died the 19 of Nov^br 1795.
Mr. Sam. Estwick the 22 of feb^ry 1797.
Mr. Henry Estwick D^o 18 of August 1797.
herd of Willowby Estwick Death the 9 of October 1799.
Henry Estwick died of a decline in the 64th foot 18 Aug. 1797.
Willoughby Estwick died of a decline in the army 9 Oct. 1799.

The Editor made the following extracts from the Register in Bridgetown :—

ST. JOHN'S.

BURIALS.

1658	Oct. 18	Frances Dau^r of Christ^r Estwicke.
1659	Aug. 12	Sarah Dau^r of Henry Estwick.
1661	Oct. 19	Christopher Estwick.
1661-2	Jan. 25	Ann Estwicke. Gap 1722—33.
1666-7	Jan. 14	John s. of Henry Estwick.
1666-7	Mar. 5	Christopher s. of Henry Estwick.
1689	Nov. 10	Mr Christopher Estwick.
1690	June 14	Mr Christopher Estwick.
1733	Oct. 28	Susanna Estwick.
1735	June 5	Christopher s. of Christ^o Estwick.
1743-4	Feb. 22	Francis s. of Richard & Eliz^th Estwick.
1745	Oct. 13	Christopher Estwick.
1753	Sep. 29	Richd Estwicke Esqr.
1754	Feb. 24	Col^o Richd Rous Estwicke.

MARRIAGES.

1663	Nov. 26	Richard Estwick and Joan Walker.
1689-90	Mar. 17	Francis Estwick and Frances Smith.
1693	Nov. 23	Thomas Sutton & Katherine Estwick.
1722	May 23	Richard Estwick & Eliz^a Rouse.
1722-3	Mar. 23	Samuel Maynard & Frances Estwick.
1737-8	Dec. 1	Christopher E. to Sarah Clark.
1749-50	Feb. 18	Col. Richd Rous E. to Mrs Sarah Haggatt.
1763	July 14	John Rous Estwick, Esqr, to Miss Mary Clarke.
1763	Sept. 23	Benj^a Mellows, Esqr, to Mrs Sarah E., Widd.

ST. PHILIP'S.

1726 Aug. 28 Elizabeth, daur. of Richd Estwick, Esq. Bur.

ST. THOMAS.

1752 Sept. 26 Christopher E., Esqr, & Mrs Harbin Hooper, widow.

Abstracts from the Island Records.

1640, May 2. Edward Estwick for 34,000 lbs. of cotton and tobacco sells 100 acres and 6 men servants. On pp. 853 and 866 his name is written " Elswicke." (Vol. I., 734.) As there is no Edward in the Estwick pedigree, the entry probably refers to the former name.

1641, Dec. 12. Richard Estwick lets his 100 acres in the parish of St. John, below the clift, for 21 years at 1000 lbs. of cotton yearly rent. (*Ibid.*, p. 926.)

1641, Feb. 21. Richard Estwick sells 8 acres under the cliff in St. John's parish. (Vol. II., 340, 404.)

1642, Aug. 25. Richard Estwicke sells 100 acres on the Windward side of the island. (*Ibid.*, 115.)

1643, Apr. 18. Mr Henry Estwicke owes the church of St. George 445 lbs. of cotton. (Vol. I., 168.)

1647, March 29. Richard Estwicke and Francis Estwicke, gentn, sell 100 acres in St. George's. (Vol. II., 104.)

Henry Estwick of the parish of St. George. Will dated 20 Jan. 1679. To my son Thomas one moiety of all my estate and to my son Richard the other moiety. My cousin Francis E., son of my brother Francis E. Sworn 25 Feb. 1679. (Vol. xiv. of Wills, p. 32.)

Bridgetown from an Old Painting.

FROM THE FIELD FAMILY BIBLE

Mrs. I. Gibbon of Belleville, St. Michael has in her possession some flyleafs of an old bible with interesting family information. The bible belonged to her grandfather Crispin Field (1813–1885) and contains entries of the births and some of the deaths of his children. He married Margaret Ann, daughter of John and Margaret Drayton in 1831. Their first child was born the next year. Margaret Elizabeth.

Attached to the two flyleafs on which is written the above information, is the title page of the Bible, with the date 1828.

One of the pages bears Crispin Field's signature but has no date.

Margaret Elizabeth was born on 18th Feby. 1832 on Saturday evening between the hours of 7 and 8 o'clock.

Samuel was born on 22nd April 1833 on Monday noon between the hours of 11 and 12 o'clock.

Louisa Ann was born on 20th December 1834 on Saturday noon at a quarter past two o'clock and died May 2nd 1863.

Emily was born on 29th October 1836 on Saturday morning between the hours of 8 and 9 o'clock.

Crispin was born on 22nd of January 1838 on Monday morning at ½ past 1 o'clock.

John Drayton was born on 12th February 1839 on Tuesday evening at 8 o'clock.

Albert was born on 24th March 1842 on Thursday morning at ¼ to 3 o'clock.

Edward was born on 16th December 1844 on Monday morning at 6 o'clock and died on 15th October 1845 at ½ past 4 o'clock. Wednesday morning.

Josephine Austin was born on 3rd July 1846 on Friday morning at ½ past 10 o'clock.

Edward Frederick was born on the 5th April 1849 on Thursday night at 10 o'clock, and died on the 10th January 1856 on Thursday noon at ½ past 12 o'clock.

C. F. (Crispin Field) born 26th November 1813 (. . . .) Sargeant died 9 May '77 at 20 after 2 p.m.

FIREBRACE FAMILY

SAMUELL FIERBRACE, CORPORALL IN CAPT. DAVICE'S COMPANY IN 1654.

This Samuell was the son of Bryan Firebrace, Merchant Tailor, of the City of London. His father went to Constantinople about 1640, leaving his wife with two children, Samuel and John, in London in poor circumstances. He died there intestate, administration being granted in London in May 1643 to Robert Cheeringe, a creditor. Her son Samuel was baptized 9 March 1634-5 at St. Margaret's, Westminster. He died in Jamaica, unmarried, and administration of his effects was granted to his mother Jane Arpe (who appears to have married again) 10 June 1657. He is therein described as " late at Jamaica in the States Service beyond sea, Batchelor."

I have been trying for many years to ascertain how and when my ancestor John Firebrace, uncle of the above Samuel, reached Barbados. It is possible he went out in the same expedition. He became a merchant and died in 1693. His will is in the Barbados Record Office.

C. W. FIREBRACE.

Danehurst, Uckfield, Sussex.

Firebrace of Barbados.

Contributed by Mr. C. W. Firebrace, who has recently returned from a visit to Barbados. A very complete tabular pedigree of the family (1543-1912), commencing with Henry of Duffield, co. Derby, has just been printed. The elder branch settled in Barbados about the reign of Charles II., then migrated to Demerara and Australia. A younger branch received a baronetcy, extinct in 1759.

BAPTISMS.

1681	Jan.	25	John S. of John and Susanna Firebrace	X^t Ch.
1685	Oct.	8	John the s. of Mr: Jno. Firebrass and Susanna his wife	St Mich.
1687	May	28	Sarah ye D. of Jno. & Susanna Firebrace	,,
1689	Oct.	22	Hannah D. of Mr John & Susan Firebrace, bo: 22d. October 1688	,,
1713	Feb.	8	Jno: ye s. of Benja. Firebrace, 20 mos: old	,,
,,	Aug.	1	Joseph ye s. of Capt: John & Mrs: Ann F. born July 12th: last	,,
1717	Nov.	—	Elizabeth D. of John and Ann F.	X^t Ch.
1723	Jan.	17	Henry Monk Lyne and Phillip the two sons of Capt: John F. decd: & Mrs: Anne his wife Henry Monk Lyne born January 11th: 1721 Phillip born 11th: of last November, Mr: Thomas Hassel & John F. by proxy for Mrs: Henry Monk Lewis & Mrs: Jane Peirce Gossips for Henry Monk Lyne, Capt. Phillip Davies Mr: John Hasel Godfathers & Alitia Thornburgh Godmother for Phillip	St Mich.
1741	June	29	Sarah Da: of Richard & Margaret F. 10 weeks old	,,
1743	Mar.	24	Ann Line Da: of Edward & Elizabeth F. born ye 9th: of last February	,,
1744	Mar.	4	John S. of Alexander and Sarah F.	St Jos.
1746	Apr.	5	Thomas, the s. of Alexander & Sarah Firebrass	St Tho.
,,	,,	23	Jane F. a child a month old	St Mich.
1747	Oct.	13	George Alexander s. of Mr: Alexander & Mrs: Sarah F. born ye 25th: of last September	,,
1768	July	9	William Newton S. of Willm & Angeletta F. Born Dec. 8th 1767	,,
,,	Oct.	6	Frances West D. of Thomas & Mary Ann F. born April the 2d	,,
1769	June	4	Edward Odwin S. of William & Angeletta F. born March the 25th	,,

1769	Oct. 20	Mary Ross D. of Thomas & Mary Ann F.	St Mich.
1771	Feb. 11	John Fielding F. S. of William F. & Angeletta his wife	"
"	Nov. 8	Samuel Thomas the s. of William F. & Angeletta F. born the 14th: Nov:	"
1772	July 8	Sarah the D. of Thomas & Mary F.	"
1774	June 12	Elizabeth Ann, D. of William & Angeletta F.	"
"	July 31	Mehitabel Christian D. of Samuel & Elizabeth Collyer Born July 4th	"
1775	Mar. 12	Angeletta D. of Wm: & Angeletta F.	"
1776	Oct. 6	Ursula Lyne Daugr: of Wm: & Angeletta F. born the 20 Sept: last	"
1778	Sep. 17	Ann Lyne the D. of William F. & Angeletta his wife born the 5th: Instant	"
1779	Sep. 6	Margarett Williams the s. of Mr William & Angeletta F.	St Tho.
1795	Dec. 6	William S. of William Newton F. & Mehetabel Christian his wife, born 10th: July last	St Mich.
1797	Jan. 6	William Edward S. of William & Sarah F. born Decr: 12th: 1796	"
"	July 30	Elizabeth Ann D. of William Newton F. & Mehetabel Christian his Wife born June 27, 97	"
1798	Dec. 6	Frances Mehetabel D. of William Newton F. & Mehetabel Christian his wife born Augt: 12th: 1798	"
1800	Nov. 23	Samuel S. of William Newton F. & Mehetabel Christian his wife, born Novr: 9th: 1800	"
1802	Nov. 13	James S. of William Newton F. & Mehetabel Christian his wife born this day	"

Marriages.

1657	Sep. 28	Stephen Bankes & Eliza Ffirebrasse* had Cert of Pub.	St Mich.
1679	Oct. 12	John Firebrace and Susanna Scott	X^t Ch.
1737	Jan. 5	John Firebrass to Frances Stevens	St Johns.
1739	Apr. 21	Alexander Firebrace & Sarah West	St Tho.
"	Nov. 24	Richard F. and Margaret Lewis Spinster	St Mich.
1741	Nov. 6	Amos Baker & Anne F. by Banns	"
1743	Apr. 2	John Boston & Elizabeth F.	St Tho.
1745	Nov. 14	Robert Turton and Ann F. Widow	St Mich.
1765	Dec. 31	John Bovell Wheeler of Saint James Parish & Ann Lyne F. of Saint Michaels	"
1766	Mar. 29	James Green to Ursella F. by J. W.	"
1767	Feb. 28	William F. to Angeletta Nusum Spinster	"
"	Apr. 18	Thomas F. & Mary Ann Roach Spinster	"
1786	Nov. 29	William Scott to Dorothy F. (Widow)	"
1790	May 15	William Newton F. to Mehitabel Christian Collier	"
1805	Sep. 1	James Morris Collier to Ann Lyne F. (Spinster)	"

Burials.

1687	Aug. 21	Sarah ye d. of Mr: John F.	St Mich.
1693	Nov. 3	Mr John Ffirebrace.	"
1715	Mar. 13	Ann Lyne F. A child.	"
1723	Aug. 2	Capt: John F.	"

* It is not known who this Eliza Ffirebrasse was, or if any relation to John Firebrace who married Susanne Scott in 1679. It is unknown when the latter arrived in Barbados, but family tradition has it that he was sent out as a Royalist prisoner. J. Camden Hotton mentions him as resident in St Michael's in 1680 with his wife and one bought servant.

1724	Jan.	18	Phillip F., a child.	St Mich.
„	Aug.	2	Mrs Anne F. Wido:	„
1725	Aug.	10	Mr Benjamin F. killed by Maj^r Frederick Feake.	„
„	„	19	James F. a child.	„
1732	Oct.	9	Mrs Susannah F.	„
1738	Aug.	15	John F.	„
1742	Mar.	11	John s. of Ric^d: F.	„
1744	„	29	Frances F.	„
1754	Oct.	6	Sarah Firebrass.	„
1763	Nov.	27	Alexander F.	„
1765	Oct.	5	Elizabeth F.	„
1766	Mar.	5	Edward F.	„
1767	Aug.	20	Edward Odwin F. infant.	„
1768	Nov.	18	Frances West F. infant.	„
1771	Mar.	2	John F. an infant.	„
1778	„	18	Thomas F.	„
„	„	29	Angeletta, d. of Wm F.	„
„	June	7	Ursula Lyne the d. of Wm F.	„
„	Aug.	7	Mary Ann F. Widow.	„
1782	June	26	George Alexander F.	„
„	July	11	Elizabeth Ann d. of William F.	„
1797	Mar.	11	William E. F.	„
1802	Jan.	27	William F.	„
„	Oct.	23	Sarah F.	„
„	Nov.	14	James F.	„
1806	Mar.	4	Elizabeth F.	„

EXTRACTS FROM WILLS IN RECORD OFFICE, BARBADOS.

John Firebrace of Barbados. Will dated 2 Nov. 1693. To my dau. Hannah
£250c. To my two sons Benj. and John, with my wife Susanna, all remainder of
my est., and maintenance for my dau. till 18 and sons till 21. My mother
Sarah F., my sister Sarah Atherton, and her 2 daus., my aunt Miller, my brother
Crofts, and his wife and 3 children, each a 20s. ring. Wife sole Ex'trix. Wit.
by Jno Felton, Jno Bushell, Nath. Smart, Rob. Shelton. Sworn by Mr R. Shelton
and Mr Nath. Smart before Gov. Kendall 8 Feb. 1693. Entered 27 Feb. 1693-4.

John Firebrace of the parish of St Michael, Barbados, gent. Will dated
30 Oct. 1721, designing to depart this Island. To my wife Ann F. all est. and
sole Ex'trix. In the p. of Wm Stevens, H. Lee, Alice Jones. Sworn by M^r W^m
Stevens before Gov. Henry Worsley at Pilgrim 11 May 1724. Entered same day.

Anne Firebrace of the Town of St Michael, Barbados, widow. Will dated
16 June..... My house to be rented out till my 1st s. Rich. be 21, then to him, he
to maintain my youngest child. Am possessed by the will of my 1. husband of
several negros, some are to be sold for satisfaction of his debts. I have a legacy
of £500 Jamaica c. due to me. To my daus. Eliz. F. and Anne F. £150 each at
16 or marriage. All residue to my children John Edward Alexander James Line
Firobrace and Phillips Firebrace at 21. I appoint John Moore, Esq., Phillips
Davies, Esq., Jas. Gohier, gent., and Sus^n Needham, wid., Ex'ors and G.
Whereas my 1. husb^d purchased a negro woman, Great Sabina, of Wm Page, gent.,
dec^d, who hath 2 ch^n, Dick and Boy, I give Sabina to Dorothy Page, Boy to
Mary Page, and Dick to Sarah Page. Bed, &c. to Ann Page that lives with me.

In the p. of Jane Peirce, Tho. Clarke. Sworn by Mr Tho. Clarke before Gov. Hen. Worsley at Pilgrim 4 Feb. 172⅘. Entered same day.

Alexander Firebrace. Will dated 1763.* Unto my wife .... Firebrace all the residue of my estate for life .... as I have herein before devised unto my said wife; unto my two youngest sons, Thomas Firebrace and Alexander Firebrace, them and their heirs and assigns for ever, they paying to their brother, my eldest son John Firebrace, now at the University of .... in the Kingdom of Great Britain, the sum of £50 currency immediately after the decease of my said wife Sarah Firebrace. I appoint my said wife Sarah Firebrace executrix, the Reverend Mr Thomas...... Proved 8 June 1764.

NOTE.—The will is continued overleaf, but is completely illegible. A note states that his son Alexander Firebrace should have been styled " George Alexander Firebrace." Witness: R^d Vines Ellacott.

Elizabeth Roach. Will dated 5 April 1775. My sister Mary Firebrace, wife of Thos. Firebrace (schoolmaster). To my nieces Mary Ross and Sarah Firebrace, D^r of Thos. Firebrace. I appoint the Rev. John Firebrace of Deptford, England, Executor in England, and my brother-in-law, Thos. Firebrace, in Barbados. Proved 13 Nov. 1772.

Richard Lindon. Will dated 4 January 1736. My dau. Susannah Lindon, son John Lindon, son Francis Lindon, nephew Edward Firebrace. Witnesses: Ed. Harnett and John Whetstone.

Geo. Alexander Firebrace of the parish of St Michael in Barbados. Will dated 20 June 1782. To my wife Dorothy F. all est. Sam. Drayton of s^d p'sh, shopkeeper, Ex'or. In the p. of W^m Ph. Poole, Phill. Mashart. Sworn by W. P. Poole before Gov. D. Parry at Pilgrim 11 Aug. 1783. Entered same day.

Adm'on 21 Dec. 1790 to Wm Scott of St Michaels of est. of above-named.

Adm'on 21 Dec. 1790 to Wm Scott of est. of Tho. Firebrace of St Michael, dec^d.

Adm'on 18 March 1791 to Wm Scott of est. of Alex^r Firebrace of this I., dec^d, with his will annexed.

William Firebrace of St. Michael, Barbados, merchant. Will dated 6 Aug. 1801. Transactions depending between the firm of Wm Firebrace & Sons and Joseph Barrow and Co., if a balance be due to latter I charge my private est. with £1000c. towards it. To my wife Angelletta F. all my est. for her life. To my dau. Line F. £500c., dau. Marg^t Williams F. £500c., and all residue to my s. Wm Newton F. My wife and son, and friend Rob. Reed, Ex'trix and Ex'ors. In the p. of M. A. Parks, Tho. Woodin. Sworn by Marg^t A. Parks before Govr Seaforth at Pilgrim 10 Feb. 1802. Ent^d same day.

---

* This is one of the wills contained in the box recently found, and is very much perished, the papers having been completely worn away at the folds, and much of the writing illegible. The later part of the will is in mere fragments.

Will of Richard Scott of the Island of Barbados, Esq., dated 8 Oct. 1719. Mentions his estate in Barbados, Great Britain, and elsewhere. His wife Elizabeth Scott, son in law Richard Lightfoot, and his now (sic) wife Mrs Jane Lightfoot, daughter Mrs Elizabeth Johnson, sister Mrs Sarah Bowles, sister Susanna Firebrace, to whom he leaves £5, John Firebrace, to whom he leaves £5, Kinsman and Godson Mr James, Friends Mr Gobeir, Thomas Maxwell, Capt. George Green, daughter Elizabeth Warner.* P. 26 Feb. 1719-20.

Robert Whitehead of Barbados. Will dated 23 July 1719. Witness: Benjamin Firebrace.

Richard Lindon of the Parish of St. Michael's, Barbados. Will dated 28 June 1736. Dau. Susanna, son John Lindon, nephew Mr Edward Firebrace, son Francis Linden, and George Gibbs and Thomas Clarke Ex'ors. Proved 4 Jan. 1736-7.

Richard Linden, Attorney at law, buried 6 Sept. 1736. (St Michael's.)

John Wheeler of the Parish of St. Peter's, Barbados. Will dated 15 June 1770. Dau. Ann Wheeler, granddau. Ann Lyne Wheeler, son John Borell Wheeler; John Borell Wheeler and Anne Wheeler Ex'ors. Proved 25 July 1770.

NOTE.—John Borell Wheeler of the Parish of St. James, Barbados, married Anne Lyne, daughter of Edward Firebrace, at St. Michael's 31 Dec. 1765.

This Indenture made 3rd January 1732 between Richard Firebrace of St Michael, Gentleman, eldest Grandson and heir at law, as well of John Firebrace, merchant, his late Grandfather, of Susannah Firebrace, widow, his late Grandmother, of John Firebrace, Gentleman, his late uncle,† all late of St Michail, Barbados, and Richard Lindon, Gentleman, for a legacy of £250 bequeathed by the will of John Firebrace the elder to his daughter Hannah Firebrace, with whom the said Richard Lindon intermarried. Witness: Edward Firebrace. Recorded 25 June 1734, vol. 129, fo. 18.

This Indenture made 1 July 1784 between William Firebrace of St Michael, and Samuel Nasum of the same, whereby William Firebrace, in consideration of his love for his wife Angeletta, and his daughters Anne Lyne and Margaret Williams, grants slaves to Samuel Nasum upon trust for William Firebrace for his life, with remainder to Angeletta and Anne Lyne and Margaret Williams the daughters, being minors at the date of the deed. If the daughters die before reaching the age of 21 years the slaves to be divided between his sons William Newton and Samuel Thomas and their mother Angeletta Firebrace.

This Indenture made 17 April 1805 between William Newton Firebrace and Samuel Thomas Firebrace, both late of the Parish of St Michael and Island of

---

* Eliz., dau. and h. of Richard Scott of Barbados, Esq., mar. Col. Edward Warner of Antigua, and died 13 Aug. 1723, aged 37. The Warners quarter her arms: *Argent, three Catherine wheels Sable.* [EDITOR.]

† Richard Firebrace was eldest *son*, not *nephew* of John Firebrace the younger, and elder brother of Edward Firebrace, the witness. This deed was copied and sent to me by the Parish Clerk of Bridgetown. The error may be a clerical error of his or of the clerk who copied the original deed.

Barbados, Esq^{res}, by Stephen Phillips their Attorney of the one part, and John Cummins of the Parish of Christ Church of the other part. In consideration of £2350 paid by the said John Cummins, the said William Newton Firebrace and Samuel Thomas Firebrace grant a piece of land in Bridgetown containing 6830½ square feet, together with a mansion and dwelling house to the said John Cummins in fee.

This Indenture made 21 Oct. 1805 between Ward Cadogan of St Michael's, Esqre, of the one part, William Newton Firebrace, late of the said Parish, but at present of the Colony of Demerara, Esquire, and Mehetabel Christian his wife, late Mehetabel Christian Collier, spinster, of the second part, and Christopher Knight of St Michail, Gentleman, as trustee, of the third part, regarding the sale of three male slaves for £500 to William Newton Firebrace and Mehetabel Christian his wife.

Deed Poll made 27 May 1806 under the hand of Angeletta Firebrace of the Parish of St Michael's, Widow, granting in consideration of the sum of £90 to be paid by Catherine Lacey, a free mulatto, a negro female slave by name Melissinda.

This Indenture made 2 Dec. 1808 between William Newton Firebrace of the Colony of Demerara, Esquire, of the one part, and William Sturge Joy of the Parish of St Michael's, Wheelwright, of the other part, regarding the sale of a piece of land in Bridgetown, containing about 13,247 square feet, for the sum of £500, together with a mansion as per plan endorsed.

This Indenture made 7 June 1810 between William Newton Firebrace of the Colony of Demerara, Esquire, of the one part, and Frances Maynard Weeks, widow, of the other part, granting to her for the sum of £650 a piece of land, together with a Dwelling House in the parish of St Michaels in a certain Street called Mare Hill St., bounding lands belonging to Mrs Duke, Mrs Dewsbury, and John Ironmonger, Esquire.

Ford.*

Edward Foord or Ford of Guildford, co. Surrey═Elizabeth . . . .

Francis Ford═Laurence, remar.	John Ford	Tho.═. . . .	Lieut. Chas.═. . .,
of Barbadoes, 14 March 1654-5	of Barba-	Ford,	Hillyard, liv-
died v.p. Chas. Rich, mer-	does, mer-	dead	"brother" ing
Will dated 17 chant (his will	chant, died	1654,	of Fra. Ford 1654.
July 1654; dated 9 March	v.p. Will	and	1654; ? of
proved 2 May 1657, 466, Woot-	proved	left a	London,
1657 (160, ton); living a	1666 (57,	will.	merchant,
Ruthen). widow 1679.	Mico).		1660, and
			Barbadoes.
			(Col. Cal.)

Francis Ford, born about 1654-5; named 1657 in the will of Chas. Rich as his son-in-law (*i.e.*, step-son); had a ticket for London 26 July 1679; named 1679 in will of Rob. Rich, brother of Chas. Rich. Will proved in Barbados 1680.

John Foord of Barba-dos, Esq., born Oct. 1616; churchwarden of St. Andrews 1680 and owner of 280 acres, 120 negros. M.I. there.

Mary═Tho. Day
Ford. of Stoke-
next-
Guild-
ford, liv-
ing 1662.

Tho. Day, aged 10 in 1662, Visitation of Surrey.

---

* Contributed by Mr. Hugh Alexander Ford, with additions by the Editor.

243

Thos. Ford of the Ridge, Barbados.⫫Eleanor, dau. of John and
He heads the Baronet's pedigree. | Susan Austin, bapt. 13 Nov.
See "Devon Notes and Queries," | 1662; mar. 24 July 1690;
i., 157. | ? bur. 8 Jan. 1754.

Francis Ford, Esq., bapt. 6 Feb.⫫Martha Barrow, dau. of Smithell⫫Helena.
1693; M. of A. for Christ Church | Matson and widow of Capt. John | 2nd
1730 and 1736; bur. 29 Dec. 1763. | Hooper; mar. 5 March 1716-17. | wife.
Will dated 26 Oct. 1748; proved in
Barbados 7 Jan. 1764.

Francis Ford of "Lears," born⫫Elizabeth, dau. of Burch Hothersall and widow
24 Feb. 1717-18; M. of Coun- | of Sam. Osborne, Esq. (whose will was dated
cil 1767; died in Portman Street | 11 Oct. 1756); mar. 28 Jan. 1758. Adm'on
circa Aug. 1772. Will dated 29 | 7 Sep. 1773 of her estate for her four children,
April 1772; proved 4 Sept. 1773 | minors.
(357, Stevens).

Sir Francis Ford, created Bart. 22 Feb.⫫Mary Anson, sister of   Martha Ford.
1793; only son and heir; born 15 Nov. | Tho., Viscount Anson;   —
1758; M. of Council; M.P. 1790. Will | mar. 1785; died 20 Jan. Anne Ford.
dated 27 Jan. 1800, codicil 2 March | 1837, aged 73. M.I.   —
1801; proved 7 Nov. (743, Abercrombie). | in Holy Trinity, Chel- Eliz. Ford.
Owned plantations in Barbados and | tenham.
Essequibo.

Sir Francis Ford, 2nd Bart.,   2. George   3. Rev. Charles Ford of Balliol Coll.,
of Christ Church, Oxford,   Ford.   Oxford, matric. 12 May 1815, aged 17;
matric. 24 Oct. 1805, aged   B.A. 1819, M.A. 1821; R. of Billing-
18; died 13 April 1839.   ford 1821—50, and of Postwick, co.
(For issue see "Baronetage.")   Norfolk, 1843 until his death 14 May
                                           1863. (Foster.)

CONFIRMATION OF ARMS TO FRANCIS FORD OF BARBADOS, 1793.

The following grant, on parchment, was purchased with a bundle of W.I.
deeds in 1909 from a bookseller. The whole of the left margin, containing the
shield, is unfortunately lost, having been cut off. The missing words, placed
within brackets, have been supplied from other grants by Heard. The grant
must have been made a few days before the grantee was created a Baronet. It
is not signed, but is apparently a duplicate, the original of which should be in the
College of Arms.

To ALL AND SINGULAR to whom these Presents shall come Sir Isaac Heard
Knight GARTER Principal King of Arms and Thomas Lock Esquire CLARENCEUX
King of Arms of the South East and West Parts of England from the River
Trent Southwards send Greeting.

𝖂𝖍𝖊𝖗𝖊𝖆𝖘 Francis Ford of Ember Court in the Parish of Thames-Ditton in
the County of Surrey Esquire Son and Heir of Francis Ford of Lears in the
Parish of Sᵗ Michael in the Island of Barbadoes Esquire deceased hath represented

244

unto the Most Noble Charles Duke of Norfolk Earl Marshal and hereditary Marshal of England that he is by tradition descended from the Family of FORD of Devonshire, and hath borne Armo[rial] Ensigns but owing to] the long residence of his Family in the said Island of Barbadoes he is at present unable;[to prove his descent therefrom] and therefore requested the favor of his Grace's Warrant for our confirming to him and [his Descendants and to] the Descendants of his said father such Armorial Ensigns as may be proper to be borne by him [and them according to the] Laws of Arms. **And forasmuch** as the said Earl Marshal did by Warrant under [his hand and seal bear]ing date the twentieth day of February instant authorize and direct Us to confirm such [Armorial Ensigns accor]dingly. **Know Ye therefore** that We the said GARTER and CLARENCEUX in [pursuance of the Warrant] of the said Earl Marshal and by Virtue of the Letters Patent of our several Offices to each of Us [respectively granted un]der the Great Seal of Great Britain do by these Presents confirm and exemplify to the said [Francis Ford the Arms fo]llowing that is to say Per Pale Gules and Or two Bends Vair, on a Canton of the second a [Greyhound courant Sab]le and for the Crest on a Wreath of the Colours A Greyhound's Head sable, erased Gules, [muzzled Or as the same] are in the Margin hereof more plainly depicted to be borne and used for ever hereafter by him [the said Francis Ford E]squire and his descendants and by the descendants of his said Father Francis Ford Esq[r] [with all due and] proper Differences according to the Laws of Arms without the Let or Interruption of any [Person or Persons whats]oever. **In Witness** whereof We the said GARTER and CLARENCEUX [Kings of Arms have to] these Presents subscribed our Names and Affixed the Seals of our several Offices [this . . . . day of] February in the thirty third Year of the Reign of our sovereign Lord GEORGE the [Third by the Grace of G]od King of Great Britain France and Ireland Defender of the Faith &c[a] and in the [year of Our Lord One thou]sand seven hundred and ninety three.

Richard Forde of Guildford, Surrey, brewer. Will dated 22 Feb. 1614. My daus. Eliz., Susan, and Sarah F. 40[l] each at 21. My dau. Agnes, wife of Rich[d] Lavie, 40s. and her children Rich., Agnes, and Wm. Lavie, 40s. each. Rich. F., s. of my s. Ollyfe F., 20s. at 21. My s. Tho. F. the fittings of the brewhouse in share with my wife Anne so long as she remain a widow, also the tenement and brewhouse now in the occupation of me, Richard Gurner, and John Champion in the p. of S[t] Mary, Guildford, except that part in the occupation of Ollife F. my s.
My s. Tho. to have lands in S[t] Nich. and Holy Trinity in Guildford, he paying to my dau. Marie Keene, wife of John K., 40s. annually. Property in occupation of my s. Ollife F. and his s. Rich. to be theirs for life, then to the heirs of my s. Tho. All residue to my wife Anne and s. Tho. Proved 9 Nov. 1614, Archd. of Surrey, 21, Stoughton. ("Genealogical Monthly," p. 64.)

Barbadoes. Francis Ford. Will dated 17 July 1654. John Ford my brother and Humphry Kent to be Ex'ors in Trust. To my wife Lawrence Ford the sugar I have sent home for London consigned to my brother Lieut. Charles Hillyard, about 34,000, also 26,000 lbs. due to me in this island. The child she goeth with. To her also the housing M[r] Wm. Johnson now liveth in. To my brother John Foord my house at the Bridge town which I purchased of Mr. Wm. Johnson. The Balance due from M[r] Mark Mortimore. My loving father and mother living in Guilford in Surrey £500 st. and the houses sold to me by my brother John Foord to remain to my said father and mother by names of Edward and Elizabeth. I give her also all my household stuff and the horse and my negro Robin. To Humphry Kent, Jun[r], the 4 acres I purchased of M[r] Wm. Johnson near Bridgetown, adjoining M[r] George Greene. To M[rs] Anne Blythe, wife of Capt.

245

John Blythe, £50 st. The legacies bequeathed by my late brother Thos. Ford to be paid. To Mr Tho. Hooper, minister, Lt.-Col. Robert Hooper, Mr Charles Rich, Mr John Parris (?), Mr Tho. Batson, Mr Henry Batson, Capt. Gabriell Gadman, M^r Wm. Wright, M^r Wm. Eastchurch, M^r Wm. Johnson, Mr Francis Clay, Capt. John Blythe, M^r Wm. Tickle, Mr John Shearland, Mr. Peter Calverd, and Humphry Kent, to each a suit of mourning. To my brother Lieut. Charles Hillyard and his wife £20 st. To my wife 5000 lbs. of sugar. To Wm. the cook that liveth with me 500 lbs. of sugar. Witnessed by John Parris, Humphry Kent. Proved 2 May 1657 by John Foord, the brother, the letters of adm'on formerly granted to Richard Batson, a creditor, being revoked; power reserved to H. Kent. (160, Ruthen.)

Transcript of the will of Thomas Foorde of Barbados, apparently a fragment. Given to my younger Brother Jo. Foord fowre hundred pounds betweene Mr. Richard Batson and ye said Tho. Foord and all ye goods yt hee hath in ye pdcamore and ye Francis and Joyce except ye black nagg, for his brother Francis Foord 500 lbs. off Gilford 3 hundred lbs., to his father and mother ye other 200, for his Brother John ye houses and land after his father and mother's decease, likewise his Brother John shall have all ye storehouses, goods, debts innye Barbados, for Henry Perrer, debtor to ye said Tho. Foord, 160 lbs., 100 lbs. he hath given ye use to his Bro. and after to be equally distributt to his children, ye 60 lbs. for his father and mother. He hath given to Mrs. Batson, Mrs. Bridgewood and Mrs. Mary Batson each 10 lbs. per peece for morneing gownes. Matthew Batson, Elizabeth Batson and Mary Foord ye younger each 5 lbs. per peece for a dimond rings=In the rounde house a box of money 20 lbs. for ye buriall of Thomas Foord, i peece of gould for Doctor Weshers, i peece for Mr. Ward, i peece for Mr. Cease, for each of them a ringe. Given to Mr. Thomas Batson i peece of gould for a ring, all his cloathes, linen and other things aborde ye pacamore for his brother John. Witness: Tho. Batson, Jacob Withers.

Tho. Foorde.

Tho. Batson appeared ye 28th Sept. 1654 and deposed he was witness to ye sealeing and delivering of ye above will and testament by Tho. Foord before me John Roberts.

[Barbados.] Entered ye 28th Sept. 1654. (13-65.)

Chas. Rich, merchant. Will dated 9 March 1657. Lands in B. My wife Lawrence. My son-in-law Fra. Foord 500^l. My brothers John and Rob. R., etc. Proved in 1658 (466, Wootton.)

John Foorde, parson, of Newtimber, co. Sussex. To my sons Francis and John and daus. Eliz. and Mary £100 apiece. Proved in 1659 (502, Pell.)

Barbadoes. John Ford of the Island aforesaid, merchant. Will dated 18 Sept. 1662. To be buried in the parish church of St. Michaels .... Unto my father and mother Edward and Elizabeth Ford all my estate in England and in Barbadoes. If both be dead .... then to be equally divided unto these persons hereafter named, that is to say, to the children of Richard Lanie per Jane Mills, to the children of my brother-in-law Henry Peryer per Elizabeth Ford, and to the children of William Leach per Mary Lanie. Thirdly, I give and bequeath unto William Bicnon, Esqr, William Poine, Esqr, D^r De Lakonce, Mr. Marinne Hales, Mr. John Fisher, Capt. John Williams, Capt. John Greene, Capt. Robert Browning, Capt. Robert Clarke, Capt. Thos. Bond, Mr. Thomas Bartlett, Mr. Richard Saywell and his wife, Mr. Jurian Barnes and his wife, Mr. Mark Mortimer, Mr. James Sparrow, Mrs. Sarah Bridgwood, Mr. Mathew Batson, to my Aunt Mrs. Mary Ford, to my cousin Mr. Edward Ford, to my cousin Mr. John Ford, to my cousin Mr. Thomas Ford, to my cousin Mr. Thomas Day and his wife, to Lieut. William Eastchurch and his wife, to Mr. Humphrey Kent and his wife, to Mr. Roger Kemys, to every one of these persons to have 25s. a piece to buy them gold rings. Unto Humphrey Kent, senior, that Four acres of land that my brother Francis Ford purchased of Mr. William Johnson, attorney to William Penoye of London, merchant, which said land adjoineth to the land of Mr. Robert Grene, deceased, and on the land of Mr. Thomas Bell, now called Gravill Hill and now in the possession of Mr. William Sharpe and others, adjoining to the Caseway near to the house and land of Mr. John Hasell and Mr. Edward Cole, which parcel of land my brother Francis Ford by his last will bequeathed to Humphrey Kent, Junior, but was not to him delivered, but now by this my last will and testament I do confirm it to Humphrey Kent, Senior. Unto Francis Ford, junior, the son of Francis Ford, Senior, at 21, 10s. Unto Lieut. William Eastchurch my diamond ring. Unto Mr. Roger Kemmys my grey gelding and my negro boy Robin. Unto Mr. Robert Howard and to his wife 400 lbs. Muscovado sugar to buy each of them a gold ring. Unto Sampson Ellis and to Thomas Laney, my servants, my wearing apparell. . . . . Unto Sampson Ellis 1000 lbs. to be shipped for London and consigned to Mr. Mark Mortemer. . . . . And lastly, I do . . . . appoint . . . . my loving friends Lieut. William Eastchurch, Humphrey Kent and Mr. Roger Kemys to be . . . . executors . . . . and in the presence of Anthony Anthony, Samuell Osburne.

[Certificate by Edward Bowden, Deputy Secretary, Barbados, that the above Will is a true copy.]

7 April 1666. Administration to Richard Batson, attorney to the executors named. (P.C.C., 57, Mico.)

Rob. Rich the elder of L., gent. Will dated 16 Nov. 1679. My cousin Fra. Foard s. to my sister Laurentia Rich 50¹. My sister-in-law Laurentia Rich, widow. Testator was a Barbados merchant. (166, King.)

Francis Foord, now in the Ship " Honor," Capt. Thomas Warren, Commander, bound for Barbados, now ill of a feavour whereof severall in our Ship have died, do this seventeenth day of March Anno. dom. 1680, make . . . . this my last will. To my loving friends Mr. Rowland Holt and Mr. Joseph Hough, now on board our Ship, five pounds sterling a piece, also to my much honored and kinde Master Mr. Francis Bond in Barbados ten pounds, which said twenty pounds I request my cousin Mr. Robt. Rich to pay them with expedition which he may safely do, I having a letter from my uncle Robert Rich other two executors in England so to authorize him and ye remaining thirty pounds in full of said Legacy I give to my sister Ann Rich. If my mother be dead since my departure from England I do bequeath whatever my said mother has left me . . . . by her will to my said sister Ann Rich. The following small debts to be first discharged. Mr. Patrick Jenkins' ex'ors £3 0s. 0d.. Dr. Birch 10s. 0d., Thos. Allen, Shoemaker, for a pair of shoes, 5s. 0d., Andrew Harbin, cousin of Joseph Harbin, who appointed me to pay in London by letter, which losing is unpaid, £1 5s. 0d.; Capt. Warren £1 2s. 0d.; Capt. Warren for a cask of Brandy containing 8 ½ gallons at 2s. 6d., £1 1s. 3d.; Samuel Carpenter, owing him for a Campaigne Coat, which if his correspondent Mr. Moore expresses not to be paid I desire may be satisfied, £2 4s. 0d. Five pounds to said cousin Robert Rich, whom I request to accept of being my executor, as also eleven pounds more which he may justly apply on my account out of the estate of the said uncle Robt. Rich, decd., his man Abraham Walrond. In the presence of Thomas Warren, R. Holt, Joseph Hough.

Barbados. Mr. Thomas Warren and Mr. Rowland Holt personally appeared 14 April 1680 before his Excellency J. Atkins and made oath.
Barbados. Entered 24 April 1680.

Rob. F. of B. My niece Margaret, Countess of Cavan. Proved 1707 (8, Poley).

Benjamin Matson, merchant. Will .dated 18 November 1712. I forgive my brother Smithel Matson debts ; Sarah Carew, now in Great Britain, £50; Margaret Carew, £50; Elizabeth Drinkwater, £300; Mr. Samuel Game, £50, and Mr. Charles Game, £50; to Christopher, son of Mr. John Fowler, £25; Benjamin Fowler, son of Christopher, £25 at age of 15. Legacies to Mr. Nath. Denham, Col. Joseph Salmon, Nath. White, Edw. Freeman, Benj. Bullard, Hon. Dudley Woodbridge, Esq., and his wife, Benj. Woodbridge (under 15), Margaret and Jane Willey, Sarah Willey (under 15), Mary Woodbridge (under 15), Dudley Woodbridge, jun^r (under 15). To my wife Margaret all my real estate for life and twenty-five negroes. The Hon. Dudley Woodbridge, Esq., and Capt. John Hooper executors; and the children of Capt. John Hooper and Capt. George Barrow, by their wives, the daughters of my brother Smithel Matson, to be residuary legatees. Witnessed by Thos Shawe, Thos Withers, Edwd Freeman, at Barbados.

8 Oct., 1723. Administration granted to Edward Lascelles, administrator of the goods of Margt. Moore *alias* Matson, deceased, while living executrix [*sic*] and residuary legatee [*sic*] of the deceased, to the use of William Moore her husband, now at Guernsey. (212, Richmond.)

Sam. Forte of St John's B., in his will proved 13 Jan. 1713 names a dau. Ursula, wife of John Ford.

Barbados. Francis Ford, of the parish of Christ Church in the island aforesaid, Esquire. Will dated 26 Oct. 1748. Unto my dear and honoured mother Eleanor Ford, widow, during her natural life my Below Rock Plantation, lands, buildings, slaves, stock, etc., to be held by her during her life in the same manner she has done in my lifetime. Unto my dear and well beloved wife Helena Ford everything that she had a right to before our intermarriage, with the crop standing and growing on her land, to be disposed of by her as she thinks proper. As I have settled an annuity upon her by way of jointure and in lieu of her dower or thirds, I do as a mark of my great esteem and regard for her give her the sum of One hundred pounds to buy her mourning and a piece of plate. All the residue and remainder of my estate real and personal I give and devise unto my well beloved son Francis Ford, Esquire, his heirs and assigns for ever, and I appoint him sole executor. In the presence of Jno. Lyte, Grant Elcock, William Duke.

Barbados, 7 Jan. 1764. William Duke appeared and swore as to the due execution of the above will.

Will of Samuel Osborne, of St. Michael in Barbados, Esquire, dated 11 Oct. 1756. I bequeath to my wife Elizabeth for life all my real and personal estate, and after her death the same to her lawful issue; in default of issue she shall bequeath the same to our most deserving relatives. My said wife to be executrix. Signed Sam. Osborne, and witnessed by Philip Gibbes, John Hothersall, William Duke.

6 Sept. 1773. Commission issued to Philip Gibbes, Esqr, one of the testamentary guardians appointed to Frances, Martha, Ann and Elizabeth Ford, spinsters, minors, the children of Elizabeth Ford, formerly Osborne (wife of Francis Ford), deceased, the said Elizabeth dying before proving the said will. (368, Stevens.)

Francis Ford, Esquire, of the parish of St. Michael in the island above named. Will dated 29 April 1772. To my mother-in-law Thomazin Ford £25 and also " her living in my dwelling house on my plantation called the Ridge." To each of my daughters Martha Ford, Ann Ford and Elizabeth Ford, £10,000, together with certain slaves (named), to be paid at their ages of 18 or on prior marriage. I give unto Miss Damaris Carter £30 per annum for life. To my esteemed friend Miss Esther Margaret Bordes, £50. To Samuel Padmore, junior, son of my manager Samuel Padmore at Lear's Plantation, £100. To Frances Baker, daughter of Alice Baker, late of Barbadoes, deceased, £18 per annum, and maintenance for life at my plantation called Lear's, so long as she shall live single. To Elizabeth Millward of the parish of Christ Church, widow, £12 per annum. It is my will that Frederick, the son of the above-named Elizabeth Millward, shall during his minority be decently maintained at the expence of my estate, and that he be put to school at proper age and have a classical education if his genius will take it; I desire that he be bound apprentice to some genteel profession at 16 years of age, and I give him £1000 at his age of 21. Manumission of certain slaves (named) and provision made for their maintenance. All the residue and remainder of my estate, real and personal, I give unto my son Francis Ford at 21 years. But in case my said son shall die under age without male issue, I will that my plantations be divided in manner following: to my daughter Martha and her heirs my plantations in this island, one called Bentley's, another called the Ridge, and the other called the Below Rock; to my daughter Ann and her heirs my two plantations called Lear's and the other called the Bay; to my daughter Elizabeth my two other plantations called Carrington's and Pickering's. But if my son leave female issue, then I give to each daughter of my said son £10,000 at her age of 18 or day of marriage. Whereas by indenture of lease dated 11 July 1771, between Alexander Sandiford, Esqr, and myself, I have let for a term of years to him my Bay Plantation before mentioned, and have covenanted to accept the sum of £13,500 as a full consideration for the said estate, now in case the said plantation should be sold and my son die under age leaving no male issue, I give the said sum of £13,500 to my daughter Ann. I do also give my daughters their residence in my dwelling house on my plantation called Lear's, each to have the sole use of a chamber to herself. Each of my executors the sum of £50. I nominate my friends John Hothersall, Philip Gibbes and John Brathwaite of the Kingdom of Great Britain, Esquires, and Thomas Hothersall and Grant Ellcock of this island, Esquires, executors and guardians of my children. And I also appoint my son Francis Ford, when he shall attain the age of 21, executor of my will and guardian of my daughters. In the presence of John Gibbes, Wm Daley, William Bayley.

[Barbadoes. Entered 12 December 1772.]

The will of Francis Ford, late of the parish of St. Michael, Barbadoes, but in the parish of St. Mary le Bone, co. Middlesex, Esqr, deceased, was proved 4 Sept. 1773 by John Hothersall, Philip Gibbes and John Brathwaite, Esquires, power reserved to Thomas Hothersall and Grant Ellcock, Esqrs., when they shall apply for same, and to Francis Ford at his age of 21. (357, Stevens.)

See *ante*, p. 199, for the will of John Austin. *

Sir Francis Ford of Marylebone, Bart. Will dated 27 Jan. 1800. To my wife Mary £700 a year over and above her dower. To each child £5000. All lands and slaves for my eldest s. Francis F. at 21. Cod. now of Essequibo 2 March 1801. All property to my s. Fra., he to pay to my wife £1000 a year. Remainder in default of issue to my sons Geo. and Chas. Proved 7 Nov. 1801 by Mary F., testator, l. of Oakedge, co. Stafford, but of Barbados (743, Abercrombie).

1640, June 10. Tho. Foard of B., planter, sells 30 acres. (Vol. I., 765.)

1675, Nov. 25. Minutes of the Assembly of B. An Act giving licence to Rich. Forde, Surveyor, to have the sole benefit of selling his plots of this island, passed. (Col. Cal., p. 303.)

1679. Tho. F. of Christ Church parish, owner of 15 acres and 9 negroes. (Hotten, 478.)

1679, July 26. Francis F. in the ship *Mallego Merchant* for London. Time out, ticket from B. (*Ibid.*, 369.)

1680. Rich. F. and wife of St. Michael's parish with 1 child and 2 slaves. (*Ibid.*, 447.)

1680. John F. an Assistant to the Scotland Court of C.P. (Col. Cal., p. 515.)

*Page 129, this volume.

1680. John Foord, Esq., of St Andrew's parish, 280 acres, 4 men servants and 120 negros. (Hotten, 469.) There was a stone to him, " John Foord, gent., b. in Oct. 1617 " (rest obliterated). (Archer, 383.)

1730 and 1736. Francis F., Esq., a M. of A. for Christ Church. (Oldmixon, I, 83, 94.)

1772, Aug. 20. Ford of the island of Barbadoes, lately arrived from thence for the benefit of his health. (" Town and Country Mag.," 448.)

1772, Sept. Francis Ford, Esq. in Portman-street, one of the council in Barbadoes. (*Ibid.*, 504.)

1801, June 7. Suddenly on his estate at B., Sir Francis Ford, bart. of Ember, Surrey, so created Feb. 14, 1793. He was f. a fellow-commoner of St. John's coll. Cambridge; B.A. 1778. (" G.M.," 859.)

1802, July 21. At Liverpool, after a long illness, Wm. F. l. of B. (*Ibid.*, 783.)

1837, Jan. 20. At Cheltenham, aged 73, Mary, widow of Sir Francis Ford, Bart., aunt to the Earl of Lichfield. She was the eldest dau. of George Adams Anson, esq. by the Hon. Mary Vernon, dau. of George, 1st Lord Vernon, was married in 1785, and left a widow in 1801, having had issue Sir Francis Ford, the present Baronet, and a numerous family. (*Ibid.*, 331.)

1839, Apr. 13. At Charlton King's, aged 52, Sir Francis Ford, Bart. of B. after a severe & painful illness of 8 years. He succeeded his father Sir Francis the 1st Bart. in 1801 ; & m. in 1807, Eliza, only dau. of Henry Brady of Limerick, esq. by whom he has left two sons. (*Ibid.*, 554.)

1839, Apr. 9. At Clifton, the Rev. G. G. Gardiner, to Fra. Mary, only dau. of the l. P. Touchet & niece to Sir F. F. Bart. (*Ibid.*, 650.)

1839, Aug. 19. In Portland-pl. the Right Hon. Eliz. Lady Colville, wife of Vice-Adm. Lord C. She was the only dau. of Fra. F. & sister of Sir Fra. F. Bart. was m. in 1790, & had issue an only dau. who d. in infancy. (*Ibid.*, 433.)

1842, Mar. 9. At Torquay, a. 22, Mary, wife of the Rev. Wm. Lionel Darell, & eldest dau. of the l. Sir Fra. F. Bart. (*Ibid.*, 450.)

1846. Oct. 31. At Brighton, Sir Fra. John F. Bart. to Cornelia-Maria, eldest dau. of Gen. Sir Ralph Darling. (*Ibid.*, 1847, 194.)

Rich. Steele, founder of the " Tatler " and co-editor with Addison of the " Spectator," m. not long after March 1705 Mrs Margaret Stretch, widow, dau. of . . . . Ford. She as h. to her brother, then lately deceased, administered to his est. at Barbados worth 850*l*. per ann. Charged with a debt of £3000. She d. Dec. 1706, and in Jan. 1707 Steele administered to her est. (" D.N.B.")

CHRIST CHURCH.

Marriages.

1690	July 24	Thomas Ford and Eleanor Austin
1716-17	Mar. 5	Francis Ford and Martha Hooper

Baptisms.

1662	Nov. 13	Eleanor Daughter of John and Susan Austin
1693	July 6	Francis Son of Thomas and Eleanor Ford
1717-18	Feb.	[*blank*] Son of Francis and Martha Ford. (This entry is between two others of Feb. 23 and Feb. 28)

Burials.

1691	July 19	Benjamin Matson
1692	Oct. 3	Thomas Son of Thomas Ford
1695	June —	Thomas Ford
1713	Oct. 23	John Austin
1754	Jan. 8	Eleanor Ford
1763	Dec. 29	Francis Ford

1654-5 Mar. 14 Laurentia Ford and Mr Charles Rich
1656-7 Mar. 27 Wm Ford & Mary Harper
1662 Oct. 2 Mr John Ford, Merchant, buried in the Church
1666 Mar. 29 Mr Humphrey Brockdon & Mrs Elizabeth Ford
1758 Jan. 28 Francis Ford, Junr, to Eliz^a Asborne [*sic*], Widow
1764 Apr. 18 Elizabeth Ford (bur.)
1745 Sept. 3 Samuel Osborn, Esq., and Mrs Elizabeth Hothersal; by Mr Carter
1678 Oct. 24 Mr Benj^a Matson & Mrs Margrett Venman
1679 Aug. 15 Jno. Carew & Eliz^a Matson
1679 Sept. 21 Eliz^a & Margrett ye Daugh^{trs} of Mr Benj^a & Margrett
            Mattson, bap.
1681 Sept. 21 Eliza the D^a of Mr Benj^a Matson, bur.

WILLIAM GRANT OF BARBADOS

AND SOME OF HIS DESCENDANTS.

1. WILLIAM GRANT. Gentleman, (b about 1620 m about 1663 Elizabeth) of Castle Grant, Barbados, said to be a cousin of Francis Grant of Cullen, and Monymusk (afterwards Sir Francis G., Bart, and Lord Cullen a law lord) and also a kinsman of James Grant of Frenchie afterwards Grant of Grant (see Barons Strathspey) arrived in Barbados about 1671. The old family tree and all old family papers were said to have been destroyed in the Hurricane of 1831. It is on record that he purchased land in 1672, and slaves at a later date. On 3 June 1680 he owned 30 acres, and had 5 white servants, and 40 negroes; he also employed three freemen, and later was possessed of a larger estate. His widow called "Madam" Elizabeth in the Census Papers of 1715 was at that date surviving him. He died in 1687, and by his Will dated 30 August 1686, proved 13 October 1687, gave his wife Elizabeth an annuity of £30 sterling (to to be paid out of the profits of his plantation) and the tenancy for life of his mansion house; legacies of £100 to his daughter Ann Moore, wife of John Moore, and £50 to each of their children Elizabeth and John. To his sister, Ann Gage, resident in England, the sum of £10 sterling yearly. To his daughters Angel and Margaret £300 sterling each, to be paid at 18 or on marriage and to have their abode in his mansion house, with education befitting them. To his son Francis at 21 the lower plantation adjoining the lands of Jacob Lucie, [1] Francis Smith, John Vaughn, Bryan Blackman deceased and Allan Mackaskell; and twenty able negroes. To his son William at 21 his upper plantation where he then lived, adjoining lands of the said Jacob Lucie, and the heirs of John Worsam. The plantations were not to go out of the name of Grant. His silver tankards to William and Francis, whom he appointed executors together with his friends Col. John Waterman, Capt Humphrey Waterman 2nd, his son-in-law John Coombs (?), and his wife Elizabeth. To each executor a ring of 40/- value, and to his son-in-law John Moore a ring of 20/-.

Issue, probably all born in Barbados:

i. ANN married John Moore, named in above Will, with their children *(i) Elizabeth* and *(ii) John.* Col. John Waterman, executor of the Will of William Grant married Elizabeth Moore, daughter of William Moore and Aunt of Sir H. Moore in Jamaica. It is probable that John Moore was a near relation of Mrs. Waterman. The Moores are said to be descended from Sir Edward More, 1st Bart of *More Hall,* co Lancashire. See Archer's M. I. p. 364,

ii. MARY married John Coombs (?) 1693 See Will of Wm. Grant.

iii. ANGEL was not 18 in 1686. d. 1763.

(1.) Jacob Lucie's plantation of 700 acres called "Mount Lucie" afterwards became the property of John Lucie Blackman and was called "Blackmans." Wm. Grant acquired a part of this plantation and added it to his lands, calling the whole "Castle Grant.

2. iv. WILLIAM,2 born 1670 died in 1712.

    v. MARGARET, was not 18 in 1686 died 17 March 1720 unmarried.

3. vi. FRANCIS, born about 1678 died in 1727.

2. WILLIAM GRANT (William[1]) of Castle Grant, b. 1670,

married 9 March 1689 Elizabeth Hunt. He was a Member of Assembly for St. Joseph 1702—1705, 1706—1711, during which time he was first Captain, then Major, and finally Lt. Col. of Militia, and a Justice of the Peace. When he first took his seat in the Assembly his return was challenged, perhaps, as has been suggested owing to his being a Scotsman, but the Attorney General and Solicitor General gave a verdict in his favour. He was Commissioner, with Hon. J. Maycock, for paying off and cancelling Bank Bills, and they had to give security in the sum of £10,000 each for the faithful performance of their duties. Lt. Col. Grant was also one of the four members of the Assembly who signed the despatch to Queen Anne protesting against the attempt to take away from the Assembly the right to appoint the Treasurer of the Island. He was also corresponding member with the Speaker, Hon. Richard Downes. William Grant with others, signed a Petition to William III dated 12 December 1700, and another to Queen Anne, 6 September, 1704, expressing their loyalty. He died on Nov. 21, 1711 about 42 years of age. By his Will, made in St Joseph, Barbados, on 2 Novr. 1711, he made provision for his wife, Elizabeth, and gave legacies of £200 to each of his children (by name) except William, to whom he devised and bequeathed the residue of his estate.[2] The Executors of his Will were his brother Francis, Thomas Miller, Dr Marmaduke Nicholls, Joseph Wooley, and his eldest son William. The Will was proved and recorded in Barbados on 18 March 1711/12.

Children born in Barbados :

  4. i. WILLIAM 3 born 1693.

  5. ii. JOHN born 1694 d. 1742.

    iii. ELIZABETH born 1697.

    iv. EDWARD born 1699, not named in his sister Mary s Will.

    v. ANN born 1704, married Edward Sayers 3, and died 1757. Her will is dated 25 May, 1757.

    vi. MARY, born 1706, died 1737, unmarried. Her will is dated 11 March, 1735

    vii. FRANCIS, born 1708 married Margaret Sayers 27 Decr. 1727.

    viii. JOSEPH, born 1709, not mentioned in his sister Mary's will.

    ix. HANNAH, born 1711 Married first......Moore and had issue

        'i) *William M.* (ii) *Francis Grant M.* (iii) *Elizabeth Grant M.* Hannah Grant married secondly   Walcott and had issue (i) *Henrietta Walcott.*

3. FRANCIS GRANT 2 (William 1) born about 1678. Married

(2.) His children were to be educated befitting their station and his sons especially in the science of the " Mathematiques "

(3) Captain John Sayers mentioned in the records of 1680 as having 2 white servants and 10 negroes. Captain James Sayers mentioned as commanding H.M. Frigate Richmond at Barbados 1748. In a dispute over the marriage of William Moore's son to Barbara Waterman 14 Sept. 1713 Nicholas Sayers signed as Counsel for Petitioner Sept. 20 1714. (C. O. 31. 9)

Christian Smitten, daughter of Patrick Smitten (who died Jany.
1732 and whose will is on record in Barbados wherein he describes himself as a Planter living in St Joseph).

Children of Francis Grant and Christian (Smitten) his wife:

    i.   LUCRETIA born 1706 m. Edward Nutt.

    ii. ELIZABETH, born 1708 died 1747. Will dated 17 Aug. 1739 in which
        she mentioned her mother Christian, sister, Lucretia, niece Christian
        Ann G. and nephew Grant Speight.

6. iii. WILLIAM[3] born 1710, of whom later.

    iv. JOHN, born 1712 married Mary Clarke 13 Feb. 1738.

    v. THOMAS born 1714, died 2 March 1771.

By his Will dated 28 August 1727, proved 25 Sept. 1727, Francis Grant mentioned his wife, Christian and all his children by
name, and appointed his brother-in-law Patrick Smitten, William Speight, and his nephew William G. and his wife and son
William, executors.

4 WILLIAM GRANT [3] (William [2] William [1]) born 1693. Married 1714, Ann Nutt.

Issue :

    i.   AMELIA, married Dr. John Williams.

    ii. MELANIA, married George Gascoigne J. P., 22 March 1753, son
        of Hon. Stephen Gascoigne who left a legacy to his kinsman
        Francis More 1688.

    iii. WINIFRED, married William Whittaker J. P., 17 February 1757.

    iv. MERCELLA, married Thomas Edey 1740.

By his Will (undated) proved 6 July, 1747, William Grant [3]
mentioned his wife (not named), gave Dr. John Williams £100
in full of any marriage portion due to his former wife, the testator's daughter, and legacies to his grandchildren Hugh, Charlotte, and Salvina Williams at 14, his daughter Mercella Edey,
wife of Thomas E. and their daughter Elizabeth at 16 and his
daughters Melania and Winifred. He appointed his wife executrix, and his cousin Francis Miller, and friends Charles Moe,
James Butler Harris, Randall Clements, and Dr. John Williams
overseers.

5. JOHN GRANT [3] (William [2] William [1]) b. 1694 md. Ann
Miller, and had issue. He was a Surgeon, and owned a house
and sixteen acres of land in St. George's parish.

Issue :—

    i.   CHARLOTTE under 18 in 1741.

    ii. ELIZABETH, md. Michael Spencer on 29 Decr. 1755, and whose
        will (proved 1759) is on record.

    iii. AGNES, married Philip St. Hill (a Devonshire family.)

Dr. John Grant died July 1742 having by his Will dated 9
October 1741 (proved 28 July 1742) appointed his brother William G. and brother-in-law Francis Miller and Thomas Whittaker and his friends Eyare Walcott and his wife Anne executors. He gave £10 to the poor of the parish of St. Joseph, and
mentions his sister, Hannah Moore, and her sons, William and

Francis M., his sister Ann Sayers, his godson Thomas Grant and his daughters Charlotte, Elizabeth and Agnes were under 18.

6. WILLIAM GRANT[3] (Francis[2] William[1]) born 1710 d. Aug 8th 1765 J.P., married Ann Bell, sister of Captain Francis Bell, son of Frances Bell who died 1739 and who was buried in Bell's Mausoleum, St. John. Philip Bell, Governor of Barbados 1641—1650, was of the same family.

Issue:

i. KEZIA, married Rev. Wm. Duke L.L.B. Rector of St. Thomas 28 August 1758 to 29 Oct. 1786, and Chaplain of the Assembly 22 August 1766 to the date of his death. Buried 30 Octr. 1786 in Family vault at St. Thomas. He was eldest son of Wm. Duke Clerk of Assembly (d. 16 August 1765) and brother of Henry Duke, Solicitor General of Barbados. The Dukes are said to be descended from the Dukes of Lake House, near Exeter.

7. ii. FRANCIS 4 born 1737 d. 1790.

iii. CHRISTIAN ANN d. 1785. Her Will is dated 26 August 1783.

iv. JEMIMA born about 1739 married 28 Nov. 1771 Dr. Reynold Skeete son of Reynold Skeete (4) who died 1721. Jemima died before 1783: see will of Christian Ann G in which Ann Bell Skeete is mentioned.

7. FRANCIS GRANT[4] (William[3] Francis[2] William[1]) born 1737, died 1790, owned *Blackman's* plantation, (5) md. Frances Walcott (6) who died 13th Feb. 1818.

Issue:

i. WILLIAM 5 born 1 Nov. 1762 died August 1765.

8. ii. FRANCIS BELL, born 1765 died Nov. 29th. 1817.

iii. THOMAS DUKE, born 1770 died 1771.

iv. HENRY DUKE, born 1772 died 11 June 1779.

v. ANN DUKE born 1776 Md. 1. Jan. 1795 J. Lewis and had issue (i) JOHN GLASGOW LEWIS (ii) a daughter who died young.

ANN DUKE LEWIS died, in 1839.

8. FRANCIS BELL[5] (Francis[4] William[3] Francis[2] William[1]) born 1765 of Blackman's and Gibbes Alleyne Estates and Tenby. Lt. Col. of Militia, St. Thomas. Justice of the Peace. Lived in England. Portrait extant of him and his family, supposed to be by Romney. Md. Ann Bell Moore, his cousin, daughter of William Moore of Canewood (See Will 24 July 1845) and Susanna Charlotte Henery.

Issue:

i. FRANCIS BELL 6 born 5 April 1792. Died 18 March 1809 in Edinburgh where he was being educated.

ii. BELL, born 1793, died in London, educated at Bath. Her will was proved in London in 1867 in which her cousin Ann Bell is mentioned.

(4.) Mary Skeete married Reynold Alleyne ancestor of the first Baronet.

(5.) Ann Grant (Francis' mother) Francis and Christian Ann Grant were all buried in the Bell Mausoleum St. Johns, Barbados. Francis Grant mentioned as one of the Grand Jury 19th June 1779 (c o. No. 31 34.) also subscribed to Institute of Society of Arts 1781.

(6.) Stephen Walcott emigrated to Barbados in consequence of being concerned in a plot against Charles II Hon Sam Walcott mentioned as Major Gnl. in Governors Council 3rd Nov 1778 See. C O State Papers. John Walcott Signed a petition to William IV as one of the Grand Jury 24th June 1791 (C. O. 31,6.)

255

iii. WILLIAM HENRY, born 29 July 1795, educated Edinburgh married Alice Musson 16 April 1835 daughter of John Musson Esq. Entered the Church and become Chaplain to Bishop Aubrey Spencer, Bishop of Jamaica, great grandson of 3rd Duke of Marlborough. Bishop Spencer md. Mrs. Grant's sister. (see Peerage) William Henry G. died 1842 in Newfoundland (See G. M.)

iv. STEPHEN DUKE horn 1797 died 1802.

v. SOPHIA born 1799, educated Bath and md. 1820 William Griffith Barrister at law of Windsor Estate and Frenches Estate and had issue :

　　1. William Brandford Griffith afterwards Sir W. B. Griffith K.C.M.G., Governor of Gold Coast who m Mary Eliza d of John Metcalf of Kirby Lonsdale and Antigua 1848 and had issue four sons and seven daughters, of whom (i) WILLIAM BRANFORD GRIFFITH afterwards Sir Wm. C.B E. (ii) HORACE BRANDFORD GRIFFITH created C M.G. Sir William Brandford Griffith was Ed. Harrison Coll. & University of London was Chief Justice of the Gold Coast and later legal adviser to Ministry of Pensions married Evelyn daughter of Penrose Nevins of Settle, and had issue (i) WILLIAM BRANDFORD Captain in the Buffs, educated Eton, married Francoise de Baude, daughter of Baron Baude of Cannes and great-niece of Count I. de la Grange (who owned the famous Derby winner Gladiateur 1865,) they had issue (i) WILLIAM b 1895 (ii) EVANGELINE, married Lt. Col. Byam Grounds of Hoe Hall Norfolk in 1916 had issue one son John Sutton Byam b. 1917 Ed. Eton E. Liverpool Regt.

vi. LUCY GLASGOW born 1803 Ed. Bath. Died in London.

vii. JOHN GLASGOW born 1805.

viii. SUSANNA CHARLOTTE born 1807. educated Bath, married Rev. Dr. Musson brother-in-law of Bishop Spencer and Wm. Grant.

ix. FRANCES born 1809 died 1889.

10. x. FRANCIS BELL born 1811 married Annette Moore daughter of Edward Henery Moore Esq. and Dorothy Frere Willoughby his wife.

xi. ELIZABETH WALCOTT born 1815, unmarried, and died in London 1890.

9. JOHN GLASGOW GRANT[6] (Francis Bell[5] Francis[4] William[3] Francis[2] William[1]) born 20th July 1805. at Blackman's plantn, educated privately and called to the Bar at the Middle Temple in 1839. He filled important Judicial positions in Barbados and in 1854 was appointed Master in Chancery which office he held for 28 years. He was offered by Sir Francis Hinckes the Chief Justiceship of Tobago which he declined for domestic reasons. However, at the request of Sir James Walker he acted for a time as Chief Justice of Barbados. Mr. Grant was elected a Member of the House of Assembly for the parish of St. Thomas on 12 Jany. 1841, but subsequently lost his seat at the General election which was controverted in January 1849, being returned Member for St. Michael in 1852 and he sat continuously for that constituency until 1858. Represented the parish of St Joseph from 13 August, 1867, until he was called to the Legislative Council on 1st April 1879. Mr. Grant was Speaker of the House of Assembly from 28 July, 1875, until he sat in Council. It was while he was Speaker that the young Princes, the Duke of Clarence and Prince George, now King George V. visited the Island. When they left, Lord Charles Scott in command of H.M.S. *Bacchante* addressed a

256

letter to Mr. Grant thanking him for all the very kind entertainments they had received, stating the officers and himself would carry away a very pleasant recollection of their visit, and all wished it had been prolonged so as to have been able to return to some small extent the kindness they had received. Some years later Mr. Grant received a very gracious personal letter from Prince George thanking him for his condolence on the death of the Duke of Clarence and referring to the Barbados visit. Mr Grant was ever diligent in the administration of Island affairs. He was a Member of almost every Board in connection with the Legislature, and Chairman of many. He eventually became the Senior Member of the Council but left for England where he resided until the day of his death. On retiring from the Legislative Council he received a despatch from the Colonial Office informing him " that while Her Majesty had been graciously pleased to accept his resignation, the Secretary was instructed to add an expression of Lord Derby's regret that Mr. Grant had found it necessary to sever his long and honourable connection with the Colonial Legislature. "

In 1861 Mr. Grant was appointed by Sir Evan MacGregor, Lt. Col. of the 7th Regt of Militia, and was aide-de-Camp to several Governors of Barbados.

During the Constitutional Crisis of 1876 (commonly called the Riots) over sixty members of various families sought refuge and protection at Mr Grant's residence Holborn House, and were hospitably received for more than a week. It was during this time that a rather amusing incident occurred. It was reported to Mr. Grant that a large and threatening crowd of blacks had assembled outside the main gate at Holborn. Mr. Grant turned out the guard of soldiers which had been sent to protect Holborn, and seizing the first stick at hand in the Hall went down with them to the gates to read the Riot Act. He read the Riot Act to the crowd and to emphasize the last words he brought the stick down smartly and as he did this the sheath flew off and left a gleaming blade pointed at the crowd. They gave one look at it, and then fled in every direction. No one was more surprised than Mr. Grant, who had without knowing it picked up a sword stick.

Mr. Grant was second in two duels, in one of which he was nearly killed. On the handkerchief being dropped, he heard the report (as he thought of both pistols) and seeing his principal standing very still he thought he had been hit and rushed to his assistance. Just at that moment the opponent fired, and the bullet passed very close to Mr. Grant's head. For this breach of etiquette, Mr Grant at once challenged the opponent; but the duel was not allowed to take place, and the opponent who was an Officer in a Regiment was cashiered. One of Mr. Grant's duelling pistols is in the possession of a descendant.

In the Constitutional crisis of 1876 Mr. Grant, then Speaker took a highly important part in defending the rights of the citizens against the threatened inroads of the Confederation party led by Governor John Pope Hennessey, which gained for him the gratitude and esteem of the people of Barbados.

In 1884 Mr. Grant was created a Companion of the Most Distinguished Order of St. Michael and St. George, on which occasion he and four of his sons (all in the Services) were presented at the Court of St. James.

Mr. Grant was a collector of old china, shells and coins, and most of his collection still remains in the possession of the family. A portrait of him, painted about the year 1836 when he was reading for the Bar, is still preserved.

He owned Canewood plantation. Holborn House and Tenby House, and also lived for some time at Warrens, St. Michael. He was author of a Report on Emigration from Calcutta (see Parliamentary Papers).

In 1842 Mr. Grant married Mary Elizabeth. daughter of John Walter,[7] of Farr's Estate, Barbados.

Children of the marriage :

11 i. FRANCIS WILLIAM SEAFIELD[7] named after his Godfather, Francis William. 6th Earl of Seafield. Born 1842.

ii. MARY ELIZABETH ARNOLD b 1844 d in 1890. Educated in Jersey. Named Arnold after maternal great grandmother.

iii. JOHN GLASGOW, born 1845, married Alice Trimingham 1872, daughter of Benjamin Trimingham, and had issue (i) Cyril Earl, born and died 1873 and (2) Lionel born 1875, married his cousin Mabel daughter of F. B. Grant and is now Auditor General of Barbados. Lionel and Mabel Grant had issue one daughter, Eileen, B. A. London University. John Glasgow G. died in Australia.

12. iv. FRANCIS BELL b 1848 married Emily Haughton of Jamaica (8) and had issue.

v. ANN BELL b 1851. Educated Jersey. Md. Septr. 1878 Rev. Sutton Moxly, Chaplain of Royal Hospital London, son of Rev. Dr. Moxly, of Glenville, Fermoy, Ireland. Rev. Sutton Moxly was author of A West Indian Sanatorium and Guide to Barbados 1868. Issue

    (1) KATHLEEN MOXLY died young.

    (2) STEPHEN HEWITT MOXLY b 1886, Lt. Commander R. N. Educated Winchester, Md. Lucy Remer daughter of R. Remer Esq. of De Vere Gardens, London,

    (3) MARY FRANCIS SUTTON MOXLY

    (4) ANN BELL SUTTON MOXLY Md. Col. A. F. Congdon, C. M. G. 1906. and has issue(1) Stephen (2) Theresa.

    (5) MADELINE SUTTON MOXLY

    (6) JOHN HEWITT SUTTON MOXLY b 1891 Educated at Oxford, Lt. in Bedfordshire Regt. killed in action in France in Great War.

    (7) JOSEPH STEPHEN SUTTON MOXLY b 1893.

vi. HENRY EUGENE WALTER b 26 DECEMBER 1855, Educated in London Barrister at Law, Inner Temple, 1896 ; formerly Private Secretary to late Governor Sir William Robertson at Barbados and Trinidad and the late Sir W. Brandford Griffith, Governor of the Gold Coast ; Resident Justice, Harbour Island, Bahamas 1897—9 ; Acting Attorney General, British Honduras, 1902—3 ; Acting

(7) See pedigree of Walter of Barbados Vol, V, Caribbeana pages 185, 917, 916, ✻ Mr. Richard Walter owned 300 acres in Barbados 1679 Captain John Walter owned 800 acres in 1674, m. Lucy Alleyne April 22nd 1697.

(8) See "Caribbeana" Jan 1919 Vol. 6 for pedigree of " Haughtons " ✻✻

*For p. 185 see p. 579, this volume.
**Pages 306-311, this volume.

Colonial Secretary 1904-5 Member Executive and Legislative Councils 1902—3, 1904—5 Acting Governor 1905 ; Colonial Secretary and Member Executive and Legislative Councils. Leeward Islands 1909—12 ; Acting Governor, 1911 ; and 1912 ; Agent and Consul Friendly Islands (Tonga), Deputy Commissioner for the Western Pacific with jurisdiction in the Kingdom of Tonga, and Judicial Commissioner for the Western Pacific for the hearing of matrimonial causes within the Kingdom of Tonga, 1912—16 ; Temporary Assistant, Admiralty, 1917—18 ; Colonial Secretary and Member Executive Council, Bahamas, 1918—25; Acting Governor, 1919—1920 and 1922. in 1887 went on mission for Trinidad to Venezuela in connection with seizure of British ships Henrietta and Josephine. Created C M.G. 1911 at Coronation of King George.

vii. WILLIAM GRIFFITH GRANT b 1858. Educated University London and R.M.C. Sandhurst ; entered Army 1878 and was gazetted to the Lincolnshire Regt. He served in S. Africa War 1902 and retired 2nd. in Command of the Regt. After retirement he was Brigade Major of York and Durham Territorial Brigade. He was Deputy Lieutenant for E. Riding of Yorkshire. On outbreak of Great War he rejoined the Army at age of 57 and was appointed Colonel of 17th Batt : Royal Fusiliers in France at the Front and later 13th Batt. Sherwood Foresters at Brockton. At end of the war he was awarded the Order of the British Empire for his services.

LT. COL. GRANT married 1898, Mary Angela 2nd daughter of Colonel Sir Robert Edis K.B.E., C.B. of The Old Hall. Norwich and had issue

    (1) John, Lt. Comd R. N. b1902 ed. Cambridge.

    (2) Elsie Mary m. Edward Young.

    (3) Margaret b. 1907.

    (4) Robert Patrick Seafield, Lieut. R.M. b. 1910.

    (5) Jean }
    (6) Ann, } Twins.

Lt. Col. Grant died at Winchester in 1933.

13. viii. ALFRED ERNEST ALBERT b.1861 of whom later.

    ix. AUBREY SPENCER b 1864 B. A., Cantab, d. 1898 was sometime Sec. to Baron Hirsch.

    x EDWARD PERCY FENWICK GEORGE b 1867 Educated H. M. S. Britannia and Royal Naval College, Greenwich. Entered the Royal Navy, Created C. B. for Services at Battle of Jutland 1916 K. C. V. O. 1920. Served in Egyptian War. 1882 Egyptian Medal, Khedive's bronze star) Lieut of Racer during Brazilian Revolution 1893 ; commanded Halcyon, Arrogant, Gibraltar, Falmouth, King Edward VII, Marlborough, Ramilles, both the last ships in the Great War. Received thanks of Australian Government for services 1910 and in 1921 ; special mission to Somaliland in command of H. M. S. Gibraltar · Flag Captain to vice Adm. Sir Lewis Bayly in King Edward VII and Marlborough ; Flag Captn. and afterwards Chief of Staff in Marlborough to Admiral Sir Cecil Burney, 2nd. in command of the Grand Fleet ; present at the Battle of Jutland (Despatches C. B) ; Commodore 2nd. Cl. 1916 ; Naval A. D. C. to the King 1918, 1929 ; Rear Admiral 1919 ; Ist. Naval Member and Chief of Australian Naval Staff 1919—1921 ; Commander-in-Chief of Australia Station 1921—22. Adml. Supt. Portsmouth Dockyard 1922—25 ; 1927 President of the Selection Board for entry of Officers into the Britannia and also President of Board for entry of officers into the Army Navy and Air Forces ; Vice Admiral 1924; Admiral retired 1928. Holds Russian Order of St Vladimir with swords

Married 11th. July 1926 Florence Gwendoline Doughty, widow of Rear-Adml. Henry Montague Doughty, C. B., C. M. G., (See Burke's Landed Gentry) and daughter of Lt. Col. Gatskill-Burr. Admiral Sir Percy Grant sat on the last Grand Jury to be held in Anglesey 1933.

10. FRANCIS BELL GRANT [6] (Francis Bell [5] Francis [4] William [3] Francis [2] William [1]) born 1811. In Orders, M. A. Durham, Rector of the Parish Church of Parham, Antigua, afterwards Rector of Christ Church, Barbados, 1859—1869. Married Annette Moore, daughter of Edward Henery Moore, and Dorothy Frere (Willoughby) his wife. Children of the marriage :—

i. FRANK, died at an early age.

ii. DOROTHY FRERE, born 10 July 1840, died 25 June 1916, Md. Hon. John Gardiner Austin (b 19 July 1838, d. 9 March 1902) nephew of Bishop Austin, Primate of the West Indies, and they had issue :

(1) Mehetabel Emma Grant Austin, born 21 August 1867, Md. 30 Decr. 1891 William Burslem, and had issue.

(2) Jeffrey Gardiner Austin, b 14 March 1870, died 5 De: cember 1872.

(3) Brigadier General John Gardiner Austin. C. B., C. M.G. late R. A. O. C. born 20 June 1871, Md. 3 May 1898 Margaret Drew Moir. second daughter of the late Rev. Charles Moir, M. A. Glasgow, and they have issue a son, John Gardiner Austin, born 19th August 1903.

(4) Arthur Piercy Gardiner Austin, born 2 August, 1873, Md. 10 June 1905, Louise Frances Watts, daughter of late Sir Francis Watts, K. C. M. G. Imperial Commissioner of Agriculture for the West Indies and first Principal of the Imperial Col. of Tropical Agriculture and they have issue four daughters and one son.

(5) Dora Helen Annette Austin, born 12 Novr. 1874, unmarried.

(6) Sir Harold Bruce Gardiner Austin, Knight, O. B. E., Speaker of the House of Assembly of Barbados, born 15 July 1877, Married 13 April 1904, Marie Lilian Dennehy second daughter of the late Charles Dennehy M. D., C. M., Principal Medical Officer of St. Lucia., and they have issue (1) Mabel Patricia, (2) Clodagh Marie..

(7) Mabel Louisa Frere Austin, born 15 Decr. 1878, Md. 18 Feb. 1903 Charles Edward Yearwood, barrister at-law, (d. 1935). No issue.

(8) Malcolm Burnett Gardiner Austin, born 24 May, 1880 Md Muriel Jane Craigan, and has issue one son and one daughter.

(9) Francis Elwin Wilday Gardiner Austin. born 10 April 1882, Md. 14 April 1909, Gwendolyn May Frances, and they have issue.—(1) Bruce Wilday Gardiner Austin (2) Geoffrey Francis Austin, (3) Aurdrie Dorothea Austin.

iii. MATILDA, born 1841, Md. J. Walton Browne M. D. C. M. of Belfast afterwards Sir Walton Browne Kt. and had issue a daughter, Dorothy, who Md. Colonel Young, R. A. M. C.

iv. EDWARD HENRY, Born at Parham, Antigua, 10 July 1843 Md. Colin

Lovesay, daughter of Judge Lovesay, Grand-daughter of Rear Admiral Edward Hoyt, Hydrographer of the Navy, and great great-grand daughter of James Baillie of Douchour, Scotland. No issue.

v. ANN ESTWICK, Md F. Preston Esq. of Manchester, and had issue (1) Ellis (2) Estwick.

Rev. Francis Bell Grant married secondly Mrs. Lange, of London ; there was no issue of the second marriage. He died in England on 29th September 1888.

11. FRANCIS WILLIAM SEAFIELD GRANT [7] (John Glasgow [6] Francis Bell [5] Francis [4] William [3] Francis [2] William [1]) b. 1842 d. 1912. Entered the Army and became a Major in Oxfordshire Light Infantry. Wounded in Ashanti War 1873, mentioned in Despatches. A.D C. to Governor of Sierra Leone and of Bahamas. Md 1875 Anne, daughter of Michael Steel, Esq. of Begbroke House, Oxfordshire.

Children of the marriage :

i.   ARCHIBALD SEAFIELD b 17 Febry. 1878. Ed. Eton. Major Black Watch. Retired 1914. Magersfontein S. Africa, despatches. D.S.O. Great War, despatches. Married 1st Lilian Bull daughter of William Bull Esq. J.P. of Hove, and had issue (1) IAN MURRAY SEAFIELD b Balthayock Perth Scotland. 1909. (Murray after Lord George Murray, now Duke of Athol Godfather). Ed. Wellington Lieut. Staffordshire Regt. She obtained a divorce and he md. 2nd Aileen daughter of Rev. Edgar Swainson from whom he obtained a divorce 1928 (no issue) and married 3rd Lillian Thompson 4 June 1930 and had issue (2) EUGENE SEAFIELD b 17 March 1930 after (Dowager Countess of Seafield, Godmother).

ii. CECIL DE MONTMORENCY (Montmorency after his Godfather Lord Frankfort) born 1879, died at sea 1907. Educated at Eton and Camb. Dist. Service S. African War. Recommended for V. C., Lieut. Norfolk Regt. After the War he joined the Jamaica Mounted Constabulary and distinguished himself during the Earthquake disaster. Died unmarried.

iii. DUNCAN WALTER born 1882, educated H. M. S. Britannia and R.N. College, Greenwich, R. N. Retired Commander R. N. Commander R. Aust. Naval Coll. as Captain 1917—19. Afterwards Chief of Staff to Adml. Sir Dudley de Chair, Govr. of New South Wales 1924—5. C. B. E. for services in Great War. Md. Beatrice Edith Payne, widow, and daughter of E. Moggridge of Wykeham, Burgess Hall, Sussex, and Woodfield Park, Monmouth.

Issue :

(1) Francis William Seafield b. 1925 Godfathers, Earl Jellicoe, Lord Strathspey. ‗

(2) Trevor John Duncan. b. 1926

iv. ALAN FRANCIS STEEL educated H. M. S. Britannia and R N. College Greenwich. Retired Comdr. R. N. b. 1884. Md. Norah Fuller-Maitland, daughter of Capt. Alexander Fuller-Maitland of Wargrave Court, Wargrave, Berkshire and has issue : (1) ANN born 1914 (2) EVE born 1917.

12. FRANCIS BELL GRANT [7] (John Glasgow [6] Francis Bell [5] Francis [4] William [3] Francis [2] William [1]) born 1848, Educated in London, Md. Emily Haughton daughter of William Haughton

261

Esq. of Jamaica and had issue:—

    i. FRANCIS, born 1884 Sub Lt, R. N. V. R. during War, died in England

    ii. MABEL, born 1878. Md. Lionel Grant.

    iii. RUBY born 1882 unmarried.

    iv. IDA GWENDOLINE, born 1888, md. V. Tatum Esq. son of General Tatum.

13. ALFRED ERNEST ALBERT [7] (John Glasgow [6] Francis Bell [5] Francis [4] William [3] Francis [2] William [1]) b 1861 d. London 14 Augt 1933 entered the R.N. 1874. Educated H. M. S. Britannia and. R.N. Col Greenwich. Md. August 1894 Evelyn Wells daughter of W.W. Wells and great niece of Lord Kinlock (Law Lord) He saw his first War service in H.M.S. *Achilles* during the Egyptian War. In command of the *Racoon* he served in S African War and took part in the blockage of Delagoa Bay. He commanded H.M.S. *Racoon, Pyrames Forte* and *Lord Nelson* and also the Gunnery School at Chatham. He was Captain Supt. of Pembroke Dk. Yard and on promotion to Rear Admiral retained the appointment. During the Great War he was at the Admiralty as President of the Committees for the Expedition of the building of Merchant ships and Motor Transport and was later appointed Admiral Supt. of ships on the Tyne. After his retirement in 1921 he became a Nautical Assessor to the House of Lords and was Chairman of the Shipwrecked Mariners Society. For his services during the War he held the Distinguished Service Medal of America. From 1913 to 1915 he was A. D. C. to H. M. George V. He was a J. P. for Kent. He had issue.

    i. DOUGLAS STAMFORD. b. 1895 (after Earl of Stamford Godfather : Sir A. Grant of Monymusk was the other) Entered R. N. Coll. Greenwich. Lt. Comdr. R. N. Md. Juanita daughter of Admiral Sir Richard Pierce, K. C. B., K. B. E. of Freehole Bath. No issue.

    ii. WILLIAM HAMILTON GRANT born 1899. Educated Haileybury. Captain Black Watch, Wounded Great War. Md. Jany 1930 Barbara Guinness only Child of Arthur Guinness Esq. of Green Norton Hall, Towcester (see Burke's Peerage under Ardilaun), and has issue.

        (1). Ian Arthur b. 28th Dec. 1930.

        (2) Diana b. 12th March 1934.

Haggatt of Barbados.

WM. YEAMANS, of Stapleton, gent. Will dated 23 Jan. 1616. My s. in l. John Haggatt an overseer and 5¹. My dau. Eliz. H., To my grandch[n] John, Marie, and Nath. H. 10¹ ea. All my law books to my son H. (17, Essex.)

ANN YEAMANS, of Bristol, widow. Will dated 2 Nov. 1664. My l. husband Wm. Y. gave to my s. Haggat's ch[n] John, Mary, and Nath¹ 10¹ ap., this to be made up to 20¹. To the rest of the ch[n] of my s. Haggat 10¹. My s. H. 10¹. My Kinswoman Mary H. the cypress chest in her father's chamber. To Mary H., dau. of Rich[d] H., gent., dec[d], 40s. (162, Hene.)

MARY YEAMANS, of Bristol, widow of Wm. Y. Will dated June 1677. My Kinsman Nath. Haggatt, Esq., my trustee. To my cozen Nath. Haggatt the legacy left me by my late M. in l. his grandmother. (55, Reeve.)

Rev. Tho. Barnard, of Eton College, co. Bucks, clerk. Will dated 28 Nov. 1782. Whereas I am seized in right of my l. wife Mary Grey of a sugar plantation and slaves in the parishes of St Peter and St Lucy in the I. of Barbadoes, containing 148 a. which was settled on T. I hereby appoint it to my s. Tho. B. and my daus. Mary Penelope Eliz. Jane, and Ann Dorothy, my ch^n by my said l. wife Mary, and whereas I am seized in fee of several pieces of land in St Mary and St Lucy and divers negros and a considerable pers. est., I charge all legacies thereon. To my daus. Mary B. and Penelope B. £100 ea. in full of a legacy left them by their l. grandf. the Rev. Geo. B. To my wife Frances £200. To Walter Waring of Edwardston, co. Suff., and John Jackson of Old Burlington St., Esq^{res}, £700 on T., to pay the Int. to my said wife and at her death to my s. George B. and such other child I may have by her at 21. All my lands and negros to T. to raise £1000 to pay the interest to my said wife then for my s. Geo. My wife and s. Tho. B. to be G. of said s. Geo. My s. Tho. and daur. Pen. to be G. of my dau. Ann Dorothy. All res. to my s. Tho. and daurs. Mary, Pen., Eliz. Jane, and Ann Dorothy. My s. Tho., my wife Fra., and dau. Pen., ex'ors. Proved 4 January 1785 by Tho. Barnard the son, and Fra. Barnard, widow, the relict and surviving Executors.

On 30 July 1821, adm'on of estate left unad. by Tho. B. and Fra. B. to Edw. Tyrrell of Guildhall, Esq., on behalf of Rebecca Langston of Bath, widow, and the Rev. Stephen Hurt Langston of Richmond, co. Surrey, limited to deceased's interest in a certain lease of 1771, of premises in Little Honwood, co. Bucks. Tho. Barnard survived the said Tho. Barnard but died intestate. (3, Ducarel.)

Othniel Haggat, of Bristol, merchant. Will dated 24 April 1718. Confirm to my wife Eliz. the settlement of the plantation at Barbados, and a negro man Rangoe and his sisters. To my son Othniel 100^l and no more, because I doubt not his Mother will make a provision for him. 50^l for charities in B'os. To every one of my negroes new cloths. To my wife all other lands I purchased since I left that I. all negros, cattle, horses, coppers, etc. To each of my daus., Abiah Baskervile and Eliz. Thruppe, 600^l. To every one of my grandchildren a broad peice of gold. My wife Ex'trix for B'os, and to give security in the the court of C.P. for St Michaels, and my said 2 daus. for G. B. If my wife die before me then all est. to my s. Othniel. Wit. by Ann Grimes, Tho. Chinn, John Becher Junr. 19 May 1718. Confirm Will. Witnessed by Robert Maundrell and the above.

Codicil, 6 Sept. 1718. 600^l for dau. Thruppe, to trustees, my son Baskervile and Mr. Stephen Hodges, also my s. Othniel if he shall come to reside in Eng. Wit. by Sarah Cooke, Ann Grimes, John Becher, Jun.

Proved 18 August 1719 by Abiah Baskervile, wife of " Jacobi" Baskerville, and Eliz. Thruppe, wife of Rowland Thruppe, the daughters and Ex'trices. (146, Browning.)

Nathaniel Haggatt, late of the Island of Barbados, now of Richmond, co. Surrey, Esq. Will dated 17 Jan. 1761. Whereas by a settlement made the 25 Aug. 1760, on the marriage of my dau. Susannah H. with Dr Edward Barnard, I have secured 6000^l as a portion which I charge on my estate. I give her my linen and china in Eng. To my nephew Wm. H., son of my brother the Rev. Wm. H. of B'os, deceased, 150^l c., and to my niece Sarah H. 100^l c. Miss Sus^n Thompson of B. 100^l c. Miss Mary Clarke residing with my dau. S. B. 100^l c. My nieces Sarah and Jane Scott 100^l apiece c. Servant Ann Williams her freedom and 10^l c. a year. All residue of est. to my s. Wm. H., but if he die before 21 to my dau. S. B., my nephew W. H. he then to pay my niece Sarah H. 3000^l. Sugars to be consigned to Edwd Clark Parish of L., merchant. I appoint him and Joseph Pickering of G^r Q. Str. Linc. Inn F., Esq., Geo. Hannay of Soberton, co.

ARMS.—*Argent, two bends Gules.*   CREST.—*A palm tree.*

....⊤Othniel Haggatt of Barbados, then of Bristol,⊤Eliz., sole
1st | merchant. Will dated 24 April 1718 ; proved | ex'trix.
wife.| 18 Aug. 1719 (146, Browning). | 2nd wife.

Abiah, born 1678 ; mar. James	Eliz., mar. Row-	Hon. Othniel Haggatt, only⊤
Baskervile of Bristol. Mar.	land Thruppe ;	son and heir, Judge of
lic. 21 June 1700, she æt. 22	named in her	Oistin's, lately dead 1732.
and he 30.	father's will.	

....⊤Hon. Othniel Haggatt, Mer-⊤Susanna, heiress to her⊤Hon. Simon Lam-
1st | chant, of Bridgetown and | dau. Mrs. Ruth Wood- | bert of Barbados
wife.| M. of C. 1726 ; Chief Baron | bridge 1748. She gave | and Bristol, died
     | of C. P. ; died 27 Nov. | the Font in St. Lucy's | 1715. 1st husband.
     | 1735 ; bur. at St. Michael's. | 1747. Bur. 17 Dec. 1751 | Arms : *Gules, a*
     | Bookplate No. 196. | at St. Michael's. | *chevron between*
     | | | *three horses Argent.*

Rev. Wm.⊤	Sarah,	Nathaniel Hag-⊤Jane Lam-	Ruth Lambert, coheiress,
Haggatt,	mar.	gatt, planter	bert, co-	mar. (as his 2nd wife)
Rector of St.	Capt.	1740 ; bur. at	heiress,	Rev. Dudley Woodbridge,
Michael's	David	Mitcham 17 Oct.	mar. 6 Feb.	Rector of St. Philip's.
1742 till his	Lewis.	1762. Will dated	1730 at St.	She died at Boston. Will
death ; bur.	—	17 Jan. 1761 ;	Michael's ;	dated 23 Dec. 1748, a
3 Oct. 1747.	Mary.	proved 4 Dec.	bur. at	widow ; proved 14 Feb.
		1762 (507, St.	Mitcham,	1749. His will was dated
		Eloy).	Surrey, 5	15 March 1747 and proved
			May 1755.	14 Feb. 1749 (65, Green-
William Sarah, ? mar. 18 Feb. 1749-50			ly).
Hag- Col. Rich. Rous Estwick at			
gatt. St. John's.			

Nathaniel	Susannah,⊤Edward Barnard,	Simon	William Hag-⊤..., dau.
Haggatt,	born 1738 ;	D.D., born at	Othniel,	gatt, born at	of ....
born	mar. at	Harpenden 28	bapt. 17	Barbados 9	Walter
1736 ; bur.	Richmond,	April 1717 ;	and bur.	Feb. 1743 ;	[? John,
at Mit-	co. Surrey,	Headmaster of	18 June	bur. at Mit-	M.P., of
cham 30	26 Aug.	Eton 1754 ; Canon	1739.	cham 18 July	Woking],
Sept.	1760, then	of Windsor 1760 ;	—	1773. Book-	formerly
1748, æt.	aged 22 ;	Provost of Eton	Mary,	plate No. 197.	of Barba-
12.	died 23	1765—81 ; Chap-	born at		dos.
	June 1764 ;	lain to Geo. III. ;	Barba-		
	bur. at	bur. at Harpen-	dos 27		
	Harpen-	den 9 Dec. 1781.	Jan.		
	den, co.	See pedigree in	1740 ;		
	Herts.	Jewers " M.I. in	bur. 28		
		Wells Cathedral,"	Aug.		
		p. 97.	1742.		

A portion of this pedigree was contributed in 1912 by Mr. H. C. Barnard of
the Federated Malay States.

Francis Haggat of⊤ Wm. Yeamans of Bristol,⊤Anne, of Bristol.
Mark, co. Somer- | gent. Will dated 23 Jan. | Will dated 2 Nov.
set. | 1646 (17, Essex). | 1664 (162, Hene).

John Haggat of Bristol, admitted to the Middle Temple 11 Dec. 1643 ;⊤Eliz. Yea-
Chief Justice of Carmarthen, Cardigan and Pembroke. | mans.

John⊤	Marie	Nathaniel Haggat, admitted=Frances Beckford,	Other
Haggat.	Haggat.	to Middle Temple 18 Feb.	dau. of Rich. Beck-	chil-
		1660-1 ; ? party to close roll	ford, Alderman of	dren.
		of 1688 relating to Barbados.	London ; mar. 17	
			Dec. 1677.	

Thomas Haggat, son of John and Eliz., bapt. at St. James, Clerkenwell,
8 Feb. 1673 ; ? bur. at St. Michael's, Barbados, 28 Dec. 1725.

Hants, Esq., Edmond Jenkyns, Gidney Clarke and John Lucy Blackman, all of
B'os, Esqʳˢ, Ex'ors and G. and 20ˡ each. My s. sole Ex'or at 21. Wit. by
Tobias Pickering, Giles Hunt, Cha. Lackington. Proved 4 December 1762 by
Ed. C. Parish, Esq., and Jos. Pickering, Esq., power reserved to the others.
(507, St. Eloy.)

John Haggatt of Somerset, pleb. Magd. Coll. Oxf., matric., 24 Nov. 1584,
a. 16. (Foster.)
    1667. Simon Lambert, Esq., one of the commissioners appointed to collect
the Acts. (Laws of Barbados.)
    1688. Close Roll. Nath. Haggatt and John Cary. (*Ante*, I., 166.)
    1700, June 21. James Baskervile, of the City of Bristol, Bach. 30, and Mʳˢ
Abiah Haggatt of same Spʳ, 22 ; with consent of her father Mʳ Othniel H. at
All Saints, Bristol, afsᵈ or . . . (Fac. Off. of Archbishop of Canterbury.)
    "Mʳ Othniel Haggatt, 1723 " Printed book label.
    1726, Aug. 8. Othniel Haggot, Esq. ; appointed one of h. M. Counsel at B.
(Hist. Register, 32.)
    1730. At a General Assembly. Present, Othniel Haggatt, Esq., and Chief
Judge of the Court of C. P. (Oldmixon, 83, 87.)
    1732, Nov. 10. Extract from a letter from Bridgetown, refers to The store of
the Hon. Othniel Haggat, Esq., where the Assembly met, and a footnote states :
"This was the Son, who had a Father of the same Name (a M. of C. likewise,
and Judge of Oistin's-Court) then lately deceased, as is now likewise the Son."
(Caribbeana i., 73, pub. in 1741.)
    1734, Oct. He was appointed Chief Baron of the Court of Exchequer. His
2ᵈ wife was Susanna, widow of Simon Lambert. ("Notes and Queries," 11 s.,
vi., 149.)
    1746. Tho. Barnard was licensed to the Plantations by the Bishop of London
on Dec. 22.
    1750. Rev. Mʳ Barnard, Rector of Bridgetown in B., a subscriber to Hughes'
History.
    1760, Aug. 25. Dr. Barnard, head master of Eton school, to Miss Haggett,
of Richmond. ("G.M.," 391.)
    1762, July 20. Rev. Tho. Bernard. His brother Canon of Windsor and
Head Master of Eton. He was Rector of Sᵗ Michael's, B'oes, and obtained leave of
absence for a year in 1756 but which was continued to 1762 for 6 years. In Ap.

1762 he returned to B. and resided 2 months, and was given a yr's leave to bring over his wife and family. (Letter from Gov. Pinfold, Fulham Palace MSS.)

1762, Oct. 18. Nath. Hagget, Esq.; at Richmond, Surrey. ("G.M.," 502.) A merchant and M. of C. (Poyer, 275.)

1766. Close Roll. Wm. H. and Jos. Pickering. (*Ante* I., 171.) "William Haggatt, Esq" Festoon arm.

Crest : *A palm tree.*

Arms. Quarterly : 1 *and* 4, *Argent, two bends Gules ; 2 and 3 Gules, a chevron between three horses Argent* [LAMBERT] ; impaling, *Argent guttée de sang, two swords in saltire Gules, debruised of a lion rampant* [WALTER]. (" W.I. Bookplates," No. 197.)

EDWARD BARNARD.—He was head master of Eton 1754—64, when he became Provost. The "D.N.B." does not mention his marriage, which is thus entered in the parish registers of Richmond, Surrey :—

"1760. Edward Barnard, D.D., a bachelor, of Eton, Bucks, and Susanna Haggatt, spinr, of Richmond ; licence, by Thos. Barnard, Minister. Witnesses, N. Haggatt, El. Parish."

In the "Allegation" his age is given as forty-three, and hers as twenty-two. Was the officiating minister the same Thomas Barnard who was consecrated Bishop of Killaloe and Kilfenora in 1780 (*vide* " D.N.B.") ?

Richmond. Albert A. Barkas, Librarian.

(" Notes and Queries," 10 s., xi., 28.)

Thomas Barnard, the officiating minister, was in all probability not the future Bishop of Killaloe and Kilfenora, but Edward Barnard's brother who became Fellow of Eton in 1772, and was also Vicar of Mapledurham (" Registrum Regale," p. 17).

Edward Barnard's wife is described in the Eton Parish Register (under notice of the birth of her son) as the daughter of Nathaniel Haggatt of Barbadoes. Cole says that Barnard, " while he was Master of Eton Schole, . . . married a West Indian lady of a good fortune, but who lived with him not many years." There was one son by the marriage, Edward, born in 1763. (*Ibid.*, 116.)

R. A. Austen Leigh.

See Brown's Somersetshire Wills, I., 29, and IV., 13, for two early wills.

Rev. Geo. Haggatt was 42 years Rector of All Saints, Ruston, N'ants.

ST. MICHAEL'S, BARBADOS.

1704 Aug.	8	Othniel Haggard, a child. Burial.
1706-7 Jan.	5	A child of Mr Othniel Haggards.
1725 Dec.	28	Mr Thomas Haggard.
1735 Ap.	22	Susannah Da. of the honble. Othiniel Haggatt Esqr
1735 Nov.	27	The honble Othinil Haggatt Esqr, a sermon.
1739 June	17	Simon Othniel s. of Nathl Haggatt Esqr, & Mrs Jane h. w. bap.
1739 June	18	Simon Othniel s. of Nathaniel Haggatt Esqr. Burial.
1742 Ap.	17	This day the Revd Mr William Haggatt was inducted into this Parish.
1742 Aug.	28	Mary Da. of Nathaniel Haggatt Esqr.
1747 Oct.	3	The Revd Mr William Haggatt, Rector of this Parish in the Chancel. (Entered also in the p. regr. of St Thomas.)
1749 Dec.	17	The Revd Thos Barnard & Mary Grey.

ST. JOHN'S, BARBADOS.

1661 June 6 L⁺ Coll. Lambert and Mary Read.
1749-50 Feb. 18 Col. Richd Rous Estwick to Mrs Sarah Haggatt.

ST. JAMES, CLERKENWELL, LONDON.

1673-4 Feb. 8 Thomas, s. of John & Elisebeth Haggett. Bapt.
1695 July 21 Mary d. of James Hagget & Alice his wife ; b. 19.

HALL
OF TULLY, CO. DONEGAL, IRELAND, AND BARBADOS

CREST—A stork statant, in its right foot a roundle.
ARMS—Vert, a chevron Or between three cranes' heads erased Arg. a border
of the second charged with eight trefoils of the first.
  The above described arms are those of HALL (Ramilton,) Co. Donegal
Ireland, and Barbados allowed by Betham 1810, granted to William Hall Esq.
of Tully.
  1. WILLIAM HALL[1] of Tully had ten sons, namely—
  (1) WILLIAM HALL,[2] named in the Will of his brother, Alexander dated 25
September 1801 as being then deceased. His daughters (not named) are mentioned in the same Will, and also a son
  (1) *Alexander,* then under age.

(2) ALEXANDER HALL, born at Tully, 28 February, 1751, died a bachelor at Bath, England, in 1802. There is a monument to his memory in Bath Abbey, North Aisle, North Wall; a tablet surmounted by an urn between two females opposite second bay:—

In Memory of ALEXANDER HALL Esqr.
Late of the Island of *Barbados,*
who was born at *Tully* in the County of Donegall
in that part of the (now) United Kingdom
called *Ireland,* on the 28th of February 1751
died in this City on the 27th of March
and was interred near this spot
on the 2nd of April 1802;
This Stone is erected by
DAVID HALL and GEORGE HALL,
as a small tribute
of grateful affection
to the best of Brothers

He was a merchant in Barbados, and made his will there on 25 September 1801, whereby he gave to his brother Robert Hall of Tully near Ramilton, Ireland, if he should survive him £2,000 stlg. To his brother Patrick Hall, £30 stlg. per annum during his life and after his death £500 stlg. to his children equally. To his niece, the daughter of his brother Samuel Hall who died in America, £500 stlg. at 21 or day of marriage. To the children of his brother, James, who died in America, £500 stlg. equally when the youngest attains 21. To his nephew, Alexander Hall, the son of his elder brother William Hall, £100 per annum until he attained 21 to be laid out by his executors on his maintenance and education and when he attained 21 a legacy of £2,000 stlg. To each of the daughters of his deceased brother William Hall, £100 at 21.

He gave to his mulatto girl, Becky, (bought of Mrs. Nihell), her freedom and manumission together with £300 Cy. to be paid to the Churchwarden of St. Michael parish to entitle her to £18 per annum and all advantages of freedom agreeable to the late Act for the Manumission of Slaves, and also all his best bedstead, bed, bedding and furniture sufficient for a chamber together with £25 Cy. and all this to be done within one month of his decease.

All the rest, residue and remainder of his estate, whether in Barbados, Demerary, Great Britain or elsewhere he gave to his two brothers, David Hall and George Hall, then with him in the West Indies, to be equally divided between them share and share alike. He appointed his said two brothers, and his friends, James Beaumont Evans and Richard Sharp to be executors, thereby empowering them to sell his estate called Perry's* in Barbados or any or all of his estate in Demerary or elsewhere. The will was witnessed by John Humpleby, Thomas Pierrepoint, William Pierrepoint, Samuel Watt, John O'Brian, Joseph Gibson and John Rd. McNeill. Proved on the Oath of Thomas Pierrepoint, 12 May 1802 before Governor Seaforth.

(3) ROBERT HALL, of Tully, mentioned in the above Will, together with his son—

(i) *Alexander.*

---

* Perry's Plantation (470 acres) in the parish of St. Joseph. The name was changed to Springfield by Mr. Richard Parris Pile when he purchased it in 1804 from David Hall for £20,500.

(4) PATRICK HALL, mentioned in the above Will, together with his son—
    (i) *Alexander.*
(5) SAMUEL HALL, died in America, mentioned in the above Will, together with his daughter (not named).
(6) JAMES HALL, died in America mentioned in the above Will, together with his children—
    (i) *Frances,* mentioned in the Will of her Uncle George Hall,
    (ii) *William,* also therein mentioned.
2. (7) DAVID HALL, born at Tully, c. 1772 married, 25 May 1811 at St. James's Church, Barbados, Margaret Salter, daughter of Hon. John Forster Alleyne of Porters and Elizabeth Gibbs (Willing) his wife.† He owned Springfield plantation in St. Joseph and Locust Hall plantation, St. George, and was a partner in the several firms of Alexander, David & George Hall, David & George Hall & Company, and George Hall & Company, West India Merchants. At the time of his marriage he had succeeded to the estates and interests of his two brothers, Alexander and George Hall. He left Barbados, apparently with the intention of permanently residing abroad in July 1811. A daughter was born of the marriage on 8 October 1818 at Clifton, Bristol, but apparently she did not survive, as he refers in his Will to his son, as his only surviving child. The son was—
3. (i) ALEXANDER HALL HALL.[3]
Margaret Salter Hall, his wife, died in London, 7 May 1823.
David Hall seems to have returned to Barbados once only after his removal to London in 1811, and that was in the year 1818 when we find him granting a new power of attorney to John Forster Alleyne, William Eversley, Thomas Law, Alexander Hall and Charles Thomas Alleyne, all of Barbados. The document is dated July 4, 1818, and the donor states that he intended shortly to leave Barbados for England.
He was also a partner in the firm of Underwood Hall & Co. of London, West India Merchants, the others being Henry Iles Underwood, Charles McGarel, and Alexander Hall. After the death of Mr. Underwood, the surviving partners carried on business at Austin Friars, London, under the firm of Hall, McGarel & Co.
David Hall resided at times at Portman Square, London, Botley's Park, Surrey, Portland Place, and finally at Park Crescent, Regent's Park, London according to his Will dated 15 March 1843, in which he stated that he intended shortly to remove to Park Crescent, where he subsequently died on 4 September 1844. By his Will he devised and bequeathed all his estate and property to his only surviving child, Alexander Hall Hall,[3] and appointed him sole Executor. The Will was proved in London on 14 Sept. 1844, and the value of his estate was sworn at under £200,000. Before his death he seems to have realised all his West Indian property and interests, and he had sold Springfield plantation in 1804 to Richard Parris Pile and Locust Hall in 1843 to William Alleyne Culpeper.
(8) A son of William Hall,[1] name unknown, but by reference to the text of the monument in St. George's Church to George Hall (see later) who is described as the Tenth and youngest son of his father.
(9) Another son of William Hall[1] name unknown, but by the same reference.
(10) GEORGE HALL, born at Tully, c. 1776, who (and possibly his brothers Alexander and David with him) had established a mercantile business in Barbados before 1805, when he gave a power of attorney to his brother David to represent him in Barbados being intended shortly to leave the island on a visit abroad.

---

† See the pedigree of Alleyne of Barbados *B.M. & H.S. Journal* Vol. IV. No. 2. The reference to Margaret Salter Alleyne's Marriage is on page 87. of Volume IV. ✻

✻ Pages 60-70, this volume.

He married Lucretia, only daughter of Joseph Ostrehan (d. 7 August 1809) and Elvira his wife (d. 12 Jan. 1848) in 1810. He owned Locust Hall plantation and appears to have had extensive mercantile interests in Barbados, Demerara and elsewhere. By his Will dated 22 July 1810 he declared that if he should die in Barbados it was his wish to be buried in St. George's Church or Churchyard. He referred to the terms of his marriage settlement dated 23 February 1810, to which his wife, Lucretia, and her mother Elvira Ostrehan were parties, and Samuel Perry and George Gibbs the Younger were trustees, securing an annuity payable to her if she survived him. In addition he gave her a legacy of £2,000 stlg. and desired the marriage settlement trustees to secure the sum of £10,000 mentioned in the settlement for the purpose of raising the said annuity against his plantation Locust Hall. To his brother David he gave his gold watch with the chain, seal, and trinkets thereto. To Frances Hall, daughter of his deceased brother, James Hall, £375 stlg. To Georgiana Hall Smith, daughter of his friends John Lucie Smith and Ann his wife £1,000 stlg. at 21 or marriage. To each of his godchildren Deborah, Mary, Catherine and John Humpleby Pierrepont, the children of Thomas and Eleanor Ann Pierrepont, William, son of the said John Lucie Smith, Baynes Reed, son of George Reed, Sarah Thomas, daughter of the Rev. Anthony Keighley Thomas, and Horatio Nelson Glentworth, son of Doctor Plunkett Fleeson Glentworth of Philadelphia the sum of £25 stlg. each to be paid to their guardians.

His executors to lay out £400 sterling to the charitable uses following—one-half to be distributed amongst persons who dwell in the vicinity of Ramilton, Co Donegal, the place where he was born, and the other moiety amongst such persons who dwelt in this Island as his executors should deem objects of charity, particularly widows of good character and orphans. To the poor of the Colony of Demerary £5 stlg. thereby excluding and debarring the Weas Kamer(?) from any interference or concern whatsoever in his affairs.

To his brother David his moiety of his faithful servant, Samuel Thornhill, with the request that his brother would set him free from all manner of slavery by deed of manumission and after that was done he gave him an annuity of £10 Cy per ann. for his life. The residue of his estate to be divided amongst his children equally or to one only. Failing any such child or children he bequeathed the following legacies— To Alexander Hall, son of his deceased brother, William, £1,000, to Alexander Hall, son of his deceased brother Patrick, £500. To William Hall son of his deceased brother James, £500. £50 stlg. to each of his other nephews and nieces not named. The residue of his estate to his brother, David, but in case of his death before the testator, then his friends, Thomas Law, merchant, and Thomas Hollingsworth, planter, both of Barbados and Richard Wace of Castle Street, Falcon Square, London, merchant, should be entitled to receive out of his estate each the sum of £1,000 stlg. for his own use, and the final residue to his nephew the said Alexander, son of William Hall, his nephew William Hall, son of James Hall, and Alexander, son of Patrick Hall, in the same proportions as the legacies thereby given to them.

He appointed his brother David Hall, and the said Thomas Law, Thomas Hollingsworth and Richard Wace executors, requesting them not to qualify as executors during the lifetime of his brother David.   )

The Witnesses to the Will were John Brathwaite, George Ostrehan, and Wm. Eversley, and the document was proved on 21 September 1810.

A monument to his memory is affixed to the North Wall of St. George's church, with helmet and breastplate in high relief, and the text on the mantling.

In Memory of / GEORGE HALL Tenth and Youngest son of William Hall of Tulley / in the County of Donegall, Ireland, of Locust Hall Estate, in this Parish/

and many years a merchant in Bridgetown / who departed this life on the 12th of Septr, 1810 / Aged thirty-four years / and whose remains lie interred within these walls, this stone is erected / by his only surviving brother, / who can truly say, that in him / with the most perfect integrity / were eminently combined / active benevolence, lively practical charity, steady efficient friendship and true piety. / The towers must share the builder's doom / Ruin is theirs and his the tomb / But better boon benignent heaven / To faith and charity has given / And bids the Christian hope sublime / Transcend the bonds of fate and time.

The monument is the work of Richard Westmacott, the London Sculptor, and is dated 1813.

The crest and arms at the beginning of these notes are shown on the above monument.

There was no issue of the marriage, and his widow, Lucretia Hall married Hon. & Rev. J. H. Gittens, Rector of St. John, by whom she had issue.

The East Window of St. John's Church was erected to her memory after her death on 14 January 1859 aged 67.

3. ALEXANDER HALL HALL[3] (David,[2] William[1]), born at Bay's Hill Lodge, Cheltenham on 11th April 1812, baptized Alexander Hall by mistake of the officiating clergyman and his godparent. After that, each male child was baptized HALL, but not females. The surname by custom became HALL HALL. Alexander Hall Hall was educated at Eton and Balliol College, Oxford, resided at Watergate, Sussex, and was a Justice of the Peace for the county. He married Caroline Hankey, daughter of Thompson Hankey. Their children.

4. i. *Charles Alexander Hall,*[4] born at Wimbledon on 21st August, 1839.

   ii. *Alleyne Hall,* born at Watergate, Sussex, on 2nd May, 1845. Married Cecilia Ellen Brochman, and had issue 2 sons and seven daughters. Died 31st July, 1937.

   iii. *Fanny,* married Robert Wilson, and had issue 4 sons, 8 daughters.

   iv. *Caroline.*

   v. *George Hall,* born 9th May, 1841; married Florence Vokes and had issue 2 sons and 4 daughters.

   vi. *Emily Maude,* born 11th February, 1850, at Watergate, Sussex, married William Down, R.N., and had issue 2 sons and 4 daughters.

   vii. *Meta,* married   Featherstone.

   viii. *Theodore Hall,* born at Watergate, Sussex, on 15th September, 1852; married Lucy Byron and had issue one son.

4. CHARLES ALEXANDER HALL,[4] (*Alexander Hall,*[3] *David,*[2] *William.*[1]) born at Wimbledon on 21. August, 1839, educated at Eton and Christ Church, Oxford, of Funtington Hall, Sussex, married first, Elizabeth Tritton, and secondly, Henrietta Vodoz. Children of the first marriage—

   i. *Charles Hall,*[5] died young.

   ii. *Margaret*

   iii. *Gertrude,* living.

   iv. *Katherine*

   v. *Blanche,* married Rev. Arnold Shaw, and has issue 5 sons one daughter.

5. vi. ALLEYNE HALL

        Children by the second marriage—

   vii. *Dorothy,* living.

   viii. *David Patrick Hall,* living.

        Charles Alexander Hall Hall died in Egypt.

   viii. ALLEYNE HALL,[5] (*Charles Alexander Hall,*[4] *Alexander Hall,*[3] *David*[2]

Sussex. Educated at Eton and Sandhurst, Captain in the Royal Irish Regiment. Married Emily Lambert, daughter of Lt. Col. Walter Lambert. Children of the marriage— of Dean's Grove, Dorset.

  i. *Elizabeth,*
  ii. *Francis Alleyne Hall[6]*
  iii. Margaret, married John de Penderill Waddington.

6.   FRANCIS ALLEYNE HALL,[6] (Alleyne Hall,[5] Charles Alexander Hall,[4] Alexander Hall[3] David Hall[2] William Hall[1].) born at London on 13th October 1914, educated at Oundle, and Clare College, Cambridge; M.R.C.S., L.R.C.P., of Medford House, Gloucestershire. Married Mary Whittaker, daughter of Major W. E. de B. Whittaker of the King's Regiment.

Children of the marriage—

  i. MICHAEL ALLEYNE HALL, born 31st. January 1954 at Mickleton Campden, Gloucestershire. *

  ii. CLARE MARGARET HALL, born at Medford House, Mickleton Close on 12th. March 1955. The first girl to be christened Hall since the days of Alexander. *

  iii. JOHN FRANCIS HALL, born at Medford House, Mickleton Close on 12th April 1956.

  iv. CHRISTOPHER HALL, born at Gloucester on 30th October 1957.

---

*For *Mickleton Close* read *Mickleton Glose.*

Hampden of Barbados.*

The following are from Abstracts of Wills, etc., at Somerset House, made by the late Mrs. Sydney Smith :—

1630, May 7. Commission to Owen Hampden, brother of Charles Ha len, late in foreign parts, bachelor, deceased.
1630, May 7. Commission to Owen Hampden, brother of Henry F den, late in foreign parts, bachelor, deceased.
1706, Aug. 18. Commission to Anna Maria Lovell, relict of Samuel ovell, late of Jamaica, deceased. Note by Mrs. Sydney Smith as follows: "This belongs to the Hampdens (Bishop of Hereford). They want a Charles Hampden of Barbados. There is one mentioned in the Census of 1679, but he is not yet otherwise found, though they have employed a professional worker."
1653-4, Jan. 24. A deed in the Registrar's Office in Barbados mentions "land in Christ Church of Mr. John Hampton."
1675-6, Jan. 7. Charles Hamden a witness to the will of Priscilla Nightingale.
1675. John Hampton. Will proved 15 Oct. 1675 (Recopies, vol. ix., 374, 375). To be buried in Christ Church. Wife Ann Hampden. Son John Hampden, jun. Cousin Marriah Elizabeth Davis.
1721, Feb. 14. Sarah Hamden of St. Peter's. Will proved 25 Nov. 1725. Five children, Mary Harris (wife of John Harris, executor), Susanna Haiden, Orian Hamden, William Hamden, and Sarah Hamden.
1715. John Hamden of Christ Church, chirurgeon. Will proved 17 Dec. 1715. Wife Eleanor. Sons Charles and John.
1715. William Hampton, late of the City of New York, but now residing in Barbados. Will dated 4 April, proved 6 April 1715. Sister Ann Hampton, living in Essel Street in London. Executors, Stephen Thomas of Barbados, merchant, Joshua Wree of New York, merchant.
1750-51. Will of Sarah Hamden of St. Philip. Daughters Elizabeth Hamden, Hester Carter; her dau. Joanna Carter. Kinsman Thomas Franklin.

* Communicated by Mr. N. Darnell Davis.

1784. John Hamden of St. John, practitioner in physic and surgery. Will proved 9 July 1784. Wife Sarah. Nephew John George Pile, residuary legatee. Sisters Frances Pile, Eleanor Hamden. Nieces Margaret Tysoe Pile and Eleanor Hampden Pile.

1735-6. Hester Hamden of St. Philip, widow. Grandsons Charles Hamden, George Hampden, John Hampden, and Wren Hampden. Granddaughters Hester and Elizabeth. Sister Mary Snow.

BAPTISMS.

1648	May 27	Elizabeth d. of John Hampton.
1650	Aug. 29	Robert s. of John Hampton.
1654	Oct. 5	John s. of John and Martha.
1661	Oct. 21	Martha d. of Charles Hamden.

| | | | Reference to Register. | | |
			Vol.	Page.	Parish.
1673	June 8	John son of John & Ann Hampton	17	100	Christ Church.
1710	Dec. 9	Hester dau. of George Hamden	22	78	St. Philip.
1714	Jan. 30	John s. of John Hamden	22	90	St. Philip.
1714	Dec. 26	Thos. son of Geo. & Sarah Hamden	22	89	St. Philip.
1715	July 27	Renn son of John & Eleanor Hamden	17	186	Christ Church.
1715	June 26	{ William son of } Mrs Hampton { Mary daug: of }	{ 22 { 22	91 } 91 }	St. Philip.
1716	Nov. 28	Elizabeth Dau: of Geo. Hampden	22	94	St. Philip.
1740	Sep. 25	John son of John & Susanna Hamden	17	233	Christ Church.
		Child of Thomas*	22	131	
1739	April 13	Charles Hambden	22	131	St. Philip.
1743	Aug. 21	Frances dau. of John & Susanna Hamden	17	239	Christ Church.
1746	Dec. 21	Eleanor dau. of John & Susanna Hamden	17	245	Christ Church.
1754	Aug. 20	Renn son of Renn & Sarah Hamden	17	252	Christ Church.
1756	Oct. 10	John son of Renn & Sarah Hampden	17	255	Christ Church.

MARRIAGES.

1672	Mar. 17	John Hampton and Ann Rushbrook.
1679-80	Jan. 16	Ezekiel Hamden and Agnes Abraham.
1694-5	Feb. 26	John Hampton & Sarah Holloway. (Licence.)
1701	Sept. 1	George Hambden & Sarah Peaver.

DEATHS.

1647	Sept. 24	Elizabeth.
1647	Sept. 30	John.
1651	July 13	William Hamden, son of Wm Hamton.
165–	April 14	Reynold son of John Hampton.
1654	Sept. 9	John Hampton.
1659	July 19	Robert son of John.
1673	June 18	Peter.
1686	Oct. 11	Charles Hamden.
1695	Feb. 17	Robert Hampton.
1714	Feb. 18	Dr John Hamden.
1715	April 5	William Hampton, Merchant.
1724	Oct. 21	Robert son of Dr Hamden.

* Index says child of Charles.

			Vol.	Page.	Parish.
1734	Dec. 26	Eleanor Hamden	21	116	Christ Church.
1759	Sep. 15	Anthony Hampton	4	106	St. Michael.
1761	Nov. 10	Mary Hamden, a child	21	133	Christ Church.
1766	April 6	Mr Thomas Hampton	29	41	St. John's.
1767	Feb. 25	.... Hamden, a child	21	139	Christ Church.
1769	Jan. 22	.... Hamden, a child	21	141	Christ Church.
1770	Oct. 23	Thos. Hampton, a child	21	143	Christ Church.
1770	Jan. 28	Elinor Hamden	25	74	St. Philip.
1774	July 1	Dorothy Hampton	21	147	Christ Church.
1779	Feb. 2	Susanna Hamden	21	153	Christ Church.
1782	Jan. 2	William Hampton	5	301	St. Michael.
1783	Jan. 16	William son of Eliz^a Hamden	5	336	St. Michael.
1789	Aug. 28	Elizabeth Hamden	5	492	St. Michael.
1790	Aug. 29	William Hamden, a child	21	165	Christ Church.
1790	Oct. 13	Sarah Hamden, a child	21	165	Christ Church.
1791	Nov. 12	Mary Hampton	21	166	Christ Church.
1792	May 26	William Yard Hamden, a child	21	167	Christ Church.

Indenture dated 21 Oct. 1774 between Wm. Hamden, S^r, of St Michael's, planter, and Susanna his wife, of the one part, and Nath. Phillips, planter, of the other, granting two slaves, Sabina and Daphne, in trust for Wm Hamden, J^r, Frances Hamden, and Eleanor Hamden, children of the said Wm Hamden and Sus^a his wife, as soon as Eleanor shall attain the age of 18 or marry. Signed and sealed by the three parties. Witnessed by Jacob Da Costa, Wm Jno Nesfield. Acknowledged before the Hon. Jas. Shepherd, chief baron of H.M. Court of Exchequer, 21 Oct. 1774. (Extracted by Mr. E. G. Sinckler, Nov. 1911.)

JOSEPH AND ALEXANDER HARBIN: TWO BARBADIAN MERCHANTS, THEIR FAMILIES AND DESCENDANTS.

By SOPHIA W. RAWLINS, B.A., F.S.A.[1]

The 1676 Census of Barbados[2] gives among the inhabitants of the parish of St. Michael, Barbados, Joseph Harbin and his wife, whose household consisted of three children, one hired servant and eight negroes, and Alexander Harbin, his wife and one negro.   It is clear from their wills that Joseph and Alexander were cousins, and that they came of a family of London merchants of west country origin can be discovered from other sources.

The fourth instalment of "Alleyne of Barbados" by Louise R. Allen,[3] begins with the marriage of Thomas Alleyne, 1733-84, fourth son of Abel Alleyne, 1699–1747, to Dorothy Harbin, daughter of John and Harbin Forster, and the present article is an attempt to trace the descent of the name Harbin from Joseph Harbin who settled in Barbados in the middle of the 17th century, to his great-great grand-daughter who died in 1814.

Joseph Harbin's will proved in Barbados in 1692, shows that he has (or had had) a brother, John Harbin, merchant, of London who had two children, Thomas and Anne.   Research into the Harbin pedigree by the late Prebendary Bates Harbin and the present writer established the identity of this John Harbin, who lived in the parish of St. Helen's, Bishopsgate, from circa 1660 till his death in 1673.   He was a merchant engaged in importing hemp and timber from France, and in supplying naval stores to the Admiralty and in 1669 an official "office of exchange" was opened in his house.   Anne, his eldest surviving child was baptised at St. Helen's, November 13, 1662; she was followed by Margaret, baptised 1668, Robert, 1669, Thomas, 1670, and Jane, 1671.   There was also another son, George, born between the two elder sisters but not baptised at St. Helen's; the 'Alumni Cantabrigienses' shows him to have been born circa 1666 and describes him as a native of Essex, a fact which is not without interest in identifying his kinsman Alexander Harbin of Barbados.

Anne Harbin married, in 1695, as his second wife, Baldwin Malet of St. Audries in West Somerset, and from their third son, Alexander, descends the present Sir Edward Malet, Bart.   Her sister Margaret had married in 1692 another widower, Sir Francis Warre, baronet, of Hestercombe near Taunton, while Jane married Richard Hawley, a grandson of Francis, first Lord Hawley.[4]   Their brother George, a non-juring clergyman and antiquarian, who died in 1744, sans prole, describes his father as of a family long settled in Somerset and used the arms—azure a saltire voided between four spearheads or, granted to Robert Harbin of Newton Surmaville, Yeovil, who had been a mercer at Blandford in Dorset and appears to have made a considerable fortune which he invested in buying a number of scattered properties in Somerset and Dorset.

It is clear, however, that Joseph Harbin of Barbados was not a son or grandson of Robert's eldest son John Harbin who succeeded him at Newton Surmaville in 1621 and died in 1638.   But in 1663, there died at Somerton, a small town about ten miles from Yeovil, a mercer named Thomas Harbin, who left four sons, John, James, Joseph, who was then 'overseas', and Thomas.   John

---

1. Neé Harbin.
2. J. C. Hotten, *Original List of Persons of Quality who went from Great Britain to the American Plantations*, p. 439.
3. *Journal of the Barbados Museum & Historical Society*, IV, p. 34.*
4. *Burke's Extinct Peerage.*

* Page 47, this volume.

Harbin of St. Helen's had a brother James who was buried there on November 23, 1672, and the evidence (with an uncommon surname) of the three brothers with the same names and of the two Josephs both overseas at the same time seems to make it probable that Joseph Harbin of Barbados was in fact the son of Thomas Harbin of Somerton. Unfortunately the loss of the Somerton registers for this period make it impossible to establish the date of his birth. Thomas Harbin's wife's name was Alice; she was probably a sister of Jerome Churchey of Somerton who is described as 'my brother', i.e. brother-in-law, in Thomas' will.[5] Moreover, Thomas had a grandson Andrew Russ, and an Andrew Russ was a servant on Joseph of Barbados' Carolina plantation in 1691. Whether Thomas Harbin of Somerton belonged to the Newton family, it has not been possible to discover. Robert Harbin of Newton Surmaville who died in 1621 aged 95, had two younger sons, Robert, a London merchant, and George of Blandford, but their wills cannot be found and it is not known if they left descendants. On the whole it seems more likely that Thomas was descended from one of the elder Robert's brothers or cousins. The name was not uncommon in Dorset at this time but the Newton family was the only one which could be described as 'long settled' in Somerset.

The statement that George Harbin the non-juror was a native of Essex may connect his family with that of Andrew Harbin of Great Parndon in that county, who was also a dyer and citizen of the City of London. He died in 1670, having made a lengthy will.[6] From this it appears that he was twice married and had two sons, Alexander and Andrew, and a daughter, Sarah; he had four brothers Zanchy, Edward, Thomas and Henry and a number of nephews, including 'John son of my brother Thomas'. Zanchy and his sons John and Robert may be identified with a linen-draper of that name of Milton Abbas near Blandford, and his sons John, who was sent to the Merchant Taylors School in London, and Robert; and Thomas and his son John may be Thomas of Somerton and John of St. Helen's, for this would account for John's cousin Alexander of Barbados. (Andrew also mentions his sister Alice Harbin—Alice was the name of Thomas of Somerton's wife, and sister and sister-in-law are interchangeable at this period).

Alexander Harbin was not buried at Great Parndon, nor is his will in the P.C.C. registers, and when we find that Alexander of Barbados had a son Andrew, the probability that Alexander Harbin of Great Parndon had emigrated to Barbados and was the Alexander whose will was proved there in 1685 is further increased.

Assuming this identification to be correct, and the writer is aware that it rests on an accumulation of evidence rather than on absolute proof, Alexander Harbin's career was as follows. He was baptised October 1, 1626, at All Hallows the Less in the City of London, probably the third but eventually the only surviving son of Andrew Harbin by his first wife Alice. He was educated at the Merchant Taylors School,[7] where he spent the years 1638-44, and was subsequently apprenticed to a merchant tailor of the parish of St. Laurence Pountney, a parish in which his cousins John, Richard, and Morren Harbin were also living during the early years of the Commonwealth.[8] By the time Alexander grew up, his mother had died and his father had married again, in 1647, Anne, widow of Adrian Dent, and daughter of James Smith of Hammersmith.[9] Whether it was the finan-

5. P.C.C. Laud 116.
6. P.C.C. Pye 73.
7. *Merchant Taylors School Register*, ed. E. P. Hart, 1936.
8. Andrew's will, and MSS. copy of St. Laurence Pountney register at the Society of Genealogists.
9. Visit of London 1664, p. 128.

cial difficulties to which his father refers in his will, or the existence of a step-mother and brother which induced Alexander to leave England one cannot tell; he may have followed the example of his cousin Joseph or of Thomas Warden of the company of Merchant Taylors, whose career is described in the *Journal of the Barbados Museum & Historical Society*. [10] Although there seems to be no reference to Alexander Harbin in the Barbados archives before 1676, he may well have been there earlier. Andrew Harbin appointed his wife executrix in 1667, which may indicate that his eldest son was then abroad, and the fact that she waited three years before proving his will, may indicate that she decided not to act until her step-son's return.

According to a manuscript note in the Society of Genealogists' copy of the Great Parndon registers, Alexander Harbin married Dorothy Moyse (possibly a sister of James Moyse who was living there in 1675); she may be the Mrs. Dorothy Harbin buried at St. Helen's, Bishopsgate, June 11, 1672. The same manuscript notes refer to a deed by which Alexander Harbin appointed John Sealey and Robert Hill to act as Trustees for his son Robert. An Andrew Harbin, who may have been Alexander's son of that name was at Merchant Taylors School 1673-4, but from this date Alexander disappears from the English records.

His half-brother Andrew died unmarried in 1680 or 1681. His will was made at Portsmouth 'when about to go overseas'—perhaps to join Alexander in Barbados—June 15, 1680, and was proved by his mother December 22, 1681;[1] she was buried at Great Parndon December 21, 1687.

If Alexander Harbin of St. Michael was identical with Alexander of Great Parndon, he had married again before the census of 1676, and he may be the Alexander Harbin of St. George, who, with his wife Elizabeth, sold 25 acres of land there to Major Paul Lyte in 1679.[12] The Alexander Harbin whose will, dated November 26, 1684, was proved in Barbados on November 12, 1685, was a widower (which he may have been for the second time) and was of St. Michael. He left his 'household stuff' to his daughter Anne, and plate and rings to his daughter Mary, wife of Thomas Low; he mentions his cousin Joseph Harbin, Sarah his wife and their sons John and Joseph, who were each left £3. to buy themselves beaver hats; and another cousin, Richard Lintott. His executor was his son Andrew, a young merchant who did not long survive his father, for on December 2, 1686, the P.C.C. in London gave administration of the goods of Andrew Harbin of 'Sherborrow apud Guyndam in partibus Celebes'—probably Sherborough on the Gold or Guinea Coast—to his sister Mary, wife of Thomas Low. Anne, the unmarried daughter, must have died about the same time, as in 1688, Joseph Harbin is described as attorney of Mary, only surviving daughter and heiress of Alexander Harbin and wife of Thomas Love (or Lowe) of London, gentleman. Robert, the son of Alexander mentioned in the Great Parndon register had presumably also died without issue; he may have been the Robert Harbin buried at St. Helen's June 16, 1684; he left a widow, Miriam, and property at Milton Abbas, which, however, makes it more likely that he was a son or grandson of Zanchy Harbin than of Andrew. It seems clear from the 1688 deed that Alexander left no descendants in the male line but there are later references to Andrew Harbins, whose connection with earlier Andrews has not been traced. An Andrew Harbin witnessed the will of Col. John Hallett of Axmouth, Devon, late of Barbados in 1698,[13] and in 1710, Olive Harbin of Barbados was acting as administratrix of her late husband Andrew Harbin.

10. Vol. I., p. 94.
11. P.C.C. North 183.
12. Barbados Deeds.
13. P.C.C. Pett 25.

To return now to Joseph Harbin. At what date or with what capital he settled in Barbados one does not know, but it is evident that he prospered there. Many west country men, particularly royalists, were going to Barbados under the Commonwealth. Joseph's brother John was certainly a royalist, for his descendants long preserved a letter written by the young James, Duke of York, in 1651, thanking John Harbin, merchant of Morlaix, for a gift of £500.[14] It is possible that Harbin was acting as an agent for other royalists in England, and that his trade with Brittany was a convenient cover for the sending of secret funds across the Channel.

If Joseph was the son of the Somerton mercer he was probably in Barbados before 1662: he married in or about 1665, Sarah, sister of Rafe Lane and a connection of the Seabury family of Duxbury in New England, by whom he had two sons, John and Joseph, and a daughter Elizabeth, who married Robert Waite. In 1665, when he was acting as churchwarden of the parish of St. Michael,[15] he was probably already a man of substance, and by the time of his death in 1692, he had become a considerable property owner. In 1682, he entered into a partnership with Charles Pope, merchant, and Joshua Smith, planter, to acquire a plantation in Jamaica, and by 1691, they had erected there 'a sugar work with good probability of making sugar there in time to come'. This plantation was called Penn and was at Port Morant.[16] He had an interest in a plantation in St. Lucy, which he sold in 1686, property in St. Michael purchased for 10,000 lb. of sugar in 1671, and a plantation in South Carolina, which is briefly referred to in his will. Penn plantation was probably named after William Penn, for by 1686, Joseph Harbin had joined the Society of Friends, and in that year he, with Thomas Fretwell, planter, and Edward Wright, chirurgeon, took a five years lease of certain property from James Ashford, including a messuage 'for a place to meet in, as it now is and hath usually been', in fact as a Quaker meeting house.

Joseph's will was dated February 15, 1691/2, and proved in Barbados, September 12, 1692, by two of the witnesses, George Forster and Thomas Bushell. His widow Sarah died in 1697, her will being dated June 28, 1697, and proved in Barbados on November 26 of the same year.

Before proceeding to an account of Joseph's sons it may be of interest to refer to another Harbin, who was probably in Barbados at the same time, although he cannot be traced in the records of the island. In 1675, William Harbin of Newton Surmaville recorded in his diary a visit from a sailor who related that he had seen William's uncle, Mr. Edward Harbin, in Barbados, and that he 'dined at Mr. Bishop's table'. William, a young man of 20, remembered having been told by his father, John Harbin, who had died in 1672, that he, John, had had a brother Edward who had gone to the West Indies some twenty years before and had never been heard of since. 'Whether it be true or no', William commented on the sailor's story, 'I cannot tell', and to this day nothing further is known of Edward Harbin's career in the West Indies, though he and Joseph were probably distantly related and may well have known each other.

Joseph Harbin in his will left £200 to his cousin (i.e. niece) Anne, 'eldest daughter of my brother John Harbin, merchant'. In 1695, as already mentioned, she married Baldwin Malet of St. Audries. The latter rented the farm of certain

14. *Historic Manuscripts Commission Report* V. Malet MSS., p. 319.
15. He appears in the churchwarden's records on various occasions from 1665—73 *Journal of the Barbados Museum & Historical Society,* Vol. XV, p. 101 *et seq.*
16. Barbados Deeds, and *Caribbeana,* II, p. 151.

taxes in Somerset and through the dishonesty of an agent became involved in financial difficulties. Tradition in the Malet family long preserved the tradition of wealthy and helpful relations in the West Indies. John Harbin, Joseph's elder son did apparently adopt Francis Malet, his cousin—Anne's second son, as he refers to him in his will as 'my kinsman Francis Malet now living with me', and left £30. a year for his education and maintenance, and £200. to come to him at the age of 21. At the date of the will (1708), Francis was about 10 years old, and nothing further is known of him. In the next generation his brother, the Reverend Alexander Malet, Rector of Combe Flory in Somerset, sent his younger son, Alexander to Barbados, where he settled and married Alice, daughter of Nathaniel Lucas of Bridgetown.

John Harbin himself had an adventurous career, for as a young man he was captured by those notorious pirates the 'Sallee rovers' and at the time when his father was making his will in 1691, 'he had long been a captive in Sallee', but at least he must have escaped or been ransomed, for within about a year of his father's death (before November 1693) he was back in Barbados taking part in the settlement of his father's estate.[17]   By his wife Philippa or Phillis (her name is spelt differently in the two probate copies of his will), he had one daughter, Mary who married, before 1719, William Gordon.   John Harbin died in 1708 or 1709, his will being dated December 8, 1708, and proved in Barbados August 5, 1709, and again in London, December 15, 1709, by Richard Diamond acting as attorney for Joseph Harbin the testator's brother.   Besides Francis Malet, he mentions his nieces Sarah and Deborah Harbin, the daughters of his brother Joseph, and his cousin Philippa and Thomasine Thornhill of the parish of St. Thomas, and Mary Harrison.   His exact relationship to these ladies has not been ascertained but from the *Journal of the Barbados Museum & Historical Society*[18] it appears that Col. Thomas Thornill married Philippa Davies and had a daughter Thomasine, who married firstly, Wardell Andrews and later William Savage of Bloxworth in Dorset, a parish, incidentally, in which another branch of the Harbin family held land at this period.   In 1711, a Philippa Harbin who may have been John's widow, was licensed in London to marry Robert Wynn.

There is (or was) a Harbin family of South Carolina who, so the present writer has been informed, were descended from 'Joseph Harbin of Barbados', and used Somerset names on their estates. It is clear, however, from their wills that Joseph Harbin of Barbados, who died in 1692, left only two sons, and that of the two John had only one daughter and Joseph two, so that the ancestor of the Carolina family must have belonged to a different branch of the family. It is quite possible that the mysterious Edward Harbin or the Andrew Harbin who died in 1710, may have left a son Joseph, perhaps named after the most prosperous member of the family in Barbados, as he seems to have been. Unfortunately, the John Harbin who died in about 1709, makes no mention in his will of the Carolina plantation which his father had left him, and he may have sold it to some Harbin kinsman, or his daughter and her husband may have done so at a later date. A Joseph Harbin of London, who was a second cousin of John Harbin of Barbados, died in 1709, but he left no will, and the administration (P.C.C.) granted to his widow Elizabeth (née Child) gives no clue as to whether he had any property in Barbados or South Carolina.

Joseph Harbin the younger, second son of Joseph Harbin the elder of Barbados was aged 48 in the Barbados Census of 1715, [19] he married circa 1687,

17.   Barbados Deeds.
18.   Vol. I. p. 94.
19.   *Journal of the Barbados Museum & Historical Society*, IV, p. 73.

Elizabeth, sister of Samuel Gallop, ('my neices Ruth and Elizabeth, daughters of Samuel Gallop' occurs in her will) and had two daughters Deborah and Sarah. Deborah married Isaac, son of Robert Thorpe of St. Philip, [20] and had a son Joseph and four daughters. The eldest daughter, Harbin, married circa 1728 when she was about sixteen, John Foster (or Forster) of Forster Hall, St. Joseph, and had one son, Isaac-Thorpe, and five daughters, of whom the second, Dorothy-Harbin, married in 1754 Thomas Alleyne and died at Dedham, Massachusetts in 1814, leaving issue.[21] Sarah Harbin married firstly, Joseph Salmon of St. Michael,[22] and secondly Thomas Baxter, Barrister-at-law. By her first husband, she had issue two daughters, Margaret who married Richard Salter and died without issue, and Harbin who was married three times, and left issue.

Joseph Harbin's will was dated August 26, 1719, and proved in Barbados on September 22, 1719, his daughters Sarah Salmon and Deborah Thorpe being executrices. Like his father, he was a member of the Society of Friends. His widow Elizabeth survived him 13 years, and died in 1732, her will being dated August 5, 1732, and proved in Barbados September 17, 1732. She mentions a number of friends and relations, but neither of her own daughters, and only one grandchild, Harbin Foster and the latter's small daughters Deborah and Dorothy-Harbin. Her residuary legatee was Mrs. Frances Austin. More might be written of Sarah Salmon and Deborah Thorpe and their descendants, but with the birth of 'the beautiful Dorothy-Harbin,' as she seems to have been known to her American descendants, the beginning of the fourth article on "Alleyne of Barbados", has been reached with which this account started.[23]

20. Barbados Deeds, 1714.
21. Barbados Deeds, 1710.
22. Dated December 1, 1790, pr. Ap. 5, 1795 P.C.C. Holman 196.
23. *Journal of Barbados Museum & Historical Society*, IV, 34—5. *

*Pages 47-48, this volume.

DESCENDANTS OF JOSEPH HARBIN OF BARBADOS

By

SOPHIA W. RAWLINS, B.A., F.S.A.*

Joseph Harbin of St. Michael's, d.1719, left issue by. his wife Sarah Gallop, two daughters, Deborah and Sarah. The following notes on their descendants in England and Barbados may be of interest in tracing the pedigrees of the families with whom they intermarried:

I. DEBORAH HARBIN, aged twenty-seven in the Barbados census of 1715, married in 1710 Isaac Thorpe aged about twenty-two, son of Robert and Katherine Thorpe, who were, like Joseph Harbin, members of The Society of Friends. The will of Isaac Thorpe of St. Philip's was dated June 19th, 1732, and proved in Barbados March 21st, 1733. Deborah, to whom he left £500 and "the living in my mansion on my Plantation" outlived him nearly twenty years. Her will was dated November 27th, 1750, and proved in Barbados December 17th, 1751.

Isaac and Deborah Thorpe had issue one son and five daughters.

(1) *Joseph*, b.c. 1717, d. August 2, 1760 "possessed of considerable real and personal estate" and leaving a holograph will, which obliged his executors, the Hon. George Walker and Christopher Moe to bring a petition to Governor Pinfold before they could execute it. It was dated December 6, 1759 and proved August 12, 1760 in Barbados. Joseph Thorpe left £500 and £50 a year with plate and china to his wife Mary, but ordered that she should not "have her living on either of my plantations or have anything to do with them after my death and this for good reasons best known to myself."

Joseph and Mary Thorpe left issue two sons and two daughters:

    i. George who was to receive £3000 under his father's will at the age of twenty-one.

    ii. Isaac, who inherited property in St. Michael's under the will of his grandmother, Deborah Thorpe.

    i. Thomasine, married—Bedford.

    ii. Deborah. She is mentioned in the will of her cousin, Deborah Forster, in 1790 as being unmarried and living in England at Taunton, Somerset.

(2) *Harbin*. B.c. 1711; married c. 1727 John Forster of Forster Hall, St. Joseph's. They had issue one son and five daughters:

    i. Isaac-Thorpe; will proved in Barbados 1775.

    i. Deborah, b. 1728, d. unmarried c. 1794. Will dated December 1, 1790, at Bristol, pr. P.C.C. April 5, 1794 (Holman 196), (B.M.H.J. iv. 34).

    ii. Dorothy-Harbin, b.c. 1731, married 1754 Thomas Alleyne and left issue—see Alleyne of Barbados B.M.H.J. iv. 34; this family continued the use of Harbin as a Christian name till at least 1890.

---

*See the article on Joseph and Alexander Harbin: Two Barbadian Merchants, their families and descendants, by Mrs. Rawlins, in this Journal, Vol, XIX p. 28. **

* * Pages 276-281, this volume.

iii. Mercy-Catherine, married John Moseley.
iv. Sarah-Harbin.
v. Elizabeth-Holder.
Harbin Forster's children are all mentioned in the will of their grandmother, Deborah Thorpe.
(3) *Catherine*, b. 1714, married Dr. William Cox.
(4) *Sarah*, married 1.—Osborne; 2. the Rev. Haynes Gibbs.
(5) *Elizabeth*, married c. 1743, William Holder of St. Thomas.

There does not seem to be any full published pedigree of the Holders. The following account, based on the notes, in Caribbeana II, 377 and V. 194 has been expanded from wills, the Gentleman's Magazine and Hutchin's History of Dorset, I. 288.

William Holder, who married Elizabeth Thorpe, was the grandson of the Hon. William Holder of St. James', d. August 11, 1705, and probably son of the William Holder whose will was proved in Barbados 1727. He seems to have lived a good deal in London, as both his sons were born there, but died in Barbados, and was buried in the burial ground attached to the Holder plantation. His will, dated August 13th, 1752, was pr. P.C.C. 1753 (Searle 47). His mother Mary Ashley survived him. She was probably the widow of John Ashley, "late of Barbados and now of Blackheath" whose will dated Oct. 9, 1750 (P.C.C. Bushy 273) and pr. October 1751, mentions his wife Mary. Elizabeth Holder, like her mother Deborah Thorpe, remained a widow for some twenty years. She died at Bristol, where she had been living in King's Square in the Parish of St. James, June 19, 1783, and was buried at Hinton Charterhouse near Bath. Will dated Oct. 23, 1782, pr. P.C.C. July 3 1783, (Cornwallis, 359).

William and Elizabeth Holder left issue two sons:
i. William-Thorpe, b. 1744, in Lincoln's Inn Fields; educated at Eton, 1759-61, matriculated at Trinity College, Oxford, Oct. 30, 1761: married c. 1765, his cousin, Philippa-Eliot, d. of Reynold Hooper of Barbados, not Philippa Eliot as in Eton Register. At about this time he bought the Langton estate at Long Blandford in Dorset from the Rev. John Coker, and was sheriff of Dorset 1769-70. Later he sold Langton to George Snow and lived near Dorking in Surrey, and in London, where he had a house in Grosvenor Place. He died there Aug. 17, 1787, and was buried in a vault in Battersea Church. Will dated Oct. 4, 1785, pr. P.C.C. 1787, (Major 411) Philippa Holder as a widow lived at 16, St. James's Square, Bath, and died at Bathford in 1813, aged 71, leaving directions that she should be buried in Battersea Church, with her husband, son and daughters, and that all her property in England and Barbados should go to her granddaughter Margaret-Philippa Holder, Will dated August 7 1813, pr. Oct. 12, 1813, (P.C.C. Heathfield 501).

William-Thorpe and Philippa-Eliot Holder had issue:
a. William-Philip. D. unmarried "in his twenty-second year, late of Dorking, Surrey, and of Grosvenor Place" Oct. 1, 1797 (Gentleman's Magazine; Caribbeana has "in his twenty-fifth year") Buried at Battersea. His will, dated July 23, 1796, pr. Oct. 26, 1797 (P.C.C. Exeter 647) left £8000 to his surviving sister Margaret.

b. John-Hooper of Cerney House near Cirencester, Gloucs. Married 1, August 5th, 1808, Elizabeth, youngest d. of the Hon. William Hewitt and niece of Viscount Lifford; she died Jan. 15, 1810, leaving an only daughter, Margaret-Philippa. 2. March 18, 1812, Anne, youngest dau. of the Rev. Jeffrey Ekins, Dean of Carlisle (According to Caribbeana, V. 194, John Holder had issue by his second marriage; I have not been able to trace the family further).

a. Philippa d. an infant; buried at Langton, 1767.

b. Philippa-Harbin. D. unmarried 1795; buried at Battersea. Her will dated March 30th, 1795, pr. June 7, 1795, (P.C.C. Newcastle 389) left everything to her sister Margaret, including her share in an estate in Christchurch, Barbados "called the Rendezvous land".

c. Margaret-Dehany. D. unmarried 1809; buried at Battersea. She lived at Bath with her mother but died at Cerney House. Her will, dated Ap. 11 1804 pr. Nov. 10, 1809 (P.C.C. Loveday 824), left £10,000 to her brother John.

ii. James-Aynesworth. B. 1746, educated at Eton, 1759-64, matriculated at Merton College, Oxford, March 27, 1765; of Ash Park, Hampshire (Eton Register 1753-90). Executor to his mother in 1783 and to his cousin Deborah Thorpe in 1794.

II. SARAH HARBIN, b. 1691; married 1. c. 1714, Joseph Salmon of St. Michael's—probably the Major Joseph Salmon aged thirty-three of St. Michael's, who appears in the 1715 census of Barbados, and was probably the son of Col. Joseph Salmon then aged sixty-six (B.M.H.J. iv. 74). Sarah married 2, in 1728, Thomas Baxter of Barbados c. 1699—c. 1749, barrister-at-law.

The Free School in Bridgetown, founded by Thomas Harrison in 1733 was built on land purchased from Thomas and Sarah Baxter. (B.M.H.J. xiii, 171).

Thomas Baxter's will, dated Jan. 4, 1748, pr. in Barbados June 12, 1749, and in London Oct. 12, 1749 (P.C.C. Lisle 304), left his wife, Sarah, executrix and residuary legatee. He left a number of personal possessions and small legacies to his friends, including "the gentlemen of the Bar", Edmund Jenkins, Robert Cholmeley, John Cowse and William Warren, and to his godson, Isaac Forster, but mentions no relations of his own.

After her second husband's death Sarah Baxter came to England and settled at Bath, where she died "at her house in Bladud's buildings", Nov. 1, 1770.

She was buried in the church of Hinton Charterhouse some miles from Bath, where her daughter Margaret Salter, placed a monument in the south side of the tower to "Mrs. Sarah Baxter of the Isle of Barbados— —the best of parents". (Caribbeana IV. 175). Above are the arms:— per bend sinister, azure (or sable) and argent, three fishes hauriant, impaling, argent a saltire. The colours are much faded but the first coat is presumably salmon and the second Harbin, which should be, azure a saltire voided between four spear-heads or. These arms were used by the Rev. George Harbin d. 1744, and his sister Margaret, second wife of Sir Francis Warre, Bart., of Hestercombe, Somerset, who were first cousins of Sarah Baxter's father Joseph Harbin. Sarah Baxter's will was dated March 28, 1768, pr. P.C.C. April 20, 1776 (Trevor 145) and recorded in Barbados in April of the same year. She is described as late of Barbados and now of the City of Bath, widow. She left half her property including that in Barbados to her daughter Margaret and the latter's husband Richard Salter, and the other half between her grand-daughters Margaret Dehany and Philippa Holder. Her younger daughter Harbin Rycraft received a small legacy and a great-grandaughter Mary Dehany some of her personal possessions.

Sarah Baxter's surviving issue were her two daughters by her first husband, Joseph Salmon, Margaret and Harbin; a third daughter, Sarah, probably died young.

(1) Margaret b.c. 1716; married the Hon. Richard Salter (1710-76) son of Timothy Salter of Barbados by his first wife, Arabella Alleyne. He matriculated at St. John's College, Oxford, Dec. 1, 1710 (Alumni Oxonienses), and was a member of the Barbados legislature. His will was dated at Bath, June 11, 1768, but he later returned to Barbados where he died, Aug. 6, 1776. (Will pr. P.C.C. Collier 398). His widow erected a fine monument by Nollekens to his memory in St. George's Church. It was illustrated in an article on Barbados Churches by Stewart Perowne in Country Life Dec. 7, 1951. The arms attributed to Richard Salter by his wife are not those of any Salter family recorded in Burke's General Armoury—possibly they were inherited in the female line. On an escutcheon is, *Harbin,* a saltire between four spear-heads quartering *Salmon,* three salmon hauriant.

Richard and Margaret Salter had no issue and on her death in 1803 Margaret left not only her own property in Barbados but the Salter plantation as well to her niece Margaret Dehany.

(2) Harbin, b.c. 1718; married at St. Michael, June 9, 1734, Reynold Hooper, only son of Daniel Hooper of St. Thomas, by his wife Philippa Eliot. Reynold Hooper was b. 1712 and matriculated at St. John's College, Oxford, Dec. 23, 1727 (Alumni Oxonienses). He died in Barbados 1749 and was buried at St. Michael's as "the Hon. Reynold Hooper of St. Thomas." Will dated at Gosport near Portsmouth, March 3, 1748, and pr. P.C.C. 1749 (Lisle 314). He left issue one son and two daughters.

Harbin married 2 at St. Thomas Sept. 26, 1752, Christopher Estwick, whose will was proved in Barbados 1755 and 3—Rycraft. The last reference to her I have found is in her mother's will in 1768.

Issue of Reynold and Harbin Hooper:

    i. Reynold-Salter-Salmon, bapt. St. Thomas, July 6, 1743. He is not mentioned in any of the wills referred to, except his He is not mentioned in any of the wills referred to, except his father's, and may have died young.

    i. Margaret-Salter; married Philip Dehany, elder son of David Dehany of Hanover in Jamaica, of a family of Dutch origin, long settled in Jamaica (Caribbeana, III, 288).

      The Dehanys left Barbados to live in England, first at Far-leigh in Hampshire, and later at Hayes Place near Bromley, Kent, which had been Lord Chatham's residence and was sold after his death. Lord Dartmouth had been the owner for some years before Philip Dehany bought the mansion and its fine grounds. Margaret Dehany died August 3, 1809 (Gent. Mag.). "Philip Dehany, esq., of Upper Seymour Street, Marylebone and Hayes Place, Bromley" died in October of the same year. (Gent. Mag.) His will pr. P.C.C. December 13, 1809 (Loveday 874) left everything to his only daughter, Mary-Salter Dehany, who had also inherited the Salter estate left to her mother by Margaret Salter in 1803. She died unmarried in 1832.

ii. Philippa-Eliot, bapt. St. Thomas Sept. 6, 1742; married her cousin William-Thorpe Holder (as above) and died at Bathford 1813, leaving surviving issue, one son John-Hooper Holder.

The Hooper dates given above are from the article on Hooper of Barbados in B.M.H.J. iv. p. 34, and from Carib. iv. 45.

Abstracts of the wills of Isaac, Deborah and Joseph Thorpe and Sarah Baxter were supplied to the writer by Mr. E. M. Shilstone without whose kind assistance this and the preceding article on Harbin of Barbados could not have been written. The wills of Reynold Hooper, Richard Salter, and William Thorpe Holder are printed in B.M.H.J. xiii, p. 184—5; the remainder of the wills quoted have been abstracted by the writer from the P.C.C. registers at Somerset House.

HARRISON OF BARBADOS.

Compiled by E. M. SHILSTONE

The HARRISON family was established in Barbados from very early times and certainly prior to the year 1638 when Edward and William Harrison are known to have been residents and landowners. With the exception of the parish of Saint Joseph, the records of all the island parishes abound in evidence of the increase and activities of this family, especially in the seventeenth and eighteenth centuries. It is remarkable, therefore, that not a single male representative of any branch of the family is now living in this island, although a sugar-work plantation in St. Lucy still bears the name Harrison's.

The main interest in the HARRISON family lies in the life and career of Hon. Thomas Harrison, who founded the Harrison Free School in the year 1732, which with unbroken continuity still exists and flourishes as Harrison College.

The ancestry of Thomas Harrison has never been established beyond question. It is presumed that he was born in Barbados and about the year 1689, in which event he may be identified with Thomas Harrison named in the Census of Barbados of 1715 as a resident of Saint Michael aged 25 years with a household of one woman—probably his wife. But his eldest living child, George, had been born on 6 September 1714 and no mention is made of him or any other child in the household, although in the case of many other families children of the tenderest age are recorded. The same census records disclose the names of two other Thomas Harrisons then resident in Barbados, namely, Thomas aged 16, the son of Philip Harrison of the parish of Saint George, who is also named in his father's Will (1725) and is not to be confused with our Thomas Harrison who is almost certainly the "Harrison" of the firm of Withers and Harrison also named in Philip Harrison's Will; and secondly, Thomas Harrison of Saint Peter's parish aged 20.

The surname of Thomas Harrison's wife, Eleanor, before her marriage is not known. Their marriage is not entered in the records, which are not necessarily complete for the period in question, but the baptisms of their children are all entered in the Registers of St. Michael. Mrs. Harrison predeceased her husband, but her burial is not recorded in the Register of the church.

A large grey marble monument with an inscription recording Hon. Thomas Harrison's virtues and attainments stands on the floor against the north wall of the parish church and cathedral of St. Michael where he was buried. We are reminded by the inscription that he "from a small and tender beginning By arts of honest industry Grew rich belov'd and honour'd" and on the strength of this assertion we cannot look for his birth and parentage in high places; but it may be of interest to some of the great number of past and present pupils of the school which bears his name to attempt to trace his ancestry; and the following records of the HARRISON family have been compiled and are now offered to readers of the Journal in the hope that they will provide materials for further research along the same lines and that if any of Mr. Harrison's descendants are still living and these lines reach their eyes they may be able to furnish particulars which are wanting.

In a list of names of the inhabitants of Barbados in the year 1638 who then possessed more than ten acres of land, given on p 51 et seq. of the *Memoirs of the First Settlement of the Island of Barbados* (London 1743) we find the names of Edward Harrison and William Harrison.

A Census of the inhabitants of Barbados taken in 1679 contains the following particulars of the Harrison families then resident in the island.

Parish of St. Philip	Acres.	White servants.	Negroes.
John Harrison who owned	8		2
John Harrison, senior,	2		
John Harrison, junior,	4		
Abraham Harrison	4		

Parish of St. John.			
Phil. Harrison			2

Parish of St. Peter.			
Captain Robert Harrison		6	
Thomas Harrison	1		

In the Militia.
Captain Harrison, who commanded a company of 103 men.
Thomas Harrison, foot-soldier.
Andrew Harrison, whose quota for the troop was 2 men.

Parish of St. Michael.
Burials, 1679. August 20. Charles Harrison.

The Census of the island compiled in 1715 gives the following names.

Parish of St. Lucy.	Men's ages	Women's ages	Boys,	Girls.
Robert Harrison and family,				
4 men, 2 women, 1 boy, 1 girl	25, 21, 23 50	48, 15	15	9

Parish of St. George.

	Men's ages	Women's ages	Boys,	Girls.
John Harrison	42			
Darius* Harrison		40		
Elizabeth Harrison				13
Mary Harrison				8
Philip Harrison	38			
Mary Harrison		30		
Thomas Harrison				16

Parish of St. Peter.

Mr. Henry Harrison	25			
Thomas Harrison	20			

Parish of St. Michael.

Thomas Harrison [and household]	25	25		
Edward Harrison [and household]	19, 40	35		17

Parish of St. James.

John Harrison [and household]	25	20, 26	1, 3, 4	

Parish of St. Philip.

Mary Harrison		64		
Mr. Andrew Harrison	26			
Susannah Harrison		21		
John Harrison	66			
Elizabeth Harrison		62		
John Harrison	21			

Harrison Baptisms, Marriages, and Burials, taken from the copied records now deposited in the Central Registry.

Parishes.	BAPTISMS, TO THE YEAR 1780.		
Christ Church	1644, Oct.	17	Eleanor, dau. of Ralph & Catharine Harrison.
" "	1646, Sep.	10	Catharine, dau. of Ralph and Catharine Harrison.
" "	1649, Apl.	3	John, son of Ralph Harrison.
St. Philip	1651, Jan.	5	Dorothy, dau. of John Harrison.
"	1653, Dec.		—— son of John Harrison.
"	1654, Nov.	11	John, son of John Harrison.
"	1654, Nov.	16	Ann, dau. of John Harrison.
"	1655, Sep.	25	Dorothy, dau. of John Harrison.
"	1660, Jan.		Elizabeth, dau. of John Harrison.

* ? Darcus.

Parishes.	Date		
St. Michael	1664, Oct.	16	John Harrison.
„	1674, Jan.	10	William Harrison.
St. Philip	1676, Apl.	12	John, son of John and Mary Harrison.
„	1677, Feb.	3	Robert, son of John and Mary Harrison.
St. Michael	1680, Nov.	19	John Harrison.
St. Philip	1680, Dec.	26	Mary, dau. of John and Mary Harrison.
„	1680, Feb.	19	Sarah, dau. of Edward Harrison.
„	1680, Jan.	2	Hannah and Margaret, children of John & Hannah. Harrison.
Christ Church	1686, Apl.	11	Marrus, son of Thomas and Ann Harrison.
St. Philip	1688, Dec.	30	William, son of John & Elizabeth Harrison.
St. Michael	1695, Sep.	18	Mary, dau. of Abraham and Margery Harrison, born 29 May last.
„	1696, Mar.	4	William, son of Abraham and Margery Harrison.
St. James	1711, May	22	John James, son of John and Rebecka Harrison, born 21 May about noon.
St. Michael	1712, Nov.	1	Jane, dau. of Mr. Thomas and Mrs. Eleanor Harrison, born 30th Oct.
„	1714, Sep.	15	George, son of Mr. Thomas and Mrs. Eleanor Harrison, born 6th inst.
„	1716, Apl.	25	John, son of Mr. Thomas and Mrs. Eleanor Harrison, born 28th inst. (?ulto.)
„	1718, Apl.	13	Eleanor, dau. of Mr. Thomas and Mrs. Eleanor Harrison, born 11th inst.
St. Philip	1719, Dec.	26	John, son of Andrew Harrison.
St. Michael	1720, Apl.	7	Christopher Harrison.
„	1722, July	1	Mary, dau. of Mr. Thomas and Mrs. Ellinor Harrison. Thomas Withers, Mary Withers, and Elizabeth Worrell, Godparents.
„	1723, Oct.	27	Sarah, dau. of Mr. Thomas and Mrs. Elleanor Harrison, born 19th inst. Hy. Dodsworth, Samuel Wadeson, Mrs. Anna White, and Mrs. Mary Anne Roberts, Godparents.

Parishes.			BAPTISMS TO THE YEAR 1780.
St. James	1723, Nov.	3	Abel Harrison about 9 years bapt. in church.
St. Philip	1725, Sep.	23	Anne, dau. of Andrew Harrison.
„	1727, Jan.	6	child of John & Mary Harrison.
„	1730, July	26	Elizabeth, dau. of John and Mary Harrison.
St. Michael	1733, Aug.	13	Josias Harrison, a child about 21 mos. old.
St. James	1734, Aug.	24	Tabitha Harrison, an adult.
„	1734, Aug.	24	Elizabeth, dau. of John James and Tabitha Harrison, about 13 mos. old.
St. Michael	1744, Mar.	17	Thomas Harper, son of Dr. George and Jane Harrison, born 14th inst.
„	1745, Mar.	3	Jane, dau. of Dr. George Harrison, born 21 Feb.
„	1745, Feb.	21	George and Jane, twins of Dr. George and Jane Harrison, born that same day.
St. James	1764, Dec.	17	Rebecca, dau. of John & Martha Harrison.
„	1767, Sep.	7	John James, son of John and Martha Harrison, born 26 May. 1766.
„	1769, Nov.	21	Thomas, son of John & Martha Harrison.
St. Philip	1772, Nov.	7	William Thomas, son of William and Elizabeth Harrison.
„	1774, Feb.	16	John, son of William and Elizabeth Harrison.
St. James	1775, June	5	Rebecca, dau. of John & Martha Harrison, 14 days old.
St. Philip	1777, Oct.	19	Elizabeth, dau. of William and Elizabeth Harrison.
„	1778, June	5	Frances, dau. of William and Ann Harrison.
„	1779, Jan.	6	George, son of William and Elizabeth Harrison, born 14 Nov. 1778.

MARRIAGES TO THE YEAR 1800.

Christ Church	1643, Nov.	2	Ralph Harrison to Catharine Jones.
„ „	1649, Apl.	10	Catharine Harrison to Matthew Mahon.
St. Michael	1668, Feb.	10	James Harrison to Elizabeth Perridge.

MARRIAGES TO THE YEAR 1800.

St. Philip	1673, May	19	John Harrison to Hannah Maccoy.
St. Michael	1674, May	30	Jane Harrison to Charles Powell
Christ Church	1674, Aug.	16	Robert Harrison to Elizabeth Austin.
St. Michael	1677, Feb.	8	Roger Harrison to Anne Skellhorne.
St. Philip	1682, Jan.	29	John Harrison to Jone Martin.
St. Michael	1685, Sep.	3	John Harrison to Mrs. Sarah Burnam.
St. Philip	1688, June	4	Mary Harrison to John Ramsden.
St. Michael	1692, Mar.	27	Mrs Ann Harrison to Rowland Hye.
St. Philip	1693, Jan.	24	Joseph Harrison to Mary Read.
St. Michael	1695, Apl.	7	Abraham Harrison to Margery Adams.
St. Philip	1695, July	31	Mary Harrison to James Mann.
St. John	1698, July	29	Sarah Harrison to Thomas Sedford.
St. Philip	1699, July	1	Ann Harrison to John Clarke, junior.
St. John	1699, Mar.	11	Mary Harrison to John Swallow.
„	1699, Mar.	17	Robert Harrison to Mary Wheeler.
St. Michael	1702, May	13	Margery Harrison to David Welcraft.
„	1704, June	29	John Harrison to Dorcas Bunyon.
St. James	1708, Mar.	6	Mrs. Mary Harrison to Henry Mills.
St. Philip	1712, Aug.	3	Andrew Harrison to Susanna Kirton.
St. James	1718, June	28	Mary Harrison to Jos. Russell.
St. Michael	1719, Nov.	23	Rebecca Harrison to Archibald Landrick.
„	1722, May	19	Captain William Harrison to Mrs. Margaret Lee.
St. Philip	1723, Feb.	16	John Harrison to Mary Bunyon.
St. Michael	1727, Jan.	9	Jane Harrison to Blenny Harper, Merchant.
St. James	1732, Oct.	1	John James Harrison to Tabitha Goring.
St. Michael	1734, Nov.	13	William Harrison to Temperance Sexton, relict of late . . . . Sexton of this parish.
St. James	1736, Oct.	8	John James Harrison to Elizabeth Goring of St. Thomas.
St. Michael	1737, Jan.	31	Mary Harrison to John Walk.

MARRIAGES TO THE YEAR 1800

St. Philip	1737, Apl.	16	John Harrison to Mary Delph.
St. Thomas	1739, Feb.		Thomas Harrison to Elizabeth Lead.
St. Michael	1740, Sep.	1	John Harrison to Elizabeth Moore, widow.
„	1743, July	10	Sarah Harrison to Elias Minville.
St. Philip	1745, Oct.	12	William Harrison to Ann White.
„	1746, Sep.	14	John Harrison to Ruth Kirton.
„	1749, Oct.	21	Ann Harrison to John Sisnett.
St. James	1754, Dec.	21	Elizabeth Harrison to Charles Stuart.
St. Michael	1759, Jan.	24	Ruth Harrison to Geo. Phillips.
„	1760, July	20	Jane Harrison to Jonathan Worrell.
St. Thomas	1760, Apl.	18	Rebecca Harrison to Thomas Favell.
„	1760, July	20	Jane Harrison to Jonathan Worrell.
St. Michael	1762, Aug.	3	Mary Harrison to Charles Nellson.
St. Lucy	1762, —		Benjamin Harrison to ———
St. Philip	1769, July	7	Sarah Harrison to Rowland Bascom.
„	1771, July	20	William Harrison to Eliza. Hunt.
St. Peter	1780, July	27	Susanna Harrison to Joshua Sandiford.
St. Michael	1800, July	7	Jas. G. Harrison to Elizabeth Bourne.

BURIALS TO THE YEAR 1800.

Christ Church	1647, Mch.	23	Eleanor Harrison.
„ „	1659, Sep.	2	William Harrison.
St. Michael	1665, Oct.	13	John Harrison.
St. John	1657, Aug.	29	Elizabeth Harrison.
St. Michael	1669, Oct.	6	Mary Harrison.
„	1670, June	15	Eliza. Harrison.
Christ Church	1671, Apl.	2	Jane Harrison.
St. Michael	1674, Jan.	15	William Harrison, a child.
„	1674, Feb.	17	John Harrison, a seaman.
„	1679, Oct.	13	Matthew Harrison, a seaman.
„	1679, Aug.	28	Charles Harrison.
„	1680, Aug.	10	Thomas Harrison.
„	1680, Mch.	3	Ann Harrison, a child.
„	1680, Nov.	28	John Harrison, a child.
St. Philip	1680/1 Jan.	6	Andrew Harrison, son of John Harrison.
„	1681, Mch.	16	John Harrison (senior).
St. Michael	1682, Dec.	7	John Harrison.

BURIALS TO THE YEAR 1800.

St. Philip	1683, Mch.	16	John Harrison, son of John Harrison (senior).
St. Michael	1684, Apl.	14	John Harrison.
„	1684, Sep.	11	Robert Harrison.
Christ Church	1684, Nov.	1	Miles Harrison.
St. Philip	1685, Aug.	23	John Harrison.
Christ Church	1690, Dec.	7	Manus Harrison.
St. Michael	1691, Feb.	28	Richard Harrison.
„	1691, Feb.	26	Jonathan Harrison.
„	1691, July	3	Andreas Harrison.
„	1695, Oct.	10	Mary Harrison, a child.
„	1696, Apl.	26	Ensign John Harrison.
„	1696, July,	12	John Harrison, marriner.
„	1696, Sep.	1	John Harrison.
„	1697, July	25	Samuel Harrison, marriner.
„	1698, Sep.	25	John Harrison, schoolmaster.
„	1699, May	23	Richard Harrison, a pauper.
„	1699, May	24	Mary Harrison.
St. Michael	1700, Oct.	5	Mrs. Dorothy Harrison.
St. John	1700, Oct.	25	John Harrison.
St. Michael	1701, Nov.	16	Thomas Harrison, marriner.
„	1702, Dec.	27	Gilbert Harrison.
„	1703, May	29	Thomas Harrison, Esq. in church.
St. James	1793, July	25	James Harrison, a carpenter.
St. Michael	1712, June	25	Capt. Thomas Harrison.
,,	1712, Dec.	7	Jane Harrison, a child.
,,	1713, Mar.	4	Capt. Anthony Harrison.
St. James	1716 —		John Harrison about 35 years from Coll. Palmer's plantation.
St. Michael	1718, Sep.	23	Richard Harrison.
„	1718, Apl.	27	John Harrison, Boatswane.
„	1718, May	20	Katharine Harrison.
St. James	1718, Oct.	15	Francis Harrison about 25 years.
St. Philip	1726, July	18	——— child of John Harrison.
„	1731, Jan.	7	Mary Harrison, wife of John Harrison.
St. Michael	1733, Aug.	14	Josias Harrison, a child.
„	1734, Apl.	4	Katharine Harrison, a child.
„	1734, Feb.	28	William Harrison, a saylor.
„	1735, Jan.	7	Temperance Harrison, wife of William Harrison.
Christ Church	1735, Apl.	16	——— daur. of John Harrison.
St. Michael	1738, June	18	Captain Thomas Harrison.
St. James	1738, Oct.	20	Abel Harrison, aged 23, died of a fever.
„	1739, Dec.	20	Jno. James Harrison aged 29, died of a polypus.

BURIALS TO THE YEAR 1800.

St. Michael	1740, Jan.	18	William Harrison, a copper smith.
„	1741, Feb.	21	Fanny Harrison, a child.
„	1742, Jan.	14	William Harrison, a child.
„	1745, Feb.	25	George, son of Dr. George Harrison.
„	1746, June	8	Hon. Thomas Harrison in the new Chancel.
St. Thomas	1746, June	8	Hon. Thomas Harrison*.
St. Philip	1749, Dec.	2	John Harrison.
„	1751, Aug.	30	—— son of John Harrison.
St. Michael	1755, Apl.	26	John Harrison.
„	1759, July	19	Sarah Harrison.
St. James	1764, Dec.	19	Rebecca Harrison, an infant.
St. John	1771, Nov.	8	John Harrison, ye President's groom.
St. Michael	1778, Nov.	8	Allen Harrison, mariner on board Ship Reynolds, Kendal master, from Lancaster.
St. Philip	1779, Jan.	5	John —————— a child, son of William Harrison.
„	1779, Jan.	25	Elizabeth, a child, dau. of William Harrison.
St. Michael	1780, Aug.	3	William Harrison, a soldier of the 86th Regt.
St. Philip	1781, Feb.	28	Elizabeth Harrison.
St. Michael	1794, Mch.	5	Edward Harrison from the 34th Regt.
St. Peter	1788	—	John Harrison.
„	1795, Dec.	9	John Harrison.
„	1798, Jul.	3	Grace Harrison.

(To be continued.)

---

* His interests in and connection with the parish of St. Thomas caused the Rector, who probably assisted at the funeral ceremony, to enter the burial in the Register of St. Thomas, although the interment took place at St. Michael.

HARRISON OF BARBADOS.

HARRISON WILLS TO THE YEAR 1800.

Will dated 13 Jan. 1669/70 of EDWARD HARRISON of St. James, gentleman.

To my daughter, Rosamond Harrison £2,000 stlg. six years after my decease and £500 more at the age of 15, also one negro girl, and her maintenance and schooling till she marries or reaches the age of 16.

To my wife, Dorothy Harrison, all the estate that I received with her upon marriage, part lies in the occupation of Ralph Fretwell, Esq., and part in the hands of Wm. Rose, also one-third part of my estate for her life and then to my son, Edward Harrison and his heirs, leaving to my wife the use of all linen etc., which was hers before marriage. The residue of my plate and household goods to be divided between my children Edward and Rosamond. My plantation to be divided and managed with the consent of my overseers. To my cousin John Harrison 40,000 lbs. of muscovado sugar and the horse he rides. To my cousin Thomas Harrison 20,000 lbs. of sugar in two instalments. To my god-son, Thomas Ince, 1,000 lbs. sugar, and my other god-son 500 lbs. To the parish of Saint James 5,000 lbs. sugar and to St. Peter 2,500 lbs. To my servant, John, the stone-cutter, to William Russell, to Isabell——, Faith Martin, Bridgett Sage, and John Banfield 500 lbs. each. To Joshua Antrobus, and to Joseph James 1,000 lbs. each.

I appoint Edward Harrison my sole executor, and likewise all my real and personal estate to him and his heirs for ever. If my son Edward and daughter Rosamond should die without issue then it shall pass to my cousin John Harrison. I appoint as overseers Samuel Newton, Esq., Robert Legard, gentleman, and John Rokeby, merchant, and I give them £10 each to buy a ring. Sgd. Edward Harrison. Witnesses : Joseph James, Udall Walker, Joshua Antrobus.

Codicil dated 17 Jan. 1669/70. The gifts to my wife to be in lieu of dower. If further issue born to my wife, I give to the same £1,500 stlg. at 16, and if it be a son then on the death of son Edward without issue, all the estate given to him, and if it be a girl then to divide the estate equally with Rosamond, and in default of issue to my cousin John Harrison. I appoint the finishing of the stone house which I am now building. Sgd. Edward Harrison. Witnesses : Robt. Legard, Joshua Antrobus.

Will and Codicil proved 15 Feb. 1669/70 before Chr. Codrington.

Will dated 15 April 1670 of MARGARET HARRISON of St. George. To my son Samuel Sedgwick my estate until my son James

296

Sedgwick shall come in proper person and lay claim on one-half, and my son Samuel the other half. My son John Sedgwick 10,000 lbs. sugar and two negro women and a pickaneny for his daughter Martha Sedgwick.

To my son Elias Sedgwick 6,000 lbs. sugar.

To my daughter Elizabeth Simkins all my wearing apparel.

To my grand-daughter Margarett Simkins my bed with 2 sheets and pillows and my saddle with a necklace of currell (coral) and pearl and the jewel belonging to it, a stone ring, my bible and a suit of mourning.

To Charles Harrison, senior, £3,000 cy. To Bartholomew Evans 20/-. To Mrs. Anne Ulright a scarfe and 20/-. To my— John Coppen one scarfe and 20/- and a scarfe to his wife. To Richard Salter and John Strode each a scarfe and 20/- to buy a ring. These legacies to be paid by Samuel and James if he comes, proportionally.

I appoint Richard Salter and John Strode overseers.

Sgd. Margarett Harrison. Witnesses: Jos: Brumidge, Wm. Spring.

Proved 28 Nov. 1670 before Chr. Codrington.

Will dated 20 June 1670 of REBECCA HARRISON of London, widow.

My estate in England, Barbados, and Nevis in America, and in the hands of Isaac Barton, John Edwards, Stephen Mitchell and Michael Smith, merchants, unto Edward Pelham, son of Thomas Pelham of Compton Valence in Dorset, of London, merchant, and appoint him executor.

Sgd. Rebecca Harrison. Witnesses: Richard Billingsby, Robert Eduse.

Not proved. Recorded 22 May 1671.

Will of JOHN HARRISON of Deptford in the county of Kent, mariner, dated 25 July 1653.

To my wife Rebecca Harrison for her life all those tenements in Deptford or elsewhere in Kent and then to the heirs of her body by me begotten. I give her all my plate and ready money and appoint her executrix.

Sgd. John Harrison. Witnesses: Will Deverge, John Steele, John Andrews, senr., Proved 9 June 1671. Recorded 11 June 1671.

Will of JOHN HARRISON of St. Peter, Barbados, dated 6 Jan. 1671/2.

To my god-daughter Margaret Rock 500 lbs. sugar.

To Sarah Millnes, daughter of John M., 500 lbs. sugar.

To Hugh Kelly 400 lbs. To my mother, Alice Harrison and my brother William, and my two sisters Alice and Mary 10,000 and my mother to have the disposal of it.

To my brother Thomas Harrison and sister Elizabeth Harrison all my land, houses, goods, etc. (before excepted) equally between them, and I appoint them executors.

Sgd. John Harrison. Witnesses: Edward Littleton, William Mullins, William Connant, Hugh Kelly.

Proved 12 March 1671/2 before Chr. Codrington. Recorded 9 Aug. 1672.

Will of THOMAS HARRISON of St. Peter, planter, dated 16 Feb. 1671/2.
To my godson William Holloway and all my other god-children 100 lbs. of sugar each. To Eleanor Butler 500 lbs. sugar. To Hugh Kelly 300 lbs. sugar and all my clothes. To Wm. Connant 200 lbs. sugar. I appoint my sister Elizabeth Harrison sole executrix and give her all my real and personal estate.
Sgd. Tho: Harrison. Witnesses: Robert Moggs, Henry Jones, Hugh Kelly.
Proved 12 March 1672, before Chr. Codrington. Recorded 9 Aug. 1672.

Will of EDWARD HARRISON the elder of St. John, planter, dated 11 March 1675/6.
To my son Edward Harrison all my real and personal estate, and failing issue, to the children of my sister Joan Smith (Harrison). To my servant Robert Browne his freedom. To Nicholas Doll 2,000 lbs. sugar. To Elizabeth a mulatto her freedom when Mrs. Ann Dixwell's lease is expired which she hath of her. I appoint Henry Walrond sole executor.
Sgd. the mark of Edward Harrison. Witnesses : Ann Dixwell the elder, Ann Dixwell the younger, Martha Dixwell.
Codicil dated 13 March 1675/6. I give to Mrs. Ann Dixwell the elder 4,000 lbs. of sugar. This bequest was made in the pre-sence of Nicholas Dall and Thomas Browne by Edward Harrison. Sgd. Nicholas Dall (his mark). Robert Browne. Will and Codicil proved 29 March 1676 before Jonathan Atkins. Recorded 13 April 1676.

Will of ROBERT HARRISON of St. Peter, All Saints, esquire, dated 4 July 1700
To my son Robert the dwellinghouse in Speightstown where-in Benj. Dillon lives and ....sq. ft. of land of the plantation where I now live to be run out by the stock pen near the seaside on the edge of the path leading away to my mansion house, to build him a storehouse. To my sons Robert and Edward my library of books. To my son Edward one dwellinghouse in Speightstown and one horse and one slave. To my son Thomas Harrison one horse, one slave. To my daughter Katharine Harri-son one horse and one girl slave. To my wife Katharine £1,500 in lieu of dower and £150 per annum out of the profits arising from my two estates situate in St. Peter and St. Lucy over the said sum of £1,500 until the same is paid. To my wife all my plate and best furniture, a horse, two slaves, and living in my mansion house where I now live on my plantation in St. Lucy during her widowhood. To my sons Edward and Thomas £1,500 each at 21 out of the profits of my estates. To my daughter Katharine £1,500 at 18. My three children to be educated out of my two estates and their abode in my mansion house. To my

son Jonas (*sic*) Harrison at 21 the plantation whereon I now live in St. Peter except the land bequeathed to my son Robert, together with the slaves and implements and the heirs male of his body and failing heirs, to my son Edward, and the heirs male of his body, and failing heirs to my son Thomas and the heirs male of his body and failing heirs to my son Robert and his heirs male. To my son Robert my plantation in St. Lucy with slaves etc., and failing heirs to Thomas, Edward, and Josiah (*sic*), in succession and failing heirs to the right heir of Robert.

Lt. Col. Thomas Maycock, Major William Timbrill (? Terrill), Wm. Burnett, gent., Wm. Elton, Walter Prott, Samuel Maverick, Esqs., executors.

Sgd. Robert Harrison. Witnesses: Thomas Lewin, Mary Lambert, Mary Chaffe. Proved 30 July 1700. Recorded 26 August 1700.

Note. This Will is twice entered, again under date 26 August 1702.

Will dated 10 November 1701 of THOMAS HARRISON, mariner. To Thomas Evans all my land and dwellinghouses situate in the town of Kirby, Essex. Also debt of £10 due me from my Uncle Stephen Buroughs of the town of Kirby, husbandman, and all sums due to me from any ships or persons, and all my real estate wheresoever, and appoint him sole executor.

Sgd. Thomas Harrison. Witnesses: Ph. Battersby, William Harman, Clement Larrier. Proved 25 Nov. 1701 before John Farmer, Presdt.

Will dated 12 January 1702, of JOHN JAMES HARRISON of St. James, practitioner in physic. To my wife Mary Harrison my riding horse called Mellowes, together with her saddle and furniture. The rest of my personal estate to be divided between my wife and my three children John, Mary, and Frances Harrison, and my real estate between my three children. My wife to have the management of my children and their estates during widowhood, otherwise to be put in the hands of Capt. Joseph Harris and Capt. Samuel Hagbourne. I appoint my wife and the said Joseph Harris and Samuel Hagbourne executors.

Sgd. Jno. James Harrison. Witnesses: George Adams, Thomas Wade, Wm. Neblett, Walter Taylor.

Proved 11 Feb. 1702 by John Farmer, Presdt.

Will dated 26 May 1703 of THOMAS HARRISON of St. Michael. To my mother, Mrs. Lydia Harrison, £80. To my mother-in-law Mrs. Mary Davies £10 to buy mourning, and I discharge her of £150. one year's interest due on £1,500 since Feb. last on my wife's marriage portion.

To my sister-in-law, Philippa Thornhill, widow and her daughter Thomazin Thornhill £10 each to buy mourning and £10 to buy a ring. To John Thornhill son of Philippa, all my wearing apparel and £20 for three years for his education. To my wife Mary all the rest of my state in Barbados and England and appoint her executrix.

299

Sgd. the mark of Thomas Harrison. Witnesses: Mary Bayley, Henry Allman, David Williamson. Proved 29 June 1703 before Bevil Granville. Recorded 29 Sep. 1703.

Will of MARY HARRISON of St. James dated 27 Nov. 1711.

To my son John Harrison my dwellinghouse, 13 acres of land and six slaves. To my daughter Mary Mills, three slaves. To my daughter Frances Harrison six slaves. To my grandson John James Harrison one slave. My son John sole executor. Sgd. the mark of Mary Harrison. Witnesses: Elizabeth Ross, Tho. Ross. Proved 11 August 1712 before Robert Lowther. Recorded 12 Sept. 1712.

Will of PHILIP HARRISON of St. George, millwright, dated 13 Febry. 1724/5.

Any sums due me from Samuel Forte to be paid towards debt due by me to Messrs. Withers & Harrison, and also moneys due me from the estate of George Walker towards payment of my debt to Messrs. Crumpton & Hassell.

To my wife, Mary Harrison, for life all my real and personal estate, and after her death I give to my son, Thomas Harrison, a girl slave, and in case of his death to my nephew, Philip Rea (? Raa); to my brother Joseph Harrison, a slave, Cuffee, and after his death to my niece Jane Raa. To my niece Ethel Gittens, wife of Samuel Gittens, a slave called Nanny; to my niece, Mary Harrison, a slave. I appoint my wife, Mary, and my kinsman Samuel Gittens executors.

Sgd. Philip Harrison. Witnesses: Joseph Gittens, Richard Boone, James Smith. Proved 13 March 1724/5 and recorded 18 March 1724/5.

Will of JOHN HARRISON of St. Philip, dated 17 August 1709.

To my wife Elizabeth Harrison all my real estate with the use of my household stuff and two cows during her life. To my son Andrew Harrison after his mother's death one-half of my land and four slaves. To my son, John Harrison the other half of my land and three slaves. I direct that Andrew shall help his brother John to build a house with the timber growing on his land and it shall be 30 feet long and 13 feet wide. My granddaughter, Mary Parsons to be put to school for three years at the expense of my estate. To my niece, Dorothy Pickering 20/-. To my grand-daughter, Mary Pickering, 20/-. To my niece, Susanna Stoute 40/-. I appoint my sons John and Andrew Harrison executors. Sgd. John Harrison. Witnesses: Joshua Gittens, John Pickering, William Pickering. Recorded 6 Aug. 1725.

Will of KATHARINE HARRISON of St. Lucy, widow of Robert Harrison late of St. Peter, dated 2 Sept. 1732.

To my son Robert Harrison one guinea of gold. To his three children, Robert, Katherine, and Mary £50 cy. each. To my niece Anne Maycock, the wife of Major John Maycock £50 cy. To her three daughters, Sarah, Anna, and Christian £25 cy. To my son Edward Harrison £1,000. To Edward and Katherine Harrison all the residue of my estate, and I appoint them as executors. Sgd.

Katherine Harrison by her mark. Witnesses: John Maycock, Thos. Maycock. Proved 3 Octr. 1733.

Will of WILLIAM HARRISON of St. Michael, Coppersmith, dated 16 Jan. 1740. To my friend, Thomas Morrison of St. Michael all my estate in Barbados and Jamaica and all I am entitled to under the Will of my brother Edward Harrison late of Kingston, Jamaica, and I appoint him sole executor. Sgd. W. Harrison. Witnesses: Samuel Game, Jno. Middleton, Richard Dennery, Reynold Gibbs. Proved 20 Jan. 1740.

Will of THOMAS HARRISON* of St. Michael, Barbados, dated 6 Novr. 1745. To my daughter, Jane Harper, my interest in her dower, being the negroes which I bought at outcry. I also give her my plantation in St. Thomas with two sugar works and negroes thereon for her life, and the use of all my household stuff on the said plantation. To my granddaughter Jane Harper £500 cy. at 18 or marriage to be paid by her mother out of the profits of the same plantation. To my sister-in-law, Sarah Worrell, £150 cy. out of the profits of the same plantation and the use of a chamber and furniture in the dwellinghouse of the same plantation during her life.

To my son John Harrison the plantation in the parish of St. Andrew called the Overhill and also my plantation in St. Peter called Ashton Hall, with the negroes, cattle, stock, etc., also the Customs house and the storehouse in Speightstown called Scantlebury's, and also all my land and buildings in Christ Church, and my land in the parish of St. Thomas formerly Bannatyne's and also all my land and buildings in the town of St. Michael not herein mentioned together with the reversion on the death of his sisters of the houses given them for life and also all debts due to me (except the debt due to me by his brother George Harrison). I also give him my shallop and shallop-negroes, subject to his paying all my debts, funeral expenses and legacies.

I give to my daughter, Eleanor Neil, widow, £100 cy, and my house in Swan Street during her life. To my daughter Mary Walke £100 cy. and my house at The Roebuck, formerly Barbara Moor's, during her life. To my daughter, Sarah Minveille £100 cy. and my southernmost corner tenement in High Street, together with the storehouse behind it, fronting Palmetto Street, for her life. To my grandchildren, son and daughters of my daughters, Mary Walke and Sarah Minveille, living at my death £100 cy. each at 21.

I give to my good friends, Thomas Withers and William Duke Esqs., to my brothers-in-law, Thomas Duke and Doctor Jonathan Worrell, to my sons-in-law, John Walke and Elias Minveille, to my sisters, Sarah Worrell and Martha Duke, and to my daughters, Jane Harper, Eleanor Neil, Mary Walke and Sarah Minveille, £20 cy. each to buy mourning.

---

* Hon. Thomas Harrison, the founder of the Harrison Free School.

To my granddaughters, Joannah, Eleanor, and Elizabeth Neil, £100 cy. each at 21 to be paid by my son, George Harrison to whom I devise my plantation in St. Michael and St. George and the residue of my real and personal estate in this island during his life and after his death to such of his children as he shall by Will appoint, and in case of no Will to my right heirs.

I appoint my sons, George and John, and my friends, Thomas Withers, and William Duke, Esqs., my brothers Doctor Jonathan Worrell and Thomas Duke executors.

Sgd. Tho. Harrison. Witnesses: Ja. Booth, Samuel Hinkson. Proved 25 June 1746 and recorded same day.

Will of GEORGE HARRISON of St. Michael, Barbados, Bachelor of Physick, dated 21 March 1745.

To my wife, Jane, my son Thomas Harper Harrison, my daughter Jane, provided I shall have no other child alive at the decease of my wife, the money that now lies at interest in the estate of Samuel Adams of Christ Church. To my son Thomas Harper Harrison all lands in Barbados, he paying thereout to my daughter Jane £2,000 cy. I appoint my father, Thomas Harrison, my brother John Harrison, and friend Wm. Duke to be executors and guardians, likewise my wife.

Sgd. George Harrison. Witnesses : Philip Lytcott, Jas. Thorne, Wm. Worrell. Proved and recorded 6 Decr. 1746.

Will of HON. JOHN HARRISON of St. Michael, Barbados, dated 14 April 1755.

To my sister Jane Sturge, wife of William Sturge of St. Michael, Eleanor Neil of the same parish, widow, Mary Walk, wife of John Walk, and Sarah Minveille, wife of Elias Minveille, my brother-in-law, John Walk, and nephew-in-law, Wm. Moore jr., and niece Jane, his wife, £50 each to buy mourning.

To each of the following nephews and nieces—Jane Harrison, daughter of my late and only brother, Dr. George Harrison, Joannah Niele, Eleanor Niele and Elizabeth Niele, daughters of my sister Eleanor Niele, John Walk, Robert Walk, Mary Walk, Eleanor Walk, Abigail Jane Walk, Jane Walk, and Sarah Walk, children of my sister Mary Walk, David Minvielle and Susannah Minvielle, children of my sister Sarah Minvielle, £500 cy each. My said nephew, John Walk to be allowed by my executors £60 per annum until 18 and £100 per annum until 23 years for his maintenance and education in Great Britain. My nieces Jane Harrison and Eleanor Niele to be allowed by my executors £60 per annum until 18 or marriage for their maintenance and education in England. To William Roberts, son of William Roberts decd. £150, and to Miss Elizabeth Roberts, daughter of the said Wm. Roberts £150. To Ann Kelly, daughter of Ann Kelly, widow, my messuage in Palmetto St., St. Michael's town, now in the possession of Samuel Moore, attorney-at-law, and £500 and my household furniture &c. (silver and plate excepted) in the house where I now live near St. Michael's town and a horse named Beauty. To Mary Kelley, widow, daughter of Mary Hooper,

302

widow, £100. To Ann Kelley Snarling, daughter of Robert Snarling £150. To my clerk Samuel Hinkson £50. To my nephew Harrison Walk 9 acres of land in St. Thomas adjoining the plantation of my brother-in-law, John Walk, called Walk . . . . (? Spring) plantation, and £60 per annum until 18 and £100 per annum until 23 for his maintenance and education in Great Britain, and in case of his death the said nine acres to my nephew John Walk. To my nephew Thomas Minvielle, my River plantation, St. Andrew, at 23 years and the storehouse in Speightstown and an allowance of £60 p.a. and £100 per annum, and in case of his death the said plantation to be sold. To my nephew Thomas Harper Harrison at 23 Ashton Hall plantation, St. Peter, and a store in Speightstown, and also Strouds plantation, St. Michael, bounding on my nephew Neil's plantation, St. George. All other plantations and properties to be sold by executors. Residue of estate to nephew, Thomas Harper Harrison, at 23, and in the event of his death before 23, Ashton Hall and Strouds plantations and the residue of my estate to my nephew, Harrison Walk, at 23, and failing him to my nephew, Thomas Minvielle, and failing him to my nephew, David Minvielle, and failing him to my nephew John Walk.

I appoint Wm. Sturge, Elias Minvielle, Hon. John Cobham and Samuel Fouchett of London to be executors and I give them £50 each for mourning.

Sgd. John Harrison. Witnesses : Robert Snarling, Martin Joyce, Robert Wadeson. Proved 30 April 1755.

Will of ROBERT HARRISON of St. Peter, Barbados, dated 19 April, 1755.

To my son Edward Harrison £400 for 3 years, a horse valued at £25, and a mulatto slave. To my son Thomas Harrison £700 at 21, a horse valued at £25 and a negro boy. To my son John Harrison £700 at 21, a horse worth £25, and a negro boy. To my daughter Katherine Harrison £700, a horse worth £25 and a negro woman. To my daughter Mary Harrison £700, a horse worth £25, a negro woman and a girl. My sons and daughters to be maintained out of the profits of my estate.

To Edward Harrison my law books and the case which contains them, and my other books, except Nelson's Justice of the Peace, which I give to Robert Harrison. Residue of my estate to Robert Harrison, and I appoint him executor.

Sgd. Robert Harrison. Witnesses : Richard Denny, Thomas Chandler, George Edwards. Proved and recorded 27 November 1755.

Will of JOHN HARRISON of St. Philip, Barbados, dated 29 November, 1755.

My three slaves (named) and 8½ acres of land bounding on lands of Mr. Nicholas Rice, to be sold by my wife, Ruth, and Captain John Best for payment of my debts.

To my wife my slave Betty and 4 acres of land and buildings for her life and then to my daughters Susanna and Rebecc

Harrison and their heirs. If they die without issue, to my sister-in-law Dorothy Sisnett.

To my daughters Susanna and Rebbeca three slaves (named) at the age of 15, with remainder to my wife for life and then to my sister-in-law, Dorothy Sisnett.

My wife, Ruth, and Captain John Best executors. Sgd. Jno. Harrison. Witnesses : William Weeks, John Norris. Proved and recorded 22 Jany. 1756.

Will of WILLIAM HARRISON of St. Philip, Barbados, dated 21 March, 1757.

To my wife Ann Harrison two slaves (named). My executors to sell my house and any of my eight slaves (named) to pay my debts, and the residue to my son William Harrison at 21. Residue of my estate to my brother-in-law, James White. I appoint James White and my wife Ann executors. (The testator died before signing the Will. It was recorded 16 June 1757.)

Will of BENJAMIN HARRISON of St. Lucy, Barbados, planter, dated 16 January, 1762.

To my nephew John Harrison £5; to my nieces, Elizabeth Stuart and Rebecca Farwell (? Favell) £15 each. To my wife Sarah my ten slaves (named) and the residue of my estate, and I appoint her executrix.

Sgd. Benjn. Harrison. Witnesses : Benja. Hinds, John Allport, Obed Boyce, George Armstrong. Proved and recorded 7 September, 1763.

Will of THOMAS HARRISON of St. Peter, Gentleman, dated 9 December 1764.

To my sister Katherine Harrison, 1 girl slave, Polly, and £180. To my sister Mary Harrison £200. To my brother, John Harrison £200. To my niece, Susanna Harrison £50. To my kinsman, Benjamin Maycock £15. To my kinswoman, Anna Maycock £15. To my kinswoman, Sarah Maycock £7. 10. To my kinswoman, Mary Maycock £7. 10. I set free my slave Rachel, and £50 to be paid to the churchwarden of St. Peter for her support, according to the Statute. Also a boarded house to be furnished her and 40/- per annum for life.

Residue of my estate to my brother, Robert Harrison, subject to my debts and legacies, and the said Robert to be executor.

Sgd. Thomas Harrison. Witnesses : Charles Kyd, George Edwards, Bishop Edwards. Proved and recorded 8 January 1765.

Will of ROBERT HARRISON of St. Peter, Barbados, dated 9 June 1766.

To my sister Katherine Harrison, one slave girl and £200, to my sister Mary Harrison £200, to my brother John Harrison £200, to my niece Susanna Harrison £200. To my cousin Anna Maycock £100. To my cousin Benjamin Maycock and to his daughters Mary and Sarah, £25 each.

I set free my negro woman Betty and give her £150 and two mulatto girl slaves, Phillis and Rachel. I set free my negro woman

Grace and give her £100 and a mulatto girl slave Mary. A house to be provided for Grace and Betty.

Residue of my estate to my brother, Edward Harrison; and I appoint him executor.

Sgd. R. Harrison. Witnesses : Thos. Whitney, Denny Gibbes, James Pooler. Proved and recorded 9 August 1766.

Will of ELIZABETH HARRISON of St. Michael, widow, dated 19 May 1763.

To my daughter Mary Duvy, wife of Andrew Duvy £220 now in her husband's hands. To my grand-daughter, Elizabeth Duvy, £50, a bed, bolster and pillows, a set of damask curtains, coverlit, two new damask table cloths, two new sideboard cloths, 8 new towels, 6 new napkins, a case with 12 silver handled knives.

To my grandson, William Duvy, £50, a silver tankard and all the rest of my real and personal estate except the following : To my grand-daughter Alice Duvy £50, a pair of holland sheets and pillow cases, 12 silver teaspoons, and a copper waiter; to my grand-daughter, Rebecca Duvy, £50, a silver salver, feather bed bolster and pillows, a pair of holland sheets and pillow cases and 8 new napkins; to my grandson, Andrew Duvy, £50 and 6 large silver spoons; to my granddaughter, Hannah Duvy, £50, a pair of holland sheets and pillow cases and 6 large silver spoons.

Appoint my son-in-law, Andrew Duvy, and my grandson, William Duvy, to be executors. Sgd. Eliza. Harrison. Witnesses : Jno. Luke, John Richardson, Mary Luke. Proved 18 March 1768.

Will of MARY HARRISON of Speightstown, St. Peter, Spinster, dated 8 July 1771.

To my brother, John Harrison, a negro woman slave, Philady and her two sons Romeo and Sandy to wait on him during his life, and after his death to my niece Susanna Harrison. £400 to be invested for my brother, John, until he shall recover his reason and be capable of taking care of himself, otherwise to fall into my estate.

£300 to be invested and income paid to my sister Katherine Maycock, wife of William Dottin Maycock, and the use and service of two women slaves. At her death the slaves for my niece Susanna Harrison. I manumit my slave Mary and give £400 to be invested for her life, and give her my two slaves Sarey and Juliet for her life.

To my friend Elizabeth Callender, widow of Smith Callender, £25. To Sarah Whitney, daughter of Thomas Whitney, £50. Residue of my estate to my niece, Susanna Harrison, at 21. Appoint Thomas Whitney and Anne Christian Payne, executors.

Sgd. Mary Harrison. Witnesses : Howard Callender, Sarah Maycock. Proved 13 May 1799.

Hawtayne.

Edw[d] Hawtaine, of the cittie of Westm[r], gt. Will dated the last of Oct. 1627. For the poor of the village of Epwell, iu the parish of Swake Cliffe, Oxfordshire, where I was born £100. My cosen Vallence citizen of L., all books. My bro. John H. of Oxfordshire and his ch[n] £200, and my sister his wife my bible. To the ch[n] of my sister Hall, of Oxfordshire £150. P. 9 Aug. 1628. (77, Barrington.)

Valentine Hawton or Haughton, of Rickall, Yorkshire, yeoman. Will p. 1657. (123, Pell.)

Rich[d] Peers of B'os, Esq. Will dated 18 Dec. 1659. My grandsons Richard Hawton 20,000 lbs., Jonathan Hawtaine and Valentine Hawtaine 10,000 lbs. each, said R[d] H. an overseer. (70, Laud.)

The will of Richard Haughton was proved in J'ca, 1694-7.

Edward Hawtaine, D[r] of physicke. Will dated 12 Aug. 1666. I constitute my wife Eliz. sole Ext'rix and to enjoy all my est. P. 9 May 1667, by E. H. (62, Carr.)

David Dehany, of Hanover, J'ca, planter. Will dated 17 Aug. 1753. Philip Haughton Senior, of Hanover an Ex'or. (271, Pinfold.)

Philip Haughton of the p. of Hanover, J'ca, planter. Will dated 1 Feb. 1763. My wife Cath. to reside on any one of my estates of Fat Hog Quarter and Green Island, both in Hanover or Retirement in the p. of S[t] James, and house negroes and furn. Plate to my 3 daus. My bro. Jonathan H. £100. Sister Ann Tharpe £100. Nephews Rob. H. and R[d] H. sons of my bro. Jonathan H., and W. Tharpe s. of my sister Ann T. £100 ea. My nieces Cath. H., Ann H. and Mary H. daus. of my bro. Val. H., ea. a negro boy and girl at 21. To my dau. Mary James ½ of the sugar pl. called Green I. and the land I purch. f. belonging to W[m] James dec[d] and ⅓ the slaves, 24 mules and 40 working steers. To my grds. Ph. H. James the other ½ at 21 and £100 a yr. till then. I give her also a piece of land patented by W[m] Pusey containing 540 a., a piece patented by Mich. Corney c. 575 a., and 2 runs patented by W[m] Dorrell of 600 a. and ⅓ of the negroes and stock belonging to my penns. To my dau. Ann Clarke my sugar pl. called Fat Hog Quarter with 60 a. I purchased of John Heath and negroes and 24 mules and 40 steers. Also 200 a. called the Cockoon to the E. of the land I purchased of W[m] Tharpe and ⅓ of the negroes, etc. belonging to my penns. To my dau. Sarah H. my sugar pl[n] called Retirement in the p. of S[t] Jas. and slaves, 40 mules and 40 steers, the

ARMS.—*Sable, three bars Argent, on a canton Or a rose and thistle.*
CREST.—*A bull.*

Gerrard Hawten of Essington,⊤Margaret, youngest dau. of Lawrence
co. Oxford, 2nd son of Edward. │ Washington of Sulgrave, co. North-
(See the Visitation.) │ ampton. He died 26 Eliz.

Henry Hawtayne of Colthorp, co. Oxford, Esq.; of⊤Mary, dau. of John Doyley
Brasenose Coll., Oxf., matric. 10 Nov. 1598, aged 18; │ of Chiselhampton, co.
student of Gray's Inn 1604. │ Oxford.

A

Thomas Hawtayne, born 1607;⊤Katherine Gerrard Hawtayne, born   Henry
of Q. Coll., Oxf., matric. 1622, │ ....   1609; of Barbados, plan-   Haw-
aged 15; of Calthorpe 1634. │   ter, 1639, then aged 30;   tayne.
                                        M. of A. 1651.

B

Gerrard Hawtayne⊤Hester   Edward   Richard Hawtayne of⊤Rebecca
of Barbados.   │ Wiltshire, Hawtayne   Barbados, grandson │ Hirst,
                │ mar. 1680.   of St. Mary's, and overseer 1659 of │ mar.
                │   Jamaica,   Rd. Peers; of Christ │ 1665.
                │   1683.   Church 1680.
Gerrard Hawtayne, bapt. 1681.

½ a. I purchased of Corbt Lawrence and Baker whereon my storehouse is built
whence I ship my sugars, a parcel of land I purchased of Wm Tharpe containing

C

Eliz., dau.⊤Richard Haughton, born 1691,⊤Eliz., 3rd dau. and   Ann Haughton,
of Geo.   │ eldest son and heir; M. of A. │ coh. of Col. James mar. William
Goodin;   │ for Hanover 1726, Custos and │ Guthrie; remar.   Tharp of Han-
died 25   │ Col.; d. 15 Jan. 1740, aged 49. │ before 1743 Ed-   over. She and
Dec. 1734,│ M.I. at H. Court estate. Will │ ward Clarke, and   her son Wm.
aged 34. │ proved in Jamaica (Archer, │ died 14 Oct. 1764,   named in the
M.I. 2nd │ 332). His 1st wife Rebekah, │ aged 53. 3rd wife.   will of her
wife.   │ dau. of Tho. James, died 27 │   brother Philip.
          │ Jan. 1722, aged 26. M.I.

D

Richard Haughton, born⊤Mary, dau.   Jonathan,   Rebecca, born 1723; mar.
1726; of Esher and Ven- │ of Geo.   Philip and Col. Tho. Reid of St.
ture, Jamaica, and of │ Ricketts of George,   James. She died 11 April
Hornchurch, co. Essex; │ Canaan;   all died   1747, aged 24. M.I. at
of Magd. Coll., Oxf., │ died 27   young.   Golden Grove (Archer,
matric. 19 Oct. 1742, │ Dec. 1749,   329).
aged 16; of the Inner │ aged 19.
Temple 1742. Will dated   —
1762 (66, Cæsar).   Mary, mar. 29 March 1743
                                                 Col. John Reid, elder
s.p.   brother of Col. Tho. Reid.

307

300 a. and the old Pasture to the W. containing 1300 a., and ⅓ of the negroes belonging to my penns at 21 or M. My 4 grdch⁴ Cath. H. J., Mary H. J., Eliz. H. J. and Ph. H. Clarke £2000 each out of sums in the hands of Mʳ Mich. Atkins of Bl. at 21. All residue to my sd. 3 daus. I appoint Montague James, Simon Clarke, junʳ, Esqʳᵉˢ and Wᵐ Tharpe of Sᵗ Jas. with my wife Ex'ors and wife sole G. of my dau. Sarah H. and in default of issue of my 3 daus., est. to Wᵐ Tharpe and Rob. H. and Rᵈ H. sons of my bro. Jonath. H. In the presence of Jas. Anderson, Geo. Cumming, Geo. Slacker. P. 2 Mch. 1767 by Simon Clarke the yr., p. r. to M. J. Esq., and Cath. H. wid. the other surv. Ex'ors. (98, Legard.)

A
─────────────────────────────────────

Edward Hawtayne, born 1616; of=Eliz. | Jonathan Hawtayne of=...., dau.
Magd. Coll., Oxf., matric. 1634; .... | Barbados, gent., mort- | of Richard
aged 18; M.D. 1660; died 19 Dec. | gaged his moiety of | Peers of
1666; bur. in Salisbury Cathe- | Charles Fort plantation, | Barbados,
dral. Will (62, Carr). | Hole Town, 1643. | Esq.

B
─────────────────────────────────────

Jonathan Hawtayne of=Temperance | Eliz. Tom-=Valentine Hawtayne=Ann
Barbados; removed to | Baker, mar. | linson, | of Barbados, removed | ....
Jamaica 1670—5. | 1669; bur. | mar. 1666 | to Jamaica, where he | mar.
[According to Archer | 1670. | in Barba- | patented 1000 acres | 1672
he mar. Mary Dehany, | . | dos. | in St. Mary's 26 | in Bar-
and was father of Col. | | | Car. II.; living 1693. | bados.
Richd., b. 1691.]

Susanna Hawtayne, | Jonathan Hawtayne, bapt. 1667=Mary Dehany of
bapt. 1670. | in Barbados. | Vere.

C ─────────────────────────────────── C

Mary Haughton, mar. | Johanna Violet,=Jonathan Haughton,=Lydia, dau. of
John Brissett of Han- | died 2 Sept. | 2nd son, born 17 Dec. | Rob. Bowen
over, planter. His will | 1733, aged 30. | 1694; died 18 Feb. | of Westmore-
dated 1740. | M.I. | 1767, aged 72. M.I. | land; born
| | | 2 May 1710:
| | | mar. 19 June
| | | 1734; died 10   E
Jonathan Haughton, | Sarah, mar. | Frances, | Rebecca, mar. | Sept. 1755,
born 1728; d. 24 June | Col. Edw. | d. unmar. | John Waller, | leaving two
1753, aged 25. M.I. | Chambers | — | nephew of | sons and two
——— | of Prosper. | Eliz., d. | John Terrick, | daus. M.I.
Mary, mar. Dr. Wood. | | unmar. | Bp. of L. ~

D

Samuel Williams=Margaret | William Haughton. | Robert=Sarah
Haughton, born 1738; | Bonella, | — | Haughton, | Gar-
at Eton 1753; of the | dau. of | Eliz. Goodin Haugh- | born | brand
Inner Temple 1755; | ? .... | ton, mar. Sir John | 29 Aug. | Barrett,
of Queen's Coll., | Williams; | Taylor, Bart., of | 1733 (sic); | mar.
Oxf., matric. 11 Oct. | mar. before | Lyssons. He died | died 25 | 2 June
1756, aged 18; | 1769. | 1786, aged 41. | June 1766. | 1763.
Speaker; died 12 | (Ante, III., | W.I. Bookplate | M.I.
Aug. 1793. | 349.) | No. 539.

Sam. Haughton, born 10 April 1776; died Dec. 1778.   Eliz. Helen.
M.I. at Anglesea Pen.

308

Edw. Clarke of Trelawney in J., Esq. Will dated 23 Aug. 1773. My s. in l. (stepson) Sam Wms. Haughton.

In the Annals of Swainswick (quoted *Ante* I., 375) testator is stated to have been b. 1716 and to have m. Eliz. Guthrie, widow of Wm. Williams and dau. of Philip Haughton, but this is incorrect.

Richard Haughton l. of Venture in the I. of J., now of Hornchurch, co. Essex, Esq. Will dated 12 June 1762. My negro servants Diego and Nancy £1 10 c. a yr. and their freedom. To my bro. in l. John Reid, Esq. all sums due from my uncles Jonathan H. and Ph. H. Esquires in respect of the pers. est. of my l. F. dec^d. To my bro. in l. Tho. Reid my Bogue est. which was settled by Norwood Whitter, Esq. during my minority and while I was in Eng. and was taken possession of by John Moor. To Ben. Harding of Hornchurch, Esq., John Reid and Tho. Reid my third share of Orange Cove plantation which I purchased of Mrs. Clarke as her dower all my negro servants, sugar works and stocks thereon and when my interest ceases to transfer them to Esher pl., I give to sd. T. my pl. of Esher with all pieces of land I purch. of Michael Petgrave and my pl. at Venture, land called Sauls Land, 100 a. called Lewens, and a parcel of 36 a. my l. F. purch. of Valentine Haughton, my ¾ Allens Land devised to me and my 3 brothers by my l. F., Linches Land which I purch. of Tho. Linch, my moiety of Friendship Est. I purchased of John Thorp, Esq. (? Tharp), buildings, negroes, stock coppers on Trust to manage until the yst. of the chⁿ of my sisters Reb. Reid and Mary Reid by their husbands Tho. R. and John R. be 21 for the use of sd. ch^{rn}, and ship produce to Mr Wm Reynolds, M^t in L. and to sell when yst. ch^d is 21 and divide all proceeds, s^d T. to be Ex'ors, and on the death of Ben Harding, Wm Reynolds to be an Ex'or, and when either John or Tho. Reid die, Mr Chas. Heorn (?). P. 23 Feb. 1763 by B. Harding, Esq., p. r. to the others. (66, Cæsar.)

C

| Valentine= Haughton, 4th son. s.p.m. | Philip Haughton, 3rd son, born= Dec. 1700; died 22 Feb. 1765, aged 64. M.I. at Fat Hog Quarter in Hanover. Will (98, Legard). | Cath., dau. of John Tharp of Green Pond; born 1716; mar. 1735; had three sons and five daus.; died 7 May 1775, aged 59. M.I. |

E

| Richard Haughton, born 2 July 1747; died 14 Jan. 1779, bachelor.

Eliz. Haughton, mar. John Patterson, M.D., s.p.
—
Rachel Haughton, born 22 Dec. 1739; died 23 Feb. 1778, unmar. M.I. | Lydia Haugh- ton, born 3 Feb. 1745; died 19 July 1746. M.I. | Mary Haughton, coheir, mar. Col. Montague James. Their issue took the name and arms of Haugh- ton before James. | Ann Haughton, coheir, born in Jamaica 14 April 174–; mar. Sir Simon Clarke, 7th Bart. Her fortune £100,000. She died at Cheltenham 19 Sept. 1800. M.I. at Tewkesbury. His will dated 29 Oct. and sworn Nov. 1777 (220, Corn- wallis). |

It is not known why the Hawtaynes of Barbados changed the spelling of their name to aughton in Jamaica. Proof is desirable.

PARISH REGISTERS OF BARBADOS.*

MARRIAGES.

1665 Richard Hawtaine and Rebecca Hirst.
1666 Valentine Haughton and Elizabeth Tomlinson.
1669 Jonathan Haughton and Temperance Baker.
1672 Valentine Hawtaine and Ann Hawtaine.
1680 Gerard Haughtaine and Hester Wiltshire.
1708 Robert Haughton, married.
1711 Ann Haughton, married.
1715 Mary Haughton and John Wake.
1721 Hannah Haughton and John Blades.
1751 Rebecca Haughton, married.
1754 Mary Haughton, married.
1762 Robert Haughton and Elizabeth Cattlewell.

BAPTISMS.

1654 Rachel, dau. of Captain Hawton.
1667 Jonathan Haughton, s. of Valentine and Elizabeth.
1670 Susanna Hawtaine, dau. of Jonathan and Temperance Haughton.
1681 Gerard, s. of Gerard and Hester Haughtaine.
1687 Elizabeth and Mary, daus. of Robert and Elizabeth Haughton.
1693 Robert and Ann, children of Robert and Elizabeth Haughtaine.
1712 Mary Haughton, dau. of Robert and Agnes.
(?1715) Thomas Haughton, baptised.
1718 John Haughton, s. of Robert and Agnes.

BURIALS.

1645 Richard Hooten.
1670 Temperance Hawtain, wife of Jonathan Hawtain.
1691 Rowland Haughton.

1638. Edward Hawton & Gerrard Hawtaine owners of over 10 acres. (Memoirs of Barbados, p. 76.)

1639, June 28. Portus South'ton, Gerrard Haughton of 30 yeares, Com Ox'on. gen', free planter of the Barbathoes. (Hotten, 298.)

1640. Bond of Garrard Hawtaine in £1000 st. (Barbados Deeds, Vol. I., p. 20.)

1643, Sept. 15. I, Jonathan Hawtayne of B., gent. sell to Capt. Daniel Fletcher of B. my moiety of ye plantation called Charles Fort by the sea in the p. of St. James near The Hole which I lately purchased of him (the whole plⁿ being of 400 acres) as by his bill of sale dated yᵉ 14th inst. with buildings and servants together with one plⁿ which I purchased of Capᵗ Chr. Codrington by deed of sale of 20 March 1641 containing 100 a. and 8 negroes, but on payment to D. F. of 30,000 lbs. of tobacco well made up in rowle and wreathe on the last day of May next these presents to be void. Confirmed by Lieut. John Holmes. Inventory of servants and goods. (*Ibid.*, p. 92.)

1651, Nov. 5. Gerard Hawtayne as a M. of A. signed the Declaration. Gerard Hawtyn of Lee in Oxfordshire, mar. Margaret dau. of Abel Makepeace of Chipping Wardon, gent. (Cavaliers and Roundheads, by N. D. D., p. 218.)

1679, Aprill the first. Gerard Hawton in the ship Expedition for London, John Harding, Comander. Time out. Barbados tickets. (Hotten, 374.)

---

* The Cavaliers and Roundheads of Barbados by N. D. Davis, p. 108, extracts having been supplied by Mʳ Geo. Hammond Hawtayne, C.M.G.

1680. Richd Hawtaine owner of 30 a. in Christ Church. (G. H. H.)

From a deed of mortgage dated 27 Sept. 1693 it appears that Sir Tho. Lynch and Valentine Haughton, Esq., on 2 Nov. 1682, became partners in two plantations of 2020 acres in St. Mary's, 1000 a. of which had been patented to V. H. in 26 Charles II., bounded on Mr Edward Haughton. On adjustment of accounts V. H. owed £855. See a fuller abstract *Ante* II., 104, 148, 151. John Peers, Esq., of B'os settled a plantation of 1000 a. on the N. side of J'ca in 1672. He probably brought over his cousins the Hawtaynes and Hawtons, and may have handed over the land to them.

In Burke's Armory the Arms of Hawten of Calthorpe, Oxf., are:— *Or, on a fesse cottised Gules, three hinds heads erased of the last, a unicorn courant Argent.*

Hawton or Houghton of L. (Heralds Coll..c. 24) bore:—*Argent, three bars. Sable, in chief two mullets pierced of the second.*

Houghton (Aldⁿ of L. d. 31 Dec. 1596). *Sable, three bars Argent.* CREST:—*A bull.*

1793, Aug. 12. In Westmorland, J., the Hon. Samuel Williams Haughton, speaker of the assembly of that island, and one of the representatives for the parish of Hanover. (G. M., 1051.)

1798, April. In Falmouth, John Robertson, Esq., of New York, to Miss Eliza Haughton. (Columbian Mag.)

1800, Jan. In Vere, at Milk River, Mr. W. Haughton, to Miss Olivia Beal, of that parish. (*Ibid.*)

Mary, dau. of Geo. Ricketts of Canaan, m. Richd Haughton of Esher, J'ca. She d. 27 Dec. 1749 aged 19. (*Ante* I., 384.)

Livingston gives a ped. proved by two chancery suits of 1744 and 1783. (Sketch Pedigrees, 46.)

Neill Malcolm· of Poltalloch co. Argyll m. Mary dau. of John Brisset, Esq., and widow of Philip Houghton of J'ca, Esq. He d. 1 Ap. 1802 and was succeeded by his only son Neill, b. 26 July 1769. (Burke's L. G.)

1919. On the 23rd Jan., at Melrose, Cross Roads, Jamaica, Roger Swire Haughton, J.P., of Kingston, Jamaica.

Analostan (Barbadoes) Island 1865.

DR JAMES HENDY

By

E. M. S.

Dr. James Hendy, the eldest son of Doctor James Hendy of Barbados and Jane (Polegreen) his wife[1], was born in St. Michael and baptised there 17 December 1750.

He went to Scotland to study medicine, and was elected to the Medical Society of Edinburgh on 26 December 1772. Influenced by the prevailing interest in the lymphatic system he devoted his researches to it. He graduated M.D. at Edinburgh University in 1774 having written and presented a thesis *Tentamen Pyhsioiogicum de secretione glandulari* which was published in Edinburgh the same year. He continued his medical education at Middlesex Hospital and wrote and published an Essay on Glandular Secretion containing an experimental enquiry into the formation of Pus: and a critical examination into an opinion of Mr. John Hunter "That the Blood is alive". London: Printed for John Bell near Exeter Exchange, Strand, MDCCLXXV. 8vo.

The above Essay written from London under date January 1775 was dedicated to the Faculty of Middlesex Hospital. It gives the result of experiments made in Edinburgh from 21 June 1774 and afterwards; and also records observations made while he was studying at Middlesex Hospital.

Not long after (1775) he returned to his native country to practise his profession. On 31 May 1776 he married Lucy Alleyne at the Parish church of St. James, the daughter of Dr. Abel Alleyne of Mount Standfast, Barbados, and Jane (Skeete) his wife.

He pursued his researches in the subject of the Glandular Disease of Barbados while practising as a physician generally and as Physician to H.M. Naval Hospital at Barbados. On 13 November 1783 he was appointed by Governor David Parry to be Physician General of all the Militia Forces in the Island—a post of great honour and distinction.

His years of experience and practice in the then prevalent glandular disease, sometimes called "elephantiasis", prompted him to compile a Treatise thereon; the author's chief intention (as he says) "was to satisfy . . . the enquiries of

1. Marriage, St. Michael's Register, 9 April 1748, Doctor James Hendy and Jane Polegreen, spinster. He is described as a merchant in his Will dated 5 July 1777, proved 22 July 1777. He was probably an apothecary with the courtesy title of "Doctor" and carried on a mercantile business as well as an apothecary's shop. His four children James, Philip, Henry and Jane and his "cousin" James Polegreen are named in his will.

strangers concerning a disorder which never fails to attract the notice of the curious." The title of the work is "A Treatise on the Glandular Disease of Barbadoes: proving it to be seated in the lymphatic system. By James Hendy, M.D. Member of the Edinburgh Royal Medical Society, Physician to His Majesty's Naval Hospital at Barbadoes and Physician General to the Militia of the Island. London: Printed for C. Dilly in the Poultry, MDCCLXXXIV". The frontispiece shows elephantiasis in a patient named Daniel Massiah. The work is dedicated in terms of affection to "the worthy and respectable inhabitants of His Majesty's Antient and Loyal Colony of Barbadoes, to whom I am greatly indebted for every comfort of life and for whom I shall ever retain sentiments of gratitude." It contains notes from his case book from June 1781 onwards.

The book was translated into French by Jos. L. J. Fr.-Ant. Allard, and printed in Mem. de la Soc. Med. d'emulation de Paris, tom IV.

The following year, J. Rollo, published a criticism of the work — "Remarks on the disease lately described by Dr. Hendy under the appelation of the glandular disease of Barbados." London: 1785. 8vo. To this criticism Hendy replied by a "Vindication of the opinions and facts contained in a treatise on the glandular disease in Barbadoes. By James Hendy. M.D. London:" 1789, 8vo. 2nd. Ed. 1790 8vo. Member of the Edinburgh Royal Medical Society; Physician during the late war to H.M. Naval Hospital at Barbadoes; Physician General to the Militia; and one of the Physicians to the General Dispensary of the Island. London: Printed for C. Kearsley. No. 46, Fleet Street, MDCCLXXXIX[2]. The book was dedicated to Sir John Gay Alleyne, Bart., Speaker of the House of Representatives at Barbadoes by the Author "having the honour by a near family union with you[3] of becoming intimately acquainted with the many amiable qualities and polite accomplishments which adorn your private character". It was subscribed by Hendy as from Bridge-Town. Barbadoes, May 16th. 1788.

The exact date and place of Hendy's death have not been discovered. It occurred sometime between the date of his Will, 20 August 1794 and that of the probate, 6 December 1794.[4] There is no record of his burial in the Church Registers. It is possible that he went to England and died there. His widow, Lucy, then of St. Michael, on 5 April 1799 gave a power of attorney (on her leaving the Island) to Hon. Jonathan Blenman and Richard Cobham to manage her affairs. She lived in England and had her residence near Bath. Her death was announced in *The Barbados Mercury* of 4 February 1815. The date of the event is not given.

Dr. Hendy and his wife had issue eleven children —

1. James Alleyne Hendy, —   b. 9 April 1777.
2. Abel Dottin Hendy, —   b. 10 April 1780. d. 7 Aug. 1780.
3. Lucy Hendy —   —   b. 7 Sep. 1781. d. 7 Sep. 1782.
4. Abel Dottin Hendy, —   b. 30 Sep. 1782.
5. Lucy Alleyne Hendy, —   b. 1 Dec. 1783
6 Henry Hendy, —   —   b.   1784. d. 6 Nov. 1827.
7. Francis Skeete Hendy, —   b. 11 Sep. 1785. d. 25 Oct. 1785.
8. Judith Hendy —   —   b. 1 May 1788.
9. Susanna Hendy   —   b. 14 Sep. 1789.
10. Elizabeth Jones   Hendy   b. 1 Mar. 1791
11. Francis Hendy   —   b. 3 Dec. 1794. posthumously.

The eldest son, James Alleyne Hendy, graduated M.D. 1802 at Edinburgh.

He was living in Chelmsford. Essex, in December 1810 when he signed a power of attorney to his brother. Henry Hendy of Bridgetown. Henry Hendy was an Assistant Commissary General in H.M. service in Barbados when he died suddenly on 6 Nov. 1827.

The Hendy family was established in Barbados late in the XVII century There is only one known male descendant now living in this island.

E. M. S.

2. Most of the above facts are from "Dictionnaire Historique de la Médicine Ancienne et Moderne" Dezeimeris. Tom. III. Pt.1. Paris 1836; and *Bibliotheca Britannica*. R. Watt, L. Edin. 1824, extracts having been kindly furnished me by Dr. J. J. Keevil of the Royal College of Physicians.

3. Dr. James Hendy's wife, Lucy, was a sister of Jane Abel Alleyne who married her cousin, Sir John Gay Alleyne—Alleyne Pedigree. B.M.H.S. Journal, Vol. 14, Page 37. *

4. Will of James Hendy of St. Michael, Doctor of Physic. To my wife (not named) £3,000. Also £3,000 of real property and estate in trust for my children born and unborn (my wife being now enceinte) at 21 or marriage. Wife to be executrix and guardian of my children; after her death, Dr. Robert Lovell of Bristol under whose kind care my son, James, now is, to be guardian of my son James, and my brother, Philip Hendy, Valentine Jones, and Richard Cobham of Barbados to be guardians.

Dated 20 Aug. 1794. Witnesses: Grant Ellcock, Samuel Hinds Jr. Saml. Perry. Proved 6 Dec. 1794.

* For Vol. 14, p. 37 (read Vol. 4, p. 35) see p. 35, this volume.

Higinbotham of Barbados.

The following records were forwarded by Mr. William M. Sweeny of the Custom House, New York City. The Editor has made abstracts of the wills to save space. The entries from the parish register are unfortunately not in full:—

17 Sept. 1649. I, Otwell Higginbotham, in the Barbadoes, being bound in a voyage for England. The £250 I am to receive by bill of exchange I bestow as follows: To my father Oliver Higginbotham and Anne my mother £20. To my brother William £10. Brother John £20. Brother Oliver £5. To William Higginbotham, son and heir of my body, £50. My daughter Anne £25. My cosen Capt. John Higginbotham in the Barbadoes £5. Cosens John, Joan, Martha, Alice, Sara and Priscilla, children of the said Capt. John Higginbotham, £30 amongst them. Cosen Mary Higginbotham, daughter to said Capt. John, £20. Katherine, wife of John Bunce, and her children, £20. Alice Zeale £5. For my funeral £20. All other my estate in England or elsewhere, land or otherwise, I give unto my son and heir William Higginbotham, and I make Nicholas Higginbotham of Cheshire in England, and Capt. John Higginbotham in the Barbadoes, who is my attorney, my executors. Witnesses: Tho. Higginbotham, Tho. Zealell. Proved 30 Jan. 1651-2 by Nicholas Higginbotham, power being reserved to the other executor. (P.C.C. Bowyer, 6.)

John Higinbotham of St Philip's, Barbados, Senr. Will dated 19 Sept. 1672. To my son Capt John H. 2000 lbs. of sugar, besides the 70 acres I settled him in, and acquit him of all accounts when I sold unto him and Left Sam. Tweney the work and 60 acres or for his voyage to Jamaica and New England. I also give him 60 feet square of land on Carlisle Bay between Mrs Griffin's house and the sea. To Chas. H, my grandson 1000 lbs., and to his two sisters Jane and Millicent 500 lbs. each at the age of 15. To my dau. Joane Waitte, widow, 2000 lbs., and to her four children Tho. Gibbs, John Gibbs, Higinbotham Gibbs and Jane Gibbs 1000 lbs. each at 21 the two sons, and 15 the two daus., and quitclaim to her the plantation whereon she now lives, being 50 acres, she giving equal portions to them at 21 only to Tho. Gibbs her eldest son to have 4000 lbs. more. To my dau. Martha Knightly 3000 lbs., and to her three children Shedon K., John K., and Martha K. all my plantation in the Thicketts where they live, about 25 acres, with the houseing built when the eldest son Shedon attains 21, and I give them the negroes Sampson and his wife Mingo, Winbar and his child Pefoe. My dau. to have the management or 6000 lbs. apiece. To my dau. Mary Townsend wife of Lieut. Richard T. 2000 lbs., and to him 500 lbs., and to my three grandchildren Tho. T., Alice T., and John T. 500 lbs. each at 15, and to the child wherewith my dau. now goeth 500 lbs. To Nicholas Buckerfield late husband to my deceased Goddau. (sic) Alice 200 lbs., and to his two sons my grandchildren Nicholas and Higinbotham B. 1000 lbs. each at 12. To my dau. Sarah H. 14 acres next to Mr Francis Dethickshire from Exors long gully square over to Dr Tho. Parkins, but my wife to enjoy one half the crop of ginger, cane or corn, and I give her one negro woman Nen Judy, and one wench Ocain, and a girl Black Jane, one bedsted of Bully tree and a cedar tester and 4000 lbs. and one year's maintenance. To my dau. Priscilla Long 3000 lbs., and to her two daus. Merandila Clenen and Mellicent Clenen 500 lbs. each at 18. To my granddau. Jane Beleffe 1600 lbs. at 21, and have her stock of cattle and sheep. To my natural brother Lt Tho. Higinbotham 2000 lbs., and my sister his wife 100 lbs., and to Margt Jones 500 lbs., and to his two children Nicholas and Eliz. each 500 lbs. at 21. To my nephews Sam. Finny and Joseph Higinbotham 500 lbs. each, and to coz. Finney's wife Mary 500 lbs., and to their son Jeffrey my grand (sic, but ? god) son 500 lbs. at 16. To my dau. Sarah H. the house and lands rented to Mrs Griffin at the Bay for which she pays 50s. by the year.

I give my dau. Priscilla Long my tenement at the Carlisle Bay wherein Mr Hampton lives and pays 50s. rent. To my son Capt. John H. my tenement on Carlisle Bay rented to Mr Robert Gibson in lieu of the 60 feet square, and the latter I give to my two daus. Joane Waite and Martha Knightly. To my wife Alice all the rest of my estate, she paying my debts and legacies, and leave her sole Ex'trix.

Codicil, 21 Feb. 1672. If wife die suddenly the Ordinary to appoint a trustee. In the presence of Tho. Parkins, David Evans, Sibbell Powell, Tho. Wormbarton. By his Excellency, the 13 Oct. 1673, Dr Tho. Parkins, David Evans and Tho. Wormbaton made oath that they did see Lt Coll. John H. seal and publish his will. Signed " R. Colleton." Entered 27 Nov. 1673.

John Higinbotham of Barbados, bound off for the recovery of my health. Will dated 21 March 1682. To my wife Jane all my estate, and Ex'trix. To my kinsmen Mr John H. and Mr Joseph H. 15s. apiece for a ring. To my good friends Major John Johnson and Mr Geo. Mason each £10 st., and to be overseers. In the presence of Will. Tusson, Edw. Cutler. By the R^t Hon. the Lt Gov., Mr Edw. Cutler appeared and was sworn. Given at Fontabelle 7 Nov. 1687. Signed " Edwyn Stede." Entered 9 Nov. 1687.

Tho. Higinbotham of Barbados and p. of St Philip. Will dated 13 July 1679. Small estate. To my son Nicholas and dau. Eliz. all my estate equally at 19, if both die then to my kinsman Sam. Finney and his three children John, Samuel and Mary, he to be sole Ex'or, and I give him and his wife a gold ring. In the presence of John Gibbs, Wm. Lewis. By L. E. appeared both witnesses and were sworn this 16 March 1679. Signed " J. Atkins." Entered 16 March 1679.

Joseph Higinbotham of Barbados and p. of St Philip, merchant. Will dated 6 April 1693. To my wife Eliz. H. all my estate, and sole Ex'trix. In the presence of Willburring Merrey, Tho. Gibbs, Sam. Finney, J^r, John Frizell, J^r, Sam. Smith. By L. E. John Frizell, J^r, appeared and was sworn 9 May 1693. Signed " Kendall." Entered 17 Aug. 1693.

Charles Hegenbotham of the p. of St Philip and I. of Barbados, gent. Will dated 17 Aug. 1732. To my wife Ann H. the negro women Folly, Cubba and Accamema, Violet and Quashebah girls, and Benn, Cuffey and Bemass boys, and all my household goods and cow. To my son Cleavor H. the reversion of the above. To my granddau. Ann Reddin a negro girl Sarah. My granddaus. Hepsibah H. and Ann H. All residue to my son John H. My wife to be sole Ex'trix. In the presence of R^d Sandford, Tho. Heggenbotham. By his Excellency Mr Tho. H. appeared and was sworn. At Pilgrim 20 May 1734. Signed " Howe." Entered 28 May 1734.

Ann Heggenbotham of St Philips, Barbados. Will dated 29 March 1740. To my son John H. 5s. as a bar against any demand. To my son Chas. H. 5s. in like manner. To my three sons Tho., Joseph and Cleavor H. £3 c. each annually for 4 years. To my son Tho. H. a negro Robinson. To my grandson John Redan at 21 £20 c. To my granddau. Ann Redan at 21 a negro woman and the land and building wherein I dwell, being 10 a., also goods and furniture, and to be Ex'trix. My friend Sam. Lashley and Roger Weeks Ex'ors in trust and Guardians. In the presence of John Irondall, Wm Peckerin. By his Excellency Mr John Irondall appeared and was sworn. At Pilgrim 28 Aug. 1740. Signed " Robert Byng."

Wm. Higginbotham of St Philip's, Barbados. Will dated 22 Sept. 1748. To my cozen Joseph Waith one negro Jack and a woman Sesley, and sole Ex'or. Signed with his mark. By his Excellency Jos. Bayley appeared and was sworn. At Pilgrim 7 April 1749. Signed "H. Grenville."

John Higinbotham of the p. of St Thomas in the East, Jamaica. Will dated 5 Feb. 1739. To my son Tho. Higinbotham Alice Nusum, 4 negro boys (*sic*). To my friend Dorothy Nusum 2 negro boys. To my son Chas. H. my riding horse. All residue to my son Tho. Higinbotham Alice Nusum. My son John H. now residing in Barbados. Dorothy Nusum to be sole Ex'trix. Signed by his mark. In the presence of John Plimly, Peter Bascom. On 26 July 1744 appeared John Plimley and made oath. Signed "Edwd Trelawny." Dorothy Nusum renounced 26 July 1744, in the presence of Tho. Mascall. Entered 26 July 1744 in Lib. 24, fo. 135. Jamaica.

1638. John Higinbotham, owner of 10 acres or more.
1666. Barbadoes. Gentlemen of the country : Lieut.-Col. Higginbottom, a stout man and fit for command. (Col. Cal., p. 413.)
John Higginbotham was clerk of the Assembly from 1670—1682. His salary was £100 or 20,000 lbs. His last letter was dated Jan. 4, 24, 1682, and at the new election of 25 April his name disappeared. The Election of his kinsman Sam. Finney for St Philip's was voided.
Census of 1680. St. Michael's. Jn° Higginbotham and wife, 5 acres, 2 servants, 3 slaves. (Hotten, 441 and 455.)
Chr. Codrington II. leased on Feb. 1683 for 11 years at the rent of £2200 st. all those 2 plantations called Didmarton and Consett of 750 acres in the p. of St. John to Capt. John Higginbotham. (See Close Roll of 1699, "Antigua," i., 153.)

EXTRACT FROM BAPTISMAL REGISTERS, 1637—1750.

Year.	Name.	Parish.
1650	Higginbotham, Bridget	St. Philip.
1655	Heginbotham (Child of)	,,
1657	Higinbotham, Joane	,,
1661	,, John	,,
1664	,, Charles	,,
1667	,, Jane	,,
1673	,, Hepzibah	,,
1677	,, John	,,
1678	,, Elizabeth	,,
1678	,, Bula	,,
1679	,, Joseph	,,
1684	,, Rebekah	,,
1686	,, Joseph	,,
1686	,, Elizabeth	,,
1689	,, Sarah	,,
1695	,, John	,,
1696	,, Charles	,,
1699	,, Thomas	,,
1701	,, Ann	

Year.	Name.	Parish.
1701	Higinbotham, William	St. Philip.
1703	„ Joseph	„
1718	„ Charles	Christ Church.
1722	Higginbotham, Sarah	St. Michael.
1722	Higinbotham, Hephzibah	St. Philip.
1724	Higginbotham, Melicent	Christ Church.
1724	Higinbotham (Son of John)	St. Philip.
1726	Higginbotham, Benjamin	Christ Church.
1726	Higenbotham (Son of Thomas)	St. Philip.
1728	Higginbotham, Susanna	Christ Church.
1729	„ Roebuck	St. Michael.
1736	„ Elizabeth	Christ Church.
1736	„ John	St. Philip.
1738	Higinbotham, Mary	„
1738	„ John	„
1739	Higginbotham, Benjamin	Christ Church.
1739	Higinbotham, Cleaver	St. Philip.
1742	Higginbotham, Esther	Christ Church.
1745	„ John	„
1747	„ Esther	„
1747	„ John	„

EXTRACT FROM MARRIAGE REGISTERS, 1643—1768.

Year.	Name.	Parish.
1674	Higinbotham, Sarah	St. Philip.
1676	„ Joseph	„
1677	„ Jno.	St. Michael.
1682	Higginbotham, Rebecca	„
1685	Higinbotham, Martha	„
1685	„ Mary	„
1688	Higginbotham, Charles	St. Philip.
1695	„ Sarah	St. Michael.
1706	„ Elizabeth	St. Philip.
1714, Jan. 11	Higinbotham, Joh^a and Henry Dewick	„
1715	Higginbotham, Thomas	St. Michael.
1717, Apr. 5	Higinbotham, John and Susanna Walker	Christ Church.
1717	„ Mary	St. Philip.
1721	Higginbotham, Thomas	„
1732	„ Cleaver	„
1754	„ Elizabeth	St. Michael.
1755	„ Susanna	Christ Church.
1763	„ Benjamin	St. Philip.

EXTRACT FROM BURIAL REGISTERS, 1644—1755.

Year.	Name.	Parish.
1674	Higinbotham, Mary	St. Philip.
1679	„ Hepzibah	„
1684	Higginbotham, Joseph	„
1684	„ John	St. Michael.

Year.	Name.	Parish.
1687	Higginbotham, John	St. Michael.
1693	Higinbotham, Jane	,,
1693	,, (Son of Joseph)	St. Philip.
1700	Higginbotham, Jno.	St. Michael.
1701	,, Mary	,,
1705	,, Henry	Christ Church.
1724	,, Margaret	St. Michael.
1726	,, Benjamin	Christ Church.
1726	,, Millicent	,,
1732	,, Elizabeth	St. Michael.
1754	,, Esther	,,
1755	,, John	,,
1755	,, Jonathon	Christ Church.

HOOPER OF BARBADOS.

CENSUS OF BARBADOS, 1679. Hooper names taken from the list. Parish of St. Michael, the Country. CHRISTOPHER HOOPER, 25 acres, one hired servant, ten slaves.

Parish of St. George. MR. ROBERT HOOPER, 219 acres, two white servants, 117 negroes.

Parish of Christ Church. JONATHAN HOOPER. 50 acres, 17 negroes.

CRISPINE HOOPER, 100 acres.

DANIEL HOOPER [no land] 2 white servants, 9 negroes.

Tickets issued by the Secretary to passengers abroad. June 17, 1679, *Hooper Daniell*, in the Ketch *Joseph* for New York, Abraham Knott, Commander.

List of Soldiers in Col. Lyne's Regiment. Owners of plantations which send men to the troop—MR. CRISPIN HOOPER, 6 men, 6 Jan. 1679. Col. Bates Regiment, freemen that serve for themselves, John Hooper, John Hooper. Col. Robinson's Troop. MR. CHRISTOPHER HOOPER.

CENSUS OF BARBADOS, 1715.

Parish of Christ Church.

	age.		age.
Jonathan Hooper	17	Robart Letts. Hooper	33
Martha Hooper	33	Sarah, his wife	32
Danniell, her son	13	Daniell, his son	12
John, her son	10	James, his son	10
Joseph, her son	8	Robart Letts., his son	7
Matthew, her son	7	John Birkett	17
Benjamin, her son	6	James Power	22
Thomas, her son	4	John Hartle	28
Elizabeth, her dau.	5		

Parish of St. George. List collected by Dan Hooper.

	age.		age.
John Hooper	40	Collo. Edward Hooper	27
Lettice Hooper	38	Anna Hooper (since	
Robert Hooper	14	decd.)	59
Sarah Hooper	12	Francis Hooper	29
James Hooper	7	Robert Hooper	4
John Hooper	6		
Lettice Hooper	3		
Edward Hooper	1		
Dan. Hooper	36	Phillippa Hooper	7
Phillippa Hooper	34	Reynold Hooper	5
Jane Hooper	12	Eleanor Hooper	3½
Daniel Elliott Hooper	10	James Hooper	1/3

Parish of St. Michael.

William Hooper, 4 men ages 26, 21, 35, 35, 1 woman 40, 4 boys, ages 20, 18, 15, 13, 2 girls, 16, 12.

Parish of St. Philip.

Elizabeth Hoopper, single woman, 30.

Mary Hoopper, 3. Joseph Hoopper 1.

HOTTEN'S LIST OF EMIGRANTS. Prisoners at Wells to be transported. In a receipt for 100 prisoners on Mr. Nepho's acct. to be sent to Barbados, 20 Septr. 1685. JOHN HOOPER. The name occurs twice in the list.

HOOPER WILLS RECORDED IN BARBADOS.

By the President. Whereas I have been informed by Mr. Roger Wotton that you whose names are underwritten have entered Caveats in the Secretary's office for several sums of sugar due to you from the estate of THOMAS HOOPER decd., and said Wotton doth desire Letters of Admin. to said estate, he being the greatest creditor: These are in His Majesty's name to command you to appear before me at my house on Monday next by three of the clock in the afternoon to show cause why Letters should not be granted to said Wotton. 8 August 1662. Sd. Hum: Walrond, President. To Mr. John Sparke, Mr. John Bowden. Mr. James Pearce, Capt. John Ryder, Lt. Christopher White, Mrs. Anne Robinson now wife of George Walton.

Note. Rev. Thomas Hooper was Minister of St. Michael from 1657 until his death in 1662. Roger Wotton complained to the Vestry that he was "burdened by the maintenance of Christopher Hooper, son of ye late Minister, his mother who was in England taking no care for his maintenance, and there being no estate of his father to relieve him". The Vestry resolved that "the Churchwarden doe put ye said Christopher Hooper an apprentice to some merchant of ye towne or other, where they shall think fit and what charges he shall be at shall be allowed by ye Vestry". He was accordingly apprenticed to Mr. John Rookeby, merchant, for eight years.
The Minister's Widow, Mrs. Ursula Hooper, petitioned the Vestry for her husband's unpaid salary amounting to 20,000 lbs. of muscovado sugar and was granted the amount. She afterwards married Mr. Henry Hutchinson.

13 March 1636 according to computation of Church of England. I ANTHONY HOOPER of city of New Sarum in Co. Wilts, Merchant. [Many pious words.] My body to be buried in the parish church of St. Thomas, New Sarum, towards the reparation of which church I give 40/-, and to the Minister of God's word there 40/-. £100 to be spent about my funeral; to 100 poor people of the city of New Sarum £10 to be equally divided amongst them.

To the Company of Merchants within the said city £10 to be bestowed as they shall think fit. Towards the reparation of the church of Ploweatt in Britain near St. Malo £6, and to the Minister there £4. To Thomas Banes, mariner, £20. To my godson, Anthony Lyne, £10. My executors to pay my brother-in-law John Le Poutre £500 which I give to the first two children that he shall have by my sister Katherine his now wife. To my sister Martha Hooper £1,000, and to my sister Mary Hooper £600, to be paid them within 6 months after their marriage days, and in the meantime for their maintenance and education, provided they marry with the consent of my executors.

To my brother, Robert Hooper, £1,000 at 21, and in the meantime for his education and maintenance and preferment in the trade of merchandising, in which course of life I desire my executors to cause him to be brought up. [Provision against his estate being diminished by loss at sea]. An abstract of my estate made by my partner, Jacob Le Gay before my last coming from St. Malo.

To my grandmother Mrs. Katherine Baines and to her grandchild my cousin Katherine Baines £5. To my friends Jacob Le Gay and John Page, merchants, resident in St Malo £5 each, and to John Windover of Sarum, gent, £3 to buy them rings. I forgive Henry Orgatt, merchant, 30/- which he oweth me, and I give him 30/- more.

Residue of my estate to my brother Thomas Hooper, whom I make sole executor; and my friends Thomas Hooper, gent, my uncle, and Barnaby Coles, gent, my said brother-in-law John Le Poutre and Thomas Batter, merchants, and Ambrose Ringwood of New Sarum to be overseers of my Will and assistants to my executor, and I give them £5 each. I appoint that £250 be paid to such of my father's creditors as shall make it appear that my father died indebted to them, to be divided proportionately to their debts. (Sd.) Anthony Hooper. Witnesses: Thomas Oviat, Jno. Windover, Giles Batter, Ambrose Ringwood.

An exemplification of the Will allowed in the P.C.C. and proved before Francis Willoughbye in Barbados states that at the time of his death Anthony Hooper was of the parish of St Nicholas Acon: in London, and was a bachelor.

19 December 1667. ROBERT HOOPER of Barbados Esq. If I die in Barbados my body to be buried in St. Philip church, and the expense of my funeral not to exceed 20,000 lbs. muscovado sugar.

I give all my lands plantations stock and other estate in Barbados or elsewhere to my only son Robert Hooper, charged with the following yearly sums. To my kinsman, Edward Hooper, of Horncourt, co. Southampton, Esq., my friend Richard King of Upham, co. Wilts, Esq., Peer Williams of Trayes June [Gray's Inn] co. Middlesex, Esq., brother-in-law to my dear wife, Katherine, lately decd., to each of them £50.

My dear brother Peer Williams shall take care of and bring up my son, and in case of Peer's death, then my said . . . Edward, and in case of his death, then my friend Richard. . . . I allow £50 a year for my son Robert's maintenance.

To my sister-in-law Mrs. Elizabeth Bramston and to Frances her daughter their living on my plantation in the same condition as they have done hitherto for so long as they shall please, and I give my said sister £26 per annum, and to her daughter Frances £24 a year for 3 years, and then £400.

To my loving friends, William Sharpe, Richard Howell, James Cowes, Robert Le Gard Esq. and Crispin Hooper, merchant, all of this Island 5,000 lbs. of sugar a piece. Friend Crispin Hooper to remain and dwell on my plantation and manage the same for the advantage of my son Robert, and to have his comfortable substance thereon and £200 a year until my debts are paid, and £300 a year until my son attains 21. My loving friends and kinsmen Edward Hooper, Richard King, and Peer Williams executors in trust for my son Robert.

If no son of mine living, then my plate to Crispin Hooper, my jewels to Frances Branston, and the plantation to be sold to Crispin at a reasonable price and the money divided between the children of my kinsman Edward Hooper, of Peer Williams, and of Crispin Hooper equally, except £500 to be paid to the poor of New Sarum.

Appoint my friends William Sharpe, Richard Howell, James Cowes, Robert Le Gard and Crispin Hooper, all of Barbados, overseers of my Will. (Sd.) Robert Hooper. MEMORANDUM. Whereas Mr. William Williams of Milk Street, merchant, unckle to my deare wife Katherine lately decd. and Mrs. Mary Williams, mother of my said wife, promised at their death to give me £500 in addition to the portion with my wife, now I will that if they shall do accordingly then I give unto Frances Branston £400 more than already given her in my will. (Sd.) Robert Hooper. Witnesses: Richard Hawkyns, Abraham Tillard, Char: Beauvoir. 13 May 1669. Proved by oaths of Col. Richard Hawkins and Mr. Abraham Tillard. (Sd.) Christopher Codrington.

I GILBERT HOOPER now resident in Barbados, mariner. To my wife, Ruth, all my estate, both that which is in co. Missenden and my wages due to me in this Island, and she to be sole executrix for herself and my children. My trusty friend John Sutten of Barbados to be overseer of my Will. Dated 1 Jan. 1675. (Sd by his mark) Gilbert Hooper. Witnesses: John Hall, Andrew Gall, Daniel Kingson. Proved Jan. 26, 1675. J. Atkins.

30 September 1685. I CRISPIN HOOPER of St. George, Barbados, merchant. To be buried in St. George's church. To the poor of West Alving, co. Devon, (being the place of my birth, £100, to be put out at interest by the churchwardens. To the poor of St. George's where I now live £25 to be divided by my overseers. To my dear friend Mrs. Thomasin Bastard (living in or near Kingsbridge, co. Devon,) in grateful love of her constancy to me £200. To my eldest sister, Elizabeth Woolcott (of same town of Kingsbridge) £25 per an. during her life. To John Woolcott, son of my said sister £50 and £150 to be divided among his children. To my sister Grace Hooper living in the parish of Avalong Ifford near the town of Kingsbridge aforesaid £200. To my half brother Gyles Hooper living in the town of Aishbertonin in Devon £50 and to his son Crispin £50 and £250 to be divided

amongst the rest of my said brother's children. To my half sister Mary Hooper living near Kingsbridge £50 and to her two children £20 each. To my niece Mary Asshe of Lanceston, co. Cornwall (dau. of my brother Henry Hooper decd.) £130. To my nephew Mr. Richard Asshe (husband of my said niece) Goldsmith in Lanceston £50 to buy him a ring to wear for my sake. To Mr. Robert Hooper, son of Coll. Robert Hooper decd. £100 and to his good wife Mrs. Ursula Hooper £50. To Mrs. Frances Martin (widow of Captn. William Martin decd.) now living in Barbados £150 and in case of her death to her son John and her dau. Elizabeth. I give 40 mourning rings to friends in Barbados at the discretion of my exors.

My exors. to purchase of Mr. Robert Hooper the freedom of the negro Kate to the end she may be free. To her little son, William, his freedom for ever, he being mine to dispose of by virtue of Mr. Robert Hooper's gift to me as appears by his letter to me of 2 May, 1684, and I desire my exors. to give him Christian education.

To Major Richard Salter living in the parish of St. George and Captn. Joseph Salmon of St. Michael £50 each.

I appoint Crispin Hooper son of Robert Hooper Esq. living in England to be my exor., and he being a minor I appoint my loving friends Richard Salter and Joseph Salmon Snr. exors. in trust until the said Crispin attains 21. If either of my exors. should die, I appoint Captn. Edward Claypoole. If Crispin should die I appoint his father Mr. Robert Hooper exor. (Sd) Crispin Hooper Witnesses: Robert Draper, Jonathan Shipley, William Griffith, James Salmon. Proved 27 Novr. 1686, before Edwyn Stede.

Codicil to Will of CRISPIN HOOPER. I give to Mrs. Frances Martin, widow, the following debts due me:— Coll. Cristopher Codrington £100, Paul Lyte of St. George's Esq. £200, John Gray of Christ Church gent and Mrs. Frances Gray widow £100. Dated 3 Novr. 1686. (Sd.) Crispin Hooper. Wits: Leolin Lloyd, Robert Wilkinson, Robert Hiensall. Proved 27 Novr. 1686.

Will of JONATHAN HOOPER of Barbados, gent. To my wife Elizabeth all my estate until my sons, Oistin H. and John H. attain 24, then she is to have one-third part of my estate out of my plantation below the Rock and also my land ten acres and house, abutting on lands of Hon. Samuel Newton lately decd., Nathaniel Kingsland, and Edward Herbert, and all my negroes for her life and widowhood. After her decease my plantation below the Rock of 42 acres Abutting on John Gunning, David Moody, Parick Cunningland, John Stripes, Eliz. Knowles, Saml. Terrill and Thos. Bunton, and the negroes thereon for my son Oistin and the heirs of his body, whom failing, for my son John and his heirs, whom failing, for my son Andrew now in England and my dau. Mary now in Barbados.

To my son John H. at 24 my plantation of 10 acres and three men and six women slaves, and failing him, for my son Oistin, and failing him for such child as my wife now goeth with, whom failing, for my son Andrew and dau. Mary.

To my dau. Elizabeth £500 at 20 or marriage, if she marries with consent of her mother. £500 to the child my wife now goeth with. To my son Andrew 20/-. My dau. Mary to have her maintenance until marriage and £50. I appoint my wife and my well-beloved brother Capt. James Oistin and Mr. John Gray overseers and £5 each to buy them rings. Dated 20 May, 1685. (Sd.) Jona. Hooper. Wits: Love Justice, Robert Wilkinson, William Smith, Isaac Ragg. Proved by I. Ragg 18 August, 1687, before Edwyn Stede.

December 5, 1699. Will of ROBERT HOOPER of St. George, Barbados, Esq. To the parish church of St. George my old and new testament with the cutts in folio in two vols. which I order to be delivered to the minister of the said parish immediately after my decease. To two poor families of the said parish £10 each. To my dau. Katherine H. £2,000 within 3 years after my decease, and £100 per an. to be paid her in England until her portion is paid. Also my negro woman Quashie and my diamond ring and £200 when she marries to buy her a coach and horses. Also £50 per ann. for life commencing 7 years from my death.

My dear wife Anna H. shall remain and dwell in my mansion house during widowhood and the use of the gardens and her accommodation at the charge of my plantation, and use of my plate and household stuff, two riding horses, and live stock, and the use of my negroes to care them, and £800 payable £100 yearly. Also my new coach and six horses, my sedan, and her saddle, and also all plate bought since our marriage with R.H.A. and her gold watch and all my English books, negroes etc., in addition to her jointure of £150 by deed, 7 February, 1693.

Residue to my son Edward H. at 21, failing him to any son I may have by my wife Anna, failing whom, to my daughter, Katherine, at 21, she paying £2,000 to any daughter I may have by my wife Anna, at 21. If no children to inherit my estate, then all to my wife for life, and then to my cousin William Poole Williams of Grogasum, Esq., he paying £1,000 to the poorest and nearest of my father Agar's relations.

My wife Anna H. exx. and guardian of my son and daughter, and my son Edward sole exor. at 21, and £150 per annum during his minority. If my wife should refuse the trusts, I appoint my loving friends Hon. George Andrews and David Ramsay, Esq., Lt. Col. George Peers, Major John Wiltshire, Mrs. Frances Eyles and

Anthony Wallinger of London, merchants, to be exors., and £10 to each exor. (Sd.) R. Hooper. Witnesses: Ann Robertson, Robert Stillingfleet, Abell Luder, Jas. Robertson. Proved 8 January, 1700 before R. Grey.

Will of CRISPIN HOOPER now resident in Barbados. To my dear and honoured grandfather Mr. Thos. Agar a silver tankard of £20. To my cousins Elizabeth and Phebe Warren, daughters of my uncle and aunt, Samuel and Elizabeth Warren, £20 each. To my sister Catharine H. a set of dressing plate of £100 value. To Mr. Cummins who was my schoolmaster and to Mr. Edward Hinton of Christ Church Coll., Oxford, who was my tutor, a ring of 20/- value. Residue to my honoured father Robert H. Esq., and to be sole exor. Dated 13 September, 1699. (sd.) Crispin Hooper. Witnesses : T. Bendyshe, John Culston, Benja. Gibbes. Proved before R. Grey 17 November, 1700.

Will of Major DANIEL HOOPER of Christ Church, Barbados, Esq., being now suddenly designed off this island.

To my two daughters, Mary Nasmith, wife of Mr. Robert Nasmith now in England, and Elizabeth Haskett, wife of Mr. Elias Haskett, £700 each. To my two daughters, Ann H. and Eleanor H. £600 each at 16 or marriage, and in the meantime £20 per annum and their maintenance and two negro slaves each.

£10 yearly for two years to the poor of Christ Church parish. £50 to Churchwardens of same parish towards the charge of placing the Creed, Lord's Prayer, and Ten Commandments with the figures of Moses and Aaron in some convenient place in the parish Church.

To nieces Sarah and Louis Dwight, daughters of sister Dwight each £10, and £10 to the youngest daughter of my said sister.

I forgive my brother Christopher H. all sums due by him to me and give him £5 and £10 to each of his children.

To my friends Hon. Col. Tobias Frere and Lt. Col. Thomas Maxwell, Esq., Capt. Philip Kirton, Capt. Richd. Rycroft, and Capt. Thos. Maxwell each a gold ring of 40/-. To friends Lt. Anthony Barker, Lt. John Holmes, Mr. Thomas Haslewood and Mr. Claybourne Haslewood each a gold ring of 20/-. To the first child each of my daughters Mary, Elizabeth, Ann, and Eleanor shall have £20. My estate to be divided into eight parts : three-eights to my son Daniel, two-eights to my son Robert Lettis H., three-eights to my two youngest sons St. John H. and William H. at 21.

Sons Daniel H. and Robert Lettis H. to be exors. Dated 1 October. 1700. (sd.) Daniel Hooper. Witnesses : Thomas Maxwell, jnr., Peter Mascoll, Samuel Dannald. Proved by Samuel Dannald 12 Feby, 1700.

Will of Captain JOHN HOOPER of Christ Church, Barbados, Esq.

To my wife Martha H. four slaves, and if she should marry, either the best horse in my stable or £130 cy. to buy her one. I gave my father-in-law, Smithell Matson of Christ Church, Esq., judgment for £1,000 cy., for payment of an annuity of £100 cy. per annum to my wife in lieu of dower, which I confirm. To my sons John, Joseph, Matthew, Benjamin, and Thomas, £500 cy. each at 21. To my daughter Elizabeth, £500 at 18 and four negro slaves. My sons to have their accommodation in my house until 14, and then bound apprentice to some good trade or calling. Residue of my estate to my son, Daniel. If all my children die, my estate to my wife, Martha, and nephew, Jonathan. My son Daniel, my wife, and Uncle Benjamin Matson, guardians. If my wife marries I appoint Major Daniel Hooper and Capt. Robert Lettis Hooper, Esqrs., Capt. Edwin Stevens and Patrick Mayeoye, gent, with the said Benj. Matson, exors and guardians. Dated 19 Octr. in 10th year of Queen Anne. (Sd.) John Hooper. Witnesses: Robert Jones, Wm. Parsons, Saml. Dannald. Proved 25 May, 1714.

HOOPER OF BARBADOS.

Will of ANNA HOOPER of St. George, widow, late the wife of Robert H. Esq. decd. To be buried in St. Michael's church with my husband.

To the parish of St. Lucy in this I. where I was born, one silver flagon, one silver cup and silver salver, communion plate for the said parish church amounting to the sum of £50 to be bought in England by my cousin John Tidcombe there.[1] To my son-in-law [? step-son] Edward H. gent., son and heir of my said late husband the books marked R.H., the gold-headed cane, the gold tooth-pick case, the gold watch, the gold shoe-buckles given me by my late husband in his Will, all my pictures and £20 to buy mourning.

To my god-daur. Anna Goode £100. To the rest of my said daur. Goode's children £200. To Mr. Bartiham Goode, my said dau's husband £20 to buy him mourning. To my cousin, Elizabeth Titus £50, my diamond ring and my crimson damask bed. To my Aunt, Katharine Thresher £50. To my Aunt, Christian Cook £50. To my Aunt Threshire's children £100. To my cousin Judith Carleton £400. To my cousin Eleanor Robertson £500. To my cousin James Robertson £100. To my cousin Joseph Carleton £40. To his children £40. To my cousin, John Cook £50. To my cousin, Samuel Warren £50. To Mr. Henry Feak £10. To my cousin, Fidelia Pulman, wife of Mr. William Pulman £30. To Mr. John Carleton £50. To my cousin, Anna Carleton £50. To my cousin, Anna Carleton, wife of John Carleton £100, and £100 to be divided amongst all her children. To all my god-children a ring of 30/ each. To Catharine Carmillo, my maid, £20. To her son Thomas Carmillo £20. My negro man Tom Curdy to be set free and I give him £5. My negro woman Jug to be set free and I give her £5. My negro woman Nanny to be set free and I give her £20. All my lands in West Hordy, Sussex, which were purchased of John Browne and Jane his wife and others be within two years after my death sold by my friend and kinsman John Tidcombe of London, merchant, and I give him £100 thereout, and he shall remit the balance to my executor.

My late husband's estate indebted to certain persons and to me. My son-in-law, Edward H., to discharge those obligations out of the plantation and estate of his late father, and to remain on the said plantation until he attains 22. I give him all my horses and negroes not otherwise disposed of. In case of his death under 22, I give to my daughter-in-law, Katherine Goode, the wife of Barnham Goode, gent. formerly Kathleen Hooper, spinster, all that I intended for Edward.

To my cousin Margery Lowe all the residue of my estate, and I appoint her sole executrix. Dated 2 July 1707. sd. A.

Hooper. Witnesses R. Wiltshire, Jno. Hall. Edward Ragg. Proved February, 11, 1715.

(1) Extract from *Barbados Diocesan History*. St. Lucy's Church. The altar vessels are of beaten silver 1721. They consist of a silver flagon 15 ins. high with a base 8 ins. diameter weighing 5 lbs. 7½ ozs., a silver chalice 9½ ins. high, 5 ins. diameter 1½ lbs., a silver patten 6½ ins. diameter, 14½ ozs., a large silver almsdish 12½ ins., 3 lbs., 2 ozs., all engraved—''The gift of Mrs. Anna Hooper by her Will to the parish of St. Lucy in Barbados, the place of her nativity, 1721''. Originally there were two chalices, one of which was given in exchange by H. Hutson Rector, with consent of the Vestry, to Mr. A. Cadogan of Pickerings for two modern chalices and one modern patten on June 17, 1895.

Will of JEAN HOOPER of town and parish of St. Michael, widow.

The bond payable to my son-in-law Richard Dearsley for £500 with interest to be paid out of moneys due me by Hon. Reynold Alleyne, and the balance of said moneys and other moneys due me by John Hall, mariner, and others be placed out at interest, and income thereof to my son John for life, afterwards the capital for his lawful children. If John shall die without issue, then said money to be equally divided between my three daughters, Mary Pare, widow, Judith Rennell, widow, and Elizabeth Mitford, widow.

To my friends Mr. John Shurland, merchant, Dr. Joseph Gamble, and Edmund Duffey, gent., the house I now live in and two storehouses and six slaves, upon trust for son John, except he shall marry anyone of ill repute, in which case the property to go to my three daughters. My old negro woman, Adinah, to be employed in light work—washing, mending etc., during my son's life, and after his death she is to be set free. To my bearers a gold ring of 20/ and a scarf each. My four daughters Mary Pare, Judith Rennell, Elizabeth Mitford, and Anna Dearsley a gold ring of 20/-. Executors: John Shurland, Joseph Gamble and Anna Dearsley, £10 each for mourning clothes. Dated 15 October 1720. sd. Jean Hooper. Witnesses: E. Smith, Wm. Palmer, John Pare.

Codicil dated December 29. There is no interest due on the bond of £500. John is to have use of my household goods for his life. The ring for Ann Dearsley is declared void. sd. Jean Hooper.

Will of WILLIAM HOOPER of St. Michael. I bequeath all my property to my brother, Daniel, and appoint him sole executor. Dated January 21, 1720. sd. William Hooper. Witnesses: Thomas Napoleon, John Remington, Richd. Goodwicke. Proved February 2, 1720.

Will of DANIEL HOOPER of St. Thomas. I give to my daughter Eleanor £1,000 at 18 and £1,000 more on 2nd August, 1730, and in case of her death the said sums for my son Reynold at 21. To Eleanor, jewels, rings, slaves, and £60 per ann. for her education, and a horse and saddle and a negro to attend her when she goes out. Also my best beds and furniture. Her guardian to assist her in getting £500 left her by her Uncle Elliott, and part of the legacy left her brother James in his Uncle's Will now devolving on her by her brother's death. My niece Ann Green to have her living on my plantation and £16 per an. until her cousin Reynold attains 22. To my brother Robert Lettice Hooper my part of the farm in East New Jersey on the Raviton River and on his death to his sons James and Robert Lettice Hooper equally and they to release my son Reynold from all claims, otherwise this gift to be void. Residue to my son Reynold, at 21, and his maintenance not exceeding £150 per an. in the meantime. If my son and daughter should die, my estate to my brother and his two sons James and Robert. My son Reynold to be sole executor, and Hon. Henry Peers Esq., George Forster Esq., John Alleyne Esq., son of Judge Reynold Alleyne decd. Thomas Gollop, Esq., Henry Lascelles Esq., Elizabeth Jordan, widow, and my cousin Major John Millington, guardians. To each guardian a piece of plate £25, and a piece of plate to each of my friends, Gelasius McMahon and Robert Warren. To the minister of the parish of St. George £10. Dated Octr. 7, 1726. sd. Dan. Hooper. Witnesses: Jno. Cox, James Cox, Richard Cox, F. Pearce. Proved 6 February 1726.

Will of FRANCES HOOPER of St. Michael, widow. My body to be buried in my family vault in St. Lucy's church. To Mrs. Ruth Haggatt 5 negroes, with all the money that is due me from the estate of Col. Simon Lambert, decd. for her own use. To Jane Haggatt, wife of Nathaniel Haggatt, Esq., 4 negroes and all that may be due me from estate of John Gibbons, decd., from Col. John Pickering and from Col. Robt. Harrison for her use. To Nathaniel Haggatt (son of Cornelia) my sleeve buttons. To Susanna Haggatt (daur. of Nathaniel H.) my gold watch, shoe buckles, gold thimble and ear-rings. To the said Jane and Ruth Haggatt all my plate and household goods with the remainder of my real and personal property. I appoint Nathaniel Haggatt my executor and Mrs. Susanna Haggatt, Mrs. Ruth Haggatt and Jane Haggatt executrices. Dated 2 Septr., 1740, sd. by her mark. Witnesses: Eliz. Wakup, William Hall. Proved 22 October, 1741.

Will of SARAH HOOPER of Christ Church. To my daur. Sarah Parris, wife of Major Edward P. one negro man. To my granddaur. Elizabeth Rycroft, daur. of my son Richard R., decd.

one negro boy to be delivered to her when my grandson Thomas Rycroft (son of said Richard R., decd.) attains 21. To my grand-daur. Sarah Rycroft, another daur. of said Richard, one negro boy. To my son Edward Parris and his wife Sarah £15 each to buy a suit of mourning. To their son John Parris £25. Residue to my grandson Thomas Rycroft at 21. Appoint said Thomas Rycroft as executor and my son-in-law Edward Parris executor and guardian in trust over the body and estate of my said grandson. Dated 9 February, 1731. sd. Sarah Hooper. Witnesses: W. Carey, Joseph Edggill, Wm. Maloney.

Proved 27 October, 1742.

Exemplification of Probate of Will of Robert Lettis Hooper, decd. from Province of New Jersey in America, City of Perth Amboy.

I ROBERT LETTIS HOOPER of city of Perth Amboy in co. Middlesex, Province of New Jersey, gentleman. Sick. To my wife Sarah (certain) slaves for her lifetime and then slaves to be freed and given for their lives 2 acres of the land bought from Charles Dunster, Esq. lying in Perth Amboy. Household effects to wife for life and then to my children, James and Isabella Hooper. To my son Robert Lettis Hooper certain slaves. Confirm deed of gift to my son and daughter, James and Isabella.

Sums due me from estate of Richard Rycroft decd. of Barbados to be divided equally between wife Sarah and James, Isabella, and Robert Lettis. Residue as to one-third for wife, one-third to James and one-third to Isabella. Appoint Reynold Hooper and Richard Wiltshire of Barbados Esqres. and Joseph Murray Esq. of city of New York, and son James executors and wife and daur. executrices, (the said Reynold H. and Richd. Wiltshire to act concerning my affairs in Barbados only). Dated 27 Jan., 1738. R. L. Hooper. Witnesses: Rebecca Legall, John Webb, P. Kearney. Recorded in Barbados 2 Novr., 1743.

WILL OF FRANCES HOOPER of St. George, widow. To my daur. Ursula H. a piece of land near St. Michael's town and to her only son, Robert. To Ursula a rose diamond ring, a gold girdle buckle. a pair of pendants, a pair of gold shoe buckles and ear-rings, pearl necklace, gold thimble that was my sister's, and she is to be maintained and educated until 21, £20 per annum and £1,000. To Jane Bannister, daur. of Peter Bannister, £15. To Alice Bannister a ring of 50/-. Residue to son and daur. Dated 22 April, 1740. sd. Fran. Hooper. Witnesses: Roger Favell, Thomas Davis, Edward Grove. Proved 19 July, 1744.

Codicil, 19 June 1744, explaining gift of £1,000 to Ursula who was entitled to money under Will of Mrs. Elizabeth Frizer and her (Ursula's) sister Frances decd. sd. by X of Frances Hooper. Witnesses: Edward Wiggins, Abrm. White, Melvin Green. Proved 19 July 1944.

Will of REYNOLD HOOPER of St. Thomas, Barbados, but at present in the town of Gosport in Hampshire, England. In pretty good health. To my son, Reynold Salter Salmon Hooper, £5,000 cy. at 21. To my daur., Margaret Salter Hooper, £1,500 cy. at 18 or marriage. To my daur. Phillippa Elliott Hooper, £1,500 Stlg. at 18 or marriage. If I have any other child, if a boy £2,000 cy. at 21, if a girl £1,500 cy. at 18 or marriage. My son Reynold to be educated in England, and for his expenses I allow £65 stlg. per an. until he is 12, £80 per an. until he is 16, and if he gives hope of succeeding in any profession then to be placed at one of the universities as a commoner or pensioner until he comes of age. I give him £100 to fit him out for the university, and allow him £130 stlg. per ann. until he comes of age. If he choses to learn the trade of a merchant, I desire him to be put with a firm of good repute in England or Holland or other part of Europe and an advance made him of his £5,000, and I allow him £100 stlg. until 21. My wife, Harbin H., the residue of my real and personal estate, in lieu of dower. I appoint my wife during widowhood, Hon. Richd. Salter Esq. and Mrs. Margaret Salter his wife, Richard Wiltshire sen., John Newton and Eliakim Palmer Esq. executors and guardians. Dated 6 Novr., 1748. sd. Reynold Hooper. Proved in Barbados on oath of Frances Pearce and Richard Husbands, 10 July, 1749.

Another certified copy of same Will recorded on 26 Jany., 1749 in Barbados.

ORDER of Ralph Weekes Esq., President of Barbados, to hear the Petition of John Lyte and Samuel Game and Mary Hooper, widow, to admit holograph will of Robert Hooper Esq.

Will of Robert Hooper Esq. of St. George. To be buried in St. Michael's church. To my wife all her linen, wearing apparel, jewellery, plate, etc. except my father's grandfather's and great-grandfather's pictures which I give to my sister Ursula Game. wife of Samuel Game Esq. To my wife, Mary Hooper, her living in my mansion house during widowhood. My chaise and chaise horse and her two saddle horses. The use of that parcel of land adjoining the house called The old Garden, comprehending the Pond to windward of the house, cocoanut trees and cassia fistula and plantain trees, and certain slaves. My friend Capt. Guy Spooner my silk sash and a ring of 50/-. An appraisement to be made of my net assets: one-sixth thereof for my daur-in-law, Elizabeth Ball [step-daur.], at 18 or marriage if she marries with her mother's consent.

To each of my executors £20 cy. to buy a suit of mourning. Residue of my estate to my wife, Mary, and my sister Ursilla Game for life, and then to her heirs. Wife, Mary, brother Samuel Game, and friend John Lyte to be executors. not signed. Proved by Capt. Guy Spooner to be in hand-writing of Robert Hooper. Recorded 20 Decr., 1754.

[The testator's widow, Mary, afterwards married Jonas Maynard who survived her and married as his fourth wife Christian Mercy Alleyne, widow of Reynold Alleyne.]

HOOPER MONUMENTAL INSCRIPTIONS IN BARBADOS.

Extracted from *The Monumental Inscriptions in the Churches and Churchyards of the Island of Barbados*, edited by VERE LANGFORD OLIVER, M.R.C.S., London, 1915.

St. Michael's Cathedral. In cross walk from south to north porch:

1. Here lies the body of / ROBERT HOOPER Esq. / late Attourney Generall / of this Island who / departed this life the 24 / of July 1700: aged forty/three Years.

Almost certainly identical with Robert Hooper, son of Robert Hooper of L. gent., of Hart Hall, matric. 15 Oct., 1674, aged 16, perhaps bar.-at-law, Gray's Inn, 1684, as son of Robert of Sarum, Wilts, esq., deceased. (Foster).

On the south wall, east corner:

59. A boldly carved monument of white marble with cherubs' heads, curtain, and swags of flowers.

ARMS.—*On a fess three annulets between two moles;* impaling *blank.* Archer gave the impaled coast as: *Per fess indented,* but that is no longer visible.

ROBERTUS HOOPER Armiger, Amicus / certus in re incerta, pius simul et / munificus notisq. amor Deliciœque / Vir haud vulgariter eruditus et egregio / Ingenii acumine ornatissimus, nec non / multos in annos Incolis hujusce Insulæ / beatis Regivs Attornatus Generalis / Obijt 24 die July AD: MDCC / Siste, Lector, quid dixi? / Non obijt, nec obire potest, sed vivet in ævum / Cum Christo in cælis, in terris ore virorum.

Parish.	Date of Baptism	Name.
St. Philip	27 March 1649	Susanna, dau. of John Hooper.
St. Michael	26 Decr. 1654	Philip, son of Mr. Thomas Hooper.
Ch. Church	30 Novr. 1673	Mary, dau. of Daniel & Eleanor Hooper.
do.	26 Septr. 1675	Elizabeth, dau. of Daniel & Eleanor Hooper.
do.	6 Novr. 1677	Thomas, son of Daniel & Eleanor Hooper.
St. Philip	10 Jany. 1678	Oistin, son of Jonathan & Eliza. Hooper.
Ch. Church	27 Novr. 1679	John, son of Jonathan & Elizabeth Hooper.
St. Michael	23 Febry. 1681	Eliza. the dau. of Mr. Xtoph. & America Hooper.
Ch. Church	30 April 1682	child of Daniel & Elizabeth Hooper born 25 Novr. 1681.
do.	23 March 1682	Elizabeth, dau. of Jonathan & Elizabeth Hooper.
do.	16 Augt. 1684	Deborah, dau. of Jonathan & Elizabeth Hooper.
do.	22 Septr. 1685	John, son of Daniel & Eleanor Hooper.
St. Michael	2 Augt. 1688	ye son of Mr............ Hooper.
Ch. Church	1 Novr. 1689	Ann, aged 1 year & 11 months dau. of Daniel & Eleanor Hooper.
do.	1 Novr. 1689	William son of Daniel & Eleanor Hooper.
St. Michael	15 Novr. 1691	Elizabeth ye dau. of Mr. Charles & Mrs. Judith Hooper.
Ch. Church	15 Novr. 1692	Jacob, son of Daniel & Ellen Hooper.
do.	15 Novr. 1689	George, son of Daniel & Ellen Hooper.
do.	14 Feby. 1694	Eleanor, aged 3 years, dau. of Daniel & Eleanor Hooper.
do.	11 Jany. 1702	Daniel, son of John & Martha Hooper.
St. Michael	6 Jany. 1704	Mary, dau. of George and .... Hooper.
Ch. Church	May 1703	Ann, dau. of Daniel & Philippa Hooper.
do.	14 Augt. 1703	Daniel, son of Robert & Sarah Hooper.
do.	Novr. 1703	John, son of John & Martha Hooper.
do.	14 Feby. 1705	Joseph, son of John & Martha Hooper.
do.	24 Feby. 1704	James, son of Robert & Sarah Hooper.
do.	12 Octr. 1706	Philippa, dau. of Robert Lettice & Sarah Hooper.
do.	21 April 1706	Matthew, son of John & Hannah Hooper.

Parish	Date of Baptism	Name
Ch. Church	June 1708	Robert Lettice, son of Robert Lettice and Sarah Hooper.
do.	6 Decr. 1708	Benjamin, son of John & Martha Hooper.
do.	29 Septr. 1710	Elizabeth, dau. of John & Martha Hooper.
do.	16 Octr. 1711	Thomas, son of John & Martha Hooper.
do.		Mary, dau. of Robert Lettice & Sarah Hooper, born August 31, 1712.
do.	21 Feby. 1714	Sarah, dau. of Robert Lettice & Sarah Hooper.
do.	28 Novr. 1715	William, son of Robert Lettice & Sarah Hooper.
do.	28 Novr. 1715	Eleanor, dau. of Robert Lettice & Sarah Hooper.
St. Michael		dau. of ....Hooper Esq. and Mrs......... his wife, born 16 March 1734/5.
St. Thomas	6 Septr. 1742	Philippa Ellis, dau. of Reynold Hooper Esq. & Mrs. Sarah.
do.	6 July 1743	Reynold Salter Salmon, son of the Hon'ble Reynold & Mrs. Sarah Hooper.
St. Michael	2 Octr. 1758	Robert, son of Robert & Joanna Hooper, born 23 Septr. 1758.
Ch. Church	28 Jany. 1760	Margaret, dau. of Joseph & Margaret Hooper.
St. Michael	25 Novr. 1761	Robert Lettis, son of Robert Lettis Hooper decd. and Joanna, his wife, born 18 Septr. 1761.
Ch. Church	19 Augt. 1777	Alice Ann, dau. of James & Elizabeth Hooper.

HOOPER MARRIAGES.

Parish	Date of Marriage	Name
St. Michael	14 Novr. 1654	Joane Hooper to John Penderr.
do.	24 Septr. 1658	Mary Hooper to John Thornton.
do.	7 Decr. 1665	Mrs. Ursilla Hooper to Mr. Henry Hutchinson.
do.	10 April 1669	Jone Hooper to William Arden.
St. Philip	28 April 1675	Robert Hooper to Dorothy Clemens.
Ch. Church	13 April 1690	Maria Hooper to Robert Nesmith.
do.	22 Feby. 1691	William Hooper to Mary Momford.
do.	4 July 1692	Elizabeth Hooper to Thomas Rich.
St. Michael	22 Octr. 1694	Mrs. Judith Hooper to Mr. George Wiltshire.
Ch. Church	19 Augt. 1697	Oistin Hooper to Margaret Markland.
do.	21 Decr. 1699	Margaret Hooper to Robert Markland.

Parish	Date of Marriage	Name
St. Michael.	22 Septr. 1700	Dorothy Hooper to William Jefferies.
Ch. Church	Decr. 1700	John Hooper to Martha Matson.
do.	2 Augt. 1702	Daniel Hooper to Philippa Elliot.
St. Michael	12 Novr. 1710	Edward Hooper to Mrs. Frances Mans.
Ch. Church	5 Jany. 1710	William Hooper to Sarah Rycroft.
do.	5 March 1716	Martha Hooper to Francis Ford.
do.	16 Feby. 1729	Daniel Hooper to Mary Cantwell.
St. Michael	9 June 1734	Reynold Hooper Esq. to Mrs. Harbin Salmon, spinster.
Ch. Church	20 Novr. 1740	Elizabeth Hooper to John White.
do.	7 Jany. 1745	Robert Hooper to Mary Ball.
St. Thomas	26 Septr. 1752	Mrs. Harbin Hooper, widow to Christopher Estwick Esq.
St. Michael	17 Septr. 1757	Robert Hooper to Joanna Rowe.
do.	30 June 1770	Lettice Hooper to William Bynoe.
Ch. Church	27 July 1774	Margaret Hooper to Thomas Buck.
do.	11 April 1776	James Hooper to Elizabeth Evelyn.
St. Michael	15 May 1788	Elizabeth Hooper to Samuel Moore.

HOOPER BURIALS.

Parish	Date of Burial	Name
St. Michael	16 Augt. 1657	Marmaduke Hooper, a seaman.
do.	21 Septr. 1661	John Hooper.
do.	20 May 1662	Thomas Hooper, Minister, in Chancell.
do.	20 Jany. 1670	Thomas Hooper, junior.
do.	6 Octr. 1673	Thomas Hooper, a lad.
do.	22 Novr. 1673	Richard Hooper.
do.	1 Augt. 1674	Margery Hooper.
do.	4 June 1674	Robert Hooper, Almshouse.
do.	31 Decr. 1675	Gilbert Hooper.
do.	7 Septr. 1683	Mrs. Urculoe Hooper.
do.	21 Septr. 1683	Samuel Hooper, mate of Captain Tanner's ship of New England.
Ch. Church	1 Octr. 1684	Sarah Hooper.
do.	7 Augt. 1687	Jonathan Hooper.
do.	12 April 1691	Mary Hooper.
St. Michael	11 May 1692	Elizabeth Hooper, a child.
do.	3 Decr. 1692	Robert Hooper, son of Attorney General.
Ch. Church	28 Novr. 1692	George Hooper, son of Daniel.
St. Michael	8 April 1693	Mrs. Ursula Hooper, in Church.
do.	18 Novr. 1694	Elizabeth Hooper, a child.
do.	14 Septr. 1695	John Hooper, free negro.
Ch. Church	5 Septr. 1696	Thomas Hooper, a child.
do.	25 Feby. 1697	Elizabeth Hooper.

Parish	Date of Burial	Name
St. Michael	13 Jany. 1698	George Hooper.
Ch. Church	15 June 1698	Mary Hooper.
	29 March 1698	Thomas Hooper.
St. Michael	23 Jany. 1699	Benjamin Hooper.
do.	25 Septr. 1699	Crispin Hooper, in Church.
Ch. Church	16 June 1699	Oistin Hooper.
St. Michael	26 July 1700	Robert Hooper, in Church.
do.	29 Jany. 1701	John Hooper.
Ch. Church	19 Octr. 1704	Joseph Hooper.
St. Michael	17 Feby. 1708	Christopher Hooper.
do.	19 Octr. 1713	Edward Hooper, a child.
Ch. Church	1 May 1713	Mary Hooper, a child.
Ch. Church	4 May 1713	Philippa Hooper, a child.
St. Michael	1 Feby. 1714	Mrs. America Hooper, widow.
Ch. Church	22 Novr. 1714	Sarah Hooper, a child.
St. Michael	7 Jany. 1715	Ann Hooper, a widow, in the Church.
Ch. Church	23 Decr. 1715	William Hooper, a child.
do.	27 Decr. 1715	Eleanor Hooper, a child.
St. Michael	17 March 1716	Mrs. Ann Hooper, a widow.
Ch. Church	27 Decr. 1720	John Hooper.
St. Michael	27 Jany. 1720	William Hooper, Captain.
do.	18 Octr. 1724	James Hooper, son of Mr. John Hooper.
do.	19 July 1725	Bernard Hooper, son of Colonel Edward Hooper, in Church.
Ch. Church	11 Octr. 1726	Thomas Hooper.
St. Michael	11 Octr. 1730	Colonel Edward Hooper, in the Church.
St. Philip	10 Feby. 1730	Elizabeth Hooper.
St. Michael	28 May 1736	Mrs. Frances Hooper.
do.	27 Septr. 1738	John Hooper, a poor Sailor.
do.	24 Septr. 1741	Frances Hooper, widow, in the new Chancel.
do.	21 June 1744	Frances Hooper, widow, in the Church.
St. Thomas	June 1749	The Hon. Reynold Hooper, buried in St. Michael.
St. Michael	19 Octr. 1754	R. Hooper.
do.	19 April 1759	Robert Hooper, a child.
do.	8 July 1762	Mathew Hooper, second mate of Captain Fisher from Bristol, consigned to Wm. Moore, Merchant.
do.	11 April 1763	Robert Hooper, son of Joanna Hooper.
do.	15 April 1763	Elizabeth Hooper, daughter of Joanna Hooper.
do.	12 Feby. 1774	Mary Hooper.
Ch. Church	3 Octr. 1774	Joseph Hooper.

HOOPER OF BARBADOS.

HOOPER DEEDS.

29 Aug. 1644. JAMES HOOPER and THOMAS HOOPER of Barbados, for 6600 lbs. of good and well conditioned tobacco, grant to Wm. Greene and Tho. Hearne of Barbados, planters, 25 ac. of land, fallen and unfallen, bounded as in original bill of sale between the lands of Capt. James Drax on the east, on the lands of Christopher Perkins on the west, on lands of James Greene on the south, and ye late plantation of Robert Bates; these being the bounds when it was 50 acs. sold us by Mr. Benyon; together with all housings, provisions, implements etc., always reserving to vendors their apparel, hamacoes, one iron pott, 2 turkeys, and 2 piggs. sd. James Hooper, Thomas X. Hooper, Wits: Roger Fisher, . . . Greene.

31 May, 1651. John Powell of Barbados, admr. of est. of John Merricke decd, and guardian of Mary M. child and hieress of J. M., to CAPT ROBT. HOOPER of Barbados, Esq., lease of Merricke's plantn., Christ Church, of ten ac., for 7 years, at 1,000 lbs. muscovado sugar per an. Wits: Archibald Johnson, Edward Williams.

7 Oct., 1651. Capt. Francis Williams of Barbados, gent., to CAPT ROBT. HOOPER of Barbados, gent., lease of 40 ac. of plantation in Christ Church, abutting on lands in the tenure of William Browne, Lawrence Price, Thomas Floyd, John Spendlove, and John Pomery, with the canes thereon; excepting 4 ac. of woodland and the bodies of mastick trees now standing which will bear 8 ins. square and upwards, with liberty to carry away the same within 2 months after the canes are planted or cut, for 7 years at 11,000 lbs. of well-cured muscovado sugar at 2 times in each year. sd. Robert Hooper. Wits: Frs. Mosse, scr., James Mullins, Lodowick Williams his mark, Ed. Williams.

28 Mar., 1654. James Drax of Barbados, Esq., to ROBERT HOOPER and Martin Bentley of Barbados, for £454 stlg. assigns one-eighth part of Ship *Samuel* and one-eighth part of Pinnace *Hope*, llately set out from England for Africa for negroes, and one-fifth part of cargo and profits. Memo. that R. H. and M. B. have purchased on their own hazard, and they shall not question the title of said J. D. thereto nor any incumbrance, nor shall J. D. be liable for any accident which may have befallen the ships since they set out on the voyage. sd. Robert Hooper, Martin Bentley. Wits: Jno. Catesby, W. Hamlyn.

30 Mar. 1653/4. ROBERT HOOPER and Martin Bentley of Barbados, Esqs., to James Drax, sale of great storehouse in Bridgetown commonly known as Vandeshurs (?) house, which the said R. H. and M. B. purchased from Peter Frederickson, on the condition that they shall permit J. D. to select for his use out of their one-eighth part of the negroes which shall be brought on the good ship *Samuel* (commdr. Samuel Cooke) to this island or elsewhere in the Caribe islands two male negroes and two female negroes, and a like number out of the Pinnace *Hope* (Commdr. William Goodlord) both of which ships are now performing a voyage to the coast of Africa and thence bound hither; and R. H. and M. B. bind themselves to pay Drax £454 stlg. on last of October or 54,480 lbs. weight of good muscovado sugar before March 1655, then this present conveyance to be void. sd. Robert Hooper, Martin Bentley, Wits: John Hamlyt, Jno. Catesby.

May 1654. Richard Gwalter of Barbados, Carpenter, to ROBERT HOOPER, sale of 9 ac. of land, bounding on lands of Richard Lee, Capt. Francis Williams, Jno. Cole, Mr. Spendlove. sd. Rich. Gwalter, Wits: Wm. Bentley, Roger Cottrell.

12 Sep., 1654. ROBERT HOOPER of Barbados, for ample satisfaction made by my well-beloved brother Martin Bentley of same Island, grant of one-half part of my plantation 200 ac. in Christ Church and St. Philip, formerly purchased of Lieut. Hugh Powell, Lieut. Thomas Lucomb, David Adams, Duby Linsey, Richard Alwainda, and Richd. Guatter. Bounded by lands of William Fortescue and Richard Rolston north, David Adams, George Pasfield and John Morrish decd. east, John Morrish and Lawrence Price, south, and Francis Williams west, and of all houses timber, stock, tools, utensils etc. according to annexed inventory; and also one-half part of land and house thereon which was lately known as Vandeseures (?) house, lately purchased by R. H. from Peter Frederickson, situate near seaside at the Bridge Town in St. Michaels, and when a new storehouse is set up on this land, same is to be in partnership equally between us. sd. Robert Hooper, Wits: William Bentley, Christopher White, Isaac Legay jnr.

Inventory: In the Mill house, 3 long goudgens, and 3 short do: with capuces, and boards and plates for the rollers. In the boiling house, 6 coppers, 3 coolers, ladles and skimmers. In the still house, 3 stills and worms. In the stables, 12 horses, mares and colts. In the smithshop, the bellows, anvill, and other smith's tools. In the cook room, several iron potts and kettles. In the overseer's room, several hoes, axes, pickaxes, and sledges, wedges, bills etc. In the curing house 1700 sugar potts, one beam, weights and scales. In the old curing house, several feet of timber for rollers. In the store house, several goods in the care of Roger Cattrell. In the house where Tho. Reo dwells sundry stock or rabbits, fowls, turkeys, and ducks. In the dwellinghouse, several bedding, hammocks, plates, pewter, linen, and household stuffe. In the pasture, as cattle, workers, cows, ewes, and fine young sheep. In the plantation, yokes, bows and chains. In the negro town, 54 working negroes and 12 children, and 35 christian men servants names as follows: [names of slaves omitted here]. Christian servants—James Corse, William Evans, Wm. Martin, Hector Main Rowe, Alexr. Roiman, Alex. Moberton, John Tweed, Wm. Mowbray, James Fentley, James Hobbs, John Watts, Martin Redman, Hugh Redman, Hugh Terrell, Robt. Forgey, Robt. Mackoghlin, John Perry, George Linn, David Bell, Wm. Linn, John Reeves, Roger Ward, Evans Allen, John Hay, Moran Carr, James Jenkins, William Heckmer, James Gordon, Wm. Craghead, Wm. Mackhoone, Wm. Burridge, Tedge Cordegan, Wm. Budd, Cullum Makary, John Horne.

24 May 1655. Martin Bentley of Barbados, merchant, to LT. COL. ROBERT HOOPER. sale of land near the Indian Bridgetown. 50 ft. breadth to street side, 90 ft. to the sea, butting on other lands of M. B. and R. H., John Futters, Thomas Vaughan, and the sea. Wits: Shershaw Carey, Christopher White, Arthur Bull, James Fontleroy.

2 Apl. 1656. THOMAS HOOPER for £60 stlg. sells to Coll. Thomas Middleton of Popler, co. of Excise(?), 5 ac. of land and wood in parish of St. George, Barbados, butting on lands of T. M. late in possession of Richard Baker south, ye land of said T. M. late in possession of John Pembroke east, and ye land of Wm. Rollock decd. west and north. sd. Thomas X. Hooper. Wts: Richard Cornish, Wm. Weldon.

25 Jan. 1658. George Passfield of Redriff, Surrey, appoints COL. ROBERT HOOPER of London, his agent to recover property from John Lewis, planter, and John Brawnson, bricklayer, both of Barbados; and to take over his Valley plantation from Richard Frewtrall (? Fretwell) overseer. sd. George Pasfield, Wts: George Sitwell, Jairus Waterer.

5 July 1658. ROBERT HOOPER of London Esq. to Peter Legay and Isaack Legay of London, merchants, grant of plantation of 105 ac. in parish of St. George, Barbados, late in the possession of Sir Antony Ashley Cooper, Bart. and now in occupation of R. H., butting on lands of Captain Gerrard Hawtaine, Thomas Spendlove, Lodowicke Williams; and another plantation of 100 ac. in St. George, late in occupation of said G. H. but

now in occupation of R. H., butting on the aforesaid plantation of Sir A. A. C., on lands of Capt. William Jarman, Thomas Wiltshire and Henry Hunt, with the canes, woods, houses, mills, coppers, utensils, and 40 able bodied working negroes etc. sd. Robert Hooper. Wits: Richard Marshall, Josiah Pike, Proved before the Lord Mayor of London, 3 Dec. 1658.

6 July 1658. Peter Legay and Isaac Legay of London, merchants, to ROBERT HOOPER of London, mortgage of the same plantations as above described to secure £1800.

15 Decr. 1660. Partition made by "my brother Mr. Martin Bentley and myself ROBERT HOOPER of our plantations and storehouses in Barbados that the said Bentley would give me £500 stlg. that he might make his choice and keep it, which proposition I doe accept of and accordingly doe set down the particulars of our lower plantation consisting of 300 acres with which shall go these things". [It seems that Bentley chose the "upper plantation" which may be identified as the plantation still called Bentley. and Hooper was left in possession of the "lower plantation", almost certainly the plantation now called *Windsor*. The inventory of appurtenances follows].

The windmill with his set of rowlers and all things thereto belonging. The cattle mill with its set of rowlers and all things thereto belonging. The boiling house with coppers that are hung and the receiver with what belongs to it. The still house with the stills, worms, and cisterns. The curing house which is now building to be finished at our joint cost, all other housing to go with it as they now are. All the earthen pots, all ye mastick which are bought abroad and not yet brought home, half of locust trees and timber which is bought abroad and not yet brought home, the free use of forge and smith's shops on our other plantation and the use of smith and farrier for one year, the great storehouse wherein Mr. John Hallett dwelleth, and all rents therefor, half the yams now growing on the plantation and the other plantations to have the other half to carry away, the beam and weights at our storehouse in Bridgetown. Him to whom the lower plantation belongs to have these things and his dwelling at our now dwellinghouse on the upper plantation for six months next after date hereof; also 40 negroes for five turns to help bring home earthern ware pots for this plantation before 15 Jan. next. This lower plantation to allow and furnish the other with 10 ac. of standing wood next adjoining to Thomas Spendlove and Thomas Wiltshire to be cut within 5 years, and to supply the other with 50 gallons of spirits or rum if desired, to be returned within two months, and the use of the lime kiln to burn one turn and to find the wood for it. "This condition made by Robert Hooper intended hereby all the land formerly of Anthony A. Cooper and Capt. Gerard Hawtaine and of Capt. Edward Thornborough commonly called Pinchback, the whole containing about 290 ac. I am contented with this lower plantation for my proper estate upon the division with my brother Martin Bentley. Witness my hand." sd. Robert Hooper. Wits: James White, Arthur Bull, John Bond, Jarius Waterer. Acknowledged by R. H. 18 July 1661 before Tho: Ellice.

13 Decr. 1667. John Bawdon of Barbados, attorney for John Sparke, releases to COL. ROBERT HOOPER of Barbados, plantation of 100 ac., 75 ac. of which (in Christ Church) Hooper had purchased from Capt. Edward Thornborough, and also thirty negroes, which Sparke and Bawdon had taken in mortgage from Hooper on 2 March 1660, in consideration of debt of £1000 paid.

1 Feb. 1675. DANIEL HOOPER of Christ Church, Barbados, merchant, for 45,168¾ lbs. muscovado sugar paid by Thomas Maxwell of said parish and island, chirurgeon, sells him 24 ac. 2 rds. 36 p. of land in Christ Church, abutting on lands of Thos: Redman, late of Philip Kirton, and on the sea southwards. sd. Danell Hooper, Wits: Isaac Ragg.

21 Aug. 1678. Mortgage from Edward Harlestan and Elizabeth his wife of Barbados to DANIEL HOOPER, for 1000 lbs. muscovado sugar, of 25 ac. in St. Philip and 10 ac. in Christ Church.

19 May 1679. ROBERT HOOPER of Gray's Inn, co. Mdsex, gent, son & heir of Robert Hooper late of Barbados Esq., decd. and also exor. of his Will to Anthony Wallinger of London, merchant, of a dwelling house and plantation in Barbados late in the possession of said R. H. decd. 347½ ac., windmills, boiling-house, curing house, still house, in St. George, 150 negroes, plantation utensils, etc., for securing £1904. 17. 7 stlg. then due. sd. Robert Hooper. Wits: John Prier, John Firebrass, John Smart, J. Browne, Judith Wallinger. Proved by John Firebrace and John Smart, merchants, before Jonathan Atkins, 20 Augt. 1679.

13 July 1683. CHRISTOPHER HOOPER of Barbados, gent. to Edmund Jeffries, sale of 10 ac. in St. Michael. butting on lands of Humphrey Kent, Col. John Hallett, and seashore. sd. Christo. Hooper. Wits: George Mason, Cornel Widnell, Edmond Ford.

25 Sep. 1684. CHRISTOPHER HOOPER of St. Michael, planter, to Col. John Hallett. £489. 3. of 34 ac. 1 rd. 6 p. of land in St. Michael. sd. Christopher Hooper. Wits: Ri: Cartwright, John Cocke, Thomas Duboys, Thos. Lawrence.

[Between the years 1685 and 1694 eleven deeds are recorded by which Daniel Hooper as Chief Deputy Marshal of the Court of Common Pleas for the Precinct of Christ Church and St. Philip conveys land sold under execution to the several purchasers thereof.]

15 Oct. 1687. ROBERT HOOPER of St. George, gent. to John Consine £451 stlg. 28 ac. 32 p. of land in St. George, butting on lands of the widow Middleton, James Bull, and widow Harman, of Robert Talbot and the high road. sd. Robert Hooper Wits: John Wiltshire, Arch. Johnstone, James Sparrow.

6 Feb. 1693. ROBERT HOOPER of St. George, their Majesties Attorney General of Barbados to Hon. John Whetstone of Christ Church, Member of Council, and Henry Feake of St. Michael, gent., grant of plantation of 350 ac. in St. George and Christ Church, together with houses, windmills and sugar works, and 134 negroes; the land bounding on lands of Major John Wiltshire, Mr. Thomas Wiltshire, Sir Martin Bentley decd. Capt. Lawrence Price, and Capt. John Cousin. sd. Robert Hooper. Witts: John Howe, Edward Allanson.

7 Feb. 1693. ROBERT HOOPER 1. John Wiltshire and Henry Feake 2 and Anna Tidcome of St. Peter All Saints, widow of Samuel Tidcome 3 Settlement by R. H. of the plantation described in the last above deed to secure a jointure of £150 to Anna Tidcombe on her then intended marriage to Hooper.

7 Feb. 1695. Anna Tidcombe 1. John Wiltshire and Henry Feake 2 and ROBERT HOOPER 3. Reciting marriage between Anna and Robert Hooper "with whom Hooper will have a considerable fortune", but excepting a sum of £3,100 cash in the hands of Sir John Eyles and Francis Eyles, London Merchants, which is to be laid out in the purchase of real estate in England and is not to be subject to the husband's control, but is to be held upon the trusts of the deed.
Wits: Edward Denny, John Howe, Edwd. Harrison, Jon. Taylor, Thos: Herbert, Ed. Alanson.

7 Feb. 1693. Same parties as in last deed. Settlement of 23 slaves upon the trusts of the former deed.

15 June 1694. Miles James of Christ Church, gent. and Elizabeth his wife, late Elizabeth Ramsden. widow, and theretofore E. Oistin, daur and co-heires of Edward O. decd., to DANIEL HOOPER of Christ Church, Esq. £83. 7. 6. paid. Sale of 27 acres of land in Christ Church, abutting on lands of Col. Richd. Elliot.

John Blagrove, decd., Margaret Bailey, Reter Baxter, on the sea, on Oistin's town, and on other lands of D. H. sd. Miles James, Eliza. James, Wits: Edwd. Harlestone, Fran. Catlin, Daniel Hooper junr.

23 July 1696. ROBERT HOOPER of St. George and Anna his wife, to John Broome of St. Lucy. £400 paid. Sale of a tract of land containing several small plantations together about 20 acres, formerly belonging to Capt. Daniel Kendall to whom Anna is daur and heiress; together with the houses and 16 slaves. sd John Broome. Wits: Wm. Cleland, James Hancock.

23 July 1696. ROBERT HOOPER of St. George, his Majesty's Attorney General, and Anna his wife to Henry Feake of St. Michael, gent., and John Wiltshire of St. George. Conveyance of 16 slaves upon certain trusts. sd Robert Hooper, Anna Hooper. Wits: Michael Glyd, Jas. Taylor, Tho. Poor.

20 Nov. 1697. MARY HOOPER to JOHN HOOPER. Conveyance of a negro girl slave. sd Mary Hooper. Wits: Elizabeth Carleton, Ann Chase.

7 Augt. 1703. James Cowse of St. Michael, attorney of James Sherry of London, merchant, to DANIEL HOOPER and ROBERT LETTIS HOOPER of Christ Church, Barbados. £132. 10. Conveyance of 13 ac. 1 rd. of land in St. George, abutting on lands of Capt. Daniel Hooper, Wm. Bulkeley, Samuel Webb, and John Hill, formerly of Sir Peter Leare. sd. James Cowse. Wits: Francis Pile, Fredk. Feake.

5 March 1702. DANIEL HOOPER and ROBERT LETTIS HOOPER, executors of Will of Daniel Hooper decd. Release Hon. Robert Bishop and his land in Christ Church, from a judgment debt of £723. 2. 4½. sd. Dan. Hooper. Robt. L. Hooper. Wits: Ann Hooper, Wm. Parsons.

29 Sep. 1698. ROBERT HOOPER of St. George, and George Peers of St. Michael, executors of Will of Col. Richard Salter, to Capt. Robert Johnston, Capt. Thomas Alleyne, and Elizabeth Salter Widow; grant of a yearly rent charge upon a plantation and boilinghouse in St. George. sd. Ro. Hooper, George Peers. Wits: John Wiltshire, William Weaver, Charles Sawyer.

22 Decr. 1700. JOHN HOOPER of Christ Church to Mary Hall, spinster, grant of a negro girl slave. sd. John Hooper. Wits: S. Matson, Samuel Donnald.

9 July 1705. DANIEL HOOPER and ROBERT LETTIS HOOPER to Thomas Taitt of St. Andrew, chirurgeon, 40 acres of land in St. Thomas, part of Fisher's Pond plantation, paying the yearly rent of one pepper-corn at the feast of St. Michael the Archangel. Sd. Daniel Hooper, Robert Lettis Hooper. Wits. Jno. Cole, Christopher Hooper.

20 May 1708. Philip Kirton of Christ Church, Esq., and SAMUEL HOOPER of same parish, Esq., sale of slaves and 49 head of neat cattle. sd. Philip Kirton. Wits: Richard Rycroft, Wm. Baron, Thomas Maude.

5 Apl. 1711. DANIEL HOOPER Esq., one of the guardians of James Elliott, an infant, only son and heir of Hon. Richard Elliot, late of Barbados decd. Reciting Will 23 Jan. 1702 of Richard Elliott, giving his estate to his son James, and appointing Hon. Col. Richard Scott, the said Daniel Hooper by the name of his son-in-law Capt. Daniel Hooper, and his friend John Gray then in England, guardians. Sale by D.H., guardian, to William Hooper of Christ Church, of a house in Oistins Bay, alias Charles Town. sd. Daniel Hooper. Wits: Tho. Carew, Wm. Parsons.

28 April 1712. CAPT. WILLIAM HOOPER of Christ Church to James Milne. £106. Sale of land in Charles Town, alias Oistin's Bay. sd. William Hooper.

28 April 1712. ROBERT LETTIS HOOPER of Christ Church to Anthony Jones of same parish. £253. Sale of 11 ac. of land in Christ Church. sd. R. L. Hooper. Wits: Robert Jones, Jno. Dempster, Jno. Durant.

17 January 1715. WILLIAM HOOPER of St. Michael to Benjamin Jemmott of the same parish. Sale of 8 negro slaves. sd. Wm. Hooper. Wits: David Rycroft, Rich. Rycroft.

12 May 1715. ROBERT LETTIS HOOPER of Christ Church to Richard Graves of same parish. £200. Sale of 6 ac. of land in Christ Church. sd. R. L. Hooper.

19 April 1716. ROBERT LETTIS HOOPER Esq. and WILLIAM HOOPER, gent., to Wm. Legall. £210. Sale of a house in Oistin's Town, with the land abutting on lands of James Elliott, Esq., Capt. John Dempster, Capt. Jno. Adams decd. sd. R. L. Hooper, Wm. Hooper. Wits: Anthony Jones, Henry Batten.

11 June, 1718. ROBERT LETTIS HOOPER of Christ Church to Richard Rycroft of same parish. £7240. sale of 80 acres of land

in Christ Church, together with all buildings and slaves thereon. sd. R. L. Hooper. Wits: Wm. Hooper, Robert Warren, Isaac Le Gay.

9 Sept., 1720. DANIEL HOOPER of St. George to James Elliott of Christ Church. £240. Sale of land in St. Thomas containing 12 acres. sd. Dan. Hooper. Wits: Philip Kirton, H. Gibbs.

23 Dec., 1727. Rebecca Legatt of New York, widow, and ROBERT LETTIS HOOPER of the same city. £10. Sale of a parcel of land in Christ Church, Barbados, containing 5½ acres. Abutting on lands of Richard Rycroft, with the house thereon. Sd. Rebecca Legatt. Wits: John Torrance, Jere. Tothill.

The following notes concerning Mrs. Anna Hooper and the acquisition by the trustees of her marriage settlement with Robert Hooper of an English estate in the terms of the settlement have been largely compiled from information supplied by Mrs. Ursula Ridley of West Hoathly, Sussex, in whose possession is a volume of accounts of the Manor of West Hoathly Rectory and other important documents relating to the period covered by Mrs. Hooper's transactions with her London Agents.

Anna Hooper was the daughter and only child of Daniel Kendall of Barbados, under whose Will dated 29 March, 1663, she became possessed of a considerable fortune. She first married Samuel Tidcombe of Barbados, who dying in 1693 left a large estate and ample provision for his widow, including a sum of £3,000 in the hands of her cousins, John and Francis Eyles, merchants, in London. Following the terms of the Hooper marriage settlement this legacy of £3,000 was laid out in the purchase of the manor and lands of the estate of West Hoathly, in Sussex, including the Priest House, a XII century building which formerly belonged to the monks of Lewes under the Cluniac Priory of St. Pancras at Lewes. The history of the Priest House is interesting and has been written by Mrs. Ursula Ridley for and published by the Sussex Archaeological Society, Barbican House, Lewes. Confiscated by Henry VIII in 1538, the manor of West Hoathly formed part of the dowry of Anne of Cleves after her divorce from the King, and was eventually purchased by Thomas Browne in 1560 whose family had for generations farmed its lands. In 1695 Mrs. Hooper purchased the property from John and Jane Browne and others who were the then owners. It is recorded that Mrs. Anna Hooper never visited England and, consequently, she never saw the estate which she had acquired, although her former husband, Samuel Tidcombe, had stipulated in his Will, that if she should think fit to go to England, his executors were to give her a "handsome provision" for her voyage at the charge of his estate. Mrs. Hooper directed the English estate to be sold after her death (she died in Barbados in January 1715 aged 59) and by that time the Priest House had become very dilapidated. In 1906 the Priest House was completely reconditioned by Mr. John Godwin King, care being taken to preserve all the features of the place, and it was restored to approximately the condition in which Thomas Browne had left it in the XVI century.

It has since been converted into a Museum, furnished almost entirely with old-world objects from West Hoathly.

The West Hoathly estate was managed at first by Sir John Eyles, who employed Nathaniel Moore as his steward. The Great House and land was let to John Rowe. Sir John Eyles and Rev. W. Griffiths, the Vicar of West Hoathly, seem to have had many passages of arms over an annual "pension" of £3. 6. 8. which the lords of the Rectory Manor had paid to the Vicars since the time of the Cluniac monks, but only when "it needs must be paid." John Browne, the former owner, and his predecessors were not called on to pay the tithe regularly, mainly because they were known to be impecunious. But the Vicar now saw a better chance of establishing his rights with the trustees of the rich Mrs. Hooper. Sir John never answered the Vicar's letters or request for payment of the tithe, and he never went to West Hoathly. But in November 1697, in spite of the almost impassable muddiness of the roads, William Griffiths, journeyed to London and demanded his tithe in person. The vicar was not successful in recovering his tithe, but he extracted a promise from Sir John that when the roads were fit for a gentleman to ride on he would go down to West Hoathly. Nothing came of this promise, but Griffiths eventually persuaded the tenant Rowe to pay him the £3. 6. 8., who hoped to be allowed to deduct it out of his half-year's rent. Sir John would not hear of this, and Rowe refused to pay another penny of the tithe. In September 1698 the impoverished vicar wrote a letter to Sir John Eyles, which is still preserved with the rest of the correspondence on the subject.

"To Sir John Eyles at Mr. ffrancis Eyles's house in Great St. Helens near the church.

Sir,

I have with patience expected your presence at Hoathly this summer according to your promise made to me in London November last but I cannot expect you now so near the winter. This is therefore to desire the favour of you to let me know what I shall depend upon as concerning the tithe due to me from your purchase in my parish. There is one half year which you owe me for your field, when Michelmas comes there will be three years due from Mr. Rowe your tenant, which he (as he pretends) refuseth to pay because you and your articles between you and him barred him from it. All which, if I be not deprived of my lawful, customary and just dues, amounts to £7 and odd money which is great deal of money in a poor vicar's pocket and would do me a great kindness if I had

347

them; but how poor or how rich person I am it is just and reasonable I should have my due. Never do I believe you intend to deprive me of a penny that is so. However yours nor any other man's promise without performance paid any debt; and therefore I desire you would be so kind to let me know what I am to depend upon, for had I not trusted to your promise of coming down and reconciling your differences or mistakes I would have fined your good tenant long ago for I know too well that delaying is too often denying, and many an honest man suffers for his patience. I have a great family to maintain and the living is small and already it hath no reason to be diminished or made less by carelessness or neglect. But as you have the report of an honest, just gentleman I doubt but you will show yourself such by ordering my dues to be paid me. So hoping shortly to have a line or two in answer to this,

Yours sir, your humble servant,

W. GRIFFITHS."

The letter did not have the desired effect, and the Vicar instituted proceedings against Sir John and Francis Eyles. Rowe, the tenant, to his great chagrin was brought into the affair, and although the result of the lawsuit is not recorded, Rowe seems to have been so worried over it that he left the Manor and farm, and it was afterwards let to Walter Bonwick.

Sir John found the West Hoathly estate a nuisance, and his cousin Anna very troublesome and unbusinesslike, and he refused to continue to act as her agent. John Tidcombe, her late husband's nephew, and then a London merchant, who had never seen Anna or corresponded with her "other than is usual with relatives at a distance" consented to act for her "purely out of regard to her as his aunt." In 1700 he rode down to West Hoathly, a journey which cost him £4. 15. He found the barns of the manor in bad repair and the old Tudor house shabby and dark because of the many blocked up windows. He agreed to do repairs to the house and barns, and the chancel of the church at a cost of £48. 7. It had been the duty of the lords of the manor from the time of the Cluniac monks to repair the chancel, and this was continued up to the year 1936.

John Tidcombe's accounts are still preserved in a large volume in the Manor House of West Hoathly, and offer some very interesting examples of Anna Hooper's expenditure on her step-son Edward Hooper, who had been sent about the time of his father's death to England to school, where his sister Katharine, who had married Barnham Goode, was living in Kingston-on-Thames. Edward seems to have spent his school holidays with his cousin Elizabeth Titus, who was afterwards named as a beneficiary in Anna's Will.

The following extracts from John Tidcombe's accounts, showing how the rents of West Hoathly were used, may be of interest:

"1702-3. ffebry 10.   To paid Queen's Tax, £12. 7. 6.

1705. ffebry 8.   — To paid the Lord's rent (to the Vicar) £1. 5.

1705-6. ffeby 8.   — To paid taxes at Hoadly for 1704 £25. 3. 9.

1707 July 1.   — By received for 1300 marles at two shillings and six pence a hundred. £1. 12. 6.

This was used for fertilizing the land.

1709-10 ffebry 6 — Recvd. ffines and admissions £3. 15.

1704-5 ffebry 28 — To paid Mrs. Elizabeth Titus for her (Anna's) son £50.

          To paid ditto on her own account £12. 10.

1705. May 8th — To paid Mr. Tully the surgeon for Edward Hooper £43.

May 22nd — To paid Doctor Taylor's bill, £8. 12.

May 11th — To paid Mr. Edward Hooper one month's pockett, 10/-.

June 30th — To paid for a box for ditto, 5/-.

          To paid for a gown for Mr. Edward Hooper £1. 2. 6.

July 2nd — To paid Mr. Goode's expenses for going to Oxford, £2. 10. 6.

          To paid Mr. Edward Hooper his pockett money going to Oxford, £1. 1. 6.

July 5. — To remittance to Mr. Hudson of Queen's College for her son, £30.

These payments occur regularly.

1705. July 17. — To paid for a suit of clothes for her son £6. 5. 8.

„   „ — To paid for peruke for ditto, £2. 3.

July 20th — To paid Schoolmaster's bill in full £20. 8. 5.

1705-6. ffebry 16. — To paid for her children's maintenance £60.

During this period we find many entries connected with an Act of Parliament which had to be passed before Robert Hooper's Plantation could be mortgaged to pay the debts he had left at his death. Many payments to lawyers include:—

"1703. Aprill 10. — To paid Mr. William Peere Williams his fee, £2. 6. 6.

1704-5. Jan. 8 — To paid Customs of a Barrell of Sugar sent Mr. Williams, 17/6.

ffebry 8 — To paid coach hire at sundry times £1. 6. 6.

1706. June 6 — To paid cash by her looking into S. Fort Plantation affair £3. 16. 8.

These expenses were paid out of West Hoathly funds along with such items as:—

1703-4. ffebry 5 — To paid customs, etc., of Cittron Water sent to Coz. Titus, 7/6.

1704-5. ffebry 28	—	To paid Customs of sundry tokens sent her friends, £3.
1707. Aprill 5	—	To paid to Mr. Barnham Goode for his wife's maintenance, £55.
1710. December 11		To cash paid charges on a box of plants and a box of seeds per Captain Swann, £1. 3. 6.
1712. July 10	—	Freight of plants from hence, £1.

Tidcombe received money from other than Sussex sources. We find many entries concerning consignments of sugar sent over for him to sell, as well as:—

1704. Nov. 4	—	By recevd a Bill of Exchange on Mr. Holder, £50.
1707. May 29.	—	By neat proceed of a jewell recevd. by the Lancaster, £149. 19.
September 13		By neat proceed of 6 hogsheads of sugar by the Francis & Elizabeth, £40. 3. 9.
1710. March 13	—	By neat proceed of 19 baggs of Cassia* per Captain Swann, £19. 13.
1706. May 30	—	By neat proceed of 19 hogsheads of sugar, £122. 15. 7.
„ „	—	By ditto of a loss of seventy five pounds on the *Somersett*, £61. 8. 5.

The risks to shipping were considerable, what with storms, pirates and French privateers who were very active in West Indian waters during the War of the Spanish Succession. Insurance rates were very high.

"1705. July 20 — To £250 insured in sundry ships, £33. 14. 6.

It was evidently wiser not to risk all one's gold in one ship. The "sundry ships" which carried Anna's trade included the *Devonshire* galley, the *Two Brothers*, the *Nesbit*.

Before leaving Oxford in 1707 Edward Hooper presented to Queen's College two silver tankards, still in use there. They bear his name and arms:—A bend charged with three annulets between three boars. They are entered in the College inventory under the date 1704, are in Tidcombe's accounts for 1707, but bear the hall mark of 1744.

Apart from the regular payments to Mr. Hudson we find in

1706. July 2nd	—	Bill remitted to Mr. Hudson for her son £100.
1707. May 2	—	To paid for linen for her son, £18. 17. 6.
May 16th	—	To paid for one month's allowance for ditto, £4. 6.
July 22	—	To paid a piece of Plate for her son for the College, £10. 10. 3.
July 27	—	To paid the shoemaker and barber and her son's monthly allowance, £6. 10. 6.

---

* Cassia fistula, one of the minor crops then exported from Barbados.

1707. October 30 — To paid her son at his going away, £4. 6.
     „   „   — To paying his ffoy (farewell party) £1. 7.
     „   „   — Carriage of his things from Oxon, £1. 1.
He went to stay with his father's people in Devonshire before
going back to Barbados and evidently cut something of a dash
there.
1707. October 30 — To gloves and capps for her son, 11/-.
      Nov. 24   — To paid the sword cutler, £1. 14.
      Dec. 13   — To paid the taylor for her son, £17. 16.
1707-8. Jan. 10 — To her son's bill on me when at Plymouth,
                   £88.
1707-8. Jan. 10 — To paid for saddle, pistolls, holster, etc. for
                   her son, £16. 4. 6.
      ffebry 4   — To her son's bill on me due to my friend
                   at Plymouth for balance, £47. 2. 6.
      March 5   — To paid for a pass for her son, £2. 11. 2.
Anna Hooper died in 1715. Her will written in her own large
handwriting, was made while Edward was still in England. Its
legality was disputed but finally allowed.

Full extracts taken from her will were published earlier in
this compilation of HOOPER Records, *ante*, page 32, Vol. vii,
November, 1939, No. 1. *

Anna's cousin, Eleanor Robertson, who received a legacy of
£500 under the will, seems to have taken an active part in
obtaining due administration of the estate, although it was very
difficult to come to any arrangement with Tidcombe owing to
the delays caused by distance. Ever since 1706 Tidcombe had
been complaining bitterly to his aunt that the rents of West
Hoathly and sales of sugar did not cover her presents and other
expenses. Her executrix ordered him to pay large legacies by
selling the property. This Tidcombe refused to do until he had
been repaid the £645. 8. which Anna's presents had cost him.
After years of litigation the courts ordered the sale of the West
Hoathly property. A purchaser was found in 1731 in Robert
Bostock of Otford, Kent, who paid £2,400 for the land and the
Manor. Tidcombe, after deducting his expenses handed over the
money to a French sea captain who got safely past Spanish men-
of-war and pirates and delivered the money at Barbados.

_____

*See p. 328, this volume.

351

CRISPIN HOOPER OF BARBADOS

By HILDA J. HOOPER

In 1668, Colonel Robert Hooper, one of the three Commissioners to Barbados "died on his last voyage". In his will dated 1667, he asks his friend Crispin Hooper, merchant of Barbados, to reside on and manage his estate in Barbados "until my only living child Robert is of age."[1]

There are a number of deeds in the Library at Exeter, Devon, and in the possession of the Devon and Cornwall Record Society, in which the name of Crispin Hooper of West Allington (or Alvington) Devon, gentleman figures, acting at times on behalf of the well-known family of Crispin, or for William Bastard of Gerston in West Alvington, from 1596 onwards. Number 1216, dated 20th April, 1690, is an Indenture of a fine levied by William Tottell of the Middle Temple and Phillip Brockdon of Dodbroke on a messuage in West Alvington for the benefit of Crispini Hooper and Elizabeth his wife, signed Crispini Hooper, and endorsed "my first wife's jointure".

There is a lease dated 1st September 1620, from William Bastard of Gerston to Crispin Hooper of Gross Park, Pinnyes Park and Lulham, for 99 years on the lives of Crispin Hooper, Elizabeth his wife and William their son, signed "Crispin Hooper"[2].

"1630–31. Henry Tothill of Paymoure to Crispin Hooper of West Alvington: Lease of a Mansion House of Paymoure [Peamore] and certain messuages and lands adjoining in the parish of Exminster, the manor of Dodbrooke, and many other lands in Devon. Lands in Dadbrooke the jointure of Elizabeth wife of Crispin Hooper of W. Alington." Assuming Crispin Hooper to be aged 21 in 1596, he would be born about 1575. He was married to his first wife Elizabeth (perhaps daughter of Philip Brockdon of Dodbroke) by April 1619, and their first son William Hooper was born by August 1620. Other children of the marriage were Henry, Crispin, Elizabeth, and Grace. Crispin Hooper married, secondly, by Exeter Marriage Licence 11th April, 1635, Rebecca Waldrob or Waldron of Dartmouth, widow, and by her had a son Gyles Hooper, or Ashburton, and a daughter Mary Crispin Hooper who died before May 1661.

His eldest son William Hooper of West Alington, Devon, gentleman, a Major in the Army, died in London in 1675, and was buried in St. Margaret's Westminster. His will, in the Perogative Court of Canterbury,[3] proved July 1675 (marked on the otuside, "Major Hoop 's will" and "Mr. Will Hooper's will"), was sealed with the coat of arms "a castle triple-towered on a gyrony of eight, armine and or".

---

1. Extracts from early Hooper wills recorded in Barbados will be found in the Society's Journal, Vol. VI, p. 198.*
   Another early Hooper will, which mentions Barbados but was not recorded there, is that of Lieut. Col. George Hooper of St. Margaret's, Westminster. This will is dated 13th August, 1648 (P.C.C. 125 Essex), from which the following has been extracted. He desires to be buried in St. Margaret's, Westminster. He leaves to Mr. Randall Warner and Isabel his wife, of Bandon Bridge, Cork, father and mother of my late wife deceased all my estate and award in Ireland settled upon me by the Parliament of England upon the rebel lands of Ireland which amount to £1,000. To my brother in law William Warner all the goods I sent him for my use in Barbados, West Indies. To my cousin Stephen Hooper in Scotland 30/-. To my cousin Elizabeth Esham here in England £80. To my cousin Aymo Govering £70. The will was proved on 25th. August by his friends David Blacke and Captain Samuel Playford.
2. Calendar of Deeds bequeathed to the Royal Albert Memorial Exeter, by J. Brooking Rowe.
3. P.C.C. 76 Dycer.
   *Page 320, this volume.

He left an annuity of £6 each to his two sisters, Elizabeth Woolcot and Grace Hooper. "To my cosen [i.e. niece] Mary Hooper of Exminster Devon, the lease of my tenement in Exminster called Court Gardens. To William Woolcot, son of John Woolcot of Dadbrooke, Devon, all my lands etc., in Dadbrooke, also goods and money in West Allington. Overseer, until he is of age 21, to be William Bastard of Garston, Esq.,—John Bare of Barescombe, Esq., and John Woolcot of Dadbrooke, trustees, William Woolcot to be sole Executor." There was a further administration in April 1677, of this will, presumably when William Woolcot came of age.

Major Hooper lodged in Westminster with "Alice Harrison, my landlady, to whom £10.," and he asked that Mr. Robert Northleigh and Mr. John Gidley of London, should arrange his funeral.

Crispin Hooper of St. George's, Barbados, merchant, by his will dated 30th September, 1685, proved in November 1686,[4] "To be buried in St. George's Church." To the poor of West Alving, co. Devon, (being the place of my birth) £100. "To my dear friend Mistress Tomasin Bastard, (living in or near Kingsbridge, co. Devon,) in grateful love of her constancy to me £200." [Perhaps this is "Thomasine, daughter of my cosen (i.e. nephew) John Bastard deceased", mentioned in the will of William Bastard of Garston 1639,[5] of the house called "Collapit" in Garston, parish of West Alington.] "To my eldest sister, Elizabeth Woolcott of Kingsbridge Devon, an annuity of £25. To John Woolcott, son of my said sister, £50., and £100. to be divided among his children. To my sister Grace Hooper, living in Aveton Gifford, near town of Kingsbridge, £200. To my half-brother Gyles Hooper living in Ashburton, £50. and to his son Crispin £50., and £250. to be divided among the rest of my brother's children. To my half-sister Mary Hooper living near Kingsbridge and her two children £90.

To my niece Mary Asshe of Launceston, daughter of my brother Henry Hooper, deceased, and wife of Mr. Richard Asshe, goldsmith in Launceston, co. Cornwall, £130. . . ." [Henry Hooper of Exminster, perhaps married 1661 (Exeter Marriage Licence) Elinor Hele of Kingsnympton, and died before 1685.]

The church registers and Bishops Transcripts of the various places in Devon mentioned in the two wills may yield further information.

Gyles Hooper of Ashburton had sons Crispin and John, and daughters Jael, Margaret, Elizabeth, and Grace, born between 19th September 1665 and 8th June 1681. Of these, Crispin Hooper has a daughter Elizabeth born 1689; and a William Hooper at Ashburton has sons William born 1688, and Crispin born 1696, and two daughters named Elizabeth, and then Maria or Mary. There are three entries in the registers of St. John's Church, Hackney, London, 1774, 1798, 1801, relating to the name of Crispin Hooper.

John Wolcot, "Peter Pindar",[6] 1738–1819, satirist, and poet, was born at Dodbrooke near Kingsbridge, son of Alexander Wolcot, surgeon, son of a country surgeon, was probably a descendant of John Woolcot and Elizabeth Hooper. There seems to be a certain resemblance in personal appearance and character between "Peter Pindar" and Alexander Woolcott, broadcaster and author of the United States, whose father was the younger of two brothers who left England in the middle of the 19th Century, "arriving in the States in 1861, aged thirteen", "born in Greenwich." If the statement that Alexander Woollcott's father was "Walter" is true, there was a Walter, son of William Thomas Woollcott, clerk to the Finsbury Savings Bank, and Catherine Ann, née Boulton his wife, born on 27th October,

4. *Journal of Barbados Museum & Historical Society*, Vol. VI, p. 201-2. *
5. P.C.C. 88 Harvey
6. *Dictionary of National Biography.*

    * Pages 323-324, this volume.

1848, at 4 Lower Rosoman Street, Amivell, Clerkenwell. There was another Walter, born in the first quarter of 1846, at Whitechapel.

There is also recorded at Somerset House a birth at Greenwich on 1st April, 1848, at 6, Sexton Place, of George John son of George Woolcott, cordwainer, and Elizabeth, née Fleming, his wife. There are very few Woolacots, Wolcots, Woolcotts, etc., born between 1845–8, and those mostly in London or Devon. It would be interesting if any connection could be traced between the two men of letters. There is a "Woolacombe" Bay North West of Barnstaple, and many names of North West Devon villages end with "cott"—the name Woolacot was probably a place name.

The name Hooper is also interesting as denoting the keepers of Hoopern or Whoopern towers (watch towers against the Danes: Anglo Saxon "Hwopan"—to threaten). In Norman times this man was called "Le Hoper" (Old French, meaning "one who calls to another from a distance"), and there is little doubt that these men had to be able to utter a high-pitched warning call, audible for a great distance. The Vikings usually entered a country by its waterways, so watch towers on the banks of the rivers were an essential form of protection, just as the Martello towers were built on the Kent and Sussex coasts in Napoleon's day. Some of these ancient towers still stand on the river Suir in South East Ireland, with the Comeragh Mountains on one side and the Slievanaman Range on the other. Other Hoopern towers would be on a height, accessible to the neighbouring population and their cattle, which were driven into the foot of the towers.

Hothersall of Barbados.

Eliz. Hothersall of L., wid. Will dated 28 Aug. 1658. My grandchild Eliz. H., dau. of my s. Theobald H., my 2 messuages in Hart Str., Covent Garden, p. of St Martin's-in-the-feilds, & her heirs, & in default of issue to my grandchild Mary H., one other of the daus. of my sd son, my grands. Robert H., s. of my sd s. To my grandchild Mary H., my messuage in Phœnix Alley in or near Hart Str., &c. To my sons John H. & Theobald H., a trunk of linen marked G. A., standing in the house of my s. T., called the Goate Taverne in Smithfeild. My dau.-in-law Eliz. H., wife of my s. T., my best diamond ring, sd grd daus. not 18. My grandson Theo., s. of my sd s. Theo., one silver tankard & porringer. All res. to grdchd Eliz. H., & sole Ex'trix. I appoint my sister, Mistris Isabella Lusher, & friend Master Rob. Smith, overseers, £5 each. Proved 21 Feb. 1658, ad' to Theo. H., the Father of Eliz. H., testx, l. of St Sepulchres. On 11 Feb. 1666, comr to Wm. Avery the G. of Eliz. H., a minor, Theo. H. being dead. (98, Pell.)

Mary Allanson of Wandsworth, wid. My dau. Eliz. Hothersall. My s.-in-l., Rich. H., dec^d, & his brother John H. Eliz. H., wife of my grandson Theobald H., citizen and vintner. P. 1653. (135 Brent.)

John Burch of Guydiehall, co. Essex, Esq. Will dated 17 Nov. 1668. Funeral not to exceed £300. To my wife Margarett B., my manor & lands of Guidiehall in the p. of Hornechurch, the house, the parke with the warren, & the Unicorne Inne for her life, then to my sister Rebeccah Hothersall. On my purchase of the s^d manor I settled a lease of 1000 years of a part of the lands in the names of Tho. Kendall, Esq., since dec^d, & of Wm. Drax, Esq., to be for my wife & sister. To my said wife £1500, books, jewells, plate, coach-horses, coach & produce, & the one moyetie of my plantation called Hogsty, in St John's p., I. of Barbadoes, cont. 500 a., negroes, cattle & stock, & the moiety of my storehouse in the town of St Michael's, & the other moiety to my sister Rebecca H., & the reversion of my wife's ½ to her, & the remainder of the whole to my 2 nephews Tho. H. & Burch H. All produce to be consigned to Mr Tho. Cooper, merchant, & whereas my brother-in-l., Thos. H., hath, in pursuance of an agreement of marriage had between Tho. Muddiforde, son of Sr Tho. M., Bt., & Frances, the dau. of the said Thos., since dec^d, contracted a debt of £1200, secured by a mortgage of some est. in the Barbadoes, I give to my six nephews & nieces, the ch^n of my s^d sister Rebeccah, £1200, to redeem the said mortgage, & to be secured to them. To my sister £500. Eliz. Clarke, my housekeeper, £100. My cosen Tho. Cave, £100. My cosen Abigall, wife of Geo. Ash, £50. Mr Tho. Cooper, £100. Governors of Christ's Hosp. £100. To my 6 nephews & neeces John, Tho, Burch, Eliz., Reb^a & Anne H., & my neece Abiah Trott, the dau. of my sister Eliz. Trott, £300 apiece at 16 or m. All residue to my wife & sister. My wife sole Ex'trix in Eng., & my loving friends Col. Sam. Barwick, Capt. James Thorpe & Lt John Sayers Exors. in T. at the B'oes., Mr Tho. Cooper & Mr Wm Drax, overseers in Eng., £30 a piece. To the chapel of Rumford, in the p. of Hornechurch, 2 silver flaggons of £12 apiece. £5 to the minister for my funeral sermon. Proved 4 Dec. 1668 by Marg^t B., p. r. to the others. (151, Hene.)

Proved also in B'os 8 Feb. 1668-9 by Chr. Codrington with a copy attested by the Lord Mayor. (Barbados Records, vol. xv., p. 66.)

Barbadoes. Dame Rebecca Bridge. Will dated 18 Nov. 1671. To be interred in St John Church. To my dear husband Sr Tobias B. all my pers. est., & Giddy Hall in Essex, for his life, now in the possession of my sister Margarett Burch, & after his death to my son John H. My husb^d to quit all disbursements laid out here on this plantation called Hothersall's Poole. He to remember my 3 daus. & grandchild Rebecca Kendall, & to be G. to my two sons Tho. & Burch H. If he die before me then I give his nephews Francis John & Tobias B. all his moneys. To my daus. Eliz. Kendall, Rebecca & Anne H., & my grandchild Rebecca Kendall, all my personal est., both here & in Eng., & plate, excepting £50 to Mr Wm Lashley, minister. Nurse Slogrove to enjoy her 3 acres & 2 to be added. My son, Thos. Kendall, sole Ex'or, & care of all est. here till my husband arrives. Signed with a cross. Witnessed by Henry Byrch, M. Leolin Loyd, Rebe^k Beale. Proved 29 March 1672 com^r to Sr Tobias Bridge, K^t. (26, Eure.)

John Hothersall of Guydyhall in the p'sh of Hornechurch, co. Essex. Will dated 30 July 1694. To my 1st s., Tho. H., all my est., r. & p., both here & in the I. of Berbados at 25. My dau., Meliora, £1200, & £300 I have put into the Million Act on the lives of my s. Thos. Burch and herself, at day of m. or 21. My

Arms.—*Azure, a leopard rampant ppr.* [Hothersall]. (Quartered by Pinder. Jewers' M.I. of Wells Cathedral, p. 278.)

Capt. Tho. Hothersall, sen., of Barbados,⊤ Justice of No. 1 Precinct 1631; purchased 1000 acres before 1641; His plantation marked in Lygon's map; bur. 2 May 1659.

Capt. John Hothersall of B. 1638.

A

Tho. Hothersall, jun., mort-⊤Rebecca Burch of Hother-⊤Sir Tobias Bridge, Kt., gages his plantation in St. John's 1658; bur. 14 Feb. 1668-9, but *query*, as he was dead at date of will of Col. John Burch 17 Nov. 1668. Will recorded in 1669.

salls Poole plantation and of Gidea Hall; bur. at St. John's Barbados. Will dated 18 Nov. 1671; proved 29 March 1672 (26, Eure).

C.-in-C. about 1662, *vide* Col. Cal.; Col. of the English Reg., Barbados, 1669; mar. 25 July 1669; M. of C. 1672.

s.p.

B

John Hothersall, born 1654;⊤Meliora of Giddy Hall 1693; matric. from Magd. Coll., Oxf., 20 Jan. 1670-1, aged 16; M. of C. 1685. Will dated 30 July and proved 30 Sept. 1694 (216, Box).

(? Drax), living 1707.

Thos. Hothersall, a minor, ? M. of C.⊤ and dead 1701.

Tho. Hothersall of Merton Coll., Oxf., matric. 14 July 1696, aged 15; ? recommended for the C. 1701.

C

Tho. Hothersall of Hothersalls Poole plantation and Gidea Hall, a minor 1694; died bachelor. Will dated 27 Feb. 1707; proved 12 July 1710 (159, Smith). At his death Gidea Hall was sold to Sir John Eyles.

Burch⊤ Hothersall, heir to his brother Tho. 1707; living 1746.

John⊤Joyce, Hother- sall. sister of John Farmer, Esq.

Eliz. Hothersall, mar. 1st Sam. Osborne, whose will was dated 11 Oct. 1756, and 2ndly Fra. Ford, who died 1772. She died 1773 intestate.

John Hothersall,⊤ nephew and coheir 1703 of John Farmer.

John Hothersall of Hothersalls,⊤Amy North, dau. and heir of Geo. N.; died 28 Esq., died 22 Nov. 1796, aged 80. March and bur. 5 April 1785, aged 60. M.I. M.I. at St. John's. Bath Abbey.

Dau., ? mar. Hon. Wm. Bishop, President of the C. She died 21 March 1816. He died in L. 21 Aug. 1801, aged 49. M.I. in St. Peter's, Barbados.

Eliza Maria Hothersall, died 1 Jan. 1771, aged 5.

Ann Isabella Hothersall, 1st dau. and coheir, mar. 30 Jan. 1766 Hon. Wm. Pinder, Chief Justice. He died 14 Dec. 1806 on his estate. M.I. at St. John's. Their son quartered the arms of Hothersall. She died April 1807, dau. Rebecca H. £1200 & £200 in the Million Act on the lives of my s. Guy & Edward, at day of m. or 21. To my sons Burch, John, Guy, Edward & Francis £1200 apiece at 21. To my wife, Meliora, £200 a year out of my est. in Eng., & £100 a year out of B'os, & to be sole G. of my s. Thos. & all my chⁿ, & Ex'trix during widowhood, but if she marry I appoint my dear brother Burch H., my bro. Nich. Prideaux, & my friends Sr John Eyles & Fra. Eyles to be G. & T. My wife to also have my plate, jewells, coach & horses. Proved 12 Sept. 1694 by Meliora H., wid., the relict. (216, Box.)

A

Col. John Burch of Barbados and Gidea Hall, Rom-=Margaret . . . ., inherited ford, Essex. Will dated 17 Nov. and proved 4 Dec. | Gidea Hall; living 1671. 1668 (151, Hene).

s.p.

B

| Burch Hothersall, born March 1664; entered Merchant Taylors' Sch. 11 Sept. 1679; M.A. Oxf. 1682; from Eman. Coll., Camb.; M. of C.; died about 1698. | Eliz. Hothersall, mar. 21 Jan. 1668-9 Capt. Tho. Kendall. — Rebecca Hothersall, spinster 1671. | Anne Hothersall, spinster 1671. | Frances Hothersall, mar. art. dated 1658 with Tho. Muddiford, son of Sir Tho. M., Bart. She was dead 1668. |

C

| Guy Hothersall, living 1707. | Edward Hothersall, living 1707. | Francis Hothersall. | Meliora Hothersall, mar. Hallett of Axmouth. died Nov. 1733. 1746 (152, Potter). | Rich. She He died | Rebecca Hothersall. |

(? Thos.) . . . . Hothersall=Hester . . . .

Ann Cath. Hothersall, great-niece 1777 of Mrs. Kath. Tunckes, wife of . . . . Harris 1781.

Tho. Hothersall of Guydy Hall, co. Essex, Esq., 1st s. & h. of John H., l. of G. H., dec^d. Will dated 27 Feb. 1707. My l. F., by will dat. about 31 July 1694, gave all his est. to me subject to payments not yet fully satisfied. I appoint John & Joseph Eyles two of the sons of Fra. E. of L., Esq., to be my Ex'ors and T., & give them my freehold estate Guydy Hall to sell & pay legacies due to my brothers & sisters, & I give them my plantation in the I. of Barbadoes called Hothersall's Poole, with negroes & stock, to pay to my Mother, Mrs Meliora H., £300 a year in satisfaction of the annual sums left by my father's will, & after discharge of all legacies to my Mother for life then to my bro. Burch H., he to then pay £50 a year to my brother Guy H. & £100 a yr. to my bro. Edward H. To Ex'ors £50 a piece. Proved 12 July 1710 by both Ex'ors. (159, Smith.)

Sir Peter Colleton of St Jas., Middx., in his will of 1693-4 appoints John H. of Gueddy Hall, Rumford, Essex, Esq., an overseer.

Mary Phillips, widow. Will proved 1705. My brother John Hothersall. My father-in-law Mr Fred Phillips of New York, merch^t. (37, Gee.)

John Farmer, Esq. Will proved 1705. My sister Joyce Hothersall. One moiety of my est. to my nephew John Hothersall, gent. My nephew Fred. Phillips. (88, Gee.)

1724, Oct. 27. Burch Hothersall's affidavit to the will of John Sampson at B'oes.

Sarah Yeamans, of B'os, widow. Will dated 11 Dec. 1724. Burch Hothersall, Esq., an Ex'or.

Joseph Hawes of Antigua, planter. Will dated 31 March 1738 in London. Witnessed by John Hothersall.

Harry Slingsby of B'os. Will dated 21 Aug. 1746. Burch Hothersall of B'os, Esq., an Ex'or. Geo. North of B'os & L. Will proved 1763. My dau. Amy wife of Mr John Hothersall. My interest in a plantation in B'os. (145, Cæsar.)

1631. Thos. Hothersall Esq., Justice of No. 1 precinct from the Windward Point to Mangrove Bridge. (Memoirs of the First Settlement, p. 16.)

1638. Thos. Hothersall and Capt. John H. then owners of more than 10 acres. (*Ibid.*)

1641, Aug. 11. Tho. H., gent., for 16,000lbs. of cotton sells to Tho. Cliff 200 acres, part of 1,000 a. Tho. H. bought of Henry Hawley. (B'os Records, vol. i., p. 171.)

1658, Apr. 20. Tho. H., of B'os, the Y^r, for £1250, pd by Wm. Sharpe of B. M^t have sold him my plⁿ of 140 a. in the p'sh of St John, bounded N. with Ferdinando Paleologus, Cap. Geo. Martain, and Col. Jno Burch ; E. by Ed. Ash ; S. by Geo. Horster and Kendall plⁿ ; W. by Cap. Tho. Hothersall, S^r, etc., with the Ingenio. ("Gent. Mag." for 1843, p. 19.)

Merchant Taylors School. Burch Hothersall, b. March 1664, entered 11 Sept. 1679.

1685, May 22. John Hothersall takes the oaths as a M. of Council.

1698, March 16. Burch Heathersall of the Council is dead. (Col. Cal. p. 137.)

1701, June 25. Govr Grey recommends for the Council Thos. Hothersall, a gentleman, whose Father had the honour to serve in Council, and who inherits his very considerable estate. (*Ibid.* p. 318.)

Close Roll, 27 Geo. III. Part 2, No. 13, 28 Feb. 1787, Ashton Warner and others. Recites the will of Kath. Tunkes, b. of St Mich. Barbadoes, widow, dated 21 Nov. 1177, by which she gave to Anne Cath. Hothersall, her great niece, £500 c. at 18 or marriage, and in case of death to Hester H. her mother, and appointed Tho. H. Esq., one of her Ex'ors, and by Ind. of 27 Apr. 1781 he has paid Anne Cath. Hothersall (now Mrs. Harris), the £500 c, (Antigua iii., 195.)

Mary, 5 dau. of Andrew Jenour of Dunmow, co. Essex, Esq. m. 1 John Hathersall, who d. s. p., and 2 John Langley of London, linendraper. (Visitation of Essex, A° 1612, p. 223.)

John Hethersoll, of Grays Inn, barr. at law, m. Martha, sister of Sir Kenelm Jenour, Bart. She rem. John Langley of L. Ald., who d. 1639. (Misc. G. et H. 2 S. iii., 169.)

A pedigree of Hothersall of H. is in Baine's *History of Lancashire*, iv. 110.

See Phillipse in Burke's *Landed Gentry* and Bath Abbey Register.

ST. JOHN'S, BARBADOS.*

BURIALS.

1659 May 2 Thomas Hothersall, Esqre.
1662 Dec. 27 William, s. of Capt Thos Hothersall.
1668-9 Feb. 14 Capt Thomas Hothersall.
1689 Oct. 20 Elizabeth, dau. of Capt Hothersall.
1752 May 25 Burch, s. of John Hothersall, Esqr.
1754 July 13 George Burch Hothersal, s. of Mr John Hothersall.
1796 Nov. 1 John Hothersall, aged 80 y^{rs}.

MARRIAGES.

1659 July 28 Mr John Lewes and Ann Hothersall.
1662 May 20 Thomas Moddiford and Ann Hothersall.
1668-9 Jan. 21 Capt Thomas Kendal and Eliz. Hothersall.
1669 July 25 Sr Tobias Bridge and Rebecca Hothersall.
1766 Jan. 30 Mr William Pindah to Miss Ann Issabella Hothersall.
1776 Apr. 18 Francis Skeete, Esqr, to Eliza Hothersall.

ST. BOTOLPH, BISHOPSGATE.

1707 Jan. 3 Thomas Hothersall, 21, bur.
1710 Feb. 21 Mary Hothersell, 60, bur.

MAR. LIC. BY BISHOP OF LONDON.

1615, Oct. 6. Richard Hothersall of St Dunstan in the West, L., Merchant Taylor, & Elizabeth Allanson of St Brides, L., spr., at St Martins in the Vintry, L.

1620, Dec. 11. Thomas Hothersall, of St Botolph, Bishopsgate, L., Plasterer, & Margery Lane, of St. Mary Colechurch, L., spr., her parents dead; at St Mary Colechurch aforesaid.

MAR. ALLEG. OF VIC. GEN.

1667-8, Feb. 22. William Avery of Gray's Inn, Gent., Bach., about 29, & Elizabeth Hothersall of Lewisham, Kent, sp^r, about 18; consent of her mother Elizabeth Freeman, wid.; at St Mary Savoy, or St Clement Danes, or St Katherine near the Tower, L.

1689, Sept. 3. Henry Hothersall (or Hethersall) of St Andrew's, Holborn, L., Gent., Bach., about 23, & Mrs Mary Scott, of St Giles in the Fields, spr., about 24, at her own disposal; at St James, Clerkenwell.

They were married on Dec. 27 as Henry Hethergale & Mary Scott.

---

* The ancient baptisms have been lost.

359

JOHN AND SARAH ANN HUMPLEBY

By E. M. SHILSTONE

John Humpleby was born Circa 1773. He is the first of the surname mentioned in the records of Barbados, and was almost certainly born in England. His wife, Sarah Ann, was the daughter of James and Mary Bascom of Barbados; born 30 November, baptised 5 December, 1770. She was the foundress of The Ladies Association for the Relief of the Indigent, Sick and Infirm.   *

Sarah Ann Bascom married first Thomas Harris of Barbados at St. Thomas Parish Church on 28 February, 1780. There is no issue of the marriage recorded. He made his Will on 27 April, 1799, wherein he is described as a merchant of St. Michael. He gave all his estate to his wife, Sarah Ann, if she should survive him; and if they should both die at sea, to his beloved sister-in-law, Mary Elizabeth Bascom; one-half to her absolutely, and the other in trust for his niece, Mary Ann Bascom, daughter of James Thomas Bascom, at 18 or on the day of marriage.

He appointed his wife, his sister-in-law, and his father-in-law, James Bascom, executors. He died sometime in 1804 (burial not recorded) and his Will was proved on 25 April, 1804.

The next record of interest is the marriage of John Humpleby to Sarah Ann Harris, widow, at St. Michael's Church on 30 May, 1805. *The Barbados Mercury* of 1 June, 1805 notices the marriage of "Mr. John Humpleby and Mrs. Sarah Harris, widow." John Humpleby was a Bridgetown merchant, and he was also the owner of one or more sugar plantations in Barbados. On 22 April, 1803 he sold and conveyed his plantation, Perry's, in the parish of St. Joseph, of 477 acres (which may be identified as the planta-

---

*For *28 February 1780* read *28 February 1790*.

tion since known as Springfield) with the slaves, stock etc. thereon along with a parcel of land containing 6165 sq. ft. situate in Middle Street and Bolton Lane, Bridgetown, with the buildings thereon[1], to David and George Hall, merchants, for the sum of £17,664. He probably owned other plantations which may be assumed from the terms of a later power of attorney which the signed on 24 April, 1811. He is therein described as "at present of the parish of St. Michael, esquire, but intending shortly to depart the same" (evidently on a visit abroad) the attorneys being John Smith, merchant, of St. Michael, and in case of his death, Alexander King, the younger, to carry on his business, manage his plantations, and, if necessary, to sell his real estate.

A son, John Humpleby, was born to him and Sarah Ann, and the following is a record of his baptism—"Parish of St. Michael, 13 June 1806, John, son of Humpleby (sic) and Sarah Ann, his wife."

The Will of John Humpleby the elder bears date 6 May, 1806.—Will of John Humpleby of St. Michael, merchant. To John Smith the sum of £100 currency. To Robert Harris £100 currency. Residue to Wife, Sarah Ann Humpleby, and she to be sole executrix. The Will was proved 28 February, 1814. His death is noticed in the *Barbados Mercury* of 29 January, 1814.—"Last night, John Humpleby esq., of this Town"; and also in the *Gentleman's Magazine*, p. 408 — "1814 January 28, in Barbados, John Humpleby Esq. many years a respectable merchant in that Island."

There is a floor stone to his memory in the Cathedral in Bridgetown. "Sacred to the Memory/ of JOHN HUMPLEBY Esquire/ who/ In the 41st year of his Age/ Fell the Victim/ of a Violent and Dreadful malady/He departed this transitory life/on the 28th of January 1814/" (2 lines). The remainder is under a pew.

In 1816, Mrs. Humpleby made a visit to England. A power of attorney from her to Henry Cheeks, Philip Caddell and John Smith all of Barbados, dated 10 June 1816, expressed to be in her own right as well as executrix of her husband's Will, was executed and recorded. She lived to the age of eighty. An obituary notice appeared in The Barbadian Newspaper of 17 June 1850—"On 13 inst. Mrs. Sarah Ann Humpleby, widow of the late John Humpleby Esq. aged 80. The lady was the well-known foundress of the Ladies Association for the relief of the indigent, sick and infirm."

By her Will dated 22 November 1849, she gave to the Treasurer for the time being of the Ladies Association $160 for the use of the said Association, and also the following other legacies, namely, to her niece-in-law, Elizabeth Bascom, wife of her nephew, Samuel Lawrence Bascom, $320; to the children of her sister-in-law, Mary Thomas, sister of her deceased husband, John Humpleby; and to the Orphan children of the late William Henry Humpleby, nephew of her late husband £25 stlg. each. To Tabitha Wood, residing in England, niece of her husband, £25 stlg. To her nephew, Joseph Straghan Bascom, $320. To each of her nieces, Sarah Racker, Margaret Richards, Mary Bascom, widow of her late nephew, George Bascom, and to Margaret Humpleby Allder, $640. To her nephew, Augustus Morris Crichlow King, the interest on the said sum of $640 during his lifetime and on his death the said sum to be divided amongst her said nieces as above stated. The residue of her estate was given to her "beloved daughter-in-law, Thomasin Humpleby." Her said daughter-in-law, and friend Conrade Adams Howell and her nephew, Joseph Straghan Bascom to be executrix and executors. The Will was signed by her mark, owing possibly to her advanced age and physical incapacity.

1. Distant plantations invariably maintained a warehouse at one of the seaport towns for storage of the sugar shipments pending the loading of the vessels. The sale of a plantation often included the town warehouse.

John Humpleby the younger was married at St. George's Church, Barbados, on 31 October 1828 to Thomasin Inniss, daughter of John Inniss.[2] They had a daughter, Thomasin Ann, baptized at St. Michael on 25 January 1830.[3] She died in infancy and was buried at St. Michael on 27 December 1831.

John Humpleby the younger died in Bridgetown on 10 August 1844 aged 38 years,[4] having made his Will on 4 April 1837 by which he gave all his estate to his wife (not named) and appointed her as executrix and her brothers, John Inniss and James Inniss as executors. The Will was proved on 8 November 1844. His widow, Thomasin, became the President of the Ladies Association in succession to Miss McBreedy who had succeeded the first Mrs. Humpleby, the foundress, as President. Thomasin Humpleby died on 2 February 1894 aged 86 years.[5] She was the last person to bear the surname HUMPLEBY in Barbados.

2. 1828 October 31. *Married*: This morning at St. George's Church by Rev. John Brathwaite, Conrade Adams Howell Esq. to Elizabeth, eldest daughter, and John Humpleby Esq. to Thomasin, second daughter of the late John Inniss Esq.—*The Barbadian Newspaper*.
3. *Birth*: On Saturday, 17 inst. at Springfield, residence of Mrs. John Inniss, the lady of John Humpleby Esq. of a daughter.—*The Barbadian Newspaper*.
4. *Died*: Yesterday at the residence of his mother, aged 38, John, only son of the late John Humpleby Esq.—*The Barbadian Newspaper*.
5. *Burial*: St. Michael, 2 Feb. 1894, Thomasin Humpleby, Relict of John Humpleby Esq. Abode Innissmoyle, Barbarees, St. Michael, aged 86.

JOHN & SARAH HUMPLEBY

Since the article on John and Sarah Humpleby appeared in the February issue of this Journal,[1] the Society has been presented with some interesting relics connected with the Humpleby family by Miss Olive Inniss, a great-niece of Mrs. John Humpleby Jnr. The first is a memorial brooch commemorating Thomas Harris, the first husband of Sarah Humpleby. The brooch is painted on porcelain and depicts two ladies, the elder of whom is probably intended to represent the widowed Sarah Harris, who points at a mother-of-pearl tombstone on which is recorded:

"T. HARRIS.
O.B. 12 Apl.
1803, AET
35."

From the mouth of the younger woman issues forth a banner, with the words "YOU PART TO MEET AGAIN." Behind the tombstone is an urn from which a bird is drinking whilst its mate flies towards the urn. Overhead, the branches of a weeping willow droop. At the base of this scene is a loose plait of hair, one end of which partly surrounds the rim of the locket.

Miss Olive Inniss informed the writer that during the French Revolution Mr. and Mrs. Thomas Harris were in France and escaped in the costume of French peasants, Mrs. Harris in the disguise of a fruit seller. Mr. Thomas Harris, who was suffering from a severe cough, was smuggled on board a waiting ship in a large coil of rope. Much to Mrs. Harris's relief, her husband was not seized by a fit of coughing during the search of the ship by the Republican Guards, or by the prodding with bayonets of the coil of rope in which Mr. Harris was concealed.

A silver snuff-box belonging to Mrs. John Humpleby Jnr., is another gift from Miss Inniss. It is oblong in shape and engraved, and bears the former owner's initials "T.H." (Thomasin Humpleby) It was made at Birmingham by Wardell & Kempson — Circa 1830; the date letter is obliterated.[2]

Three pencil drawings by Mrs. John Humpleby Jnr., presented by Miss Inniss, show much artistic talent, although these appear to be copies. It was Mrs. John Humpleby Jnr., who started her great-niece, Miss Dora Howell,[3] (1867—1954), on her career as an artist by teaching her to copy the work of other artists.

Miss Inniss has also presented a copy of a poem written by Mrs. John Humpleby Jnr., after the death of her infant daughter Tomasin Ann, who died in 1831. The poem is dated 1837 and three further verses were added by Mrs. Humpleby in 1887, seven years before her own death. After Mrs. Humpleby's death in 1894, the poem was discovered among her private papers.

Lastly, Miss Inniss states that the two watercolours in the possession of the Ladies' Association for the Relief of the Indigent Sick and Infirm, which now hang in the sitting-room of the Association's Home are both of Mrs. John Humpleby Snr.,[4] one of which was presented to the Association by Miss Amy Bascom and the other by Miss Olive Inniss.

1. By E. M. Shilstone, O.B.E., *B.M. and H.S. Journal* Vol. XXIV pp. 65—66. *
2. Wardell & Kempson's mark was registered in 1816. It is unlikely however, that this is the date of the snuff-box.
3. Miss Howell, well known locally for her watercolour paintings and painting on china, later received instruction from Ernest Bowen—a Barbadian artist, and in England. It is hoped later in the year to hold a memorial exhibition of the work of Dora Howell. The Director of the Museum will be glad to hear from owners of watercolours or paintings on china by Dora Howell who will be willing to lend exhibits for this purpose.
4. See "A miniature Communion Set and The Ladies' Association for the Relief of the Indigent Sick and Infirm," by Neville Connell, *B.M. and H.S. Journal*, Vol. XXIV, p. 62, *footnote* 28.

*See pp. 360-362, this volume.

MAJOR NATHANIEL KINGSLAND.

MAJOR NATHANIEL KINGSLAND, owner of Kingsland plantation in Christ Church parish, Barbados, and resident in
the island from at the latest 1645 until his death in 1686, had a
large estate in the Colony of Surinam before its rendition to the
Dutch, and also had a grant of a plantation from the Proprietors
of New Jersey lying between the junction of the Hackensack and
Passaic Rivers.

His parentage and place of birth have not yet been traced,
so far as we are aware, but he must have come to Barbados
within at most seventeen years of its first settlement by the
English. He was thrice married and had children by his second
and third wives. He was one of the representatives for the
parish of Christ Church in the House of Assembly from about
1666 to about 1677 and held the appointment of Captain and
then Major in the Militia.

In the Calendar of State Papers for 1668 and following years
is given the account of his ill-treatment by Governor Lord
Willoughby and his son Lt. Genl. Henry Willoughby in the matter of his estates in Surinam. It seems that in 1664 Kingsland
leased his plantation in Surinam, with the slaves, stock, etc.
thereon, worth £10,000, to his nephew William Sandford for five
years. On the rendition of that Colony to the Dutch the territorial rights of owners and lessees were preserved to them, but
in contravention of this arrangement Sandford was evicted by
Governor Byam and Kingsland's estate was seized by Lt. Genl.
Henry Willoughby. Willoughby's soldiers by his orders took
possession of the slaves and stock which were brought to Barbados and offered for sale. Kingsland petitioned Lord Willoughby
for relief but without success, and he (Kingsland) thereupon
caused the bellman of Bridgetown to publish a notice that the
sale of these chattels was illegal: Willoughby's soldiers who had
a share in the booty, determined not to be cheated of their
rights, "grew into a great mutiny" and one of them shot a
musket at Kingsland. For the offence against the Governor's
dignity in attempting to stop the sale, Lord Willoughy had
Kingsland imprisoned, but after three days he was released at
the request of the Assembly, on the ground that he was one of
their number and entitled to his liberty. In the meantime,
Henry Willoughby had sold the plantation in Surinam to a
Dutchman and "a great house in the town" to a drinkseller.

Kingsland petitioned the King in Council for "Royal Letters
Mandatory to Lord Willoughby to cause speedy Justice to be
done to the Petitioner", whereupon the King wrote to Lord
Willoughby expressing his just resentment at his and his son's

actions, and ordering him to restore all Kingsland's goods to him. The King's orders were not obeyed, and Willoughby went so far as to cancel the Commissions which Kingsland held, and forced him to accompany him to England for an adjustment of their differences before the King. On 6 April 1669 Kingsland and his nephew William Sandford laid their Petition before the King in Council in which their grievances against Lord Willoughby were stated. Lord Willoughby filed his answer on 23rd of the same month, and it is rather provoking to find that the Calendar of State Papers makes no further mention of the matter, so that we are completely in the dark as to the outcome of the affair. However, there is ample evidence to show that Kingsland was not eventually deprived of his Commission and public rights. Until his death he resided at his plantation Kingsland, which passed under his Will to the younger of his two surviving sons, Nathaniel, and eventually came into the possession of Thomas Applewhaite, a cousin. Through the intermarriage of the Applewhaite and Eversley families the plantation passed into the ownership of the Eversleys from whom it was purchased about fifty years ago by Mr. Thomas Birt Evelyn, whose descendants are still the owners of that and other plantations of the Kingsland group of estates.

The Kingsland ownership of large tracts of land in the State of New Jersey in the United States seems to have continued through several generations of the American branch of the family and still excites the interest of many of their descendants. Mr. Daniel F. de Beixedon, a descendant of Gustavus Kingsland, nephew of Major Nathaniel Kingsland, who is compiling genealogical details of the family, has promised for publication a transcript of the deed of 15 August 1688 by which Mary Kingsland, widow and executrix of Major Nathaniel Kingsland, transferred title to Isaac Kingsland, devisee under her husband's will of one-third interest in the New Jersey estates. Any other information relating to the family which our readers may be disposed to contribute will be published in this Journal.

Among the Society's records is a newspaper cutting (evidently of American origin, but the name of the newspaper is missing), with the date pencilled as 9 August 1925, and under the title of "Museum gets Historic Stone—Old Kingsland Manor stone finds a resting place in Hackensack". It states that the old Kingsland Manor House corner stone (evidently the house had been demolished) had been deposited in the Bergen County Historical Museum.

There is only one Monumental Inscription to the Kingsland family in the churchyards of Barbados, and that is on a stone lying near the walls on the south side of the present Chancel of the parish Church of Saint George. It seems that when the chancel was rebuilt in 1924, the workmen found a tombstone under the floor, but no evidence of a grave, with the following inscription :

Here lyeth interred ye body
of NATHANIEL Son of
ROBERT KINGSLAND obijt ye 16th
day of Sept anno dom. 1689.

The deceased was the grandson of Major Nathaniel Kingsland of Kingsland plantation, named in the latter's Will for a legacy of £250. The stone was removed and laid in the churchyard.

The records of baptisms, marriages, and burials in the parish of Christ Church for the period covering Nathaniel Kingland's lifetime are almost complete. Unfortunately, the records of St. George's parish are non-existent, hence the failure to obtain particulars of his son, Robert Kingsland's marriage and issue, since he seems to have settled in St. George's parish at an early time and to have owned estates there.

Appended are copies of the only three KINGSLAND Wills on record in Barbados, and extracts from the Christ Church parish Register showing the entries relating to Nathaniel Kingsland and his family. Extracts from the early deeds recorded in Barbados are also included, as they throw considerable light on the family's ownership of property in this Island.

BARBADOS WILLS.

Will dated 6 October 1682 of ROBERT KINGSLAND of St. George, gent. Whereas my wife Martha Kingsland is with child at my now going off this Island, and if the child shall be a male then I bequeath all my estate real and personal to my son Nathaniel Kingsland and unto such male child as aforesaid and their heirs to be equally divided between them when each is 18. But if the said child is a female, then I give such child £200 to be paid at 18 or sooner if my executrix pleases, provided my son Nathaniel is still living, but if he dies without issue then I give the whole estate to such female child and her issue for ever Failing her, the said estate to my wife if she marries again and her issue, and if she dies without issue to my brother John Kingsland and his heirs for ever.

I appoint my wife sole executrix and she is to provide for my child or children till 18 years old.

I appoint my friends, Captain Richard Sutton, and Captain Edward Claypoole overseers of my will and to see to the education of my child or children.

(sd) Robert Kingsland. Wits: Tim. Mascolls, Hen. Harding, Emanuel Mandeville, Geo. Mason, Thomas Miller.

Proved by witnesses Thomas Miller and Emanuel Miller 28 June 1683 before John Witham, Governor. Recorded 22 May 1687.

In 1679 Robert Kingsland was the Commander of the ship *Judith* which traded between Barbados and London.

Will of NATHANIEL KINGSLAND of Christ Church, Barbados, dated 14 March, 1685 [that is, according to new style of reckoning 1686].

To my nephew Isaac Kingsland and his heirs for ever one-third of my plantation in New Jersie near to New York with the third part of all the houses and slaves and live stock which shall be thereon at my death; the other two-thirds of my said estate in New Jersie to all my sons and daughters and their heirs for ever to be equally divided between them, namely, my sons John Kingsland and Nathaniel Kingsland, my daughters Isabelle Harding, wife of Henry Harding, my daughter Carralyne Barrow, wife of John Barrow, junior, my daughter Mary Walley, wife of William Walley Esq., and my daughter Hester Applewhaite, wife of Henry Applewhaite Esq.

It is my will that whereas the estate of Major Philip Kirton decd. is indebted to me in about £1500 secured by deed of sale dated 9 April 1672 of his plantation, sugar work, negroes, cattle, etc. from him to me and Richard Noake, sureties for him in the Secretary's Office, I bequeath the same to my son John to be recovered by him immediately on my death and my executrix to deliver the said deed to my son John.

Whereas I have already given my son-in-law, William Walley Esq. about £1000 with his now wife Mrs. Mary Walley: now I give him £1000 provided he make a jointure for his said wife of £200 per annum, to be paid him six months after his making the said jointure, and if he shall not do so, then I give my said daughter £1000 to be paid in two equal instalments in two years.

To my daughter Carralyne Barrow £100 to be laid out in negroes.

To my grandson, Nathaniel Kingsland, son of Robert Kingsland decd., £250 to be paid out of my estate when he is 21.

To my trusty servant, Abraham Bueno, £1000 to be paid in three years after my decease, and if he will live upon my estate until my son Nathaniel shall come of age to keep the accounts and manage my estate as he doth at present and render an account every half-year to my executrix and my good friend James Fauntleroy Esq. whom I do appoint to receive the same, then the said Abraham Bueno to receive £40 yearly during the term he shall live upon my plantation.

I bequeath my whole estate in Barbados, i.e. the plantation on which I now live, with all the houses, sugar work, windmill, coppers, stills etc. together with all the negro slaves, cattle, horses and stock, as also another plantation which I purchased from Aaron Barwick formerly part of the plantation belonging to Sir Robert Haskett, unto my son Nathaniel and his heirs lawfully begotten of his body for ever, my debts and legacies hereby bequeathed first paid, and not until the death of his mother my executrix; but my executrix shall allow him during his minority what is convenient for his education, and after his coming of age what she thinks convenient; but if she dies before he is 21 then my executors in trust shall allow him what is convenient, and the estate to be his at 21. If Nathaniel shall die without issue, the said estate to my son John and his heirs for ever, and for want of issue to my four daughters aforesaid and their heirs for ever.

To my daughter Isabelle Harding £50 two years after my decease.

My friend James Fauntleroy to inspect my plantation every six months to make up the accounts with my said servant Abraham Bueno until Nathaniel shall receive the estate, and to assist my executrix in writing to my correspondent in England and to manage all law suits etc. and to receive £40 yearly.

I appoint my wife Mrs. Mary Kingsland my sole executrix to whom I give my whole estate real and personal except what I have bequeathed to my son John during her life if she remains unmarried and pays my debts and legacies. If she shall marry again her powers shall cease and to have only one-third part of my estate for her dower and my executors in trust to be guardians of the body and estate of my son Nathaniel and to take the other two-thirds of my estate into their possession and manage the same for my said son and to pay my debts etc.

To my said wife one-third of all my household plate jewellery etc. and the other two-thirds to my son Nathaniel.

I appoint my friends James Fauntleroy and Charles Buckworth executors in trust and in case my wife shall die then to be sole executors of my will and guardians of my son Nathaniel until he comes of age and I give them £10 each to buy a ring.

(sd.) Nathaniel Kingsland. Wits: Thomas Neale, Samuel Gasalee, Henry Rushbrooke, Abra. Bueno and James Fauntleroy.

Proved before the Governor Edwyn Stede, 1 April 1686 by Neale, Gasalee and Rushbrooke as witnesses. Recorded 1 April 1686.

Will dated 5 December 1693 of MARY KINGSLAND of Christ Church, widow.

My body to be buried near the body of my husband Nathaniel Kingsland.

I give to my daughter Mrs. Hester Applewhaite, wife of Henry A. Esq. my green damask curtaines and vallins together with the bedstead and what belongs unto it. To my friends Mrs. Whetstone, wife of John Whetstone Esq. and to Mrs. Dameris Browne wife of Captain Stephen Browne and to Mrs. Mary Hart wife of Doctor Hart a mourning ring each.

To my friend Charles Buckworth of Christ Church gent all those negroes which I bought from William Rawlins and Coll. Tho. Maxwell together with all my cattle etc. due me from the estate of my husband Nathaniel Kingsland and all arrears of dower and also all my plate jewells etc. and I appoint the said Charles Buckworth executor of this my Will.

(sd.) Mary Kingsland. Wits: James Mashart, Gerrott Herbert, and John Heddoe.

Proved by Marshart and Herbert 19 July 1694 before Governor Kendall.

KINGSLAND BAPTISMS TO 1700.
All in Christ Church Parish.

1650 October 25	Nathaniel, son of Nathan Kingsland
1651 November 13	Ann, daughter of Nathan & Hester Kingsland
1653 June 7	Susanna, daughter of Nathan & Hester Kingsland
1654 September 7	Hester, daughter of Nathan & Hester Kingsland
1655 August 23	John, Son of Nathaniel & Hester Kingsland
1656 September 20	Francis, son of Nathan & Hester Kingsland
1658 January 29	Isabelle, daughter of Nathan & Hester Kingsland
1659 August 11	Hester, daughter of Nathaniel & Hester Kingsland
1661 May 29	Caroline, daughter of Nathan & Hester Kingsland
1666 April 1	Mary, daughter of Nathaniel & Mary Kingsland
1667 February 8	Hester, daughter of Nathan & Mary Kingsland
1668 May	Frances, daughter of Nathaniel & Mary Kingsland.
1669 October 10	Lucinda, daughter of Nathaniel & Mary Kingsland
1674 February	Henry, son of Nathaniel & Elizabeth Kingsland

KINGSLAND MARRIAGES TO 1700
All in Christ Church Parish.

1648 August 13	Nathaniel Kingsland & Hester Lewis
1668 December 3	Nathaniel Kingsland & Mary Coleman
1673 March 6	Henry Harding & Isabella Kingsland
1678 June 2	William Watts & Caroline Kingsland
1682 December 26	William Walley & Maria Kingsland
1684 November 27	Henry Applewhaite & Hester Kingsland

All in Christ Church Parish.

1645 October 14	Wife of Nathaniel Kingsland
1653/4 March 9	Susanna, daughter of Nathan Kingsland
1654 December	Hester, daughter of Nathan Kingsland
1656 September 9	Francis, son of Nathan Kingsland
1660 April 27	Hester, daughter of Nathan Kingsland
1661 October 23	Nathaniel, son of Nathan Kingsland
1663 November 13	Hester Kingsland
1670 September 2	Lucinda, daughter of Nathaniel Kingsland
1672 September 5	Judith, daughter of Nathaniel Kingsland
1674 February 21	Henry, son of Nathaniel Kingsland
1684 August 27	Francis Kingsland
1686 March 26	Nathaniel Kingsland
1686 November 24	John Kingsland
1694 July	Mary Kingsland

BARBADOS DEEDS

20 Novr. 1654. John Routh of Barbados, planter, sole heir and next-of-kin of Thomas Wilkinson of Barbados decd. in consideration of 30,000 lbs. of musc. sugar paid by Nathaniel Kingsland of Barbados gent sells him one-third part of 168 acres in Christ Church on which the said N.K. is now living, together with all houses etc. sd John Routh.
Witnesses: John Mackerness, John Davies, Henry Baldwin. Recorded 4 December 1654.

7 July 1655. Michael Anderson of Barbados, planter, in consideration of 2,450 lbs. musc. sugar paid by Nathaniel Kingsland of Barbados gent sells him one yoke of oxen black & white. sd. Michael Anderson.
Witness: Henry Baldwin. Recorded 10 Aug. 1655.

7 Novr. 1661. Thomas Pead of Barbados, gent., and Sarah his wife, in consideration of 5,200 lbs. musc. sugar paid by Captain Nathaniel Kingsland of Barbados, sell him a plantation of 45 acres of land in Christ Church adjoining land of Mr. George Rushbrooke, north, on William Kirton Esq. west, on other lands of said Thomas Pead, south, and on land of Mr. Thomas Davis now in the possession of the said N.K. east. sd. Thomas Pead, Sarah Pead. Witnesses : Richd. Buckworth, Hugh Powell, Thos. Hatton.

12 April, 1662. Elizabeth Kingsland of the Island of Barbados wife of Henry Kingsland now resident in England as Attorney for the said H.K. under a power dated 20th May 1662, for 10,000 lbs. muscovado sugar paid by John Jones of the parish of St. Philip, Barbados, Gent., sells him 10 acres of land in St. Philip, butting on Edward Wood west, Capt. John Thomas and Capt. William Pooles (?) east, John Chester north, Thomas Bomfield south, and fronting upon the lands of Captain Ferdinando Bushell.

X the mark of Elizabeth Kingsland. Witnesses: John Clockton, Hen. . .(missing). Recorded 25 June 1662.

3 May 1662. Edward Cranfield of Barbados gent., in consideration of a valuable sum of sugar, sells to Nathaniel Kingsland, gent. 360 ac. of land in Christ Church, Barbados, butting on lands of Robert Newman, Christopher Clarke, Robert Cole, Estate of Robert Mills, & William Cooper north, of Thomas Cloake John Cooke decd., & Robert Saunders west and on the sea south. Sealed in the presence of Thomas Hatton.

Above is meant to convey that if the said E. Cranfield when required shall pay to Capt. N.K. the sum of £150 and 9,000 lbs. musc. sugar with all costs and interest, then the said bill of sale to be void.

sd. Nath. Kingsland.

3 June 1669. Robert Gutteridge of Barbados, planter, and Mary his wife, for £112. 10 sell to Nathaniel Kingsland 12 acres in Christ Church, butting on lands of Lieut. Col. Samuel Newton, George Oker, Richard Bridgswick and Robert Ample and said N.K., together with all houses, woods, underwoods etc. sd. Robert X Guttridge, Mary X Guttridge. Witnesses: Wm. Scrape, Thomas Booths. Recorded 17 June 1669.

5 Octr. 1669. Robert Amp of Barbados planter, and Susanna his wife, for 4,000 lbs. good musc. sugar sell to Nathaniel Kingsland of Barbados Esq., 6¼ acres of land in Christ Church, butting on lands of Coll Samuel Newton north, of Doctor Daniel Gilbert east, of the said N. K. west and south, with all houses etc. sd. Robert Amp, Susanna X Amp. Witnesses: Emnl. Mandeville, Thomas Booth. Recorded 22 Oct.1669.

20 May 1678. Margaret Clarke of Christ Church, Barbados, widow, one part and Nathaniel Kingsland, Esq., and James Oistin gent of the same place of the other part. In consideration of a marriage proposed between William Watts of the said parish, gent, only son of Margaret, and Carolina Kingsland, daughter of the said N. K. and of £750 English money to be paid by N.K. as a marriage portion and for settling an estate on the said W. W. and Caroline and their children to be gotten, she the said Margaret Clarke settles one-half of her plantation with its appurtenances situate in Christ Church containing one thousand and twenty acres, butting on lands of Ralph Parrott, Coll Samuel Newton, John Redman late of Thomas Clarke, John Searle, James Lee, William Blanchard, with one-half part of six coppers, three stills and the buildings on the said plantation, and one-half of fifty negroes, upon Wm. Watts and Caroline and their issue.

sd. Margaret Clarke. Witnesses: Daniel Searle, Jo. Rowny, Richd. Seawell. Recorded 3 Septr. 1679.

7 April 1680. Robert Kingsland of St. George, Barbados, gent., and Martha my wife, for £450 Stlg paid by Nathaniel Kingsland of Christ Church, Esqre, sell him 23 negroes, men, women and children whose names are mentioned in the schedule hereto. sd. Robert Kingsland, Martha Kingsland. Witnesses John Menzies, Ralph Britton, Thomas Deacons. Recorded 28 May 1680.

8 Dec. 1680. Isaac Barton, Mariner, now resident in Barbados, owner of two-thirds of the Ketch called the *Amity of Boston*, 40 tons, now at anchor in Carlisle Bay, and now master of the said Ketch, for £25, grant unto Nathaniel Kingsland two-thirds of the Ketch for the space of one year and one day, the purpose being that if the said Isaac Barton shall repay on 8 April 1681 the sum of £25, then this deed shall be void. sd. Isaac Barton. Witnesses : Robert Hole, Abraham Bueno de Mesqt. Recorded 30 June 1684.

1 May 1684. Indenture between Mrs. Martha Kingsland of the parish of St............(missing). Widow, and David Lewis of the parish and Island chirurgeon and practr. in Physick, lease of plantation in St. George of 36 acres, butting north on lands of Captain Richard Sutton, south on lands of James Toones, west on lands of Capt. Thomas Watson, east on lands of Capt. Henry Harding, with dwellinghouse etc., for 7 years, £145 Stlg rent. Mrs. K. to have one board room and chamber at south end of the dwellinghouse during the term of the lease with full right of egress, ingress etc. Tenant to have the right to cut cherry and loblolly trees and any other trees not suitable for timber, except four mastick and one cedar tree growing on said land.

sd. David Lewis. Witnesses : Henry Harding, Marmaduke Niccolls, Thomas Estwick, James Fauntleroy. Schedule of 21 negroes, average value £20, women £14 — 30, boys £8 — 10, girls £3—5. Furniture : 2½ doz. joynt stools £3. 6. 0. 1 doz. turkey leather chairs £5. 5. 6., great tables £11, 1 sideboard table 18/-.
Recorded 19 June 1684.

13 March 1687. Henry Applewhaite Esq., to Hon. Col. John Hallett. Assignment of two sums of £2,000 each held against Mary Kingsland widow and exx. of Will of Nathaniel Kingsland decd.

sd. Henry Applewhaite, John Hallet, Mary Kingsland. Wits. : Joseph Alford, Abra: Bueno de Mesqa : , Nicholas Sayers.

6 February 1704. Indenture between Nathaniel Kingsland, late of Barbados, gent, but now of City of London, England, son of Major Nathaniel Kingsland heretofore of the parish of Christ Church, Barbados, Esqre decd., and Mary his wife, of the first part, Thomas Lemon of the parish of St. Paul Shadwell, Mdlsex. Mariner, and Captain John Kirton late of the Island of Barbados but now of the parish of St. Mary Le Bon, London, of second part and william Vaux of Clements Inn in co. of Mdlesex, gent., and George Tilden of Clements Inn aforesaid gent., of third part. To bar the entail created by the late N.K., the said N.K. and Mary his wife covenant with the said T.L. and J.K. and their heirs to levy fines before the feast of Easter next of all that capital messuage or tenement called Kingsland plantation and two stone mills with their appurtenances one boiling house with 8 coppers, 1 still house with 3 stills, cisterns, and 2 curing houses and all other houses, gardens, yards, etc., and also all those lands now planted with sugar canes near adjoining the messuage

372

and therewith now or late demised used occupied or enjoyed containing by estimation 235 acres, also 90 negroes, men, women and children to the said plantation belonging, all lying in the parish of Christ Church, Barbados, in America, and were the estate and inheritance in fee simple to him the said N.K. the father in his lifetime, and the same with the said negroes now are or late were in the tenure of the said N.K. (party hereto) his under tenants or attorneys, which said lands abut on lands of Major Thomas Maxfield [?Maxwell] south, the plantation of Mr. William Carter west, the plantation of Mrs. Elizabeth Sherman north, the plantation of Mr. John Wheatson, Mrs. Gunnett Wheatson north, James Callender decd. east, Mr. Thomas Newton east, Mr. William Parsons and Mr. Henry Risbrooke south, Mrs. Elinor Osborne north, all of which said lands etc. in the parish of Christ Church in the Island of Barbados (to wit) in the parish of All Saints in Hastings in the co of Sussex; and the parties shall stand seised of the same to the use of the said N.K. his heirs and assigns for ever. sd. X the mark of Nathaniel Kingsland, Mary Kingsland. Tho Lemon, John Kirton, Wm. Vaux, George Tilden. Witnesses : Tho. Maycock, Edmd Giles Hooper, John Day.

Barbados. By His Excellency Hon. Thomas Maycock Esq., one of the witnesses made Oath that he did see the said parties to the said deed sign etc. 27 July 1715. Robt. Lowther (Governor).

24 March 1723-24. Nathaniel Kingsland of St. Margaret Westminster, gent, to Thomas Applewhaite of Barbados Esq. Whereas T.A. and Edward Pare of Barbados gent, and George Lascelles of London, merchant, on behalf of and a surety for T.A. by bond dated 16 Sept. 1719 became bound to N.K. for £700 to secure an annual sum of £100 for his life. And Whereas in consideration of such bond N.K. on 15 Sept. 1719 conveyed Kingsland plantation and all his estate in Barbados to T.A. And Whereas E.P. and G.L. both reside in Barbados and N.K. required security given him in London. George Newport of London merchant for account of sd. T.A. hath agreed to give security £1,500 to secure the annuity, and T.A. now required further assurance of the said plantation and premises from N.K. In consideration of the new bond N.K. conveys unto T.A. Kingsland plantation, 160 acres in Christ Church butting on lands of William Carter Esq., Thomas Maxwell Esq., Conrade Adams Esq., Richard Callender and other lands of T.A. formerly part of Kingsland, together with mills and buildings and all other plantations in Barbados, white servants, negroes, cattle, horses, sheep, pigs, and utensils and implements. sd. by Robert Warren, attorney of N.K. Wits. : Humphrey Cockeram, R. Morris. Endorsed. Letter of Attorney to Robert Warren and Henry Lascelles of Barbados Esqs. to execute the deed.

sd. 11 Jan. 1723 Nathl. Kingsland. Wits. : Thomas Hawys, Simon Clarke, Tho. Newson, Tho. Tryon, John Page. Proved in Barbados by Thomas Newson. Recorded 31 March 1724.

Kirton of Barbados.

Wm. Kirton of the parish of Christ Church, Barbados, Esq., 11 November 1669. To be buried in the parish church. To my wife Margaret £1200 sterling due from Mr. Tho. Applewhaite of St. Tho. parish, and make Richd. Buckworth, Esq., Mr. Nich. Prideaux, and Mr. Richd. Seawell Exors. as to that sum. I give her also the use of half my house and sheep, poultry, etc., and one third of all my goods and household stuff, 2 negro men and women, a parcell of linen to come from Holland by Capt. Edwd. Kirton, 3 horses and my coach, and 20,000 lbs. of muscovado sugar yearly. Digorie my eldest son by my first wife 12,000 lbs. yearly, having paid many unnecessary sums for him, and £400 sterling after 5 years. My son Francis 6000 lbs. yearly to be apprenticed, then 35,000 lbs. yearly, and Mr. Tho. Cheavely of L., merchant, to receive for him 50,000 lbs. at 20 and 50,000 lbs. at 21. My daughter Dorothy Kirton 8000 lbs. yearly and 50,000 lbs. at 16 or marriage, and 50,000 lbs. the following year. All my Brookhaven plantation to my son John Kirton, which I had in marriage with his Mother my late dear wife Eliz., and confirmed to me by the late Wm. Lord Willoughby, then to Philip my second son, then to Francis my third son. My son John to have 6000 lbs. yearly till 16. To my eldest son Philip by my second wife Susanna all the plantation I purchased of Wm. Chapman, Tho. Hackleton, Geo. Hanbury, Henry Russell, John Frenicke, and Mr. John Nevinson, then to my son Francis, then to my son John. To my son Degory a silver tankard that was my late wife's Eliz., a silver sugar dish, and a spoon. To my now wife a silver tankard and half the rest of my plate, the other half to my son Phillip, my daughter Dorothy, my

Dr. John Kirton of St. Michael's parish, Barbados. Will dated 30 May 1728; proved at Barbados 22 February 1728-9. =Anne, sister of Walter Caddle; born 1700; died 7 August 1765, æt. 65. Will dated 28 May, proved at Barbados 15 Oct. 1765.

Dr. Alexander Kirton of St. Michael's, Surgeon, 1765. =Barbara, 1st dau. of Michael Anderson of Tushielaw by Janet, 4th dau. of Sir James Naesmyth of Posse, Bart.; remarried William Carter, and in 1786 succeeded her uncle in Tushielaw; died 1790.

Mary Kirton, only dau. s.p. =Philip Simmons of Barbados, dead 1765. =Rebecca ....

John Kirton-Anderson of Barbados and Tushielaw and of Albion Place, co. Surrey, born 1758; died 1816. Will dated 27 Dec. 1815; proved 20 February 1816. =Angel, dau. of .... Price, and relict of .... Maloney; Ex'trix to her husband. s.p.

Anne Kirton, married 1772; married 2ndly, in 1785, John Allen Olton of Barbados, and had a dau. Rebecca Olton who married, 1810, Sir R. A. Alleyne, Bart. =Henry Peter Simmons of Barbados, died 1779.

Philip Simmons, born 1774; died 1800. =Vernona Estwick, dau. of .... Rowan; married 1796; died 1805.

Henry Peter Simmons, died a bachelor 1845.

Benjamin Thomas Gaskin, 1st son of Colonel Gaskin of Barbados; married 1818; died 1818. 1st husband. =Anne Vernona Simmons of Tushielaw, born 1797; died 1837. =Rev. Thomas Gordon Torry, youngest son of Bishop of St. Andrews; married 1829; died 1856. 2nd husband.

Benjamin Thomas Gaskin-Anderson, born March 1819 posthumous. =Emily Claxton Callender, his cousin, of Barbados, married 1841; died 1887.

Patricea Jean Torry, died 1836.

Vernona Thomas Christian Torry,* married 1852. W. I. Genealogist. =Richard Sidney Smith, Captain R.N., died 1880.

Benjamin Thomas Gaskin-Anderson, born 1842, Colonel of Scottish Borderers. =Amelia Passmore, 1st dau. of Major William Rous Newlyn, married 1865.

son Francis, and my son John. To Eliz. Phillipps the youngest now living with me 3000 lbs. at 14. Dr. John Wharton £20. To the parish of Christ Church £20 for plate. Jewels to my wife. To my said three T. the £1600 due from Mr. Tho. Applewhaite. £100 to said Dr. J. Wharton. £300 to my daughter

* Mrs. Vernona Smith was a very enthusiastic collector of W. I. pedigrees, and sent me these Kirton notes some years ago. Her Jamaican pedigrees were, I believe, acquired by the British Museum. Others are in private hands. Will any reader supply the date of her death?

Dorothy, and the rest to pay the debt to Mr. Edwd. Boddy and Mr. Nath. Kingsland. Said three T. to be overseers. To each Exor. £10 and appoint my son Phillip one.

Witnesses: Eliz. Bainham, Doctor Wm. Dunne, Capt. Wm. Eyton.

Proved 23 November 1669; sworn before Chr. Codrington, President.

Entered at Barbados 27 November 1669.

John Kirton of St. Michael's parish, Barbados, practitioner in physick and chyrurgery, 30 May 1728. To my wife Anne all my estate, and Ex'trix.

Witnesses: M. Duncan, Wm. Murray, John Richards.

Proved 22 February 1738 in the presence of Ja. Dottin, President.

Barbados, entered 22 February 1738.

Ann Kirton of Christ Church, Barbados, widow, 28 May 1765. All my 99 acres and house in Christ Church, 12 negro men, 8 women, 8 boys, 11 girls to Jas. Simmons, Benj. Nicolls, Walter Caddle, Junior, and Henry Peter Simmons on T. To Mrs. Susannah Frettor £10 c. a year. My son Alexr. of the parish of St. Michael, surgeon, the use of my plantation for life and subject to the education and care of my granddaughter Ann Kirton and my grandson John Kirton, his children, after their Father's death, to his said two children, viz., two thirds to John at 22 and one third to Ann. If my said grandson John die then two thirds to Ann and one third to my daughter Mary Simmons, widow. If Ann die first then all to John; if both die then all to my daughter Mary Simmons; if all three die then the plantation to be sold and then £200 to my sister Eliz. Purchase or her son Alex. Purchase, £200 to Mrs. Cath. Miller of Christ Church or her daughter Ann Miller, £100 to each of the children of my brother Walter Caddle, Esq., and £50 to my nephew Anderson Stanton. £50 to my niece Anne Bend his sister, and £50 to each T., and all the rest to the said Wr. Caddle, Junior, and Hen. Peter Simmons. Henry Beckles, Esq., Tho. Woolford, and Richd. Wiltshire, Esq., Exors.

Proved 15 October 1765 before Chas. Pinfold, President.

Barbados, entered 15 October 1765.

Rich\d Kirton of New Windsor, 19 October 1748. My wife Keturah. My daughter Keturah Kirton. My sister Susannah Hathaway.

Proved 17 November 1748.

Additions and Corrections

Page 66. *

Johannes Kirton, Americanus ex Insula Barbados, 9 Aug. 1720. (Peacock's "Leyden Graduates.")

From a stone at Christ Church it appears that John Kirton, M.D., died 15 July 1738 (Archer, p. 380), so the probate of the will 1728-9 may be an error for 1738-9.

Mr. B. P. Scattergood of 7 and 9 Cookridge Street, Leeds, has acquired some forty volumes of the late Mrs. Vernona Smith's MSS., which relate mostly to families in the W.I. They are unfortunately badly arranged, and without any index. Her last letter to the Editor was dated 25 October 1899 from 125 White Hart Lane, Barnes.

---

*Page 375, this volume.

THE EARL OF HAREWOOD, K.G. AND THE RELATIONSHIP OF THE LASCELLES FAMILY WITH BARBADOS

(From Notes Contributed by Mr. E. M. Shilstone.)

Lord Harewood arrived in Barbados on a visit to his son's estates on 25th November 1936. Lord Harewood is a Trustee of many Museums including the British Museum and the South Kensington Museums in London. It was therefore natural that he should take a great interest in our own Museum. He visited the Barbados Museum on the 1st December when, in company with Mr. E. M. Shilstone and the resident Curator, Mr. Howell Clarke, he made a tour of inspection of the Galleries.

Lord Harewood was much impressed with the achievements that had already been made and was very interested in the further plans for extension and development. He made a detailed examination of the exhibits and gave most helpful advice for improvements in methods of display and labelling. He was particularly interested in the exhibits of Barbados coral and fossils and agreed that a more ambitious display of marine zoological exhibits would be valuable and instructive both to residents and visitors to the island.

Lord Harewood left Barbados for England on 8th December but, before his departure, he made application for Life Membership of the Society, and has since been elected.

The Lascelles family have been associated with Barbados since the early part of the 18th century. The brothers Henry and George Lascelles, sons of Daniel Lascelles (1655-1734), were merchants residing in Barbados. Henry Lascelles was also Collector of H.M. Customs in Barbados, an office which was later held by his half-brother, Edward Lascelles, from whom the Earls of Harewood are descended. Subsequently, Henry Lascelles became a West India Merchant in London and became Member of Parliament for North-allerton as his father had been before him. His first wife, Mary Carter, was a daughter of Edwin Carter of Barbados, and his second wife was also a Barbadian lady, Janet, daughter of Hon. John Whetstone, Deputy Secretary of Barbados.

Henry Lascelles owned *Lascelles* Plantation in St. James and this estate remained in the family until the 19th century. Henry Lascelles was survived by his three sons:

1. Edwin, afterwards first Baron Harewood.

2. Daniel, of Goldsborough, Yorkshire, a very rich West India Merchant who was in partnership with William Daling and Gedney Clarke. Daniel was divorced from his wife and his fortune passed to his brother Edwin, Lord Harewood.

3. Henry, who died without issue in 1786.

Edwin, Lord Harewood, was twice married but there was no

issue of either marriage and on his death in 1795, the barony became extinct. His large estates in England and the plantations in Barbados which then included the *Mount* in St. George and *Kirtons* (now *Kent*) in Christ Church passed to his cousin Edward Lascelles. Edward was the eldest surviving son of Edward Lascelles, the Collector of Customs in Barbados. He was in turn created Baron Harewood in 1796, and Viscount Lascelles, Earl of Harewood in 1812 and was the ancestor of the present Earl.

Edward Lascelles, the Collector of Customs, married Frances Ball, daughter of the Hon. Guy Ball of Barbados who survived him. (She married, secondly, Frances Holbourne, Admiral of the White Squadron). Their son, Edward, first Earl of Harewood, was the only son to marry and leave issue and all the family fortunes became concentrated in the Earl who had also succeeded to the estates of the family of the half-blood.

The *Belle* plantation in St. Michael and the *Mount* plantation in St. George are now the only estates in Barbados held by the family. In 1918, the *Thicket* and *Fortescue* plantations were sold by the present Earl's father, the 5th Earl of Harewood; under whose will the *Bell* and the *Mount* were devised to his second son, Major Edward Lascelles, D.S.O., for life. Major Lascelles died in 1935 and the estates are now held in trust for the Hon. Gerald Vincent Lascelles, second son of the Earl and the Princess Royal on whom they are entailed.

In the Council Chamber, Bridgetown, there are two large portraits in oils of Edwin, Lord Harewood, of the first creation and of Edward, Baron Harewood of the second creation who was afterwards Earl of Harewood. The portrait of Edwin, Lord Harewood, bears the following legend—"As a mark of respect to their native country this portrait of the Right Hon. Edwin Baron Harewood is presented by Edward, Earl of Harewood to the Colony of Barbados. A.D. 1818."

The other portrait is inscribed beneath as follows:—"This portrait of the Earl of Harewood, Painted for the Legislature of Barbados in grateful testimony of their high esteem is by their order placed as a companion to that of his ancestor. 1820."

The expression "ancestor," is, of course, an error for, as already pointed out, the first Earl (the subject of the portrait) was a cousin of the first Baron Harewood.

THE NEW ARCHBISHOP OF CANTERBURY.

The Most Rev. William Temple, D.D., the Lord Archbishop of York and Primate of England, has been appointed to succeed the Most Rev. Cosmo Gordon Lang, D.D., as Archbishop of Canterbury and Primate of all England.

Some of His Grace's ancestors had associations with Barbados, having been born and lived in the island. His mother was a member of the Lascelles family.

During the first half of the eighteenth century his ancestor, Edward Lascelles, son of Daniel Lascelles, M.P., for Northallerton, became collector of customs in Barbados. He married a Barbadian lady, Frances, daughter of Guy Ball at St. Michael's Church (now the Cathedral) on January 1st, 1732. Their son Edward, who was baptised at the present font in St. Mchael's Cathedral, was destined to have a notable and distinguished career.

He joined the army and rose to the rank of Colonel. At an early age he became M.P., for Northallerton, his grandfather's constituency. In 1796 King George III created him Baron Harewood of Harewood in Yorkshire, and in 1812 made him Viscount Lascelles and Earl of Harewood.

The family became landed proprietors in Barbados, and the Belle Plantation is still in the possession of the family. The following is the genealogical line of His Grace of Canterbury from Edward Lascelles, collector of customs in Barbados :

Edward Lascelles, m. Frances dau. of Guy Ball of Barbados.

Edward, 1st Earl of Harewood m. Anne dau. of William Chaloner.

Henry. 2nd Earl of Harewood, m Henrietta dau. of Lt. Genl. Sir John Sebright.

Rt. Hon. Wm. Saunders Sebright Lascelles, m. Lady Caroline Howard. dau. of George 6th Earl of Carlisle.

Beatrice Blanche Lascelles, m. Most Rev. Frederick Temple, Archbishop of Canterbury.

William Temple, Archbishop of Canterbury, 1942.

𝕷𝖆𝖜𝖗𝖊𝖓𝖈𝖊 of 𝕭𝖆𝖗𝖇𝖆𝖉𝖔𝖘.*

WILLS.

1675, July. Nicholas. Mother Mary. Sister Elizabeth (wife of Nicholas Hope). Sons, Jekyl and Thomas.

1678, May 10. Nicholas, Planter, St Thomas. Daughters, Anne (wife of James Gardner; child Ephan), Sarah Lawrence. Wife Ephan.

1681, May 9. Henry, junior, St James. Wife Lydia. Daughter Lydia. Sons, Edward, Henry, Herbert, Thomas.

1712, April 4. Thomas, St James. Son Herbert. Daughters, Margaret, Mary, Eliza. Nephew Edward Lawrence. Brother Henry.

1725, Aug. 4. Henry the younger, St Michael's Town. Sons, William, one posthumous. Father and Mother, Henry and Ann. Sister Ann, wife of Robert Piggott. (Her sons, Henry Piggott West, Thomas Piggott, John. Her daughter Barbara.) Kinsmen, John Shurland, William Noblett.

1726/27, Feb. 28. Henry, St James. Daughter Ann, wife of Robert Piggott. Sons, Henry and Thomas. Daughters, Barbara, Jane, Ann Piggott. Grandson William Lawrence. Kinsman John Noblett. Witness to will, Edward Lawrence.

1743, Nov. 17. Edward, St James, Carpenter. Wife Elizabeth. Children, only Henry named. Kinsman Thomas Noble.

1746, Sept. 4. Mary, Widow, St Michael's. Grandson and heir Thomas Hope. (He seems to have been the son of Jekyl and Elizabeth Hope.)

1751, June 13. Herbert, Planter, St Michael's. Sons, John, Herbert, Bartholomew. Brother Samuel Farnell.

1754, Jan. 28. Thomas, St. Michael's. Wife Alice. Son William (son Thomas and daughter Agnes). Daughters, Sarah, Ann, Susannah, Mercer. Granddaughter Elizabeth Foster (daughter of Dampley (?) Foster).

1756, March 25. Catherine, Widow, St Michael's Town. Sons, Joseph, Nathaniel, Francis, and Benjamin Borden.

---

*Communicated by N. Darnell Davis.

BARBADOS RECORDS

LEE FAMILY. '

The family is represented here in some of the earliest records. Among the names of owners of more than ten acres of land in the year 1638 we find Richard Lee, John Leigh, Joseph Lee, John Lee, Robert Lee, Adam Lee, Richard Loe (Lee?).

In St. Michael's Cathedral graveyard there is a blue marble headstone with decorated floral borders, and an altar with figures at top, with the inscription —

Here lyes interr'd / the body of / CAPT. GEORGE LEE / of Boston, New England / aged 31 years, who / died Septr. ye 17th 1737.

The corresponding burial entry says—1737 Sep 18 Capt Thomas (sic) Lee of Boston.

EXTRACTS FROM RECORDS OF LEE OR LEA WILLS
recorded in the Registry at Bridgetown.

ROBERT LEE, late of London, in the parish of St. Martins, vintner, but beyond the seas, deceased. Probate granted by Oliver, Protector of the Commonwealth of England, Scotland and Ireland and the Dominions to Henry Lee brother of the deceased, as sole executor.

The Will bequeaths his body to the dust from whence it came, there to be decently buried if he dies in England; but if beyond the seas, his body to stand to the curtesye of some well-minded Christian. All his estate to his brother, Henry Lee, of London, who is to be sole executor.

Dated 7 August 1641. sd. Robert Lee, Witnesses : John Whitehood, Wm. Adames, John Gibson. Proved 31 January 1654/5, in England. Recorded in Barbados 23 Augt 1655.

LIEUTENANT JOHN LEE of Barbados, gent.

Wife, Margaret, to see his body buried in Christian manner.

To wife, and five children, namely, eldest daughter Mary, second daughter not named, sons, Richard, Charles and John, all real and personal estate in sixths.

Wife to be exx. Friends, Henry Thrall and John Panton to be overseers of will.

Dated 30 Septr 1657 : sd. John Lee. Wits : Gabriel Aldworth, John Garaway.

Proved by both witnesses's Oath, 16 Nov. 1657. Recdd next day.

JOHN LEA. Deposition of Jane Fudgwell, senior, aged 42.—

1. Went with her daughter to house of John Lea one night.
2. John Lea was very ill, had a fit, deponent thought he would die.
3. When he came to himself she said to him "Jack, one of these fitts will carry thee away", and she enquired whether he had disposed of his property.
4. John Lea called for the widow Waterland, and before me and my daughter he said "She is my heir and sole executor : I give her all I have, except the mulatto boy Cullee, whom I desire to be apprenticed to a cooper or to any thing else he likes and to set him free, and a mulatto Betty to be set free also and put to school.

5. The said John Lea took by the hand the same Widow Waterland, and said—"woman Waterland give me a cup of wine;
I make no other Will, the cup of wine shall seal my will".
6. The said John Lea was sensible at the time.
Sworn to by the said Jane Fudgwell 27 May 1663 before Humph.
Walrond, President. She made her mark. Deposition of Mary Barber
age 20, daughter of the said Jane Fudgwell, to the same effect.

ROBERT LEA of city of London, gent., now resident in Barbados.
To wife, Mary, and daughter, Rachell Jeffreys, both of London, all
his personal estate, subject to debts. To son-in-law, Lawrence Hannaton,
of Barbados, gent., £20. To kinswoman, Sarah Fowler, senior, of London,
£10. To her daughter, another Sarah Fowler, £5. To his kinsman,
Thomas Ceanne, of Mostlicke, Middlesex, linen draper, £5 To brother,
Thomas Lee, of parish of Croxham, Somerset, shoemaker, my signet
ring to be conveyed to him with all speed after his decease. Appoints
Thomas Ceanne and John Bawden, merchant, to be overseers and executors in trust. To ancient poor people of St. Michael (Barbados) £10. sd.
Robert Lea. Witnesses: Anthony Young, George Boughton, Gilbert
Innings, William Spring. Proved 18 December 1665.

JOSEPH LEE of St. Peter's All Saints parish, Barbados. Christian burial.
To god-daughter, Elizabeth Deakers, daughter of Roger Deakers, and
Anne Deakers his wife, 10 ac of land situate in St. Andrew Overhills par-
ish, Barbados, butting west on Lawrence Sanders, north upon John Legg,
decd., south upon Joseph Lea, east on the sea, with houses thereon. sd. by
his mark. Dated 1 Jany 1669/70.
Witness: Richard Manderff (mark), Wm. Molley, Wm. Perreman, (mark),
Charles Greenling. Recorded 28 June 1670.

ELIZA LEE (of Barbados). Desires Christian burial. Sister, Mary
Horne, nee Lee, but being married she has since been called by name
of . . . . and being now Daniel Horne's wife, to be sole exx. of all left to me
by my father, John Lee, and to have the same, except what I give to my
brother, Richard Lee of Virginia, provided he comes personally to claim
the same within two years of my death : otherwise the same to go to said
sister Mary. None of the rest of my kindred is to have any right to anything
that belongs to me. sd. by her mark Eliza Lee.
Dated 26 June 1674. Wits: Anthony Prince, Alexander Allen.
Proved 20 Sept 1674. Recorder 6 Oct 1674.

CAPTAIN THOMAS LEE, late of St. Peter's parish (Barbados).
Deposition of Major William Forster, aged 48 years, taken 31 July 1679,
1. The said Thomas Lee being sick, desired the deponent and Robert
Breviter esqre, decd., being brothers-in-law to the said Lee, to care for his
wife and children.
2. The deceased had little estate, save his household stuff and two
young negro children of his wife's negro Jenny, whom he desired his wife
to have during her life.
3. After wife's death the negro boy to go to his (testator's) daughter,
Anne, and the negro girl, to daughter Katherine; and if the said negro girl
should have a child, it should go to his daughter Margaret.
4. He desired the deponent and Brevitor to see his will carried out.
Sworn by deponent 31 July 1679.

FRANCIS LEE of St. Michael's parish, Barbados, gentleman. Debts
to be paid To my wife (no name) all my real and personal estate absolutely

382

in full confidence that she will provide for my children : wife to be exx. sd. Fras. Lee. Dated 9 September 1727.
Witnesses : Robert Jocelin, John Willoughby, Patrick Graham. Proved 17 January 1727/8 by Oath of John Willoughby. Recdd. 17 Jan. 1727/8.

JOSEPH LEE of St. Michael, Barbados, jeweller. To eldest son, Joseph, second son, John and third son Edward, an equal share of his estate at 21.

To eldest daughter, Margaret Leanford Lee, equal share at 18 or marriage; to second, third and fourth, and youngest daughters, Elizabeth, Barbara, and Anna, £50 at 18.

To friends, Captain Daniel Wildey and John Tead Rushbrook a ring of value 20/- each. To wife, Mary, several slaves, and residue of estate absolutely.

Appoints wife and friends, D. Wildey and J. T. Rushbrook, to be exx and exors. and guardians of children. sd. Joseph Lee. Dated 22 April 1747. Witns : Wild. Dowling, Nat. Clarke, Conrade Mashart. Proved 28 Sept. 1747 by oath of C. Mashart.

THOMAS LEE (or Lees) of town of St. Michael, Barbados, goldsmith. To Thomas Clarke £5. My executor to sell my slaves and household goods etc. To niece Mary Lees, daughter of my brother Edward Lees, who commonly resided with my sister, Ann Cortius (? indistinct) née Lees of Uxbridge Middlesex, Widow, one-half of my estate after debts paid, and in case of her death to her brother Lees. To John and George Gascoign, sons of my friend George Gascoign esq. equally the other half of my estate. George Gascoign to be executor. sd. Thomas Lee. (Apparently he called himself Lee). Dated 29 Febry 1747 Wits: Wm. Reece. and Thomas Clarke. Proved 28 July 1748 by T. Clarke, gent.

JOSEPH LEE, late of St. Mary Magdalen, Bermondsey, Surrey, decd. mariner, now chief mate of the Pretty Betsy in Lower Thames.

To wife, Ann Lee of the parish of St. Mary Magdalen all real and personal estate. Dated 5 March 1752. sd. Joseph Lee. Wits: Joseph Houghland. Thos. Chappell. Proved in Prerogative Court of Canterbury 26 March 1783. Letters Testimonial issued 7 April 1783. Recorded in Barbados 11 June 1787.

LEE BAPTISMS TO 1750.

Parish	Date		
St. Michael	1650 Oct.	13	Elizabeth, dau of Randall Lee
St. Philip	1652 Jan.	30	Thomas, son of Thomas Lee
do.	1661 June		Child of Josh Lee
do.	1661 Dec.		Margaret, dau of James Leigh
St. Michael	1662 Nov.	16	Sarah, dau of Peter Lee
St. Philip	1675 Aug.	22	James, son of James & Margaret Lee
St. Michael	1677 May	3	William, son of Charles & Martha Lee
do.	1678 Mar.	13	Sarah, dau of Charles & Martha Lee
do.	1683 Oct.	18	Charles son of Charles Lee ye Marshall
do.	1685 Feb.	7	James son of Thomas Lee
do.	1686 June	30	Dorothy, dau of John Leigh & Dorothy Leigh
do.	1700 Nov.	22	Mary dau of Tim and Johanna Lee, born 10 Mar 1696
do.	1700 Nov.	22	Edward son of Tim & Johanna Lee.

			born 12 Feb 1698
St. Michael	1700 Nov.	22	James child of Tim & Johanna Lee, born 16th
Christ Ch.	1702 Sep.	22	Henry son of Nathaniel & Alice Lee
St. Michael	1705 July	10	3 children of Mr. Leigh's
do.	1710 Sep.	15	Joseph son of Tim Lee
do.	1711 June	8	John son of Tim Lee
do.	1712 Nov.	9	Thomas son of Francis & Mary Lee, born 6 Feb 1711
do.	1712 Nov.	9	Francis child of Francis & Mary Lee born 5 Nov 1712
do.	1712 Dec.	6	Joanna dau of Tim & Joanna Lee, born 5th
do.	1714 Jan.	6	Joseph, son of Francis & Mary Lee
do.	1714 Jan.	22	Jonathan son of Timothy & Mrs. Lee, born same day.
do.	1719 Oct.	29	William Henry child of Frances Lee
do.	1719 Oct.	29	Frances child of Frances Lee
do.	1720 Feb.	11	Mary dau of Thomas Lees
do.	1726 July	6	George, child. Ed. Randell and Robert Dawe, godfathers, Mary Durridge and Elizabeth Rogers, godmothers
do.	1731 Feb.	21	Samuel, son of William & Mary Lee, born 17 Mar 1730
do.	1738 June	25	Elizabeth, dau of Joseph & Mary Lee, born 12 May
do.	1740 April	6	John, son of Joseph & Mary Lee, born 1st
do.	1742 June	16	Barbara, dau of Mr. Joseph & Mary Lee, born 28 May
do.	1744 Oct.	15	Edwin son of Joseph & Mary Lee, born 8th
do.	1745 Oct.	5	Deborah Lee child of William & Mary Lee, born 29 Decr 1740
do.	1745 Oct.	5	Margaret, child of William & Mary Lee, born 1 Oct 1743
do.	1746 Oct.	24	Anna Maria, dau of Joseph & Mary Lee born 21st.

MARRIAGES TO 1750

Parish	Date		
St. Michael	1653 Sep		Mary Lee to John Rogers
do	1655 Aprl	16	Elizabeth Leigh and William Davis
do	1655 July	23	Cissley Leigh and Oliver Bacon
St. John	1658	22	Mary Lee to Thomas King
Christ Ch.	1660 July	1	Joan Lee to Dermott Morphew
do	1662 Jan	16	John Lee to Mary Forchildren
St. John	1664 Sep	18	John Lees to Jane —
St. Michael	1665 Sep	21	Mary Lee to Francis Dean

St. Michael	1666	Jan	31	Mary Lee to John Hartwell
do	1667	Oct	26	Peter Lee to Susanna Puddiford
do	1707	Dec	23	Francis Lee to Mary Burnell
do	1720	Jul	27	Alice Lee to John Blagrove
do	1722	May	19	Margaret Lee spinster to Capt Wm. Harrison
do	1730	Dec	1	William Lee to Ellenor Banfield
do	1731	Jul	18	Elizabeth Lee spinster to Arundell Burton
do	1733	April	1	Thomas Lee* to Mary Giles, spinster
do	1739	Dec	1	Johannah Lee to Wm. Lawder
do	1739	Nov	26	William Lee to Mary Homeyard spinster.
do	1750	Feb	10	Richard Lees to Deborah Smith.

* Thomas Lee is said to have settled in Charleston, South Carolina, in 1734, and to have been the progenitor of the numerous Lee descendants in America.

BURIALS TO 1750

Christ Ch.	1645	Feb	7	John Leigh
St. Michael	1650	Sep	5	Walter Lee, servant
Christ Ch.	1650	Jun	23	John Lee, servant to Richard Peers
St. Michael	1654	Oct	24	Mr. Lee
do	1654			Thomas Lee
do	1657	Oct	1	Lt. (Lieutenant) John Lea
do	1663	Aug	27	Henry Lee, merchant
do	1665	Decr	7	Robert Lea
do	1667	July	9	Thomas Lee
do	1667	May	4	Lidia Lee
do	1667	August	14	Laurence Lee
St. John	1665	July	11	Ann, dau of John Lee
St. Michael	1669	October	26	John Lee
do	1670	June	25	Peter Lee
do	1670	April	28	Cornelius Lee, a lad
do	1674	Feb	9	Mary Lee
do	1674	Sep	8	Elizabeth Lee
St. Philip	1676	Feby	16	Margaret, dau of James Lee
St. Michael	1677	August	23	Mary Lee
do	1678	August	17	William son of Charles & Martha Lee
Christ Ch.	1678	July	19	William Leigh
St. Michael	1679	April	2	Sarah, dau of Charles & Martha Lee
Christ Ch.	1679	Novr	8	Thomas Lee
St. Michael	1680	April	10	Cullen Lee
St. Philip	1681	July	5	Margaret wife of James Lee
do	1681	January	7	James son of James Lee
St. Michael	1682	May	31	Charles Lee
Christ Ch.	1683	Aug	24	James Lee junior
St. Michael	1684	Octr	3	Charles son of Charles Lee
Christ Ch.	1684	January	8	James Lee
St. Michael	1685	January	21	Mary Lee, parish pauper, wife of one Thomas Lee
do	1685	January	25	John Lee son of foregoing Mary

St. Michael	1685 Febry	12	Martha wife of Charles Lee
do	1685 March	5	Elizabeth dau of Charles Lee
do	1685 March	18	Owen, son of Charles Lee
do	1686 July	1	Dorothy dau of John & Dorothy Leigh
do	1687 March	14	James son of Thomas & Mary Lee
do	1689 Dec	15	George Lee, musician
do	1689 May	2	Grace, wife of Charles Lee
Christ Ch	1689 Feb	5	Dorothy Lee
St. Michael	1690 April	2	John Lee mariner
Christ Ch	1690 Dec	30	Edith Lee
do.	1691 Jan	26	Agnes Lee
St. Philip	1693 April		Mary Lee
do.	1693 Jun	27	William Lee
St. Michael	1695 July	27	Anthony Lee
do.	1696 Oct	26	Elizabeth wife of Charles Lee
Christ Ch.	1696 Jan	7	Sarah Leigh
St. Michael	1697 July	5	Charles Leigh
do.	1697 Octr	16	George Leigh
do.	1699 Jany	28	Joseph Lea mariner
do.	1699 Oct	26	Capt William Lee
do.	1701 Sep	6	Elizabeth Lee, widow
do.	1701 June	28	William Lee mariner
do.	1703 Octr	20	Christopher Lee
do.	1705 Oct	15	John Leigh man-o-war-man
do.	1705 Oct	12	Thomas Lee
do.	1705 Aug	3	John Lee
do.	1710 April	6	Benjamin Lee man-o-war-man
do.	1710 Aug	22	Joseph Lee, merchant
do.	1710 Sep	20	Joseph Lee, infant
do.	1710 Octr	1	Mary Lee spinster
do.	1711 June	8	John Lee, a child
do.	1711 Feb	11	Hannah Lee
do.	1713 Nov	12	Francis Lee a child
do.	1713 Jan	21	Nathaniel Lee, of ye Train [Band]
Christ Ch.	1714 July	28	Moses Leigh
St. Michael	1719 Octr	4	Margaret Lee
do	1719 Octr	29	Francis Lee
do	1730 Octr	6	Henry, son of Thomas Lee
do	1725 March	29	Mary Lee, a child
Christ Ch	1726 June	29	Christiana Lee
St. Michael	1727 Septr	12	Francis Lee, attorney-at-law
do	1730 Jan	16	Thomas Lee, parish pauper
do	1734 Nov	10	Samuel son of William Lee
do	1735 April	26	Mary Lees, spinster
St. Michael	1735 May	22	Elizabeth wife of Thomas Lees
do	1737 Septm	18	Captain Thomas Lee of Boston
do	1738 January	25	Joannah, wife of Timothy Lee
do	1739 Septm	3	Dr. Joseph Leigh
do	1742 Septm	13	John Lees
do	1742 Septm	20	John Lee, saylor
do	1744 March	11	Theophilus Lee, almshouse

do	1746 Dec	9	Mary, daughter of William Lee
do	1747 October	19	Anna Maria, daughter of Joseph Lee deceased
	1747 July	7	Timothy Lee, shipwright
do	1747 August	30	Edwin Lee, son of Joseph Lee
do	1748 July	11	Thomas Lee, gunsmith.

CENSUS RECORDS 1679.

Charles Lee and wife,	Town of St. Michael, 1 slave.
Sarah	daughter of Charles & Martha Leigh, baptized 13 March 1678 in St. Michael.
William,	son of Charles & Martha Leigh, buried 17 August 1678 in St. Michael.
Sarah,	daughter of Charles & Martha Leigh, buried 2 April 1679 in St. Michael.
Sarah Leigh,	living in Christ Church, owned 172 acres of land, 52 negroes.
James Lee,	living in Christ Church, 4 negroes.
William Leigh,	buried 19 July 1678 in Christ Church.
Katherine Lee,	living in St. Philip, 5 ac. of land.
Edward Lee,	do. St. Lucy.
John Lee,	Commander of Ship White ffox, sailed 5 May 1679 for London.
do	Commander of Ship White ffox, sailed 20 March 1678 for London.
Henry Lee,	departed 1 April 1679 for Virginia in the ketch Unity James Rainy Commander.
Richard Lee,	departed 17 July 1679 for Virginia in the pinke Rebecca Thomas Williams, Commander.
Henry Lee,	departed 25 Octr 1679 for London, in the ship Happy Returns, Isaac Hand, Commander.
James Lee,	in Col. Christopher Lyne's Regiment and under command of Capt. Robert Bowcher, 6 Jan. 1679.
Mrs. Lee,	was providing three men in Col. Lyne's Regt. on 6 Jan 1679.
Stephan Lee,	soldier, under command of Capt. John Thurbane, in Col. Baylie's Regt.
Charles Lee,	soldier in Capt. Ely's company in Col. Bate's Regt.
Charles Leigh,	Sergeant in Capt. Norris's Company in Col. Bate's Regt.
Cully Lee,	soldier in Capt. Burrows' company in Col. Bate's Regt.
Mrs. Sarah Leigh,	provides one soldier in Col. Samuel Newton's troop of horse 1715.
Francis Lee,	living in St. Michael, with household, 1 man 30 years; 1 woman 26 years, 3 boys, (15y, 3y. and 18 months) 2 girls (16 yrs., 14 yrs.)
Timothy Lee,	living in St. Michael, with household of 1 man, 42 years, 1 woman, 42 years; 4 boys (17 yrs, 16 yrs, 11 yrs, 9 mos.) 3 girls (13 yrs, 8 yrs, 3 yrs.)

SAM LORD AND HIS CASTLE

Compiled by

COLONEL A. H. WIGHTWICK HAYWOOD,

C.M.G., C.B.E., D.S.O.

It was not until February this year (1963) that an opportunity occurred for me to go to Barbados with the object of investigating the story of Sam Lord's life and his connections with my family. Since the days of my boyhood the subject had intrigued me, for my parents had kindled the imagination of us children by fairylike tales of a Castle and fabulous estates in Barbados which should have been inherited by my father, but for some unexplained reason passed out of the family.

My interest in the matter was again aroused much later in life when after the death of both parents, a diary came into my possession, written by my grandfather, James Haywood, being an account of his journey to Barbados in 1845—46 to make inquiries about Sam Lord's estate after the latter's death in 1844. The diary described the result of his inquiries up to a certain point, but then ended abruptly without stating how the property was finally disposed of. It was from this point that my investigations had to proceed.

The diary mentioned that Sam Lord's favourite niece, Frances Lord, had married a Captain Charles Trollope and had a substantial interest in the estate. I, therefore, decided first to trace any descendants of this marriage with a view to ascertaining how they had benefitted and what information might be helpful before going to Barbados.

Captain (later Major–General Sir C.) Trollope, was a younger son of Sir John Trollope, Bart. With the aid of an old Baronetage I discovered there were two surviving direct descendants viz., Angela and Sylvia, Grand–daughters of this Captain Trollope. By a lucky chance I was able to locate the younger, Sylvia Trollope through the London Telephone Directory, and established the family connection. It appeared that her elder sister, Angela had married a Mr. Giffard. Their son, Peter, was now the senior male descendant of the Frances Lord who had married Captain Charles Trollope. To him I was referred by his aunt, Miss Sylvia Trollope.

By this means I was able to pick up some useful information, as well as being supplied with introductions to a few influential people in Barbados.

LUCY LORD *née* WIGHTWICK   SAMUEL HALL LORD

After miniatures by an unknown artist by kind permission of
Colonel A. H. W. Haywood, C.M.G., C.B.E., D.S.O.

PLASTER MASK OF SAMUEL HALL LORD AT LONG BAY CASTLE
By kind permission of Sam Lord's Castle Ltd.

Thus the way was prepared to enable me to start my investigations on arrival in Barbados, where I duly landed on 24th February after an uneventful voyage in the M. V. *Brunsdeich* of the Geest Line, a ship of 4,500 tons under Dutch ownership, but chartered * to a German Company for the Banana trade with the West Indies.

Having installed myself in a comfortable Guest House, "The Torrington," at Worthing near Bridgetown, the capital of Barbados, I made use of Peter Giffard's introductions to meet Sir John Chandler, the President, and Mr. Neville Connell, the Curator, of the Museum. From both of them I received a warm welcome, as well as sound advice on how to proceed with my investigation.

Research work at the Barbados Registry resulted in the discovery of the Wills of Sam Lord and his elder brother, John Thomas Lord, as well as numerous indentures and documents relating to the estates owned by them. I also made a thorough search in the Public Library of books containing references to Sam Lord, his ancestry and life. While in back-files of the Barbados Newspaper *The Advocate*, with the courteous help of their staff, I was able to collect much useful information about Sam Lord's life and activities.

My warmest thanks are due to Sir John and Lady Chandler and to Mr. and Mrs. Armel Yearwood for their hospitality which enabled me to meet so many Lord connections. Nor must I omit to mention the many interesting drives they took me to visit Sam Lord's Castle and his Sugar Plantations, as well as other places of note in the Island. Finally I would like to say I have found Lady Chandler's Memorandum "Sam Lord's Castle" both interesting and helpful in compiling this brochure.

FAMILY HISTORY OF THE LORD FAMILY.

The earliest mention of the name of Lord in Barbados is of Henry Lord, described as a 'Minister,' who owned more than 10 acres of land in 1638. Two years later, on 1st September 1640, James Lord, a planter, buys 15 acres of land in Christ Church from John Maunsell. There is no evidence to show that either of these men was an ancestor of Samuel Hall Lord.

The Lord family were in possession of the Long Bay property from the 18th century. It produced cotton and aloes, but no sugar cane owing to the shallow depth of the soil and the force of the N.E. Trade Winds.

Our earliest authentic information of the Lord family is of John Lord, married to Bathsheba Hall Serjeant, who died in 1799

---

*For *Dutch ownership, but chartered to a German company* read *German ownership, but chartered by a Dutch company.*

leaving 2 sons, John Thomas and Samuel Hall[1] and four daughters, Mary Bathsheba[2] married to Dr. Richard Keen Austin, and Sarah, Bathsheba and Elizabeth Sarsfield, unmarried. They lived in a mansion house built in 1780 on Long Bay Estate of only 145 acres in extent. The family was not wealthy. On his death, John Lord left the property equally to his two sons after their mother's death. The unmarried daughters were each left £1,500. At their father's death the sons were 23 and 21 respectively. Two of the daughters died early. Sarah in 1816 aged 33 and Bathsheba in 1818, also aged 33 and both unmarried.

Bathsheba Lord, the widow of John Lord did not die until 1820, aged 72.[3] Elizabeth Sarsfield continued to live at the family mansion Long Bay Castle, until her death in 1851. She had survived all her brothers and sisters.[4]

1804—1816, MARRIAGE OF SAM LORD TO LUCY WIGHTWICK.

Samuel Hall Lord was baptised at St. Philip's parish church on 23rd November 1788. In 1804 he embarked for England. He was then 26 years old, ambitious, eager to see the civilized world and determined to build up his fortune. It is said that he modelled his manner of life on the Regency Buck, making his debut in London and Bath Society, probably with the object of marrying a young lady of fortune. Presumably his income was derived from Long Bay Estate.

According to my parents' version of the affair, my great–grandmother, Lucy Wightwick, met him at a ball in Bath, was apparently overwhelmed by his dashing appearance and manner; and determined to marry him against her father's wishes. She was then probably about 20 years of age. Her father, Thomas Dewey Wightwick, at the time owned Hewelsfield Court, near Chepstow, Bushbury, Staffs; and Capel Court, Gloucestershire; he also probably had property near Wolverhampton. From Sam Lord's point of view her prospects were therefore attractive. The miniatures I have of the couple about the time of their marriage show Sam as a good–looking young man dressed in Regency style, while Lucy's features are homely rather than pretty.

During his temporary residence in Bath, Sam resided at "Orange Grove." The marriage took place on 28th February, 1808, at Abbey Church, Bath. This may indicate that Lucy's parents were not present and it was a run–away match, otherwise the wedding would probably have been held at the Wightwick's country home. The rest of the year 1808 was spent in England, but whether in Bath or at her parents' home is not known.

On 27th January 1809 Lucy's first child, a son, Oceanus, was born on the voyage to Barbados.[5] He only survived two and a quarter years and was buried in the family vault at St. Philip's parish church in the Island. Emma Lucy was born at Long Bay on 22nd April, 1811, she also died shortly after,[6] and was buried in the family vault.

At the latter end of June, 1812, owing to her husband's ill-treatment, Lucy left Long Bay, arriving at her father's house in August. There her third child, Cecilia, was born on 17th November 1812. Sam was present at the time. The christening took place shortly after at Hewelsfield Church.

About June 1814, Lucy returned to Long Bay with her husband on the understanding that the child should be left in England. However, in April 1815, in consequence of hearing her husband had sent to England for the child, and being apprehensive that the climate would prove fatal to its life, she again voluntarily, and without her husband's knowledge, returned to her father's house. On 6th October, 1815, a deed of agreement was entered into and it is recorded that although Sam Lord had absented himself from her he now agreed to live with Lucy on condition that he paid her an annuity of £300 a year which was to be increased to £500 if he died before her. Her father Thomas Dewey Wightwick of Bushby, Staffs., and Stubbs Wightwick of Trinity College, Oxford, were also parties to this agreement and the annuity was to be paid by Sam Lord or his executors half yearly to them, in the Dining Hall of Lincoln's Inn, for the benefit of his wife. She agreed to surrender her right of dower and was given absolute guardianship of their daughter Cecilia. Further, she was free to leave Sam if he ill-treated her again. In May 1816, Lucy left her husband on account of his ill-treatment and she never lived with him again.[7]

1804—1820, LIFE AND DEATH OF JOHN THOMAS LORD; CHARGES OF FRAUD AGAINST SAM LORD.

Sam's brother John Thomas Lord, was baptised early in September, 1776. He is said to have been of a very different character to his brother. The impression one gets is that he was of a steady plodding disposition, probably honest and unassuming. His marriage to a Miss Sarah Marshall took place on 1st November, 1804. When Sam and his bride arrived in Barbados in 1809 presumably the two families lived together at Long Bay with their mother and sisters. The arrangement could not have been a happy one owing to Sam's ill-treatment of his wife, Lucy. He is reputed to have beaten her and locked her up in a slave's dungeon before she ran away in 1815, but how much is fact and how much is fancy is hard to say. She is also reported to have been so short of money that she had to bribe a slave with her gold necklace to secure her release, using the diamond pendant to pay for her passage on the ship.

In June 1813, the Pool Estate, St. John, was purchased by John Thomas Lord and Sam Lord from an absentee proprietor, Hon. Thomas Graham, of Oldbury Court, Gloucester. As the Lord brothers were unable to pay the purchase price it was agreed that the owner would accept a mortgage on the property of £18,000 — a fairly frequent method of purchasing plantations. It comprised a sugar cane plantation of 366 acres with mill for crushing the cane and slaves.[8]

It is thought that after Pool was bought, John Thomas and his family lived there while Sam continued to live at Long Bay when he came back from England with his wife in 1814. Although John Thomas Lord represented the parish of St. Philip as a member of the House of Assembly from 1809 until his death in 1818, his residing at the Pool seems to be borne out by the baptism of his daughter Frances, at St. John's parish church on 17th April 1717, whereas his other children were baptised at St. Philip's parish church.

In 1817, legal proceedings were taken against Sam Lord on charges of forgery and perjury,[9] the details of which I was unable to ascertain, however, early in 1820 the charges were dropped and the case rescinded by order of the Attorney General, presumably for lack of evidence.

The legal ramifications of the Lord family are not easy to follow and this has been further complicated by the ravages of time and deteriorating records. According to the Deeds Index, in 1809, there was a conveyance from Sam Lord's mother, Bathsheba Lord to John Thomas Lord and Samuel Hall Lord; it has not been possible to examine this document, but it was possibly some arrangement whereby she conveyed Long Bay to these two sons who were entitled to it after her death under their father's will, in exchange for an annuity as long as she lived. If this were not the case, how would it have been possible for the sons to deal freely with their half shares in Long Bay, as they did, without her assent?[10].

Whether as the result of Sam's difficulties in connection with the charges of fraud, or in anticipation of these, on 21st February, 1817, by indenture, Sam Lord conveyed to his sister Elizabeth Sarsfield his half-share in Long Bay and his half-share in the Pool for the sum of £35,000. Further, Elizabeth Sarsfield confessed a general judgment to Sam Lord for this amount. Now this was probably a legal device, for we know that Elizabeth Sarsfield never paid a penny towards the purchase price of £35,000 or any interest thereon, as this is recited in a deed of 1834, when Sam's half-share of Long Bay and the Pool is reconveyed to him by Elizabeth Sarsfield.

On the 28th November 1818, John Thomas Lord is buried at
St. Philip's church, at the early age of 42. He left a wife, Sarah and
4 children — John born on 29th March, 1807, and 3 daughters,
Adriana, born 8th April 1805, Elizabeth, usually called Eliza,
born 18th May 1811, and Frances born 8th February 1817. There
had been other children of the marriage who had died in infancy.[11]

By his will, dated 8th April, 1818, he left his wife, Sarah
an annuity of £60 for life. To each of his 3 daughters he left
£3,000 to be paid at the age of 21 or on marriage, in the case of
any of these dying the share to go to the suvivors or survivor.
To his son, John at 21, he left his half-share in Long Bay and the
Pool. He expressed the wish that if his sister Elizabeth Sarsfield,
would sell her half-share in these properties that it should be purchased out of his estate and added to his half-share for his son
at 21. In the event of his son John dying before the age of 21,
his property was to be equally divided between his brother Sam and
his surviving children. Sam was appointed one of the executors of
the will.

In 1820, Mrs. Lord Snr., Sam's mother, died as also did
Adriana, John's eldest daughter. During this year the building of
Long Bay Castle, erected on the site of the old mansion of Long Bay,
which had been begun with slave labour two or three years previously,
was completed. The Castle stood with its four corners at the
cardinal points of the compass, surrounded by massive stone walls
with crenelated battlements, in every way a most imposing edifice,
which is said to have cost £20,000 — £30,000.

Aspinall in his account of the Castle, now known as Sam
Lord's Castle, says "In August 1831, one of the worst cyclones
recorded on the Island swept away part of the roof and scaffolding,
but left the walls intact, a tribute to their strength. The ceiling
took three and a half years to complete and was the work of the
Englishman, Charles Rutter, and two Italian Workmen, formerly
employed in decorating Windsor Castle."[12]

1821—1829, SAM LORD CONSOLIDATES HIS POSITION.

Having built himself a fine castle at Long Bay, Sam began
to live and entertain there on a lavish scale. At law, his position
as Master of Long Bay Castle is interesting. His sister Elizabeth
Sarsfield is supposedly the owner of one half of Long Bay and the
Pool and his brother's estate owns the other half share. In 1821,
John, Sam's brother's only son, died somewhat mysteriously it was
said, although no proof of other than death from natural causes
was produced.[13]

By the terms of his brother's will, Sam and the surviving
daughters Eliza and Frances at 21, were to become entitled to

the half share of Long Bay and Pool. In 1826, Eliza died at sea,[14] and her share was added to that of Frances who was still a minor. So that Frances now owned two–thirds of a half share and Sam one–third of a half share. The remaining half share was held by Elizabeth Sarsfield until 1834, when she conveyed this half–share n Long Bay and the Pool to Sam in his own right and not as Executor of his brother's will. This made Sam the owner of four–sixths and Frances two–sixths of the estates.

Sam was anxious to consolidate his land between Long Bay and the Pool. With this in mind he bought in 1822 Bowmanston Plantation of 214 acres with a mansion. Later, in 1829 he bought the Ruby estate of 356 acres and added to it until it was 399 acres in extent, thus joining up his whole territory, to form one solid block from North to South.

In 1828 Sam, having gone to England, saw Lucy by appointment at her lodgings in Bristol. According to James Haywood's diary she then offered to return to Barbados and live with him, but he replied, "It would not suit his present habits." Again to quote from the diary, he was suspected by his sister, Elizabeth Sarsfield, of living an immoral life, although no proof of this was given. If this was a fact his reply may have been the reason for refusing to take Lucy back to Barbados. However, about November of the same year Sam made another appointment with Lucy at Wolverhampton at which he asked her to return, but then she refused.

Although Sam had never paid Lucy any allowance, which he should have done under the Agreement of 5th October 1815, he had paid for his daughter's education at Miss Webb's Seminary at Clifton. In October 1828 her mother took Cecilia to Paris to finish her education; in 1834, Mr. Daniel, through Miss Stuart, was authorized to allow £100 a year for the purpose. This was only paid for one year after which he said he could not afford it, but he wished his daughter to travel with him in America. Who were Miss Stuart and Mr. Daniel[15] and what may have been Sam's purpose in wishing to go to America? To these questions I have no clue, but they have been culled from the Diary.

1830 — 1844 WRECKS ON COBBLERS REEF. HURRICANE OF 1831 AND ITS CONSEQUENCES.

Before 1st May, 1875, when the lighthouse at Ragged Point was built, wrecks on Cobblers Reef were frequent. Even after the lighthouse was built sailing ships continued to be wrecked. In calm weather crews could usually get ashore easily; in stormy weather ships were generally driven on to the rocks and over them into shallow water, not far from the beach at Long Bay.

Persistent rumour was current that in many cases Sam Lord was the author of these wrecks, which he engineered by the device of hanging lanterns on trees and the horns of cattle; these swayed about in the wind and appeared to be the lights of Carlisle Harbour, thus misleading ships as to its whereabouts.

Captain Wish, R. N.[16] has classified the wrecks which occurred at this period and an endeavour has been made to show if, and when, Sam Lord could have been accused of responsibility for them. The wrecks are divided into two catergories:—

(a) 1820 — 1834; 5 wrecks (b) 1835—1841; 16 wrecks.

(a) 1820—1834.
1. In 1826 the *Shipley* a Military Transport was lost with many lives.
2. Between that date and 1832 an unnamed vessel was wrecked.
3. In 1833 the Barque *Wanderer* was wrecked.
4. On 10th December 1834 the Brig. *Regina* was lost.
5. On 17th December 1834 the *Seven Brothers* was wrecked.

But Sam Lord was away from 1824 to 1827, and therefore could not have had a hand in the case of No. 1. He was in residence in 1833, but actually entertained the Captain of the *Wanderer* at the Castle for a couple of weeks, so is unlikely to have been the cause of his shipwreck.

From 1834 to early 1839 Sam was absent in the United Kingdom, thus he could not have been responsible for wrecks Nos. 4 and 5. This leads to the conclusion that the only case in doubt is No. 2, but at that period Sam, having got virtual possession of the Long Bay and Pool properties was unlikely to have need to resort to wrecking to add to his wealth.

(b) 1835—1840

From 1835 to early 1839 Sam Lord was in the United Kingdom, or on the voyage back to Barbados. Amongst the wrecks classified by Captain Wish the names of two are noted towards the end of the period. On 28th June, 1840 the Brig. *Susan Crane* was lost on Cobblers Reef, and on 13th July, the Barque *Emerald* sank there. In the former case Sam had hardly got back to the Castle while in the latter case he was entertaining the Trollopes, his niece and nephew–in–law, as bride and bridegroom, there, it cannot therefore be supposed he could have acted as a wrecker in their presence.

On the above evidence it appears there is no shred of justification in attributing any of these wrecks to Sam Lord. Moreover, when a wreck occurs it is compulsory for the Captain of the ship to be summoned into Court to give an account of the circumstances, when there is little doubt that the facts would have been fully disclosed.

Rumour has said that a subterranean tunnel existed connecting the beach with the Castle by which plunder was carried into its dungeon. No trace of such a tunnel has, however, been found.

HURRICANE OF 1831.

In the account of the building of Long Bay Castle reference was made to the hurricane of 1831 showing how stoutly its walls were fashioned. Although his Castle stood firm, a vast amount of damage was done throughout the island and most plantations, including those of Sam Lord, suffered severely. In order to give financial assistance to farmers who had lost their crops the Government issued Exchequer bonds, guaranteed by mortgages on their lands. Sam was obliged to apply for many thousand pounds worth of mortgages, which did a great deal to undermine his financial position.[17] These mortgages, combined with his extravagant mode of life, helped to accumulate a load of debts under which he was severely hampered during the latter part of his life.

1840 — 1844. MARRIAGE OF FRANCES LORD AND DEATH OF SAM LORD.

On 21st March, 1840, Frances, the only surviving child of John Thomas Lord, Sam's elder and deceased brother, was married to Captain Charles Trollope, 70th Foot, later to become Major-General Sir Charles Trollope, K.C.B. He was the younger son of Sir John Trollope, Bart., of Casewick, Lincolnshire. The couple were married at St. Mary's, Bryanston Square, London and accompanied Sam Lord on his return to Barbados on their honeymoon.
It was during this visit that Frances made the sketch of Long Bay Castle from which the lithograph was made by P. Gauci.[18] At the end of the visit the Trollopes returned to England where Captain Trollope resumed his military career.

Frances held, as is related earlier a one-third share in Long Bay and the Pool. She agreed to relinquish her rights in these estates during her uncle Sam's lifetime in exchange for an annuity of £1,000 per annum. This annuity was never paid. The terms of this marriage settlement became the subject of litigation after Sam Lord's death; this resulted in the Trollopes getting possession of Long Bay and Pool after purchasing outstanding interests from mortgagees in 1847.

In 1844, Sam Lord made his final will on 8th July before leaving Barbados for England on 10th July, in the *Eleanor*. Under this will, after certain bequests, he left his property on trust, to be administered by his sister Elizabeth Sarsfield, his niece Mary Frances,

Harvey,[19] and his friend Thomas Lee, a merchant of Liverpool. The trust was to operate for 500 years with provision for continuance of the executors as each one died or refused to act any longer. The trust was to be administered for the ultimate benefit of his eldest grandson, my father, then aged one year, the child of Sam's daughter, Cecilia Haywood, wife of James Haywood. It is to be recollected that Cecilia was in any case entitled to receive the allowance of £300 — £500 per annum under the Deed of Agreement drawn up on 5th October 1815, not a penny of which had been paid.

Sam Lord died in London on 5th November, 1844 and was buried in Kensal Green Cemetery. The notice of his death appeared in *The Gentleman's Magazine*, No. 104, of that month, which was probably inserted by James Haywood, his son–in–law.

In connection with Sam's death the following account was given by his coachman, Rolestone,[20] when the latter returned from London. "The last day had been little different from the others. The master's coach had been ordered from Jermyn Street. We drove to some unidentified spot in London; a hall–porter ushered Sam Lord in, while I drew the coach to one side. Hours passed, he did not come out; I went to the hall–porter to ask for my master; he replied 'I would never wish you to be as your master is now; you will never see him again; take back the carriage'."

1845 — 1847. WINDING UP OF SAMUEL HALL LORD'S ESTATE.

My endeavours to obtain the accounts for the final winding up of Sam Lord's estate proved fruitless. I was told in the Bridgetown Registry that none could be traced. As the period in question was over 100 years old it was more than likely any papers dealing with them would have been destroyed many years ago.

I ascertained, however, from some indentures and agreements found in this Registry that James Haywood had, during his visit to Barbados, either in 1845, or at a later date, succeeded in getting himself, a solicitor called Samuel Husbands, and a Mr. Charles Prettejohn, appointed to administer the Trust in place of Elizabeth Sarsfield, Mary Frances Harvey and Thomas Lee, who had all resigned as Executors. It therefore seemed most unlikely that James Haywood would have left any stone unturned to collect any assets available for the trust.

It is on record that debts amounted to some £18,000, including Bank overdrafts and individual creditors (by 1847) no less than seventeen judgments for debts were made. There is no means of telling whether James Haywood ultimately got any redress for his wife, Cecilia, or succeeded in making the trust solvent, but it seems to say the least of it doubtful. It is known that Bowmanston Estate was advertised for sale by Thomas Lee, one of the original executors.[21] Ruby must also have been sold, but the buyer I was unable to trace. While, as already stated the Trollopes purchased outstanding interest from the mortgagees in possession of Long Bay and Pool and acquired them. Although there is no question that in law, and by reason of Sam Lord's will, my father, Lt. Colonel Walter Wightwick Haywood was the rightful inheritor of the bulk of Sam Lord's at one time considerable estate, owing to the accumulation of liabilities his inheritances proved practically valueless.

ASSESSMENT OF SAM LORD'S CHARACTER.

Although we may acquit Sam Lord of being a wrecker, or even of being responsible for the deaths of any of his brother's children, yet there are other charges which must be laid against him, they are dishonesty and cruelty in his family life. On the other hand he was both ambitious and energetic, while it is likely he had a charm of manner particularly for women.

His ambition for wealth and power probably caused him to administer his brother's estate unscrupulously and for his own benefit and not for that of his nephew.

Undoubtedly he treated his wife very cruelly, making it impossible for her to live with him. He gave her no allowance and did little towards financing his daughter's education and up-bringing. It is true that the 1831 hurricane and the slave eman-cipation bill of 1833, were causing him and all planters considerable losses at this time, but government loans for the former and the £10,000 compensation Sam received for the latter, helped considera-bly to mitigate the consequent depreciation of his income.

The outstanding monument to Sam Lord's fame is undoubtedly the Castle he built at Long Bay. Schomburgk's History calls it "an oasis in the desert."[22] It most certainly eclipses any mansion in Barbados in beauty of design and its power of defying the pass-ing of the years. The taste he showed in modelling the interior is particularly noteworthy, although the methods he used to help to defray the cost of building must be condemned.

NOTES.

1. John Lord's eldest son, Richard Sergeant Lord, predeceased his father by 4 months, dying on 2nd June 1799. He is, therefore, not mentioned in his father's will, but his 5 children, Thomas, John, Richard Sergeant, Mary and Bathsheba are each left £100 by their grandfather. A fourth son of John Lord, named Thomas died in infancy in 1782.

2. Not named in her father's will, but two of her daughters, Bathsheba and Caroline Austin were left legacies.

She was therefore born about 1747, but her baptism has not been traced. There are entries in the Register of Baptisms (Vol. 22/143) of 1753 described as "From fragments without date of year or order" one of which reads "Dau. of John and Ann Sergeant." Children were often baptised when a few years old and this entry may refer to her baptism. Her will, dated 15th May, 1820, mentions the following grandchildren; Caroline, Sarah, Mary Frances, Sarah Bathsheba and Lucy Whytick (*sic*) Austin; Mary, Bathsheba, Thomas *alias* Jones, and Richard Sergeant, children of Richard Sergeant Lord; and Elizabeth, Frances and John, children of John Thomas Lord.

Buried on 2nd June 1851 at St. Philip's parish church, aged 64, described as of Long Bay Castle.

He was baptised at St. Philip's parish church on 21st March, 1809, and his name is entered as 'Orechus', Register 22/14; but his name is correctly given as Oceanus when his burial is recorded on 5th May 1811.

Baptised 25 July 1812, name entered as Emma Lacey instead of Lucy, buried 16 April, 1814, St. Philip's parish church.

Deeds, 306/504.

Deeds, 289/109 *et seq*.

A warrant was issued for Sam Lord's arrest with reward of £100 for his apprehension on 5th February 1817. *The Barbados Mercury*, 8th February 1817. See also "Sam Lord Fact or Fiction" by Derek Bickerton, *Advocate*, (*Magazine Section*) 9th, 16th, 23rd, 30th April 1961.

Index gives Reference as 244/158.

Haynes Elizabeth born 10th May, 1809, buried 6th August, 1810; Mary Franklin born 15th March 1813, buried 16th April 1814. The baptisms and burials of these two took place at St. Philip's parish church.

A Pocket Guide to the West Indies by A. Aspinall, pp. 94—5.

There is no record of his burial, he may have died in England or, if he died in Barbados, he must have been buried either at Long Bay or the Pool. The same is true of his sister Adriana.

Died on board the ship *Venus* on her passage from Bristol to this island, Miss Lord, daughter of the late John T. Lord Esq. *The Barbadian Newspaper* 17th February, 1826. According to the recital in a deed the date of her death was 2nd February 1826. Deeds 289/110.

Probably Mr. Thomas Daniel an absentee proprietor and sugar merchant of London.

"Sam Lord — Fact of Fiction" by Derek Bickerton. *Advocate* (*Magazine Section*) 7 May, 1961.

£6,600 on Long Bay and Pool; £3,000 on Bowmanston and £3,400 on Ruby Estate.

The lithograph shows part of Sam Lord's herd of deer and the legend reads: "Drawn from nature by Fanny Trollope."

19. Née Austin married, on 17th August 1837, at St. Philip's parish church, Lt. William Harvey K.C.B. *The Barbadian* 19th August 1837.

20. Thomas Rolestone of Bowmanston was married to Elizabeth James Lord, also of Bowmanston, on 8th April 1839, by licence at St. John's parish church. One of the witnesses of this wedding was Samuel Hall Lord. It was rather unusual for a plantation owner to be present at one of his servants marriage. There were, however, slaves at Long Bay and Pool with the surname Lord, a practice which was later more common of taking the surname of the owner as slaves had none. In 1836, Thomas Rolestone, a labourer and a minor, petitions by Elizabeth Sarsfield Lord, his next friend, that his reputed father Thomas Rolestone, who was illegitimate and unmarried made a will about 1827. By this will, Thomas Rolestone bequeathed his 2 board and shingled houses in Bridgetown to his reputed wife Kitty Blenman for her life and at her death the smaller house to her reputed son, John Rolestone, and the larger house to her reputed sons Robert Rolestone and the petitioner to be equally divided between them. The testator appointed Samuel Hall Lord executor, to whom the will was delivered by John Edghill who had drawn up the same. Sam Lord had omitted to have the will proved and the will was lost. In 1836 Sam Lord was in England. Thomas Rolestone, Sam Lord's coachman, returned to Long Bay after his master's death, for in January 1850 we find him witnessing a conveyance from Elizabeth Sarsfield Lord to Mary Frances Harvey, her niece. By Sam Lord's will he left the sum of £30 currency per annum to Thomas Rolestone and his wife Elizabeth James for their joint use and then to the survivor.

21. *The Barbadian*, 25th February, 1846.

22. *History of Barbados*, by Sir Robert H. Schomburgk, 1848, p. 219.

THE ANCESTRY OF DR. NATHAN LUCAS

IN the Society's Journal of May 1940, Vol. VII. No. 3 a short account was given of the life of Dr. Nathan Lucas (1761—1828) scion of an old Barbados family, the compiler of numerous Ms Volumes of records of old Barbados the majority of which are preserved in the Public Library in Bridgetown.

The ancestry of Dr. Nathan Lucas has been definitely traced from Richard Lucas, who was resident in Christ Church parish in 1662, but the family appears to have been established in Barbados from much earlier times, although the connecting links are not complete. Nicholas Lucas, who was buried in Christ Church on 30 September 1650, was a landowner as early as 1638. There is no evidence to prove how or when Mount Clapham plantation came into the possession of the family, but it passed under the Will of Nathan Lucas (died 1771) to his son, Dr. Lucas, and it is quite probable that it formed part of the estate of the latter's grandfather, Dr. Nathan Lucas (died 1723) who is known to have owned property in Christ Church.

The ancestry of Hon. Nathan Lucas, the antiquary, so far as it can be proved is appended.

1.   RICHARD LUCAS of Christ Church, died July 5, 1684.
     Married Elizabeth Stokes, 20 December 1662.
     Issue:—

         1. Samuel, baptised April 11, 1664.
     2. 2. Nathan, baptised May 4, 1666.
         3. Elizabeth, baptised November 23, 1668. Died Nov. 30, 1668.
         4. Richard, baptised Febry. 19, 1671.
         5. Henry, baptised October 9, 1673.
         6. William, baptised July 10, 1676.
         7. Theophilus, baptised Novr. 26, 1678. Died Octr. 17, 1705.

2.   NATHAN LUCAS, died December 1692.
     Married Sarah (Surname unknown).
     Issue:—

3. 1. Nathan, baptised February 5, 1689.
   2. Philip, baptised April 27, 1690. Married Ann Pritchard August 10, 1712, Died January 20, 1719.
   3. Thomas, baptised December 12, 1692.

3. Dr. NATHAN LUCAS, died March 15, 1723.
Married Mary Taylor, daughter of George and Alice Taylor of St. Philip, December 19, 1718.
Issue: —

    1. child, (name not recorded), baptised October, 26, 1719.
4. 2. Nathan, born March 2, 1722, baptised Jany. 24, 1723.

4. NATHAN LUCAS, died 1771.
Married Sarah Jordan.
Issue: —

    1. Sarah, born September 1753. Married Edmund Eversley August 26, 1774.
    2. Mary Taylor Lucas. Married Richard Haslewood August 29, 1775.
    3. Alice, married Alexander Malet, April 5, 1785.
    4. Ann Jordan, born April 14, 1757.
5. 5. Nathan, born January 9, 1761.
    6. Joseph Jordan, born 16, 1763.

5. NATHAN LUCAS, Surgeon, Member of H.M. Council, Chief Judge of the Common Pleas for the Precinct of St. Michael, sometimes presided as Chief Justice of the Court of Grand Sessions, Compiler of the Mss. which bears his name, and an authority on scientific and agricultural subjects. Died February 20, 1828.
Married Mary Crookenden of The River plantation, Saint Philip. She died November 27, 1825.
Issue: —

    1. Mary, born 1787. Married Charles Kingsley, and they had issue Rev. Charles Kingsley, Author of *Westward Ho!*, *At Last!* and other works.
    2. Elizabeth, born November 10, 1788. Died July 25, 1789.
    3. Sarah Ann, baptised January 11, 1791. Died January 12, 1791.
    4. Nathan, baptised October 1, 1792. Died at Tours in France September 23, 1813.

Ch. Ch.	1643 Sep.		Joan, d. of Nicholas & Joan Lucas.
„	1646 Nov.	20	Elizabeth, d. of Nicholas & Joan Lucas.
St. M.	1656 Feb.	15	Joane, d. of Christopher Lucas.
Ch. Ch.	1664 Apl.	11	Samuel, s. of Richard & Elizabeth Lucas
„	1666 May	4	Nathan, s. of Richard & Elizabeth Lucas.
„	1668 Nov.	23	Elizabeth, d. of Richard & Elizabeth Lucas.
St. M.	1669 Oct.	3	Lucas.
Ch. Ch.	1671 Feb.	19	Richard, s. of Richard & Elizabeth Lucas.
„	1673 Oct.	9	Henry, s. of Richard & Elizabeth Lucas.
„	1676 July	10	William, s. of Richard & Elizabeth Lucas.
„	1678 Nov.	26	Theophilus, s. of Richard & Elizabeth Lucas.
„	1684 Nov.	25	Richard, s. of Samuel & Johaddan Lucas.
St. Phil.	1685 Dec.	27	Mary, d. of Charles and Ann Lucas.
Ch. Ch.	1686 Oct.	7	Elizabeth, d. of Samuel & Johaddan Lucas.
„	1686 Dec.	19	Elizabeth, d. of Nicholas & Sarah Lucas.
St. Phil.	1688 Sep.	16	Alice, d. of Charles and Ann Lucas.
Ch. Ch.	1689 Jan.	31	Thomas, s. of Samuel & Johaddan Lucas.
„	1689 Feb.	5	Nathan, s. of Nathan & Sarah Lucas.
„	1690 April	27	Philip, s. of Nathan & Sarah Lucas.
„	1690 Dec.	6	Richard, s. of Richard & Elizabeth Lucas.
„	1692 Dec.	12	Thomas, s. of Nathan & Sarah Lucas.
„	1693 June	28	Thomas, s. of Samuel & Johaddan Lucas.
St. Phil.	1698 Dec.	25	Charles & Margaret, s. & d. of Thomas Lucas.
Ch. Ch.	1700 Dec.	22	Ann, d. of Theophilus & Sarah Lucas.
„	1703 Nov.		Zachariah, s. of George & Wilhelmina Lucas.
„	1713 Oct.	8	Conrad, s. of Nathan & Catherine Lucas.
„	1713 Aug.	8	Richard, s. of Philip & Ann Lucas.
St. M.	1717 Dec.	25	William Lucas, a young man about 23 yrs. old. The Rev. Mr. Thos. Napleton & Charles Peyton, his chosen witnesses.

BAPTISMS TO YEAR 1800 *(Continued)*

Ch. Ch.	1717 June	11	.... d. of Richard & Mary Lucas.
„	1719 Oct.	26	.... c. of Nathan & Mary Lucas.
St. M.	1720 Jan.	6	Anna Lucas, in church.
„	1723 Jan.	24	Nathan, s. of Dr. Nathan & Mrs. Mary Lucas of St. Philip's parish, born the 2nd day of last March Benja. Poor, the said Nathan, godfathers, and Martha Taylor, godmother.
„	1733 Sep.	3	William Lucas, a child.
„	1740 Dec.	2	Charles Lucas, a child 13 months old.
Ch. Ch.	1740 Dec.	25	William Lucas, a young man of about 23 yrs. of age, Rev. Mr. Thos. Napleton & Charles Peyton his chosen witnesses.*
St. M.	1741 June	29	Mary Lucas a child, died same day.
„	1753 Sep.	17	Sarah, d. of Nathan & Sarah Lucas, born 10 inst.
„	1757 April	16	Ann Jordan, d. of Nathan & Sarah Lucas, born April 14, 1757.
„	1761 Jan.	11	Nathan, s. of Nathan & Sarah Lucas, born Jan. ye 9th 1761.
„	1763 June	16	Joseph Jordan, s. of Nathan & Sarah Lucas, born this day.
„	1763 Aug.	11	Hanna Ritta, d. of Joseph & Sarah Lucas.
„	1768 Dec.	5	Frances Eveling, d. of Joseph & Hannah Lucas, born 2nd.
Ch. Ch.	1770 April	26	Richard, s. of Richard King & Barbara Lucas, born Feb. 18.
„	1771 Jan.	1	Mary Ann., d. of Henry Eveling & Sarah Lucas.
„	1772 Nov.	15	Frances d. of Henry Eveling & Sarah Lucas.
St. M.	1773 Oct.	7	Joseph, s. of Joseph & Sarah Lucas.
Ch. Ch.	1775 April	17	Joseph James, s. of Henry and Sarah Lucas, born Novr. 13, 1774.
St. Phil.	1777 April	15	Sarah Elizabeth, d. of Henry & Sarah Lucas.
„	1780 Jan.	5	Harriott, d. of Henry Lucas and his wife.
„	1781 Dec.	25	Nathaniel, s. of Henry Evelin Lucas and Sarah his wife, in Church.
St. M.	1782 Novr.	21	Jane, d. of Jos. Lucas & Loetitia his wife, b. 16 inst.
St. Phil.	1784 Octr.	24	Rebecca, d. of Henry Evelin Lucas & Sarah, his wife.

---

* See a similar entry in the St. Michael's Register under date 25 Decr. 1717, evidently inserted at the later date.

Ch. Ch.	1786 Jany.	22	Mary Ann, d. of Joseph & Letitia Lucas, b. Sep. 7, 1784.
St. Phil.	1786 June	5	Angel, d. of Henry & Sarah Lucas.
Ch. Ch.	1787 April	7	Jacob & Frances, s. & d. respectively of Joseph & Letitia Lucas, born 5 instant.
St. M.	1788 Decr.	25	Elizabeth, d. of Nathan & Mary Lucas, b. 10 Novr.
Ch. Ch.	1788 Jany.	12	Josiah Phillips, s. of Christopher & Mary Lucas.
St. P.	1789 Mch.	10	Henry, s. of Henry Evelin & Sarah Lucas.
Ch. Ch.	1790 June	20	Letitia, d. of Josias & Letitia Lucas, b. 15 inst.
Ch. Ch.	1791 Jany.	11	Sarah Ann, dau. of Nathan & Mary Lucas.
Ch. Ch.	1792 Decr.	4	Nathan, son of Nathan Lucas and Mary his wife, born October 1, 1792.

LUCAS MARRIAGES TO 1800

Ch. Ch.	1651 June	1	Joan Lucas to Henry Price.
St. M.	1659 Octr.	12	Richard Lucas to Elizabeth Darrow.
Ch. Ch.	1661 June	21	Ann Lucas to Matthew Yateb.
„	1662 Decr.	20	Richard Lucas to Elizabeth Stoakes.
„	1662 Novr.	11	Joan Lucas to Richard Beard.
„	1670 July	28	.... Lucas to Mary ....
St. Phil.	1680 April	11	Thomas Lucas to Ann Wahabb.
Ch. Ch.	1690 Feby.	2	Richard Lucas to Elizabeth Robinson.
St. Phil.	1692 Aug.	7	Ursula Lucas to John Russell.
St. M.	1696 April	16	Elizabeth Lucas to Richard Lane.
„	1698 Decr.	23	Mary Lucas to Arthur McSwain.
„	1700 Mar.	18	William Lucas to Sarah Sheephard.
Ch. Ch.	1702 Octr.	8	George Lucas to Wilhelmina Harris.
„	1713 Decr.	28	Nathan Lucas to Catherine Legay.
„	1712 Aug.	10	Philip Lucas to Ann Pritchard.
St. M.	1713 Sept.	13	Sarah Lucas to William Thornhill.
Ch. Ch.	1714 Novr.	21	Richard Lucas to Mary Rushbrook.
St. M.	1715 April	17	William Lucas to Margaret Ennis.
Ch. Ch.	1718 Decr.	19	Nathan Lucas to Mary Taylor.
St. J.	1712 Aug.	11	Joseph Lucas to Mary McClean.
„	1724 Feb.	2	Joseph Lucas to Frances Evelyn.
„	1724 Nov.	16	Charles Lucas to Margaret Scroggs.
St. Jon.	1727 Nov.	8	Ann Lucas to Edward Butcher.
St. Phil.	1728 April	22	William Lucas to Catherine Ingram.
St. J.	1732 June	20	Sarah Lucas to John Drayton.
Ch. Ch.	1735 May	23	Elizabeth Lucas to William Bynoe.
„	1736 July	31	William Lucas to Margaret Fenty.

MARRIAGES TO YEAR 1800 *(Concluded)*

St. M.	1737		Frances Lucas to ....
„	1738 Oct.	19	Mary Lucas, Spinster, to Robert Barbridge Reeves.
St. J.	1753 July	4	Joseph Lucas to Dorothy Baxter.
St. J.	1755 Sep.	23	Elizabeth Lucas to William Boyles.
„	1756 April	21	Ann Lucas to Elisha Luke.
St. M.	1774 Aug.	26	Sarah Lucas to Edmund Eversley.
„	1775 Aug.	29	Mary Taylor Lucas to Richard Haslewood.
Ch. Ch.	1778 June	8	Frances Burnett Lucas to Thomas Pollard.
St. M.	1780 Mar.	26	Sarah Lucas to John Smith.
„	1781 Oct.	13	Joseph Laticia Dennis.
St. Phil.	1785 Dec.	16	Nathan Lucas to Mary Crookenden.
St. M.	1788 April	5	Alice Lucas to Alexander Malet.
St. M.	1790 April	16	Mary Lucas to John Flannagan.

LUCAS BURIALS TO 1828

Ch. Ch.	1647 Sep.	27	Elizabeth Lucas.
„	1650 Sep.	30	Nicholas Lucas.
St. J.	1666 July	19	Henry Lucas.
Ch. Ch.	1668 Nov.	30	Elizabeth, d. of Richard Lucas.
St. M.	1669 Oct.	6	one Lucas.
„	1669 Aug.	1	James Lucas.
„	1671 April	17	Joseph Lucas.
Ch. Ch.	1684 July	5	Richard Lucas.
St. M.	1689 May	7	John Lucas, mariner from on board Admirall Hewtson.
„	1690		John Lucas.
„	1691 Aug.	24	John Lucas, mariner.
Ch. Ch.	1692 Dec.		Nathan Lucas.
„	1695 Jan.	15	Samuel Lucas.
„	1695 May	23	Richard Lucas.
„	1696 Sep.	5	one Lucas.
„	1700 Feb.	8	Philip Lucas.
„	1703 Nov.	1	Wilhelmina Lucas.
„	1703 Nov.	4	Zachariah Lucas, a child.
„	1705 Oct.	17	Theophilus Lucas.
„	1708 Dec.	27	Johaddan Lucas.
„	1709 Nov.	28	Thomas Lucas.
„	1711 Dec.	19	Mary Lucas, a child.
„	1713 May	28	Ann Lucas.
„	1717 July	21	Mary Lucas.
St. M.	1718 Aug.	25	Katharine Lucas.
Ch. Ch.	1719 Jan.	20	Philip Lucas.
„	1719 May	19	Richard Lucas.
St. M.	1720 Dec.	16	James Lucas, a child.

St. M.	1720 Oct.	2	Sarah Lucas.
„	1720 Feb.	11	Nathaniel Lucas son of Nathaniel Lucas.
„	1723 Mar.	15	Dr. Nathan Lucas.
„	1725 Jan.	2	Mrs. Mary Lucas.
„	1730 April	2	Elizabeth Lucas.
Ch. Ch.	1731 July	20	Thomas Lucas.
„	1733 Jan.	1	Mrs. Lucas.
St. M.	1736		George Lucas.
Ch. Ch.	1737		Child of Joseph Lucas.
St. M.	1740		Charles Lucas.
„	1743 Aug.	28	Ann Lucas a spinster.
Ch. Ch.	1746 Jan.	19	Charles Lucas.
„	1747 Jan.	3	Joseph Lucas.
„	1747 Sep.	20	Margaret Lucas.
St. M.	1750 Nov.	25	Mary Lucas.
„	1752 May	5	Alice wife of Nath. Lucas.
Ch. Ch.	1755 Feb.	26	Margaret Lucas.
„	1755 Oct.	8	Mrs. Frances Lucas widow.
St. M.	1756 Aug.	18	William Lucas.
Ch. Ch.	1759 Mar.	15	Thomas son of Thomas Lucas.
„	1759 May	28	Joseph Lucas.
St. M.	1768 Aug.	11	Frances Lucas, an infant.
Ch. Ch.	1768 Feb.	27	Mr. Lucas.
St. M.	1773 Nov.	28	Henry Lucas.
St. M.	1773 Oct.	9	Joseph, son of Joseph Griffith.
„	1775 Jan.	31	Margaret Lucas.
St. Phil.	177 June	9	Barbara Lucas, an infant.
Ch. Ch.	1787 Dec.	9	Jacob Lucas.
„	1787 Dec.	10	Frances Lucas.
St. M.	1789 July	25	Elizabeth, daughter of Nathanl. Lucas.
Ch. Ch.	1790 April	1	Widow Lucas.
St. M.	1791 Jan.	12	Sarah Ann daughter of Nathan Lucas.
Ch. Ch.	1793 Nov.	16	Dorothy Lucas age unknown.
„	1793 Nov.	25	Thomas Lucas aged 37 years.
„	1794 Jan.	10	Eliza Lucas age unknown.
„	1794 Aug.	14	George Parris Lucas age unknown.
„	1796 Jan.	2	Elizabeth Lucas aged 21 years.
„	1797 Aug.	8	Mary Lucas aged 64 years.
St. M.	1798 May	7	Letitia Lucas.
Ch. Ch.	1797 July	12	Christopher Lucas.
St. M.	1799 May	27	Elizabeth Lucas.
„	1800 June	25	Margaret Lucas.
„	1803 Dec.	10	Thomas Lucas, a mariner.
Ch. Ch.	1804 Dec.	28	Angel Lucas.
„	1804 Jan.	11	Frances Lucas aged 30.
„	1805 July	19	Henry Lucas aged 60.

Following entries omitted until

St. M.	1825 Nov.	25	Mary Lucas, Christ Church, aged 70.
„	1828 Feb.	21	Nathan Lucas, Christ Church aged 68.

LUCAS WILLS RECORDED IN BARBADOS.

Will of NICHOLAS LUCAS of Christ Church, Barbados. (no date).

To the Minister of the parish of Christ Church 100 lbs. of sugar. To the church of Christ Church 100 lbs. of sugar to be disposed of by the Churchwarden.

To my (blank) Nicholas Lucas all that my plantation adjoyning to Lieut. Christian Brookhaven provided he pay unto his two sisters Ann and Joane 1000 lbs. of cotton, sugar, or tobacco, or the value thereof when and so soone as they shall attain 18 years or are married.

To my goddaughter the eldest daughter of James Lee five shillings stlg. To my loving friends Mr. Richard Isham, Lieut. Michaell Witherall, Ensigne John Jackson and Owen Roberts 20/- a piece to buy each of them a ring. All the rest etc. to my wife Joana Lucas to be disposed of by her for the use benefit and education of my said three children. My wife to be executrix, Lieut. Witherall and Jackson to be supervisors.

(signed) P.me Nicho. Lucas. Witnesses: Owen Roberts, Tho: Powdrell. Deposition of Owen Roberts aged 31 taken 7 Oct. 1650. (Will written by him) Jurat coram me, Wm. Kirton. Deposition of Thomas Powdrell aged 24 years. Deposition of John Davis aged 30 years taken 8 Oct. 1650.

Will entered in the Registry 4 Oct. 1650.

Nuncupative Will of DEGORY LUCAS. Deposition of Urban Streete aged 35 years and Matthew Holmes aged 21 years taken before Governor Hen: Willoughby on 9 April 1666. Witnesses stated that they were in the home of John Allen, well-digger, on 10 April 1666, wherein Degory Lucas lay very sick, and they heard the said Lucas express himself thus: I give all my estate whatsoever to the said John Allen, desiring him to have me handsomely buried; and less than half hour after the said Degory Lucas died.

Will of JAMES LUCAS of Barbados, dated 8 June 1669.

My wife Ann is to be my sole executrix, and I give her all my real and personal estate whatsoever in Barbados or in England, provided she will pay my debts. (signed) James X Lucas. Witnesses : John Skining, John Griffin, John Banister. Entered 4 Aug. 1669.

Will of RICHARD LUCAS of Barbados, dated 11 June 1684.

All my estate to my wife Elizabeth for her life, and after her death I give to my son Nathan my mansion house I now live in and the land thereto and also the smithshop, stables, etc. and also one acre of land called Woolfsland and one negro Mingo. To my son Samuel the remainder of my estate. To sons Richard and Theophilus £50 each at 21. My wife Elizabeth to be sole executrix.

Witnesses: Wm. Clement, Saml. Gaselee, Isaac Ragg. Entered 23 Sep. 1684.

Will of RICHARD LUCAS of Christ Church, Barbados, Gent. dated 23 April 1719. To my daughter Elizabeth Lucas all my estate and in case of her death before me to my sister Elizabeth Lucas. My daughter Elizabeth to be executrix. My brothers, Mr. Francis Pile and Mr. Stephen Pile to be guardians of my infant daughter. Witnesses: Theo. Pile, Wm. Price, Samuel Dame .... Entered 22 May 1719.

Will of WILLIAM LUCAS of St. Michael, Barbados, dated 7 Nov. 1747. To my wife, Margaret, all my real and personal estate and to be executrix. (signed) Wm. Lucas. Witnesses : Ar. Upton, Thom. Hothersal. Entered 24 Aug. 1756.

Will of NATHAN LUCAS of town and parish of St. Michael, Brazier, dated 14 May 1765.

My wife Sarah Lucas £200 cy. yearly for her life charged on my sugar work plantation Clapham, and to have the living on my estate during her widowhoold. Also all household or town negroes commonly employed about the work of my townhouse (names of 14 slaves follow) and also house in Bridgetown wherein I now live and furniture, chaise, and chaise horse.

My eldest son Nathan Lucas £10,000 cy. charged on my estate.

Daughter Sarah Lucas at 18 years or marriage, my slave Mingo and £1,500 cy.

Daughter Mary Taylor Lucas at 18 or marriage, slave Prudence, and £1,500 cy.

Daughter Alice Lucas, at 18 or marriage, slave Willoughby, a woman, and £1,500 cy., and a slave to be bought for £80 and given to her in satisfaction of what is due to her from me for a legacy under the Will of Benjamin Poore.

Daughter Ann Jordan Lucas at 18 or marriage £1,500 cy. and a slave to be bought for £80.

To the child my wife is expectant of if a son £2,500 cy. and if a daughter £1,500 cy.

To my sister-in-law, Ann Jordan, £50 cy.

An inventory to be taken of my shop in Bridgetown and also of all copper, brass, pewter, and lead that may be in my coppersmith shop and brazier shop. My wife to be executrix, and my brothers-in-law, Hon. Edward Jordan and Joseph Jordan Esq. and friend Hon. John Lyte to be executors.

(signed) Nathan Lucas. Witnesses: James Burke, John Clinton, William Carr. 3 June 1771.

Codicil. To my wife £100 per annum more. My four-wheel carriage and four horses thereto belonging with two negro men, Yea and Nay. Wife to have her living on either of my estates.

Daughter Sarah Lucas additional legacy of £500 cy.

Daughters Sarah Lucas, Mary Taylor Lucas, Alice Lucas, and Ann Jordan Lucas, to have additional legacies of £500 each.

Wife and Hon. Edward Jordan, Joseph Jordan, William Duke, and John Prettyjohn Esqrs. to be executors and my sister-in-law Ann Jordan executrix. The mark of Nathan Lucas. Witnesses: Philip Jackman jnr., William Bynoe, James Burke. Proved and recorded 11 June 1771.

Will of SARAH LUCAS, St. Michael, Barbados, dated 2 Jany. 1774.

My house in Bridgetown to be sold by my executors and a small house purchased by them for my four daughters, Sarah Lucas, Mary Taylor Lucas, Alice Lucas, and Ann Jordan Lucas, while unmarried.

Gifts of slaves to said four daughters and son Nathan Lucas. Legacy of £80 to Mary Taylor Lucas.

My marble slab with the cistern to my son, one pair of silver candlesticks thereto belonging, also the following articles (record blank)............ at the dwellinghouse at the plantation of my............ called the Spring, to wit, a pair of mahogany sconces, ... Beaufelt, a large glass fishpot, all the prints, the cases of silver-handled knives and forks and spoons and the two-handle silver cup. To my daughter, silver teaspoons and strainer, and the furniture not disposed of to be sold, as well as my chaise and four horses. My sister Ann Jordan.

To my two housekeepers, Mrs Joanna Le Count and Mrs. Ann MacAndrew £10 each.

To my brothers Hon. Edward Jordan and Doctor Joseph Jordan, my friend Hon. Richard Cobham and sister Ann Jordan, executors.

(signed) Sarah Lucas. Witnesses: Ann King, Edmund Eversley, Joseph King. Entered 3 May 1774.

Will of NATHAN LUCAS of Barbados, dated 27 Sep. 1816.

All my estate to my wife Mary during her life and after her death as she shall by deed or Will appoint; and in default of appointment I devise all my estate to Gibbes Walker Jordan and Matthew Coulthurst Esqs. in trust for sale and conversion, and one-half thereof for my son Nathan for life and after his death for his children equally and if no child in trust for my daughter Mary Kingsley, wife of the Rev. Charles Kingsley. And as to the other moiety of my estate in trust for my said daughter Mary Kingsley during her life and after her death in such manner as she should by deed or will appoint, and in default of appointment between her children equally.

(signed) Nathan Lucas. Witnesses: W. Garnett, Henry Woolford jnr., William Husbands, D. Secty.

Proved 25 Febry. by W. Husbands, Deputy Secretary, before J. B. Skeete, President.

EARLY DEEDS RECORDED IN BARBADOS.

9 March 1641. Thomas Lewis to Nicholas Lucas of a plantation of 20 acres in Christ Church. Thomas X. Lewis. Witnesses: Henry Wooton, John Batt, Ferdinand Eyton.

18 March 1641. Nicholas Lucas and William Salt of Barbados, Bond to William Pead of Barbados. 3,000 lbs. cotton wool. (sgd.) Nicho. Lucas, Wm. Salt. Witnesses: Tho. Gay, Martin Lynton.

28 Dec. 1641. Francis Toebast of Barbados, planter, have received from my kinsman, Hendricke Lucas in the province of Holland, mariner, £200 stlg. and 10,000 lbs. of well conditioned merchantable tobaccoe in role. Sell him all that plantation whereon I now live lying at Black Rocke in St. Lucie, Barbados. Witnesses: Robert Loyd, Jno. Wood.

25 March 1664. Nicholas Lucas of Barbados, Planter, to Tho. Lewes, Gent, sale of "my plantation whereon I now live, which I formerly purchased of said T. Lewes." (sd.) Nicho. Lucas. Witnesses: Henry Wooton, Peter Joanes.

10 June 1645. John George of Barbados, gent, for 2,000 lbs. tobacco sell to Nicholas Lucas the younger of Barbados, sonne unto Nicholas Lucas of the said island, 5 acres part of the land I purchased of Henry Austine, bounded with the land of Lieut. Pead, windward, and Lieut. Christian Brookhaven, leeward, and lying at ye foot of the wood and Henry Russell's land. George covenants that Nicholas Lucas the elder shall have the use of the land aforesaid until his son Nicholas Lucas the younger shall come of age. (sd.) John George. Witnesses : Walter Barrett, Tho. Trigge.

22 March 1711. Col. Joseph Browne of Barbados, planter, for £50 cy. paid by Nathan Lucas of Christ Church sells him 3 acres in Christ Church near the Batterre called St. Joseph's Batterre. Witnesses: William Verhulst, Richard Lucas, Stephen Browne.

.... **1722.** Frederick Feake, Sergeant at Arms of the Court of Chancery of Barbados to Nathan Lucas of St. Michael, Practitioner in Physick and Surgery and Mary his wife, formerly Mary Taylor, spinster, one of the daughters of Alice Taylor late of the parish of St. Philip widow. An order obtained by them for costs against Samuel Richards of St. James, planter, administrator of the estate of the said Alice Taylor, for £59. 12. 9. cy., to satisfy which Order the Sergeant at Arms conveyed to them 3 ac. 3 rds. 12¾ p. of land in Christ Church. Witness : Robert Austin.

KINGSLEY FAMILY

The search for information concerning Dr. Nathan Lucas, the Barbados Antiquary, (1761-1828) by means of original letters, memoranda, etc. still continues. A likely and important source of information should be through the descendants of the KINGSLEY family. Lucas's daughter, Mary, married Rev. Charles Kingsley, and their children were—Rev. Charles Kingsley, the Author, (1819-1875), Dr. George Henry Kingsley (1827-1892), Gerald Kingsley, Henry Kingsley, the Author, (1830-1876), and Charlotte who married Chanter.

Rev. Charles Kingsley, the son, died leaving issue; Dr. George Kingsley married Mary Bailey (1860) by whom he had a son, Charles, and a daughter Mary, who married Rev. W. Harrison. rector of Clovelly, and wrote under the pen name of Lucas Malet; Henry Kingsley married his second cousin, Sarah Maria Kingsley.

It is supposed that the descendants of Rev. Charles Kingsley (1819-1875) or some of them settled in the United States.

---

* The marriage took place in the Island of Guadeloupe during the period of the English occupation of that island, 1810-14. A notice of the event appeared in the Gentleman's Magazine for 1811 (page 188),—
"August 1811. Lately. At Guadeloupe. Lieut. Cumming, to Baroness Judith De Bretton, eldest daughter of Baron Frederick De Bretton of St. Croix."
Her designation on the monumental inscription as "third daughter of Baron de Bretton" (not the eldest) is probably the correct one. Ed. Journal.

Lyne of Barbados and Jamaica.

Christopher Lyne of Barbados, Gent. Will not dated. My brother Edward Lyne £100 if my estate be over £1000. My sister Alice Lyne £100. Kinswoman Sarah Andrews, wife of John Andrews, £50, my dear friend Mrs Barberye Waldin, dau. of Edmund Waldin, deceased, Executrix, my Father in law Mr Francis Raynes Overseer. Witnessed by Richard Hawkins, Simon Lynde, Thomas Ellacott, Clem. Starr, 17 Mar. 1650. Sworn by Mr Thomas Ellacott, aged about 23, and Mr Simon Lynde,* aged about 27. Recorded in Barbados.

Will of Colonel Christopher Lyne of Jamaica in the Parish of St Thomas, dated 27 Feb. 1689-90. My son Captain Richard Lyne of Barbados and Parish of St George's, all my estate in England, Barbados, Jamaica, and elsewhere. My dau. Mary, wife of John Batten, £1500 Barbados c., wife Elizabeth Lyne £150 a year and a dwelling house in Barbados, son Richard Lyne Ex'or. Michael Bond and James Stretch to be trustees in Jamaica until my said son comes or sends from Barbados. Witnesses: Modyford Freeman, Lewis Evans, John Campion, John Clarke. Proved 25 Sept. 1690. Recorded in Spanish Town, Jamaica.

Testator in 1679 owned 272 a., was Col. of a foot reg., and had a licence to go to Jamaica. (Hotten and "Colon. Cal.")

Elizabeth Lyne of Barbados. Will dated 16 Nov. 1690. My dau. Mary Bratten "one Cabbanett," sister Mary Wale "a new morning gownd and a petticoate and £5," cousin Elizabeth Hasell "my seddan," grandson Christopher Lyne "one silver tankard marked C. L., and two mourning rings, one that was his grandfather's, and another his father's," grandson Richard Lyne £100 at the age of 18, grandson Christopher Lyne "all the rest of my estate, but in case he die before the age of twenty-one years then to my grandson Richard Lyne," "a pair of pearle braseletts to my daughter Mary Bratten, and after her decease to my granddaughter Elizabeth Lyne, provided my daughter have no issue," "my granddaughter Elizabeth Lyne," and "my daughter Anne Lyne," my kinsman Samuel Hasell £5. Proved 2 Nov. 1693. Recorded in Barbados.

There is nothing to shew the relationship between the Christopher Lyne of 1650 and Col. Christopher Lyne who died in 1693. There is no record of the death of Christopher Lyne in 1650, nor of the marriage of Christopher Lyne and his wife Elizabeth in Barbados Registers, nor of the baptisms of any of their children.

Anne Lyne, daughter of the testator above, and of Col. Christopher Lyne, married Capt. John Firebrace of St Michael's.

---

* His pedigree is given in "N. and Q.," 68, iv., 390, where it is stated that he was born in 1624, and went to Boston in 1650. From the above will he must have gone to America viâ Barbados. It is not stated what relationship he bore to the testator.

414

MIDDLETON FAMILY AND BARBADOS.

The name Middleton is "derived from the lands of Middleton, or Middle-toun, county Kincardine, Scotland, which that family possessed for more than 450 years. The Middleton family rendered distinguished service to the Crown. John Middleton was Lieutenant-General of Horse in the royal armies during the Civil War. At the Restoration, he was created Earl of Middleton, Baron Clermont and Fettercairne by Charles II. The second Earl of Middleton, Charles, was an ambassador at the Court of Vienna, and a principal Secretary of State of Charles II. Lord Middleton accompanied James II to exile in France after the Revolution of 1688, and he managed the affairs of the Jacobite shadow-court at St. Germains until his death. Lord Middleton's title was forfeited in 1695, because of his allegiance to James II.

George Middleton, nephew of the 1st Lord Middleton, was the grandfather of Charles Middleton, who afterwards became the 1st Lord Barham. Charles Middleton's naval career is of especial interest to Barbadians. He was born in 1726, and entered the Royal Navy at an early age. He rose to be a Captain, and saw service in the West Indies from 1757-61, during which time he commanded the following ships: **Speaker**—1757-8; **Barbados**—1758-9 **Arundel**—1759-60, and **Emerald** 1760-1.

In the mid 18th century, the Caribbean waters were infested by French privateers. While in command of the **Speaker**, a brigantine of 20 guns, Captain Middleton destroyed a number of French privateers which were harassing commerce in the Caribbean. One of the prizes he captured was a privateer which had been haunting the coast of Barbados. This earned him the gratitude of the island.

The Minutes of the House of Assembly for 25th October, 1757, record: "On the Motion of Francis Bell Esqr. seconded by John Lyte Esq. It was ordered **Nemine Contradicente,** that the Clerk prepare an address to his Excellency in Council for an Order on the Treasurer for payment of One hundred Pistoles to Charles Middleton Esqr. Commander of his Majesty's Brigantine called the **Speaker** to buy him a sword for taking a French Privateer infesting the Coast of the island, and for other good services done on his Cruises, which are duly regarded by the Publick: And that a Copy of this Minute be delivered to Mr. Middleton by the Clerk.

The Clerk having presented the said Address the same was read & passed **Nemine contradicente."**

On 22nd November, 1757, the Clerk of the House of Assembly "presented to the House a Letter signed by Charles Middleton Esqr., Commander of the **Speaker,** which he desired might be presented and the same being read was ordered to be entered and is as follows:

Gentlemen,

It is with the greatest Satisfaction and Acknowledgement, that I have received from Mr. Duke, Secretary to your Assembly, their Minute of the 25th of October, so much in my favour, and I beg leave to take this opportunity of expressing the just sense I have of their Kindness; to which I can take no other merit than a good Inclination, to do justice to the Commission I am entrusted with, and a strong desire of continuing my services to this Island in particular, by all the means and methods, which the small Command I have will admit of.

The present you intend me, is of that nature which leaves me not at liberty to accept it, and I hope from the Goodness you have already favoured me with, that my excusing myself from such an Acceptance may be received with a favourable Construction, and not lessen the Esteem, the Publick have already honoured me with.

The Minute of the house, I shall carefully preserve as a Mark of their Regard and Approbation—A far more valuable Consideration to me than any other; and I hope my future conduct will convince more than words how much I have the interest of this Island and their favour at heart.

I am,

Gentlemen

Your most obliged and most obedient humble servant,

CHAS. MIDDLETON.

Speaker in Carlisle Bay
October the 28th—1757

Then John Gay Alleyne Esqr.* expressed himself as follows (Vizt)
"Mr. Speaker,
So laudable a Spirit as Captain Middleton has discovered on this occasion must not be passed by either unnoticed, or unhonoured in this Assembly, I therefore move that it is the opinion of this house that Captain Middleton has shewn no other than a noble Principle of Conduct by this refusal to accept the Sum of Money offered him in Acknowledgement of his Services, and has expressed himself entirely to the satisfaction of this House by his Apology—And that such an early Specimen of Heroick Vertue in this young Commander, should not fail of all due Honour and Attention, I further move that, in lieu of the 100 Pistoles which We had voted him before, We should now send to England for a gold-hilted Sword of that value to be presented to Captain Middelton, as a thing more worthy his acceptance and which We shall desire may be worn by him as the Instrument of his own Glory, and our Publick Gratitude."
And his Motion was seconded by Richard Hall Esqr. and being unanimously concurred in
Ordered that the Treasurer of this Island remit the One hundred Pistoles made payable to Mr. Middleton, to the Agent for this Island in Great Britain to be by him laid out in purchasing a gold-hilted sword to be presented to Mr. Middleton.
Captain Middleton married Margaret, daughter of James Gambier, and sister of Vice-Admiral James Gambier, who became Governor and Commander-in-Chief of Newfoundland in 1802. Captain Middleton was created a Commander in 1871. In 1805, he became an Admiral, 1st Lord of the Admiralty, a Privy Councillor, and was created Baron Barham, with remainder to his only child Diana, the wife of Sir Gerard Noel-Noel. Lord Barham's son-in-law was the heir of Henry Noel, Earl of Gainsborough, to which title he later succeeded. The Barham barony became merged with the Gainsborough earldom, so that the present Earl of Gainsborough is also Lord Barham. Lord Gainsborough still has in his possession the gold hilted sword studded with diamonds presented to his ancestor by the House of Assembly, Barbados.
The name Middleton was not unknown in Barbados prior to the days of the gallant Commander of the Speaker. Christopher Middleton is named amongst those who owned more than 10 acres of land in Barbados in 1638, and, Ligon in

---

* J. G. Alleyne, junior member of the House of Assembly represented St. Andrew's parish. He afterwards became Speaker, and was created a baronet in 1769.

416

his **History of Barbados,** published in 1657, records that he drew a plan of a house for Captain Middleton. The records of this island contain wills for the name of Middleton, but not for a certain John Middleton, a cousin of the 1st Lord Barham, who emigrated to Barbados. To the son or grandson of John Middleton, whose name is also John, Lord Barham left £100 by the codicil of his will of 1808 (proved in 1813): "Not having it in my power to save John Middleton of Barbadoes from his want of education, I leave him one hundred pounds. Commissioner Thomson will find him through Capt. Wolra." This family of Middletons are the heirs of the forfeited Middleton Barony.

BARBADOS HILL IN WALES: MORRIS FAMILY

As the river Severn widens out to merge imperceptibly with the Bristol Channel, the Wye enters it from the north, and at the junction of the two rivers is the market town of Chepstow. The Wye forms the boundary between the Welsh county of Gwent (formerly Monmouthshire) and the English county of Gloucestershire. Five miles upstream from Chepstow is the village of Tintern, best known because of the ruins of Tintern Abbey, which is one of the oldest, as well as one of the most beautiful, of the Cistercian foundations in Britain. The Abbey itself is close to the river bank; behind it and slightly to the north is a hill which bears the name Barbados Hill.

Enquiries in Gwent as to the origin of the name elicited little information except that it was very old. However, a chance discovery suggested that it might be connected with two brothers, Lewis and Richard Morris, who lived in Barbados in the seventeenth century and were the sons of William Morris of Tintern. Lewis was born there about 1601, and Richard about fifteen years later.

Lewis had a varied and adventurous career, the first part of which cannot be traced in detail. In his early life he seems to have been a seafarer, and for several years from about 1630 he was employed in the Puritan settlement on Providence Island in the south-western Caribbean off the coast of Central America. By 1638 he had become a landowner in Barbados, where he married his first wife, the widow of Thomas Barton. He was in England for at least part of the Civil War (though there is a story of an expedition to Algiers), and he was second in command of the Parliamentary forces at the siege of Chepstow in 1648. He must have returned to Barbados soon after that, because in 1650 he was one of the twenty Roundhead leaders whose arrest and trial was demanded by Humphrey Walrond. Nicholas Foster says that some of them left the island to escape arrest, and Lewis Morris was obviously among them.

In 1651 Lewis returned to Barbados with the Ayscue expedition, and he commanded the attack on the fort at Holetown. During the governorship of Daniel Searle he was elected to the House of Assembly, and was then very quickly appointed a member of the Council. As was the case with several other men in public life in Barbados, his identification with and support for the Cromwellian regime did not prejudice his relations with the Government after the Restoration.

At some date that cannot be fixed Lewis became a Quaker. William, Lord Willoughby, described him as 'an honest man, though a Quaker', and later, in 1668, as 'a severe Quaker'. In spite of this, Willoughby continued to employ him and sent him with a military expedition to the Leeward Islands, and he was known as Colonel Lewis Morris to the end of his life. Lewis entertained George Fox when the latter visited Barbados in 1671, and he shared in the severe persecution that the Quakers suffered at that period.

Richard Morris had joined his brother in Barbados, probably soon after the Restoration, but little is known of his career here except that he was a planter. In 1670 he emigrated to New York, where he purchased a large area of land, now part of the Bronx, which he called Morrisania. His son, Lewis Jr, was born there in 1671, and within two years both parents were dead. Lewis Sr. was appointed guardian of his namesake and nephew.

Lewis Sr. did not leave for New York until about August 1675; he later returned to Barbados, from which he departed finally in 1679. He bought a large tract of land in Monmouth county, New Jersey, and he also acquired or established an ironworks, which he called Tintern Ironworks; the name still exists in a corrupt form in Tinton Falls.

Lewis Morris died in 1691; he had married twice but left no children, and his whole estate went to his nephew, Lewis Jr. The latter had a distinguished career, and at the time of his death in 1746 he had been Governor of New Jersey for eight years. His grandchildren included the Lewis Morris who was one of the signatories of the American Declaration of Independence and Gouverneur Morris, who was prominent in American politics during the American Revolution.

Lewis and Richard Morris had been born and brought up in the shadow of Barbados Hill at Tintern, and their family may well have owned it. Even now Tintern has only about 700 inhabitants; in the seventeenth century the population must have been very small indeed. The Morris connection with Barbados is therefore likely to have been the reason for the name Barbados Hill.

Nightingale of Barbados.*

WILLS.

1669. Edward Nightingale of St. Philip's Parish. Probate 28 Jan. 1668-69. Brothers, Jeffery, Tamahill,† and Granado (residuary legatee). Sisters, Ann Berrisford, widow, and Theodora Todd. Sister and Brother-in-law, Katherine and Edward Michell.

1676. Priscilla, wife of Granader Nightingale, gentleman. Her maiden name was Webb. Probate 21 March 1676. Granader Nightingale, junior, son of Granader Nightingale. Thomas and James Nightingale. Robert and Christopher Webb, sons of Robert Webb, deceased. Kinsman, Richard Lowe. Charles Hamden a witness to the will.

1736-37. Nathaniel Nightingale, Planter, of Christ Church. Probate 17 March 1736-37. Sons, Nathaniel, Granado, John, Gamaliel. Daughters, Katharine, Susannah.

OLTON FAMILY RECORDS.

The following records were copied from an old Bible, printed by Thomas Baskett, Printer to the Un. of Oxford, 1747. Inscribed on the title page—John Olton 1749. The entries are on the backs of the printed pages.

* Communicated by Mr. N. Darnell Davis, C.M.G.
† ? Clerical error for Gamaliel.

JOHN OLTON son of Gera & Margaret Olton was md. to Mary Oistin, dau of James & Sarah Oistin 23rd of Aug. Thursday 1750 by Rev. David Saer Esq. of ye psh of Ch. Ch.

The above John Olton was born 30 d of Mar 1722 in the p of St Joseph.

The above Mary Oistin was born & bap. ye July 1732 as appears by the Ch book of ye p of St. Michael.

My son John Allen Olton was born ye 1st July 1751 about 10 O'c in the morn (Monday) Mrs. Mary Lytcott midwife, and was bap. 25 Augt following by Rev. David Saer Esq. of ye p. of Ch. Ch. Charles Maynard & Allen Sharrett Godfathers, Margaret Bascom & Christian Grame G. mothers.

My dau Sarah Olton was b. 22 Sep. 1753 Saturday about 6 o'c p.m. Mary Lytcott Midwife & was bap. 5 Apl. 1754 by Rev. David Saer Esq. of p. of Ch. Ch. Thos. Burton Godfather & Margaret Olton & Rebecca Oistin G. mothers. The said Sarah d. 9 Apl. 1754 about 5 o'c a.m. & was buried in p. of Ch. Ch. in ye new Cyd.

My da Sarah Lintott Olton was b 11 Feb. 1755 about ¾ hr. after 11 in ye a.m. Tuesday Mary Lytcott midwife—bap. 13 Feb. 1755 in ye even. by David Saer Esq. Mary Allder & Rebecca Oistin G. mother and myself G. father & d. 25 Decr. 1756 & was burd in Ch. Ch. by Rev. David Saer in new Chyd.

My son Gera Olton was b 8 Jan. 1756 about 9 o'c p.m. & was bap. 26 June 1757 by Rev. David Saer Esq. of Ch. Ch. & Henry Crichlow & Edmund Brandford Gfathers & Mary Charnock & Mary Austin Gmothers.

My son Henry Olton was b 3 Aprl. 1758 (Monday) about 3 a.m. & was bap. 16 of same mo. by Rev. David Saer Esq. of p Ch. Ch. Chas Burton & Chas Brandford Gfathers & Mary Burney widow & Eliza. Warren Gmthrs.

My father John Olton d. on Sunday Jan 12 1800 & was bd at noon in S. M's Chyard aged 75 years.

My mother Mary Olton d on Monday Dec 18 & was buried next day at noon in S. M's Chyard aged 78 years.

My brother John Allen Olton was married to Ann Simmons widow of Henry Peter Simmons and theretofore Ann Kirton Spr at her pltn in St. Phillip psh by Hon & Rev Robt Brathwaite Rec on Thursday Sep 29 1785. He survived his wife (who died in England) & died on 1 Aug 1810 leaving 1 son & 3 daus viz—(1) Margaret Anne Olton, b on Tuesd, Sep 5 1786 & was Md to Cap Wm. Whitmore of the Royal West Indian Rangers Brevet Major Aide de Camp to Major General Munro & son of John Whitmore Esq. of Old Jewry London at Cabbage Tree in S. James pash by Rev Mr Henry Caddell Rec of St Peter on Easter Sund Apl 14 1811. Cap Whitmore d. s. p. at the Island of S Thos in his passage with his wife to England in the mo July 1815. (2) Mary Olton 2nd da of above John Allen & Anne was b May 18 1789 & was married in Eng. sometime in yr 1809 to Thomas Dunkin Esq then Lieut of 13th Dragoons but now of 18th Hussars. They have 3 children. (3) John Allen s of above John Allen & Anne Olton was b 14 Oct 1790. He remains unmarried. (4) Rebecca Olton yst d. of above John Allen & Anne Olton was b. 23 Aug 1792 & md to Sir Reynold Abel Alleyne Bt then of 16th Regt of Foot only surviving son of Hon Sir John Gay Allenyne Bart at Harrow pltn St Phil. by Rev Mr. Henry Caddell on Thurs 20 Sep 1810. They have now two surviving daughters.

My brother Gera Olton was md to Mary Ann Crichlow the eldest da of Dr. Samuel & Mary Crichlow of p of St. Phil at her father's house by Hon. & Rev. Robt Brathwaite on 10 Dec. 1778. She d on Thurs. 24 June 1796 & was buried on Sat. 26 noon in St. M's chyard leaving 2 daus & 1 son (surviving many others) viz—(1) Mary Anne the eldest da was b on 25 Oct. 1779 & was md to Edward James Yard, yst son of Thomas & Mary Yard sometime (I think in Apl) in yr 1703 at S. Thos. Ch. by Rev. Mr. Henry Quintyne Rec. Mr. Yard soon left her a widow with 3 children, Edward, Mary, & Elizabeth, and she afterwards md in England 18.... to Joseph William Waith of the Pine plantn by whom she has now two children William & Josephine. (2) Gera Olton was born 13 Nov. 1780 & was md. sometime in the yr 1809 in Engl. to Maria Wharton Goldpap, a da of John George Goldpap Esq. of the 1 of St. Christopher, formerly of the Army. They haw now 2 surviving daus—Maria Goldpap & Georgina. (3) Johannes Olton was born 24 Feb. 1784 & was md to Thos. Carter Cox s of her uncle & aunt Thomas Gretton & Elizabeth Cox at Rockley in Ch. Ch. sometime in the morning June 1805. They have now three surviving children—Elizabeth, Thomas & Mary.

I Henry Olton was married to Sarah yst of 3 daus of Bollingbroke & Dorothy Curll at her mother's house over the old Bridge by Rev. Thos. Wharton D.D. on Thursday 12 June 1783. (A later entry inserted here) 12 June 1816 33rd year of our marriage.

My bro. Gera died on 18 Apl 1855 after having married Mrs. Elizabeth Cox widow of Wm. Cox by whom he had no children & was buried in St. Michael's Chyard the next evening.

Memorandum. May 13 1776 Monday My niece Mary Allder departed this life in my house in Ch. Ch. buried in the new chyd by Rev. Robt. Bowcher Esq.

Memorandum. Oct. 6 1777 Monday my sister Mary Allder the mother of the above Mary Allder d and was bd 7 Oct. by Rev. Robt. Bowcher in the new Chyd in Ch. Ch.

Memorandum. Nov. 27 1782. Wed. a.m. about 11.30 my sister Margt. Olton d at Mrs. Sarah Allder's & was bd. 28 in new chyd by the side of Ann Collynns midwife by Rev. Mr. Jno Duke about 1 o'c at noon.

Memo. My father Gera Olton d March on Sat. 1735 & was bd in S. Jos. Ch. by Rev. Mr. Brown of S. Andrew. His text was 15 Ch of St. John & 15 verse.

Memo. My Mother Margt. Bascom dep this life 23 Oct. 1769 being Monday in a.m. & was bd in New Chyd at Ch Ch with my bros Gera & Ralph Olton 24 day by Rev. David Saer Esq.

My nephew Gera Olton only survg s of my bro Gera Olton d between 10 & 11 o'c at night in Friday 9 Feb. at Balls pltn in Ch. Ch. the ppty of Renn Hampden Esq. & was brought to my house bet 10 & 11 o'c next night & from thence buried in S. M's chyd at 8 o'c on Sunday morn by Rev. Mr. King Curate of S. M. sd Henry Olton.

(In another hand)

My father Gera Olton son of Ralph & Mary Olton was b ye 23 March 1689 my mother Margaret Olton who was Margaret MackKew was b 17 Feb. 1693 & was md to my father Gera Olton 7 Feb. 1716.

My sister Mary Olton d of Gera & Margaret Olton was b 21 Oct. 1718.

My bro Gera Olton was b. 30 Mar 172........

Myself John Olton was born 30 Mar 1724.

My sister Margaret Olton was born 2 June 1726.

My bro Ralph Olton was born 23 Sep. 172........

My sister Eliza. Olton was born 6 Aug. 1731.

My brother Wm. Olton was born 26 Aug. 1734.

The above William Olton died   & was buried in S. Joseph's Ch. The sd Wm Olton at Salter's estate in S. George parish.

My bro Ralph Olton d at my house in p of Ch. Ch. 31 Jan. 1760 & was buried at Ch. Ch. by Rev. Mr. David Saer.

My bro. Gera Olton d 24 May 1763 in the Glebe House in Ch. Ch. & was buried in Ch. Ch. yd by Revd. Mr. David Saer.

(On a fly leaf in a later hand)

Mary Elizabeth Curll June 19 1854.

Edward Bollingbroke Curll the eldset son of Henry & Mary Curll b 24 Mar 1804 was md to Mary Ironmonger the only dau of John & Mary Ironmonger on 13 May 1809.

Mary Elizabeth the eldest d of Edward B. & Mary Curll born 16 Decr. 1831.

Sarah Agnes 2nd d of above born 2 Feb. 1834.

Emily Jane third dau of above born 26 Feb. 1837.

Helen Catherine 4 dau born 16 June 1839.

Ann Rothwell 5 dau born 29 June 1842.

Edwardine Marie 6 dau born 21 Novr. 1843.

OLTON-YARD

Captain E. C. Yard of Stepney, Barbados, draws attention to
an error in these records published in the *Journal* for August
1942, page 202. The Bible entry gives the date of Edward James
Yard's marriage to Mary Ann Olton as the year 1703 which is
manifestly an error for 1803. Captain Yard says: According to
family repute, Edward James Yard was the eldest and not the
youngest surviving son of Thomas Yard who married Mary Elvira
Cox, Edward is alleged to have married without the consent of
his parents, and his Uncle, Benjamin Alleyne Cox, the owner of
Forster Hall, Cottage, and Groves plantations, marked his disapproval by leaving the estates by his Will to the younger nep-

hew, Thomas Yard, who married Elizabeth Skeete Pinder of Hothersall plantation. (See Captain Timothy Pinder of Barbados, and some of his descendants, *Journal*, Vol. 1 August 1934, page 197 *et seq.*)

Like many other of these family traditions, the records prove that there is no foundation for this statement. It is abundantly clear from the records that Thomas Yard was the eldest surviving son of the marriage (9 April, 1774) between Thomas Yard (d. 1780) and Mary Elvira Cox, (d. 1790), although the date of his birth is not recorded. This fact is supported by the circumstance that Thomas Yard's name appears before that of his brother Edward James Yard in all the relative Wills.

Mary Elvira Cox was the only child of John William Cox whose wife was Elvira Thorne to whom he was married on 2 June 1754. John William Cox's Will dated 31 October 1772 (Proved 26 October 1773) mentions his brothers James Cogan Cox and Benjamin Alleyne Cox as executors; his wife Elvira, and his daughter Mary Elvira His widow, Elvira Cox, by her Will dated 5 August 1792 (Proved 7 September 1792) appointed her brother-in-law Benjamin Alleyne Cox and Anthony Barker as executors, and gave most of her estate to her grandchildren, Thomas Yard, Edward James Yard, and Mary Elvira Yard.

Benjamin Alleyne Cox married Sarah Harbin Forster on 14 April 1754 He afterwards settled in England and died there in 1802. He was buried in the Abbey Church at Bath 15 December 1802, and a monument with arms—Argent, a chevron gules between three Cocks—with inscription recording the burial was erected in the south choir aisle of Bath Abbey by his nephew Thomas Yard. By his Will dated 27 February 1801, Benjamin Alleyne Cox (who appears to have been childless) gave legacies of £2.000 each to his nephews, Thomas and Edward James Yard and his niece Mary Elvira Yard, and placed his estate comprising his seat called Green Hill with other land named Harris's his plantation Groves's and a place called The Retreat, and his plantation Forster Hall in the parishes of St. John and St. Joseph in trust, entailing them on his nephew Thomas Yard and his sons in succession, and failing him or his issue, for his nephew Edward James Yard and his sons in succession, and failing him or his issue, on his niece Mary Elvira Yard and her sons.

THOMAS YARD of Barbados.

Captain Yard has also kindly furnished the following information concerning Thomas Yard, son of Thomas and Mary Elvira (Cox) Yard.

THOMAS YARD was born in Barbados. It may be here recorded that Edward James Yard, his brother was born in 1776. His baptism at the parish church of St. Michael was recorded on

424

7 October 1776. The baptisms of his brothers and sisters (other than the same Thomas Yard) are all entered in the same parish register, who all died in infancy, with the exception of Mary Elvira, his sister.

Thomas Yard's father, Thomas Yard, died on 30 December 1780, and his mother, Mary Elvira (Cox) Yard, died on 23 January 1790. Thomas Yard (the younger) having inherited his Uncle's estates, married Elizabeth Skeete Pinder, and they seem to have visited England in the years 1805, 1812, and 1815. In 1812, Thomas Yard was a Lt.-Colonel in the Barbados Militia. Finally he and his wife and children went to reside permanently in England, living at various times at Bath, London, Teddington, at 10 Brunswick Terrace, Brighton, and at Bucklands Grange, Ryde, Isle of Wight ,after the death of his wife on 14 February 1836. She is buried in Hove Church, Ryde. Thomas Yard used the arms of Yard of Bradley, Devon; but on his Uncle's death the tinctures were altered, and three cocks added on a chevron, and the Alleyne-Cox crest assumed.

The children of Thomas and Elizabeth Skeete Yard were :
1. Adelaide, born in Barbados 2 January 1807, died 13 September 1885, unmarried.

2. Mary Elvira, born 18 May 1808, died 4 June 1808.

3. Eliza, date of birth unknown, died July 25, 1887 unmarried.

4. Alleyne Cox Yard, who succeeded his father in the ownership of the Barbados estates, was baptised in Barbados 10 June 1809. Married Henrietta Saunders of Fern Hill, Ryde. He was of Buckland. Their children were—

> (1) *Henrietta*, married John Nicholas Hathway, Quanhurst, and Ryde, d. 1923.

> (2) *Alleyne Cox*, died unmarried in India when serving with Warwickshire Regt. (47th) as major, 14 July 1887.

Alleyne Cox Yard, the father, died 20 March, 1858 and was buried at Ryde. On his death the Barbados estates devolved upon his son Alleyne Cox Yard, and on the latter's decease his sister Mrs. Hathway became entitled to them.

5. Rev. Canon Thomas Yard, born in Barbados 10 December 1810, baptised in St. George's Church 14 February 1811. Anthony K. Thomas, Garrison Chaplain was then Rector; a former Rector being Rev. W. L. Pinder, brother of Elizabeth Skeete (Pinder)

Yard. Thomas Yard was sent to England in 1815; was educated at Eton, a captain of the Oppidans, collecting "salt" at the last occasion but one. Later of Exeter College, Oxford. B.A. 1832, M.A. 1839. Ordained Deacon 21 December 1834, Priest 20 December 1835, by Bishop of Chichester. Curate of St. Nicholas, Brighton, 1834; of Felcham, near Leatherhead 1836; of Redhill, Havant, Hants, 1838; Rector of Eshwell, Rutland, 1850; Honorary Canon of Peterborough Cathedral 1870; Proctor in Convention 1875. He retired in 1892, living in the New Walk, Leicester. Rev. Canon Thomas Yard and his brothers were all educated at Eton.

Rev. Thomas Yard married in England, Mary Johnstone Bevan. Their children':

(1) *Mary Louisa*, died unmarried in 1901 and buried at Bath.

(2) *Thomas Charles*, Worcester Regt. (29th). Died a bachelor, 14 November 1874, and buried at Bury, St. Edmunds.

(3) *Charles Edward*, married October 1875, Mary Atter, and had issue (1) Edward Charles Yard, born 5 February 1877, now of Cottage & Groves plantations, Barbados, the present names of the family estates, of which he became the proprietor after the death of Mrs. Hathway in 1923. (2) Margaret Elvira, born 2 April 1878, died unmarried.
Charles Edward Yard died 1 June 1888.

6. George Beckwith, born in Barbados, 6 October 1812. Married Agnes Hawkins of Bignor Park, Sussex, who died 14 October 1858. No issue. He was for many years Vicar of Wroxby, Lincolnshire, and died in London in 1873.

7. Charles, born in Barbados, May 1815. Died 12 November 1869. (His baptism is not recorded in Barbados).

8. Frederic, born in England. He saved a school fellow from drowning near Rothly, Leicester. He was Major in 32 Regt.

* * * *

ORDERSON FAMILY RECORDS

By E. M. SHILSTONE

The earliest mention of the ORDERSON family in Barbados is to be found in the Census Records for the year 1715. John Orderson, age 23, and Ann (presumably his wife) aged 22, are entered as living in the parish of St. George. The next record in point of time is the Will of the same John Orderson, which was proved in 1741. The Will discloses that Orderson had some right or interest in Cape Fear in North Carolina, which suggests that he may at some time have been resident in that country.

Facts relating to the family taken from the public records and various printed sources have been compiled in the following narrative.

1. JOHN ORDERSON[1], born c. 1692; md. Ann . . . .
    Children—
    2. (1) John[2]
        (2) Ann
        (3) Elizabeth, md. (before 1740) Randal Clement of St. Joseph and had issue — (1) Randal, (2) Henry, (3) Irenaeus, (4) Mary, (5) Susanna, (6) Elizabeth, who (with the exception of Randal) are named in the Will dated 30 Aug., 1784 of their father Randal Clement. Randal, the son, predeceased his father, and died in St. Michael in February or March 1765, leaving a widow, Mary, and two infant daughters, Elizabeth Ann and Mary. His Will, dated 12 Feb., 1765, discloses that he was a stationer and bookbinder, and that he bequeathed his "statutory ware, books, and accompting house furniture" to his brother, Irenaeus, and his Uncle, John Orderson, equally. To Mr. Joseph Manning of St. Michael, cordwainer, he gave "so much of the leather I shall have by me at my decease as he shall make choice of to the value of £4 currency". He appointed his brother, Irenaeus, and John Orderson as executors, and the witnesses to his Will were William Walker[1], William

---

1. William Walker and George Esmand were partners in the printing business of Esmand & Walker, publishers of the *Barbados Mercury*.

Brown and George Esmand, the last named being the witness proving the execution of the Will on 27 March 1765. John[1] Orderson died early in 1741 at the age of 49. By his Will dated 6 Dec. 1740, he gave his wife, Ann, 2½ acres of land with house thereon in St. George[-] as also the money due to him by Dr. George Keyser. He gave legacies to his son John and his daughters, Elizabeth Clement and Ann Orderson, and to his grandson, Randal Clement, fifty shillings to buy him a pair of gold buttons and a Bible. To his children "all the right title and interest which I might have in Cape Fair [Fear] or elsewhere". He appointed George Hall of St. George and his son-in-law, Randal Clement executors. The Will was proved and recorded on 14 April, 1741. There is no record of the baptism of his children, of his burial or that of his wife, or of the marriage of his daughter, Elizabeth, to Randal Clement.

2. JOHN[2] (John[1]) md. Mary Stafford at St. Michael, 17 Oct., 1754.
Their children were—
    (1) Elizabeth Ann, born c. 1755; died a spinster 12 Aug., 1829, aged 74.
3. (2) John Edward,[3]. eldest son,
    (3) James Robson, d. May, 1789.
4. (4) Isaac Williamson,[3] born 28 May, 1767.
5. (5) Thomas Harrison,[3] born 10 Sep., 1769.
    (6) Mary, md. James Fraser jr. 2 Oct., 1796.
    (7) Frances Boaz, born 22 Dec., 1772, died a spinster, 19 Jan., 1855.

John[2] Orderson and his sons were the proprietors of *The Barbados Mercury* and the printing business in Bridgetown. Orderson seems to have succeeded Esmand and Walker in the ownership of the newspaper. *The Barbados Mercury* is said to have commenced publication in 1762. The issue of the paper for 5 April, 1783, states that it was then being printed by John Orderson and Company at the New Printing Office, Marl Hill, Bridgetown. On 20 Sep., of the same year, Orderson gave notice that on 17 Oct., the then partnership of John Orderson and Co., would expire and a new partnership would commence as John Orderson and Son. Orderson acknowledged the patronage he had enjoyed for eleven years, which indicates that his connection with the newspaper commenced sometime after it had been established. His sons, John Edward and James Robson were taken into partnership in 1783, and the three of them continued as Editors of the paper. The father and the two sons were involved in an accident which caused injuries to several people at Mr. Brown's New Theatre in Bridgetown, early in December, 1783. After the second act of the play, several persons retired to the gallery of the playhouse which gave way and many were injured by the fall. But none suffered so much as the Editors of the paper; John Orderson, the father, had his left leg broken and received severe blows in the head. His eldest son, John, was dangerously wounded in the tendon Achilles which was nearly divided, and his son James, severely wounded in his hand.

Besides his printing business, John Orderson held the appointment of Clerk of the Parish of St. Michael, to which he was appointed on 12 May, 1774, at a salary of £60. a year, and he served in that capacity until his death.

The Ordersons were the publishers of "Orderson's Barbados Almanac". An advertisement of the forthcoming publication for the year 1788 appeared in the *Mercury* of 5 Dec., 1787, which states that the Almanac was "calculated by Mr. Thomas Donohue, teacher of the mathematics in Bridgetown"

---

2. The deed of conveyance to Orderson for this land is on record in the Registration Office, Bridgetown, and shows that the land adjoined the Glebe land of the parish.

John Orderson died in 1798. The entry of his burial in the Register of St. Michael is as follows: "1798 Nov. 5, John Orderson, Parish Clerk, who had acted in that capacity for 24 years 5 months and 11 days". His widow, Mary, survived him until 28th Jan., 1818, on which date she was buried at St. Michael. His son, John Edward Orderson seems to have continued alone as Editor of the paper some time before his father's death. Then in 1787 John Edward and Isaac Williamson, were named as the editors of the paper. After John Edward's death in 1795 Isaac Williamson was the sole proprietor, but as will be seen, he severed his connection with the business at the end of the year 1810 at which time control of the newspaper finally passed out of the hands of the family.

3. JOHN EDWARD,[3] (*John*[2], *John*[1].) md. 4 Nov. 1784, Elizabeth Smith.
Their children—
(1) John, b. 20 Aug., 1785; d. 17 June, 1786.
(2) Anna Maria, b. 14 Jan., 1787; md. Benjamin Storey, 31 Jan., 1805.
(3) William, b. 2 Sep., 1788.
(4) Robert, b. 20 June, 1790; d. 21 June, 1790.
(5) Thomas Spencer, b. 21 Sep., 1792; d. 11 June 1802.

John Edward[3] died 10 Feb., 1795, being survived by his widow, Elizabeth, who died 4 Sep., 1816. There is a monument to her memory in St. Peter's churchyard —

I.H.S. Mrs. ELIZABETH ORDERSON/who survived her husband J. E. ORDERSON / 20 years of irreproachable widowhood/ lies buired here/.

Mrs. Elizabeth Orderson made her Will on 20 Sep., 1815, being then of the parish of St. Thomas. She gave to her daughter Anna Maria Storey, wife of Benjamin Storey, £300; to her grandson, Benjamin Edward William Storey £500; to her grand-daughters Anna Maria Storey and Mary Elizabeth Storey £150 each at 18, to her son, William Orderson, £100. She directed that her land in or near the old market in the town of St. Michael be sold. To her mother-in-law, Mary Orderson, and to her sisters-in-law, Mary Fraser, Elizabeth Ann Orderson and Frances Orderson, £10 each. She appointed her daughter Anna Maria Storey and the latter's husband as executors. The Will was proved on 3 Decr., 1816.

4. ISAAC WILLIAMSON[3] (*John*[2], *John*[1]) born 28 May, 1767; md. 10 Sep., 1798, in England, Frances Toosey, niece of Philip Prior Esq., of Great Russell Street, London, (*Gent. Mag.* 198). She died 20 July, 1810, on her passage from Barbados to England[3]. I. W. Orderson md. secondly 1 Aug., 1812, at Brighton, England, Theodosia Eleanor Lambe.

There are no details available of his early life or how and where he obtained his education. For many years he was the Editor of *The Barbados Mercury* and either part or sole proprietor of the printing business. He was the author of "Directions to young Planters for the care and management of a sugar plantation in Barbados", published in London in 1800. The imprint does not bear his name but the identity of the author is well recognised. In ascribing the authorship to him (by the name of *J. W. Orderson*) Ragatz[4] says — "The author was a member of a well-known Barbadian family. A complete treatise on sugar cultivation. The duties of plantation officials, the proper care of negroes, agricultural methods, each month's work, rules for sugar making and rum distilling, and cautions to be observed with respect to live-stock are fully set forth. Also contains receipts for West Indian drinks".

---

3. Barbados Mercury. 8 Sep. 1810. 4. Ibid. 22 Sep. 1812.
4. *A Guide for the Study of British Caribbean History.* 1763—1835, *including the Abolition and Emancipation Movements*: Compiled by Lowell Joseph Ragatz, Washington 1932.

This literary effort leads one to the conclusion that Isaac Orderson must have had some training and practical experience in agriculture in Barbados.

Soon after his first marriage in England in 1798, he returned to Barbados with his wife, accompanied by her sister, Mary Toosey, who did not long survive. A monument to Mary Toosey's memory is on the south-east wall of the nave of the Cathedral and Parish Church of St. Michael. Above the inscription is a female mourning over an urn, with a cherub at each top corner. "Sacred to the Memory/of MISS MARY TOOSEY/who departed this life May 23rd 1799/universally lamented/Aged 24 Years. Erected by her brother William Toosey as a tribute to his affection". Her death was noted in the *Gentleman's Magazine*, 621:— "1799 May 23, At Barbados, Miss Toosey, late of Tavistock St., Bedford Square".

After his first marriage, Orderson continued as Editor and Proprietor of *The Mercury*, the name of which was changed to *The Barbados Mercury and Bridgetown Gazette*. Owing to the condition of his wife's health, they took passage for England, but she died during the voyage on 20 July, 1810. Her memory is preserved in a monument placed under that of her sister in the Cathedral. It consists of a tall narrow tablet surmounted by an obelisk, on which are a medallion of the deceased and two figures:—

"This Monument/As a melancholy Tribute of Conjugal Affection is erected/To the Memory/ of MRS. FRANCES ORDERSON/who in the 31st year of her age/on 20 July 1810/ on her Passage to England (her native Country)/Died at Sea/and whose Body, during an awful Calm was/committed to the unfathomable deep/. (Thirteen lines follow.) Below three ships are carved in low relief.

At the end of the same year a notice appeared in *The Mercury* of 29 Decr., 1810, that "Mr. Orderson, (in name Isaac) here hands over this newspaper to William Walker & Co." It may be assumed that he had returned to Barbados by that time. On his leaving for England in the following year, he signed a power of attorney dated 25 April, 1811, giving power to his brother the Rev. Thomas Harrison Orderson of Christ Chuch and John Inniss of St. Michael to conduct his affairs.

His second marriage was mentioned in *The Mercury* of 22 Sep., 1812 — "At Brighton, England, on 1st ulto. by the Rev. Dr. Carr, Isaac W. Orderson Esq., late Proprietor and Editor of this paper, to Miss Theodosia Leonora Lambe, daughter of . . . . Lambe Esq., Inspector of Taxes for the County of Sussex".

In 1816 he published a pamphlet in London entitled "Cursory remarks and plain facts connected with the question produced by the proposed Registry Bill." The author's name is given as "J. W. Orderson", late of Barbados[5].

The Molehead or Pierhead in Bridgetown having been destroyed by the hurricane of 1780 and not extensively repaired, the legislature decided to rebuild it according to plans made by Lt-Col. Sir Charles Smith, Commanding R.E., who laid the first stone on 22 Feb., 1826. The work was done under the supervision of Isaac Orderson who gave an account of the work done by the year 1828 to the Editor of *The Barbadian Newspaper*, Details of the construction of the Pier are given in the issue of Sep. 9 of the newspaper.

At the age of seventy-five, Isaac Orderson wrote and published a volume entitled "CREOLEANA: or, Social and Domestic Scenes and Incidents in Barbados in days of Yore." The imprint states that it was by J. W. Orderson of

5. Noted in *Bibliography of the West Indies* by Frank Cundall, F.S.A., Kingston, Jamaica, 1909, page 127, item 2539. It is remarkable that this pamphlet and his later work *Creoleana* both bear the name *J. W. Orderson* as that of the Author. One wonders why Orderson did not substitute the initial I for J. when correcting the proofs of the work.

Barbados, and that it was published in London by Saunders and Otley, Conduit-Street, in 1842.

In 1827, Orderson published a pamphlet entitled "Treatise on the Education of the Poor in Barbados" which received the commendation of the House of Assembly by resolution moved at a meeting of the House on 2 Oct., 1827, by Gabriel Jemmott, thanking Orderson "for his laudable and judicious pamphlet."

It is interesting to note that the columns of *The Barbadian Newspaper* for 9 April, 1842, contain a suggestion by Mr. Orderson for establishing a Barbados Institute and Colonial Museum, although no interest in the project was awakened at the time.

Isaac Williamson Orderson was in his eighty-first year when he died on 6 December, 1847. He was the last of his immediate family; dying without leaving issue and his younger brother, the Rev. Thomas Harrison Orderson predeceasing him.

Commenting on Orderson's death, the Editor of *The Barbadian Newspaper* in its issue of Dec., 1847, says — "Isaac William Orderson Esq., a gentleman who was universally respected and whose patriotic acts and intentions for the prosperity and welfare of his native country must be remembered with gratitude. For many years he was Editor and Proprietor of *The Barbados Mercury* which under his able superintendence obtained a circulation far exceeding any that colonial papers now enjoy. Many of our countrymen and friends who have gone before him experienced his liberality, benevolence and hospitality when he was in the days of his prosperity; and those who knew him in adversity highly appreciated his character and talents, and looked up to him with reverence and respect as one of the most patriotic men of his day. He was followed to his resting place in the Cathedral Churchyard by many of our most respectable citizens, by five of the clergy, and a large number of ladies, a circumstance unusual at the funeral of a gentleman, but it was his particular wish, for he always delighted in the Society of ladies."

Evidently the wife of his second marriage predeceased him as no mention is made of her in the newspaper obituary. There is no Will of his on record, and it is evident that towards the close of his life he fell into straitened circumstances, and had no estate of which to dispose.

4. THOMAS HARRISON[3] (*John*[2], *John*[1]) born 10 Sep. 1769 md. (date unknown) Dorothy Ann Fee, daughter of Richard Fee of Barbados.[6] There are no details available as to the date and place of his Ordination as a Clerk-in-Holy Orders. He was instituted as Rector of St. Andrew, Barbados, 1 April. 1802; and the following year he was transferred to the Rectory of Christ Church, the Rev. W. M. Payne being inducted to the living of St. Andrew in his place on 30 June, 1803. The Church Records show that he entered upon his duties in Christ Church on 31 May, 1803, and continued therein until 11 Dec., 1820, from which date he was absent until 26 Dec., 1822, when he again signed the Registers and continued to do so until 9 June, 1833. During the period of absence referred to, he and his wife visited her sister, Mrs. Miller, in Philadelphia for some time, and later moved to Cooperstown, New York, where he filled a vacancy at Christ Church in that town for several months, eventually returning to Philadelphia before leaving finally for Barbados. While he was officiating at Christ Church, Cooperstown, the honorary degree of D.D. was conferred on him by the faculty

---

6. Richard Fee married Dorothy Evans, who bore him two daughters (1) Margaret, who married Captain Miller and (2) Dorothy Ann, Mrs. Orderson. The Millers emigrated to the United States and lived in Phildelphia.

of Union College of Schenectady, N.Y.[7] He and his wife returned to Barbados in December 1822, when he resumed his duties as Rector of Christ Church.

Rev. & Mrs. Orderson left Barbados in July 1833, once again bound for Philadelphia. Evidently he was ill at the time of his departure, for he died on 15 August, 1833, at the age of 64 and was buried in Christ Church Burial Ground in Philadelphia.

The gravestone bears the following inscription:
In this grave is deposited
the body of
the Revd. Thomas Orderson D.D.
a native of the Island of Barbados
in which he officiated 30 years as
Rector of the Protestant Episcopal
Church in the Parish of Christ Church.
He was eminently distinguished for
his classical and Theological learning
his fervent piety and the possession of
every moral virtue which could adorn
and dignify the character of the Divine,
the Gentleman and the Christian.
Born September 10th, 1769, died August 15th 1833
Aged 64 years.
This Monument is erected to his Memory
by his bereaved and affectionate wife.
Blessed are the dead who die in the Lord.

Before his last voyage to America began, he made his will on 10 July, 1833, giving all his estate to his wife, and failing her to Mrs. Anna Maria Husbands[8] widow of Pennsylvania, and appointing Dr. Henry John Cutting M.D. as executor. The witnesses to the Will were Robert Reece and Benjamin H. Jones. The Will was proved on 11 March, 1835.

---

7. Founded 1795 as Union College, in 1873 it became Union University.
8. She was the widow of Joseph Dottin Husbands.

A PALEOLOGUS IN BARBADOS

by

Enno Franzius,

Author of *History of the Byzantine Empire*

As the sun rose on 29th May 1453, the last Roman Emperor, Constantine XI Paleologus, fell, sword in hand, vainly striving to stem the Turkish tide that poured through the crumbling walls of Constantinople. With him the Roman Empire and the Paleologus dynasty that had ruled it since 1259 expired. Two and a quarter centuries after his death and seven thousand miles distant, Ferdinand Paleologus was buried in Saint John's Church on the verdant isle of Barbados.

The fall of Constantinople, the last capital of the pitiably shrunken Roman state, founded over two thousand years earlier on the banks of the Tiber, sent a shudder through Christendom. There survived two remnants of that state, which for ages had ruled the Occident and repelled, annihilated, or converted the fiercest tribes of three continents.

One of these fragments was the Empire of Trebizond on the southern coast of the Black Sea, which had led a separate existence since the fateful year of 1204. It was to fall to the Turks in 1461.

The other imperial vestige was the Despotate of the Peloponnese. It was ruled by two brothers of the fallen Emperor, Demetrius and Thomas. Demetrius governed the southeast and pursued a pro-Turkish policy, while Thomas controlled the northwest and followed a pro-Latin course. Together with other Christian rulers of the general area, the two Despots acknowledged the suzerainty of the conquering Sultan, Mehmet II, and paid him tribute. There was frequent strife between the brothers, and they were unable to raise the instalments for Mehmet. At length, he determined to terminate their sway and in May 1460 appeared in the Despotate at the head of a large army. Demetrius surrendered at his hill capital of Mistra. Thomas held out briefly in Messenia, but in July took ship for the Venetian possession of Corfu. By the following summer Mehmet had completed the conquest of the Peloponnese except for Monemvasia, two Venetian footholds, and Maina. The inhabitants of this precipitous peninsula claim the ancient Spartans as ancestors, resisted Christianity until the ninth century, soon after the expulsion of the Paleologi recognized as leader a man claiming descent from the last Emperor of Trebizond, and for centuries continued to delight in fierce feuds and piratical plunder.

In the interim, the Sultan had given Demetrius an Aegean town and some islands to govern. In 1467, however, he deprived him of these holdings. The former Despot and his wife, Zoe, entered cloisters in Adrianople, where they died in 1470. Their only child, Helen, had already breathed her last.

As for Thomas, already in 1460 he left the Island of Corfu for Italy,

433

taking with him the presumptive head of Saint Andrew from Petras, where the Apostle is believed to have been crucified on an x-shaped cross. He presented the precious relic to Pope Pius II, ceded him his rights to Monemvasia and adopted the Roman Catholic faith. Not to be outdone, the Holy Father, who was none other than the renowned humanist Aeneas Silvius Piccolomini and was an ardent proponent of a crusade to recover Constantinople, bestowed on him a pension and the Order of the Golden Rose. In 1465 Thomas died at the age of fifty-six, and the three youngest of his four children, whose mother had departed this life in Corfu, were adopted by the Papacy.

Thomas' daughter Helen, the widow of the Despot of Serbia, Lazar III Brankovitch. by whom she had three daughters, died in 1473 in a convent on the Ionian Isle of Leucas.

For Thomas' daughter Zoe, who was probably born in 1456, Pope Sixtus IV arranged wedlock to Ivan III, Grand Duke of Muscovy. The wedding took place in 1472 in the Vatican, Ivan being represented by proxy. His Sanctity hoped that this marriage might lead to the union of the Roman Catholic and the Russian Orthodox Churches and to a combined crusade against the Turks. His dream was not realized. Zoe was rebaptized Sophia and reconverted to Orthodoxy. As husband of the daughter of the legitimate successor of Constantine XI, Ivan III, the first national ruler of Russia, adopted the title of Czar (Caesar), the double-headed eagle of the Paleologi, and Byzantine court ceremony. Thereafter the Czars considered Moscow the third Rome and never abandoned their ambition to retrieve the fallen second Rome on the Bosporus.

Thomas' elder son, Andrew, heir to the imperial purple, was born in 1453. He married a woman of ill repute. Furthermore, he borrowed a large sum of money from Pope Sixtus IV to reconquer the Peloponnese, but used the funds for other purposes. He also sold his imperial rights to Charles VIII of France, retaining only the Peloponnese for himself. After Charles' death, he resold his claims to Ferdinand and Isabella, who, however, omitted to pay for them. He died in 1502, and his handsome son Constantine became head of the papal guard. Constantine's later career and the date of his demise are unknown.

As for Thomas' younger son, Manuel, born in 1455, he returned to Constantinople, probably in 1477, accepted a pension and an estate from Mehmet II, married, and had two sons. One died young. The other became Moslem and an official of the Sublime Porte. It is not known whether he had offspring.

It seems certain that at this time Thomas had no more than four legitimate children.[1] Yet among the ancestors of the man who lies buried in

---

(1) Runciman. **The Fall of Constantinople** (Cambridge. 1965), p 231. Originally he had five children, but a daughter died in childhood. See Papadopulos, **Versuch einer Genealogie der Palaiologen** (Munich, 1938), pp. 65-66.

Barbados there is listed a John Paleologus as son of Thomas. This John must have been either his natural son or a kinsman not in the direct imperial line. He did not go to Rome with Thomas' legitimate children, and either he or a scion of his migrated from Corfu to the Adriatic town of Pesaro. From him were descended his son Theodore, his grandson Prosper, his great grandson Camillo, and his great great grandson Theodore.

The last named, a man of great stature with an aquiline nose, early married a woman also bearing an imperial name, Eudoxia Comnena, by whom he had a daughter in 1594. Eudoxia must have died before the end of the century, and Theodore for a time fought for the Dutch in their war of independence against Spain. Then he repaired to England.

Here in 1600 he was in the entourage of the Earl of Lincoln at Tattershall Castle in Lincolnshire. Because of his superior erudition and expert horsemanship, he was chosen to approach an eccentric young man of twenty, who was living as a hermit in the adjacent woods, consuming much venison, and reading the works of Marcus Aurelius and Machiavelli. Apparently both his learning and his equitation so impressed the young recluse that he consented to abandon his sylvan abode for Tattershall. He was later to gain fame in the New World as Captain John Smith.

Later, Theodore Paleologus married Mary Balls of Suffolk, by whom he had five children. In 1628 he seems to have been in straitened circumstances, for he wrote the Duke of Buckingham shortly before that stateman's assassination, to request employment. During his last years he and his family lived in the home of Sir Nicholas Lower [2] at Clifton in Cornwall. By the time of his death in 1636 he had a long white beard. He was interred in the church in Landulph.

A brass tablet on the wall of the church displays the double-headed eagle of the Paleologi and records:

Here lyeth the Body of Theodoro Paleologus of Pesaro in Italye descended from ye Imperiall lyne of ye last Christian Emperors of Greece, being the sonne of Prosper, the sonne of Theodoro, the sonne of John, the sonne of Thomas, second brother to Constantine Paleologus, the 8th of that name [and last of ye lyne yt raygned in Constantinople untill subdewed by the Turkes, who married with Mary ye Daughter of William Balls of Hadlye in Souffolke, Gent., and had issue 5 children, Theodore, John, Ferdinando, Maria, Dorothy, and departed this life at Clyfton ye 21st of January, 1636.[3]]

Theodore's daughter Mary died single in 1674, while Dorothy married William Arundell and died in 1681. In the interim, war had erupted between

(2) Sir Nicholas' sixty-eight-year-old wife Elizabeth died in 1638. A brass plaque on the wall of the church in Landulph, her last resting place, celebrates her sterling qualities, including her "amiable subjection to her husband (a vertue rare and high)." See Rogers, **The Strife of the Roses** (London, 1890), p. 199

(3) Quoted from Schomburgk, **The History of Barbados** (London, 1840), p. 229

Parliament and Charles I. Theodore's son Theodore served Parliament under Lord Saint John, was killed in 1644, and buried in Westminister Abbey. John and Ferdinand joined the King's forces and fought at Naseby, where in 1645 the King was decisively defeated and presumably John lost his life.

With the decline in royal fortunes, Ferdinand, a man of gigantic stature, sailed to Barbados, where his mother's family had land. Britishers had first settled this uninhabited island in 1627. For sustenance they had obtained seeds, roots, and plants from the Dutch in Guiana. During the conflict between King and Parliament, the settlers were practically independent, traded with the Dutch, prospered, and by 1650 numbered over thirty thousand. While they included followers of both the King and of Parliament, they deliberately pursued a policy of salutary neutrality. As royalist hopes waned in the latter 1640s, more of the King's adherents emigrated to Barbados. The increase in royalist numbers led to a decline in the spirit of neutrality, and in 1650 the royalists seized power, proclaimed Charles II their King as successor to his beheaded father, and banished the leading partisans of the Commonwealth.

As a result, a Commonwealth fleet blockaded the insurgent island. After a few months' resistance, the Barbadians capitulated in January 1652 on terms acknowledging their right to trade freely and to be taxed only with the consent of their elected representatives. The home government, however, did not abide by the promise of free trade. Despite Barbadian protests, it subjected Barbados to its mercantilist policy, preventing direct trade with foreigners, buying all Barbadian exports (of which sugar was already the most important), and forcing the Barbadians to procure their imports only from or through the mother country.

Of Ferdinand's reactions to these events there is no trace. Possibly he was a militant royalist, since he bequeathed a gray mare colt to Edward Walrond,[4] whose family had played a leading part in the rising against the Commonwealth in 1650. At all events, he had a small cotton plantation in the eastern part of the island, and in memory of his Cornish home he named his house Clifton Hall. It was on the heights near the Anglican Church of Saint John, of which he was a staunch supporter. Already in 1649 he was a vestryman, in 1655 a churchwarden, in 1657 a trustee. Nor did he confine his public activities to the Church. In 1654 he was lieutenant and in 1660 surveyor of the highways. Little else is known of him. Although the traditional date of his death is 1678, it would seem that he died in 1670.[5]

His wife, Rebecca, and a young son, Theodore, survived. In 1684 Theodore married Martha Bradbury, returned to England, settled in Stepney, served in the royal navy, and died off Corunna in 1693. The same year his daughter, Godscall, was baptised. Of her all trace has been lost.

---

(3) Quoted from Schomburgk, **The History of Barbados.** (London, 1840), p. 229 **Historical Society,** Vol. 7, 1940, pp. 165-166

(5) Shilstone, pp. 166-168

Yet knowledge of the British Paleologi appears not to have been restricted to England and the Antilles. It is related that when in the 1820s the Greeks uprose against Turkish rule, the revolutionaries wrote to the authorities in Barbados that they had traced the Paleologi from Italy to Cornwall and Barbados and that if a male scion were still there. they would gladly furnish him with the means to come to Greece and would proclaim him their sovereign.[6]

Some years later, an anonymous voyager in Barbados heard that in the remote recesses of the interior there dwelt a modest tenant, who was descended from "the Greek prince from Cornwall." His efforts to discover this individual were without avail, and the most that he could learn was that he was ignorant and illiterate.[7] Even today there is rumor in Barbados of Paleologi progeny in or near the coastal town of Bathsheba within view of Ferdinand's grave.

In Britain too, the destiny of the English Paleologi continued to arouse interest. The register of Saint Giles-in-the-Fields reveals the marriage of an Andrew Peliologus in 1633. In 1803 a lieutenant William Constantine Paleologus was reported with the army in India. In 1854 it was recorded that a Dr. W. J. Paleologus was proceeding to the theater of war in the Crimea. In 1867 it was recounted that there lived in Cornwall miners bearing the corrupted name "Palligy." Though of humble condition, they were said to be aware of their imperial descent. In 1923 a family with the name of Paleologus was said to have been living in Somerset. These Paleologi were probably descendants of Greek migrants from Spain and Italy who came to England during the reigns of Charles I and Charles II and were unrelated to the imperial family. In this connection, it might be noted that some Greek parents gave their children the name of an imperial dynasty, such as Comnenus, Cantacuzenus, or Paleologus. Persons so baptized frequently either dropped their own surname or transposed their names.[8]

Meanwhile, in Barbados the great hurricane of 1831 had demolished the Church of Saint John. Beneath its ruins, in the vault of Sir Peter Colleton under the organ loft, was Ferdinand's leaden coffin. In accordance with Orthodox practice, his head lay to the west and the corpse was embedded in quicklime. Thus, though a practising Anglican, Ferdinand had apparently left instructions that he be buried according to the faith of his fathers.

With the erection of a new church in 1835-1836, his coffin was placed in the vault of Joseph Heath in the churchyard. In 1906 a public subscription provided the funds to erect an upright Portland tombstone, now showing signs of deterioration and bearing the inscription:

(6) Zakythinos, **Le despotat grec de Morée** (Prais, 1932), I, 296

(7) **Desultory Sketches and Tales of Barbados** (London, 1840) p. 197

(8) **Notes and Queries**, 3rd ser., Vol. I, 1862, p. 179; 1st ser., Vol. 10, 1854, p. 494; 3rd ser., Vol. II, 1867, p.485; 3rd ser., Vol. 12, 1867, p. 30; Burke; **Vicissitudes of Families** (London, 1869), I, 115; Karadja in **Bulletin de l'Institut pour l'etude de L'Europe sud-orientale** Vol. 10, 1923, p.115

Here lyeth ye body of
FERDINAND PALEOLOGUS,
descended from ye Imperial
lyne of ye last Christian
Emperors of Greece,
Churchwarden of this Parish,
1655-1656,
Vestryman twentye years,
Died October 3, 1678.

No other Paleologus, even during the two centuries that the family occupied the imperial throne, was interred in a more striking site. On a cliff eight hundred feet high, Ferdinand's sepulcher overlooks the Atlantic, whose soundless breakers form a pristine white border for the fresh verdure of the windward coast. Graceful palms wave gently in the breeze. Delicate pink petals fall on the grave from a frangipani tree. And when the zephyrs become stronger, there begins the chatter of the hardened pods of an overhanging tree, somewhat ungraciously known as the Woman's Tongue Tree,

BIBLIOGRAPHY

ANON. *Desultory Sketches and Tales of Barbados.* London, 1840
Barbados Diocesan History, ed. by J. E. Reece and C. G. Clarke-Hunt. London, 1928
BRADFIELD, HENRY J. "The Last of the Greeks; or Ferdinando Paleologus." *Gentleman's Magazine*, January 1843
British Empire in America Oldmixon, Vol. II. London, 1741
BURKE, BERNARD. *Vicissitudes of Families,* Vol I. London, 1869
Chambers Edinburgh Journal, No. 419, N. S., 10 January 1852
CHATTERTON, E. KEBLE. *Captain John Smith.* London, 1927
DAVIS, N, DARNELL. *The Cavaliers & Roundheads of Barbados, 1650 – 1652.* Georgetown, British Guiana, 1887
DUNKIN, EDWIN H. W. *Monumental Brasses of Cornwall.* London, 1882
Great Britain. *Calendar of State Papers, Domestic Series, of the Reign of Charles I, 1628 – 1629.* London, 1859
HARLOW, V. T. *A History of Barbados, 1625 – 1685.* Oxford, 1926
JAGO, VYVYAN. "Some Observations on a Monumental Inscription in the Parish Church of Landulph." *Archaeologia*, Vol. 18, 1817
KARADJA, CONSTANTIN J. "Une branche des Paléologue en Angleterre." *Bulletin de l' Institut pour létude l'Europe stud-orientale*, Vol. 10, July-December 1923

LAWRENCE-ARCHER, J. H. *Monumental Inscriptions of the British West Indies.* London, 1875

LEIGH FERMOR, PATRICK. *The Traveler's Tree.* London, 1955

LIGON, RICHARD. *A True & Exact History of the Island of Barbadoes.* London, 1673

LYNCH, LOUIS. *The Barbados Book.* London, 1964

MEDLIN, WILLIAM K. *Moscow and East Rome.* Geneva, 1952

Notes and Queries, 1854, 1862, 1867

OLIVER, VERE L. *The Monumental Inscriptions in the Churches and Churchyards of the Island of Barbados.* London, 1915

PAPADOPULOUS, AVERKIOS TH. *Versuch. einer Genealogie der Palaiologen, 1259 – 1453.* Munich, 1938

POYER, JOHN. *The History of Barbados.* London, 1808

ROGERS, W. H. HAMILTON. *The Strife of the Roses.* London, 1890

RUNCIMAN, STEVEN. *The Fall of Constantinople, 1453.* Cambridge, England, 1965

SCHOMBURGH, ROBERT H. *The History of Barbados.* London, 1848.

SHILISTONE, E. M. "Ferdinand Paleologus." *Journal of the Barbados Museum and Historical* Society, Vols. 7-8, 1940-1941; Vol. 14, 1946-1947

SMITH, BRADFORD, *Captain John Smith.* New York, 1953

STANLEY, ARTHUR P. *Historical Memorials of Westminister Abbey.* London, 1876

ZAKYTHINOS, D. A. *Le despotat grec de Morée,* Vol I. Paris 1932

Peers of Barbados.

Richd Peers of the I. of Barbados, Esq. Will dated 18 Dec. 1659.

To my son John P. all my plantacon *Lebanus or Renderee**containing 600 acres, with the houseing, six of my best horses, all the negroes, coppers, stills, suger potts, 30 cattell, hogs and fowles, household stuffe, also my mannors, lately bought of Sr Walter Pye called Liner's Ockell, in Herefordshire, as also 50 sheepe, 20 goates, my bason and ewer, two silver tankards, large saltseller, moneys, jewells, coach and harnes. To my son Edward all that my plantation whereon I now live containing 300 acres, with the houses, coppers and stilles belonging to the sugar worke and 30 cattell. To my dau. Eliz. £2,000 st., to be paid out of such moneys as I have in my brother-in-law Capt James Hawley's hands. To my dau. Susan Jones 10,000 lb. of sugar and the use of 30 acres whereon she now liveth and the use of my 5 servants thereon. To my dau. Mary, the wife of Nich. Boate a parcell of land in Eng. valued at £60 per annum, purchased by my order for y^t use by my brother Hawley of Brainford. To my grandchild Richd Hawton 20,000 lbs. To Jonathan Hawtaine and Valentine Hawtaine 10,000 lbs. each. Onto my cozen Anne Payce 70,000 lbs. and to have her maintenance in my dwelling house until paid. I make my son John P. my heir and Exor. To my servants Philip Darby, Will. Parsons and Antho. Purson 1,000 lbs. apicce. I constitute my friends Mr. Francis Sadler and my grandchild R^d Horton, my cozen Anne Payce and Mr. John Ashcraft overseers and 2,000 lbs. each. I entreat my loveing friends Coll^o Henry Hawley and Coll^o Edmond Read to be supervisors to call my overseers to accompt once every 3 months sugers to be consigned to my brother Capt^t James Hawley. I appoint Coll^o Henry Hawley, Coll^o Edmond Reade and James Hawley of New Brainford, Esq., to be G. of my two sons, John and Edward till 17. My friend Mr. Rob. Tothill to be an overseer and 2,000 lbs. In the presence of Tho. Modyford, John Ashcraft, Phillip Darby. By the President appeared J. A. and P. D. and were sworn this 2 April 1661. Hum. Walrond. P. 14 May 1662 by John Peers. (70, Laud.) Recorded also in Barbados.

John Pierse (in margin Peers) of Strettum, co. Surrey, esq. Will dated 16 March 1688. All my estate in the B'oes and elsewhere beyond the seas to my friends Col. Richd Guy, R^d Howell, esq., and R^d Barrow of Covent Garden gent. on trust. To my s. John £100 a year. My s. Tho. the like. My dau. Mary P. the like. To my 3 daus. Eliz., Frances and Anne by my 2^d wife £60 a year till 14 then £100 a year, and I commit their education to my friend Mistress Eliz. Hill and give her £40 a year. To Mistress Dorothy Spendlove and her son John and her dau. Anne £100 a year. My nat. child Frances £25 a year and £40 to bind her apprentice. To Eliz. Ashcroft & her 3 sons John, R^d and Edwd and her 2 daus. Susⁿ & Eliz. £20 a year each. Susan Mingo a black and her 3 chⁿ Judith, R^d and Hester £10 a year each. Kath. Campnell my last wife's servant £20 a year. Mistress Anne Broughurst £25. To my 3 daus. by my 2^d wife all the plate and jewels of their mothers. My s. Rich^d my coach and 4 horses. Overplus to him and his heirs male, they to be Ex'ors. £200 for my funeral. The lease of my house at Stretham, the rent to be paid out of my est. On 31 July 1689 commission to Rob. Chaplain M^t the Guardian of Rich^d, Mary, John and Tho. Peers, minors, the Ex'ors renouncing. On 24 July 1695 comⁿ to Mary Peers the dau., she now having attained the age of 21. On 27 Nov. 1705 comⁿ to R^d P. the son, Mary P. the dau. now dead. On 27 April 1714 comⁿ to Han.. P. the wid. and relict and administratrix of R^d P. the son. (102, Ent.) Recorded also in Barbados.

---

* Rendezvous.

ARMS.—. . . . *A bend cottised* . . . .

Thomas Peers of Barbados, M. of C. 1629—38.

These may be two distinct families, as they bore different arms.

Richard Peors of Barbados, Dep. Gov. 1633—38; a commissioner for Lord Willoughby 1652; M. of A. 1651—56. Will dated 18 Dec. 1659; proved 14 May 1662 (70, Laud). Brother-in-law of Gov. Henry Hawley.

Hester, dau. of Sir Thos. . . . . of co. Hereford; bur. 15 Sept. 1678 at Christ Church, Barbados. M.I.at St. Michael's.	John Peers, born 1644, of Christ Church, Barbados; M. of C. 1674—1683; settled 1000 a. in Jamaica 1672; later of Streatham, co. Surrey; died 17 March 1688, aged 43. M.I. there. Will dated 16 March 1688; proved 31 July 1689 (102, Ent).	Frances, dau. of Sir Jonathan Atkins, Knt.; bur. 5 Apr. 1685 at St. Michael; sister of Mrs. Eliz. Walrond.	Edward Peers, died intestate. Adm'on in B'dos 2 July 1667 to his brother John.

Mary, born 1674; died 1705.

Richard Peers, born 1684.	Hanna	John Peers. ? Will recorded in 1745 at B.	Thomas Peers.	Eliz., under 14 in 1688. — Frances. Will dated 3 Mar. 1758, then of St. Andrew, Holborn; proved 17 June 1760 (254, Lynch); died 16 June 1760.	Anne, mar. Capt. Hale.

John Peers of Hammersmith, Esq., born 1700; died 7 April 1761, aged 62. M.I. at Streatham. Will dated 10 May 1758; proved 18 April 1761 (143, Cheslyn).	Tho. Peers.	Richd. Peers. heir to his brother John.

Richd. Peers.

Capt. Geo. Peers of the parish of St. Michael's in the Island of B'es. Will dated 2 Nov. 1689. To my s. Henry P. all my est. r. and p. in this Island, Eng. or J'ca. My wife Martha and friends Tho. Bread and Benj. Matson of this Island, M[rs] to be Guardians, and all 3 Ex'ors till my son be 21. In the presence of Chr. Terry, Mathew Ling, Benj. Fletcher. Proved 1 Oct. 1713 by Henry Palmer the attorney of Henry P., esq., at B'es, the s. of the Hon. G. P. (231, Leeds.)

Frances Peers of St. Andrew, i. lborn, co. Middlesex, spr. Will dated 3 March 1758. To be buried by the remains of John P., esq., my father at Stretham, co. Surrey, under the marble stone where he is. I give the money due from my nephew, M[r] Tho. P., upon bond to him, he paying £500 thereout to my godson Rich[d] P. (s. of my nephew M[r] Rich[d] P.) at 21. I give my s[d] godson my own picture and the two of Lady Milman. £500 to my nephew M[r] Rob. P., and the like sum to my niece Mrs. Richardson, wife of the Rev. Dr. R., and the like to my niece Mrs. Lacy, widow, if she die before me, to her dau. Fra. Ann Eliz. Lacy at 21. To my aunt Mrs. Jane Atkins, £20. To Mr Wm Richardson brother of the sd Dr R., 10 gs. To my two servants £5 apiece. To the trustees of the charity school of St. Geo. the Martyr £20. All residue to my nephews Mr John P. and Mr Richd P. and to be Ex'ors. Proved 17 June 1760 by John P. and Rd P., esquires, the nephews. (254, Lynch.)

A

| Eliz. | Mary, mar. Nich. Boate. | Capt. Geo. Peers of Barbados, M. of C. Will dated 2 Nov. 1689; proved 1 Oct. 1713 (231, Leeds). =Martha .... |
| Susan, mar. .... Jones of Barbados 1659. | A dau., mar. Jonathan Hawtayne. | |

| Arms.—*Argent, an inescutcheon.* | =Henry Peers, born 1683, only son and heir; M. of A. 1706; Speaker 1727 till his death 4 Sept. 1740, aged 57. M.I. at St. George's. Worth £150,000. Will recorded at Barbados. Arms.—*A lion rampant, in its paw a staff raguly.* Crest.—*A lion's head erased.* | = ... Arms.—*A chevron between three cocks.* |

| Henry Peers, born 1712; matric. from Q. Coll., Oxf., 16 Dec. 1729, aged 17; barr.-at-law of Inner Temple 9 July 1736; bur. in the Temple church 12 Aug. 1736. | ...., dau. and coheir, mar. John Lyte, Speaker 1740, later M. of C. He died 17 May 17-7, aged 61. M.I. at St. George's. | ...., dau. and coheir, mar. Tobias Frere, M. of A. 1740. |

John Peers of Hamersmith. Will dated 10 May 1758. To my bro. Tho. P. £100 yearly. To Ann Mills who lives with me £30 a year. All residue to my brother Richd P. and sole Ex'or. Sworn 10 April 1761, test. J. P., esq. Proved 18 April 1761 by Rd P., esq. (143, Cheslyn.)

CHRIST CHURCH, BARBADOS.

*1650, Aug. 1. Henry s. of Richard Peers, buried.
*1678, Sept. 15. Hester wife of John Peers, buried.
1678, Sept. Hester the wife of Jno Peerse, esq., buried ye 15th. (494, Hotten.)

ST. MICHAEL'S, BARBADOS.

1678, Sept. 15. Elisabeth ye wife of John Peers, esqr, buried. (*Ibid.*, 429.)

TEMPLE CHURCH.

The Honble. Henry Peers, esq., a Barrister of the Inner Temple, was buried in the Middle Temple vault on Thursday the Twelfth day of August Anno Dom. 1736.

* I took these two entries from the copy of Register in Bridgetown. Hotten must have copied his from the transcript in the P.R.O., London.

1629, Feb. 23. Mr Thomas Peers a member of the first Council. (Memoirs of the First Settlement.)

1631. On 11 April Gov. Henry Hawley appointed Tho. Peers to the Council.

1633, Apr. 3. Hawley appointed his brother-in-law, Richard Peerce or Peers, Dep. Gov. during his absence. Peers again acted on 1 Sept., 1635, and was next year President. (Schomburgk, 265-6.)

1638. Tho. Peers, Esq., and Richd Peers, Esq., Dep. Gov., owners of more than 10 acres.

1639-40, Jan. 20. Richard Peers, Gent., of St Dunstan's West, Widower, 42, and Mary Payne of same, sp^r, 19, dau. of Chr. Payne, Gent., who consents ; at St Nich. Cole Abbey. (Mar. Lic. by Bishop of L., p. 247.)

1652, Jan. 9. Francis, Lord Willoughby appointed Sir Richard Pearce as one of his commissioners to treat with Sir Geo. Ayscue. There is no record of his knighthood.

1656. R^d Peers as a M. of A. signs Address to the Protector. (Thurloe iv., 651.)

1660. Sir Richd Peers a M. of C. at the Restoration. (Col. Cal., 494.)

1671, Dec. 17. Sir Tho. Lynch writes from Jamaica : " Esquire Pierce from Barbadoes came to see the island." (Col. Cal., 300.)

And 1672, July 5. " Esquire Peirce has sent blacks and servants to begin a plantation on the north side, &c." (*Ibid.*, 386.)

1673, May 28. John Pierce has 1,000 a. in Barbadoes. (*Ibid.*, 497.)

1674, Feb. The King's commission to John Pears and others to administer the oaths to Sir Jonathan Atkins, Govr in Chief of Barbadoes. (*Ibid.*, 554.)

1674, Ap. 13. John Peirce recommended to be of the Council of B. (*Ibid.*, 575.)

1680. John Pearse a M. of C. (*Ibid.*, 515.)

1680. X^t Ch. John Pears, Esqu^r, 910 a. 8 white servants. 180 negroes. (Hotten, 483.)

1683, Aug. 6. Dep. Gov. John Witham writes : . ho. Walrond and John Peers, both of the C^l, married to 2 sisters. (Col. Cal., 406.)

Tho. Peirse (Peers) s. Edw. of Barbados, arm. of X^t Ch. Oxf. matric. 23 Nov., 1693, a. 17.

Vis^t Howe to the Duke of Rutland at Belvoir Castle. 1733, June 28, Barbados. " I have desired Page to introduce to you Mr Peers, son to the Speaker of the Assembly, who is worth above 150,000*l.*" (Hist. MSS. Rep. rt, 12th Report, Vol. II., p. 194.)

1736, Aug. Henry Peers. Esq ; Barrister at Law, and King's Council of Barbadoes, at the Temple. (Historical Register, 47.)

" 1740, Sept. 4. Dyed Henry Peers, Esq ; who was first elected a Member of the Assembly, the 6th of Aug., 1706, and from the 18 July, 1727, was constantly chosen Speaker.

He had been Colonel of the Royal Regiment of Foot Guards, made Brigadier General by Mr. Worsley, and Lieutenant General, and Master General of the Ordnance by Lord Howe. For many years before his Death, he had a greater Share of Popularity than any Man before him had ever enjoyed, tho' he wanted a liberal Education, and had never been but once (and that a short Time) off the Island.

And if a strict Discharge of every Trust ; a lenative Disposition to his Debtors ; a zealous Endeavour to prevent Extentions, and to keep Estates together ; an indefatigable Industry to serve his Friends ; a Forbearance to procure any lucrative Office in Government to himself or to his Family, to reimburse the large Sums he expended on Account of the Publick ; a steady, undisguised Conduct in the Exercise of his Power and Authority ; his not oppressing any that differ'd from him in Politicks ; but offering his Advice for continuing many in high Offices, from which he might easily have had them

443

removed, were Virtues in him deserving Commendation; he must notwithstanding his Failings, be allowed a worthy Patriot.

The Assembly on his Death, chose, and have continued his Son-in-Law, John Lyte, Esq; their Speaker, and the Freeholders of the Bridge Parish elected, and have continued in his Stead, his other Son-in-Law, Tobias Frere, Esq; one of their Representatives. The Conduct of those Gentlemen shew that they fully intend to imitate the Example of their worthy Father."

[Memoirs of the First Settlement of Barbados, App. 4-5.]

There is also an account of his election as Speaker in 1735-6 in the original "Caribbeana," II., 133.

1740, Oct. 9. John Lyte chosen Speaker of Barbadoes vice Henry Peers, Esq., deceased, his father-in-law. (G.M. 55.)

Minutes of C^l at Barbados.*

2 July, 1667. Berry and Cunningham. John Pierse, Esq., petitioned to have the adm'on of his brother Edward P's est. Granted and the letters of admon. gr. to Capt. John Berry and afterwards to Capt. Alex. Conyngham recalled and made void.

Pearse v^s Berry. 10 March, 1667. Upon the complaint of Rich. Howell, Esq., and Mr Rich. Guy, att^y to John Pearse, Esq. Appraisement of the land of the s^d J. P. attached for Capt. John Berry declared wholly illegal. New writ of appraisement ordered to be issued by the Judge of the C^t of C. P. for Christ Ch. and St Philip.

Peers v^s Berry. 9 Oct., 1668. Ordered that John Peers, Esq., by a sworn surveyor and at his own costs and charges do runn out the Plantacon now in the possession of Capt. John Berry lately in the possession of the s^d J. Pierse adjoyning the Randevous Plantacon and all ye land above 100 a.

Peers v^s Berry. 14 Oct., 1668. Petition of John Peers re s^d Plantation Rendezvous.

STREATHAM, CO. SURREY.

On a blue marble slab in the passage of the south aisle. A stone step to the chapel rests on the upper part of the shield.

ARMS: .... *a bend cottised* ....

HERE LYETH THE BODY OF THE HONORA^{BLE}
IOHN PEERS ESQ : WHO WAS ONE OF THIER†
MAJESTIES COUNCELL IN THE ISLAND OF
BARBADOS WHO DEPARTED THIS LIFE
17 MARCH J688 IN THE 44 YEAR OF HIS
AGE.
ALSO OF HIS DAUGHTER
FRANCES PEERS
WHO DIED IUNE 16TH
1760
LIKEWISE IOHN PEERS ESQ^r
GRANDSON OF THE ABOVE
JOHN PIERS† ESQ^r
WHO DIED THE 7TH APRIL 1761
AGED 62 YEARS

---

* Extracted 20 Nov. 1911, by E. G. Sinekler and forwarded to me by Mr Oscar Berry of Monument Sq., London Bridge, E.C., 19 Feb. 1912.   † *Sic.*

CAPTAIN TIMOTHY PINDER OF BARBADOS AND SOME OF HIS DESCENDANTS.

CONTRIBUTED By E. M. SHILSTONE

In the Census Papers of Barbados for the year 1679 the only Pinder name recorded is that of Richard Pinder who is mentioned in Col. Lyne s Regiment of Militia; while in the Census taken in the year 1715 there are four distinct families bearing the name. The names and ages of the Pinders in the latter Census are as follows: In the parish of Christ Church, Richard Pinder, 38, and Ann, his wife, 40; Nathan Pinder, 40, and Ann, his wife 40 ; John Pinder, 41, and Jean, his wife, 36, with their children Ann, 16, Margaret, 13. Mary, 9½, Prudence, 6, Richard, 3, John, 1. In St. Michael, Timothy, 31, with a household consisting of males, two (19 and 2) females two (26 and 27) and John Pinder 35, whose household comprised three women 35, 18, 14, three boys 12, 8, 2½. and one girl 6. There are no contemporary records now existing by which the relationship of the several families may be established

Richard Pinder who is mentioned in the Census of 1679 may have been the progenitor of all those named in the 1715 list. His original Will which is stated in the Index of Wills to have been recorded in Barbados in the year 1697, is now missing from among the records.

1. CAPTAIN TIMOTHY PINDER [1] of Barbados was born about the year 1683, and almost certainly in Barbados. He married Katherine Cheesman, sister of Thomas Cheesman of St. Michael, Barbados, in whose will (dated 10th. February, 1740 and recorded 2nd March, 1741) his nephew Timothy Pinder [2] and his (Timothy's [2]) children, Timothy [3], Thomas Cheesman, George Lake, William, and Francis, and his (the testator's) niece Sarah Pinder, are named as legatees of £50 each.

Issue of Timothy [1] and Katherine (Cheesman) Pinder, born in Barbados :—

   i. TIMOTHY [2], born 1713, baptized at parish church of St. Michael, on the 28th August, 1913.

   ii. KATHLEEN OR KATHERINE baptized at St. Michael, 19th March, 1716. not mentioned in her father's will, and probably died 9th October, 1720,

   iii. SARAH, born the 6th January, 1721 married John Carter on the 5th September 1741 and had issue:—

(1) Elizabeth Carter	(5) Katherine Carter
(2) Thomas Lake Carter	(6) Timothy Cheesman Carter
(3) Henry Carter	(7) William Carter
(4) Forster Carter	

John Carter owned **Highgate, St. Michael,** and his will is dated 12th September 1767 in which his children are named as above. Timothy Pinder[1] died in St Michael 4th October 1723 aged 40 years. and was buried at the parish church ; Burial Register 1723, October 5th.—Captain Timothy Pinder. In the paving of the church there is a stone with the inscription " Here lyeth the body of Mr. Timothy Pinder who departed this life the 4th day of October A. D. 1723 aged 40 years. Also here lyeth the body of Mr. Thos. Cheesman who departed this life the 16th day of February, 1740, aged 48 years." By his will dated 3rd October 1723, Timothy Pinder [1] gave his wife (not named) one-third of his estate : to his daughter Sarah £1500 currency at 18 or marriage ; to John Webb, son of Captain John Webb and Jane his wife £100, to his cousin and godson John Pinder £100 currency ; to his brother-in-law Thomas Cheesman £100 currency to buy him a suit of mourning, to his son Timothy the residue of his estate. He mentions "All my brothers and sisters." Wife and Thomas Cheesman Executors. His will was proved 11th October 1723. He probably owed his rank of Captain to his service in the Barbados Militia. Katherine, his widow, married secondly, 19th of July 1724 Thomas Lake, a wealthy merchant and landowner in St. Michael who had no children. He lived at Lake's Garden near the Old Church Yard, where he owned extensive properties. "Lake's Folly " is named after him. By his will dated 6th June 1758, proved 7th August 1758, he gave most of his fortune to the children and grand children of his wife Katherine by her first marriage with Timothy Pinder. She pre-deceased him the 18th December 1754.

2. TIMOTHY PINDER[2] *(Timothy)*[1] born 1713, married Frances and had issue born in Barbados :—

   i. TIMOTHY [3]

   ii. THOMAS CHEESMAN, owned Walkers Plantation, which he sold to Joseph Jordan before his death. He d. s. p. 1788. His will is dated 9th August 1788 (Pd. 25th August 1788) by which he gives his gold seal with family arms to his brother William, and most of his estate, including Lake's Garden, to his sister Katherine Redwar.

   iii. GEORGE LAKE, d. s. p. 7th June 1771. Will dated 28th July 1770. Gives his sister, Katherine Lake Redwar, her daughter Elizabeth, brother Thomas Pinder, nephews and nieces—Francis Ford Pinder and Amy North Pinder, son and daughter of brother William Pinder ; Elizabeth, James Shepherd, and Francis. daughter and sons of sister Katherine Lake Redwar, £200 each. Brother William Pinder and Ann Isabella his wife, sisters Katherine Lake Redwar and Francis Brenan, and friends the Hen : Iraeneus Moe, and Cheesman Moe ten guineas each to buy a ring. Residue to brother Thomas and Executors Thomas Pinder and Iraeneus Moe.

3. iv. WILLIAM.

   v. FRANCIS.

   vi. KATHERINE LAKE married Richard Redwar, and had issue born in Barbados.

   vii. FRANCES, married Brenan and had issue born in Barbados.

446

Timothy [2] was a Merchant in Barbados. His will is dated 19th May 1746 (Pd. 18th September 1750). His wife, Frances, and his children are all named therein, except the youngest daughter, Frances, who was born afterwards, and she received a share of his estate under a codicil dated 19th July 1750. He was buried at St. Michael on the 24th July 1750. His widow Frances died 1767. In her will dated 5th June 1767 (Pd. 8th August 1767) she names all her children, and also Francis Ford Pinder, son of her son, William Pinder, and gives a great deal of silver plate and family portraits to her daughter Frances.

3. WILLIAM PINDER[3] *(Timothy [2] Timothy [1])* was married in 1776 to Ann Isabella, youngest daughter of John Hothersal of Hothersal Plantation, Barbados. Under the will of John Hothersal (undated 1796. Pd. 8th December 1796) William Pinder became entitled to a large portion of Mr. Hothersal's estate, including Hothersal (then called Hogstye Plantation.) He also owned Ayshford Plantation in St. John, Barbados. Became a member of Council of Barbados in 1782, and had a place at that Board and presided as Chief Justice of the Common Pleas until his death on 16th December 1806. He is buried in the family Burial Place in the Churchyard of St. John, Barbados, which is marked with a stone inscribed "Sacred to the memory of John Hothersal Esq. who died November 22nd A. D. 1796. Also William Pinder Esq, who died 16th December 1806 and Anne Isabella, his wife. eldest daughter of the above mentioned John Hothersal who died in April 1807. Also Francis Ford, infant son of the Revd. John Hothersal Pinder, M. A., and Anne Brathwaite, his wife who died August 14th A. D. 1824.

Issue born in Barbados.—

4. i. FRANCIS FORD 4, born 31st March 1767.

5. ii. JOHN HOTHERSAL

iii. AMY NORTH, baptised at St. Michael, Barbados, 11th May 1770. married Gibbs Walker Jordan 15th February 1786 and had issue. He was M. A., F. R. S., one of the Benchers of Inner Temple, and Agent for Barbados. Died 15th February 1823 at Portland Place.

iv. MARY JANE HOTHERSAL born 6th July 1772, baptised St. Michael, Barbados, 21st July 1772, married 10th February 1790, to Richard Straker Wickham, and had issue six sons and three daughters. She died at Barbados 2nd January 1830 Aged 57 years 6 months.

v. ROBERT HOTHERSAL born 12th September 1774, baptised 20th September, not mentioned in his Father's will.

vi. ELIZABETH SKEETE born 4th March 1778, married Thomas Yard.

vii. ANN ISABELLA, married 6th July 1805 at Barbados to William Maundy Harvey, Col. of 79th Regiment of foot, and had issue.

6. viii. WILLIAM LAKE born 1782.

ix. MATTHEW, born 18th January 1784 baptised at St. Michael 20th January. Married 12th April 1806 at St. John Barbados to

447

Francis Skelly Tidy then Capt. of the 1st Royals and A. D. C. to Governor Beckwith, (Governor of St. Vincent), and afterwards Col : of 14th Regiment of foot.

x. GEORGE PARRY BISHOP, born 19th February 1787, baptised at St. Michael 12th March 1787, not mentioned in his father's will, and probably died before 1806.

By his will dated 29th September 1806, Pd 15th January 1807, the Honourable William Pinder gave his widow an annuity of £400 currency, charged on his plantation Hogstye. and her living thereon. To his son the Rev. Wm. Lake Pinder £4000, and to each of his three daughters Elizabeth Skeet Yard, Isabella Harvey, and Matthew Tidy £2,500 currency, when each of his sons-in-law (their husbands) should possess sufficient landed estate to vest the same and settle it upon them. These legacies were charged upon his plantation Ayshford. To each of his daughters Amy North Jordan and Mary Jane Wickham £2, 000 currency charged upon Hogstye Plantation with same provisions as regards settlement of real estate; £500 already given to each of said two daughters on marriage. To son John Hothersal Pinder, his plantation Ayshford with slaves, etc., charged with legacies. To son Francis Ford Pinder. Hothersal Plantation charged with legacies and also all residue of his estate.

4. FRANCIS FORD PINDER (*William*[3] *Timothy*[2] *Timothy*[1]) born the 31st of March 1767, was Member of Assembly for St. John from 20th December 1798 during that session; later member of Council. Married first 12th April 1790 Elizabeth Christian, born 22nd November 1769, daughter of Jonas Maynard and Christian Mercy (Clarke) his wife, and brother of Hon George Maynard.

Issue :—

7. i. WILLIAM MAYNARD [5] born 7th July 1792, baptised 2nd September. St. Michael.

8. ii. JOHN HOTHERSAL, born 27th April 1794, baptised 9th May, St. Michael.

Elizabeth ChristianPinder died 9th December 1799. On the west wall of the nave of St. John's Church, Barbados is a white marble monument bearing the figure of a woman standing nursing a babe, with a small child beside her, and the inscription " This marble transmits to posterity the virtues of Elizabeth Christian Pinder, wife of the Honourable Francis Ford Pinder and daughter of Jonas and Christian Mercy Maynard, who animated by the unfading example of her excellent mother, shown forth thro' life one of its brightest ornaments, distinguished by unaffected piety, Christian humility. and active benevolence, after ten years of uninterrupted felicity, passed in the endearing society of her beloved husband, her tender frame and delicate constitution fell a victim to the slow but fatal progress of a disease which,

448

ELIZABETH PINDER

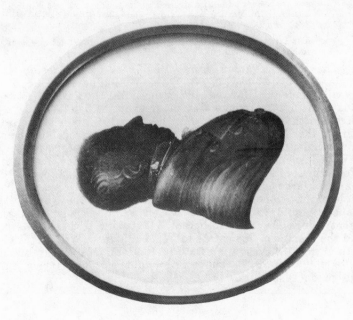

FRANCIS FORD PINDER

undermining her invaluable health and yielding neither to the tender assiduities of an adoring husband. the united skill of the most experienced physicians, nor the influence of a more genial climate, removed her in the bloom of youth to the regions of eternal bliss on the 9th December 1799 aged 30 years."

The Honourable Frances Ford Pinder married secondly Elizabeth Senhouse, daughter of William Senhouse of the Grove, St. Philip, and Elizabeth Ward Senhouse his wife, at St. Philip, Barbados 21st. November, 1802. Her brothers were Sampson Senhouse and Humphrey Fleming Senhouse and she was a niece of Sampson Wood. She was entitled under her father's will to £3600 which was settled on her marriage.
Issue on the 2nd marriage :—

i. FRANCIS FORD, of Trinity College, Cambridge, Rector of Gosforth, Cumberland. Born 23rd Nov. 1803. Died unmarried. 31st August 1861.

9. ii. HUMPHREY SENHOUSE.

iii. GEORGE, born 18 Jany. 1809, Colonel in 15th Regiment, died unmarried, 14 Jany. 1881.

iv. ELIZABETH WOOD, born 1806, died unmarried in England 15th January 1847. Her will was made 19th November 1846 at 5 Marlborough Street, Bath, by which she gave her brothers the Rev. F. F. Pinder, Rector of Gosforth, Cumberland, Rev. Humphrey Senhouse Pinder, Rector of Bratton Fleming, Devon, George Pinder a Major in 15th Regt. of foot, William Maynard Pinder of Brookfield, Weston, near Bath and the Rev. J. H. Pinder of Wells, Somerset, the legacy of £2,000 left her by her father charged on Hothersal plantation, and also £3,280 in the stocks, besides all her furniture and plate etc , and her leasehold messuage in Marlborough Street, Bath,—Will P. C. C. 12 Nov. 1847, Pd. B. 9 August 1848.

v ANN ISABELLE. born Nov. 1806, died 15 Jany. 1847, not mentioned in her father's will.

The Hon. Francis Ford Pinder went to reside in England, and died at Gay St., Bath, 27th January, 1843. By his will made in England 10th June 1840, he gave the two sons of his first marriage £4,400 currency which he had received with his first wife. To his sons William Maynard Pinder, the Reverend John H. Pinder, the Reverend Francis Ford Pinder, the Reverend H. S Pinder and George Pinder, he gave large sums of money, and to his daughter Elizabeth Wood Pinder, a legacy of £2,000 and an annuity of £100 besides a large share of his furniture and silver plate. To each of his grandchildren by name (except the youngest, Isabella) children of his eldest son W. M. Pinder, £50 at twenty one. He left Hothersal Plantation with stock etc, and the residue of his estate to W. M. Pinder. Will Pd. C. C. 11th March 1843, and his estate in England was sworn under £10,000. Will Pd. Barbados 10th January 1845. His second wife predeceased him.

5. JOHN HOTHERSAL PINDER, [4] (*William*, [3] *Timothy*, [2] *Timothy* [1]) of Ayshford, St. John, Barbados, was born about the year 1768. Married Thomasin, daughter of Robert Haynes, who was Speaker of the Assembly in Barbados (from whom she had a marriage portion of £7,000). He was Major in Barbados Militia, and also Member of General Assembly for St. John 1803—1820. He went to reside in England, and died suddenly while at Service at All Saints Chapel, Bath, Sunday 11th March 1821. Monument to him in Walcot Church, Bath. See Carib. I 124. His widow married Lt. Col. Christian F. Lardy at St George, Barbados on 4th December 1823. By his will dated 13th January, 1821 (he was then residing in Bath) he gave his widow £150 per annum in addition to £600 per annum settled on her Marriage; and her all his plate except his large silver two-handled cup and cover with arms on cup and crest on cover which he bequeathed to his brother the Reverend W. L. Pinder, at her death; he gave his wife power to appoint by will £8,000 out of £10,000 secured against Ayshford Plantation (which he had sold in December 1817 to Wm. Matson Barrow for £35,000) His slaves to his wife for life and then to his brother W. L. Pinder, — legacies to nephews Rev. J. H. Pinder, William Harvey, son of Col. Harvey of 79th Regiment of foot, and his late sister Ann Isabella, to Goddaughter, Ann Campbell Higginson, daughter of John Higginson Esq., of Everton, near Liverpool ; to friend William Matson Barrow £50 to be allowed him on the first interest due by him ; to sister M. J. H. Wickham wife of William Straker Wickham ; to nephew Francis Wickham at twenty one ; to sister Matthew Tidy, wife of Col. Tidy of the 14th Regiment of foot ; to his brother F. F. Pinder ; to niece, Isabella Wickham youngest daughter of sister. at eighteen ; residue to F. F. Pinder. Rev. W. L. Pinder. sister Amy North Jordan, sister M. J. H. Wickham, Elizabeth Skeete Yard and Matthew Tidy equally. Witnesses—Dowding Thornhill, Samuel Taylor, Wm. Foderingham,—Pd. in England by Samuel Taylor of City of Bath 22nd March, 1821. Pd. Barbados 29th May 1821.

6. THE REVEREND WILLIAM LAKE PINDER [4] (*William* [3] *Timothy* [2], *Timothy* [1]) born circa 1781—M.A. In Holy Orders. Rector of St. George, Barbados 1820—1841. Married 8th June, 1808 Harriet Wilson, daughter of Dr. Charles Wilson.
Issue :—

   i. ELIZABETH MAYNARD, born 1809, married Capt. John Wilson of 93rd. Regiment. Died of fever at Rowans, B. 27th October 1841 Aged 32.

   ii. Henry

   iii. WILLIAM CHARLES, born 1815. Lieut. 55th Regiment. Died of fever at Fort William Calcutta, 18th February 1841, aged 26.

451

Mrs. Pinder died at Easington Hall Rectory, York, 24th February, 1836, aged 52. Rev. W L. Pinder died of fever at Rowans, St George, 4th July 1841 aged 60 years. An upright grey marble slab set in masonry was erected over their tomb in St John's Churchyard on 26th May 1843 "by the only survivors of the family.'' By his will made in B. 14th May 1838, the Rev. W. L. Pinder gave his daughter E.M. Wilson, the sum of money which was her mother's nearly £600 Stlg., £10 to Capt. John Wilson, and residue to his sons Henry and William Charles.

7. WILLIAM MAYNARD PINDER, [5] (*Francis Forde*, [4] *William*, [3] *Timothy*, [2] *Timothy*, [1]) Born 8th July 1792 at Barbados, Pembroke Coll: Camb, Barrister at Law, Member of Assembly for St John 1820-24. Resided at Hothersal Plantation, and obtained six months leave from Assembly and sailed for Liverpool with his family July 1824. Married Ann Applewhaite, daughter of Edward Applewhaite, 7th September, 1820 at St. George, Barbados.

Issue :—

i. FRANCIS FORD, born 2nd April, 1822, Barrister-at-law, Inner Temple, died in England unmarried, 3rd November 1876. His will dated 17th December 1873 (Pd. in England 16th December 1876. B. 15th June 1900) by which he gave Hothersal Plantation to his brother Rev. North Pinder and the residue of his estate to his four surviving sisters equally.

ii. ELIZABETH MAYNARD, Married Rev. Canon Francis Witts of Upper Slaughter, Gloucester.

iii. EDWARD, born 20th August 1825, died unmarried, 2nd October 1859. In Holy Orders.

iv. NORTH, born 16th December 1828. Fel. Trinity Col: Oxford, Rector of Rotherfield, Greys. Md Frances Jane, daughter of the Rev. William Hopkins, Rector of Nuffield, Oxford. Hothersal Plantation passed out of his possession by sale through the Court of Chancery on 4th July 1900.

v. CATHERINE, Married Rev. George Thompson.

vi. ANN.

vii. MARY HOTHERSAL.

viii. ISABELLA, died unmarried 29th June 1863.

William M. Pinder died at Brookfield. Bath, 16th July 1869. His will dated 20th December 1862, and two Codicils of 8th February and 10th November, 1866 were made in England and proved there 11th September, 1900. Hothersal Plantation passed under his will to his eldest son, Francis Ford Pinder.

8. JOHN HOTHERSAL PINDER, [5] (*Francis Ford*, [4] *William*, [3] *Timothy*, [2] *Timothy*, [1]) born 27th April 1794 at 9 o'clock on Sunday morning, baptised 8th May at St. Michael. M. A. Caius Col. Camb: Chaplain to Society's Estates B. 1818-27. First Minister of St. Mary's Church, Chaplain to Bp. Coleridge. Sent as Commissary to British Guiana 1827. Appointed Prin-

cipal of Codrington College 1830. Resigned 1835. After five years in England he assumed first Principalship of Wells Theological College founded 1840. Married Ann Brathwaite, daughter of Scawen Kenrick Gibbons, at St. Andrew's Church, by Rev. W. L. Pinder 16th August 1819.

Issue :—

i. FRANCIS FORD, born 28th July 1824 at Hothersal. Died 14th August 1824. Buried at St. John, See M. I. on page 198.

Rev. J. H. Pinder died at West Malvern on 16th April 1868. His widow died at Maynard Cottage, West Malvern, 15th January 1892. Her will dated 29th September 1891 was Pd. 12th March, 1892 P. P. R. and Pd. in B. 16th September 1892.

9 HUMPHREY SENHOUSE PINDER, 5 (*Francis Ford,* 4 *William,* 3 *Timothy,* 2 *Timothy,* 1). Born 3 April 1805, died April 1888. Fel. of Caius College, Cambridge. Rector of Bratton Fleming. Married first Harrietta Bowdler who died within a year without issue , married secondly 1848, Marianna, daughter of James Gould Esq.

Issue :—

i. HUMPHREY FLEMING, born 22 Febry., 1851, married 3 April 1913 Katherine Isabel Neale. Died 16 Novr. 1916, buried Patshal. Salop. No issue.

ii. JAMES GOULD. In Holy Orders. Born 15 March 1857. Married Mabel, daughter of Col. Ozzard, 2 August 1886. He was Chaplain to H. M. Forces, and died 31st May 1890, leaving issue two sons.

   (i) Albert Humphrey, born 9 May 1887, killed in action (Somme) 15 Septr. 1916.

   (ii) Harold Senhouse, born 21 April, 1889, married Lilian Edith, daughter of Charles Archibald Murray of Taymount Stanley, Perthshire, 10 July 1919 and has issue one son one daughter.

iii. MARIANNA AUBREY Married in 1881 Sir Lewis Tonna Dibdin, Kt. K.C. Dean of the Arches. She died 1927 and left issue.

iv. ELIZABETH SENHOUSE, died unmarried 27 May, 1890.

v. FRANCES, born and died 1859.

vi. JOHN HOTHERSALL born 22 March, 1862. Died unmarried 1914.

vii. FANNY GEORGINA, (twin sister) born 22 March, 1862, married 1905 Hugh Stanley Vaughan. No issue.

PINDER OF BARBADOS.*

Since the publication of the article "Captain Timothy Pinder of Barbados and some of his descendants" (ante, Vol: 1 No. 4 pp 195—202) further information has been discovered concerning Ann Isabella Pinder. daughter of Chief Justice William Pinder, who married Col. Wm. Maundy Harvey in Barbados on 6 July 1805.

In September, while visiting the historic Port of Sandwich in Kent. I noticed a tablet in the wall of the ancient parish church of St. Peter, which not only records the death of Mrs. Harvey. but furnishes some interesting details of her husband's family

The inscription is as follows : —

In a vault on the outside of this wall are deposited the remains of Katherine Harvey youngest daughter of Samuel Harvey Esq. and Katherine his wife, who on the eve of her intended marriage was suddenly attacked with the alarming symtoms of a rapid decline which closed her prospects of earthly felicity, separated her from all family and endearing connections and terminated her existence in this world by removing her to a better on the 28th day of May 1807 aged 23 years. Likewise were removed into the same vault the remains of Ann Isabella the wife of Lt. Col. Harvey, only son of Samuel and Katherine Harvey and daughter of William Pinder Esq of the Island of Barbados, who also died of a decline on the 4th day of February 1807 in the 28th year of her age leaving issue one son.

Let the Young and the cheerful learn from hence that sublunary happiness is vain and uncertain. and that only beyond the grave true joys are to be found.

Also to the memory of William Maundy Harvey Esq. Lieut. Colonel of the 79th Regt. of Foot. Colonel in the British Army, Brigadier General in the Portugese Service and a Knight Commdr. of the Portuguese Order of the Tower and Sword : he died at sea on his passage home from Lisbon on the 10th day of June 1813 aged 38 years and was buried in the Atlantic Ocean in Lat. 45.37 Long. 9.42

There is also a Memorial tablet in the same Church recording the death of Samuel Harvey, late one of the Jurats of the Town of Sandwich, who died 2nd Augt. 1813 aged 67 years, and of his wife Katherine who died 18 Nov. 1835 aged 79 years.

Mrs. Samuel Harvey was the only child of Wm. Maundy, a merchant of Sandwich (d. 6 Feb 1790 aged 69 years) and Mary his wife (d. 2 Nov 1756 age 36 years) whose tombstone in the Church of St. Mary, Sandwich, records the above details.

E. M. SHILSTONE.

---

* Pages 445-453, this volume.

WILLIAM POLLARD OF DEVON AND THE WEST INDIES AND SOME OF HIS DESCENDANTS

By W. B. POLLARD, B.A., D.Sc.*

William Pollard, the progenitor of the Barbados family was the third son of Sir Hugh Pollard of Kings Nympton, Devon. By the middle of the 16th century the descendants of Walter Pollard, who settled at Way Barton, Devon, in 1242, had formed a number of branches. The senior branch was seated at Horwood in Devon, and there were two other branches in the same County at Langley Barton and at Kings Nympton. There were also branches at St. Hillary in Cornwall, Nuneham Courtney in Oxfordshire, Castle Pollard in Ireland and elsewhere.

The visitation of Devon in 1620 only recorded the Langley branch of the family. The pedigrees of the Horwood and Kings Nympton branches are recorded in Thomas Westcote's *Pedigrees of Most of the Devonshire Families* and are shown in J. L. Vivian's *Visitations of Devon*.

The Kings Nympton parish registers were destroyed in Exeter during the last war. The Bishops' Transcripts from these are in the Exeter City archives and from them the baptisms which took place in the generation following William Pollard, have been recovered.

Family tradition alleged that William Pollard first emigrated to Virginia, but research has shown that it was to Bermuda and not Virginia that he went.

In 1898 the late Col. Lowsley, R.E., printed a pedigree sheet of the Barbados Pollards. This had been prepared from family records and from information contained in the St. Michael's parish register in Barbados. Since then additional information has become available. This consists of wills, the census returns for Barbados in 1715 and other information published in the *Journal of the Barbados Museum & Historical Society* and elsewhere. This new information has been used to check the Lowsley pedigree and to amend and extend it.

1. Sir Hugh Pollard of Kings Nympton, Devon, England. Living there in 1568, Sheriff of Devon 1587. Married, first, Dorothy 4th dau. of Sir John Chichester of Youlston, Devon; second, Elizabeth, dau. of Sir George Speke.
Children of Sir Hugh Pollard and Dorothy his wife:—

  2.   i.   Lewis,[2] Born 1578. Eldest son.

        ii.   Francis, 2nd son, md. Ann only dau. and heiress of Thomas Dourish of Heath Barton, Devon (T. Westcott's *Devonshire* p. 618).

  3.   iii. William.

       iv. Susan. md. 10 Aug. 1596, John Northcote of Yewton, Devon, by whom she had 12 sons and 6 daughters. Bur. 5 June 1634.

        v.   Anne. md. 9 April 1604, at Ashton, James Welsh Esq. Brass in St. Peter's, Barnstaple. Died 1621 (*Memorials of the Church of St. Peter* by J. R. Chester).

       vi. Gertrude. md. 20 June 1616, Gilbert Davy at Newton St. Cyres.

      vii. Margaret. md. first — Widdon; secondly, Robert Dodson of Hayes Co. Cornwall, 26th Dec. 1609 at Ashton.

At the time of the Armada Sir Hugh Pollard was Colonel commanding 800 men of the North Division Co., (*Historical MSS Commission Report* 15, Appendix Part VII. page 5).

---

* The writer would like to express his gratitude to E. M. Shilstone Esq., O.B.E., for the help which he has given me in the compilation of the following account of the Pollard family.

He was appointed to farm the Tobacco Tax in England 7 Oct. 1611. The
Lord Deputy & Council to Sir John Davies:—
"Whereas for the increase of his Majesty's revenue in this Kingdom we have
thought it fit to lay an imposition of 18d. lawful money of and in England upon
every pound of tobacco that is now within this Kingdom or that hereafter shall
be imported or brought into the same, and also for every gross of tobacco pipes
2s. like money and so ratably for every dozen that now is in this Kingdom which
imposition we have thought meet to set to farm to our well beloved Sir Hugh
Pollard Kt. and his assigns for the term of 7 years beginning at Michaelmas last
he or they paying unto his Majety his heirs and successors the rent of £20
English yearly during the said time". (*Historical MSS. Commission Report*, 78,
Vol. IV. page 41).
"Warrant upon surrender to be made by Sir Hugh Pollard, Kt. Farmer of
the Taxes on tobacco and tobacco pipes of a fiant of grant to be made unto
Thomas Dowrish of Heath Barton Co. Devon Esq. to be farmer of the said
taxes." 6 Dec. 1614 (*Calendar of State Papers relating to Ireland* 1611—1614,
page 530). Thomas Dowrish was the father-in-law of Francis Pollard, 2nd son
of Sir Hugh Pollard as shown below.

    2.   Lewis Pollard[2] (Hugh[1]) Born 1578. Matriculated at Broadgate Hall,
Oxford 12 Dec. 1595. (J. Foster). Barrister at law. Married Margaret. dau.
of Sir Henry Berkeley of Bruton, Co. Somerset. Deputy Lieutenant of Devonshire, 14 Oct. 1623. (*State Papers Domestic*). Created a Baronet, 31st May
1627. (G. E. Cokayne, *Complete Baronetage*). Buried in Kings Nympton
Church 19 Nov. 1641. (Bishops' Transcripts of Kings Nympton Parish Register).
    Children of Sir Lewis Pollard and Margaret his wife:—

4.   i.   Hugh[3], Born about 1605. 2nd Baronet (*Dictionary of National
Biography*).
    ii.   Lewis, Bapt. 30 Nov. 1607. (B.T. Kings Nympton).
    iii.   John, Bapt. 2 Oct. 1608 (B.T. Kings Nympton). Not mentioned
by Westwood or Vivian.
    iv.   Barkley, Bapt. 27 June 1610. (B.T. Kings Nympton). Matricu-
lated Wadham, Oxford 30 Oct. 1629. (F. Foster).
    v.   Margaret. Bapt. 10 Sept. 1611 (B.T. Kings Nympton).
    vi.   Amyas. Born 1616. 3rd Baronet. Deputy Lieutenant of Devon,
20 Dec. 1676. Barrister at law. With his death on 5 June 1701
the Baronetcy became extinct. (G. E. Cokayne's *Complete
Baronetage*). M.I. in Abbots Bickington Church. Will and
Administration, (British Record Society). He left a natural son
Thomas, who married Sarah, dau. of Jonathan Prideaux 25 June
1702. M.I. in Abbots Bickington Church.
    vii.   George. ob. S.P. 15 Jan. 1687. M.I. in Fremington Church.
Will proved 29 April 1687. (C. Worthy's Devon: Wills).
    viii.   Mary. md. John Amory mar. lic. 28 April 1641, Exeter.
    ix.   Catherine, named in the will of her brother-in-law Sir John
Chichester, living unmarried 1669. M.I. in Yarnscome Church.
    x.   Elizabeth, mar. Sir John Chichester of Hall. bur. 20 July 1661,
at Bishops Tawton. Devon.
    3.   William Pollard[2] (Third son of Hugh[1]) was born about 1583. He is
known to have arrived in Bermuda in 1616, because at the Assize held there, in
1618, the Church wardens presented the said William Pollard 'for that he hath
contrary to religion and the discipline of the Church of England refused or
neglected to receive the Holy Communion ever since he came into the land

which is about two years since'. (*Memorials of Bermuda* by General Sir J. H. Lefroy, Vol. 1, pp.151, 683). He had probably been in the Army because on his arrival he was appointed a captain of the forts. His status and position can be gathered from the previous Assize in 1617, at which the baylie of the Pembroke tribe, Mr. Pollard (for so was the baylie named) being a gentleman bred up and sent over by the Earl of Pembroke had used these words to certain people of the tribe that:—'rather than his folk should go up to work at the forts, he himself would lie in irons for them." Mr. Pollard was tried together with Mr. Rich (a Kinsman of the Earl of Warwick and baylie of the Southampton tribe). On confessing their errors they were pardoned and restored to their former commands.

The baylies had the position of Justice of the Peace. They were supervisors of the labour and manners of the people within their tribes or parishes and were remunerated with a thirtieth of the landlord's profits. In 1621 the post of baylie was abolished but Pollard remained on as representative of the Earl of Pembroke (*History of Bermudas* by General Sir J. H. Lefroy pp. 98—103).

On June 26th 1620, William Pollard bought a share from Sir Francis Parington in the Virginia Company, from which the Bermuda Company was an offshoot. *Records of the Virginia Company* by S. M. Kingsbury Vol. 1. p. 378; Vol. 111 p. 62).

William Pollard's signature has been preserved on a document which he, together with nine others of the principal inhabitants of Bermuda signed in 1622. In this document they set out six grievances for which they held the Governor, Captain Butler, responsible (MSS. of the Duke of Manchester, *Historical MSS. Commission Report VIII*, Part 2, Paragraph 295).

From a letter written by Capt. Henry Woodhouse without date but probably June 1625, it is known that William Pollard was then in England with the Earl of Pembroke on business connected with Bermuda and was expecting to return there shortly. (*Memorials of Bermuda* by General Sir J. H. Lefroy, Vol. 1, p. 346).

Captain William Pollard was still living in Bermuda in 1629 and is mentioned in a letter from Captain Philip Bell (then Governor of Bermuda) to Sir Nathaniel Rich dated 28th April of that year. MSS. of the Duke of Manchester; *Historical MSS. Report VIII*, Part 2, Paragraph 416.

After the death of the Earl of Pembroke in 1630, intestate and with liabilities amounting to £80,000, his Bermuda estate was sold to two London merchants. William Pollard then emigrated to Barbados. The exact date is difficult to fix as most of the early Barbados records were lost in the fire which destroyed Bridgetown, the capital, in 1668. Other factors which may have influenced his decision to leave Bermuda were the strained relations which he had with three succeeding Governors during the time he was there. A number of energetic and discontented Bermudians came to Barbados at this time. Between 1629 and 1638, there were grants of 67,387 acres of land to 700 odd persons, an average of less than 100 acres each. (H. Wilkinson's *Adventurers of Bermuda*, p. 260 and *Journal of Barbados Museum and Historical Society* Vol. XIII, Part 4, page 106).

He was living in Barbados in 1638 and his name appears in a list of persons holding 10 acres of land and over. (*Memoirs of the First Settlement of Barbados*). This is presumably the estate of about 100 acres known as Pollards which remained in the elder branch of the family till about 1798 when it passed to Thomas McIntosh Branch Esq. William Pollard's will has not survived. His children, most of whom must have been born in Bermuda, are chiefly known from their wills as the Parish Registers of St. John in the Pembroke Tribe, Bermuda, covering their period are lost. See also Capt. John Smith's *History of Virginia*, pages 367 & 374 and note 1907 Edition.

5.   I.   Hugh Pollard[3], Eldest son.
6.   II.   James Pollard.
7.   III.   Thomas Pollard.
8.   IV.   Richard Pollard.
9.   V.   George Pollard.
10.   VI.   John Pollard.
     VII.   Sarah Pollard, mentioned in the wills of James, Thomas, Richard and John Pollard, married John Butcher.
Issue:—
George and Walford Butcher.
Sarah Butcher was aged 70 at the St. Michael's Census of 1715.
     VIII.   J'one Pollard. Married Thomas Little 3 Oct. 1643, at St. Michael, Barbados, perhaps a daughter of William Pollard[2].

4.   Hugh Pollard[3] (Eldest son of Lewis[2], Hugh[1]). Born about 1605. Married probably about 1626 Bridget (G. E. Cokayne's *Complete Baronetage*), relict of Francis Norris, 1st Earl of Berkshire, who committed suicide on 29 Jan. 1622. She was the 2nd dau. of Edward Vere, 17th Earl of Oxford and a granddaughter of Lord Burleigh. She was born 6 April 1584, and had by her 2nd husband Hugh Pollard an only daughter Margaret. She died between Dec. 1630 and May 1631. (*Complete Peerage* Vol. 9 page 648).

Lady Bridget was the sister of Susan Vere who married on 27th Dec. 1604, Philip Herbert, Earl of Montgomery to whom Barbados and other Islands had been granted in 1627.

Hugh Pollard was implicated in May and June 1641 in the first army royalist plot, was imprisoned and expelled from the House of Commons in which he sat for Beeralston, Devonshire. For this offence his father decided to disinherit him. Hugh Pollard petitioned Parliament and obtained their permission to visit his dying father and was forgiven. He became 2nd Baronet on 19th Nov. 1641, on the death of his father.

Returning from Holland, in search of levies for the King's Service, he was pursued by the Parliamentary ships but escaped. He defended Dartmouth against Fairfax but was wounded and taken prisoner. At the Restoration, he was sworn a Privy Councillor and made Controller of the Household. He was appointed a member of a committee to consider all business relating to foreign plantations. (Acts of the Privy Council (Colonial) 1662, pp. 544 and 572). He died, 27 Nov. 1666 and was buried in Westminster Abbey. (Westminster Abbey Burials, Harleian Society's Publication, Cokayne's *Complete Baronetage*, and *Dictionary of National Biography*)

5.   Hugh Pollard[3] (eldest son of William[2], Hugh[1]) of Barbados. Married, Elizabeth Geoffrey, 1645 (Lowsley Pedigree). This marriage has not been found. It may have been taken from a family Bible or similar source. Thomas Jeffrey of Barbados and All Hallowes, Lombard Street, London, made a will 18 June 1656 (Berkley 218) and proved in 1656, in which he mentions his mother Elizabeth and his son Thomas and others. There are also in Barbados, the wills of Edmund Jefferies 1683 and John Jefferies 1685, who held land as shown in the 1680 register. Persons of that name are found at an early date in many of the Islands, and in W. Berry's *Pedigrees of the County of Sussex*, 1830. William Jefferies is mentioned as being in New England in October 1611.

Children of Hugh Pollard and Elizabeth (Geoffrey) Pollard, his wife:—
11.   I.   John Pollard[4].
12.   II.   Geoffrey Pollard.

III.	Daniel Pollard, married Zyzima Magnalimore, a Greek lady in 1693 at St. Michael.
IV.	Richard Pollard married Frances Harding, 28 Nov. 1695, at St. Philip. He died in 1704 and she in 1708, both were buried at St. Michael.
Issue:—
(1) Richard, baptised 1698 at St. Michael. Died unmarried 1730, buried at St. Michael.
(2) Mary, baptised 10 April 1699 at St. Michael.
V.	Francis Pollard, a musician. Married Elizabeth 5 Nov. 1693 at St. Michael. He died in 1700 and she in 1720 and both were buried at St. Michael. Issue:—
(1) Richard, baptised 6 Dec. 1694, St. Michael, aged 21 at St. Michael Census 1715.
(2) Francis, baptised 23 Sept. 1697, St. Michael.
(3) Joyce, baptised 14 Jan. 1698, St. Michael and buried there the same year.

6.	James Pollard[3] (William[2], Hugh[1]). Mentioned in the will of his brother Thomas. No evidence that he was ever married. Will of James Pollard of St. Michael, Barbados, Gent. Weak. To sister Sarah Pollard, my negro woman (named) and the residue of my estate to my brothers and sister Thomas, George, Richard, John, and Sarah Pollard. Signed by mark James Pollard. Dated 6 Oct. 1670. Proved 21 April 1671.

7.	Thomas Pollard[3] (William[2], Hugh[1]). No evidence that he was ever married. Buried at St. Michael 1676. Will dated 4 Feb. 1675, proved 1677. Abstract:—My brother John Pollard all the land which was left me by my brother James Pollard, deceased: and then to go to his eldest son James Pollard. My brother Richard. My sister Sarah. My nephew George Pollard.

8.	Richard Pollard (William[2], Hugh[1]), planter, mentioned in the wills of his brothers, James, Thomas and John. Buried at St. Michael 1681. Unmarried. He had 3 acres of land in 1680 as shown in the St. Michael Register. His will was proved in 1682. Abstract:— My nephew and godson George Butcher. My 'brother' and sister John and Sarah Butcher. My nephew George Pollard son of my brother George Pollard decd. My brother John Pollard. If George Butcher die: to be paid to his brother Walford Butcher. Executor:— Brother John Pollard.

There is an entry "William, son of Richard Pollard, Christ Ch. bapt. 23 Dec. 1663", but no mention of any children or wife in the above will.

9.	George Pollard[3] (William[2], Hugh[1]). Left no will but was mentioned in the wills of his brothers James and Richard Pollard. Buried at St. Michael in 1674. Married and had issue:—
13.	I.	George Pollard[4].
II.	John Pollard, executor of his brother's will.

10.	John Pollard[3] (William[2], Hugh[1]), of St. Michael Parish. Mentioned in the wills of his brothers, James, Thomas and Richard. Married Anne, daughter of John Clare of St. George Parish. At the St. Michael census in 1715, she was aged 64. Her will is dated 17th July 1716 and was proved 7 Nov. 1722. Will of Anne Pollard, widow, of St. Michael, Barbados:— To my granddaughter Mary Bunyon one negro woman. She is to be sole executrix. At the Census in 1680 John Pollard had 5 acres of land, and no bought servants or negroes.

John Pollard's will is dated 5 Oct. 1685 and was proved in 1687. Abstract:—My son James Pollard the 3 acres of land left me by my brother Thomas Pollard, also money in his grandfather John Clare's Estate in the Parish of St.

George. My 2nd son, Richard, the 3 acres of land left him by my brother Richard Pollard. My son John Pollard, a share of what was bequeathed me by my brother-in-law Wm. Clare. My daughter Sarah Pollard for ever and my daughter Anne Pollard. My wife Anne Pollard executrix. Children of John Pollard and Anne (Clare) Pollard his wife:—

    I.   James[4] (eldest son) born 29 Dec. 1677, at St. Michael. Mentioned in his uncle Thomas's will. Probably died young.

    II.   Richard, bapt. 27 Sept. 1683, at St. Michael..

    III.   Sarah, born 30 Dec. 1675. Bapt. 8 Jan. 1677, at St. Michael. Married Thomas Adamson, 12 Oct. 169?, at St. John.

    IV.   Anne, born 7 Jan. 1676. Bapt. 8 Jan. 1677, at St. Michael. Married Philip Bunyan, 10 April 1694. Issue: Mary Bunyan, mentioned in her grandmother Anne Pollard's will (7 Nov. 1722).

14. V.   John, mentioned in his father's will.

11.   John Pollard[4] (eldest son of Hugh[3], William[2], Hugh[1]). Born 1649 (Lowsley) Married Emlyn. The marriage is confirmed by the St. Michael Parish Register entry of 21 Nov. 1683, "Eliza, daughter of John and Emlyn Pollard." Emlyn Pollard, widow was buried in 1712 (St. Michael's Parish Register) aged 78, and was, therefore, 49 when Elizabeth was born. There is a monumental inscription to her at St. Michael recorded by V. L.. Oliver in *Monumental Inscriptions of Barbados* No. 203, p. 35.

Here lyeth interred the body of Emlin Pollard who departed this life June 21st 1712 aged 78 years, and the bodyes of John Pollard, Samuel Pollard, Mary Pollard and John Pollard junr. children of Doctr. John Pollard. Also Mary Pollard (cement). (wife?) of the sd. Dr. John Po...... who departed this L.... May 26tt 1733 aged 45.

Children of John Pollard and Emlyn Pollard his wife:—

15. I.   John Pollard[5]. Mentioned in the deed of sale by his sister Elizabeth.

    II.   Elizabeth Pollard, born 20 Nov. 1683, bapt. 21 Nov. 1683. St. Michael's. Will of Elizabeth Pollard of St. Philip, Spinster. To my nephews John Polard and Henry Armell Pollard 3 acres in St. Michael, and if both should die under 21 to my niece Mary Culpeper. To Mary Culpeper 1 negro slave and a cow Betty and also a slave for Mary Culpeper's child to be born. To Mary Culpeper my interest in the estate called Kirtons.... To Dr. Nicholas Franklin's son Jonathan a cow called Cherry.... Appoints Alleyne Culpeper and Dr. N. Franklyn exors. Dated 26 Feb. 1754 N.B. On 23 March 1755, Elizabeth Pollard made a deed of sale to her brother John Pollard for the within 3 acres of land in St. Michael for £100. Proved 6th Aug. 1755.

12.   Geoffrey Pollard[4], (Hugh[3], William[2], Hugh[1]). He was a witness to the will of Edward Prince of London and Barbados, dated 11 March 1690. Proved 1691 (Vere 193). *B.M.H.S. Journal,* Vol. XIII, No. 1 & 2 p. 77.. From this it can be assumed that he was probably born not much later than 1670. Married Phoebe 1st wife, by whom he had a son.

    I.   Alraisa, bapt. 27 Sept. 1701 at St. Philip "Son of Jeffrey and Phoebe Pollard". Mrs. Phoebe Pollard died in 1702 and was buried at St. Michael.

Geoffrey Pollard then married Mrs. Ann Penn, 2nd wife, on 20 Jan. 1704 at St. Michael. Issue:—

I. John, bapt. 1705 at St. Michael "ye son of Geoffrey and Mrs. Ann Pollard".

At this time he was clerk to the St. Michael's Vestry, as shown in their Minutes of 8 May 1704 and 30th Aug. 1705.

After the death of Mrs. Ann Pollard, he married Rebecca Curtys, 28 April 1709, at St. Philip. Her family came to Barbados at an early date and the name of John Curtis is among the persons recorded in the *Memoirs of the First Settlement of Barbados* who held 10 acres of land and over in 1638. In Philip Lea's map of Barbados dated 1685, the Pollard and Curtys estates are shown adjacent to each other in the St. Philip parish. Children of Geoffrey Pollard and Rebecca (Curtys) Pollard, 3rd wife:—

       I.   Mary Pollard, born 1712, bapt. 8 April 1726, aged about 14 years, at St. James.

16.   II.   Thomas Curtys Pollard[5], eldest son.

      III.   Sarah Pollard, born 17 Aug. 1723, bapt. 8 April 1726 at St. James.

17.   IV.   Robert Pollard, bapt. 26 July 1736 at St. Joseph. His will is signed Robert Jeff Pollard.

13.   George Pollard[4] (eldest son of George[3], William[2], Hugh[1]). Born in Barbados in 1646 (Lowsley Pedigree). Mentioned in the wills of his uncle Richard and Thomas Pollard.

Married Mrs. Elizabeth Pawton, 22 Dec. 1670, at St. Michael. Children of George Pollard and Elizabeth Pollard his wife:—

       I.   Sarah Pollard. Born 1672. Buried at St. Michaels 1673.

      II.   Elizabeth Pollard. Born 1673. Buried at St. Michaels 1673.

18.   III.   George Pollard[5], Eldest son, born 1674. Aged 41 at the 1715 Census.

Will of George Pollard[4]. To my son George Pollard, To my wife Eliza Pollard, To my child that is to be born boy or girl to have an equal share. My brother John Pollard, executor. Proved 1688.

14.   John Pollard[4] (3rd son of John[3], William[2], Hugh[1]) of St. Michael. Married and had issue:—

19.   I.   John Pollard[5] (eldest son) of St. Lucy. Mentioned in his father's will.

      II.   Joseph Pollard. Mentioned in his brother John's will.

      III.   George Pollard. Mentioned in his sister Sarah's will.

      IV.   James Pollard. Executor of his sister Sarah's will.

      V.   Sarah Pollard. Spinster. Will of Sarah Pollard of St. Michael. Dated 14 Nov. 1740. To my brother George Pollard certain slaves. Brother James slaves and money due to me. Brother James exor. Proved 5 Sept. 1744.

His will made at St. Michael, Barbados and dated 28 Dec. 1734, was proved 20 May 1736.

Abstract:— To all his children shown above he left slaves and appointed 'my above said sons and daughter to be my Executors and Executrix of this my last Will and Testament'. He also directed that they should have the use of his house till they alter their condition'.

15.   John Pollard[5] (Eldest son of John[4], Hugh[3], William[2], Hugh[1]). Planter of St. Philip Parish, Barbados. Married Sarah Barry, 25 May 1705, at St. Michael. She was living in Barbados in 1731 and witnessed a baptism at St. Michael of Avis Freeman in that year. The Barry family were among those which settled in St. Andrew's Parish, Jamaica, in 1633.

Children of John and Sarah Pollard his wife:—

       I.   Sarah Pollard, bapt. 20 April 1706, at St. Michael.

21.   II.   John Pollard (Eldest son). Mentioned in his Aunt, Elizabeth Pollard's will. Bapt. 17 Jan. 1710, at St. Michael.
22.   III.   Armell Henry Pollard, 2nd son mentioned in his Aunt, Elizabeth Pollard's will.
        IV.   Mary Pollard. Married Alleyne Culpeper 1752, at St. Philip. Mentioned in her Aunt's will.
        V.   Ann Pollard, married Dr. Nicholas Franklin 1752, at St. Philip. Mentioned in her Aunt's will.
        VI.   James Pollard. Bapt. 16 May 1717. Married Mary Bynoe, 21 Aug. 1748, at St. Michael.
        VII.   Richard Pollard, born 26 April 1722. Bapt. 2 June 1722 and buried at St. Michael's the same year.

Will of John Pollard[5]. Abstract:—

To my daughter Mary Culpeper, wife of Alleyne Culpeper formerly Mary Pollard. £200 and my largest silver salver. To my grandson Abel Alleyne Culpeper, son of Alleyne and Mary £100. To my granddaughter born last Sunday 25 Sept. instant and not yet christened, £100.

To my daughter Ann Franklin, wife of Nicholas Franklin formerly Ann Pollard £250 and my other silver salver. To my grandson Jonathan John Franklin son of the said Nicholas Franklin and Ann his wife £100 and to the child expected to be said Ann £100. Residue to my two sons John Pollard and Armell Henry Pollard when the latter attains 21. If both die under 21, I give my estate to two grandsons, Abel Alleyne Culpeper and Jonathan John Franklin. Executors and guardians of my sons, Mr. Henry Edey and Mr. William Butler. Dated 29 Sept. 1757. Proved 3 Jan. 1758.

16.   Thomas Curtis Pollard[5] (Geoffrey[4], Hugh[3], William[2], Hugh[1],). Born about 1714. Buried 1770 at St. Michael. Married Thomasine Williams, 20 June 1741, at St. Joseph.

He was given a warrant by the Governor of Barbados to practise as a surveyor of lands, he having satisfied William Webster, the Surveyor General, of his proficiency, 10 March 1732. In June of the same year, Thomas Curtis Pollard, (at the request of the vestry of the parish and by virtue of his Excellency's warrant), made an accurate survey of the old St. Michael church yard and from thence discovered considerable encroachment to have been made within the old bounds; the particulars of which are shown by his certificate. (The 1st Survey was made in 1658 (*B.M.H.S. Journal* Vol. XX, p. 34).

Children of Thomas Curtis Pollard and Thomasine Pollard his wife:—
        I.   Thomas Curtis Pollard[6]—eldest son. Born 1749. Married Mary Ann Henry at St. Michael 1772.
        II.   Rebecca Curtis Pollard ⎫
        III.   Minerva   ..   ., ⎬ Triplets. Bapt. 1743 at St. Joseph.
        IV.   Eleanor   .,   ,, ⎭
        V.   William   ..   ,,   Bapt. 1751 at St. Michael.
        VI.   Thomasine Williams Pollard. Married Daniel Donovan, 24 April 1783 at St. Philip.
23.   VII.   Nathaniel Curtis Pollard.
24.   VIII.   Henry Curtis Pollard.

17.   Robert Geoffrey Pollard[5] (Geoffrey[4], Hugh[3], William[2], Hugh[1]). Baptised 26 July 1736, at St. Joseph. Married Joanna. Children of Robert Geoffrey Pollard and Joanna Pollard his wife:—

462

25. I. James[6] (eldest son) Named in his father's will.
    II. Rebecca, baptised 15 Dec. 1756, at St. Philip.
    III. Robert   } Baptised 15 Aug. 1759, at St. Philip |
    IV. Sarah   { Baptised 15 Aug. 1759, at St. Philip } Triplets
    V. One Other   } Not baptised. |
    VI. Elizabeth baptised 13 Oct. 1762, at St. Phillip.
    VII. Mary baptised 8 Feb. 1764, at St. Philip.
    VIII. Sarah baptised 8 Feb. 1764, at St. Philip.

Will of Robert Geoffrey Pollard of St. Philip's Parish Barbados. Abstract:—
The money that I have out, to be immediately collected to pay my debts and the balance to be put out at interest together with the money which shall accrue from the sale of a chaise and gelding and all my shop medicines and such interest money with my negro labour and the profits of my land shall be applied to maintain my children. To my wife 2 slaves and To my son James my land and buildings to be given him when my two youngest daughters attain 21 or marry. To my son James and my daughters Rebecca, Elizabeth, Mary and Sarah, certain slaves equally. My wife to be executrix. Dated 15 Feb. 1767. Robt. Jeff Pollard. Proved 27 March 1767.

18. George Pollard[5] (eldest son of George[4], George[3], William[2], Hugh[1]). Married Ann. Children of George and Ann Pollard:—
    I. John, bapt. March 1702 at Ch. Ch. Probably died before 1715.
    II. A daughter.
    III. George[6] (eldest son) baptised March 1710. Ch. Ch.
    IV. William, bapt. 3rd Jan. 1713, Ch. Ch. At the St. Michael's Census of 1715 the family were aged, 41, 40, 16, 14 and 12 respectively.

19. John Pollard[5] (John[4], John[3], William[2], Hugh[1]). Will of John Pollard of St. Lucy, sick.
To my loving cousin Mary Pollard, wife of John Pollard for life and then to my cousin John Pollard junior. To my cousin George Pollard, father of the said John Pollard 2 acres of land in St. Michael with part of a dwelling house thereon, butting on lands of Daniel Wildey, R. Estwick and Samuel Dunckley for his life and then to my cousin Armell Henry Pollard son of John Pollard. To my brother Joseph Pollard 5/-. To my aunt Sarah Bonyan £5. Cousins George Pollard and John Pollard Exors. Dated 4th July 1744.
Proved 23rd Nov. 1744.

20. In addition to the John Pollard's named in the will there was at this period a Dr. John Pollard married to another Mary Pollard née Gould. He probably belongs to the senior branch of the family. The evidence for his exact place in the pedigree has not been found.
Note. Mary (Gould) Pollard died in 1733.

20. Dr. John Pollard[5]. (not known[4]). Died 1740. Buried at St. Michael's. No evidence has been found concerning his parentage or training as a Doctor. Married Mary Gould 21 July 1719, at St. James. Mary (Gould) Pollard died in 1733 and was buried in the family vault at St. Michael's. Children of Dr. John Pollard and Mary his wife:—
    I. John Pollard, eldest son, baptised 8 Feb. 1720, at St. Michael's, buried there in 1725. M.I. on Pollard tomb at St. Michaels.
    II. Emerline Pollard. Mentioned in her father's will. Married Thomas Pierce, 26 Feb. 1735, at St. Michael's. He was Clerk of the St. Michael's Vestry, 25 March 1751. At the time of her marriage Emerline cannot have been more than 15.

III. Edward Pollard. Born 22 Oct. 1722 and baptised the same day. Buried at St. Michael's in 1736. Mentioned in his father's will.
26. IV. Thomas Pollard. Born 13 July 1726 and baptised 17 Aug. 1726, at St. Michael's. Mentioned in his father's will.
V. Samuel. M.I. in St. Michael, Pollard tomb.
VI. Mary Pollard. Baptised 26 July 1730, at St. Philip. M.I. on Pollard tomb.
VII. John (Jun.) M.I. on Pollard tomb in St. Michael.

Dr. John Pollard was appointed on 15 Jan. 1721, as Doctor to the Almshouses in succession to Dr. Sidney, at the Vestry meeting on that date. He still held the post in 1737.

Will of John Pollard of the town of St. Michael, practitioner in physic and surgery.

To my son Edward Pollard the house and land in the country and also one two-handle silver cup. To my son Thomas Pollard my dwelling house in Reid St. and one Silver Tankard. To my daughter Emerline (sic) Pearce 5/-. Residue of my estate to my sons Edward and Thomas Pollard equally when my youngest son Thomas attains 21, and in the meantime he is to be properly educated and brought up out of the profits of my estate. £10 is to be distributed to some poor families in St. Michael's Parish. Proved 25 Aug. 1740.

21. John Pollard[6] (eldest son of John[5], John[4], Hugh[3], William[2], Hugh[1]). Baptised 17 Jan. 1710, at St. Michael. Married Susanna Taylor, 1 May 1765, at St. Philip. Children of John and Susanna Pollard his wife:—
   I. Mary Gould Pollard. bapt. 8 April 1766 at St. Philip. Presumably died an infant.
   II. Mary Gould Pollard, baptised 21 Aug. 1767. Probably named after Dr. John Pollard's wife Mary Gould. Mary Gould Pollard married on 20 Jan. 1785 her cousin Jonathan John Franklin (mentioned in her grandfather John Pollard's will, proved 3 Jan. 1758).
   III. John Robert Pollard, bapt. 1 Oct. 1772 at St. Philip. In the register of baptisms the name John is omitted, but in his father's will he is twice called John Robert and in an old family pedigree he is shown as "John Robert". No further information has been found concerning him. At his father's death he would have been head of the family in Barbados, but the old pedigree, mentioned above, shows that the descent passed from his father to his father's brother, Armell Henry Pollard. It seems probable that he died before coming of age.

Will of John Pollard of St. Philip parish, Barbados. Abstract:—

To my wife Susannah Pollard, she maintaining my children during their minority: all my lands, buildings and slaves for her life and at her decease to my daughter, Mary Gould Pollard, six slaves (named) at 21, and also £500 to be paid her 3 years after my son John Robert Pollard shall come into possession of my estate. To my wife the interest on money due to me by Captain John Smith during her life. and after her death I give it to my said daughter Mary Gould Pollard £300 and slaves to be sold to make up her legacy to £800.

After my wife's death to my son John Robert Pollard at 21 all the residue of my estate and failing his issue one half to my wife and one half to my natural daughters, and if wife not then living, then to all natural born daughters. Dated 21 Nov. 1777.

Witnesses:— Nathaniel Curtis Pollard, Jonathan Franklin Snow. Joseph Taylor, Jesias King. Proved 19 March 1778.

22. Armell Henry Pollard[5] (John[5], John[4], Hugh[3], William[2], Hugh[1]). Mentioned in the wills of his father, and in that of his aunt Elizabeth Pollard. Married Mary Shepherd, 3 April, 1761, at St. Philip.
Children of Armell Henry Pollard and Mary Pollard his wife:—
    I.   Elizabeth Pollard, bapt. 31 Dec. 1761, at St. Philip. She married Abel Alleyne Culpeper, 6 Nov. 1781, at St. John's. She died of smallpox aged 33 and was buried at 'Easy Hall' plantation burial place 25 Dec. 1793. (V. L. Oliver, *Monumental Inscriptions of Barbados*, p. 194).
27.   II.   Armell Henry Pollard, born 1764 (Lowsley) eldest son.
28.   III.   John Pollard, bapt. 20 May 1765, at St. Philip.
    IV.   Mary Shepherd Pollard, bapt. 30 Dec. 1768, at St. Philip.
    V.   Susannah Moore Pollard, Died 1804. S.P. Buried at St. Michael.
    VI.   James Shepherd Pollard of the Colony of Demerara appoints his brother Armell Henry Pollard, gent., of Barbados, with powers of attorney, 13 Sept. 1795.
        Will of James Shepherd Pollard of St. Michael Barbados. Abstract:— To my brother John Pollard £25. To brother Armell Henry Pollard certain slaves, £75 and all the balance of my estate, and appoint him executor. Dated 17 April 1795. Proved 16 March 1799.

23. Nathaniel Curtis Pollard[6] (Thomas Curtis[5], Geoffrey[4], Hugh[3], William[2], Hugh[1]).
Married 1st Mary Tabitha McCarty, 13 Feb. 1799, at St. Philip.
Issue:—
    I.   John Penn Pollard.
        John Penn Pollard of St. George's Grenada appoints father Nathaniel Curtis Pollard of St. Michael, Barbados, with Powers of Attorney to sell three slaves, 13 Sept. 1806.
        Signed John Penn Pollard. Witnesses:—M. Campbell, Miss (sic) Thomasine W. Pollard.
        2ndly, he married Frances Nightingale, 14 Dec. 1800, at St. Philip.
24. Henry Curtis Pollard[6] (Thomas Curtis[5], Geoffrey[4], Hugh[3], William[2], Hugh[1]).
Married Rebecca Strong, 17 April 1770, at St. Philip. Issue:—
    I.   Elizabeth Rebecca Curtis Pollard, bapt. 2 Feb. 1772, at St. Philip.
    II.   **Henry Hugh Curtis Pollard, bapt. 11 Aug. 1774, St. Philip.**
    III.   Elly Anne Curtis Pollard, bapt. 5 Aug. 1776, St. Philip.
    IV.   Frances Curtis Pollard, born 14 Oct. 1774, bapt. in 1777, St. Philip.
    V.   **Hugh Curtis Pollard, born 10 Nov. 1777, bapt. 27 Feb. 1781, St. Philip.**
    VI.   Henry Curtis Pollard. Born 8 March 1779, bapt. 27 Feb. 1781, St. Philip.
    VII.   Robert Curtis Pollard, bapt. 24 April 1783, St. Philip.
Henry Curtis Pollard (Jr.) of Demerara appoints Thomas Chandler of Barbados with Powers of Attorney, 2 May 1808.
Henry Curtis Pollard of Demerara appoints Abel Edwards of Barbados with Powers of Attorney 28 Feb. 1822.
25. James Pollard[6] (eldest son of Robert Geoffrey[5], Geoffrey[4], Hugh[3], William[2], Hugh[1]).
Married Ann, dau. of Richard Kettlewell, 28 March 1775, at St. Philip.
Children of James Pollard and Ann Pollard his wife:—
    I.   Sarah Pollard. Bapt. 10 Nov. 1777 at St. Philip.
    II.   Robert James Pollard. Bapt. 9 May 1779 at St. Philip.

III. Rebecca Pollard. Bapt. 1 Dec. 1780 at St. Philip.
IV. Robert John Pollard. Bapt. 15 Nov. 1781 at St. Philip.
V. Harriet Pollard. Bapt. 17 Feb. 1785 at St. Philip.
Will of James Pollard of St. Philip Parish, Barbados, Sick..
To nephew William Crawford and my niece Mary Crawford £25 each. To nephew Robert James Stout a red cow. To my wife Ann Pollard residue during her widowhood with the incumbrance of my mother's free access and living in the place and to be provided for out of the same as in my lifetime. I direct Mr. Richard Kettlewell, father of my wife, does not trouble himself in the affairs of my estate as in that case I give the same to my nephew Robert James Stoute, he paying to each of his brothers Thomas Stoute and Edward Stoute £100 each. And after my wife's death or marriage, I give my estate to my nephew the said Robert James Stoute.
I appoint my wife and my trusty friend Mr. Brian Tayler as executrix and executor.
Dated 24 October 1789. James Pollard. Edward Stoute. John Gibbs. Proved 20 January 1790.
26. Dr. Thomas Pollard[a] (3rd son of Dr. John[b]).
Baptised 17 Aug. 1726, at St. Michael's. Medical training unknown. Married first, Ruth Stearn, 25 April 1748, at St. Michael's. Children of Dr. Thomas and Ruth Pollard his wife:---

    i. Ann Stearn Pollard, Born 1751 (Lowsley). Married Joseph Mayers 3 Feb. 1774, by whom she had a son John Pollard Mayers. Born 20 April 1777. Baptised 1777 at St. Michael's. She died 20 April 1777, in childbirth and was buried at St. Micahel. John Pollard Mayers held a commisison in the Royal Regiment of Militia Barbados for 13 years and was Colonel for 9. He was a member of the House of Assembly from 1802---1817. From April 14th 1829 till 1848 he was Agent in London for Barbados. He owned Staple Grove Plantation. Barbados, and also had an estate at Brasted in Kent where he died in 1853. B.M.H.S. Journal, Vol. XII, p. 83.

29. II. John Pollard (eldest son).
30. III. Walter Pollard (2nd son).
    IV. Ruth Pollard. Baptised 25 Oct. 1755, at St. Michael. Died at Bath, 5th Feb. 1797. Married The Rev. Dr. J. Gardiner by whom she had a daughter, born about July 1795, probably at Taunton.
    V. Thomas Pollard. Baptised 2 July 1757, at St. Michael. A doctor of Medicine. Died about 1785. A letter to his brother Walter dated 7 June 1777 is preserved in Hardwicke MSS. 35655. Secondly he married Mrs. Caroline Henrietta Bedford of Boston U.S.A. 1 Sept. 1775, at St. Michael. He retired to Bath, Somerset, in July 1783, where he died 26 March 1786 and was buried in Clifton Churchyard. His wife died there 11 Nov. 1808. Probate issuing out of Prerogative Court of Canterbury on 10 April 1786, of the Will of Thomas Pollard of the City of Bath, Dr. of Physic granted to daughter Ruth, spinster, one of the executors.

Ruth Pollard of Bath, spinster, executrix and residuary devisee then appointed John Tucker, Paul Bedford and Thomas Peerce all of Barbados with Powers of Attorney 17 April 1786. On Ruth Gardiner's death 5 Feb. 1797, Mrs. Caroline Henrietta Pollard of Bath widow and relict of Thomas Pollard deceased, and surviving executrix, appointed Joseph Mayers, Paul Bedford and Francis Workman 27 July 1797, with Powers of Attorney.

Will of Dr. Thomas Pollard:— To my wife Caroline Henrietta Pollard, all her jewels, plate and wearing apparel that she was possessed of at the time of her marriage and since given to her. I have by deed granted to my son Walter Pollard my equal ½ part of two parcels of land in Virginia which were drawn in the lottery of Colonel Bird between John Tucker, Esq., of the parish of St. Michael Barbados and myself. I hereby confirm the gift and also £20 most sincerely regretting it is not in my power to make a more ample provision for him, the very narrow and limited state of my fortune totally putting it out of my power.

My executrices named to sell any part of my residuary estate. And whereas I have received and used considerable sums of money the property of my said wife, I direct the money arising from such sale to be equally divided between my said wife and my daughter Ruth Pollard, and I appoint them executrices of my will. Dated 10th March 1786. Proved 10 April 1786. Allowed in Barbados 1 June 1786 and again recorded there in 1798.

27. Armell Henry Pollard[7] (eldest son of Armell Henry [6], John [5], John[4], Hugh[3], William[2], Hugh[1]). Born 1764 (Lowsley). Married Jane Weekes Branch, dau. of Thomas McIntosh Branch. 2 May 1797 at St. Michael. Children of Armell Henry Pollard and Jane Weekes Pollard his wife:—

    I. Armell Henry Pollard.[8] Born 1797 and bapt. 16 Jan. 1798, at St. Michael, and died an infant in the same year.

    II. Elizabeth Frances. Born 1798. Bapt. 2 Oct. 1799, at St. Michael. Married 1st ——Kirton, 2nd J. D. Newsum.

At the death of Armell Henry Pollard[7], his brother John Pollard's line became the senior branch of the Barbados family.

28. John Pollard[7] (second son of Armell Henry [6], John[5], John[4], Hugh[3], William[2], Hugh[1]). Bapt. 20 May 1765, at St. Philip. Married Elizabeth Gittens Branch, dau. of Thomas McIntosh Branch, 26 Jan. 1788, at St. Michael. Elizabeth Gittens Pollard was born 4 Oct. 1770 and died 3 Sept. 1838 John Pollard died 30 Nov. 1810. Children of John Pollard and Elizabeth Gittens Pollard:—

    I. Thomas McIntosh Pollard. Born 9 Feb. 1789. Eldest son. Died 13 March 1854. Unmarried.

    II. **John Henry Pollard. Born 14 Aug. 1790. Bap. 30 Sept. 1790** at St. Michael. Died 24 Dec. 1818. Unmarried.

    III. Samuel Branch Pollard. Born 24 Aug. 1792. Bapt. 26 Jan. 1797, at St. Michael, died in 1798

31.   IV. Nathaniel Weekes Pollard[8]. Born 24 Aug. 1792. Bapt. 26 Jan. 1797, at St. Michael. A twin brother of Samuel Branch.

    V. Mary Jane Pollard. Born 19 May 1794. Bapt. 26 Jan. 1797, at St. Michael. Died 1811. Unmarried.

    VI. Armell James Pollard. Born 24 April 1796. Bapt. 26 Jan. 1797, at St. Michael. Died 6 June 1806.

    VII. Elizabeth Anne Pollard. Born 5 Nov. 1797. Bapt. 1 March 1798, at St. Michael. Died 12 July 1860. Married George William Wells. who was born 4 Aug. 1798; the son of Richard and Catherine Wells. The marriage took place in Demerara, 12 June 1832, where G. W. Wells died 26 March 1866. Issue:—

      (1) George Pollard Wells. Born 17 March 1833. Died 21 Oct. 1869 at sea on the way to England. Unmarried.

      (2) William Hustler Wells. Born 22 March 1835. Died Feb. 1837.

      (3) William Nathaniel Wells. Born 8 June 1837. Died 9 June 1837.

      (4) John Richard Branch Wells. Born 8 June 1840. Died 15 Oct. 1844.

VIII. Agnes Danson Pollard. Born 30 Sept. 1799. Married 6 Nov. 1815. George Hannah Bagaley. No issue.
IX. Philip Lewis Pollard. Born 29 Sept. 1801. Died in 1804.
X. George Danson Pollard. Born 5 Oct. 1804. Died in March 1826.
XI. Charlotte James Pollard. Born 18 Jan. 1806. Unmarried.
32. XII. William Branch Pollard[8]. Born 15 Aug. 1807.
XIII. Martha Jane Pollard. Born 17 Aug. 1809. Unmarried.

The first seven children were baptised in Barbados, but, about 1797, John Pollard emigrated to Demerara as may be seen from the Powers of Attorney which he gave to his representatives in Barbados. 'John Pollard of St. Michaels Barbados, but intending shortly to go to the Colony of Demerara, appoints brother Armell Henry Pollard of St. Michael Barbados with Powers of Attorney.' 7 March 1796.

John Pollard, native of the Island of Barbados but now residing in Demerara, appoints Lynch Thomas of Barbados with Powers of Attorney. 24 Aug. 1807.

He is said to have owned an estate known as "Spring Hall" on the East Coast Demerara.

His will has not been found either in Barbados or Georgetown, Demerara. All the dates of births and deaths are from family records made by W. B. Pollard[8] for the period 1788—1877.

29. John Pollard[7] (eldest son of Dr. Thomas[6], Dr. John[5]). Born 1753. Entered Eton 7 Sept. 1761 to 1771. Matric. at Oxford from Queens College 7 June 1771, but never graduated. Admitted to Inner Temple 2 Sept. 1769. Died young of consumption, after 30 Jan. 1774 and before 3 May 1774. Buried in Clifton Churchyard. (Foster, *Alumni Oxon.* V. L. Oliver's *Caribbiana* and Eton College Register). A number of his letters to his brother Walter are in the Hardwicke MSS. 35655 in the British Museum and cover the period 27 May 1771—30 Jan. 1774.

30. Walter Pollard[7] (2nd son of Dr. Thomas[6], Dr. John[5]).
Baptised 25 Oct. 1755 at St. Michael. Eton 1761—1766, then Harrow 1770—1771. With Crooke and Parnell he drew up a petition to the Governors at Harrow School objecting to the appointment of Dr. Heath of Eton as headmaster. There followed the riots at which the Governor's coach was stoned, rolled down the hill to the common, and there smashed to pieces.

The Governors sent the School home for a week and expelled the ringleaders altogether. Among those mentioned above was Richard Wellesley, the future Governor General of India.

Walter Pollard then went to the Rev. Dr. Parr's School at Stanmore. He was admitted at Emmanuel College, Cambridge, 27 Oct. 1772, where according to Maurice's Memoirs "by his ingenuous temper, his sportive humour, his sprightly manners, his virtuous principles and his literary attainments he gained the love and admiration of all his fellow collegians." He left Cambridge without taking a degree.

He was admitted to the Inner Temple on 20 Jan. 1772 and was called to the Bar on 21 Nov. 1777.

Towards the end of 1779 Walter Pollard decided to visit his father and with the help of friends, obtained a passage to Barbados with Admiral Rodney's fleet, arriving there early in 1780. He experienced the hurricane of October the 10th of that year about which a friend wrote:— "Walter Pollard and family have lost everything. He has nothing else left, and they only could not be shaken by the wind or blasted by the lightning."

After the destruction of his father's estate he returned to London and practised at the Bar. In December 1783 he left for America and landed at Charlestown in February 1784. He first moved to Richmond, Virginia, where he attempted to obtain possession of some land which his father had won in a lottery. He also attempted to practise his profession at Camden, South Carolina. In both these projects he seems to have been unsuccessful. The war of Independence had left much ill feeling except in Philadelphia to which he moved later.

On the 12th April 1788 he sailed for Barbados, where he suffered recurring fevers and finally returned to England about June 1789, with his health broken and little or nothing achieved. His old friends rallied to his assistance and by their influence he obtained a post in the Customs as second assistant to the Surveyor of the King's Warehouse in the Port of London from 16 Dec. 1791. Again in July 1794, his friends Hardwicke and Abercorn came to his help and he was appointed to a better post as Controller of the Exchequer Bill Pay Office. He still held this post on 25 Aug. 1812. In 1796 he resided at Bench Buildings, Inner Temple.

Walter Pollard left a vast correspondence which his friend Philip Yorke, afterwards 3rd Lord Hardwicke, preserved among the Hardwicke MSS., now at the British Museum. These are numbered 35655 and 35656 and cover the period 1771—1812.

In his last letter he mentions a daughter "threatened by most fatal consequences" and in his will be mentions a son Edward and his wife Mary. His will ((Ellenboro' 36) is signed Walter Pollard, Chelsea, Kings Parade, dated 13 Feb. 1818 and proved 20 Jan. 1819. Abstract:—

"I give to my said wife such of my furniture as she may find convenient, the rest of my effects, my good books, are to be sold except such as may be serviceable to my son Edward for his education, and of that money arising from the sale and of whatever I may be worth at my death, one third I leave to my wife and the remainder to my son Edward Pollard."

Proved at London by the oath of Mary Pollard, Widow.

Calender of Inner Temple Records, Vol. V, 1751—1800.
Eton and Harrow School Registers.
Harrow by P. H. M. Bryant.
Venn's *Alumni Cantab.*
The Gentleman's Magazine, 1825, I, 367.

31. Nathaniel Weekes Pollard[8] (fourth son of John[7], Armell Henry[6], John[5], John[4], Hugh[3], William[2], Hugh[1]). Born 24 Aug. 1792. Bapt. 26 Jan. 1797, at St. Michael, Barbados. He died of cholera in France, 17 Aug. 1834, and was buried in a vault in St. Mark's Church, Middleton Square, London. In 1813 he married first Sarah Alleyne Bush, (née Mansfield); relict of Henry Bush. Her mother Sarah Alleyne Culpeper, who was born in Barbados 10 Aug. 1774, married William Mansfield.

Children of Nathaniel Weekes Pollard and Sarah Alleyne Pollard his wife:—

33. I. Nathaniel Weekes Pollard (eldest son).
    II. Sarah Maria Pollard. Born 6 Dec. 1815 and died 6 June 1891, in Georgetown, Demerara. Married Abel Alleyne Burrows, 9 July 1834, in London. Issue:—
       (1) Abel Alleyne.
       (2) Marian, mar. James Hill.
       (3) Emily, mar. Frank Conyers.
       (4) H. Aglimby, mar. — Spence 1872.
       (5) Stanley, mar. Jane Crawford.
       (6) Fitzherbert.

III. Mary Jane Pollard. Born 10 July 1819 in London. Married Charles Lidiard in Demerara. Issue:—
  (1) Peregrine.
  (2) Charles.
IV. John Henry Pollard. Born 24 Nov. 1820 in Demerara. Bur. in Repentir Cemetery, Demerara, 24 April 1871. M.R.C.P. He married Jane, who was born 29 Jan. 1820, dau. of Richard Williams of the Burncoose Co. Cornwall branch of that family. Her marriage took place in June 1842. Buried at Hove Church, Sussex, 30 Jan. 1875.
Children of John Henry Pollard and Jane Pollard his wife:—
  (1) Ada Mansfield, born 15 June 1846. Married 28 Jan. 1873, Lieut B. Lowsley, R.E., at the Cathedral Georgetown British Guiana. He died 25 July 1905. Issue:— See Burke's Landed Gentry 17 Edition. Lt. Col. Lowsley drew up the pedigree which is quoted throughout this work.
  (2) John Henry, born in Demerara.
  (3) Alice Josephine Cory. Born in Georgetown, 8 June 1850. Married 4 July 1871, at Georgetown, Demerara, Francis Hinks, son of Sir Francis Hinks, C.B., K.C.M.G., sometime Governor of Barbados and British Guiana. Issue:—
    i. Francis Stewart Hinks. Born 23 Nov. 1872, in Canada.
    ii. Grace Alice Geraldine Hinks. Both at Montreal, 20 Nov. 1876. Married Mark Whitfield Wooding 15th June 1896, at Savannah, U.S.A.
V. Edward Alleyne Pollard. Born 1822. Married in Australia.
  After the death of his first wife on 15th April 1824, in Demerara, Nathaniel Weekes Pollard married secondly Jane Williams Culpeper, 28 Feb. 1830, at St. Anne, Blackfriars, London. There was only one child of this marriage.
34. 1. William Branch Pollard.
  Will of Nathaniel Weekes Pollard, dated 26 March 1834, proved 2 Oct. 1834. Abstract:— I leave to my heirs Nathaniel Weekes, Sarah Maria, Mary Jane, John Henry, Edward Alleyne and to my son William Branch Pollard Jun. as also any further issue of my present wife Jane William Pollard, share and share alike.
  It is my earnest wish that my timber concern should be continued and carried on by my executors herein named as long as it appears that the return made thereon is commensurate with the capital employed. My wife Jane Williams Pollard and my brother William Branch Pollard to be Executrix and Executor and with Mrs. Jane Culpeper, Guardians over my minor children.
  Nathaniel Weekes Pollard owned two sugar estates, De Weavers and Susanna's Rust in Demerara.
32. William Branch Pollard[8] (Eighth son of John[7], Armell Henry[6], John[5], John[4], Hugh[3], William[2], Hugh[1]). Born 15 Aug. 1807. Married at the Cathedral, Demerara, 26 May 1841, Elizabeth dau. of Richard Batty, who came of a Yorkshire family, and Frances Straghan (Henry) Batty. His wife, Elizabeth, was born 24 Aug. 1816 and died 23 April 1869, in Georgetown, Demerara. William Branch Pollard died 9 Dec. 1879 and was buried at Repentir Cemetery, Georgetown. He was Auditor General of British Guiana, and an official Member of the Court of Policy.

470

At the meeting of Court of Policy after the Auditor General's death, the Attorney General said:--

"There were many of his duties that did not come directly before the notice of the public, but for the execution of which he was entitled to the highest credit.

I will merely allude to one of them, the laying out of the Sinking Fund. No one as far as I know ever asked how it was laid out, but we find that everything connected with the money was done to the best advantage. I may also mention the excellent manner in which he carried out the details of the Immigration Loan. No one ever interfered with Mr. Pollard in this respect, and it was his proudest boast to say that while he had the charge of the laying out of the funds, not a single cent had ever been lost to the Colony.

Your Excellency, I have lost my oldest colleague, and I can scarcely say how greatly I regret his loss. I have known him and esteemed him through a great number of years, and I now remain the oldest member of this Court.

In accordance with Your Excellency's instruction, I will now introduce the following resolution:

The Court deeply regret the loss which the Colony has sustained by the death of the Honourable William Branch Pollard, and desires to record their high appreciation of the long and valuable services rendered by him to British Guiana both as Auditor General and as a member of this Court."

The Colonist, 27th December 1879.

Children of William Branch Pollard and Elizabeth Pollard his wife:—

I. William Fox Pollard (eldest son). Born 4 March 1842. Died 5 Feb. 1900. Buried in Ramsgate (Kent) Cemetery. Unmarried. Government Medical Service, British Guiana.

II. Charlotte Elizabeth Pollard. Born 10 Sept. 1843. Died 28 Nov. 1843.

III. Frances Pollard. Born 15 Aug. 1844. Died 27 Aug. 1922 in Demerara unmarried.

IV. Agnes Wells Pollard. Born 6 July 1846 in British Guiana. Died 10 April 1934. Married 10 April 1872, Fredric Augustus Winter, Civil Servant in British Guiana, who died there 10 Oct. 1902.
Issue:—

(1) Ethel Marion, born 30 Dec. 1872 in British Guiana. Died 1894 in British Guiana.
Married the Rev. Frank Pringle, who died in 1916.
Issue:—
i. Ethel Marion, Born in British Guiana, 10 June 1894. Married 17 Dec. 1917, Hugh Chester Humphrys, Q.C. Born 1890.

(2) William Cecil, Born 8 April 1874, in British Guiana. Guy's Hospital, M.R.C.S.; L.R.C.P. Government Medical Officer in British Honduras, where he died, unmarried.

(3) Leila Agnes, Born 14 Aug. 1884, in British Guiana. Died 26 Feb. 1954, in British Guiana. Married Cecil Farrar, Company Director, who was born 6 March 1875 and died 17 Dec. 1948.
Issue:—
i. Leila Everald Agnes, Born 11 Dec. 1905. Married 12th Dec. 1931, Arthur Barron, Bank Manager, born 13 July 1899 in England, and educated at Brighton College.

ii. Cecil Frederick, Born 31 Dec. 1907. Chartered Accountant. Married Mabel Eileen Austin in Barbados 24 Oct. 1934.

    (4) Elliot Edward. Born 1884 in British Guiana. Educated at Queens College, British Guiana and McGill University. B.Sc. Geologist. Married Mabel Gill. Born 1891 in Barbados. Issue:—

        i. Eric Elliot. Born 1921 in Barbados. Lodge School and McGill University, B. Eng. Research Dept. Atomic Energy of Canada. Married Helen Hall, born 1924 in Canada.

        ii. Frederick Elliot. Born 1922. Lodge School and McGill University, Ph. D. Assist. Professor of Archaeology, Toronto University. Married Joan Hay of Canada.

        iii. Phyllis Elliot, Born 1925 in Barbados. B.Sc., McGill. Married Philip Freed. Born 1925 in U.S.A. B.A. Science Teacher N. York Public School.

    (5) Armine Ursula. Born 9 Sept. 1890 in London. Married 25th April 1923, James Farrar Irving. Born 20 Jan. 1891. Educated at Edinburgh Academy. Served in the K.O.S.B. and awarded the M.C. British Guiana Civil Service (Retired). Issue:—

        i. Ethel Jean. Born 17 April 1924, in British Guiana. Married William Ian Gordon, 30 Oct. 1942. He was born in Trinidad and educated at Strathallan.

        ii. Nicola Jean. Born 16 Oct. 1943, in British Guiana.

        iii. Sheena. Born 12 Oct. 1944, in British Guiana.

        iv. Joanna Katherine. Born 12 Oct. 1950, in British Guiana.

        v. William Neil Irving. Born 11 Aug. 1957, in British Guiana.

35. V. George Richard McIntosh Pollard.

    VI. Ellis John Pollard. Born 17 Oct. 1851. Died 4 July 1856.

    VII. Margaret Cornelia Pollard. Born 6 Oct. 1853. Married her cousin W. B. Pollard, Jun., 9 Oct. 1877 as shown elsewhere. Died 29 Aug. 1935. Buried at St. John's Church, Crowborough, Sussex.

    VIII. Edward Bickersteth Pollard. Born 26 July 1855. Married Sarah Ann Hill. He died 4 June 1923, at Bisley, Surrey. Issue:—

    (1) Edward Hill Pollard. Born 20 June 1893. Married Edith Hannaford at Mitcham, Surrey.

    (2) Richard Batty Pollard. Born 29 April 1896. Killed at Tel el Quelifa, Palestine 4 Nov. 1917.

    IX. Ellen Jane Pollard. Born 3 July 1857. Died 6 April 1941, at Leigh, near Reigate, unmarried.

    X. Mary Eliza Rosalie Pollard. Born 26 Nov. 1858. Bapt. at Christ Church, Highbury, London. Died 6 Oct. 1937, at Portarlington, Ireland. Married Dr. F. C. Fisher in Demerara. Issue:—

    (1) Madison Branch Fisher. Born 1883 in Demerara. Living 1957. Unmarried.

    (2) Hariet Cary Fisher. Born 1884 in Demerara. Married C. B. Harwood. Issue:—Winifred Rosalie Harwood.

    (3) Frances Margaret Fisher. Born 1886 in Demerara. Died 1947. Unmarried.

    (4) Frank Charles Fisher. Born 1889 in Demerara.

    (5) Muriel Agnes Fisher. Born 1890 in Demerara.

    (6) Arthur George Fisher. Born 1891. M.B. Capt. in the R.A.M.C., M.C. The citation stated:—"He went forward to the front line

under very heavy fire to locate some wounded, whom he later succeeded in rescuing. He has previously done very fine work." Died 1954. Unmarried.

(7) Richard Headly Vicars Fisher. Born 1895. Died 1950.

(8) Robert Lucius Cary Fisher. Born 1900 in Ireland.
Wing Commander R.L.C., R.A.F., M.S. Retired. Married Ethel Genul and had issue:—
    i. Patricia Rosalie. Born at Quetta, 1 Aug. 1931.
    ii. Lila. Born 12 May 1939.

XI.   John Elliot Troughton Pollard. Born 30 June 1860. Died 7 Aug. 1872 in Demerara.

33.   Nathaniel Weekes Pollard[9] (Eldest son of Nathaniel Weekes[8], John[7], Armell Henry[6], John[5], John[4], Hugh[3], William[2], Hugh[1]). Born 6 June 1814. Educated at Charterhouse 1826—1828 and then Sherbourne which he left in 1829 (School Registers). Trained as an engineer.

Late superintendent in the Public Works Trinidad and Special Agent of that Colony in the U.S.A., for emigration. He emigrated to Australia, where he contributed a paper to the Melbourne Chamber of Commerce (1856) on National Communications and another on manufactures from the raw materials produced in Victoria for the Government (1860). He also wrote on Victorian Institutions and Establishments (1861). He married Mary Elizabeth Hillier in London.

Children of Nathaniel Weekes Pollard and Mary Pollard his wife:—

I.   Rhoda Branch Pollard. Baptised 14 Dec. 1841, at St. Michael, Barbados.

II.   Fanny Pollard. Married Edward Fitt in Trinidad.

III.   Edward Fox Pollard. Baptised 17 April 1844, at St. Michael, Barbados.

IV.   Henry Pollard.

V.   Mary Pollard.

34.   William Branch Pollard[9] (Nathaniel Weekes[8], John[7], Armell Henry[6], John[5], John[4], Hugh[3], William[2], Hugh[1]). Born 25 June 1833, in Demerara, British Guiana. He served in training as a Civil Engineer, under the firm of M'Clean & Stileman, and was for six months Assistant Engineer on the Furness Railway. Returning to British Guiana, he was appointed Assistant Colonial Civil Engineer. He was elected an Associate of the Institution of Civil Engineers 3 April 1860.

In January 1863, he was appointed Colonial Civil Engineer and Overseer of Public Works for the Colony of British Guiana. On 6 Nov. 1868, he became a full Member of the Institution of Civil Engineers. He had then constructed various coast defences, groynes, sea-walls etc., and built several gaols, hospitals and police stations.

He was Captain commanding the British Guiana Artillery. His chief interest was music and he played the organ.

He married, first, Elizabeth Ann Blackley, in Liverpool, 16 Sept. 1869. She was born 30 Oct. 1841 and died in Demerara, 22 Feb. 1872. Only child of the marriage of William Branch Pollard and Elizabeth Ann Pollard his wife:

36.   I.   Amy Elizabeth Rosalie Pollard[10].

Secondly, he married his cousin, Margaret Cornelia Pollard, dau. of William Branch Pollard[8], 9 Oct. 1877. Issue:—

37.   I.   William Branch Pollard[10].

II.   Marguerite Muriel Culpeper Pollard. Born 15 Oct. 1879, at Georgetown, British Guiana. B.A., B.Litt., Oxon. Died 24 Oct. 1939. Buried at Oxford Cemetery. Unmarried.

William Branch Pollard[9] retired from the Government Service in British Guiana in 1880, as a result of a sunstroke. He settled at St. Leonard's, Sussex.

where he died 9 December 1889 and was buried at Ore Cemetery. His widow Margaret Cornelia Pollard, died 29 Aug. 1935 and was buried at St. John's, Crowborough, Sussex.

35. **George Richard McIntosh Pollard**[9] (2nd son of William[8], John[7], Armell Henry[6], John[5], John[4], Hugh[3], William[2], Hugh[1]). Born 1 Feb. 1850 in Georgetown, British Guiana. Accompanied Charles Barrington Brown, the discoverer of the Kaietur Falls, on his second journey there for the purpose of making collections for the Museum of the Agricultural Society in Georgetown, British Guiana. (*Canoe & Camp Life in British Guiana* by C. Barrington Brown). Came to England and studied Medicine at Guy's Hospital, M.R.C.S., L.R.C.P. He married Grace Husband, dau. of the Rev. Dr. McFarlane of Clapham, 25 July 1876. Practiced Medicine at Ramsgate and retired to Moffat, where he died 19 June 1923.

Children of Dr. G. R. M. Pollard and Grace Pollard his wife:—
38.   I.   William John McFarlane Pollard.
     II.   Jenny Grace Pollard. Born 9 Feb. 1879. Living 1957.
     III.   Armell Richard Pollard. Born 20 Oct. 1880. B.A. Cantab. Trinity 1900. Chief Engineer Central Provinces India and later of Gwalior State. Married Eva Mary, dau. of John Hill of Payette, Idaho, U.S.A. He died 9 March 1947 in California. Issue:—
       (1) Elizabeth Mary Grace. Born 3 Feb. 1930, at Bilaspur, C.P. India. Married David Bigbee of California Nov. 1950. Issue:— one daughter and one son.
       (2) Edward John Pollard. Married Elizabeth Allan of California, Sept. 1952. Issue:—
         i. Allan Richard. Born 2 March 1955.
         ii. Katherine. Born 2 Sept. 1956.
     IV.   Edward Branch Pollard. Born 1 March 1883. 1st Lieut. 8th K.O.S.B., attached to R.E. Mining & Tunnelling branch. Died of wounds 26 July 1915, at Abbeville, France. Associate of the Royal School of Mines, London. Unmarried.
     V.   Helen Elizabeth Pollard. Born 6 Feb. 1885. Living 1957.

36. **Amy Elizabeth Rosalie Pollard**[10] (William[9], Nathaniel Weekes[8], John[7], Armell Henry[6], John[5], John[4], Hugh[3], William[2], Hugh[1]). Born 4 Oct. 1870, in Demerara, British Guiana. After the death of her mother in 1872, she was brought to England and lived with her mother's relations and later took their name of Imrie.

On coming of age she became a Catholic and joined the Franciscan Order of Poor Clares.

As Sister Mary Clare, she was the Foundress of Sclerder Abbey, near Polperro, Cornwall, and became its first Mother Abbess. Sister Mary Clare also built the Church of St. Mary of the Angels in Liverpool. She died 4 April 1944, and was buried behind the High Altar at Sclerder Abbey.

37. **William Branch Pollard**[10] (Only son of William[9], Nathaniel Weekes[8], John[7], Armell Henry[6], John[5], John[4], Hugh[3], William[2], Hugh[1]). Born 10 Aug. 1878, in Georgetown, British Guiana. Clare College, Cambridge 1898—1901. B.A. Government Laboratory, London 1903—5. Egyptian Government Laboratory, Cairo, 1905—1924. D.Sc., London 1938. Married Joyce, dau. of Henry Nicholas Corsellis, 4 Oct. 1910. Issue:—
     I.   William Branch Pollard[11], only child. Born 12 May 1913, at Bulaq Dakrur, Egypt. Educated at Oundel 1927—1931. Clare College,

Cambridge 1931—1934. B.A. Flying Officer R.A.F. 1941—5. Film Director.

Married Barbara Mary Spencer Nowill, only dau. of Ernest Spencer Nowill, at Sutton, Surrey 28 Sept. 1940. Issue:—
    (1) Richard William Pollard. Born 27 June 1942, at Sutton, Surrey. Educated at Westminster 1955.
    (2) Sarah Barbara Pollard. Born 22 July 1943, at Rudgwick, Sussex.

38. William John McFarlane Pollard[10] (Eldest son of George[9], William[8], John[7], Armell Henry[6], John[5], John[4], Hugh[3], William[2], Hugh[1]). Born 22 July 1877. Entered Guys Hospital. M.D. London. Joined the Medical Service West Africa. Croix de Guerre Avec Palm. He married Mary Campbell, dau. of Robert Makenzie Fraser of Epi, New Hebrides. He died 26 Sept. 1939, at Cheltenham.

Children of Dr. William John McFarlane Pollard and Mary Pollard his wife:—
I. Armell Richard Pollard. Born 9 March 1919. Cheltenham College which he left in 1937. Entered Pembroke College, Oxford, in 1937. Enlisted in 1939. Captain in 9 Durham L.I. Killed on the Mareth Line having volunteered to carry a message 22 March 1943.
II. Jocelyn Mary Mellis Pollard. Born 18 June 1922, at Edinburgh. Married Dr. William Thomson M.D., Edinburgh, 17 June 1952. Issue:—
    (1) Gillian Mary. Born 19 June 1954.
    (2) Jocelyn Margaret. Born 11 Oct. 1955.
    (3) Andrew William Pollard. Born 4 Nov. 1957.
III. John Fraser Pollard. Born 18 July 1925, at Edinburgh. Cheltenham College which he left in July 1943. 2nd World War, S.A. Baluch Regiment. Mentioned in Dispatches. Pembroke College Oxford, 1947—50. M.A. Athletics Blue. Assistant Conservator of Forests, Nigeria.

Porter of Barbados.*

WILLS.

1679. Proved Jan. 20, 1679-80. John. Wife Jone. Sons, John and James.

1750. Proved Oct. 10, 1753. John. Mother Elizabeth. Nieces, Susannah and Sarah Reeves, Elizabeth Porter. Brothers, Robert and Charles.

1753, Sept. 27. Samuel. Wife Jane. Children, ..., William, Jane Goodridge (her daughter Jane). Grandchildren, Samuel and Martha Greaves. Daughter, Martha Greaves. Sons-in-law, Samuel Goodridge, Joseph Greaves.

1769, Aug. 1. Charles Thomas. Son Thomas. Brothers, Thomas Oxnard and Edward Harris Porter.

1782, Sept. 25. Thomas Westbury. Sons, Thomas Reason Porter, William. Daughters, Margaret, Elizabeth, Mary (wife of Anthony Gilkes). Relations, William Harris Porter and Edward Thomas.

1786, 20 Feb. William. Wife Elizabeth. Children, Joseph, John, Samuel. Daughter Margaret Roach (sons, Samuel Porter Roach, Wm. R., and daughters Elizabeth R., Martha R.).

1786, 20 Feb. William. Sons, Joseph, Benjamin, John, Samuel. Wife Elizabeth. Brother John. Daughter Margaret Roach (her son William, daughters Elizabeth and Martha Roach).

1796, Feb. 15. John. Nephew Joseph. Sister Jane Goodbridge. Nieces, Sarah and Mary Goodbridge, Martha Greaves. Wife Alice G.

1796, July 25. Alice, widow. Sisters, Sarah and Jane Pierce, spinsters. Brother Thomas Ibbott Pearce.

MARRIAGES.

Year.	Christian Names.	To whom Married.
1649	William Stokes	Jane Porter.
	Jane Stokes	Wᵐ Porter.
1660	John	Eliz. Terrill.
1663	Nicholas	Mary Smith.
1663	Richard	Ann Perry.
1665	Amy	John Searing.
1667	Elizabeth	Thōs Woodbine.
1672	William	Elizabeth Puckering.
1675	Robert	Jane Warner.
1682	Alice	Thōs Cox.
	Ann	Thōs Burton.
1684	Maria	James Morrisor.
1692	Jane	Giles Burnside.
1696	Marmaduke	Hannal Elles.
1697	Robert (C.C.)	Margaret Whetlawe.
1701	Hannah	Jeremiah Cattelee.
1706	Thomas	Elizabeth ....
1713	Abigail.	
1722	John	Susannah Giles.
1722	Mary	John Reeves.
1727	John	Alice Martin.
1729	John	Branch (Widow).

* Communicated by Mr. N. Darnell Davis, C.M.G.

476

Year.	Christian Names.	To whom Married.
1730	John	Marshall.
31	Robert	Eliz. Phillips.
34	Margaret	James Legay.
34	Richard	Alice Gibson.
37	Charles	Alice Ferris.
39	Jane	Thomas Magrath.
45	Susanna (Widow)	William Wallace.
47	Cornelia	Barnard Jones.
50	Thomas Wokebury	Eliz. Relsen.
51	John.	
52	Jane	James Roberts, John Porter.
57	Eliza	William Lascells.
60	William	Judith Courtney.
62	Thomas Oxnard	Mary Kills.
65	Charles Thomas	Sarah Robinson.
65	Sarah	Francis Mose.
66	Edward Ferris	Ann Dempster.
67	Mary	John Benjamin Richards.
68	Philip	Esther Taylor.
76	Martha	James McCaskel.
78	Mary	Anthony Gilkes.
82	William	Lucy Ann Nessfidd.
83	Margaret	Thomas Gilkes.
84	John	Alice Pierce.
85	Elizabeth	Samuel Gittons.
88	John	Eliz. Emptage.
93	John	Rebecca Jones.
95	Wm Harris	Margaret King Belcher.
1804	Wm Harris	Eliza Jane Butcher.

1643, Aug. 6. Thomas Porter of London, Merchant, Attorney of Morgan Davis of London, Merchant. ·(See folio 28 of Vol. I. of " Recopies.")

BIRTHS.

Year.	Christian Names.	Parents.
1664	John, Christ Church	Thomas and Mary Porter.
64	Anne	Robert and Anne.
66	Mary	Robert.
67	Jeremiah	Francis.
68	Sarah	Nicholas.
69	Eliz.	
70	Robert.	
72	Charles.	
78	Peter	Robert and Jane.
78		Do.
83	Thomas	Do.
85	Philip	Porter and Ann.
1700	James	Robert and Mary Ann.
02	Eliz.	Do.
07	Mary	Thōs and Eliz.
08	Thomas	Robert and Mary.
11	Richard, born August 1709 b. 5 Sept. 1710	John and Eliz.
11	Rebecca	
16	Charles	Thōs and Eliz.
18	John	Do.

Year.	Christian Names.	Parents.
1719	Mary, about 5 years old	John and Eliz.
19	Sarah, about 4 years old	Do.
19	Elizabeth, about 2 years old	
23	Ann, about 2 years old.	John and Eliz.
27	Thōs.	
27	Abraham.	
32	Thōs Westbury	Thos., Jr, and Mary.
33	William	Robert and Eliz.
34	Mary	John and Susanna.
35	,,	
38	Richard	Richard and Alice.
39	Edward	Charles and Alice.
40	Mary	Do.
43	Thōs Oxnard	Thōs Westbury and Eliza.
51	Eliz.	Charles and Alice.
52	Mary	Thomas Westbury and Elizabeth.

DEATHS.

1658	Henry.	1758	Mrs.
1658	Arthur.	58	Richard.
65	Robert.	61	Charles.
68	Anne.	62	Sarah.
68	Jeremiah.	62	Robert.
68	Elizabeth.	63	Wm.
75	Nicholas.	64	John.
86	Wife of John.	65	Mary.
91	William.	65	Alice.
91	Robert.	67	Eliz.
93	William.	69	Thomas Oxnard.
95	Mary.	69	Charles Thomas.
95	Richard, Esqre.	69	Edward.
1706	Josiah.	70	Mary.
14	Robert.	71	Margaret
18	Wm.	71	Susanna.
30	Robert.	73	Ann.
36	Mary.	74	Mary.
36	Eliz.,	76	Thomas.
36	John.	78	Elizabeth.
39	Edward.	79	John.
40	John.	80	Charlotte.
41	Agnes.	80	Esther.
44	John.	82	Ann.
46	John.	82	Wm.
47	Thomas.	82	Thōs Westbury.
48	Thomas.	84	Daniel.
50	John.	85	Wm.
52	William.		Philip.
52	Richard.		Elizabeth.
55	Alice.	88	Samuel.
56	Margaret.	89	Edward Huronis.
56	Robert.	89	Lawrence.
56	Margaret.	89	Benjamin.
56	Robert.		Mary.
57	Eliz.	90	Mercy.
58	John.		Eliz.
58	Eliz.		

Rawdon of Barbados.

The following notes have been made from Add. MS. 15,556, British Museum, which is labelled "Abstracts of Titles, 1687—1800 ":—

By deed poll dated 3 April 1652 and recorded at Barbados 31 March 1653, James Holdip of the said Island, esq., sold to Dame Eliz. Rawdon, Tho. Rawdon, esq., Eliz. Forster, widow, and Robert Swinnerton, merchant, all of London, a moiety of that plantation called Fisher's Pond, containing 350 acres; also that parcel of 300 acres part called Rawdon plantatious in the parish of St Michael.

It appears that between 1653 and 1666 the 300 a. was leased out by Col. Tho. Rawdon without Mr Swinnerton, who d. 1674, being consulted. Fisher's Pond (the other moiety having been conveyed to Col. Tho. Rawdon by John Waldoe of the said Island, esq., by deed of 8 Sept. 1653) was in consideration of £13,000 st. conveyed by Col. Rawdon to Edward Thornburgh. The present claimant, Joseph Keeling, esq., married Hester, only child of Marmaduke Rawdon, esq., the last heir male, who by lease and release of 14 and 15 Oct. 1750, recorded 30 April 1762, conveyed Rawdons Rents, otherwise Rawdous plantation, to the said Joseph Keeling and Esther and to the longest liver now devolved on Mr Keeling by survivorship. (fo. 111.)

Schedule of Ind'res granted by Col. Tho. Rawdon, 1654 to 1665, taken from the Sec. Office at Barbadoes in 1762. 22 names are given. (fo. 110.)

Appended (fo. 109) is a short tabular pedigree of 5 generations down to Mrs Hester Keeling.

Marriage Licences.

1610-11, March 16. Marmaduke Rawdon, Clothworker, of All Hallows Barking, Bach., 29, and Elizabeth Thorogood, of Hodsden, Herts, Maiden, 19; consent of father Thomas Thorowgood of same, Gent.; at Broxborne, Herts. (Bishop of London.)

1672, Sep. 17. Christopher Sparke of Inner Temple, Gent., Bach., about 30, and Elizabeth Rawdon, of Hoddesdon, Herts, Sp^r, about 18; her mother's consent; at Hoddesdon afs^d. (Vicar-Gen. of Archb. of Canterbury.)

1672, Dec. 16. Marmaduke Rawdon, of Broxbourne, Herts, Esq., Bach., about 25, and Hester Corsellis, of Stepney, Midd., sp^r, about 24, her parents dead; at St Cath. Coleman, St Dunstan in the E., or St Olave, Hart Str., London. (Faculty Office.)

1681, July 19. Nathaniel Brent, of Hodsdon, Herts, Bach., 30, and Eliz. Roydon, Spr., 18, dau. of Marmaduke R. of same, who consents; alleged by Henry Crew, of St Olave's, Hart Str., L.; at Hertford, Stapleford or Amwell, co. Herts. (Faculty Office.)

1689, Dec. 9. Marmaduke Rawdon, of St Mary Magdalen, Bermondsey, Surrey, Mariner, Bach., about 35, and Mrs Margaret Peverell, of the same, spr., about 20, at own disposal, no parents or guardians; at St Mary Magd. afs^d. (Vicar-Gen. of Archb. of Canterbury.)

ALL HALLOWS' BARKING.

Baptisms.

1612 Mar. 29 Thos Rawdon s. of Marmaduke Rawdon and Elizabeth his wife.
1618 Apr. 9 Elizabeth dau^r of Marmaduke Rawdon and Eliz^h his wife.

ARMS.—*Argent, a fess between three pheons, all Sable.*
CREST.—*On a mural coronet a pheon with a laurel branch issuing thereout.*

Rafe Rawdon of Stearsby in Yorkshire═Jane, dau. of John
1568. He heads the pedigree in the │ Brice of Stilling-
Visitation of London of 1633—5. │ ton, Yorkshire.

A

Laurence Rawdon of York,═Margery, dau.   Robert Rawdon, citi-═Katherine,
born at Bransby; freeman │ of Wm. Bar-   zen and fishmonger │ dau. of
and grocer 1593; Sheriff │ ton of Cawton   of London, died 15 │ Tho.
1615; Alderman 1624; bur. │ Hall; died 17   Sept. 1644. Will │ Hacker of
in Crux Church 6 July 1626, │ April 1644,   (204, Fines). │ London.
aged 58. Arms on blue stone. │ aged 74.
Will dated 6 and proved 21
July 1626 at York.

B

Roger   Robert Raw-   Marmaduke Rawdon, bapt. at   Margery, mar.   Mary,
Raw-   don of Mit-   Crux 18 March 1609-10; mer-   Sir Roger   and a
don.   cham, co. Sur-   chant in the Canaries; died   Jaques of El-   3rd
   rey, died   bachelor 6 Feb. 1668. M.I. at   vington, Knt.   dau.
   1644 and left   Broxbourne. Will (22, Coke).
   issue.   See his Life and "D.N.B."

Marmaduke Rawdon═Hester, 4th and youngest dau. of Abraham Cor-   Thomas
of Hoddesdon, 1st │ sellis of London, brewer; mar. lic. dated 16 Dec.   Rawdon,
son and heir; died 30 │ 1672, then aged 24; died 7 July 1719, aged 75.   2nd son,
Oct. 1681, aged 35. │ M.I. at Broxbourne. Will (169, Browning).   1666.

Charles   Dorothy, dau. of═Marmaduke Rawdon of Hoddesdon, only═Rebecca
Rawdon, │ John Freeman of │ son and heir, attorney-at-law of Colches- │ . . . .
died │ Colchester, co. │ ter; purchased Fingringhoe manor in │ 2nd
young. │ Essex; mar. 3 │ 1707; had claims to Fisher's Pond and │ wife.
   Feb. 1705; living │ Rawdon's Rents in Barbados; died 31
   1712. 1st wife. │ Oct. 1752, aged 72. M.I. at Broxbourne.
      │ Will (286, Bettesworth). Last heir male.

C

s.p.

Doro-   Robert Plumer═Hester Raw-═Joseph Keeling of Barking,═Alice Sla-
thy,   of Great Am- │ don, only sur- │ Esq., bapt. at St. James,   ney, sister
died   well, High She- │ viving child │ Clerkenwell, 4 July 1724;   of John
young.   riff of Herts; │ and heir, died │ mar. 25 July 1744; J.P.   Slaney of
   died 11 Jan. │ at Fingring- │ Essex and Middlesex; Col-   Norwich,
   1740, aged 52. │ hoe, near Col- │ lector of Customs at Barba-   Esq. His
   M.I. at Great │ chester, 5 │ dos; owned Rawdon's plan-   will (405,
   Amwell (Cus- │ Sept. 1756. │ tation; died 9 Aug. 1792.   Bevor).
   sans, ii., 128). │ Will (18, │ Will (436, Fountain). See
      │ Herring). │ W.I. Bookplates, No. 208.

s.p.   s.p.

Joseph Keeling.   John Keeling.   William Keeling.   Mary, mar. . . . . . Tooke.

1621 Aug. 29 Marmaduke sonne of Marm^ke Roydon and Eliz^h his wife.
1622 Dec. 19 Martha dau^r of Marmaduke Roydon and Eliz^h his wife.
1624 Apr. 25 Katherine dau^r of Marmaduke Roydon and Eliz^h his wife.

(A long notice of Sir Marmaduke is given in the History of the parish, pp. 66-67.)

A

Sir Marmaduke Rawdon, Knt., bapt.=Eliz., only dau. and heir of Tho. William
at Brandsbie 20 March 1582, aged Thorogood of Hoddesdon in Rawdon,
29 in 1610-11, of All Hallows Bark- Broxbourne, co. Herts; mar. 7 4th son.
ing; a great merchant adventurer; April 1611; lic. dated 16 March —
M.P. Aldborough 1627; Lieut.-Col. 1610-11, then aged 19; her for- James
of City Bands 1629; Master of Cloth- tune was £10,000; sole ex'trix Rawdon,
workers' Co.; owner of plantations 1646 of her stepmother Mrs. 5th son.
in Barbados 1627; fined for Alder- Martha Molesworth. Had 10
man 1639; raised a regiment for the sons and 6 daus. Will dated 27
King 1643; Govr. of Farringdon, Feb. 1666; proved 5 March
where he died 28 April 1646, and 1668 (36, Coke).
was buried.

D

Col. Thomas Rawdon of Bar-=Magdalen, dau. Marmaduke Raw-=Sarah, 2nd
bados, born 20 and bapt. 29 of Randolph don, 2nd son, born dau. and
March 1612 at Barking; F.C. Crew of Hatham 16 and bapt. 29 coheir of
Trin. Coll., Camb., 1624; Barne, co. Kent, Aug. 1621 at Hugh
resided in Portugal 1630—8; Esq.; mar. 21 Barking; F.C. of North of
Envoy there and Col. of Horse April 1642, aged Jesus Coll., Camb.; Tewin, co.
1644; retired to Canaries for 15. Will dated a merchant; heir Herts.
two years; resided in Barba- 3 Nov. and and ex'or 1668 of (Cussans,
dos until 1662; bur. 3 Aug. proved 2 Dec. his cousin Marma- ii., 13).
1666 and M.I. at Broxbourne. 1675 (130, Dy- duke.
Will (136, Mico). cer).

B

George Raw- Eliz., 1st dau., mar. Chr. Sparke of Magda- Martha. Kathe-
don, 3rd son, the Inner Temple; mar. lic. dated 17 lene. rine.
1666. Sept. 1672, he aged 30 and she 18.

C

Magdalen, mar. Hester, proved her Elizabeth, mar. Sam. Bagnal of London,
Geo. Lysons of mother's will in salter. She died 11 Dec. 1712, aged 34.
Gray's Inn. 1719. M.I. at Broxbourne.

Marmaduke Rawdon and Edmond Foster were two of those London merchants, who obtained from the Earl of Carlisle a grant of 10,000 acres in Barbados in 1627-28. This company sent out a ship the Marygold, John Jones
master, with Capt. Charles Wolferstone and Capt. John Swan as their agents,
which arrived in Carlisle Bay on 5 July 1628. ("Memorials of St. Lucia,"
p. 474.) The 10,000 acres are shewn in Lygon's map of about 1650.
1686, Sept. 2. Ind're between Tho. Rawdon of Hoddesden Hartfordshire
Esq. and Capt. Wm. Mott of Barbados gent. concerning certain lands near the
Indian Bridge in St. Michael's parish belonging to Dame Elizabeth Rawdon
widow of Sir Marmaduke Rawdon. (New Eng. Reg. for 1914, p. 181.)

1756, Sept. 5. Mrs. Hesther Keeling, Colchester, Essex. ("London Mag.," 452.)

1756, Sept. 13. Wife of Jo. Keeling, Esq.; at Fingringhoe, Essex. ("G.M.," 451.)

1792, Aug. 9. At Barking, Essex, Joseph Keeling, esq. collector of the customs for Bridgetown, Barbadoes, and in the commission of the peace for Essex and Middlesex. (*Ibid.*, 774.)

The manor of Westbury in Barking was owned by Blackburne Poulton, attorney at law, who died 1749, leaving it to his nephew Poulton Alleyne, from whom it descended to Joseph Keeling, Esq. (Wright's "Essex," ii., 481.) A pedigree of Keeling was entered in the Visitations of London and Staffordshire. For other authorities see Clutterbuck's "Herts," ii., 64, 74; Cussans' "Herts," ii., 190; Wotton's "Baronetage," iv., 470; Wright's "Essex," ii., 734; "Mis. Gen. et Her.," 5 S., i., 19; the "Life of Marmaduke Rawdon of York," Camden Soc. Pub., 1863; "Visitation of York"; Calendar of State Papers, Domestic, 1628-29; Illustration of Rawdon book-plates in Ex Libris Soc. Pub., vol. vii., 10.

Robert Rawdon, citizen and fishmonger of L. Will dated 7 Aug. 1644. £700 I owe my son-in-law Nich. Raynsford by bond of £1000 to be first paid.

D   D

Bevell Rawdon, 3rd son, a merchant at Surinam 1666.	Robert Rawdon, 9th son, godson 1644 of his uncle Robert; died a bachelor in the Canaries.	Elizabeth, 1st dau., bapt. 9 April 1618 at Barking; mar. Edmond Forster, partner of Col. Tho. Rawdon, and a grantee of land in Barbados 1628; Capt. of City Bands 1633. She living 1666.	Martha, 2nd dau., bapt. 19 Dec. 1622 at Barking; mar. Tho. Williams of Layton, co. Essex; a widow 1666.

Katheren my wife shall have ⅓ of my personal estate. My s^d son-in-law N. R. and Eleanor his wife and my s. Wm R. shall have ⅓, and the testators ⅓. I will as following. To my s. W^m £20. To my bro. Marmaduke R. my best cloke and £3 for a ring. Rob. R. my godson, his son, £5 at 21. My cozen Raphe Trattle £3. Cosen Mary Trattle £3 at marriage. My part of the good ship the "Marmaduke" to my 4 grandch^n Rob., Edwd, Marm. and Nich. Raynsford. My grandchild Kathtryne Raynsford £20. Poor of Magnus parish 40s. Poor of Magd. Bermondsey £3. All residue to Katheryne my wife and my said son-in-law N. Raynsford and Ex'ors. To my wife the house on the bancksyde which I purchased of Mr Edwd Gryffen in St Saviour's, Southwark, for her life, then to s^d son-in-law. To my dau. El^r Raynsford those 3 tenements I lately bought of John Pope in Mitcham, co. Surrey. I give that house I bought of Harryson Eatlaffe in Burnham, co. Essex, to my 2 Ex'ors. My brother Marm. and cosen Raphe Trattle to be overseers. Proved 8 Oct. 1647 by Kath. R. the relict and Nich^s Raynford. (204, Fines.)

Martha Molesworth of Hoddesdon, co. Hartford, widow. My 1. husband Pryn's gods. Wm P. of Lincoln's Inn, Esq. I give unto Marmaduke Rowdon son of my Ex'trix £100. To Bevill Rowdon her son £200. Rob. R. her son £200. To Marm. R. s. of Tho. R. £200 at the age of 7. Cozen Anne Forster. Widow Martha R. dau. of my Ex'trix £1000. To the 2 daus. of my grandson Edward (*sic*) Forster of L., march^t, to Eliz. the eldest £150, and Martha 2^d dau. £150, in discharge of all promises bills made unto the s^d Edmond (*sic*) F. To Edmond F. s. of s^d Edmond F. £200. My dau.-in-law Eliz. Lucey my gold ring with 5 diamonds. Martha her dau. a gold chain. To my s^d grandsons Edmond F., Wm Bowyer

482

and Henry Crewe £10 each. All residue to my dau.-in-law Dame Eliz. Rowdon al's Rawdon al's Thorowgood and sole Ex'trix. Tho. Thorowgood, my late dec^d husband and father of the s^d Dame E. R., left me a plentiful estate. I do love her and her children. 19 July 1646. Proved 26 Oct. 1646 by Dame Eliz. Rowdon al's Rawdon al's Thorowgood. (148, Twisse.)

Testator's 3^d husband was Bevile Molesworth, whose will was proved in 1636. (Vivian's "Visitation of Cornwall," i., 327.)

1653-4, Jan. Sr Roger Jaques, Kn^t. Adm'on on the 21st to Dame Mary Jaques, relict of Sr R. J. of the city of York, alderman. fo. 623.

Tho. Rawdon of Hoddesdon, co. Hertford, Esq. Will dated 1 April 1664. All my estate in the Isle of Barbadoes to my six younger children, viz., Thos., Geo., Eliz., Magdalen, Martha and Kath., equally at 21 or day of marriage; to be educated and brought up by their mo:her. To my s. Thos. all suger and sums due to me from my brother Bevill R. which I sent him towards the setling of his plantation in Surrinam. All residue to Magdalen my wife and sole Ex'trix. My trusty friends Sr John Colleton, B^t, and Benj. Sheppard, scriveno^r, overseers, and £10 apeece. In the p. of Wm Rawdon, etc. Proved 25 Sept. 1666 by M. R. the relict. (136, Mico.)

D

Katherine, 3rd dau., bapt. 25 April 1624 at Barking; mar. W^m. Gamble *alias* Bowyer of Laytonstone, Esq. He died 22 Sept. 1658, aged 43. M.I. at Broxbourne. (Cussans, ii., 183.) She living 1668.	Jane, mar. Ralph Trattle of Greenwich.	...., dau., mar. Henry Crewe of Bristol, Surveyor of Customs. He died 4 March 1685, aged 69. M.I. at Broxbourne. (Cussans, ii., 196.)

Marmaduke Raudon of L., merch^t, s. of Lawrence R. late of the city of York, alderman. If I die near York to be buried in Crux church in the chancel where my dear father and mother and most of my family have been buried. If I die at Hodsden to be buried in the chancel of Broxborne church near my cossen Bowyer. To the sons and dau. of Sr Roger Jaques, viz., Roger, Henry, W^m, Robert and Grace, 20s. each. To my aunt the Lady Raudon £10. To Coll. Tho. R., to his son Marmaduke, his dau. Eliz., and to his wife £30, and to his son Marmaduke my emerald ring with the R.'s arms. My cossen Bevill R. my great ring of diamonds with the King's picture in it and one of my Spanish rapers. My cossen Mrs Kath. Bowyer my cup of pure gold and great cup of mother of pearl set in silver and £10. Mrs Eliz. Forster £10. Mrs Jane Crew and her husb^d £20. Mrs Martha Williams £50 and £10. Her son Mr David W. £10. Cossen Allington and his wife £10, and his sister Kate and other brothers £5 apiece. Cossen Mr Wm Bowyer £5. Mr Tho. Boycott and Mr Nath. Fen his brother £5 each. Cossen Wm Rawdon and his wife £20, and to her £100, and each of his sons £50 only. To my godson Lawrence £100, and to each of his daus. £20. Cossen Rapho Trattle and his wife £10 each. Cossen Mrs Mary Fellowes £5. Cossen Mrs Jane Tice £5. Cossens Chr. Hebden, Wm Hebden and Tho. White each a silver tankard with my arms to be engraven thereon, and to every of their children 20s. Cozen Mrs Ann Brice, wife to Mr Fra. B., my ring with 5 diamonds. To the eldest child of Mr John Harrison of Bransbie £5, for the love I had for their uncle my Stuart [*sic* ? steward] Marmaduke Harrison. Cossen Mrs Eliz. Templer my oriental emerald ring. My Lady Hewley, wife unto Sr John Hewley, my great jewel of gold with K. David his picture. To the parish of Crux, York, where I was born, £100, to be imployed in land and penny loaves given every Sunday to the poor. £60 to the citty of York for a gold chain to be worn by the Lady Maioress, and £400 for buying those houses which belonged to M[r] Scott next Allhallows to be pulled down and to widen the pavement and to make a cross or shelter for the market people that sell meal and corn, also a cup of pure gold of £100 with the citty's and my arms engraven on it, also a silver chamber pot of £10 for the L[d] Mayor. To the poor of Bransby and Stersbie where my dear father was born, and parish of Canton where my good mother was born, £5 each, to be disposed by my cossens Hebdens of Stersbie and cosen Barton of Canton. To Mary How, once servant to my sister the Lady Jaques, £5. Towards repairing the chapel in the town of Hodsden £10. Gods. Marmaduke R. s. of Rob. Raudon of York Pinner £10 and £50 at 21. My nephew M[r] W[m] Jaques and M[rs] Margt. Brown £10 each. Cossen Raphe Trattle the Elder my fur coat with 4 doz. pure gold buttons upon it. £100 upon a monument in Broxborne church in that E. window where M[r] Baily lieth buried, which may correspond with the monument of S[r] Rob. Cock on the other side, which I give in memory of my ever honored Unckle S[r] Marmaduke Rawdon; also hard by the great window in the chancel, to correspond with my cossen Bowyer's monument, £20 or £30 in a small monument in memory of me and recording my travels in Holland, Flanders, France and Spain. All residue to my loving cossen Marmaduke R., 2[d] son of S[r] Marmaduke R. of Hodsden, Kn[t], and sole Ex'or.

In London this 19 June 1665. M[r] Hugh Hassall my plain gold ring with the King's picture and £5. Proved 9 Feb. 1668 by M. R. (22, Coke.)

Magdalen Rawden of Hoddesden, co. Hartford, widow. Will dated 3 Nov. 1675. To my dau. Magd. R. £900. My son Geo. R. £700. My son Thos. R., having advanced, I give only £10. My household goods in the house at H. to my son Marm. My brother and sister Crew and sister Price £10 each. My children Marm., Eliz. Sparke and her husb[d] Geo.,* Magd., and to my son Marmaduke's wife £10 each. Magd. dau. of my son Marm. £10. My negro Frances £10. To my dau. Magd. all arrears of rent for my joynture. Whereas I have granted to my son Sparke rents in Hartfordshire of £15 2s. 6d. for £200, this sum to be repaid. To my son Marm. £5 to buy 2 silver trencher plates. My son Geo. R. and my dau. Magd. R. Ex'ors and the residue of personal estate. To be buried in the parish church of Broxborne near my late husb[d]. Proved 2 Dec. 1675 by Geo. R., the son and surviving Ex'or. (130, Dycer.)

Dame Eliz. Rawdon of Hodsdon in the parish of Broxbourne, co. Hertford, widow. To be interred in the parish church of Broxbourne. To my grandson Marmaduke R., eldest son of my son Tho. R., dec[d], all my messuages, lands in the parish of S[t] Antholin's within the walls of the city of L., also my messuage the white hinde and the messuage and toft adjoining in the town of Hodsdon, also my copyhold messuage called the upper house in the parish of Waer, co. Hertford, and 5 acres, also my copyhold land and tenem[t] within the manor of Nasingbury, co. Essex. My said houses in S[t] Antholin's was burnt by the late great fire I give £500 towards the rebuilding of them. To Marm. R., my 2[d] son, my messuage in Hodsdon, the Cock with the 2 other decayed tofts adjoining, and 7 acres and 1 acre of meadow lying in Dutch meade, 2 acres called Chadwell meade. To Bevell R., my 3[d] son, my messuages in the parish of S[t] Mary Matfellon al's Whitechappell, co. Midd[x], for his life, and at his death to return to my s[d] grandson Marm. R., and failing him to my grandson Geo. R., 3[d] son of my eldest son Tho., dec[d]. To my dau. Martha William, widow, £600, to be laid out by my dau. Kath. Bowyer in land for an annuity, and at her death to my s[d] grandson Marm. R. To my godson (sic) Tho. R., 2[d] son of my eldest son Tho., dec[d], £50 at 21. Geo. R., the youngest son of my 1st son Tho. R., dec[d], £50 at 21. To each of my sons and daus. £5 for mourning, viz[t], my dau. Magdalen R., son Marm. and Sarah his wife, Eliz. Foster my dau., Henry Crew my son-in-

* His name was Christopher.

484

law and Jane his wife, Martha Williams my dau. Gifts to servants. Poor £10. Forgive debts due from my dau. Martha W. or her husbᵈ Tho. W., decᵈ. I have left in writing several legacies to my sons and daus. not incerted in this will. All residue of lands and goods to my son Bevell R., at present on the plantation of Surenam beyond the seas, and my right in that plantation called Barbados. My sᵈ son and dau. Kath. Bowyer, widow, joynt Ex'ors. 27 Feb. 1666, 19 Chas. 2ᵈ, in the presence of Henry Alington, Wᵐ Bowyear, Wᵐ Turner. Proved 5 March 1668 by K. Bowyer the dau.; power reserved to B. R. (36, Coke.)

Hester Rawdon of Hodsdon, co. Hertford, widow. Will dated 17 Dec. 1712. To be buried in Broxbourne Church. To my s. Marmaduke R. and my dau. Hester R. all my household goods (except all such as were my sister Anne Williamson's which I give my sᵈ dau.). To my s. Marm. all family pictures and £800, but if he die before me the sᵈ sum to my cousins Nich. Corsellis of Layer Marney, co. Essex, Esq., and Marm. Allington of Linc. Inn, Esq., and my sᵈ dau. upon T. to invest with the approbation of my dau. Dorothy R., wife of my sᵈ son for the use of my granddau. Hester R. his dau. and any other dau. To my granddau. Anne Lysons 20 gs. she having a very plentiful est. Of the residue ⅓ to my s. Marm. R., ⅓ to my dau. Hester R., ⅓ to my s. Sam. Bagnall of L., salter, and my dau. Hester R. on trust for my 3 grandchildren Sam. B., Eliz. B., and Hester B. Whereas my sister Anne Williamson, decᵈ, by her will dated 27 Oct. 1709 gave me and my s. Marm. £800 in trust for the use of my dau. Eliz. Bagnall and her children, and my dau. is dead leaving 3 children. No accounts to be demanded for my sᵈ sisters boarding with me. My s. Marm. Rawdon and dau. Hester Rawdon Ex'ors. In the p. of Nic. Corsellis, Tho. Bagnall. Proved 26 Sept. 1719 by both Ex'ors (169, Browning).

Marmaduke Rawdon, late of Hodesdon in the p. of Broxborne, co. Herts, now of Kentish-Town, p. of Pancrass, co. Middx., Esq. Will dated 17 Oct. 1750. To be buried in the Church of B. where my Father and Mother were laid. To my dau. Esther, wife of Joseph Keeling of Barking, co. Essex, Esq., all my lands in the I. of Barbadoes or Eng. and all moneys yet in arrear for the purchase of one plⁿ in B'oes called Fisher's Pond, which was sold by my grandf. Tho. R. shortly before his death, and for which a judgment was obtained as by my box of writings relating to the est, and to one other called Rawdon's Rents or plⁿ, which last I have conveyed to my son-in-law Joseph K. and Esther his wife my dau., to be delivered to her also the picture of my Father and grandf. To my wife Rebecca plate and arrears of rent and one annuity from the Exchequer, all furn. and personal est. My son-in-law Joseph K. and my wife Ex'ors. Proved 4 Nov. 1752 by Joseph K.; power reserved to Rebecca R., the relict (286, Bettesworth).

John Keeling of the parish of St. James, Clerkenwell,* co. Middx., brewer. Will dated 21 March 1753. To be interred in my family vault in Leigh, co. Stafford. Mʳ Jas. Reynolds late of Sᵗ Jas., C., butcher, £100. My brother Joseph K., Esq., £250. Bro.-in-l. Tho. Hughes £100. My wife Ann £100 and ½ my furniture. All residue of personal estate in trust to pay £200 a year to her and to carry on the business of brewing until my son John K. be 21, then all to him, if he die ½ to my brother Joseph and ½ for my wife. All real estate to son John and in default to my sᵈ brother.
Codicil. Cousin Mary wife of Rᵈ Prerst £50. 9 Jan. 1755. On 28 May 1759 appoints Jos. K. of Sᵗ Jas., C., Esq. Proved 30 May 1759 by Ann K., wid., etc. (174, Arran.)

Hester the now wife of Joseph Keeling of Fingringhoe, co. Essex, Esq., late Hester Rawdon, spr. Will dated 21 Aug. 1756. All my real estate in England

---

* Testator, 2nd son of John and Mary Keeling, was bapt. 25 May 1721.

or elsewhere to my loving husband Joseph Keeling and his heirs absolutely, also all personal estate and sole Ex'or. Proved 20 Jan. 1757 by J. K. (18, Herring.)

John Slany of the city of Norwich, Esq. Will dated 3 Sept. 1787. To Trustees £3000 bank stock, £1600 3 per cent. bank annuities, £54 per ann. bank long annuities, £100 short annuities and £500 5 per cent. annuities to pay the interest to my s^d sister Alice Keeling for her life, and at her death the interest of ¼ for her husb^d Joseph K. for his life.

Codicil. 4 Oct. 1790. Plate, linen, china and glass to my s^d sister.

Proved 30 Aug. 1791. (405, Bevor.)

No Slanys are named, only nieces Kath. Hunt and Mary Cooke.

Joseph Keeling of Westbury House in the parish of Barking, co. Essex. Will dated 6 Jan. 1792. Infirm of body. To my wife Alice all my farms and lands in Great Britain, bank stock and consols, plate, furniture, horses, chariot for her life, to be disposed of by her by will to such of her ch^n as she thinks proper. My snuff box and gold watch to my dau. Mary Tooke. The new gold watch to my dear son Capt. John K. with the seal of arms of K., Rawdon and Slaney. Whereas my son has been most cruelly treated and neglected by his late uncle John Slaney, Esq., who has taken no notice of him in his will, and I am entitled to a moiety of a mortgage of £1000 from Lord Cahir of Irel^d, the interest being payable to my wife and at her death to go to her son and dau., and my son having disposed of the post obit to Mr Playters for £100, w^h I purchased, I bequeath it to him. I give him my claim on my lands in the parish of St Michael, I. of B'oes, conveyed to me by my late F.-in-l. Marm. Rawdon, Esq., for which I have expended large sums endeavouring the recovery thereof without effect, but have recovered part which I have called Rawdon Place, consisting of 3 houses and lands adjoining the fort called Greenwill fort to the Leeward of Bridge Town. My wife Alice sole Ex'trix. If I die in Barking to be interred in that part of the ancient symmetry (*sic*) w^h I have ordered to be enclosed and set apart as a burial place for myself and family next the chy^d of Barking, the wall of w^h I shall break a gateway fronting the N. door. If I die at Buxton or near Leigh in Staffordshire, in w^h chy^d I have a family vault, to be interred there with my ancestors.

1 Aug. 1792. *Codicil.* Whereas I have £500 stock of the Bank of England worth £1000, my wife to have it, but sh^d my son succeed in his application for the Harwich packet, the stock to be applied towards fitting that out and having £1300 or £1400 at my bankers, let that be applied towards the annuities of my nephew John Keeling and his wife, and the copyhold malthouses in the manor of Cannonbury, Kingston, may be sold.

Proved 20 Aug. 1792 by Alice K., wid., the relict. (436, Fountain.)

WILLIAM REECE OF ST. THOMAS, BARBADOS, AND SOME OF HIS DESCENDANTS.

1. **WILLIAM REECE** (1) of St. Thomas, Barbados, is thought to nave been born in England, but there were several well-established families in that parish in the Seventeenth and early Eighteenth centuries, and it is probable that he was a descendant of one of those families. He married Sarah [? Skinner] but there is no record of the marriage, nor does the baptism of their first child William (2) appear. William's (1) will is dated 1 April 1795 in which all his children are named. Will was proved Barbados 10 Feb. 1806 There is no record of his burial and no obituary notice in newspapers. On 15 February 1806 his widow Sarah and her children William (2), Robert, Mary, and Judith, joined in a deed to sell to her son Abraham the life estate of Sarah for £30 to be paid annually, and the estate in remainder of the children for £400. in 14 acres of land in St. Thomas, bounding on lands of Charles Padmore, William Cleland Moore, and the estate of Abel Hinds deceased, together with the dwellinghouse. The deed states that the parties to the deed were the children of William (1) surviving him. Sarah, his widow, went in later years to reside at Gibbons plantation which had been acquired by her son William (2). She was injured in the hurricane of 1831 and died on March 27, 1832, aged 86 years. Their children were :

    2.   i.   William (2)
    3.   ii.   Robert, b. 19 July 1780.
    4. iii.   Abraham.
         iv.   Isaac, b. 26 Jan. 1783.
          v.   Mary, twin sister of Isaac.
         vi.   Judith. b. 7 Oct. 1787.
        vii.   Elizabeth, bap. 11 Apr. 1792 ? d. 29 May 1802.
       viii.   Charlotte, bap. 21 Apr. 1794, d. 5 Oct. 1804.

2. **WILLIAM** (2 (*William* (1)) married Elizabeth Bascom on 23 Dec. 1802, and he seems to have acquired with her a considerable number of slaves and land in St. John. He owned Pilgrim and Gibbons plantations in Christ Church, and he gave the land on which Providence Chapel stands, besides assisting in erecting the building. He fell ill, and went to England in 1835, where he remained until November 1835. He sailed from Liverpool 11 Nov. 1835, but died on the voyage. By his will dated 27 April 1835, his widow was to have half the profits of his plantation Pilgrim Place during her life. The Wesleyan Society also benefitted considerably — the remainder of his property went to his brother Robert and sisters Mary and Judith—the shares of the sisters to devolve on his nephews and nieces children of his brother Abraham. All his slaves on his two plantations were to have half-an-acre of land during their lifetime. He died s.p. His will

was proved Barbados Reg. 28 Dec. 1835. His widow Elizabeth died at Pilgrim Place 14 Dec. 1853 aged 74 years.

3. ROBERT (2), *(William* (1) *)* was born 19 July 1780 in St. Thomas. He married Sarah Knight on 26 September 1805. He owned Hope, Bannatyne and Egerton plantations. He went to reside in England at 13 St. Mark's Crescent, Regents Park, but was in Barbados again late in 1853. He was then blind, and was living at The Hope with the Manager Mr. Gall. His will, dated 2 May 1853, was made in England. He gave his wife Sarah half the profits of The Hope for her life. His daughter Elizabeth, wife of Robert Haynes of Thimbley Lodge, Yorks, was to have £3000 charged on Egerton plantation. The rest of his estate was for his son Robert. He died in England in 1858. His widow Sarah died at Bannatyne aged 84 years on 24 November 1868.

Their children were :

    5. i. Robert (3) b. 9 July 1807
        ii. Elizabeth b. 18 March 1809, married Robert Haynes Junior on 26 Sept. 1825, and had issue.
       iii. James b. 5 Oct. 1811.

4. ABRAHAM (2), *(William* (1) *)* Married Sarah Elizabeth Bayley daughter of Elijah Bayley, 2 Jan. 1802. Resided in St. Thomas or St. James and was murdered on his way home 21 July 1816. Buried St. Thomas. The story is that he had borrowed a white mare from one Allamby, a neighbour, to visit his brothers in Christ Church. The negroes hated Allamby and were lying in wait for him in a gully somewhere in St. Thomas, which is still called Reece's gully. In the dark the negroes mistook Mr. Reece for Allamby and stoned him when he entered the gully. His body was left under a rock until found later. His widow continued to live on the small plantation in St. James for a few years and leased the land, but in 1821 she moved with her family to Goodland in Christ Church. She died in July 1865.

Their children were:—

      i. *Mary Elizabeth* (3) b. 31 May 1803, bap. 8 June 1803. Her father was then described as Manager of Buttals plantation. She was killed in 1831 storm at Gibbons plantation, Christ Church where she lived with her grandmother and aunt.
      ii. *Charlotte*, bap. 12 Aug. 1805. Married Rev. John Philp 12 March 1834. He was a Wesleyan Minister. They went to live in England, and he was Minister at Carmarthen. d. 91 years old s.p. buried Bristol Cemetery.
  6. iii. *William James*, bap. 23 Nov. 1807.
      iv. *Sarah Frances*, bap. 6 Mar. 1810 d. unmarried in 1897 at Ellerton, St. George, and buried in Christ Church.

6 (a)   v.   *Judith*, bap. 13 Sept. 1812, married John William Estwick Gall 16 May 1829.

    7. vi.   *Abraham*, b. 14 Sept. 1814.

    8. vii. *Isaac*, b. 27 Jan. 1817, posthumous.

    5. ROBERT [3] (*Robert* [2] *William* [1]) b. 9 July 1807 Barrister-at-law Inner Temple. Provost Marshal of Barbados. He lived at Bannatyne and owned that plantation and The Hope. Married first Caroline Ann Spellen on 19 July 1834, who died 13th Oct. 1839, 23 years old; and secondly Louisa Kirkman, in England, who survived him. She was a daughter of the Piano Manufacturer. Robert [3] died in England in 1874. He lived at No. 33, Lansdown Crescent, Nottinghill. His will dated 27 Jan. 1872. Proved 18 Jan. 1875. He was the Author of a handbook on Agriculture in Barbados entitled "Hints to Young Barbados Planters". Published in 1857 by Israel Bowen, Barbados.

Children of Robert Reece [3] by his first wife, born in Barbados were:

    i.   *Elizabeth Ann* [4] bap. 17 July 1835. Married William Thomas Henry Effingham at Barbados 10 Feb. 1853.

    ii. *Sarah Isabella* bap. 29 April 1836.

    iii. *Robert*, b. 2 May 1838 The Dramatist. He matriculated at Balliol College 28 Jan. 1857, B.A. 1860, M.A. 1864. Student Inner Temple 1860 not called. Short time Medical Student; 1861-63 Extra Clerk in office of Ecc. Commissioners; 1864-68, Extra Clerk Emigration Commissioners. Meanwhile wrote comic pieces for the Stage with fair success. See D.N.B. Died 10 Cantlowes Road, Camden Square, London, on 8 July 1891. Buried Kensal Green. He married and had issue.

Children of Robert Reece [3], by his second marriage, born in England :

    i.   *Henry* [4]

    ii. *Elizabeth*—married Lyttelton Horton Leslie s. of the Countess of Rothes.

    6. WILLIAM JAMES [3] (*Abraham* [2] *William* [1]) bap. 23 Nov. 1807. He lived at Wilcox Plantation married Elizabeth Tinling, d. of Isaac John Tinling, Judge of the Assistant Court of Appeal, 10 Sept. 1833. She was killed at Windsor Station, Barbados, in getting out of the train at night.

Their children were :

    i.   *William James* [4] bap. 15 Oct. 1835.

    ii. *Mary Elizabeth* bap. 1837 d. 1884.

    iii. *Isaac John* bap. 21 Mar. 1840. Married Jessie Georgina Gorringe 5 May 1869 and had issue 4 sons and three daughters.

    iv. *Robert* b. 27 Oct. 1847 d. 3 Apr. 1907. Married Josephine Evelyn—Issue :

i. Evelyn Adelaide
ii. Mary Louise—Married Arnold Reece and has issue 3 sons and 3 daughters
iii. Edward Bertram—Married and has issue 1 daughter
iv. Annie Gertrude—(died)
v. Florence May
vi. Robert Cecil—Married and has issue 2 sons and 1 daughter
vii. Minnie Grey
viii. Gracie Lee
ix. Isabel—(died)
v. *Abraham Arnold* b.
Married Kate Mapp. Issue :
i. *Arnold* married Louise Reece his cousin and has issue
ii. *Kate* married William Drayton and has issue 2 sons.
iii. *Lewis* married Helena (Minnie) Crouch). No issue
iv. *Nellie* married Wakeford Elliott. No issue.
vi. *Frederick St. Aubyn.* Married first Evelina Rowena Zelina Springer
i. Eardley Reece. Married Julia Swindell; no issue. He was drowned during the Great War when the vessel in which he was travelling from Africa to England was sunk by the enemy.
ii. Edith Reece. Married John Crandall. No issue.
F. A. Reece's first wife died and he married secondly Nellie Bourne and had issue a boy who died in infancy.
vii. *Charlotte Philp,* b. 25 Dec. 1841. Married Isaac Bruce Gall. Issue.
i. *Isaac Bruce Gall*—Married.
ii. *Reece Gall*—Married. Died.
iii. *Lottie Gall*—Married Coleridge Seale. No issue.
iv. *Edward Gall*—Married Edith Legall. Died.
v. *Isaac Gall*—Married Maud Legall. No issue.
vi. *Olive Gall*

7. ABRAHAM [3], (*Abraham* [2], *William* [1]), bap. 14 Sept. 1814. Born in St. James, Barbados. Went to reside with his mother and sisters at Goodland, Christ Church, sent to Grammar School in Bridgetown 1828. The house in which he was staying in Town was blown down in 1831 storm. In 1834 was Medical Student. Entered Codrington College 1st Term 1835. In long vacation 1837 went to England returning in October. Passed final Testamur. Ordained deacon by Bishop Coleridge 1838 Jan. 6, Epiphany, at St. Michael's Cathedral. Licensed Curate Holy Innocents, St. Thomas, before the Chapel was completed. At end of 1838 removed to St. Bartholomew. Married Elizabeth Bynoe Evelyn, daughter of Capt. George James Evelyn, R.N., 3 April 1838. Built a house near St. Bartholomew. In 1839 Festival of St. Philip and St. John admitted to Priesthood. In 1840 health failing, Bishop granted him 6 months' leave to go to England.

Left Barbados 25 April. During the voyage his second child was born 11 May. Landed Liverpool 21 May. Left England 15 September and reached Barbados Oct. 1840. In 1842 his first child died of fever after a few days' illness (d. 17 Sept.) In 1845 he went to Worthing, Christ Church, and his third child born there on 27 Dec. 1845 (Abraham Daniel). Appointed to District of St. Matthias, including St. Lawrence on 20 June 1848. St. Matthias not completed until end Oct. 1848. Rectory of Christ Church, April 1853, to act for Rev. C. C. Gill who had left for England, but retired April 1854. Abraham Reece left for England and arrived in May 1854, returning to Barbados 1 Aug. 1855. On the voyage to England the youngest child died aged 6 months, off Banks of Newfoundland. 30 April 1855 left London by ship *Candidate* Capt. Pearce. Arrived 15 May 1855. Went back to St. Matthias. Established Hastings Grammar School—Master Mr. Talkeld, who died of fever, succeeded by Mr. Williams of Wadham College, Oxford, who was drowned while bathing near School. Rev. T. Greenidge was appointed to succeed him. School closed 1857. June 1857 went to England on leave—family and two nieces with him. Left England by S.S. *Atrato* 1858 Sept. 17 accompanied by his brother and his wife, ten in party. Arrived Barbados 6 Oct. 1858. Appointed Rector of Christ Church 1859 on death of Rev. C. C. Gill. Left Barbados 2 June 1868 and arrived in England 17 June accompanied by wife, daughter Janette, nephew T. B. Evelyn, Jr. Visited his daughter Mrs. Phillips. Two sons at Cambridge. Wife died at Kibworth, Leicestershire, 9 July 1868. Buried parish church. Tombstone erected. Left England 2 April 1869, arrived and resignea Rectorship and left for England Aug. 9, 1869. He married Ellen Wakeman in England in 1871, by whom he had issue a daughter. Rev. Abraham Reece died in England 1905 Dec. 12 aged 91.

Children by first wife :

i.   Abraham b.   d. 17 Sept. 1842 of fever.

ii.   b. 11 May 1840.

iii.   Abraham Daniel [4] b. 27 Dec. 1845 M. A. St. John's College, Cambridge. Married Elizabeth Ann Lutley. He was Clerk in Holy Orders, Vicar of West Hatch, Somerset d. s.p. in 1904. His widow Elizabeth Ann Reece died in February 1940 at the age of 95.

iv.   James Ebenezer b. 5 Mar. 1847. M. A., St. John's College, Cambridge. Master of Trent College, England, 6 years. Vicar of St. Bartholomew for 3 years; of St. Luke's for 2 years. Inspector of Schools from 1885 to 1911. Canon of St. Michael's Cathedral. Secretary to Bishop Parry in 1872. Chaplain to Bishops Bree, Swaby, Berkeley and Bentley. Married Charlotte Ann Evelyn 1872. No issue. Died 3rd Dec. 1931 at the age of 84 while attending evening service at St. David's Church while kneeling before the Communion Table after having pronounced the final words of the blessing.

7(a) v. Frances Elizabeth Ann—Married Rev. Abel Phillips, Missionary in Rio Pongo, Vicar of Trinity Yeovil. Died in 1900. Left issue.

7(b) vi. Sarah Janette b. 4 Dec. 1849, married Rev. E. C. Lutley. She died in 1886. Rev. E. C. Lutley died February 1940. Aged 92 years.

vii. ....died aged 6 months in 1854.

7(a) Frances Elizabeth Ann (4) (*Abraham* (3), *Abraham* (2), *William* (1)) married Rev. Abel Phillips.

Issue i. Theodore Evelyn Reece Phillips, M.A., F.R.A.S., F.R.Met. Soc., Sec. Roy. Ast. Soc. 1919-1926. President 1927-28. Rector of Headley since 1906. b. 28 March 1868. Married 1906 M. A. Kynaston, Croydon. Educated Yeovil Grammar School, St. Edmund Hall, Oxford. Ord. 1891. (See Who's Who). Has issue one son, John Phillips, who is Vicar of Seend in Wiltshire.

ii. Ernest Augustus Phillips. Unmarried. Vicar of a church in Croydon.

iii. Alice Elizabeth Annie Phillips, married Rev. Edgar A. Luff and has issue (1) Cyril, (2) Evelyn, (3) Gytha.

iv. Ethel Margaret Phillips. Unmarried.

v. Arthur Herbert Edmund Phillips. Married Louisa Baldwin; issue two sons.

7(b) Sarah Janette (1), (*Abraham* (3), *Abraham* (2), *William* (1)) maried Rev. E. C. Lutley.

Issue i. Evelyn Janette Lutley. Died 1938.

ii. Muriel Lutley. Unmarried.

iii. Daisy Lutley. Married Dr. Ernest Travers-Stubbs. No issue.

iv. Edward J. R. Lutley. Married Eleanora Dundas-Bruce and has issue a daughter, Rosemary.

v. Cyril Lutley, married Emily Crewes; issue one son, one daughter

vi. Harold E. B. Lutley. Married Daisy Slater and has issue two sons.

8. ISAAC (3) (*Abraham* (2), *William* (1)) b. 27 Jan. 1817. Married Elizabeth Mary Greenidge 4 April 1837. Owned Egerton, Pilgrim and Gibbons plantations. Will dated 17 May 1884. Proved 14 Mar. 1890. He built the Middle School on Pilgrim Place.

Issue i. Elizabeth Frances b. 30 Dec. 1840.

ii. Isaac Richard b. 6 Feb. 1847. Married Marion Hollinsed 11 Mar. 1873. Issue :

(i) Cyril.

(ii) Louisa. Married Philip Bovell and has issue.

(iii) Reece Hollinsed. Married.

iii. William, b. Clerk in Holy Orders. Married Maud Humphrey and has issue. Died.

iv. Abraham Llewellyn, b.   **Dr. of Medicine.**
Married a lady of French origin, resided in America,
and had issue, one son. Died.

v. Judith, b.   Married Jas. H. Inniss. No issue.

vi. John.

vii. Charles, b.   Married Helen Hollinsed, (she
was killed in Jamaica Earthquake) and had issue 4
children.

viii. Sarah, b.   Married Harry O'Brien. No
issue. Died.

9. **WILLIAM JAMES** (4) (*William James* (3), *Abraham* (2),
William (1)). Married first Elizabeth Gall. Issue :

i. William James Reece. Married Ida Gall and had
issue a son, Beresford St. Aubyn Reece.

ii. Harry Reece. Died.

iii. Estwick Reece.

iv. Ernest Reece.

v. Mary Elizabeth Reece. Married Arnold Outram :
Issue 2 daughters, 3 sons.

vi. Eustace.

vii. Maud.

viii. Amy.   Married Coleridge Gill;
Issue :

(i) *Mabel Gill,* married Elliott Winter.

(ii) *Helen,* married Charles Armstrong.

(iii) *Walter,* married Grace Crick.

William James Reece married secondly Elizabeth Greenidge.
Issue :

i. Eustace Reece.

ii. Isobel Reece, married Stanley Hawkins and has
issue: 1 son, 2 daughters.

iii. Douglas Reece, married Eva Rock and has one
daughter Dorothy.

iv. Nigel Reece, married first Nellie Rock and has issue :
5 daughters and one son. She died and he
married secondly Ethel Rock. No issue of the
second marriage.

WILLIAM REECE OF ST. THOMAS AND SOME OF
HIS DESCENDANTS.

Rev. Canon J. C. Wippell, D.D., Principal of Codrington College writes :

"May I presume to suggest an addition to your interesting article on the Reece family?

At the bottom of page 121, (Vol. VII, May 1940; No. 3)[*] you mention 'William (*Isaac* (3), *Abraham* (2), *William* (1)) Clerk in Holy Orders, has issue.' It should be recorded that one of his sons, Humphrey Stanley Reece, born 1892, theological student at Codrington College 1911-1915, left Barbados to serve in the Great War early in 1915. Became lieutenant in the Gordon Highlanders. Won the Military Cross March 1916 'for conspicuous gallantry during operations when leading the attack. When his company commander was killed he took charge and drove off an enemy counter attack. He came back over the open frequently to report to "Battalion Head Quarters". Died of wounds April 2, 1916'.

---

[*] Page 492, this volume.

THE KINDRED OF BEZSIN KING REECE (1765—1838) OF ST. MICHAEL, BARBADOS.

By MAJOR H. M. REECE

A descendant of Bezsin King Reece, now living in England, was told forty and more years ago by his great-aunt who had been born at Merton Lodge, Collymore Rock, St. Michael, Barbados, that he was descended from an early settler (1627) of this island.

The Barbados records of the first two hundred years show one hundred marriages and one hundred and fifty baptisms of persons recorded under the surname REECE. Of these, two each belong to the 17th and sixty marriages and one hundred and twenty baptisms to the 18th century. Over this period extracts from forty wills are available. A study of these records shows they are not complete. Research is further complicated by the popularity of such names as William, John, Thomas, Margaret, Mary, and Elizabeth. They married young and had large families but, unblessed as they were by modern medical knowledge, many died young and few lived to see their children grow to manhood.

One is left with a deep impression of their courage and the faith they had in the future.

It is known that none of Bezsin King Reece's family in the male line lives in Barbados today. There are, however, members of another family of Reece living in the Island whose pedigree is given in the *Journal of the Barbados Museum and Historical Society,* Volume VII, May 1940, page 116.*

The genealogical tree of the kindred of Bezsin King Reece (1765—1838) so far as the records disclose, is set out in the following paragraphs. It can be traced in the records to William Reece of the Parish of St. James, who had a family of eight children, whose baptisms are entered in the Church records of that Parish between the years 1712 and 1731.

In the Memoirs of an Early Settler of Barbados (Royal Empire Society Library) one Thomas is said to have set up business as a carpenter and builder. He is thought to have also built boats. He may have been of the kindred of an early 18th century fisherman on the River Usk in Monmouthshire, who by his substance more probably owned a fishing fleet and whose family came from Western Herefordshire. (Bradney's *History of Monmouthshire*).

It is likely that William Reece was the scion of one or other of the families already established in the Island in the 17th century such as that of Bartholomew Reece (d.1685) who owned Chalky Mount Plantation of some 250 acres in St. Andrew Parish and sixty negro slaves, who was succeeded by his grandchildren; or perhaps that of Lawrence Reece, planter of John's Parish who left five young children when he died in 1684.

In the absence of direct evidence of any such relationship it is proper to commence the pedigree from—

1. WILLIAM REECE of St. James, whose wife, Christian, (surname unknown) had eight children—
    i. *JOHN,* b. 28 April 1712, married Mary Tyldesley 1737 and had children—
        (1) *Mabel,* bap. 24 Jan. 1739, and
        (2) *Mary,* who m. John Arthur 1757.
    ii. *THOMAS,* b. 27 Mar. 1714, married Hannah Tyldesley 1737, and had children—
        (1) *Edward,* b. 1744; married Catherine Wharton 1774; children, John, b. 1777, and Hannah, b. 1780,

---

*Page 487, this volume.

(2) *Henry*, b. 1745, married Elizabeth Morris, 1785
(3) *Richard*, b. 1749, married Isabella Leach 1794.
iii. *ELIZABETH*, b. 1716, married Jonathan Russell 1737.
iv. *MARY*, b. 1718.
v. *WILLIAM*, b. 28 Oct. 1722.
    These five children were all baptised at St. James Church on 29 Oct. 1722.
vi. *RICHARD*, b. 1723; alive 1756.
2. vii. *WILLIAM*, b. 23 Nov. 1725.
    Richard and William baptised together at St. James, in 1727.
viii. *ANN*, b. 25 Oct. 1731, baptised at St. James Church 28 Oct. 1731; m. James Barrow 17 Aug. 1751.
2. WILLIAM[2] (William[1]) of the parish of St. Thomas, b. 23 November 1725; married Mrs. Mary Harper 22 Oct. 1748.
On 26 Dec. 1767 he was in the Island of Antigua and appointed William Barrow his attorney in Barbados. It is thought that he and the Barrows were concerned in West Indian inter-island commerce. His son, Bezsin King, later m. Sarah Barrow.

    Children of William.[2]
i. *John Harper*, bap. 15 Nov. 1753; m. Margaret Branch 24 Aug. 1776. A daughter, Mary Harper. b. 24 Sept. 1779, m. John James. 30 July, 1814.
ii. *William Downes*, bap. 4 Oct. 1755; m. Margaret Mounter 24 June, 1780. Their daughter, *Margaret Downes*, m. Edward Brace Terrill, junior, 17 Dec. 1809.
iii. *Jonathan*, m. Ann Wilfe, 20 April 1781. A son *Jonathan James*, bap. 29 Jan. 1786, d. in infancy.
iv. *Margaret*, m. John Gaskin 22 Apl. 1773. Her children were (1) *Mary*, (2) *Margaret*, and (3) *Thomasin* who married Edward Brace Terrill, senior.
3. v. *Bezsin King*, b. 1765. Jonathan, Margaret and he were probably born in Antigua. The name *Bezsin* is said to be derived from the Welsh word for a shoal (of water). His name being taken from one of a line of shoal-draught ships sailing between Islands of the West Indies. The name implies a "Sandpiper"; a wader bird who frequents shallow coastal waters.

The Will of William[2] (date indistinct) was made in 1769 and was proved 16 Feb. 1769. He directed his executors to sell the plantation of 98 acres which he had bought from his father's executors, together with the buildings and utensils, 29 negroes, 18 head of cattle and 4 horses. His wife, Mary, to have his horse *Welch* to draw her chair, and one-fourth part of all his monies after the sale, besides the use of his house and land and six slaves for her lifetime. His daughter to have eleven slaves and their issue.

His son, John Harper, at 21 to have his blacksmith's shop and three skilled slaves. His sons, William, Jonathan and Bezsin, to have a negro slave each and £100 at 21 and an equal division of the residue at their mother's death.

His widow, Mary Reece, made her will 14 April 1784, and the same was proved on 14 May. Her children and grand-children named in her Will are—her daughter Margaret Gaskin and grand-daughters Mary Gaskin, Thomasin Gaskin, Margaret Harper Gaskin, and Margaret Downes Reece. Her sons, Bezsin King, John Harper and his wife Margaret, and William Downes, are all named, but her son Jonathan and his wife Ann are not mentioned.

3.   BEZSIN KING[3] (*William*[2], *William*[1]) Merchant of St. Michael; m. Sarah Barrow 27 Dec. 1794.
  Children of Bezsin King and Sarah Reece,
    i.   *John*, b. 27 Aug. 1795, bap. at St. Michael, 25 Sep. 1795. A power of attorney dated at Barbados 27 Apl. 1832 shows that he intended shortly to visit the United States. Another power indicated that he was in Barbados on 10 April 1839 and was about to leave for England. By the Will of his father he had a legacy of £5000, and it is believed that he died in Kensington, London, without issue.
4. ii.   *Bezsin*[4] (*Bezsin King*[3] *William*[2] *William*[1]). b. 23 Aug. 1796.
   iii.   *James* b. 4 Mar. 1799, died in infancy.
  Bezsin King[3] Reece carried on business as a merchant in Bridgetown for forty years. He was one of the town's most prominent citizens and at his death in 1838 he was the oldest surviving merchant in the town. A few weeks before his death he was present at the laying of the foundation stone of St. Barnabas School which was to be built on two acres of land adjoining Pickerings estate (later merged in the Pine plantation) and given by him for the purpose. He was buried in St. Michael's Parish Church and Cathedral in Bridgetown where there is a mural tablet in the nave to his memory and also a stone marking his grave in the western porch.
  The inscription on the mural tablet reads:—
  In the western porch of this Cathedral/are deposited the remains of/BEZSIN KING REECE/Who departed this life on the 23rd day of September 1838/after a short illness age 73 years. (13 lines follows: erected by his grandchildren.)
  In the western porch. ledger: Here lie the remains of/BEZSIN KING REECE/ who departed this life on the/23rd day of September 1838 aged 73 years.
  By his will, proved 3 Oct. 1838, he gave to his son John £5,000; to the five children of his son Bezsin £500 each; to three daughters of his sister, Margaret Gaskin, £100 each; and the residue to his son, Bezsin. His faithful female slaves Mary Ellen, Elizabeth and Diana to be bona fide free subjects after his executors receive compensation money from the British Government and these slaves to be paid immediately the proportion of the compensation money awarded for each.
4. BEZSIN[4] (*Bezsin King*,[3] *William*,[2] *William*[1].) b. 23 Aug. 1796. m. 12 June 1822, Mary Elizabeth Olton, daughter of Michael Olton of Merton Lodge, Collymore Rock, St. Michael, Barbados. Their children were—
    i.   *Mary Bezsin*, b. 1826, d. young.
5. ii.   *John Deane*[5], b. 1828.
   iii.   *Sarah*, bap. 28 Nov. 1829. d. young.
   iv.   *Bezsin King*, bap. 2. Dec. 1830, d. 3 May 1831.
    v.   *Elizabeth*, b. 28 Dec. 1831. m. Lieut. Col. Furlonge, No issue. She died at Bath, 23 Feb. 1914.
   vi.   *Margaret*, bap. 14 Jan. 1833. d. 21 Jan. 1834.
6. vii.   *Bezsin*[5], bap. 10 Apl. 1834.
  viii.   *Elvira* bap. 18 Aug. 1835. m. (1) Dr. Fleming. 4th Dragoon Guards who died, and (2) Richard Murdock, Actor, whom she divorced. She died at Bath 1915 without issue.
   ix..   *Catherine Garrett*, md. John Torrance Haynes of Barbados, Planter. At one time he managed Yorkshire Estate, and he owned Bush Hall plantation.
  Children of John Torrance Haynes and Catharine Garrett Reece—
        (1) *Louise Newton*, md. Gabriel Lafitte, and had issue a son, Cecil Alexander Lafitte.

(2) *Kate Isabella,* md. William Lindsay Harbourne Haynes, issue—
    (a) Lindsay Harold, md. (1) Eileen DaCosta and (2) Annie
    Garret Exley Haynes.
    (b) Kathleen Isme, md. Vernon Smith.
(3) *John Exley,* md. Annie Gaskin Rose, Issue—
    (a) Henry Torrance Exley,
    (b) Annie Garrett Exley,
    (c) Mary Exley,
    (d) Agatha Exley,
(4) *Mary* d. aged 12 years.
(5) *Helen Furlonge,* md. Patrick Norman Hadow, and has issue
    a son Douglas Patrick.
(6) *Earwaker Carrington,* md. first, Elizabeth Reece Beckles and
    had issue a son, Edward John Earwaker Haynes; md. secondly,
    Gertrude Jones who survived him.
(7) *Arthur Felix,* md. Louise Elizabeth Quiller.
(8) *Agatha,* d. aged 4 years.
  x. *Louise* bap. 14 Mar. 1840, m. Arthur Ruddock, blind organist
    of St. Paul's Cathedral. She died without issue, 23 Nov. 1908.

Bezsin[4] owned the 498 acre plantation known as the Pine Estate in St. Michael parish and also the Yorkshire Estate in Christ Church. He had the reputation of being much liked and respected by his slaves on account of his kind treatment and gentle manners. He was delicate in health and visited Bath, England, in 1823 and subsequently a number of times. Finally after the birth of his daughter, Louise, at the Pine in 1840, he moved with his family to 7 Sydney Place, Pulteney St. Bath, a mansion overlooking Sydney Gardens. There he lived in some style with several negro servants.

His Barbadian Estates were managed by Edward Brace Terrill and Henry Dummett. In 1842 he returned to Barbados on business but died at sea on the return voyage, aged 46 years. A tablet to his memory in St. Michael's Cathedral reads—

    To the dear and beloved memory of / Bezsin Reece / who (on his
    voyage to England from this Island / for the benefit of his health / in
    the R.M.S. Packet *DEE*) departed this life the 22nd Septr. 1842 after
    an illness of severe suffering / leaving a widow and eight children.

By his Will, proved 23 Nov. 1842, he left his estate equally between his sons, John Deane and Bezsin, at 21.

He charged the Pine plantation with an annuity to his widow of £500 sterling per annum and £150 per annum for the maintenance of his daughters, Mary, Sarah, and Elizabeth, and with £3000 each at 21. Yorkshire Estate was similarly charged for his daughters Elvira, Catherine and Louise. He appointed his friends Henry Dummett and George Abel Dean as executors. By a codicil to the will he says — "Whereas there are signs that the value of West Indian property may deteriorate . . . I value my plantations at £50,000 cy. and same to be appraised at my death and if the appraised value thereof is less than that sum, then the legacies to my daughters are to abate in proportion that such appraised value bears to £50,000. His executors were empowered to sell his estates, houses and stores in Bridgetown.

His widow, Mary Elizabeth married Henry Dummett 31 August 1844 at St. Alphege, Kent, and she died at Bath in 1894.

i5. JOHN DEANE[5] (*Bezsin*[4], *Bezsin King*[3], *William*[2], *William*[1].) b. 1828. He was 14 years of age when his father died. In early manhood he returned to Barbados where it is apparent that he had no livelihood in the depressed state of the West Indian sugar industry. On 29 Dec. 1848 he was appointed Ensign in the 2nd. West India Regiment. At Jamaica, having attained the age of 21, he appointed John Heyes of Barbados his attorney to call for accounts from his father's executors of his inheritance. The Pine Estate had been sold about 1845; a few years before property reached its lowest value. His mother and sisters continued to live at 7 Sydney Place in style and each sister received her £3000 at the age of 21 or marriage.

His brother, Bezsin[5], died in 1864 and his widow and her daughter had to be provided for; so that about this time the remaining interests in Barbados were sold. His mother moved to a small house in Daniel Street, Bath, in 1867. In all he received less than one-tenth of his father's estimate of the value of his property.

In 1868 he was on leave from West Africa and on 9th February he married Cecelia Ann Newman, daughter of Dr. George Newman, 17, Queen's Square, Bath. He had served in Jamaica with her brother Arthur, 2nd West India Regiment; and with her brother, Humphrey, 6th Regiment of Foot, who as an Ensign of 19 years, had been killed there in 1864. His regiment presented Bath Abbey with a stained glass window in his memory.

In 1871, he returned to command at Cape Coast Castle: he was taken ill and died at Sierra Leone on 2 April 1871, aged 43 years.

His record of service was—Appointed Ensign 2nd West India Regt. 29 Decr. 1848; promoted Lieutenant 28 Aug. 1849; Captain 28 Jan. 1853; Major by Brevet 9 Feb. 1855; Major 13 Aug. 1868; Lieutenant-Colonel 19 March 1871.

He had two sons—

    7.   i.   *Bezsin King*[6], born 10 Dec. 1869.

    8.   ii.   *John Deane*[6], born 12 Oct. 1871.

6.   BEZSIN[5], (*Bezsin*[4], *Bezsin King*[3], *William*[2], *William*[1]).

He was baptised 10 April 1834 and was eight years of age when his father died. By the time he came to age the Pine Estate and the stores in Bridgetown had been sold to provide for his mother and sisters. He and his brother John shared Yorkshire and the Pine House.

He entered the Royal Military College, Sandhurst, in 1852 and was commissioned an Ensign in the 37th (North Hampshire) Regiment of Foot on 3 Sep. 1853. He was stationed in Ceylon and served in India during the Mutiny, receiving the Queen's Medal.

In 1860 he was at Devonport and married Mary Woods. They had two children.

    i.   *Bezsin* who died aged 5 months and

    ii.   *Mary*

He died at Dover, aged thirty, 30 Oct. 1864. By his Will, proved 21 Feb. 1865 he left his interest in Yorkshire and The Pine House to his widow for her life and then to his daughter Mary. She died a spinster in Bath in 1915.

7.   BEZSIN KING[6], born 10 Dec. 1869, m. Ada Louisa Pittman, and had issue—

    i.   *Elvira Bezsin*, Spinster, b. 1 Aug. 1896 who lives at South Stoke, Combe Down, Bath, Somerset.

    ii.   *Wynifrede Bezsin*, widow, b. 26 Oct. 1901, m. Lieut.-Colonel James Radcliffe Cooper, a shipping agent. Their children—surname Cooper—

        (1)   *Richard*, b. 15 Feb. 1933 and

        (2)   *Ursula Bezsin* b. 8 Aug. 1929, m. Owen Rundle, 31 Mar. 1955.

Bezsin King[6] Reece was of delicate health and lived all his life in Bath and owned The Chalet. South Stoke, Combe Down. He died 21 Aug. 1929, aged 50 years and his widow on 4 Feb. 1957, aged 84 years. They are buried in the Newman Burial ground in Locksbrook Cemetery, Bath.

8. JOHN DEANE[6] (*John Deane*[5], *Bezsin*[4], *Bezsin King*[3], *William*[2], *William*[1]) b. at Bath, 12 Oct. 1871. Entered Royal Military College, Sandhurst, 1891, and commissioned 2nd Lieutenant Royal Dublin Fusiliers 20 Feb. 1892. He subsequently transferred to Indian Army, Carnatic Light Infantry, and was promoted Lieut. 5 June 1895, Captain 10 June 1901, Major 20 Feb. 1910, Served Mesopotamia 1916/7, Lt. Col. by Brevet 1 Jan. 1918, retired 5 Apl. 1920.

He married Constance Lilian, daughter of Revd. Woolaston Goode, Barrister-at-Law, and Vicar of Paignton, South Devon and grand-daughter of Sir Charles Munro, 9th Bart. of Foulis, on 16 Aug. 1902 at Bath. He died 1 May 1949 aged 77 years and his widow 10 Mar. 1951 aged 75 years. They are buried together in the Hawthorn Road Cemetery, Bognor Regis, Sussex.

Their children are—

i. *Humphrey Munro*, b. Kampti, C. P. India, 31 July 1903, Entered Royal Military College 1 Sep. 1921; Commissioned 2nd Lieut. The South Wales Borderers 30 Aug. 1923; Served in India and Aden; 1923—29; Captain 24 Jan. 1934; Seconded Nigeria Regiment Royal West African Frontier Force, 1932—38, Major 30 Aug. 1940; retired 1 June 1948. Married Ethelwynn, daughter of Surgeon Captain A. Lavertine R.N., 14 Nov. 1936. No issue.

ii. *Dorothy Constance Deane*, B. Kampti, C.P. India, 9 Feb. 1905, m. 18 Jan. 1926 at St. Georges, Penang, Thomas Edward Upton, rubber planter, and a member of the Federation and State Council of Malaya, 1948—52. Two daughters—Surname Upton.

   (1) *Rosemary*, b. Malaya, 25 June 1931.

   (2) *Elizabeth*, b. Malaya, 24 June 1941.

iii. *Barbara Deane*, b. Hove, 20 June 1911, m. Robert Kaan Austrian Engineer at Felpham, Sussex, 10 Sep. 1938.

   Two sons—Surname Kaan.

   (1) *Richard* b. Vienna 25 Aug. 1940.

   (2) *Roger*, b. Vienna, 20 Dec. 1942.

iv. *John Deane* b. Bexhill, Sussex 20 Apl. 1916, served with Royal Engineers in Normandy and North West Europe 1944/45. Bachelor.

RESPICE FUTURUM.

QUAKER RECORDS

SETTLE—TAYLOR

Richard Settle, undoubtedly of English birth and parentage, seems to have been resident in Barbados within a decade after the Quaker doctrine had been brought to the island by Mary Fisher and Ann Austin in 1655.

He is numbered among those who suffered punishment at the hands of the authorities for refusing to conform to the laws and regulations of the island of the period. In the year 1669 according to Besse[1] penalties were inflicted on him for not sending his servants into arms; and a marshal of the Regiment and two sergeants invaded his abode and took away 4 shoats[2] of about 60 lbs. each, and two bigger hogs of about 140 lbs. each, all to the value in sugar of 1040 lbs., in execution to satisfy the fines.

Richard Settle died early in the year 1671, leaving a widow, Frances, who had been previously married to—Taylor, by whom she had a son, Robert Taylor. Richard and Frances had a daughter Sarah, who married Thomas Morris. The Taylors were definitely Quakers, but it is uncertain whether Sarah and Thomas Morris followed in the faith.

Settle was the owner of two small plantations, the particulars of which may be traced from the will of his widow, who disposed of the estate under powers given to her by her husband's will which follows.

Barbados. This nineteenth day of the 8th montn called October, 1670, I Richard Settle being very ill and weak in body. To Margery Moulins, [3] wife of Richard Moulins, my wife's kinswoman, 10 acres of land which I bought of Timothy Terrill in St. Andrew's and St. Joseph's parishes whereon she now liveth and one negro now in her possession during her natural life and then to her son Francis Boulton, and if he should die to my daughter, Sarah Morris.

To my brother Peter Settle in England, one hhd. of good muscovado sugar to be shipped to him clear of all charges, only freight and duty in England which he is to pay. To my sister, Judith Settle, one hhd. of the like sugar (on the like terms). To Peter Settle's children £20 each at 21.

To men friends in London £60 stlg. to be disposed of by them as they shall think good upon the account of truth. To men friends in Barbados 3,000 lbs. sugar towards buying and building a meeting house and a piece of land for a burying ground for friends upon the Cliff, [4] either about Pie Corner or any other place near thereto where men and women friends do judge convenient (if they do build a house as aforesaid) the sugar to be paid within three months after the ground is bought and the house begun to be built.

To my cousin, Thomasin Morris, sister to my son-in-law, Thomas Morris, 2,500 lbs. sugar or one negro woman about 15 or 16 years of age to be paid within two years of my decease if she shall be then living in Barbados.

To Alexander Carnes (5) Robert Taylor's son-in-law, 500 lbs. sugar 5 years after my decease, and to his mother Judith Taylor 20/- stlg.

---

1. A Collection of the Sufferings of the People called Quakers, by Joseph Besse (London) 1753. Vol. II. Chap. 6, p. 281.
2. Young pigs.
3. The name is indistinct. It is most likely Mulineux, of Mullineux, a Quaker name. One of the family is named in Robert Taylor's Will, *post*.
4. In St. Philip, which is later referred to in Robert Taylor's Will.
5. The name in indistinct. It may be a corruption of "Cornish" a name which occurs among the witnesses to Robert Taylor's Will, *post*.

To my son-in-law, Thomas Morris, the Rushia leather couch and chairs which he hath in his possession at my house in Bridge Town.

To my daughter, Sarah Morris, all that my house and land wherein they now dwell at the Bridge Towne during her life, and after her decease to her children, only that end of the said house which is next to M[oisers [6] the Jew which I except for my loving wife during her natural life to make use of, and after her decease to the said Sarah and her children. My wife, Frances Settle, to be sole executrix, and I give my whole estate to her during her life and then to be at her disposal to give it to whom she pleases if she be capable of making a will, otherwise all my estate to my daughter, Sarah Morris, during her life, and then to her children. To my grandchild, Frances Morris, my daughter Morris's eldest daughter, £20 stlg. to be laid out in plate 5 years after my decease and her name to be engraved on the plate.

I appoint my loving friends, John Holder, senior, and Thomas Foster and my son-in-law, Thomas Morris and Robert Taylor to be overseers and £5 to each of them.

Sd. Richard Settle. Wts: John Holder, jun., Henry Baismore. Proved 14 March 1671,

The widow Settle is named in a list of Barbados women Quakeresses in 1677 preserved in London at Friends Reference Library [7]. She was a member of the Spring Meeting which was held at Porey Spring, St. Thomas.

Her Will is dated "the sixteenth day of the eleventh month called January, 1677", i.e. 1678 by modern reckoning, and she is therein described as widow and relict of Richard Settle late of the island, planter, deceased, and sole executrix of his will, which left all his estate at her disposal.

She gave her /plantation of 68 acres in the parish called St. Joseph and 34 negroes thereon and another plantation at "Chaulky Mount" in the parish called St. Andrews containing 50 acres, besides all her other estate and property to her son-in-law, Thomas Morris, merchant, and her daughter, Sarah, his wife, provided they release to her son, Robert Taylor, of the same island, planter, and Jane his wife, one-half of the plantation whereon the said Robert dwelt, with the negroes, horses, mules, cattle, and stock thereon.

Her will contained a schedule of the property intended to pass thereunder. It is of interest as an indication of the adequate but simple furnishings of a household of Friends of the period, in keeping with their mode of life.

THE SCHEDULE

10 men negroes, 11 women, 13 boys and girls, 4 cows, 2 young bulls, 1 heifer, 3 calves. One stone dwellinghouse tyled, one round stone pigeon house tyled, one stone kitchen, one chimney tyled, one row of stone houses 100 ft. in length, all tyled, containing houses for poultry etc., all with half story for several uses, 7 negro houses of stone and tyled, one kiln house with brick pillars and tyled, one large pott-house to make dry earthern wares in, and one boarded spring house.

3 tables, 6 joint stools, 1 couch of rushey (Russia) leather, 6 chairs of ditto [evidently those given by Richard Settle's Will to his son-in-law, Thomas Morris] 3 chests, two trunks. one chest of drawers, 3 bedsteads, 3 beds, 2 of feathers, one of flocks, 3 bolsters, 2 pair of pillow sleeves, 2 ruggs and covering, 2 setts of curtains, 4 pair of sheets, 3 pair of pillow sleeves, 2 doz. napkins, 2 tablecloths, 1 pair of fire irons with brasses, 1 pair of andirons, shovell and tongs, 2 brass kettles, 3 skillets, 4 iron potts, 2 pott hangers, 1 brass chafing dish, 2 brass scummers, 1 brass ladle, 1 brass nose bellows, 1 doz. pewter dishes, 1 doz. plates. 1 pair pewter candlesticks, 1 pair brass candlesticks and 1 warming pan.

The testatrix took the unusual course of appearing before the Governor, Sir Jonathan Atkins, and acknowledging the Will, and recording it in her lifetime, that is, on 10 April 1678. Consequently, the record does not give the date of

6. The name is indistinct.
7. Copied in "186 Barbados Quakeressess in 1677", By Henry Cadbury: *Journal*, Vol. 9, p. 197. (Pages 680-682, this volume.)

her death, but it seems that she predeceased her son, Robert Taylor. Even so, he did not long survive her, as his will was proved in the month of June, 1680.

Will of Robert Taylor of St. James Planter.

To Richard Ford, surveyor, Joseph Borden and Thomas Pilgrim, merchants, and Ralph Fretwell, planter, £20 each. To Edward Wright, William Mullinex and Ralph Weeks, chirurgeons, and Henry Burch, physician, £10 for the use of the chirurgeons meeting of friends called Quakers.

To the four eldest of my sister Morris's children £10 each and to the youngest £8. To my daughter, Mercy Taylor, all my lands, houses, etc., except those I have settled on her mother my wife, Jane, viz. one-half of the plantation which I purchased of my brother and sister Morris; the other half of the plantation which I had of my father-in-law, [8] Richard Settle, and all my estate in this island I give to the management of my friends Ralph Fretwell, Edward Wright, Thomas Pilgrim and Samuel Hancock of Barbados, Christopher Taylor. near Waltham Abbey and Ezekiel Woolley, in or near Spitfields in London in Old England and appoint them executors and guardians of my only daughter, Mercy, until she is 18, and then all my lands etc. to be vested in her.

My dwellinghouse on this my plantation shall be as formerly for the use of my friends called Quakers. I also desire that the vault which we have begun in friend's burial place on tne Cliff may be finished quickly wherein I desire my father and mother and my former wife's bones with mine own may be decently put as soon as may be and that it be a burial place for my family as we formerly intended it. [9]

I have set my hand and seal twenty-first day of the twelve month called February, 1679 (1680). Sd. Robert Taylor. Wits: Martha Cornish, William Simpson, Sarah White, Humphrey Wheelwright, John Teague, John Mussicke, Tho. Cornish, John Parrotts, Elizabeth Benny. Proved by the Oaths of T. Cornish, J. Merrick, J. Parrot, and H. Wheelwright, 8 June 1680. Recorded 14 September 1680.

Thomas Morris survived his wife, Sarah, and died about January 1696. His Will dated 2 March 1695 names his eldest son, Robert, as executor and guardian of his young brother and sisters. The other children named are Frances (then Frances Terry, married, with two infant daughters, Sarah and Frances) Dorothy and Thomasin and Richard the youngest child who was to be sent to England to the University. The testator names his friends, Colonel Richard Salter and Lt. Colonel Thomas Merrick as advisers to his son as sole executor. The will was proved on 16 January 1696, and it bears no evidence that Thomas Morris was adherent to the Quaker faith.

8. Step-father.
9. This burial place is most certainly identical with the old Quaker burial ground near the edge of the cliff in the village near St. Philip's Church. There is a stone wall enclosure with an iron gate leading to 9 tombs hewn out of the rock. Two are marked with the letters R.W. and G. respectively. One is known to be the tomb of Ralph Weekes, but it is uncertain if the other lettered G. is that of the Gretton or the Gittens families.

Skeete of Barbados.

The following notes were taken from the Record Office at Barbados by Mr. N. Darnell Davis, C.M.G., and kindly presented to the Rev. R. Skeete, at present Rector of the Parish of St. Peter (1914).—E. L. Skeete.

Captain Francis Skeete was the founder of this family. His sister appears to have married Colonel Reynold Alleyne, who was one of the early settlers in Barbados, and a leading man on the Parliament side when the struggle arose between the Cavaliers and Roundheads. Captain Skeete appears to have been allied (I think by marriage) to Colonel William Hilliard, another prominent colonist and large landowner.

Captain Skeete died young and apparently without making a will. His children were then looked after by Alleyne and Hilliard.

On the 9th of August 1642 Captain Francis Skeete, gentleman, sold 20 acres of land to Ensign Michael Cooke. (Deeds, vol. i., p. 132, N. D. Davis.)

Francis Skeete of St. Thomas. Will dated 6 March 1710-11. Wife Margaret. Children Edward, Elizabeth, Martin, Reynold, Ann, Francis, and the child my wife now goeth with. Brothers Edward and Reynold. Kinsmen the Hon. Thomas Alleyne and Reynold Alleyne, Esquire. Proved 20 May 1712.

Edward Skeete of St. Thomas, Esq. Will dated 3 June 1715. Wife Ann. Children, only Francis is named. Brother Reynold. Kinsmen Benjamin, Timothy, John (senior), and the Hon. Abel Alleyne. Proved 1721-22.

Reynold Skeete of St. Andrew. Will dated 28 Oct. 1721. Wife Ann. Son Edward. Daughters Margaret, Isabella, Ann, Elizabeth. Brothers-in-law Lieut.-Colonel Wm Sandiford, John Wilde. Kinsmen Hon. Reynold, John, and Reynold Alleyne, Esquires. Proved 15 March 1721-2.

Francis Skeete of St. John's. Will dated 11 Sept. 1740. Left all to Mrs Sarah Walwin. No Skeetes mentioned. Proved 25 Nov. 1740.

Edward Skeete of St Thomas. Will dated 31 July 1748. Son Francis. Daughter Elizabeth. Wife's father Wm Copp, dec^d. Proved 27 Oct. 1748.

Margaret Skeete of St. Thomas, widow. Will dated 3 June 1748. Sons Edward, Reynold. Daughters Elizabeth, wife of Thomas Earl, Ann, wife of Richard Reece. Granddaughter Elizabeth, daughter of Edward. Nephew Francis Skeete. Executor Dr. Reynold Skeete. A witness Wm Reece. Proved 1 Sept. 1748.

Jean Skeete of St. Philip, widow. Will dated 23 April 1743. Son Wm Wheeler Skeete. Daughter Frances D. Harley (her children John, Edward, Benjamin, Jane, Mary, Frances, Sarah). Daughter-in-law Bridget Skeete. Kinswomen Frances Skeete, Sarah Rollstone. Proved 26 Nov. 1743.

Elizabeth Skeete of St Michael, spinster. Will dated 18 Dec. 1748. Mother Ann Skeete. Brothers Francis (St Peter's), Reynold (St Thomas). Nephews Reynold and Edward, sons of brother Reynold Skeete. Nieces Ann Moore, Susannah and Mary, daughters of brother Reynold, Jean, daughter of brother Francis. Proved 9 Jan. 1749-50.

William Wheeler Skeete of St. John's. Will dated 4 Dec. 1748. Wife Bridget. Daughter-in-law (step-daughter?) Bridget Moseley (her daughters Bridget and Isabella Moseley). Nephews William, Benjamin, John, Edward Arthurley—a Sir John Arthurley—Francis Skeete, Senior, and Dr Reynold Skeete. Sisters Frances Arthurley (her 4 daughters, Jane, Mary, Frances and Sarah). Kinswoman Sarah Rollstone (her sister Frances Skeete). Witnesses : Edward Skeete, Robert Moseley and J. Noett. Proved 15 Aug. 1754.

Frances Skeete of St. Peter's. Will dated 18 April 1758. Sons Thomas, Abel, Alleyne, Edward. Daughters Marion Alleyne Skeete, Christian and Jane Skeete. Brother Reynold. Cousins Robert Skeete and Robert Clinton. Proved 18 June 1759.

Edward Skeete of St. Peter's, Practitioner in Physics and Surgery. Will dated 22 March 1759. Wife Elizabeth. Sons Francis, John, Brathwaite. Daughters Rebecca, Elizabeth. Proved 20 April 1759.

505

Roberta Skeete of St. Thomas. Will dated 30 May 1766. Sister Elizabeth. Proved 2 Feb. 1770.

⚭ Elizabeth Skeete of St. Thomas. Will dated 6 Dec. 1773. Cousins Ann and Martin, daughters of Mrs Reynold Skeete, Mrs Benjamin Atherley, Ann Williams, Thomas, son of George Williams, George, son of George Williams, Major Richard Reece, Francis Reece. Relatives: Thomas Reece and Margaret, wife of George Williams. Hannah Reece a witness. Proved 5 Jan. 1774.

Reynold Skeete, the Elder, of St. Thomas, Planter. Daughter Ann. Sons William, Edward (his son Francis), Thomas. Proved 28 Oct. 1783.

Elizabeth Skeete, late of the City of Bath and of St. Peter's, Barbados, spinster. Will dated 26 July 1784. Niece Kitty Gibbons, daughter of Scawen Kenrick Gibbons. " Mother and Uncle." Proved Aug. 1794.

Ann Skeete, widow. Will dated 9 Jan. 1781. Sons Reynold and Edward. Daughter Susanna, wife of Thomas Reece. Granddaughter Elizabeth Murray *alias* Esmon. Witnesses: John Atherly, William Porter. Proved 26 June 1781.

John Brathwaite Skeete of St. Peter's. Will (dates omitted by Mr. N. Darnell Davis). Wife Agnes. Son John Brathwaite (only child named). Uncle John Brathwaite. Brother-in-law William Harris.

William Edward Skeete of St. Thomas. Will undated. Wife .... Father Reynold Skeete, Esquire. Eldest son Frank (other children's names not given). Sister Ann. Proved 28 July 1795.

MARRIAGES OF SKEETE IN VARIOUS PARISHES OF THE ISLAND.

Date.		Skeete.	To.
1668	June 28	George	Alice Ayshley.
1676	Feb. 27	Margaret	Frances Kirton.
1696	Aug. 14	Francis	Margaret Martin.
1704	Aug. 24	Reynold	Ann Jones.
1717	Oct. 8	Edward	Mary Collins.
1724	April 23	William Wheeler	Bridget Smith.
1735	Dec. 4	Ann	Richard Reece.
1739	June 9	Elizabeth	Thomas Earl.
1740	Oct. 23	Francis (Doctor)	Mary Martindale.
1748	May 28	. . . .	Elizabeth Brathwaite.
1748	June 30	Ann	William Moore.
1755	April 5	Mary	John Murrey.
1756	Nov. 4	Elizabeth	Edward Butler.
1771	April 28	Francis	Elizabeth Jones.
1771	Nov. 28	Reynold (Jr.)	Jemima Grant.
1773	Sept. 16	Edward	Rebecca Rudder.
1774	Mar. 24	Thomas	Christian Williams.
1778	May 25	Reynold	Rebecca Matterson.

Date.			Skeete.	To.
1778	May	2	Reynold	Rebecca Matison (widow).
1779	Nov.	27	William Edward	Rebecca Atherly.
1782	Jan.	17	Rebecca Tate	Patrick Dogood.
1783	Nov.	20 (?)	Christian	Scawen Kenrick Gibbons.
1786	Dec.	28	Frances	Samuel Taylor.
1788	May	3	Edward	Elizabeth Lake Hinds.
1791	April	28	Jane Martindale	John Herbert.
1793	Oct.	12	Mary Martindale	Samuel Stoute.
1794	Jan.	18	Elizabeth (widow)	Hon. Wm Bishop, President.
1794	Mar.	10	Reynold	Sarah Mellowes.
1799	Nov.	11	John Brathwaite	Mary Bishop.
1799	Dec.	16	Agnes	Bonham Pinson.
1799	April	27	Elizabeth-Ann-Rebecca	John Wickham.
1800	July	31 (?)	Anna Marian	Edward Austin.
1806	Dec.	23	Frances	Mary Elizabeth Lewiss (?).
1807	May	30	Edward	Christian Mounter.
1809	Mar.	11	Rebecca Ann	John Lawrence.
1810	April	21	Edward	Mary Gibson.
1810	Mar.	31	Edward	Margaret Lloyd.
1810	Nov.	8	Ann Bell	Michael Howard.

The Editor has added the following notes :—

Reynold Alleyn of St. Philip's, gent. Will dated 25 Oct. 1675. Eliz. and Edward Skeat, children of Col. Edward Skeat. Mrs. Mary Skeat.

Tho. Alleyne of St James'. Will dated 1 June 1713. My cousin Edward Skeete, Esq., £20, and to his son Francis my godson £50 at 21.

Benj. Alleyne of St. James'. Will dated 1 June 1715. My kinsman Edward Skete, J^r, son of Capt. Edward Skeete, the Eldest, £150.

1643, Jan. 20. Capt Wm. Hilliard, Esq., for the great love to my nephews Edward Skeete and Renold Skeete sons of my beloved brother Capt. Francis Skeete deceased, assign 370 acres in the p. of St Philip part of ye plantation called Three Houses of 570 a. l. in the possession of the said Fra. S. also 60 a. in Christ Church called Four Square plantation ⅗ to Edward the Elder and ⅖ to Reynold and in default of issue to Roberta their Mother now wife of Edward Pye merch^t. (Vol. I. of Deeds, p. 291.) On p. 574 there is a sale of 70 acres by the Skeetes.

Skeete. Eton 1760—68. Francis s. of Edward of London, entered 16 Sept., admitted pensioner Trin. Coll., Cam., 21 April 1768, aged 18, scholar 1768, re-adm. Fell. Com. 29 May 1770, did not graduate. Francis, eldest s. of Edward, l. of Barbados, esq., deceased, adm. Inner Temple 12 Nov. 1770.

On his tomb in St. Michael's churchyard he is styled Fra. Skeete, Esq., eldest son of Edw. and Eliz. Skeete, died 4 May 1777, aged 28.

1788, March 5. In Charter-house-sq. a. 63, Tho. Skeete, esq ; l. of B. ("G.M.," 275.)

Eliz. S., dau. of Edw. S., Esq., and Eliz. of B., died 10 May 1792, a. 34. M.I. in Bath Abbey. (*Ante*, 1., 26.)

~ 1800, Jan. 26. At Bridgetown. B., Lieut.-col. Benham, of the 69th foot, to Miss Agnes S. niece to the Hon. Wm. Bishop, gov. of that island. ("G.M.," 588.)

General Pinson Bonham, of Great Warley Place, co. Essex, b. 1762, m. Agnes, dau. of John Brathwaite S., President of B. Bookplate with arms of Bonham impaling Skeete: *Or, a chevron between three fleurs-de-lis Gules.* ("W.I. Bookplates," No. 170.)

1810, Oct. 16. Died Miss Margaret Skeete. St. Michael's. ("Barbados Mercury.")

1816, Sept. 26. At her son's estate, Mangrove, B., Mrs. Skeete, relict of the late John Brathwaite S. esq. of that island. ("G.M.," 566.)

1816, Nov. 9. Yesterday, Wm. Skeete, Esq. & his remains were this morning interred in St Michael's Church. ("Barbados Mercury.")

1818, Jan. 27. In St Thomas's, Dr Thomas Skeete. (*Ibid.*)

1840, Sept. 1. At Wells, S. L. Gower, of Little Hemspton, Devon, to Agnes Bonham, 3d dau. of the late E. Skeete of B. ("G.M.," 424.)

1843, July 5. At Mangrove Plantation, B., Mary Bishop, 3d dau. of the late President Skeete, & wife of Wm. B. Gibbons. (*Ibid.*, 334.)

1846, May 5. At Norton Bavant, Wilts, Capt. Walter Caddell, 36th Reg. Bengal Army, to Ellen, yst. dau. of the l. Hon. J. B. Skeete, President of H.M. Council of B. (*Ibid.*, 87.)

Capt. Chas. Kyd Skeete, b. in B. 17 Jan. 1824; served in the 19th reg. 1842—1852.

John Braithwaite Skeete, 1 s. of Henry Bishop of B., W.I., cler. Non-Coll., matric. 16 Oct. 1868, aged 20, B.A. 1873, a student of Linc. Inn 1869.

Francis de Courcy Skeete, 3 s. of Henry Bishop of Brighthall, B., cler. Non-Coll., matric. 18 Oct. 1873, aged 21; B.A. 1887.

ST. JOHN'S.

1667 Nov. 10 Reynold Skeete and Margt Culpeper.
1698 Aug. 26 Capt Edward Skeete & Jane Graves.
1739 July 4 Reynold Skeete to Frances Dalvin.
1776 April 18 Francis Skeete Esqr to Eliza Hothersall.

ST. THOMAS.

There are several baptisms of Dr. Reynold Skeete's children.

ALL SAINTS. (Archer, 401.)

Capt. Edward Skeete, b. 13 June 1639, d. 14 May 1727, a. 88. (M.I.)

MANGROVE, ST. PETER'S.

John Brathwaite Skeete, Esq., d. 15 Nov. 1794 in 43d year. (M.I.)

Sober of Barbados.

Robert Sober of S[t] Andrew Overhills. Will dated 31 Oct. 1685. My wife Mary. Proved 1686. (Recorded at Barbados.)

Lawrence Trent of S[t] Peters, Barbados, Esq. Will dated 2 July 1742. To the children of my nephew John Sober, Esq., £100 each. (278, Edmunds.)

John Sober, late of the p. of S[t] Peter in the I. of B'es, now of Little Burstea, co. Essex, Esq. Will dated 12 Oct. 1751. My father-in-law Nich. Wilcox of B'es, Esq., Edw[d] Clark Parish of L., Esq., Abr. Carleton Cumberbatch and Joseph Lindsey, both of B'es, Esq[res], on T. all my sugar work plantations and personal estate. 200 negroes, 100 cattle and 10 horses to be kept on my estate, 60 a. to be planted in provisions, negroes to be well fed and clothed, and casks to be made. My s[d] father-in-law Nich. Wilcox and Mother-in-law Marg[t] Wilcox, Ed. C. Parish, A. C. Cumberbatch, J. Lindsey and my brother-in-law Nich. Wilcox £50 each. My nephew and niece W[m] and Sarah Timbrill, ch[n] of my late sister Eliz. T., wife of Wm. T., dec[d], £500 each at 21 and £40 a year each till then. My friend Rob. Wadeson £10. My wife Mary S., late Mary Wilcox, dau. of s[d] Nich. W., Esq., £1500, our mar. sett. dated 25 Oct. 1743, and £100 for mourning, all my plate with the coat of arms of her father, her riding horse, jewels, use of my house in B'es until my eldest son be 21. My father-in-law Abr. Cumberbatch has by his will lately made broke his contract in regard to four of my ch[n], Sarah S., Abr. S., Mary S. and Cumberbatch S. I give them each £3000 c. at 21. My co[u]in Joseph Pickering, now in L., £10. My eldest son John at 21 all my real estate and residue of personal estate; power to heir to charge estate with joynture of £200 c. Son John to go to Oxford at 17. T. to be Ex'ors.
Codicil. Late f G. B., now of B'es. My father-in-law Nich. Wilcox has died. To my wife my coach and 6 horses, the use of my house called the Castle on my pl[n] in S[t] Peters and use of house-negroes and £150 a year if she 'o not dwell there. My aunt M[rs] Reb[a] Almond of S[t] Lucy £50 c. To poor of S Peter £10 a year for 10 years. My wife, my bro.-in-law N. W. and friends Hon. Ph. Gibbes of S[t] Jas., Esq[res], and Rev. Jonathan Dennis, Fellow of Q. Coll., Oxf., with Edw. C. Parish and Jos. Lindsay Ex'ors and T. and G. of my 5 ch[n]. Revoke app. of A. C. Cumberbatch. Jon. Dennis £100 for his care of my 3 sons and £50 for mourning. Ph. Gibbes £50. Dated 16 Nov. 1755 in the presence of Geo. Lavine, Edw. Willson, Ph. Lovell. B'es by the Presid[t] Ph. Lovell was sworn at Pilgrim 2 Dec. 1755, Ralph Weekes. A true copy 28 May 1762. Rich. Husbands, D. Sec[y]. Proved 3 March 1763 by Mary S., widow, the relict, and Nich. Wilcox, Esq.; power reserved to E. C. P. and J. L., Esq[res], surviving Ex'ors, and Hon. Ph. G. and Rev. J. D. (152, Cæsar.)

Abraham Sober of Kensington, Esq. Will dated 30 March 1772. My Mother-in-law Mrs Mary Sober £300. My sister Sarah Sandiford, wife of Dr S. of B., £1000. All residue to my sister Mary Sober and my brothers John Sober and Cumberbatch Sober, Ex'ors. Proved 16 June 1772 by Mary S., spr., power reserved to the others. (234, Taverner.)

Mary Sober. Will dated 28 July 1792. To be buried at S[t] Faiths under S[t] Pauls with my dear Mother M[rs] Mary S. To my sister M[rs] Sarah Frewin £30. M[rs] Judith S. £30. Mary Cumberbatch Cumberbatch £25 a year. Sarah S. £500. Johannes S. £500. Elletson S., now in the E. I., £2000. Penelope

509

ARMS.—*Ermine, a saltire Gules, on a chief Sable three crescents Or.*
CREST.—*Out of a crescent Or a lion's head Gules.* (Book-plate of John Sober.)

John Sober of Barbados 1638.   Tho. Sober of Barbados 1638.

Robert Sober of St. Andrew's.=Mary
Will dated 31 Oct. 1685; . . . .
proved 1686.

Abr. Cumberbatch of St. An-=drew's, Esq. Will dated 22 Nov. 1750; proved 1753 (8, Searle). (*Ante*, II., 84.) Names his grandchildren Sober.

John Sober= of Barbados, gent.

Lawrence Trent of St. Peters, Esq. Will dated 2 July 1742; proved 1 Sept. 1746 (278, Edmunds). Uncle of John Sober.

1. . . . .=John Sober of The Castle=2. Mary Wilcox, dau. of
Cumber- | in St. Peter's, Esq., and of | Nich. W., Esq., and
batch. | Little Bursted, co. Essex, | Margt. (he died 1751—
| born 1715; of Q. Coll., | 55); mar. sett. made 25
| Oxf., matric 24 Aug. 1731, | Oct. 1743; of Welbeck
| æt. 16; died in B'os 1755. | Str.; bur. in St. Paul's
| Will dated 12 Oct. 1751; | crypt. Will dated 27
| cod. 16 Nov. 1755; sworn | July 1789; proved 21
| 2 Dec. 1755 (152, Cæsar). | June 1791 (302, Bevor).

Eliz. Sober, mar. Wm. Timbrill of St. Michael's Town, Barbados, merchant. His will dated 25 July 1743; proved 1743 (530, St. Eloy).

s.p.

Penelope Blake, dau.=John Sober, 1st son and heir, of Sober=Martha Bersheba.
of Maj. Martin B. of | Castle, born 1739; of Q. Coll., Oxf., | Will dated 26
A.; mar.6 Nov.1760; | matric. 8 Apr. 1756, æt. 17: n.; pre- | Apr.1795; proved
died 29 Jan. and bur. | sented font to St. Peter's in 1767; | 7 Jan. 1797
2 Feb. 1774 in Bath | named in 1772 in the will of his | (49, Exeter).
Abbey. M.I. (*Ante*, | brother Abr.; dead 1795; bur. in St. | 2nd wife.
II., 231.) 1st wife. | Faith's under St. Paul's Cath.

s.p.

Hope Elletson Sober, in the E. I. in 1789; ? left natural children by an Indian woman.

John Sober of= Latheron near Dunbeath, Scotland.

Abr. Cumber-=Ann, dau. of
batch Sober, | Tho. Kemp,
born 1771; | M.P.for Lewes,
Capt. Dragoon | who died 3 May
Guards; died | 1811. She died
in L. 7 Dec. | in 1855.
1813, æt. 42. | (" G.M.,"
(248, Bridport.) | i., 331.)

Penelope Wentworth Sober.

John Middleton Sober.

Mary Esther Sober, died in L. 16 Oct. 1832, æt. 18.

Abr. C. Sober the younger, 1791.

W.I. Bookplates,
No. 235
(reduced).

John Sober

A

Abr. Sober, bur. in crypt of St. Paul's Cath. Will dated 30 Mar. and proved 16 June 1772 (234, Taverner.)	Cumberbatch Sober, born 1742; of Barbados 1772; heir 1792 to his sister Mary; of U. Geo. Str., Marylebone; died 13 Jan. 1827, æt. 85. ╤ Judith	Sarah Sober, wife of Dr. Sandford of Barbados in 1772; wife of .... Frewen 1792.	Mary Sober, died 24 Aug. 1793; bur. in St. Paul's Cathedral crypt. Will dated 28 July 1792; proved 6 Sept. 1793 (478, Dodwell.)

Sampson Wood Sober of the Polygon, Southampton, later of St. Peter's, Barbados, only son and heir, died 4 March 1811 v.p. in U. Geo. Str. Will dated 18 April 1799; proved 22 April 1811 (198, Crickitt.) ╤ Jennett, niece to Tho. Walke of Barbados; died in L. 1 Dec. 1815, æt. 42. Will dated 22 Nov. and proved 15 Dec. 1815 (624, Pakenham).	John Sober, ? died 1816. M.I. St. Peter's Font, Barbados.	Mary Cumberbatch Sober, mar. Abr. Cumberbatch, who was born 1754 and died 16 June 1796. She re-mar. 20 Aug. 1797 Wm. Smith Forth of King's Dragoon Guards.	Sarah Sober, mar. Samson Wood, Jr. He was at Eton 1762—8; adm. to Mid. Temple 1768.

Harrison Walke Sober, heir 1800 to his great-uncle Tho. Walke, then under 16; at Eton 1811; of 14th Hussars; died shortly before 1863.	Judith Sober, born 18 March 1794; mar. 19 Feb. 1818 at St. George, Hanover Square; died 1871. ╤ Francis Onslow Trent, Lieut. 14th Light Dragoons; died 10 April 1846.	Eliz. Jennett Sober, died 26 Dec. 1795, aged 18 months and 19 days. M.I. at St. Peter's.

Harrison Walke John Trent-Stoughton, ╤ Rose, youngest dau. of Wm. Plunkett
Col. of 68th L. I., great-nephew of | and widow of Tho. Anthony Stoughton
John Sober, who died 1816; mar. 1889; | of Owlpen, co. Glouc., and Ballyhorgan,
of Ashton Hall plantation 1891; died | co. Kerry, who died 1885.
1899.

511

Wentworth S. £3000, plate, linen, furniture. To John S., now in Scotland, £20 a year. Abr. Cumberbatch S. £20 a year. All residue in money, land or negroes to my brother Cumberbatch S. and his son Sampson Wood S. equally and Ex'ors. On 5 Sept. 1793 appeared Daniel Coxe of John Str., St Geo., Han. Sq., Esq., Cumberbatch Sober of Welbeck Str., Esq., and Judith Sober his wife, and Penelope Wentworth Sober of the same place, spr. P. W. S. swore her aunt died 24 of last month and sealed the will with her arms. Cumb. S. is the brother of dec^d. Testx. of St Mary le bone, sp^r. Proved 6 Sept. 1793 by C. S., Esq., the brother; power reserved to S. W. S., Esq. (478, Dodwell.)

Martha Bersheba Sober. Will dated at Margate in ye Isle of Thanet 26 Apr. 1795. All my freehold and personal estate in the I. of B'oes which came to me by the will of my late husband unto Hope Elletson S. for his life, he paying to his next brother Alr. Cumberbatch S. and his sister Penelope Wentworth S. £100 per annum each, and at the decease of H. E. S. I give my estate to his next brother John S. and his heirs male, he then paying to Abr. C. S. £200 a year and to his sister P. W. S. £150 a year, remainder to his younger brother Abr. C. S., then to my dau.-in-law Pen. W. S. I appoint Sir John Gav Alleyne, Bart., Speaker of the Assembly, and Wm Bishopp, Esq., of Spring Hall, Trustees and Ex'ors, with Tho. King, Esq., of Chiswick Mall, co. Middx., Ex'or for Eng. To be bur. at St Peters.

Codicil, 26 April 1795. Lord Harewood's mortgage on Sober Castle estate not quite liquidated all sugars must be consigned to Messrs. Elliott Adams and Whalley in Hylords Court, Crutched Friars. If any Ex'or be dead Nathl Elliott, Esq., Merch^t, Crutched Friars, to be Ex'or for W. I. affairs. I have left my estate to Hope Elletson Sober for his life only, as I believe his attachment to the Indian is not legal and his chⁿ are illegitimate in justice to the rest of my husband's family. His handsome legacy from his grandmother and aunt. Ex'ors £100 each.

Codicil, 27 April 1795. My own £5000 in the 4 per cents. £2800 for Mr Sober's private debts the estate has cleared. The legacy of my father. To Mrs Eliz, Middleton of Kensington Palace £1000 for life and at her death to my cousin John Gowan, Esq., of Chichester, and the portrait of my father by Gainsborough, then to J. G. To Mrs Gowan an enamelled miniature of my father and to J. G. a crayon portrait of our relation Sir Jas. Napier. To Sir J. N. a ring. My carriage to my sister-in-law Juliana King. To Sir J. N. the gold medal of H.M. given my F. when he was P. of Wales. My late husband's chⁿ as follows: To Hope E. S. £500 for his little Eliza. To John S. his next brother £100 and to his son John Middleton S. also £100. To Abr. C. S. £100 and Pen. W. S. £100 and £1000. Mrs John S. a silver pencil. Mrs Grace Marler of Starpoint Ho., Powderham in Devonshire, £50 and the portrait of my mother and miniature picture of our dear sister Reading with one of Mrs Middleton. Rob. Ladbroke, J^r, Esq., £200. My sister-in-law Mrs Juliana King £100 the locket of her brother (? Edw. Gascoigne), and the ring left me by her mother. My bro.-in-law Tho. King, Esq., of Chiswick Mall my Ex'or for Eng. If I die in L. to be bur. in the chapel of St Faiths under St Pauls n^r my late husb^d Mr Sober. At West Horseley Place, Surrey, are two chests of mine to be sold for the poor there. The things I left at Kensington Palace. Account of leg. John S. of Scotland and his wife Ann. Latheron n^r Dunbeath. Sworn by Abr. C. S. of Baker Str. 16 Jan. 1797. Test. I. of Kensington Palace, after of Margate, but late of Pall Mall, widow. Proved 7 Jan. 1797 by Abr. C. S. the residuary legatee. (49, Exeter.)

Mary Sober of Welbeck Str., Cav. Sq., co. Middx., widow. Will dated 27 July 1789. To be bur. in St Faith's Church under St Paul's Cath. in or near the grave of my son Abraham S., Esq. Funeral £50. My dau.-in-law Sarah

512

Frewen £50. My son-in-law Cumberbath (*sic*) S., Esq., now in the I. of B'oes, £100. My friend and pastor the Rev. Jacob Duch'. e of Sloan Str. £50. My friend Mʳ John Pedder of Chatham Place £100, if he die to his four chⁿ Sarah Ainslie, John P., W. P. and Mary P. To my dau.-in-law Mʳˢ Judith S. of B'oes £25 and to her daus. Mary Cumberbatch Cumberbatch, Sarah Sober and Johannas Sober £25 each. To my great-grandson Abr. Cumberbatch the yʳ £25 for a ring. My friends Mʳˢ Barbara Kennedy 5 gas. Mʳˢ Mary Ashley 5 gas. and the silver bread basket she gave me when with me in Sᵗ James Place. Mʳˢ Sarah Knight 10 gas. Miss Eliz. Redwar, now living at Sir Philip Gibbes's, 10 gas. Mʳˢ Ringston 5 gas. Mʳˢ Alicia Wilcox, widow of my decᵈ brother, 10 gas. My goddau. Mʳˢ Mary Pringle £20. My godson Wᵐ Sturge Moore, Esq., £30. My grandson Elliston Sober, now in the E. Indies, £1000, if he die then £500 to his sister Penelope, £250 to his brother John S. and £250 to his brother Abr. S. To my Ex'or £1000 on Trust for my granddau. Pen. S. at 25. My grandson John S. £500. My grandson Abr. S. £200. To the ch. wardens of Christ Ch., B'es, £10 c., also of Sᵗ Peters £10 for poor widows. My grandson Samson Wood Sober £100. My friend Sir Philip Gibbes, Bart., 10 gas., and John Brathwaite, Esq., 10 gas. Release my dau. Mary Sober and granddau. Pen. Sober from all sums owing for their board and lodging with me. All residue to my dau.-in-law Mary Sober. My sᵈ dau. and Sir Ph. Gibbes, John Brathwaite, Esq., and my grandson Samson Wood Sober, Ex'ors. Proved 21 June 1791 by Mary S., spr., the dau. On 18 Feb. 1794 proved by John Brathwaite, Esq.; power reserved to Sir Ph. Gibbes and S. W. Sober. (302, Bevor.)

Samson Wood Sober of the p. of Sᵗ Peter and I. of B'os. Will dated 18 April 1799. My wife Jennett S. £1000 and plate. My dau. Judith S. at 18 £3000. My dau. Eliz. Jennett S. £3000 at 18. To my son Harrison Walke S. my sugar work plantation in Sᵗ Peter with the slaves, and all residue remʳ to my 2 daus. My wife, my father Cumberbatch S., Esq., my wife's uncle Tho. Walke, Esq., Ex'ors and G. In the presence of Jnᵒ Howell, P. W. Sandiford, Wᵐ Cadogan. Proved 22 April 1811 by Jennett S., wid., and C. S., Esq., the father. (198, Crickitt.)

Tho. Walke of the I. of B'os, Esq. Will dated 5 April 1800. To my wife Eliz. Jennett W. £1200 a year from my bank annuities in lieu of dower, to reside on my plantation of Asheton Hall, power to bequeath £8000, if she marry then only £300 a year. My niece Jennett Sober £1000 a year for her support and the education of her son Harrison Walke S. (not 16). To Judith S. and Eliz. Jennett S., daus. of my sᵈ niece, £5000 each at 21. My niece Abigail Jane Thomas, wife of Mʳ Wᵐ Carter, T. formerly A. J. Dunckley, spr., the follᵍ sums due to my late brother Harrison W., Esq., viz.: £3090 due from Cumberbatch Sober, Esq., on judgment dated 15 May 1793; £1852 due from Mʳ Jacob Goodridge on judgment dated 26 Aug. 1795, and £1300 due from Mʳ Eyare Pile on judgment dated 26 Aug. 1795, making £6242 c. To Eliz. Jennett T. and Mary Jane T., daus. of sᵈ W. C. T. and Abig. Jane T., £3000 each at 21. My niece Mary Harrison Dunckley £12,000 annuities. I remit to Miss Dorothy Lisle and Miss Margᵗ Warren Lisle all sums due including £310 secured by their late Mother's note, and to Doro. L. £200 a year, and to bequeath by her will £4000. To Margᵗ W. L. £400 a year with power by her will to dispose of £4000. My godson Tho. Harrison Walke Wharton, son of Mʳˢ Mary W., wid., £150 a year until 18, £200 a year till 23, then £1000. To his M. £50 a year. Mʳˢ Mary Walke, wid. of my late brother John W., decᵈ, £50 a year. My godson Tho. Walke Lemar Wood, son of Samson Wood, Jʳ, and Sarah his wife, formerly Sarah Sober, £500 at 21. My godson Edwᵈ Beaufoy, son of Wᵐ Henry B. and Agnes his wife, formerly Agnes Payne, £200 at 21. Godson Tho. Daniel the Yʳ of Bristol, Mᵗ, £1000. My godson Tho. Daniel, son of sᵈ Tho. D. the Yʳ, £1000

513

at 21. My goddau. Maria Daniel, d. of s^d Tho. Daniel the Y^r, £500 at 21. John Daniel of Mincing Lane, M^t, £1000. Mrs Ann Cave, wife of Mr Stephen C., £100. John Cave, son of s^d Stephen C. by Ann his wife, £500 at 21. Mrs Eleanor Belfield, wife of Rev. Finney B., £200. Mrs Eleanor Gell £100 and her sons John G. and Wm G., Edw. Gell and Tho. G. and Chas. G. £100 each at 21. To Miss Joan Worrell, dau. of Edw. W., Esq., dec^d, £250. To my wife Eliz. J. W., Tho. Daniel the Elder of Mincing Lane, M^t, Tho. Daniel the Y^r, John Daniel and Wm Cartor, Thomas and Wm Prescod of B'os, Esq., my sugar work plⁿ in the p. of St Tho. heretofore belonging to the Hon. Jas. Carter, Esq., dec^d, also my Ashton Hall plⁿ in St Peter, my plⁿ of Overhill in St Andrew with the houses, mills and slaves to the use of Harrison Walke Sober, the eldest son of my niece Jennett S., at 23, remainder to the sons of my nieces Abig. J. Thomas and Mary H. Dunckley, etc., 130 slaves to be kept on Carters, 130 on Ashton Hall and 115 on Overhill. To each child of my s^d 3 nieces £3000. All sums in the hands of Messrs. Tho. Daniel and Co. of L. or Tho. D. and Son of Bristol, and all residue to T. for H. W. S. Trustees to be Ex'ors. In the presence of Tho. McIntosh, Renn Hamden, Wm Welch, Sam. Moore. Proved 3 Nov. 1800 by E. J. W., wid., Tho. Daniel the Elder, Tho. D. the Y^r and John Daniel; power reserved to the others. (826, Adderley.)

Abraham Cumberbatch Sober. (Will very short and not dated.) My wife Ann the dau. of the late Tho. Kemp, M.P. for Lewes, co Sussex, all my estate and sole Ex'trix, she paying to each of my brothers and sister 100 gas. Proved 7 April 1814 by Ann S. (248, Bridport.)

Jennett Sober. Will dated 22 Nov. 1815. All sums due from the £1000 left me by my husband, the £1000 annuity left me by my uncle Tho. Walke, the £300 c. annuity left me by my uncle Harrison Walke and my jointure of £600 st. to my mother Mrs Mary Walke. £100 to my father-in-law Cumberbatch Sober, Esq., for Eliza Rice, late Allison, for the support of Emily Allison her child. Plate equally to my three chⁿ Harrison Walke Sober, Judith Sober and Eliza Jennett Sober. My father-in-law sole Ex'or. In the presence of Jennett Sober, Eliza Branthwayt, Joan Trent. Proved 15 Dec. 1815 by C. S., Esq. (624, Pakenham.)

ST. JOHN'S, BARBADOS.

1734-5 Feb. 18 Thomas Sober to Jane Redman.

ST. JOSEPH'S, BARBADOS.

1738-9 Mar. 2 John Sobers to Margaret Ceeley.

ST. GEORGE'S, HANOVER SQUARE.

1818 Feb. 19 Francis Onslow Trent, Esq., B., of this parish. & Judith Sober, S., of St. Marylebone. Lic.

1638. John Sober and Tho. Sober, owners of more than 10 acres. (Memoirs of the First Settlement, p. 82.)

1760, Nov. 6. John Sober, Esq., of Barbadoes, to Miss Pen. Blake of Sevenoak, Kent. ("G.M.," 542.)

514

1774, Feb. 2. Bath. Sat. died at her lodgings in this City, the lady of John Sober, Esq., of the island of Barbados. ("Bath Chronicle.")

1802, Feb. 15. At her father's house, the wife of A. C. Sober, esq. a still-born dau. ("G.M.," 181.)

1805, July 6. Mrs. Hannah Sober, St. Michaels. ("Barbados Mercury.")

1805, Dec. 24. Mr. Aaron Sober to Miss Sarah Elizabeth Wilkie, St. Michael's. (*Ibid.*)

1811, March 7. In Upper George-street, Portman-sq. Sampson Wood Sober, esq. of the Polygon, Southampton, only son of Cumberbatch Sober, esq. ("G.M.," 397.)

1811, Apr. 23. On the 4th ulto. at his father's house, London, Sampson Wood Sober, Esq., of this island. ("Barbados Mercury.")

1813, Dec. 7. Aged 42, Abraham Cumberbatch Sober, esq. ("G.M.," 700.)

1815, Dec. 1. In Blandford-st. aged 42, Mrs. Jennett Sober, relict of the late S. W. Sober, esq. of the Polygon, Southampton. (*Ibid.*, 642.)

1827, Jan. 13, In Upper George-st. Bryanston-sq. aged 85, Cumberbatch Sober, esq. (*Ibid.*, 92.)

1832, Oct. 16. In Torrington-sq. aged 18, Mary-Esther, youngest dau. of late Abraham Cumberbatch Sober, esq. (*Ibid*, 482.)

Tho. Kemp of Lewes Castle and Hurstmonceaux Park, co. Sussex, M.P., left a son Tho. R. Kemp, born 1782, and a dau. Anne, who mar. 1, Rev. Geo. Bythesea, R. of Ightham, co. Kent, and 2, Capt. A. C. Sober of the Dragoon Guards. (Burkes "Landed Gentry.")

Eton, 1811. Harrison Walke Sober, formerly of the 14th Hussars, died lately. (Eton School Lists, published in 1863, p. 73.)

THORNHILL OF BARBADOS.

Extracts from the Census records of 1679 and 1715.

1679.	Parish	Inhabitants.	Servants.	Acres.	Slaves.
	St. James	Col. Timothy Thornehill	7	268	150
	do.	Captain Timothy Thornehill	10		
	St. Andrew	Captain Timothy Thornehill 1		170	150

List of the most eminent planters:

Colonel Timothy Thornehill   500 acres.

Forces in the Island.

Colonel Timothy Thornehill, Regiment of Foot, 655 men.

„ „ „ 3 officers, 104 men.

Captain Timothy Thornehill 1 officer, 83 men.

1715.	Parish	Inhabitants.	Ages.
	St. George	Timothy Thornhill	24
		Catherine Thornhill	18
		Henry Thornhill	¼
	St. Thomas	Phillippa Thornhill	45
		Mrs. Mary Thornhill	16

BARBADOS WILLS.

Colonel TIMOTHY THORNHILL. Will dated 7 June 1681. To be buried in St. Thomas Church either in or near as possible to ye grave of my deceased wives both called Susannah.

To my daughter Ann, my eldest daughter unmarried, £1,000 at 18 which will be 4 May 1682, or marriage.

To my youngest daughter Judith £1,000 at 18, which will be on 29 March 168........[indistinct], or marriage.

To my son Henry, £1,500 at 21, which will be 26 Feby. 1689, and £200 at 14 or 15 to bind him out to some honourable apprenticeship.

To my youngest son Thomas, £1,500 at 21, which will be the last day of March 1691, and £200 to bind him out apprentice, to some honourable profession.

To Susannah Strode, Sarah Strode, Elizabeth Strode, John Strode, Ann Strode and Mary Strode, children of John Strode by my eldest daughter, Mary, £100 each.

To the poor of the parish of St. James, 20,000 lbs. of Muscovado sugar. To my son-in-law, Captain John Samson and to my daughter, Susanna, his wife, and to my son-in-law, John Strode, and to my daughter Mary his wife, and to my son, Captain Richard Salter and Elizabeth my daughter, his wife, each a mourning suit.

To my eldest son, Timothy, all my estate and he to be sole executor. My son-in-laws John Strode and Captain John Richard Salter to be trustees of my four children minors.

To my brother [?in-law] Major John Hawkesworth and to Mr. Charles Legard, minister of the parish of St. James, each a mourning suit.

To Hon. John Reid £20 to buy him and his lady mourning, and £5 for................daughter Agnes Reid.

(Sgd.) Tim. Thornhill. Witnesses: Thomas Fuller, Philip Morgan, John Dubey. Proved 10 August 1681 by Oaths of Futter and Morgan before Richard Dutton, Governor.

TIMOTHY THORNHILL of St. Lucy, gent. Will dated 2 March 1726.

My loving wife, Katherine, £100 per annum, slaves, horse and saddle, living in my house and care of my children.

My sons Timothy and Dowding £750 cy. each at 18.

My daughters Elizabeth and Judith £500 cy. each at 18.

To my son Henry and his heirs all rest of my estate at 21, but in the event of his death, then to my son Timothy and his heirs at 21, and failing him to my son Dowding and his heirs.

My brother Colonel Dowding Thornhill, Mr. John Poyer, and Mr. Hurdis Jordan, executors.

X the mark of Timothy Thornhill. Witnesses: Timothy Salter, D. Thornhill, John Alleyne. Proved by Hon. Timothy Salter Esq. 16 March 1726/7 before Hen. Worsley, Governor.

THOMAS THORNHILL of St. Thomas, esquire. Will dated 10 Feby. 1730.

My whole estate to my mother, Phillipa Thornhill, and she to be sole executrix.

(sgd.) Tho. Thornhill. Witnesses : J. Amson (?), Robt. Warren, Edw. Doldarne. Proved 18 March 1730 before Hen. Worsley, Governor.

DOWDING THORNHILL of St. Lucy. Will dated 2 November 1732.

To my wife Jane, two negro wenches with their issue for her life, also one-half of my household stuff, plate, jewels, etc. Also one-half of my estate real or personal which I am possessed of or which may fall to me on my mother's death or otherwise, for her life.

To my daughter Mary two negroes and the other half of my household stuff, jewels, plate, etc. together with the residue of my estate and the reversion of my wife's half thereof. If my wife shall have a child, if a boy my Will is that my estate bequeathed to my daughter, except the negroes and household stuff, shall be for such male child at 21, allowing £1,500 for Mary out of my estate at 18 or marriage; if a girl child, £500 for her at 15 or marriage.

In case of failure of issue I give my estate to my nephew Henry Thornhill.

To my mother and mother-in-law 40/- to by two mourning rings.

To my nephew Henry £100 at 21, and to my other two nephews, Timothy and Dowding and my neices Elizabeth and Judith £25 each at 21 to buy a negro.

I empower my executors to sell as many acres of the out-skirts of my estate for payment of my debts especially that of grandmother Dowding's in the parish of St. Peter, bounding on Matthew Grey Esq. and others and whereon Charles McCarty now lives as tenant, and of 16 acres bounding on George Hannay and John Poyer and Thomas Gilkes, and of 13 acres whereon Nicholas Chandler now lives and John Hollingsworth lived as tenant, and to sell as much sugar and rum crops off my estate over and above my wife's one-half as must fit. I appoint Reynold Alleyne senr. and Major John Alleyne esq., Lt. Col. Wm. Sandiford, John Poyer and Hurdis Jordan esqurs. and Mr. John Trent executors. and my wife Jane (during widowhood) executrix.

(sd.) D. Thornhill. Witnesses: Charles McCarty, Daniel Yates, Samuel Beron. Proved 19 January 1732 before President James Dotin.

PHILIPPA THORNHILL of St. Thomas, widow. Will dated 16 Feby. 1733.

To Elizabeth Whetstone, spinster, £100 and the black chest of drawers in my bedchamber with all my clothes therein. Residue of my estate and the whole estate of my late kinswoman Philippa Evans deceased to my son-in-law Edward Doldarne, merchant, and he to be sole executors. During his absence from the island I appoint Robert Warren esq. my executor.

517

(sgd.) Philippa Thornhill. Witnesses: Benjamin Clarke, Sarah Doldarne, Lydia Anderson. Proved 5 April 1734 before Lord Howe.

JANE THORNHILL of St. Lucy. Will dated 3 April 1739. To my grand daughter Mary Thornhill Bonnet £500 and 4 negroes at 21. To my grand daughter Jane Waldron Bonnet £200 and a negro girl. To my grand daughter Thomasin Bonnet £100 and one negro. To my nephew Henry Thornhill £50. The estate of my late husband Dowding Thornhill. To my daughter Mary Bonnet, provided she survives her husband Edward Bonnet, if not surviving, to her children.

If my daughter and grand children die I give to my brothers Major Michael Terrill and Col. William Sandiford each £50. To my 3 nieces Cornelia Sandiford, daughter of Colonel Sandiford, Jane Terrill, daughter of Major Terrill, Cornelia Yearwood, daughter of Samuel Yearwood, and residue of my nephew Henry Thornhill.

I appoint my brother Colonel Wm. Sandiford and Lt. Col. Hillary Rowe, Captain John Waite, and Mr. Jacob Scott executors in trust.

(sgd.) Jane Thornhill. Witnesses : Elia Goulding, John Griffith, Mary Jordan. Proved 7 October 1739 before James Dottin.

TIMOTHY THORNHILL of Christ Church. Dated 7 December 1758. To my son Timothy 4 negroes. To my son Dowding 4 negroes. To my daughter Henrietta 4 negroes, a bed, bolster, pillows etc., chest of drawers, dressing table, and glass thereon, chamber table and hair trunk, set of china and small mahogany round table and the apparel of her deceased mother. Residue to be divided between by sons Timothy and Dowding. My brothers Henry and Dowding Thornhill to be executors and guardians. (sgd.) Timothy Thornhill. Witnesses : Jno Carter, Alexander Butcher, jr. Proved 31 March 1759, before Charles Pinfold.

DOWDING THORNHILL of St. George. Will dated 25 April 1770. To my wife Jane 6 negroes, furniture, (plate excepted) carriage, two horses, her riding horse and saddle, with £60 per annum and her living on my plantation, but if my son Henry marries the annuity to be increased to £100.

To my son Dowding jnr 5 negroes and he to be kept in England and educated at the expense of my estate until 16 and then to return to Barbados to be apprenticed to some linen and dry goods way at £30 per annum and £1,000 to be put in trade. If he dies before 21 £500 to be paid to my daughter Jane Ann Terrill Thornhill.

To Jane Ann Terrill Thornhill 4 negroes and £30 per an. until 21 and £1,000 after the death of my wife £200 more. If she dies before 21 then £600 of her legacy to my son Dowding. She is to have her living on my estate.

My son Henry to be kept in England five years and allowed 100 guineas per annum, and at the end of five years to receive all the residue of my estate, failing him to son Dowding jnr. who shall pay Jane Ann Terril Thornhill £1,000 and failing her to my wife Jane.

I appoint my brother Hon. Henry Thornhill and nephews Henry Thornhill and Hon. Hillary Rowe jnr. and Mr. Gabriel Ford executors.

To Mrs. Elizabeth Pickett £5 for a ring, and the same to Thomas White.

(sgd.) Dowding Thornhill. Witnesses : William Eversley, Samuel Benskin, Thomas White.

Codicil dated 25 April 1770 directing money left after paying annual expenses to be paid towards debts.

Will and codicil proved 4 July 1770 before Wm. Spry.

HENRY THORNHILL of St. George. Will dated 28 July 1769.

To my wife Mary during her widowhood her living on my estate Locust Hall with all my plate and household furniture. Also my chariot and pair of horses and use of my town negroes during her life. Our marriage settlement £400.

To my son Alexander £2,500 at 23 and until then £100 per an.

If my wife should bear another child I give it £2,500 at 23 and my town negroes at my wife's death. To my grandson Henry Clarke £1,000 at 21. To my granddaughter Cornelia Thornhill Rowe at 21 £1,000. To my son Hon. Henry Thornhill £50 to buy mourning and a large estate in St. Lucy already provided with stock. To my daughter Jane Rowe, wife of Hon. Hillary Rowe, jnr., £50 for mourning and she is already provided for at the time of her marriage.

To my two sons in law William and Edmund Eversley £50 for mourning.

To my son Timothy my estate Locust Hall in St. George with all stock thereon and all residue of my estate, he paying my debts and legacies. To my son Timothy sole executor.

(sgd.) Henry Thornhill. Witnesses: John Ramsey. Thomas White.

Proved 17 September 1770 before Wm. Spry.

HENRY THORNHILL of St. Thomas. Will dated 10 June 1780.

To my wife Elizabeth Adams Thornhill £100 per annum and living on my estate Lion Castle until my son Henry attains 21.

To my son Henry at 21 residue of my estate. If he dies under 21 then to my wife Elizabeth Adams she paying my mother Mrs. Jane Thornhill £100, my sister Mrs. Jane Gibson £100 and my brother Dowding Thornhill £100. I appoint my wife executrix, Hon. Robert Burrowes and Benjamin Bostock executors and guardians.

(sgd.) Henry Thornhill. Witness: Thomas White, Thomas White junr., Benjamin Farley. Proved 17 December 1781 before James Cunninghame.

519

TIMOTHY THORNHILL of St. Michael. Will dated 11 February 1811.

To my wife Elizabeth Sedgwick Thornhill £4,000 and 16 slaves, my household furniture, one-half of my plate, horse and chaise. All sums due to me by Messrs. Barrow, Lousadas & DaCosta, John & Richard Inniss, and Dr. Cutting to be assigned to my wife as part of her legacy of £4,000.

Whereas my father Henry Thornhill, snr., on marriage of my brother Henry Thornhill gave him an estate in St. Lucy called Harrisons subject to a mortgage to David Parris for £3,000 or £4,000 and a debt due to Richard Ellcock upon a solemn verbal promise that he would pay the said debts, and also to his son-in-law Hillary Rowe a debt due to him, and to Jacob Hussey a debt due to him, which several debts remain unpaid owing to the improper conduct of the said David Parris who having foreclosed the said mortgage declared at the sale of the said mortgaged premises by the Master that whosoever should bid more than he and which was less than the amount of the mortgage money should be obliged to pay immediately the whole sum due to him, well knowing from the melancholy state, the island had been in and was then that it was not in power of any person at that time in Barbados to raise so large a sum, he therefore became the purchaser of the plantation. To do away with any unfavourable opinion of my father from the aforesaid debts being still unpaid, I give unto the legal representatives of the said Richard Ellcock the sum now due to me by Dr. Grant Ellcock on note and also due me by Hon. Joshua Gittens on execution and note and the sum of £1,200. I give to the legal representatives of the said Jacob Hussey £600 and I declare such gifts are in satisfaction of all debts owing to them from my said Father.

I give the residue of my estate to the child my wife may be expecting at the time of my death, if no such child, then residue be divided as follows. To William Thornhill debt due from him to me, and £1,000 due me from Hamlet Wilson, Esq. I give to each of the children of my niece Deborah Piggott £200 at 21. To my great nephew Timothy William Thornhill £2,000 at 21. If he dies without issue then £1,000 to nephew William Thornhill. To my great nephew Hillary Rowe £1,000 at 21. To my cousin Jane Dowding Gibson £200. To cousins Dowding and Henry Thornhill £50 each. To Elizabeth Thornhill daughter of Dowding Thornhill £100. To friends Rev. John Brome and Mr. John Inniss ten guineas each. Residue to great nephews Hillary Rowe and Timothy William Thornhill at 21.

I appoint my nephew Thomas Rowe and cousins Dowding Thornhill and Henry Thornhill and my friends Rev. John Brome and John Inniss executors.

(sgd.) Timy. Thornhill. Witnesses : John Howell Todd, Samuel Games.

Codicil dated 7 February 1813. To my wife £100 in addition. To cousin Jane Gibson £100. Adjustment necessary on Hamlet Wilson having paid £1,000. Directs £500 part of sum now due of late nephews Hillary Rowe's sealed note to Samuel Ramsden decd., and to me to be applied in part payment of sum given to representatives of my brother-in-law Hillary Rowe, and surplus to nephew Hillary Rowe.

Will and Codicil proved 11 May 1831 before Governor Beckwith.

THORNHILL BAPTISMS TO 1850

Ch. Ch.	1646 Decr. 22	Mary d. of Timothy and S u s a n Thornhill.
Ch. Ch.	1648 Feby. 13	Susan d. of Michael and ....Thornhill
Ch. Ch.	1650 Novr. 7	Susan d. of Timothy Thornhill.
S. Jas.	1697 Octr. 23	Henry s. of Lt. Col. Thomas and Phillippa Thornhill.
S. Jas.	1698 Octr. 4	Mary d. of Col. Thomas and Phillippa Thornhill.
S. Luc.	1754 Feby. 17	Gibbons Williams s. of Henry and Mary Thornhill, born 16 January.
S. Luc.	1756 Feby. 8	Cornelia d. of Henry and Cornelia Thornhill, born 17 Novr., 1755.
S. Thos.	1756 July 18	Mary Ann Jane Tyrel d. of Dowdin Thornhill.
S. Luc.	1757 June	Thomas s. of Henry Thornhill and Cornelia, born 16 June.
S. M.	1768 Decr. 30	Henry Clarke s. of Henry and Deborah Thornhill, born 25 Octr.
S. M.	1770 April 12	Gedney s. of Henry and Deborah Thornhill.
S. M.	1771 Decr. 19	Timothy s. of Henry and Deborah Thornhill, born 16 Octr.
S. Luc.	1775 April 11	William s. of Henry and Deborah Thornhill, born 11 April.
S. M.	1778 June 2	Deborah d. of Henry and Deborah Thronhill, born 20 July, 1776.
S. Pas.	1782 March 31	Henry s. of Henry and Elizabeth Thornhill.
S. Jas.	1796 Decr. 26	Dowding s. of Dowding and Thomasin Ann Thornhill, born 1 Decr.
S. Jas.	1799 March 10	Henry s. of Dowding and T. Ann Thornhill, born 6 February.
Ch. Ch.	1800 Sept. 12	Deborah d. of Gidney and Sarah Thornhill, born 7 Aug.
S. Jas.	1801 May 10	Robert s. of Dowding and T. Ann Thornhill, born 23 Decr.
S. M.	1803 Feby. 28	Timothy William s. of Gidney and Sarah Thornhill, born 14 Septr., 1801.
S. Jas.	1803 Augt. 14	Elizabeth Jane d. of Dowding and T. Ann Thornhill, born 18 March.
S. Jas.	1806 July 22	Thomasin Ann d. of Dowding and T. Ann Thornhill, born 5 Novr. 1805.

S. Jas.	1808 March 13	Jane Terril d. of Dowding and T. Ann Thornhill.
S. Jas.	1810 Novr. 13	Mary d. of Henry and Sarah Thornhill, born 13 August
S. Jas.	1811 May 21	Francis d. of Dowding and T. Ann Thornhill, born 21 May.
S. Jas.	1813 Decr. 26	Timothy s. of Dowding and T. Ann Thornhill.
S. Jas.	1814 June 20	Jane Elizabeth d. of Henry and Sarah Thornhill.
S. Jas.	1815 Novr. 29	Thomasin Ann d. of Dowding and T. Ann Thornhill, born 8 April.

THORNHILL MARRIAGES, TO 1850.

Ch. Ch.	1647 May 28	Peter Thornhill to Eleanor Gardner.
St. M.	1672 Decr. 5	Ann Thornhill to Maj. John Hawkesworth.
St. M.	1713 Septr. 13	William Thornhill to Sarah Lucas.
S. Thos.	1728 Novr. 7	Mary Thornhill to Edward Doldane.
S. Luc.	1762 May 20	Jane Thornhill to Hillary Rowe.
S. Luc.	1762	Dowding Thornhill to Jane Terrill.
St. M.	1767 Octr. 8	Henry Thornhill, jnr. to Mrs. Deborah Clarke, Spr.
S. Thos.	1777 Augt. 7	Francis Gibson to Jane Ann Terrill Thornhill.
S. Jas.	1779 June 24	Henry Thornhill to Elizabeth Adams Burrowes, spr.
S. Luc.	1780 July 27	Henrietta Thornhill to Rev. Thos. Harris.
St. M.	1794 Decr. 30	Timothy Thornhill to Jane Spry Backhouse, widow.
S. Jas	1795 Novr. 25	Dowding Thornhill to Thomasin Ann Burrowes.
Ch. Ch.	1799 Sept. 15	Gidney Thornhill to Sarah Cumberbatch.
S. Phil.	1803 Mar. 12	Capt. Timothy Thornhill to Elizabeth Sedgewick Garner.

THORNHILL BURIALS.

St. M.	1660 Dec. 28	Isaac Thornhill.
St. M.	1661 April 21	Isaac Thornhill.
St. M.	1698 Sep. 22	Col. Thomas Thornhill.
S. Jas.	1698 Sep. 22	Lt. Col. Thomas Thornhill.
St. M.	1703 July 5	Timothy Thornhill.
St. M.	1714 May 3	John Thornhill:
St. M.	1730 Feb. 26	Thomas Thornhill.

THORNHILL DEEDS

Barbados. Whereas a difference depends between Capt. Tymothy Thornhill now resident in the Island and John Boyce of County of Middlesex, Mariner, and now resident in Barbados, which difference was referred to us Lt. John Holmes, George

Read, Christopher Thomson and John Maniford as arbitrators by document 1 July 1643 We therefore award Tymothy Thornhill 1229¾ lbs. tobacco or cotton to be paid by John Boyce; and Tymothy Thornhill to give John Boyce power to receive £11 sterling from Roger and Lucanion of Boston, New England, part of a bond of Ensign Hall and other St. Christopher planters. Dated 6th July, 1643.

Edward Harris of Barbados, gentleman, sells Sgt. Major Tymothy Thornhill of Barbados a moiety of 150 acres land with half of negroes, cattle, etc. situate in St. Thomas called *Mangrove* plantation Butting and bounding on lands of Mr. William Thomas, Captain John Barker, Captain Peter Edney and ye glebe land.

Dated 17th May 1654. Edward Harris, Wits.—Mott, Thornhill—rington. Pd. 30 May 1654 by Edw. Harris before Thos. Noell.

Whereas William Phillips of Barbados gentleman deceased left considerable estate in Barbados—plantations, lands, houses, stock, servants, etc., which came to Anne his widow and relict now the wife of John Thornhill of London, Merchant, by virtue of certain Letters of Administration granted her. Appoint my loving brother and friend Coll Tymothy Thornhill, Captain John Webster, Captain Lawrence Hallstead, and Mr. John Horne, all of Barbados, authority to collect.

Dated 20 January 1658—John Thornhill, Ann Thornhill.

Witnesses: William Smith, Easter Hallstead.

Proofs before Lord Mayor of London. Produced L.A. under seal of Court of Commonwealth for probate of wills.

Whereas by deed by Mr. James and Martin Noell of London, Merchants, 8 August 1654, we: Thomas Noell of Barbados Esquire, and Richard Buckworth of Barbados, gentlemen, together with John Bayes and John Maniford of Barbados, merchants, are empowered to grant estate in Barbados held by James and Martin Noell and Stephen Noell deceased and particularly plantation çalled Black Rock owned by them—we grant unto Sgt.-Major Tymothy Thornhill Black Rock plantation in St. James 150 acres, house, etc.

Dated 29th May, 1656.—Tho. Noell, Richard Buckworth.

Witnesses: John Webster, John Naylor, Robt. Drye, Tho. Middleton. Pd: 29 May 1656 before John Hawkeridge.

Thomas Abbott of Barbados, Merchant, grants to Major Timothy Thornhill of Barbados, gentleman, the plantation I formerly lived on and now in possession of Mr. John Partridge of Barbados, Merchant, containing 46 acres in St. James, Bounded leeward on land of Mr. Dorrill, windward on land of Capt. Philip Miller and one end by a parcel of land belonging to William Land and the other end by the sea, with 7 Christian servants,........ negroes, 4 assinegoes, 1 featherbed and bolster, 2 pillows, and a chest of drawers, 2 tables, 2 formes, 2 bedsteads with 2 pair of curtains and vallens, 15 butter dishes, 1 dozen of great plates, 10 small plates, 2 flagon potts, 2 candle sticks, 2 sallet dishes, a pewter basin, a stewpan of brass, 2 brass skellets, a pair of

523

tongs, and a fine shovel of brass, a chaffing dish, 3 brass lamps, 3 quart pots, a pint pot, a half-pint pot, a pewter salt, a marble salt, a wax candlestick of brass, a new three-breadth hammock, 40 swine small and great, a stone jug with kiverlid, 3 chests, 2 trunks, a small pewter vinegar bottle, a brass pestle and mortar, a smothing iron with 2 heaters, a brass kettle, 3 iron pots, a baking stone, a frying pan and brass ladle.

Dated 2nd January, 1656—Tho. Abbott.

Witnesses : John Partridge, John Thornhill, Robert Dea, Thos Hughes.

Acknowledged before John Hawkeridge 13 January 1656.

Joseph Lowe of Barbados, Chirurgeon, and Dorothy his wife formerly called Dorothy Clinckett, widow and relict and administratrix and principal devisee of John C. Clinckett of Barbados deceased. £1800 Sterling paid by Hon. Sir Tymothy Thornhill, Barbados, sells one-third part of sugar plantation 230 acres in St. Peter and St. Andrew Butting and bounding on lands of Rev. Wm. Walker, Clerke, Robert Johnstone, other lands of Sir Tymothy Thornhill, lands late of Henry Clinckett decd. George Gray, Robert Maxwell and John Hurst one-third stone mill, boilinghouse 9 coppers, 3 stills, dwellinghouse, 28 cattle, which John Clinckett had in common with his brothers Abraham Clinckett and Benjamin Clinckett.

Dated 19 April 1686. Sgd. Joseph Lowe. Dorothy X D. L. Lowe.

Witnesses: Wm. Forster junr. John Legard. Ack: 19 April 1656 before Wm. Forster.

Anthony Dyer and William Russell of Barbados, planters, for certain sugar paid, do grant to Major Timothy Thornhill of Barbados one plantation commonly called the ten acre plantation Butting and bounding Capt. Wm. Thomas, Raymond——, Lieut, Richard P—— and S. Thomas.

Dated 28 July 1655. Anthony Dyer. Wm. P. X Russell.

Witnesses: John Stretton. Ack. 28 July 1665 before John Colleton.

17 March 16— Timothy Thornhill of Saint James demises to George Hurst of St. Andrew, gentleman, all that his plantation in St. Peter containing 20—— Bounding east on Jeremiah Savory, north on lands of Clincketts, west on lands of Richard Parker, Elias Luke and Meletiah Holder, and south on Wm. Hawkesworth and Cap. Thomas Hothersall and one other parcel of land butting n.e. on the land of John Wayte s.w. on Thomas Johnstone s.e. on the River and n.w. on lands of Abel Alleyne with windmill (wall sided?) boiling house, coppers, etc., still house, still wormes and worm tubs, curing house, dwellinghouse, and also 100 negroes and 16 meat cattle, for 11 years from 1 July next at the Assurance office Royal Exchange London £700 sterling. If mill and buildings destroyed by hurricane Timothy Thornhill will pay half cost of workmen's wages and find timbers and stuff for repairs. Timothy Thornhill to cut timber for use of his other plantation called the Black Rock

plantation. To grow and leave 60 ac. of first crop canes with one box of dung in each cane hole. Sgd. George Hurst.

Witnesses: George Payne, Richard Middleton. Ack: by George Payne 23rd February 1682 before Will Howe.

List of negroes and value of each.

Memo regarding children slaves who were to remain on the said four hills plantation.

15 December 1681—Lt.-Col. Andrew Afflick St. James, Barbados, and Major Timothy Thornhill of same parish £1500 paid. Sells his plantation in St. James 100 acres Bounding Mr. John Hooker, the land of Mr. Thomas, the salt sea, on Mr. Philip Gibbes, and on lands now——Yeamans widow. Stone windmill for grinding sugar canes at and making of sugar. 64 negro slaves, —Andrew Affleck.

Witnesses: John Farmer, William Chester, William Kirkham. On 3 March 1683 Lt. Col. John Farmer, and Mr. Will Chester gentlemen appeared before Hon. Wm. Howe, Chief Justice for His Majesty's Court of Common Pleas held for St. James and St. Thomas and swore they saw Affleck sign. Will Howe.

25 October 1683. Laughlan Constantine, labourer, St. James, Barbados, and the Hon. Sir Timothy Thornhill of Barbados, sells 8 acres St. James, Bounding and butting John Martin, Robert Harris, Abraham Harrison, —Moll and 2 slaves in consideration of his support of Constantine during his life and decent burial etc. X Laughlan Constantine—Witnesses:J. Legard, Saml. X Apthorp, John Hall.

Major Thomas Helme of St. James Barbados, sells to Sir Timothy Thornhill, Bart. of St. James, Barbados, all his lands and buildings situate in Towne of *Speights Bay*, alias *Little Bristol*.

Dated 15 October 1683. Thomas Helme.

Witnesses: J. Legard, John Browne. Ack: 1 November 1683 by Thomas Helme before John Reid.

Dated 15 October 1683—Hon. Sir Timothy Thornhill of St. James, Barbados, Dame Thomasin his wife and Jacob Scatteby of St. Peter, Planter, sells plantation of 71 acres in St. Peter Butting and bounding on lands late of Major John Stoute deceased, Anne Kelsall, lands late of Capt. John Maynard deceased, Henry Williams deceased, and Robt. Goldstone; 1 other parcel of land 6 acres near above Butting and bounding on lands of Major John Stoute deceased, Col. Alexr. Riddocke deceased (formerly in occupation of May Jarvey deceased). Signed Timothy Thornhill, Thomasin Thornhill.

Witnesses: Wm. Chester, John Doughtye, Charles Legard.

Ack: 1 November 1683. John Reid.

Dated 13th October 1683. Sir Timothy Thornhill of St. James, Bart. and Dame Thomasin his wife convey above land to Major Thomas Helme.

Witnesses: J. Legard, John Browne, Ack: 1st November 1683 by Sir Timothy Thornhill and Dame Thomasin his wife before John Reid.

Dated 15th October, 1683. Hon. Sir Timothy Thornhill of St. James, Barbados and Dame Thomasin his wife and Liuet.-Col. John Farmer and Major Thomas Helme All those plantations called Four Hills containing in the whole 250 acres being lands which said Timothy Thornhill lately demised to George Hurst (now deceased) situate in St. Peter and St. Andrew Butting and bounding on lands of Jeremiah Savary, on lands now or late of said George Hurst, deceased, lands of the Clincketts, Richard Parker, Elias Lake, Melita Holder, Wm. Hawkesworth, Thomas Hothersall, being the major part thereof. Bounding on lands of John Waite, Thomas Johnson, and on a river, and Major Abel Alleyne,—windmill, boilinghouse, and 120 negro slaves (names in schedule) *to the use* of Sir Timothy Thornhill and his wife. for their lives and survivor and after the decease of Sir Timothy Thornhill and Dame Thomasin to use of the heirs of their bodies and in default of issue to use of Sir Timothy Thornhill if he survived his wife, and if she survived to the use of herself for a jointure, and to the use of Sir Timothy Thornhill. If Dame Thomasin predeceased without issue to have right to will £1000. Sgd. Tim Thornhill Thomasin Thornhill.

Witnesses: Charles Legard, John Doughty.

Ack: 1st November 1683 before John Reid.

15 October 1683. Counterpart of above signed by John Farmer and Thomas Helme in the presence of Samuel Farmer, Joshua Foxley, Samuel Lanethorne—List of Slaves.

526

SOME RECORDS OF TRENT, CARLETON, AND CUMBERBATCH FAMILIES OF BARBADOS.

Contributed by E. M. SHILSTONE.

COMPLETE pedigrees of the Trent, Carleton, and Cumberbatch families, all connected by marriage, would seem to be wanting. A pedigree of SOBER of Barbados published in V. L. Oliver's *Caribbeana,* Volume V, p 251, records the connection between that family and Abraham Cumberbatch's descendants; and in 1866 a compilation entitled 'Collections for a Genealogical Account of the Family of Cumberbatch' was published in London by George W. Marshall, Ll.B. Neither of these compilations gives much of the available records of the Barbados family.

COMBERBACH or CUMBERBATCH appears to have been a Bristol family. Abraham Cumberbatch of Bristol married Ann Lord of St. Philip's parish, Bristol. The marriage allegation bears date 15 May 1675. He was probably the same Abraham Cumberbatch whose will was proved 1690 (88 Duke)* and he may have been the father of Dr. Josias Cumberbatch, Abraham Cumberbatch, and Ann Cumberbatch who are the first persons of the surname mentioned in the Barbados records in the early eighteenth century.

The TRENT family seems to have had an earlier connection with Barbados. Lawrence Trent does not figure in the Census records of 1679, but not many years after he and his family of four sons and two daughters were established in Speightstown.

The family of CARLETON was of the parish of St. Thomas as early as 1670. Edward Carleton of the third generation married Ann, one of the two daughters of Abraham Cumberbatch of Cleland and The Farm plantations. Her sister, Mary Cumberbatch married John Sober of The Castle, St. Peter, thus causing the union of those three families in one generation. The connection with the TRENT family came in the next generation with the marriage of the son and only child of the marriage between Edward Carleton and Ann Cumberbatch with Elizabeth, the daughter of Lawrence Trent and Jane his wife. In the meantime, this son of Edward Carleton, Abraham by name, had become entitled under the Will of his grandfather, Abraham Cumberbtach, to Cleland and The Farm plantations and by the direction of the testator had assumed the surname Cumberbatch.

There are no longer any descendants in the male line of any of these three families in Barbados. On the distaff side there are descendants of the Carletons through their connections with the Walrond and Howell families.

The plantations Cleland, The Farm, and Ebworth which once belonged to the Cumberbatch brothers have since passed out of

---

* I have not seen the Will.

the family ownership. Nicholas plantation, St. Peter, is now the sole remaining link with the past history of the family. The plantation with the fine old mansion known as Nicholas Abbey still belongs to Captain C. J. P. Cave of Hampshire, England, a grandson of Charles Cave who married Sarah, daughter of Edward Carleton Cumberbatch, who with his brother, Lawrence Trent Cumberbatch, purchased it in the year 1811.

TRENT WILLS.

LAWRENCE TRENT of Parish of St. Peter, Barbados, Esquire, bound for Kingdom of England.

To my eldest son John T. the house in town of Spights Bay in which Wm. Browne now lives and one shade [shed] opposite to it, two lusty men negroes and one woman negro and £1,000 Stg. provided he marry with approbation of my executors, Wm. Forster and Wm. Cleland Esquires, when he shall accomplish 21, and if he marry without their consent £500 only at 25.

To my second son William T. the house that James Nore now lives in, and one negro boy and £500 Stg. at 21, also his maintenance in England whilst he remain there or if he shall return here until he shall accomplish his age. To my third son Andrew T. the house that Dr. Sherman now lives in upon Spights Bay together with one negro boy and girl and £500 at 21 and in the meantime to have his schooling and maintenance. To my fourth son Lawrence T. ye house in Spights Bay in which Mr. Ward now lives and one negro boy and one negro girl and £500 at 21 and in the meantime his maintenance and schooling. To my two daughters, Elizabeth and Agnes, £600 each within 12 months of their respective marriages and one negro boy and one negro girl each. Executors £10 each for mourning. To my god-daughter Sarah Forster ye daughter of Col. Wm. Forster ye sum of £40 Stg. All residue of my estate to be divided between my sons and daughters equally. My trusty friends Col. Wm. Forster and Capt. Wm. Cleland executors and guardians of my estate. Dated 11 July 1692. Law: Trent. Witnesses: Sam. Lambart, Edwd. Forster. Sworn by Edward Forster. 23 March, 1692/3.

JOHN TRENT of St. Peter, Barbados, Merchant.

To my four grandchildren, children of my daughter Susannah Pickering late wife of Col. John Pickering, viz. John, Joseph, Elizabeth, and Sarah P. each £400 Cy., being money now due to me from said Col. J. P. and to remain in his hands for their use at 8% interest until grandson John attains 21 and my granddaughters at 16. If either of them should die I bequeath his or her legacy to my son Lawrence Trent. To my daughter Sarah Yeamans £400 Cy. and to her son my grandson Robt. Yeamans £400 cy. To my three grandchildren Edward Denny,

Trent Denny and Elizabeth Denny, children of my daughter Elizabeth Denny, widow of Mr. Edwd. Denny late dec'd £400 each at 21. To my six grandchildren, children of my daughter Agnes Denny wife of John Denny, viz: John, Samuel, Lawrence, Edward, Thomas and Susannah £400 each at 21, and also £400 to the child now to be born of my said daughter Agnes Denny. I appoint my brother Mr. Andrew Trent have his accommodation in my house as he now hath, and the keeping of a horse and boy during his natural life. I appoint my sister Agnes Burgess hath her accommodation in my house with the keeping of the negro she now hath during her single life. I bequeath unto my apprentice Elizth Rash £5 Cy. the day she is free. To Col. Jno Pickering, my daughter Sarah Yeamans, Mr. Jno Denny £20 each for mourning. To my brother Andrew Trent and sister Agnes Burgess £10 each for mourning. To my granddaughter Elizabeth Timbrell and her husband Wm. Timbrell one suit of mourning each. To Rd. Mills £10 Cy. to buy mourning. I devise and bequeath residue of estate to my son Lawrence Trent and appoint said son, my brother Andrew Trent, friend Hon. James Bruce Esq., son-in-law Mr. Jno. Denny and late apprentice Rd. Milles to be exors. Dated 4 February 1734. John Trent. Wit: Bowden Fercharson, Wm. Delahantey, Anthony Jones. Sworn by A. Jones 2 June 1735.

ANDREW TRENT, of St. Peter, Barbados, Gentleman.

To my natural son Andrew T. £50 Cy. To my sister Agnes Burgess £150 Cy. Residue to nephew Lawrence T. and appoint him executor. 4 Decr. 1735. Andrew Trent. Wit: John Lindsey, Rd. Milles. Sworn by Rd. Milles 22 Oct. 1736.

WILLIAM TRENT of Biddenden, Kent, England. (Browne 259.) Will dated 1 May 1737.

To Mary wife of Joseph Disney of Cranbrook, and Matthew, William and Mary her children. My sister, widow Burgess of Barbados. Thomas Ross of St. Kitts. Servants Mary Leeds, Richard Giles who married Martha El Gillet. Sarah Oliver wife of William Oliver and her sister Elizabeth now living in Cranbrook. Godson William, son of Mr. Moreton, Curate of Staplehurst. Mrs. Honor Astlake, goddaughter of my late wife. Mr. and Mrs. Disney. Nephew Laurence Trent in Barbados. The grandchildren of my late brother John Trent.

Witnesses Julia Jenkin, Richd. Beace, Peter Parton.

Probate granted to Edward Sommers, attorney of Laurence Trent, now of Barbados, nephew of William Trent, Clerk, deceased. 1747. Ap. Admn. granted to Abel Dottin, executor of Lawrence Trent decd.

LAWRENCE TRENT of St. Peter, Barbados Esquire.

My wife Jane T. £1000 Cy over and above £2600 secured to her by marriage settlement, also furniture and plate, my chaise and horse, her riding horse and saddle her watch etc., three slaves and £50, for mourning. Her living in my dwellinghouse in Speightstown and use of my negroes so long as she continues my widow or resides in this island unmarried. To my daughter Elizabeth T. £3000 Cy at 16 or marriage and seven slaves and my household plate, my silver tea-kettle coffee pot and waiter. I give to the child of my wife now to be born £5000 at 21 if a boy or £3000 at 16 or marriage if a girl, six slaves, my large silver tankard and two large silver salvers. My daughter Elizabeth and said child now to be born to be handsomely maintained and educated out of profits of my estate here or in England. I give £100 Cy to be distributed among as many poor people in this island as my exors shall think fit. I give to Col. John Pickering £20. To Rev. Wm. Dowding for himself and wife £20. To Elizth. Denny widow for herself, eldest son and daughter £30, and to Mr. John Denny for himself, wife, eldest son and eldest daughter £40. To my son John T. my silver cup with two handles and cover, one other silver cup with handles and cover whereon are engraven several gents names and my silver watch and all rest, residue etc. of my estate real and personal at 21; and it is my desire he be sent to England so soon as he be thought to be a proper age by my executrix. (Several remainders over of property in case of decease of his children without issue); finally, to the children of Col. John Pickering by my sister Susannah his late wife. The child of Mr. Edward Denny dec'd by my sister Elizth now his widow and child of Mr. John Denny by my sister Agnes his now wife. To each of them who shall then be living at the time of this contingency £100 Cy. To children of nephews John Sober Esq. £100 Cy. and residue to following viz: children of Col. John Pickering by my sister Susannah his late wife, children of Edward Denny dec'd by my sister Elizabeth his now widow, and children of Jno Denny by my sister Agnes his wife to be equally divided between them. Appoint Uncle Edwin Somers of London, merchant, friend Hon. Abel Dotton Esq., nephew Jno Sober Esq. friend Walter Caddle, Merchant, all of this Island, guardians of bodies and estates of my said son John Trent and the child my wife now goes with and exors. of this my will until my son John or such other sons as I may have be entitled to my estate attain 21 years from which time I appoint him sole exor. I give each exor. £25 for mourning. 2 July 1742. (sd) Lawrence Trent. Wit: Joseph Callender, Richard Milles and Wm. Richardson. Sworn by Rd. Milles 26 September 1743

Codicil 9 July 1742 giving £1000 Cy to every child of any son entitled to residue of his estate in case such son dies before attaining 21 (Sd.) Law: Trent Wit: John Sober and Rd. Milles. Sworn by Rd. Milles 26 September 1743.

JOHN TRENT of Clarges St. St. George, Hanover Square, London.

Aunt Rebecca Knight £50 p.a. for life; to servant Ann King £50. To my relation and friend Jas. Phipps of Peterborough, Northants, Samuel Estwick of Berkeley St., Portman Square, Abraham Cumberbatch the father and Abraham Cumberbatch Jnr. both now resident in Barbados and Stephen Welch of City of Bath £60. All residue of Estate to son John Trent and if he dies before 21 I bequeath the following to Sam'l Estwick £2000, to niece Anne Sandiford of Barbados relict of Wm. Sandiford dec'd £2000, niece Jane Welch of Barbados £2000, to sister Laurentia Lavine relict of Isac Lavine dec'd £2000. Residue to nephews Abraham Cumberbatch Jnr., Lawrence Cumberbatch, Edward Cumberbatch and John Cumberbatch all of Barbados Exors. James Phipps, Sam'l Estwick, Abram Cumberbatch, Stephen Welch and Abram Cumberbatch Jnr. 7 October 1784. Witnesses: Wm. Withers, Jno. Brett, John Trent, John Fulbrook. Sworn 29 April 1786 by Wm. Withers of Camberwell, Surrey, Merchant, that he was a witness to will in deceased's late counting house in Fenhill St. London. Exemplification issuing out of P. C. C. dated 3 May, 1786.

JOHN TRENT. To my wife...................Trent £200 during her natural life in addition to her jointure. To my younger children £6000 each when they come to 21. Appoint Jno. Hanning, Wm. Hanning and Constantine Phipps as trustees. X John Trent. Wit: Robt. Strike, Francis Phipps, X John Tucker, Wm. Hanning (Sd) at Dillington this 5 August 1796. I do give Robt. Strike £50 beyond his yearly.................. It is Mr. Trent's wish that if either of his estates must be sold that Dillington estate be first sold. *Codicil.* £6000 to child to which Mrs. Trent is now pregnant at 21. John Trent *N.B.* when Mr. T. signed will he was unable to sign name but recovered to sign codicil. Proved 3 September 1796. Will of John Trent late of Dillington in Somerset who died on 6 August 1796.

JOHN TRENT. Exemplification P.C.C. of John Constantine Trent of Lownes St. Belgrave Square, Middlesex, a Captain in H.M. Regt. Horse Guards and Major in H.M. Army. Administration with will annexed granted 6 February 1847 to Jenette Eliza Trent, Spinster, one of children of Francis Onslow Trent dec'd. C. E. Trent and the sd. F. O. Trent the brothers and executors of testator's will having died in his lifetime and testator having died without leaving any children.

Will of John Constantine Trent of 41 Lownes St. Whereas on my marriage in 1834 with my wife Frances Sophia, theretofore F. S. Swainton Strangewayes, spinster, I agreed to provide her with a jointure of £500 to be charged upon an estate in Barbados then belonging to me, and whereas I have lately sold estate for £10,000 and my wife has released same from her jointure and I have executed an indenture dated 27 May inst. made between myself and my wife of one part and Wm. Speke, Nash Vaughan, Edwards Vaughn, and my brother Constantine Estwick Trent and Francis Onslow Trent of the other part whereby I have covenanted to pay her an annuity of £500 if she survive me; Whereas I am at present without issue. Furniture etc. to wife, plate to any child of mine failing whom to my brother C. E. Trent, to my sister Eliza Julia, the wife of Charles Fox Champion-Crespigny, my half-sister Eliza Jennette, wife of Philip Champion Toker and my old friend Charles Cave of Mincing Lane and my friend Archibald Ham late surgeon in Royal Horse Guards. Failing issue, estate to nephew and godson John Trent, son of my brother Francis Onslow Trent at 21. My brother C. E. Trent and F. O. Trent in equal shares and to issue of either of said brothers if they die before me, 30 May 1844. Sd. John Constantine Trent. Wit: Charles Druce Jnr. 10 Billiter Square, London, Chas. Clarridge Druce.

CARLETON WILLS.

Will dated 2 May 1671 of JOHN CARLETON of parish of St. Thomas, Barbados.

My wife Margaret Carleton for her life and then to my first born son and his heirs, and if no son, to my brother Josias Carleton's first born son by his wife Elizabeth, and if no son, to my wife for ever. My wife Margaret executrix; brother Josias Carleton, Capt. Paul Lyte and John Rootes to be overseers. Sgd. John Carleton. Wits: John Lambert, John Rootes. Proved 13 February 1672.

Will dated 19 April 1682 of JOSIAS CARLETON of Parish of St. Thomas, Barbados.

To my friends Lieut. Robert Ashford and William Williams, Junr., my plantation in St. Thomas of 24 acres in trust. I commit the care of my children to my friend Jane Cooke, namely Elizabeth, John, Mary, Josias, and Judith Carleton.

To my son John one negro man and two negro women slaves, my feather-bed with pillows, my colt, silver hilted rapier and my seal with my coat of arms. The land given by will of my late brother John Carleton to my son John. My sister Lambert. Robert Ashford and William Williams junr. to be executors. sd. Josias Carleton. Wits: Tho. Lowe, Roger Spratt, Henry Thomas Hart. Proved 30 June 1682.

Thomas Williams of St. Thomas, gent., and Thomas Carleton of town of St. Michael, merchant, administrators of estate of William Williams, jnr., decd. release Hon. William Sharpe from all demands etc. in respect of the said estate. Dated 19 September 1710.

Will of JANE CARLETON of St. Thomas, widow.

My daughter Judith Carleton; grandson Josias Carleton, granddaughters Elizabeth, Anne, Judith Carleton. Appoint my daughter-in-law Judith Carleton sole executrix. sd. Jane Carleton. Wits: Elizabeth Grove, Thos. Elcock, and John Carleton. Proved 13 May 1717.

Will of JOHN CARLETON of St. Thomas, Barbados, dated 5 January 1726.

To my wife Anna one-third of my estate in lieu of dower, and in case of her marriage the remaining two-thirds be placed in hands of my son Josias for maintenance of my children Josias, John, Richard, Edward, James, Benjamin, and Christian Carleton. Legacies to children and residue to son Josias, but in the event of his death to sons in succession and to daughter Christian. Wife Anna executrix. sd. Jno Carleton. Wits: Tho. Williams, Ed. Spencer, John Reed. Proved 18 January 1731.

Will dated 6 August 1763 of JOHN CARLETON of St. Thomas, Barbados.

To wife Rebecca all my estate until my son Edward is 21, and an annuity to wife until marriage again. Provision for child whose birth was expected. My sisters Anna and Elizabeth Carleton. Wife Rebecca executrix during widowhood, Uncle Edward Carleton, cousin Honble Abraham Cumberbatch, brother-in-law John Rouse, and friend Dr. Jno. Worrell executors. sd. John Carleton. Wits: Rob. Ashford, W. Worrell, Christo. Ford. Proved 3 October 1763 by William Worrell.

Will dated 6 July 1738 of EDWARD CARLETON of St. James, Barbados.

Son Abraham £10. Residue to wife Susannah Carleton and appoint her and James Robinson executors. sd. Edw. Carleton. Wits: B. Bostock, James Cockes, William Clinkett. Proved 6 August 1765.

Will of BENJAMIN CARLETON of St. Michael, Practitioner of Medicine.

Give to my heir-at-law two shillings and no more. My daughter Elizabeth Wiltshire Best wife of Joseph Palmer Best my house, land and slaves for her life and then to my granddaughter Jane Carleton Best daughter of the said Elizabeth Wiltshire Best.

Appoint James Palmer Best and Elizabeth Wiltshire Best executors.

Sd. Benja. Carleton. Wits: Nathl. Phillips, Jno Grassett, Solomon Smith. Proved 2 October 1772.

Will dated 17 November 1777 of EDWARD CARLETON of St. Thomas being at present 19 years of age and upwards.

To my Mother Rebecca Carleton all my estate and appoint her executrix. sd. Edward Carleton. Wits: John Duke, James Thos. Rous Hackett. Proved 13 April 1778.

533

Will of SUSAN CARLETON of St. Peter, widow, dated 2 December 1780.

Estate to my three daughters, Elizabeth Denny, Ann Prieliaux and Eleanor Worrell. Kinsman Mr. Andrew Wade to be executor. The mark of Susan Carleton. Wits: Francis Ford, Jno. Hendy, W. Wade. Proved 6 January 1781.

Will dated 25 June 1797 of REBECCA CARLETON of St. Michael, widow.

Legacy of £300 to be divided between Benjamin Walrond, George Walrond, Agnes Walrond, Benjamin Walrond, junr., Mary Judith Walrond, Susanna Dorothy Walrond, Renn Hampden Walrond, Nicholas Hunphrey Walrond, Rebecca Rous Walrond. Sisters-in-law Anna and Elizabeth Carleton left to them by Will of my husband. Niece Judith Elizabeth wife of Benjamin Walrond and their daughter Susanna Dorothy Walrond. Nieces Rebecca Howell and Agnes Rous Howell. My nephew John Howell deceased. Nephew and Godson Conrade Adams Howell. My nephew Thomas Rous Howell. My sister Agnes Howell. Niece Elizabeth Johannes Howell daughter of the said John Howell decd. Children of my nephews Nicholas Prideaux Howell, Thomas Rous Howell and Conrade Adams Howell, Residue of estate to sister Agnes Howell, and appoint her, my nephew-in-law Benjamin Walrond and nephews Thomas Rous Howell and Conrade Adams Howell executors. sd. Rebecca Carleton. Wits: John William Sobers, James Fowler Neblett, Wm. Alder. Proved 19 July 1802.

CARLETON BAPTISMS TO 1800.

1708 May 24	Sarah, daughter of Thomas and Dorothy Carleton, born 17 December 1707.
1709 May 10	Elizabeth, daughter of Edward and Judith Carleton,.
1726 March 23	Mercy, child 3 or 4 years old.
1726	Abraham, son of Edward and Anne Carleton, born 12 inst.
1733 August 25	William Carleton, born 13 September 1731.
1733 November 4	Elizabeth, daughter of Edward and Susannah Carleton, born 3 inst.
1734 March 7	Anna, daughter of Edward and Susannah Carleton, born 9th last month.
1733 June	Anna, daughter of Josias and Elizabeth Carleton.
1735 December 15	John, son of Josias and Elizabeth Carleton.
1736 July 26	Thomas Carleton, a child.
1736 June 6	Philip Scott, son of Edward and Susannah Carleton, born 4 inst.

1737 March 29	Elizabeth, daughter of Thomas and Hannah Carleton, born 17 inst.
1737 November 13	Eleanor, daughter of Edward and Susannah Carleton, born 8 inst.
1738 January 11	Ann, daughter of Edward and Susan Carleton, born this day.
1739 July 3	Elizabeth, daughter of Josias and Eliza Carleton.
1739 May 2	Helenah, daughter of James and Hester Carleton.
1740 April 9	John, son of Major Edward and Susan Carleton, born 6 inst.
1741 April 25	Thomas, son of Mr. Thos. and Mrs. Hannah Carleton, born 15 Feb. 1740.
1741 September 17	Eleanor, daughter of Edward and Susan Carleton, born 9 inst.
1743 April 7	Susanna, daughter of Col. Edward and Susan Carleton, born 23 September 1742.
1749 September 12	James and Ann, son and daughter of James and . . . . Carlton.
1758 November 5	Edward, son of Dr. John and Rebecca Carleton.

CARLETON MARRIAGES, TO 1800.

1705 March 17	Thomas Carleton to Dorothy Campion.
1707 November 25	Mr. Edward Carleton to Mrs. Judith Mellows.
1720 December 3	Ann Carleton, spinster, to James King.
1724 May 1	Mr. Richard Carleton to Mrs. Elizabeth Martin.
1726 May 23	Mrs. Elizabeth Carleton, spinster, to Mr. Richard Rowland, merchant.
1726 June 5	Mr. Edward Carleton to Mrs. Ann Cumberbatch.
1726 August 20	Dr. Josias Carleton to Mrs. Mary Hollaway.
1730 August 2	Mrs. Christian Carleton, spinster, to Mr. James Robertson.
1730 May 21	Mr. Thomas Carleton to Mrs. Hannah Ellacott, spinster.
1731 January 28	Mr. James Carleton to Mrs. Hester Blount.
1731 July 18	Dr. Josias Carleton to Mrs. Elizabeth Martin.
1732 November 16	Edward Carleton to Susan Scott.
1742 December 17	Dr. Benjamin Carleton to Mrs. Jane Grassett.*
1742 December 27	Benjamin Carleton to Jane Grassett.*

* This duplicate entry under different dates seems inexplicable.

1749 September 3	Mrs. Judith Ann Carleton to Mr. Christopher Estwick Gall.
1752 March 28	Susanna Carleton to John Robinson.
1752 September 28	Elizabeth Carleton to John Denny.
1753 September 12	Judith Carleton to Thomas Campbell, by license.
1753 December 13	Christian Carleton to Benjamin Reed.
1756 February 12	Dr. John Carleton to Rebecca Rouse.
1761 September 18	Eleanor Carleton to William Worrell, by license.
1763 November 27	Ann Carleton to Samuel Prideaux, by license.
1769 July 27	Elizabeth Wiltshire Grassett *alias* Carleton to Joseph Palmer Best.
1778 December 24	Susanna Carleton to William Ennis.

CARLETON BURIALS, TO 1800.

1685 March 18	Peter Carleton, a servant of Coll. Hallett's.
1671 February 17	Susanna Carleton, a child.
1694 August	George Carleton.
1701 November 11	Edward Carleton, a mariner.
1705 January 27	Thomas Carleton, a child.
1702 December 17	Richard Carleton, mariner.
1708 November 4	Mrs. Eliza Carleton.
1709 May 11	Eliza Carleton, an infant.
1725 November 22	Ann Carlton, wife of Edward Carlton, died of consumption.
1727 November 10	Capt. John Carleton.
1727 September 12	Mrs. Ann Carleton.
1728 May 25	William, son of William Carleton.
1726 March 27	Mercy Carleton, a child.
1728 June 26	Dr. Josias Carleton.
1731 September 4	Elizabeth Carleton, an infant.
1733 February 9	Mr. John Carleton.
1735 March 28	William Carleton.
1737 November 16	Eleanor Carleton, aged 8 days, died of fitts.
1740 September 18	Dr. Josias Carleton.
1741 July 21	Thomasine Carleton, daughter of Ann Carleton.
1742 March 17	John Carleton, aged 3 years, died of convulsions.
1743 July 7	Mr. Thomas Carleton.
1747 December 8	Richard Carleton, buried in the church.
1752 December 6	James Carleton, a child, buried in the church.
1753 January 7	Robert Carleton.
1753 October 9	Elizabeth Carleton aged 78 years.

1754 November 23	Frances Carleton.	
1754 September 12	Anna Carleton, aged 18 years.	
1754 August 17	Mrs. Mary Carleton, buried in Holloways plantation.	
1755 April 15	James Carleton, buried in the church.	
1763 August 15	Thomas Carleton.	
1763 August 16	Dr. John Carleton.	
1765 July 25	Edward Carleton, aged 61 years.	
1766 October 22	Elizabeth Carleton.	
1769 November 10	Hannah Carleton.	
1770 September 8	John Carleton, aged 6 years.	
1772 January 5	Jane Carleton, wife of Benjamin Carleton.	
1772 June 10	Capt. Benjamin Carleton.	
1778 February 16	Edward Carleton.	
1780 December 30	Susannah Carleton.	
1783 January 3	John Carleton, mariner.	
1799 September 16	Rebecca Carleton.	

CUMBERBATCH WILLS.

Will dated 8 July 1732 (Bedford 202) of ESTHER CUMBER-BATCH of Bristol, widow.

My nieces Mary and Rachel Wilcox, their father Thomas Wilcox of Gloucester, upholder, my brother-in-law. Parnell Williams all my wearing apparel. Wits. Sarah Webb, George Adderley. Proved 1732.

Will dated 7 October 1741 (Boycott 194) of MARY COM-BERBATCH of Bristol widow.

My daughter Mary wife of John Morse of Bristol, apothecary. My daughter Anne Cumberbatch. Wits. John Taylor, Henry Byndloss. Proved 1743.

Will dated 24 May 1739 of JOSHUA COMBERBATCH of St. Thomas, Barbados.

To my daughter-in-law, Mary Hussey £40 per an. during the life of my sister Ann, and then my house and land in St. Thomas and six negroes and all the plate that was her father's. To the poor of St. Nicholas parish in Bristol £25 stlg. to be divided as the Vestry shall think proper. To two infirmaries in Bristol £25 stlg. each.

To my niece, Mary Sober, £100 cy. To my niece, Sarah Comberbatch £100 cy. If my nephew Abraham Carleton shall attain 22 years I give him £50 cy. To the poor of St. Thomas parish £10 for five years. To my kinsmen John and George Mission (after my sister shall take out such medicines as she shall think fit) all my wearing apparel, medicines, instruments and physical books, and the debt due from George Mission to me to be equally

divided between them. To Hon. Abel Dottin £50 cy. To my god-son Samuel Collier, £20. To my godson Thomas Cobham £10.
My negro man Mercury his freedom and two acres of my outside land and £6 per an. To my sister Ann Cumberbatch two-thirds of all my estate and one-third to my brother Abraham.

Executors—sister Ann, brother Abraham, and Hon. Abel Dottin. sd. Joshua Comberbatch. Wits. Thomas Williams, Jacob Luke, Tixtover Carter. Proved 10 July 1739.

Will dated 22 November 1750, of ABRAHAM CUMBERBATCH of St. Andrew, Barbados.

Mr. Edward Clarke Parish of Great Britain, Col. Wm. Gibbons, Col. Edmund Jenkins, Wm. Sturge, Esq., my grandson Abraham Carleton, and Wm. Ross to be executors and trustees.

My plantation to be kept stocked with 250 negro slaves, 100 head of cattle.

To my kinswomen, Ann Sandiford £500, Mary Sandiford £200. To my sister Ann Cumberbatch £25. To my kinswomen, Mary Mors, wife of John Mors of Bristol £200, and Ann Cumberbatch sister of Mary Mors £100. To each of my kinsman, Dr. George Mission's children which he has by the daughter of Joseph Leacock £150 at 21. To my godson Abel Collier £100 at 21. To my friend Edward Jones who lives with me £100. To my kinsman Dr. John Mission an annuity of £12. To my kinsman Mr. Alexander Cumberbatch £10 stlg. per an. To my granddaughter Sarah Sober £3,000 cy. at 18. To my grandson Abraham Sober £3,000 cy. at 21. To my granddaughter Mary Sober £3,000 at 18. To my grandson Cumberbatch Sober £3,000 at 21 in satisfaction of an agreement made between me and their father John Sober dated 1 February 1742. To my grandson John Sober who is unprovided for by said articles £1,000 at 23. £50 to each of my trustees. Residue to my grandson Abraham Carleton for life and then to his heirs in tail male and to take the name of Cumberbatch and failing him and his issue to my grandson John Sober and his heirs in tail male, failing him to my grandson Abraham Sober and failing him to my grandson Cumberbatch Sober. sd. A. Cumberbatch. Wit: Isaac Skinner, George Alleyne. Thos. Sullivan, Jno. Moseley. Proved 8 January 1751.

Will dated 18 November 1752 of ANN CUMBERBATCH of St. Thomas, Barbados, spinster.

To my friend Mr. Patrick Rose, Rector of St. Thomas £12 for his fees of burial of me. Also £30 stlg. for a pulpit clock for St. Thomas church. £30 to the poor of the said parish. To my cousin Alexander Cumberbatch of Great Britain £100 stlg. To my cousin Mary Morse of Great Britain £50. To my cousin Ann Brice, sister of said Mary Morse of Great Britain £50 stlg. To each of the sisters of my said cousin Alexander Cumberbatch £30.

£150 to be place at interest for my cousin John Mission and the principal for his children. £150 for my cousin Dr. George

Mission and then for his children, George, Sarah, and Mary. To my cousin Mary Sandiford daughter of Col. Richard Sandiford deced. £30. To my cousin Ann Mission wife of Dr. George Mission £30. To my grandniece Sarah Sober my pearl necklace, and to my grandniece Mary Sober a pair of diamond earrings and my gold watch and one-half of my plate to them. To my grand nephews and nieces, John, Abraham, Cumberbatch, Sarah, and Mary Sober, children of my deceased niece £1,000 cy. To my nephew Edward Carleton £50. Residue to my grand nephew Abraham Cumberbatch, formerly Abraham Carleton.

I appoint Edward Carleton and Abraham Cumberbatch executors. Wit. Jona. Worrell, Richard Cobham, John Barnwell. Proved 11 October 1757.

Will dated 26 April 1785 of ABRAHAM CUMBERBATCH of Saint Andrew, Barbados, intending shortly for England. To my wife Eliza £3000 cy. in full of our marriage articles, and the further sum of £1000 cy. All my plate and that of my grandfather Abraham Cumberbatch to my wife and six negroes and one-half my furniture. The other half of my furniture to my son Abraham. All my lands in the parish of St. Peter to be purchased by my son Abraham and my stonewall house in Speightstown and the money to go to pay the legacy to my wife. The residue to be divided between my sons Lawrence Trent Cumberbatch, Edward Carleton Cumberbatch, and John Trent Cumberbatch.

WHEREAS my grandfather Abraham Cumberbatch directed that 250 slaves be kept on his plantation: I direct all others to be sold and the money divided between my three sons.

On the marriage of my said daughter Ann Sandiford with Mr. William S. I promised £3000: I direct any balance due to be paid to her. To my two grandchildren Alexander and Abraham Cumberbatch Sandiford, children of my said daughter Ann.

I appoint my wife Elizabeth and son Abraham executrix and executor. sd. A. Cumberbatch. Wit: Wm. Craigg, Wm. Bovell, Wm. Cadogan. Proved 15 December 1785. by Oath of Wm. Bovell before Governor D. Parry.

Will dated 7 May 1795 of ABRAHAM CUMBERBATCH of St. Andrew, Barbados. To my wife Mary Cumberbatch £180 per an. in addition to £3000 settled on her by Release of CLELANDS and THE FARM plantations and as much sugar and other provisions so long as she remains my widow.

To my brothers Lawrence Trent Cumberbatch, Edward Carleton Cumberbatch and John Trent Cumberbatch £1000 each out of the profits of my estate. To my sister Ann Sandiford, widow of William Sandiford, £500. To my nephew Abraham Cumberbatch Sandiford, son of Mrs. Ann Sandiford £50.

Residue to my son Abraham Parry Cumberbatch, and if he should die under 21, in order to comply with the wish of my great-grandfather, Abraham Cumberbatch from whom the estates were handed down and who seemed to desire that they be kept in the family and named, I direct that my brother, L. T. C. take possession and stock kept up and profits divided between my three brothers, allowing my sister Ann Sandiford £300 per an. Should L. T. C. die then my brothers E. C. C. and J. T. C. to take possession in turn and the heirs of the survivor to inherit.

I appoint my wife, and my three brothers executors and guardians of my son Abraham Parry Cumberbatch.

sd. A. Cumberbatch. Wits. Benja. Sandiford, Thomas Sandiford.

Proved 5 August 1796.

Will dated 13 July 1821 of EDWARD CARLETON CUMBERBATCH of St. Peter, Barbados, now resident at Clifton in co. Gloucester, Esq.

To my daughter Sarah Cave, wife of Charles Cave Esq £4000 to be paid to her five years after my decease. To Stephen Cave of Clifton aforesaid and the said Charles Cave £1000 upon trust for my grandson Stephen Cave, son of the said Charles and Sarah Cave, at 21, and in the meantime for his education.

To my brother John Trent Cumberbatch in Barbados £500 cy. To my sister Ann Sandiford, widow, of Barbados £100 per an.

Subject to a bond of £4000 due to my said daughter on her marriage with Charles Cave, I give to my brothers L. T. C. and J. T. C. all that my one-half part of Saint Nicholas estate in St. Peter and also another plantation and estate called Ebworth and all other estates in St. Peter or elsewhere with the stock etc. to the use of the said L. T. C. and J. T. C. upon trust as to £400 per an. to my son Edward Carleton Cumberbatch for five years after my death and then for my son absolutely, and if he die within the period leaving no issue, upon trust for my daughter Sarah Cave. And if my said son should marry any daughter of Andrew Ash of Bath, musician, at any time during the said five years, the trusts to be void and I allow him £300 per an. for life.

sd. Edwd. C. Cumberbatch. Wits: R. Hampden of Barbados, Esq., Thomas Barton of Bristol, mariner, and Jer. Osborne, solicitor of Bristol. Proved 18 February 1822 by Oath of Hon. R. Hampden.

Will dated 17 September 1821 of JOHN TRENT CUMBERBATCH of St. Peter, Barbados.

To my sister Ann Sandiford £30 per an. Residue of plantations etc. to my brother Lawrence Trent Cumberbatch, and appoint him executor and my sister Ann, executrix. sd. Jno. Trent Cumberbatch. Wits: Thomas Challenor, John Goodridge, John Henry Leacock. Proved 19 November 1822.

Will dated 31 March 1829, of LAWRENCE TRENT CUMBERBATCH of St. Peter Esq.

To my nephew Edward Carlton Cumberbatch an annuity of

£300 and all silver plate given my deceased sister Ann, except a silver bread basket. The annuity in addition to that payable to him by me under the Will of his deceased father Edward Carlton Cumberbatch. To my grand-nephew Lawrence Trent Cumberbatch, son of my nephew E. C. C., £1000 at 21. To my grandniece Laurentia Trent Cumberbatch daughter of my said nephew E. C. C. £500 at 18. To my grand-nephew Stephen Cave, son of my nephew-in-law and niece Charles and Sarah Cave of England £500 at 21. To my grand-nephew L. T. Cave, son of the said Charles and Sarah Cave £1000 at 21. To my overseer Thomas Smith Harding £100. To the said Charles Cave my chronometer, chain, and appendages. I direct my slaves (named) to be manumitted. To Mary Laurentia Lavine, Francis Lavine, Abraham Lavine, George Beckwith Lavine and Lizzie Lavine, house in Speightstown and £100 each. To John Edward Cumberbatch and Richard Cumberbatch a house in Speightstown and £100 each. Residue to my niece Sarah Cave.

Appoint Charles Cave sole executor. sd. Lawrence Trent Cumberbatch. Wits. Jno. Eversley, Edmund J. Eversley, Conrade A. Howell.

Codicil. I give my nephew Edward Carlton Cumberbatch £1000 in token of his having entered into Holy Orders, and to Rosalie Geraldine, his daughter, £500 at 18, she having been born after my Will was made. Dated 15 January 1833. sd. Law: Trent Cumberbatch. Wits. W. H. D. Rollack Thos. Connell. Proved 6 January 1834.

CUMBERBATCH BAPTISMS TO 1800.

1784 November 29	Abraham Parry, son of Abraham Cumberbatch and Mary his wife.
1795 July 15	Edward Carlton Cumberbatch, son of Edward Carlton Cumberbatch and Sarah his wife, born 3 June.
1797 October 31	Sarah Cumberbatch, daughter of Edward Carlton and Sarah Cumberbatch, born October 10.

CUMBERBATCH MARRIAGES TO 1800.

1784 February 17	Abraham Cumberbatch to Mary Cumberbatch Sober.
1726 August 20	Ann Cumberbatch to Dr. Josias Cumberbatch.
1794 September 9	Edward Cumberbatch and Sarah Howell.

CUMBERBATCH BURIALS TO 1800.

1739 June 4	Dr. Joshua Cumberbatch Esq.
1757 October 10	Mrs. Ann Cumberbatch.
1794 January 26	Elizabeth Cumberbatch.
1797 October 14	Sarah Cumberbatch.

TRENT.

LAWRENCE TRENT of Speightstown, St. Peter, place of origin unknown. Left Barbados for England shortly after making his Will on 11 July 1692. His second son William was then being educated in England. Name of his wife not known ; he was probably then a widower. It seems likely that he never returned to Barbados. His Will was proved in March 1693.

His children were all under age, namely,

1. JOHN, born in 1674, of whom later.
2. WILLIAM, who was of Corpus Christi Coll. Cambridge in 1698, and took Holy Orders. On 28 June 1698 he signed a Power of Attorney in favour of his brother John in connection with his share of his father's estate, probably about the time he attained his majority. He lived at Biddenden in Kent, and it would seem from his Will, dated 1 May 1737, that he died a widower.
3. ANDREW, born in 1678, lived in St. Peter, Barbados, and died in 1736 a bachelor.
4. LAWRENCE, of whom nothing is known besides his being named in his father's Will.
5. ELIZABETH, named in her father's Will, but not in later Wills of the family.
6. AGNES, married . . . . Burgess, and was a widow living in Barbados in 1737. Her brother John provided for her accommodation in his house during her widowhood, and her brothers Andrew and William left her legacies.

JOHN TRENT, eldest son of Lawrence Trent. Lived in St. Peter and was a merchant in Speightstown. Name of wife unknown. She predeceased him, probably dying before 1715 when he is mentioned in the Census records as living in St. Peter with his three daughters, aged 20, 17, and 13, respectively, and his brother Andrew, aged 37. He died in 1735 at the age of 61.

His children were :—

1. LAWRENCE, of whom later.
2. SUSANNAH, who married Colonel John Pickering and died before 1735, leaving issue four children, namely, John, Jean, Elizabeth and Sarah.
3. SARAH, who married first Robert Yeamans and had a son, Robert, and afterwards married Rev. William Dowding.
4. ELIZABETH, who married Edward Denny and had issue, Edward, Trent, and Elizabeth, and became a widow sometime before 1734.
5. AGNES, who married John Denny, and had six children at the date of her father's Will, namely, John, Samuel, Lawrence, Edward, Thomas, and Susannah.

LAWRENCE TRENT, eldest son of the abovenamed John Trent, survived his father by only eight years, leaving his wife, Jane, (surname unknown) and two, if not three children him

542

surviving. Lawrence Trent was living in Speightstown at the date of his Will (26 September 1743) and judging from the contents of that document, he was extremely prosperous. He had already settled £2,600 (a considerable sum in those days) on his wife at the time of their marriage, and he added more to her fortune by his Will. His two infant children were left to the care of his nephew John Sober*, his uncle Edwin Somers of London, and Hon. Abel Dottin, his friend, until they attained their majority. His Will was proved on 26 September 1743.

His children were:—

1. ELIZABETH, who was under sixteen in 1742. She married, with a substantial fortune, Abraham Carleton, son of Edward and Ann Carleton, who had by then assumed the name of Cumberbatch on inheriting Cleland and The Farm and more of his grandfather's fortune.

   For particulars of her children and issue see under the pedigree of Cumberbatch *post*.

2. JOHN, a child in 1742. He and his sister were educated in England, and later he made his home there. He was living in Clarges Street, St. George's Hanover Square in 1786 at the time of his death. He married Mary Phipps at St. Marylebone, London, before 1769. She was a daughter of Constantine Phipps of St. Kitts, Member of Council there. (See V. L. Oliver's *Caribbeana*, Vol. I p. 69). He had one child, John, who married and had issue, dying at Dillingham in Somerset on 6 August 1796.

3. A child expected at the date of Lawrence Trent's Will, and from the will of John Trent dated 7 October 1786 it may be gathered that she was—

   LAVINIA, who married Isaac Lavine. The marriage articles, dated 6 February 1766 of Lavinia Trent with Isaac Lavine are recorded (Vol. 40/68), from which it appears that he settled Reids Bay plantation on her and the issue of the marriage. Her brother-in-law, Hon. Abraham Cumberbatch and Stephen Welch were the trustees of the settlement. She was a widow in 1771.

CUMBERBATCH

According to Oliver, (*Caribbeana*, Vol. I p. 228) the family arms are:

CREST.—*An eagle's head erased.*

ARMS.—Gules, an eagle displayed between three trefoils Or.

MOTTO.—NE TENTES AUT PERFICE.

ABRAHAM CUMBERBATCH of Cleland and The Farm plantations, Barbados. His wife's name is not recorded. He had a considerable fortune and no son to carry on the name. His two daughters were—

1. ANN, who married Edward Carleton on 5 June 1726 and had one child only and died on 12 September 1727. Their child was Abraham Carleton who was born 1727, of whom later.
2. MARY, who married John Sober of The Castle, St. Peter. They had issue:—
   1. John Sober, born 1739, married first Penelope Blake, daughter of Major Martin Blake by whom he had issue, and secondly Martha Bersheba. He died 1795 and was buried in St. Faith's under St. Paul's Cathedral.
   2. Abraham Sober, died 1772 and buried in the crypt of St. Paul's.
   3. Cumberbatch Sober, born 1742, died 13 Jany. 1827 aged 85.
   4. Sarah Sober, wife of Dr. Wm. Sandiford of Barbados.
   5. Mary Sober, died 24 August 1793, and buried in the crypt of St. Paul's.

ABRAHAM CARLETON, son of Edward and Ann Carleton. He inherited Cleland and The Farm plantations and other estate under the Will of his grandfather, Abraham Cumberbatch. He assumed the surname Cumberbatch in fulfilment of the terms of the said Will. Married Elizabeth Trent, daughter of Lawrence and Jane Trent. He was a Member of the Council of Barbados for thirty years. He made his Will on 26 April 1785 intending shortly to leave for England. He died there on 25 July 1785 and was buried in Bristol Cathedral by the Precentor on 30 July. A tablet to his memory erected on the north wall of the Choir Vestry of the Cathedral records that he bore a long and painful illness with uncommon patience and fortitude, and came to England in hopes of receiving benefit from a change of climate. (See M. I. Oliver's *Caribbeana,* Vol II, p. 84.

His children were—
1. ABRAHAM CUMBERBATCH, born 1754, who married Mary Cumberbatch Sober, daughter of Cumberbatch Sober. She was his second cousin. After his death she married 20 August 1797 William Smith Forth of the King's Dragoon Guards.

   Abraham Cumberbatch inherited Cleland and The Farm, and was for some years a Member of Council of Barbados. He went to live in England and died of a malignant fever at his seat Fairwater, near Taunton, on June 16, 1796 in his 42nd year. A tablet to his memory is on the north wall of the north choir of Bristol Cathedral. Erected by his widow. His only child and heir was—

   ABRAHAM PARRY CUMBERBATCH, born in Barbados, baptised 29 November 1784. He married Charlotte, daughter of Robert Burnett Jones on 31 October 1805. She died 15 January 1818, and he married secondly, Caroline Chaloner by whom he had issue. Abraham Parry Cumberbatch died at Tunbridge Wells October 1840 aged 56. A tablet to the memory of his first wife, Charlotte, is on the north wall of the north gallery of St. Mary, Paddington. See Oliver's *Caribbeana*, Vol I. p. 228.

2. LAWRENCE TRENT CUMBERBATCH, died a bachelor in 1834 in Barbados.

3. EDWARD CARLETON CUMBERBATCH. Part owner with his brother John Trent Cumberbatch in Nicholas and Ebworth plantations. He married Sarah Howell on 9 September 1794, and had two children. He died at Clifton, Bristol; on 9 August 1821, and is buried in Bristol Cathedral.
His children are—
   1. Edward Carleton Cumberbatch, of whom later.
   2. Sarah Cumberbatch, of whom later.

4. JOHN TRENT CUMBERBATCH of St. Peter, Barbados. Part owner of Nicholas and Ebworth plantations. He died a bachelor in Liverpool on 19 November 1822, leaving the bulk of his estate to his brother Edward Carleton Cumberbatch.

5. ANN CUMBERBATCH, married Dr. William Sandiford and had issue two sons.

EDWARD CARLETON CUMBERBATCH, son of Edward Carleton and Sarah (Howell) Cumberbatch, was born in 1795. He was educated at Harrow and Trinity Coll. Cambridge. Under the terms of his father's Will, he was disinherited by his marriage on 6 August 1822 to Mary, Gertrude, daughter of A. Ashe Esq. of Belvidere, Bath. He took Holy Orders and was Headmaster of Hitchin Grammar School. He died at Reading on 15 October 1835 aged 40.

There were three children of the marriage—

   1. LAWRENCE TRENT CUMBERBATCH, born 1 May 1824, married Anne Cave, daughter of George Cave. Resided at 25, Cadogan Square, and was a Surgeon. He died in 1889, leaving five children.
   2. LAURENTIA TRENT CUMBERBATCH, died 10 May 1851 unmarried.
   3. ROSALIE GERALDINE, died unmarried 9 October 1851.

SARAH CUMBERBATCH, daughter of Edward Carleton Cumberbatch and Sarah (Howell) his wife. Born 1797. Married 1 May 1818 Stephen Cave of Cleve Hill, Gloucester. She inherited Nicholas and Ebworth. They had issue two children:—

   1. Stephen Cave who marrieed Jane Haviland.
   2. Lawrence Trent Cave who married Lucy Greenwood. He died in 1899. They had issue two sons and two daughters. The eldest son of the marriage is Charles John Philip Cave, the present owner of Nicholas plantation in Barbados.

Corrections

Errata. In the notes on Trent, Carleton, and Cumberbatch families which were published in the Journal for November 1941, two errors have been noted. On page 50, the record of Sarah Cumberbatch's marriage should read—Married 1 May 1818, Charles, second son of Stephen Cave of Cleve Hill, Gloucestershire. And on the same page it is stated that Lawrence Trent Cave and Lucy, his wife, had issue two daughters. In fact, there were three daughters of the marriage. *

---

*See above.

TRENT OF BARBADOS

Mr. H. B. Thomas of Bexhill-on-Sea, Sussex, England, has kindly sent us copies of some interesting Monumental Inscriptions in the church of Biddenden, Kent, and other records of the TRENT and other families with Barbadian associations. He writes—

In the parish church of Biddenden, Kent, there is, mural on the east wail of the south chancel, a white marble tablet which reads:

M.S.

GULIELMI TRENT
In Barbadâ Insulâ Americanâ nati.
E. Collegio C.C. apud Cantabrigienses A.M.
Hujusce Ecclesiae Rectoris Cui per Annos 36 Fidus invigilavit Pastor
Pietatis & Virtutis ubique (praesertum Hic) Monitor Assiduus et flexanimus:
Nec Magis Parochiam bene institutendi Studiosus
Quam Eidem et Vicinitati dilectus,
Ob Probitatem Animum erectum, generosum,
Et lepidam quandam in Colloquio Affabilitatem
Uxorem duxit MARIAM filiam GULIELMI DYER Mercatoris
Insulae predictae Indigenam Feminam Optimam, Pietate & Prudentiâ eximiè
ornatam
Quam cum mors abripuisset
Dies erat Martii 12 s An: Dom. 1735 Aetat: 64)
Secundis nuptiis sibi adjunxit MARIAM Filiam Richardi Beale
De hac Parochia Generosi Eamq. Superstitem reliquit
Januarii 25 mo An. Dom: 1739 Aetat 64
MARIA uxor supradicta decessit
Octob. 4 to. A. 1780 Aetatis 74
Defunctorum juxta Reliquias
(Quae infra sub Marmore locum indicante conduntur)
Sepulta est CHARLOTTA MARIA GULIELMI WALKER Amigeri
Filiola vix biennis
Quam matre orbam (obnixe efflagitantibus Patre & Aviâ) Amicitiae causa
Sibi in Domum recepterunt
Affectu vere Parentali
Vivam fovebant
Mortuam lugebant
Et secum hic memorari volebant
Haecce obiit
Maii llmo An: Dom: 1718
LAURENTIUS TRENT Armiger
GULIELMI (a JOHANNE fratre Natu majore) Nepos et Haeres
Pietatis et Observantiae ergo
Ponit curavit.

In the floor of the quire of the church are two blue marble stones marking burial vaults and engraved:

(i)
H S S
Exuviae GULIELMI TRENT Rectoris
A dextra jacet
MARIA TRENT

(ii)
H S S
Exuviae
MARIAE TRENT GULIELMI uxoris
Filiae GULIELMI DYER. A sinistrâ jacet
CHARLOTTA MARIA WALKER

Venn, Alumni Cantabrigienses, gives the following particulars—

"WILLIAM TRENT, Adm. pens. at Corpus Christi, 1693, of London. Matric. Lent 1694. B.A. 1696—7. M.A. 1700. Perhaps admitted at Leyden 14 Oct. 1699. Ord. priest (London) 23 Aug. 1700. V. of Chislet, Kent, 1700—5 ,R. of Biddenden 1704—40. Died 15 Jan. 1740 aged 64."

He was inducted into the Rectory of Biddenden on 9 June 1704 on the presentation of Archbishop Tenison.

The Parish Registers of Biddenden have the following entries:

Baptism: 10 May 1706. Mary, daughter of Mr. Richard & Elizabeth Beale. Born 7 May 1706. (In 1737 she became the second wife of Mr. Trent. The Beales were a prosperous family of clothiers and land owners long established in Biddenden).

Burial: 15 May 1718. Charlotta Maria Walker ob. 11 May circ Hor. 2—3 antelue. J.S. ad. oscula Xti. rapta (which may perhaps be translated that she died 11 May about 2—3 hours before daylight: taken to the embraces of Christ. J.S. may be "Jesu Salvatore").

Burial: 18 March 1734/5 Mary Trent wife of William Rect.

Marriage: 13 September 1737 William Trent Rector and Mrs. Mary Beale of this parish by Licence.

Burial: 23 January 1739/40 William Trent Rector of this Parish. (This is two days before the date of his death as given on his memorial tablet. It is not impossible that the burial date is at fault, for scrutiny of the Register suggests that the entry may have been written in some months later.)

Burial: 10 October 1760 Mrs. Mary Trent widow.

Possibly relevant to Barbados is another entry:

Marriage: 26 October 1727 Joseph Disney Vicar of Cranbrooke to Ann Rosse of this Parish by Licence.

An Historical . . . Account of the Weald of Kent by T. D. W. Dearn (published at Cranbrook, 1814) p. 87, in describing the Parish Church of Cranbrook (an adjoining Parish to Biddenden), notes:

"Against the wall in the north aisle is a tablet to the memory of the Rev. Joseph Disney, A.M., vicar of Cranbrooke & Appledore who died August the 3rd 1777, aged 82 having been respected as a gentleman, distinguished as a scholar, and exemplary as a clergyman, as also of his wife Ann, daughter of Mr. Ross of Barbadoes, & their eldest son, the Rev. Matthew Disney, B.D. who 'having proved himself worthy of such parents died March the 9th 1768 aged 37' ".

Mrs. Ann Disney died in 1782 aged 77. A son, William, Rector of Pluckley, Kent, from 1777 to 1807, and a daughter survived her.

It may be inferred that the Rev. William Trent had no children by either of his wives: and this is confirmed by the absence of any baptismal entries in the Biddenden Registers. He and his wife perhaps made the rectory at Biddenden a home for visitors from the West Indies. Following the death of her mother, they had adopted the infant Charlotta Maria Walker, and they felt her death, when she was hardly two years old, very keenly. It may well be that her father was settled in Barabdos. Ann Rosse was doubtless married from the Trent's home.

We are able to add from the Barbados records the following notes on the above information supplied by Mr. Thomas.

The TRENT family had early connections with Barbados. For extracts of Wills and other records of the family see 'Some records of Trent, Carleton & Cumberbatch Families of Barbados" in the *Journal*, Vol. IX, p.32. *

Rev. William Trent, Rector of Biddenden, was the second son of Lawrence Trent of Barbados, who by his Will dated 11 July 1692 made in Barbados on the eve of his departure for England where he died in the following March, provided for his son's education and maintenance in England until he should arrive at the age of 21, when he was to receive a legacy of £500, the gift of a house and land in the island, and an equal share with his brothers and sisters in the testator's estate.

Extracts from the Rev. W. Trent's will dated 1 May 1737 are given in the article in the Journal above referred to. Persons named as beneficiaries in the Will are, Mary, wife of Joseph Disney, of Cranbrook, and Matthew, William and Mary, her children; William Trent's sister, the Widow Burgess of Barbados; Thomas Ross of St. Kitts; Sarah Oliver, wife of William Oliver and her sister Elizabeth then living in Cranbrook; Godson William, son of Mr. Moreton, Curate of Staplehurst; Mrs. Honor Astlake, goddaughter of his late wife; and his nephew Lawrence Trent of Barbados and the grandchildren of his late brother John Trent.

Lawrence Trent, nephew of Rev. W. Trent, to whom he left the bulk of his estate was the son of his eldest brother, John Trent of Barbados. This Lawrence Trent caused the memorial in the church at Biddenden to be erected to the memory of his Uncle and others therein named.

The testator also referred in his Will to his "late wife", but as it bore a date earlier than the date of his second marriage, there is no reference to the lady who became his widow. The statement in the Trent pedigree on page 47 of the volume of the *Journal* above referred to that "it would seem from his will dated 1 May 1737 that he died a widower" must be corrected in the light of the information supplied by the Biddenden records.

Mary Dyer, his second wife, was born in Barbados. Her father was William Dyer, merchant, who came from the village of Nether Stowey in Somersetshire and settled in Barbados.

---

*Pages 527-545, this volume.

548

Trollope of Lord's Castle, Barbados.

Mr. W. H. Trollope, referring to the accompanying illustration of his coat-of-arms, writes, "I have had it designed by Mr. Hare and carried out in fibrous plaster painted, and am sending it out to Barbados to be hung in our dining-hall in Lord's Castle.* The arms are: *Vert, 3 bucks courant Argent, attired Or, within a bordure of the second* [TROLLOPE]; *impaling Argent, a saltire Sable, on a chief Gules three cushions Or, in base a human heart ensigned with an imperial crown proper* [JOHNSTON, of Carnsallock, co. Dumfries] in right of my wife Louisa Charlotte Campbell, only dau. of the late Capt. Frederick Johnston, R.N., fourth son of the Right Hon. Sir Alex. Johnston, of Carnsallock, co. Dumfries, Chief Justice of Ceylon.

I succeeded to Long Bay Castle estate, St. Philips, and the Pool plantation, St. John's, by the will of my late brother, Col. F. C. Trollope, Grenadier Guards, in 1913, and he had it from my father, Gen. Sir Charles Trollope, K.C.B., in right of my mother Frances, only child of John Lord and niece of Samuel Hall Lord. My father was a son of Sir John Trollope, 6th Bart., of Casewick, Lincolnshire, and brother of the 1st Baron Kesteven.

Long Bay Castle was built in 1820 replacing an earlier structure."

5 Montagu Square, W.   W. H. TROLLOPE.

---

*See p. 550, this volume.

TROTMAN OF BARBADOS

From pedigrees compiled by F. H. Trotman.

1. ROGER¹ ROBERT TROTMAN, in a deed signed 16 May,1648, sold land
    in St. James. In counter deed, 22 July, 1643, described as landowner.
2. WILLIAM¹ TROTMAN, planter of St. James. In counter deed dated 22
    July, 1643, described as Planter of St. James, & in deed, 16 Sept., 1644, sold
    land in St. James. Son, Thomas ² Trotman.
3. THOMAS ² TROTMAN (William¹), buried at St. Peter   1679. Wife,
    Constant, as widow in census 1679 in St. Thomas. Sons:—
    - i. ? Thomas ³ Trotman, born c. 1667, aged 48 in census of 1715
      in St. Thomas. Wife not named, probably deceased before
      1715. Son, Thomas ⁴ Trotman, born c. 1702; in census of 1715
      in St. Thomas, aged 13.   ? Will entered 3 March, 1757. Wife,
      Patience, dau . . .Lovell, married at Christ Church, 10 Sept.,
      1726. No further descendants.
    - 4. ii. Henry ³ Trotman.
4. HENRY ³ TROTMAN (Thomas ² William ¹), son of Thomas ² Trotman
    and his wife Constant. Not named in census of 1715, presumably then
    dead. Married at Christ Church, 7 March, 1695, to Elizabeth, dau. of
    . . .Dilley, named in census, 1715, in Christ Church, as widow, aged 48.
    Exx. of son Thomas's will.
    Children:—
    - i. Constant Trotman, baptised at Christ Church, April 1697,
      aged 2 years; named in census 1715, in Christ Church.
    - ii. Thomas Trotman, baptised 1700, aged 6 months. In census
      of 1715, in Christ Church, aged 14. Will dated 13 Dec., 1728,
      entered 13th March, 1729. Died unmarried.
    - 5. iii. Henry ⁴ Trotman, baptised at Christ Church, 1703, named in
      census of 1715, aged 13.
    - iv. Robert Trotman, baptised at Christ Church, 25 Dec., 1707; in
      census of 1715 in Christ Church, aged 8. Named in will of
      [?] cousin, Thomas ⁴ Trotman, entered 1757. Wife, Sarah, and
      2 sons. Youngest son baptised at Christ Church, Oct., 1751 &
      named in will of said Thomas ⁴ Trotman, 1757.
    - 6. v. William ⁴ Trotman, baptised at Christ Church, 1710; named in
      census 1715, aged 4.
5. HENRY ⁴ TROTMAN (Henry ³ Thomas ² Willam¹), 2nd. son of Henry ³
    Trotman and his wife Elizabeth. Baptised at Christ Church, 15 Aug.
    1703; named in census of 1715, aged 13; will dated 11 Nov. 1773; entered
    2 Nov., 1776.
    Twice married; 1st. Frances . . . . ., & had issue:—
    - i. Ann Trotman, baptised at St. Michael, 24 March, 1742. Will
      dated 8 Nov., 1775; entered 2 Nov., 1776. Unmarried, named
      in father's will.
    - ii. Daniel Trotman, baptised at St. Michael, 24 March, 1742.
    - 7. iii. Henry ⁵ Trotman, baptised at St. Michael, 24 March, 1742.
    - 8. iv. Nathaniel ⁵ Trotman.
    - [?] v. Frances Trotman, wife of Robert Gibson, married at St.

Michael, 23 Sept., 1773.

Married, 2ndly. Mary ...... named in husband's will & had issue:—

9. i.   Robert 5 Trotman.
    ii. A daughter, wife of .... Mason, named in wills of father and of half-sister, Ann, respectively.
    iii. Sarah Trotman, wife of Conrade Davis, married at St. Michael, 4 Jan., 1767. Named in wills of father and of half-sister, Ann, respectively.

6. WILLIAM 4 TROTMAN (Henry 3 Thomas 2 William 1), of Ridge Plantation, Christ Church, and St. Michael. Fourth son of Henry 3 Trotman and his wife, Elizabeth, baptised at Christ Church, 17 Dec., 1710; named in census 1715, aged 4. Will dated 14 Aug., 1756, entered 13 Aug., 1757, names wife, Sarah. Had issue:—
    i.   Mary Trotman, wife of Dr. Thomas Storey, married at St. Michael, 10 Dec., 1772. Named in wills of father and of sister, Susanna, respectively.
10. ii. Henry 5 Trotman, born c. 1736.
    iii Susanna Trotman, will dated 5 Oct., 1794, entered 4 Nov., 1794. Unmarried; named, a minor, in father's will, 1756.

7. HENRY 5 TROTMAN (Henry 4 Henry 3 Thomas 2 William 1), 2nd. son of Henry 4 Trotman and his 1st. wife, Frances. Baptised at St. Michael, 24 March, 1742. Named in his father's will. Wife Jane; had issue:—
    i.   Mary Trotman, named in will of grandfather, Henry 4 Trotman, 1773, & in will of aunt, Ann Trotman, Spinster, 1775.
11. ii. Henry 6 Trotman, born 31 Dec., 1767.
    iii. Thomas Trotman, named in wills of grandfather, and of aunt, Ann Trotman, respectively.

8. NATHANIEL 5 TROTMAN (Henry 4 Henry 3 Thomas 2 William 1), 3rd. son of Henry 4 Trotman and his 1st. wife, Frances. Witnessed father's will, 1773, & will of sister, Ann Trotman, spinster, 1775. Married Eleanor, widow ...Walrond, at St. Michael, 30 March, 1776, and had issue:—
    i.   Nathaniel James Trotman, born 17 Jan., 1768; baptised at St. Michael, 29 Feb., 1768.
    ii.   Sarah Ellen Trotman, baptised at St. Michael, 24 Sept., 1771.
    iii. Christian Trotman, baptised at St. Michael, 24 Sept., 1771.
    iv.   Robert Trotman, baptised at St. Michael, 28 Jan., 1776. Member of House of Assembly for Parish of St. Goerge, 1803.
    v.   James Trotman, born 4 Jan., 1776; baptised at St. Michael, 28 Jan., 1776.
    vi.   Eleanor Trotman, baptised at St. Michael, 12 March, 1778.
    vii. James Carleton Trotman, born 21 April, 1782, baptised at St. Michael, 5 May, 1783.

9. ROBERT 5 TROTMAN (Henry 4 Henry 3 Thomas 2 William 1), of Baldwick Estate, St. John, and of St. Michael. 4th. son of Henry 4 Trotman, and 1st. child by his 2nd. wife, Mary. Named in father's will, & in will of half-sister, Ann Trotman, Spinster. His will dated 27 June, 1791, entered 18 Aug., 1796. Executors sold the Baldwick estate to Gen. Robert Haynes*,

_____

* The Baldwick Estate was renamed "Haynesfield" by General Haynes and is now called "Wakefield".

9 Aug., 1804. Married twice, & had issue by 1st. wife:—

    i.   Sarah Trotman, wife of John Marsh, married at St. Michael, 7 Dec., 1775. Named in father's will.

    ii.   Elizabeth Trotman, wife of Wm. Hughenos, married at St. Philip, 30 March, 1777. Named in father's will, and in will of brother, J. C. Trotman.

    iii. James Crichlow Trotman, of Olive Grove Plantation, St. Joseph, and Nebacho Plantation, Demerara. Died 7 Nov., 1809. Will dated 31 May, 1809, entered 10 May, 1810. Named in father's will. Died without issue.

    iv.   William Trotman, named in father's will. Wife Eleanor, widow of St. Michael, died 30 March, 1813. Will dated 5 Octr., 1812, entered 17 April, 1815. Only child, Eleanqr, wife of Benjamin Jones of Demerara, married at St. Michael, 16 Aug., 1798. Named in will of mother and grandfather, Henry [4] Trotman, respectively.

Married 2ndly, Mary Ann, dau. of ..... Bourne, at St. Michael, 23 June, 1775, and had issue:—

    i.   Samuel Henry Trotman, born 16 Dec., 1775; baptised at St. Michael, 18 Jan., 1776. Will dated 22 Oct., 1818, entered 28 Aug., 1819. Married Joannah Sarsfield; will dated 18 June, 1831, entered 30 June, 1831. No issue.

    ii.   Mary Trotman, wife of ...Portmans. Named in will of grandfather, Henry [4] Trotman, & in will of brother, H. G. S. Trotman, 1804.

    iii. Henry George Steele Trotman, baptised at St. Philip, 1777. Will dated 9 Feb., 1804, entered 14 Nov., 1804. Unmarried.

10.   HENRY [5] TROTMAN (William [4] Henry [3] Thomas [2] William [1]) of Valley & Hill Plantations in St. George. Only son of William [4] Trotman of Ridge Plantation, Christ Church. Born c. 1736. Member of House of Assembly 1795/6 & 1804. Died 8 Dec., 1804, aged 68. Will signed 14 July, 1804, entered 24 Dec., 1808. M. I. in St. George. Named in father's will, 1756, and in wills of sister, Susanna Trotman, Spinster, 1794, and of cousin, Ann Trotman, Spinster, 1775, respectively. Wife, Elizabeth, born c. 1730. Died 26 Aug., 1790, aged 60. M. I. in St. George. Had issue

12.   i.   Thomas Clarke [6] Trotman

13. ? ii.   John [6] Trotman

    iii. Mary Trotman, baptised at St. Michael, 17 April, 1763. Wife .... Mahon. Named in father's will, & in will of aunt, Ann Trotman, Spinster, 1775.

    vi.   William Robert Trotman, baptised at St. Michael, 28 Feb., 1768.

    v.   Richard Trotman, baptised at St. Michael, 6 May, 1771.

11.   HENRY [6] TROTMAN jnr. (Henry [5] Henry [4] Henry [3] Thomas [2] William [1]), eldest son of Henry [5] Trotman and his wife Jane. Born 31 Dec., 1767; baptised at St. Michael 17 April, 1768. Married Joanna, dau. of Samuel Brandford, at St. Michael, 28 Oct., 1800. Her burial registered at St. Michael, 11 June, 1832. Had issue:

    i.   Joanna Trotman, wife of .... Walrond. Named in will of brother S. B. Trotman 1873/82.

    ii.   Brandford Trotman, baptised at St. Michael, 1804. Will dated

4 July, 1890, entered 24 July, 1890. Named in will of brother
S. B. Trotman. Spinster.

   iii. Susanna Trotman, born 6 Dec., 1810, baptised 29 Feb., 1812.
Wife of .... Evans. Named in wills of sister Brandford Trotman & brother, S. B. Trotman.

   iv. Henry Trotman, named in will of sister, Brandford Trotman,
1890.

   v. Samuel Brandford Trotman, born 12 Dec., 1811, baptised at
Michael, 29 Feb., 1812. Will signed 6 April, 1873 & 3 codicils,
last dated 14 Sept., 1882. He is described as "Formerly of Barbados, now of De Kenderen's Plantation in Demerara". Will
and annexed instruments allowed on 26 March, 1886, by Chief
Justice in Barbados.

12.   THOMAS [6] CLARKE TROTMAN (Henry [5] William [4] Henry [3] Thomas [2]
William [1]), of Bulkeley Estate, Valley & Carmichael in St. George. Col.
in St. George's Regt. of Militia in 1804, Member of House of Assembly
1795/6, & 1815/16. Retired to York Place, Clifton England. Died 7 May,
1826. Will proved P.C.C. 1 July, 1826, entered Barbados 9 March, 1827.
M.I's. with Arms in Clifton Parish Church & at St. George, Barbados.
Named in wills of grandfather,, William [4] Trotman, of Ridge, Ch. Ch.,
1756, & of aunt, Ann Trotman, Spinster, 1775. Married Ann, dau. of ....
Hamilton, at St. Michael, 16 Oct., 1794. She died at 6 York Place, Clifton,
24 Jan., 1874, aged 98. Her will dated 19 Feb., 1867, proved 18 April, 1874.
M.I's. in Clifton Parish Church, & St. George, Barbados. Had issue:—

14.   i. Henry [7] Trotman, born c. 1790.

   ii. Mary Hamilton Trotman, wife of Rev. Wm. Drake Sealy.
Named in father's will, and in will of sister, Ann Trotman,
Spinster, 1882.

   iii. Ann Trotman, born 1798; died, unmarried, 28 Aug., 1887, at
7 Mendian Place, Clifton. Will dated 15 June 1882, proved
28 Oct., 1887. M.I's. in Clifton Parish Church & St. George's,
Barbados.

15.   iv. Simon Lee [7] Trotman, born 23 Jan., 1802.

16.   v. Joseph [7] Trotman, born 21 July, 1804.

17.   vi. Thomas [7] Trotman.

18.   vii. William Clarke [7] Trotman, born 1811.

   viii. Philip Phipps Trotman, named in mother's will, & ni will of
sister Ann Trotman. Wife Ann, named in will of sister Ann
Trotman. Had issue, 2 daus., Kate died c. 1936, and ...., wife
of .... Manning.

13.   JOHN [6] TROTMAN ? (Henry [5] William [4] Henry [3] Thomas [2] William [1])
of Wilcox Plantation, Christ Church. Presumed to be a son of Henry [5]
Trotman of Valley & Hill Plantations in St. George. Named in will of
aunt, Susanna Trotman, Spinster 1794. His burial registered at St. Michael,
10 Dec., 1815. Married 1st. Elizabeth Ann, dau. of James Williams, baptised at St. Thomas, 1770; died 6 Sept., buried at Bath Abbey 13 Sept.,
1793. M.I. Bath Abbey. Had issue:— One child. Married, secondly
Elizabeth Hinds, eldest daughter of General Thomas Williams of Welchman's Hall, St. Thomas, and Woburn, St. George, Bapt. at St. Thomas,
1782. Married at St. Thomas, 29 Jan., 1801. Had issue:—

i. John Trotman, born at St. Pancras, London 20 Aug., 1803.

ii. Thomas Williams Trotman, born 31 July, 1809, baptised 1 Jan. 1812, at Christ Church. Assistant to Dr. J. W. W. Carrington of St. Thomas. Sailed to Liverpool 1837. Later, practised medicine in Florence. Died of typhus in Italy, July 1862. Will signed 14 March, 1834, proved 30 July, 1869. Married Elizabeth Wilhelmina Bellingham, dau. of Samuel Ffennell Esq., of Cahir, Tipperary, and his wife Frances Grenville Bindon. Her will dated 1 June, 1876, then living at No. 7, Victorio Emanuale, Florence. Died 2 March, 1891. Will proved 23 March, 1892. Named in husband's will, & in will of Ann Trotman, Spinster, 1882. No issue.

iii. Elizabeth Prescod Williams Trotman, born 12 May, 1810. Baptised 1 Jan., 1812, at Christ Church. Married at St. George, 1 Dec., 1831. Died 1895. Wife of Thomas [7] Trotman, of Bulkeley. Will dated 21 Oct., 1891, entered 15 Feb., 1895. M.I. in St. George's Churchyard. Named in will of Brandford Trotman, Spinster, 1890, and in will of brother T. W. Trotman, 1834.

iv. Margaret Williams Trotman, born 15 March, 1814. Wife of Dr. John William Worrell Carrington of St. Thomas. Married at St. George, 6 March 1832. Died 1881.

14. HENRY [7] TROTMAN (Thomas Clarke [6] Henry [5] William [4] Henry [3] Thomas [2] William [1]), eldest son of Thomas Clarke Trotman of Bulkeley, Valley & Carmichael in St. George. [?] Born c. 1790. Matric. Queen's College 16 Dec. 1812, aged 22. Inherited Hill House. Member of House of Assembly for Parish of St. George 1817/19. Died 1 March 1857, aged 66. Married Elizabeth Ann, dau. of .... Brandford, born 20th. June, 1794. Married at St. Michael, 7 Oct., 1819. Died 23 Feb. 1831, in St. Michael's. Buried at St. George 24 Feb., 1831. Had issue:—

i. Malvina Williams Trotman, eldest dau. Died at Clifton, Bristol, 18 May, 1840.

ii. John Warren Trotman, born 23 Oct., 1820. Baptised at St. George, 12 Nov., 1820. Matric. 1831, at St. Alban's Hall, Oxford.

iii. Thomas Clarke Trotman, born 30th. Jan., 1822; baptised at St. George 8 Jan., 1824. Living in 1857. Deceased when his widow made her will. Married Augusta, dau. of .... Crichlow, 1846. Her will dated 12 Sept., 1890, proved 20 May, 1892. No issue.

iv. Margaret Brandford Trotman, baptised at St. George 22 Nov., 1826. Wife of .... Crichlow. Named in will of sister-in-law, Augusta Trotman, widow 1890, and in will of brother J. W. W. Trotman, 1870.

v. James Thomas Williams Trotman, baptised at St. George 22 Nov., 1826. Will entered 29 July 1870. ? No issue.

vi. Henry Trotman, born 20 Aug., 1829, baptised at St. George 28 Aug., 1829. Died 3 Sept., & buried at St. George, 4 Sept., 1829. M.I. in St. George's Churchyard.

16.   JOSEPH [7]TROTMAN (Thomas Clarke [6] Henry [5] William [4] Henry [3] Thomas [2] William [1]), 3rd. son of Thomas Clarke Trotman of Bulkeley, etc. in St. George. Born 21 July, 1804, baptised at St. George,1804. B.A. 1827. M.A. 1829 'at Worcester College, Oxford. Barrister-at-Law. Owner of Forster Lodge, St. George. Later lived at Warrens. On death of wife moved to 22 Pulteny St., Bath, where he died, 21 Dec., 1868. Will dated 10 Dec., 1866, proved 12 Oct., 1869. Left Warrens to daus., and Cane Garden to sons. Named in father's & mother's wills respectively. Wife, Susanna, born c. 1815, dau. of Thomas William & Frances Bradshaw, married 22 April, 1835. Ward of Dr. Hewitt who left her Warrens & Cane Garden. Died at Warrens, 22 April, 1852. M.I. in St. George. Had issue:—

  i.   George Hewitt [8] Trotman, retired as Colonel, 60th. Rifles. Took part in Roberts's march from Kandarhar to Kabul. Later of Newtown House, Bantry, Co. Cork. Died 11 April, 1916. Will dated 17 May, 1914, proved 18 July,1916. Named in will of grandfather, Thomas Clarke Trotman, 1826 & in father's will.

  ii.   Ellen Louisa Trotman, died 8 Dec., 1918. Admon., 4 Feb., 1919, "of 12 Burlington St.. Bath". Named in father's will, & in will of aunt, Ann Trotman, Spinster, 1882. Unmarried.

  iii.   Josephine Trotman, wife of Herbert Hope Keighley. Named in father's will, & in will of aunt, Ann Trotman, Spinster, 1882.

  iv.   Edward Perch Trotman, of Cane Garden, St. Thomas. Died 6 Aug., 1896. Will dated 2 Nov., 1888, proved 21 Jan., 1897. Unmarried.

  v.   Frederick Hamilton Trotman. At time of marriage, gent., of King St., Bath. Died at Imber, Co. Wilts., 31 Aug., 1881. Will dated 5 March 1870, proved 27 Sept., 1881. On death certificate, aged 44, Bank Clerk, of Founder's Court, Lathbury, & 1 Sharstead St., Kennington Park, Surrey. Named in father's will. Wife, Louisa Caroline, dau. of John Hayman, Hotel Keeper. Married at Parish Church of Trinity, Bath, 31 Jan., 1865, aged 20. Named in.husband's will. Had issue, children named in father's will.

  vi.   William Mends Forte Trotman, Lieut. Col.. Gloucestershire regt. Later of 18 Henrietta St., Bath, & then of Fairtown, Buckland, Monachorum, Devon. Will proved 13 July, 1926. Died 25 Nov., 1925. Named in father's will. Wife, Mary Ann Beatrice, dau. of Dr. Nash of Bath. Died 8 April, 1953. Will dated 4 July, 1950, proved 25 June, 1953, and described as "of 30 Belvedere, City of Bath." Refers to marriage settlement of 1884, & that she did not have issue.

  vii.   Susan Frances Hinds Trotman, died unmarried, 8 Dec., at 18 Russell St., Bath. Named in Father's will, & in will of aunt, Ann Trotman, Spinster, 1882.

  viii.   Anne Hamilton Trotman, wife of Capt. Piers Edgcombe. Married 2ndly., Col. William Wood. Named in father's will, & in will of aunt, Ann Trotman, Spinster, 1882, & of brother, George Hewitt Trotman, 1914, respectively.

  ix.   Sarah Isabella Trotman, wife of Seymour Kane. In 1919, widow, of 14 Russell St., Bath. Named in father's will.

17.   THOMAS [7] TROTMAN, (Thomas Clarke [6] Henry [5] William [4] Henry [3]

Thomas [2] William[1]) of Bulkeley's, St. George; 4th. son of Thomas Clarke Trotman of Bulkeley, Valley & Carmichael, in St. George; and his wife Ann. Named in mother's will, 1867. Estate sold to William Mason in 1866. Wife, Elizabeth Prescod Williams, dau. of John & Elizabeth Hinds Trotman; born 12 May 1810, baptised at Christ Church, 1 Jan. 1812. Married at St. George, 1 Dec., 1831. Died 1895, cp. M.I. on Williams Memorial in St. George's Churchyard. Will dated 21 Oct., 1891, entered 15 Feb., 1895. Named in will of her brother, Dr. Thos. Williams Trotman, 1834, & in will of Brandford Trotman, Spinster, 1890. Had issue:—

[?] i. Thomas L. [8] Trotman, buried at St. George, 2 Aug., 1931, aged
ii. Elizabeth Lee Trotman, born 5 Oct., 1832, baptised at St. George, 14 Oct., 1834. Wife of Tom Sealy.
iii. John Hamilton Trotman, baptised at St. George, 14 Oct. 1834. Named in wills of Aunt, Ann Trotman, Spinster, 1882.
iv. Mary Catherine Hinds Trotman, unmarried. Named in mother's will, and in wills of Aunt Ann Trotman, & of Dr. T. W. Trotman 1834.
v. Thomas Lee Trotman, died suddenly at Bulkeley, 19 Nov., 1862. Buried at St. George's.

18. WILLIAM CLARKE [7] TROTMAN (Thomas Clarke [6] Henry [5] William[4] Henry [3] Thomas [2] William [1]), M.D., M.R.C.S., Edinburgh, 5th. son of Thomas Clarke Trotman of Bulkeley, etc., in St. George. Born 1811. Freeholder of Cross Farm, Badgeworth, Glos., & of "Energlyn". Died 30 May, 1893. Will dated 13 May 1892, proved 30 June, 1893. Named in mother's will, 1867. Wife, Margaret, died 16 March 1891, at Energlyn, 41 Canynges Rd., Clifton. Will dated 10 July, 1875, proved 10 Aug., 1891. Had issue:— 1 dau., Anna, wife of John Hancock Selwyn Payne. Inherited father's house & estate. Named in father's will.

THE HOUSE OF THE SEVEN GABLES

THE TURNERS OF NEW ENGLAND
AND BARBADOS.

By G. ANDREWS MORIARTY, A.M., LL.B., F.S.A.

THE Turners offer a rare and interesting example of a family with one branch established at Salem in the Colony of Massachusetts Bay in New England and another in the Colony of Barbados. Each branch attained a prominent position in its respective Colony. In 1668-69 John Turner of Salem built the house, still standing, which has been made famous as the "House of the Seven Gables" in Nathaniel Hawthorne's romance of that name. It is a fine example of XVIIth century New England architecture.

In 1912 this writer contributed an article upon the Turners of Salem to the Essex Institute Historical Collections (Salem) for that year and in 1913 an additional article upon the Barbadian family based upon searches made by him in the Spring of that year in the archives at Bridgetown. As these articles, printed in a local New England historical publication, are not likely to be known to Barbadian antiquaries it has seemed to him of some interest to combine these two articles and present them to students of Barbadian history.

The original home of the Turners in England has not, as yet, been ascertained but there are some very slight indications that they may have come from the Eastern part of Suffolk. The Barbadian and New England families descend from two brothers, Peter and Robert Turner respectively. The former is known only from a mention of him in the will of his brother, Robert Turner of Boston, Mass., who left a legacy to "Abigail Death, daughter of my brother Peter Turner", while the will of Capt. John Turner of "Three Houses", St. Philip's parish, Barbados, left a bequest to "my beloved sister, Abigail, now the wife of William Death". The new England family retained a tradition of their connection with Barbados but, as is usual in such cases, it was wrong in its details, as it made Capt. John Turner of Salem (son of Robert of Boston) the son, instead of the cousin, of Capt. John Turner of Barbados.

1.————TURNER, living in England at the beginning of the XVIIth century. He had, probably with other issue:

    2. i. *Peter,* born about 1600.

    3. ii. *Robert,* born about 1611. Of New England.

2. PETER,[2] ————)[1] TURNER. Nothing is known about him except from the reference to him in his brother's will. Married and had issue:

    4. i. *John,* born about 1622. Later of Barbados.

       ii. *Abigail,* born about 1627. Married William Death, gentleman and planter of St. Philip's Parish, Barbados, about 1650. She is mentioned in the will of her uncle, Robert Turner of Boston in 1651, as the daughter of his brother, Peter Turner. The will of William Death of St. Philip's was dated 9 Feb. 1701/2, proved 15 July 1702 (Barbados Probate).

They had issue three daughters: 1. Elizabeth, married Thomas Todd of St. John's Parish, died before 1687; 2. Patience married John Taylor, who died before Feb. 1701/2; 3. Abigail married as his 2nd. wife George Braithwaite of St. Philip's Parish.

     5. iii? *Richard*,[3] born about 1630.

    3. ROBERT[2] (———[1]) TURNER of Boston, Mass. Born in 1611, died in 1651. He was a shoemaker and merchant. Came to New England from London in the "Blessing" in 1635 aged 24 years (Hotten's Lists ed. 1874 p. 93). He was admitted a townsman at Boston on 25: 2 mo.: 1642 and became a member of the First Church at Boston on 17 (12) 1643/4 (Pope's "Pioneers of Massachusetts" p. 465). In 1643 he joined the Boston Artillery Company (History of the Ancient and Honorourable Artillery Company of Boston, Vol. 1, p. 134). On 1 : 10: 1644 Valentine Hill of Boston, merchant, (his brother-in-law) conveyed to Robert Turner of Boston, shoemaker, a house and garden in Boston on what is now Court Street in that city. (Suffolk Deeds) and on 30: 4 mo.: 1651 he sold the same to Thomas Roberts of Boston, feltmaker (ib.). His will dated 14 Aug. 1651 was proved on 3: 10: 1651. The inventory, taken on the same day, shows an estate of £384: 04: 11. In this will he names his wife Elizabeth, his sons John and Habakkuk, his daughter Elizabeth and an unborn child. He left a legacy to Hannah Hill, "daughter of my wife's sister Frances Hill" and to "Abigail Death, daughter of my brother, Peter Turner", also to John Spurr's wife. One of the overseers was "my loving friend, Mr. Valentine Hill" (Suffolk Co. Mass. Probate; New Eng. Hist. Gen. Reg. Vol. IV, p. 285).

    Married about 1642 Elizabeth, daughter of Richard Freestone, woolen draper of Horncastle, Co. Lincs. by his wife, Margery, daughter of Robert Freestone of Brinkhill, Co. Lincs. and sister of Robert Freestone M.D. of Thimbleby, Co. Lincs. (B.A. Emanuel College Cambs. 1610 and Fellow Commoner, M.D. 1628). Elizabeth was baptized at Horncastle on 17 Oct. 1619 and joined the First Church at Boston on 7 (1) 1646, after her marriage to Turner. The proof of this unrecorded marriage is complicated.

    Capt. John Turner of Salem, son of Robert and Elizabeth of Boston, had a daughter Freestone Turner, born at Salem on 25 Oct. 1677 (Salem Vital Records). On 9 (9) and 28 (10) 1634 Anne and Frances Freestone, "kinswomen of our brother William Hutchinson" were admitted as members of the First Church at Boston (Pope's Pioneers of Massachusetts, p. 176). On 26 Oct. 1640 Elizabeth Freestone spinster of Boston (Mass.), formerly of Alford, Co. Lincs., daughter of Richard Freestone of Horncastle woollendraper deceased, gave a power of attorney to John Hutchinson of Alford to collect certain moneys due to her from the estate of her grandmother Mary Cuthbert and also from the estate of her uncle Robert Freestone deceased, executor of the will of her grandfather Robert Freestone, who was one of the executors of her father (Lechford's Note Book, p. 181). An examination of the "Lincolnshire Pedigrees" compiled by Canon Madison and published by the Harleian Society shows that George Freestone of Horncastle married, as her first husband, Mary, daughter of John Hutchinson, Major of Lincoln in 1564; she married 2ndly.—Cuthbert (cf. New England Historical Genealogical Register, Vol. XX, pp. 357-359). They were the parents of Richard Freestone named above, whose wife Margery is shown by the entry in Lechford to have been identical with Margery, daughter of Robert Freestone (brother of George) baptized at Brinkhill, Co. Lincs. on 18 June 1587, who was buried, as the wife of Richard Freestone, at Horncastle on 23 June 1625, Richard and Margery Freestone had, among other issue, Frances, bapt. 13 Oct. 1610, Anne, bapt. 12 Nov. 1615 and Elizabeth, bapt. 17 Oct. 1619, all at Horncastle. It is clear that these three young women must have come to Boston in New England with their cousin William Hutchinson of Alford, Co. Lincs. (son of Edward, the son of John the Mayor of Lincoln) in 1634. His wife was the famous Anne Hutchinson, who caused such a political and religious turmoil in Boston in 1636; she was a near relative of John Dryden the poet. Frances Freestone is clearly identical with Frances the first wife of Valentine Hill an early Boston merchant and the overseer of the will of Robert Turner. Frances, the wife of Valentine Hill, died on 17 Feb. 1645/6 and their only child, who survived, was a daughter Hannah bapt. at Boston on 17 March 1638/9 at the First Church; she is the "Hannah Hill daughter of my wife's sister Frances Hill" named in the will of Robert Turner. Nothing further is known of the third sister Anne Freestone.

    Children of Robert and Elizabeth Turner (all born at Boston):

    i. *John* born 28 April 1643, died young.
6. ii. *John* born 8 Sept. and bapt. 15 Sept. 1644.
7. iii. *Habakkuk* born 18: (2): 1647.
    iv. *Elizabeth* bapt. 18: (4): 1648. Married Eleazer Gedney of Salem merchant on 9 June 1665. Left issue.
    v. *Frances* bapt. 26 (6) 1650 aged about 6 days. Died young.
    vi. *Robert* born 17 May 1652, died in July 1652.

    4. CAPT. JOHN[3] (*Peter,*[2] ———[1]) TURNER of "Three Houses" St. Philip's parish, Barbados. He was born about 1625 and appears to be identical with the John Turner who was a merchant at Boston, Mass. between 1644 and 1649. Aspinwall's Notarial Records contain a number of references to his commercial activities in Boston at this time. On 30 (10) 1647 John Turner and Benjamin Gillom sold the ship "Expectation" and her cargo to Stephen and Adam Winthrop (i.e. sons of Gov. John Winthrop of Massachusetts). On 5 (6) 1650 a bill concerning this transaction was attested by Aspinwall as a power of attorney was given by Mr. Adam Winthrop to Francis Robin-

son of Barbados, merchant, to act for him against John Turner, who by this date had settled in Barbados (Aspinwall's Notarial Records, pp. 119, 313). On 16 Aug. 1653 John Turner gave a bond to John Richards of Boston to deliver 22,848 lbs. of muscovado sugar at the "Indian Bridge" or at the 'Hole" in the Island of Barbados (Suffolk Co., Mass. Deeds). As "John Turner of St. Michael's" he sold nine acres in that parish, where he lived, to Robert Scott on 19 Sept. 1659 and Abel Alleyne witnessed the deed (Barbadian Deeds). On 9 Jan. 1652 Sir George Ayscue wrote to Lord Willoughby to arrange for a meeting of the Peace Commissioners at "Mr. Turner's house, the sign of the Mermaid at Oistin's" (Cal. of State Papers Am. & W. I.). On 12 Oct. 1666 "John Turner of St. Phillip's Parish merchant" conveyed to Abel Alleyne of St. Michael's Parish, gent. for £5,728 the moiety of his plantation of 421 acres in St. Andrew's parish (Barbadian Deeds). He represented St. Philip's Parish in the Assembly in 1666 and on 28 March 1667 he was a member of the Council (Cal. State Papers Am. & W. I. 1661-68). On 9 Jan. 1667/8 he bought of John Turner mariner of Salem in New England ¼ part of the new ketch "Speedwell" then lying in Salem harbor (Essex Co. Mass. Deeds). The will of John Turner of St. Philip's Parish gentleman dated 6 Oct. 1673 was proved 26 Nov. 1673. He left an annuity to his daughter Anne to be administered by her sister Mrs. Mary Rouse and her brothers Abel and Reynold Alleyne. He gave an annuity of £50 to "my beloved sister Abigail, now the wife of William Death" and annuities of £50 each to her daughters Elizabeth, Patience and Abigail. The residue he left to his two daughters Abigail and Mary Turner and made his two sons-in-law (i.e. step sons) Abel and Reynold Alleyne, overseers of his will and guardians of his daughters. Reynold Alleyne was to manage his estate for two years. (Barbadian wills). His estate was a very large one.

Married, after 16 June 1650 and prior to 1656, Mary Skeat, widow of Col. Reynold Alleyne, who was slain in the Parliamentary forces of Sir George Ayscue in their attack upon the island.

Children:

    i. *Anne* born after 1653. Probably died unmarried.

   ii. *Abigail* born about 1656, bapt. an adult at St. Philip's Parish on 17 Sept. 1676. Married on 19 Sept. 1676 Tobias Frere Esq. of Christ Church Parish. Children: 1. John bapt. 17 July 1677 at St. Michael's; 2. Tobias bapt. 7 Feb. 1680/81 at Christ Church, and buried at St. Philip's 22 Aug. 1681; 3. Thomas bapt. 28 April 1684, buried 25 April 1687/8 at Christ Church.

  iii. *Mary* born about 1658, baptized an adult at St. Philip's 17 Sept. 1676. Married 18 Feb. 1676/7 Col. Thomas Spyar Esq. of Mount Standfast, St. Andrew's Parish. His will, dated 28 Nov. 1682 was proved 4 Dec. 1682. Children: 1. Mary, 2. Elizabeth, 3. Rebecca. The latter married William Ter-

rill Esq. of Cabbage Tree Hall and had issue an
only daughter Mary Terrill, who married John
Alleyne Esq. of "Four Hills", St. Andrew's Parish
and Magdelen College Oxford. They were the ancestors of the present Baronets (cf. Burke's Peerage).

5. RICHARD³ (? *Peter*,² ——¹) TURNER of St. Philip's
Parish Barbados. He had a son Richard bapt. on 14 Dec. 1662
and is probably the Richard Turner, who married at St. Philip's
Parish on 2 Jan. 1678/9 Dorothy Compton and had Peter bapt.
28 March 1680/1; John bapt. 8 April 1683 and Elizabeth bapt. 8
March 1683/4.

6. CAPT. JOHN³ (*Robert*², ——¹) TURNER of Salem, Mass.,
on 9 Oct. 1680 "aged 36 years" (M.I. in Charter St. Cemetery,
Salem, Mass.). He removed early in life to Salem, Co. Essex,
Mass., where he became a wealthy merchant trading with Barbados. On 17 Aug. 1668 he purchased from Ann Moore, widow,
a house and lot on Salem harbor at the foot of Turner's Lane
(now Turner Street) and the following year he erected a mansion house, which is still standing and known as "The House
of the Seven Gables". It was the scene of Nathaniel Hawthorne's
famous romance of that name. He owned and operated the
ferry from the foot of Turner's Lane to Marblehead, Mass. He
leased from the town Baker's Island at the entrance to Salem
harbor for one thousand years and erected a warehouse thereon, later he purchased the island outright (Essex Co. Deeds).
On 12 March 1673/4 he was Constable of Salem and on 28:9:1676
he had a license to retail strong drink. On 13: 1: 1678/9 he was
a Selectman of Salem (i.e one of the town's governing body).
In 1679 he was at Barbados and on 29 April of that year he had
a ticket to go to Boston on the ship "Nathaniel" (Hotten's Lists,
p. 411). On 9 Jan. 1667/8 John Turner of Salem 'marrenear"
sold to Capt. John Turner of Barbados one fourth part of the
new ketch "Speedwell" then riding in Salem harbor (Essex Deeds
op. cit.; Perley's Hist. of Salem, Vol. II, p. 370). He died intestate leaving a large estate in lands, ships, goods &c. He was
buried in the Charter Street Cemetery at Salem under a large
flat stone with the folowing inscription: "Here lyeth the body of
Mr. John Turner aged 36 years, who dyed on ye 9 Day of October in ye year Our Lord 1680". Administration on his estate
was granted to his widow Elizabeth on 13 Oct. 1680 (Essex Co.
Court Files, Vol. XXXIV, p. 85; Essex Co. Prob. Bk. 301, p. 169).
After her death and that of her second husband a new administration was granted to his son John Turner, who had just
come of age, in 1692 and on 6 June 1693 he presented a new
inventory of the estate (Essex Prob. Vol. 303, pp. 98-99). The
estate was finally divided among the children on 22 March
1696/7 (ib. Vol. 305, pp. 289-292).

He married on 2: 10 mo.: 166-(1668) Elizabeth, daughter of
Thomas Roberts feltmaker and merchant of Boston, Mass. She
was bapt., in the First Church at Boston on 11: 4 mo.: 1648.
She married 2nly. at Salem on 19 June 1684 Major Charles Red-

563

ford, a wealthy Salem merchant, who died while on a visit to Barbados and was buried at St. Michael's on 11 Aug. 1691. His wife predeceased him. The will of Major Bedford aated 29 April 1691 made his step hon. John Turner one of his executors. He left the bulk of his estate to his Turner step-children, as he died without issue. (Essex Co. Prob.).

Children of John and Elizabeth Turner:

    i. *Elizabeth* born 20 April 1669, died April 1671.

8.   ii. John born 12 Sept. 1671.

  iii. *Elizabeth,* born 15 Dec. 1673, married, as his third wife, Benjamin Gerrish Esq. of Salem, a rich merchant and Deacon of the First Church at Salem, on 24 Sept. 1696. Children: 1. John born 23 June 1698; 2. Eunice born 12 Nov. 1699, died 29 Aug. 1700; 3. Lydia born 22 June 1701.

  iv. *Eunice* born 1 Jan. 1675/6; died in or before 1706; married as his first wife, Hon. Col. Samuel Browne of Salem on 19 March 1695/6. He was a very wealthy merchant and Deputy from Salem to the Massachusetts General Court, Judge of the Court of General Sessions and that of Common Pleas in the County of Essex and a member of His Majesty's Council for the Province of Massachusetts Bay. They had an only child, Mary bapt. at Salem on 4 Jan. 1701/2, who died in infancy. The son of Col. Browne by his 2nd wife was Hon. William Browne of Salem (A.B. Harvard 1729) also Judge of the Court of General Sessions and a member of the Council. He married Mary, daughter of William Burnet Esq. Royal Governor of New York and Massachusetts Bay, and the granddaughter of the famous Gilbert Burnet, Bishop of Salisbury, who was so prominent in the time of William III. A grandson of Col. Samuel Browne by his 2nd wife was Hon. William of Salem, Judge of the Superior Court of Massachusetts and one of the Mandamus Counsellors just prior to the American Revolution Being a Royalist he went to England and was made Governor of Bermuda.

   v. *Freestone* born 25 Oct. 1677, died 14 June 1714. married on 30 March 1699/00 Major Walter Price of Salem (A.B. Harvard 1695) a prominent merchant and soldier in the French War. In 1708 he was in command of the Haverhill (Mass.) garrison when that town was attacked by the French, whom he succeeded in driving off with considerable loss. Children: 1. John born 29 March 1700/1; 2. William born 22 March 1701/2, died 31 Aug. 1702/3; Sarah born 4 Feb. 1709/10 married Joseph Bartlett ; 4. Elizabeth born 9 May 1714, married Mitchell Sewell.

vi. *Abial* born 14 Oct. 1680, living in 1718 a spinster.

7. HABAKKUK[3] (*Robert*[2]............[1]) TURNER of Salem, Mass. He also removed from Boston to Salem and was a merchant trading with Barbados. Married Mary, daughter of Lieut. George Gardner a merchant of Salem, Mass. and Hartford, Conn. on 30 April 1670.

Children:

    i. *Robert* born 25 April 1671, removed to Weathersfield, Conn., where he married and had a numerous family.

    ii. *Mary* born 25 (11) 1672, died 14 (8) 1674.

    iii. *Habakkuk.* He was a Salem merchant and died unmarried in 1754.

Mary (Gardner) Turner married 2ndly on 15 Sept. 1686 John Marston of Salem.

8. COL. JOHN[4] (*Capt. John,*[3] *Robert,*[2] ....[1]) TURNER of Salem. He is usually styled in the records "Hon. Col. John Turner Esq.". He was a very wealthy merchant, magistrate, soldier and a great man generally. He was born on 12 Sept. 1671 and died 4 March 1741/2. In 1692 he was appointed administrator on the estate of his father and was executor of the will of his step-father, Major Charles Redford. He was Constable of Salem on 14 March 1695/6. As Captain of a troop of horse he made an expedition into the wilderness above Andover, Mass. against the French Indians and is reported to have been successful, bringing back 40 scalps, which gruesome relics are said to have hung long in the attic of "The House of the Seven Gables". This was in 1703 (Felt's Annals of Salem). On 11 June 1704 he went out with Major Stephen Sewell in a shallop and the Fort Pinnace against the pirate Quelch, whom they captured off the Isles of Shoales with some of his ill gotten gold and brought him into Salem (Diary of Judge Samuel Sewell, ed. Mass. Hist. Soc.). On 28 March 1706 he sent out a vessel to retake his sloop, which had been captured by the French and taken into Port Royal. On 14 June 1707 he commanded the Essex Horse in a fight with the French and Indians near Haverhill and on 27 Aug. 1708 he fought a desperate engagement with the enemy in the wilderness, near what is now Manchester, New Hampshire, who were under the command of the famous voyageur Hertel de Rouville and inflicted considerable loss upon them. On 15 Oct. 1716 Col. Samuel Browne (his brother-in-law) and Major John Turner commanded the Essex troop of horse, which went to Lynn, Mass. and accompanied the Royal Governor, Col. Samuel Shute, to Salem. Later he became Colonel of the Essex County Regiment, thus rounding out his military career.

In civil life he was equally prominent. He was a Selectman in 1705; in 1712 he was the Deputy from Salem to the General Court and was a member of His Majesty's Council from 1721-1741. He was a Justice in 1712 and in 1714 Judge of the Massachusetts Court of Common Pleas for the County of Essex. He was a very active and successful West Indian merchant. In the latter part of his life he erected an elegant mansion on Essex Street in Salem and removed thither from "The House of the Seven Gables". He left a very large estate for those days, which was divided on 24 April 1745. His plate alone was valued at £534 (Essex Co. Probate).

Married at Salem on 22 May 1701 Mary, daughter of Robert Kitchen Esq., a prominent Salem merchant, by his first wife, Mary, daughter of Major William Boardman of Cambridge, Mass., Steward of Harvard University. She was living a widow in Salem in 1764.

Children of Col. John and Elizabeth Turner:

   i. *John* born 8 Aug. 1702, died 13 Aug. 1703.

   ii. *Elizabeth* born 14 June 1704, married Hon. Thomas Berry, Esq. of Ipswich, Mass., Judge of Probate for Essex Co. on 2 May 1728.

   iii. *Mary,* born 1 Nov. 1706, married 15 Aug. 1728 Capt. Ebenezer Bowditch, a merchant of Salem. They were the grandparents of the eminent Nathaniel Bowditch LL.D., the famous mathematician and the author of "Bowditch's Navigator", which is still in use, and of Deborah Bowditch, who married Capt. Thomas Moriarty of Salem, the ancestors of the compiler.

9. iv. *John* born 20 May 1709, died 19 Dec. 1786.

   v. *Eunice* born 17 April 1713, married 1st. Benjamin Browne Esq. of Salem on 19 June 1729 and 2ndly. Nathaniel Balston Esq. of Boston, Mass. Left issue. Her picture, painted by Smibert is still in existence.

   vi. *Robert,* bapt. 20 Nov. 1715. Mariner and merchant of Salem died in 1761.

   vii. *Habakkuk.* Merchant of Salem. Died 1753-1764.

   viii. *Bethia* bapt. 2 March 1717/8.

9. JOHN[5] (*Col. John,*[4] *Capt. John,*[3] *Robert,*[2] ——[1]) TURNER Esq. of Salem, merchant. Born at Salem 20 May 1709, died 19 Dec. 1786. He was Deputy from Salem to the General Court and Naval Officer and Collector of the Port of Salem. In the Revolution he sided with the Crown and was an addresser of General Gage on 11 June 1774, when he arrived in Salem (Stark's Loyalists of Massachusetts", p. 131), but, as he did not take an active part in that struggle, he escaped the Confiscation Act of 1778 and remained in his native town until his death. His portrait painted by Smibert is now in Boston.

Married Mary Osborne of Boston on 8 June 1738 and had a large family. One of his daughters Mary* bapt. 1 Jan. 1743/4, married 3 Feb. 1763 Daniel Sargent of Gloucester, Mass. and Boston. They were the ancestors of the distinguished Boston family of that name. It is not proposed to carry on the family further in this paper.

[FOOTNOTE] * Her portrait painted by J. Singleton Copley is now owned by a descendant in Washington, D.C.

A LETTER FROM BARBADOS 1672.

by

G. ANDREWS MORIARTY, A.M., LL.B., F.S.A.

THE RECORDS of the coastal towns and counties of New England contain many references and papers relating to Barbados in the XVII and XVIII centuries, the period when the commercial and social ties between the two places were very close.

The following letter, dated at Barbados 21 Jan. 1671/2 is preserved among the papers in the case of *Clifford vs. Turner* in the Essex County Quarterly Court Files in the office of the Clerk of the Essex County Court at Salem, Mass. This was a suit by John Clifford of Salem against Capt. Habakuk Turner of the same town, Master of the ketch "Return" of Salem, for his refusal to give Clifford a receipt for the delivery by him of four hogsheads of salt fish shipped by Clifford in the "Return" and consigned to Mr. Anthony Tolman in the Barbados. The case was heard in the June term of the Court, 1672.

The plaintiff John Clifford was a rope maker and merchant of considerable means in Salem. He came from Boston, Mass., as a young man, and was admitted an inhabitant of Salem 15 Feb. 1663/4. His house stood in the middle of Derby Street on the West side of English St. in Salem. He owned considerable real estate in the Eastern part of the town near the river and harbour and he had a large farm in the adjoining town of Lynn close to the Salem line. He filled various local offices and soon after 1680 he removed to his Lynn farm, where he died on 17 June 1698. He was a Quaker in his religious views. He left an only daughter Elizabeth, who became the wife of Capt. Jacob Allen of Salem and later of Sewee, South Carolina. They were the ancestors of many of the prominent merchant families of Salem in the XVIII century. From the letter it seems probable that John Clifford came to New England from Gloucestershire via Barbados. The list of men able to bear arms in Gloucestershire in 1608 contains numerous persons of the name in various walks of life. They probably descended, more or less remotely, from the ancient and knightly house of Clifford of Frampton, a cadet branch of the great Anglo-Norman family of Clifford, which remained in Gloucestershire when the elder line removed to the North of England, after its marriage with the Vipont heiress in the middle of the XIII century.

Capt. Habakuk Turner was a cousin of Capt. John Turner of "Three Houses", St. Philip's parish, Barbados (c. f. Journal of the Barbados Hist. Soc. Vol. X., pp 9, 13.) *

The letter now follows :

"Barbados.

31 January 1671-2

Lo : Cousin :

Mine and my wifes love to you and y'r wife and daughter hoping you are in good health as I w'th my wife and children are at ye writing hereof. I have re'cd y'r letter and re'cd by John Gardner[1] w't two hundred seventy and eight p'ds of ffish and sixty foure p'd of onions. I gave a re'ct to Jno. Gardner for thirteen pound of onions more than I have or did receive w'ch mistake I desire may be rectified I not having ye w't of ye fish and onions have not re'cd any goods yet, but by the first opportunity I shall send ye some goodes, y'r ffish came to a very bad markett here being as much and a man may buy as good Codfish as neede to be spent for a p'd of sugar a p'd. I shall by the next send ye more at large I borrowed a bagg of Jn'o Gardner to bring up the onions and not having an opportunity to carry it down as soon as I should therefore I desire y'u to make my excuses. If he be come away but I purpose to send y'r letter w'th him. I spake with Anthony Tolman about y'r fish and he doth acknowledge ye rec't thereof & saith y't he has sent y'u severall letters & y'r accompt w'ch he makes no doubt but y'u have rec'd. If you can by any convience send sum barr'lls of Pickled oysters, I shall make y'u honest returns w'ch is ye needful at present from

Yo'r Lo: ffrd & kinsman

GEORGE MAGGS

Yo'r Uncle William Shingleton is dead & Uncle ffrancis Carter & Uncle Tiss are all dead and your sister Jean is married to one Dobbs and lives Just und'r ye Shopp at ye beare he is a barber Surgeon I do expect newes every day from Glost'r no more at present".

Cannot some of our Barbadian antiquaries shed some light upon the persons mentioned in the postcript to the above letter and upon George Maggs the writer ?

On reference to the Chairman of the Department of Historical Research of the Society, the following information has been given. *Ed. Journal.*

Footnote 1. Capt. John Gardner (1624-1706) was a prominent sea Captain and merchant of Salem. He later removed to Nantucket, where he was a leading citizen and the chief magistrate.

*Pages 561 & 565, this volume.

Like his correspondent, John Clifford, the writer of the letter, George Maggs, was also a Quaker. He died in 1677 in Barbados a few days after making his Will which was proved on 25 June 1677. The Will is dated "17th. day of ye 4th month called June, 1677," when the testator described himself as being sick and weak.

He expressed the wish to be buried in some convenient place at the discretion of his executors, and bequeathed to his wife, Ann, his real and personal estate either in Barbados or in England or elsewhere, and appointed her executrix. In the event of her death, he appointed his grandson, Walter Stiles, as sole executor and gave him all his property if he should attain the age of 21. Failing that, everything should go to and equally between his grandchildren Sarah, Ann, Elizabeth, and Edward Mayo, children of Edward and and Sarah Mayo. Edward Mayo to be executor in trust to see his will performed.

His daughter Sarah Mayo was to receive "one gold diamond cut ring" and his daughter Mary Clarke, the wife of Roger Clarke "one gold ring with a red stone in lieu of one shilling"

He stipulated that his son-in-law, Edward Mayo's testimony should be received without an Oath, being well satisfied of his fidelity. (This was in reference to the Oath required of an executor for the due performance of his office : a difficulty which every Quaker had to face in view of his intolerance of an Oath of any kind. The testator intended that Edward Mayo should administer the estate without the usual formalities being complied with.)

The Will was witnessed by Philip Foussier, George Lister, Sarah V. Hope, and John Seed, three of whom afterwards testified to the due execution of the Will for probate purposes.

Note that Maggs evidently intended to cut off his daughter, Mary Clarke, with a shilling, (or its equivalent) presumably because she had married one not of the Quaker faith. And yet it appears from the marriage records, that his daughter Sarah, had been married in the parish church of Christ Church on 2 September 1666 to Edward Mayo (who is named in error as Edward Mays). It is probable that Edward Mayo and family afterwards seceded, and embraced Quaker principles before the Will of Geore Maggs was made.

As to the other persons named in the postscript to the letter; there are no burial entries in the church records concerning either William Singleton, Francis Carter, or "Uncle Tiss", neither do we find the record of the marriage of Jean Clifford and "one Dobbs"; which is not surprising, as they all probably belonged to the Society of Friends (Quakers) whose congregation in Barbados at that time was numerous.

Walcott of Barbados.*

John Alexander Walcott, son of Benjamin Walcott and Dorothy his wife, formerly Dorothy Carrington Williams, spinster, was born January 24th, 1766, and was married December 14th, 1792, to Caroline daughter of John Walcott and Mary Anne his wife, formerly Mary Anne Henry, which said Caroline was born Feb. 1766, and died October 4th, 1805. They had these five children : Mary Jane, born Oct. 3rd, 1793, and married to Mr Richard Linton. John Alexander, born 19th June 1796, died Jan. 19th, 1806. Caroline Frances, (sic) April 18th, 1799. Benjamin Edward, born Dec. 6th, 1801, died October 14th, 1816, and Dorothy Slicombe, born May 28th, 1804, died Sept. 25th, 1805. He, John Alexander Walcott the elder, departed this life March 1818.

William Walrond the younger and Caroline Frances Walcott were married September 17th, 1818, by the Rev. Francis King, officiating for Mr Garnett, Rector of St Michael's.

Caroline Frances, daughter of the above, was born 27th August 1819 and was baptized 17th September following by the Rev. R. F. King.

Jane Anne the second child was born 27th April 1822.

William Walrond died by a very rapid decline November 13th, 1832, and was buried at The Cathedral.

Caroline Frances, eldest daughter of the aforesaid William Walrond and Caroline Frances, was married to Joseph Straughan, 4th son of Dr James Sarsfield Bascom, March 31st, 1840. Died July 19th, 1851.

Joseph William, first son of the above Joseph Straughan and Caroline Frances, born June 6th, 1841, baptized June 30th and died August 1st same year.

Joseph Humpleby, second son of the above, born Nov. 10th, 1842, was baptized Dec. 14th, 1842, and was married in December 1869 to Angelique Landry of Demerara. He died in George Town, Demerara, May 1875.

Aubrey Carleton Joseph, 1st son of the above, born April 15th, 1871. Remond James, 2nd son, born Sept. 15th, 1872, died the same year. Florence Beatrice, born Nov. 5th, 1873.

James Alexander, 3rd son of the above Joseph Straughan and Caroline Frances, born August 8th, 1844, baptized Sept. 25th, 1844, was married in Demerara July 14th, 1881, to Louise Catherine Younger, of Viewfield House, Edinburgh.

Isabella Munro, only child of the above, was born in Demerara July 5th, 1882. The above James Alexander died September 15th, 1883.

---

* 1818, Ap. 26. At Bristol, Mrs. Eliz. Walcott, widow of the late Robert J. W. esq. of B. ("G.M.," 571.)

THE WALRONDS, CO-HEIRS OF ANCIENT BARONY.

By H. G. HUTCHINSON.

THE WALRONDS were an old English county family. The original ancestor was Robert of Bradfelle in Devonshire. His grandson Richard was also living at Bradfelle in 1154. It was about this period that surnames were coming into use, and early in the reign of Henry III his grandson Richard, the son of another Richard de Bradfelle, assumed for the first time the surname of Walrond by which his descendants in the male line, and his unmarried descendants in the female line, have been known ever since.

This Richard Walrond was the ancestor of Colonel Humphrey Walrond who eventually settled in Barbados.

Colonel Walrond had rendered loyal aid to Charles I in the struggle between King and Parliament, and according to Captain Nicholas Foster, a contemporary writer, had come to Barbados "Towards the latter end of the Warrs when the Sun of the Cavaliers expected conquest."

Colonel Walrond became the leader of the Royalist Party in Barbados, and for the part he took in that struggle the reader is referred to the Journal of the Barbados Museum and Historical Society for August 1943.

When the Parliamentary party gained the upper hand the leaders of the Royalist party were banished, and among these was Colonel Walrond, their leader. He resorted to Spain where he must have displayed the same gallantry as he did in England and Barbados, for the King of Spain, Philip IV, conferred on him the titles of Marquis of Vallado, Conde de Valderonda, Conde de Parama and a Grandee of Spain of the First Class "for service rendered to the Spanish marine."

At the restoration of the monarchy Colonel Walrond returned to Barbados, and received a mandamus from the King, appointing him President of the Council, of which he had been a member in pre-Cromwellian times.

From 1660 to 1663 he was Deputy-Governor of the Island. In addition to the plantations which he owned he purchased the Guinea plantation in St. John during this period. The parish church of S. Michael, now the Cathedral, which was destroyed in 1780 by hurricane, was being built during this period.

Beside his Spanish honours Colonel Walrond was one of the co-heirs of the ancient Barony of Welles. As it is the object of this article to trace the co-heirs of this barony in Barbados it may be just as well to give an account of how this honour came to be in the Walrond family, and to say something of the said title.

On February 6, 1299, King Edward I made Adam de Welles a baron. His representative descendant, Lionel the 6th Lord Welles, was slain at the Battle of Towton fighting on the side of the Lancastrians. When a baron leaves no sons and more than one daughter, the title descends to each daughter, but as only one is allowed to assume the title, each sister is a co-heiress of the barony, and her representative descendant is the co-heir, co-heiress or co-heiresses in case a co-heir should leave more than one daughter, but no sons.

Lionel, the 6th Baron de Welles, left a son who succeeded him, but who died without issue; and in consequence of which his sisters became co-heiresses in the barony.

Among these sisters was Eleanor de Welles who married Sir Thomas Hoo, Baron of Hoo and Hastings. Lady Hoo and Hastings had a daughter and co-heiress Elizabeth, who married Sir John Devenish, whose eventual descendant and representative Elizabeth married Henry Walrond, a member of the Inner Temple, London, and the grand-father of the Colonel Humphrey Walrond, his representative, who emigrated to the Island of Barbados.

Colonel Humphrey Walrond married Elizabeth, the daughter of Sir Nathaniel Napier of More Critchel, by whom he had among other sons his "son and heir," as described in a deed of 1656, Captain George Walrond.

It may assist the reader to state that Colonel Walrond had four representatives in succession by the name of George, then a Benjamin, and then another George.

Colonel Humphrey Walrond's eldest son, George[1] Walrond had fought for Charles I as a Captain of the Horse Guards, and had lost an arm in so doing. He had accompanied his father to Barbados. The Census Papers of 1679 show that "Captain George Walrond" was the only Walrond who had an estate in S. Philip's parish and it was there that the last years of his life were spent. He died in 1688 and apparently had lost his wife Frances, the daughter of William Coryton, M.P. for West Newton, as there is no mention of her in his will.

His will shows that he had three married daughters and two sons who were minors, viz:

    I George[2] Walrond
   II Theodore[1]. He married Elizabeth, sister of Captain
       Smith, and had issue:—
         I Mary
        II Theodore
       III George

Theodore[1] Walrond died in 1706, and was apparently survived by his elder brother as there is a George Walrond who is a witness of his will. Captain Walrond's elder son, George[2] Walrond, continued to live in St. Philip's parish on the estate which his father had left him. From his son's will in 1743 we gather that he (i.e. George[2] Walrond) sold some of the land of the estate, as his son desired that what his father had told should be bought back. From the records of his children's baptisms in S. Philip's parish we gather that George[2] Walrond's wife's name was Mary, but her surname has not been traced.

George[2] Walrond died intestate before the Census of 1715, as his wife Mary Walrond is described as a widow of S. Philip's parish in that census.

By Mary, his wife, George[2] Walrond left one son and three daughters, viz:

I   George[3] Walrond

II   Mary, born Oct. 27th, 1695, baptised Oct. 28th, 1695

III Elizabeth, born Sept. 15th, 1698, baptised Sept. 20th, 1698. She died in 1752, and mentions in her will her three nephews George[4] Walrond Snr. and Theodore[2] and George[5] Walrond Jnr. (born 1751), and her niece Martha Sandford.

IV Martha, born Oct. 26, 1699, baptised Oct. 30, 1699.

The baptisms of the sisters were all recorded together at St. Philip in 1701.

As George[3] Walrond succeeded his father as a co-heir of the Barony of Welles it might be advisable to give his baptismal record at S. Philip's church, which is as follows:—

1696. Oct. 14 George son of George and Mary Walrond Oct. 3." He continued to live on the family estate in St. Philip which his grand-father Captain Walrond had left to his son George[2] Walrond "to him and his heirs for ever."

On July 9th, 1724, he married Dorothy, the daughter of John and Dorothy Puckering, at S. Philip's church, and the baptism of their eldest son George[4] Walrond is recorded at the said church on March 1st, 1726.

By his wife, Dorothy, he had issue five daughters and the following three sons:—

I   George[4] Walrond

II   Thomas Walrond

III Theodore[2] Walrond. Theodore[2] entered into a business co-partnership with his brother George[4] in Broad St., Bridgetown, as he himself states in his will of 1769. He marries, but leaves no issue. In his will he leaves his gold-headed cane to his brother George[4] Walrond's son, Benjamin Charnock Walrond.

George[3] Walrond left money to his five daughters, and his sons Thomas and Theodore[2]. To his son George[4] Walrond he leaves his 'Whole Estate' after the death of his wife, Dorothy Walrond.

George[4] Walrond became a merchant in Broad Street, Bridgetown, as already stated, in co-partnership with his brother Theodore[2] Walrond, and left S. Philip's parish for St. Michael's parish in which Bridgetown, the capital of Barbados, is situated.

George[4] Walrond was married to Mary Garratt at S Michael's Church on February 22nd, 1750. The following year their son George[5] Walrond was born—the "George Walrond, Jnr." of his Great-Aunt Elizabeth's will in 1752.

George[4] Walrond was for several years a member of the S. Michael's Vestry. It was during his time as a member that the terrible hurricane of 1780 which did so much damage to buildings, and destroyed most of the parish churches, and among them that of S. Michael took place. The writer has some recollection of having been shown by Mr. E. Fitz-patrick, an antiquarian, some record in which George[4] Walrond served on the committee for the rebuilding of these churches and among them S. Michael's church, which subsequently became the Cathedral of the Diocese.

George[4] Walrond also served on the committee for the rebuilding of Harrison's Free School of which he was the Treasurer.

Before S. Michael's Church was completed in 1789, "Mary the wife of George Walrond" died in 1788, and was buried at that Church.

George[4] Walrond survived his wife many years, and died at a good age in 1806. He too was buried at S. Michael's Church on June 8th, 1806, and by a co-incidence his grandson, another George[6] Walrond was also buried at the said church (then the Cathedral) on June 8th, 1845. George and Mary Walrond ("née Garratt") had a deed drawn up in 1782, in which the names of two daughters are mentioned and their son's name Benjamin Charnock Walrond, but this deed was not recorded until after George[4] Walrond's death in 1806. By then he had only one surviving child, Benjamin, and it is most probable that he had it done.

George[4] and Mary Walrond had three sons, viz.,

I   George[5] Walrond, baptised at S. James on June 23rd, 1751. The marriage is recorded of George Walrond Jnr., to Ann King on July 26, 1774 at S. Michael's church. On January 25th, 1785, the burial is recorded Husband of Ann Walrond. On Oct. 6th, 1790 the burial is recorded of Ann Walrond, Widow at S. Michael's church. Both husband and wife die intestate, and there are no baptismal records of any children, nor any other kind of record of any.

II Benjamin[1] Charnock Walrond, born August 27th, 1756, and baptised on October 28th, 1756 at S. Michael's Church.

III Theodore Smith Walrond, born July 7, 1757, baptised at S. Michael's Church on August 2nd, 1757. On Oct. 10th, 1757 there is recorded at S. Michael's church the burial of "Theodore Smith Walrond a child."

As his elder brother died without issue before his parents, Benjamin[1] Walrond succeeded his father as co-heir of the ancient Barony of Welles. He was one of the masters of Chancery for the Island of Barbados.

He married Judith Elizabeth, the daughter of Nicholas Howell. It is a matter of interest that through the Rous family on her mother's side, she was descended from Lt. Thomas Rous, the Island Parliamentarian or Roundhead, who is mentioned in Nicholas Foster's book "The Horrid Rebellion in Barbados 1650." Through the Rous family she is also descended from another famous Island Roundhead, viz. Colonel Revnold Alleyne, who led the Island Parliamentary forces against the Royalist party in 1652. Thus the descendants of Benjamin and Judith Walrond are descended from the leaders of the Cavaliers and Roundheads in **Barbados.**

Benjamin[1] Walrond did not long survive his father as he died in September, 1810. His wife followed him in 1813. They both were buried at S. Michael's Church.

Benjamin and Judith Walrond were the parents of a numerous family, which they both mention in the folowing order in their wills :—

 I   George[6] Walrond.
 II   Agnes Walrond.
 III   Benjamin[2] Walrond, a colonel of the militia. He was the grand-father of Mrs. A. D. Gill.
 IV   Mary Judith Jackson, "wife of Wm. Jackson, Esq., formerly Mary Judith Walrond". She was the mother of the Rt. Rev. Wm. Walrond Jackson, Bishop of Antigua 1860—96. It may be of interest to record that when Judith Walrond died in 1813 she left her grandson, the future bishop, a slave.

  After her husband's death Mary Judith Jackson married Abel Clinkett, Esq., the Editor-Proprietor of *The Barbadian* Newspaper, whose portrait adorns the walls of the Barbados Museum.
 V   Renn Hampden Walrond.
 VI   Nicholas Humphrey Walrond.
 VII   Rebecca Rous Walrond.
 VIII   Ann Walrond.

The eldest son, George[6] Walrond, who succeeded his father to the co-heirship of the Barony of Welles, was a Major of the Militia. He commanded the Four Companies of the Royal Miltia which lined the street from Trafalgar Square to S. Michael's Cathedral on January 29th, 1825, for the enthronement of Bishop Coleridge, the first Bishop of Barbados.

George[6] Walrond was twice married. In 1810 he married Maria Shepheard. They had two children—a daughter called Maria who died young, and a son, George[7] Walrond who died without issue in May 1845. He mentions his father George[6] Walrond in his will, as well as his father's second wife Catherine Elizabeth Walrond. He used to live at S. Helen's in S. George.

George[6] Walrond was married for the second time to Catherine Elizabeth Skinner, of S. Peter, on June 8th, 1824. They used to live at Fauxbourg, Black Rock, until their deaths. His married daughters continued to reside there, and some of their children were married from there. By his second marriage George[6] Walrond had an only son Benjamin[3] Walrond who was drowned while quite a young man. He was deeply religious, and one Sunday insisted on going to Church although it was raining heavily. He was swept out by the beach by Joes River on his horse. His body was never recovered, but his hat and Prayer Book were picked up at Brandon's, not far from Fontabelle. George[6] Walrond was buried at S. Michael's Cathedral on June 8th, 1845, and his second wife was also buried there nine years later on July 14th, 1854.

George[6] Walrond was succeeded by his two surviving daughters as co-heiresses of the ancient barony of Welles. They were the last of the Walronds to have this ancient honour, for they both married brothers by the surname of Inniss (changed to original name of Innes by one of the sons), and so the co-heirship of the barony of Welles passed into the Inniss or Innes family. The two surviving daughters of George[6] and Catherine Walrond of Fauxbourg,, Black Rock, were :—

I   Maria Shepheard Walrond.

II Thomasin Ann Walrond m Joseph William Inniss. Thomasin Ann, the younger daughter, was born on October 10th, 1834. She lived at first at Fauxbourg, her father's residence and afterwards at The Ark in Fontabelle. She died on June 18th, 1899—seven centuries after the creation of the Barony of Welles. She was buried in the Inniss burial spot at S. Michael's Cathedral where her husband was also buried in 1903.

The surviving issue of Joseph and Thomasin Inniss were four sons and three daughters, viz.:—

I   Walter Inniss (d August 25, 1920) m. Ella Dunscombe, and had along with three daughters, an only son, Howell Inniss b 1892, m 1920 Aveline Mayers, and has issue. Both father and son were co-heirs of the barony.

II   Harold Inniss m Amy Lawrence, and has issue.

III Hubert Inniss m Ida Seifert—no issue.

IV   Archibald de Lisle Inniss m Lelia Springer, has issue.

V   Agnes Inniss m Herbert Jackman, and has issue.

VI   Maggie Inniss m Fred Skinner, and has issue.

VII Isabel Inniss.

The elder daughter of George[6] Walrond and his heiress, Maria Shepheard Walrond, was born on April 10th, 1825. She continued to live at Fauxbourg after her father's death in 1845, and spent her married life there. Her marriage to Thomas Dixon Reid Inniss in 1855 was a remarkably happy one. They had been lovers from childhood. He was one of the leading masons of the Scotia Lodge, being a master. After her husband's death in 1882 she continued to live at Fauxbough until the marriage of her only surviving daughter. Priscilla to the Rev. W. G. Hutchinson in 1892 when she went to live with them at Boscobel Vicarage until her death on May 29th, 1898.

In accordance with the .wish of her husband she was buried in his grave at S. Michael's Cathedral; the committal being performed by her son-in-law at the burial place of the Inniss family, and not far from the spot where his own body was laid to rest in January, 1943.

For three generations all her fore-parents had been buried at this church.

The surviving children of Thomas and Maria Inniss were:—

1.   Thomas Walrond Inniss (changed name to Innes).

2. Wm. Hothersall Inniss m Ethel Ashby, and left issue
3. Priscilla Inniss m Rev. Wm. Gordon Hutchinson, of the Clan Donald, and has issue
4. Ernest Allder Inniss b Ida Cummins, and has issue.

The eldest son, who succeeded his mother to the co-heirship of the Barony of Welles, was the first of the Inniss family to have the honour.

He went to Mauritius where he managed the large estate of Britannia. A pleasant reminiscence of his stay there was the visit of H.R.H. the Duke of York. His company entertained the Duke, and he had to undertake the entertainment. The Duke was one of the crack shots of England, and a shooting match was arranged, and he had the pleasure of witnessing the Duke's skill.

He took an interest in cricket, and once played in a friendly match captained by the famous W. G. Grace. He finally retired to live in Surrey, England, and was a non-playing member of the County Cricket Club. He re-visited the West Indies on a few occasions, and died at his English home in Caterham, Surrey, on January 20th, 1943.

By his marriage to Laura Browne of England he left two sons, viz.:—

1. Laurence Walrond Innes, F.R.C.S.
2. Major Leslie Walrond Innes. He served in the Great War 1914-18, finally as a Major. He won the Croix-de-Guerre. He was an engineer, and had completed a magnificent bridge at Hong Kong just before the present war, only to have the disappointment of seeing it wrecked by the Japanese. He served as a Major in the fight against the Japanese, and both his wife and himself are prisoners-of-war in the hands of the Japanese. Their only son John is in the R.A.F.

The elder son, Laurence Walrond Innes, F.R.C.S., who succeeded his father, is a surgeon in Plymouth, and has rendered service to his country in both the Great Wars. In the Great War of 1914-18 he served as a Captain.

He is the elder representative of Colonel Humphrey Walrond.

He married Dorothy Pidgeon of England, and had by her three children, viz.:—

1. Anthony.
2. Hazel.
3. Heather.

Note by Editor. The claims, if any, of the descendants of the Barbados branch of the family to the barony as outlined by Mr. Hutchinson have never been put forward, and the barony still remains in abeyance. On the other hand, it is on record that in the year 1832, Bethell Walrond, a collateral descendant with Humphrey Walrond as common ancestor, petitioned the King to terminate the abeyance in his behalf. The Petition was referred to the Attorney General of England who reported in favour of Bethell Walrond's claim. The line of descent of the barony is given in Burke, and has hitherto been accepted as correct. Mr. Hutchinson disagrees.

𝔚𝔞𝔩𝔯𝔬𝔫𝔡 of 𝔅𝔞𝔯𝔟𝔞𝔡𝔬𝔰.*

Charles Walrond married Elizabeth Walrond, spinster. Had issue :—
Second child William Walrond, born Aug. 14, 1766, married Dec. 22, 1791, to
Sarah Elizabeth Lake, daughter of Abraham Mullyneux and Angel his wife,
formerly Angel Washington, widow (previously Angel Hughes, spinster).
Sar. Eliz. Lake Mullyneux died Nov. 1811.
Abraham Mullyneux and Angel Mullyneux had issue :—
    Sarah Elizabeth, born Oct. 8, 1792.
    Charles Humphrey, born June 2, 1794.
    William, born Feb. 23, 1796.
    Ann Hughes, born Oct. 1798.
    Lake (daughter), born 1800.
    John Walcott, born March 20, 1802.
    Mary, born Feb. 8, 1806.
                                                            **

Benjamin Walrond married Dorothy Skinner July 28, 1808. Had issue :—
    Hannah Hall, born Nov. 18, 1809 ; married John Munro† 1838.
    Dorothy Rollock, born June 2, 1811 ; died Nov. 30, 1814.

    Benjamin Walrond, born March 16, 1813 ; married 11th Dec. 1838 Ann
        Walcott.
    Mary Tucker Walrond, born 30th April 1814 ; married to James Punch
        17th July 1834.
    Judith Elizabeth, born 5th July 1815 ; married to P. Milne 21st July 1836.
        Died 1st September 1836.
    Agnes, born 3rd December 1816. Died 25th March 1832.
    John Ince, born 19th April 1818. Died 27th August 1820.
    Sarah Rollock, born 14th November 1819. Died 5th Oct. 1831
    George, born 19th March 1821.
    Conrad Adams Howell, born 19th January 1823.
    Margaret Ann, born 29th November 1824.
    Nicholas Humphrey, born 6th August 1826.
    Dorothy, born 6th September 1828.
    Adelaide Louisa, born 1st Aug. 1830.
    Agnes Sarah, born 26 August 1832.

Benjamin Walrond married Ann Walcott.
    Mary Jane, born 1838 ; married John Inniss Howell.
    Elizabeth Ann, born in 1839.
    Hannah Ince married Conrad Adams Howell.
    Mary Tucker married Thornhill Howell.
    Benjamin Walrond married . . . . Aitkin.
    Helen Louise married Joseph Howell.
    James Walcott.
    Clara Margaret Winifred married John Manning.
    Gerald Nicholas married . . . . Walcott.

---

* From family records. Communicated by Mr. Bascom of Barbados.
† 1853, Nov. 17. At Greenwich, a. 17, Margaret-Walrond, yst. dau. of the l. John Munro,
B. ("G.M." 1854, p. 106.)

** Benj. Walrond, Provost Marshal General, died at Barbados 16 July 1844,
aged 57. The writer of the obituary notice in the "Gent. Mag." describes him
as descended from Col. Humphrey Walrond, the Royalist Governor in 1660.
He was married as B. Walrond, Junr., on Jan. 28, July being an error in copying.

Walter of Barbados and South Carolina.

John Walter, Esqr, of Woking, co. Surry. Will dated 30 Dec. 1734. I appoint my eldest son Abell W. sole Ex'or, and his Mother my wife G. to my young ch^n, and to my s^d son Abell I devise all my manors and lands in G^t Britain and I. of B'oes, and also my pers. estate in T., to sell to pay £400 a year to my wife for her life, but I give her and her heirs for ever my mansion house at Hoebridge and all else purchased by me of Jas. Feild, Esq., dec^d, and of R^d Bird and Cath. his wife and all plate and furniture, coach and pair of best horses, and 100 gns. To my s. Henry W. the moiety of my lands purchased in Grenvill Co. in S. Carolina from Capt. Douglas with 20 negroes now on the same, also 1000 acres which I hold by grant from the Crown, being part of the Baroney lying at Days Creek in the said co. To my s. Wm W. the other moiety of said lands, 20 negroes, 1000 a. part of s^d baroney, and £1250. To my sons Jas. W., Alleyne W., and Meynell W. each 2000 a. in s^d co., part of the Barony granted me by the Crown, and to each £2000. To my 2 daus. Lucy and Mary £2000 each at 18. My Ex'or to manage 1000 acres part of my said Baroney, with 20 negroes, for my s. John W. for his life. To my s. Richd W., who has already rec^d a fine fortune from me, 1000 a., part of said Baroney, and £500. To my grandson John W., the s. of Abell W., Esqr, all my lands in Goose Creek, South Car., called Red Bank, and all the remainder of my Baroney, being 2000 acres. To my dau. Eliz. Dottin £500. My dau. Lucy W. £500 more at 21. If my s. Henry W. do not settle in S. C. I revoke the gift of land and give £1500 Barb. c. in lieu thereof, to be p^d by Mr Wm Walker, and the moiety of Douglas' lands I give to my s. W^m in lieu of the 1000 a. and the 2000 a. taken from my s. Henry and W^m. I give to my yr. sons Jas., Alleyne and Meynell equally. Whereas I may have 100 negroes in Car. I w^d have them valued and put on the land of Jas., Alleyne and Meynell, and the value deducted from their legacies. To my grandson John W. £2000 to stock his lands. Witnessed by Tho. Bunde Alleyne, Benj. Maynard.

Codicil, dated 18 March 1735. To my s. Henry W., if he shall settle in S. C., £1250. Sons Jas., Alleyne and Meynell £40 a year till 18. All residue to my s. Abel W. Proved 5 June 1736 by Abel W., Esqr, the s. and sole Ex'or. (142, Derby.)

Edward Baron of Abergavenny. On 27 Oct. 1724 commission to Gideon Harvey, Esq., the Guardian of Lady Cath., dowager Baroness of Abergavenny, a minor, the widow and relict.

Abel Walter of Baddesley, co. S'ton, Esq. Will dated 13 Aug. 1767. Weak in body. Whereas I have by deed poll dated 12 of this present month of Aug. executed a power for raising portions for my younger sons and daus. I confirm it, and my wife Jane being entitled to a joynture of £800 a year, I give all my real and personal estate to my s. John W. of Farley Hill, co. Berks, Esq., in T. to sell and to pay to my wife £500, and as to certain plate and furniture for my wife, and to sell the remainder and divide proceeds into 6 parts for my dau. Ann 2-6th, my dau. Charlotte 1-6th, my s. Neville 1-6th, my s. George 1-6th. My s. John sole Ex'or. (Signed with a cross.) Proved 24 Oct. 1767 by John W., Esq., the son. (397, Legard.)

Jane Walter of Badsley in the p. of Bolder in Hampshire. Will dated 20 Sept. 1769. My dear children John W. and Anne W. to be trustees, and all real and personal estate. £20 for funeral. To my s. John all my family pictures.

ARMS.—*Or, guttée-de-sang, two swords in saltire Gules, over all a lion rampant Sable.*

Richard Walter of Barbados, merchant and planter 1678 ;⊤⊤
Donor of the font in 1684 in St. James's ; M. of C. 1698 ;
bur. at St. James' 17 Aug. 1700.

John Walter of Barbados, then of Woking, co. Surrey, M.P.⊤Lucy, dau. of the
Surrey 1719 and 1722; bur. at Woking 5 May 1736. Will │ Hon. Abell Alleyne
dated 30 Dec. 1734; proved 5 June 1736 (142, Derby). │ of Barbados; died
Owned a barony of 12,000 acres in S. Carolina. │ 1738.

Abel Wal-⊤Hon. Jane	Henry	William Wal-⊤	James⊤Eliz. Hillman
ter, 1st son │ Nevill, dau.	Walter,	ter of Wampee │	Walter, │ of Salisbury,
and heir, of │ and even-	sold his	plantation of │	Capt., │ co. Wilts,
Badsley in │ tual heir of	lands at	1000 a. in Ash- │	under │ mar. at Wok-
Boldre, co. │ Geo., 11th	Woking	ley Barony, S. │	18 in │ ing 28 Oct.
Southamp- │ Baron	in 1761.	Carolina. │	1734. │ 1749 by lic.
ton ; sold │ Aberga-			
his manors │ venny, who			
in Surrey ; │ died 1720-1.			
bur. in Bath │ She died 19	John⊤Jane, dau.	Elizabeth Walter, │ Capt.	
Abbey 15 │ Mar. 1786.	Alleyne │ of Dr.	mar. in England │ John	
Oct. 1767. │ Will dated	Walter, │ David	Wm. Haggatt of │ Abel	
Will dated │ 20 Sep.	Lieut. in │ Oliphant	Haggatt Hall of │ Walter,	
13 Aug., │ 1769 ;	Col. Moul- │ of S. Caro-	1300 a. in Ashley │ cousin of	
and proved │ proved 2	trie's regt.; │ lina ; mar.	Barony, S. Caro- │ John,	
24 Oct. │ May 1786	succeeded │ at Charles	lina. He was born │ 1806.	
1767 (397, │ (314, Nor-	to Wam- │ Town	1743, and died │	
Legard). │ folk). W.I.	pee plan- │ *circa* Feb.	1773. (*Ante*, IV., │	
│ Bookplates,	tation. │ 1774.	168.) │	
│ No. 744.			

John Walter, 1st⊤Newton *	Rev. Neville	George	Charlotte Walter, mar.
son and heir, of │ Walker,	Walter, born	Walter.	5 May 1768 at St.
Farley Hill, co. │ mar.	1737; of Christ	—	George's, Hanover
Berks, 1767, later │ at St.	Church, Ox-	Ann	Square, Ascanius Wm.
of S. Badsley in │ George's,	ford ; matric.	Walter.	Senior of Bray, co.
Boldre ; owner of │ Hanover	24 May 1753,		Berks, where he died
Mount Wilson and │ Square,	aged 16 ;		24 Oct. 1789. M.I.
Apeshill, Barba- │ 17 Nov.	B.C.L. 1784 ;		Will (559, Macham).
dos. Will dated │ 1757.	R. of Bergh		She was sole heir of
19 July 1806; │	Apton, co.		her brother John. Her
proved 4 May 1811 │	Norfolk ; died		will (554, Crickitt).
(263, Crickitt). │	Dec. 1802.		(*Ante*, IV., 281.)

The money I owe them. When the legacy of £500 left me by Mr Shirk is rec^d, I give my children Neville W. and Charlotte Senior £50 each. All residue to my dau. Ann W. Witnessed 19 June 1770. Proved 2 May 1786 by John W. the son and Ann W., spr., the dau. (314, Norfolk.)

* Newton Walker was only child & heir of Alex. Walker of Barbados, Esq., and died 1772. Wm. Walker, attorney-gen., was of Mount Wilton plantation in 1722.

John Walter of South Badsley in the p. of Boldre, co. S'ton, Esq. Will dated 19 July 1806. To M[rs] Helen Anstey wife of John Anstey, Esq., and dau. of the late Ascanius Wm. Senior, Esq., my gold watch. My cousin Capt. John Abel Walter £50. To Tho. Berkley of Lymington, co. S'ton, Esq., and Chas. Harbin of Ringwood, gent., my plantations in the I. of B'oes called *Mount Wilson* and *Apeshill*, with the negroes, and my dwelling house in Albemarle Street, St. George's, Hanover Square, now in the occupation of Wm. Erle on Trust to sell. I give them also my freehold and leasehold messuages in S. Badsley and Sharpurcks to sell to pay all interest to M[rs] Charlotte Senior of Bath, widow of Ascanius Wm. Senior, Esq., for her life, and at her death to pay the interest to Jane Long wife of the Rev. Rob. Churchman Long of Denston Hall, co. Norfolk,

A

Sarah, dau.=Rev.Alleyne Wal-=Bridget		John	Lucy	Elizabeth Wal-
and coheir of	ter, born 1724;	Butler,	Walter.	Wal-	ter, mar. Abel

Sarah, dau.⹀Rev.Alleyne Wal-⹀Bridget	John	Lucy	Elizabeth Wal-
and coheir of | ter, born 1724; | Butler,	Walter.	Wal-	ter, mar. Abel
Rich. Bird of | of Christ Church, | mar. at	—	ter.	Dottin of Eng-
Woking; | Oxford, matric. | Sunning-	Meynell	—	lish, co. Ox-
widow of | 24 Oct. 1740, | hill, co.	Walter.	Mary	ford, and of
Rich. Winch | aged 16; B.C.L. | Berks,	—	Wal-	Barbados. His
of Bray, co. | 1748; D.C.L. | 24 Oct.	Richard	ter.	will was dated
Berks, whom | 1752; R. of Crow- | 1759.	Walter,		19 Nov. 1759;
she mar. 15 | combe, co. Som.; | 2nd	bapt.		proved 3 Jan.
Feb. 1742; | died April 1806, | wife.	1 Sept.		1769
mar. lic. dated | aged 82. |	1698 at		(9, Lynch).
7 Aug. 1754. | |	St. James,		Their only son
1st wife. | |	Barbados.		Abel was born
| |			1737.

and at her death to divide the principal among her children. Trustees to be Ex'ors. Witnessed by Sarah Burrard of Lymington, etc. Proved 4 May 1811 by both Ex'ors. (263, Crickitt.)

1643, July 8. Tho. Walter, gent., sells 20 acres. (B'os Records, vol. i., p. 228.)

1678. The "Constant Warwick" returning to B'os as she came near the Island took an Interloper, commanded by one Capt. Golding, and bound to this I. with Negroes. The Ship belonged to Mr. Richard Walter, a Merchant there, and M[r] John Bowden, a Merchant in L. (Col. Cal., 36.)

1680. S[t] James. Richard Waltors. 3 servants, 206 acres, 140 negroes. (Hotten, 506.)

1687-8. Mr. Rich[d] Walter, a considerable planter. (Col. Cal., 43.)

1697, Oct. 28. Mandates were given by the King in 1695 for the appointment of Rich[d] Walter (and others) to the Council of B'os, tho' owing to the miscarriage of the mandates by sea these gentlemen have never been admitted. (*Ibid.*, p. 2.)

1698. Rich[d] Walter, Esq., then a M. of C. (*Ibid.*, p. 60.)

1699, Jan. 25. Capt. John Walter appointed assistant to Judge Hooker. (*Ibid.*, p. 31.)

1720. John Walter, M.P. for Surrey, and M[r] Alleyne his brother in law, men of great interest in B'os, were heard by the Lords Justices in the complaints against Gov. Rob. Lowther. (Oldmixon, ii., 69.)

1736, May 12. John Walters, Woking, M.P. for Surrey. ("G.M.," 292.)

1745, April 14. John Walter, Esq., at Worcester Park, Surrey. (*Ibid.*, 220.)

1758. Hugh Hamersley by John Walter and Newton Walter his wife. (Close Roll.)

1786, March 19. In Hampshire, the hon. Mrs. Walter, dau., and at length sole heiress, of Geo. Nevill, Lord Abergavenny, first baron of England, wife of Abel W., esq. ("G.M.," 270.)

1802. Lately (Dec.). Rev. Neville Walter, rector of Bergh-Apton, and the moiety of Holveston, Norfolk, in the gift of Lord Abergavenny. He was of Christ Church, Oxford; B.C.L., 1784. (*Ibid.*, 1226.)

1806, April. At Crowcombe, co. Somerset, of which he was rector, in his 83rd year, the Rev. Alleyne Walter, LL.D. (*Ibid.*, 388.)

Duncan Grant, Lieut. R.N., wrote 21 Oct. 1913 from Australia that his grandmother was a Miss Mary Eliz. Walter of the Barbadian family.

ST. GEORGE'S, HANOVER SQUARE.

1768 May 5   Ascanius William Senior of Tewin Place, Herts, Esqr, W., and Charlotte Walter of this p., S. Married by Nevill Walter, Clerk, L.A.C. Witnessed by John Walter and Nassau Senior.

1757 Nov. 17   John Walter of this p., Esq., B., and Newton Walker of St Mary le Bowe. Lic.

BATH ABBEY, CO. SOMERSETSHIRE.

1767 Oct. 15   Abel Walter, Esq., buried.

ST. JAMES', HOLE TOWN, BARBADOS.

1679 July 4   Alice ye Wife of Thomas Walter; buried.
1698 Sep. 1   Richard the S. of Cap^{tn} John and Lucy W.; bap.
1700 Aug. 17   The Honb^{le} Richard W., Esqr; buried.

SUNNINGHILL, CO. BERKS.

The Reverend Alleyne Walter, D.L., of Woking in the county of Surrey, Clerk, and Mrs Bridget Butler of this parish were married by Licence, Oct. 24th, by me J. Thistlethwaite. 1759.

MARRIAGE LICENCES OF COMMISSARY COURT OF SURREY.

1740 Oct. 28   James Walter of Wokeing, captain, and Eliz. Hillman of Salisbury, co. Wilts, at Woking. Rev. Alleyne Walter of Chobham, clerk. (Vol. ii., 268.)

1754 Aug. 7   Alleyne Walter of Chobham, abode several years, LL.D., clerk, bach., 29, and Sarah Wynch of Woking, abode several years, wid., 29; at Woking. (*Ibid.*, p. 322.)

Chobham.—The Duke of Cleveland sold the manor to John Walter, Esq. In 1748 this gentleman's son Abel Walter obtained an Act of Parliament enabling the Crown to sell him the Freehold of this, with Bisley and Woking (see Vol. 1., p. 126), which was done accordingly. Of this family it was purchased, in 1752, by Lord Onslow's Trustees. (iii., 193.)

Bisley.—The Duchess of Cleveland died 9 Oct. 1709. In 1715 her interest was sold to John Walter, Esq. Mr. Walter died 12 May 1736, and was succeeded by his son Abel, who in 1748 obtained an Act of Parliament enabling the Crown to grant him the Freehold, which was done, and in 1752 he sold it to Lord Onslow's Trustees. (*Ibid.*, 189.)

The Manor of Fosters *alias* Windlesham.—In 1717 it became the property of John Walter, Esq. About 1744 it was bought of him by the Trustees of Lord Onslow. (*Ibid.*, 82.)

The Manor of Bagshot.—It came into the hands of John Walter, Esq., probably as purchaser of the Zouch Estate (see Woking). It was sold in 1748 to the Trustees of Lord Onslow. (*Ibid.*, 83.)

Woking.—In 1715 this estate was purchased by John Walter, Esq., of Busbridge in Godalming . . . . in 1719 was elected one of the Knights for this Shire in Parliament, for which also he was a second time returned at the General Election in 1722 . . . . the estate was sold in 1752 by Abel W. (*Ibid.*, i., 126.)

Manor of Brookwood.—Tenement called "The Hermitage." Mrs Cath. Wood inherited from Jas. Zouch. She, after Mr Wood's death in 1708, married Rd Bird of Woking, yeoman, by whom she had two daus. Cath. and Sarah. Cath. married Tho. Lambourn of Woking, yeoman. Sarah married (1) Rd Winch, gent., of Bray Wick, co. Berks; and (2) Rev. Alleyne Walter, LL.D., who purchased the other moiety and sold the whole. (*Ibid.*, i., 129.)

Hough Bridge in Woking.—Purchased in 1730 by John Walter, Esq. In 1735 he devised it to Lucy his wife, who in 1738 devised it to Abel and Henry her sons, who sold in 1761 to Alleyne W., LL.D., their brother. He sold in 1763.

Busbridge, a capital messuage in Eashing, a hamlet in Godalming.—Laurence Eliot sold it about 1710 to John Walter, Esq., of the Island of Barbadoes. (*Ibid.*, i., 618.)

John Walter married Lucy dau. of . . . . Alleyne, Esq., of Barbadoes, and left Abel his s. and heir, who sold this estate in 1737. (*Ibid.*, p. 620.)

WOKING, CO. SURREY.

1742 Feb. 15 Were married Mr Richard Winch of the parish of Braywick in the County of Berks, and Mrs Sarah Bird of this Parish.

1749 — Captain James Walter and Miss Elizabeth Hillman were married October 28th.

BURIAL.

1736 May 5 Was buried John Walter, Esqr, of Hobridge.

[There is no memorial in old Woking Church.—ED.]

Alex. Skene, to whom Sam. Wragg sold 3000 a. in 1721, was also a man of prominence in the Province.

He had originally come from Barbados, and was a M. of C. with Sam Wragg in 1717 .... He early conveyed away a tract of 1000 a. from the southern part of his purchase to Wm. Douglas, who transferred it to John Walter of Woking Park or Tooting, County Surrey, England .... 1300 acres Skene continued to hold. He apparently called his plantation " New Skene," and at his death it passed to his son John Skene. John Skene died in 1768 .... His real and personal property he devised to his friend Wm. Wragg, Esq., who in 1770 sold the 1300 a. to Wm. Haggatt, who renamed it " Haggatt Hall." Wm. Haggatt was an Englishman, who married Eliz. Walter the dau. of Wm. Walter and granddau. of John Walter of Woking Park. She had been educated in England, where she married Haggatt.

After Haggatt's death the property was acquired by Sam. Wainwright, who further subdivided it .... The name " Haggatt Hall " still survives locally, but corrupted to " Hackett's Hill " ....

The 1000 a. acquired by John Walter was called " Wampee " plantation, and was devised to his son William. John Walter owned considerable real estate in S. Carolina, viz., a plantation called " Red Bank " on the Copper River, and a tract of 12,000 a. called Walter's Barony, on Day's Creek or New River in Granville, now Beaufort County. Wm. Walter devised the " Wampee " plantation to his son John Alleyne Walter, who was for a time a lieutenant in Col. Wm. Moultrie's regiment, and married Jane Oliphant the dau. of Dr David Oliphant, a member of the Council of Safety, a prominent figure in the Revolutionary councils. (S. Car. Hist. and Gen. Mag., vol. xi., p. 89—91. An excellent map accompanies the article.)

1774. Jno Allen Walter, Ash: River (married to) Jane Oliphant, S. C. Town. (*Ibid.*, 102.)

The Washingtons of Barbados.*

Although no connection has yet been established between the Washingtons of Barbados and the Washingtons of Virginia, it may be well to place on record such information as is attainable respecting the Barbadian family, who held a good position in that Island.

In the October Number of the "Register of the New England Historic Genealogical Society" (Boston, Mass) was printed a letter from Theodore Pargiter of London, dated 2 August 1654, in which the writer refers to John Washington of Barbados as his cousin. This John Washington has not, so far as one knows, been properly identified, and Mr. Waters makes scant reference to his existence on p. 32, and in a footnote thereto, in the "Ancestry of Washington," published at Boston, U.S.A., in 1889. At the same time it is to be noted that at the date of John Washington's presence in Barbados, families mentioned in the "Ancestry" as connections of the Virginia family were living in the Island and doing business with it from London. There were Pargiters (pp. 25, 31, 32, 43), Rumballs (32, 33), and Tyrrells (42). The notable family of Codrington was connected with the Washingtons, through the Guises of the Baronetage. The first Virginian settler married a Pope, and there was a family of Pope in Barbados. In each

* Communicated by Mr. N. Darnell Davis.

case the Popes were of Bristol. In 1633 a Philippata Curtis died in Guiana, who was probably of the family of Philip Curtis of Islip, near Banbury, whose daughter married Sir John Washington (see Commission, 9 Dec. 1633, to Roger North, a Creditor of Philip Curtis, late in Amazonia, in parts, deceased, at Somerset House).

It may have been from a traditional interest of their family in Barbados that Lawrence and George Washington visited the Island in November and December 1751, rather than Jamaica or some other Island of the Caribbeans, when they sought a change of climate for the elder brother, then a dying man. Lawrence, it must be remembered, had also served in the West Indies as a British Naval Officer, under Admiral Vernon, in whose honour he had named his grant of land Mount Vernon.

Subjoined are some extracts from the Records of Barbados, made by Mr. Sinckler and another, to whom access has been readily granted by Mr. Lindsay Haynes, the Registrar of the Colony, in whose keeping the old documents have loving care.

WILLS OF WASHINGTONS.

Richard Washington of the Parish of St. Michael's and Island aforesaid, Gent. Will dated 21 April 1734. All my Estate either in this Island or in Great Britain to my wife Elizabeth Washington, to be by her disposed of to and amongst my children as she shall think fit, and appoint her sole Executrix.

RICHARD WASHINGTON. (Seal, but no arms.)

Witnessed by Ruth Rumball, Jno: Fowler, Mary Rumball.
Sworn by Mrs. Mary Rumball before Governor Thomas Robinson 29 Dec. 1744.
Barbados. Entered 29 Dec. 1744, fo. 66.

Elizabeth Washington of St. Michael's, Barbados, Widow. Will dated 4 March 1744. All my Estate real and personal which I am possessed of or entitled to in Great Britain as Executrix of my dear husband Richard Washington unto Richard, Mary, Eliza, George, John, and Eleanor Washington, children of ye said Richard Washington, to be equally divided between them share and share alike. Unto Richard Washington and Mary Washington their parts to be paid "immediately at the Recovery." Unto my 3 children George, John, and Eleanor Washington, all my estate real and personal in this Island to sons at 21 and dau. at 16, and to be educated out of the profits of my said Estate. Lastly I appoint Ralph Nowden, Merchant, of Great Britain, and Thomas Lake of Barbados, Merchant, and my loving Sister Mary Rumball, Spinster, Executors and Executrix.

ELIZ. WASHINGTON. (Seal, no arms.)

Witnesses: Wm Lindsey, Benj: Biddle, Ruth Briston.*
Sworn by Ruth Briston 4 July 1745 before Governor Thomas Robinson.
Barbados. Entered ye 4th July 1745, fo. 118.

George Washington. Will dated 27 January 1769. To my wife Angel Washington all my Estate, and appoint her sole Executrix.
Richard Vines Ellacott and Alex: McKenzie appeared before Governor William Spry 25 Sep. 1769, and swore that they knew George Washington, late of

---

* Marriage at St. Michael's 6 Oct. 1743. Walter Briston and Ruth Rumbold.

586

the Parish of St. Michael, that the above will was written throughout in his hand-writing, and the signature to the will was his.

Barbados. Entered 25 Sep. 1769.

On 18 Oct. 1769 administration was granted by Governor Spry to George Forbes of St. Michael's, Barbados, Merchant. Sureties, William Forbes and Thomas Woodin.

ST. MICHAEL'S.

BAPTISMS (1637 to 1806).

1761 Mar. 26   Theophilus Ashton Gordon, son of Theophilus & Mary Washington, born July 26, 1758 ; also George Ashton Gordon, son of Theop: Gordon and Mary Washington.

MARRIAGES (1643 to 1802).

1738	Aug. 27	Washington,	Richard, M^r, to Mrs Elizabeth Rumbold.
1762	Nov. 27	,,	George, to Ann .... (Spinster).
1765	Dec. 23	,,	George to Angel Hughes, Spinster.
1776	Jan. 14	,,	Angel, to Abraham Mullineux.

BURIALS.

1754	Sep. 5	Washington,	Mary ....
1756	May 27	,,	Eliz^a Parish ex O. C.
1756	Nov. 9	,,	Mary.
1763	July 25	,,	Ann.
1769	Mar. 21	,,	George.
1769	April 24	,,	John (Seaman).

ST. JAMES.

BURIALS (1637 to 1801).

1736	Feb. 20	Washington, Robert, aged about 10 years, son of Richard Washington. Apoplexy.
1744	Mar. 10	Washington, Elizⁿ, aged 43 years, died of a fever & lax.
1746	Aug. 1	Washington, Richard, aged 49 years ; died of a " vomitting."
1746	June 4	Washington, John, aged 13 years.

1653, Oct. 17. For 15,000 lbs. of good and well-cured Muscovado Sugar, Jonathan Andrewes, Thomas Andrewes, and Thomas Wardell, Merchant, sell to Captain Robert Rumball, Gent., of the said island, a parcel of land "lyeinge near the Indian Bridge Town in the Parish of St Michael in the said Island, bounded on the lands where the Old Sessions House stood, Southward ; upon the lands of the heirs of Robert Greene, deceased, Eastward ; and upon the land called Merchants' land, Northward and Westward. (Re-copies of Deeds, Registration Offices, Bridgetown, vol. iv., part 2, fol. 922.)

1656, May 14. Captain Robert Rumboll, gent., sells certain Land and Buildings at the Indian Bridge Town to Charles Rice or Rich.*

* Charles Rich of Lambeth, Merchant, died 1658, having married Laurentia, relict of Francis Ford of Barbados, Merchant. Charles's brother Robert was of the same Island (will proved 1679, 166 King), also two of his nephews, Robert and Edward, with their families. [EDITOR.]

"This 31st day of May 1656, appeared before me Captain Robert Rumball and Anna his wife, and acknowledged the Within Bill of Sale to be their free and voluntary act and deed. Acknowledged before me

THO. NOELL."

(Vol. iii., p. 16, 31 May 1655.)

Robert Pope of Barbadoes. Will dated 26 March 1659. My sisters Mary, Anne, and Sarah. To my Mother Mrs Eliz. Batty I leave my mansion house in Shelford, Cambridge. My wife Anne.
Witnessed by Nathaniel White, Elinor N. Brookes. Proved 27 April 1659. Barbados. Entered vol. ii., fo. 261.

BURIALS AT BARBADOS (name of Parish not given).

1657 Aug. 12 Joseph Pope.
1659 April 12 Robert Pope.

George Pope at Barbadoes. Mem. that on 1 Sept. 1659 Geo. Pope of Bristoll, Merchant, being sicke, declared his last will nuncupative that his cousin John Pope should be his Ex'or and heir. In the presence of John Pope S^r, Grace Taylor.
"The Keepers of the Liberty of England by authority of Parliament" . . . . Know ye that on 30 Sept. 1659 the will was at London proved and adm'on granted to John Pope. Signed R. Hankey, Wm. Jones, Mark Cottle, Reg^r.
Barbadoes. By the Govr approved. Mr James Haymon, attorney to Mr John Pope j^r, the Ex'or, being sworn to bring into the Secretary's office an Inventory. This last of Feb. 1659. Danyell Searle.

Charles Pope, now residing in Barbadoes. Will dated 24 March 1691 (? 1690-1). My estate in Jamaica. My dau. Mary. My brothers Chr., Rich^d, and Edwd Pope of Butleigh, co. Som., all estate. Sarah dau. of Geo. Harlin of this I., Merchant, Jas. Pinnock of Liganea, Jamaica. Hon. Geo. Lillingston, Wm. Bushe, Benjamin Hole to be Ex'ors for this I., and Edward Stanton, James Pinnock, and John Wilmot for Jamaica. Barbadoes. Entered 12 January 1691-2.

WATTS BIBLE RECORDS.—From records entered in a family Bible now in the possession of Mrs. E. Shirley Taylor.

Wilhelmina Dalzell Fowle Watts was born 1 June 1854 and died 12 July 1932

Mary Matilda Watts was born 10 March 1858.

7 August 1862. Died of haemorrhage of the lungs at Coronmense Protestant College, City of Liege, Belgium, where he had been acting English and Mathematical Professor, Jonas Wilkinson Watts Esq., aged 24, Scholar of Pembroke Coll., Oxford, eldest son of Frederick Watts Esq. Police Magistrate, St. Philip. (Newspaper cutting from *The Globe* 8 Sep. 1862).

Died on Thursday morning last at Dodds Estate, Mr. Frederick Coleridge Watts at the early age of 23 years, son of Frederick Watts Esq. Police Magistrate of St. Philip. This young gentleman had for a long time been a great sufferer, but his end was peace. Buried in the family vault at St. Philip's Church on Friday last. He was the second son. (From a cutting in *Barbados Globe* Newspaper of Monday 3 Sep. 1866).

Frederick Watts died 24 February 1878.

Death on Friday last of Mr. Aubrey St. John Watts, late Police Magistrate of District C. Mr. Watts was held in high esteem for his urbanity of manners and uprightness of character, and his death is generally regretted. (Newspaper cutting). Date added in ink—12 January, 1894.

Charlotte M. Watts, died 6 April 1897.

Frederick Watts was married to Charlotte Maria, second daughter of Jonas and Charlotte Wilkinson on 18 December, 1834.

Jonas Wilkinson Watts was born 18 September, 1835. Died 30 October 1835.

Jonas Wilkinson Watts, the second, was born 28 October 1836.

Frances Ann Watts was born 28 September 1838.

Frederica Philippa Watts was born 26 January 1841. Died 2 August 1926.

Frederick Coleridge Watts was born 31 August 1843.

Aubrey Saintjohn Watts was born 15 July 1846.

Charlotte Maria Watts was born 5 June 1848. Died 31 March 1916.

Edward Gascoigne Watts was born 6 October 1850.

Thomas Fowle Watts was born 18 November 1854.

Wilhelmina Dalzell Fowle Watts was born 1 June 1854.

Mary Matilda Watts was born 10 March 1858.

Funeral of Dr. Watts of Princeton, late Medical officer of Dartmoor Prison took place yesterday. Relatives of the deceased present were—Dr. Wilkinson, an Uncle, and Mr. Wilkinson, a cousin of London; Dr. Watts, Watford; and Mr.

Phillips, Portsmouth. (here follows an account of the service of burial) Dr. Watts was only thirty-two years of age. Church-warden of Princeton Church and Superintendent of the Church Sunday School. (Inserted in ink—He died 23 October 1884).

The Reverend Thomas Watts, M.A., Rector of Herbrandston, Milford, Pembrokeshire, and a Prebend of St. David's, only brother of Frederick Watts Esq. Police Magistrate of St. Philip. The Rev. gentleman was for 15 years Headmaster of the Lodge School and Chaplain to the Society's Estates as well as Chaplain to Bishops Coleridge and Parry. We copy from the Pembrokeshire Herald of 29 July 1864 a brief sketch of Mr. Watts's life. On Sunday last (24th) at Dairy Park, the residence of his son................He became a divine early in his life, and went out to Barbados. On his return to England he became the incumbent of the Vicarage of St. Mary in this town where he continued to serve until about December 1858, when he was presented to the valuable living of Herbrandston.—Was in his 59th year. He was several years Magistrate of the County, of late years Chairman of Quarter Sessions. Buried on Thursday in the family vault in St. Mary's burial ground.

On Tuesday last at Dodd's estate, St. Philip, the residence of her son-in-law, Frederick Watts Esq. Police Magistrate, Mrs. Wilkinson relict of the late Jonas Wilkinson Esq. of Bayfield and Holborn House and mother of Dr. Wilkinson, M.D. late of this Island. The deceased expired on her birthday on which she completed her 81st year. (Newspaper cutting from The Globe of 25 August 1864).

Died on 20 inst at Dairy Park in this County at the advanced age of 79 years. Mrs. Watts, Mother of the late Rev. Thomas Watts M.A. Rector of Herbrandston and Canon of St. David's and Chairman of Quarter Sessions and of Frederick Watts Esq. Police Magistrate Barbados, W.I. (Pembrokeshire Herald August 26, 1864.)

Note. Rev. Thomas Watts died July 1864.

His mother died 20 August 1864.

Mrs. Wilkinson died 23 August 1864.

On 20 October 1893 at 35 Gloucester gardens, Hyde Park, T. Lyte Wilkinson M.D.

Died. Edward Gascoigne Watts, 3 August 1900.

*   *   *   *

WILLIAMS OF WELCHMAN'S HALL,

BARBADOS. 1675—1825.

The popular family legend of the Williams family of Welch-man's[1] Hall states unequivocally:—[2]

"General William Asygell Williams and Dorothy, his wife were among the first settlers in Barbados. They were from Wales. He was a General in command of an old Welch Fusilier Regiment in Cromwell's time; he went against Cromwell and joined the Government party i.e. Royalists. Cromwell seized him, and all his 1,000 men made them prisoners in Bristol, and sent them all out to Barbados and other West Indian Islands. The old General built a house and a vault on Welchman's Hall land. He had 4 sons."

"General William Asygell Williams begat
Thomas,   who begat
William,   who begat
George,   who begat
Thomas,   well known as
Genl. Williams, of the Barbados Militia,who begat
George ,   who begat
Charles,   who died in the U.S.A.,
without issue."

Unfortunately, the sources of his family legend are completely unidentified, and without dates attached until c. 1730. Research in various Histories of Barbados, and other local historical records some of which give lists of prisoners consigned to Barbados by Oliver Cromwell in 1653, and also in 1657—58, furnish no clue to the identification of General William Asygell Williams of the Welch Fusiliers; neither can he be identified, as such, in any of the officially registered records of the Williams family in Barbados, of which there are a great many, dating from c. 1640. It is not possible, therefore, to explain t h e inconsistencies which arise between the family legend and the official records which have been traced concerning the founders of this family of Williams of Welchman's Hall.

Local records give a great deal of information of the Williams family in Barbados, 'gents' merchants, planters, masters of vessels, seamen etc., from Wales, Gloucestershire, Bristol, etc., buying and selling land and merchandise, from 1640; marriages, from 1648; wills, from 1649; and baptisms, from 1658.

The property of the Williams family in Barbados is first shown on Philip Lea's map of 1685, situated in Christ Church, probably that of 406 acres registered in the census of 1679, held by Major Richard Williams, a member of the Assembly for Christ Church in 1680.

Other property of the Williams family is shown on William Mayo's map of 1715—1720, among which is definitely that situated in the region of Welchman's Hall,[3] in the Parish of St. Thomas, adjacent to the Worrell property, in the region of t h e present Sturges Plantation.

On 16th July, 1675, a deed dated 4th June, 1675, is recorded of the purchase by William Williams, for £332.13., of a property of 21¼ acres, in St. Thomas, formerly belonging t o John Paige, and bounded on the north by lands of William Worrell'.

On 1st December, 1675, the marriage is recorded in St. Michael, of William Williams to Mrs. Dorothy Grant.

The co-incidence of names, and the property described, indicate that these Williamses can be definitely identified as the first William and Dorothy Williams of Welchman's Hall. This conclusion is supported by the sequence of the dates of the succeeding generations of this family.

Mr. William Williams is registered in the census records of 1679 as the owner of 67 acres in St. Thomas.

The burials are registered in St. Michael of William Williams, on 5th Oct., 1681, and of Dorothy Williams, on 12th May, 1682, but these records cannot be definitely identified as referring to William and Dorothy Williams of Welchman's Hall.

General William Asygell Williams, of the family legend, must have been either a very young General during the Protectorate, in England, or quite an elderly man when he acquired his property in Barbados, married, and founded the family of t h e Williams of Welchman's Hall. There is also the possibility of his having been previously married.

On 26th June, 1677, the baptism is registered in St. Michael, of *Isabella*, daughter of William and Dorothy Williams, but no baptism records can be identified of any of the 4 sons referred to in the family legend.

In 1682, a William Williams, Jnr., of St. Thomas, is named in the will of Josias Carleton, of St. Thomas, as friend and assignee in trust of the testator's plantation in St. Thomas. Carleton properties in St. Thomas, one shown as a Mansion House, and the other as sugar works, are marked on Mayo's map (1717—20), situated to the south of the Williams property.

In 1710, a deed is recorded in which Thomas Williams, gent., of St. Thomas, and Thomas Carleton, merchant, of the town of St. Michael, are named as administrators of the estate of William Williams, jnr., decd. Taking the names and dates into consideration the Williams men here named could have belonged to the earliest Williams family of Welchman's Hall, if William Williams jnr., was the son of an earlier marriage of General William Asygell Williams.

In April, 1677, the marriage is registered in St. Michael of William Williams jnr., to Mrs. Eliza. Fercharson, and in 1687 the will is recorded of William Williams, naming his wife Elizabeth.

No other records concerning the Williams family of St. Thomas can be identified before 1715.

The census returns for St. Thomas in 1715 name 6 Williams men as belonging to 4 separate households:—

(1) William Williams, aged 31;
(2) William williams, aged 36;
(3) Alexander Williams, aged 60, with (4) Alexander Williams, aged 16;
(5) Thomas Williams, aged 34, with (6) Henry Williams, aged 34.

After examining all the available records pertaining to Williams families of this period,[4] it has been concluded that, of these men named in the census returns for St. Thomas, in 1715, only THOMAS WILLIAMS, aged 34, can be assumed to be the son of Gen. William Asygell Williams, named in the family legend.

2. THOMAS[2] WILLIAMS of Welchman's Hall (William Asygell[1]).

Following the family legend, Thomas Williams, born c. 1681, aged 34, in the census returns for St. Thomas, in 1715, is identified as the son of Gen. William Asygell Williams of Welchman's Hall. As Thomas Williams, gent., of St. Thomas, administrator of the estate of William Williams, jnr., decd., he is probably identified in a deed recorded in 1710; and also as Thomas Williams, witness to the will of John Carleton of St. Thomas, dated 5 Jan., 1725/26, and proved by sd. Thomas Williams before Samuel Barwick, in 1731.

There is no record of the marriage of Thomas[2] Williams, but his wife may be identified as Judith Williams, aged 31, in the census of 1715, in St. Thomas, and in the baptisms, registered at St. Thomas, of 2 daughters of Thomas and Judith Williams.

On 9th Jan., 1741, the burial is registered, at St. Thomas, of Captain Thomas Williams, buried in a vault in his garden. This is corroborated by family records, and is the first official reference to the family vault built by General William Asygell Williams, according to the family legend. Through the ensuing years this vault has been the subject of popular legend and many a family anecdote.

No records of the baptisms of any sons of Thomas[2] Williams have been found, but following the family legend, a household of 4 boys in the census returns for St. Thomas in 1715, with William as the eldest, has been identified as the family of Thomas[2] Williams of Welchman's Hall.

After careful consideration of the available records of this period, the following have been identified as the children of Thomas² Williams of Welchman's Hall.

3. i. WILLIAM³ WILLIAMS, aged 12, in census 1715, in St. Thomas.
    ii. THOMAS WILLIAMS, aged 10,
    iii. JAMES WILLIAMS, aged 8,
    iv. JOHN WILLIAMS, aged 5,
    v. *Judith Williams*, aged 3, in census, 1715, a single girl in a household.
    vi. ELIZABETH WILLIAMS, baptised in Jan. 1715, at St. Thomas, daughter of Thomas and Judith Williams.
    vii. *Dorothy Williams*, baptised in Feb. 1729, daughter of Thomas and Judith Williams.

Before continuing with the senior line of the Williams of Welchman's Hall, through William² Williams, an account will be given of the families descendant from the younger children of Thomas² Williams.

   ii. THOMAS³ WILLIAMS, named in the census of 1715, aged 10, is identified as the 2nd son of Thomas² Williams of Welchman's Hall. As Thomas Williams, of St. Thomas, he is named in a Deed recorded in 1745, as administrator of the estate of Thomas Williams, Esq., in the sale of a piece of land in St. Thomas, bounding on the lands of the sd. Thomas Williams Esq., decd. This identification accords with the fact that his elder brother William³ Williams, predeceased his father, Thomas² Williams. Other records of Thomas³ Williams are not so clearly identified.

   On 19th Aug. 1728, the marriage is registered at St. Thomas, of Thomas Williams to Mary Treasure. The name 'Treasure' is found in association with the Carrington families of St. Thomas, who were neighbours of, and related by intermarriage, with the Williams family of Welchman's Hall.

   The baptism of 3 daughters of Thomas and Mary Williams are registered at St. Thomas, namely— *Mary*, baptised in June 1728; *Thomasin*, born in Oct. 1734, and baptised in April 1735; and *Barbara*, baptised in Jan., 1738/39. No. subsequent references to these daughters, nor to any sons of Thomas² Williams have been found.

   iii. JAMES³ WILLIAMS, aged 8 in the census of 1715, as the 3rd son of Thomas² Williams of Welchman's Hall, presents many problems in regard to his subsequent identification. The burial of James Williams is registered at St. Thomas in Feb. 1734, and there is no previous record of his marriage. Subsequent records, however, present an arresting significance in the coincidence of the sequence of dates, and in the use of the family name, James, in a well identified family of 3 brothers and a sister, who could be the children of James[3] Williams. This family consisting of the brothers *William, Thomas* and *James*, with sister *Ann*, are all named in each others wills, respectively, with their children and other relatives. The Williams families descending from these brothers are traced well into the 19th century, and subsequent references indicate their relationship to the original family of Williams of Welchman's Hall.

It is possible that one of the *Legends of Old Barbados*, attached to the Williams family of Welchman's Hall, may belong to this period. The story, as related by the late Mr. E. G. Sinckler, might well account for the abscence of marriage and baptism records, and the lack of contemporary references to this family of children, evidently orphaned when very young. The Legend mentions neither names nor dates, but relates how one of the sons of the family at Welchman's Hall married an Italian lady who was a Roman Catholic, and the family strongly objected to the marriage. This lady was a fine horse-woman, and also did much to improve the grounds of the family mansion house, planting many valuable fruit trees. The lady died, and was buried in the family vault. At some time later, when the vault was opened again, the coffins were found in the utmost disorder with that of the old General standing upright by itself! The coffins were then arranged in order again, with that of the old General placed at the bottom, and the others on top of it, but the next time the vault was opened, the old General was upright again!

The family presumed to be the children of James[3] Williams:

(1) *William[4] Williams* (James[3], Thomas[2], Wm. Asygell[1]), in will of *William Williams of St. Thomas*, entered 20th April 1774, naming his brothers Thomas and James, his sister Ann, and, significantly, Wiltshire Hooper Williams, the son of John Williams, brother of James[3] Williams.

William[4] Williams appears to have married twice. On 12 June, 1760, the marriage of William Williams to Elizabeth Corrigel Williams is registered at St. Thomas. Elizabeth Corrigel Williams was the sister of Wiltshire Hooper Williams, named in will as aforesaid. The baptism of Elizabeth, daughter of William Williams, is registered at St. Joseph, on 27 May, 1763. The will of John[4] Williams, dated in 1769, and entered in 1770, names his grand-daughter, Elizabeth, daughter of William and Elizabeth Corrigel Williams, but neither she, nor her daughter, are named in the will of her mother in 1777/78.

On 18 Jan. 1771, the marriage of William Williams to Jane Hayes, widow,[5] is registered at St. Thomas. His burial is registered on 22nd March 1774. The will of William Williams, entered in 1774, names his wife, Jane, and his daughter Elizabeth. His widow subsequently remarried twice.

The numerous instances of intermarriage in these Williams families is very noticeable.

(2) *Thomas*[4] *Williams* (James[3] Thos.[2] Wm. Asygell[1]), in will of *Thomas Williams of St. Andrew*, planter, dated 24th Nov., 1775, and entered 17 Sept., 1783, naming his wife Sarah, his daughter, Ann Skeete Williams, and his son *Thomas*[5] *Williams* as minors. Also named in this will are, sister, Ann Williams, nieces and nephews, children of brother William and James, and, as ex'tors brother, James Williams, and cousin, Wiltshire Hooper Williams, the same named in the will of his brother, William[4] Williams, in 1774. The naming of this relation is significant in identifying this family with the Williams family of Welchman's Hall. There is no record of the marriage of Thomas[4] Williams, nor of his connection with the contemporary Skeete[6] families, suggested by the use of the name 'Skeete' for his daughter. An interesting note arising from the will of Thomas Williams of St. Andrew, dated 1775, is his reference to a set of silver spoons marked *"T.E.W."*[7] There are no baptism records of any children of Thomas[4] Williams and his wife, Sarah.

Thomas[5] *Williams*, (Thos.[4] Jas.[3] Thos.[2] Wm. Asygell[1]) son of Thomas Williams of St. Andrew is identified in the will of *Thomas Williams of St. George*, dated 28th July, 1823, entered 9th April. 1827. The will names his 2 children, Lucretia Skeete Williams and James[6] Williams, minors; also his wife, as ex'trix, with his brother-in-law, Aaron Sober Robinson. The marriage of Thomas Williams to Jane

Robinson, spinster, is registered at St. Michael's on 10th Oct., 1801. In Oct., 1803, the baptism is registered, at St. Michael's, of a daughter, Margaret Ann, born in July 1802, who is not mentioned subsequently. In May 1805, the baptism of daughter Lucretia Skeete Williams is registered at St. Joseph's. No record is found of the baptism of son James. A deed recorded in 1817, of Thomas Williams of St. Joseph, planter, and his wife Jane, formerly Jane Robinson, shows that Thomas[5] Williams was a planter, at that time in St. Joseph. Another deed drawn previously in 1815, but not entered until 1819, records the sale of a small property in St. George by Thomas Williams, planter, of St. Andrew. In his will of 1823, Thomas[5] Williams names his wife's 2 sisters, Christian and Charlotte Robinson, and his own 2 sisters, Ann Skeete Williams and Sarah Benjamin Williams. The latter is not named in her father's will. The will of Sarah Benjamin Williams, of St. Michael, spinster, is recorded in Nov., 1829. She names as nieces and nephews the children of her decd. sister, Margaret White, and as ex'tors, nephew Thos. White, and Saml. Thos. Austin, none of whom have been otherwise identified.

Lucretia Skeete Williams, daughter of Thomas[5] Williams married Joseph Leacock, at St. George's, in Jan. 1827. Of *James[6] Williams*, son of Thomas[5] Williams, no further records have been traced.

(3) *James[4] Williams* (James[3] Thos.[2] Wm. Asygell[1]), is identified in the will of *James Williams of Christ Church*, planter, dated 4th June 1787, entered 7th March, 1788, naming as nieces and nephews the children of his decd. brothers, William and Thomas Williams, and his sister, Ann Williams, spinster. His wife, Elizabeth, and his daughter Elizabeth Ann, a minor, were to be maintained and have their residence in the dwelling house of his plantation, but this property is not named. His son *James Thomas[5] Williams*, was to inherit the property at 21. The marriage of James Williams to Elizabeth Goddard, spinster, is registered at St. Michael's on 7th July, 1768. He died at Bath, England, on 3rd Oct., 1787, aged 47 years. A tablet to his memory, and to that of his daughter, Elizabeth Ann Trotman, who died in 1793, aged 22 years, is erected in Bath Abbey. The

marriage of his daughter, *Elizabeth Ann Williams,* to
John Trotman of Wilcox plantn. in Barbados, is not
recorded locally. This marriage was the first of
other connections between the families of Trotman
and Williams of Welchman's Hall descent. In 1801,
John Trotman of Wilcox married, secondly, Elizabeth Hinds, eldest daughter of Gen. Thomas[5] Williams of Welchman's Hall.

James Thomas[5] Williams (James,[4] Jas.[3] Thos.[2]
Wm. Asygell[1]), son of James[5] Williams of Christ
Church, married Margaret Elizabeth Brandford, at
St. Michael's, on 8 May, 1894, and had 2 daughters
and 1 son. His eldest daughter, *Elizabeth Ann Williams* was baptised at Christ Church on 27 April, 1795,
married Henry Trotman, jnr., at St. Michael, on 7th
Oct., 1819, and had issue, one of whom was Henry
Clarke Trotman of St. Michael, administrator of the
estate of his decd. grandmother, Elizabeth Ann
Trotman, in 1857. *James Thomas[6] Williams,* baptised at Christ Church, 22nd April 1797, and *Margaret Smith Williams,* baptised at Christ Church,
28th Dec., 1799, the son and younger daughter of
James Thomas[4] Williams, died unmarried. This
family is commemorated on a memorial tablet at
St. George's Church, naming:

James Thomas Williams, Snr., born 1 May, 1769;
died 4 Sept., 1815. Margaret Elizabeth Williams,
born 25 Jan., 1779; died 3 March, 1836. Elizabeth
Ann Trotman, born 26 June, 1794; died 23 Feb.,
1831. James Thomas Williams, born 16 Feb., 1797;
died 4 Sept., 1821. Margaret Smith Williams, born
31 Aug., 1799; died 15 Nov., 1803.

(4) *Ann Williams,* spinster, the youngest of the family of
James[3] Williams, named in the wills of her 3 brothers,
and also in several records of the Skeete families of
St. Thomas, died in 1815, aged 82. Her obituary
notice appeared in the *Barbados Mercury* of 26
Sept., 1815.

iv. JOHN[3] WILLIAMS, (Thomas[2] Wm. Asygell[1]) the 4th son
of Thomas[2] Williams of Welchman's Hall, named in the
census of 1715, in St. Thomas, aged 5, is identified in the
will of John Williams of St. Michael, dated 5th Oct.,
1769, and entered 14th June, 1770, naming his wife,
Elizabeth, and 6 of their 7 children, all of whom are
identified by their baptisms and other records. The
marriage of John Williams to Elizabeth Nurse is regis-

tered at St. John's on 13th. July, 1732, and the baptisms of 5 of their children at St. Thomas. The burial of Mr. John Williams is registered at St. Thomas on 28th Oct., 1769, as 'buried in private lands,' referring, no doubt, to the family vault at Welchman's Hall. The will of his widow, as Elizabeth Williams, widow, of St. Michael, dated 5th Feb., 1777, and entered 26th Jan., 1778, names 2 sons and 3 daughters. There is a long line of descent from this branch of the Williams family of Welchman's Hall, which has not, at present, been traced beyond c. 1825. A brief account of the children of John[3] Williams and his wife Elizabeth, and their descendants, is given here.

(1) *Judith Williams*, baptised at St. Thomas, 19th Nov., 1734; unmarried, and named as residual legatee in the will of her mother in 1777.

(2) *Fearnot Williams*, no baptism record, but named in the wills of both parents; married John Cox, at St. Thomas, 20 Oct., 1759.

(3) *Dorothy Carrington Williams*, born 15 May, 1738, baptised at St. Thomas, 6 July, 1744; named in the wills of both parents as the wife of Dr. Benjamin Walcott; their son, John Alexander Walcott, born 24 Jan., 1766.

(4) *Elizabeth Corrigel Williams*, born 10 June, 1740, baptised at St. Thomas, 6th July, 1744; married her first cousin, William[4] Williams, on 12 June, 1760, at St. Thomas (*cp. ante*). She predeceased her husband but the record of her burial has not been identified.

(5) *Alexander Walker Williams*, born 22nd June 1742, baptised 6th July, 1744; not named in his parents' wills, and presumed to have died young.

(6) *Wiltshire Hooper[4] Williams* (John[3] Thos[2]. Wm. Asygell[1]) born on 31st May, and baptised at St. Thomas, 6th July, 1744; named in his parents' wills in 1769 and 1777, respectively, and as cousin in the will of Thomas Williams of St. Andrew, in 1775 (*cp. ante.*) is identified in the will of *Wiltshire Hooper Williams, planter, of St. Lucy*, dated 6th Oct., 1781, entered 30th April, 1783, naming his wife, Mary Anna, and 2 children, minors; his 2 nephews, sons of his brother, Lewis Williams; and his brothers-in-law, William Prescod and Samuel Hinds. The Marriage of Wiltshire Hooper Williams to Mary Anna Prescod is registered 31st December 1772, at St. John's, in which parish her brother, William Prescod, was the owner of Kendall plantation, as stated in the will of

the sd. William Prescod in 1815.[8] One of her sisters married Samuel Hinds of St. Peter, a prominent landowner of his era, whose daughters married into the families of Williams and Worrells of St. Thomas, thus furnishing another example of the pattern of intermarriage in groups of families, as so often found in Barbados of the 18th century. Property named in the will of Wiltshire Hooper[4] Williams is 10 acres land in Black Rock, with buildings, and a house in Speightstown tenanted by John Poyer[9] The burial of Wiltshire Hooper Williams is registered at St. Peter's, 26. Feb., 1783. No subsequent references to his daughter, *Elizabeth Hinds Williams* named in his will have been found.

His son, *John Prescod[5] Williams*, (Wiltshire Hooper[4] John[3] Thos.[2] William Asygell[2]) born, 10 June, 1775, and baptised at St. James on 21st Jan., 1776, is named, as a minor, in his father's will of Oct. 1781. He married his first cousin, Sarah Prescod Lewis, daughter of John Edward Lewis and his wife, who was a sister to the mother of sd. John Prescod Williams. The marriage of John Prescod Williams is registered at St. Lucy's 9th Aug., 1810. There were 4 children of the marriage — *Wiltshire Hooper[6] Williams*, baptised at St. James, 25 Jan. 1812; *Elizabeth Prescod Williams*, Baptised 18th March, 1813 at St. James; *Sarah Prescod Williams*, and *John Prescod[6] Williams*, whose baptism records have not been found. As a beneficiary under the wills of his uncle, William Prescod, in 1815 (cp. note 8.) John Prescod Williams was refunded the amount he owed sd. uncle, for the purchase of the plantations Westmoreland and Water Hall. The will of John Prescod Williams of St. James, dated 5 May 1818, and entered 8th December 1823, names his wife and 4 children (as above), with other friends and relatives. His plantations, Westmoreland and Water Hall, in St. James, were to be sold and the capital invested in Gt. Britain. Legacies bequested amounted to over £30,000

Research into this branch of the Williams family has not been continued beyond this period.

(*To be continued.*)

Footnotes

[1] 'Welch' is the spelling used in the designation of certain regiments, not including the 'Welsh' Guards. Oxford Dictionary.

² Communicated to E. M. Shilstone, Esq., President of the B. M. & H. S., by a member of the Carrington family of St. Thomas, descendants through intermarriage, of the Williams' family of Welchman's Hall.

³ This property is marked by a house, and not by a windmill. which denoted a 'sugar work' plantation.   c.p, reference in the family legend to the house built at Welchman's Hall by Gen. Wm. Asygell Williams.   Eventually the property became a sugar-work plantation.

⁴ (1) &(2) No further reference to these Wm. Williamses can be identified; cp. previous ref. to Wm. Williams, jnr., of St. Thomas, as possibly of family of Welchman's Hall.   (3) & (4) Alexander Williams and his descendants are named in records of earlier Williams families in St. James and the Northern parishes.   (6) Henry Williams is identified as son, named in will of Hugh Austin, of St. Andrew, 1691/1700, whose descendants are traced in the family line of Williams in St. Joseph.   In this family, the name 'Hugh' Williams occurs in each successive generation, and is associated with the Austin families of Barbados.

⁵ First married as Jane Adamson, to Thos. Hayes, in Sept., 1753, at St. Thomas; 3rd marriage as Jane Williams, wid., to Richard Hunt, in Aug., 1782, at St. Thomas; and 4th marriage, as Jane Hunt, wid., to George Williams, Esq., in Jan. 1786.

⁶ Thos. Skeete of St. Thomas, married Christian Williams, in 1774.   Skeete records of this period have several references to various Williamses.

⁷ In the Museum there is a silver spoon with similar initials, but the silvermark dates this specimen as London 1811.

⁸ Will of Wm. Prescod, Esq., late of B'dos, now of Growei St., Bedford Sq., Mdlsx., entitled to plants.   Kendalls, in St. John, Sion Hill, Rock Dundo, Small Hopes and Carleton, in St. Peter; Searles, Territts and Dayrells in Christ Church. Properties assigned in trust to Wm. Hinds of Speightstown, Esq., and John Gay Gooding, decd. mercht. Beneficiaries — Wm. Hinds Prescod, Francis Prescod, Mary Ann Prescod children of bro. Francis Prescod; Samuel Hinds Prescod and William Prescod, sons of decd. brother, Wilson Prescod; nieces, Mary Anna Goding, wife of John Gay Goding, Hannah Prescod Clarke, and her sister, Mary Grazett; nephews, John Prescod Williams and Samuel Lewis, son of John Edward Lewis, Samuel Hinds of St. Michael Esq., and his son Samuel Hinds; also, the children of Abel Hinds, late of B'dos, and Samuel Jackman of B'town, and his son, John Abel Jackman.   A legacy also to Susey Prescod, a free mulatto woman.

⁹ Possibly the historian, author of Poyer's *History of Barbados*, published in 1808, with a supplement, printed in Bridgetown, for W. Williams & Co., 1808.

WILLIAMS OF WELCHMAN'S HALL, BARBADOS. 1675—1825

*

(Continued from Vol. XXIX, page 75, the family of John³ Williams, 4th son of Thomas² Williams of Welchman's Hall)

(7) *Lewis⁴ Williams* (John³ Thos.² Wm. Asygell¹) is named in the will of his father, John Williams of St. Michael, in 1769/70, with a legacy of £400 in the estate of George Hayes, and also in his mother's will, in 1777/78, and in those of other relatives. There is no record of his baptism, nor of his marriage to his wife, Margaret, named in his will. The will of *Lewis Williams of St. Joseph*, dated 1 May, 1793, entered in June, 1793, names his son *John Archibald Williams*, '...and all my children,' of whom there were 3 others, all named in baptism records. Also named as friends, are Samuel Hinds and Francis Prescod, and as witness, Paul Carrington. The children of Lewis Williams and his wife, Margaret, are identified as follows—

> *John Archibald⁵ Williams*, baptised 7 July, 1771, at St. Joseph; unmarried; as John Archibald Williams of James, his will is entered in May, 1795. He names his St. brothers, and sister, Elizabeth Clarke, wife of James Sandiford.
> *Elizabeth Clarke Williams*, only daughter, baptised at St. Joseph's on 29 May, 1774, and married James Sandiford, at St. Peter's, on 4 April, 1795.
> *Francis⁵ Williams* (Lewis⁴ John³ Thos.² Wm. Asygell¹) baptised at St. Joseph's on 25 February, 1776; married Margaret Whitney, at St. Peter's, 4 January, 1798, and had 2 daughters, Elizabeth, baptised at St. Peter's in December 1799, and Sarah Jane, baptised 17 January, 1801, and married Henry Thornhill in October 1819, registered at St. Michael's and at St. James. The will of *Francis Williams of St. Michael* is dated in June 1807, as '...intending to depart this Island for the colony of Demerary' [sic]. There is no mention of his wife, whose death may be identified in the notice appearing in the 'Barbados Mercury,' of 15 March, 1806, of the death, in St. Michael, of Mrs. Williams, wife of Mr. Francis Williams. The will of Francis Williams of St. Michael was not proved and entered until 30th August, 1819. On 22 September 1808, the marriage of Francis Williams to Elizabeth Parris Clarke is registered at St. Michael's On 23 May 1815, the 'Barbados Mercury' notes '...Died on Sunday last, Mrs. Ruth Clarke, mother-in-law of Mr. Francis Williams.'

*See p. 600, this volume.

John Prescod Williams, (Lewis[4] John[3] Thos.[2] Wm. Asygell[1]) youngest child of Lewis Williams of St. Joseph, born 10 June 1775, baptised 21 January 1776, at St. James, and possibly identified in the marriage of John P. Williams to Mary Artey, in April 1820, at St. James.

Research into the records of this branch of the Williams family has not been carried beyond this period.

Before continuing with the main line of the Williams families of Welchman's Hall, some further reference must be made to Elizabeth, daughter of Thomas[2] Williams of Welchman's Hall.

vi ELIZABETH WILLIAMS, daughter of Thomas and Judith Williams, baptised at St. James. 3 January 1715, married William Carrington, at St. Thomas, on 2 October 1746. The Carrington families of St. Thomas, from whom the family records mentioned in this account are derived, claim their descent from General William Asygell Williams of Welchman's Hall through this marriage. William and Elizabeth Carrington had 8 children, of whom the 4th son, Richard Williams Carrington, born in 1751, married Jane, daughter of Dr. John Worrell of St. Thomas. on 3 June 1797, at St. Michael's. Richard Williams Carrington and his wife Jane were the parents of Dr. J. W. W. Carrington, of St. Thomas, and his brother, N.T.W. Carrington Esq., of St. Joseph, of whom there are descendants in Barbados at this present time. In 1840, Dr. J. W. W. Carrington bought the old Williams family home of Welchman's Hall from Mr. Ellis, of St. Thomas, to whom this property had been sold by the last Williams owner in 1826. Dr. Carrington died in 1866, but Welchman's Hall continued to be the Parent Home of this family until the death of his widow in 1881, when the property was sold, in 1882, to Mr. Charles West.

William Carrington of St. Thomas died in 1787, and his widow Elizabeth in 1793. Paul Carrington, their 6th son, is named as a witness to the will of Lewis Williams of St. Joseph, as previously noted.

3. WILLIAM[3] WILLIAMS (Thomas[2] Wm. Asygell[1]), in the senior line of descent of the Williams family of Welchman's Hall, was the eldest son of Thomas[2] Williams of Welchman's Hall. Born c. 1703, he is named, aged 12 years, with his 3 brothers, Thomas, James and John, in the census returns for St. Thomas in 1715. There is no record of his baptism. William[3] Williams married Mary, daughter of George Worrell, eldest son of John Worrell, the first owner of the Worrell property adjacent to that of the Williams at Welchman's Hall. This was the first of a series of intermarriages between the families of Williams, Worrells and Carringtons, adjacent landowners in the parish of St. Thomas during the

18th century. The marriage of William Williams to Mary Worrell is registered at St. Thomas on 12 September, 1730. This is the first instance where the 'family legend' is supported by registered records in the Island, and is taken as justifying the lines of descent as traced in the present record. The burial of William Williams is registered at St. Thomas on 2 December, 1735/36, [sic] as '...son of Capt. Thomas Williams, buried in his father's vault' ...i.e. the family vault at Welchman's Hall. He left no will. His widow, Mary, married secondly, – – – Wilson, as identified in the will of her mother, Mary Worrell, widow, of St. George, in 1757. There are no baptism records of any children of William[3] Williams and his wife Mary, but 2 of such are clearly identified in subsequent family, and other records, namely,

4.   i.   GEORGE [4]WILLIAMS, whose family line is traced subsequently

> ii.   MARY WORRELL WILLIAMS, as named in various family records, married Nathaniel Devonish, at St. John's, 3 January, 1754, and had a son, John Parrott Devonish[1]. This family was associated with Chalky Mt. plantation in St. Andrew and St. Joseph, as indicated in a deed of 1803, recording the sale of Chalky Mt. plantation by John Parrott Devonish and Thomas Williams. The name 'Devonish' is still familiar in Chalky Mt. district.

4.   GEORGE[4] WILLIAMS of Welchman's Hall (William[3] Thos.[2] Wm. Asygell[1]), son of William[3] Williams and his wife Mary, nee Worrell, was born in or about 1734. There is no record of his baptism, but he is clearly identified in subsequent family and other records. His marriage, as George Williams, gent., to Miss Margaret Reece, is registered at St. Thomas, 22 April, 1756. Margaret Reece, born in 1736, was the daughter of Richard and Ann Reece, and sister of Thomas Reece of 'Bezin's' now Hopewell plantation. Her mother, Ann, was the daughter of Francis Skeete, of St. Thomas, and his wife Margaret, daughter of Dr. John Martin of the same parish. George Williams and his wife Margaret, with their sons Thomas and George, are named in contemporary records of their Skeete relatives in St. Thomas. The baptisms of the 3 sons of George and Margaret Williams are registered at St. Thomas. The burial of Mrs. Margaret Williams wife of George Williams, is registered at St. Thomas, 29 December 1783. George Williams married, 2ndly, Jane widow of Richard Hunt, on 1 June, 1786, at St. Thomas. Jane Hunt, widow, had been married, and

widowed, 3 times previously. Her 2nd marriage as Jane Hayes, widow, to William Williams, in 1771, has already been noted. He was a 1st cousin of her 4th husband, George[4] Williams. The burial of George[4] Williams is registered at St. Thomas, 1 March, 1791. He was 57 years old. Family records state that he and his 1st wife, Margaret, were buried in the family vault at Welchman's Hall but make no reference to his 2nd wife, Jane. The burial of Jane Williams is registered at St. Thomas on 26 September, 1807.

The sons of George[4] Williams and his wife Margaret —

    i. *Williams Williams*, baptised 29 December, 1756, at St. Thomas and died after baptism, as recorded in the register at the same time.

5.   ii. THOMAS[5] WILLIAMS, known as Gen. Thomas Williams, of the Barbados Militia, whose family line is traced subsequently.

    iii. *George Worrell Williams*, baptised at St. Thomas, 26 December, 1762 and died in 1776. His burial is registered at St. Thomas, 15 January 1776, as '...Master George Williams, buried in family vault...' i.e. the vault at Welchman's Hall.

Pertaining to this period (1789) is another legend of Old Barbados centered around the Williams family of Welchman's Hall. This legend, like many others, although founded on fact, tends to be very confused as to the identity of the persons concerned. This story (cp. *B.M. & H. S. J.* IX, p. 51, 'As Dead as Cage') relates how a certain Mr. Forte[2] a young gentleman of a good family of high social position in the Island, having killed a young Lieut. Cage, of the 49th Regt., in a duel, sought refuge with his friends, the Williams of Welchman's Hall. Here, he hid during the day in a cave in Social Rock Gully, in the lands of the plantation, and was fed and cared for at the Mansion House at night. At that time, continues the Legend, the old General Williams had been long since dead, and the household was under the direction of '*Aunt Peg*,' one of his elderly spinster daughters, who, by her ingenuity and quick presence of mind, was able to outwit the Regimental search party, by cleverly concealing young Mr. Forte, when he happened to be at the Mansion House at the time of the sudden and unexpected arrival of the Troops.

In the family's version of the story, as told by Carrington descendants, '*Aunt Peg*' is said to have been, Margaret, the 2nd daughter of General Thomas Williams. This is im-

possible. The date of the duel is certified by the burial of
Lieut. Cage registered at St. Michael's Cathedral on 18
July, 1789.   At that time George⁴ Williams was the owner
of Welchman's Hall, and had no spinster sister, nor maiden
aunt, who can be identified in all the numerous records which
have been searched. His son, General Thomas Williams,
was a young man of about 30, in the year 1789. He was
married, and had several young children, among whom was
his 2nd daughter, Margaret, about 5 years old at this time.
Thus the identity of 'Aunt Peg the lady who hid Mr. Forte'
remains a mystery.

5. THOMAS⁵ WILLIAMS of Welchman's Hall (Geo⁴ Wm.³ Thos.²
Wm. Asygell¹) generally known as General Williams,
of the Barbados Militia, was the 2nd son of George⁴ Williams
and his wife Margaret, nee Reece, whose eldest son, William,
died in infancy On succeeding to the family property,
General Williams is said to have built a new Mansion House
at Welchman's Hall, on a different site from the original old
mansion built by General William Asygell Williams. This
2nd house was destroyed in the hurricane of 1831, and nothing remains to-day to show where these old houses were
situated, although the original family vault still survives.
Thomas⁵ Williams was baptised on 27th December 1759, at
St. Thomas.   There is no record of his marriage to his wife
Elizabeth Prescod nee Hinds, who is identified in the will of
her father, Samuel Hinds, the Elder, of St. Peter, entered in
1808, as daughter, Elizabeth Prescod Williams, legacy of
£500 '...which I have in a sealed note against my son-in-
law, Thomas Williams, her husband...' The several intermarriages between the families of Prescods, Hinds and
Williams have been referred to previously (cp. ante, p. 75).
The noticeable practice of using the same names for members
of different branches of these families, tends to make subsequent identification confusing. Since the parochial records
of St. Peter are missing before c. 1780, no records of this
family of Hinds, in St. Peter, can be traced. This includes
the marriage of Elizabeth Prescod Hinds to Thomas Williams.
For a period of 66 years, continuously, from 1773 to 1839,
the family of Samuel Hinds of St. Peter³ father, sons and
grandsons, represented the parish of St. Peter in the House of
Assembly and Council of the Island, holding various offices
in the Government during that period. As a representative
for St. Thomas Hon. Thomas Williams, Major-General of
the United Battalions (Militia) of St. James and St. Thomas,
was associated with them in the Legislature of the Island

from 1795 to 1821. During the years 1803 to 1819, General Williams was joined in the Assembly by his son, known as Major George Williams, as the junior member for St. Thomas. In 1805 General Williams was appointed Chairman of Committees of the Assembly.

Like so many of the old land-owning families in Barbados, the Williams family of Welchman's Hall appear never to have been associated with their property as planters. A Deed recorded in 1811 shows that, at some time previously, Gen. Thomas Williams had been in business with the late Alexander Hall, of Barbados, merchant, as merchants under the firm of Williams and Hall. In this Deed David Hall, '...now voyaging to America...' is named as executor to the will of the said Alexander Hall, decd. Previously to this, in a Deed recorded in 1803, David and George Hall, of St. Michael, are named as the purchasers of part of Chalky Mt. Plantation in St. Andrew and St. Joseph, 140 acres with Mansion, windmill, boiling house, etc., sold to them by Thomas Williams and John Parrott Devonish. Other Deeds record that at various times General Williams sold portions of the land of his property in St. Thomas. In 1821 the sale of such land to Nathaniel Carrington shows that the Carrington family of St. Thomas, related by marriage to the Williams family of Welchman's Hall, were owners of property adjoining Welchman's Hall, hence the district in that locality known as Carrington's Village at the present time. By a Deed recorded in 1803, Benjamin Hinds of St. Michael, with his wife Ann, daughter of Thomas Maxwell, decd., conveyed to Hon. Thomas Williams of St. Thomas, (his brother-in-law), as Trustee and Attorney, for the benefit of the said Benjamin Hinds, a certain property[4] in St. Michael, together with the sum of £1,000, the same being legacies to the said Ann Hinds under the will of her father, Thos. Maxwell, decd. This Deed had its sequel in 1825, when; "being bound by a Judgement conferred in the Court of Common Pleas in 1823, to Ann Hinds, widow, and executrix to the will of her late husband, Benjamin Hinds, decd., in the penal sum of £23,920. 17s. 11d., for securing payment of the sum of £11,960. 8s. 11½., besides charges, unto Ann Hinds, as executrix, as also for securing the payment of interest on the last mentioned sum of money from 1st September, 1823, at the rate of £6 per cent, until the whole be fully paid," General Williams sold to William Grant Ellis, Esq., of St. Thomas for £19,500 the sugar-work plantation known as Welchman's Hall in St. Thomas, containing 177 acres, with mansion, mill, boiling house, etc., and 67 slaves, with the agreement that Wm.

Grant Ellis should pay off the debt to Ann Hinds, as part of the purchase money, paying Thomas Williams £1,545. 17s. 6d. on account, leaving a balance due him, of £5,000, secured to him by said Wm. Grant Ellis. Thus Welchman's Hall, the original property and family home of the Williams family of St. Thomas for over 150 years, passed out of their possession.

In the following year, 1826, General Thomas Williams died at his residence, Woburn, in St. George, where he had been pre-deceased by his wife in 1809. The burial of Elizabeth Prescod Williams, aged 45, wife of General Thomas Williams, is registered at St. Thomas on 27 March, 1809, and that of Thomas Williams, late of Welchman's Hall, aged 66, on 31 July, 1826. Both were buried in the family vault at Welchman's Hall. When General Williams acquired his property of Woburn, in St. George, has not been ascertained, but it is evident that he was living there long before the sale of the old family home of Welchman's Hall.

The occasion of General William's death was marked by a long and laudatory obituary notice in *The Barbadian* newspaper of 1 August, 1826, speaking of the General as '...a gentleman amiable in private life and estimable in a public character, who will be long remembered with affectionate feelings. A high sense of honour and a manly independence, an undeviating integrity of conduct, peculiarly distinguished his performance of his public and private duties. While his very engaging social qualities endeared him to a numerous circle of friends, his country looked up to him with confidence as one of her most fearless and zealous supporters and defenders of her rights and interests...'

General Thomas Williams was survived by only 4 of his large family of children. In his will, dated 7 November, 1825, entered 28 August, 1826, he left to his son, George Williams, of U.S.A., Esq., a legacy of £100, and to his 3 daughters, Elizabeth Hinds Trotman, widow, Margaret Williams and Malvina Williams, spinsters, residual legatees, his dwelling -house with all appurtenances and the land attached, with his slaves. This was the property, Woburn, in St. George, where his daughters named had resided with him. A miniature portrait[5] of General Thomas Williams, wearing a blue coat, said to be the uniform of the Militia, is in the possession of a Carrington descendent now resident in the U.S.A. This miniature had been handed down from mother to daughter in 3 generations of the female descendants of Gen. Williams' eldest daughter, Elizabeth Hinds Trotman, when the last owner in Barbados donated it to her senior male Carrington relative in the U.Ş.A., in or about 1930.

Contemporary with Gen. Thomas Williams and his wife Elizabeth, of Welchman's Hall, there was another Thomas Williams[6] and his wife Elizabeth, of the parish of St. Thomas. In some instances, therefore, it is difficult to identify, with certainty, parochial records, and other references to children of 'Mr. Thomas Williams' and/or 'Thomas and Elizabeth Williams'', where no other information is available. With such help as can be obtained from family notes and records, the following have been identified as the children of Thomas[5] Williams, and his wife Elizabeth Prescod, nee Hinds:

6. i. GEORGE[6] WILLIAMS, whose record will be traced subsequently.

ii. *Samuel Hinds Williams*, baptised 4 March, 1781, at St. Peter's, son of Thomas and Elizabeth Williams; died 17 March, 1794, aged 13, as ref. family records; burial registered at St. Thomas, 18 September, 1794.

iii. ELIZABETH HINDS WILLIAMS, baptised 28 September, 1782, at St. Thomas, daughter of Mr. Thomas and Elizabeth Prescod Williams; Reference in family records as married to John Trotman, of Wilcox, in 1801. The marriage of Elizabeth Williams is registered at St. Thomas, 29 January, 1801, but the name of the bridegroom is omitted in the record. This was the 2nd marriage of John Trotman of Wilcox, whose 1st wife, Elizabeth Ann, daughter of James Williams of Christ Church, died at Bath, G.B., in 1793 aged 22 (cp. ant:, p. 72). John Trotman died in 1815. His widow, Elizabeth Hinds Trotman is named in the will of her father in 1826, as residual legatee with her 2 unmarried sisters, of the property of Woburn in St. George. The burial of Elizabeth Hinds Trotman has not been identified.

Of the daughters of Elizabeth Hinds Trotman, *Elizabeth Trotmant* born in 1811, married Thomas Trotman of Bulkeley, and *Margare, Williams Trotman*, born in 1814, married Dr. J. W. W. Carrington of St. Thomas, on 6 March, 1832, at St. George's Church. Dr. J. W. W. Carrington was related to the Williams family of Welchman's Hall by the marriage of his grandparents, William Carrington and Elizabeth Williams in 1746 (cp. ante. p. 94).

iv. MARGARET WILLIAMS, baptised 8 August, 1784, at St. Thomas; unmarried; named with her sisters, Elizabeth Hinds Trotman, and Malvina Williams, spinster, in the will of her father, General Thomas Williams, as previously related. By a deed of 1827, Margaret and Malvina Williams of St. George, spinsters sold to Elizabeth Gall of St. John, spinster, for £600, a dwelling house with lands attached in St. James, adjoining Lascelles plantn., the property of Randall Phillips, and other property of the said Elizabeth Gall. This property joined part of the residual estate of Thomas Reece, of St. James, Esq., deceased (cp. ante, p. 95) left to his nephew, Hon. Thomas Williams and his heirs. Hon. Thomas Williams left same to his daughters Margaret and Malvina Williams. The will of Margaret Williams of St. George, spinster, dated 25 April 1863, entered 10 February, 1871, names her Trotman relations, the children and

609

grandchildren of her sister Elizabeth Hinds Trotman, but not any of their Carrington cousins, by whom she is referred to as '...Aunt Peg, the lady who hid Mr. Forte!...' (cp. ante p. 96).

v. MALVINA WILLIAMS, baptised 29 May 1786,at St. Michael's; unmarried, named in her father's will in 1826, and subsequently, with her sister Margaret Williams, as previously recorded. Malvina Williams died at Woburn, St. George, 14 November, 1854, aged 68, and was buried in the family vault at Welchman's Hall.

vi. *Margaret Elizabeth Williams*, baptised 25th September, 1787, at St. Joseph's, daughter of Thomas and Elizabeth Williams; identified in the death noted in the family records, on 13 October, 1792, of Thomas Williams' daughter, aged 5 years.

vii. *Rebecca Williams*, baptised 17 February, 1788, at St. Thomas, daughter of Thomas and Elizabeth Williams; identified in the death noted in the family records, on 26 June, 1792, of Thomas Williams's daughter, aged 4 years.

viii. *Thomas Williams*, no baptism record; noted in the family records, on 9 December, 1791, Mr. Thomas Williams's son died, aged 25 months, burial registered at St. Thomas.

ix. THOMAS WILLIAMS, baptised 2 September, 1792, at St. Thomas, son of Thomas and Elizabeth Williams, was a young doctor, as whose apprentice Dr. J. W. W. Carrington started his medical career in 1817. Dr. Thomas Williams, aged 27, and his younger brother, Samuel Hinds Williams, aged 21, were both drowned at Bathsheba on 5 July, 1819. *The Barbados Mercury* of 6 July, 1819, notes the death of '...Dr. Thomas Williams and Mr. Samuel Hinds Williams, the much esteemed sons of Thomas Williams Esq., of St. Thomas, while they were bathing yesterday morning at Tenby.' Their burial is registered at St. Thomas on the same day, as 'drowned together and interred at the same time in the family vault in this Parish.' There is no evidence that young Dr. Thomas Williams was married.

x. *Robert Hinds Williams*, baptised 5 July, 1795, at St. Thomas; burial registered at St. Thomas, 10 February, 1817, aged 22 years and 7 months.

xi. *Katherine Ann Hinds Williams*, baptised 23 April, 1797, at St. Thomas; no further references found.

xii. SAMUEL HINDS WILLIAMS, baptised 17 June, 1798, at St. Thomas; drowned at Bathsheba, on 5 July, 1819, aged 21, with his brother Dr. Thomas Williams, as previously recorded.

6. GEORGE⁶ WILLIAMS (Thos.⁵ Geo.⁴ Wm.³ Thos.² Wm. Asygell¹) baptised on 31 January, 1780, at St. Thomas, son of Mr. Thomas and Elizabeth Prescod Williams, was the eldest child of his parents. Like his father, George⁶ Williams was never a planter, and he never became the owner of the old family property of Welchman's Hall. Sometimes referred to as Major George Williams, there is no evidence as to his occupation, or profession, other than that of the sale and purchase of landed property, of which there are many Deeds recorded. By a Deed registered in 1801, General Thomas Williams conveyed to his son George, then aged 21, 12 acres of land in St. Thomas, part of the lands of Welchman's Hall. At the session of the House of Assembly 1803/4, George

Williams was returned as the junior member for St. Thomas, in place of Mr. Samuel Forte. His father, General Thomas Williams, had already represented the parish from the session of 1795/96, and together, father and son served their Parish in the Legislature of the Island until the end of the session of 1818/19, after which George Williams left the Island, and his place in the Assembly was filled by Mr. Nathaniel Forte.

On 10 June, 1802, the marriage is registered at St. Thomas, of George Williams to Elizabeth Whitfoot, daughter of Charles and Elizabeth Whitfoot born 29 August, 1785, and baptised at St. Peter's, 26 January, 1786. Family records infer that George Williams and his wife Elizabeth, resided at their plantation, Orange Hill, in St. Peter, which he sold on leaving the Island to settle in the U.S.A. Orange Hill may be identified with the plantation called 'Dear's' containing 212 acres, bounding on the plantations called 'The Rock' and 'Four Hills' in St. Peter, which is named in Deeds recorded in 1815 and 1816, as the property of George Williams, Esq., of St. Peter, and his wife Elizabeth. No Deeds have been traced to show when George[6] Williams acquired this plantation, but he was the owner of property in St. Peter in 1803, when, by a Deed recorded in January of that year, he bought 5 acres of land from James Fenty of St. Peter, adjoining other lands of George Williams. In a Deed registered in June 1803, George Williams is named as of the parish of St. Thomas, but in Deeds registered in 1807, and subsequently, he is always named as George Williams of St. Peter.

During the years 1803—1819 there are numerous Deeds recording George Williams of St. Peter as engaged in business transactions dealing with the buying, selling or leasing of sugar plantations and other landed property, as well as slaves, of which transactions the following records are examples. A Deed of 1807 records the purchase, for £3,500, and re-sale for £2,525, from and to Joseph Leacock, an executor under the will of Benjamin Leacock, deceased, of a small plantation of 35½ acres, with dwelling house and sugar works, adjoining Colleton's Leeward Plantation in St. Lucy, part of the estate of said Benjamin Leacock, deceased. In 1815 and 1816 a series of Deeds record transactions by George Williams and his wife Elizabeth, concerning the plantation called Dear's in St. Peter, which they conveyed, at the beginning of 1815, to Thomas Williams, Esq., of St. Thomas, for 1 year, and at the end of that period, to Charles Kyd Bishop, of St. Peter. This transaction is immediately followed by Deeds concerning the sale of Dear's plantation to Charles Kyd Bishop, for £25,710, and the arrangements by the latter, for part payment of the purchase money by assigning to George Williams and his wife Elizabeth certain debts vested by law in the said Charles Kyd Bishop against the respective estates of certain persons named. The plantation called Dear's was probably that known as Orange Hill, which was sold when George Williams was leaving Barbados. But evidently he did not leave the Island immediately. In 1817 he bought Heywood's plantation in St. Peter, for £20,000 from Ruth Whitfoot, spinster, of St. Peter. No subsequent transactions concerning this property have been traced. In 1819, George Williams Esq., having previously contracted with Charles Kyd Bishop, Esq., both of St. Peter, for the purchase of Merton Cottage for £1,720, sold the same to John Henry Leacock, M.D., of St. Peter, for £2,000. Merton Cottage was a small property consisting of a dwelling house, store house and other buildings, with about 3 acres of land, on the road leading into Speightstown.[7] The Deed of Sale of Merton Cottage is the last reference to George[6] Williams as living in Barbados. The final transaction in his name, through his attorney Hon. Philip Lytcott Hinds, of St. Peter, is recorded in 1823, when George Williams was resident in U.S.A This Deed concerns the conveyance of Reid's Bay[8] plantation in St. James, with mortgages attached, first, from Henry Peter Simmons to Charles Kyd Bishop, next, from the latter to George Williams, and finally from George Williams to Abraham Rodrigues Brandon, with mortgages attached as from 1 July 1815.

Family records state that Major George Williams and his wife settled at Montevideo, in Minnesota, U.S.A., and that he was survived by 1 son, Charles, who died without issue. No references have been found as to the dates of the death of George[6] Williams and his wife, nor to that of their son, Charles Williams, with whose passing the senior line of this family of Williams,the founders and owners of Welchman's Hall for 150 years, came to an end.

The children of George[6] Williams and his wife, Elizabeth, nee Whitfoot:—

    i. *Thomas Williams*, no baptism recorded; named in family records as having died on 9th May, 1804, aged 8 months.

    ii. *Thomas Williams*, born 15 February, 1805, baptised at St. Peter 5 February 1811; died aged 11; no burial record found.

    iii. *Ruth Williams*, born 19 September 1808; baptised at St. Peter, 5 February, 1811; no other reference found; may have accompanied parents to U.S.A.

    iv. CHARLES WHITFOOT[7] WILLIAMS, born 5 September. 1810; baptised at St. Peter, 5 February, 1811; accompanied his parents to U.S.A., returning to Barbados on a visit in 1840. He survived his parents and died without issue. No further references have been found.

v. *Katherine Ann Hinds Williams*, baptised at St. Thomas, 4 July 1813. No further references found.

vi. *George Williams*, born 22 March, baptised 22 October, 1813. at St. Peter; burial registered 27 October, 1813, at St. Thomas, as son of Major Williams of this Parish, about 5 months old.

FOOTNOTES

1. From Dr. J. W. W. Carrington's notes:—
"......John Parrott Devonish had 3 sons, John Parrott, Joseph and William. and 2 daughters, Martha, the wife of — Richards, and Mary Catherine who remained a spinster. John Parrott Devonish, jnr., married 1st, an Englishwoman, by whom he had 3 daughters: Mrs. Nick Walrond, who was the widow Hall, Mrs. Nick Howell, and Mrs. James Crichlow. His wife died, and he married 2ndly, Eyre Coot Walrond who left no issue......"

2. Possibly Mr. Samuel Forte, member of the Assembly for St. Thomas from1787/88 —1802/03. Named as Dr. Samuel Forte, he was the senior member for the parish, with Hon. Thos. Williams (Gen. Thomas Williams) as the junior member, during this period.

3. Hon. Samuel Hinds the Elder, of St. Peter, member of Assembly 1773—1799; sometime owner of Maynards and Gibbes plantns. Will 1808, His sons: Hon, Wm. Hinds of St. Peter, member of Assembly 1800—1816; Hon. Saml. Hinds, M.D., of St. Michael, member for St. James, 1797—1802, member of Council from 1802, owner of Warrens Plantn., will 1824; Hon. Benjn. Hinds of St. Michael, member for St. Peter, 1795 to death in 1807, Hon. Treas. of Is. from 1805, C. J. Court of Common Pleas in St. Peter, will 1807; and Abel Hinds. Grandsons:— Hon. Philip Lytcott Hinds of St. Peter, son of Hon. Sam. Hinds, M.D., member for St. Peter. 1817—1822; Hon. Saml. Hinds, jr, son of Abel Hinds?, member for St. Peter 1823 —1839, Hon. Speaker 1837—1839. Daughters of Hon. Saml. Hinds the Elder. Anna Maria, wife of William Graham; Rebecca Wilson, wife of Jonathan Worrell of Frampost, Sussex, formerly of Highland, St. Thos, Barbados;.....wife of Richard Skinner of St. Peter? ; Eliz. Prescod, wife of Hon. Thos. Williams of St. Thos.

4. Named as 'The Retreat' in St. Michael, in the will of Benjamin Hinds, 1807.

5. A contemporary family portrait is the Worrel miniature, illustrated facing p.18, B.M.H.S.J. XXIX,. (See p. 629, this volume.)

6. In 1807 the will is recorded of Thomas Williams, arithmetic master of St. Thomas, naming his wife, Elizabeth Williams, and 5 children, the baptisms of 3 of whom are registered at St. Thomas. This Thomas Williams has been identified as belonging to the line of Williams families of St. James, whose connections, if any, with the Williams families in St. Thomas has not been discovered. Baptised in 1768, this Thomas Williams was about 9 years younger than General Thomas Williams. In tracing the family of the latter, the dates involved, and references found in the notebooks of Dr. J. W. .W. Carrington of St. Thomas, (decd. 1866) have been taken into account in identifying the children named in this record.

7. If not continuously from this time, 'Merton' (Cottage) was again the residence of the P.M.O. for St. Peter when it was occupied by Dr. Campbell Greenidge from c. 1870, and afterwards, in the early part of the present century, by his son, Dr. Oliver Greenidge.
In 1929 it became the site of the Alexandra Girls' School, founded in 1894, and formerly housed in an old building in Queen's Street, Speightstown.

8. Reid's Bay plantation owned by the Bishops of St. Peter, a prominent family during the 18th century, when Hon. Williams Bishop was for many years President and C. in C. of the island. His brother John Bishop, died c. 1790, was then the owner of Reid's Bay. Charles Kyd. Bishop was his son.

A FORGOTTEN TRAGEDY

In the month of August of this year, a silver tea-service consisting of three pieces, tea-pot, cream jug, and sugar-basin, was offered for sale at an auction of furniture, plate etc., at a private house in Bridgetown. Made in the reign of King George III, each piece of plate bears the London silver hall-marks for 1807-8, being of "acanthus leaves" decorative design and otherwise heavily chased. The makers mark is that of Thomas Halford.

A crest—a bull's head couped at the neck—is engraved on the base of each piece; and on the opposite side in old English letters the initials "F.F.P.". The initials are certainly a later addition, as the more recent history of the ownership of the silver as told to the writer will prove.

Greater interest in this set of silver lies in another inscription in script characters which was added nearly fifty years after the silver was made and which reads "H.W. Obt. 16 May, 1853". These words are engraved on the bottom of each article. The owner of the silver could give no information concerning the facts leading to the record of the death of H.W. thus commemorated, or even the name of the deceased.

A search among the records in the Registry in Bridgetown disclosed the fact that on 17th May 1853 Henry Williams of Hastings District was buried in St. Matthias Churchyard, Hastings, Barbados, aged 25 years. His place of burial is marked with a stone bearing the following words—

To the memory of / Henry Williams Esq. B.A. / of Wadham College Oxford / and master of the / Hastings Grammar School / in this island/who departed this life / the 16th May 1853 / Aged 25 years.

His is one of three similar tombs side by side at the north-east corner of the churchyard. The first is marked with an inscription to the memory of Thomas Salkeld Esq. late master of Hastings Grammar School, who died 12 October, 1852, aged 25 years placed there by his pupils as a tribute of affection. The second also bears lettering recording the burial of William French who died 10 Decr. 1852 aged 24, a native of Bloxham, Oxfordshire, and master of the Highgate School in this island, and was placed over his remains by his widow. The third is the tomb of our Henry Williams.

Henry Williams's death is recorded in the *Barbadian* Newspaper for Wednesday, May 18, 1853, in the following words:—

It is with deep regret that we record the awfully sudden death of a valuable member of society, that of Mr. Henry Williams, the able master of the Grammar School at Hastings, lately under the charge of the lamented Mr. Salkeld. The deceased unfortunately went into the sea the night before last.

between seven and eight o'clock, expecting to enjoy a bath, but alas he, at the second plunge into the water, disappeared. After some time his body was recovered; medical assistance was rendered by gentlemen of the Garrison and every effort made to restore animation, but life was totally extinct.

From all that we have heard of Mr. Williams' character, his attainments and his remarkably happy manner of communicating knowledge, we think the school sustains an irreparable loss.

An inquest was held on the body and a post mortem examination made by Dr. Herron of the Army Medical Staff. We have not heard what the verdict was, but we understand that the opinion was that the unfortunate gentleman died of apoplexy. We think this very likely to be correct, as he imprudently went into the bath with a full stomach, having perhaps dined heartily.

Oliver's Monumental Inscriptions of Barbados (p. 121) adds a note to the inscription on the tomb, stating that he was the sixth son of Robert Williams of Llangewny, co. Brecon, gentleman, and he matriculated from Wadham Coll. 26 June. 1846, aged 18, B.A. 1850.

The Hastings Grammar School was founded about the year 1851-2 by Rev. Abraham Reece, Curate of St. Matthias and afterwards Rector of Christ Church. The death of two of his masters in quick succession may have contributed to the closing of the school in 1857.

It is possible that the parents of the deceased young man, desiring to perpetuate his memory at the school, presented the service of plate to the Institution, hence the inscription recording his death. At the time of its presentation, the tea-service was nearly fifty years old, doubtless a "family piece". Has the crest—a bull's head—any connection with the donor's family?

CHARLES WILLING 1738—1788

The portrait of Charles Willing 1738—1788, which appears on the opposite page, is in the collection of The Historical Society of Pennsylvania and is here published by kind permission of that Society to whom we are indebted for information. To Miss Anna Ruthledge we are also indebted for kindly calling our attention to the portrait and for sending us the photograph. Charles Willing, of Pennsylvania was the second son of Charles and Anne (née Shippen) Willing and was a merchant of Barbados. Charles Willing the younger was born on 30th. May 1738, he married in Barbados on 24th. May 1760 Elizabeth Hannah Carrington, born 12th. March, 1740 and died 12th. October, 1795. Charles Willing predeceased his wife by dying on 22nd. March, 1788.

CHARLES WILLING, 1738—1788.

By permission of THE HISTORICAL SOCIETY OF PENNSYLVANIA.

Elizabeth Hannah Willing, née Carrington, came of a family long settled in Barbados. She was the daughter of Paul Carrington, (1706—1750) and his wife Mary, née Gray, of St. Michael. Mrs Willing was one of several children. Her grandfather was Dr. Paul Carrington, of St.Philip, Barbados, who was presumed to have died at sea in 1716. Her grandmother, Mrs. Hemingham Carrington was born in 1671. No marriage has been traced between her grandparents and it would appear that Dr. Paul Carrington was married in 1687 to Thomasine Waterland who died in 1727. Both Dr. Paul Carrington in 1716 and Mrs. Thomasine Carrington in 1727 mention certain of their joint issue. In his will, however, Dr. Paul Carrington describes Mrs. Hemingham Carrington as his wife and mentions certain of his issue who are also mentioned in the will of Mrs. Hemingham Carrington in 1745. Amongst those described as a son is Paul and his daughter Elizabeth Hannah is also mentioned.

Whatever may be the real truth of Dr. Paul Carrington's marriages [?], two of his sons, like his granddaughter Elizabeth Hannah Willing, went to live in America. George Carrington, baptised at St. Philip's Church in 1711, settled in Virginia in 1727. He married first in 1732, Anne Mayo, the daughter of William Mayo, the celebrated map-maker of Barbados. His second marriage was to Frances, daughter of Enoch Gould, who had issue who married into the Cabell family of Virginia. Another son, Edward Carrington, baptised at St. Philip's Parish Church in 1715, signed his will on 5th May 1736, intending a voyage to Virginia. His wife, Jane, née Gibbs, whom he married in 1734 is not mentioned in his will and is therefore presumed to have died before that date. Edward Carrington's will was entered at Barbados in 1745.

Of the marriage of Charles and Elizabeth Hannah Willing, the second child Elizabeth Gibbes Willing born in 1762, married in Barbados in 1782 John Foster Alleyne of Porters, St. James. She died in Barbados in 1832 and her descendants owned Porters until the beginning of this century. The elder daughter Ann Willing became the wife of Luke Morris.

Little appears to be known of Charles Willing except that he was a successful merchant. The portrait was formerly in the possession of Mrs. Eliza Littell of Baltimore, who bequeathed it to St. Luke's – Germantown Church , with a request that it be given with other paintings to the Historical Society of Pennsylvania. Whilst the painting was in Mrs. Littell's possession it was attributed to William Johnston* by Dr. J. Hall Pleasants. This attribution has subsequently been disagreed with by the Frick Art Library of New York.

---

*See "William Johnston, American Painter, 1732—1772", by Neville Connell *B.M.* & *H.S. Journal*, Vol. XXIV, pp. 152—160.

THE WORRELL FAMILY IN BARBADOS

Several spellings of the name Worrell are to be found in British West Indian records from the mid 17th century. Vere L. Oliver, the learned Editor of *Caribbeana*, brackets these spellings Worrall, Worral, Worrell, as belonging to the same family. He records the name Warrell separately, but families of this name in Nevis were contemporaries of the Worralls and Worrells of the same island, and it is possible that these were also of the same family. In Barbados, the name is usually spelt Worrell, but the spelling Werrill and Worrall, and other minor variations are also found. Apart from Nevis, the name Worrell also occurs in Jamaica, but so far it has not been possible to link the Barbados branch with either of these.

The earliest Worrell mentioned in the records of this island is Richard Worrell, son of Christopher Worrell, baptised in St. Michael's Church in 1658. It has not been possible to connect either of the above with the pedigree which begins with John Worrell, 1655—1718. Other members of the Worrell family mentioned in local records, who also remain unconnected with the Worrell pedigree, are as follows —

1661 Ralph Worrell of St. Peter leased a plantation of 90 acres to John Howard of the same parish for 32 years.

1673 Thomas Worrell, gent., is mentioned in a deed of conveyance as trustee of his natural sister, Dorcas, wife of Richard Binyon of St. George.

1677 Mary Worrell, widow, buried at St. Philip's parish church.

1680 Unnamed Worrell, buried at St. Philip's parish church.

1680 Samuel Worrell, buried at St. Philip's parish church.

1683 Dr. William Warrell, "of the ffrancis ffrigate," buried at St. Michael's parish church.

1685 Joseph Worrel, "of Capt. Thos. Downes" buried at St. John's parish church.

1715 Richard Worrell married Rebecca Butler at St. Michael's Church and also a Richard Worrell of St. Michael, age 46, is named in the census of 1715.

No Worrells however are named in the census of 1679.

The arms of the Worrell family as depicted on the family burial place at Sturges plantation are as follows :—

Three covered cups; on a chief — 2 lions passant.

Crest: A lion's jamb, erased, holding a covered cup.

The Crests of the Worrell (Worrall) families as recorded by Duval are:

(i) In a lion's gamb erect & erased, Argent, a cross-crosslet of the same.

(ii) In a lion's gamb erect & erased, Sable, a (covered) cup Or.

The arms of the Worrall family of Clifton, Bristol, (1872) are described in *Caribbeana** as quartered, 1 & 4, i.e. the arms of the chief family being, 'Gules, a chevron Or between 3 crosses-crosslet, in chief a lion passant.' The crest being (i) as previously described. The Worrell Arms as depicted appear to embrace the main features of the arms of both the Butler family and Harrison family.

The Butler families of Nevis, of which one of the more prominent members was Captain Gregory Butler, a Commissioner under General Venables, c. 1645, bore arms as recorded by *Caribbeana*†:

---

* Vol. II, P.372.

˙ Vol. II, P. 60.

'Or, on a chief indented Azure, 3 covered cups of the first.

Crest: Out of a ducal coronet as eagle rising from plumed feathers.'

Duval records this crest as belonging to the families of Irish nobility and gives several other crests used by other Butler families.   Among these the crest of Butler families of London, Durham and Scotland is that of a covered cup.

The Harrison family of Barbados was connected by marriage with both the Worrell and the Butler family.   The Arms of Harrison College, presumed to be those of its founder, Thomas Harrison are:

Or, 2 lions passant, Gules, on a chief of the second, 3 covered cups, Or,

Crest: In a lion's gamb, erect & erased, Gules, a covered cup, Or:

1. JOHN[1] WORRELL, name as 'taylor' in deed of 1692.

Born c. 1655; named in census of 1715 in St. George, aged 60, with wife Bathsheba, aged 58, and daughter Martha, aged 16.   Deed recorded 1692, headed 'In Nevis', states that John James of St. Thomas, planter, was bound to John Worrell of St. Thomas, tailor, in the sum of £600, and in his will of 1718, John Worrell bequeaths to son George the plantation he bought from John James, situate in St. Thomas, containing 16 acres.

Deeds of 1709 and 1710 record the purchase of land adjoining his property, and slaves, attached from the property of William Cole deceased.

Other property bequeathed to son George is named as '5 acres adjoining [above mentioned property] formerly belonging to John Northeast; also my upper land purchased from Elizabeth Speed, situate in St. Thomas, containing 9 acres; also my plantation purchased from Evan Andrews situate in same parish containing 4 acres.'

Worrell property is not shown on any map before that of William Mayo in 1720.   In this and subsequent maps it is shown in the vicinity of the present Sturges plantation which became the property of the Worrell family through the marriage of Jonathan [3] Worrell to Jane Harrison, owner of the same, in 1760.

"Sturge's" plantation is first named as Worrell property in a deed of 1789.   In 1840 it was sold out of the Worrell family, and in Schomburgk's map of 1845 the name Sturges is used in place of the name Worrell of earlier maps .

The name "Cole's Cave" identifies the site of Worrell property bought from William Cole in that locality.

John Worrell left his property to his eldest son George, and failing an heir to George, then to his 2nd son William.

The children of John Worrell and wife Bathsheba are named in his will of 1718 — namely:—

2.   i. George Worrell, b. c. 1685

3.   ii. William b.c. 1692

4.   iii. Nathan b.c. 1694

5.   iv. Jonathan b.c. 1698

v. Sarah, spinster, of St. Thomas.   Will proved 1758, naming nieces, Mary Walke, Snr., Eleanor Wooding, Sarah Duke, Eleanor Elridge Mary Worrell, Snr., Bathsheba Worrell, Eleanor Daniel, Elizabeth Worrell, and great nieces Mary Butler and Susannah Minvielle. Also great nephew William Sturge Moore.   Residual legatee and executrix, Jane Sturge, niece.   Executor: William Moore, son-in-law of Jane Sturge.

vi. Martha b.c. 1699; named in census 1715 in St. George. Married Thomas Duke; daughter Sarah Duke named in will of aunt, Sarah Worrell, 1758.

vii. Eleanor, not named in father's will. Married Hon. Thomas Harrison, named as son-in-law in will of John[1] Worrell; founder of Harrison's Free School [now Harrison College]. Their children:

    i. Dr. George Harrison, baptised 1714, St. Michael; will proved 1746; wife Jane Cobham. Children: Thomas Harper Harrison, died a minor, and Jane, married Johnathan[3] Worrell 1760.

    ii. Jane Harrison, married (1) Harper, deceased in 1746; married (2) William Sturge. Named in will of aunt Sarah Worrell. Her daughter Jane Harper, married William Moore, Jnr., executor to will of said Aunt. Gd.son William Sturge Moore named in said will. Other grand-sons — Daniel, John Harper, Blaney and Thomas Moore.

    iii. Hon. John Harrison, baptised 1716; will 1755. Unmarried; member of Vestry St. Michael.

    iv. Eleanor, baptised 1718; married (1) John Neil named as Eleanor Neil, widow, in will of brother John (above named): Her daughter, Joanna Neil, married William[3] Worrell, 1755. Other daughters Eleanor and Elizabeth Neil. Eleanor Neil, widow, possibly married (2) . . . Wooding, as named in will of aunt Sarah worrell, 1758.

    v. Mary, baptised 1722; married John Walke of Walke Spring, St. Thomas. Named in will of aunt, Sarah Worrell. Children, John, Robert, Harrison, Thomas, Mary Abigail, Sarah and Jane Walke.

    vi. Sarah, married Elias Minvielle. Named in will of aunt, Sarah Worrell. Children — Thomas, David and Susannah Minvielle named in will of aunt.

2. GEORGE[2] WORRELL (John[1]), eldest son of John and Bathsheba Worrell, born c. 1685; named in census of 1715 in St. Thomas, aged 30 with wife Mary aged 28.

There are no baptism records of his children who are identified by the will of his widow Mary Worrell in 1757. The burial of George[2] Worrell is registered in July 1738 at St. Thomas. " . . . buried in his garden" which is taken to be the first reference to the Worrell family burial place situated in a field of the present Sturges plantation. George Worrell inherited the property of his father John Worrell, in St. Thomas, which, failing an heir to George, was to go to his brother William.

George Worrell had no son, but during his lifetime he bought and sold property in St. Thomas, some of which, according to the boundaries given, was adjacent to the original Worrell property, thus enlarging the same.

In 1712 he sold to George Hows of St. Michael, for £5. 2. 4. ten acres of land and premises thereon, to be conveyed by Edward Skeete, Churchwarden of St. Thomas.

In 1712, bought for £7. 7. 10½., 19 acres of land formerly belonging to estate of William Cole, deceased, attached from Mrs. Joane Harris for parish dues. Said land bounded on north by lands of Mr. William Bryant, John Worrell and Richard Merrit respectively; on west, by lands of Captain Thomas Williams [i.e. Welchman's Hall]; on south by lands of Mr. Henry Feake [Ayshford]. Bryant property is shown on Moll's map of 1717; Williams, Worrell and Ayshford, on Mayo's map of 1720 [cp. "Cole's Cave" for site of Cole property].

1720: Sold to Nathan Worrell of St. Michael, merchant (his brother) for £540, 30 acres land, with houses etc., in St. Thomas; also to John Charles of St. Michael's, gent., for £60, 3 acres land in St. Thomas, bounding on lands of George Worrell as described in 1712.

Bought, in 1720, from Margaret Barclay of St. Thomas, for £200, 7 acres land, bounded on north, east and south by lands of George Worrell, and on west by lands of Captain Thomas Williams.

The information given in these deeds indicates that the original Worrell property consisted of lands which were eventually incorporated in the present Sturges plantation.

The death of Mary, widow of George[2] Worrell, is identified in the burial, registered in 1756 in St. John, of Mrs. Mary Worrell, from St. George, and by the will of Mrs. Mary Worrell, widow of St. George, recorded in 1757, naming her daughters — Mary Wilson, Elizabeth King and Eleanor Elridge; also grand-daughters — Mary Ann Elridge, Mary Devonish, Mary Ann Smith, and Mary Elizabeth and Martha King. Executors: Son [in-law] Eyare King, daughter, Mary Wilson and Kinsman James Mahon.

The children of George[2] Worrell and his wife Mary, as identified by the above will and by later family records:

    i. Mary, born c. 1707. Married (1) at St. Thomas 1730 William Williams; their daughter Mary Worrell Williams married Nathaniel Devonish and had issue John P. Devonish et al. Married (2) . . . Wilson.

    ii. Elizabeth, married Eyare King, named as executor and had issue— daughters also named in mother's will as above.

    iii. Eleanor, baptised 1728, St. Thomas. Married . . . Elridge named in will of aunt Sarah Worrell, 1758. Had issue — daughter named in mother's will.

3. WILLIAM[2] WORRELL (John[1]), born c. 1693, aged 22, census of 1715, Christ Church. Died c. 1737; will recorded 1737, of William Worrell, planter of St. Michael.

Wife Ann named as residual legatee and sole executrix and guardian of children [all minors] during widowhood, otherwise brother Dr. Jonathan Worrell, and brothers-in-law Hon. Thomas Harrison Esq., and Thomas Duke Esq., to be executors in trust and guardians.

In 1761, the burial is recorded in St. Michael of Ann Worrell, aged 60.

Children of William and Ann Worrell named in will of William[2] Worrell, 1737:—

    6. i. John[3] Dr., St. Thomas.

    7. ii. William.

    8. iii. Edward.

    iv. Ann; possibly buried St. Michael, August 1765.

    v. Sarah; buried, St. Michael, September 1781.

        Will of Sarah Worrell of St. Michael, spinster, proved September 1782. Legacies to:— sister-in-law, Catherine Worrell (wife of brother Edward); niece, Joanna Worrell, daughter of brother Edward. Executors, brothers William and Edward, and Thomas Phillips, one of the attorneys of Edward Worrell.

    vi. Elizabeth, baptised Christ Church, 1730.

        Named in will of aunt, Sarah Worrell, 1758; also in will of Elizabeth, widow, of her uncle Nathan Worrell, 1762. May be identified in the Power of Attorney dated March 1756, recorded July 1766, of Elizabeth Worrell 'late of island of Barbados now of city of Bath . . .' to Thomas Workman Esq., of island of Barbados . . . 'to collect from executors of Hon. Edward Jenkins, Esq., £50 legacy under Jenkins' will.

vii. Bathsheba, burial registered August 1780, St. Michael. Will of Bathsheba Worrell of St. Michael, spinster, proved September 1780. Legacies to — sister Sarah Worrell; niece Joanna Worrell, daughter of brother Edward; niece Eleanor Worrell daughter of brother William. Executor, brother, William Worrell.

In the event of his brother, George [2]Worrell, being without male issue, William [2]Worrell was named as legatee of the property of his father, John[1] Worrell, of St. Thomas. William, however, predeceased his brother George, and there is no record that any of the said property passed to his sons.

4. NATHAN[2] WORRELL (John[1]), born c. 1694; named in census, 1715, in St. Michael, aged 21, with 2 women, aged 20 and 36, and 2 boys, aged 1 year, and 6 months. Also named in his father's will, and as witness to the will of [his son-in-law] William Butler in 1747.

There is no record of his death, nor of any will. He pre-deceased his wife.

The baptism is registered in St. Michael, 22nd September 1716, of '. . . Elizabeth, wife of Nathan Worrell, aged about 19 years . . .' [Since the term 'about' is used, the discrepancy noted in the ages given in this and that of the census record may not be important.]

The death of Elizabeth Worrell, aged 65, is registered 16th June 1762, in St. Michael, and the will of Elizabeth Worrell of St. Michael, widow, relict of Nathan Worrell Esq., deceased, recorded on 12th July 1762, naming children and grand-children.

The children of Nathan[2] and Elizabeth Worrell are identified by baptism records and by references in the will of Elizabeth Worrell.

    i. Dr. John [3]Worrell, of St. Michael; cp. reference in census 1715, boy aged 1 year.

    ii. Richard, baptised 3rd August 1715; cp. reference in census 1715, to boy aged 4 months. Burial registered in St. Michael, 17th November 1716. 'Richard Worrell, a child. . . .'

    iii. Ann, baptised St. Michael, October 1716, died 1720, burial registered St. Michael.

    iv. Eleanor, married William Carney Butler, 1738, St. Thomas. His will is recorded in 1747 . . . 'William Butler of St. Michael, suddenly setting off for Jamaica . . .' Naming wife, Eleanor; witness, Nathan Worrell. This reference may indicate the connection with the eminent Butler family in Jamaica whose armorial bearings so closely resemble those of the Worrell family in Barbados and of the Harrison family (cp. Harrison College Arms).

        The will of Eleanor Butler, widow, recorded 1751, names son, Nathan, and daughters Mary, named in will of great-aunt, Sarah Worrell 1758, and Elizabeth named in the will of her grand-mother, Elizabeth Worrell, widow, in 1762. Guardians of children to be her mother, Elizabeth Worrell and her brother Nathan[3] Worrell.

9. v. Nathan,[3] baptised 22nd October 1728, St. Thomas.

In 1719, Nathan [2]Worrell sold to Benjamin Smith of St. Philip, watchmaker, for £45. 13. 7. 330 7/10 square feet of land and such part of house and long store as is on it. No reference is made to the site, but it is presumed that it was in St. Michael. The following year, 1720, Nathan Worrell of St. Michael, merchant, bought from George Worrell (his brother), for £540 a property of 30 acres, with houses etc., in St. Thomas, and the baptism of his son, Nathan, and the marriage of his daughter, Eleanor, are registered in St. Thomas.

The will of his widow, Elizabeth Worrell of St. Michael, in 1762, names, with certain legacies, her grand-daughters, Elizabeth Worrell and Mary Hurst (daughters of Dr. John Worrell of St. Michael), and grand-daughter Elizabeth Butler, as residual legatee. Also named is her deceased son, Nathan Worrell, and his sons Nathan, William and Jonathan. From the debt due her from deceased son Nathan, £100. to be raised for grand-daughter, Mary Hurst, and £150. to be equally divided between her 3 grand-sons abovenamed, which sum is '. . . to be unproved until each attain 21 years . . .' Nephew William Cobham to be sole executor and guardian. Elizabeth Butler recommended to his friendship and protection.

It may be noted that no reference is made to the property of deceased husband, William Worrell, in St. Thomas.

5. JONATHAN² WORRELL (John¹), of St. Thomas, Practitioner in 'Physick and Surgery' (as designated in will), was the ancestor of the last, most wealthy and most fully documented family of Worrells in Barbados. There is no record of his baptism but from his tombstone it is deduced that he was born in 1697. His burial is registered in 1753 in St. Thomas '. . . in family vault . . .' His monumental inscription transcribed by Dr. J. W. W. Carring-ton in 1853 reads:— "To the/ Memory of/ Doctor Jonathan Worrell/ Who closed an/ Useful life/ on the 21st September 1753/ aged 56. This stone is/ deposited by an/ affectionate and only/ Son.

The marriage of Jonathan Worrell of St. Thomas to Mary Bryan [t] of St. James is registered at St. James in 1721. Mary Bryan (Bryant, Briant) was the daughter of William and Mary Bryant, whose monument in St. Thomas Churchyard was erected by their grandson, J. Worrell.

The baptisms of only 2 of the children of Dr. Jonathan and Mrs. Mary Worrell are registered in St. Thomas, Jonathan: baptised 9th June, 1734 and Martha: baptised 16th September, 1739. The burials of 2 children are registered in St. Michael. William, son of Dr. Jonathan Worrell, 19th November 1738, and Martha, daughter of Jonathan Worrell, 20th September 1746. The surviving children of Dr. Jonathan² Worrell are named in his will of 1753.

      i. Sarah, cp. marriage 1757, St. James, to Edward Leamington of St. Joseph.

     ii. Mary, wife of John³ Worrell (John¹ William²) of St. Thomas, practitioner in 'Physick and Surgery.' Married, St. Thomas 21st December, 1746; buried in St. Michael 1797; will 1797. Dr. J. W. W. Carrington, her grandson, in his diaries, gives her age as 75 at the time of her death, which places the date of her birth in 1722.

10. iii. Jonathan³.

There is no mention of the property of Dr. Jonathan Worrell, thus it is difficult to determine whether he inherited the original property of his father John¹ Worrell willed 1st to eldest brother George² Worrell, and 2nd, failing an heir to George, to his next brother William² Worrell, William predeceased George, but left a son John³ Worrell, who married Mary, daughter of Dr.

Jonathan Worrell. Certainly his burial at Sturges seems to indicate that he resided on the original Worrell property.

6. JOHN[3] WORRELL (William[2] John[1]), Practitioner in 'Physick and Surgery', of St. Thomas. Identified as the eldest son of William[2] and Anne Worrell of St. Michael, named as a minor in the will of his father, William, in 1737. The marriage of Dr. John and Mrs. Mary Worrell is registered in St. Thomas on 21st December, 1746.

His wife Mary Worrell was his first cousin, daughter of his father's youngest brother, Dr. Jonathan[2] Worrell, in whose will of 1753, both Dr. John and his wife Mary are named.

There were 10 children of this marriage, the baptisms of 7 of whom are registered at St. Thomas, and the other 3 named in the wills of their parents, respectively:—

    i. Ann, baptised 1748; married John Marshall, St. Thomas, 1st January, 1778. Named in the will of her mother Mary Worrell, 1797, with her children: Mary Marshall, John Worrell Marshall, Samuel, William and Thomas Marshall.

    ii. Mary, baptised 3rd October 1749: Will of Mary Worrell of St. Michael, spinster, dated 26th March 1827, proved 16th August 1828, names, with legacies, her sisters, Martha Alleyne and Sarah Alleyne; her nephews Thomas Marshall (executor to will) and his wife Margaret Elizabeth and children Margaret Ann and Thomas Clarke Marshall. Also nephews John Edward Worrell Alleyne, son of sister Martha, and John William Worrell Carrington and his brother Nathaniel Thomas Worrell Carrington, sons of sister Jane.

    iii. Martha, no baptism recorded, but her nephew, Dr. J. W. W. Carrington, records her death on 9th August 1849, at the age of 101 years. It is possible that she may have been one of a twin with her sister Mary. The marriage of Martha Worrell to Dymock Alleyne is registered at St. Thomas, 11th September 1794. They had 1 son John Edward Worrell Alleyne, named in the will of his grand-mother, Mary Worrell in 1797, and in the will of his aunt, Mary Worrell, in 1827. Dr. J. W. W. Carrington records the death, on 4th September, 1799, of Dymock Alleyne, aged 36, by suicide with a gun.

    iv. Jonathan Worrell, baptised 9th April 1752, at St. Thomas. Identified with Jonathan Worrell of Barbados, died 26th November 1773, aged 22 years. Monumental Inscription in Bristol Cathedral [cp. *Caribbeana* Vol. II, p. 81].

    v. William Worrell, baptised 9th April 1756. Named as legatee of his father's estate in the latter's will, 1779. Since no subsequent reference is found concerning the said William Worrell, it is presumed that he died in 1779, his burial being that of William Worrell recorded in St. Michael in 1779.

    vi. Jane, baptised 23rd December, 1759 at St. Thomas; married Richard William Carrington, 3rd June, 1797, at St. Michael. Named in her mother's will in 1797, with her husband executor to said will. Their 2 sons, John William [s] Worrell Carrington and Nathaniel Thomas Worrell Carrington, are named in the will of her sister, Mary Worrell, spinster, of St.

Michael, in 1825 Dr. J. W. W. Carrington records the death of his mother in 1813, aged 52, buried in the family burial place at Sturges plantation. His father died in 1817, aged 66.

vii. John Worrell; no baptism recorded; named as a minor, in the will of his father in 1779, to be an executor of the same at 21. No further references have been identified and it is presumed that he died young.

viii. Elizabeth, baptised 6th December 1761, at St. Thomas and not subsequently named. Identified in the burial of Elizabeth Worrell, a child, at St. Thomas, 4th October, 1763.

ix. Eleanor; no baptism recorded. Burial of Eleanor, daughter of Dr. John and Mary Worrell registered 29th December, 1782, at St. Thomas.

x. Sarah; born 31st March, baptised 3rd April, 1768 at St. Thomas. Married Benjamin Alleyne, 6th September 1798, at St. Michael. Named, before marriage in her mother's will, 1797, and subsequently in the will of her sister, Mary, in 1825.

The burial of Dr. John Worrell is registered at St. Thomas on 27th September, 1785. His grandson, Dr. J. W. W. Carrington of St. Thomas records that he was buried in the Worrell family vault at Sturge's plantation. His will, dated 20th May, 1779, was signed and sealed, but not attested. After his death, on the petition of John Marshall of St. Thomas his son-in-law, one of the appointed executors, the will was admitted by H.E. David Parry, Esq., Governor, and was proved and recorded on 13th October, 1785.

The location of his property, left to his son, William, is not indicated. At the time of his death only one of his daughters, Sarah, the eldest, was married, and a legacy of £100. was left to her daughter, Mary Marshall at 21. His wife and unmarried daughters with his younger surviving son, John, were to live in his house, or have a 'decent habitation near the estate' rented for them; and certain legacies in cash at 21. His expressed wish was that 'my family shall live in peace and harmony with each other and render to each other and every other person every service in their power . . . I am to be buried in a plain and frugal manner without any kind of parade . . .'

His appointed executors were his sons William and John (at 21), his son-in-law John Marshall, Thomas Walke, (a relative, the son of his father's 1st cousin Mary née Harrison), and Gabriel Ford. His wife to be executrix during her widowhood.

The will of Mary Worrell of St. Michael, widow, is dated 19th August, 1797. She names her daughters, Ann Marshall, Martha Alleyne, and their respective husbands and children also daughter, Jane Carrington and her husband, and daughter, Sarah Worrell, as yet unmarried. Appointed executors were her 3 sons-in-law, previously named, witnesses:— Eleanor Gill [daughter of her husband's brother, William Worrell], Joanna Worrell [daughter of husband's brother Edward Worrell], and Antipas Carrington [relative of son-in-law, Richard William Carrington].

7. WILLIAM³ WORRELL (William² John¹), the 2nd son of William and Ann Worrell; no baptism recorded, but named as a minor in his father's will in 1737.

2 marriages are recorded of a William Worrell of this period —
(1) St. Michael, 19th December 1755: William Worrell to Joanna Neil. Joanna Neil was the daughter of Eleanor Neil, née Harrison, 1st cousin to William[3] Worrell. There is no further record of a Joanna Worrell at this period.
(2) St. James, in 1761: William Worrell to Eleanor Carleton. Wife Eleanor is named in the will of William[3] Worrell in 1785, and 3 daughters, the baptism of only 1 of whom is recorded in St. James in 1762 (born 1761). William Worrell was appointed attorney to his brother Edward Worrell, formerly of Barbados, now of St. Christopher. Power dated 24th October, 1780, recorded 14th February, 1782.

In 1784 William Worrell was appointed by William Senhouse, Surveyor-General, to supply the place of the said Edward Worrell, during his absence, as Deputy Waiter of H.M. Customs at the port of Bridgetown. Power dated 22nd November, 1784; recorded 1788.

The burial of William, 'husband of Eleanor Worrell' is registered in St. Michael, 28th September, 1785. The will of William Worrell is dated 17th September, proved 30th October, 1785. He does not specifically name his property, which was to be appraised after payment of all debts and charges, ⅓ of such appraisement to go to daughter Eleanor, wife of John Gill, merchant of Barbados, subject to her paying ⅓ of his wife's annuity of £30 per annum, and ⅓ of the legacies to his grandsons, John and William, sons of daughter, Eleanor.

The residue of his estate to his daughters Susan and Elizabeth, who were to be executors with his wife . . . with the advice of his brother Edward, now in Great Britain, his son-in-law, John Gill, his kinsman John Walke, Charles Padmore and other friends named.

By a deed recorded in 1810, Eleanor Worrell sold to Hon. John Spooner of St. Michael, for £30, 1 parcel of land in St. Michael containing 2 roods 6 perches, bounding on land of Eleanor Worrell, Mary Parsons, said John Spooner and the Broad Road . . . with appurtenances thereto belonging.

The burial of Eleanor Worrell is registered in St. Michael in 1810. The children of William[3] Worrell:—

    i. Eleanor Worrell; no baptism recorded. First named as residuary legatee in will of aunt, Bathsheba Worrell, 1769, as . . . 'niece Eleanor Worrell, daughter of brother William Worrell . . .' 1st marriage recorded in St. Michael 22nd May, 1777, Eleanor Worrell to John Lewis;* died 1779; had daughter, Joanna Lewis. 2nd marriage recorded in St. Michael, 1781 to John Gill; named as wife of John Gill, merchant, in her father's will 1785, with 2 sons John and William Gill.

    ii. Susan Worrell; born 8th September, 1761; baptised St. James, 10th October, 1762. Named in father's will, 1785.
(cp. baptism St. Michael, 17th July, 1805, of Anna Samuel, natural daughter of Susan Worrell?)

    iii. Elizabeth Worrell; no baptism recorded; named in father's will, 1785. Married 2nd January, 1788, St. Michael, to Samuel Padmore Jnr., (cp. Charles Padmore, named as friend in will of father William, 1785.

* John Lewis was appointed in 1779 as an attorney to Edward Worrell, uncle of said Eleanor Worrell.

8. EDWARD[3] WORRELL (William[2] John[1]), 3rd son of William and Ann Worrell, named as a minor in the will of his father in 1737. Edward Worrell was twice married — 1st as recorded in the baptism in St. Michael of Joanna, daughter of William and Elizabeth Worrell, born 28th March, baptised 7th April, 1761. Joanna Worrell is named subsequently in the wills of 2 of her father's sisters.

2nd marriage recorded 9th February, 1766, in St. Michael: Edward Worrell, gent., to Katherine Niccolls, spinster, by Revd. Mr. John Carter.

Katherine Worrell is named as sister-in-law in the will of her husband's sister Sarah in 1782. The burial of Katherine Worrell is registered in St. Michael in 1805.

Edward Worrell was a Waiter of H.M. Customs, at the port of Bridgetown. During the years 1763-1784 he was frequently if not continuously away from Barbados. It is possible that his 1st wife, Elizabeth, died abroad. In 1777, 1779 and 1780 Edward Worrell was in St. Christopher. In 1784 his daughter Joanna was in Plymouth, Co. Devon, having been formerly in St. Christopher. In 1785, Edward Worrell was in Great Britain, as referred to by his brother William. It is probable that he died in Great Britain.

Of the children of Edward Worrell, only daughter Joanna is definitely identified. In 1810, a deed of sale of slaves to Hon. John Beckles of St. James is recorded by 3 Worrell spinsters of St. Michael, whose names suggest they were the daughters of Edward and his wife Katherine Worrell (sometimes spelt Catherine).

    i. Joanna, baptised in St. Michael 1781; daughter of Edward and Elizabeth Worrell; named in will of aunt, Bathsheba Worrell, 1769, and as residual legatee in the will of her aunt, Sarah Worrell in 1782.

       In 1784, Joanna Worrell, sometime of St. Christopher in West Indies, now of Plymouth, County Devon, appointed attorneys in Barbados to sell her slaves. Deeds of 1803, 1805 and 1809 record the sales of slaves by Joanna Worrell, spinster, of St. Michael. The three spinsters mentioned above were:

    ii. Williama Wells Worrell.

    iii. Catherine Edward Niccolls Worrell.

    iv. Eliza Julia Ward Worrell.

9. NATHAN[3] WORRELL (Nathan[2] John[1]), the only surviving child of Nathan and Elizabeth Worrell, baptised at St. Thomas, 22nd October, 1728; married Mary West, in St. Michael, 26th January, 1752; buried in St. Michael 8th January, 1762.

The will of Nathan Worrell is dated 6th January, 1762, and he died without being able to sign it. It was made for him by William Duke, and read to said Nathan, who declined to execute same, saying that he had nothing to make a will about, but agreeing that it was right for his wife to adminster his estate according to the terms of the will. Probate was allowed of the unsigned will, on 12th January, 1762.

The 4 sons of Nathan and his wife Mary Worrell are named in the will of their grandmother, Elizabeth Worrell, in 1762.

    i. John: born 22nd November, 1753; baptised 1754 in St. Michael.

    ii. Nathan: born 19th January, 1756; baptised 27th April, 1757, in St. Michael.

iii. William Cobbah (*sic*): no baptism recorded.

iv. Jonathan: no baptism recorded.

(No subsequent reference to these children has been found).

10. JONATHAN[3] WORRELL (Dr. Jonathan[2] John[1]), baptised 9th June, 1734 at St. Thomas, only son of Dr. Jonathan Worrell and his wife Mary, née Bryant, was 19 years old at the time of his father's death in 1753. Having matriculated at Glasgow University in 1752, his father willed that he should continue studying Physic until he was 25 years old, with an allowance of £125. per annum until he finished his studies. At the age of 25 he was to inherit his father's estate, but no property was named.

It is not known whether he finished his studies, but he was never a Practitioner of Physic. He returned to Barbados and became the wealthiest landed proprietor of all the Worrell family in this island.

Jonathan[3] Worrell was twice married and had 10 children of whom the baptismal record of only one has been found.

His first marriage to Jane Harrison is registered at St. Thomas on 20th July, 1760. Jane Harrison was the daughter of Dr. George Harrison of St. Michael, the eldest son of Hon. Thomas Harrison and his wife Eleanor, sister of Dr. Jonathan Worrell.

There is no record of the death of Jane, first wife of Jonathan[3] Worrell, nor of his marriage to his second wife, Catherine, who survived him. In 1780 Jonathan Worrell was in Ipswich, Suffolk, but when he left Barbados is not known. He never returned to the island, but acquired the property Juniper Hall, Mickleham, Surrey, where he lived until his death in 1814. His burial place is in the churchyard of the parish Church there, with his wife and one of their daughters, as recorded on the monumental slab:—
"In this vault/are deposited the Remains/ of Jonathan Worrell Esq./ of Juniper Hall in this Parish/who departed this Life/the 26th January 1814/ Aged 79 years./ ALSO/ the remains of Bridgetta/ Daughter of the above/ and wife of Henry Knight Esq., who died at Brightelmstone/ 19th November, 1815/ Aged 43 years./ ALSO/ the Remains of/ Mrs. Catherine Worrell/ Relict of the above/ Jonathan Worrell, Esq./ Died September 1st 1835/ Aged 87 years."

Jonathan[3] Worrell was evidently a man of considerable wealth. Besides his father's estate, he was also the residual legatee of the estate of his grand-father, William Bryant of St. James, by the latter's will in 1757. William Bryant was the owner of plantations in St. James, St. Thomas and St. Andrew, in each of which parishes he left an endowment for the education and clothing of 2 poor boys and 2 poor girls.

The legacies to his Worrell grandchildren and great-grandchildren were numerous and valuable. The names of the various plantations owned by William Bryant are not known, but it is likely that Sedgepond in St. Andrew, named as the property of Jonathan[3] Worrell, was one of them.

Jane Harrison, first wife of Jonathan[3] Worrell, was also heiress of considerable property, in possession of her husband during his lifetime and reverting to their son, William Bryant Worrell, at his death. Among this property was the plantation Sturges, of 115 acres, named for the first time in 1789.

Other plantations named as the property of Jonathan Worrell were Neils, in St. George and St. Michael, The Spring in St. Thomas and the

Jonathan Worrell. 1734 — 1814, by
Ozias Humphry.
By permission of the late Mrs. A. E. Sealy.

Arms of the Worrell Family; Azure,
3 covered cups, Argent; on a chief,
Or, 2 lions, passant, Sable.
Crest: In a lion's gamb, erect and
erased, a covered cup.

Mrs. Jonathan Worrell as Hebe by Benjamin West (1738 — 1820).
Oil on canvas, 50 x 39½ inches.
By permission of the Trustees of the Tate Gallery, London.

Hill (or 'Scotia') in St. Andrew and St. Peter. These 3 plantations were at one time in the possession of the Harrison families.

In addition to his considerable landed property in Barbados, some of his interests in which he disposed of in 1800, in 1803 and 1804 Jonathan[3] Worrell purchased certain tracts of very valuable land in Prince Edward Island, in the Gulf of St. Lawrence, amounting to some 24,700 acres in all.

By his will of 1811/14 Jonathan[3] Worrell left handsome endowments to his 8 surviving children — 5 sons and 3 daughters none of whom had children themselves. Of these, several were themselves generous bene- factors, as shown by their respective wills. Among their various bene- ficiaries were Dr. J. W. W. Carrington of St. Thomas and his brother N. T. W. Carrington of St. Joseph, with their wives, respectively, referred to as being "next of kin" to the Worrells in Great Britain. These Carringtons appear to have valued this family relationship as is shown by the use of the name 'Worrell' for nearly all of their children.

Except for the first, there are no baptisms recorded of any of the other children of Jonathan[3] Worrell, and but for this first child, and his son William Bryant Worrell, there is no indication as to which were his children by his first wife, Jane, née Harrison, and which, if any, by his second wife Catherine. The children of Jonathan[3] Worrell:—

     i. Mary, baptised 1761 St. Thomas, daughter of Jonathan and Jane Worrell.

11. ii. William Bryant[4] Worrell, identified as eldest son of Jonathan and Jane Worrell.

12. iii. Jonathan, born c. 1766/7; died at Frampost, East Grinstead, Sussex, 1843, in 77th year.

13. iv. Charles, born c. 1770; died in London in 1858, aged 88; unmarried.

     v. Harriet, born c. 1771; died in London, 1858, aged 88; buried in the family burial place in Mickleham (Mitcham).

        The will of Harriet Worrell of 43 Jermyn Street, St. James, Westminster, London, spinster, is dated in 1838, with 7 codicils following — the last dated 1858. It contains much interesting information. In the 1st codicil, dated in 1851, she refers to the portrait of ". . . our late mother" to be preserved by her remaining brothers and sisters, and after their deaths to be given to ". . . one or other of the National Picture Galleries, in order that it may be handed down to posterity as a specimen of the painting of that eminent artist the late Sir Benjamin West and likewise of female beauty of the last century . . ."

        Also referred to in this codicil is her ". . . . father's miniature portrait, set around with diamonds . . ." left to her sister, Mrs. Boulton. In July 1856, however, Harriet Worrell sent this miniature, with the following note: 'A good likeness of my own father, presented with my kindest love to Mrs. Doctor Carrington, as the wife of our next of kin' (in Barbados). This miniature has been handed down through the female descendants of Dr. J. W. W. Carrington to a great grand- daughter of the present day. The miniature is by Ozias Humphry, R.A. (1742-1810). The portrait of Mrs. Worrell by Benjamin West, R.A., is in the collections of The Tate

Gallery, London, and is reproduced by permission of the Trustees.

vi. Bridgetta, born c. 1772; married Henry Knight, Esq.; no issue, died in 1815; aged 43; buried in the family burial place at Mickleham, cp. Monumental inscription.

Bridgetta Worrell was the constructor of a model of Juniper Hall, which was much prized by her brothers and sisters. In the first codicil of her will 1851, Harriet Worrell refers to this model as having been in her 'undivided care for 40 years, and is in perfect condition and in my opinion worthy of a place in the Great Exhibition of 1851'. This family treasure eventually passed, in 1865, to Mrs. Boulton, the sole surviving member of this family.

14. vii. Septimus, date of birth not identified. Died in 1856, buried at Mickleham (Mitcham).

viii. Thomas, born c. 1776; died at Highland Plantation in St. Thomas, Barbados, the property of his brother Jonathan, in 1802, aged 26.

15. ix. Edward, born c. 1786, died in London, 1865, aged 79; buried at Mickleham (Mitcham).

x. Cecilia (or Celia) Maria: date of birth not identified. She was not married in 1811/12 (the dates of her father's will) and was a widow in 1842, so named in the will of her brother Jonathan. The name of her husband is not mentioned. Mrs. Boulton (or Bolton) survived all her brothers and sisters, and with the death of Dr. J. W. W. Carrington in 1866, their nearest relative in Barbados, all contact with the Worrell family and Barbados seems to have ended. The date of her death has not been identified.

11. WILLIAM BRYANT[4] WORRELL (Jonathan[3] Jonathan[2] John[1]), eldest son of Jonathan Worrell and his first wife Jane, née Harrison, and sole heir of his mother's properties. No records of his birth or baptism, nor of his education have been identified. He left Barbados in or about 1789, and in 1792 was 'now of Inner Temple, London.' In 1816 William Bryant Worrell late of Parish of St. Clement Danes, Middlesex, Barrister-at-law, and member of Hon. Society of Inner Temple' was 'at present residing at Probats Hotel, King Street, Covent Garden, but intending shortly to reside at Rouen in France'. He married a French woman, Marie Anne Elizabeth Catherine Amand, but the date of his marriage has not been identified. He owned a property in the Commune of Canmont, Dept. of the Eure. consisting of a house, farm and effects, bought from a Mrs. Morris. In 1824-25, William Bryant Worrell was 'living upon his income, residing at No. 27 Crosne Street, City of Rouen' where he made his first will in 1824, and his last in 1825. He died on 14th March, 1832, when residing at No. 20 Beffroy Street, Rouen. After his death, his widow seems to have spent some time with his family in London. In 1841, she was resident in Jermyn Street, London, where her sister-in-law, Harriet Worrell was living at the time. She died in Rouen on 21st April, 1853. There were no children of the marriage.

There are numerous records concerning the property of William Bryant Worrell in Barbados. From his mother he inherited Sturges plantation in

632

St. Thomas, containing 155 acres, as well as a small property called Somerville in the same parish, a small property in St. Andrew, a house and land in Speightstown, and "The Retreat" in St. Michael. On leaving Barbados in or about 1789, he instructed his attorneys to sell all or any of this property, and only the plantation Sturges seems to have been left unsold at the time of his death in 1832.

By his father's will of 1814, William Bryant Worrell inherited the plantations Neils in St. Michael and St. George, "The Spring" in St. Thomas and "The Hill" in St. Andrew and St. Peter. [The latter has been identified with the plantation formerly known as 'the Overhill, and in the earliest days as "Scotia" or "Skeetes."]

His widow was the sole legatee of all of the property of William Bryant Worrell, both in France and in Barbados. His will, proved in London in 1832, was not allowed or recorded in Barbados until 1840, when the legatee was 'deemed an alien' and the properties, Neils, Sturges and the Hill, were escheated to the Crown and put up for sale by the Receiver General of Casual Revenue. John Montefiore bought Neils for £8,266.13.4; Eyare King and Christopher Gill bought Sturges for £9,933.6.8; and James Corbin bought The Hill for £3,864.8.4. [Messrs. King and Gill were relatives of the Worrell family.]

No reference to the plantation 'The Spring' has been identified.

In 1841, upon a petition by the widow, Madame Marie Anne Catherine Worrell, to H.M. Commissioners of Treasury, a grant of the purchase money was made over to her.

12. JONATHAN[4] WORRELL (Jonathan[3] Jonathan[2] John[1]), born c. 1766/67, but whether a child of his father's first marriage or of his second, has not been identified. He left Barbados in 1816 and bought the property Frampost, in East Grinstead, Sussex, where he lived until his death in 1843, in his 77th year. In an obituary notice published in *The Barbadian* newspaper of 29th March, 1843, it is said of him 'in kindness of heart, generous hospitality, charity and plain unsophisticated manners, Mr. Worrell was a perfect example of the "old English gentleman'." He was survived by his wife Rebecca Wilson Worrell, who was the daughter of Hon. Samuel Hinds, the Elder, of St. Peter, named in his will, entered in February 1808. There is no record of his marriage. Also named in the will of Jonathan Worrell is Rebecca Worrell Clarke, wife of George Elliott Clarke, Esq., and probably the only child of Jonathan and his wife Rebecca Wilson Worrell.* His widow, Rebecca, died at Frampost in 1851, aged 75.

Jonathan[4] Worrell remained in Barbados longer than the other members of his family. In 1796, he bought Highland plantation in St. Thomas for £10,000. Here his brother Thomas died in 1802.

By his father's will in 1814, Jonathan Worrell inherited 5,000 acres of land and property in Prince Edward Island, besides a legacy of £3,000, and was appointed one of the executors in trust of his father's property in Barbados.

In 1816, he left the island to live in England, where he bought his property, "Frampost." In 1821, he had recently sold his plantation Highland, in Barbados, to Thomas McIntosh of Bridgetown, planter.

By his will made in 1842 Jonathan Worrell left his freehold property of Frampost in trust for his wife, after her death, to (their daughter ?) Mrs. Rebecca Worrell Clarke, then to her husband G. E. Clarke, then to

* This assumption is based on the testator's references to his sister as Cecilia *Worrell* Bolton (sic).

their eldest daughter, Rebecca Worrell Clarke and after her for her children as tenants-in-common.

His share in Sedgepond plantation, and all his other real estate in Barbados he left to his surviving 3 brothers, Charles, Edward and Septimus, and 2 sisters, Harriet Worrell and Cecilia Worrell Bolton [*sic*] as tenants in common.

13. CHARLES[4] WORRELL (Jonathan[3] Jonathan[2] John[1]), born c. 1770; unmarried; died at his residence in London, 17 Mitford Street, Edgeware Road, aged about 88. For many years Charles[4] Worrell lived in Prince Edward Island, where his father owned extensive properties, acquired in 1803 and 1804.

Records show that Charles was living in Prince Edward Island from c. 1811, and possibly before, until 1841, or possibly later. The date of his return to England is not known. His will was made and signed in 1855 at his "country residence of Hope House, Kew Green, Surrey." His residence in London, where he died, is first mentioned in 1856.

By his father's will (1811), Charles Worrell was left an equal share, with his younger brother Edward, of a certain tract of 20,000 acres of land in Prince Edward Island, 'very valuable property', and also 1/7 share of the plantation Sedgepond in Barbados and a legacy of £3,000.

In 1841, he sold his 1/7 share in Sedgepond to his brother Edward.

He died on 6th January, 1858, and his will was proved in London on 12th March, 1858. His will, dated 1855, directed that his estate should be sold and the proceeds invested and income to be paid to Malvina Amanda Mary Ann Butler Friend, wife of George Friend, for her life, and the capital and income to such of her children as she should appoint. Legacies were left to London Hospital, and to certain relatives and friends, including £500 to Dr. J. W. W. Carrington of Barbados, 'the grandson of my father's sister, Mary Worrell.'

14. SEPTIMUS[4] WORRELL (Jonathan[3] Jonathan[2] John[1]), date of birth not identified; name suggests that he was the seventh child, but whether by his father's first or second marriage is unknown.

He was unmarried and died in May 1856; buried at Mickleham (Mitcham).

Septimus Worrell is named in numerous records of deeds pertaining to the family properties, etc.

He was an officer of the Regiment of H.M. Coldstream Guards, but his rank is not mentioned.

With his brothers and sisters he was equally endowed under his father's will of 1814, with a share of 4,000 acres of the property in Prince Edward Island, a share in the plantation Sedgepond, cash legacy of £3,000, etc.

From his sister-in-law, widow of his deceased brother, William Bryant Worrell, he inherited a share in the proceeds of the sale of Sturges plantation in 1841.

In 1845, with his brother Edward Worrell, as executors etc., 4/5 of the family property of Sedgepond in Barbados was sold to Alexander Corbin of Barbados, 1/5 being retained by Septimus Worrell, then the last Worrell proprietor of real estate in the island, until his death in 1856, when it was bought by the same Alexander Corbin.

By his will (and codicils) dated in 1854 and 1855, Septimus Worrell left generous legacies to many of his old friends in the Guards Regiments, or their dependants, as well as to numerous other persons, among them being a legacy 'of £1,000, to be applied for the benefit of Carrington Worrell of Barbados, West Indies, and his family, provided that evidence be established that he is a relative of my late father'. [No Carrington Worrell has been identified, but there were several Worrell Carringtons.] Doctors, hospitals, and many persons in adverse circumstances were also among the beneficiaries.

His share in Sedgepond plantation, previously mentioned, went to his 2 surviving brothers, Charles and Edward, and 2 sisters, Harriet Worrell and Cecilia Boulton.

His collection of paintings, etc., were left to the care of his executor and friend Erskine Tustin, 'knowing he will keep them together and dispose of them satisfactorily at his death'. No further information as to this collection, or its merits, has been discovered.

15. EDWARD[4] WORRELL (Jonathan[3] Jonathan[2] John[1]), born c. 1786; unmarried; died in London, 27th February, 1865, aged 79; buried in family vault at Mitcham (Mickleham).

From a reference in his will, Edward Worrell was a member of the firm of Messrs. Drummond, Bankers, of Charing Cross, to whom he left a sum of money to be divided between such clerks as had been in their service for 7 years previous to his death.

As with his brothers and sisters, Edward[4] Worrell was equally well endowed by his father, and various deeds, etc., show that he had a prominent part in the management of the family affairs.

In 1845, he received from his sister-in-law, Marie Worrell, widow of his deceased brother William Bryant Worrell, ½ of the trust fund derived from the sale of the Worrell estates, Sturges, etc., in Barbados, which had been her husband's property. In 1855, Edward Worrell conveyed this share, valued at £4,599.8.4. with 2 years interest in arrears, to the recently widowed wife of N. T. W. Carrington, of Barbados, brother of his relative Dr. J. W. W. Carrington.

By the year 1853, Edward Worrell had become possessed of 4/5 of the remaining Worrell property in Barbados — Sedgepond plantation 226 acres, in St. Andrew and St. Peter, which he sold for £2,400 to Alexander Corbin of St. Peter. Up to the time of his death in 1865, Edward Worrell kept in close touch with his Carrington relatives in Barbados, with frequent gifts in money or kind, as recorded by Dr. J. W. W. Carrington.

Edward Worrell died suddenly, at his residence, 71, St. James's Street, London, on 27th February, 1865, survived only by his sister Mrs. Boulton, appointed as his residuary legatee, to whom he left the portrait of his mother by Sir Benjamin West, for her life, and thereafter to the trustees of the 'National Gallery of Pictures in Trafalgar Square.' A very large number of beneficiaries are named in his will — relatives, friends, employees, public institutions, poor relief, etc.

Among his relatives are named:— Dr. J. W. W. Carrington, of Barbados, J. E. W. Alleyne†, then of Prince Edward Island and his 3 sons. After the death of Edward[4] Worrell in 1865, and that of his relative Dr. J. W. W. Carrington of Barbados in 1866, no further references to these Worrells have been traced.

---

† The son of Martha and Dymock Alleyne of Barbados. His mother was Martha Worrell, sister of Jane, mother of Dr. J. W. W. Carrington.

SOME BARBADOS RECORDS OF THE WRONG FAMILY

Will of JACOB WRONG dated 24th June 1704, of the parish of St James. To wife Eliza Wrong two slaves by name, stock and household furniture and all rest and residue of Estate for her life. At her death as follows, To John Steward and Eliza Steward his sister, the children of John Steward, my house and land whereon I now dwell equally to be divided. To the said John Steward, my gun and sword. To Anne, daughter of Joseph Russell dec'd a slave girl, Sarah. To John Smith son of Thomas Smith a slave by name. To Isaac Wright one gold ring 20/–. To my four bearers to the grave one gold ring 20/– value each. Wife Eliza Wrong to be sole executrix.

Witnesses: John Leach, Thomas Robinson, William Teague.

Proved 22nd October 1704.

Will of HENRY WRONG, carpenter, of the parish of St. James. To son Henry Wrong one negro slave and "all my plantations of lands and buildings whereon I now live" at 21 or marriage. All rest, residue of estate to children, John, Elias, Sarah and Mary Wrong at 21 or marriage. In case of death of any child respective share to be divided amongst survivors. Brothers John Wrong, Jacob Wrong, William Carter and Daniel Robinson to be executors.

Dated 28th March 1735

Wits: William Stewart, Samuel Browne.

Proved 27th August 1735.

Will of JOHN WRONG of the parish of St John. To my son John Wrong and Mary Wrong (sic) all estate real and personal to be equally divided between them and their survivors forever. My father Elisher Moore, brother William Smith and cousin John Wrong to be executors and guardians of my children.

Dated 21st October 1737

Wits. Bryan Ellis, John King, Jno Ellis.

Proved 5th November 1731.

Will of JACOB WRONG of St Peter's All Saints Parish. To cousin John Goodridge's three children Mary, Thomas and Sarah Goodridge £100 that lies in the hands of Mr. Thomas Treasurer, until the eldest is 21. To godson Thomas Weir £25 at 21. To cousin Felix Goodridge's chiln Jacob, Mary and Sarah Goodridge £5 each. To cousin Richard Nurse's chiln, Mary and Sarah Nurse £5. To cousin Samuel Marshall's son John £5 at 21. To wife Katherine Wrong the remainder of my estate for life and at her death to cousin William Marshall son of Samuel Marshall, house land and slaves. Wife Katherine to be executrix and two friends James Hackett and Felix Goodridge executors.

Dated 1st May 1749.

Wits: Richard Nurse, Samuel Goodridge.

Proved 21st June 1749.

Will of ANN WRONG of the parish of St John. To dau Mary six slaves by name, bedstead and furniture of chamber. Also "a part of two negro slaves now in possession of my grandmother, Ann Rudder which I come in as co-heir for with my sister Mary Yearwood". In case of daughter's death to son Rich-

ard Wrong. To Richard all rest residue. In case of both children's death then to sister Mary Yearwood. Lastly I nominate Richard Wooding, John Mitcham and Dr Francis Prinne (?) executors.
Dated 12th Oct 1762
Wits: William Cragg, John Smith, Josias Arthur.
Proved 3rd Jany 1763.

Will of KATHERINE WRONG of St. Peter. Remainder of money after expenses are paid to niece Katherine McDonald and goddaughter Elizabeth Agard. Slaves to be sold and money to educate nephew and niece Anguish and Katherine McDonald the chiln of Anguish and Elizabeth McDonald. Slaves to be sold and money entrusted to friend Philip Gibbes Jr. To slave Diana £5. Friends John Agard, Thomas Middleton and Jacob Scott executors.
Dated 5th March 1762.
Wits: William Holland, Joseph Price.
Proved 14th March 1763.

Will of ISAAC WRONG of St Peter's. To wife Mercy Wrong £200 and one-third of real and personal estate. Money to be collected and paid to son John Wrong at 21. £40 per ann. to be given to wife Mercy Wrong. All estate to be divided between son John Wrong and daughter Ann Christian Wrong to be put out to interest. Remainder of estate to be divided between brother John Wrong and sister Sarah Wrong, sister Alice Leacock and niece Elizabeth, daughter of Thomas and Mary Denny. Then goddaughter Sarah Goodridge, goddaughter Rebecca Armstrong £50. Wife Mercy Wrong, brother in law John Wrong friend Joseph Leacock and friend Benjamin Yearwood to be executors.
Wits: Harris Drayton, Moses Olton, Joseph Arnold.
Dated (sic) May 1768.   Proved 25th Nov. 1772.

Will of JOHN WRONG of St. James. To wife Sarah Wrong estate real and personal as long as she remains my widow: at her death to be divided between children Henry, John, Isaac, Christian and Sarah Wrong; in case of death to their heirs. Wife Sarah to be executrix, Sons Henry Wrong and John Wrong executors.
Dated 17th June 1779.
Wits: Henry Piggott, John Marshall.
Proved 16th November 1782.

Will of ISAAC WRONG of St. James. To wife Olevy Rains Wrong whole estate as long as she remains a widow and at her death to be divided among surviving children. In case of wife's remarriage estate to be divided among surviving children. Wife Olevy Raines Wrong to be executrix and sons John, Henry, Isaac, Robert Bassett and James Wrong executors.
Dated 4th August 1812
Wits: J. B. Williams, Henry C. Bayley, Edward Henry Whitehall.
Proved 24th April 1820.

Will of JOHN WRONG of St Michael. All estate real and personal to wife Elizabeth Ann and her heirs forever. Wife to be executrix and friends Thomas Granger Nicholls and Conrade Adams Howell executors.
Dated 25th October 1841.
Wits: Cragg Gowdey, John P. Smith.
Proved 28th November 1845

Will of ELIZABETH ANN WRONG of St. Michael widow. £41. 13. 4
to the Ladies Association for the Relief of the Indigent Sick and Infirm. To
the St. Michael Clothing Society £41. 13. 4. To my sister-in-law Mary Gibbs
Hinkson £166. 13. 4. To each of my sisters-in-law Esther Francis Wrong,
Christian Broadhead wife of John Broadhead and Sarah Ann Wrong £83. 6. 8.
To each of my nieces in law Olivia Christian Bayley, Frances Ann Clive wife
of Joseph Clive, Ann Leacock Broadhead, Maria Catherine Broadhead, Sarah
Eliza Broadhead, Susan Rebecca Broadhead, Mary Elizabeth Broadhead, Frances
Olivia Hinkson, Maris Luisa Wrong, Frances Elizabeth Wrong and Cordelia
Ann Wrong at 21 £208. 6. 8. To said niece in law Frances Olivia Hinkson
my mahogany wardrobe. To doctor Wm. Clarke £41. 13. 4. To Elizabeth
Thornhill Howell, Letitia Jane Howell, Thomasin Ann Howell, and Anna Louisa
Howell, daus of my friend Conrade Adams Howell £83. 6. 8. at 21. To Avis
Padmore £125 and all household furniture. To Mary Spencer and Carola Martha
Willoughby £10. 8. 4. To Catherine Smith widow of John Smith £20. 16. 8.
To Elizabeth Lorenza Whittaker Yearwood dau. of John Washington Yearwood
£80. 6. 8. at 21. To Olive Fitt, Agnes Branch Fitt, Elizabeth Frances Fitt,
Mary Ann Fitt, Sarah Christian Fitt, Charlotte Jane Healis, daughters of Robert
John Fitt £10. 8. 4. each at 21. To Sophia Amelia Burton daughter of Thomas
William Burton £20. 16. 8. at 21. Shares in West India Bank to Robert
Bassett Wrong of British Guiana. Land in Hole Town to sister-in-law Mary
Gibbs Hinkson. Dr. William Clarke, Conrade Adams Howell executors.
Dated 16th April 1851.
Wits: W. H. Allder, Edward Wason.
Codicil dated 5th January 1853, for disposal of property recently acquired in
St Michael.

EXTRACTS OF POWERS OF ATTORNEY

JOHN WRONG of the parish of St John, merchant, intending suddenly to
depart this island for North America . . . appoint wife, Elizabeth Wrong, and
friend Thomas Whitney attorney-at-law to be my attorneys . . .
Dated 1st July 1773. Recorded 12th May 1774.

British Guiana,
County of Demerara.
I, Maria Louisa Wrong of the county and colony aforesaid appoint
Isaac Wrong at present residing in the island of Barbados to be my true and
lawfull attorney . . .to receive from the executors of the Estate of the late
Elizabeth Ann Wrong . . . the sum of £208. 6. 8. and such other sums due me
under the will of the said Elizabeth Ann Wrong.
Dated 14th November 1861.
Wits: Thomas Hunt, William Wharton.
Proved 30th November 1861.

ISAAC WRONG of the island of Barbados Esquire, but intending shortly
to depart the same, appoint Thomas Stone Eve of the parish of St Michael, merchant, to be the substitute attorney of Maria Louisa Wrong of the county of
Demerara in the colony of British Guiana........in her place to act....according
to the Letter of Attorney of the said Maria Louisa Wrong given to the said
Isaac Wrong.
Dated 31st December 1861. Wits: Samuel Gibbes Busby.

MONUMENTAL INSCRIPTION

St Michael's Cathedral graveyard. South of walk around chancel, single
grave with inscription—
JOHN WRONG / departed this life / November the 14th. 1845 / Aged
55 Years.

Yeamans of Barbados.

Blanch Yeomans of the cittie of Bristoll, widdow, l. the wife and Ex'trix of the will of John Y., l. of the same, brewer, deceased. Will dated 30 April 1647. To be buried in the church of Redcliffe near my husband, £20 as a stock for the poore to be paid yearly in bread. To the poore of S[t] Thomas £3. My kinsman Phillipp Benfield £5. £10 amongst the 5 ch[n] of James Walton, cooper, deceased. My kinsman Fra. Yeomans £10 and to his sisters Sarah Rider and Eliz. Owen 40s. apeece. I nominate my s. Rob. Y. and my sons-in-law John Pope, John Woory and Peter Hyley Ex'ors and £5 apiece. To my sons Geo., John, Robert, Joseph and Rich[d] Y. £200 each. To my s. Wm. Y. £100. To my daus. Eliz. Pyett, Mary Wathen, Anne Warren, Patience Woory, Sarah Pope, Martha Tomlinson and Johane Hiley £200 each. To my granddau. Marie Wathen £100. My s. Joseph hath given bond to my s. Rob[t] for £100 he owes me, that bond and the debt of £60 my s. Rob. owes me to be accompted part of my estate. To the poor of Temple parish £6. All residue to my 13 ch[n] and my granddau. Mary Wathen. Sealed this 4 May 1647 in the presence of Fra. Y., not. pub. and others. Proved 20 July 1647 by Rob. Y., J. Pope, J. Woory and P. Hiley (160, Fines).

George Yeomans of London, Merchant. Will dated 19 Sep. 1653. Bound on a voyage to parts beyond the sea. My cargo in the "Golden Lion" whereof Rich. Husbands is Master. Bound to Barbados. I give all goods to my friends Geo. Vaughan, merchant taylor, and Wm. Andrews, dyer, on trust to pay my Mother Rachell Y. 20s. and my brother Edw[d] Y. 5s. My trustees to be Ex'ors. Wit. by Jo. Smith at the Angell in Birchen Lane, Edmund Butcher, W[m] Bower, sc[r]. Proved 2 March 1656 by both Ex'ors (106, Ruthen).

This 12 April 1662 appeared Coll[o] John Yeomans and Margaret his wife, the relict of Coll[o] Benj. Berenger, l. of B., deceased. Her 4 children by the said L[t] Col. B. B., viz., Mary b. before 1656, Symon, John and Margaret (posthumous). B. B. d. Jan. 1660 and was buried in the church of All Saints in S[t] Peters. His nuncupative will. Several depositions. (Barbados Wills, vol. xv., p. 11.)

Sir James Browne, Baronet. Will dated 16 Dec. 1665. To be buried in the church of S[t] Peter. My daus. Willoughby B. and Secunda B. all my estate. My 2 nephews John B., esq., and M[r] W[m] B. Sworn 5 March 1666 at Barbados. (Ibid., p. 52.)

John Leaver of Barbados, merchant. Will proved in 1668. My goddau. Rachel Yeomans £25. M[r] Edward Yeomans and his wife 1000 lbs. of sugar. (5, Hene.)

S[r] John Yeamans, Barron[t], ready to imbarque to y[e] province of Carol. Will dated 20 May 1671. To my wife y[e] Lady Margaret in lieu of dower 30,000 lbs. of sugar annually the use of my house and 45 acres bounding upon y[e] lands of Hen. Mills, Esq., Tho. Merricke, Esq., and of the late L[t] Coll. Berrenger, and also these negroes Jupeter and her children, 8 milch cows and stock, plate, jewells, linen, etc., coach and 4 horses, a riding horse, and the negroes that L[t] Col. Berringer possessed that came to her by right of administracon the custody of all my children unmarried and under 21. To my dau. Willoughbie 120,000 lbs. within 10 years after her m. or when she arrive at 21. My son Ro. . . . 200,000 lbs. at 21. My dau. Anne 120,000 lbs. within 2 years after her m. or when 21. My 2 sons George and Edward each 150,000 lbs. at 21. My wife's dau. Margaret

639

John Yeamans of St. Mary Redcliffe,=Blanche Germain, mar. 29 June
Bristol. brewer. Will dated 12 June | 1610 at St. Mary Redcliffe.
and proved 7 Nov. 1645; recorded at | Will proved 20 July 1647 (160,
Bristol. | Fines).

. . . .,=Sir John Yeamans, Bart., 1st=Margaret (? dau. of=Hon. Benj. Beringer
? dau.	son, bapt. at St. Mary Red-	Rev. John Foster),	of Barbados, a cava-
of....	cliffe 28 Feb. 1611; of Bar-	remar. 11 April	lier and M. of C.
Limp.	bados 1638 and 1643; free of	1661; had a grant	1651; Lieut.-Col.;
1st	the City of Bristol 31 Aug.	of 1070 acres in	died Jan. 1660; bur.
wife.	1649, then a merchant; Col.	South Carolina in	at All Saints. Nun-
	and M. of C. 1660; created	1674-5; ? remar.	cupative will at Bar-
	a Baronet 1664-5; Gov. of	Col. Jas. Moore,	bados. Adm'on to
	South Carolina 1665—74;	Govr. of South	his widow.
	died at Barbados Aug. 1674.	Carolina. She was	
	Will dated 20 May 1671;	alive in 1711 at	
	sworn 1 Dec. 1674 and re-	Goosecreek.	
	corded at Barbados and South		
	Carolina.		

Sir Wm. Yeamans, 2nd=Willoughby,dau.   A son,   Frances Yeamans, mar. be-
Bart., Major 1664; | of Sir James   killed in   fore 1663 Sir Rob. Hackett,
in 1665 acted for the | Browne, Knt.and a duel   Knt., M. of A. and Major
planters who removed | Bart., who was   1668   1653; knighted at Whitehall
to Carolina; sole ex'or| bur. 11 March   by John   23 Nov. 1677. He was bur. 3
to his father 1675. | 1665; guardian Colle-   Mar. 1678-9. M.I. at Adams
                      | 1677 of her son. ton.   Castle estate, Christ Church,
                                                     Barbados. =

Sir John Yeamans,=Margaret, dau. of Ph.   Wm. Hackett. 1st son, matric. from
3rd Bart., a minor | Gibbes; aged 45 in   Christ Church, Oxford, 27 May
28 April 1677; | 1715; remar. Wm.   1680, aged 17; died 17 Nov. at
dead 1715. | Foster.   Merton College, and there bur. 19
                                                Nov. 1708.

Sir John Yeamans, 4th Bart.,=Anne Scantlebury, spinster, mar. in
aged 26 in 1715. | Barbados; aged 26 in 1715.

Sir John Yeamans, only son, at Barbados 1771.=

Rev. Sir Robert Yeamans, Vicar of Fittleworth, co. Sussex,
1776 till his death s.p. 19 Feb. 1788. Title extinct.

Sir Robert Yeamans of Bristol, Bart. Will dated 24 Jan. 1686. My 3 houses
in Redland for my loving kinsman Robert Y., now resident in Barbadoes, s. of
my late brother Sir John Y., deceased. (71, Foot.)

17,000 lbs. after her m. or at 21. My wife's son John 40,000 lbs. 3 years after
21. My dau. Mrs Frances Hackett, now wife of Rob. H., Esq., within 4 years
20,000 lbs. for a ring. My wife's dau. M^{rs} Ma. . . . Maycoke 5000 lbs. for a ring.
My wife's son Symon the choice of my horses. My nephew Sam. Woorey
20,000 lbs. in further lieu of his time with me. I make my s. Wm. Esq. sole
Ex'or. Wit. by Will. Browne, Tho. Bamfield, Nich. Carteret.

My wife to have my ketch the "Hopewell," now in a voyage to Virginia, and
2 parcells of land of 10 a. each, the one I bought of Phelps bounding on
Mrs Sandiford and on Tho. Jones the other of Jas. Masters and Henry Jones
bounding on Mrs Gay, my brother Foster and Rob. Clinton.

By H. E. Jonathan Attkins, Gov. of Barbados, appeared Mr Wm Browne, and
was sworn 1 Dec. 1674. Testator l. of Carolina. Proved by S^r Wm. Y., Barr^t,
s. and h., with letter of attorney dated 16 June 1675 to Col. Jos. West and Lt Col.
John Godfree. Approved of by Col. Jos West, Gov. of North Carolina 14 Sept.
1675.

[I have made the above abstract from a copy of the will which appeared in the
South Carolina "Hist. and Gen. Mag.," vol. xi., 112, in an article contributed by
Mr. M. Alston Read.—ED.]

Hon. Col. Robert Yeamans, born	=Eliz., dau.	George Yeamans.	Edward Yea-
1666; heir 1686 to his uncle Sir	of Elisha	—	mans.
Robert Yeamans of Bristo' Bart.;	Mellows	Willoughby Yea-	—
bur. at St. James, Holk Town,	(Burke).	mans, ?mar. 1stly	Anne Yea-
7 July 1728, aged *circa* 62;		.... Smith, and	mans.
? mar. 7 Sept. 1701 Eliz. Neal.		2ndly Ph. Gibbes;	
		ex'trix of latter in	
		1697.	

Col. Robert Yea-=Mary Ferchar-	Capt. John=Mary Walker,	Philip=Mary,
mans, jun., ?mar. son, dau. of	Yeamans, dau. of Alexr.	Yea- dau. of
Sarah, dau. of .... Ferchar-	named Walker, Esq.,	mans. Joseph
John Trent. She son; mar. 15	1742 in the Judge of Bar-	Gibbes,
remar. Rev. Wm. Oct. 1726.	will of his bados; mar. 9	Esq.
Dowding M.I. in St.	brother-in- June 1734 at	
(Burke). Michael's.	law Alexr. St. Thomas.	
	Walker.	

Robert Yeamans, died 7 Nov. 1740, aged 10.   Walker Yeamans.

.... Yeamans. (Perhaps Edward, brother of John of 1645)=Rachel.

Edward Yeamans of Barbados, ?bro. of George=	George Yeamans of London,
1653; Ensign 1662, Capt. 1665, and signed to	merchant. Will dated 19
go to Carolina, still of Barbados, 1668, Major	Sept. 1653, bound to Barba-
1675; ? Prov.-Marshal of Jamaica 1677—83.	dos; proved 2 March 1656
	(106, Ruthen).

Rachel Yeamans, bapt. 9 Nov. 1662; goddau.	Christopher Yeamans,
1668 of John Leaver of Barbados, merchant.	bapt. 25 May 1665.

Sarah Yeamans of St Michael's, Barbados, widow. Will dated 11 Dec. 1724. To my dau. Sarah 3 negros, and in default of issue to my dau Barbara, then to my Kinsman Wm. Wheeler Skeet. To my dau. Sarah at 21 £720 c. To my niece Sarah Walwin £100 at 21. All my remaining slaves to be sold and all residue to my 2 daus. equally. My friends Burch Hothersall, Esq., and Geo. Howe, merchant. Ex'ors and Guardians. Witnessed by Tho. Harrison, James Hasel, John Tyache, Barbados. By Henry Worsley, Esq., Gov., etc., appeared Wm. Webster, Esq., Dep. Sec., who swore to the copy. Entered 22 Dec. 1725. Proved 30 May 1727. Com. to Henry Palmer, the attorney of Burch Hothersall and Geo. Howe. (128, Farrant.)

Alexr Walker of Barbados, Esq. Will dated 19 May 1742. My brother-in-law Capt. John Yeamons £50 c. yearly and my riding horse. Proved 1758. (59, Hutton.)
He d. 23 May 1757 aged 60, and was buried in Westminster Abbey. (Chester, 390.)

Tho. Maycock of St Lucy's, Barbados, Esq. Will dated 1730. My estate in Gloucestershire, which I purchased of Col. Robert Yeamans. Recorded in Barbados.

ST. MICHAEL'S, BARBADOS.

1662	Nov.	9	Rachel the Da of Ensign Edw. Yeomans, bap.
1665	May	25	Xtopher the s. of Capt Edw. Yeomans, bap.
1667	Aug.	24	Christopher ye s. of Capt Edward Yeomans in ye chicell, bur.
1727	July	31	Mrs Sarah Yeamans in Chancel, bur.

ST. JOHN'S.

1661	Apr.	11	Coll. John Youmans and Margt Bellinger [sic].
1670	Nov.	12	Capt Archd Henderson and Elizabeth Yeamons.
1667	May	23	Capt Thomas Maycock and Mary Beringer.
1665	Mar.	11	Sr James Browne, Kt & Bart.

ST. JAMES.

1701	Sep.	7	Coll. Robert Yeamans & Mrs Eliz. Neal.
1726	Oct.	15	Coll. Robert Yeomans, junr, Esqr, & Mis Mary Fercharson, spinster.
1728	July	7	The Honble Coll Robert Yeamans, Esqr, aged abt 62 years.

ST. THOMAS.

| 1734 | June | 9 | Mr John Yeamans & Mrs Mary Walker. |

1637, Oct. 25. Wm. Hall of B., planter, binds himself to serve Arthur Yeomans, gent., for 4 years for lodging, food, etc., and 400 lbs. of cotton or tobacco. (Vol. i., p. 798.)

1640, Nov. 26. Arthur Yeomans, gent., sells to Wm. Y., gent., 20 a. in St Michael's. (Vol. ii., p. 351.)

1643, Dec. 4. John Yeamans, gent., sells 10 a. Witnessed by Jon. Yeamans. (Vol. i., p. 679.)

1643, Jan. 3. Arthur Yeomans, gent., sells 30 a. (*Ibid.*, p. 95.)

1643, Feb. 17. Also 60 a. in St Michael's for 5000 lbs. of cotton. (*Ibid.*, p. 305.)

1644, July 2. Arthur Yeomans mortgages his plantation purchased of Joseph Lee. (*Ibid.*, p. 906.)

1644, March 14. Robert Yeamans gives security for 7000 lbs. of tobacco for 3 negroes. (*Ibid.*, p. 591.)

1645, Apr. 4. John Yeamans and others (not named) sign a request for the payment of ministers. (*Ibid.*, p. 601.)

1653, May 16. John Yeamans. gent., for 30,000 lbs. of sugar sells to Capt Tho. Merrick 50 a. (Vol. ii., p. 72 .)

ABSTRACTS FROM THE CALENDAR OF STATE PAPERS, AMERICA AND WEST INDIES, 1661—1668.

1661, Jan. 2. Minutes of the Cl. Present John Y. p. 1

1663, Aug. 18. Present. p. 154. Nov. 23 as " Col." p. 169

1664, Mar. 28. Present. p. 195.

1665, Jan. 7. Agreemt betw. the Lords Proprietors of Carolina and Majr Wm. Y. of B. on behalf of Sir John Y. his father and 84 others (named), adventurers to the sd Province, granting 500 a. for every 1000 lbs. of sugar to settle in the cos. of Clarendon, Albemarle and Craven. Edwd Y. occurs in above list, also Rob. Hackett. p. 267

1665, Jan. 1. Petn of Sir Rob. Y., Kt, for licence for the Great Charles of Bristol with 30 mariners bd to Barbadoes freighted with servants and horses. pp. 259 and 265

1665, Jan. 11. Comn from the Lords Proprietors app. Sir Jno Y. Gov. of co. Clarendon, nr Cape Fair in Carolina, and granting him 6000 a., and saying that they have prevailed with H.M. to confer a baronetcy upon him. p. 269

1666, Jan. 23. Lt.-Col. Wm. Y., M. of A. for St. Peter's, B. p. 352

1666, Sep. 29. John Y. present at a Cl at B. p. 413

1667, Feb. 15. Sir J. Y. present at a Cl at B. p. 446

1667, Feb. 18. Warrt to Capt. Edw. Y. to impress the Gilded Lion prize at B. p. 447

1667, Mar. 5. Lt.-Col. Wm. Y. elected a M. of A. p. 452

1667, July 9. The charges of the Assembly against Sir J. Y. pp. 478 and 593

1668, Sep. 15. " A s. of Sir John Colleton's last week killed a s. of Sir J. Y. in a duel." In the Index this has been given in error as relating to Lt-Col. Wm Y. p. 613

1638. John Yeomans, Tho. Yeomans & Rob. Yeamans of Barbados.

Census of 1676—80. St James's, Elizabeth Y. St Lucy's, Dame Willoughby Y. St Peter's, The Lady Willoughby Y.

Census of 1715. St Peter's, Dame Margt Y., 45, a son 13 and a dau. 18. Sir John Y. 26, his lady 26. St Mich., Mrs Sarah Y. St James, Col. Rob. Y.

APPENDIX A: Genealogical Notes

Notes and Queries

ARCHER : WICKHAM.

Query.—Margaret Archer married Captain Henry Wickham, R.N. (1665—1735). The only note of her in family papers is that she was "of Barbados". Captain Henry Wickham of the "Diamond" was returning from the West Indies in charge of a convoy of Merchantmen in 1693 when he was attacked off the Coast of Ireland by two French frigates and overpowered. He was fined £1,000 and sentenced to 10 years imprisonment. After. his release he lived at Heslington, Yorkshire, with his wife Margaret. He died in 1735 and she died in 1751, and they were both buried in York Minster. *Major J. L. Wickham.*

Note supplied.—Margaret, daughter of John Ogilby of Bridgetown, married Hugh Archer 2 Jan. 1681. A son, Hugh, and a daughter, Elizabeth, were born of the marriage. Hugh Archer who died 6 May 1689 had married first Dorothy Cullum in 1671, who died 13 Dec. 1680.

A Power of Attorney dated 5 January 1698/9 from Henry Wickham and Margaret his wife was recorded in Barbados 5 April 1699. Henry Wickham, one of the sons of Rev. Tobias Wickham, D.D., and Dean of York, appoints Major John Pilgrim of Bridgetown, Barbados, to be the attorney of said Henry Wickham and of his wife, Margaret, relict and. executrix of Hugh Archer deceased with authority to pay John Ogilby of Bridgetown, father of Margaret, a yearly sum of £20, and revoking a prior power to John Sale, Gentleman, and Elizabeth his wife. Sgd: Hen. Wickham, Margaret Wickham. Witnesses. Francis Clarke, Richard Metcalfe William Vevers (?)

BROUGHTON.

Query.—Information required concerning the ancestry of John Broughton (b 1692) who went to New England from Barbados and married Sarah Norman at Marblehead, Mass., U.S.A. about 1718, and died there in 1729.   *Mrs. E. D. Coddington.*

Note Supplied.—Baptisms, Christ Church, Barbados.

> 5 Nov. 1644. Elizabeth, daughter of William and Catharine Bloughton (? Broughton).

> 26 Dec. 1680. Elizabeth, daughter of Alex and Israel Bloughton (? Broughton).

Marriages, Christ Church.

> 16 June 1650, Henry Broughton to Sarah.

11 April 1717, Mrs. Ann Broughton, widow, to Mr. Richard Dearsley, Merchant.

Burials :—

St. Michael, 11 Dec. 1678, William Broughton.
> Christ Church, 14 Feb. 1667, Sarah Broughton, wife of Henry Broughton.
> St. Michael, 11 Dec. 1678, William Broughton.
> St. Joseph, 22 August 1720, Jeremiah Broughton.

Will of Symond Broughton now resident in the Barbados.

To be buried in church or church-yard of St. James. My son, James Broughton, I do make my heir. My daughters Elizabeth and Rebecca 3000 lbs. tobacco each. If my wife Arise Broughton, mother of my son James, shall keep herself a widow until the heir comes of age he is to give her 4000 lbs. tobacco, or else sufficient meat and drink as the plantation will afford, and clothes as long as she lives, and one private room to herself. Dated 13 June 1652. Sgd. X the mark of Symond Broughton. Proved 21 Dec. 1652.

Deeds:—1644   Simon Broughton to Roger Sturdinant.
          1644   do.   to Thomas Barnett.
          1655   Henry Broughton to Robert Binbury.
          1659   Thomas Broughton to Richard Cooke et al.
          1673   Henry Broughton to John Ruck.
          1641   Sympson Broughton from Thomas Perkins.
          1643   Simon Broughton from Francis Tobast.
          1645   George Broughton, Charter party.
          1654   Henry Broughton from George Johnson.
          1673   Henry Broughton from Edward Oistin.

DUBOIS.

Query.—Any information concerning Dubois required. Katherine, wife of Hon. Guy Ball of Christ Church, Bart, was the daughter of Thomas Dubois (or Duboys) of St. Michael, Merchant.

Note supplied.—Wills recorded in Barbados:—

1687 Elizabeth Dubois.   1700 Thomas Duboys.
1692 John Duboys.   1741 John Dubys.

21 Jan. 1686 Elizabeth Dubois, Spinster,: my body to be buried at the discretion of my father-in-law John Halse. All my estate to the said John Halse and Edith his wife for life and then to their daughter, Susanna. I appoint my said father executor. X mark of Elizabeth Dubois. Witnesses: Tho: Phillips, X Elizabeth Ramsay, Thos. Cox, John Newton. Proved 2 June 1687.

18 Nov. 1692. John Duboys of St. Michael Esquire. My wife Elizabeth to have the care of my two children John and Richard and the profits of my real estate for their maintenance. If she marries again my brother, Thomas Duboys, to have the care of children. To son Richard £700 left me by David Ramsay. Residue to my son John and if he die under 21 without issue to my wife Elizabeth and my niece Catherine, daughter of my brother Thomas. Brother Thomas guardian of my children, and if he should die before they attain 21, my friends George Poore and John Mills and my wife to be executors and guardians. Gold rings to George Poore, John

Mills, Aunt Amy Kelly, and sister Katherine Duboys, Philip and Margaret Duboys, and brother in law Capt. William Kirkham.

Sgd: Jno. Duboys. Witnesses: John Hallett, James Denham, John Hallett, Jnr. Pd. 7 Dec. 1692.

8 April 1699. Thomas Duboys of St. Michael Esquire being suddenly bound off for Kingdom of England.

My executrix shall forthwith sell my shares in ships and all my merchandise and chattels to pay following legacies:—Daughter Katherine £2000 to be put out at interest by my executrix and Hon. George Andrews, Robert Hooper Esq. and Mr. William Godman, Merchant for her use to be paid her at 16 or marriage, and one-half my plate &c. To my nephew John Duboys, son of my brother Major John Duboys deceased and Elizabeth his wife £50. To my nephew Richard son of my said brother John £200. To my brother in law Thomas Trent Esquire and my sister Ann his wife £50 each and £50 to each of their children. To my brother and sister Townsend £10 each. To Captain John Garvey and Mary his wife £10 each. To Benjamin Alford son of Joseph Alford deceased £25. To my sister Baker £10 to buy her mourning. To John Hallett Esq. my large silver sword and my best bullet gun, and to Major George Peers my largest gun. My servants William Coggin, Edward Morris, Elizabeth Harris, £10 each. £20 among the poor housekeepers of St. Michael's parish. To Dr. Henry Byrch and his wife, and Capt. John Garvey and Mary his wife, gold rings of 40/- each. To my wife Katherine £1500 and one-half my plate &c. and certain slaves by name. My wife to be executrix until my son Thomas arrives at the age of 21 if she continues my widow. Hon. Geo. Andrews, Robert Hooper, William Godman, to be overseers in Barbados, and my friend Mr. Francis Eyles, Merchant in London, to assist my wife in managing my estate in England. Residue to son, Thomas and to be sole executor at 21. If Thomas dies under 21, my wife to have £500 and daughter £1000 and residue to nephews, John and Richard, sons of Major John Duboys. Sgd. Thomas Duboys. Witnesses: Nicholas Prideaux, John Parkinson, Walter Thomas Ward.

The Probate discloses that Thomas Duboys died on his passage to England, and the will was transmitted to his widow by Hon. George Andrews by letter dated 15 August 1699 from "The Russia" (Andrews plantation) where he resided. The Grant P.C.C. was made May 1700 to the widow, Katherine Duboys, for use of John and Richard Dubois, residuary legatees, by which it appears that the testator's son Thomas had died under 21.

2 Oct. 1742. Will of John Duboys. Although much reduced by a sad lax and sad thrush and sourness out of my stomach, I give to Katherine Dubys for her services and living with me upwards of 19 years a negro crooked wench and her two boys Jack and Harry and all my personal estate. To my cousin Joseph Ball, my real estate and make him and Katherine Dubys executor and executrix. Sgd: John Dubys. Proved 10 Oct. 1741.

Query.—What is the origin of the expression, "As hot as Mapp's mill-yard." *Information required :*

HUSBANDS PLANTATION, ST. JAMES.

A stone above the arched doorway of the old mill wall bears the following inscription

```
D
1 x A
JAN. 17.
1729.
```

I (or J) and A.D. are the initials of Joseph Dotin and his wife Ann, who owned the plantation in 1729. The estate was then called *Jordans*, to which Ann Dotin had become entitled through her father, Edward Jordan who died in 1728 leaving all his estate to her. Joseph and Ann Dotin had four daughters—Susanna, Ann, Elizabeth, and Christian; and one son, Edward, who died in 1736 at the age of eleven years—"of a malignant fever". The daughters were thus co-heiresses of their father, and Susanna, who married Samuel Husbands, took *Jordans* plantation and its name was changed to *Husbands*. Ann married Edward Jordan; Elizabeth married Wm. Blennman; and Christian married Sir John Gay Alleyne, and brought him *Nicholas* plantation which she had inherited from her father. Joseph Dotin died 1735 at 45, and his widow, Ann, married secondly Rev. Dudley Woodbridge. See M.I. in St. James' Church, Holetown, to the Jordans and Dotins.

YEAMANS.

Ann Yeamans, one of the daughters of Sir John Yeamans by his second marriage to Margaret Berringer, widow of Colonel Benjamin Berringer, was married three times. She was first the wife of Rev. Mr. Norvell, secondly of one Jemmott, and lastly of Richard Farnum of St. Peter, Barbados, Planter. These facts are stated in a deed dated 13 May, 1724, from George Nicholas of St. John, Barbados, to Richard and Ann Farnum, at page 122 of Volume of Deeds recorded in Barbados in 1724.

PLAXTON.

Query.—Information desired concerning Hon. George Plaxton, Treasurer of the Excise in Barbados.

Note Supplied.—He was Treasurer from 1725 to 1732, and appears to have been associated in business with Edward Lascelles and George Maxwell. He left Barbados for England in April 1734, appointing Arthur Upton and George Maxwell as his attorneys here. More information desired.

Readers' Queries

C. 162. SMELT. About 1745, William Smelt (senior) was appointed Receiver of Revenues, Barbados. When did he relinquish the appointment? Is there any trace of the death of his wife Dorothy; or of the baptism of any children of his son William (junior) and the latter's wife Ursula between 1743 and 1750.

    No record of the appointment. There are no entries in the church records of burials, 1740—1775, and baptisms 1740—1750.

R. 162. ROWE. *Wanted*: Names and dates of baptism of all the children of Rev. Thomas Rowe, Minister of St. Matthew's Chapel, Barbados, and Sarah Elizabeth his wife.

    The following entries of their children's baptisms are found in the Church register.

    Mary Jane, born 5 Oct. 1841, bap. 28 Dec. 1841.
    Maria, born 15 Oct. 1842, bap. 25 Nov. 1842.
    Robert Hillary Wedgewood, born 14 Sep. 1844, bap. 18 Oct. 1844.
    Edwin Augustus, born 20 Feb. 1846, bap. 23 Apl. 1846.
    Alice Emily, born 19 Dec. 1847, bap. 16 Mar. 1848.
    Reginald Perch, born 3 June 1849, bap. 31 July 1849.
    Matilda Blanche, born . . . bap. 3 Jan. 1851.
    George Perch, born 3 April 1852, bap. 2 June 1852.
    William Augustine Edward, born . . . bap. 12 Jan. 1854.

Sh. 162. HARRIS. Is there any record of the sojourn in Barbados of Thomas Harris, a wealthy Quaker Merchant who went to Rhode Island in 1658.

Si. 162. ANDREW NORWOOD, mariner and surveyor, son of Richard Norwood, one of the early residents in Bermuda. *Wanted,* definite records of his marriage, children etc.

The name Andrew Norwood occurs about the year 1664 in early Barbados documents, plans of land etc., where he is described as a surveyor of land. There is no record of his marriage.

Bu. 162. BURNHAM. Information concerning Thomas Burnham, who embarked from England in 1635 for Barbados. Burnham records wanted.

Only one will is recorded—Will of Thomas Burnham of Barbados, merchant. To brother, Anthony (if living) 10,000 lbs muscovado sugar. To sister, Sarah Burnham (if living) 10,000 lbs sugar. To servant George Bread, if he will assist my dear wife in making up all accounts, 6,000 lbs sugar. Residue of estate, houses, slaves, etc. to wife, Frances, and she to be executrix. Friends, Philip Travers, merchant, and Edward Cripp to be overseers, and to each of them 2,000 lbs sugar to buy them mourning. To have six bearers at funeral, namely, Ralph Hassell, senr. William Mackerness, senr. John Legay, Will Fletcher, Robert Huse, George Brickhead, and to each of them a ring of 10/- value.

Dated 18 July 1674. Witnesses: Gab. Newman, George Birkhead (or Brickhead), Thomas Fercharson.

Proved and recorded 1 Sept 1674.

BAPTISMS

Parish of St. Philip, 1662, Augu. 14, John son of Edward Burnham, 1665, March 18, Francis, son of Edward Burnham.

MARRIAGES

Parish of St. John. 27 June 1670. Thomas Burnham and Frances Holdipp.

BURIALS

None.

Ha. 159. HANDY. Records of John Handy and Samuel Handy wanted.

BAPTISMS to 1700. None.

MARRIAGES, St. Michael, 6 Jan. 1682, Kathn. Handy and William Bradbournier.

BURIALS, St. Michael. 11 August 1675. Susan Handy.
,,   10 June 1680, Elizabeth, daughter of John and Eleanor Handy.
,,   28 April 1682. John Handy.

John Handy of St. Michael, Barbados, gent. To have Christian burial. To William Handy, son of Samuel Handy in the Kingdom of England, £100 'two years after my decease. To Edmund and Frances, son and dau. of Francis Turton £10 each at 18. To godson John Fowler, son of John F. decd. £10. To the parish of St. Michael, £20 "for the putting forth of some 'prentices at the discretion of my executors". To Richard Guyton, John Crisp, Capt. William Davis, Thos. Peers, Thomas Leare, and Capt. Thos. Watson, a gold ring each of 20/- value and a mourning scarfe, and these to bear up the pall at my funeral. Estate real and personal to my granddaughter, Susan Mackey, at 18. Wife Lardi (?) Handy to be executrix during widowhood until my granddaughter is 18, but if she marries again to have one-third of the estate and no more. Friends Capt Thomas Watson, Thomas Peers "gouldsmith" to be executors. Dated 24 April 1682. If granddaughter should die under 18 then whole estate to William, son of Samuel Handy of England, after the decease of wife. Wits. Edmund Strafford, Nicholas Mortimer, Phillis Mahon, Ellinor Paddison. Proved 4 May 1682.

We. 159. TIMBRILL. William Timbrill of Barbados, merchant, purchased two lots of land in Water Street, Chestertown, Maryland, in 1736, and returned to Barbados in 1743, and died there. Are there any Barbados records relating to the family?

BARBADOS WILLS

Will of Thomas Timbrill of St. Andrew, Barbados. My funeral expenses not to exceed £20. To my sister, Diana Summerhays, £20 to buy a ring. To my cousin, Charles Summerhayes, £10 to buy a ring. My sister Ann's son £5 to bind him apprentice and £15 more when out of his time. To my Uncle John Timbrill 3/- per week during his life. Residue of my estate in Barbados or elsewhere to be divided between my wife, Margaret, and my two sons Thomas and William, and they to be executors. No date. sd. Thos Timbrill. Wits: Mary Laming, Jehu Cordle. Proved 14 April 1730.

Will of William Timbrill of town of St. Michael, Barbados, merchant. To my son William two negro women, Kate and Hannah. To daughter, Sarah, a negro Thisbee. Whereas I am seised of two lots of land in Chester Town on Chester River in Maryland in America and household furniture and other goods in possession of John Bullen of Maryland, and also of five other negro slaves in Barbados, besides merchandise, plate, furniture etc. and other real and personal estate to be disposed of for uses of my two children William and Sarah, my son at 21 and my daughter at 18.

To my dear mother, Margaret Timbrill, my brother Thomas Timbrill, my uncle William Breedy, all of the Kingdom of Great Britain, and my uncle Lawrence Trent, my brother-in-law, John Sober; and my friend Walter Caddell, each a gold ring of 20/- My Uncle Lawrence Trent, my brother-in-law John Sober, and my friend Alexander Murray and Richard Carter to be executors sd. Wm. Timbrill. Dated 25 July 1743. Wits: Thomas Morrison, Richard Carter, Edward Grove. Proved 25 August 1743.

BURIALS. St. Michael. 27 July 1743. Mr. William Timbrill.

POWERS BOOK. William Timbrill of St. Michael, merchant, being suddenly bound off this island for North America, appoints Walter Caddell of the same parish and Dr. William Bruce of St. Andrew to be his attorneys. Dated 27 July 1736. Wits: John Thomas. John Dapwell jr.

John Sober of Barbados in his will (1751) names his nephew and niece William and Sarah Timbrill, children of his sister Elizabeth, wife of William Timbrill.

Sh. 156. ROUSE. Nathaniel Rouse of London, merchant, was the owner of plantations in Barbados. Are particulars available?

A power of attorney dated 10 Oct. 1698 from Nathaniel Rouse in which he is described as above, to Charles Egerton of Barbados, planter, to manage *HALTON* plantation in Barbados is recorded in Vol. 29 of Powers.

Miscellaneous Notes

AMBLER RECORDS, BARBADOS.

Burials—St. Michael, 27 May 1766, John Ambler.*

* John Ambler was born at James Town, Virginia, 31 December 1735, son of Richard Ambler (b. 1690) and Elizabeth (Jaquelin) his wife. John was burgess in James Town and Collector of the district of York River.

Will of SAMUEL AMBLER of Barbados. Dated 4 February 1772. Proved 16 October 1776. Wife Charity and friend Thomas Ostrehan Senr. my largest house in Bridgetown for my grandson, Cornelius Barry, at 18 which will be on 11 July 1788. To Ruth Francklin, wife of Benjamin Francklin, daughter of my wife Charity, my other house in Middle Lane.

WHERE IS THE TOMBSTONE BEARING THE EARLIEST DATE IN THIS ISLAND?

The oldest tombstone of which there is any visible evidence may be seen in the old church-yard at Christ Church; *not* the site of the present parish church, but an ancient burial-ground on a low, rocky, promontory by the sea in the neighbourhood of the district now known as Dover. It lies adjacent to the house called Nova Lisboa.

The first church in the parish was built by the early settlers on this site, but it appears from a record in the minutes of the Island Council in January 1670 to have sometime previously fallen into decay (perhaps it was seriously damaged in the hurricane of 19 August 1667) and the record includes a report from the Vestry of the parish of (I quote) "great. . . inundations lately upon the chiefest place for burial at the parish church having washed the earth from off the corpses." The great inundations mentioned in the Vestry's communication to the Council had lasted four days. The flood washed 150 coffins into the sea and rendered the church so insecure that it was decided to erect a new church on another site.

A portion of the old church yard remains up to the present time, but only seven vaults with monumental inscriptions now mark the resting places of pioneers who settled in that part of the Island. Unhappily, the place is unprotected and not cared for, as respect for the dead as well as interest in the history of the Island both demand.

A tablet on one of these vaults has the following inscription:

HERE LYETH/WILLIAM BALSTON ESQ/DECD the 26 OCTOBER Ano Dom 1659.

This tombstone bears the earliest date of burial of any person whose memory is perpetuated in the burial grounds and I should say that it is the oldest visible tombstone in any burial-ground in Barbados.

Just a word or so about William Balston. His name is mentioned in a list of inhabitants who, in the year 1638, (that is the eleventh year of the first settlement) owned more than 10 acres of land, and doubtless he had settled here at an even earlier date. His will is recorded in the Registry here and we gather from it that he was the owner of a plantation in Christ Church parish and he was survived by his wife Jane and his daughter Damaris.

CHAMBERLAINE v. HEWETSON

13 Oct. 1694. Orator Willoughby Chamberlaine, late of Barbadoes and now of London, Esq., one of the sons of Edward Chamberlaine, late of Barbadoes, who made his will 21 July 1673.

Orator's mother Mary married Sir John Witham.

Orator's eldest brother Segrave Chamberlaine.

Orator's sisters Butler Chamberlaine and Tanquervill Chamberlain.

Def'ts Thomas Hewettson, Butler Chamberlaine *alias* Hewettson, Sir Francis Windham, and Hester Windham.

(Chancery Proceedings before 1714, Ham, 361-41. Answer filed, Hamilton, 59-48.)

13 Nov. 1695. The answer of Thomas Hewettson to the complaint of Willoughby Chamberlaine.

The Compt is son of Edward Chamberlaine, late of Barbadoes, Esq., deceased, who made his will and left his wife Mary guardian of his children.

Compt's elder brother Seagreave Chamberlaine under 21.

The other def't Butler Chamberlaine had a legacy of £3500 and went to Barbadoes.

Sir Francis Windham, Bart., who married the widdowe of Mathew Ingram.

(Chancery Proceedings before 1714, H. 59-48.)

Col. Edward Chamberlaine of Barbados, born in co. Leicester, died 23 July 1673, aged 50, having married Mary, dau. of Col. Edward Butler. (Archer, 362.)

His two sons were both at Merchant Taylors' School. Seagrave, born 15 Jan. 1661, entered March 1674-5, and Willoughby entered June 1675 (School Register).

Willoughby C., born in Barbados, s. of Edw. C., Esq., matriculated from Christ Church Coll., Oxf., 25 Nov. 1681, aged 18, and joined the Middle Temple the same year. (Foster.) Described as a Colonel he was knighted at Kensington 6 Feb. 1695, and died s.p. at Little Chelsey 1697 distracted, and his widow Oliana remarried Capt. Mitford Crowe (Le Neve). In his will he names his wife *Oriana* (259, Lort).

Pedigrees were entered in the Visitations of Leicester and Warwick 1619 and London 1634. Crowe was later Governor, and the Editor has his engraved portrait.

FAMILY of the name CLEMENT

We have an enquiry from the Chairman of the Standing Committee for Preservation and Protection of Historical Monuments and Archaeological Sites in British Guiana for information concerning SUSANNA CLEMENT whose death and burial are recorded on a tombstone now lying in a cane-field aback of plantation Providence on the east bank of the Demerara River.

The inscription on the tombstone is as follows:—

Sacred to the Memory of Susanna Clement, wife of Richard Clement Esqr., of the Island of Barbados and their eldest son, John Clement. She died in August 1786 Age 26 years. Also sacred to the memory of Joanna Dougan who died in May 1816 and was the eldest sister of Susanna Clement.

The marriage records in Barbados have been searched without any information concerning the parties resulting.

COLLIER OF BARBADOS.

These notes were taken by myself in Barbados in 1904. Mehetabel Christian Collier was my great-grandmother, and I am anxious to find out their earlier history, and whether they belonged to the Dorsetshire family, as their arms lead one to suppose. The inscription was difficult to read, and it may be that Jane Miller, whose register entry does not tally with the tombstone, may have been daughter of Joseph and Elizabeth *Miller*, and not Collier. William and *Jane* Collier of the tombstone seem to have been living at the same time as William and *Mary* Collier of the register. It is rather puzzling.

INSCRIPTION ON A TOMBSTONE IN THE CHURCHYARD OF ST. MICHAEL'S CATHEDRAL, BRIDGETOWN, BARBADOS.

Here lie the Bodies of | ABEL COLLIER who died | Aug. 4 1775 aged 34 years. | SAMUEL COLLIER | Sept. 12 1786 aged 50. | JAMES K. COLLIER | Ap. 7th 1793 aged 50 | and JANE COLLIER Jan. 26 1800 | aged 67 all of this parish | Sons and Daughter of WILLIAM | and JANE COLLIER of | St Andrews Parish deceased |

Also the bodies of WILLIAM | Son of aforesaid SAMUEL COLLIER | and ELIZABETH his wife who died in 1777 | aged 5 months. JANE MILLER | Feb. 14 1796 aged 20 years | daughter of JOSEPH and ELIZABETH | COLLIER and great-grand-daughter | of aforesaid WILLIAM and JANE | COLLIER. | ABEL BANNISTER . . . . | of aforesaid WILLIAM and JANE | COLLIER | Aged 22 years.

Other children of Samuel and Elizabeth Collier were:—

MEHETABEL CHRISTIAN COLLIER, born 4 July 1774; bapt. 21 July following at St. Michael's, married there 15 May 1790 William Newton Firebrace, Chief of the Legislative Council of Demerara. She died in Tobago in Aug. or Sept. 1822.

JAMES MORRIS COLLIER,* married 1 Sept. 1805 at St. Michael's Anne Lyne Firebrace, daughter of William Firebrace of St. Michael's, Barbadoes, and sister of the above-named William Newton Firebrace.

The Collier family bore for their Arms: *Gules, on a chevron between three wolves' heads erased Argent, as many roses of the first, stalked and leaves vert.* CREST.—*A demi-unicorn Argent, almed, maned, and hoofed.* (From the impression on a seal in my possession.)

In Burke's "General Armoury" these arms are ascribed to Collyer of Dorsetshire. (There is no evidence of this in Hutchins.—EDITOR.)

The following entries are from the Registers in the Record Office, Bridgetown, Barbados:—

Jane daughter of William and Mary Collier, b. Jan. 4, 1730-1; bapt. Aug. 20, 1733.

Mary daughter of William and Mary Collier, b. 17 Aug. 1733; bapt. Aug. 20, 1733.

Jane daughter of Elizabeth Miller, buried Feb. 15, 1796.

(Note.—The latter entry does not tally with the inscription on the tombstone.)

C. W. FIREBRACE.

Danehurst, Uckfield, Sussex.

* 1812, Feb. 15. On the 5th inst. at Tobago the Lady of Hon. J. M. Collier, Speaker of the House of Assembly of that Island, of a son. ("Barbados Mercury.")
1853, Oct. 6. In Great Ormond-st. aged 59, Catherine-Gregorie, widow of the late James Morris Collier, of the Island of Tobago. ("G.M.," 650.) [EDITOR.]

De BRETTON

The reference made to the family of Baron de Bretton of the Island of Santa Cruz in the Journal for February 1948 (Vol. xv. No. 2 p. 105) in relation to the memorial stone to Judith (de Bretton) Cummins which was recently discovered in St. Michael's Cathedral has brought the following contribution from Mrs. Douglas C. Armstrong of Christiansted, St. Croix, V. I. U.S.A. Mrs. Armstrong writes:— **

The Baron Frederick de Bretton was apparently originally of French descent. When the island of St. Croix was acquired by the Danes in 1733 the baron and his family were living there. Their original town house, a fine mansion of three stories, is still standing. Baron Frederick de Bretton had two sons—Peter and Lucas, who both bore the title of baron.

Judith de Bretton, who afterwards became the wife of Captain Cummings, was the third daughter of Baron Lucas de Bretton, and was at an early age involved in an exciting scandal of the times. The story goes that when Judith was of the tender age of 13 years, an old friend of the family persuaded her to elope with him at midnight, only to be cast out into the streets a few hours later on his point blank refusal to marry her. Her brother, another Lucas de Bretton, discharged a pistol twice at his sister's assailant.

An account of the affair was reported to the Danish authorities, and as a result, Lucas de Bretton was banished from St. Croix his plea for leniency on the ground of his noble descent having failed.

The stigma of the scandal of Judith's elopement and subsequent events having spoilt her chances of an alliance with any respectable St. Croix family, it is supposed that the marriage to Capt. Cummings, a complete stranger to the Island was the result of the bridegroom's ignorance of the facts. It is probable that Cummings was stationed in St. Croix during the British occupation from 1807 to 1815. when his acquaintance with his future wife was made.*

The de Brettons, or Van Brettons, as the name was sometimes used, were in St. Croix as late as 1850, when a certain Dr. John de Bretton, Baron de Bretton, was living there with his two daughters. Both daughters married and died childless.

The family name is not now represented in the Island of St. Croix.

---

* The marriage took place in the Island of Guadeloupe during the period of the English occupation of that island, 1810-14. A notice of the event appeared in the Gentleman's Magazine for 1811 (page 188),—"August 1811. Lately. At Guadeloupe, Lieut. Cumming, to Baroness Judith De Bretton, eldest daughter of Baron Frederick De Bretton of St. Croix."
Her designation on the monumental inscription as "third daughter of Baron de Bretton" (not the eldest) is probably the correct one. Ed. Journal.

** Page 673, this volume.

HAVILAND OF BARBADOS.

Information and parentage are wanted of Miles Haviland, who is described as receiving a ticket to go from Barbadoes to Rhode Island in 1679. There was a William Haviland living in America at the time, and until a few years previously at Newport, Rhode Island, after which he removed to Flushing, Long Island. This William was the founder of the Haviland family in America, and believed to have been the son William (baptized 7 September 1606 at St. Thomas's Church in Salisbury, Wilts) of James Haviland, Mayor of Salisbury 1602-3. It is possible that, knowing his kinsman William was living in America, Miles may have gone to visit him. If so, what was the relationship, and what became of Miles?

In 1680 there was a Captain Mathew Haviland who owned servants in Barbadoes. This Captain Mathew was undoubtedly the son of Mathew Haviland of Payton and Wellisford Manors, co. Somerset, and Elizabeth Payne his wife, who was married to Elizabeth Webber; for John Haviland, son of last-named Mathew, in a letter to John de Haviland of Guernsey dated 31 March 1709, mentions a " brother call'd Mathew who dy'd in ye East Indies [West Indies—Barbadoes ?] about 20 years since " [1689]. Miles could not have been his son, for Captain Mathew Haviland, as also his only and twin brother John, was born 3 June 1661, and could not have had a son born even at that date. Nor is there a Miles in any anterior generation to Mathew, his father.

HAYNES OF BARBADOS.*

A short history of this family has just been published, which makes a very welcome addition to our scant West Indian genealogies. The first portion comprises the notes made by General Robert Haynes (1769—1851). These consist of memoranda relating to his family, interspersed with bits of local history, and are very interesting and valuable. The second portion contains a genealogy sent by an American gentleman, but this is so full of incorrect dates and other errors as to be quite unreliable.

The pedigree of the family can be proved from Richard Haynes of Newcastle in St. John's Parish, who was there married to Elvy Thorne on 30 July 1718. A certain John Haynes, Constable of that parish in 1661 and Surveyor of Roads 1671, is supposed to be identical with one of those names, formerly of Barbados, then of New York, merchant, born 1639, who died 9 December 1689, and in his will, dated 24 August 1689, named his wife Eliz., his son John, then at Barbados, and his son Andrew, also his brother Robert Haynes in Barbados. This Robert was presumably identical with the man of those names who was sidesman of St. John's 1683-4, Surveyor of Roads 1684—8, and of the Vestry in 1695. The above-mentioned Richard was probably descended from one of these two brothers John and Robert, but search will be necessary to establish this.

The parish register of St. John's commences—Marriages from 16 August 1657, Burials from 10 August 1657, and several entries are given from these, but no Baptisms. Let us hope that when further data have been secured, and abstracts of wills and indentures made from the Registrar's Office at Bridgetown, a revised and fuller edition, with a tabular pedigree, may be published.

---

* " Notes by General Robert Haynes of New Castle and Clifton Hall Plantations, Barbados, and other documents of family interest." Edited by the late Edmund C. Haynes, A. Percy Haynes, and Edmund S. P. Haynes. (Argus Printing Co., 78 King William Street, London, E.C. (No date.) Pp. 32, 8vo, paper cover.

HEWETT OF BARBADOS.

Indenture made 27 Sept. 1671 between John Hewett formerly of Barbados now of London cooper on the one part and Tho. Martyn of London merchant on the other Witnesseth that John Hewett sells to Tho. Martyn for a competent sum all that plantation with the storehouse heretofore built by Capt. Tho. Eagle and sold by Tho. Eagle to Chr. Lyne and by Chr. Lyne to John Hewett and by John Hewett let to Geo. Orpen servant to John Hewett in the year 1653 near Austen's Bay bounded on the one side by Capt. Edny and on the other by Capt. Thornhill. (Abstract from a deed which passed through the Editor's hands.)

In Hunter's " Familiæ Minorum Gentium," p. 1030, is a pedigree of Hewet, from which it appears that John Hewet, D.D., Chaplain to King Charles, and beheaded in 1658, had a son John, " merch¹ in Barbadoes, who had afterwards a place of £200 a year in the Exchequer," married Mary dau. of Major Roe of Windsor, and had a son John, Rector of Harthill.

MASONIC RECORDS.

In view of the impending bi-centenary of the death of Alexander Irvine, founder of Freemasonry in Barbados, the following inscription on his tomb in the eastern portion of the graveyard of the Cathedral is of interest.

Large altar-tomb. On the top slab is a Jacobean shield with mantling in sunk circle:—

CREST.—A tower over W. and H. ARMS.—On a chevron between three Towers a pair of compasses. MOTTO.—LET BROTHERLY LOVE CONTINUE.

To the Memory of / ALEXANDER IRVINE Gent / The Founder of Free Masonry / in Barbados / who lived Beloved and died / Lamented by all who knew him / the Brethren of Saint Michaels Lodge / of which he was the First Master / have placed upon his remains this Stone / to be a monument of his Merit / and their Gratitude / He departed this life the 13th / day of November 1743 / in the 49th Year of his Age.

There is no corresponding burial entry in the Church Register.

The Founder of Scotia Lodge, No. 340 Scotch Registry, which will celebrate its 150th anniversary of its foundation in 1944, is buried in the same graveyard near the west porch of the Cathedral. On his tomb is inscribed a circle, the sun in centre, compasses above it, with the following inscription:—

In Sacred Memory / of Departed Worth / This Tablet is Erected / By the Past Masters / Wardens and Members of / the Scotia Lodge / No. 340 Scotch Registry, / as a mark of Respect / for the Distinguished / Talents and Virtues / in the Cause of Masonry / and in Remembrance of / Our Respected Brother THOMAS WATSON / Past Master and Founder / of the above Lodge / who Departed this Life / on the 2nd Septr. 1854, / Aged 52 Years.

The register of marriages solemnized in the parish of St. James in the island of Barbados in the year 1698 contains an entry under date February 24, of the marriage of "Capt. JOHN NANFAN, (Governor of New York) and Mrs. ELIZA CHESTER." The record is signed by Charles Irvine, rector of the parish.

Captain John Nanfan was commissioned as Lieutenant-Governor of New York, 1 July 1697. He was recommended for the post by his relation the Earl of Bellomont on the latter's appointment as Governor of New York and New England, who described him as of Sir John Jacob's regiment of foot and "an experienced good officer who has served the whole war."

Bellomont sailed from England for New York in the winter of 1697, but being driven off the coast by a gale, found himself in January 1698 in Barbados, having parted company from every ship of the little squadron that had sailed with him. It is evident that Captain Nanfan was one of the Earl's *entourage* and sojourned in Barbados until the former's departure in the month of March 1698. During this visit, he married Mrs. Eliza Chester.

The Earl and party reached New York at the end of March and he and the Lieutenant-Governor were sworn in on 2nd April, 1698.

Lord Bellomont reported to Secretary Vernon on 6 December 1700, that he had consented to Nanfan's departure for Barbados to look after his wife's fortune there, the leave of the King requested about a year previously never having been granted. Nanfan was in Barbados when Lord Bellomont died suddenly on 5th March, 1701, and did not reach New York until 19th May following.

Who was Mrs. Eliza Chester? Was her marriage to Nanfan the result of their chance meeting in Barbados?

The Will of Richard Nanfan, late of the parish of St. Mary, Whitechapel, London, master of the merchant ship Puttoxon, dated 2nd January 1937, was proved in England, 23rd November 1737, and recorded in Barbados on 30th May 1740. He left everything to his wife, Elizabeth, and appointed her sole executrix. There are no details of his property and Barbados is not mentioned, but the testator's connection with the island is evident by the necessity for proving the will there. Was he son of Captain Nanfan and Mrs. Eliza?

PEARD OF BARBADOS AND PLYMOUTH.

Mr. H. Tapley-Soper, F.S.A., Librarian of The City Library, Exeter, has contributed the following note on Justinian Peard, Mayor of Plymouth, 1644-5, extracted from Volume XVII, (1937) page 325, of the Transactions of the Plymouth Institution—a paper by C. W. Bracken entitled Romance of some old Plymouth Deeds".

Justinian Peard was Mayor of Plymouth, 1644-5, and played an important part during the Seige. A copy of his will and the Archbishop's Certificate appointing his executrix are preserved among Group A. He left, after the death of his wife Jane, a dwellinghouse in Nutt Street, Cann House, to his nephew Oliver, the Maudling House, garden and three fields to his nephew John. To his wife Jane among other bequests he left £100 to be paid out of his plantation at the Barbados. To the Free School in Plymouth (the Corporation Grammar School) he left £10 "to buy books for the use of poor boys and to remain in the said School to begin a Library".

"The Will is witnessed but undated, nor is any executor named. By the original Certificate preserved, the Archbishop of Canterbury (by his Registrar) appointed Elizabeth Peard, relict of Justinian, as executrix, on the application of the two nephews (*nullum omnino fecerit et constituerit executorem*). The apparent confusion between the names Jane and Elizabeth is solved by these extracts from St. Andrew's Registers: January, 1668-9, Mrs. Jane, wife of Mr. Justinian Peard, buried, October 5, 1669, Mr. Justinian Peard and Mrs. Elizabeth Jeffrey married. October 15, 1669, Mr. Justinian Peard buried."

The mention of the Maudlin House at Mutley where the original Plymouth Maudlin or Leper Hospital once stood, of Peard's business transactions in the West Indies, and of his gifts to the old Plymouth Grammar School are of interest".

Justinian Peard's name occurs twice in the Barbados Records, but there is nothing to suggest that he was ever present in this Island. Two other members of his family, namely, Simon Peard and George Peard were residing here, as appears by the local records. In 1655 Justinian Peard and Richards Evans of Plymouth, Merchants, acquired land in the parish of St. James, being then owners of other lands on which the same was bounding, doubtless the plantation to which Justinian referred in his

Will. The deed of conveyance is dated 28 August, 1655; the consideration for the purchase was 5,600 lbs. of muscovado sugar, and one of the witnesses is Simon Peard, who was probably Justinian's agent in Barbados.

George Peard was a London Merchant, but residing in Barbados when he made his will on 17 May 1662. Simon and George Peard were nephews of Justinian Peard and brothers of Oliver and John who were beneficiaries under Justinian's will.

These facts and others of value in tracing the family history are clearly stated in George Peard's will, the terms of which were as follows. His mother, Mrs. Alice Peard, a widow, was to enjoy the profits of the annual value of £20 of his estate in New Port, Devon, for her life and then to devolve on his brother Simon. Also, one-half of all his lands recovered or to be recovered since the death of his brother Charles. The other half to go to his brother Oliver. To Simon, all the reast of his lands. To his brother John the net proceeds of 2 butts of muscovado sugar shipped in the Exchange of Plymouth, consigned to his Uncle Justinian.

To his sister Mary Peard, £10. To Justinian Peard £1, and to his Aunt (Justinian's wife) £1. Various small gifts to John Worsam, Richard Evans, John Evans, and his mother Alice Peard. His mother and John Worsam executors.

The Will, dated 17 May 1662, was proved in Barbados 22 July 1662.

*   *   *   *

SIMMONS OF BARBADOS.

Can any of the readers of "Caribbeana" refer me to a Scottish or Barbadian newspaper of 1777 to 1780, containing the announcement of the birth of a son to the wife of Henry Peter Simmons of *Harrow* Plantation, Barbados?

H. P. C. SIMMONS.

Hastings, Barbados.

THE EARLIEST WILL OF BARBADOS.

John Symons of the Barbadies, Labourere, 10 June 1627, 3 Charles. To John Dudman my wages due from Capt. John Powell. Richard Leonard to be sole Ex'or and I give him all monyes due in England. + of testator. Wit. by Fraunces Cox, + Will. Browne.

Proved 10 Dec. 1628. Comⁿ to Peter Hull, one of the creditors of J. S., late in foreign parts, deceased, during the absence and with the consent of R. L. (109, Barrington.)

TOPPIN OF BARBADOS. (Add. MS. 31, 228, fo. 44.)

MARRIAGES.

1676	Mʳ Miles Toppin & Mʳˢ Scotanglinder Maxwell.	Xᵗ Church.
1687	Oct. 11 Scotanglinda the wife of Capᵗ Miles Toppin, buried.	Sᵗ John's.
1698-9	.... 4 Majʳ Miles Toppin & Mary Dickenson.	Sᵗ John's.
1693	Edmund Burke & Eliza Toppin.	
1706	Mʳ Jas. Toppin & Mʳˢ Mary Seawell.	Xᵗ Ch.
1711	Mʳ John Toppin & Mʳˢ Angeletta Destin.	Xᵗ Ch.
1728	Philip Taylor & Eliza Toppin.	Sᵗ John's.
1731	Miles Toppin & Sarah Pearce.	
1741	Thos. Herringham & Christiana Toppin.	Xᵗ Ch.
1736	Wm. Serlius & Eliza Toppin.	Sᵗ John.
1745	Anthony Evan & Jane Toppin.	Xᵗ Ch.
1748	John Gall & Mary Toppin.	Sᵗ John's.
1752	Thos. Toppin & Susanna Nurse.	Xᵗ Ch.
1764	George Ince & Susanna Toppin.	
1773	Chas. Tyrwhitt Lewis & Mary Toppin.	
1778	Thos. Ingram & Elizᵗʰ Toppin.	
1793	Francis Butcher Carter & Rebecca Toppin.	Sᵗ John's.

APPENDIX B:

NEW ENGLAND AND BARBADIAN NOTES.

By

G. ANDREWS MORIARTY A.M., LLB., F.A.S.G., F.S.A.

*

The Journal for February 1947 contains a number of references of interest alike to the antiquaries of New England and Barbados and it occurs to me that a few notes upon them may be of interest to Barbadians.

1. JOSEPH and ANNE BORDEN (pp. 9-10).

Joseph Borden was a native of Portsmouth, Rhode Island and the member of a prominent Quaker family in that Colony. He was born there on 3 July 1643, the son of Richard and Joan (Fowle) Borden of Portsmouth, who came to New England from Headcorn, co. Kent about 1638 (Records of the Portsmouth Quaker Meeting, *ex penes* Newport Hist. Soc.). Richard was an Assistant in 1653-4 and was General Treasurer of Rhode Island 1654-5, he died 25 May 1671. He belonged to a family of prosperous Kentish yeoman, which had been settled in Headcorn since the fourteenth century and his direct line has been traced to Edmund Borden of Headcorn, who died in 1539. The family has been prominent in Rhode Island and the adjoining parts of Massachusetts for the last three centuries. A brother of Joseph, Benjamin, removed to Burlington, New Jersey and became the ancestor of the Bordens of New Jersey and Pennsylvania. In the eighteenth century a member of the Rhode Island family settled in Nova Scotia and became the ancestor of the late Canadian Premier, Sir Robert Borden.

Joseph married Hope—and had Sarah born 17 April 1664, William born 31 Dec. 1667 and Hope born 26 Dec. 1673, all at Portsmouth. Soon after this last date Joseph removed to Barbados. The Anne Borden, who witnessed the marriage of Joseph Kirle and Mary Brett, was probably a second wife of Joseph, married in Barbados or she may have been an unrecorded daughter.

Joseph's mother, Joan Fowle, was the daughter of Richard Fowle yeoman of Frittenden and Headcorn, co. Kent and the niece of Francis Fowle, a wealthy clothier of Cranbrook in that county, who died without issue in 1632.

(For an account of the Bordens see Austin's Genealogical Dic. of Rhode Island pp. 23-24: New Eng. Hist. & Gen. Reg. Vol. 84, pp. 70—84, 225—229. For Fowle see Register Vol. 75, pp. 226—233.)

---

*This apparently refers to the second of two articles on the Turner family of Barbados and New England, which have been reprinted on pp. 559-569, this volume.

2. JOSEPH HARBIN, his son JOSEPH JR. and THOMAS HARBIN (pp. 9—10).

Joseph Harbin was a well to do merchant of St. Michael's, who owned plantations in Jamaica and South Carolina. His wife Sarah was a cousin of the children of Samuel Seabury of Duxbury, Plymouth Colony. Samuel's father, John of Boston, Mass., in 1639, removed after 1642 with his eldest son John to Barbados. Samuel was the ancestor of the American family (c.f. Register op. cit. Vol. 67, p. 363).

Thomas Harbin was probably a brother of Joseph, and the ——Harbin, who married Elizabeth, sister of John Emperor of St. Michael's and of Capt. Francis Emperor of Lower Norfolk county, Virginia. Another sister, Sarah Emperor, married on 1 March 1659 Edward Oistin Jr. gent. of Christ Church and 2ndly. William Lee, on 3 Aug. 1670 at St. John.

The will of Elizabeth Harbin, "late of Barbados but now of Princess Ann co. Va.", dated 30 Dec. 1693, was proved 4 Nov. 1696 (Princess Ann was set off from Lower Norfolk in 1692). She left bequests to her cousin, Elizabeth Ramsden, daughter of "my sister Sarah Lee in Barbados" and to the latter's children Elizabeth and William Ramsden, to "my cousin Mr. Francis Emperor and his son Francis", to her cousin Mrs. Sarah Emperor, wife of cousin Francis Emperor, to kinsman Mr. Tully Robinson and made Mrs. Sarah Emperor (i.e. Sarah, wife of Francis Tully Emperor of Barbados and Lower Norfolk co. Va. and the daughter of Edward and Sarah (Emperor) Oistin of Christ Church) her executrix. Her Barbadian property was in the hands of Thomas Sherman and Joseph Hough at Barbados (Princess Ann co. wills). The Virginia Emperors were also Quakers.

Sarah, daughter of Edward and Sarah (Emperor) Oistin of Christ Church married on 25 Sept. 1679 her first cousin, Francis Emperor, later called Francis Tully Emperor, son of Capt. Francis Emperor of Lower Norfolk co. Va. This Francis Tully Emperor lived both in Barbados and Lower Norfolk and Princess Ann counties. His will, dated 26 May 1698, was proved 20 July 1711 in Princess Ann. His wife's will, dated 20 March 1701/2, was proved 25 Oct. 1709 at Barbados. She names her daughter Elizabeth and the Ramsden and James children of her sister Elizabeth, then the wife of Miles James.

Tully Robinson, named as a "kinsman" in the will of Elizabeth Harbin, was the ancestor of a prominent family on the Eastern Shore of Virginia.

John Emperor of St. Michael's, brother of Capt. Francis of Virginia, probably had a son Thomas, who was the father of Capt. John Emperor of St. Michael's (bapt. 1 July 1672 at St.

Michael's). This Capt. John married Amerinthia, daughter of Bernard Schencking of Christ Church. Both Schencking and his son-in-law, John Emperor, migrated to South Carolina, in the Barbadian emigration to that colony, between 1693 and 1695. Capt. Emperor died without issue at Charleston. The Emperor family is now extinct, but the name long survived as a given one among the old families of Lower Norfolk and Princess Ann. Elizabeth, sister of Capt. John, married Thomas Farr of Barbados. They also went to South Carolina, where Elizabeth died at Charleston on 15 Nov. 1725 leaving issue.

These Emperors appear to have gone to Barbados and Virginia from Norwich, England, where a family of Emperors appear among the Flemish refugees, who settled in Norwich during the Spanish wars in the Low Countries towards the close of the sixteenth century. The name, originally de Keyser, was translated "Emperor" at Norwich (cf. Records of the Walloon Church at Norwich, pub. by the Huguenot Soc.).

(An account of the Emperors, Oistins and Harbins will be found in the Virginia Hist. Mag., pub. by Va. Hist. Soc., Vol. XXI, pp. 417—420, Vol. XXIII, pp. 438—440).*

3. TOBIAS and LUCY FRERE (p. 31).

Lucy was evidently the second wife of Tobias Frere of Christ Church and London, as Tobias married at St. Phillip's on 19 Sept. 1676 Abigail, daughter of Capt. John Turner of "Three Houses" in that parish. (cf. Journal Vol. X, p. 10).

4. CONSTANT SILVESTER (p. 41).

He was a London merchant, who, before 1657, emigrated to Barbados. On 9 June 1651 he, together with his brother Nathaniel, purchased from Stephen Goodyear, the grantee of Lord Stirling, Shelter Island near Montauk Point, the easterly end of Long Island, New York. In 1674 re-established Dutch Government at New York confiscated Constant's share and sold it to Nathaniel, whose descendants, after the English reconquered New York, held the island as lords of the manor of Shelter Island. (Considerable information regarding these Silvesters will be found in the New Eng. Hist. & Gen. Reg. Vol. 37, pp. 381-87 and Vol. 45, pp. 295-96; cf. also Savage's Gen. Dic. of New England·Vol. IV, pp. 98-99). The Silvesters were also Quakers.

5. REV. DUDLEY AND RUTH WOODBRIDGE (p.44)

The Rev. Dudley Woodbridge descended from one of the most distinguished families of Massachusetts, which came from

---

Stanton in Wiltshire. His father, Dudley Woodbridge A.B. (Harvard 1696), was born at Windsor, Conn. on 7 Sept. 1677, the son cf the Rev. Benjamin and Mary (Ward) Woodbridge. His maternal grandfather, the Rev. John Ward of Haverhill Mass., was one of the most distinguished clergymen of early New England. The elder Dudley removed to Barbados prior to 1702 and on 30 June 1707 he was appointed Judge of the High Court of Admiralty at Barbados and died in London, 13 Feb. 1719/20. In 1711 he wrote to Benjamin Coleman of Boston that he had intended to send his eldest son Dudley (the testator of 1747) to New England "but now resolve him for London." This son matriculated at Oxford in 1723 and became rector of St. Philip's Barbados. A younger son, Benjamin, went to Boston Mass. in 1716 and was killed in a duel on Boston Common in 1728 by Henry Phillips. The first New England ancestor of the family, John Woodbridge of Newbury,, Mass., was educated at Oxford and by his uncle the Rev. Thomas Parker of Newbury a noted New England minister. He was the son of the Rev. John Woodbridge of Stanton, Wilts. The wife of John Woodbridge of Newbury, whom he married about 1639, was Mercy, daughter of Thomas Dudley, the early Governor of Massachusetts, who, prior to his emigration to New England in 1630, had been Steward to the Earl of Lincoln.

The Judge of Admiralty at Barbados was painted by Sir Godfrey Kneller and several mezzotints made from the picture survive. One of these is reproduced in the excellent biography of the Judge in Sibley's Harvard Graduates (Vol. IV, pp. 317-20).

The Judge's daughter Mary married Abel Alleyne of Mount Standfast.

There is a genealogy of the family, compiled by the distinguished New England antiquary, Miss Mary K. Talcott of Hartford, Conn.

MORE NOTES ON NEW ENGLAND AND BARBADOS

By

G. ANDREWS MORIARTY, A.M., LL.B., F.S.A.

DAVENPORT

By reference to the August 1947 issue of the **Journal** (Vol. XIV, No. 4 p. 173 passim) it will be seen that Humphrey Davenport was a member of the St. Michael's Vestry 1660-1661 and Churchwarden in 1659 (p. 177) Humphrey Davenport from Barbados settled in Dorchester, Mass., about 1666, where a Thomas Davenport, possibly a relative, had been residing since 1640. He married Rachel, daughter of Thomas Holmes, a brother of Major William Holmes of Scituate and Boston, Mass. He soon removed to Hartford, Conn., where his wife was convicted for card playing by the pious or bigoted Puritan magistrates. Thereupon, he removed to the more liberal atmosphere of the Dutch colony of New Amsterdam (New York) and in 1674 he was living on the West side of Broadway, below Rector Street. He was the ancestor of the Davenports of Westchester Co., New York, and Western Connecticut. He was, undoubtedly, the Humphrey Davenport, who was commissioned clerk of Ulster Co. N.Y. (Savage's Genealogical Dictionary of New England 11/12; N.E. Hist. & Gen. Reg. XXXIII 26; Bolton's Hist. of Westchester Co., N.Y.; Blake's Hist. of Putnam Co., N.Y.; Ouderdonk's Hist. of Long Island).

WHITE-VASSALL.

The will of William Vassall of St. Michael's, dated 13 July 1655 is on file in the Barbados Record Office. He left 1/3 of his estate to his son John and 2/3 to his daughters Judith (wife of Resolved White of Scituate and Marshfield, Mass.), Frances (wife of James Adams of Marshfield), Anne (wife of Nicholas Ware, merchant of St. Michael's, formerly of Virginia), Margaret (wife of Joshua Hubbard of Scituate and Hingham, Mass.) and Mary (single at Barbados in 1655). The son, John Vassall, was of Scituate until 1661, when he sold his estate and removed to the West Indies, probably to Jamaica or Barbados. In 1667 he was engaged in the settlement of Cape Fear, North Carolina, when he wrote to New England asking aid for that colony.

William Vassall was a wealthy and important planter in both New England and Barbados. The family are said to have been Huguenot refugees in London, descended from the de Vassalls, barons of Guerden in Querci, Perigord.

John Vassall, Alderman of London, in 1588 fitted out and commanded two ships of war in the Armada Fight, which was commemorated in the family crest of a ship with sails and masts proper. This John had two sons Samuel and William. Samuel was one of the original patentees of the Massachusetts Bay Company in 1628; he was an officer of the Company and an Alderman of London. In 1640 Samuel Vassall, clothier, was M.P. for

London. He was active on the side of the Parliament and in 1646 he was one of the English Commissioners for the conservation of peace with Scotland. Samuel never came to America, but his son John settled in Jamaica and was the ancestor of the Vassalls of Jamaica and Massachusetts. Their fine Georgian mansion on Brattle St. ('Tory Row') in Cambridge, Mass., was later the residence of the poet Longfellow. In the American Revolution the family were loyalists and went to England. Lady Holland, the famous Whig hostess of the last century, descended from this family.

William Vassall, the other son of John the Alderman was the settler in New England and Barbados. He came to Massachusetts in the Winthrop fleet in 1630, but soon returned to England. In 1635 he came back to Massachusetts bringing his family with him and settled in Roxbury, Mass., whence he soon removed to Scituate in Plymouth Colony (part of Massachusetts since 1692) where he was the leading citizen. Of pronounced Presbyterian views he soon became embroiled over religious and political matters with the Congregational rulers and in 1646 he went to England to petition for redress against the government, intending to return soon. He never came back, but in 1648 he settled in St. Michael's Barbados, where he was a prominent merchant and planter. All his daughters except Anne and Mary married and remained in New England (White).

Among the mutilated deeds in the Barbados Record Office, at Bridgetown is one whereby "Resolved White of Scituate in New Plymouth in New England and Judith his wife, daughter of William Vassall of this Island Esq." conveyed to Nicholas Ware of St. Michael's, merchant, all his one-fifth of two-thirds of William Vassall's plantation in St. Michael's, "on the West side of ye gulf or river" and all other lands inherited from the said Vassall, except the land where the said Vassall formerly lived in New England, lying in the townships of Scituate and Marshfield in New England. Dated 17 March 1656/7; acknowledged by Judith, wife of Resolved White, 20 March 1656/7; entered 24 March 1657. Resolved White also witnessed a deed of sale from Mary Vassall of Barbados to her brother-in-law, Nicholas White of St. Michael's, merchant, for her share in her father William Vassall's plantation in St. Michael's on 11 May 1657.

Resolved White was of Scituate and Marshfield, Plymouth Colony, and later of Salem, Mass. He was the son of William and Susanna White, who were members of the congregation of Brownist exiles at Leyden, Holland. On 11 Feb. 1611/2 William White "Englishman", woolcarder, and Anna (Susanna) Fuller were married in Leyden and on 1 Dec. 1616 they resided in the Uiterstegracht Street in Leyden. Their son Resolved was born in Leyden in or about 1616 (he deposed in the Essex Co. Mass. Court in 1679 "aged about 63 years"). In the Summer of 1620 he embarked, with his parents, on the famous voyage of the Mayflower, which brought the first permanent settlers to New England. His brother, Peregrine, (an ancestor of the writer) was born in the cabin of the Mayflower in Cape Cod harbour in Dec. 1620 and was the first English child born in New England. After the death of his wife, Judith, Resolved White removed to Salem, Mass., where he remarried and died shortly after 1680.

William White, the father of Resolved and Peregrine, died in the first terrible Winter of the Plymouth Plantation in 1620/1 and his widow Susanna, remarried Edward Winslow, afterwards Governor of the Plymouth Colony. Edward Winslow was a member of a gentle family of Droitwich, co. Worcs. As a young man he was sent to finish his education with a Continental tour and falling in with the Brownists at Leyden he became converted to their views and thereafter cast his lot with them. He also came in the Mayflower in 1620. Edward and Susanna were the ancestors of one of the most distinguished families of New England. A portrait of Gov. Winslow now hangs in "Pilgrim Hall" at Plymouth, Mass. The descendants of Resolved and Judith (Vassall) White are very numerous in the United States.

The deed, above cited, is of considerable interest as it proves the actual presence of a Mayflower passenger in Bridgetown in 1657. Resolved White and Judith had undoubtedly gone to Barbados in connection with the settlement of her father's estate.

(cf. New Eng. Hist. Gen. Reg. XVII/56-61; LXVII/369; Am. Gen. XVII/193-206; Dexter's "The Pilgrims in England, Holland and New England").

MAVERICK.

Among the Barbadian deeds is an agreement made 14 Jan 1649/50 between Nathaniel Maverick of New England gent. and Capt. George Briggs of "ye Barbados Esq.". It recites that Capt. Briggs has bought of Nathaniel Maverick, with the consent of his father, Mr. Samuel Maverick and with the advice and consent of his friends, Mr. Richard Vines[1] and Mr. John Turner[2], who have received a like order from Mr. Samuel Maverick, an island, known as Nodles Island, and Capt. Briggs binds himself to pay before 1 Sept. 40,000 lbs. of white sugar at some convenient storehouse at the Indian Bridge or at the Hole.

Among the same deeds is an indenture dated 31 July 1656 between Samuel Maverick of New England gent. and his son and heir Nathaniel Maverick on the one part and Col. John Bury of Barbados Esq. on the other. Shows that by deed dated 15 Feb. 1649/50 Samuel and Amias Maverick assigned to Capt. George Briggs an island, commonly called Nodles Island in Massachusetts Bay in New England and the said Briggs by deed of 28 Oct. 1650 conveyed the said island to the said John Bury. A difference having arisen between John Bury and Samuel Maverick, the Massachusetts General Court on 7 June 1653 ordered the said Bury to pay the said Maverick 700 lbs. at the storehouse next the sea in good well cured Barbados Muscovado sugar.

---

1 Mr. Richard Vines above named went to Maine in the service of Sir Ferdinando Gorges, Lord Proprietor of Maine in 1616, being one of the earliest Englishmen in New England. He was a Councillor of the Maine Government in 1635 and Steward General (Deputy Governour) after the departure of Thomas Gorges. Vines resided at Biddeford Pool, near the mouth of the Saco River. On 20 Oct. 1645 he sold his patent and removed to Barbados. He was buried at St. Michael's 19 April 1651.
2 For Mr. John Turner see my article on the Turners in the Journal, Vol. x No. 1. November 1942.

(Pages 559-566, this volume.)

On 1 Sept. 1656 John Parris[3] of Barbados, merchant, sold to Nathaniel Maverick of the said Island, merchant, one-half of a store house at the Indian Bridge (Barbados Deeds).

The will of Nathaniel Maverick of St. Lucy's parish Esq., dated 16 Aug. 1670, was proved 24 Feb. 1673/4. To be buried by his son, Moses Maverick near the South East window of St. Lucy's church. To daughter Mary Maverick 40,000 lbs. of muscovado sugar at her marriage or eighteen years. If his father came to the island he was to be maintained out of his estate . . . . Residue to sons John, Samuel and Nathaniel under twenty one years of age. Sons Samuel and Nathaniel to be educated and bound as apprentices under able merchants. Overseers Col. William Yeoman, Major Samuel Lidcombe and Capt. John Stearte. Witnesses: John and Samuel Maverick, William Lemon and Richard Springer. Codicil 3 Sept. 1672. To mother Amias Maverick £10 stirling per annum for life. To sister Mary Hooke[4] 1,000 lbs. of sugar for a mourning gown. On 8 Jan. 1673/4 Mr. Miles Scottow was made an overseer in place of Col. Lidcombe. Proved 24 Feb. 1673/4. (Barbados Wills).

Nathaniel Maverick was the son of Samuel Maverick, one of the earliest settlers of Massachusetts and was a prominent figure in that Colony. The Mavericks were a clerical family from Devonshire; and their ancestry has been traced to Robert Maverick, clerk, of Awliscombe, who was buried there 14 Nov. 1573, through his son Peter Maverick, Vicar of Awliscombe, who died shortly before 3 Feb. 1616/7, the Rev. John Maverick and his son Samuel, abovenamed.

The Rev. John Maverick, father of Samuel and grandfather of Nathaniel, received his B.A. degree at Exeter College, Oxford in 1599, M.A. 1603. After serving as curate to his uncle the Rev. Radford Maverick, vicar of Ilsington, co. Devon, he was inducted into the living of Beaworthy, co. Devon in 1615. In March 1629/30 he was chosen one of the teachers of the Puritan church organized at Plymouth and sailed for New England in the Winthrop Fleet soon after, arriving in New England on 30 May 1630. A zealous Puritan he became minister of the church at Dorchester, Mass. and died 3 Feb. 1635/6.

Samuel Maverick, his son, had preceded him to New England and arrived there in 1624. He settled on Noddles Island in Boston Harbour

---

3   John Parris of Barbados, merchant, was evidently the brother of Thomas Parris Esq., of Barbados, whose will, dated 21 Aug. 1673, was proved 2 Sept. 1673. He names his eldest son John "now in England," his brother-in-law Mr. John Oxenbridge of New England and his son, Samuel, to whom he left all his estate in Barbados, including his house at Reed's Bay. This Samuel Parris became a cleric and went to New England, where he was settled as the minister at Salem Village (now Danvers, Mass.). He attained an unsavory notority as a leader in the witchcraft delusion in 1692. The will of John Parris of Barbados Esq., dated 15 May 1660, was proved 23 Oct. 1661 (cf New Eng. Hist. & Gen. Reg. XXXIX/337; LXVII/365—67; LXIX/146—159; Essex Institute Hist. Coll. (Salem) XLIX/354—355).

(now East Boston, where the name Maverick Square preserves his memory). In 1625 he built his house and fortified it with "a Pillizado and fflankers and gunnes both belowe and above in them". This house was still standing in 1660 "the Antientest house in ye Massachusetts Government". Unlike his father, Samuel was a Churchman and a zealous Royalist. He was noted for his open house and lavish hospitality. John Joseleyn, the traveller, who visited his brother in Maine in 1638, records in his book "An Account of Two Voyages to New England, published in London in 1674, that on 10 July 1638 "I went a shore upon Noddles-Island" and he adds that Mr. Maverick was the only hospitable man in all the country". Shortly before the Restoration he went to England to complain of his treatment at the hands of the Puritan magistrates. In 1664 he returned, as one of the Royal Commissioners sent out by Charles II to curb the Puritan magistrates of Massachusetts and to reduce the Dutch at New Amsterdam (New York). When the other Commissioners returned to England, after their failure to shackle the Massachusetts Government; Samuel Mayerick remained behind and settled in the recently acquired Colony of New York. He resided in New York in a house "on the Broadway", which he had received as a gift for his fidelity to the King, where he died between 1670 and 1676. The descendants of his brothers and sisters are numerous in New England.

Nathaniel Maverick, his son and heir, removed to Barbados shortly before 1656 and was a planter and merchant in St. Lucy's. There are a number of wills of the family in the Probate Office at Bridgetown and some entries of the family in the St. Michael's parish register. In 1664 he was one of the group of Barbadians who joined in an agreement to settle in Carolina (Coll. S.C. Hist. Soc. V/29) and although he never left Barbados it seems that some of his descendants, perhaps his son John, was the ancestor of the South Carolina Mavericks. The family in Texas, which became so prominent there in the last century, descend from the Carolina Mavericks. (There is a good account of the family in the N.E. Hist. Gen. Reg. XCVI).

ST. MICHAEL'S CATHEDRAL, BARBADOS

DURING the execution of repairs to the flooring of the pews in the north aisle of the Cathedral nave, five large tombstones were uncovered which have not seen the light of day for a century, or more. It is, therefore, interesting to be able to add particulars from the inscriptions on these ledgers to the information supplied by Oliver's Monumental Inscriptions [1] in this ancient edifice.

At the eastern end of the aisle, the entire stone which covers the tomb of the honourable JOHN PILGRIM is now visible. The excellent carving in the blue marble slab of the deceased's crest and coat of arms shows to advantage in the strong light of the adjacent window.

On sunken oval, mantling, helmet and wreath:—

Crest: A dexter arm in armour holding a scimitar.

Arms: Two bears' heads (**Frere**) impaling three pilgrim's staffs (**Pilgrim.**)

Adding the details which were missing from Oliver's M.I. No. 49, the inscription reads as follows:—

HERE LIES YE BODY OF YE / HONBLE JOHN PILGRIM ESQRE, / ONE OF HIS MAJESTY'S COUNCIL / IN THE ISLAND OF BARBADO'S / WHO DIED YE 25th OF DECEMBER 1715, / AGED 63 YEARS & SEVEN MONTHS.

The burial record says—1715 Dec. 26 The Honble Jno. Pilgrim in the Chancel.

He married Elizabeth Frere and left a son, Joseph.

Five ledgers, each covering the full length and width of the bricked vault underneath, lie end to end along the aisle. Going west—

1. Blue marble ledger — Here Lyeth interred ye body of / PETER CHARLOTT / Obijt the 18th day of January / Anno dom 1689. / Also the body of SAMUEL BATEMAN / Obijt ye 21st day of March 1694/5 Aged 45 years / Also the body of HENRY CHARLOTT / Obijt the 19th of August 1705 / Aged 61 years.

---

1   The Monumental Inscriptions in the Churches and Churchyards of the Island of Barbados, British West Indies, Edited by Vere Langford Oliver, M R C S , &c. London: Mitchell Hughes and Clarke, 140, Wardour Street, W. 1915.

Burial Record — 18 Jan. 1689/90, PETER CHARLOTT, [2.] Gent, in ye church. This entry could hardly be discovered by reference to the Index of Burials in the Registration Office, since it is indexed under the letter G as GEM, PETER CHARLOTT. The copyist obviously misread the word "gent" after the deceased's name in the original entry

Burial Record. 20 August 1705. Mr Henry Charlot in ch(urch).[2.]

Burial Record. 22 March 1695. Capt Samuel Bateman in ch(urch). Captain Bateman married Peter Charlott's widow, Frances, at St. Michael on 29 December, 1692.

Frances, daughter of Peter Charlott and his wife, Frances, married Mr. Henry Lintott at St. Michael on 5 June, 1707.

2. Blue Marble ledger broken across and in four pieces.

Arms— Three talbots heads erased between ten black cross crosslets (HALL) impaling a fleur-de-lis.

HERE LYETH INTERRED YE BODY OF CHRISTIAN / ELY DAUGHTER OF ARTHUR HALL[3] AND/KATHARINE HIS WIFE. SHE WAS BORN IN / BRAZIL YE 9th OF APRIL 1653 AND DYED THE 16th OF FEBRY 1671/2.

THES (sic)

ALSO JOHN LUFTON YE SON OF JOHN LUFTON / AND CHRISTIAN HIS WIFE DYED YE 12th OF / AUGUST 1673.

Christian Hall married, first, John Lufton. Their son John, whose name figures in the inscription, was born before 1671. Her husband, John

2   CHARLOTT WILLS RECORDED IN BARBADOS.
  Barbados. Memo. that Mr Peter Charlotte in sound mind, memory and judgment did in the presenc of Mr John Kenny, Mr Jedidiah Hutchinson, Mr John Wate, Mr (?s)   Hinks, Mrs Charity Springham, give his whole estate to his beloved wife, Frances Charlott to her and her heirs for ever, on the 17 day of Jany. 1689(90)
  Barbados. By the Hon the Lt. Govr. Mr John Kenny, Clarke, (Clerk-in-holy Orders) Mr Jedodiah Hutchinson, and Mr John Waite, appeared and made Oath that they were present and did hear Mr Peter Charlott say and declare what is contained in the above memo. (etc. etc) Proved 21 January 1689 (90) before Edwyn Stede
  Will of HENRY CHARLET of psh .of St M. merchant, (sick). Gives his niece, Frances Charlott of St M., the only daughter of his late bro, Peter Charlott of the said Island decd. his whole estate, and she to be sole exx. Dated 17 August 1705 mark of Henry Charlott. Witnesses : Will ? Moore, Ad. Justice, Charles Peyton. Proof — Appeared the reverend Adam Justice and made Oath (etc.) 24 August 1705. Bevill Granville
  3   Will of Arthur Hall.
  Arthur Hall of Town of St M   To be buried in the old churchyard of the Psh. of St M and my funeral to be only such as shall become a Christian according to the discretion of the Overseers of my Will
  To my son Francis Hall and my dau. Christian, now the wife of Mr John Lufton, mercht., my household goods in equal shares
  To my son Francis one cask or barrell bound with iron having thereto a cover with a padlock, and all the treasure it contains Also one negro boy by name Gunner, and one piece of plate commonly used for a lemonade cup containing in wine measure two quarts and in weight 30 ozs of silver, and my hatband of gold in weight one oz. or better.
  To my sisters-in-law (the sisters of my late wife Katharine Hall deceased) now living in Holland or elsewhere, one oz of dust gold apiece, and to that of my sd wife's sister, Marram Honning a crucifix of silver which my wife bought in her lifetime intentionally for her. To Mr Wm. Tickle who hath been entrusted with the keeping of my accounts, 30/- stlg. that he be assisting to my overseers of my will.
  Residue of my estate in England, Holland, or elsewhere to my son, Francis, and my dau. Christian, now the wife of Jno Lufton mercht. equally
  I appoint Capt John Hallet, merchant, Mr Edward Barton, merchant, and my son-in-law John Lufton merchant and Mr Humphrey Kent, gent., overseers, Hallet and Barton to have administration of affars until my son comes to 21   £5 to each overseer.   mark of Arthur Hall. Wits Joost Boey, Aungener Bond, Rich. Glascock, Scr.
  8 Feb. 1668, appeared Richard Glascock, scrivener, and Joost Boey, limner, and made Oath etc

Lufton, died 5 Febry 1671. She married, secondly, Dr. James Ely[4] on 4 April of the same year.

Burial Record — 5 Feby. 1671 Mr John Lufton in church.

Marriage record — 4 April 1671 Mr James Ely to Mrs Christian Lufton Burial record — 13 August 1673 Jno Lufton a child in Ch(urch).

3. White marble ledger—Sacred / to the Memory of / a beloved and honoured Mother. Mrs. ANNA MARIA CLINTON / who died March 20 1820 / Aged 61 / and of / a much beloved and ever lamented / Sister / JANE KATHARINE CLINTON / who departed this Life / April 16 1817 Aetat 27 / Over their respective ashes / is placed / this Tribute / of / sincere affection / and / lasting regard.[5]

C. ROSSI.[6]

4. White marble—SACRED / To the Memory / of JUDITH CUMMINGS / Wife of Capt / CUMMINGS Dy At Q.M. Genl. / and / third daughter of Baron de Bretton / of the Island of Santa Cruz / who departed this life on the 12th July / A.D. 1821 / Aged 32 Years.

5. White Marble—Here lieth the Body / of WILLIAM DOWLING Esqr. / Who passed through life / Esteemed and Respected / For the Practice of / Many virtues / A Social Companion / A fast Friend / an honest man / In humble Resignation to / The Will of God / On the 16th day of May 1769 / In the 65th Year of his Age / He breathed out / His last Moments / In this pious Strain / O! that Men would therefore praise the / Lord for his Goodness and the Wonders / he doeth for the Children of Men.

4 Will of Dr James Ely
James Ely of St Michael (sick). My children Ann, Elizabeth, and James at 21 or marriage; failing whom, to my sister Ann Ely of KingsBridge in the co. of Devon, spinster, £50
All my late wife's linen &c to my two daughters, Ann & Elizabeth; and to my son all my linen &c. Request my very loving friends, the honble Richard Salter of this Island Esqr. Captain Richard Barrett, & Capt George Keyzar to be executors
Dated 8 October 1688. s. James Ely. Wits: Wm. Beresford. ffras. Draycott, Thos. Huh., Robt. Heimpsall. Proved 17 Oct 1688
5 Marriage—1784 April 28. John Clinton to Anna Maria Grasett.
Baptism—1785 July 29, son of John Clinton and Anna Maria, his wife, born 1 July 1785 and buried 26 Sep. 1785
   do. —1788 June 18. Elizabeth Grasett, dau. of John Clinton and Anna Maria his wife, born 12 March 1788
   do. —1789 Sept. 26—Robert John, son of John Clinton and Anna Maria his wife, born 17 Sept 1789
   do. —1790 Nov 27. Jane Catharine, dau. of John Clinton and Anna Maria his wife, born Oct 1790
6 Sculptor. He executed several other works in Barbados. See the Wall tablet (Oliver M I No 55) in the south-east wall of nave of the Cathedral to Major JOHN WYNNE FLETCHER, 4th King's Own Regt. and ADC to Governor Sir Henry Warde, who died 24 Oct 1824 It seems likely that he was one of the Italian artists imported by Samuel Hall Lord to execute the mural and ceiling decorations for which Long Bay Castle is famous

SOME MONUMENTAL INSCRIPTIONS

AT ST. MICHAEL'S CATHEDRAL

On 13th. April, 1964, workmen engaged in raising the level of part of the south floor of St. Michael's Cathedral, between the second south window and the south door under the gallery, removed a wooden floor which had previously covered two large marble gravestones and part of a third. The inscriptions on two stones are not recorded in *The Monumental Inscriptions in the Churches and Churchyards of the Island of Barbados* by Vere Langford Oliver, London, 1915. Two of these stones were covered when Oliver made his transcriptions, for he gives part of the third, that of John Humpleby, of which he notes that the remainder was under a pew.

The first gravestone is of grey marble and the inscription occupies only about one–third of the stone. It reads: HERE LIE THE REMAINS OF/ BENJAMIN IFIL ESQUIRE,/ WHO DIED/ ON THE 1ST DAY OF SEPTEMBER 1835,/ AGED 60 YEARS./ Benjamin Ifill is also commemorated by a monumental inscription on the south wall, between the first and second windows, which is recorded by V. L. Oliver.

To the west of the above gravestone is one of grey marble which is broken across, the bottom portion of the stone reads: JAMES

PAYNE SON OF/ JOHN & MARTHA PAYNE DIED MAY
16TH 1809/ AGNES BEAUFOY PAYNE DAUGHTER/ OF
THE REVEREND WILLIAM MAYNARD/ & ELIZA ANN
PAYNE/ DIED JANUARY 16TH 1849./ On the upper part
of the stone is inscribed: Here Lyeth the Body/ of Mr. John
Bufhell/ Merchant Aged 63 years/ or there about, who depar/
ted this Life the 29th of/ November in the year of/ our Lord
1680./

Beneath this inscription to John Bushell and above that of
the much later inscription to James Payne, there is a Crest (of
Bushell or Busshell, Cheshire): *A Cherub's head proper*, and, Arms:
A Chevron, below in base an antique crown.

John Bushell was an early settler, for in 1638 he owned more
than 10 acres of land in Barbados. In the census of 1679, John
Bushell Snr. and his wife Rebecca are mentioned with 2 children
and 7 negroes. His will was made on 1st October, 1680, and is
recorded in the Registration Office, Bridgetown. He mentions
3 daughters, Rebecca (married Lane), Sarah (married Depay),
Martha (unmarried) and a son, John. He made a bequest to the
poor of Fradsame, in the County Palatine of Chester and to the poor
of St. Michael, Barbados.

To the west of the previous gravestone is one of white marble,
of which the first 11 lines had been exposed in the cross-aisle and
are therefore, more worn than the remainder of this long inscription,
which was under the wooden floor. The exposed portion was recorded by V. L. Oliver, who noted that the remainder was under a
pew. It reads: Sacred to the Memory/ of JOHN HUMPLEBY
Esquire/ Who/ In the 41st. Year of his age,/ Fell the Victim/
of a Violent and Dreadful Malady./ He departed this transitory
life/ on the 28th. of January 1811:/ Mourned by his Relatives/
Lamented by his Friends/ And, Regretted by all the Good and
Just that knew Him/ Large was his allotted portion of Private
Virtue./ The Kind and Affectionate Husband./ The Fond and
Tender Parent./ The Mild and Indulgent Master/ were united in
Him./ Faithful to his Friend./ Generous to his Afsociate./
Humane to Mankind/ He lived not for Himself Alone;/ But,/
Prompted by sweet Benevolence,/ His generous Bosom glowed
and felt for All./ Let then this Lettered Marble,/ Which,/ In
Justice to his Revered Name./ His Disconsolate Widow/ Raises
over the Mouldering Body/ Remain:/ A Monumental Record./
of Deceased Worth./

John Humpleby was probably an Englishman by birth.
He was a merchant in Bridgetown and the owner of one or more
plantations. He married in 1805, Sarah Anne Harris, née Bascom,
the widow of Thomas Harris of Barbados. John Humpleby had

675

issue a son, John, baptised in 1806. Mrs. Sarah Anne Humpleby was the foundress, in 1825, of the Ladies Association for the Relief of the Indigent Sick and Infirm, now in St. Michael's Row.*

---

* See "John and Sarah Humpleby" by E. M. Shilstone, *B,M. & H.S. Journal* Vol. 24, pp 65—67 and 132—3. A portrait sketch of Mrs. Sarah Ann Humpleby appears in Vol. 24, facing page 52. **

**The sketch of Mrs. Humpleby and the two articles by E. M. Shilstone are found on pp. 360-363, this volume.

APPENDIX D:
LISTS OF BARBADOS QUAKERS

BARBADOS QUAKERS—1683 TO 1761.
PRELIMINARY LIST.

By HENRY J. CADBURY.

THAT the Society of Friends called Quakers was once quite numerous in Barbados is clearly evidenced both by the records of that sect and by the records of that island. Nowhere, however, has been published even a tentative list of such persons. We scarcely expect Quakers to be separately designated in the census lists of 1679 or 1715. Only by certain characteristics in language when they themselves are quoted, as for example in wills, can the names of some of them be discovered from the legal records. The search for them would be a very slow process. On the Quaker side no records of local meetings are known to be extant on the island. They probably used in their graveyards no stones at all, certainly few inscribed stones.

The nearest thing to a list of Barbados Quakers ever published is in Volume 11, Chapter 6, of *A Collection of the Sufferings of the People called Quakers*, by Joseph Besse (London, 1753, pp. 278—351). Here are given in detail the fines or other punishments inflicted by the authorities on individual Quakers between 1658 and 1695. The names are conveniently alphabetized in The Fourth Index of the same volume and amount to over 225, excluding names repeated because misspelled, and excluding also the names of passing visitors to the island.

In the hope that in the near future various studies of Quaker history in Barbados may be published, whether in this Journal or elsewhere, it has seemed worthwhile to offer here a preliminary list of Barbados Quakers, derived from certain material which may be described as follows: When Quakers in good standing remove, the meeting where they have been visiting, or where they have been members, usually sends with them to the meetings to which they expect to come some kind of letter or certificate of recommendation or transfer. Among collections of such minutes received by Friends in Philadelphia (now at 304 Arch Street, in books numbered I.15 and I.16) are some fifty minutes from Friends in Barbados. They are signed by two or more persons, up to twenty five in some instances, and they are of course dated. The earliest are from 1683; the last from 1761. Thus though they begin twenty five years later than Besse's record, they also extend two generations later. The signers moreover may generally be regarded as Friends well esteemed and of some influence, whereas the sufferers in Besse in some cases had little connection with organized Quakerism. As in Besse, a few names are those of visitors; that is, Friends from abroad who happened to be present when the certificate was signed. Thus, of the names below it is probable that Thomas Chalkley, William Edmundson, William Fisher and Leonard Snowden represent the non-Barbadians. The list includes many persons of whom much else could be told and for whose Quakerism we have other evidence. Those which occur in Besse's *Account* have been marked with an asterisk. It has seemed useful to add the date of the certificate on which the signature appears; or, if the same Friend signed more than one of these certificates, as is often the case, to add the dates of the earliest and latest. Though other material for lists of Barbados Quakers is known to be in existence, some of it in England and temporarily unavailable, this partial list is offered as a beginning.

Anderton, Samuel	1706	Clement, James	1716–38
*Andrews, Edward	1683–87	Rebecca	1740
* William	1683	*Collins, Philip	1696
*Ashford, James	1683–86	Collyns, Benjamin	1727–33
*Barnard, Robert	1696	Sarah	1740–48
Bartlett, Thomas	1702–06	*Cotten, Benjamin	1687
Winifred	1706	*Currer, Henry	1683
*Beek(e), John	1683–96	Curtis, Nathaniel, Jr.	1696
Bidou, John	1727–32	Dawes, Mary	1726–40
Booteman, James	1686	Robert	1726–29
* Robert	1686–96	*Deeth, William	1696
Borden, Ann	1702–06	Dennis, Jonathan	1696
* Joseph	1683	Dury, Andrew	1732–61
Katherine	1740	Mary	1740
Bushell, John	1740–49	* William	1696–1729
Byrch, Ann	1748	Dynmyne, Dennis	1696
Hannah	1748	*Edmundson, William	1683
* Henry	1702–06	Ellacott, Hannah	1702–06
Mary	1748	Henry	1696–1740
Temperance	1702–06	Ellicutt, Margaret	1686
Callender, Ann	1749	Fisher, William	1749
Benjamin	1740–60	Floyd, Mary	1740
Elizabeth	1740	* Nathan	1683–87
Hannah	1726–40	Samuel	1729–50
John	1740	*Forde, Richard	1683
Mary	1726–40	French, Ann	1726
Richard	1729–49	Joseph	1727–40
William	1728–54	*Fretwell, Dorothy	1686
Chace, Elizabeth	1706	* Ralph	1686
* John	1683	* Thomas	1683
Chalkley, Thomas	1732	*Gamble, Frances	1683
*Christopher, William	1683	Joseph	1716–50
*Clark, Thomas	1686–96	Rebecca	1740–48
*Clarke, William	1696	Gibbes, Thomas	1720

678

Gibson, Alice 1740
John 1731-60
Rowland 1738-59
Sarah 1740-48
Thomas 1760
*Glover, John 1683
Gowith, Richard 1687
*Gray, George 1683-87
Hannah 1687
Gretton, Elizabeth 1686
Griffin, Ann 1726
*Griffith, Herbert 1683
Grove, John 1696-1716
*Grove, Joseph 1696
* Rebecca 1706
*Habbin, Thomas 1696
Harrison, Edward 1726-54
Elizabeth 1740-48
Hillary, William 1748-50
Holder, Alice 1686
Hooten, Thomas 1732
*Hooton, Martha 1702
* Oliver 1683
Hoskins, Hester 1687
* Richard 1683
*Hunt, Edward 1683-96
Elizabeth 1702-06
Hutchins, Rebecca 1687
* William 1683-87
Jackman, Hannah 1740-48
Joseph 1733-61
*James, John 1686
Sarah 1686
Kelsall, Ann 1687
Kiths, Margery 1726
Lawrence, Mary 1686
* William 1683
Lewes, Elizabeth 1740
John 1727-40
Luke Elizabeth 1740
Jacob (Jr.) 1730-42
John 1740-61
Mary 1748
*Marshall, Cuthbert 1696
Mein (e), Patrick 1727-29
Mellor, Augustine 1749-60

Morris, Elizabeth 1706
Sarah 1726
William 1727-30
Nevinson, Ann 1706
Oxley, Ann 1740
John 1720-42
John, Jr. 1740-43
Sarah, 1726-48
*Parsons, Edward 1683-87
*Pearcey, Benony 1683-96
Pearcy, Elizabeth 1740
Pedder (?), John 1759
*Pilgrim, Thomas 1683-96
*Plumly, John 1696
*Poor, Richard 1702-27
Richards, Samuel 1727-40
* Thomas (Jr.) 1683-87
Winifred 1687
Richardson, John 1742-60
Mary 1726
*Robinse, Thomas 1683-92
Scott, Sarah 1687
Sharp, Peter 1727
Sheren, Alice 1746
Smith, John 1716-20
Mary 1726
Snowden, Leonard 1744
*Sutton, Richard 1683
Swinsted, Sarah 1687
*Taylor, George 1696-99
* John 1696
Samuel 1716
* Walter 1687
*Thilston, William 1696
Thomas, Margaret 1686
*Thorpe, Robert 1683-86
Treasure, Ann 1687
*Waite, John 1687
Priscilla 1686
Walker, Ann 1686
Warner, William 1749-50
Waterman, Margaret 1686
*Weekes, Ralph 1683-96
*Wright, Edward 1683-86
Elizabeth 1686
*Wynne(e), John 1683-1706
Sarah 1706

186 BARBADOS QUAKERESSES IN 1677.

By HENRY J. CADBURY.

ONE feature almost distinctive of early Quakerism was the importance given to women in Church affairs. Special women's meetings were organized in England within a decade of the rise of the Society of Friends. When George Fox came to Barbados in 1671, he promptly arranged for women's meetings there, and they were evidently held at the chief Quaker centres on the island as well as for the island as a whole. A list of women Friends in Barbados arranged by the local meetings to which they belonged is preserved in London at Friends Reference Library among some papers belonging to the Box Meeting of London women Friends. It is dated 1677, it was addressed to Rebecca Travers, and signed by Ralph Fretwell. The names of the meetings and the number of names under each are as follows:—

Plantation Meeting	41
Thicketts and Clift Meeting	21
Windward Meeting	31
Bridge Meeting	40
Spring Meeting	30
Champion Ground Meeting	23

Except for "Clift" and "Windward" all these meetings can be located and their houses show upon the ancient maps. In the following list the arrangement by meetings has been replaced by a single alphabetical list, the initials P, T. W. B. S and C being used respectively to indicate the meeting to which the Friend belonged. P. was in St. Peter's parish, Bridge is in Bridgetown The Spring near Porey's Spring in St. Thomas, The Champion Ground meeting house was near Pumpkin Hill now in St. Lucy's parish. Names mentioned also by Joseph Besse in his account of Sufferings of Quakers in Barbados are marked with an asterisk. The names are as follows:—

T	Adamson, Jane	B	Borden, Hope
W	Archer, Eliz.	T	Bowman, Mary (or Marg.)
W	Ashby, Mary	*W	Braister (i.e. Brewster),
P	Baker, Eliz.		Margaret
B	Baraman, Judith	W	Braithwaite, Avis
B	Barnes, Eliz.	B	Brett, Mary
W	Barry, Mary	B	Browne, Eliz.
B	Beedle, Marie	S	Cade, Mary
P	Benn, Rebecak	C	Cammell, Alice
B	Birch, Temperance	B	Chace, Eliz.
S	Bissek, Ann	T	Carter, Eliz.

B Bockett, Mary
P Clavan, Eliz.
T Cole, Sarah
C Collins, Alice
W Cooper, Susanna
B Cope, Eliz.
*W Curtis, Marie
P Dewsbury, Mary
C Dotten, Ruth
S Dry, Dorothy
S Earle, Dorothy
S Edwards, Sarah
B Ellis, Margett
P Emblin, Rebecka
B Emes, Joane
W Evans, Marie
P Feake, Ann
B Fell, Lydia
T Fitch, Jane
W Foorde, Grace
T Fortescue, Mary
T Foster, Hester
*S Fretwell, Dorothy
T Frizzol, Eliz.
*S Gallop, Ann
W Gamble, Margery
P Gamble, Sarah
C Garrett, Sus.
*C Gay, Eliz.
C Gay, Eliz., Junr.
P George, Ann
S Gibbs, Margarett
W Gittings, Hannah
W Gittings, Hannah
P Glover, Eliz.
B Grace, Marg. (or Mary)
P Gray, Hannah
P Gray, Mary
T Griffin, Alice
S Gritton, Eliz.
P Guliame, Abigail
*T Gunston, Ursula
P Habbin, Elizabeth
P Hacksworth, Eliz.
B Hall, Sarah
S Hancock, Grizell
P Harrison, Abigale
C Harvey, Katherine

T Christopher, Sarah
W Hart, Dorothy
B Harvey, Ruth
B Hasell, Eliz.
S Heelie, Ann
W Hilton, Deborah
S Hinshow, Hester
P Holder, Deborah
S Holder, Alice
P Holder, Joan
W Homeyard, Kath.
P Hood, Rachel
C Hoskens, Hester
P Howard (now Cooper),
    Constant
B Huett, Barbara
B Hunt, Eliz.
T Hunt, Frances
T Hunt, Francis
B Hunt, Martha
P Hutchings, Rebecka
*W Hutton (i.e. Hooton),
    Martha
C Jackson, Margret
W Jales, Marg. (or Mary)
S James, Ann
*S Jay (alias Cooke), Hannah
P Jennings, Sarah
C Jones, Alice
S Jones, Ann
P Jones, Eliz.
C Keen, Mary
P Kelsall, Ann
W Kerne, Alice
S Lawrence, Mary
S Lewis, Gertrude
W Loftus, Frances
B Lovell, Edith
B Loyd, Rebecka
P Luke, Rebecka
B Lumlie, Sarah S.
S Mansfield, Elinor
B Marshall, Bridget
B Martine, Ann
P Martine, Ruth
C Minnes, Joan
W More, Anchoret
P Morres, Marie

B	Moulder, Christian	T	Sutton, Eliz.
P	Moulder, Dorothy	P	Swan, Mary (or Marg)
P	Mulinax, Elizabeth	C	Swinsted, Eliz.
W	Neale, Eliz.	P	Swinsted, Sarah
B	Newby, Eliz.	C	T———, Olive
C	Newton, Marg.	S	Taite, Eliz.
W	Norton, Katharine	P	Taylor, Grace
S	Owen, Mary	S	Taylor, Jane
P	Pearcie, Bridget	W	Taylor, Mary
S	Peele, Mary	P	Thorpe, Alice
C	Pennyman, Susan	C	Tilston, Ann
B	Perrin, Eliz.	*W	Titchburne, Winifred
*S	Pershouse, Eliz.	T	Todd, Eliz.
B	Persons, Joan	W	Todd (Codd), Rebecka
B	Pilgrim, Barbara	P	Treasurer, Ann
C	Pinke, Kath.	B	Venner, Ann
W	Pinner, Alice	S	Waite, Mary
B	Poole, Eliz.	C	Waite, Susannah
B	Pore, Susanna	S	Walk, Ann
B	Quidden, Ann	B	Walker, Sarah
T	Rice, Lucea	W	Warren, Winifred
P	Richards, Ann	P	Weale, Marie
S	Richards, Marg. (or Mary)	P	Webb, Martha
B	Ridgway, Martha	W	Weeks, Agnes
T	Robbins, Ann	B	White, Ann
P	Robinson, Eliz.	*W	Whitehead, Winifred
S	Rootsey, Ann	T	Whitlock, Eliz.
T	Rous, Elenor	P	Wickham, Alice
C	Sandes, Kath.	P	Willmot (alias Davis),
*C	Savory, Eliz.		Eliza
C	Scanterbury, Eliz.	T	Wood, Eliz.
S	Settle, Frances	C	Wood, Marg.
B	Sidgwick, Ann	S	Wright, Eliz.
*P	Smith, Marie	B	Wright, Margret
W	Street, Eliz.	W	Wyber, Dorothy
T	Sutton, Eliz. (wid.)		

WITNESSES OF A QUAKER MARRIAGE IN 1689

by HENRY J. CADBURY.

WHEREVER QUAKER records are preserved they prove a valuable source of biographical information almost unequalled. These dissenters, just because they neither baptized infants, nor "married by a priest," nor interred their dead in sacred ground, were careful to record births, marriages and deaths with regularity and completeness. Such record books certainly once existed for Barbados Quakerism. Their loss is therefore keenly felt by anyone who would recover the history of this important element in the island's early English history.

Probably a list of members was rarely made. The membership is rather inferred from these other full records. The fullest list for the period up to 1695 is in Besse's *Collection of the Sufferings of the People Called Quakers*, 1753 (see the fourth index to the second volume). In earlier issues of this *Journal* I published two other lists, in 1941 a preliminary list of "Barbados Quakers—1683-1761" (IX. 29-30), and in 1942 a list of "186 Barbados Quakeresses in 1677" (IX. 195-197) . *

Another source of information is represented here by a single marriage certificate. The Quaker marriages were elaborately safeguarded. At two prior monthly meetings the principals gave notice of their intentions to the meeting, which was asked to authorize the marriage. Then when the ceremony occurred a certificate was provided which was signed by most of those present as witnesses. These original certificates were preserved by the principals but they were also copied in a book provided for the purpose. Such a book doubtless existed in Barbados and has been lost; but in the present case since the groom was of Pennsylvania another copy was entered in the book of Marriage Certificates of Philadelphia Monthly Meeting and also in a book there entitled "Copies of Marriage Certificates which were not recorded in the Meeting Records at the time the Marriages were solemnized.." Both these books are in the Department of Records, 302 Arch Street, Philadelphia.

The principals are described as "Joseph Kirll of Pennsylvania & Mary Brett, daughter of John and Mary Brett of Michael's Parish in the Island of Barbadoes." The date is "the ninth day of the month called October, 1689." The place is a "publicke assembly of the people called Quakers met together at the house of John Brett in the parish of Michael's aforesaid."

---

*Pages 677-682, this volume.

The men and women who signed the certificate are listed below. Most of them are known to be Friends, including some of the most influential Friends, and probably others were Friends also. But non-Quakers were not excluded from attending and witnessing a Quaker marriage and one may conjecture that the groom being a mariner was accompanied by some shipmates from off the island. In the lists an asterisk is used as in the previous lists to indicate names that appear in Besse, sometimes, however, with a difference in spelling due perhaps to the copyist of the marriage certificate. Those which appear in the two earlier lists of this journal are marked 41 or 42 according to the year of publication.

First come the signatures of the bride and groom and of the bride's family.

> Joseph Kirll
> Mary Brett now Kirll
> *John Brett
> Mary Brett   42
> John Brett, Jr.
> Rebecca Brett

Then over thirty each of men and women in separate lists or columns.

MEN.	WOMEN.
*John Sutton	Mary Tudor
Thomas Rudgard (Rudyard, proprietor and deputy Governor of New Jersey until he left in 1685 for Barbados.	Ann Mellowes
	Elizabeth Weale
	Kath. Norton 42
Thomas Homer	Barbara Hewett 42 (wife of Robert)
Francis Gibbon	
James Denham	Mary Neale
John Bates	Bridget Peaney 42 (Pearcey)
Cha. Pope	*Margaret Brewster 42 (wife of Thomas)
* Richard Fford 41	
*Tho. Pilgrim 41	Sarah Jennings 42
*Jose. Harbin	Elizabeth Chace 41 42 wife of John)
*Richard Hoskins 41	
*Thomas Clark 41	Eliza Morris 41
*Joseph Borden 41	Sarah Hall 42 (wife of Hugh)
*John Weale	Eliz. Clay
*Emanuel Curtis	Eliz. Wilson
Augt. Hall (Perhaps Hugh Hall).	Ann Curtys
	Jane Ostrahan (spelled also Austrihan)
Elisha Mellowes	Hannah Smith

*John Beeke 41
*Benony Peaney 41 (Correct spelling is Pearcey)
*Walter Taylor 41
*Tho. Habbin 41
Wm. Copp, Junr. (also spelled Cope)
+John Jones
*Jose. Harbin, Jr.
Richard Goddard
John Weale, Jr.
+John Plumley 41
*Robert Weale
*John Hutton
John Hunt
*John Newland
Nathan Floyd.

Susanna Plumley
Ann Borden 41
Hester Cotton
Grace Taylor 42 (wife of Walter)
Mary Peaney (probably Pearcey)
Ann Grace (wife of Benjamin)
Rachel Pilgrim
Eliz. Sutton 42
Ann Parker
Abigail Harrison 42
Ann Chace
Ann Taylor
Mary Coates
Margaret Morris
*Mary Curtis 42
Rebecca Ford
Mary Hall (daughter of Hugh)
Eliz. Hunt 41 42 (wife of Edward)
Ellen Morris
Sarah Tode (probably Todd)

Though our present interest is in the Barbados witnesses a few words may be added about the groom. Joseph Kirle (Kirll or Curle) continued his trade and was a member of the party, in fact the master of the barkentine *Reformation*, which sailed from Jamaica and was shipwrecked off the coast of Florida on September 23rd, 1696. An account of this wreck and the subsequent experiences of its survivors as captives of the Indians, written by another Quaker merchant aboard, Jonathan Dickinson, was published in 1699 under the title *God's Protecting Providence*. It was reprinted many times later; including editions in German and Dutch, and it has been most carefully edited by C. M. and E. W. Andrews and published in 1945 by the Yale University Press. Joseph Kirle repeatedly appears in the exciting story as one of the *dramatis personae*.

His name is subsequently met wtih both as a sea captain and as a Pennsylvania merchant. In 1703 he owned extensive tracts of land in Bucks County there. A letter of his in the same year from Philadelphia to Jonathan Dickinson in Jamaica shows that he kept up his old association. It also mentions his wife (Logan Papers at the Historical Society of Pennsylvania). There was other correspondence and business dealing between Kirle and Dickinson, and he was called upon to attest the truth of the now famous narrative (Andrews, *op. cit.* p. 115).

QUAKERS IN BARBADOS IN 1687

by Henry J. Cadbury

There are three extensive lists of Quakers in the island of Barbados in the Seventeenth Century. Two of them cover a number of years, one is for a single date but confined to women. The oldest is the index to the Chapter of Joseph Besse, Collection of Sufferings of the People Called Quakers, 1753 II , 278 - 351, viz. The Fourth Index, Ibid. p. 626-628. They amount to over 225 persons excluding names of passing visitors to the island. They cover the years 1660-1695.

The second is based upon the signatures to the some fifty certificates for Friends removing to Philadelphia from Barbados 1682 and 1761. Omitting again temporary visitors they add up to 150. They were listed with the date or with first and last dates in this periodical. [1]

The third is 186 Barbados Quakeresses in 1677 from a contemporary list preserved at Friends Library in London and divided among the six meetings on the island. This also I published in this periodical arranged alphabetically with the name of the meeting indicated by its initial: Bridgetown, Champion Ground, Plantation, Spring, Thickets, Windward. [2]

Recently I have come upon a shorter list. It is dated Bridgetown 13 April 1687 and is "from our General Monthly Meeting of Men and Women Friends at the Bridge Town in Barbados" and contains 68 names. It is a certificate on behalf of Roger Longworth, a Friend from Lancashire who had arrived there from Ireland about three months before as a travelling minister and

1.   B. M. & H. S. Journal Vol. lX, 1941, pp. 30f. , Vol. XlV, pp. 8-10
2.   B. M. & H. S. Journal Vol. lX, 1942, pp. 195-197. *

*These three articles are found on pp. 677-685, this volume.

who was about to depart for mainland America. The
signers recommend him to the faithful Friends, brethren and sisters in America.

The certificate was signed by sixty eight Friends,
thirty nine of whom were men and twenty nine women,
eight of the latter being widdows " and twenty five of
the women having their names signed for them[3] in an
identical handwriting.

The men's names occur all of them except three in
Besse's Index mostly among those most recurrent there.
John Eckley was probably the Pennsylvania Quaker of
that name, only transiently present on the island. Most
of the men were also signers of the certificates used in
list 2 above. At least half of the women are in list 3
above, but few of them as members of Bridgetown
Meeting, which suggests that the signers of this certificate included persons from other meetings in the
island.

I give below the names of the women and the men
separately arranged in alphabetical order:

Austrahan, Joan	Kelsey (? Kelsall), Ann
Brett, Mary	Mansfield, Ann
Brewster, Margaret	Morris, Eliz.
Cotton, Hester	Murrell, Margaret
Ford, Grace	Norton, Kathryn
Ford, Susannah	Pearcey, Bridget

3. This is the description in W. I. Hull, William Penn and the Dutch Quaker
Migration to Pennsylvania, 1933, p. 374. .
He gives the full text of the certificate but none of the names of the signers. Dr. Hull said that this was the only record of Longworth's work on
the island. He evidently did not know, that in addition to many other letters by Longworth which he used, there are three written in Barbados in
12 mo 1686 (February 1687) to London or Amsterdam in the Benjamin
Peter Hunt Collection in the Boston Public Library, Nos. 4, 5, and 6.

Fretwell, Dorothy
Grace, Ann
Grace, Margret
Gray, Hannah
Hall, Sarah
Holder, Alice
       Martha
Hutton, Ruth
Huett, Barbara

Peters, Olive
Robbins, Ann
Savery, Eliz.
Scott, Sarah
Swinstead, Sarah
Taylor, Grace
Waite, Priscilla

- -

Beeke, John
Borden, Jos.
Braithwaite, John
Brett, John
Clarke, Thomas
Clarke, William
Cotten, Benj.
Currer, Henry
Curtis, Emanuel
Eckley, John
Ford, Richard
Fretwell, Thomas
Gibbes, Stephen
Gowith, Richard
Gray, George
Grove, Joseph
Griffith, Herbert
Habbin, Thos.
Hall, Hugh
Huett, Robt.

Hunt, Edw.
Laurence, Wm.
Pearcey, Benony
Pilgrim, Thos.
Plumley, John
Poor, Richd.
Richards, Thos.
Robinson, Jos.
Rodman, John
Savery, Jeremie
Taylor, George
Taylor, Walter
Thorpe, Rob't
Sutton, Rich'd
Waite, Wm.
Weale, John
Weekes, Ralph
Wright, Edward
Wright (?) John

An Epitaph on the late Dr. Gamble, one of the
Denomination of Quakers, in Barbados [4]

Beneath yon turf lies Gamble's duft,
Without a marble, ftone, or buft;
Distinguifh'd only, when alive,
By ev'ry virtue heav'n could give:
Who envying none their honours here,
Did good to all, within his fphere:
Modeft, and meek, with fenfe refin'd,
An humble, yet a foaring mind:
Its cafe now mixt with common clay,
He'll rival kings, at the laft day.

John Smith of Burlington, New Jersey (1722-1771)
wrote: Joseph Gamble and Elizabeth his wife were a
worthy aged couple and treated me with great friendship when I was in Barbados on account of trade in 1741.
They lived at a place called Fontabell about a mile from
Bridgetown, were wealthy, yet humble and plain in carriage and dress, diligent in frequenting meetings and
of good report among all sorts of people for their uprightness and benevolence. She died some years before her husband. He was a Doctor of Physic and had
great practice for many years, in which he was humane
and noted for taking much pains and to be as ready at
all times to visit the poor as the rich, and the bless-
ings of many of them were upon him. [5]

The household of Joseph Gamble in the Census of
1715 consisted of 2 men, aged 37 and 37; 1 woman aged
31; 3 boys, aged 18, 17, and 16; 1 girl, aged 9. [6] In his

4. Gentlemen's Magazine, Vol. xxlx, p. 283, London, June 1759.
5. Manuscript Memorial of Deceased Friends, Vol. 2, p. 5, at Haverford College.
6. B. M. & H. S. Journal, Vol 111, p. 161. (Page 26, this volume.)

will he mentions no children of his own. Dr. Gamble is mentioned in the will of Jane Hooper, widow, of St. Michael in 1720 as one of 3 executors and he was left £10. for "mourning clothes." [7] He was a witness to the will of Elizabeth Alleyne, the wife of Abel Alleyne in 1746 and in 1753 he was a signatory to the Address[8] of the Quakers to Henry Grenville, Governor of Barbados, dated 4th. April 1753.[9]

Dr. Joseph Gamble died in 1756, aged 78. His will is dated 11th, March 1756. He left bequests to 3 nieces, one nephew and a great nephew, his nephew was the son of his sister Sarah Jackman, named Joseph Jackman, who I regard as my eldest son. He Dr. Gamble named as his sole executor.[10]

7.   Ibid, Vol. VII, p. 33. (Page 329, this volume.)
8.   Ibid, Vol. III, p. 114. (Page 17, this volume.)
9.   Ibid, Vol. XX, p. 80.
10.   Shilstone MSS., Notebook 10, p. 105-106.

698

700

701

703

713

716

727

728

Lord, Samuel Hall 389,
390, 391, 393, 398,
401, 549, 673
Sarah 391, 394, 400
Sarah Bathsheba 400
Thomas 399, 400
Loscombe, Joseph 177
Lot, Mary 109
Lother, Gov. Rob. 581
Lousadas, Mr. 520
Love, Alfred 184
Rev. Edward 184
Oswald 184
Roxana Bostock 184
Thomas 278
Lovell, (?) 551
Anna Maria 273
Edith 681
Edward 142
Ph. 509
Dr. Robert 314
Samuel 273
Lovesay, Judge 261
Colin 260, 261
Low. See Lowe.
Lowe/Low, Dorothy 524
Dorothy D. L. 524
Elizabeth Mary 66, 82,
83
Joseph 66, 82, 83,
524
Margery 328
Mary 278
Richard 419
Tho. 532
Thomas 278
Lower, Elizabeth 435
Sir Nicholas 435
Lowle, Ava 67
Lowsley, Col. 455
Lt. Col. 470
Lieut. B. 470
Lowther, Robert 300
Robt. 176
Gov. Robt. 373
Loyd, M. Leolin 355
Rebecka 681
Robert 412
Lucanion, (?) 523
Lucas, (?) 404, 406, 407
Dr. 402
Mr. 408
Mrs. 408
Widow 408
Alice 280, 403, 404,
407, 408, 410, 411
Angel 406, 408
Ann 404, 406, 407,
408, 409
Ann Jordan 403, 405,
410, 411
Anna 405
Barbara 405, 408
Catherine 404
Charles 404, 406, 408
Christopher 404, 406,
408
Conrad 404
Degory 409
Dorothy 408
Eliza 408
Elizabeth 402, 403,
404, 406, 407, 408,
409, 410
Frances 405, 406, 407,
408
Frances Burnett 407
Frances Eveling 405

Lucas, George 404, 406,
408
George Parris 408
Hanna Ritta 405
Hannah 405
Harriott 405
Hendricke 412
Henry 402, 404, 405,
406, 407, 408
Henry Evelin 405, 406
Henry Eveling 405
Jacob 406, 408
James 407, 409
Jane 405
Joan 404, 406
Joana 409
Joane 404, 409
Johaddan 404, 407
John 407
Jos. 405
Joseph 405, 406, 407,
408
Joseph Griffith 408
Joseph James 405
Joseph Jordan 403,
405
Josiah Phillips 406
Josias 406
Katharine 407
Letitia 406, 408
Loetitia 405
Margaret 404, 408,
410
Mary 403, 404, 405,
406, 407, 408, 411,
412, 413
Mary Ann 405, 406
Mary Baylor 403, 407,
410, 411
Nath. 408
Nathan 402, 403, 404,
405, 406, 407, 408,
409, 410, 411, 412
Dr. Nathan 402, 403,
405, 408, 413
Nathaniel 280, 405,
408
Nathan'l. 408
Nicholas 402, 404,
407, 409, 412
Philip 403, 404, 406,
407
Rebecca 405
Richard 402, 404, 405,
406, 407, 409, 410,
412
Richard King 405
Samuel 402, 404, 407,
409
Sarah 402, 403, 404,
405, 406, 407, 408,
410, 411, 522
Sarah Ann 403, 406,
408
Theophilus 402, 404,
407, 409
Thomas 403, 404, 406,
407, 408
Ursula 406
Wilhelmina 404, 407
William 402, 404, 405,
406, 408, 410
Zachariah 404, 407
Lucey, Eliz. 482
Martha 482
Lucie, (?) 174
Messrs. 173
Eliz. 175

Lucie, Jacob 174, 175,
252
Lucomb, Lieut. Thomas
339
Lucye, Jacob 119
Luder, Abell 326
Luff, Cyril 492
Rev. Edgar A. 492
Evelyn 492
Gytha 492
Lufton, Christian 672,
673
John 672, 673
Luke, Elias 524
Elisha 407
Elizabeth 679
Jacob 538, 679
Jno. 305
John 679
Mary 305, 679
Rebecka 681
Lukumb, Lt. Thomas 7
Lumbert, Lt. Col. 268
Lumlie, Sarah S. 681
Luntly, Margaret 124
William 124
Lusher, Isabella 354
Lutley, Cyril 492
Daisy 492
Rev. E. C. 492
Edward J. R. 492
Elizabeth Ann 491
Evelyn Janette 492
Harold F. B. 492
Mcriel 492
Rosemary 492
Lycott, Mary 115
Lygon, (?) 481
Lynch, Anthony 20
Antoinette 218
Dominick 218
Elizabeth 54, 218
Louis 439
Patrick Joseph Dottin
218
Sir Tho. 221, 311,
443
Lynde, Simon 414
Lyne, Col. 320, 387, 445
Alice 414
Anne 414
Anthony 321
Chr. 657
Christopher 414
Col. Christopher 387,
414
Edward 414
Elizabeth 414
Henry Monk 237
Mary 414
Richard 414
Capt. Richard 414
Lynn, Jos. 228
Lynton, Martin 412
Lyon, Sir James 58
Lysons, Anne 485
Geo. 481
Lytcott, Mary 420
Mercy 110
Philip 111, 181, 302
Lyte, Mr. 37
Jno. 248
John 20, 21, 136,
332, 333, 410, 415,
442, 444
Paul 324
Capt. Paul 532
Maj. Paul 278

734

Pollard, Eleanor Curtis
462
Eliza 460, 461
Elizabeth 456, 459,
460, 461, 462, 463,
465, 470, 471
Elizabeth Ann 473
Elizabeth Anne 467
Elizabeth Francis 467
Elizabeth Geoffrey
458
Elizabeth Gittens 467
Elizabeth Mary Grace
474
Elizabeth Rebecca Cur-
tis 465
Ellen Jane 472
Ellis John 472
Elly Anne Curtis 465
Emerline 463
Emlin 460
Emlyn 460
Fanny 473
Frances 471
Frances Curtis 465
Francis 456, 459
Dr. G. R. M. 474
Geoffrey 458, 460,
461, 462, 465
George 456, 458, 459,
461, 463, 475
George Danson 468
George Richard McIn-
tosh 472, 474
Gertrude 455
Grace 474
Harriet 466
Helen Elizabeth 474
Henry 473
Henry Armell 460
Henry Curtis 462, 465
Henry Hugh Curtis 465
Hugh 456, 458, 459,
460, 461, 462, 463,
464, 465, 467, 469,
470, 473, 474, 475
Sir Hugh 455, 456
Hugh Curtis 465
James 458, 459, 460,
461, 462, 463, 465,
466
James Shepherd 465
Jane 470
Jane Weekes 467
Jane William 470
Jane Williams 470
Jeffrey 460
Jenny Grace 474
Joanna 462
Jocelyn Mary Mellis
475
John 456, 458, 459,
460, 461, 462, 463,
464, 465, 466, 467,
468, 469, 470, 473,
474, 475
Dr. John 460, 463, 464
466, 468
John Elliott Trough-
ton 473
John Fraser 475
John Henry 467, 470
John Penn 465
John Robert 464
Jone 458
Joseph 461, 463
Joyce 459
Katherine 474
Lewis 455, 456, 458

Pollard, Sir Lewis 456
Margaret 455, 456,
458
Margaret Cornelia
472, 473, 474
Marguerite Muriel Cul-
peper 473
Martha James 468
Mary 456, 459, 460,
461, 462, 463, 464,
465, 469, 473, 475
Mary Eliza Rosalie
472
Mary Gould 463, 464
Mary Jane 467, 470
Mary Shepherd 465
Minerva Curtis 462
Nathaniel Curtis 462,
464, 465
Nathaniel Weekes 467,
469, 470, 473, 474
Philip Lewis 468
Phoebe 460
Rebecca 463, 466
Rebecca Curtis 462
Rebecca Curtys 461
Rhoda Branch 473
Richard 458, 459, 460,
461, 462
Richard Batty 472
Richard William 475
Robert 461, 463
Robert Curtis 465
Robert Geoffrey 462,
463, 465
Robert James 465
Robert Jeff 461, 463
Robert John 466
Ruth 466, 467
Samuel 460, 464
Samuel Branch 467
Sarah 458, 459, 460,
461, 463, 465
Sarah Alleyne 469
Sarah Barbara 475
Sarah Maria 469, 470
Susan 455
Susanna 464
Susannah 464
Susannah Moore 465
Thomas 407, 456, 458,
459, 460, 461, 464,
466
Dr. Thomas 466, 467,
468
Thomas Curtis 462,
465,
Thomas Curtys 461
Thomas McIntosh 467
Thomasine 462
Thomasine W. 465
Thomasine Williams
462
W. B. 455, 468, 472
Walter 455, 466, 467,
468, 469
William 455, 456, 457,
458, 459, 460, 461,
462, 463, 464, 465,
467, 468, 469, 470,
472, 473, 474, 475
Capt. William 457
William Branch 468,
470, 471, 473, 474
William Curtis 462
William Fox 471
William John McFar-
lane 474, 475
Dr. William John Mc-
Farland 475

Pomery, John 338
Poole, Eliz. 682
W. P. 240
Wm. Ph. 240
Pooler, James 305
Pooles, Capt. William
370
Poor, Benja. 405
Richard 679
Rich'd. 688
Tho. 344
Poore, Benjamin 410
George 645
Thomas 172
Pope, (?) 585
Anne 588
Cha. 684
Charles 279, 588
Chr. 588
Edw'd 588
George 588
J. 639
John 482, 588, 639
Joseph 588
Mary 588
Rich'd 588
Robert 588
Sarah 588, 639
Susanna 682
Porter, (?) 477
Mrs. 478
Abigail 476
Abraham 478
Agnes 478
Alice 476, 478
Alice G. 476
Amy 476
Ann 476, 477, 478
Anne 477, 478
Arthur 478
Benjamin 476, 478
Charles 476, 477, 478
Charles Thomas 476,
477, 478
Charlotte 378
Cornelia 477
Daniel 478
Edward 478
Edward Ferris 477
Edward Harris 476
Edward Huronis 478
Eliza 477, 478
Elizabeth 476, 477,
478
Esther 478
Francis 477
Hannah 376
Henry 478
James 476, 477
Jane 476, 477
Jeremiah 477, 478
John 476, 477, 476
Jone 476
Joseph 476
Josiah 478
Lawrence 478
Margaret 476, 477,
478
Maria 476
Marmaduke 476
Martha 477
Mary 476, 477, 478
Mary Ann 477
Mercy 478
Nicholas 476, 477,
478
Peter 477
Philip 477, 478
Rebecca 477

Raynsford, Kathtryne 482
  Marm. 482
  N. 482
  Nich. 482
  Rob. 482
Rea, Philip 300
Read, Coll. Edmond 440
  George 522, 523
  John 118
  M. Alston 641
  Mary 268, 292
  William 135
  Wm. 118
Reade, Col. Edmond 440
Reading, (?) 512
Reason, Thomas 124
Redan, Ann 316
  John 316
Reddin, Ann 316
Redford, Maj. Charles
  536, 564, 565
Redman, Hugh 340
  James 192
  Jane 514
  John 371
  John Isaac 55
  Martin 340
  Thomas 52
  Thos. 342
Redward, Eliz. 513
  Elizabeth 446
  Francis 446
  James Shepherd 446
  Katherine 446
  Katherine Lake 446
  Richard 446
  Rev. Thomas Rochford
    159
Reece, Mr. 488
  Abraham 487, 488, 489,
    490, 491, 492, 493,
    494
  Rev. A'raham 491, 615
  Abraham Arnold 490
  Abraham Daniel 491
  Abraham Llewellyn 493
  Amy 493
  Ann 496, 505, 604
  Annie Gertrude 490
  Arnold 490
  Barbara Deane 500
  Bartholomew 495
  Beresford St. Aubyn
    493
  Bezsin 496, 497, 498,
    499, 500
  Bezsin King 495, 496,
    497, 498, 499, 500
  Catherine 498
  Catherine Garrett 497
  Charles 493
  Charlotte 487, 488
  Charlotte Philp 490
  Christian 495
  Cyril 492
  Dorothy 493
  Dorothy Constance
    Deane 500
  Douglas 493
  Eardley 490
  Edith 490
  Edward 495
  Edward Bertram 490
  Elizabeth 487, 488,
    489, 496, 497, 498
  Elizabeth Ann 489, 491
  Elizabeth Frances 492
  Elvira 497, 498
  Elvira Bezsin 499

Reece, Ernest 493
  Estwick 493
  Eustace 493
  Evelyn Adelaide 490
  F. A. 490
  Florence May 490
  Frances Elizabeth Ann
    492
  Francis 506
  Frederick St. Aubyn
    490
  Gracie Lee 490
  Maj. H. M. 495
  Hannah 495, 506
  Harry 493
  Henry 489, 496
  Humphrey Munro 500
  Humphrey Stanley 494
  Isaac 487, 489, 492,
    494
  Isaac John 489
  Isaac Richard 492
  Isabel 490
  Isobel 493
  James 488, 497
  James Ebenezer 491
  Janette 491
  John 493, 495, 497,
    499
  John Deane 497, 498,
    499, 500
  John Harper 496
  Jonathan 496
  Jonathan James 496
  Judith 487, 489, 493
  Kate 490
  Lawrence 495
  Lewis 490
  Louisa 492
  Louise 490, 498
  Mabel 495
  Margaret 496, 497,
    604, 606
  Margaret Downes 496
  Mary 487, 495, 496,
    498, 499
  Mary Bezsin 497
  Mary Elizabeth 488,
    489, 493, 498
  Mary Harper 496
  Mary Louise 490
  Maud 493
  Minnie Grey 490
  Nellie 490
  Nigel 493
  Reece Hollinshed 492
  Richard 496, 505, 506,
    604
  Maj. Richard 506
  Robert 432, 487, 488,
    489
  Robert Cecil 490
  Sarah 487, 488, 493
    497, 498
  Sarah Frances 488
  Sarah Isabella 489
  Sarah Janette 492
  Susanna 506
  Thomas 495, 506, 604,
    609
  William 487, 488, 489,
    490, 492, 493, 494,
    495, 496, 497, 498,
    499, 500
  William Downes 496
  William James 488,
    489, 493
  Wm. 383, 505
  Winifrede Bezsin 499

Reed, Baynes 271
  Benjamin 536
  George 271
  John 533
  Dr. R. 210
  Rob. 240
Reese, John 15
Reeve, Mary 64
  Thomas 145
Reeves, Henry 170
  John 340, 476
  Robert Barbridge 407
  Sarah 476
  Susannah 476
  William 170
Reid, (?) 65, 79
  Mr. 175
  A. 136
  Agnes 516
  John 309, 516, 525,
    526
  Col. John 307
  Mary 309
  Reb. 309
  Tho. 309
  Col. Tho. 307
Relsen, Eliz. 477
Remer, Lucy 258
  R. 258
Remington, John 329
Rennell, Judith 329
Rennter, Henry 131
Reo, Tho. 340
Reynolds, Jas. 485
  Wm. 309
Rice, Charles 587
  Eliza Allison 514
  Lucea 682
  Nicholas 303
Rich, Mr. 457
  Ann 247
  Charles 246, 251, 587
  Chas. 243, 246
  Edward 587
  John 246
  Laurentia 247
  Lawrence 246
  Sir Nathaniel 457
  Rob. 243, 246, 247
  Robert 247, 587
  Thomas 335
Richards/Richard
  (?) 613
  Ann 19, 682
  James 141
  Jane 183
  John 376, 562
  John Benjamin 477
  Marg. 682
  Margaret 361
  Martha 613
  Mary Judith 182
  Richard 17
  Samuel 16, 19, 182,
    412, 679
  Samuel Munckley 182
  Thomas 182, 679, 688
  William Edward 182
  Winifred 141, 679
Richardson, (?) 119
  Dr. 442
  Mrs. 442
  Rev. Dr. 442
  John 59, 305, 679
  Mary 679
  Wm. 442, 530
Rickets. See Ricketts.
Ricketts/ Rickets, Gov.
  40, 61

739

740

743

Willey, Edward 23
  Jane 23, 248
  Margaret 248
  Sarah 248
William III, K. of Gt.
  Brit. 253, 564
William IV, K. of Gt.
  Brit. 255
Williams, (?) 169, 308
  Gen. 591, 605, 606,
    607, 608
  Maj. 613
  Mr. 349, 491, 615
  Mrs. 602
  Alexander 593, 601
  Alexander Walker 599
  Ann 264, 506, 595,
    596, 596, 598
  Ann Skeete 596, 597
  Barbara 594
  Charles 591, 612
  Charles Whitfoot 612
  Charlotte 254
  Christian 506, 601
  David 483
  Dorothy 591, 592,
    594
  Dorothy Carrington
    570, 599
  Ed 338
  Edward 338
  Eliz. Guthrie 309
  Eliz. Prescod 613
  Elizabeth 207, 593,
    594, 596, 597, 598,
    599, 602, 603, 609,
    610, 611, 612, 613
  Elizabeth Ann 554,
    597, 598, 609
  Elizabeth Clarke 602
  Elizabeth Corrigel
    596, 599
  Elizabeth Frere 60,
    73
  Elizabeth Goddard
    185
  Elizabeth Hinds 554,
    598, 600, 609
  Elizabeth Prescod
    600, 606, 608, 609,
    610,
  Elizabeth Whitfoot
    612
  Fearnot 599
  Francis 51, 339, 602
  Capt. Francis 338,
    339
  George 506, 591, 601,
    604, 605, 606, 608,
    609, 610, 611, 612,
    613
  Maj. George 607, 610,
    612
  George Worrell 605
  Henry 525, 593, 601,
    614
  Hugh 133, 254, 601
  Isabella 592
  J. B. 637
  James 554, 594, 595,
    596, 597, 598, 603,
    609
  James Thomas 597, 598
  Jane 470, 596. 597,
    601, 605
  John 594, 595, 596,
    598, 599, 600, 602,
    603
  Capt. John 246

Williams, Dr. John 254
  John Archibald 602
  John P. 603
  John Prescod 600, 601,
    603
  John W. 209
  John Worrell 207
  Judith 593, 594, 599,
    603
  Katherine Ann Hinds
    610, 613
  Lewis 599, 602, 603
  Lodowick 338, 340
  Lucretia Skeete 596,
    597
  Malvina 608, 609, 610
  Margaret 602, 604,
    605, 606, 608, 609,
    610
  Margaret Ann 597
  Margaret Elizabeth
    598, 510
  Margaret Smith 598
  Martha 483, 484, 485
  Mary 53, 131, 133,
    323, 594, 604
  Mary Ann 133
  Mary Anna 599
  Mary Worrell 604, 621
  Parnell 537
  Peer 322, 323
  Rebecca 610
  Richard 470
  Maj. Richard 591
  Robert 73, 615
  Robert Hinds 610
  Ruth 612
  Sa. 169
  Salvina 254
  Sam'l. 192
  Samuel 129
  Samuel Hinds 609, 610
  Sarah 73, 596
  Sarah Benjamin 597
  Sarah Jane 602
  Sarah Prescod 600
  Tho. 482, 485, 533
  Thomas 133, 206, 387,
    506, 532, 538, 591,
    592, 593, 594, 595,
    596, 597, 598, 599,
    602, 603, 604, 605,
    606, 607, 608, 609,
    610, 611, 612, 613
  Capt. Thomas 593, 604,
    620, 621
  Dr. Thomas 206, 610
  Gen. Thomas 554, 598,
    605, 606, 607, 608,
    609, 610, 611, 613
  Thomasin 594
  Thomasine 462
  Thos. 600, 603, 613
  W. 601
  William 323, 532, 591,
    592, 593, 594, 595,
    596, 597, 599, 603,
    604, 605, 606, 621
  William Asygell 593,
    600
  Gen. William Asygell
    591, 592, 593, 603,
    606
  William Peers 349
  William Poole 325
  William W. 53
  William Wiltshire 53,
    54
  Williams 605

Williams, Wiltshire
  Hooper 595, 596, 599,
    600
  Wm. 309, 601, 610
  Wm. Asygell 595, 596,
    597, 598, 599, 602,
    603, 604, 606, 610
  Gen. Wm. Asygell 601
Williamson, Anne 483
  David 300
Willing, Mrs. 617
  Abigail 65
  Ann 617
  Anne 67
  Anne Shippen 615
  Charles 61, 64, 65,
    207, 615, 616, 617
  Elizabeth 66
  Elizabeth Gibbes 47,
    61, 64, 65, 67,
    617
  Elizabeth Gibbs 270
  Elizabeth Hannah 61,
    65, 617
  Joseph 67
  Thomas 67
Willis, Eliza 76
  Henry 76
Willmot, Eliza 682
Willoughby, (?) 222, 364,
  465
  Gov. Lord 364
  Lord 7, 364, 365, 441,
    562
  Carola Martha 638
  Dorothy Frere 256, 260
  Lord Francis 443
  Gov. Hen. 409
  Lt.-Gen. Hen. 222
  Henry 364
  Lt.-Gen. Henry 222
  John 383
  Lord Wm. 221, 222, 374,
    418
Willoughbye, Francis 322
Willson, Edw. 509
Wilmot, John 588
Wilshire, John 129
Wilson, (?) 604, 621
  Anthony 200
  Carlvon 63
  Dr. Charles 451
  E. M. 452
  Eliz. 684
  Dr. George 49
  Hamlet 520
  Harriet 451
  Capt. John 451, 452
  John Grant 49
  Mary 621
  Robert 272
Wiltshire, George 335
  Hester 307, 310
  John 343, 344
  Maj. John 325, 343
  John Bayley 145
  Margaret 145
  Maria 145
  Mary 145
  R. 329
  Rebecca 145
  Richard 331, 332
  Rich'd 376
  Thomas 145, 341, 343
  William 145
Winch, R'd. 583
  Richard 581, 583
  Sarah 581
Windham, Sir Francis
  652

Windham, Sir Francis,
  Bart. 652
  Hester 652
Windover, John 322
Wingfield, Lady Frances 4
  Col. Frederick Bassett
  83, 101
Winslow, Gov. 668
  Anne 25
  Catharine Isabella 25
  Edward 28, 668
  Col. Edward 25
  Rev. Edward 25, 60
  Elizabeth 25
  Isabella Catherine 25
  Jane Isabella 25, 27
  Susanna 668
Winston, Jane Isabella
  24, 27
Winter, Armine Ursula
  472
  Elliott 493
  Elliott Edward 472
  Eric Elliot 472
  Ethel Marion 471
  Frederick Elliot 472
  Fredric Augustus 471
  James 52
  Leila Agnes 471
  Phyllis Elliot 472
  William Cecil 471
Winthrop, (?) 667
  Adam 561
  Gov. John 561
  Stephen 561
Wippell, Rev. Canon J. C.
  494
Wisdome, John 3
  Margaret 3
Wish, Capt. 396
Witham, John 366
  Dep. Gov. John 443
  Sir John 652
Witherall, Lieut. 409
  Lieut. Michaell 409
Withers, (?) 175, 287
  Mr. 300
  Jacob 246
  Mary 290
  Thomas 290, 301, 302
  Thos. 248
  Wm. 531
Withsmith, Thomas 197
Withy, Rev. Henry 36
Wittingham, Timothy 146
Witts, Rev. Canon Fran-
  cis 452
Wolcot, Alexander 353
  John 353
Wolfe, Emanuel 169
Wolferstone, Capt. Chas.
  481
Wolra, Capt. 417
Wood, Dr. 308
  Mr. 583
  Cath. 583
  Edward 370
  Eliz. 682
  Henrietta 66
  Henrietta Maria 83,
  101
  Jno. 412
  Judith Frewin 114
  Marg. 682
  Capt. Matthew 119
  Rev. R. 66
  Rev. R. Kendall 101
  Richard 45
  Sampson 177, 450

Wood, Samson 50, 511,
  513
  Sarah 116, 513
  Tabitha 361
  Tho. Walke Lemar 513
  William 17
  Col. William 556
Woodbine, Thos. 476
Woodbridge, Benj. 248
  Benjamin 665
  Rev. Benjamin 665
  Dudley 23, 91, 248,
  665
  Rev. Dudley 265, 647,
  664
  John 665
  Rev. John 665
  Mary 13, 23, 24, 26,
  248, 665
  Mary Ward 665
  Ruth 265, 664
Woodfall, Foances Wil-
  helmina 164
Woodhouse, Capt. Henry
  457
Woodin, Tho. 240
  Thomas 587
Wooding, (?) 620
  Eleanor 619
  Mark Whitfield 470
  Richard 637
Woodley, (?) 96
  Mary 96
Woodroffe, G. T. 101
Woods, Mary 499
Woodward, (?) 9
Woolcot, Elizabeth 353
  John 353
  William 353
Woolcott, Alexander 353
  Elizabeth 323, 353
  Elizabeth Fleming
  354
  George 354
  George John 354
  John 323, 353
  Joseph 253
Woolfe, (?) 232
Woolford, Henry 411
  Tho. 376
Woollcott, Alexander
  353
  Catherine Ann Boul-
  ton 353
  Walter 354
  William Thomas 353
Woolley, Ezekiel 503
Woolvin, Wm. 19
Woorey, Sam 641
Woory, J. 639
  John 639
  Patience 639
Wooton, Henry 412
Wootton, N. 179
Worcester, Countess of
  224
Workman, Francis 466
  Thomas 621
Wormbarton, Tho. 316
Wormbaton, Tho. 316
Worme, Sarah Francis
  195, 202
  William Benjamin 196
Worrel, Joseph 618
Worrell, (?) 592, 618
  Mr. 633
  Mrs. 631
  Ann 621, 622, 624,
  625, 627

Worrell, Anna Samuel 626
  Anne 624
  Bathsheba 619, 620,
  622, 626, 627
  Bridgetta 632
  Carrington 635
  Catherine 621, 627,
  628, 631
  Catherine Edward Nic-
  colls 627
  Cecilia Maria 632
  Celia Maria 632
  Charles 634, 635
  Christopher 618
  Edw. 514
  Edward 621, 622, 625,
  626, 627, 632, 634,
  635
  Eleanor 534, 620, 621,
  622, 623, 625, 626
  Eliza Julia Ward 113,
  627
  Elizabeth 290, 619,
  621, 622, 623, 625,
  626, 627
  George 603, 619, 620,
  621, 622, 623
  Harriet 631, 632, 634,
  635
  J. 623
  Jane 207, 603, 624,
  628, 631
  Jane Harrison 631, 632
  Dr. Jno. 533
  Joan 514
  Joanna 621, 622, 625
  626, 627
  John 603, 618, 619,
  620, 621, 622, 623,
  624, 625, 627, 628,
  632, 633, 634, 635
  Dr. John 603, 622,
  623, 624, 625
  Johnathan 620
  Jona. 539
  Jonathan 293, 613,
  619, 623, 624, 628,
  629, 631, 632, 633,
  634, 635
  Dr. Jonathan 301, 302,
  621, 623, 624, 628
  Mrs. Jonathan 630
  Katherine 627
  Marie 635
  Marie Anne Catherine
  633
  Martha 619, 620, 623,
  624, 635
  Mary 603, 604, 618,
  619, 620, 621, 623,
  624, 625, 627, 628,
  631, 634
  Nathan 619, 620, 621,
  622, 623, 627
  Ralph 618
  Rebecca 633
  Rebecca Wilson 613,
  633
  Richard 618, 622
  Samuel 618
  Sarah 301, 619, 620,
  621, 622, 623, 625,
  627
  Septimus 632, 634, 635
  Susan 626
  Thomas 618, 632, 633
  W. 533
  William 533, 536, 592,
  619, 620, 621, 622,

751

Worrell, William, cont.
623, 624, 625, 626,
627
William Bryant 628,
631, 632, 633, 634,
635
William Cobbah 628
William Wells 113, 627
Wm. 302
Worsam, John 252, 660
Richard 121
Worsham, John 119
Worsley, Mr. 443
Hen. 23, 516, 517
Gov. Hen. 240
Henry 175, 642
Gov. Henry 239
Wotton, Roger 321
Wragg, Sam. 584
Wm. 584
Wree, Joshua 273
Wright, Edward 279, 503,
679, 688
Eliz. 682
Elizabeth 679
Isaac 636
Ivan FitzHerbert 69
John 688
Kenneth Hepburn 69
Margret 682
Rev. Phineas 60
Thomas 183
Wm. 246
Wrong, Ann 636
Ann Christian 637
Christian 637
Cordelia Ann 638
Elias 636
Eliza 636
Elizabeth 638
Elizabeth Ann 637,
638
Esther Francis 638
Frances Elizabeth 638
Henry 636, 637
Isaac 637, 638
Jacob 636
James 637
John 180, 636, 637,
638
Katherine 636, 637
Maria Louisa 638
Maris Luisa 638
Mary 636
Mercy 637
Olevy Raines 637
Olevy Rains 637
Richard 636, 637
Robert Bassett 637,
638
Sarah 636, 637
Sarah Ann 638
Wyber, Dorothy 682
Wynch, Sarah 582
Wynn, Robert 280
Wynne, John 679
Sarah 679
Wynnee, Sarah 679
Yard, Capt. 423, 424
Mr. 421
Adelaide 425
Alleyne Cox 425
Charles 426
Charles Edward 426
Capt. E. C. 423
Edward 421, 423
Edward Charles 426
Edward James 421, 423,
424

Yard, Eliza 425
Elizabeth 421
Elizabeth Skeet 448
Elizabeth Skeete 425,
451
Elizabeth Skeete Pin-
der 425, 426
Frederic 426
George Beckwith 426
Henrietta 425
Margaret Elvira 426
Mary 421
Mary Elvira 424, 425
Mary Elvira Cox 424,
425
Mary Louisa 426
Thomas 421, 423, 424,
425, 426, 447
Rev. Thomas 426
Rev. Canon Thomas 426
426
Thomas Charles 426
Yateb, Matthew 406
Yates, Daniel 517
Yea, Georgiana 62, 66,
75, 77
Walter 76, 77
Sir William 75
William Walter 75
Wm. 66
Yeamans, (?) 525
Ann 263, 647
Anne 639, 641
Barbara 642
Christopher 641
Capt. Edw. 643
Edward 639, 641
Edw'd 643
Eliz. 266
Elizabeth 642, 643
Foster 641
Frances 640
George 639, 641
John 640, 641, 642,
643
Capt. John 641, 642
Sir John 640, 643,
647
Sir John, Bart. 639,
640
Sir John, 3rd Bart.
640
Sir John, 4th Bart.
640
Jon. 643
Margaret 640
Lady Margaret 639
Marg't. 643
Mary 263
Philip 641
Rachel 641
Ro. 639
Rob. 643
Col. Rob. 643
Sir Rob. 643
Robert 542, 640, 641,
643
Col. Robert 641, 642
Rev. Sir Robert 640
Sir Robert 640, 641
Robt. 528
Sarah 358, 528, 529,
642, 643
Walker 641
Willoughbie 639
Willoughby 641
Dame Willoughby 643
Lady Willoughby 643
Wm. 263, 266, 641

Yeamans, Lt. Col. Wm.
643
Maj. Wm. 643
Sir Wm., Bart. 641
Sir Wm., 2nd Bart.
640
Yearwood, Armel 390
Mrs. Armel 390
Benjamin 637
Charles Edward 260
Cornelius 518
Elizabeth Lorenza
Whittaker 638
John Washington 638
Jonas 126
Mary 636, 637
Samuel 518
Yeo, William 44
Yeoman, Col. William 669
Yeomans, Arthur 643
Blanch 639
Christopher 642
Ens. Edw. 642
Edward 639
Capt. Edward 642
Edw'd. 639
Fra. 639
Geo. 639
George 639
John 639, 643
Col. John 639
Joseph 639
Margaret 639
Rachel 639, 642
Rachell 639
Rich'd. 639
Rob. 639
Robert 639
Col. Robert 642
Tho. 643
Wm. 639, 643
Xtopher 642
York, Duke of 577
James, Duke of 279
Yorke, Philip 469
Youmans, Col. John 642
Young, Adm. 40
Col. 260
Anthony 382
Edward 259
Joseph 143
M. 143
Margaret 143
Margret 139
Mary 139
Sarah Fvances 195
Younger, Louise Catherine
570
Zakythinos, D. A. 439
Zeale, Alice 315
Zealell, Tho. 315
Zouch, Jas. 583

People with single names;
probably slaves, servants,
or Indians.

Accamema 316
Adinah 329
Becky 269
Bemass 316
Benn 316
Bess 19
Betty 303, 304, 305, 381
Betty Jane 50
Billey 199
Billy 12
Black Jane 315

Boy 239
Bristol 29
Cogo 198
Cubba 316
Cubbah 178
Cuffee 300
Cuffey 316
Cullee 381
Daphne 275
Dennis 113
Diana 171, 497, 637
Dick 239
Diego 309
Elizabeth 298, 497
Folly 316
Frances 14, 111, 484
Frank 17
Gabriel 12
Grace 199, 305
Great Sabina 239
Gunner 672
Hannah 650
Hannibal 28
Harry 22, 23
Jack 171, 317
Jane 169
Jean, child of Ubballi
    12
Jenny 24, 382
John 296
Jug 328
Juliet 305
June 29
Jupeter 639
Kate 324, 650
Katie 19
Little Sarah 198
Maria 171
Mary 305
Mary Ellen 497
Mate 199
Melissinda 242
Mercury 538
Mingo 315, 409, 410
Moll 152
Molly 109
Nancy 309
Nanny 181, 300, 328
Nay 410
Ned 17, 181, 199
Nen Judy 315
Ocain 315
Patience 28, 29
Pefoe 315
Peggy 23
Peter 109
Philady 305
Philip 29
Philips 12
Phillis 304
Polly 304
Pothena 23
Pretty Boy 24
Prudence 410
Quashebah 316
Quashie 325
Rachel 304
Rangoe 264
Robin 245, 247
Robinson 316
Romeo 178, 305
Rose 171, 198
Sabina 239, 275
Sambo 109
Sampson 315
Sandy 305
Sarah 316, 636
Sarey 305

Sesley 317
Sofiah 109
Sue 197
Thisbee 650
Tipp 29
Tom 50
Ubballi 12
Violet 316
Will 17
William 324
Willoughby 410
Winbar 315
Yea 410

ADDENDA

Elliot, Philippa 336
FitzHerbert, Sir Henry 56
    Mary 17
    William 56
Lascells, William 477

753